Cheddi Jagan
AND THE COLD WAR
1946–1992

Cheddi Jagan
AND THE COLD WAR
1946–1992

CLEM SEECHARAN

For Ruby, my great friend for love, Clem flip 3/2/24

For Russell, I hope this book is an inspiration love, Clem 3/2/24

IAN RANDLE PUBLISHERS
Kingston • Miami

First published in Jamaica, 2023 by
Ian Randle Publishers
16 Herb McKenley Drive
Box 686
Kingston 6
www.ianrandlepublishers.com

© 2023, Clem Seecharan

National Library of Jamaica Cataloguing-In-Publication Data
Name: Seecharan, Clem, author.
Title: Cheddi Jagan and the Cold War, 1946–1992. / Clem Seecharan.
Description: Kingston : Ian Randle Publishers, 2023. | Includes
    bibliographical references.
Identifiers: ISBN 9789768286611 (pbk). ISBN: 9789768286802 (hbk).
Subjects: LCSH: Jagan Cheddi. | Guyana – Politics and government –
    1803–1966. | Guyana – Politics and government – 1966-. | World
    politics – 1945–1989.
Classification: DDC 988.1 -- dc23.

Cover and book design by Ian Randle Publishers
Printed in United States of America

Contents

Acknowledgements.. *ix*

Abbreviations... *xi*

1. The Making of Cheddi Jagan's Marxism: Landscape,
   Port Mourant, 'Bitter Sugar,' and the Indo-Guyanese Narrative..... 1

2. The Sources of Cheddi Jagan's Communist Mission:
   Anatomy of His Longevity.. 46

3. Divergent Nationalisms: African and Indian Identities in
   Colonial Guyana, 1920s–40s, with Special Reference to the
   Idea of an Indian Colony.. 78

4. Race, Class, and Colonial Stagnation: 'Bitter Sugar,'
   the MPCA, Governor Lethem, and the Emergence of
   Cheddi Jagan 125

5. The Political Affairs Committee, Race, and the General
   Elections of 1947 148

6. Jagan's Emerging Marxism, Enmore, and Its Aftermath:
   The Late 1940s... 190

7. Jagan's Marxist Vision in the Context of the Cold War – I,
   with Special Reference to the Suspension of the Constitution,
   1950–54 222

8. Jagan's Marxist Vision in the Context of the Cold War – II:
   Race, Ideology, the Cuban Revolution, and Jagan's Fatal
   Encounter with President Kennedy, 1955–61 278

9. Anti-Communism at Home and Abroad: The Decline and
   Fall of Jagan in the Context of the Cold War, with Special
   Reference to Anglo-American Complicity, 1962–64..................... 338

10. Burnham, Jagan's Communism, Billy Strachan and the
    Communist Party of Great Britain: The MI5 Files, the Early
    1950s–1961 418

11. The Cold War and Jagan's Politics of Futility, 1965–69 460

12. 'Scientific Foresight': Jagan's Utopian Marxist Vision and Burnham's Amorphous Socialism 502

13. 'I am a Socialist; You are not a Socialist' – I: Burnham's Cooperative Socialism v Jagan's Marxism-Leninism..................... 539

14. 'I am a Socialist; You are not a Socialist' – II: The Absurdity of Jaganism and Burnhamism, 1976–79................ 594

15. 'What I Stand for Is Winning in the World': Dedicated Man, Inflexible Mind, 1980–91 633

16. The Fall of Communism and the Jaganite Mission 667

Conclusion: A Journey to Nowhere.. 701

Select Bibliography 715

Index 731

Acknowledgements

The idea of this book was given to me by Oscar Ramjeet over six years ago. It has taken far longer than I could have envisaged. Researching and writing require time and money. It is very hard work. I could not have written this book without Oscar's indefatigable effort in persuading a few distinguished entrepreneurs and professionals to contribute towards this project.

The book is dedicated to two eminent friends and sponsors, both of whom have been unfailingly supportive of my work. I am eternally grateful to Mr Imran McSood Amjad, chairman of NAGICO Insurance and MOTORWORLD Group of Companies (St Maarten, Netherlands Antilles), and Mr Komal Samaroo, executive chairman of DEMERARA DISTILLERS LIMITED (Georgetown, Guyana).

I am equally indebted to the following accomplished Guyanese professionals and entrepreneurs without whose generosity this marathon project could not have been completed: Dr Hughley Hanoman (Trinidad), Mr Seenath Jairam, SC (Trinidad), Mr Brian R. Ramphal (San Diego, California), and Mr Chris Thakoorpersad of Regency Paint and Body Shop and Electronics Division (Orlando, Florida).

It is essential for me to stress that my sponsors do not necessarily empathise with the views expressed in this work. And I do appreciate the freedom I've had to pursue my studies without any constraints whatsoever from them or any other source.

I also wish to thank Oscar for several interviews he conducted in Georgetown in May 2017; these have been very useful in comprehending, from some of the older as well as contemporary politicians, aspects of Guyanese political history. He, in turn, would like to thank Mr Bish Panday of P&P Insurance Brokers for his help with the interviews in Guyana.

Dr Baytoram Ramharack and the late Professor Brinsley Samaroo (1940–2023) read the manuscript and made perceptive comments on specific aspects of it. I have paid particular attention to their wise counsel in making extensive revision.

I have consulted numerous sources in many countries, over several decades, which have made this study possible. But I wish to recommend two that have been indispensable at all stages of this project. The online documents of the Cheddi Jagan Research Centre (Georgetown) is a superb mine of information. I appreciate the admirable work they are doing; and I hope that they will be assisted to continue to enhance their collection and disseminate it widely. I have also benefited immeasurably from Professor Frank Birbalsingh's uniquely valuable book, *The People's Progressive Party of Guyana, 1950–92: An Oral History* (Hansib, 2007), as is evident throughout the study. I am also grateful to the staff at Senate House, University of London, for giving me access to the Billy Strachan Papers in the Institute of Commonwealth Studies Collection.

My friend, Ian McDonald, has been a great source of inspiration to my work for several decades. I'm deeply indebted to him. I also wish to thank Faiyaz Ali, David Dabydeen, Riyad Insanally, Tom Kharran, John Mair, and Andrew Wright for their moral support. They, too, are not necessarily empathetic with my arguments.

My wife, Chris, gives me the love and the freedom to pursue my work, despite the selfishness, obsession and chronic absent-mindedness with respect to routine domestic chores, spawned by this lonesome and demanding exercise.

I owe a special debt to Ian and Christine Randle for taking on the monumental task of publishing this big book.

Abbreviations

AIFLD	American Institute for Free Labour Development
ASCRIA	African Society for Cultural Relations with Independent Africa
ASRE	African Society for Racial Equality
BG	British Guiana
BGEIA	British Guiana East Indian Association
BGLU	British Guiana Labour Union
CJRC	Cheddi Jagan Research Centre
CLC	Caribbean Labour Congress
CO	Colonial Office
CPGB	Communist Party of Great Britain
CPSU	Communist Party of the Soviet Union
CPUSA	Communist Party of the United States
DLM	Democratic Labour Movement
EIYMS	Wesleyan [later Susamachar] East Indian Young Men's Society
encl	enclosure
GAWU	Guyana Agricultural Workers' Union
GIWU	Guiana Industrial Workers' Union
HMG	Her Majesty's Government
ICFTU	International Confederation of Free Trade Unions
ICJ	International Commission of Jurists
INC	Indian National Congress
LCP	League of Coloured Peoples
MPCA	Manpower Citizens' Association
NAM	Non-Aligned Movement
NPC	Negro Progress Convention
PAC	Political Affairs Committee
PCD	Patriotic Coalition for Democracy
PNC	People's National Congress

PNP	People's National Party
PPP	People's Progressive Party
PR	Proportional Representation
PYO	Progressive Youth Organisation
RACS	Royal Agricultural and Commercial Society
SLO	Security Liaison Officer
SPA	Sugar Producers' Association
TNA	The National Archives
UF	United Force
UNIA	Universal Negro Improvement Association
USG	United States Government
WFDY	World Federation of Democratic Youth
WFTU	World Federation of Trade Unions
WIDF	Women's International Democratic Federation
WPA	Working People's Alliance
WPC	World Peace Council

1.

The Making of Cheddi Jagan's Marxism
Landscape, Port Mourant, 'Bitter Sugar,' and the Indo-Guyanese Narrative

Imperialism was powerless to arrest the unfolding of the laws of social development discovered by Marx and Engels. Numerous peoples, representing one-third of the world's population, won the right to embark on the building of socialism.

> – Editorial, *Thunder*, January–March 1975

Marxism-Leninism is a science, not a dogma.

> – Cheddi Jagan (1990)

Marxist literature gave me a total understanding to fit everything together.

> – Cheddi Jagan (1992)

To the East Indian population, he has become almost a myth, and is compared with 'Mahatma' [a sage]. He is the 'Nehru' of British Guiana. His picture is cut out of newspapers…and pinned on walls. They feel that Jagan has liberated them.

> – Ved Prakash Vatuk (1963)

Cheddi Jagan was born on Friday, March 22, 1918, at Plantation Port Mourant, Berbice, British Guiana (Guyana since May 26, 1966). His parents were taken to the colony as babies in 1901 by their mothers, indentured labourers ('bound coolies') from India – neither of their fathers accompanied them. The eldest of eleven children, Cheddi trained as a dentist in the US, between 1936 and 1943. He became engaged politically shortly after his return to the colony: first, as founder of a Marxist study group, the Political Affairs Committee (PAC), in late 1946; as a legislator from late 1947 (aged twenty-nine); then founder, in January 1950, of the first major political party in the colony, the People's Progressive Party (PPP). He was one of the leaders of the short-lived multiracial government of 1953 (the other was Forbes Burnham, the foremost African in the party), which was suspended by the British, after 133 days, fearing it was driven by communist goals, irreconcilable with the Waddington Constitution and a gradualist approach to responsible government. Jagan was re-elected in 1957 and in 1961 because of the overwhelming support of the larger Indian segment of the electorate, comprising Hindus (the majority), Muslims, and Christians – descendants of indentured labourers from India taken to the colony to work on the sugar plantations after the end of slavery. His defeat, in December 1964, was engineered through the instrumentality of President John F. Kennedy. He exerted relentless pressure on the British prime minister, Harold Macmillan, to effect a change of the electoral system from first-past-the-post to proportional representation (PR), specifically to oust the communist Jagan from power before independence was granted by the British.[1]

Humiliated by the Bay of Pigs debacle of April 1961 (the American invasion to overthrow Fidel Castro), Kennedy was tormented by the distinct possibility that Jagan would establish 'another Cuba' in the Hemisphere if the British gave him independence in 1962, as was virtually assured. The Americans, therefore, were totally responsible for the election (by virtue of a coalition), in December 1964, of Forbes Burnham (1923–85), the African leader in Guyana.[2] Kennedy was fully aware that Jagan's hold on the imminently decisive Indian electorate was unassailable. Burnham's subsequent flagrant rigging of elections – in 1968, 1973, 1980, and 1985 (the latter by Burnham's successor, Desmond Hoyte) – initially with the complicity of his American sponsors seduced by his orchestrated anti-communism was deemed imperative (and utterly defensible) to arrest the virtual inevitability of Indian political and economic ascendancy.

Rigging was regarded as sacrosanct to the racial security of Africans, who were imbued with the conviction that the legacy of their enslaved ancestors (over two centuries) entitled them to priority in governing the country. Jagan's Indian supporters were effectively disenfranchised, as he became mired in a sterile, unreconstructed pro-Moscow communist vision. Burnham himself would affect an affinity for Marxism, in 1975–76, thus effectively stealing Jagan's thunder and compounding his rudderlessness. But Cheddi's 'Made in Russia' brand was decidedly unpalatable to the US, as it was to all the governments in the Anglophone Caribbean (CARICOM), unwaveringly anti-communist save for the Maurice Bishop aberration – unelected – in Grenada between 1979 and 1983. Burnham's routine rigging of elections would be accommodated – indeed, conspicuously overlooked – by his 'brothers' in the region, as well as by governments in the West, notably the US.

Yet through all these dark years, Indian support for Cheddi Jagan never faltered, thus confounding the fact that virtually entire Indian villages were on the move, migrating (legally or illegally) to the capitalist world: Canada, the US, England, Suriname (then to Holland), Trinidad, and other islands in the Caribbean – anywhere that would take them. This was ironic on two counts: they were passionately drawn to precisely the lands of the 'imperialists' that Jagan viscerally despised; moreover, the Indians who fled, as well as those who stayed, rarely deserted Jagan. Yet at the end of the Cold War, and primarily because of the intervention of Jimmy Carter, free elections were held in October 1992, the first such exercise since December 1964. Thirty-nine years after the PPP was first elected, in April 1953, Jagan became president of Guyana, a post he held until his death on March 6, 1997. For fifty years he had monopolised Indo-Guyanese political empathy, deeply flawed though his communist political philosophy, his tactics, and strategy in the context of the Cold War. He has no parallel in the political history of the Indian diaspora – eclipsing even the eminent Sir Seewoosagur Ramgoolam (1900–1985) of Mauritius by virtue of his all-consuming antagonism to American and British imperialism, and the intensity of their concerted machinations in subverting his political career because of his communist creed. His ideological indefatigability and political longevity apart, most would concur that he was incorruptible: he did not steal; he did not abandon his Marxist creed although the cost of his resolve was political suicide. Even the ignominious collapse of his glorious ideological beacon, the Soviet Union, did not diminish his certainty that 'scientific socialism' or communism – often camouflaged by the ambiguous 'socialism' – was still the most perfect instrument for the ultimate liberation of humankind.

I.   The Need for El Dorado

What manner of man was this? What was the source of his uncompromising Marxist creed? To comprehend his passion and inflexibility, on one hand, and Indo-Guyanese unfaltering loyalty, on the other, requires an exploration of the nature of the Guyanese landscape: its peculiar sugar plantation culture; Jagan's own experience of plantation life, colonial society generally; in addition to the perennial Guyanese albatross: ethnic insecurity. To assess his failure, one must explore his Marxist approach to the race question, or lack thereof: his inability to reach Africans, to allay their insecurities. This was exacerbated by the Cold War and America's paranoia regarding the rise of a 'second Cuba' in the Hemisphere.

The late Jamaican novelist, John Hearne (1926–94), sees a link between landscape and the shaping of a people's temperament: '[W]e must never underestimate the significance of landscape on our lives and perceptions. Like the first stories of childhood, it fashions us in a thousand secret ways.'[3] As the

Venn Commission of 1949 reminded Guyanese, the reclamation of their narrow coastland where over 90 per cent of the population lives was achieved only after astounding hydrological inventiveness: '[E]very square mile of cane cultivation involves the provision of 49 miles of drainage canals and ditches and 16 miles of high-level waterways. If these figures are raised to cover the whole area under cane the sum approaches 5,000 miles.' They dramatised the monumental effort expended making this surreal landscape: one hundred million tons of stiff, heavy clay were dug manually by enslaved Africans.[4] The maintenance of this complex system of drainage and irrigation (the two are inseparable) demanded eternal vigilance, at great cost. No El Dorado, this strip of land on the north-eastern shoulder of South America!

The environmentally inhospitable coastland of British Guiana gave slavery its peculiar brutality, culminating in the Berbice Slave Rebellion of 1763 and the Demerara Rebellion of 1823, which hastened the end of the inhuman system. The unforgiving land had bred pessimism among early African farmers after the euphoria of the 1840s–50s, when they spent over $1 million acquiring land. Despair, fed by alternating floods and droughts and the absence of a comprehensive drainage and irrigation system, perpetuated the dark memories of slavery and aggravated bitterness towards the plantocracy, who bent the colony to their Procrustean mould. Only the large plantations had the resources to remake the land and maintain it, in order to grow sugar cane. Their 'empoldered' or reclaimed land stood in stark contrast to the vulnerable African and Indian villages on its periphery, lacking the complex hydraulic system to cope with the inescapable floods and droughts. The modern sugar plantation, necessarily under corporate ownership, thereby could never elude the inevitable stain of slavery and indentureship. In Trinidad, however, where the land demanded no exorbitant hydraulic works, African and Indian small farmers became cane-growers – partners in sugar. By the 1920s, 44 per cent of the cane was produced by them. In British Guiana, 95 per cent of the cane was grown on large plantations. By the late 1930s, one British company, Booker, owned most of these. Consequently, the plantation was imprisoned by its malevolent 'otherness,' the focus of Guyanese antipathy.[5] But antipathy towards the plantocracy never did eradicate mutual racial insecurities among the subordinate groups: first, African resentment of Portuguese commercialism; then the entrenched – and arguably ineradicable – African-Indian incomprehension. The starker economic vagaries in Guyana aggravated these insecurities, hardening the stereotypes, towards the end of Empire when the devolution of power became contentious and fiercely contested. Indeed, it is plausible that slavery notwithstanding, African Guyanese had ultimately arrived at a less antagonistic posture towards

'King Sugar' because, unlike Indo-Guyanese, they were substantially less engaged in plantation labour by the 1940s–50s. Africans tended to be employed as skilled workers, technicians in the sugar factories, or as employees of Booker commercial enterprises in Georgetown. Most of the minority of Africans in the sugar industry, therefore, were on a higher economic and social plane than the predominantly Indian field workers. 'Bitter sugar' was not a plausible mantra to them in post-War British Guiana.

Only the Dutch, with their peerless mastery of land reclamation, could have crafted this bewildering tapestry of drainage canals and fields of clean rectangles, veined with ordered drains, ditches, seawalls, and dams. This geometrical miracle spoke of Holland in the Tropics. The feat is truly astounding, for the Atlantic sits above the land while water from the rainforest of the backlands also is a perennial threat. Paradoxically, it was this hydrological wonder, with the storage of vast bodies of fresh water, that rendered the colony a haven for malarial mosquitoes. Guyana needed El Dorado; it lessened despair because it engendered visions of the conquest of the unimaginably remote rainforests of mesmeric vastness, watered by mighty rivers that, surely, must lead to mountains of gold. Regularly locating pockets of gold and diamond – always alluring tasters – kept the fantasy alive. The millennium is ever round the next bend. The inaccessibility of the interior, the paucity of roads or tracks, the hazards of navigating the big Amazonian rivers, impeded by waterfalls, heightened the fantasies and rendered the interior almost imaginary. Very few ever got there. It was ripe for the El Dorado myth; its ongoing inaccessibility perpetuated it.

The pork-knocker, the intrepid prospector and dreamer of his own El Dorado who animated the African Guyanese imagination, gave it special resonance, a motif of deliverance that fed the notion of this somewhat mythical space as an area of freedom – away from the coastland: its plantations with resilient images of enslavement; indentureship; villages of despair, the cemetery of many dreams. The Indian, a latecomer to the colony, was not claimed by the pork-knocker's yearnings. He rarely ventured into the interior, but he, too, could not transcend the uses of fantasy in sustaining effort on this capricious land. Fantasy – grandeur masking the commonplace, the ordinary, the lack of wealth, bar the recent 'Oil Dorado' – is a salient constituent of the temperament of all Guyanese. In Trinidad, the resources on the ground have been more impressive (a sugar industry with a major peasant component; oil and natural gas); the tone of political discourse markedly less grandiloquent – ideas more run-of-the-mill, somewhat boring.[6]

In October 1953, at the time of the suspension of the Constitution, Jock Campbell (1912–94), chairman of the Booker Company, the colossus of British Guiana, cautioned the Guyanese against millenarianism – the seductive appeal of the grandiose Marxist politics of Cheddi Jagan. He reasoned that it is a miracle life is at all possible on the hazardous coastland. And he sketched the context of Booker's predominance while counselling caution to avoid alienating foreign investment and reaping the whirlwind:

> British Guiana is a most imperfect place. But its imperfections are of nature – not Britain or Bauxite or Booker, who are doing their best in formidably difficult physical and economic conditions. The wonder is not that life in British Guiana is not Utopian, but that life and production can exist there at all. Its coastal belt lying below sea-level, a man-made environment reclaimed from the sea by great technical skills and at huge capital expense, fighting a perpetual battle against water, and for years against starvation prices for colonial produce – it is remarkable that inhabited British Guiana can support its ever-growing population at even the present standard of living, low as it is compared with more fortunate countries…Owing to its physical uniqueness there can be no alternative in British Guiana to large-scale planned agriculture. Destroy confidence, drive out capital and skills, and you leave nothing but swamps and starvation.[7]

II. The Roots of Jagan's 'Bitter Sugar' Mission and Its Limitations

Jagan rejected Campbell's claim that foreign capital was indispensable. As he wrote in early 1953, on the eve of the first general elections under universal adult suffrage, British Guiana did not need Booker, 'the sugar gods'; foreign capital was utterly expendable; it was necessarily a yoke of imperialism. Nationalisation was imperative for the winning of genuine freedom, he argued, in his evocatively titled pamphlet, *Bitter Sugar*:

> Booker is the symbol of British imperialism in B.G. [British Guiana]…It is represented in all phases of the economic life, so much so that B.G. is sometimes colloquially referred to as Booker's Guiana. It controls a greater part of the sugar estates, and has a dominant position in commerce…The workers are sweated and millions of dollars produced by them find their way into the pockets of 'sugar gods' in England...**As a socialist party** [Jagan's PPP: he meant communist], **nationalisation of the sugar industry, and indeed all major industries, is our objective.** In the interim, while we are still tied to British imperialism with limited constitutional powers, certain reforms have to be undertaken to break the back of imperialism… Join the fight against sugar imperialism [emphasis added].[8]

'Bitter Sugar' encapsulated Jagan's mission in politics: a veritable crusade against imperialism and its supporting cultural and philosophical underpinnings. As Jock Campbell explained to me frankly, several times (many years later) in the early 1990s, the allure of the Marxist utopianism of Cheddi was rooted in Guyanese antipathy to Booker's 'latifundism' (Jock's word):

> Anywhere else in the West Indies [Trinidad for instance] the sugar industry and business had nothing like the perceived power of Booker because the sugar industry had a lot of small cane farmers; they had a lot of people who diversified and fragmented it. In British Guiana Booker practically owned the colony; it was a state within the state. Barbadians ran the estates in Barbados whereas they were all absentee proprietors in Guyana, apart from the Brassingtons and Vieiras. Booker actually commanded a state within the state.[9]

Jagan's Marxist vision of human perfectibility simplified Guyana's problems, and it intersected with the millenarian El Dorado reflex, subliminal yet etched on the imagination of the diverse peoples of Guyana. This enabled Jagan to virtually theorise out of existence his country's ingrained racial aggregation of identity with its accompanying segmental insecurity. He postulated the inevitable primacy of class-consciousness over racial, religious, tribal, linguistic, or any other cultural or ethnic expression of identity – 'epiphenomena' that are, by virtue of his belief in historical materialism, inevitably supplanted in the struggle for working-class cohesion. 'Bitter Sugar' could be saddled with all the sins of the colony's historical pain, as Michael Swan, who met Jagan in Georgetown in 1955, observed:

> [Jagan] denies that the Colony's difficulties arise from the problems of its geography. This is an excuse invented by the imperialists to explain why they have not made greater success of the Colony. The difficulties are "man-made and made by alien control"...**Dr Jagan's answer is ruthlessly to destroy the power of "King Sugar". He was himself born and brought up on a sugar plantation** [Port Mourant]...**and his political principles are guided by a violent hatred of the sugar interests**...Generally a courteous and pleasant man in conversation, he will become excited, indignant and lose all powers of proper reasoning when the subject of sugar is discussed [emphasis added].[10]

However, Jagan's steadfast anti-Booker crusade unwittingly endowed his Marxist mission with indelible ethnic stains, an irrevocable flaw in this loosely integrated, 'half-baked' colony plagued by chronic ethnic insecurities. In 1911, 48 per cent of Indians lived on sugar plantations (most owned by Booker); by 1931, 46.8 per cent still resided there. In 1946, the year Jagan founded the Political Affairs Committee, 38 per cent of Indo-Guyanese were still resident there; in fact, Indians comprised 90 per cent of the population on sugar plantations.[11] The minority were predominantly White or light-coloured administrative or highly skilled technical staff; some were the socially lower overseers. The capacious homes of the Whites at the highest level, as well as the less pretentious ones of the overseers, were set apart from the insanitary 'logies' or generally derelict ranges of the Indian labourers. Very few Africans still lived on the plantations. Therefore, Jagan's 'bitter sugar' mission encapsulated a peculiarly Indian social and political sensibility, although Booker's 'latifundism' did have implications for all Guyanese.

Africans were disinclined to see Booker or the 'sugar gods' as the main source of their current oppression if a problem at all. Their real fear has been Indian ascendancy: long-standing, with robust roots feeding back into Emancipation and its aftermath – the contentious state-assisted system of indentureship from India that commenced in 1838 and lasted until 1917. Consequently, it is practically unimaginable that African Guyanese could renounce their conviction that the Indian is a pampered interloper, who vitiated their legacy earned by virtue of their enslavement for more than two hundred years. Indian indentureship pales in comparison with the interminable trauma inflicted by the latter. Moreover, the impressive rise of an Indo-Guyanese middle class, businessmen and professionals after the Second World War, exerted an unwholesome impression on the African sensibility – yet (ironically) 'bitter sugar' remained peripheral to the contemporary African Guyanese angst. Cheddi Jagan, his Marxism notwithstanding, encapsulates the perceived historical and contemporary African dispossession. This radical hero, of humble sugar plantation provenance yet embodying the Indo-Guyanese ascendancy, could arouse virtually no empathetic niche in the African Guyanese imagination.

Jagan's boyhood was shaped decisively on the sugar plantation with its uncompromising narratives of physical and mental oppression inflicted by the European bosses. His paternal and maternal grandmothers were taken to British Guiana in 1901 as indentured labourers when his father was two and his mother eighteen months. His grandmothers were allegedly separated from their grandfathers by the *arkatis*, the infamous recruiters in India. An 'uncle' apparently accompanied his paternal grandmother to British Guiana. His parents became child-labourers: his father at Albion, one of Jock Campbell's family's estates; his mother at Port Mourant, where Cheddi, the eldest of eleven children, was born on March 22, 1918, and grew up. His people originated in Basti District, in eastern Uttar Pradesh, and were of Kurmi caste, one of the lower cultivating shudra castes (designated as one of the Other Backward Classes [OBC]). He has remarked that there was no rebel like him in his family tree.[12] What made this extraordinary rebel in British Guiana? What were the limitations of his rebellion?

Jagan saw nothing remarkable in his caste provenance, neither did he enquire beyond the bare facts retrieved from the ships' registers regarding his antecedence. Yet colonial officials in the United Provinces (today's Uttar Pradesh) were effusive in commending the agricultural proficiency of Kurmis, although most were immemorially landless and ritually despised by the higher castes. These officials were impressed with the Kurmi's versatility: thrift, refined husbandry (especially the meticulous farming methods of the women), consistency of effort, and their ingenuity in utilising several occupational niches simultaneously. In 1897, four years before Cheddi's people left India for British Guiana, an agricultural expert observed of Kurmi women:

> Among a large section of the cultivating tribes [castes] the women freely assist the men in field labour; in fact, the effectiveness in husbandry may be to a large extent measured by the degree to which this is the case. You will constantly see the wife of the Kurmi or Jat sowing the seed grain as her husband ploughs, weeding or assisting in irrigation by distributing the water from one little patch to another, if she does not take a more active share in the work by helping to empty the well-bucket or raising the water-lift.[13]

A more recent source expressed similar sentiments on the Kurmi's attitude to money and the land, in Basti (eastern UP), the home district of Cheddi's grandmothers:

> Most moneylenders amongst the tenantry are Kurmis. It is reported from one registration office in the Basti district, where the Kurmis are particularly strong in number, that of the total sum which passes from lender to borrower in a certain tahsil (sub-district), the Kurmi contributes a full half. Generally, his own indebtedness is small, and he has money to put by at the end of the year…The Kurmi is always planting whether his crop lives or dies.[14]

Kurmis winnowing padi (unhusked rice) in Uttar Pradesh (UP), 1916. They are a lower caste of enterprising and thrifty peasants, from which Cheddi Jagan's family originated. They were from Basti District, in eastern UP.

These were some of the principal qualities Cheddi's grandmothers and his parents cultivated in the new land. Janet Jagan gives a sketch of Bachaoni (Cheddi's mom), in a story she wrote for her grandchildren: 'When Grandpa Cheddi was a Boy.' She clearly inherited the strength of character exhibited by many Kurmi women in Basti in the late nineteenth century.

Janet recalls:

> Great grandmother, Bachaoni, was very small, very quiet, except when one of her children was bad; then she would talk to them hard. They learned early that size isn't what counts, and they all behaved well and listened to her. Life wasn't easy for her. She had eleven children, six boys and five girls, and brought them all up to be strong, healthy and hard-working...Grandpa Cheddi had to help in the kitchen garden, weeding and watering the plants. When there was enough for market, he used to go with great grandmother Bachaoni and sell the greens and fruits at the Port Mourant market.[15]

And Cheddi recalled for me succinctly, in 1992, the formative influence of his mother, Bachaoni: 'She taught me the rudiments of finance, of thrift, of how to get along and make do, to survive.' But he had explained earlier, in his memoirs of 1966, how that abstemious boyhood on the sugar plantation shaped his life and his partiality for the underdog:

> At [Plantation] Port Mourant, poverty was intense – I didn't wear shoes until I was about twelve. From an early age I had to undertake various jobs to supplement the family income. As the combined income of my parents from work in the fields was inadequate even to meet the barest necessities of life, our family diet was not only always very simple and modest but also monotonous...I often had to take time off school to work in the rice fields at both planting and harvest, and on Saturdays to go and help my father cut and fetch canes. Cutting grass for our cows, helping with the kitchen garden and at times even selling produce from the latter in the open-air plantation market, became part of my routine. My mother had been clever enough to give me a kind of incentive bonus; she allotted to me part of the kitchen garden, and anything produced there was mine... From my mother I learnt the elements of finance. While my father was bold and flamboyant, my mother tackled the more mundane and difficult task of balancing the family budget. These experiences were to stand me in good stead in later life.[16]

And like Cheddi's imaginatively frugal Kurmi ancestors of eastern Uttar Pradesh, his father's earnings as a 'driver,' a field foreman at Port Mourant, were supplemented by rice cultivation, a few heads of cattle, and the produce of their kitchen garden. It was from his 'bold and flamboyant' father that Cheddi acquired his leadership qualities. Jagan (1899–1960) rose from the ranks of a menial cane cutter at the age of fourteen to a 'driver' or field foreman, on merit. Cheddi said his dad was a good cane cutter, a strong man, and an even-handed

Jagan (1899–1960), Cheddi's father. He was taken to British Guiana as a baby by his mother in 1901 (unaccompanied by his father); she was indentured to Plantation Port Mourant in Berbice, where Cheddi was born on March 22, 1918.

'driver,' but he had reached the summit of his mobility on the plantation. The next step up, as an overseer, was reserved for White or very light 'coloured' men. Consequently, he was determined that his son's ambition must not be similarly thwarted. Cheddi was proud of his father's vision: 'He sacrificed everything to give me an education; he realised the value of education. If you want to get out of the estate [the sugar plantation], you had to be educated, so he sacrificed everything to give me a high school education, to go to Queen's College [in Georgetown, in 1933–35], and then later on, to give me enough money to go abroad [to America, in 1936] – a small amount but to him it was a lot of money.'[17]

There is much here to suggest Kurmi pedigree in Cheddi's own predilection for hard work; a sincerity of purpose that was repelled by graft or any form of self-aggrandisement; in addition to circumspection regarding money, an amazing frugality, even when it involved his personal access to state funds while in office. The abstemious boyhood planted in him revulsion to extravagance, the trappings of high life, which most people in power take for granted. He was incapable of stealing or squandering public resources. He was essentially Gandhian in this respect.

As far as I know, he was not a drinker or smoker; neither did he dress extravagantly in the slightest; he was disinclined to entertain; he never flew business class and was known to have taken circuitous routes to save on airfare (as David Dabydeen elaborated for me), even after he became president of Guyana in 1992. But the spartan upbringing also imbued Cheddi with a conception of learning that was ineluctably utilitarian. It bred a propensity for formulaic thinking that limited the imagination – learning was received and internalised uncritically, rather than apprehended eclectically and argumentatively. On the contrary, eclecticism, in his Marxist frame of reference, connoted sloppiness of thought: a paucity of theoretical rigour and doctrinal clarity.

On the other hand, providing his doctrinal mould was in place, Jagan felt infallible in proclaiming the universal truth that inspired his political mission – the building of communism in pursuit of the perfectibility of humankind. He was therefore not encumbered by the perils of original thought, critical engagement with conflicting ideas (often inchoate and in flux), hence the imperative to compromise – to rethink, reassess, and modify one's stated position strategically. So, paradoxically, Jagan's Marxist illumination in the mid-1940s emerged from essentially conservative promptings: an instinctual disinclination to compromise; to give and take; to tactically reassess and reformulate in the heat of political vicissitudes – the fundamentals of statesmanship.

This would prove to be Jagan's Achilles' heels: his doctrinal purity that precluded ideological and political flexibility. He would listen to his critics in a civilised manner, yet he was preternaturally incapable of meeting them halfway, including the best and brightest of long-standing in his party. This was the source of the periodic defection or desertion, over several decades, of virtually all his able lieutenants. And this debilitating ideological fixity of Cheddi's was not subject to modification or moderation because of the generally unquestioning fidelity of his Indo-Guyanese supporters: the grassroots and the elite. At home, as well as in their substantial diaspora in the capitalist West, Indo-Guyanese saw little or no flaw in Cheddi's Marxist strait-jacket of nearly five decades. They could not go beyond what they construed as the unimpeachable mission of progress and racial security of their basically honest and humble hero, however obstinate and misguided.

The humble abode of Cheddi's family at Plantation Port Mourant

Jagan's resolve as a politician was illimitable. The constraints on his father's ambition and mobility on the plantation had a lasting impact on young Cheddi. He attended the elite Queen's College, in Georgetown, from 1932 to 1935, but he had to return to Port Mourant for a year, having failed to procure a job in the colonial civil service because of 'a paucity of godfathers.' Such jobs often went to light-skinned, coloured people, with the right family connections. The 'coolie' from the plantation was not in this frame; for the rural Indian, the wall of prejudice, on racial and class premises, was virtually impenetrable. But on his own plantation, too, Port Mourant, he considered the manager, J. C. Gibson, an Englishman, 'czar, king, prosecutor and judge': an awesome figure. The paths to the planter's mansion and the workers' ranges (logies) did not intersect. This bred in Cheddi a consuming curiosity, later a compulsion, to penetrate and dismantle the world of the supreme 'other.'

He often recalled a powerful tale from his boyhood, six or seven years after the termination of Indian indentureship, as if it were the signature of his humiliation:

> I recall vividly my curiosity about the manager's mansion. I wanted to know what it felt like to be inside the gate. I wanted to know what was going on inside. I must have been about eight or nine years old [1926-27]. I joined the creole [child-labour] gang and went to share in the largesse of the manager. The manager's wife, Mrs [Isabella] Gibson, stood at the window of the top floor of this imposing mansion. She threw coins down to us and enjoyed seeing the wild scramble for the pennies. This is the way our manager's wife offered gifts to worker's children at Christmas time on a sugar plantation.[18]

Was this the seminal moment, fused in Cheddi's memory, that would trigger his passionate hatred of the 'sugar gods'? The image of Mrs Gibson tossing pennies to child-labourers in a frenzied scramble must have lodged in his imagination: the motif of his crusade against 'bitter sugar.' This, in conjunction with the impenetrable racial barrier that strangled his able father's aspirations on the plantation, nurtured the rebel in Jagan, to alleviate the lot of the underdog. Although his father was a field foreman, he had deftly straddled the universe of the predominantly Indian workers as well as that of the White overseers. He recalled that his dad 'never completely identified' with the authorities; he always sided with the workers 'in his own quiet way, without jeopardising his position.'

Cheddi told me that he acquired courage and resolve, in addition to a moral frame of reference of right and wrong and an aptitude for hard work and sacrifice, from his indomitable father, but he repudiated his passion for hard drinking completely. Cheddi was not a drinker, unlike Forbes Burnham who smoked, drank, and entertained lavishly: a very gregarious man! Not one for small talk or banter, Cheddi was even disinclined to entertain or be entertained. Besides, he was famously scrupulous with money: his, the PPP's, and the state's. Surely an enigma – even among his comrades! In this land of big drinkers and garrulous men (as in the Soviet Union), asceticism is not an asset. Cheddi never really acquired personal friends; he was not one for intimacy, although he was always polite, humble, and charming, unfailingly possessed of an infectious smile and genuine courtesy and humility.

But the immutable plantation hierarchy, and accompanying attitudes, left its mark on Cheddi. He tended to assess people by their class background (as he perceived it) – an ideological instinct that precluded a more nuanced appraisal of the merits or limitations of individuals: little room for give-and-take. It was categorical in its political assumptions, with a ruthless tendency to exclude if one did not measure up readily. Cheddi's built-in inflexibility was not conducive to forging alliances, neither was it propitious to exercising statesmanship. The latter is predicated on situational adaptability: adroitness of timing and foresight, even a capacity for tactical flexibility regarding fundamental principles. This explains why, within Jagan's own PPP, virtually all his able comrades, between the 1950s and the 1970s, found it impossible to work with him after they had dared to challenge some sacred precept or another, invariably defecting to another party, creating their own short-lived party or splinter group, or abandoning politics altogether for greener pastures in the capitalist world.

Cheddi's father's comparatively better social status later, as a 'driver' (field foreman) on the estate, did not strain his own relationship with less privileged boys at Port Mourant. He continued to play cricket with them, a robust bond between boys his age. His father's improved status, though stuck in the lower-middle stratum on the sugar plantation, gave him ambition – a sense of possibilities; at the same time, his dad's sustained empathy with workers' grievances (however muted) provided him with a durable moral compass. Cheddi was the first in his family to go to high school, at Port Mourant then the reputable Queen's College in Georgetown. He was probably the first from his plantation to attend the latter. The pressure to succeed would have been unrelenting. The financial burden on his family, the massive expectation on the plantation – with the accompanying fear of failure – filled him with an intense purpose.

There could be no deviations or distractions, no broader interests. He did not wander beyond the academically stilted colonial curriculum that was notoriously oblivious of the Guyanese environment, its history, and diverse culture. His education at Queen's College was about preparing for and passing the examination set in England – to get a good job, preferably a profession to escape the stifled horizons ascribed by plantation norms, and also to help his ten siblings do the same. His constricted, primarily utilitarian, educational frame of reference did not challenge the intellect into critical thinking; it did not provide the means of self-assessment. It could not have alleviated the insecurities of a 'coolie boy' from the backwoods of the Corentyne Coast in Berbice, bereft of a literary tradition and with little or no acquaintance with his people's history. Besides, thrust overnight, in 1933, from Port Mourant into an unfamiliar and intimidating social environment in Georgetown, Cheddi (aged fifteen) lacked social confidence because of his material insecurity, aggravated by his being uneasy with British colonial mores.

Moreover, in Georgetown, as a Kurmi (low agricultural caste) lodging in the home of a high caste ('twice-born') Kshatriya, Cheddi was quickly made to know his place. He had to sleep on the floor although there was a spare room with a bed in the house. When he moved to the home of another Hindu, his many chores before and after school included 'cutting grass for goats.' He hated it. This was the first time he had encountered the pernicious effect of the caste system. He 'deeply resented' such entrenched and debilitating Hindu ascription of hierarchy, and he 'rebelled against it in many ways.'[20] Cheddi's mother was a dedicated Hindu, but she was not a fastidious devotee. Rituals were performed in the home and at the temple, festivals celebrated communally, but there was no punctilious adherence to daily rites: the children could lapse and catch up when necessary. Yet **those seminal humiliations in Georgetown, at the hands of high caste Hindus, arguably alienated Cheddi from all religious precepts, for good.** It was the source, surely thereafter, of his estrangement from his Hindu-Indian frame of reference, rendering him signally depleted of any religious, and Indian cultural, mooring. A massive void had lodged in the young man's soul: he would never endeavour to retrieve or manifest a compensatory religious/cultural frame of reference. His Hinduism, if not rooted out, was vitiated irreparably; it would become purely instrumental – tendentious capital exploitable for his political mission.

Cheddi (Premier of British Guiana) and his mother, Bachaoni, Georgetown, 1961

Cheddi left Queen's College in 1935 with an Oxford and Cambridge School Certificate. He claimed he was 'relatively unscathed' by the experience. Not so. In fact, he had retreated into his schoolwork, totally unaware of the potentially enriching cultural and educational strands that were being threaded through the Indian community by a small, but vibrant, middle-class elite in Georgetown. I pointed out to Cheddi that during his sojourn in the city (1933–35), several Indian organisations were flourishing

Cheddi (back row, centre), with his mother, Bachaoni, and his ten siblings

there. I noted that the [Wesleyan] East Indian Young Men's Society, led by an Indian intellectual, Peter Ruhomon, was opened to all Indians whatever their religion. They debated cultural and political issues and were drawn to a resurgent India through literature on its ancient achievements, as well as to the contemporary Gandhian revolt against British rule, covered copiously by all local newspapers (at least four in the early 1930s). I referred also to the British Guiana East Indian Association, with a high profile since 1919 on local Indian matters, in addition to engaging continually with the nationalists in India. Cheddi replied casually that he was ignorant of any such activities, read no newspapers, and had little or no curiosity in the Indian nationalist campaign. He had no access to Indian history; he nurtured no inquisitiveness in the land of his ancestors. He was immersed in his prescribed school texts – nothing more! Anything beyond this could not reach him:

> There was no bridge at all, no association – I was just going to Queen's College to pass exams; there was no way to mobilise young people like me into that kind of stream. Things were happening, but at that stage my consciousness and awareness weren't developed.[21]

Cheddi was being certificated, and the utilitarian education was geared to that end exclusively. Martin Carter (1927–97), the poet and Jagan's young Marxist protégé in the late 1940s to early 1950s, tried to grasp what Cheddi's experience in Georgetown, in the mid-1930s, must have meant to him. He offered this to V.S. Naipaul (1932–2018), in 1991:

> The sheer area of experience was too much for a young man from a plantation background to deal with. We were even more remote than we are today from so-called metropolitan centres. You could imagine – "Martin Carter looks for a word" – the lostness of a young man in those days coming out of a background without a literary culture.[22]

This Georgetown 'lostness' imposed on Cheddi a narrow educational compass; it also impeded potential wellsprings of intellectual or cultural nutrient. It shut out whatever appeared to lack any readily perceived utility; it stunted the imagination, rendering it oblivious of intimations of potential Indian cultural and religious enrichment. Necessarily, it also precluded empathy with Africans, their cultural dynamics, aspirations, fears, and anxieties. This was magnified by the fact that Cheddi grew up at Plantation Port Mourant (on the lower Corentyne District in Berbice), which was almost exclusively Indian by the early twentieth century. Therefore, when he took his Marxist certainty to the political arena in the late 1940s, he did not possess the resources to apprehend how mortally afraid Africans were of Indian domination, which he himself would ironically come to embody by the mid-1950s, when the principal African leader, Forbes Burnham, split from Jagan and the PPP to form his own party. He would even alienate

Sydney King (Eusi Kwayana), arguably Jagan's closest disciple since 1947, engendering in him an Afrocentric antithesis to Jagan, whom he henceforth regarded not as a Marxist-Leninist primarily, but as the racial embodiment of Indian ascendancy over Africans.

The 'lostness' of Cheddi never dissipated. He did not acquire the rudiments of a literary culture (Western or Eastern). He was therefore unable to comprehend the complexities and the imponderables – the futility even – of the human condition that could have inculcated scepticism of dogmas as well as received certainties. Therefore, his rejection of Hinduism and its sacred texts was never really mediated or compensated by aspects of the Western intellectual tradition. And his rejection of Western imperialism, liberal democracy as a whole, meant that Marxism-Leninism – with the millenarianism at its core: virtually a secular religion – took the place of Hindu rituals and texts.

As Sydney King asserts, if Cheddi had absorbed a modicum of Hinduism, he might not have become so enchanted with Marxism-Leninism – uncritically. But it was a measure of the Guyanese futility that even Jagan's devotion to his communist creed, as the 'scientific' instrument to eradicate racism, did not wash with most Africans, including Kwayana after he left the PPP in late 1956. Cheddi and Janet's skills at *realpolitik*, mobilising Indian support virtually in its entirety, thus guaranteeing the PPP an unassailable majority under the first-past-the-post system, was recognised as a substantially more potent threat to African interests (encapsulated by Burnham's PNC) than Jagan's communist links to the Soviet Union and Castro's Cuba.

In October 1963, Sydney King responded to a letter by Janet Jagan in a foreign magazine, *Asian and African Review* (September 1963), in which she indicted him with fomenting 'partition' and 'racial division' in British Guiana:

> ...his racial spoutings became so offensive that even the PNC [Burnham's party] could tolerate it no longer, and he was eventually ousted from the party some years ago [July 1961]. Now without a party and without any substantial support, except for a few deluded Buxtonians [from his native village, Buxton], Sydney King seeks a political comeback. He is climbing on the bandwagon of race and the appeal to ignorance and emotionalism in the manner of all demagogues. Backing him up to this most disruptive of all devices is the pro-imperialist, anti-progressive United Force [of Peter D'Aguiar]. The UF sees in partition a further delay of Independence, a further splintering of the nation....[23]

King answered Janet with palpable acrimony – evidently there was nothing left of their robust comradeship of the late 1940s to early 1950s:

> Ever since Mrs Janet Jagan came to British Guiana, she began to appeal to the deep racial instincts of the East Indian population...I

state plainly that the PPP is an East Indian party in socialist dress, allied with Eastern European powers for the furtherance of the economic interests of the Indian people. All its election manifestoes since 1957 have been programmes of naked capitalism and nothing else. I speak this time not as a demagogue, but as a keen student of economics. The PPP is a capitalist East Indian party with foreign communist alliance...

Cheddi Jagan is a racialist who said that he could not join the West Indies Federation because 'almost 100% of the East Indians' in British Guiana were opposed to joining. This same Cheddi Jagan and his internationalist wife now want Guiana's Africans to consent to their rule. How very socialist and progressive![24]

King was also accused by Janet of 'party-hopping.' He took umbrage at this, alluding to her alleged marital infidelity frequently bandied about in the colony. Such was the degradation of the political culture – and the racial antipathy – spawned by the consuming African fear of permanent racial subjugation by Indians towards the end of Empire. No antidote has yet been found for the poisoning of the soul engendered by the racism and futility of Guyana's pre- and post-independence politics. King countered Janet:

Mrs Jagan speaks of party-hopping. I have done no more party-hopping than her husband. In my life I have belonged to two parties, the PPP and the PNC. I left the PPP [in 1956] when I saw that Indian racialism was its chief dynamic. Cheddi Jagan first came out [started] in the British Guiana Labour Party and left it [before the general elections of 1947] because he was not given a certain seat. Moreover, Mrs Jagan, there are worse hoppings than party-hopping. A mere party-hopper does not need to hide from the electorate and seek a seat in the Senate, but some hoppers I know [Janet did not contest the 1961 general elections] find this a very useful 'device.'[25]

It was not widely recognised at the time, but Forbes Burnham and the PNC did receive priceless ammunition from two sources with which they appeared to have had little active or concerted collaboration. The first was Peter D'Aguiar's United Force (UF), which was less agitated by permanent Indian dominance after independence than the PNC. In fact, D'Aguiar would have collaborated readily with any known Indian party likely to lead the colony to independence, even the PPP, were it not for Jagan's devotion to his communist creed. The UF was rabidly anti-communist, but they could not identify, even conceive of, a parallel extremism within the PNC of Forbes Burnham; henceforth, they were inclined to accommodate whatever variant of 'socialism' the latter espoused. The PNC, on the other hand, was not apprehensive of Jagan's communism primarily (if at all), but (like Sydney King) of his racial leadership of Indians on the threshold of British Guiana being granted independence. Besides, Burnham did not wish to be perceived as a dyed-in-the-wool anti-communist, although he did view with approbation that the UF was immersed in an anti-communist crusade, against Jagan, since late 1960, with the rise of Castro. The latter was congruent with America's hemispheric obsession, while simultaneously degrading Jagan's political capital in the contentious ideological context of the Cold War. No 'second Cuba' in the Hemisphere was the American mantra!

D'Aguiar's UF embraced that mission passionately, but the principal beneficiary was Burnham. Secondly, the fear of African domination by Indians was not articulated as vehemently by the PNC as would have been expected. This onerous undertaking, to persistently dramatise the perils of perceived Indian racism, required a measure of brazenness, and it was executed stridently and efficaciously by a single force – Sydney King – belonging to no political party yet rendering vital iconic racial solidarity with Burnham. He showed no circumspection in admonishing Jagan as a racist and the PPP as a racial party committed to Indian domination in an independent Guyana. Independence under Indian rule must therefore be averted, by partition if necessary, unless a multiracial coalition, sharing the power to govern, could be constitutionally forged. D'Aguiar and King played a decisive role (not adequately recognised) in consolidating the foundation that facilitated Burnham's anointment as America's non-communist man, chosen by US President Kennedy to lead British Guiana to independence. Burnham was, beyond doubt, massively indebted to D'Aguiar and King for his unanticipated political ascendancy in 1964. Of course, Burnham's biggest debt is to his communist foe, Cheddi Jagan, his racial counterpoint.

By and large, Indians lacked the political sensibility to go beyond Cheddi's 'bitter sugar' mantra. Few indeed could foresee the menacing implications of his communist creed in the context of the Cold War, in 'America's backyard.' They had no means of fathoming the consuming promptings of Peter D'Aguiar's anti-communist crusade and its potential for creating monumental trouble for Jagan. Burnham appreciated this to its core – D'Aguiar's anti-communist crusade was indispensable to his prime political objective: stopping the Indian juggernaut before independence. He would ride on D'Aguiar's coattails adroitly. Burnham also maximised the political capital emanating from Sydney King's candid espousal of African self-interest and his repudiation of the *bona fides* of Cheddi Jagan and his Indian devotees for national leadership. King did immeasurable service to his African race – unexampled in cultivating racial pride and self-belief, in adverse circumstances. And Burnham always appreciated the centrality of King's unique mission to his own political resurrection after 1961.

Naipaul argues that most Hindus in the Caribbean are not possessed of the means for critical thinking regarding their own religious and cultural inheritance specifically, unless they are (like himself) re-educated through a firm grounding in the prism of the Western intellectual tradition. Besides, he had, in his formative years, been exposed also to his family's Brahmin universe of prescribed texts and rituals, however inadequate an instrument for critical thinking and self-assessment. This initial orientation, too, was important to his intellectual grounding, even if he did not quite see it that way. However, Naipaul had to transcend his restricted Hindu provenance, with its ritualised certainties and aversion to inquisitiveness and exploration (because potentially subversive) to make sense of the wider world. Jagan and his Indian supporters – a minority in the region – were not appropriately primed to cope with the political complexities of the region and beyond.

There is much of relevance to this Indian inadequacy in what Naipaul says below. Despite (or because of) Cheddi's rejection of Hinduism, he could not 'penetrate' what amounted to 'darkness' in his immediate environment. Jagan's Marxist-Leninist creed was not an asset. It compounded his alienation without offering 'ideas of inquiry...the tools of scholarship':

> We were people of ritual and sacred texts. We also had our epics... we heard them constantly sung or chanted. But it couldn't be said we were a literary people. Our literature, our texts didn't commit us to an exploration of our world; rather, they were cultural markers, giving us a sense of the wholeness of our world, and the alienness of what lay outside...
>
> I had a better idea of Indian history and Indian art than my grandparents had. They had possessed rituals, epics, myth; their identity lay within that light; beyond that light there was darkness, which they won't have been able to penetrate. I didn't possess the rituals and the myths; I saw them at a distance. But I had in exchange been granted the ideas of inquiry and the tools of scholarship...I could carry four or five or six different cultural ideas in my head. I knew about my ancestry and my ancestral culture....[26]

Naipaul did possess a reasonable grasp of his Hindu-Indian antecedence which, however understated, enhanced his frame of reference, thus augmenting his self-belief. Cheddi admits to none of this 'self-knowledge,' curiosity, or inquisitiveness. This could have facilitated an approximation to Naipaul's critical and provocatively astute means of judging, allied to his acute analytical rigour (evident in the quote above). Colonial prejudice and injustice – the limitations of his colonial education and that of the plantation generally – left an indelible scar on Cheddi: a resilient inferiority complex. He felt he always had to hit out against those deemed to be oppressors or superior. He was never really at ease with anyone defined as an enemy, whether a capitalist, imperialist, or neo-colonialist. And even when the latter did seek to make credible overtures, to meet him halfway, he felt as if the passion that sustained his mission, to dismantle all instruments of oppression, would be impaired by the mildest compromising of his Marxist creed. One must never sup with the devil.

A charming man in many ways, he knew not how to win allies, and even with allies of long-standing, he could fall out purely on a doctrinal premise that he considered sacrosanct. The history of his PPP is a tale of continual falling out between him and his best 'comrades' – the interminable haemorrhaging of the best and brightest. In the end, by the 1980s–90s, Cheddi was left with a coterie of true believers, two or three decades younger than he and his wife: essentially a pro-Soviet communist sect. Yet most of his Indian supporters, at home and abroad (most of the latter doing very well under American and Canadian capitalism), rarely deserted him. Despite his obdurate devotion to Soviet communism, they were inclined to despise those who dared to challenge their flawless hero. Ved Prakash Vatuk (cited earlier) was right that they had made of Cheddi a 'mahatma' (a sage) and a veritable Nehru.

III.   The Making of a Rebel: Leaving Port Mourant for America – and Cheddi's Discovery of Janet

But Cheddi was no push-over, even as a young student. He always had the resolve to succeed; he could not let his parents down: so much was invested in him. He worked his way through his training as a dentist in America, at prestigious Northwestern University (founded in 1851 in Chicago) – yet not a likely context in which the intellectual lacuna could be redressed. Even the course he took in social science at YMCA College in Chicago, after he had graduated as a dentist, could not remedy it. But it did stimulate a lifelong compulsion – an enduring passion to change colonial Guyana and the world. Yet the earlier utilitarian mould was ineffaceable. Arguably, it reinforced his resolution for finding the correct, comprehensive answer for the wrongs of the world. Final solutions that would lift the underdog to the plain of ultimate freedom. The world is black and white – the oppressed in the unremitting struggle against the oppressor. Marxism-Leninism was the 'bible' that, for him, guaranteed the success of his mission to right all wrongs.

It is noteworthy that the seemingly somnolent colonial society that Jagan departed in 1936, for America, had started to stir. A discernibly rebellious spirit was taking shape. A trade union representing predominantly Indian sugar workers, founded by an Indo-Guyanese jeweller, Ayube Edun, would emerge in 1937. Labour troubles had engulfed the plantations of British Guiana in 1935, the year before Cheddi left to study dentistry in America. The avalanche of protest, fanned by abysmal sugar prices during the depression, hit Port

Mourant as well. J. C. Gibson was still the manager; he had held the post since 1908. Jock Campbell (the head of Booker) knew Gibson well. As a young man learning the ropes on their neighbouring family plantation, Curtis Campbell's Albion, Jock visited him often in 1932–33. He concurs with Cheddi that Gibson had an authoritarian temperament and adds that Mrs Gibson was 'a terrifying woman.' But he reveals another dimension of the man: though paternalistic and authoritarian, he was a most able administrator. He was 'a tough manager,' but he was 'a just man.' Unlike the Scottish managers who were predominant in British Guiana, primarily 'rough Highlanders' (as Jock put it), Gibson (though Scottish by ancestry) was brought up as an Englishman of some sophistication and empathy, in the rural south-east (very much like Jock in Kent). He was 'feared,' but the workers at Port Mourant respected him. Campbell respected him, too; he was 'a class ahead of the others.'[27] During his thirty-three years as manager of Port Mourant, Gibson helped to shape an independent persona among his workers; this, arguably, bred an inclination on the part of the latter to go beyond boundaries, social and economic. This, paradoxically, was an element in making Cheddi's subversive persona, his courage and resolve – his single-minded abhorrence of 'the sugar barons.'

Mrs Ivy Jailall, all her life a devotee of Cheddi, was born at Port Mourant in April 1924 (six years after Cheddi) and grew up there in the 1930s. She knew Cheddi's father well and remembers him as a compassionate man, who often horsed around with the kids. Impressively moustachioed, he possessed a remarkable presence: clearly a kind of charisma (not her word!). She also remembers J.C. Gibson – everybody of her age did. Auntie Ivy recalls vividly that he always allowed his workers to fish in the canals, collect firewood, gather wild vegetables, and myriad supplementary sources of sustenance on the estate. Besides, he provided them with water to irrigate their rice fields on the plantation. But he was very cross if they abandoned unwanted small fish on the dam, instead of returning them to the canals. She, too, thought he was a strict but 'just man,' who did assist his workers to improve their lives.[28]

Gibson made land available for workers on the estate to cultivate rice and rear cattle; housing was generally better than on other sugar plantations, many having built their own cottages with earnings from their supplementary farming activities. He had also constructed a narrow-gauge railway to transport workers to the canefields several miles in the backlands. He was a keen cricketer and promoted the game with discernible zeal on the plantation, having created a splendid ground with admirable facilities, the best in the district and beyond. As early as the 1920s, Port Mourant had a flourishing cricket club that was a formidable competitor in the county of Berbice, winning the Davson Cup about 50 per cent of the time (the symbol of cricket supremacy in Berbice since

1925), more than any other club. The people, inspired by Gibson's initiative and empathy, pursued the game with fervour and panache; many were already technically competent and versatile cricketers. Although under the general supervision of Gibson, the committee (comprising primarily mid-range Indian workers on the plantation) exerted considerable autonomy in running the club.[29]

It is not fortuitous that Port Mourant would yield several gifted West Indies Test cricketers from the late 1940s: John Trim (1915–60), Joe Solomon (1930–), Basil Butcher (1933–2019), Ivan Madray (1934–2009), Rohan Kanhai (1935–), and Alvin Kallicharran (1949–). The annual horseracing meeting at Port Mourant, on August 1 (Emancipation Day), had become a national event; the governor always travelled from Georgetown to open it. By the early 1930s, arguably the healthiest plantation in an infamously malarial colony, Port Mourant had shaped a markedly independent, confident, and courageous Indian worker. J.C. Gibson's contribution was paramount in this process. Jock Campbell elaborated for me:

> Port Mourant was a very, very well-run estate. [The people] were [physically] big, and they were healthy in that area because of the salt air [off the Atlantic]. There was no doubt about it, they were particularly healthy, and the malaria was less serious. I think I told you that when we started ['peasant'] cane farming in my day [late 1950s], the Port Mourant cane farmers were way ahead of any other workers in the industry – they were a marvellous people. The labour force was confident.[30]

This spirit of independence, in conjunction with the festering hurt, must have quickened whatever rebellious instincts had taken shape in Cheddi Jagan. His father's 'boldness' and 'humanity,' he told me, stayed with him, but his father's life spoke also of hope and its negation, as eloquently as the plantation evoked social and racial distances. As noted earlier, the older Jagan had elevated himself from a menial canecutter to 'driver' (field foreman), but he had hit the mobility ceiling purely because of his race, being Indian. This lodged in Cheddi's colonial mind, as did the fact that he was unable to get a job in the colonial service after he left Queen's College in 1935, for the same reason. But he did not have the intellectual acuity to comprehend his colonial environment and its limitations: the raw emotions were submerged; the shape of the hurt stubbornly incoherent; the passions blazing, but inarticulate. It was out of sheer frustration, but impelled by a burning ambition, that he left for Howard University (Washington, DC) in 1936, aged eighteen, to study dentistry. Naipaul, paraphrasing Martin Carter, reflects: 'Cheddi had no literary culture, nothing that would have helped him to see and understand, and put things in their place. He had simply taken things as they had come.'[31]

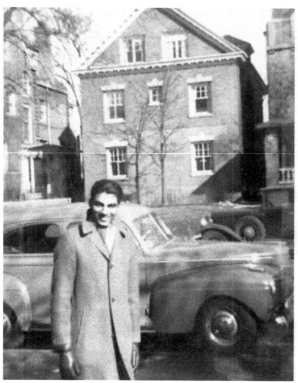

Cheddi Jagan, undergraduate at Howard University, Washington DC, late 1930s

But the passion, fed by the hurt in childhood, was resilient – the perceived gnawing injustice of the plantation and the wider colonial society. Jagan also possessed an intensity and a resolve that make for single-mindedness. He was not susceptible to despair. It is conceivable that he was animated by the raw emotions of the underdog and a lack of inhibition, an irrepressible energy and fortitude that, arguably, was a consequence of his not being overly circumspect. Besides, the comparatively progressive character of Port Mourant also endowed him with a vision of possibilities: ambition. The millenarian El Dorado reflex of the Guyanese psyche arguably bred an instinct for escape, flights of the imagination. It gave rise to the hyperbolic, a bravura persona – masks for fear and self-doubts rooted in the hazards of the land with its perennial vagaries and the incomprehension among its diverse peoples.

Cheddi carried a cardinal strand of Plantation Port Mourant to America, playing cricket in New York in the summers of 1937 and 1938

The literary void, the moderate capacity for self-assessment and critical evaluation, left Cheddi with little facility for analytical rigour, judging on merit – filtering things. The imagination and flexibility were not there, but the passion and sincerity of purpose never waned. The thinness of the former, in conjunction with the solidity of the latter, would sustain his political mission for over fifty years, including twenty-eight years in the political wilderness. He has no parallel in the Anglophone Caribbean and very few anywhere in the world. No matter how futile the situation, he never failed to convey the impression that he possessed the ultimate answer – that he was right; and that everything would be all right. His shortcomings were many, but he was a truly exceptional man.

His energy was astounding, even in his later years. The intensity of focus never slipped, neither did the effort. Indeed, the struggle to survive while he trained in dentistry in America, between 1936 and 1943, hardened it, but the narrow utilitarian thrust of his education was reinforced. He admired Gandhi and Nehru who sparked palpable pride in his Indian antecedence, but he was devoid of Indian culture. He had no Hinduism, no conception of, or feel for, the secular gifts of that ancient tradition: its poetry, art, architecture, music, philosophy – the rich cultural legacy of India, including its Islamic and Buddhist dimensions. He was just as bereft of Guyanese history and its diverse cultures: very little had been written even as late as the 1970s. In any case, he was not inclined to read beyond the strictly utilitarian, what was not prescribed by the curriculum. Therefore, he had no frame of reference to endeavour to make sense of things.

Cheddi became extremely ill in 1943, in Chicago, and was sent to a sanatorium to recuperate. The enforced solitude made him reflect on the limited intellectual horizons of his functional education. He decided to go part-time to Central YMCA College in Chicago. (This College existed between 1924 and 1945: 25 per cent of its twenty-five hundred students in 1944 were Black; one-third were Jews. It was superseded by Roosevelt University.) There, inspired by Professor Sinha, an Indian, Cheddi soon became interested in political science. He read on the American War of Independence. *Robber Barons* made him understand how American capitalism worked. He also read *Toward Freedom*, Nehru's autobiography; this made an immediate impression on him: empathy with the nationalist endeavour, in addition to the consuming sacrifice and intensity of purpose essential to the anti-colonial crusade. As Cheddi told Naipaul: 'Whatever I do, I do very intensely.' The social science course deepened that intensity. He was going beyond the mould of dentistry; he earnestly wanted to discover how 'capitalism worked,' but there was no room for eclecticism, for works of the imagination, for exploration of the complexity, the sheer elusiveness of human motives or individual motivation. Only a precise formula for comprehending the evils of capitalism would do because all problems have their source in the barbarism of the system. The conquest of capitalism was the key to eradicating all the ills of society.

That is why literature – the probing of deeper personal recesses, inquiry into complex human responses, frailties, self-deprecation, and a sense of the absurd – meant little to him. The world of the imagination, the intellectual probing into political nuances, the exploration of culture, religious complexities and their power to endure, did little for him. Cheddi was comfortable only with total knowledge; he had a passion for certainties, manuals: *How to Win Races; How to Play Bridge.* The urgencies, the Procrustean demands of a hard boyhood, the massive expectations and the fear of failure as a student, in Georgetown, Washington, and Chicago – he was the first child (of eleven); so much was invested in him – bred in him a narrow, rigid, utilitarian mental frame. It also gave him the drive, the sense of mission, the sincerity, and consistency of motives – the inflexibility, too. His Marxist creed would be his undoing, having staked everything on it by entering the Cold War on the side of the Soviet Union (and Cuba). He embraced it uncritically, with religious zeal, precisely because he perceived it as a science, the key to human transformation: the map to the perfectibility of humankind.

In 1943 Cheddi met and married Janet Rosenberg (1920–2009) in Chicago. She was a young Jewish American of East European ancestry. Janet's beauty ('love at first sight,' Cheddi recalls) and her initiating him into 'scientific socialism' struck a chord with him instantly. Like many young people during the depression of the 1930s, Janet was disillusioned with American capitalism. She possessed a rebellious streak; she became a communist, a member of the Young Communist League. But it is not clear how deep that calling was if, indeed, she did read any of the Marxist texts. Cheddi's course at Central YMCA College had given him a 'peep into socialism,' but, as he told Professor Frank Birbalsingh in October 1984, it was Janet who provided the seminal impetus to his lifelong political orientation:

> My wife Janet was a member of the Young Communist League in the US, and I was able, through her, to get Marxist-Leninist literature – Lenin's booklets and *Das Kapital.* The radical politics in which I was involved in the US began to gain clarity from these books, clarity from a working-class perspective.[32]

He would soon to be given the means of comprehending the world, having married this 'exceedingly beautiful woman.' Both the creed and Janet would augment his inchoate fortitude and confidence, giving shape to what became a lifelong mission against the 'sugar gods' and their allies in British Guiana: the plantocracy. He observed that on the sugar plantations 'intermarriage was strictly forbidden.'[33] He had already violated their code: his crusade against 'King Sugar' was about to be joined.

Cheddi spoke to me, in 1992, of the ideological awakening – and Janet – in equipping him for his war against the plantocracy: 'Marxist literature gave me a total understanding to fit everything together…Janet's influence was on the moral side: she was fed up with middle class emptiness…middle class American values, the consumerism, the whole emptiness of it.' One gets the impression

Cheddi and Janet Jagan on the day they were married in August 1943

that notwithstanding his passion, without his discovery of Janet and through her, Marxism – the acquisition of total knowledge – he would have remained just another ascendant Indian middle-class professional in British Guiana (like the Luckhoos), despite his visceral hatred of the 'sugar barons.' It is arguable, therefore, that Janet's political instinct, support, and her frequently acclaimed capacity for organising (the Achilles' heels of many organisations, political and otherwise, in British Guiana) transformed Cheddi's passion and sincerity of purpose for radical change into a credible and effective political project imbued with a mission – a veritable crusade.

A political partnership: Janet, a young, photogenic and gifted organiser, without whom Cheddi's mission could have floundered

He told me that Janet was the foremost reason why 'I did not betray my class; money was not my motivation or hers in politics.' He meant his working-class background. Besides, her generosity towards Cheddi's many siblings (ten of them) was a major factor in their professional success; and for this she earned the unstinting admiration of Cheddi's mother, Bachaoni, who often remarked that if Cheddi had married an Indian woman her other children would never have received the pivotal support Janet rendered unstintingly to them.[34] Janet's communist vision was shaped by the Communist Party of the USA (CPUSA); at the height of its influence in the 1930s–40s, it had a membership of seventy-five thousand. These were not only working-class or marginalised ethnic minorities but also people of Janet's middle-class background, motivated to want to change the world in the aftermath of the Great Depression.

Vivian Gornick has explained why the CPUSA made such a lasting impression on even young middle-class people, such as Janet, in the 1930s–40s:

> ...the educated middle class (teachers, scientists, writers) joined because for them the party was possessed of a moral authority that lent concrete shape to a sense of social injustice made urgent by the Great Depression and World War II...It is perhaps hard to understand now, but at that time, in this place, the Marxist vision of world solidarity as translated by the Communist Party induced in the most ordinary of men and women a sense of one's humanity that made life feel large: large and clarified. It was to this inner clarity that so many became not only attached but addicted. While under its influence, no reward of life, neither love nor fame nor wealth, could compete.[35]

Cheddi and Janet were married on Thursday, August 5, 1943, and he returned to British Guiana shortly thereafter. Janet joined him later that year, in December. She brought him some Marxist primers, which gave him 'total understanding of the world.' In 1991, Cheddi recalled for Naipaul, in a clean, rehearsed narrative, the illumination of nearly fifty years before:

> It was Janet who, when she came here in 1943, brought me Little Lenin Library books – little tracts, pamphlets. It was the first time I had read Marxist literature. And then – as with the bridge books – I began reading Marxist books like mad. I read *Das Kapital* after the Little Lenin series. And that helped me to have **a total understanding** of the development of society. Until then, all the

various struggles – Indians, blacks, the American people – had been disjointed experiences. To put it in a way that was **totally** related to a socio-economic system came from reading Marxist literature. For instance, **the woman question was dealt with in Engels's book, *The Origins of the Family*.** The Marxist theory of surplus value brought a *totally* new understanding of the struggle of the working class – not only that they were exploited. It was exciting to me, an intellectual excitement, because a whole new world opened to me, **a total understanding of the world** … [emphasis added].[36]

Many have argued that Cheddi became a Marxist while studying in America. This is not true. It was after he returned to British Guiana, in 1943, that Janet brought him those pamphlets from the Little Lenin Library, the source of his Marxist illumination. This literature gave him the 'total understanding' that would sustain him in his political mission of more than fifty years. In 1975, the twenty-fifth anniversary of the founding of the PPP, Cheddi recalled the lasting influence of Lenin on his politics:

I read avidly. Lenin's ideas began to shed light on the dark corners of my thinking. My experience on the sugar plantations in Guyana [in the late 1920s to early 1930s] and in the ghettoes of the USA [in the late 1930s to early 1940s] began to take on a new meaning. **The struggle of classes, I began to see with Lenin, was 'what lies at the bottom of events.' I began to relate politics, economics, race, and culture from the Leninist postulates that the economic structure formed the basis, the foundation upon which was built the political and ideological superstructure; that the political superstructure, in turn, exerted a reciprocal influence on the economic basis** [emphasis added].[37]

Cheddi was deeply impressed with the 'fundamental truths' that underpin Lenin's ideas, hence their power to remake societies all over the world. It was a seminal strand of his sustaining vision:

Lenin's ideas not only fired the blood of the exploited workers and peasants in the days of Czarist tyranny. They conditioned them for the sacrifice necessary for the building of the Soviet Socialist State. Above all, they have helped to liberate other areas of the world and to instil hope and create confidence in those remaining countries where colonialism, neo-colonialism, and imperialism still hold sway.[38]

Because Janet was a member of the Young Communist League in the US when she and Cheddi met in early 1943, there prevails a tendency to exaggerate her ideological impact on him. But it is true, as Cheddi acknowledged from time to time, that she did provide him with much of his early reading material on Marxism-Leninism – indisputably, she was a formative influence in his Marxist orientation. Yet, as is transparent in her voluminous journalistic writings for PPP publications (newspapers and booklets) over five decades, Janet was not inclined to theoretical rigour or doctrinal fastidiousness, nor did she wear her Marxism on her sleeve. Though a communist, she was remarkably non-ideological, as Martin Carter pointed out to Professor Frank Birbalsingh in December 1994:

Birbalsingh: What role has Mrs Jagan played in the life of the party and its leader?

Carter: It is wrong to suggest that Cheddi is controlled by his wife: that's not true. What is important is that she is a good organiser; she doesn't have a political bent [Martin probably meant she was not inclined to be overly ideological].

Birbalsingh: Assuming that Dr Jagan has the vision and Mrs Jagan the organisation, she might still be able to influence his vision.

Carter: Yes, but I still don't think that she had the influence that some people seem to think she had.[39]

David de Caires, too, does not see Janet as an ideologue, but he feels that Cheddi's political mission might not have been sustained, decade after decade, without her exceptional capacity to fix things – the quintessential coordinator:

> She kept the party together. She was the brilliant organiser and indispensable companion. He was the charismatic leader and, to some extent, ideologue. 'She was the gutsy party worker doing what had to be done: making the arrangements, keeping things in shape, paying the bills, keeping the shop going. I see her as having played an absolutely vital role in his career.'[40]

IV. Theoretical Fantasy and the Erasure of Ethnic Identity

Yet there is no evidence that Janet ever repudiated, or even mollified, Cheddi's lifelong, and profoundly contentious, devotion to his pro-Moscow brand of communism. Cheddi told Naipaul: 'There has always been a division between Janet and me. At the end of the day, she can drop everything and read a novel. I take my work home.' He could never see the lighter side: 'Whatever I do, I do very intensely.'[41] An anti-colonial reflex laid dormant in him for several years; it ignited towards the end of the 1940s. Deeply rooted in 'bitter sugar,' it was marked by a fixity of thought and a predilection for rejecting virtually everything that sprang from the colonial encounter – the necessarily tainted legacy of the imperialists, as he perceived it.

Marxism gave him the illusion of 'total' knowledge; its formulaic construction was accepted unreservedly as the science of human development – the road to perfectibility. What is knowable was now known. He did not have to be lumbered with the perils, anxieties, or uncertainties of creative thinking. He could virtually by-pass the vagaries of intellectual inquiry. Janet, on the other hand, because of her firmer grounding, her home-grown radicalism, an authentic component of the American youth culture of the late 1930s, and her exposure to a more rounded, eclectic intellectual milieu, did not have to wear her Marxism on her sleeve. It was there and would become a pillar of their anti-colonial crusade, but it was invariably understated, less dogmatic: allusive yet firm. She could read novels and appreciate diverse sensations beyond Cheddi's austere Marxist mould, with its pretensions to 'scientific' validity.

Brindley Benn, one of Jagan's few confidants until he, too, quit the PPP in 1965 (the two others being Janet and Ramkarran, himself estranged from them at one point), has remarked on the stubbornness of Jagan. I think he meant that although Jagan often canvassed diverse opinions, his *modus operandi* in decision-making was invariably indecisive – stymied – because he was disinclined to depart from sacred assumptions rooted in his immutable Marxist creed. This must have been unbearably agonising for him when in office from 1957 to 1964, as Governor Sir Ralph Grey noted time and again. It is most likely that Jagan was in a state of perpetual perplexity, endeavouring to square the Marxist circle while accommodating the *realpolitik* of governance in a British colony, in the context of the Cold War. This is how Brindley Benn, based on solid experience, assessed it:

> Cheddi had a way of examining every aspect of an issue in great detail. He would agonise over things sometimes until you became impatient with him. That doesn't mean that he was easily influenced. He had to be convinced. That's why Janet's influence on him is no more or less than that between any husband and wife. They were soul mates in the sense that they had similar beliefs and aspirations [Marxism/Leninism]. It is unfair to suggest that she was some kind of evil genius who corrupted her innocent but good husband. Besides… he could be very stubborn.[42]

Fortified by the 'total understanding' received from Marxism-Leninism, Cheddi calculated the 'degree of exploitation' or 'the rate of surplus value' of sugar workers at 142 per cent. He argued that in a ten-hour day the worker's remuneration (wage) was, in fact, covered by four hours of work, the sale of his labour power; the other six hours constituted 'surplus value,' profit extracted by the 'sugar gods': exploitation.[43] As early as 1946 (at the dawn of his mission), he asserted that the capitalist was superfluous to production; only the root-and-branch dismantling of capitalism and the building of the communist society could bring genuine freedom to the working class: 'All these parasitic exploiters are sharing among themselves…the surplus labour value created in production by the wage-earning working class. Only with the complete elimination of the capitalist mode of production and distribution, and its consequent surplus value and the substitution of socialistic means of production and distribution will this exploitation cease.'[44] He would never deviate from this basic mantra – the source of his indecision and his stubbornness. Dr Fenton Ramsahoye (Jagan's attorney general, 1961–64), alluding to himself and Balram Singh Rai (also in Jagan's cabinet in the early 1960s), told me that Jagan was always sceptical, if not dismissive, of any counsel emanating from 'capitalist roaders,' no matter how reasoned or persuasive. He concluded: 'He was a man of faith. Marxism was like a religion to Cheddi Jagan.'

In 1948, Cheddi identified the new 'People's Government' in Czechoslovakia, headed by the Communist Party, as a model eminently worthy of emulation for eradicating 'bitter sugar' in Guyana. He deemed it a 'new and genuine democracy' and was repelled by its being characterised as totalitarian. Apparently, they were in the process of redistributing land to the peasantry; no one could own more than 125 acres. Jagan could therefore envisage the demise of the 'sugar gods' in a similar kind of communist state.[45] He could not visualise the potential hazards of small farmers embarking on the cultivation of sugar cane in a hydrologically challenging environment, certainly the most daunting in the region – necessitating maintenance of a costly and complex drainage and irrigation infrastructure.

It is not widely known that in 1958 and 1960 Jock Campbell, the chairman of Booker, did seek (informally) to meet Jagan halfway. He proposed to him, personally, the option of the state, trade unions, and local interests owning 51 per cent of Booker, while the company would retain the rest and continue to manage the business. He listened, promised to consider the offer, but never responded. Joint ownership went against the grain of Marxist economic orthodoxy. His true position on the matter of joint ownership emerged much later, in 1972, as Leader of the Opposition. He was pressuring the Burnham regime to nationalise 'the commanding heights of the economy...foreign-owned and controlled mines, plantations, factories, banks, insurance and foreign trade.' The whole hog! Jagan argued that 'the erosion of imperialist strength and power universally had forced them to devise a new economic strategy, an aspect of their neo-colonialism – joint ownership.' He had no time for this ruse, the 'involvement of nationals and even governments as partners in imperialist companies as with Booker Stores, Demerara Company, etc...Local people are involved as shareholders, managers, and directors, who ultimately defend foreign rather than national interests and reinforce foreign domination. In Guyana, while the imperialists control the commanding heights of the economy...the government indulges in tokenism and state capitalism.'[46]

By 1975, Forbes Burnham had completed the nationalisation of the bauxite industry, given diplomatic recognition to Cuba (in 1972), and even claimed to have adopted Marxism-Leninism. (Jagan was the first leader in office, in the Western Hemisphere, to recognise Castro's Revolution, having visited him twice in 1960.) The wily Burnham had stolen Jagan's thunder. The PPP was in a quandary – rudderless – and forced into giving 'critical support' in 1975, allegedly at the behest of their Cuban comrades, to the fraudulently elected, therefore illegitimate, Burnham regime. Yet Cheddi was unrelenting in his resolve to pressure Burnham to nationalise the sugar industry and the few remaining private sectors of the economy, bar the small farmers and small locally owned commercial houses and stores. But the biggest prize would be the 'evil' (Jagan's term) Booker – the ultimate vindication of his creed:

> It must be noted that while the PNC has been forced to take some steps against imperialism, it does not have a consistent, firm anti-imperialist position. Witness that the Booker monopoly remains intact, and the PNC has declared its intention of working in partnership with it. The foreign banks and insurance companies still have a great influence in the field of finance and credit…Today many evils like the Booker monopoly still persist…[W]e do not see the attainment of socialism [communism] without first completing the anti-imperialist process by the nationalisation of the Booker monopoly, the banks and the insurance companies.[47]

Burnham nationalised Booker the following year (1976); soon 80 per cent of the economy was under the inexperienced and incompetent control of the Burnham state and clearly on the road to ruin. Yet the more Burnham was perceived to be moving to the left, to be embracing 'socialism,' the more Jagan felt that he had to demonstrate the authenticity, the purity, of his own Marxism. This was aggravated by Castro's conferring Cuba's highest national award on Forbes Burnham in April 1975 (the José Martí National Order). Consequently, as if to preserve his reputation among 'fraternal' communist parties, Jagan would continually assert the PPP's claim as the true bearer of the mantle of the Soviet Union and Cuba – the inheritors of the pure Marxist legacy, the only genuine communists in Guyana. He would become imprisoned by the absurd rhetoric, marooned in a sea of received jargon, while straining at the same time to justify his 'critical support' for Burnham's increasingly dictatorial regime.

V.   Pride in Building a Communist Party although a Racial One

On the twenty-fifth anniversary of the PPP, in 1975, Jagan counselled his communist comrades:

> As Marxists-Leninists we must be scientific and dialectical. This means taking an objective view, seeing things not on the basis of how we feel but how they really are [discoverable by the laws of scientific socialism]. This means not being dogmatic, rigid, or inflexible. If the situation demands it, then we must be fearless in changing our political line...Critical support [for Burnham] does not mean unconditional support. It means just what it says – giving support for any progressive measure, opposing any reactionary moves, and criticising all shortcomings...We are glad the PNC has been forced to swallow its anti-communist anti-Cuba sentiments and to advocate Marxism-Leninism.[48]

Ten years later, in August 1985, a couple days before the death of Forbes Burnham on August 6, the PPP Congress passed a resolution proclaiming their arrival in the 'promised land.' They were celebrating their being awarded the ultimate honour – recognition as a Communist Party by the 'fraternal' parties of the Soviet Union and its satellites – while proudly tracing their ascent to the pinnacle:

> [T]he Party decided in 1969 to commence a process of transformation from a loose, mass party into a disciplined Marxist-Leninist organisation, capable not only of widely disseminating Marxist-Leninist ideology but also of more effectively organising and uniting all working people in the struggle for a socialist Guyana...
>
> Since 1969 a series of steps have been taken to reorganise the Party's structure, promulgate a Programme, develop a disciplined core of cadres and membership imbued with the ideology of Marxism-Leninism, undeviatingly apply the principles of Marxism-Leninism to everyday problems, apply the principles of democratic centralism and criticism and self-criticism and such other principles as were necessary to achieve our objective. In this regard since our decision to transform the Party, our work on the ideological front of the class struggle has been strengthened in the fight against right and left deviationism...
>
> Our international work is based on proletarian internationalism... **We are generally recognised as and accorded the status of a communist party by all other fraternal parties** [in the Soviet bloc]...**The prestige of our Party both locally and internationally has never been higher. We can say with confidence at this 22nd Congress that our Party has been transformed into a Communist Party** [emphasis added].[49]

Their arrival did not lessen the obfuscation of the cascading dogmas. Though preposterous, it gave the leadership of the party – a sect of tightly-knit 'comrades' two or three decades younger than Cheddi and Janet – the satisfaction that they now possessed the truth that went to the heart of the creed: a philosophical superiority and moral irreproachability. No belated, bogus Burnhamite affectation of Marxism-Leninism! For many of these young Indian 'comrades' (they were overwhelmingly so), the impenetrable dogmas compensated for palpable intellectual limitations, including a modicum of theoretical rigour. Some facility with the Marxist vocabulary, therefore, did impress them as reflective of higher learning, possession of the universal truth. A kind of religious faith.

It is conceivable that the gravitas of the idioms of the creed had taken the place of Hindu mantras – a replication of the journey to Marxism-Leninism of their learned and infallible leader, Comrade Cheddi. This was augmented by rituals associated with Congresses; hosting delegates from 'fraternal' parties; paid guided tours to the USSR, GDR, Bulgaria, Cuba, or Mongolia (even the Gobi Desert, as Cheddi once told me), to witness socialism in action. They belonged to the chosen – a family of true believers. As the PPP proclaimed in 1977: 'Communism is the goal of all mankind. It represents peace, freedom, equality, brotherhood and plenty – material and spiritual…Under communism all class distinctions of society will be eliminated.'

There was a religiosity in the *modus operandi* of the PPP, discernible in Cheddi's repudiation of the 'eclectic,' 'opportunist' Marxism of the Working People's Alliance (WPA), the party of the late Dr Walter Rodney (1942–80), Eusi Kwayana (1925–), Rupert Roopnaraine (1943–), Clive Thomas (1938–), Andaiye (1942–2019), and Moses Bhagwan (1935–). The aim was to demonstrate the Marxist un-impeachability of the PPP over the ideological eclecticism of the WPA. It was nonsense, but the doctrinal tone – the received high-sounding vocabulary of the creed – would have impressed Cheddi's disciples, many tutored at the PPP's ideological school (Accabre College), where the pure communist learning was absorbed. Their chief mentor was the PPP's Marxist theoretician (1958–76), schooled initially in the pro-Moscow Communist Party of Great Britain (CPGB), Ranji Chandisingh (1930–2009). He had defined his pivotal educational role in the PPP thus: 'My task [in the PPP] is to help develop cadres with a communist outlook, loyal to Marxism-Leninism and the principles of proletarian internationalism [world revolution].' Marxist theoretician of the PPP, Chandisingh, converted to Marxism/Burnhamism and defected to the PNC in 1976, having vindicated Burnham's supposedly authentic Marxist credentials.

Preposterously, all three parties in Guyana were now vying for the true Marxist-Leninist mantle, hence the following gobbledygook from the PPP was paraded for them to appear cleverer than their ideologically flawed rivals:

> Marxist-Leninist science teaches that 'class dictatorship' exists in a bourgeois (capitalist), a transitional (petty bourgeois, bureaucratic and military strata), and a proletarian (working class) state. 'Dictatorship of the proletariat' is a specific form of state rule at a particular period in the revolutionary process, the transition period from capitalism to socialism. In essence, it is a higher type of democracy than bourgeois democracy (dictatorship of the minority capitalist class) since it has

replaced the rule of the minority capitalist class by the majority working class and its allies, the peasantry (farmers) and other non-proletarian strata of working people. This revolutionary process evolved, as in the Soviet Union, into a socialist democracy, a state of the whole people.[50]

This cascade of competing Marxist dogmas clogged the Guyanese mind, even those with no political allegiance. Yet barely a word about the debilitating racist instinct of most Guyanese! Meanwhile, Jagan's PPP was also engaged in earnest pursuit of 'bourgeois democracy,' continually and correctly impugning Burnham's PNC with rigging the general elections flagrantly, aided by the American imperialists. But interestingly, it was not from Cuba, the USSR, or the fraternal socialist countries of Eastern Europe (now Burnham's friends as well) that Jagan sought solidarity for some form of redress for free and fair 'bourgeois' elections, but the human and civil rights organisations in the lands of the 'imperialists' that he relentlessly disparaged.

Most Indians were oblivious of the theoretical and political morass in which the PPP was marooned, yet primarily for reasons of instinctual racial identification and security, their loyalty to Jagan was undiminished. Meanwhile, entire villages, with deep ancestral roots yet despairing of the Guyanese futility, were migrating with relative impunity to their perceived capitalist utopia, America and Canada. If Jagan was perturbed by the flight of a substantial segment of his flock to the heartlands of capitalism, it never showed. He did not desist from wallowing in the Marxist ideological nullity, deemed 'scientific' and endowed with the means to resolve even the monumental ethnic problem in Guyana. But by the 1980s, there were very few Africans left in his communist party. This was the most catastrophic aspect of Jagan's Marxist mission: one by one, virtually every African of note had quit the PPP, estranged by what they deemed its Indian bias, even racism, which alienated them from a movement ostensibly devoid of any racial predilection.

VI. Eusi Kwayana on African Apprehension of Indian Supremacy

Eusi Kwayana (formerly Sydney King), an African inclined towards Marxism, had been instrumental in garnering crucial African support for Cheddi Jagan, as early as the general elections of 1947; he was a highly valued confidant of the Jagans in the early 1950s. An austere, learned, and very political man, yet strangely indifferent to power and wealth, Kwayana came to embody African alienation from Jagan's predominantly Indian PPP. He explored for me, in 1992, the lacuna pertaining to Africans within Cheddi's mission:

There are these racial insecurities. The two major groups have certain conceptions of each other. Africans tended to see Indians not only as clannish but as having more money and having an interest in land. A lot of them were selling out their land [to Indians] when they went broke, and although they were doing it voluntarily, it also alarmed them. Then there was this rumour that someone from India had come and said that those who owned the land owned the country. You hear this up to now among older people…A lot of Africans were unable to go beyond that. **[A legacy of the idea of the creation of an Indian Colony in British Guiana in the 1920s: see chapter 3.]** And they would look at the behaviour of Indians near to them in judging the PPP. The PPP does not understand this until now. So, if there is an aggressive [racist] Indian member of the PPP in their district, Africans tended to see the PPP through him.

Kwayana makes another crucial point, posing a seminal problem that no one, layperson or scholar, has addressed publicly as far as I am aware:

Jagan never deals with these [ethnic] issues – he never does. Essentially, he has a lot of rage against imperialism, but at the subjective level the problem of African insecurity was never dealt with. This was one of the reasons why I left the PPP [in 1956] …The psychology of the leader is crucial. We had to fight to get Africans to accept an Indian leader. He didn't have that problem. He never had to accept a leader of another race. So, he doesn't know what it's like. He speaks about the problem of revolution, but there was no personal revolution – within himself – therefore, he could not deal with the problem of ethnicity. The theory was enough.[51]

It is conceivable, therefore, that the millenarianism (the El Dorado syndrome), a robust, if subliminal, strand in the Guyanese imagination, also, was instrumental in Cheddi's uncritical absorption of the Soviet creed. For him, the theory was infallible, offering 'a total understanding of the world,' with the promise of a virtual utopia. The question of racial insecurity, despite its bedevilling centrality to the Guyanese social and political reality, would be eliminated when the society, inevitably, embraced Marxism-Leninism. Everything would be all right under communism. It was science (after all), 'scientific socialism,' not a dogma or pseudo-science. As early as 1947 he had expressed his simplistic formula thus:

Labour [he meant a local short-lived 'party' of that name, of which he was a member briefly]…will have to solve the question of race. **This it can do by replacing the question of race by the one of class.** The rich and the poor of one particular race do not have the same interests. It is the poor and exploited of all races who have a common interest – that of improving working and living conditions [emphasis added].[52]

In fact, in early 1953, amidst the euphoria surrounding the tenuous multiracial alliance that was the People's Progressive Party of Cheddi Jagan and Forbes

Burnham, the assistant general secretary of the PPP, Eusi Kwayana (then Sydney King), had cautioned both that they should not contest more than eight seats in the general elections in April of that year. He feared that they would win the elections outright if they contested all the constituencies, and because the party – a tenuous coalition – was being superimposed on a still racially unconsolidated country, the deeply rooted racial insecurity among Africans and Indians would have negative reverberations within the party (with ominous implications for the smouldering Jagan-Burnham rivalry).

King's explication of the problem is the most revealing I have encountered about race and the much vaunted, but fragile, unity of 1953:

> I had moved in the PPP Executive that we should not win a majority. And my reason was the country was not sufficiently united. (I think only Martin Carter and I supported the motion)…We should not go for a majority; I knew we would win a majority, but I don't think the party was prepared for it. The racial unity was not there; it was a kind of coalition; it was not well-grounded – very tenuous, shallow foundations…After I went through the country, I told Jagan and Burnham: 'We will win this election.' They said maybe we will win eight seats. I said, perhaps, we should win about eight seats [one-third of those available]. And I moved a motion that we should fight about eight seats and try to do in a multiple of eight what Jagan alone was doing [as a legislator since 1947] – and really unite the country.[53]

King believes that the Indo-Guyanese triumphalist response to India's nationalist crusade had political ramifications locally – at variance with the African Guyanese and engendering palpable fear of their political emasculation – after the Second World War. This was exacerbated in the aftermath of India's independence in August 1947. Jagan was first elected to the legislature of British Guiana in December of that year. Kwayana recalls:

> I lived among very poor [African] people all my life. They were very political. But I knew they had a lot of ethnic suspicion although nobody wanted any racial confrontation; that was not there then, not mature enough…But **I knew** [also] **that they** [Africans] **did not have strong feelings against colonialism – no strong feelings against colonialism – or against Booker because of their monopoly or their treatment of people…Even the whole idea of rejecting Britain was not very firm.**

> Indians had it a lot firmer because of the Indian nationalist movement [led by Gandhi and Nehru]. They had a kind of ideological and cultural resentment against colonialism…[They were exposed to] people coming from India to lecture. Africans did not have this. The link [with the African homeland] was broken [emphasis added].[54]

Indians in Guyana had, indeed, arrived at a discernibly robust self-perception with Indian independence in 1947. It also sprang from Indian success with rice, cattle (generally), and elite advances in the esteemed professions of law, medicine, and commerce. Therefore, Jagan was sowing in an enriched soil, with his mission enhanced immeasurably by his 'bitter sugar' campaign and his perceived sincerity of purpose. It resonated powerfully with most Indians, including the middle class, by and large. This essentially eliminated overnight the older, more conservative, politicians of the British Guiana East Indian Association (such as Dr J. B. Singh), shaped profoundly by the consuming nationalist passions in India. But Jagan's formulaic Marxist thinking, fortified (paradoxically) by a buoyant Indian sense of possibilities and enhanced by the euphoria over India's independence, precluded his anticipation – even recognition – of the recrudescence of the deep-seated African fear of Indian domination.

Kwayana believes that the PPP, animated by its energised Indian majority base (decisive under the first-past-the-post electoral system), ignored the fundamental reality that the alleviation of African racial insecurity is indispensable to the making of a nation in Guyana. It was inescapable, worthy of priority over the obsessive Jaganite hankering after early independence. But hardly anyone had (or has) the courage and resolve to confront this unpalatable reality: a monumental long-term project. Indeed, to raise the question of racial insecurity in the party was 'to be divisive…to deviate from accepted policy,' although, as early as 1951, it was 'not absent from the life of the party.' On grounds of race and ideology, 'sections of the party had considered a change in leadership important.'

Kwayana explains further the basis of African fear of Jagan's leadership, and the context in which Burnham joined the PPP in 1950:

> The basic misgiving in the minds of the Afro-Guyanese working people was not the policy of Jagan as such, but their uncertainty of the linkages between him and the defensive Indo-Guyanese politicians and public figures of the day. He had been active in the B. G. East Indian Association. Secondly, many did not feel 'equally yoked' without a prominent Afro-Guyanese of equivalent social standing or status. Forbes Burnham, Guyana Scholar, returning from law studies in England [in 1949], fitted the bill…[He] had been head of the West Indian Students' Union in England at a time when it fought many liberation struggles, and came home with a reputation.

> His often-empty oratory held masses of people spellbound. Burnham's entry into the all but established PPP as its first Chairman [It is not clear that Jagan was, indeed, the leader.] sent waves of relief among Afro-Guyanese…[He] played a leading role in persuading the sections still omitted from the mass movement that a common agenda had arrived. A certain impatience with depth marked the campaigning of both leaders [in 1953] to whom an anti-colonial victory was more immediate than a consolidating of a deep non-racial understanding. The main area of education [by the PPP] should have been the racial

question and arrangements should have been made inside the party for power sharing.[55]

The PPP won the elections with eighteen of the twenty-four seats, but Kwayana's apprehensions were realised immediately. The delicate multiracial coalition of 1953 did not endure; it was already on the ropes months before the suspension of the Constitution in October 1953, as Burnham challenged Jagan's asserted claim to lead the newly elected government. Burnham quit the PPP in February 1955. The two race-based parties, the PPP (Jaganite) and PPP (Burnhamite), the latter renamed the People's National Congress in October 1957, became entrenched: leviathans of chronic ethnic disaggregation. Politics would degenerate into the racial carnage of the early 1960s, as Africans and Portuguese, aided and abetted by President Kennedy and the CIA, resorted to violence in 1962–63, to make the colony ungovernable under Jagan, to delay independence. Indians retaliated in 1964, after proportional representation (PR) was introduced following the intervention of President Kennedy, who pressured the Macmillan government forthrightly to ensure that the communist Jagan did not lead British Guiana to independence. African-Indian incomprehension was reinforced.

Yet Jagan never did tackle the race issue squarely; his treatment of it was in the abstract, precluded from clarity of exposition by his Marxist platitudes. In 1974, for instance, he wrote an article captioned 'Race, Class and Ideology' – he was still 'replacing' race with class, as he had counselled the transient local Labour Party in 1947. The intractable problem could be theorised into nullity by virtue of the infallibility of his creed, 'scientific socialism':

> What is the reality? Those who see only race in politics see only a part of the reality. The 'two monolithic racial blocs' idea, like the 'two super-powers' idea, interprets reality quantitatively, and not qualitatively. **Side by side with race, and more fundamental is class.** What is often forgotten is that the Indian and African racial groups in Guyana are not homogeneous, are not uni-class. At the bottom of each group, consisting the bulk, are workers and farmers; at the top, a small percentage of middle-class professionals and capitalists – mainly commercial and industrial capitalists (tied up in some cases with landlordism) in the case of Indians, and mainly bureaucratic-capitalists in the case of Africans…

> From a mass vanguard party…[the PPP] is being transformed into a Marxist-Leninist party. As a mass vanguard party of the working class, it recognises that apart from the working class, there are other classes and strata – the farmers, intellectuals, students and petty bourgeoisie – which can take an anti-imperialist position…[I]t will work assiduously for action against racism and state-monopoly capitalism.[56]

In February 1974, one of Cheddi's most loyal Marxist disciples and a confidant, Ramkarran (1919–90), the treasurer of the PPP for nearly forty years, explained to students at the University of Guyana how the race question would inevitably be resolved by the PPP's 'scientific ideology.' In fact, this was his master's voice:

> Though at a certain stage…[race] might be the dominant force in politics, this can only be a temporary phase. Eventually the economic base and the scientific laws of political economy will assert themselves; and the political situation will be transformed. For this transformation to take place and for it to be accelerated, there is the need for a vanguard party such as the PPP. At the ideological level it must put a scientific (Marxist-Leninist) ideology in place of an emotional and/or unscientific and utopian (cooperative socialist [a reference to Burnhamism]) ideology. It must pose an anti-imperialist, pro-socialist programme in place of the PNC's racist, anti-working class and pro-imperialist programme…Only by the attainment of working-class power and the complete transformation of the economic structure [nationalisation of the means of production] will racism and the influence of race in politics be finally brought to an end. This has happened in the Soviet Union and in Cuba. It will also happen in Guyana under the leadership of the PPP.[57]

'Guyana has always been a land of fantasy. It was the land of El Dorado,' says V. S. Naipaul. It is also a land where Indians have no knowledge of their real Indian antecedence – the reasons for leaving; the places whence their ancestors came; the tendentious, exaggeratedly constructed persona of the *arkatis*: the infamous recruiters in India, who allegedly tricked or kidnapped all the indentured labourers; the high incidence of women who went alone, unaccompanied by any relatives, to British Guiana – about two-thirds. It was a past of darkness in India; and a utilitarian forgetfulness – a collective amnesia – was instrumental in alleviating the pain and the agony of revisiting that past and its secrets, with the potential to subvert every inch of self-respect garnered in the new land. Ignorance persists about that past and always will, but the mythical India of the Hindu classic, the *Ramayana*, depicting a golden age in Lord Rama's kingdom of justice and plenitude – when there was no poverty, no disease – has filled that void in the Indo-Guyanese imagination. No memory of eastern Uttar Pradesh and western Bihar, their original homes in India (primarily), survives, although abundant primordial promptings of a cultural nature still resonate among them.

Fantasy, as I have argued, is at the heart of the Guyanese sensibility, and among Indo-Guyanese the received El Dorado reflex is augmented by the escapism offered by the *Ramayana*.[58] A millenarian strand has coiled itself inextricably in the Indo-Guyanese imagination. Cheddi's own lack of religious empathy and his Marxist utopianism, therefore, may not have been as incompatible with their 'instinctive, ritualised' lives, with the need for escapism, as it may appear. His fantasies belong. They would remain virtually inexhaustible to the end.

Indians in Guyana today continue to vote overwhelmingly for the PPP, as Africans do for the PNC, at periodic elections – ethnic censuses rather than an expression of the healthy vagaries of the democratic impulse. Parties that endeavour to transcend the racial mould soon disappear. Racial insecurity is virulent in this land of fantasy – a measure of its futility, a journey to nowhere. It is seventy-six years since Cheddi and Janet Jagan founded the Political Affairs Committee, on November 6, 1946, with the aim of 'establishing a disciplined and enlightened Party, equipped with the theory of scientific socialism [communism].' Yet hapless Guyana remains a land marked by racial bigotry, many of its people impoverished, lacking proper education – washed up – a vast amount of its best and brightest having fled into voluntary exile. Jagan's model of perfectibility – nationalisation of the commanding heights of the economy to counter the essential 'evil' of private capital – which he promulgated, with religious fervour, for nearly half a century, is now a handful of dust. Yet, by 1990 (with the collapse of the Soviet Union), Cheddi was miraculously transformed, arguing that 'foreign capital and certain methods of liberal capitalism...[did not] undermine the social gains of socialism.' Strangely, he was claiming affinity with the idea of a 'new partnership with foreign private capital, as the PPP has always advocated for Guyana [sic].'[59] Not true! He twice rejected, or ignored, Jock Campbell's bold initiative towards joint ownership of Booker, in 1958 and 1960.

In 1991, the year before the PPP was returned to government after nearly twenty-eight years in the wilderness, Cheddi told businessmen in Georgetown that his party rejected 'winner-takes-all politics...and intends to form a plural democratic government to tackle the tasks of reconstruction.'[60] Hitherto slightly endowed Guyana could not do without foreign capital, as Jock Campbell counselled in 1953. With the recent discovery of vast reserves of oil off the coast of the country, El Dorado is no longer a myth. But after fifty-seven years of freedom from British rule, Guyana is still not a nation. Therefore, this projected bonanza could, indeed, become a handful of dust unless Guyanese can summon the resolve and the imagination to erase their ingrained racist frame of reference with the ultimate aim, however protracted and tormented the project, of forging a nation and ensuring that the abundant wealth is not stolen or squandered, and that it is utilised wisely for the good of all its peoples. The legacy of Jaganism and Burnhamism is hollow, and the future is potentially calamitous without a wider conception of governance and the pursuit of a genuine commonweal.

I end this chapter with a judgment on Jagan's Marxist-Leninist mission by Moses Bhagwan, the former chairman of the PPP's youth arm, the Progressive Youth Organisation (PYO), 1962–65, and a PPP legislator. Like virtually every one of Jagan's disciples of the 1950s–60s, Bhagwan quit the PPP in 1965:

Dr Jagan was not very creative ideologically. But he persevered with his Marxist-Leninist approach believing that if he made the economy right and put poor people into jobs, he could eliminate poverty and all social problems. It is a point of view that I never shared because of the underlying ethnic problem which, I thought, had its own dynamic...In other words, the problem of race would persist in Guyana whether people were poor or rich.

It is a major failure of the PPP, in its early days, that it did not regard the Indian-African problem with due seriousness. I think Dr Jagan's greatest political contribution was made between 1943, when he returned from America, and 1953, when his first government was dismissed. From then, the impact of Jagan and Burnham, whether individually or jointly, has been negative.

...the PPP only gave up Communism at the end of the Cold War, after the collapse of the Soviet Union [around 1991]...They have always been on the wrong side of every fundamental issue.[61]

Yet, as Cheddi Jagan proudly proclaimed in 1975, the twenty-fifth anniversary of the founding of the PPP, he was confident they had made no mistakes in their pursuit of his communist vision:

The main burden of their attack is that we should not have openly espoused Marxism and given support to the Cuban Revolution. What they fail to note is that had we not taken a firm patriotic position, a worldview [Marxism-Leninism: communism] we would not have been able to win over the masses [presumably African Guyanese as well: a fantasy!] from the traitors and collaborators [Burnham's PNC, by then an ally of Fidel Castro and the Soviet Union].[62]

Notes

1. For an autobiographical sketch and his version of these events, see Cheddi Jagan, *The West on Trial: My Fight for Guyana's Freedom* (London: Michael Joseph, 1966).
2. There are two exceptionally fine academic texts, based on a substantial body of official sources, that address the subject of American and British subversion of Cheddi Jagan: Stephen G. Rabe, *US Intervention in British Guiana: A Cold War Story* (Chapel Hill, North Carolina: The University of North Carolina Press, 2005), and Colin Palmer, *Cheddi Jagan and the Politics of Power: British Guiana's Struggle for Independence* (Chapel Hill, North Carolina: The University of North Carolina Press, 2010). For an excellent collection of interviews with many of the participants in the post-War politics of Guyana, see Frank Birbalsingh, *The People's Progressive Party of Guyana, 1950–92: An Oral History* (London: Hansib, 2007). I have relied heavily on the latter. I have dealt with some of these events at length in my *Sweetening 'Bitter Sugar': Jock Campbell, the Booker Reformer in British Guiana, 1934–66* (Kingston, Jamaica: Ian Randle Publishers, 2005).
3. See John Hearne, 'What the Barbadian Means to Me,' *New World Quarterly* 3, nos. 1–2 (1966–67): 165.

4. *Report of the Commission of Inquiry into the Sugar Industry of British Guiana* (J.A.Venn, Chairman) (London: HMSO, 1949), 9.

5. This theme is developed in my article: Clem Seecharan, 'The Shaping of the Indo-Caribbean People: Guyana and Trinidad to the 1940s,' *Journal of Caribbean Studies* 14, nos. 1–2 (Fall 1999/Spring 2000): 61–92.

6. Ibid.

7. Jock Campbell to the Editor, the *New Statesman and Nation*, October 24, 1953.

8. Cheddi Jagan, *Bitter Sugar* (Georgetown: The author, n.d., [1953]).

9. Interview with Jock Campbell (Lord Campbell of Eskan; 1912–94), Nettlebed, Oxfordshire, May 9, 1990.

10. Michael Swan, *British Guiana: The Land of Six Peoples* (London: HMSO, 1957).

11. Seecharan, 'The Shaping of the Indo-Caribbean People,' 69.

12. C. Jagan, *The West on Trial*, 13–15.

13. William Crooke, *The North-Western Provinces of India: Their History, Ethnology and Administration* (Karachi: OUP, 1972 [1897]), 229–30.

14. E. A. H. Blunt, *The Caste System of Northern India with Special Reference to the United Provinces of Agra and Oudh* (London: OUP, 1931), 266.

15. This story is in Janet Jagan, *When Grandpa Cheddi was a Boy and Other Stories* (Leeds: Peepal Tree Press, 1999).

16. Jagan, *The West on Trial*, 22–23.

17. Interview with Cheddi Jagan, University of Warwick, Coventry, England, May 10, 1992.

18. C. Jagan, *The West on Trial*, 18–19.

19. J. Jagan, *When Grandpa Cheddi was a Boy and Other Stories*.

20. C. Jagan, *The West on Trial*, 23–24.

21. J. Jagan, *When Grandpa Cheddi was a Boy and Other Stories*.

22. V. S. Naipaul, 'A Handful of Dust: Return to Guyana,' *The New York Review of Books*, April 11, 1991, 18.

23. *Sunday Chronicle*, October 27, 1963.

24. Ibid.

25. Ibid.

26. V. S. Naipaul, 'Our Universal Civilization,' *The New York Review of Books*, January 31, 1991, 22, 24.

27. Interview with Jock Campbell, Nettlebed, Oxfordshire, July 23, 1992.

28. Interview with Ivy Jailall, Palmyra Village, East Berbice, Guyana, February 10, 2003.

29. Interview with Jock Campbell, Nettlebed, Oxfordshire, July 23, 1992.

30. Ibid.

31. V. S. Naipaul, 'A Handful of Dust: Return to Guyana,' 18.

32. Frank Birbalsingh, 'Interview with Cheddi Jagan,' in *The People's Progressive Party of Guyana, 1950–92: An Oral History* (London: Hansib, 2007), 30.

33. C. Jagan, *The West on Trial*, 23–24.

34. Ibid., 62–63, 19.

35. Vivian Gornick, 'What Endures of the Romance of American Communism?' *New York Review Daily*, April 5, 2020. This is adapted from her introduction to a new edition of her book, *The Romance of American Communism* (London: Verso, 2020 [1977]).

36. J. Jagan, *When Grandpa Cheddi was a Boy and Other Stories*.

37. Cheddi Jagan, 'How I came to Know Lenin,' (mimeo.), 1975, 3.

38. Ibid.
39. 'Interview with Cheddi Jagan,' in *The People's Progressive Party of Guyana, 1950–92*, 56.
40. Ibid., 148.
41. V. S. Naipaul, 'A Handful of Dust: Return to Guyana,' 19.
42. 'Interview with Cheddi Jagan,' in *The People's Progressive Party of Guyana, 1950–92*, 62.
43. C.O. 946/1 [Colonial Office], Evidence of Cheddi Jagan to the Venn Commission (Georgetown), January 14, 1949.
44. *PAC Bulletin*, no. 2, November 20, 1946.
45. *PAC Bulletin*, no. 25, April 14, 1948.
46. Cheddi Jagan, *A West Indian State: Pro-Imperialist or Anti-Colonialist* (Georgetown: The author, 1972), 59, 53–54.
47. Cheddi Jagan, 'Address Delivered to the 25th Anniversary Conference on behalf of the Central Committee of the People's Progressive Party, 3 August 1975,' *Thunder* (September–December 1975): 14–15, 25, 30.
48. Ibid., 25, 27–28.
49. 'PPP is Marxist-Leninist,' *Thunder* (Third Quarter, 1985), 6.
50. Cheddi Jagan, 'No Future for Pragmatism and Rightist Opportunism,' in *Yes to Marxism – No to Rightist Opportunism* (pamphlet issued by the PPP [1985]).
51. Interview with Eusi Kwayana, Georgetown, September 22, 1992.
52. *PAC Bulletin*, no. 20, December 17, 1947.
53. See note 39.
54. Ibid.
55. Eusi Kwayana, 'More than Survival: Afro-Guyanese and the Nation,' *Mimeo*, July–August 1988, 57–58; Kwayana, 'More than Survival: A View of the Indo-Guyanese Contribution to Social Change,' *Mimeo*, May 1988, 38–39.
56. Cheddi Jagan, 'Race, Class and Ideology,' in *Race and Politics in Guyana*, by Cheddi Jagan and Ram Karran (Georgetown: The authors, 1974), 4, 8.
57. Ram Karran, 'Race and Politics,' in *Race and Politics in Guyana*, by Cheddi Jagan and Ram Karran (Georgetown: The authors, 1974), 16.
58. See my introductory essay, '*Girmitiyas* and My Discovery of India,' in *Girmitiyas: The Origins of the Fiji Indians*, 2nd ed., ed. Brij Lal (Suva, Fiji: Fiji Institute of Applied Studies, 2004).
59. Cheddi Jagan, *Tracing our Path in a Changing World!* (PPP pamphlet), August 1990, 14.
60. Cheddi Jagan, 'Our Footsteps and our Vision for a Free Guyana,' Georgetown, *Mimeo*, June 8, 1991, 11.
61. Moses Bhagwan (New York), personal correspondence, March 2019.
62. Cheddi Jagan, 'Address Delivered to the 25th Anniversary Conference on behalf of the Central Committee of the People's Progressive Party.'

2.

The Sources of Cheddi Jagan's Communist Mission:

Anatomy of His Longevity

Sir Jock Campbell [1912–94], Chairman of Booker, wanted to work with Cheddi, but Cheddi wouldn't give him an opportunity...He needed to make a concession to Booker, one that didn't need anything substantive in terms of money...But he couldn't think of anything at all that would compel them to come into his camp. They [Booker] didn't like Burnham, but they couldn't go with Cheddi either because he was so dogmatic.

Cheddi was really quite unrealistic in terms of policy formation. He was very much under the influence of international socialists [communists]. That was his great weakness. He was a very nice man. He wasn't like Burnham at all. You could take a different point of view from him. But he would hold on to a few dogmatic positions and would not budge...He would hold to his position. It was very hard to persuade him. I think Janet was a very bad influence on him.

– Lloyd Best (2001)

I.   Ideological Inflexibility: Indians, 'Bitter Sugar,' and the Marxist Illusion

Working with the United Nations Development Programme (UNDP) in Georgetown, British Guiana, during the turbulent years of the early 1960s, Oxbridge-educated Lloyd Best (1934–2007), a Trinidadian, was one of the clever young regional economists who tried to counsel Jagan away from his stubborn idealism – towards moderation and pragmatism on development issues. For this Best was censured by Janet Jagan, who arguably was the single greatest influence on Cheddi. Janet was no visionary, no intellectual, but she was obdurate in her conviction that Marxism-Leninism had all the answers for the perfectibility of humankind. Best assesses her political role in a manner that has eluded most: 'I don't think she had any insight into the complexity of the Guyanese situation, and she was the biggest buttress of Cheddi's intransigence in Guyana. She was very hostile to dissent. In my judgement she was a person who believed if you were not for me, then you were against me.'[1]

Janet, in effect, had virtually deserted her own family and her community – her Jewish frame of reference – for the political vocation in a remote colonial backwater of which she knew virtually nothing. Cheddi also was alienated from his family's Hindu world view. Therefore, they both needed something of robust transcendence to fill the void occasioned by their mutual cultural self-evisceration. The communist utopia was that illumination; it gave them 'total knowledge' (as Cheddi put it to Naipaul) – paradoxically, a kind of divine comprehensiveness – to compensate for their yawning identity lacuna, conceivably the source of a submerged angst.

Lloyd Best makes a shrewd observation:

> Cheddi always saw Guyana in the context of the Cold War. All his references would be drawn from outside Guyana. You cannot understand Cheddi's errors and stubbornness unless you understand that. He saw the world in two camps, and he was in one camp [the Soviet or communist]. There was nothing you could do to get him to adopt another perspective.[2]

Best was an eminent scholar of the plantation economies of the Caribbean and elsewhere. But he does not explain why Jagan, his legendary intransigence, and his quixotic beliefs in the superiority of Soviet communism notwithstanding, was able to survive nearly three decades of political marginalisation. Was his widely perceived 'impracticality' congruent with his being enraptured by his Soviet communist creed? This was exploited to the hilt by Forbes Burnham, and it rendered Jagan's People's Progressive Party (PPP) a virtual sect, as it languished in opposition for nearly twenty-eight years, although he personally retained undiminished Indian racial support until his death in March 1997.

Indeed, because of Jagan's doctrinaire Marxist beliefs, Burnham was often at his oratorical best when ridiculing and belittling him as a poodle of the Soviet communists. Meanwhile, in the region and around the world (particularly in the Non-Aligned Movement), Burnham sought to cultivate a redemptive heroic image as a champion of African liberation and a 'new international economic order' – no less anti-imperialist than Jagan – yet perceptibly moderate by temperament and unfailingly statesmanlike. But, through it all, Jagan retained his overwhelmingly Indo-Guyanese allegiance, although his communist ideology was fundamentally at variance with their core beliefs – their durable religious convictions (Hinduism and Islam); their predisposition to individual initiative (in the context of the joint family) and instinctual apprehension of collective enterprises; their residual caste reflex with a predilection for hierarchy and lightness of skin – certainly not enamoured of egalitarianism; and their ancient antipathy to the *sarkar*: any constituted centralised authority that impinges on the autonomy of the family. Indians are arguably not 'party animals.'

That Burnham and his successor, Desmond Hoyte, rigged the elections in 1968, 1973, 1980, and 1985, as well as the referendum in 1978 to change the Constitution thus giving Burnham untrammelled domination of his country, contributed immeasurably to the perpetuation of Indian loyalty to Jagan. The perception by Indians that Cheddi had been wronged (in the 1962–64 period and thereafter), by Burnham and his 'imperialist' sponsors, the British and the Americans, redounded to his advantage. The perceived injustices against Cheddi, though largely of his making because of his communist creed in 'America's backyard,' were absorbed by his Indian support base as a concerted racial humiliation. It sustained him in his political vocation to the end of his life, despite his glaring political ineptitude.

Moreover, Indo-Guyanese internalisation of 'king sugar' and the 'sugar gods' as their historical oppressor par excellence – purveyors of a virtual slavery, hence Jagan's mantra: 'bitter sugar' – was enduringly unresponsive to a nuanced reinterpretation. Only large companies, with access to substantial capital and endowed with sophisticated technical and managerial capacity, could prosper in the sugar industry of coastal Guyana because of its formidable hydrological problems. And before the guaranteed prices and quotas facilitated by the Commonwealth Sugar Agreement (CSA) of 1951 (Jock Campbell was a leading architect), such prosperity could be precarious because of a volatile international sugar market – rampant fluctuation of prices being the norm. This was the context of the predominance of Booker, habituated to the environmental hazards of the colony since 1815; no one else would dare to invest in sugar in British Guiana on the scale they did.[3]

'Bitter Sugar', the motif at the heart of Jagan's communist mission

Jagan's 'bitter sugar' mantra is certainly pertinent in accounting for his political longevity, yet it must be viewed in conjunction with the power of the Indo-Guyanese master narrative – that they were tricked into indentureship in British Guiana: a 'new slavery'; that they were mercilessly oppressed and 'punished' (struggled to survive) on the sugar plantations in the colony; and that Cheddi Jagan, virtually single-handedly and heroically (another Nehru in the Indo-Guyanese imagination) fought 'the Goliaths of privilege' to eradicate their chronic exploitation and dehumanisation. It is a tale permeated by suffering – of 'slaving' for the 'sugar gods' in a veritable *narak* (hell), with no rewards. The sugar industry is virtually extinct, yet notions of the downtrodden Indian – a veritable slave during indentureship and thereafter – are not susceptible to an intellectual revisiting, thereby defying erasure.

However, this narrative is incomplete at best, given its silence on the ancient and resilient caste prejudices that are at the foundation of the immemorial poverty of India and its curtailment of the human spirit, juxtaposed with the untrammelled enslavement, for over two centuries, of Africans on West Indian plantations. It does not accommodate the context of introducing Indian indentured labour into the colony, largely superseding freed African labour on the plantations – historically perceived by African Guyanese as subversive of their welfare. This has never ceased to rankle among the latter – the subliminal source of a durable antipathy. Consequently, the widely recognised achievement of Indo-Guyanese, astoundingly comprehensive, remains barely examined in the public domain for fear of African resentment, however unconsciously. Perhaps it is largely taboo, also, because of its inherent subversion of the 'new slavery' thesis and its modern variant – Jagan's 'bitter sugar' message. Therefore, even the belated, but far-reaching, culture of reform pursued by Jock Campbell's Booker (in the 1950s to early 1960s) to ameliorate the condition of sugar plantation workers – an imaginative response to Jagan's crusade against the 'sugar gods' – could not lessen Indo-Guyanese visceral hatred of Booker. The Jaganite mantra of 'bitter sugar' would endure, averting scrutiny by the PPP's racial political constituency of the consequences of Jagan's enthralment with Soviet communism. 'Bitter Sugar' encapsulates the source of his political longevity as the unchallengeable Indo-Guyanese leader. But as Eusi Kwayana has observed, this narrative of sugar and Booker did not resonate with African Guyanese; neither did Jagan's increasingly impenetrable Marxist dogmas in his later years in the political wilderness (1964–92).

Racial loyalty – at any cost – is a cancer in Guyanese society. As recently as May 8, 2021, *Kaieteur News* observed: 'Guyana remains a society smouldering with racial anxiety and animus.' To endeavour to comprehend it would drive even the Gods to despair. It must be encoded in one's DNA, and no endeavour at logic and rationality can neutralise the intuitive, ineluctably visceral, emotions triggered when a group's racial security or self-interest is deemed to be infringed. Maybe, racialism – exacerbated by the extraordinary reach of social media with its incredible viciousness – has perplexed everyone. Yet, as early as the late 1970s, every major political party in the country was seeking validation as authentically Marxist-Leninist: the PPP, the Working People's Alliance (WPA) of Walter Rodney – even Burnham's People's National Congress (PNC), engineered into power (in 1964) by the imperialists because of its declared anti-communism. Perhaps this Marxist absurdity – inconceivable and unknown anywhere else – was a means of deflecting, however superficially, from the enervating futility of the Guyanese racist frame of reference (deeply rooted, as I argue in the next chapter). One could thereby luxuriate in theoretical fantasies that 'scientifically' project a Guyana in which class would not merely triumph over race, but where primordial aggregations of difference, breeding seemingly illimitable dissonance, would dissolve when the communist utopia, of necessity, materialises. Guyana's El Dorado syndrome?

In October 1984, in an interview with Professor Frank Birbalsingh in Toronto, Cheddi Jagan (nearly twenty unbroken years in opposition, with Burnham effectively a dictator for life) still had no regrets or reservations regarding his Marxist political mission and his *modus operandi*:

Birbalsingh: What would you regard as your greatest regret over your long career of almost forty years? What did not work as you had planned, or as you had hoped?

Jagan: I have not many regrets, to tell you the truth. I am a revolutionary and I have confidence, revolutionary confidence, in the future, because **what I stand for** [Soviet communism] **is winning. It took a long time in Guyana, but it is winning in the world as a whole.**

Birbalsingh: You have been in opposition for a long time.

Jagan: That does not matter because **I am not only fighting for the people of Guyana. I am fighting for the people of the world. I am contributing to that struggle. That struggle is winning.** That is why the United States is so hysterical at the moment, because of that very fact, that what I stand for is winning [emphasis added].[4]

Six years later, in 1990, with the collapse of the Soviet empire and the demise of the communist system, *Stabroek News* asked Jagan whether communism was dying. He gave a typically doctrinaire answer:

> In Eastern Europe it was not communism (from each according to his ability to each according to his need) but its first phase, socialism (from each according to his ability to each according to his labour), that ran into trouble. Communism, as a system, has not been tried in any country and remains a highly moralistic and humanistic ideal and destination. Even for the most advanced socialist society [the Soviet Union] it will remain an ideal or goal for the twenty-first century, as admitted distortions and deviations have forced the USSR to literally start all over again along the path of socialism...**The goals of socialism and the virtues of Marxist doctrine must not be confused with the failures of those who tried to implement socialism** [emphasis added].[5]

The creed could not be profaned! It is reasonable to assume, therefore, that for Cheddi Jagan the fact that possibly five hundred thousand Guyanese had already fled Guyana because of his and Burnham's flawed 'socialist' experiments, primarily to capitalist America, Canada, and England (ironically), hardly merited a footnote. The struggle would be prolonged; the rewards or reversals could be dispiriting at times, downright soul-destroying after the fall of the Soviet system, but the mission (a preternatural crusade) is inviolable, and beyond susceptibility to despair. No sacrifice is too great for ultimate peace and eternal happiness under the inevitable communist order; the utopia is predicated on scientific truths rooted in universal moral imperatives. Consequently, political expediency, tactical manoeuvring to secure incremental political power dispensed by the tainted hands of the doomed imperialists, was morally indefensible. Pragmatism (as exercised by the ever-slick Forbes Burnham) is short-sighted at best, for in the higher scheme of things, the golden age in the social evolution of society – the communist utopia – is unstoppable.

II. Soviet Enlightenment and the Allure of Castro's Revolution: Signing up to the Cold War

The year 2018 was the centenary of the birth of Cheddi Jagan (1918–97), one of the two most passionate communist leaders in the history of the Caribbean (the other being Fidel Castro [1926–2016]). Cheddi was a phenomenon: an American-trained dentist turned politician, with a White wife (a communist of Jewish extraction); the first notable political leader of Indian ancestry in the region; the only communist to lead a government in the English-speaking Caribbean (before Maurice Bishop [1944–83] in Grenada, 1979–83). Jagan was, in fact, the first communist to become the head of a government in the Western Hemisphere, albeit in a colony. Not only did he and Bishop espouse Marxism, but they also fervently embraced Soviet communism as the tested 'scientific' instrument and exemplar for the radical transformation of former colonies ravaged by exploitation under imperialism – from poverty and chronic underdevelopment to the 'sunlit uplands' of 'peace, freedom and socialism.' It was a mission driven by a millenarian reflex. Yet, its messianic strand apart, there was another bedevilling feature of Jagan's politics: its ideological inflexibility. From the beginning of his political mission, in the late 1940s, he did not really conceal his conviction that communism is infinitely superior to capitalism and that he subscribed to the former as it was pursued in the Soviet Union and the so-called Peoples' Democracies, the Soviet satellites in Eastern Europe.

In March 1953, the right-wing Indo-Guyanese lawyer and politician, Lionel Luckhoo (1914–97), introduced the Undesirable Publications Bill (popularly called the Subversive Literature Bill) in the Legislative Council. It was a measure conceived specifically to terminate Jagan's importation of communist literature into British Guiana. However, during the debate in the Council, Cheddi took conspicuous pride in extolling the utopian vision that was the fount of his political mission – building the communist paradise in a post-colonial Guyana. The promised land, as adumbrated by him, was eerily resonant of the abominable Stalinist regime of terror in the USSR, yet he would have dismissed the horrendous totalitarianism of the latter as a malevolent slander fomented by imperialism and its local agents. I quote Cheddi at length, as he sought to re-educate his fellow legislators, all being unreconstructed 'capitalist roaders' by his definition:

> When communists refer to force, they refer to what is known as the repressive force of society. What is that force? It is not the shooting of somebody or the murdering of people in cold blood. [What did he make of Stalin's notoriously brutal *modus operandi*?] No, the force they refer to is the force of the state which makes the law...

> In our society, in fact, in any capitalist society, we talk glibly about freedom and liberty which we must exercise eternal vigilance to preserve, but we know that in a capitalist society the state machinery is in the hands of the capitalist class, and in those hands, force is reposed. They are the ones who are using force against the people. In a socialist society, on the other hand, the table has been turned upside down. Laws are not made by the chosen few...the laws are made by the people's representatives [from the unelected Communist Party]. The state machinery is in the hands of the people's representatives who own the means of production, distribution, exchange and communication. That is the socialist society.

> ...to set up socialism one has to maintain an army, a police force, and the law to see that the former exploiters behave themselves, and if they do not, they are apprehended and tried in the People's Courts. It is the same state force, but the emphasis has been changed.

> In one instance the machinery of the state is used by the capitalist
> class against the working class and the oppressed...in the socialist
> society, the state machinery is used by the working class to see to it
> that the former capitalists behave themselves. It is from that stage
> that communism comes in a higher form of society, in which we
> have People's Councils, People's Police, People's Militia and People's
> Courts.[6]

Pragmatism never could find a niche in Cheddi's political imagination. His faith in communism was not susceptible to moderation, persuasive though the argument for it in America's sphere of influence, in the amplified heat of the Cold War after Castro's Revolution in 1959. Jagan's rage against imperialism probably has its origins in his penchant for formulaic thinking, his immersion in 'scientific socialism' – Marxist mantras, a kind of religiosity – allied with his unshakeable belief in the superiority and infallibility of the Soviet example, the universal model for the remaking of humankind: communist man! A cardinal strand was his faith in a definitive Soviet enlightenment – their communist empathy and 'proletarian internationalism' – as a disinterested benefactor unswayed by self-interest and readily accessible for Guyana's radical social and economic transformation after independence. Thus did Jagan casually, but consciously, take his little country (still a British colony) into the Cold War on the side of America's foremost enemy (the USSR) in 'their own backyard.' His political inflexibility, his doctrinaire ideological mindset, his dearth of statesmanship would prove calamitous for Guyana.

The British and the Americans agonised relentlessly, in the 1950s to early 1960s, over Jagan's predilection for communism, conjecturing whether his accession to power was likely to moderate his politics – in harmony with the acceptable social democratic ethos of most British West Indian leaders. Many were sceptical that Jagan could ever be disabused of his romanticism and naivety. Would he ever grow up? Both Lloyd Best and Jock Campbell were of the firm belief that his wife, Janet Jagan, also, was a communist and no less inflexible, although she was not inclined to venture into the theoretical quagmire Cheddi found seductive. The Jagans had a proprietorial hold on the PPP; their primary goal always was its transformation into a 'disciplined' communist party 'of the Leninist type,' in the mould of the Communist Party of the Soviet Union and its satellites. Despite the persistent racial chasm in Guyana, they sincerely believed that such a proven instrument for executing the people's will, based on scientific premises (laws) and dedicated to empowering the working class, would root out the most pernicious manifestations of 'false consciousness' engendered under capitalism – even the bedevilling racial bigotry that had degenerated into communal violence in the early 1960s.

As Jagan observed in 1966 (at the termination of British colonial rule), the future was bright despite his being ejected from office by the imperialists. He now had the time and freedom to spread his Marxist-Leninist illumination to all the people of Guyana. He was not disenchanted by imperialist machinations in his electoral defeat in 1964, because the inevitable triumph of communism would, in due course, eradicate the evils fomented by 'decadent' capitalism and imperialism. Of this he had no doubts, just as he was certain of the capacity of his PPP to cultivate and eventually secure the integration of the African and Indian people under his resolute Marxist leadership:

> The United States may be wealthier and more powerful [than Britain], but what they both stand for [capitalism] is wrong. They only present the illusion of omnipotence, for the system they uphold is decadent. Now that we are out of office…we have the opportunity of uniting the working class, of healing the racial breach…To those pessimists who say that the Indian and Negro workers cannot be united, I say look back to the situation before the 1950s. Then, too, it appeared that the two ethnic groups could not be united. John Carter then, as Burnham now, ruled in Georgetown. In the same way that the workers then marched united behind the PPP, they will soon march again.[7]

A fantasy! He reposed total trust in the 'scientific' attributes of Marxism-Leninism (his intellectual property, so to speak) to eradicate the virus of racism. However, he never did secure the electoral support of Africans in Guyana, even after twenty-eight years, when he regained power in 1992 – paradoxically because the Americans had intervened to terminate the rigged electoral process, they were partly instrumental in devising, in 1967–68, to perpetuate Burnham's rule, deemed anti-communist. Jagan is correct that many Africans voted for the PPP in the general elections of April 1953. But that is attributable primarily to their loyalty to the charismatic young lawyer, Forbes Burnham (aged thirty and already recognised as the principal custodian of African interests) – not to Cheddi Jagan or the appeal of his Marxism-Leninism. Yet never did he waver in his faith that Soviet communism was imbued with the 'scientific' means of creating the classless society that would, of necessity, extirpate racial chauvinism. After all, he was captivated by the fiction that the USSR had solved its daunting nationality problem inherited by virtue of the far-flung empire of the czars. This was the source of Jagan's resolve and his longevity – also the foundation of his tragic political career: an irrepressible cold warrior, on the wrong side in the Western Hemisphere. Indeed, as Cheddi got older and still languishing in opposition, he consciously brought the Cold War home, confident in the invincibility of his pro-Soviet vision. It evoked in him a kind of religious fervour – a sense of purpose, too. His faith in communism was unassailable: 'what I stand for is winning'!

Jagan was categorical about this at the time of the American invasion of Maurice Bishop's Grenada, in October 1983:

> Anti-communism and its modern garb, anti-Sovietism, must be combatted...For the small Caribbean states, it is suicidal to preach the doctrine of 'Caribbean exceptionalism' and 'reliance on one's own forces.' Close links must be forged with the Soviet Union and other socialist [communist] states. Experience has demonstrated that the imperialists will use all means to attain their ends of domination. Material, moral, and political support from the world socialist community [the Soviet bloc] is essential to attain political power... Despite the temporary setback in Grenada, the democratic and peace forces in the Caribbean will overcome. The Caribbean revolution cannot be stopped. The 'Marxist virus' cannot be destroyed.[8]

When the Sino-Soviet split became transparent, from the mid-1960s, the Jagans never vacillated in affirming the Soviet example as sacrosanct (of universal applicability), although Janet had been accorded individual private meetings with Mao Zedong and Zhou Enlai in August 1962. She was especially impressed with Zhou, with whom she chatted for two hours, late into the night. He was, unlike Mao, a cosmopolitan, 'fascinating personality' who spoke with Janet in English, 'with great charm and ease.' Earlier, in May 1960, she had a private meeting with the seductively handsome 'Che' Guevara. Janet recalls the encounter: '... the most outstanding event [of the trip] remains in my memory – my visit to 'Che' Guevara...While his face is firmly planted in my memory, I cannot recall a word of our conversation...'[9]

In November 1998, the former chairman of the youth arm of the PPP (1962–65), the Progressive Youth Organisation, Moses Bhagwan, spoke with Professor Frank Birbalsingh of the PPP's special relationship with the Communist Party of the Soviet Union (CPSU):

> Janet Jagan in particular and the leaders of the party were pro-Russian. Our contacts with China were always rather loose. The real reason for my expulsion from the party was because I appeared to be anti-Russian. The Russians would not tolerate anyone within the leadership with whom they were not comfortable. I've always enjoyed my relationship with Cheddi and found him respectful of other people's feelings and sensitivities. But in Third World [communist] parties, as soon as differences arise, somebody has to go.[10]

Bhagwan was confirming that dissent from the orthodox pro-Moscow stance of the Jagans could never be accommodated and that the principal arbiter in such matters was the formidable keeper of the flame, Janet Jagan. Whoever dared to challenge her judgement or the PPP's mantra on Soviet omniscience regarding Marxism-Leninism was finished. It made for inflexibility, the stifling of debate, regimentation of thought – a fear to dare to think independently of the domesticated Soviet orthodoxy – the source of the periodic haemorrhaging of the best and the brightest in the PPP, from the mid-1950s to the mid-1970s.

The history of the party is permeated by irreconcilable internal differences and the incremental defection or resignation of key leaders and activists, whatever their ethnicity. And the precipitating factor was invariably divergence from the pro-Moscow orthodoxy of Cheddi and Janet Jagan. This was exacerbated after the PPP lost power in December 1964. Only three of the leaders from the 1950s and 1960s stayed: Cheddi, Janet, and their loyal servant, Boysie Ramkarran, the treasurer of the PPP for most of his long political life. Janet praised the latter for his 'utter honesty, integrity and loyalty.' After all, he must have known where the funding was coming from and how much, yet he divulged nothing. But it was discovered later that even Ramkarran had major difficulties with the Jagans, becoming estranged from them at different times, so it is a miracle that he did stay with the PPP to the end of his life. On the birth centenary of Ramkarran (2019), the *Thinker*, organ of the Cheddi Jagan Research Centre observed of him:

> Although regarded as a loyalist, he had many major disagreements with the leadership, both in government and in opposition, which were not known outside the PPP. On several occasions, he threatened to resign from the Government and on two occasions he withdrew altogether from political life, once for as much as four years in the late 1960s to the early 1970s. But there was always a reconciliation of sorts.[11]

The only decade when very few comrades defected from the PPP was the 1980s: by then the most able were long gone, and those who stayed were young true believers. Essentially lightweights, nearly all twenty-five or thirty years younger than the Jagans, they were the object of continual ridicule by Forbes Burnham, but no threat whatsoever to his dictatorship. The remaining young loyalists of the PPP were devotees of the Jagans and the communist system dominated by the Soviet Union – a communist sect. They lacked the intellectual rigour, the flexibility of mind or independent livelihood to question the received dogmas; therefore, they were perceived as safe comrades. A fetish of sorts was made of the not too formally educated devotees of the creed, the salt of the earth, as distinct from the smart-asses with the potential to create trouble, apart from their susceptibility to the brazen enticement of Burnham to defect to his governing party.

By the mid-1970s, Guyana was awash with Marxists of one sort or another. The Jagans, Burnham supposedly (no label stuck to him!), Ranji Chandisingh, Brindley Benn (former chairman of the PPP, a Maoist), Walter Rodney, Eusi Kwayana, Rupert Roopnaraine, and Clive Thomas, just about every local politician was proud to be deemed a Marxist. Some enigma for a society steeped in racism. The pro-capitalist United Force (founded in 1960 by Portuguese businessman Peter D'Aguiar) was no longer a credible force; therefore, unlike the rest of the Anglophone Caribbean, no political party wished to be defined as pro-capitalist, pro-American, or even social democratic – a pale shadow of the authentic Marxist stuff! This probably reflected the futility of the endeavour to forge a national identity. Marxism offered a built-in theoretical rationale for not confronting the intractable ethnic albatross: defining it out of existence – an effective evasion – as the Russians did in the USSR. Yet the tenacity of Guyanese racism makes the pursuit of democratic party politics inherently flawed because general elections are largely ethnic censuses.

Why then any lingering vacillation, or incredulity, regarding the Marxist or communist credentials of Cheddi Jagan? I know for sure that the Americans and the British, based on an avalanche of intelligence reports, knew all along that he was a communist. Besides, Jagan was, by far, the most prolific writer among politicians in the region; he wrote voluminously, unlike Burnham who wrote comparatively little, although he did contribute (in a non-ideological vein, betraying no trace of communism) to *Thunder* in the early 1950s. Jagan considered himself a serious thinker, a partisan of Soviet communism, with much to contribute towards popularising the theory and practice of Marxism-Leninism. He believed that his PPP had to prioritise the imparting of ideological consciousness to the workers and peasants in colonial Guyana; and that the most effective way to undertake this was by means of political education, with the party's organ, *Thunder*, the paramount instrument.

After 1956, as Jagan's PPP sought to reconsolidate itself as a nationalist movement for independence (following the split of February 1955 and the flight of Burnham and his predominantly African supporters), there was no mistaking its communist thrust, its hostility to capitalism. In a newsletter to party workers from the Education and Research Committee of the PPP – Lesson 2: Definition of Terms (dated July 15, 1956) – this is how capitalism and communism are explained:

> Capitalists are people who own the factories, sugar estates and so on. They exploit the working class by using its labour and paying back only a part of the value produced to the real producers, the working men. This is how the capitalists make profit (surplus value). The Booker Company is a capitalist concern...and the owners who live abroad drain the wealth out of the country...In our fight against Imperialism we will always have the foreign capitalists against us... Our major fight is against the foreign capitalists and the imperialists who protect them.

On the other hand, for the PPP, communism – the most effective instrument of realising total freedom – was indispensable to the liberation of the working class:

> Communists work to intensify the class struggle, to strengthen the trade unions, to assist in every way to bring about a change for the better…In British Guiana the Government and the newspapers try to frighten the people away by telling a lot of lies about communists… In the struggle for more land, in the struggle for better wages, the communists see the movement of the forces that in the end will change society.[12]

This political re-education exercise was augmented and formalised later, from the mid-1960s, by the party's ideological school, Accabre College. Like the CPSU and other 'fraternal' communist parties around the world, Marxist-Leninist 'propaganda' was a fundamental task of the political mission. (The word 'propaganda' was imbued with connotations of communist enlightenment: a nobility of political purpose.) It was essential for every comrade to experience a transformation in consciousness, tantamount to a kind of religious awakening. Therefore, comrades had to strive tirelessly for ideological clarity, guided by the infallible principles of Marxism-Leninism, to mobilise the working class for the protracted 'class struggle' – the metamorphosis from the evil, exploitative, and unredeemable capitalist system to the half-way house of socialism, then, finally, to the exalted 'sunlit uplands' of the communist utopia.

No sacrifice was too demanding or hazardous in the endeavour to achieve this 'heaven on earth.' Inevitable though the victory of communism over a moribund capitalism, yet it had to be 'struggled' for in the context of the universal class war against the enemies of the working people, guided by 'proletarian internationalism.' Jagan had no Hinduism, Christianity, or Islam, but he had acquired the gift of Marxism-Leninism (scientific socialism), which may be profaned by the imperialists and their local 'lackeys,' but it was unconquerable. In early 1975, his party's theoretical journal, *Thunder*, editorialised thus: 'Imperialism was powerless to arrest the unfolding of the laws of social development discovered by Marx and Engels.' As late as 1990, Cheddi pronounced: 'Marxism-Leninism is a science, not a dogma.' His passion and capacity for hard work were inexhaustible, his sincerity of belief irrepressible, and his political vocation of fifty years could not be extinguished, however elusive the attainment of the communist utopia. His supporters, primarily Indian, appreciated his honesty of purpose, his total rejection of politics as a means of personal gain. Despite his communist philosophy, the implications of which few of his supporters apprehended, they stayed loyal to a man they adored as humble and incorruptible. He did not enrich himself in any discernible way during his fifty years of political engagement.

If one examines Cheddi Jagan's enormous corpus of writings during his long political career (these could easily constitute one hundred hefty volumes or more), the judgement that his Marxist-Leninist creed was his primary inspiration from the inception is incontestable. Moreover, his thinking was unfailingly in harmony with whatever variant of that philosophy was sanctioned by the CPSU. He concurred readily with the vagaries of the CPSU's canonical pronouncements on any issue, contemporary or historical. In addition, his party's bookshop (renamed Michael Ford Bookshop in 1964) was always copiously stocked with communist literature, the bulk of it emanating from the Soviet Union and Eastern Europe through the Communist Party of Great Britain's (CPGB's) principal repository in London, Central Books. In later years (after Jagan officially joined the world communist movement, in 1969, in Moscow), the PPP was represented on the editorial board of one of the main communist journals, reflecting the core beliefs of the Communist Party of the Soviet Union and subsidised by it: *World Marxist Review* (1958–90). It was based in Prague, Czechoslovakia; Cheddi was a regular contributor. (The former president of Guyana, Donald Ramotar [1950–], was on its editorial board from 1983 to 1988.) It is noteworthy, too, that until around 1967–68, the PPP bookshop also stocked literature from Communist China (such as *Peking Review*, *Red Flag*, and the writings of Mao); this ceased shortly before the PPP officially joined the Soviet Bloc, in June 1969.

The year 1960 was the ideological watershed for Cheddi Jagan. He was fortified in his creed by the rise of his regional exemplar, Cuba's Fidel Castro, to whom he offered fulsome recognition as 'the greatest liberator of the 20th century.' Consequently, he sought to build an alliance with Castro even before the Kennedy administration, through the CIA, initiated its subversion of Jagan's government in 1962–63, following his visit to the White House on October 25, 1961. Jagan was proud that despite being the leader of a mere colony, his government was a unique case in the Hemisphere of open declaration of support for the Cuban Revolution; moreover, he also defied the American trade blockade against Castro. He was most grateful for the assistance he received from the Cuban and Soviet governments when the CIA intervened in British Guiana to subvert his government:

> The Soviet Union and Cuba helped to break, in 1963, a CIA-imposed airlines and shipping blockade of Guyana, which was directed at strangling the country and crushing the PPP government. Fuel (gasoline and kerosene), cut off from neighbouring Trinidad, was supplied by the Caribbean socialist state [Cuba]. And a Soviet ship brought wheaten flour and other goods.[13]

Even after Jagan lost power in December 1964, by virtue of Anglo-American duplicity, he was not deterred, having dramatised as early as January 1966 his defiance of American imperialism by attending Fidel Castro's Tri-continental Conference in Havana. The cardinal aim of the conference was to accelerate the spread of Marxism-Leninism (communism) in the Hemisphere, in the wake of the 'disappearance' of 'Che' Guevara from Cuba in 1965, to foment revolution in Bolivia and elsewhere. In March 1966, Cheddi reflected on that 'revolutionary' experience (in *Thunder*, the organ of the PPP), reaffirming his commitment to the communist creed and, by implication, his active engagement in the Cold War:

> The delegates had, above all, a clear-cut objective – how in the face of a ruthless and immoral enemy [America] to unite all the progressive [communist] forces for simultaneous confrontation…a symbol of ideological unity. The Cuban Revolution encompasses, in a brief period, revolutionary nationalism, socialism and communism.

Jagan also wrote on the Tri-continental Conference for *Labour Monthly*, the journal edited by R. Palme Dutt, the chief theoretician of the CPGB:

> …the conference put on record its debt of gratitude to the people of the socialist countries [the Soviet Union and its satellites] who 'succeeded in abolishing exploitation of man by man by the establishment of socialism, giving with their example and aid a valuable impulse to the struggle of the peoples oppressed by imperialism.'[14]

It must have been immeasurably cathartic for Jagan to use the term 'communism' without having to look over his shoulder, but it also reflected the magnitude of the impression the Cuban Revolution had on him, in such a short time, that he felt it merited that noble designation. Therefore, when he declared at the conference of the communist parties of the world, in Moscow in June 1969, that for him it was 'a kind of homecoming,' it did indeed represent his political arrival – freedom at last to embrace the sacred beliefs permeating his political vision since 1946. There was no equivocation regarding Cheddi's stance on the Cold War, although he did have to assume a degree of circumspection when in office (1957–64). This necessitated his resort to euphemisms: 'progressive,' 'socialist,' or even 'Marxist' when probed ritualistically about his political philosophy. And it often engendered tortuous obfuscation: fodder that his many enemies, particularly Burnham, never failed to kindle.

III. A True Believer: Passion and Continuity in Jagan's Embrace of the Communist Creed

Yet Jagan was essentially consistent in espousing his communist creed. He was elected to the Legislative Council in November 1947 (aged twenty-nine), and he quickly became a passionate, fearless, and iconoclastic legislator: always well-prepared, fortified by apt quotes from official reports, blue books, and journal articles, supplemented by an avalanche of statistics to enhance his arguments. That august body had witnessed no such precedent. This lodged in the minds of many Indo-Guyanese, evoking seminal admiration for their vibrant young hero that was never erased, although his limitations as a politician and statesman did surface in due course. At the core of many of Cheddi's contributions to the debates were his Marxist beliefs, such as in his marathon speech (cited earlier) opposing the Subversive Literature Bill of 1952 piloted by Lionel Luckhoo, his archenemy. He did not sublimate his acclaim for the Soviet Union and Communist China – his conviction that these communist states constituted a change in the tide of human affairs: the ultimate liberation of humankind from the immemorial oppression of slavery, feudalism, and capitalism.

In the following excerpt Jagan is commending the socialisation of children for the new challenges of the communist order:

> … under which we take the children of the former capitalists and big landlords, and the children of the workers and farmers and send them to school where they are educated, not according to the methods of the sectarian [denominational] schools, which are mostly interested in preserving the old order…In the socialist society the children of the exploiters and the exploited are sent to the same school where their minds are moulded differently…In schools controlled by the socialist State where they are taught the true Christian philosophy to live and let live, and to behave like brothers one to another: the ultimate aim of communism being 'to each according to his needs, from each according to his ability.'

> I am sure that those who are opposed to communism today, some without any knowledge of what it is, will not object to that definition of communism…The fundamental difference between socialism and communism is that under socialism it is 'to each according to his labour; from each according to his ability.' But in the higher state of communism, it is 'from each according to his ability, to each according to his needs.'[15]

Jagan then invoked the authority of the Marxist-oriented dean of Canterbury (probably a communist), Rev Hewlett Johnson (1874–1966) – an uncritical exponent of the Soviet experiment – in validating his supposition that the post-war reality in Eastern Europe (under Soviet hegemony) was more compatible with Christian precepts than most would dare concede. The dean's reputation as an apologist of Soviet communism under Stalin was so widely known that few (if any) of Jagan's colleagues in the Legislative Council would have lent any veracity to his views on the subject. Cheddi argued:

> Some people are shouting about Christianity and how they are prepared to fight for Christianity against communism, as if to say that

socialist principles or communist principles are opposed to Christian principles. Those people, I submit, are wolves in sheep's clothing... The Dean of Canterbury has said that what is happening today in the so-called communist countries is much nearer to Christianity and Christian principles laid down by all the millions, and I think he should know. He is a qualified engineer and has been behind the 'Iron Curtain' on many occasions. He has written about what he has seen there, but because he dares to tell the truth the same people who are crying 'Christ' and 'Christians' today want to crucify him...I submit that people like the Dean of Canterbury and others in British Guiana [like himself] are trying to sow the seeds of socialism [communism] and fighting to establish a standard of morality and the good things that all men respect, no matter in what age they are living.[16]

Cheddi Jagan had, indeed, embarked on a mission. The communist calling, exemplified by the mighty Soviet Union, was noble and divine in its own right. Its monumental goal – creating the perfect communist man – transcended the corroded moral compass of ancient religious traditions. Yet paradoxically (perhaps necessarily), his uncritical absorption of the secular communist vision of utopia probably had its origin in his virtual abjuring of his family's Hindu creed, with its residual notions of caste, which he treated with disdain. Marxism-Leninism, therefore, must have evoked in him a higher compensatory quasi-religious prompting – pursuit of the ultimate good for humankind, unimpeachable, because of its roots in 'scientific socialism.' As he saw it, his conception of the flawless communist society was not grounded in dubious religious mysticism; it came out of an intellectual apprehension of the radical transformation of society informed by the 'scientific' premises of Marxism-Leninism – the instrument for the perfectibility of humankind. Cheddi was deeply impressed by the putative 'scientific' foundations of the theory.

The class struggle was therefore grounded in a precise science, dialectical materialism (the conflict of social forces activated by material needs), which would, inevitably, be resolved in favour of the working class – henceforth eliminating 'epiphenomenal' aberrations (by nature transitory), such as racism, religious bigotry, tribalism, linguistic chauvinism, and other manifestations of 'false consciousness' under capitalism. The latter tends to conceal the intrinsic exploitative social relations between classes. Yet there is nothing 'the dictatorship of the proletariat' – the highest form of democracy – could not resolve: led by the vanguard Communist Party representing the interests of all in the classless communist society, obviously free from any imperfections. It was a fundamentally flawed thesis, but its simplistic assumptions of egalitarianism and human perfectibility (with subliminal religious associations) were appealing to many, given Cheddi's sincerity, humility, charisma, and passion in articulating his message at the grassroots.

For Indians on the sugar plantations (in the villages, too), the simple binary between the White 'sugar gods' and themselves, the 'coolie' underdogs, and the promise of ready deliverance, rendered a youthful, good-looking, and energetic Cheddi Jagan an irresistible politician, quickly eclipsing his Indo-Guyanese rivals, seen as imprisoned by the old order. Dr J. B. Singh (1889–1956), Ayube Edun (1893–1957), Jainaraine Singh (1908–1998), Dr J. P. Lachmansingh (1896–1960), Sir Lionel Luckhoo (1914–97), and (later) Balram Singh Rai (1921–2022) could make no impact on the Indian electorate after Cheddi Jagan had become established as their leader (a virtual Mahatma) by the early 1950s. 'Bitter sugar' was incontestable as the slogan of Indo-Guyanese redemption and revival; its principal exponent would have no credible rival from that community for the rest of his life.

On January 1, 1950, the Political Affairs Committee (Cheddi's Marxist study group) was superseded by the People's Progressive Party (PPP), and the *PAC Bulletin* by *Thunder*, the organ of the party (edited by Janet Jagan). A central vein of Marxist thinking pervaded the latter publication as well, despite the PPP being a rather loose coalition of anti-colonials of diverse political outlooks. But those identified as communists (the Jagans, Sydney King [later Eusi Kwayana], Martin Carter, Rory Westmaas, Brindley Benn and Ramkarran) were in a majority in its executive committee. And like all parties so inclined, around the world, the PPP's organ usually offered the best means of assessing its ideological thrust. *Thunder* reflected this, as both Cheddi and Janet Jagan were among its most prolific contributors. As noted earlier, Janet was no intellectual or Marxist theoretician, but her skills as an editor and a journalist were central to the project, specifically with respect to its organisation and the articulation and dissemination of its political message in British Guiana. *Thunder* reveals that the Jagans never deviated from the orthodoxy of Soviet communism – arguably the principal factor in the continual haemorrhaging of the PPP's best minds over several decades.

But there was also a dynamic international context of 'struggle' to which Cheddi Jagan's conceptualisation of the Guyanese reality was often subsumed, if not subordinated: 'proletarian internationalism.' The lacuna – the dearth in treatment of Guyanese racism – is striking in his writings. I cannot recall seeing anything of note written in the early heady years, in the 1950s, on the intractable racial insecurities in British Guiana, not only by the Jagans and Burnham, but even by the more independent Marxists, Sydney King, Martin Carter, and Rory Westmaas (the so-called ultra-left). It was as if this bedevilling issue, erroneously framed in any case according to the Marxist tenets, would dissolve of its own volition when the golden communist order came to fruition. It is true, however, that Sydney King did consider the problem serious enough that he raised it in the executive of the PPP, but it was brushed under the carpet.

And, as far as Jagan was concerned, Stalin's thesis on the so-called nationalities question was the gold standard, of specific relevance to British Guiana, having borne fruit abundantly in the USSR: Georgians, Armenians, Azerbaijanis, Uzbeks, Tajiks, Kazakhs, Turkmens, Kyrgyz, myriad Siberian tribes, and Muslim ethnicities of the Caucasus – its astoundingly diverse peoples – were supposedly already marvellously integrated, metamorphosed by virtue of their common noble pursuit of a pure communist order, guided by the revered CPSU, the fount of all wisdom.

Jagan was fortified in his faith in the power of 'scientific socialism' to erase ethnic insecurity and chauvinism while building a communist society in which diverse nationalities interact freely, thrive economically and socially – enhancing their distinct cultural attributes in the process, thereby enriching society as a whole, as in the Soviet Union. Moreover, when this utopian vision was corroborated by the infallible Rev Hewlett Johnson, the dean of Canterbury (Cheddi read all his books), he embraced it as impeccable: gospel from an Anglican clergyman of high rank in England.

The following on Stalin and the resolution of the nationalities question is taken from the dean's book of 1939, *The Socialist Sixth of the World*, written after the butchery of millions (including a multitude of devoted comrades) perpetrated by the dictator in his insanely barbaric purges of the late 1930s. I quote the dean of Canterbury at length because Cheddi invoked his 'wisdom' religiously, over several decades, as a flawless authority regarding the enlightened transformation of the Soviet Union, inspired by Comrades Vladimir Lenin and Joseph Stalin:

> The Russian Empire of pre-revolution days has not inaptly been called 'the prison of the peoples.' Every species of oppression was practised…Nationalities were purposely divided and purposely joined up with hostile peoples to foment enmity and oppression and inter-tribal strife. In other areas pogroms, on a wide scale, were organised.

> Joseph Stalin swept the whole of this aside and taught a new way with minorities. His actions in this respect constitute one of his unique contributions to the new socialist experiment. With Lenin and his fellow-communists he accepted the common economic basis of socialist economic life: the abolition of exploitation, profit-making, and competition. He perceived, however, that it was possible that national cultural ideals can co-exist side by side within a single economic order and within a single political state in which the same ideal was held.

> There was nothing…to prevent workmen of Georgia, who accepted the socialist thesis of a non-exploiting, non-profit-making society, from living under the same widespread economic ideal with workmen

of Belorussia in the extreme west, Sakhalin Island in the extreme east, or Uzbek[istan] in the centre, and yet each of them freely thinking, speaking, and writing in their own language and possessed of liberty to develop their own culture and institutions.

It is no more necessary to force national minorities to accept the national cultural ideal of the majority within the same economic system than it is necessary for an Indian to divest himself of Indian national culture when he plays cricket with an English team. One thing only is required of an Indian cricketer: he must observe the rules of cricket. And one thing only is required of a Georgian, Belorussian or Uzbek: he must observe the economic law of socialism....[17]

The dean was a zealous advocate of Stalin's USSR, accepting at face value the Soviet narrative of their flawless communist society in the making, moulding an unfettered humanity. Therefore, the various nationalities simply had to fall in line, to become beneficiaries of a comprehensively fulfilling life afforded by the 'Plan,' conceived in the spirit of the infallible 'laws of scientific socialism':

The economic interest of those who believe in production inspired by service and not profit and live under a Plan which considers the needs of each and all upon an equalitarian basis, is the same whatever the nationality may be. The State is based upon that economic interest and political plan; and not upon the nationality of any part predominant in numbers.[18]

The dean of Canterbury was, in essence, articulating the classic Marxist theory of causation: the primacy of the economic base or substructure in determining super-structural features, such as race, religion, and other social variables. The communist society, heralding the end of exploitation of man by man and the consequent access to equality of opportunity for all, necessarily, had the ultimate means to eradicate all forms of false consciousness, such as racial prejudice or racism – expendable superstructural accretions. This had a profound impact on Cheddi's attitude to race. I think he genuinely believed that the apparent dominance of the race factor in Guyana was an aberration, a transitory one; and that Marxism-Leninism, as practised in the Soviet Union and which he espoused as gospel, would ultimately win over most African Guyanese to his communist crusade. He embraced unreservedly whatever the CPSU enunciated on just about every subject; he was sure that the successful Soviet experiment would be replicated in Guyana, radically transforming the society to the advantage of all ethnic groups, while eradicating the narrow prejudices fostered historically by rapacious capitalism under colonialism.

It is noteworthy that although Jagan was gravely antagonised by the British intervention and removal of his government in October 1953, because of his alleged aim of creating a communist state (as the British rationalised it), he saw nothing reprehensible in the Soviet invasion and thwarting of the initiatives for reform in Hungary in 1956 and in Czechoslovakia in 1968 – a kind of rehearsal for *perestroika* and *glasnost*. Kimani Nehusi has remarked on Jagan's uncritical approbation of Moscow's rationalisation of its hegemonic excesses, and its impact on the PPP in 1956. He attributes the flight of Sydney King [Eusi Kwayana], and possibly the other so-called 'ultra left' members (Martin Carter, Rory Westmaas, and Lionel Jeffrey) from the PPP, partly to their revulsion at the Soviet invasion of Hungary in October 1956:

> Dr Jagan's wooden, inflexible and received notion of Marxism demanded that the Moscow line be followed religiously. This mode of thinking…led the PPP leadership into passive and silent complicity with Soviet action that was identical to that previously suffered by the PPP itself…when the British invaded the colony in 1953 and evicted the PPP from office…[Then] the PPP leadership had condemned, in the harshest possible terms, the British invasion of Guyana in a disagreement over the Guianese interpretation of democracy, but [they] complied with Soviet *diktat* when the Soviet Union invaded Hungary in a dispute over the Hungarian interpretation of socialism.[19]

Kimani is right: whatever interpretation of events emanated from the Soviet Union, bearing the seal of approval of the inviolable authority of the CPSU, was sacrosanct to Cheddi and Janet Jagan.

The late eminent Polish philosopher, Leszek Kolakowski (1927–2009), an ex-Marxist, argues that ideology was crucial to Soviet communism, not as a philosophical rationale, but primarily because it was the *raison d'etre* – in the context of the Cold War – of the USSR being the exemplar of radical transformation to the perfect communist society – the beacon of world revolution. The fact that pro-Soviet communists around the world (like Cheddi Jagan) accepted this fiction unreservedly was crucial to the need for continual validation of the Soviet system through recurring crises of self-confidence, however camouflaged by its ritual statistical affectations of superiority over moribund capitalism. Surprisingly, inordinate credibility was rendered to the mirage of Soviet invincibility, when such affirmation originated in a colony or a young nation with vibrant aspirations to radical transformation. The ideological architecture, says Kolakowski, was grounded in the

> doctrine that the Soviet Union embodies the interests of…the working class everywhere, that it represents their desires and aspirations, and that it is the first step towards a world revolution that will liberate the toiling masses wherever they may be…This is not to say that the policy of the Soviet state at any given moment is determined by ideology, but the ideology must be there to justify it when required.[20]

Moscow – the secular Rome to many communists around the world! And the dissemination of Marxist-Leninist literature was pivotal to sustaining the faith – and the myth.

Therefore, it was paramount to embed the doctrine of Marxism-Leninism as indispensable to the Soviet system; the legitimacy of the USSR and its satellites was predicated on it. In other societies, such validation is derived from periodic elections or the charismatic, quasi-religious attributes of the hereditary monarchy. This is what I mean by the communist calling possessing quasi-religious elements: tenets and rituals, such as periodic congresses at home and in Moscow or Havana, what true believers, like the Jagans, deemed inviolable. Cheddi Jagan's philosophy, therefore, was based on faith in the omnipotence of Soviet communism – considered 'scientific,' but virtually a divine formula. Yet his vision of the emancipation of the dispossessed, rarely went beyond 'bitter sugar': the challenges of a complex, inchoate multiracial society, with discrete segments manifesting robust sectional loyalties, never did find a niche in his analysis. His inspiration, of 'scientific socialist' provenance, was premised exclusively on class conflict and the primacy, and inevitability, of working class or proletarian triumph in the class war – it minimised, if not erased, ethnic/racial and cultural susceptibilities.

Professor Kolakowski debunked the Soviet myth early, stressing the fragility of the system. On his first visit to the Soviet Union, in 1950, he apprehended it readily as a place of 'material and spiritual desolation'; its Marxism-Leninism was decorative – bogus; its grandiose assertions of victory in the making of communist man diverged conspicuously from the stark reality of a materially and spiritually impoverished Soviet man. Kolakowski was unsparing in his indictment:

> The only medicine communism has invented – the centralised, beyond social control, state ownership of the national wealth and one-party rule – is worse than the illness it is supposed to cure; it is less efficient economically and it makes the bureaucratic character of social relations an absolute principle...I do not believe that human culture can ever reach a perfect synthesis of its diverse and incompatible components. Its very richness is supported by this very incompatibility of its ingredients. And it is the conflict of values, rather than their harmony, that keeps our culture alive.[21]

With the collapse of the Soviet Union, Kolakowski revisited the inherent fragility of a Marxist frame of reference, in an essay of 2002, 'What is Left of Socialism?' He argues:

> One of the causes of the popularity of Marxism among educated people was the fact that in its simple form it was very easy...Indeed, **they enjoyed having one key to open all doors, one universally applicable explanation for everything,** an instrument that makes

it possible to master all of history and economics without actually having to study either.[22]

This is congruent with Cheddi's clarification to V. S. Naipaul in 1991, regarding his Marxist illumination: **'To put it in a way that was totally related to a socio-economic system came from reading Marxist literature...a whole new world opened to me, a total understanding of the world** [emphasis added].'[23] 'One key to open all doors'! This is how Professor Kolakowski encapsulates this very flawed 'scientific' instrument for comprehending reality.

Yet to defy the 'science' of Marxism – an extremely dangerous manifestation of false consciousness – under Stalin's reign of terror in the USSR, was to court repression, starvation, and death (slowly and painfully or summarily), as it was tantamount to subversion of the authority of the 'proletarian' state. But given the proclaimed intrinsic infallibility of the Stalinist dispensation, even mild dissent constituted not just subversion but also insanity, meriting isolation in the Gulag on psychiatric grounds, even if the butcher's hand were temporarily stayed. The historian, Jochen Hellbeck, has documented the untrammelled power of the Stalinist state to bend everyone to its will – evoking a gnawing personal sense of guilt and betrayal if one dared to manifest individual autonomy, however minimally and unobtrusively, in resisting subordination to the imposed draconian collective will. But interestingly, he also attributes this angst to a predilection for perfectibility – a utopian vision – that inheres in the ethos of the Russian intelligentsia that preceded the Bolsheviks.

Hellbeck explores this phenomenon based on diarists under Stalin's rule, one being Zinaida Denisevskaya (1887–1933):

> [Her] self-reflection predated the Soviet order; she entered the revolution of 1917 with developed and articulated notions of her own 'personality.' It was precisely from this vantage point that she criticised the Bolsheviks as uncultivated and faceless. And yet over the years she came to trade her personal autonomy for a value that appeared infinitely higher, larger, more meaningful...

> Throughout her life Denisevskaya retained a commitment to cultivate her personality, thereby revealing her engagement in the ethos of the Russian intelligentsia, that group of educated and critically thinking individuals which defined itself above all by a commitment to the creation of a perfect social order inhabited by harmoniously shaped, fulfilled, and integrated human beings. The continued pursuit of her diary was in some measure an expression of Denisevskaya's sustained aspiration toward such an ideal type of personality. In light of this longer-term commitment, Bolshevik ways of thinking and acting on the self appear less original, and more situated, as variants of a preoccupation with working on and perfecting the self that characterised larger segments of Russian culture – late imperial and revolutionary as well as Soviet.[24]

Yet, despite the moral fragility of his pro-Soviet political philosophy, Cheddi Jagan had no reservation in entering the Cold War against the Americans. He had no regrets, he asserted time and again, calamitous though the consequences for him and those who believed in him or gave him the benefit of the doubt – most Indo-Guyanese. It was a natural progression from the subliminal El Dorado syndrome embedded in the Guyanese psyche to his possession of 'total knowledge' (Marxism-Leninism) and his unwavering pursuit of the millennium. Languishing in opposition for twenty-eight years and marginalised by Burnham's blatantly rigged elections, Cheddi was even more transfixed by 'the absurdities of world revolution,' as Eric Williams once said of his erstwhile friend, C. L. R. James. And in this exercise in futility, Cheddi received the approbation of Janet Jagan, whose part in sustaining his utopian vision and political inflexibility has been minimised, if not obscured, by the common perception of her as an able and pragmatic organiser. She was much more than that: the keeper of the flame!

In fact, as Lloyd Best observed, Janet was 'a very bad influence on Cheddi.' Jock Campbell told me that he once said to Janet that if they did adopt a rabidly anti-capitalist policy regarding development (after independence), it could eventuate in widespread poverty and hunger, even the death of many. He recalled her flippant response that to achieve revolutionary changes, real freedom, people often have to die. She was the editor, for extended periods, of the main publications of the PPP (newspapers and booklets), where their belief in Marxism-Leninism and nationalisation of 'the commanding heights' of the economy were articulated openly: articles of faith. A central plank of Jagan's programme of 'almost total centralised planning and control' was the eradication of the virus of private capital – foreign and local. One of his fundamentals for radical change was 'nationalisation of the commanding heights of the economy – foreign and local "comprador" capitalist-owned and controlled factories, mines, plantations, banks, insurance companies and foreign trade.' Janet and Cheddi sang from the same hymn sheet on this key issue. Their disciples, such as C. R. Jacob (minister of finance, 1961–64), were alert to the chorus. This is an excerpt from his interview on local radio of March 24, 1961: 'We hold the view that the commanding heights of the economy must be publicly owned. In other words, state control for and by the people is the aim of the party.'

Jagan was confident that he was in possession of the 'scientific truth,' the 'correct Marxist-Leninist approach…essential for success'; moreover, that his 'struggle' in Guyana was but a fragment of his mission within the world communist movement – proletarian internationalism – guided by the unimpeachable precept of the glorious Soviet Union. I am quoting Cheddi at length:

Those who take an anti-communist position and attack the Caribbean vanguard [his PPP being at the forefront] for importing a 'foreign ideology' [Soviet communism] must be told that Marxism is not a lifeless dogma, not a completed, ready-made, immutable doctrine, but a living guide to action. **It is a science; it requires a concrete analysis of a concrete situation. Its guiding principles are the instruments which permit a correct interpretation of objective reality, and an evaluation and understanding of historical development...A Marxist-Leninist revolutionary party [like the PPP] is accountable not only to its own working class and people but also to the international working class and to mankind as a whole**...Lenin observed that 'capital is an international force. To vanquish it, an international workers' alliance, an international workers' brotherhood, is needed....

Charges of Soviet 'imperialism' are closely related to the specious idea that imperialism and socialism [communism] have some 'common features.' One hears, in response to the specific charge of conditional, 'tied' aid from the western imperialist states, that all nations have egotistic objectives and are motivated primarily by self-interest. This observation does not take into consideration that **the policies of the socialist countries are influenced by the trenchant dictum of Marxism that 'no nation can be free if it oppresses other nations** [emphasis added].'[25]

IV. The Invariable Imperative: Maintaining the PPP's Indian Electoral Base

Despite Jagan's pro-Soviet obsessions, traceable to the beginning of his political engagement in 1946, the solidity of his Indian political base was never jeopardised. From the 1920s, Indians in Guyana were energised by Gandhi's spiritual force and virtual sainthood – his moral irreproachability in his anti-colonial crusade against British colonialism, culminating in India's independence in August 1947 (the abominable travails of partition notwithstanding). This was augmented by the iconic stature of Jawaharlal Nehru, a seminal influence on Cheddi because of his legendary sacrifice in the Indian nationalist movement, immortalised by his nearly nine years in jail. Framed pictures of Gandhi and Nehru were, somewhat ritualistically, mounted on the walls of most Indian homes in British Guiana. Besides, the post-War consolidation and expansion of Indo-Guyanese engagement in rice, cattle, and commerce, enhanced their self-esteem and made them receptive to Jagan's anti-colonial mission. It was a spirit of hope and a notion of possibilities, primarily among Indians, that ignited Cheddi's 'bitter sugar' political mission, not a sense of despair or the agony of chronic deprivation.

By the end of the 1940s, Indians had cultural, economic, and political momentum in their favour. While astutely riding this wave of Indian self-esteem and expanding self-worth, Cheddi was also shrewd in ensuring that his racial support was never jeopardised. This was the propitious context in which Jagan was deftly crafting his crusade against 'king sugar' and the 'sugar gods,' imbued with emotive racial potency by the five Indian 'martyrs' of Plantation Enmore in June 1948 (see chapter 6). The eradication of malaria after the Second World War, largely through the herculean effort of the malariologist, Dr George Giglioli (1897–1975) of the Sugar Producers' Association (SPA), precipitated a sharp increase in the birth rate of Indians. This, paradoxically, constituted ample political capital for Jagan's anti-sugar/anti-Booker mission, championing workers' genuine grievances on the sugar plantations.

Janet Jagan was clever at harnessing Cheddi's abundant charismatic gifts to ensure that his racial support base (Indian) was unfailingly mobilised and consolidated. She brought decisively stellar attributes to Jagan's political mission: her capacity for hard work; an aptitude for organisational acuity (hitherto rudimentary within the political culture); her journalistic skills, enhanced by the widely popular perception of her, among Indo-Guyanese, as a beautiful young White woman dedicated to their cause against the 'sugar gods' (hitherto unexampled!). Indians do have a peculiar affinity for whiteness or lightness, rooted in the ancient Hindu texts and resilient caste notions premised on hierarchy and colour. This is true of Muslim Indians, too, with their susceptibility to Middle Eastern/Islamic conceptions of perfectibility, including the lightness or whiteness of the Arabs. This is rarely assessed, but it should not be underestimated. In any case, Janet was a priceless asset to Cheddi's political mission.

The split in 1955, the departure of Forbes Burnham and his segment of the PPP, did undermine the party's multiracial posture, irreparably, yet it was transformed shortly thereafter into a vibrant Indian party through and through. Cheddi's relentless fight against 'bitter sugar' and Janet's aptitude for maximising his political appeal (she was editor of the party's organ, *Thunder*), thus consolidating their Indian political base, are at the core of the phenomenon, following the dismembering of the tenuous alliance with Burnham of the early 1950s. They were thereby fortified, certain of victory by virtue of the Indian ethnic preponderance and Cheddi's invincibility under the first-past-the-post system. They were also beneficiaries of Burnham's discernibly lacklustre approach to the mobilisation of his rural African base, initially, in the aftermath of the split. Consequently, Jagan's PPP was returned with a majority in the general elections of August 1957, and they won again in August 1961.

Furthermore, Jagan's failure to join the West Indies Federation (1958–62) primarily because Indians were afraid that the colony would be 'swamped' by unemployed Black people from the islands, magnified African Guyanese suspicions of him. Jagan recalled that the Black West Indian leaders were coercing him to join the West Indies Federation, with the threat to curtail or terminate the market for Guyanese rice in their territories. Access to the Cuban market in the early 1960s, because of his ideological affinity with Castro and the Soviets, therefore, apart from satisfying Jagan's Indian supporters (the principal rice producers), was simultaneously an effective counter to the apparent West Indian campaign to pressure him to join the Federation. His stature among his own supporters was thereby enhanced immeasurably. No federation! But a secured market for rice in Cuba! As C. R. Jacob, executive member of the PPP, remarked in March 1961: 'Cuba has offered us a price for rice higher than that now being paid by the West Indies. This means more money for the rice producers.'[26]

Meanwhile, Africans perceived the further expansion of the rice industry in the early 1960s, facilitated by the extensive Black Bush Polder Scheme settling one thousand seven hundred families (mainly Indian) on thirty-one thousand acres (funded by the British and opened in 1961 around the time of the general elections) and the comparatively lucrative rice trade with Cuba; the incremental growth of an Indian middle class in commerce and the professions in addition to far-reaching reforms on the sugar plantations (under Jock Campbell's progressive leadership of Booker in the 1950s-early 1960s), as vindication of Jagan's partisan agenda – to elevate Indians to an unassailable position economically and politically. Moreover, Africans were demoralised by two resounding defeats at the polls, exacerbated by the likelihood of imminent independence under Jagan. They could not have envisaged, after the defeat of Burnham's PNC again, in 1961, that they would be rescued by the Americans. Jagan had made it clear that he was a communist, and that he had effectively joined the Cold War on the side of the Soviet Union and Castro's Cuba, having visited Castro twice in 1960. His meeting with President Kennedy, at the White House on October 25, 1961, was a disaster that convinced the president that Forbes Burnham was their man in their determination to preclude the emergence of a 'second Cuba' in the Hemisphere.

Despite having all the trumps in his hand, loyalty to his communist allies would cost Jagan the game. This tragedy has no parallel in the former British West Indies, indeed, anywhere. Guyana itself remains an enigma: an artificial creation that is still a geographical expression – not a political entity that could be considered a nation, more than fifty-seven years after Independence.

V. Sylvia Wynter's Repudiation of Jagan's Marxist Paradigm

I conclude this reflection on Cheddi Jagan's consuming Marxist passion, with the sobering verdict of the Jamaican cultural theorist and novelist, Sylvia Wynter (1928–). She and her then husband, the Guyanese writer and long-time friend of the Jagans, Jan Carew (1920–2012), went to British Guiana in the early 1960s to work for Cheddi's colonial government. Sylvia was, in fact, in Cheddi's residence, 'Red House,' virtually under siege, as supporters of Forbes Burnham and Peter D'Aguiar (Africans and Portuguese primarily) were burning and looting the commercial centre of Georgetown on Friday, February 16, 1962: 'Black Friday.' CIA-backed riots were unleashed in order to abort what seemed like the inevitability of the colony's independence under Jagan, sometime later that year.

Sylvia Wynter (1928–), the Jamaican-born intellectual. She and her husband, Jan Carew (1920–2012), the Guyanese novelist and friend of Cheddi, worked in British Guiana in the early 1960s

Sylvia Wynter remarks that her traumatic Guyanese experience had a transformative impact on the rest of her life:

> I realised a tragedy of enormous proportions was arising in Guyana… [because] the division between the black and Indian groups was profound. And I also realised, as I lived there, that however much the blacks struggled, they were eventually going to be displaced. I tried to speak with Cheddi. I said that whilst I'd love to continue working there it seemed that the greatest emphasis was to see if we could begin to build a common history, place the emphasis on creating a sense of a shared community, of solidarity, because that did not exist. But Cheddi was a very orthodox Marxist, and to even suggest that the superstructure was not automatically determined by the mode of production but was *constructed*, so that you can *reconstruct* it, that would have been heresy for him, genuinely…and so I said to him that I'd have to go. So, I went back to Jamaica because I was of no use any longer in Guyana…
>
> Up until then I was a Marxist because Marxism gave you a key which said look, you can understand the reality of which you're a part. This was my thinking until then. But from that moment I said, no, there is something important that this paradigm cannot deal with. A lot of my rethinking came out of that experience.[27]

Yet Sylvia could not forget, despite the chaos, violence, fear, and despair, Cheddi's generosity of spirit to many of those who were seeking shelter in 'Red House,' as Burnham and D'Aguiar's belligerent supporters marched menacingly towards the building:

> I remember Janet Jagan calling me and asking could I come over and write some radio scripts that would explain what the [Kaldor] budget was about [February 1962; the ostensible cause of the riots]. So, I took my little typewriter, and I was escorted through back roads and back doors and back gates to get to this Red House [on High Street, Kingston, Georgetown]. I'll never forget that! Because of one thing – what I remember is the gentleness of Cheddi Jagan as a person. A lot of people had taken refuge in there, and I remember him going around, concerned for the babies, if they had enough milk – an extraordinary kind of human being.
>
> Yet as I looked out of the window…what was traumatic for me was the stark nature of the divide between black and Indian — you had a black policeman at the gate, but you had a sharp-shooting Indian from the coast with a rifle aimed at him from the upstairs window. And outside you had the masses of people streaming towards 'Red House'; and Georgetown is burning…and riots![28]

This is an aspect of Cheddi's personality that people all over the world, including many who were repelled by his politics, still remember him by: his generosity of spirit; his sincerity of purpose – his fundamental humility. Yet the ultimate aim of this book is to comprehend the passion and inflexibility of a man who had all the trumps in his hand and still lost the game, in the context of the Cold War. What was it about his mental universe that made it impossible for him to recognise that the prize was there for the taking? All that was required was to know how to wait. But at the core of the Guyanese tragedy is the ethnic chasm: it cannot be papered over; it is at the heart of the social composition, as well as attitudes to power, of this difficult former colony. Marxism-Leninism could not eradicate it.

Sylvia Wynter says, 'there is something important that this paradigm cannot deal with.' She meant the power of racial, tribal, linguistic, and religious identities as discrete instruments of political articulation and mobilisation. This was diametrically opposite to Cheddi Jagan's conception of the Marxist-Leninist paradigm, based on the assumption that such divisive aggregated political segments stem from false consciousness that would be eliminated with the resolution of the class struggle, between the workers and the 'sugar gods,' for example, and the consequent empowerment of the working class: 'the dictatorship of the proletariat.'

In 1964, Jan Carew (Sylvia's husband) published a novel, *Moscow is Not My Mecca*, based on his experience of the Soviet Union as a guest of the Union of Soviet Writers in 1961–62, facilitated through the instrumentality of Billy Strachan and Cheddi Jagan. But he was clearly not enamoured of Cheddi's long-standing Soviet model, his blueprint for the advancement of an independent British Guiana. Russian thugs consider the African protagonist 'uncultured,' and dub him a 'Black monkey,' beating him up because he has a White girlfriend. Besides, Carew provides the following thought to one of his more reflective Russian characters:

> We have been told again and again that your people are hungry and illiterate victims of imperialist greed and oppression …We were never told that some of you had travelled to New York, Rome, London, Paris, and that we would envy you your clothes, your way of talking freely about things we don't dare to mention.[29]

Carew had found Cheddi's vision of utopia materially and spiritually impoverished. I did ask Cheddi about Carew's book, and he said that it could be bought for ten cents in the US, shortly after its publication there, because it was subsidised by the CIA. For Cheddi it was all water off a duck's back!

On the centenary of Lenin's birth, in 1970, Jagan wrote an article in which he restated his position on the primacy of the class struggle:

> In Third World countries the society is torn asunder by race, tribe, language, religion and cultural and economic backwardness or underdevelopment. Consequently, it is easy for the imperialists, their puppets and their agents to play on emotions, to bribe and corrupt, to divide and rule, and to subvert and overthrow…Unity in such a situation can be achieved only on the basis of the Marxist-Leninist doctrine of the class struggle. It is this scientific outlook which must be contraposed against ignorance, superstition and prejudice…
>
> The right deviationists [led by Forbes Burnham], not having a Marxist-Leninist approach, but a racialist one, not recognising that the economic structure forms the basis, the foundation upon which the political and ideological superstructures are built, see compromise with US imperialism as the only way out.[30]

Therefore, the tenacious African-Indian incomprehension in which Guyanese politics is immersed would dissolve in due course, with the construction of the communist society – the perfect universe – the realisation of which Cheddi had no doubts whatsoever. As he perceived it throughout his long political life: 'Difficulties there will be; the battle will be long and hard. But win we will. History and time are on our side!' This mantra was the source of his political resilience; the foundation of his fatal errors too. However, as Moses Bhagwan, the former head of the PPP's youth arm in the early 1960s (the Progressive Youth Organisation), has explained to me, Jagan survived despite the continual fissures within the PPP and the supposed strength of his ideology. He owed his political longevity to the loyalty of his Indian constituency – the persistence of Guyanese racism – not the 'purity' of his Marxism:

> It was a mechanistic reaction of communist parties to rationalise inner party struggles and fissures as a cleansing process because the party's core principles and philosophy survive a challenge and this

yields greater unity and cohesion and, therefore, the loss of cadres at this level, paradoxically, makes the party ideologically stronger.

This nonsense, applied to Guyana, is even more nonsensical. In the first place, it raises a second or third level abruptly into leadership. The party loses experience and quality and makes a virtue of it.

I have never seen the PPP leadership go to the masses in triumph and extol the victory of Marxism-Leninism in the Party. For the commanding idea that held the constituency intact was not ideology or the purity of it, but the fear of making the other side stronger. The enemy on the other side is the PNC, carrying the flag for African Guyanese.

The PPP's comfort with loss of cadres at that level is fictional, but they did not suffer dire consequences because ethnic solidarity was unshakeable, and in fact the splits served to fortify the solidity of ethnic support. The Indian masses had insulated themselves from the shock of expulsions and resignations, of left or right.[31]

Notes

1. Interview with Lloyd Best, May 1, 2001, in Frank Birbalsingh, *The PPP of Guyana, 1950–92: An Oral History* (London: Hansib, 2007), 89.
2. Ibid., 88.
3. See my *Sweetening 'Bitter Sugar': Jock Campbell, the Booker Reformer in British Guiana, 1934–66* (Kingston, Jamaica: Ian Randle Publishers, 2005), 290–98.
4. Birbalsingh, *The PPP of Guyana, 1950–92*, 34); Frank Birbalsingh, Interview with Cheddi Jagan, October 24, 1984.
5. Cheddi Jagan, *Tracing our Path in a Changing World!* (Georgetown, Guyana, 1990), 14, 23.
6. Cheddi Jagan, 'Debate on the Undesirable Publications Bill (1952),' in *National Assembly Speeches, Vol 2, 1952–53* (Leeds: The Caribbean Press, 2011), 309–10.
7. Cheddi Jagan, *The West on Trial: My Fight for Guyana's Freedom* (London: Michael Joseph, 1966), 452–53.
8. Cheddi Jagan, *The Caribbean: Whose Backyard?* (Published by the Author, n.d. [1985]), 314–15, 330.
9. Janet Jagan, 'Editor's Notebook: Chairman Mao,' *Thunder*, September 29, 1962 [CJRC, call no: 5100]; Janet Jagan, 'Reminiscence: Che...' [CJRC, call no: 6434].
10. Frank Birbalsingh, Interview with Moses Bhagwan, November 7, 1998, in Frank Birbalsingh, *The PPP of Guyana, 1950–92*, 115, 118.
11. 'Birth Centenary: Boysie Ramkarran (1919–2009),' *The Thinker*, Vol. 2 (July–December, 2018), 90.
12. This document is in the Billy Strachan Papers (BSP), Institute of Commonwealth Studies Documents, Senate House Library, University of London.
13. For the wider context of Soviet-Cuban aid to the beleaguered Jagan government, during the CIA-backed general strike of 1963, Jagan, *The West on Trial: My Fight for Guyana's Freedom*, chapter XIII.
14. Cheddi Jagan, 'The Havana Conference,' *Labour Monthly* (March 1966): 117.
15. Jagan, 'Debate on the Undesirable Publications Bill (1952),' 310.
16. Ibid., 319.

17. Hewlett Johnson, *The Socialist Sixth of the World* (London: Victor Gollancz, 1939), 294–96. For a fine biographical study of Johnson, an apologist of much that was discreditable about communism, see John Butler, *The Red Dean of Canterbury: the Public and Private Faces of Hewlett Johnson* (London: Scala, 2011).

18. Johnson, *The Socialist Sixth of the World*, 296.

19. Kimani Nehusi, *A People's Political History of Guyana, 1838–1964* (Hertford: Hansib, 2018), 524.

20. Leszek Kolakowski, *Main Currents of Marxism* (New York: W.W. Norton, 2005 [1978]), 859.

21. Ibid.

22. Professor Kolakowski's article of 2002, 'What is Left of Socialism?' may be accessed at: https://www.firstthings.com/article/2002/10/what-is-left-of-socialism.

23. V. S. Naipaul, 'A Handful of Dust: Return to Guyana,' *The New York Review of Books*, April 11, 1991, 19.

24. Jochen Hellbeck, *Revolution on my Mind: Writing a Diary under Stalin* (Cambridge, Massachusetts: Harvard University Press, 2006), 116–17.

25. Cheddi Jagan, 'Address to the 18th PPP Congress on behalf of the Central Committee,' *Thunder* (October–December 1974): 21, 26, 31.

26. This document is in the Billy Strachan Papers (BSP), Institute of Commonwealth Studies Documents, Senate House Library, University of London.

27. David Scott, 'The Re-Enchantment of Humanism: An Interview with Sylvia Wynter,' *Small Axe*, no. 8 (2000): 141–42.

28. Ibid., 140–41.

29. Jan Carew, *Moscow is Not My Mecca* (London: Secker and Warburg, 1964), 90.

30. Cheddi Jagan, 'Lenin and Our Time,' *Thunder* (January–June 1970): 48, 50.

31. Moses Bhagwan, personal correspondence, March 2019.

3.

Divergent Nationalisms

African and Indian Identities in Colonial Guyana, 1920s–40s, with Special Reference to the Idea of an Indian Colony

I.   J.A. Luckhoo's and Dr Wharton's Pursuit of the Idea of an Indian Colony in British Guiana

Cheddi and Janet Jagan did not grasp the forbidding complexity of Guyanese society when they embarked on their political mission in 1946; they certainly could not apprehend the depth and resilience of mutual racial insecurities. It was as Indian or African or Portuguese, not Guyanese, that most people identified themselves in British Guiana in the twentieth century. Even a liberal thinker like A. R. F. Webber (1880–1932), editor of the *Daily Chronicle* in the early 1920s and the *New Daily Chronicle* in the late 1920s to early 1930s, continually counselled the engendering of 'race consciousness' – communal identity – as a prelude to the shaping of a Guyanese national identity, in the long-run. In August 1926, for instance, Webber contemplated the differential communal pride within the African and Indian communities respectively. The latter, he argued, had benefited immeasurably from continuous engagement with their Indian legacy, whereas Africans manifested a spasmodic, less coherent and arguably ambivalent, relationship regarding their African heritage: 'more talk than anything else,' he dismissed it rather uncharitably. African consciousness was not a quotidian reality. It was deemed 'only a mild enthusiasm'; fragile, it could dissipate easily. Webber observed: 'there is nothing inherently wrong in developing the racial consciousness of any one group of our cosmopolitan community. Properly directed, race consciousness is a very fine thing.'[1] Webber's comparison was an invidious one, for he was underrating the impact of Garveyism and eclectic constructs of the African homeland on African sensibility in the colony in the 1920s. However, his apprehension of the comparative robustness of the Indian cultural synthesis, sustaining a recurring affirmation of Indo-Guyanese identity, is incontestable.

But it was the idea of the creation of an Indian colony in British Guiana, actively pursued by J.A. Luckhoo (1887–1949), the most prominent Indian politician in the colony in the 1920s, and Dr William Hewley Wharton (1869–?), the first Indian in British Guiana to graduate as a medical doctor (University of Edinburgh, 1899), that really gnawed at African self-esteem and ignited implacable fears for their very existence in British Guiana. It was planted in their imagination as the dominant motif of the Indian's resolve to dominate African Guyanese.

At the inaugural meeting of the revamped British Guiana East Indian Association (BGEIA) on April 24, 1919 (the original was founded by Joseph Ruhomon (1873–1942), Edward Luckhoo (1878–1959), and others in New Amsterdam in 1916), presided over by Dr Wharton and addressed by J.A. Luckhoo, the plausibility of an Indian colony was quietly

J.A. Luckhoo (1887–1949), the first Indian legislator in British Guiana (1916). He advocated the creation of an 'Indian Colony' there in the context of a Colonisation Scheme that did not come to fruition, despite his going to India twice and meeting with Mahatma Gandhi

corroborated. The source of the idea was Governor Sir Wilfred Collet (1856–1929) who reportedly counselled the Indian leaders thus:

> The great need [in British Guiana] is for a population of 10,000,000… He hoped that the East Indians in this colony would make the Indian Government thoroughly understand that what they wanted here were more East Indians as permanent settlers, because unless they increased the population, they would not increase their influence in the colony. It had been suggested that British Guiana was to India what Canada was to the U.K…The East Indians who came here and settled had got opportunities for advancement and their children still greater opportunities than they could possibly have had if they had remained in their own country ….[2]

The latter is incontestable (whatever one's view of the renewal of Indian immigration), as the indentured labourers were primarily low or outcaste (untouchable) impoverished people, who found infinite scope for mobility in British Guiana compared with their caste-ridden villages of despair.

The idea of the colony accommodating millions of settlers, after the end of indentureship (terminated in April 1920), was repeated by Governor Collet at a West India Committee dinner in London on August 29, 1919:

> British Guiana is as big in area as Great Britain. There would be no difficulty in finding room for 15,000,000 people, and at present the population is only a little over 300,000.'³ Earlier that month, the *West India Committee Circular* (August 7, 1919) had editorialised on the subject, noting that 'in British Guiana there are over 9,000,000 acres easily accessible for beneficial occupation and suitable for tropical cultivation.

J.A. Luckhoo and Dr Wharton were at the dinner in London, on the eve of their departure for India to persuade Gandhi of the agricultural potential of British Guiana and its capacity for the permanent settling of many more Indians. But, ominously for Africans, the Indian delegates also envisaged that they could, in the process, create an Indian colony there. Dr Wharton reportedly defined the aim of their mission (the Colonisation Scheme) thus:

> [They are going to] prove to their countrymen [in India] that British Guiana is one of the few places in which there is no prejudice, and where everyman stands on an equal footing and receive equal rights of citizenship – political and otherwise. He hopes they would be able to induce many of their fellow countrymen to join their forces, which already numbered 140,000 out of 300,000, and that they would be able to form a colony of Indians. The value of the Indian labourer is well known in the colony. He has proved himself to be the agriculturist of the country.

Not many today are aware of J.A. Luckhoo's and Dr Wharton's advocacy (however preliminary and imprecise) of an Indian colony in British Guiana in the early 1920s. Yet Luckhoo has been linked by a few Indians, including Jagan, with a 'retrograde' step to 'continue Indian immigration,' in league with the sugar planters.³ These have tended to calumniate him as a quisling, who sought to reintroduce indentureship. This is now an aspect of Indian lore: a distortion probably rooted in the contemporary perception by many Indians of some members of the Luckhoo family (such as E. A. Luckhoo and his son, Lionel) as anti-Indian collaborators with the plantocracy and, later, with the African leader in Guyana, L. F. S. Burnham, against their Indian hero, Cheddi Jagan. However, the idea of an Indian colony in British Guiana did plant pernicious tentacles of Indian domination in the psyche of African Guyanese – a potent, if subliminal, source of their enduring insecurity – J.A. Luckhoo's advocacy of it merits scrutiny. It is submerged, yet arguably at the root of the failure of Jagan's radical politics – after fifty years of his Marxist-Leninist mission – to forge even minimal working-class consciousness between Africans and Indians.

As early as 1911, C. M. Hale, a planter long resident in the colony, adumbrated the concept of the colonisation by India of British Guiana (and the British West Indies). He argued that Indo-Guyanese history was characterised by 'continual progress and improvement,' or, more dramatically, by an 'upward march in the scale of civilisation.' And he observed that creole Indians (those born in the colony) were no longer 'exotic'; they were, in fact, even inclined to regard India as a foreign country. They identified themselves as 'Guianese rather than Asiatics' and were already exhibiting 'an awakening national sentiment' towards the colony. Hale endorsed the initiative on the part of a few educated Indo-Guyanese to be relieved of the strictures of the Immigration Ordinance: the paternalistic 'protection' of the immigration agent-general, framed in the context of indentureship. But he envisaged incremental cultural renewal, and racial augmentation, of the community through migration from India, culminating in their eventual domination of the colony: **'Continually reinforced by the arrival of fresh immigrants from India, the race keeps vigorous and pure, while the Negro and Portuguese elements, already inextricably mixed, slowly perish and die out** [emphasis added].'[4]

Hale would have provoked palpable foreboding in African Guyanese, having anticipated their physical demise while the ascendant Indians colonised British Guiana comprehensively, in addition to other British possessions in the region. Indian supremacy, therefore, was being postulated on the presupposition of African social degradation and their incremental physical extinction:

> The memory of five years' wholesome discipline [indentureship], to a very large extent handed down from its original recipient to his posterity, combined with an almost automatic disappearance of that insuperable bar to progress, caste, has made the…Indian as being superior and preferable to his counterpart in Hindustan…In their stead are vigorous, self-respecting, and self-reliant colonists…There has recently been some talk of colonising the remainder of the British West Indies with East Indians. Surely the lesson of British Guiana, which owes the continued existence of her main industry [sugar] and the inception of another [rice] to these immigrants, should sweep away any hesitation…**Transplanted to Western lands, the East Indian displays a faculty for absorbing Western ideas and civilisation, without the ghastly moral degeneration the Negro has undergone in the same process** [emphasis added].[5]

J.A. Luckhoo was the first Indian elected to the colonial legislature, in 1916; he became president of the British Guiana East Indian Association (BGEIA) in 1919. He was emphatic that the organisation must assume political responsibilities: 'those [Indians] who were lucky enough to be placed in good positions should help their fellows and look after their interests,' especially the labouring class. Only one of their 'own nationality' could conceivably empathise with the feelings and grievances of Indian labourers.[6] He believed the termination of indentureship constituted a psychological watershed for Indians, and he deemed it apposite that their 'intellectual and political awakening should almost synchronise with the fall of the system.' Luckhoo felt his community had reached 'the turn of the tide'; therefore, it was incumbent on the BGEIA to cultivate and extend the spirit of civic responsibility emerging among Indians, to educate them to assert their political rights.[7]

In an interview in India with the *Madras Times*, on December 26, 1919, Luckhoo observed that 40 per cent of the potential voters in British Guiana were Indians, and if they were all registered 'no community would have equal influence at the [general] elections' as they could. They would outnumber Africans, who were 'less industrious and thrifty than the Indian community, and less anxious to acquire property.'[8] The franchise was based then on property and income criteria. Luckhoo also wished to strengthen the bond with the 'motherland' (India) so that she may be sensitised to, and thereby empathise with, 'the great destiny' that awaited Indians in the colony. British Guiana's Indians were, he thought, 'the object lesson' of what could be accomplished in colonial development, providing drainage and irrigation schemes were executed by the government.[9] He also asserted that it was widely acknowledged in the colony that its development was contingent primarily upon Indian enterprise; moreover, that the foundation was already laid for Indian predominance in wealth, education and politics. 'In the colony,' he concluded, 'the Indian labourer is recognised to be the best cultivator and, on the whole, the best citizen.'[10]

Despite Luckhoo's buoyant anticipation – even hubris – with respect to Indian preponderance in British Guiana's future, he conceded that they felt like 'scattered sons of India' because they constituted only 40 per cent of the population. And in a tactless intervention, earlier (on August 7, 1919), at a meeting in London of the multiracial British Guiana Colonisation Deputation with Lord Sinha (1863–1928), the under-secretary of state for India (an Indian), Luckhoo implored him to facilitate the creation of an Indian colony in British Guiana by sanctioning the resumption of immigration from India to the colony. It is irrefutable that African anxieties and insecurities, triggered by perceived expanding Indian hegemony, were exacerbated by Luckhoo's idea of an Indian colony, with irreparable consequences for the future of Guyana. It must be stressed that his extraordinary plea for an Indian colony, at the India Office, was made in the presence of all the African Guyanese representatives on the deputation: Hon A.B. Brown, Hon P.N. Browne, Rev E.R.O. Robertson, J. McFarlane Corry, as well as the light 'coloured' delegate, Hon E.G. Woolford.

J.A. Luckhoo was probably emboldened to make the potentially combustible request, openly, because Lord Sinha (chair of the meeting) had earlier expressed eagerness for the creation of an Indian colony in East Africa. Yet inexplicably (given the multiracial composition of the Guyanese delegates at the meeting), Luckhoo made no secret of his principal aim:

> **In British Guiana, although we form 40% of the population, we feel and we have always felt that we are scattered sons of India, and that India should stretch her hands across to us and try and help us and lift us up. The only way of doing this is to increase our numbers in the colony…We hope that in the future British Guiana will become a great Indian Colony. We appeal to the Head of the India Office** [Edwin Montagu], **and to the leaders of Indian authority and opinion to give us their help. We feel that you have our destiny in your hands, and we ask you to remember that these people who emigrate to British Guiana will have the same rights, and that if they come in sufficient numbers we shall be able to build up an Indian Colony which will be a credit to India and the Empire** [emphasis added].[11]

The idea of an Indian colony in British Guiana was replicated in a pamphlet produced by J.A. Luckhoo and Dr William Hewley Wharton; the latter accompanied Luckhoo, Parbhu Sawh (another Indian) and the attorney general of British Guiana, J. J. Nunan, on the first Colonisation Deputation to India in 1919–20. This document, *British Guiana Imperial Colonisation Scheme*, was published in London in September 1919. Luckhoo and Wharton argued:

> The resident Indians in British Guiana would like to embrace the opportunity now offered by the Government to make British Guiana an Indian Colony. They would like to encourage the settlement in the colony of every class and trade. At present the labouring and agricultural classes can materially improve their general condition by migrating to the colony and would in a short time be able to amass sufficient competence to make them independent.[12]

Earlier, in March 1919, in his address to the British Guiana East Indian Association, Luckhoo advocated the migration of higher classes of Indians, people who were obviously crucial to the legitimacy, administration and economic viability of an Indian colony, although he did not mention the idea of such a colony on that occasion. But the germ of that grand vision, however illusory, was discernible:

> We in British Guiana feel it incumbent on us to rise to the occasion and make ourselves worthy of the great race to which we belong. We feel that the time has arrived when we must collect our forces together in one grand effort to achieve the high and noble destiny to which we feel we are now called. The only remedy I could suggest is the voluntary emigration of higher classes, gentlemen in learned professions, merchants, skilled artisans and others whose social position will entitle them to respect.[13]

Luckhoo received endorsement for his idea of an Indian colony from the attorney general, J.J. Nunan, when the deputation met Sir George Barnes, secretary to the government of India in the Department of Industry and Commerce, on December 5, 1919. Nunan sought to refute the contention doing the rounds that the Colonisation Scheme was tantamount to indentureship by the back door:

> It is not a labour scheme or a project for securing cheap labour... It is based upon free immigration of Indian agricultural families... [T]hose who engage in agricultural work either for an employer or on their own behalf for three years will receive reward grants of five acres of land on nominal terms...There is to be no trace of the old indenture system. There is no compulsory residence or service or other element of compulsion. Settlers can choose their own employers...**As our population is now 45% Indian (145,000) and as our constitution involves political equality of all races, we are really offering India a colony of its own on the north-eastern coast of South America, with fertile soil and a healthier climate than that of India**...[emphasis added].[14]

The Indian colony was also advanced in an article by Luckhoo, Dr Wharton and the other Indian member of the deputation, Parbhu Sawh, which appeared in the official organ of the Indian National Congress (INC) at its Amritsar Congress, in December 1919 (it also carried the address of the chairman, Pandit Motilal Nehru, Jawaharlal's father). The grand idea of the Indian colony, which would remain in the Empire while being of 'vast political and national advantage' to India, was permeated by the millenarian El Dorado reflex in the Guyanese psyche:

> We are in a position definitely to state that the Indians now resident in British Guiana comprise about 45 per cent of the entire population... No barrier of any kind is erected against Indians [in the colony], as in the case of Natal, South Africa, etc. Here they enjoy equal rights and privileges in the truest sense of the words – on the principle of 'Man and Brother'...In other words the Indians like the rest of the community are treated on a footing of complete equality. There is no race feeling.[15]

These Indo-Guyanese advocates apparently did not envisage any contradiction between the creation of an Indian colony, on one hand, and upholding the rights of Guyanese of other ethnic groups, on the other, specifically the descendants of enslaved Africans, their predecessors on the plantations. However, the latter felt they had special claims based on prior residence, in conjunction with their being, by far, the most dehumanised segment in the making of the colony. But the enduring El Dorado reflex could transport Guyanese to heights of grandiloquence, transcending seamlessly the bedevilling racism, chronic malaria, and the formidable problem of drainage and irrigation:

> We…now formally state that it is our desire, aim, and our object, if possible, to induce more Indians from the Motherland to join our ranks, increase our numbers and so help us to make British Guiana an Indian Colony. This is really the Empire's clarion call to India. The potentialities of British Guiana are immense, and the local Government is now prepared to offer such unconditional terms in the country as would, if properly known to the Indian public in India, make them co-operate with us by coming over to British Guiana, and sharing with us some of the great benefits which we ourselves enjoy. British Guiana is a land of freedom, equality, liberty and prosperity for one and all….[16]

Luckhoo, Wharton, and Sawh continued, buoyantly, on their triumphal march to El Dorado:

> The wonderful resources of the colony…would in a very short time enable British Guiana alone to defray the Empire's present indebtedness to the United States, which was incurred in order to win the World War for freedom and liberty…In the very near future the colony will be in a position, by the introduction of Indian agriculturalists and Indian capitalists, to place British Guiana in the front ranks of British colonial possessions. The vast political and national advantage to India of having an Indian Colony on the South American continent need not be emphasised. We would then have hundreds of prosperous villages and thousands of square miles of flourishing crops springing up from the fertile soil of the colony, and by the exploitation of the Gold, Diamond and Aluminium…and other mineral and forest wealth of British Guiana, the three-century old dream of Sir Walter Raleigh regarding our Magnificent Province, the fabled land of El Dorado, will be realised.[17]

Dr Wharton entreated the INC delegates at Amritsar to approve their quest for an Indian colony:

> We are anxious that a branch of the Congress should be established in British Guiana so that it may form a connecting link with the mother country. The Indian Colony would thus not be left isolated or forgotten. British Guiana as an Indian Colony would indeed be a great asset to India, the importance of which it is needless to emphasise.[18]

The *Delhi Morning Post* carried an interview with Dr Wharton shortly thereafter, which was reproduced in the *Daily Chronicle* of British Guiana. It was captioned boldly – AN INDIAN COLONY IN THE MAKING: '**Dr Wharton intends visiting all important centres of India to get voluntary immigrants, and thus ultimately to make British Guiana an Indian Colony out and out** [emphasis added].'[19]

It is probable that Luckhoo was motivated (erroneously) by two key factors in promulgating his case for an Indian colony in British Guiana: that the Indian nationalist leaders, Gandhi in particular, would be receptive to it as a viable alternative, given that Indians in East and South Africa were subject to blatant discrimination by Europeans, their civil and political rights gravely circumscribed; likewise, by the salutary official stance (though clearly invidious) that Indians were designated the ideal colonists to propel this backward, neglected colony forward to abundant prosperity. Indeed, Governor Collet had expressed preference for 'East Indian' over 'West Indian' (African) immigrants, extolling the Indian's 'natural inclination' to cultivate reclaimed lands, allied with their industry, thrift, and apparent willingness to pay a rent for such lands to secure a livelihood. He conceded, however, that some West Indians (Africans) could find employment in places where they 'would not be available as casual labourers to coastal plantations,' an allusion to the sparsely settled interior of the colony.[20]

Implicit in the governor's preference for Indian immigrants was his assumption of their availability as 'casual labourers' on the sugar plantations. Therefore, Luckhoo's idea of an Indian colony, coming on the heels of indentureship, was fated to be stigmatised as a ruse to alleviate the labour predicament on the plantations, in the wake of the termination of the controversial and much-maligned system. It was also indefensible in a multiracial society where the Negro Progress Convention (NPC), the principal African Guyanese organisation founded in 1922, had promulgated their dictum with respect to maintaining 'ethnic balance' in the colony at all costs. The Colonisation Scheme, though largely inspired by the plantocracy, elicited diverse expectations, including a genuine belief after the Great War that British Guiana was on the threshold of a comprehensive development programme. For Luckhoo and Wharton, the Colonisation Scheme was considered a potent instrument to realise their idea of an Indian colony. With the support of the planters, the government, and local advocates of opening up the interior, they were confident that immigration could be resumed and a scheme devised for settling people on the land, thus augmenting the Indian segment of the population to a level where they would necessarily become paramount in the social, economic, and political evolution of the colony. In fact, even before the Colonisation Deputation left for London, *Indian Opinion* (organ of the BGEIA) had boasted in May 1919 that with the effectual registration of Indian voters 'it is possible for us to enlarge the electorate to such an extent as to enable us very easily to put any member of our own race in the Legislature despite the most strenuous opposition of any rival candidate of any nationality whatsoever.'[21]

II. The Negro Progress Convention's Repulsion at the Idea of an Indian Colony: Their Insistence on the Primacy of 'Ethnic Balance'

Such tactless triumphalism inevitably exacerbated African fears, and it strengthened their determination to repudiate both the idea of an Indian colony, as well as the Colonisation Scheme – unless there was parity of numbers between potential African and Indian immigrants: 'ethnic balance,' as they termed it. Shortly after J. J. Nunan and Luckhoo left for India in late 1923, on the second Colonisation Deputation, the Negro Progress Convention, frustrated by the government's inaction in acceding to their request for a parallel deputation to West Africa to attract immigrants of their race, addressed a memorandum to the secretary of state for the colonies. They submitted that if Africans were not procured on the same scale as Indians, the scheme would be interpreted as 'a distinct act of discrimination.' The NPC contended that it would 'materially reduce the status of the Negro to one of dependence,' with deleterious political consequences for them and the colony as a whole.

The pernicious resonance of Luckhoo and Wharton's idea of an Indian colony lodged in the African Guyanese imagination. Indissoluble!

> It would tend to rob them [Africans] of their political potentialities as they would be in the minority in any voting contest – the Indian voters would become more than or equal to the votes of any two of the other sections of the community; it would be detrimental to good government and the preservation of the peace of the country, and would further tend to create a monopoly for fostering or laying the foundation for class labour and would place the Government in a state of embarrassment in times of stress…All this makes it necessary that **the different sections of the subject races should be as near as possible balanced** [emphasis added].[22]

This was the context in which the NPC suggested the recruiting of Black South African migrants, who 'are hungering for better and freer labour conditions.' They also reiterated their argument with respect to the despatch of a deputation to West Africa and the West Indies – consonant with their 'right to first consideration,' being the 'pioneer settlers' on account of their enslavement.[23] In this environment of aggravated mutual angst regarding racial domination, it is understandable why, by 1923–24, J.A. Luckhoo had become discernibly reticent about his idea of an Indian colony. But the fact that the director of agriculture (Bombay Presidency), G. F. Keatinge, the sole English member of the three-man deputation to British Guiana, in 1922, assigned to scrutinise the prospects for colonisation would soon express approbation of Luckhoo's idea of an Indian colony, in his minority report, must have revitalised his grand plan despite its reprobation by the NPC. On the other hand, it would have revived aversion to the idea among the leaders of that organisation, as well as African Guyanese generally.

The second Nunan-Luckhoo Colonisation Deputation to India, in 1923–24, also proved ill-fated. The government of India had informed the India Office categorically: 'With the advent of the *swarajists* [home rulers led by Gandhi] the temper of the Emigration Committee…is likely to be very different to its predecessor [in 1920]. We trust, in the circumstances, the delegation will not sail as proposed.'[24] In fact, the whole Colonisation Scheme was doomed. Gandhi and the INC were engaged in an all-consuming anti-colonial crusade, and ending Indian indentureship had assumed a moral dimension at the core of their campaign, dramatised graphically by allegations of a spate of sexual assaults of Indian women on sugar plantations, particularly in Fiji. They were therefore disinclined to condone immigration from India, in any form, in the aftermath of the abolition of the system in 1917; neither was the government of India likely to resume immigration, even if radically modified, thereby presenting Gandhi with enhanced political ammunition. The idea of an Indian colony never did have a chance of coming to fruition, given the emotions it readily provoked within the Indian nationalist crusade. But it has left a bitter legacy among African Guyanese that is not amenable to erasure. It engendered a chronic misgiving of Indo-Guyanese motives as inherently injurious to African aspirations – methodical Indian domination of British Guiana, aimed at decisive economic, cultural, demographic and, ultimately, political hegemony. The idea of an Indian colony and the fear and anger it generated, arguably, is seminal to the enduring African-Indian incomprehension.

I began this chapter with A.R.F. Webber's reflection (in August 1926) on African identity, as a transparently less robust construct, juxtaposed with the sanguinity of Indo-Guyanese with respect to their emerging identity. Webber was probably alluding to themes of racial self-criticism that the president of the Negro Progress Convention (NPC), E.F. Fredericks (1876–1934), routinely accentuated at their annual conferences, on Emancipation Day (August 1): racial pride, self-help, the imperative of thrift, and planning for the future. On their fifth anniversary, in August 1926, Fredericks spoke in the same vein, while stressing that the rampant extravagance of Africans redounded to the economic advantage of Indians. However, one of the potential hazards of 'race consciousness' (advocated by Fredericks and Webber), a negative flipside, was the escalating antipathy between Indians – generally maligned as ruthlessly crafty – and Africans, who saw themselves as victims of the latecomers' (interlopers') ferocious acquisitiveness.

The African predicament, as depicted by Fredericks, was framed by debased cultural parameters: the loss, in creole society, of 'tribal instincts' of solidarity and responsibility – the fracturing of the African predilection for communal initiative, effort and the resolution of problems:

> Presently we stand at the foot of all peoples in material resources, not so much because of circumstances which exist outside of ourselves, but because, among and between ourselves, there exist certain practices and influences that are baneful. Our tribal instincts are shattered, our father's communal commingling and sharing are gone, community interest and community concerns are things of the past... We produce a fair quantity of wealth in our...labours in the interior of our country [in the gold and diamond fields], but the distribution of this production is wasteful and aimless.
>
> Instead of the distribution being made with an eye single to the future happiness and prosperity of the producer, it is made with an uncontrollable desire to satisfy either vanity or appetite [wanton extravagance]. This distribution therefore destroys the very sinews which should be in order to sustain the racial body...In a mixed community, the distribution of one set in the community goes to the benefit of the other set; but, in order that the whole distribution may go to the good of the whole community, the separate units of the community must produce equally in proportion to their numbers, wants and necessities.[25]

This problem was compounded in the early 1930s as the Great Depression bit and economic options evaporated. In any case, Fredericks's recipe for self-improvement amounted to the adumbration of an idealist socialist dispensation unattainable there or in any other society. And by posing the problem in this manner, he was reinforcing the widespread impression held by Africans of the Indians' single-mindedness in amassing wealth, often by sordid means and unmitigated miserliness. Rendered plausible by repetition, it was conducive to 'race consciousness' being distorted to foment racial discord and racism. Fredericks also counterposed the Indian's presumed predisposition to a longer view with the African's supposed

Hon. E.F. Fredericks (1874–1934), founder of the Negro Progress Convention (NPC) in 1922. He categorically rejected J.A. Luckhoo's idea of an 'Indian Colony' in British Guiana, apprehensive that it would entrench Indian demographic and political preponderance. Fredericks also tirelessly sought to inculcate thrift and initiative in self-enhancement among his African people

short-sightedness: 'The former is less able physically to do the labour the latter can perform, but man for man, the Indian, by steady resolution to future prosperity, produces comparatively more and brings about a happier distribution than the Negro.'[26]

Inspired by Garveyism in the 1920s (though not Garveyite), the NPC and the African Guyanese newspaper in the 1930s, *Tribune*, both fervently postulated the economic underpinning of race pride, as they sought to inculcate consistency of effort, thrift, and financial prudence in their people. In January 1930, for instance, 'Enterprise,' a regular correspondent to *Tribune*, expressed foreboding of unrestrained Indian economic ascendancy:

> In villages like Plaisance, Beterverwagting and Buxton [East Coast Demerara], where once the Negro held financial supremacy, their position is deplorable. **The Negro is being ousted week by week by the wily East Indian.** Why? Because the new Negro ignores the road to the…banks, because he is a lover of dice, because he has developed a penchant for the daughters of Rahab company [prostitutes] who reside around Bartica and in the city of Georgetown…

> He suffers from no want of opportunity to amass money, but his dissipatory proclivities act as a barrier to the practise of thrift, and as a consequence he finds himself supplanted by one who comparatively earns less than himself but who is thrifty [the Indian]…Something will have to be done, for Negroes in the villages are slipping at a rate that broods no good to the race as a whole. **Behind them is a race that has the mysticism, subtilly [sic] and crafty wiliness of the unchanging East, who are determined to place [elevate] themselves at all cost** [emphasis added].[27]

In March 1930, another regular correspondent to *Tribune* cited E. F. Fredericks while imploring Africans to practise thrift and abjure profligacy in order to hold on to their land:

> Is it not a common experience that houses and land are mortgaged and remain unredeemed only to secure money for some passing pleasure? Have not large areas of land, once the proud possession of the Negro, passed into other hands [primarily Indians] from sheer indifference and carelessness? Can the children of Africa continue in these extravagances and become a worthy class of citizens?

The dread of an encroaching Indian hegemony – conceived as a veritable financial juggernaut – was a recurring motif in the deliberations of the NPC. It was rooted largely in the incremental haemorrhaging of hard-earned ancestral African land in the villages, mainly to Indians.[28]

It is comprehensible, therefore, why a Guyanese national identity failed to cohere, while a robust bifurcated ethnic identity was in the making: discretely African and Indian. A creole sensibility – what Richard Burton calls Afro-Creole[29] – an amalgam of African and European elements with the latter arguably determinative was already consolidated. But Indians in British Guiana, steeped in their own cultural reverences continually adapted from 'many imagined Indias,' were disinclined to be absorbed by, or assimilated to it. The Afro-Creole paradigm was too redolent of African cultural syncretism, potent though the European component (Dutch then British), to render it amenable to Indian approbation. Consequently, a transcendent creole sensibility, definitive in the British West Indies, barring Trinidad with its substantial Indian segment also, did not materialise in this ethnically diverse milieu. A genuinely inclusive creole sensibility in British Guiana would have required a synthesis of Indo-Guyanese and Afro-Creole cultures – rare magnanimity and abundant generosity of spirit on both sides. This proved elusive. Although Indians were becoming increasingly creolised, it was largely creolisation from within, primarily on their own terms. Kamau Brathwaite has called this 'in/culturation.'[30] Indo-Caribbean people, he argues, experienced 'selective creolisation': an eclectic but enduring Indian master narrative conditioned and enriched their encounter with the Afro-Creole paradigm.

The Marxism-Leninism of Cheddi Jagan and the 'cooperative socialism' of Forbes Burnham would later prove inadequate to the monumental task of reconciling the highly politicised bifurcated cultural traditions.

Although an emerging Indo-Guyanese middle class sought earnestly to belong to, and engage with, colonial society, for the most part their endeavour was refracted through the spirit of an awakened, assertive India in revolt against imperial rule. Even as they adapted to the colonial milieu (most, relatively seamlessly), they were drawn ineluctably to 'Mother India' from the 1890s to the 1940s, at all stages of her nationalist crusade. Brian Moore has explained the process:

> Creolisation for the Indian immigrants was more a process of the adaptation of their traditional values, customs and behavioural patterns to prevailing customs in the alien social environment than the adoption of Creole culture patterns [Brathwaite's 'in/culturation']. Of course, there was some measure of interculturation [between Africans and Indians]…but it is evident that this was confined to the peripheral aspects of cultural life and did not penetrate into the belief systems, religious observances, the family structures, etc. of either group.[31]

III. Garveyism and the 'Race First' Philosophy

By the mid-1930s, against the backdrop of the Italian invasion of Ethiopia (Abyssinia), African Guyanese were experiencing an awakening regarding a resurgent Africa of the imagination. This would reinforce bifurcated nationalist promptings, further vitiating any embryonic sense of a Guyanese identity. In February 1935, *Tribune* asserted that Africans in the homeland were making 'firm and steady' steps, and they envisaged the congealing of a revolutionary temper that would drive the European colonisers from their lands: '[I]t may not be long before they turn the tables upon those who have carved for themselves, for the purpose of exploitation and enrichment, large slices of African territory.' They also discerned a more enlightened attitude in the homeland conducive to the pursuit of education and wealth. Yearning to canalise this perceived new ancestral vigour, the paper counselled African Guyanese to expend their time and energy efficaciously, as the various niches of mobility in the colony were 'the peculiar heritage' of Africans – an allusion to their being 'pioneer' settlers, entitled to that legacy because of their unrecompensed exploitation during two centuries of enslavement.[32]

Earlier, in July 1934, on the centenary of the Emancipation Act, *Tribune* implored Africans to patronise their own people in their commercial and professional transactions: 'race first' was the clarion call. Evoking the spirit of Garveyism, *Tribune* affirmed forthright discrimination in favour of, and loyalty towards, African enterprises: '...in a practical manner they should give preferential support and respect to their own and to particularly support professional members of the race [doctors and lawyers], and any enterprise, commercial or otherwise, already existing or that may be launched by any negro without stopping to institute comparison as to dimension or price.'[33]

The 'race first' philosophy, by Africans as well as Indians, was rarely challenged in British Guiana. In September 1926, for instance, Luckhoo remarked that it was not true that he opposed the migration of Africans to the colony. However, he was reportedly unapologetic that he 'certainly [would] like to see more of his own people [Indians] in the colony under a colonisation scheme; but who could blame him for it, or blame any other for wanting members of his own race in the colony?'[34] When Fredericks, the founder-president of the NPC, died in April 1934, *Tribune* proudly underscored what he represented to Africans: 'the greatest Negro personality in British Guiana,' who 'dedicated his life to the service of his race.'[35] The paper also memorialised his life of benevolent service in stimulating African self-respect and solidarity:

> The great work he...initiated in the organisation of the Negro Progress Convention will live and finally bring about that race consciousness and Negro solidarity for which he strove with might and main. A greater, a more sincere, and a more enthusiastic lover of his race, the colony has never seen; and it is no exaggeration...that for the benefit and upliftment of his race he sacrificed his health and his slender income.[36]

By early 1936 the Ethiopian issue, the Italian invasion of that country, had so galvanised African Guyanese that several of their organisations were immersed in a colony-wide campaign, raising awareness as well as funds, for the cause. The British Guiana Labour Union (BGLU) had its Abyssinia committee; the Universal Negro Improvement Association (UNIA: the branch of Marcus Garvey's movement) had its Ethiopian Hospital Fund; there was also an Ethiopian Red Cross Fund.[37] In February 1936, the UNIA was scheduled to hold a meeting in Georgetown. The event was advertised thus: 'A large Ethiopian flag with a lion bearing Ethiopia's standard will be unfurled. Pictures of great African men and women will be exhibited.'[38] In May 1936, the UNIA held a 'mass' meeting at Bourda Green, Georgetown, where a resolution was passed denouncing the Italian invasion.[39]

Fredericks had counselled his people in 1924 to prepare themselves for citizenship through learning and racial harmony. He also proffered a millenarian challenge to them to embrace the pan-African ideal, a redemptive philosophy, demanding sacrifice and purity of motives: 'There shall be one whole united Africa – a purgatorial Africa – when her sons having passed through cleansing fire will leave the dross behind in the flames and emerge a wonderful product of the God of all mankind.'[40] A little over a decade later, amidst the Italian invasion of Ethiopia in 1935, one of only two independent countries in Africa (the other was Liberia), African leaders in British Guiana felt transgressed. They were consequently emboldened into repudiating the conduct of Great Britain, for whom they had fought gallantly in the Great War – her silence on Mussolini's abrogation of Ethiopian sovereignty was tantamount to complicity.

Ethiopianism runs deep in the imagination of Africans in the Americas. It was instinctual for those in the diaspora to arbitrarily designate anywhere in Africa as constitutive of the imagined homeland. Even relative accuracy pertaining to their places of origin was deemed immaterial. A Yoruba, Fulani, or Zulu could not so randomly transpose or appropriate any African space with putative ancestral essence: authenticity of origin was not negotiable in their case. They had retained their discrete cultural symbols, indeed, all the instincts of a people made by the peculiarities of their respective lands, particularly the power of landscape to evoke memory and foster continuity in sustaining identity. For Africans in the Americas, descendants of peoples wrenched irretrievably from their ancestral lands and landscapes, such primordial moorings had to be imagined – the tradition, says Eric Hobsbawm, must be 'invented.' They could be loose with historical markers, hardly preoccupied with factual or contextual veracity in constructing narratives of the past to anchor the putative homeland. Africans in British Guiana, like Indo-Guyanese, could be infinitely less fastidious about the authenticity of memory grounded in geography, history, ethnicity, or any other index for validating ancestry. Therefore, Ethiopia or Abyssinia answered the void eloquently, as no other African space conceivably could in the context of the 1930s.

The sheer antiquity of Ethiopia, resonant with biblical associations and historical conquests, including its rule in the Arabian Peninsula, evoked racial pride among Africans in the diaspora, immersed in a universe of Eurocentric Christian iconography. The fact that Ethiopian royalty was reputed to have consanguineal links with King Solomon, endowed the place with sanctity: an ancient African kingdom considered an architect of Christianity in its own right. Ethiopia's provenance, then, was seminally Christian. Africans in the diaspora were, in reality, returning to their ancestral moorings by embracing Christianity. They were not merely recipients of the crumbs off their White master's table. Ethiopianism was enhanced immeasurably, in the imagination of Africans in the Americas, by the fact that (Liberia notwithstanding) Abyssinia was the only African country to retain, and successfully defend, its sovereignty in the aftermath of the European 'scramble for Africa' in the 1880s. Moreover, her stature as a concrete source of African identity, an inviolable repository of African pride and self-esteem, had been etched in their consciousness by her victory over earlier Italian invaders at the Battle of Adowa (Adwa) in March 1896.

For West Indians in particular, the victory was claimed as their own as it occurred in the decade of the 1890s, in the context of the near fatal decline of the sugar juggernaut of the region. The latter had precipitated an upsurge in African reassertion, manifested in the writings of the so-called 'coal-black' Jamaican doctor, author, medical missionary in the Congo and traveller in West Africa, Dr Theophilus E.S. Scholes (1858–1940), and the Bahamian-born, American-educated and Jamaican-based journalist and politician, and editor of the *Jamaica Advocate*, Dr J. Robert Love (1839–1914), in conjunction with the embryonic quest for political honours by a sprinkling of Black West Indians, such as Hon A. B. Brown in British Guiana, and the Pan-Africanist, Henry Sylvester Williams (1869–1911), a Trinidadian. Ethiopianism, whether acknowledged or not, epitomised African cultural antiquity, magnificence, and resilience. It offered continuity with self-esteem.[41]

Ethiopia's place in the African Guyanese imagination would be enhanced in November 1930, when Haile Selassie was crowned Emperor. This event had special resonance in the British West Indies, where it became enmeshed in, and magnified by, Garveyite imagery of 'return' to the homeland (literally and metaphorically). Ethiopia or Abyssinia conjured up African biblical provenance, prophecy, and deliverance – redemption. As anthropologist Kevin Yelvington argues:

> Although by the mid-1930s the UNIA's and Garvey's influence had diminished, partially as the result of the efforts of British and

American authorities to financially ruin and socially discredit him, many working class blacks in the West Indies continued to be influenced by Garvey's vision and teachings...Thus a remark he [allegedly] once made came not only to become enshrined in folk legend but was elevated to the status of religious prophesy by 'true believers' for whom it formed the basis of the Rastafari religious cult. According to oral tradition, he said: 'Look to Africa, where a black king shall be crowned, for the day of deliverance is near'... So to those so disposed, Garvey's words indeed seemed prophetic when Ras Tafari of Abyssinia (Ethiopia's ancient name) was crowned Emperor on November 2, 1930, and took the name Haile Selassie at his coronation. Secular prophesy met with biblical ones....[42]

Although only a microscopic minority of West Indians (Garveyites included) became Rastafari – those who see Haile Selassie (Emperor of Ethiopia) as God – the second invasion of Ethiopia by Italy, in October 1935, was experienced by most Black West Indians as an outrage to their African sensibility. As Dennis Forsythe, a Rastafari, explains, the impact of this event on West Indians of African descent was necessarily far-reaching:

Ethiopia was known and was felt to constitute the Heartland of ancient black pride, dignity and independence. Ethiopian civilisation was the only one from the era of the Roman Empire that survived into modern times with unbroken political continuity, or with substantial resemblance to its classical state. Of all the countries in Africa, Ethiopia had a coherence that other African countries lacked.[43]

In November 1935, *Tribune* carried an article captioned boldly: 'BRITAIN BETRAYS COLOURED RACES.' They contended that the White countries tend to close ranks whenever one of them is engaged in a conflict with a 'coloured' country. This was manifested in 1905 during the Russo-Japanese war, won by the latter. Now, argued the correspondent, it was transparent that Britain was prepared to let the Italian dictator, Benito Mussolini (1883–1945), have his way in Ethiopia providing her stipulated vital interests were not jeopardised:

[Britain] fears that a defeat for Italy will serve as an inspiration to the coloured races in the Empire – Indians, Arabs, Egyptians and Africans, to throw off the yoke of white domination. For this reason, Sir Samuel Hoare, British Foreign Secretary [1935], instructed Sir Eric Drummond, British Ambassador in Rome, to inform Mussolini not to be worried, as Britain has no intention to put any serious obstacles in his way, as long as he is prepared to guarantee Britain the right to the waters of Lake Tsana [the largest lake in Ethiopia], the source of the Blue Nile, which supplies water to the British-controlled cotton plantations of the Sudan.[44]

The editor of *Tribune*, H. Aaron Britton, spoke for most African people, repelled by the Italian invasion of this ancient African kingdom, when he deemed it a 'shameful' expression of European colonialism, another manifestation of White imperial arrogance:

> The whole of the black man's land has been confiscated by others, and he has been left with but two small strips: Liberia, on the west, and Abyssinia, on the east, and now they are trying to take away Abyssinia…This is both disgraceful and shameful! The Emperor of Abyssinia says he would fight to the bitter end rather than concede one inch of his land to strangers. This is right and we believe he will stick to that…This brush between these two countries [Italy and Ethiopia] has been going on for a considerable time, and it was known to European statesmen too…[It is] a dispute between a white and a coloured race, and no coloured people should stand in equality with a white.[45]

Africans in British Guiana were stridently censuring their British imperial masters for failing to repudiate what they saw as the racist Italian spoliation of the iconic African nation – central to the identity of Africans at home and abroad. Therefore, the British as well were complicit in the crime and guilty of racism. The British Empire, for which they had made immense sacrifices, fighting and dying during the Great War, on the presumption they were engaged in the noble task of extirpating German 'barbarism,' now appeared diametrically at variance with their conception of self-pride and prejudicial to their aspirations. Black people in British Guiana, inspired by Garveyite 'race first' ideology and the self-affirmative work of the Negro Progress Convention since 1922, were shaping a new identity, arguably less robustly grounded in their African homeland than Indo-Guyanese were in 'Mother India,' but palpably African, nonetheless. The imagined homeland was no less germane to their quest of self-definition, however eclectic or spasmodic.

Writing in 1936, Professor W. M. Macmillan (1885–1974), who had recently completed a study-tour of the British West Indies, remarked with empathy on the process of creolisation among Africans:

> The West Indians for all their imposed and inherited disabilities are now a distinct people with well-marked characteristics of their own…[They] have absorbed after their own manner the European outlook and 'culture.' Practically all now profess Christianity…[But] Africans the great majority of the people still are unmistakably, in appearance, in temperament, in aptitudes – even if their tribal system and distinctive culture or cultures have totally disappeared. His book was appropriately, and prophetically, titled *Warning from the West Indies*.[46]

The Great Depression and the Abyssinian issue, in conjunction with residual Garveyite promptings, would give shape to their hurt and precipitate the militancy that set the whole of the British West Indies ablaze, between 1935 and 1939. Two examples from 1935 (the year before Cheddi Jagan left British Guiana to study in the US) exemplify the palpably more assertive political attitudes spawned by the heightened awareness. In February *Tribune* was reflecting expansively on the 'awakening' in Africa – a contagious 'spirit of progress' gaining ground, from Ethiopia to Zanzibar. Not only were Africans emancipating themselves from 'superstition,' they were also liberating their minds, to lay the foundation for the industrial take-off of their economies. The paper was imbued with a spirit of optimism for Africa, citing its legacy of statesmanship and its classical heroes of 'lasting merit,' while challenging African Guyanese to engage with their illustrious antecedence:

> The hour has struck when all of African descent should get busy building up themselves in every way possible...Africa that has given us Makeda, the lady who visited King Solomon, Mtessa, the emperor who did so much for his people in Central Africa and who was eulogised by Stanley, the explorer, is rising, rising not upon hot air, but upon work of sterling lasting merit. Men of African descent, natives of British Guiana, what are you doing?[47]

In December 1935, the resurgent pride in the achievement of African people worldwide was reflected in the following caption in *Tribune*, in connection with a play on the Haitian Revolution by 'West Indian journalist C. L. R. James,' in London:

A NEW NEGRO PLAY BY WEST INDIAN
PAUL ROBESON TO STAR AS HAITIAN LIBERATOR
LONDON TO SEE TOUSSAINT L'OUVERTURE ON STAGE

The release continued: 'The life and revolutionary activity of the slave, Toussaint L'Ouverture [1742–1803], who liberated the Negroes of Haiti, has been dramatised by a West Indian journalist, C. L. R. James, and will be presented by the British Stage Society in London this winter. Mr Paul Robeson, the well-known American Negro actor, will play the leading role of Toussaint....'[48] The rebel spirit was being celebrated, and *Tribune* was fostering an appreciation of a Pan-African pantheon of heroes from the homeland and the diaspora.

Even on the plantations of British Guiana, among a minority of fieldworkers comprising non-resident African cane cutters, this spirit of heightened self-awareness and resistance ignited a mildly insurrectionary interlude in October–November 1935. These 'high-season' workers, small farmers in their own villages for most of the year, were more independent than resident Indian workers, circumscribed in their resistance by the fact that they still lived rent-free in generally derelict ranges (logies), some built during slavery and patched up ever since. The seasonal African workers, by comparison, were fortified in agitating against perceived long-standing grievances. The Commission of Inquiry which investigated the riots on several sugar estates observed: 'A feature of the disputes and disturbances...is that while the resident population is still predominantly

East Indian [approximately 54,000 of 136,000 Indians in the colony: 40 per cent], the most active parts, particularly in the disturbances, were taken by Black villagers.'[49]

Many observers concurred that these Black rebels were partly stirred into militancy by a consuming external factor – the Abyssinian issue, which day after day dominated the front pages of the four newspapers in the colony in 1935: *Daily Argosy, Daily Chronicle, New Daily Chronicle*, and *Tribune* (the Black weekly). The pent-up passions thus triggered found expression in a daring, violent collision with White authority on sugar plantations, such as Ogle and Lusignan, on the lower East Coast Demerara, accessible to Garveyite activists from Georgetown. The utter humiliation of Hares, a White overseer, by a 'mob' of African workers led by Daniel Pollard at Lusignan, encapsulates the withered hopes accompanying the Great Depression and the rebellious temper, kindled by Garveyism and the Abyssinian debacle: 'Of about 400 Blacks, from beginning to end, Mr Richards [the Manager of Lusignan] said he never saw an East Indian taking part in the disturbances....'

The violent incident, in October 1935, was narrated to the commission thus:

> Pollard [the black labourer] ordered Mr Hares [the white overseer] to wade across the trench that separates the field from the dam, and when he refused to do so, wrestled with him and tried to push him into the trench. Failing in this, he stepped back and attacked Mr Hares with his stick. Mr Hares...could only ward off the blows with his left arm which Pollard eventually broke cutting it to the bone... Pollard permitted him to leave the field by way of the 'stop-off' instead of wading through the trench. Here he was met by...a mob [Africans] armed with cutlasses and sticks and one man with a sword. They marched along with him in military formation and ordered him to carry a [red] flag at their head. At first Mr. Hares refused to do this, but after they had 'hunched' him with their sticks and threatened to strip him naked if he did not comply, he did so.
>
> After a while the flag came away from the post it was attached to, upon which the mob became infuriated with him stripping him naked from the waist up. They were shouting: 'Bad Abyssinia – all you white bitches got no business here – our country – you go back where you come from.' Proceeding in the direction of the order bridge, one of the ring-leaders, a man named Murray, beat a drum at his feet and ordered him to dance. Mr Hares said he did not know how to dance, whereupon Murray said he would show him and gave an African exhibition of dance. They then marched him on, the crowd doing a 'war dance' round him, but when they reached the order bridge and saw the armed police in the distance, they let him go.[50]

A *Tribune* journalist, who covered the strike on the sugar plantations in late 1935, testified to the widespread 'expression of solidarity with Abyssinia.' It is worth noting that during simultaneous disturbances, in Georgetown, rumours were disseminated around the city that Italian sweet vendors were selling 'poisoned goods' to Black schoolchildren. Many mothers rushed to the schools demanding their children be released 'for safety.' Another rumour soon spread that an Italian doctor [Dr Cesare Romiti] had injected 'poison serum' into Black children. Such was the ferocity of the anti-White passions spawned by the Italian invasion of Ethiopia.[51]

As *Tribune* reported, even the Archbishop of Canterbury felt impelled to reflect (at the banquet of the Royal African Society in London) on the consequences of the Abyssinian war on 'the minds of Africans and people of African descent in America and the West Indies where many disturbances had already occurred.' The 'disturbance of the African mind,' provoked by the outrage over the Italian invasion of Abyssinia, was the catalyst for inflaming the insurgent temper: 'I am sure that self-consciousness is being stirred…by the unhappy events which are occurring in Abyssinia…I am satisfied by evidence I have received that the situation in Africa is being watched with great eagerness and intensity.' The Archbishop offered a telling synopsis of the affronted African sensibility ignited by Abyssinia: 'The natives see a great White race attacking with all dreadful apparatus of modern warfare the one centre of independent African rule.'[52]

In British Guiana, this vibrant 'race consciousness' did not precipitate any known conflict between Africans and Indians. The assumption was that the shaping of discrete African and Indian identities, anchored in constructed images of homelands – essentially Africas and Indias of the imagination – was a legitimate endeavour. And although African Guyanese were apprehensive of perceived Indian economic ascendancy, with designs on political hegemony (the legacy of the idea of the Indian colony), because the shape of any post-colonial order in British Guiana was indeterminable, that conceivably volatile issue remained unexamined – a site for future contestation. No one sought to impugn the premises on which racial self-assertion was being formulated.

Yet the long-term utility of an enlightened and imaginative cultivation of segmental identities – a prelude to the necessarily slow, and at best incremental, shaping of a national identity (as A.R.F. Webber and J.I. Ramphal envisaged in the early 1930s) – never did receive the discursive treatment it merited. The mutual mistrust within ethnic cocoons (as if quarantined) just simmered, most obviously oblivious of its implications for a post-imperial political order – studiously papered over later, by the principal politicians, with Marxist rhetoric on the primacy of class over race. A site of intense and simmering racism, however contained, with a patina of Marxism-Leninism!

It was not simply a legacy of 'divide and rule' provoked by the imperialists. Indians and Africans originated in hierarchical and socially segregated societies (based on caste and tribe), often immersed in, and stunted by, ancient pejorative definitions and hatred of each other, centuries before their encounter with Europeans. To hate and kill 'the other' isn't a recent thing. It's human! Guyanese intolerance and bigotry are not unique, yet it is surprisingly moderated.

In May 1936, the president of the British Guiana East Indian Association (BGEIA), H.B. Gajraj, announced the imminent arrival of a scholar from India, P. Kodanda Rao, M.A., secretary of the Servants of India Society. Despite the deep-seated African angst over the possibility of an Indian colony or a Greater India (another version), *Tribune* endorsed the visit. But their magnanimity was predicated on the assumption that Indo-Guyanese embrace of their Indian 'fatherland' [*sic*] would stimulate the 'revival' of a parallel engagement of Africans with their 'fatherland.' It was a replication of the imperative of 'ethnic balance' engendered by the Colonisation Scheme and the idea of an Indian colony in the 1920s:

> It is...to be deplored that visits by such distinguished persons are so very few and far between; therefore, we are in whole-hearted sympathy with the resolution passed...[by the BGEIA], calculated to bridge the gap and offer more frequent communication between here and India. The achievement of that for Indians will automatically mean the revival of communications between here and West Africa, so that the two numerically stronger groups will restore frequent communications with their fatherland [*sic*] – India and Africa – a very substantial proportion of whose inhabitants profess the Muslim faith. Apart altogether from the fact of distinguished and fearless Indians visiting the colony, there have been domiciled here at one time or another, Drs Bezbora [Bezbarao] and [Ram Narain] Sharma and Mr Bechu [an indentured labour, radical letter-writer and critic of the plantocracy], whose example in public matters is worthy of emulation by all Indians.[53]

'Ethnic balance' in all matters pervaded the discourse regarding the future of British Guiana. The problem, though, was that African identity in the colony was being shaped by a largely reactive stimulus embodied by the Abyssinian issue: no visitors (scholars or religious leaders) from Africa visited British Guiana to prompt a spirit of parallel cultural and ethnic resurgence. The ancestral links were ruptured in the context of slavery, and new perspectives on an imagined homeland could not obliterate the trauma, however submerged, of that abominable wrenching and dislocation. In addition, the latter secreted a seething anger not only against European slave traders and slaveholders, but (conceivably) a sublimated bitterness towards many Africans complicit in the European slave trade. Besides, as noted earlier, Africans in British Guiana were inclined to see Indians as predatory interlopers: usurpers of their ancestral lands; cunning, commercial exploiters, with alien habits – heathens. They had already reached a state of irreconcilable political dissonance over the Colonisation Scheme, exacerbated by grave foreboding that an Indian colony was being thrust upon them.

By 1936 that fear was still potent. For the third time, *Indian Opinion*, organ of the British Guiana East Indian Association, was resurrected; it would contribute immeasurably to cohering an Indian identity in the colony. Salutary conceptions of 'Mother India,' nurtured by the robust Gandhian crusade for independence by the Indian National Congress, evoked a strikingly more aggrandising Indo-Guyanese self-image. The momentum was indisputably with them. For Africans, however, their racial assertiveness, though enhanced appreciably in the latter half of the 1930s, was still enmeshed in a narrative of victimhood: enslavement; post-emancipation usurpation of their deserved entitlements by Madeiran Portuguese and 'bound coolies' from India; growing Indian acquisition of their land; the subliminal fear of an Indian colony – now Abyssinia!

As the Cambridge-educated African Guyanese scholar, Norman Eustace Cameron (1903–83), argued in the early 1930s, the idea of the African homeland, though subject to periodic reaffirmation, was still refracted inordinately through self-deprecating constructions that conjured up darkness – internalised associations with the 'primitive' or the 'savage' – subversive of racial solidarity. Cameron framed this dilemma against a backdrop of the palpably robust cultural and religious moorings of Indo-Guyanese:

> Intercourse between the Negroes of the Americas and the Africans has been restricted, as contrasted with that between the East Indians [Indo-Guyanese] and their native India. This was originally due to the conditions under which the Africans were brought to these parts and not necessarily to an initial lack of interest in their mother country...Mutual misconceptions have long characterised the attitude of each towards the others. The [African] Americans think of those of the West Indies as 'natives' and jocularly call them 'monkey-chasers,' while the West Indians conceive of the [African] Americans as braggart and crude rather than efficient. Both of these groups think of the Africans as ugly, 'raw' and barbarous, while the Africans conceive of the others as a spiritless race – 'slave pickneys.'[54]

Yet Cameron could perceive a redemptive apprehension of Africa taking shape in the West Indies – an incremental erosion of the shame of identification, a lessening of self-contempt:

> Slowly the mind of the West Indian is being made to adopt a juster attitude towards the African. He himself has been maligned...by visitors to his country. So, he realises he must be a little more cautious in accepting travellers' tales of Africa. Again, he gets into contact with his own people who have lived among the Africans, some of whom have been able to see further than the simple exterior of native life to high intelligence and a human soul.

> Then finally the West Indian is reading more of Africa and finds that...half of the story has not been told. Hence, he is beginning to see in Africa not merely an ancestry which is assigned to him whether he likes it or not, but an ancestry in which he may well take a sympathetic interest, and for which he need feel absolutely no irksomeness in recognising his attachment to it; or, to put it positively, one in which he will learn to take just pride.[55]

That problem – a tenacious ambivalence as regards Africa – had been reinforced by an avalanche of patriotic imperial propaganda, during the First World War, to sustain the war effort; in conjunction with a tutored, if tenuous, West Indian identity with the 'mother country': Great Britain. Thus mediated, and with a hinterland of self-deprecation, it was by no means straightforward to embrace the African homeland, as Norman Cameron (with ample self-knowledge) did concede. But the perceived implacability of the Ethiopians, in the teeth of unprovoked Italian military aggression, was instrumental in drawing out a more empathetic affinity with the continent of their ancestors. Africa could be conceived less in terms of darkness, but as a pioneer in many spheres of human enterprise. Indo-Guyanese, on the other hand, manifested no such ambivalence in identifying with a resurgent 'Mother India,' led by Gandhi and Nehru in its anti-colonial crusade.

IV. 'Mother India's' Shadow in British Guiana and *Tribune's* Response

The distinguished scholar from India visiting British Guiana in mid-1936, P. Kodanda Rao (of the Servants of India Society), observed that Indians in the Caribbean (British Guiana, Suriname, and Trinidad mainly), 'even those who were born in these countries and have never been to India,' continued to 'display a tender love for [her],' despite their motherland failing to do anything to merit the imperishable loyalty of 'her children abroad.' He elaborated:

> [Indian] Immigration to these countries began nearly a century ago [1838]. During the great part of this period, till almost a decade ago, no cultural mission arrived from India to these countries. The charge cannot be denied that through all the long decades during which Indians were allowed to migrate to these countries, unofficial, cultural India had neglected to maintain and strengthen the cultural tie between India and her children abroad. The emigrants from India were recruited...mostly from the poorest, the least educated and cultured class in India...
>
> **If, in spite of these appalling disabilities, the Indians in these colonies have made the progress they have, and sustained their cultural heritage with amazing tenacity, it was all through their**

own self-effort and not due to any cultural assistance from
India. Even in the matter of their education, they owe more to
the Christian Missions from Europe and America than to any
help from India [emphasis added].[56]

Mother India's indifference notwithstanding, Indians in British Guiana
did embrace 'many Indias' in reshaping their identity in the new land. These
definitions of India were necessarily imagined, yet often consciously constructed,
a compound of the mythical as well as the more-or-less real homeland of ancient
times, coupled with the contemporary, readily apprehensible, insurgent Gandhian
India. This tendentious exercise in self-affirmation did not require the guidance
or the approbation of the motherland, although the latter, though miniscule,
was cherished. The imagined homeland was fundamental to reconstructing an
identity among 'her children abroad.' It offered a sustaining vision; it assuaged
'a hunger in their soul,' a yearning for antecedents of excellence and grandeur:
civilisation – particularly after the emergence of a small, status-conscious, middle
class, from the 1890s. The termination of indentureship in 1920 hastened the
diminution of a corrosive psychological burden while expanding the quest for
intimations of ancestral excellence. Indo-Guyanese were, in great measure,
energised by the nationalist fervour in India generated by the Indian National
Congress since 1885, and, after 1915, rendered noble (even divine), yet readily
accessible, by their revered sage, Mahatma Gandhi (1869–1948).

The fact, too, that indentured labourers from India were taken to British
Guiana as late as 1917, while a few resident Indians did continue to visit or
maintain correspondence with relatives in India, enhanced the notion of 'Mother
India' as seminal to their identity and shaping their own nationalist aspirations.
Therefore, the belated visits of several Indian scholars and missionaries from
India, in the 1920s–30s and the recent commitment of the Indian National
Congress to 'creating and maintaining contacts with Indians overseas,' as R. B.
Gajraj, secretary of the British Guiana East Indian Association observed in 1936,
constituted a dramatic change in attitudes by the motherland, reflective of her
growing self-assurance:

Mr P. Kodanda Rao…has assured us of the growing interest which
political leaders in the Motherland are showing in the welfare
of Indians overseas. Our distinguished brother's visit is in itself a
practical demonstration of this interest, and we look forward with
pleasant anticipation to more frequent visits in the future. We are
fully aware how much there is for our people yet to accomplish in
order to attain the *Purna Swaraj* [full freedom: independence], and
we can sympathise with the Mahatma in wanting all India to work for
and attain complete independence before directing their energy and
attention to Indians abroad…We feel sure that this is the beginning
of a new era for our people. In this colony we are becoming nationally

stronger every day, desiring to keep and maintain close touch with progressive India. Here is our opportunity to learn of and follow the Motherland's progressive lead.[57]

However, this perceptibly vibrant transformation that nourished Indian 'race consciousness' evoked fear among their African compatriots in British Guiana, already apprehensive of their growing numerical strength (42 per cent by the late 1930s). Moreover, it engendered suspicion that Indo-Guyanese identity with a resurgent, manifestly confident India was potentially injurious to the long-term security of Africans. The idea of an Indian colony in British Guiana still cast a long shadow among them; it hardened as Indian nationalism reached its zenith by the late 1930s. African insecurities would be magnified by the avalanche of triumphal, Indocentric journalism disseminated locally, around the centenary of Indian arrival in the colony: May 5, 1938. To African Guyanese, the powerful narrative of an insurgent India on the threshold of national independence, of the imperial yoke soon to be jettisoned, magnified their foreboding of an impending racially supreme Indian state emerging in British Guiana. This, coupled with the perceived economic and social ascendancy of Indians in agriculture, business, and the professions (law and medicine in particular), exacerbated anti-Indian attitudes. The festering African insecurities were never really addressed (not even, later, within the multiracial PPP of the early 1950s), therefore they could not be allayed. These, arguably, remain at the core of the contemporary mutual incomprehension that has stunted the political culture of Guyana.

By the early 1930s, the Indo-Guyanese personality was rooted firmly in the growing self-assurance and captivating optimism of the nationalist movement for independence in India. In October 1930, the *Daily Argosy* carried an article, captioned 'Gandhi: A Study,' which explained why Indians in British Guiana, although they were themselves in pursuit of material prosperity, could still repose trust in the ascetic Mahatma Gandhi as the custodian of their national aspirations:

> Gandhi believes no person should possess more property than is necessary for his simplest needs. Although originally fairly wealthy by Indian standards, Gandhi and his wife have given away their property and own nothing except their clothing, some books and a few necessities...He is Mahatma (great soul)...This is the man who is opposing the strength and majesty of a powerful Empire, and who set in motion one of the greatest political movements in the world's history – the Indian National Movement – which is a veritable revolution without arms...The movement advanced rapidly and in 1928 the Madras Congress declared independence as the goal of India. The Lahore Congress in 1929 confirmed it...Both in India and abroad it is recognised that Gandhi will rank in history as one of the great leaders of mankind, and the first to lead a revolution without arms based on non-violence.[58]

Yet a few months earlier, in June 1930, the *Argosy* had reproached the British Guiana East Indian Association for its unanimous resolution on behalf of all Indo-Guyanese, endorsing the Indian National Congress in their 'firm resolve' to gain independence for India. The paper underestimated the rich vein of empathy permeating the community, asserting that the 'misguided sympathy' did not reflect the sentiment of most Indians in the colony, engrossed in their material well-being and evincing no interest in 'politics or any abstract discussion.' With respect to the nationalist crusade in India, the *Argosy* alleged, erroneously and superciliously, that Indo-Guyanese existed in 'a perfect state of ignorance'; and it proceeded to 'strongly deprecate' the conduct of the Association (including that of 'a King's Counsel [J. A. Luckhoo]'):

> The civil disobedience campaign together with the declaration of independence of India by the Indian [National] Congress is in plain language an act of rebellion against the Raj [British rule]. And this is the attitude which the local East Indian Association applauds... [B]y their own precipitate and ill-advised action...[they have] done more than any of the remaining sections of the community to damn themselves in the eyes of the discerning public....[59]

The hectoring reproach of the *Argosy* probably fortified Indo-Guyanese in their affinity with Indian nationalism, as did a tone of self-deprecation permeating *Tribune's* assessment of the Gandhian crusade for freedom. In January 1931, for example, the paper offered a deeply pessimistic proposition about India's independence. They affirmed the school of thought predicated on climatic causation in explaining European domination of 'coloured races' – 'the energy of the North,' shaped by the struggle for survival in an inhospitable habitat, thereby stimulating their imagination into habitual scepticism, scientific curiosity and a predilection for inventiveness. Conversely, *Tribune* perceived a pervasive lassitude among tropical peoples, from whom a similar punctiliousness and precision regarding time, in coping with forbidding climatic hazards – foresight, flexibility, rigour, innovation – is not required. Consequently, non-Europeans tend to remain 'dormant and rusty' – unchallenged, unenergetic, and bereft of a nimbleness of intellect. European colonialism, therefore, was indispensable to the awakening of the sluggish South:

> The White Man must exercise his faculties, not because it is inherently his nature to do so, but because of the demand which nature makes upon him. He must build houses, he must cultivate, he must force nature, he must lay up stores or perish. On coming to the South, he finds many opportunities for progress which to the coloured man were unobserved. Thus, we are confronted with the fact that without the energy of the North, the South cannot be developed...The presence of the White race in the tropics is therefore absolutely necessary for the improvement and development of the races indigenous to those

parts because they bring with them the energy of the North to dispel the lethargy of the South.[60]

No imperialist could have propounded the argument for preserving the Empire – the White man's burden – with greater clarity and conviction! Therefore, *Tribune* counselled Indo-Guyanese leaders to prevail upon their compatriots in India to concede the futility of their nationalist fervour – to accept the necessity of the rule of 'the English in India' or face extinction. It is plausible that this definition of the situation was actuated, in the main, by the fragile self-confidence, if not self-contempt – the despair of the counsellor – rather than the folly of the counselled:

> It is plain that without the energy of the North (the English in India), India will perish and disappear from the map as a nation within the next generation. She cannot return to the pre-British times and cannot remain indifferent to the world which she has entered. India and Indians, therefore, would be well advised to consider Britain as her best friend and guardian. To remove the protection and prestige of England would be to doom her to destruction by forces within and without. Not a thousand Gandhis would be able to save her from humiliation....[61]

Sour grapes? It is conceivable that *Tribune's* defeatist evaluation of Indian nationalism was precipitated by African angst over palpable Indian ascendancy in British Guiana, particularly their self-assurance, arguably partly attributable to India's pursuit of *swaraj*, independence, from the late 1920s:

> Let India beware that she is not being misled in seeking independence from Great Britain; let all liberty-loving Indians in the country [British Guiana] write to their party in India [the Indian National Congress] and counsel them that this demand for an Indian Republic, as gaudy as it may sound, is not a movement in the best interest of the land they so much love. The separation from Britain is not beyond the realm of possibility, but it is lamentably undesirable because without the energy of the people of the North, the South will never, by their own effort, be able to find a place in the sun.[62]

This despairing judgement of 'native' potentialities, particularly the Indian quest for independence, had its origin also in the dismal economic condition of many Africans in British Guiana, where the 'energy of the North' was transparently anything but stellar. This gave rise to a rawness of emotions: anger, desperation, futility, and possibly the very presentiment at the core of *Tribune's* message. Though rarely vented openly, African apprehension of Indo-Guyanese economic progress (after the Great War) with land ownership, rice, cattle, commerce, and even the professions (hitherto the stronghold of Africans), cannot be underestimated. Their foreboding was exacerbated by the Great Depression of the 1930s, as it conceivably was by their abiding association of

Indian independence with the forbidding idea of an Indian colony in British Guiana.

Yet in the next issue of *Tribune*, in February 1931 (in a leader unabashedly captioned, 'Our Enemies'), as if to recant and soothe hurt Indian sensibilities, they attributed African Guyanese woes, paradoxically now, to 'those would-be Europeans,' the small White and very light-coloured minorities, who were so afraid of their shadow that they feared that Black people were ever on the verge of reverting to savagery: 'with machete and gun in hand…awaiting the opportunity to rise and slay the "puny" trembling White population,' the presence of the armed forces to protect them notwithstanding.

This precipitate, radically revised, stance was partially prompted by the presence of two British war ships in Georgetown, at a time of heightened anxiety among the White elite that lawlessness would be unleashed with the return of a few hundred volatile African miners, actuated by acute privation, from the interior of the colony. *Tribune* was, in effect, repudiating its celebration of the 'energy' of those from the 'North,' only a week earlier venerated as indispensable to tropical civilisation. Now those deemed inherently gifted with energy and foresight were summarily dismissed as being devoid of the 'ability to look ahead'; moreover, British Guiana must be developed in the interest of non-Whites, the legitimate inheritors of the country. Overnight, they were so rabidly anti-British that the Indian nationalists were rendered pale by comparison:

> [L]et us stand attention to the duty of making this colony the El Dorado of South America and Georgetown the Great White City of the Atlantic seaboard…We stand on the platform that this country must remain the heritage of the Aboriginal Indians and subject races, and that their interest must at all times be paramount to every other consideration.[63]

Some U-turn!

In July 1931, *Tribune* carried an article by a regular columnist, 'Brittanicus,' captioned 'One Hundred Years of Union,' to mark the centenary of the creation of British Guiana from the two colonies of Essequibo-Demerara and Berbice. He was even more unsparing in repudiating the character of British rule. Those Europeans who went to British Guiana were clearly deficient in the 'energy of the North.' The government was not possessed of 'foresight' and 'initiative'; it was 'emasculative'; the colony had 'retrograded.' British Guiana could not touch the level of other colonies, presumably the White ones, in their mastery of 'modern civilisation.' The columnist denounced the British ruling class for racial discrimination, the foremost reason for unequal development in the Empire.

Even Gandhi and the 'misguided' nationalists in India could not have conceived a more damning critique of colonial rule:

> Those advancements [in the white dominions] have not, we are sure, been due to greater ability to absorb the lessons, but rather to the apparently unchangeable belief among persons of the Anglo-Saxon race that government must forever be the inalienable rights of the white races; and that all peoples other than they must remain serfs. We, on this account and by reason of the fact that race superiority is a fallacy which is based entirely on ignorance and prejudice, hope that the new century of British administration in this colony will take upon itself a change compatible with the will and desires of its inhabitants....[64]

The 'will and desires' could be construed as a yearning for, even the threat of independence. The 'loyalty' of *Tribune* to the British Empire rang hollow now. It is conceivable, therefore, that if the anti-colonial movement – given worldwide resonance by Gandhi's asceticism and non-violence – had originated within the African segment of the British Empire, *Tribune* would never have contemplated counselling the indispensability of loyalty to the latter. Their original stance, predicated on the 'energy of the North,' was probably prompted by African Guyanese reservations regarding the moral unassailability of Gandhi's anti-colonial crusade, which had already stimulated nationalist excesses among Indians in British Guiana – the pernicious idea of an Indian colony. The centrality of racial self-definition and the absence of a national frame of reference were, and remain, ineluctably at the heart of the Guyanese political tragedy.

It was to counterbalance Indian ardour, by stimulating self-pride and an equivalent cultural awakening among African Guyanese, that *Tribune* made the visionary case for the study of African history. They deplored their 'ignorance of the history of Africa...the land of their forefathers' – 'a severe handicap.' The paper implored Africans that they commit themselves to rectifying this loss by asking: 'Who is the Negro? Where did he come from? What has been his contribution to the world's advancement? Whither are his steps tending?' They observed that 'a people ignorant of their own history, hazy as to the achievements of the distinguished ones of the Fatherland can make real progress very slowly.'

A people's history and their culture are pivotal to their self-esteem and their ultimate progress. Therefore, *Tribune* sought to turn the tables, depicting the African homeland as a contributor to the civilising of Europe. It had produced its men of intellectual distinction, pioneer scholars comparable with the much-celebrated European ones. Amidst the cascading assertion by Indo-Guyanese of the magnificent heritage of their motherland, the paper beseeched their people to learn about, and celebrate, Africa's ancient legacy and to be energised by the probability of an imminent political and cultural resurgence in their homeland:

> [Only] a small minority of people of African descent in British Guiana knows that St Augustine, one of the great doctors of the

Holy Catholic Church, was a BLACKMAN, and that Tertullian was another…[T]he Star of Africa is rising…the gold of Ophir, that attracted the Nordic people to her shores will ultimately prove their undoing and pave the way for an African people who will again blaze a trail to a civilisation transcending the one given by their forefathers to Europe.[65]

In addition to African misgivings regarding Indian cultural and nationalist triumphalism in British Guiana were the raw anxieties provoked by their presumption of unbridled Indo-Guyanese economic ascendancy, in conjunction with fear of a creeping political hegemony, embodied by the residually haunting idea of an Indian colony. Consequently, in tandem with the Negro Progress Convention, *Tribune* implored Africans to pursue the restitution of sober ancestral habits of self-improvement. They censured many in the colony for being thriftless ('a notorious vice') and challenged them to relinquish their supposed penchant for 'all forms of sport':

> It is surely no pleasure to us to animadvert on one of the notorious vices of our people, the excessively unnecessary indulgence in all forms of sport [partying] to which is attached their love of dress and display. This species of mimicry of modernised Western civilisation is a sure cause of so much of 'the suffering from within' among the middle classes of our people; and the masses are drifting heedlessly headlong into the same abyss. The members of the Negro Race… have the brawn and the muscle to work; but…we have to admit that their reckless penchant for spending all which they earn is one of the most conspicuous failings as well as one of the prime causes of financial suffering which they experience within their own ranks.[66]

V.   Garvey's Visit to British Guiana (1937): A Fiasco

With respect to racial susceptibility, it is essential that the symbolic representation of other people's identity is treated with the utmost sensitivity and empathy. Because so much of it is 'invented' – constructs – an ethnic group's complex definition of self may not be readily apprehensible to outsiders, even where communities exist side by side. Therefore, many Indians in British Guiana probably could not appreciate the critical impact of the Abyssinian issue, in 1935–36, on African Guyanese – the racial agony of the humiliation precipitated by the defeat and flight of Emperor Haile Selassie. Neither could they fathom why the balkanisation of Africa was a source of ongoing angst and why, indeed, many Pan-African initiatives to 'invent' a united African homeland were of West Indian provenance. The idea of homeland, rooted in fact or 'more-or-less fact' (to paraphrase Nehru), as well as fiction and fantasy are integral to making communal identities. To violate even one of its internal reverences –

often elusive to external discernment – could be virtually sacrilegious, therefore susceptible to political exploitation and potentially productive of violence. Identity is a most delicate fabric, a patchwork stuck together by myriad discrete symbolic representations; herein also resides its power to aggregate and inflame group responses.

By 1936, a distinct Indo-Guyanese identity had emerged, shaped by the moral influence of Gandhi's non-violent crusade and the incremental progress of Indian nationalism, which was universally recognised as transformative. This identity was also influenced by the economic, cultural, and educational achievements of the Indo-Guyanese in the colony, especially after the end of indentureship in April 1920. In contrast, it was difficult to make the same claim for African-Guyanese identity. The decline of Garveyism by the early 1930s was a bitter blow, and this despair was compounded by Ethiopia's defeat by the Italian fascists and the exile of Emperor Haile Selassie to London in 1936, who was already considered a god by some in Jamaica. Both Selassie and Marcus Garvey, now exiled in England, had been central to the construction of black identity in the 1920s and 1930s, but by 1936, a very dark cloud had descended over this firmament. This situation was further complicated by the relatively fragile commercial and agricultural foundations of the African-Guyanese community.

However, these two prime wellsprings of resurgent African Guyanese self-esteem – in contrast with the pre-eminent Mahatma Gandhi and Jawaharlal Nehru in the nationalist crusade in Mother India, the fount of a triumphal trajectory in Indo-Guyanese identity – were now enmeshed in images of defeat: vanquished by White power. This narrative was vitiated irreparably by a disastrous visit to British Guiana by Marcus Garvey in October 1937. The principal African organisation in the colony, the Negro Progress Convention, apparently had nothing to do with the visit, and they were only marginally represented at the functions organised for Garvey. The debacle had its origin in raging factionalism within Garvey's Universal Negro Improvement Association (UNIA), in Georgetown, which had reached him in London, and he demanded forthwith that an independent reception committee, headed by Dr S. I. T. Wills, be constituted. But the president of the UNIA in the city, T. A. Wright, and others in his organisation, refused to countenance their exclusion or marginalisation from the momentous occasion. Consequently, the factionalism, which Garvey endeavoured to circumvent or dissipate resurfaced throughout his visit with undiminished ferocity.

The day Garvey arrived at the wharf in Georgetown, he mistakenly entered the car provided by the UNIA; he was then asked to vacate it quickly for the one provided by the ad hoc 'control committee' of Dr Wills. Garvey was the guest of the latter and stayed at his home.[67] But at the main meeting of the UNIA, at Bourda Green, Georgetown, the chronic petty disputes within the organisation were vented with such vitriol that it precluded Garvey from delivering his scheduled speech. It was clear that dark clouds were hovering when the local president of the UNIA, T. A. Wright, assumed the chair for the proceedings: a young lady scheduled to render a song did not appear; neither did another who should have recited a poem; and a section of the UNIA division billed to do a song also stayed away.

Wright then proceeded to indict several people in the organisation, including F.C. Archer, who allegedly was disrupting the work of the UNIA. Garvey was so exasperated that he rebuked Wright for his behaviour:

> Look here, Mr Wright, I have come here to speak to members on matters of importance and not to hear the history of anything leading up to conflict in the UNIA. You have submitted a programme to me, and I ask you to be good enough to stick to it. I don't want to hear anything of that kind. This is a conference of UNIA members for the purpose of meeting me as their leader.

Wright continued his diatribe, seeking now to clear up the confusion over Garvey's car when he arrived in the colony. Garvey then issued a forthright warning to him that if he did not cease his 'tirade,' he would 'go away immediately.'

Wright complied, and Garvey admonished them: 'If the behaviour you have adopted today is the one you will adopt always, it is better that your division be disbanded for we cannot afford anyone to bring disgrace to our Association.' Wright tried to speak once more, and 'disorder again broke out.' A Black Cross nurse came forward and asked Wright to apologise to 'His Excellency.' Wright again sought to address the meeting, but Garvey said: 'If you do not sit down, I will leave this hall at once.'[68]

It was a disgraceful, self-destructive event, and it left Garvey with no time or inclination to address matters of relevance to the future of the UNIA. It is interesting, however, that he did make a 'lengthy reference' to the Ethiopian issue, arguing that Haile Selassie 'had forfeited the confidence of his people and of the Negro race in general because he deserted them at a time when his services were most needed.'[69]

Not only was Haile Selassie's reputation diminished, but Garvey's was also further undermined by his visit to British Guiana in 1937. African Guyanese self-esteem could not have emerged unscathed towards the end of the 1930s.

VI. The Indian Centenary in the Colony (1938), Gandhi's Nationalist Crusade, and Indo-Guyanese Triumphalism

On the other hand, a spirit of optimism and unbounded possibilities pervaded the celebration of the centenary of the Indian presence in British Guiana a few months later. It diverged strikingly from the reactive bleakness in which the African Guyanese identity project appeared to be enmeshed. In his speech to mark the Indian Centenary, on May 5, 1938, C. R. Jacob, a member of the Legislative Council since 1935 and president of the British Guiana East Indian Association, was sanguine about the Indians' capacity to enhance their self-esteem, imbued with a vision shaped by their ancient Indian heritage and an 'awakened national consciousness':

> We have brought with us to this country our religious customs, traditions and cultural standards. These, combined with our awakened national consciousness and subtle, silent forces at work among us, do not permit the surrender of our identity as a distinctive racial group. This desire, however, to remain as a separate and distinct community would in no wise interpose difficulties in the way of a hearty co-operation with other racial groups in a common purpose aiming at the development of the country and the welfare of the inhabitants.[70]

Not for the first time, little consideration was apparently given to the feelings, indeed the fears, of Africans: any new reference to a 'Greater India' or an 'Indian colony' could only have heightened their insecurity, with the potential for discord, if not conflict, whenever the incremental devolution of power by the British commenced. It is arguable, however, that the Indian leaders were endeavouring to make the colony irreversibly Indian-dominated in advance of any such devolution. In his Centenary speech, C. R. Jacob had demanded an agent-general from India to safeguard Indian interests in the colony. The *Daily Chronicle* saw the pitfall in this measure and quickly reprimanded Jacob, (notably) a member of the local legislature: 'The first patriotism of our Indians must be to British Guiana...we have no patience with them when they place India first and British Guiana second.'[71]

In praising Indian progress on the Centenary, the *Daily Argosy* also alluded to the basis of African insecurity:

> Frugal and thrifty even to the verge of parsimony, and existing in a state of simplicity in which their needs were few and comparatively easily satisfied, the Indians rapidly amassed wealth in the colony. They acquired cattle, they engaged in, and in fact were responsible for, the establishment of the rice industry. They evinced practically a hunger to own land...How well the Indians in the colony have succeeded can now easily be observed. **In the country districts they**

invariably own the lands which Africans, or persons of African descent, inherited from their forefathers [emphasis added].[72]

I wish to stress that the El Dorado complex – fantasy shaped, and necessitated, by the hazardous malarial coastal belt (below sea-level) requiring a costly and intricate hydraulic system of drainage and irrigation – is deeply rooted in the Guyanese imagination. Among Indo-Guyanese, this was magnified by the millenarian reflex inspired by the great text, the *Ramayana*, which entrenched escapist promptings in the Caribbean: exile, ideas of the golden age and redemption, even the notion of triumphal return. The eminent Indian historian, Romila Thapar (1931–), argues that the rule of Rama is 'symbolic in social memory with a mythologised utopian period of prosperity and well-being reflected in the phrase *ram-rajya* [the rule of Rama].' She explains why Tulsi Das's version of the text (the *Ramcharitmanas*) has an enduring appeal in north India (including eastern UP and western Bihar, the home of most of the indentured labourers taken to the Caribbean):

> For Tulsi the golden age lay in the past, in the reign of Rama, which he hoped would return; Tulsi's version endorses a millenarian dream. Interestingly, this millenarian strand became ideologically significant to peasant resistance, protesting against British colonial rule and landlordism in parts of India as recently as a few decades ago.[73]

The definitive place of this text among Indians in the Caribbean has fostered a millenarian vision there as well, a *rama-rajya* complex, in the minds of many thinkers and politicians as did the Gandhian revolt against British colonialism. In colonial Guyana, the joint influence of the El Dorado syndrome and the notion of a return to a golden age in the *Ramayana* has bred a predilection for utopianism: the idea that the political vocation or the great messianic political leader could open the way to eternal happiness on earth. Several Indo-Guyanese politicians in the 1930s–40s manifested this tendency, such as the trade unionist and founder of the MPCA and nominated legislator, Ayube Edun, and the president of the BGEIA and elected legislator, C.R. Jacob.

Although Cheddi Jagan was an atheist, it is conceivable that he was claimed by the powerful strand of utopianism threaded through the Indo-Guyanese political imagination, its predisposition towards the El Dorado syndrome. In fact, Jagan exemplified this tendency more comprehensively than anyone else: the eradication of 'bitter sugar' and 'the sugar gods' being the mantra for the communist utopia. But it is also true that Jagan's Marxism-Leninism had much in common with Gandhiism with its own utopian strand, encapsulated in his notion of *rama-rajya*, despite its origin as a Hindu idiom. Indian historian Charu Gupta argues that Gandhi appropriated it to reflect an inclusive millenarian vision that inheres in the Indian tradition:

> Gandhi declared *rama-rajya* to be 'a moral government based upon truth and non-violence, in other words universal religion,' and a rule under which 'the poor will be fully protected, everything will be done with justice, and the voice of the people will always be respected.'
>
> While using a symbol that could potentially spell alienation for some [particularly Muslims], he nonetheless appropriated it to signal a long utopian tradition in India and then cleverly intermeshed it with contemporary political desires of a just, equal and free society.
>
> Rejecting *Hindutva's* exclusivist interpretation, Gandhi's conception encompassed not only the mythical, ancient rule of Rama, but also the medieval, Mughal [Muslim] system of urban production and economy, and then went beyond it to provide a language of hope, dignity and rights for all.[74]

In July 1936, the editor of *Indian Opinion* (organ of the British Guiana East Indian Association), Mohamad Akbar, argued that Mother India's pursuit of freedom would soon be the inspiration for releasing the hitherto submerged political aspirations of Indo-Guyanese. He perceived their participation in the public domain as being inextricably intertwined with the success of the nationalist movement in India. In fact, because Hindus and Muslims shared a common indentureship and many continued to live together, largely in harmony, in the logies or ranges on the sugar plantations, a very strong bond developed between many Hindu and Muslim families. This was certainly my own experience of the camaraderie that prevailed between my own family and several Muslim families towards whom we shared a virtual consanguineal relationship. My own paternal great-grandmother was Muslim; she and my paternal great-grandfather (a Hindu) had grown up on the same plantation (Albion, in Berbice, owned by Jock Campbell's family). This would have been unthinkable in eastern UP/western Bihar, whence originated most of the Indian indentured labourers to Guyana.

It is comprehensible, therefore, that Mohamad Akbar (a Muslim Indo-Guyanese) would locate Gandhi's nationalist mission at the core of the emerging Indo-Guyanese political awakening:

> Mahatma Gandhi, a volcanic personality, an incomparable moral genius of our age, has shown India that freedom comes from within... We over here must try to catch and spread the spark of national feeling [from India] and fan it into a great blaze. It is the great reservoir of releasing energy and intensifying enthusiasm before which our grievances would find ready annihilation. Observe that when the will of a vast number of people gives expression to certain wants, the power would surpass even the power of the Kaieteur Falls [on the Potaro River in Guyana, with a perpendicular drop of 741 feet].[75]

There was an element of the El Dorado syndrome in Akbar's comment. But this was compatible with the Guyanese sensibility, permeated by excesses in the imagery: a grandiloquence in the messianic politics of Indo-Guyanese, leaders and led. The bombast permeates this excerpt from the Indian Centenary address by C. R. Jacob on May 5, 1938. El Dorado, the promise of the golden age, is transparent, as is the eternal foe, 'King Sugar'; so, too, the potential for the simmering African angst, over the idea of an Indian colony, to seek volatile expression:

> Looking far into the future we see Indian villages rising from among the ruins of once prosperous sugar estates, where once our fathers toiled, suffered and gave their lifeblood, and every man sitting in peace under his own fig-tree, smoking his pipe of peace, with no rude hands to disturb the quiet security of his life. Here and there a lofty chimney will be seen to remind him of the past but, as far as the eye can reach, the refreshing greenness of the land will speak of other industries being brought into existence by these humble sons of toil and Demerara as its entrepot will become as famous for its rice, cattle and other products as it is now famous for its sugar. In dim perspective we also see lines of communication established between this country and Mother India, and new blood infiltrating our communal arteries, keeping alive the cultural heritage of a glorious past and inspiring us to newer adventures.[76]

So powerful was the impact of Indian nationalism on Indo-Guyanese conception of self, they could not envision that the trajectory of their identity construction was essentially inimical to the making of a wider Guyanese identity. In May 1938, Peter Ruhomon, the Indo-Guyanese intellectual, was advocating the 'building of Greater India.' This idea also would have triggered alarm in the minds of African Guyanese – the vision of an independent India exerting suzerainty over its Indo-Guyanese-dominated appendage – the Indian colony. Ruhomon argues:

> The time has certainly arrived for us to give serious attention to the problem as to whether we are going to remain as an overseas community, in complete isolation from the Motherland [India] and her great and venerable institutions or, being one with her, in thoughts, feelings and aspirations, shall become identified with her and the silent revolutionary forces that are at work leading to the golden age of the future predicted by her sages…

> A new outlook is now dominating the minds of our leaders in the Motherland, and they are thinking in terms, not of India alone, but of her children overseas, and this wider outlook is bound to result in the mutual good of both…We manifest a justifiable pride in our history, culture and civilisation. We talk of our past glories and…of good times to come when the Motherland shall advance to the full measure of self-government…

> If we are to remain as Indians in the Colony and not lose our racial identity, I am loath to think we can work out our own destiny, unaided by the Motherland. Our brethren have awakened to the fact, and they are stretching their hands to us across the seas…In

this spirit and in this manner, the Greater India may be built up not only for ourselves but for the peace, happiness and contentment of generations yet unborn.[77]

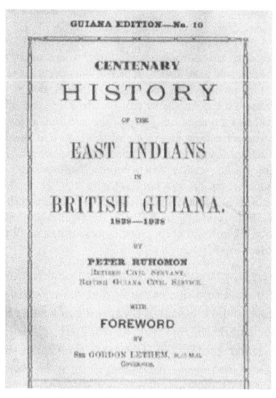

Peter Ruhomon's book chronicling the first hundred years of the Indian presence in Guyana (1838-1938) – a seminal achievement. He, his brother Joseph, and J.I. Ramphal were the pioneer Indian intellectuals in the colony. Peter compiled an admirable weekly column for many years in the Daily Chronicle, *titled 'Indian Intelligence by the Pandit'*

VII. Post-War Reforms on the Plantations and in the Villages: The Shaping of Cheddi Jagan's Radicalism

In early 1939, the West India Royal Commission (chaired by Lord Moyne) visited the region, including British Guiana. On February 13, the British Guiana East Indian Association appeared before it. The following exchange between Lord Moyne and C. R. Jacob, the president of the BGEIA, could not have allayed the apprehensions of African Guyanese of a resurgence of the idea of an Indian colony in British Guiana, his apparent concession to West Indian immigration notwithstanding:

The Chairman [Lord Moyne]: You speak of further settlement of Indians on the land, is this to be primarily for Indians who are already here, or do you wish to see more Indians brought here?

Mr Jacob: We should like to see those who are here permanently settled, and if it becomes necessary – at the moment it is not necessary – we should like to get more people from India as well as from the West Indies.

The Chairman: What, in your opinion, would constitute such a necessity — shortage of population here or poverty in India seeking for an economic outlet?

Mr Jacob: I think it would be both. This country has enormous resources. If we double the population, we would find our position would be better off…We are not satisfied that the drainage and irrigation obstacles are insurmountable. We believe that with proper attention and guidance the coastal lands could be made profitable.[78]

Therefore, by the late 1930s to early 1940s, on the eve of India's independence, the cultural momentum was decisively in favour of Indo-Guyanese; so, too, was the economic impetus and buoyancy regarding small farming, based on rice and cattle, as well as their demographic leap in the aftermath of eradicating malaria at the end of the 1940s. But the emergence of an Indian middle class, in commerce and the professions of law and medicine, also lifted their social and economic stature immeasurably. The underdogs were on the threshold of heightened political influence, if not domination. On the other hand, African Guyanese lacked a parallel comprehensive source of cultural affirmation to match Mother India; neither did they possess a parallel economic foundation to energise their social and political aspirations. This constituted a yawning lacuna among African Guyanese towards the end of Empire – signally detrimental to the creation of a nation in an independent Guyana.

India got its independence from Britain in August 1947, but partition was a dismal aspect of the dawn of a free India. This, conceivably, could have precipitated the compartmentalisation of Hindus and Muslims in British Guiana into irreconcilable camps. Yet the mutual Hindu-Muslim savagery in the immediate aftermath of the creation of Pakistan, did not provoke the dismal repercussions some might have envisaged. One reason for this is that many Hindus and Muslims (about 40 per cent in the late 1930s–40s) continued to reside on the sugar plantations (much more so than in Trinidad), routinely sharing residential space in the infamous logies or derelict ranges. Consequently, they never did relinquish their target of common resistance: the plantocracy, Cheddi's 'sugar gods.'

Equally consequential was the emergence of Cheddi Jagan, from the late 1940s, as the premier Indian leader, espousing a Marxist and secular politics – decidedly non-religious but not anti-religion. And the Enmore tragedy in June 1948, when five Indian workers were shot by colonial police, rendered Cheddi's radical politics, encapsulated by 'bitter sugar,' an enduring symbol of Indian cohesion and resistance. Yet, despite the working-class trajectory of his political mission, it was (from the inception) so definitively shaped by the specificity of the Indian plantation 'struggle,' that his capacity to empathise with, and assuage, African fears of his new order was transparently minimal. In fact, from the late 1940s, Jagan (unwittingly) epitomised Indian passion for adult suffrage (with the potential for political ascendancy), on one hand, with its obverse, African apprehension of his 'bitter sugar' mantra, as well as his anti-colonialism and crusade for independence, on the other.

African insecurity was, indeed, aggravated by Jagan's politics of rapid constitutional advance: the likelihood of universal adult suffrage by the early 1950s – coincidental with the escalation of the Indian population, following the eradication of the malarial scourge by the end of the 1940s. Between 1911 and 1920, the death rate of Indians and Africans was 31.7 per and 29.7 per thousand, respectively; between 1931 and 1935, it was 25.4 and 21.5 per thousand, respectively. With the eradication of malaria, the death rate in 1946–50 of Indians and Africans was reduced significantly: 13.9 and 16.7 per thousand, respectively. As the politics of the colony became polarised between the two ethnic segments (after the split in the PPP), between 1956 and 1960, the death rate of Indians and Africans was 9.7 and 12.5 per thousand, respectively.[79]

Indian birth rate had increased to forty-eight per thousand by 1948–49; African birth rate was lagging at thirty-five per thousand. The Venn Commission of 1949 commented on the demographic revolution:

> … when it is considered that on the sugar estates, and therefore among 21 per cent of the colony's population, the birth rate has well-nigh doubled [in a couple years], and infant and child mortality halved, the population problem for the future is evident and clamant.[80]

This would have a profound impact on how Indians perceived themselves, increasingly confident that they were no longer 'coolies' at the margins of the colony's affairs; they were moving centre stage as principal actors in their own right. I have remarked on this subject elsewhere, what I have termed a 'revolution in demographic patterns' among Indians after 1948:

> The implications of this demographic revolution for the social, economic and political evolution of the colony were astounding…the eradication of malaria represents the most important achievement in the country in the twentieth century. For Indians, it marked a

profound change in self-perception, opening the door to active politics: the rise of Cheddi Jagan.[81]

But the economic foundation of the emerging Indian self-confidence is also astounding. The expenditure of the government's funds on the chronic problem of drainage and irrigation in British Guiana was truly remarkable. Indeed, 63 per cent (£1,918,268) of the total Colonial Development and Welfare grant expended in the colony in the 1940s was allocated to drainage and irrigation. The principal beneficiaries were the predominantly Indian rice farmers. Anne Cook did a doctoral thesis on social policy and the economy in British Guiana. She explains the consequences for the rice industry of the priority funding of crucial hydraulics works in the 1940s–50s. The acreage under rice increased from 57,859 in 1940 to 93,637 in 1950 and to 153,000 by 1955:

> Between 1943 and 1944, Colonial Development and Welfare funds were used to undertake drainage and irrigation schemes which increased the land available for rice cultivation by 50%. In addition, experiments were made with the introduction of machinery for cultivation and threshing. The future of rice in Guyana, in the short-term at least, was made more secure in 1946 when Caribbean [British West Indian] governments contracted with the Rice Marketing Board, sole supplier since its establishment in 1939, to accept at least 80% of their requirements from that source at a fixed price for five years. The war-time initiative in rice continued. By 1952 [just two years after the birth of Jagan's PPP] the acreage in rice for the main harvest [October-November] had risen to 133,970 from 76,500 in 1944, largely as a result of the government's investment in drainage and irrigation.[82]

It is obvious that the Colonial Development and Welfare programme, as implemented in Guyana towards the end of Empire, redounded to the advantage of Indian rice growers primarily. And when this reality is allied with the declared policy of wide-ranging reform, pursued under the progressive leadership of Jock Campbell (the chairman of Booker) in the sugar industry, it is incontestable that the principal beneficiaries of this culture of reform in the colony, in the aftermath of the Moyne and Venn Commissions, were Indian rice farmers and Indian sugar workers, resident or non-resident on the plantations. It was quite common for many small rice growers to work part-time on the sugar plantations, usually as seasonal canecutters. Therefore, most Indian rice-growing and cattle-rearing villages remained loosely integrated with, and were buoyed by, the social and economic transformation on these plantations. This spirit of change had significant implications for Jagan's political mission from the late 1940s to early 1950s.

But this was an aggregation of communal passions, which provided the political habitat for Jagan to mount his 'bitter sugar' crusade. It came out of possibilities for change – not despair. It also substantiates, I believe, Eusi Kwayana's claim that, by and large, African Guyanese, at this juncture, harboured no strong feelings against sugar or Booker, neither did they possess the anti-colonial conviction and drive of Indo-Guyanese, inspired by India's independence and energised by the culture of reform initiated after the Second World War. The goal of the Colonial Development and Welfare programme of the Colonial Office was to minimise the possibilities of social unrest, in addition to stimulating a culture of political moderation – the incremental transfer of power in these small British colonies, within a liberal democratic framework. To a great extent, those aims were realised in the British West Indies, yet colonial Guyana, mired in its escalating racial bigotry, defied those expectations.

Anne Cook draws a sharp political insight from the peculiarity of the Indo-Guyanese community that would make the task of Cheddi Jagan, from the late 1940s, markedly feasible and its impact lasting. She explains why the radical (communist) Jagan was a beneficiary of these changes in the Indian villages and on the plantations – the foundation of his 'bitter sugar' mission. Interestingly, by the late 1940s, incremental improvement of the condition of the Indian rice grower and the Indian sugar worker (to a lesser degree) imbued both with the notion that their economic circumstances were no longer irretrievable; indeed, that this was indicative of illimitable possibilities for a metamorphosis of their condition. Therefore, their attraction to Jagan's Marxist mission of radical transformation was prompted by palpably improved conditions – not by a sense of despair and strangled aspirations. 'Bitter sugar,' ironically, was sustained not by chronic deprivation but by belief in the scope for even greater reform:

> The position of rice relative to developments in the sugar industry was of particular importance. Historically rice had been encouraged to develop as a supplement to wages earned on the estates and had later been grown as an alternative to estate wages when estate work could not be had or when wages made rice growing more attractive… The price for rice rose from $46.60 per ton in 1939 to $81.35 in 1942 [during the War], thereby offering a return to labour which compared favourably with estate work. Whilst rice growing did not cause many to abandon estate work altogether, it made workers less reliant on sugar wages and thus likely to decrease the number of weeks they spent on work on the sugar crop.[83]

Jagan's 'bitter sugar' crusade resonated with Indian sugar workers resident on the plantations, as well as those who lived in the villages, as some of the latter were both sugar workers as well as small rice farmers. The social and economic link between plantation and village, among Indians, was never totally ruptured. Jagan's narrative of 'bitter sugar,' therefore, would retain its appeal to both, as it was grounded in the master narrative of Indian indentureship as 'a new system of slavery.' It was an indispensable defence mechanism, what I have termed 'double-billing in the historiography of oppression.' It was deemed paramount in challenging the enduring African Guyanese narrative that they were deprived of their patrimony from enslavement because 'the coolies took the bread out of their mouths' after emancipation.

And as Anne Cook argues, the organic link between Indians in the village and on the plantation provided Jagan's 'bitter sugar' crusade with rich soil in which to plant, cultivate, and perpetuate his Marxist appeal. But it was a racial appeal that did not, probably could not, win African Guyanese empathy:

> The constitutional changes of the period were engineered to give experience both to an emerging political leadership and an expanding electorate in the 'responsible' exercise of political power...[But] the success of the PPP and the orientation of its leadership indicated the failure of the Colonial Development and Welfare programme to fulfil those aims...in Guyana, as compared to Jamaica, Trinidad and Barbados where similar programmes had been launched...One difference between Guyana and the islands mentioned...lies in the structure of the labour force. In Guyana a large sector of the work force was concentrated on one industry – sugar – and its workers shared working and living conditions on the plantations which in itself made the task of radical politicians easier [essentially Cheddi Jagan]. Further, the close relationship between the rice and sugar industries made for the extension of the radicalisation of the sugar workers to the peasantry [both overwhelmingly Indian]. The economies of Jamaica, Barbados and Trinidad were, by 1950, more diversified and in none of them was there a single industry with a comparable concentration of workers. Lastly, the peasantry in these countries was, perhaps, less open to radical influence.[84]

Therefore, universal adult suffrage, the Colonial Development and Welfare's disproportionate expenditure on drainage and irrigation, the culture of reform on the sugar plantations pursued by Jock Campbell's Booker, the secured market for Guyanese rice in the British West Indies, the demographic leap facilitated by the eradication of malaria by the late 1940s, in conjunction with the self-esteem spawned by India's Independence in 1947, were all instrumental in heightening the self-confidence of Indo-Guyanese by the early 1950s. African Guyanese, on the other hand, had little or no comparable sources of self-affirmation to reassure them that an independent Guyana, dominated by Indians, was conducive to their long-term security. It was, indeed, a pitch made for the radical politics of young, energetic, and self-assured Cheddi Jagan and his passionately driven, beautiful American wife, Janet: a gifted organiser.

In 1954, the Robertson Commission Report (on the suspension of the Constitution in October 1953) observed that the highly touted ethnic cohesion in the early 1950s inside the PPP, led by Cheddi Jagan and Forbes Burnham, was exaggerated. The suspicion harboured by Africans of the perceived ascendancy of Indians, in addition to their aspirations to ultimate dominance, was deep-seated. Yet it remained unexamined by the PPP:

> We...confirm from our experience that the Indian element in the population has now shaken off its lethargy and is beginning to play a major part in the life of the Colony. Education is now eagerly sought by Indian parents for their children; many Indians have important shares in the economic and commercial life of the Colony; the rice trade is largely in their hands from production to marketing. Their very success in these spheres has begun to awaken the fears of the African section of the population, and it cannot be denied that since India received her independence in 1947, there has been a marked self-assertiveness amongst Indians in British Guiana.
>
> Guianese of African extraction were not afraid to tell us that many Indians in British Guiana looked forward to the day when British Guiana would be a part not of the British Commonwealth but of an East Indian Empire. The result has been a tendency for racial tension to increase, and we have reluctantly reached the conclusion that the amity 'with which,' as the Waddington Report [of 1951] said, 'people of all races live side by side in the villages' existed more in the past; today the relationships are strained [arguably always so]; they present an outward appearance which masks feelings of suspicion and distrust. **We do not altogether share the confidence of the Waddington Commission that a comprehensive loyalty to British Guiana can be stimulated among peoples of such diverse origins** [emphasis added].[85]

Prophetic, indeed!

Notes

1. Leader, *Daily Chronicle*, August 17, 1926.
2. *Daily Chronicle*, April 25, 1919.
3. See Cheddi Jagan, *The West on Trial: My Fight for Guyana's Freedom* (London: Michael Joseph, 1966), 338.
4. C. M. Hale, 'An Indian Colony,' *The Imperial and Asiatic Quarterly Review* XXXI, 3rd series (1911): 346–48.
5. Ibid., 349–50.
6. *Daily Chronicle*, March 16, 1919.
7. J. A. Luckhoo, 'The East Indians in British Guiana,' *Timehri*, 3rd series (September 1919): 63–64.
8. CO111/635, (C. W. Doorly), no. 12776, March 9, 1920, encl.
9. Luckhoo, 'The East Indians in British Guiana,' 65.
10. CO111/635, (C. W. Doorly), no. 12776, March 9, 1920, encl.
11. IOR [India Office Records, British Library], L/E/7/1254 – J&P 5169/1919, encl. no. 4.
12. CO111/636, (Nunan), March 24, 1920, encl.
13. Luckhoo, 'The East Indians in British Guiana,' 65.

14. 'British Guiana: A Colony for India,' 20 – in CO111/636, (Nunan), March 24, 1920, encl.
15. Ibid.
16. Ibid.
17. Ibid.
18. *Daily Chronicle*, March 2, 1920.
19. *Daily Chronicle*, February 10, 1920.
20. IOR, L/E/1254 J&P 5169, Collet to Milner, April 25, 1919.
21. *Daily Chronicle*, May 9, 1919.
22. CO111/652, Thompson to Thomas, confidential, April 9, 1924.
23. Ibid.
24. CO111/651, Colonial Office to Governor Thompson, telegram, December 24, 1923.
25. *Daily Chronicle*, August 4, 1926.
26. Ibid.
27. *Tribune*, January 12, 1930.
28. *Tribune*, March 23, 1930.
29. See Richard Burton, *Afro-Creole: Power, Opposition and Play in the Caribbean* (Ithaca, NY: Cornell University Press, 1997).
30. See Kamau Brathwaite, *Contradictory Omens: Cultural Diversity and Integration in the Caribbean* (Kingston, Jamaica: Savacou, 1974).
31. Brian L. Moore, *Race, Power and Social Segmentation in Colonial Society: Guyana after Slavery, 1838–1891* (NY: Gordon and Breach Science Publishers, 1987), 28.
32. *Tribune*, February 10, 1935.
33. *Tribune*, July 29, 1934.
34. *Daily Chronicle*, September 3, 1926.
35. Leader, *Tribune*, April 15, 1934.
36. *Tribune*, April 8, 1934.
37. See, for example, *Tribune*, February 9, 16; May 24, 31, 1936.
38. *Tribune*, February 16, 1936.
39. *Tribune*, May 24, 1936.
40. Quoted in *Tribune*, March 23, 1930.
41. See my *Muscular Learning: Cricket and Education in the Making of the British West Indies at the End of the 19th Century* (Kingston, Jamaica: Ian Randle Publishers, 2006), chapter 3: 'The Making of a West Indian Intelligentsia: The Culture of Protest in the 1890s.'
42. Kevin A. Yelvington, '"West Indian Blacks Rally to the Fatherland": Ethnicity and the West Indian Reaction to the 1935 Italian Invasion of Abyssinia,' (mimeo.), 7–8.
43. Ibid., 9.
44. *Tribune*, November 24, 1935.
45. *Tribune*, December 22, 1935.
46. W. M. Macmillan, *Warning from the West Indies: A Tract for the Empire* (Harmondsworth: Penguin Books, 1938 [1936]), 52.
47. *Tribune*, February 10, 1935.
48. *Tribune*, December 1, 1935.
49. CO111/732/60036 [1936], 'Report of the Commission of Inquiry into the Disturbances [of 1935],' (Legislative Council Paper, No. 15 of 1936, Appendix 1).
50. Ibid.
51. *Tribune*, November 17, 1935.

52. *Tribune*, December 1, 1935.
53. *Tribune*, May 24, 1936.
54. Norman E. Cameron, *The Evolution of the Negro, Vol. 1* (Westport, Connecticut: Negro Universities Press, 1970 [1929]), 124, 126.
55. Ibid., 128.
56. P. Kodanda Rao, 'India and Indians Abroad,' *Indian Opinion*, June 1936, 3.
57. Rahaman B. Gajraj, 'India and her Nationals Overseas,' *Indian Opinion*, June 1936, 14.
58. *Daily Argosy*, October 12, 1930.
59. Leader, *Daily Argosy*, June 5, 1930.
60. Leader, *Tribune*, January 25, 1931.
61. Ibid.
62. Ibid.
63. Leader, *Tribune*, February 1, 1931.
64. *Tribune*, July 19, 1931.
65. *Tribune*, August 16, 1931.
66. Leader, *Tribune*, August 23, 1931.
67. *Daily Argosy*, October 23, 1937.
68. Ibid.
69. *Daily Argosy*, October 24, 1937.
70. *Daily Chronicle*, May 6, 1938.
71. Ibid.
72. Leader, *Daily Argosy*, May 5, 1938.
73. Romila Thapar, 'Epic and History: Tradition, Dissent and Politics in India,' *Past and Present*, no. 125 (1989): 21.
74. Charu Gupta, 'Gandhi on Cow, Ram-Rajya and Hindutva,' accessed at: nationalheraldindia.com/opinion/gandhi-on-cow-ramrajya-and-hindutva.
75. Mohamad Akbar, editorial, *Indian Opinion*, July 1936.
76. *Daily Chronicle*, May 6, 1938.
77. Peter Ruhomon, 'The Building of Greater India,' *Indian Opinion*, May 1938.
78. *The Royal Commission in British Guiana, 1939* (Georgetown: The Daily Chronicle Ltd., 1939), 203.
79. Jay R. Mandle, *The Plantation Economy: Population and Economic Change in Guyana, 1838–1960* (Philadelphia: Temple University Press, 1973), 97.
80. *Report of a Commission of Inquiry into the Sugar Industry of British Guiana* (J.A. Venn, chairman), Col. No. 249 (London: HMSO, 1949), 114.
81. See 'Burning the "Bridge to the Grave": Dr George Giglioli and the Eradication of Malaria, 1933–48,' in *Sweetening 'Bitter Sugar': Jock Campbell, the Booker Reformer in British Guiana, 1934-66* (Kingston, Jamaica: Ian Randle Publishers, 2005), 373.
82. Anne Patricia Cook, 'Social Policy and the Colonial Economy in Guyana,' (PhD Thesis, University of Surrey, Guildford, June 1988), 198.
83. Ibid., 201, 208.
84. Ibid., 227–28.
85. *Report of the British Guiana Constitutional Commission, 1954*, Cmd 9274 (London: HMSO), 15.

4.

Race, Class, and Colonial Stagnation
'Bitter Sugar,' the MPCA, Governor Lethem, and the Emergence of Cheddi Jagan

I.   J.I. Ramphal's Vision of Gradualism Regarding National Identity Supplanted

In August 1936, the Indo-Guyanese intellectual, J.I. Ramphal (1903–66), under the pseudonym, Lala Lajpat, reflected on the imponderable project of shaping and making a Guyanese identity. He did not subscribe to 'sectarianism' or 'sectionalism'; he believed in the principle of 'Guianese first, Indian after.' But he felt it was unrealistic to presume that they could eliminate or even elude references to 'racial problems…for yet a while' in British Guiana. He explained that local attitudes were profoundly shaped by ethnic peculiarities; this, therefore, often required internal/sectional resolution:

> Absence of thrift is so patently peculiar to the Negro community that there is a great work for the Negro Progress Convention [to persevere with]. Illiteracy and political indifference are so painfully manifest among Indians that there is [continued] scope for an Indian Association [the British Guiana East Indian Association].[1]

J.I. Ramphal believed ethnic cultural peculiarities (with their accompanying fears and insecurities) must be recognised, understood, and even discretely promoted in the short run, in the formidably protracted and tortuous process of creating a Guyanese national identity. A monumental project anywhere! It cannot be ignored or swept under the carpet; to do so would be tantamount to assembling combustible material that was bound to ignite conflict between the various segments, particularly Indians and Africans, in due course. A long-term undertaking, it is essential that it be prioritised as fundamental to the political cohesion of an ethnically complex, if not stubbornly disparate, society. The notion of being a Guyanese was still at a rudimentary stage, and Ramphal recommended a gradualist approach to national cohesion – the pursuit of a studied incremental integration:

> We want the Negroes [Africans] of the country to have *a real* Negro consciousness until they find their footing. After that they will be qualified for a real Guyanese consciousness...[But] we want Negro-controlled organisations to work for the benefit of British Guiana, giving expression to the peculiar contribution which that race is endowed to give to the world. We want Indians and other races to give their peculiar contribution also.

But J.I. Ramphal cautions:

> In a mixed community like this...the process of country [national] consciousness is necessarily slow, and in our opinion has to pass through the stage of section-consciousness to country-consciousness. What we can do is to minimise as much as possible the time at the sectarian stage and proceed quickly to the greater and better stage. It is only then that British Guiana can come into its own...When these problems will have been solved and racial equality in letter and law established, then he who talks of race and racial organisation will be an obsolete anachronism. Then we shall have mutual respect, and mutual love will follow. Then there will be a true Guianese [Guyanese] consciousness. **Until then the term Guianese is only a wish** [emphasis added].[2]

Easier said than done! Eighty-seven years after J. I. Ramphal made this argument and fifty-seven years since Guyana's independence, the country is still marooned in a quagmire of communal bigotry. It did not even attain 'a real' section-consciousness (by Ramphal's definition) because virtually every politician and opinion shaper, with the notable exception of Eusi Kwayana and Moses Bhagwan, circumvented, minimised, or ignored it as a prelude to national consciousness. When, on rare occasions, a sprinkling did espouse Ramphal's dictum, such daring individuals (the foremost being Sydney King [Eusi Kwayana]) were forthwith dismissed as racists. Yet Cheddi Jagan and Forbes Burnham, who dominated Guyanese politics for five and three-and-a-half decades, respectively, never did become anything but sectional or racial leaders, who unashamedly manipulated racial sentiments while claiming to be Marxists of one sort or another. It is not surprising, therefore, that racism still permeates virtually every transaction between the two main ethnic groups in Guyana. As I observe earlier, the three principal political leaders in the late 1970s, Jagan, Burnham, and Walter Rodney, had all assumed an ideological posture – bizarre anywhere in the world – that a variant of Marxism-Leninism or communism was the efficacious means to rapid economic transformation. Moreover, the underlying assumption was that its supposed infallibility, because of its grounding in scientific premises, would neutralise the discordant prejudices that emanate from primordial loyalties.

J. I. Ramphal's notion of gradualism in the shaping of national cohesion had no chance of coming to fruition because Guyanese leaders lacked the courage and moral fortitude to forthrightly challenge the bedevilling persistence of racism at the heart of Guyanese politics. Kwayana was calumniated by most Indians and rebuked as a racist. However, he believed that a political compromise on the governance of Guyana must be predicated on the will to resolve the historic, and widely recognised, ethnic insecurities permeating African and Indian relations, rooted in their deep-seated fear of domination by the other. As Dr Fenton Ramsahoye (Jagan's attorney general, 1961–64) told me in an interview in London (July 25, 1992), racism always pervaded Guyanese politics, despite the pretensions of Jagan and Burnham to being national leaders when, in reality, they exploited the ethnic factor adroitly in their pursuit of power:

> Jagan survives because he has racial support; he survives on racism, in the same way Burnham [head of the government for nearly 21 years] survived on racism. Burnham did not survive because of his intelligence…neither does Jagan. They are racist leaders. Jagan [then nearly 28 years as leader of the Opposition] owes none of his political longevity to Marxism.

Yet from the beginning of his political career, Cheddi Jagan was inclined to delegitimise the fundamental question of ethnic insecurity. He propounded his 'scientific' Marxist tenets to eliminate race from public discourse – deemed superfluous, or at best a peripheral factor – in comprehending the science of the evolution of society towards the inevitable communist state. Yet he and his People's Progressive Party (PPP) were skilful in aggregating Indian racial and political sentiments in enhancing his political career, particularly after Burnham quit the PPP in 1955. Indeed, Jagan deftly mobilised Indians across a potential religious chasm in British Guiana (between Hindus and Muslims), with the partition of India and the creation of Muslim Pakistan. By repudiating Hinduism or any other religious identity (unlike the ingrained Brahmin leadership in Indo-Trinidadian politics: Ashford Sinanan, Lionel Seukeran, Bhadase Maraj, Rudranath Capildeo, Stephen Maharaj, Basdeo Panday, and Kamla Persad-Bissessar), Cheddi was perceived as impartial to, if not agnostic toward, both Hindu and Muslim Indo-Guyanese religious sentiments. He was unreservedly secular; this was pivotal to the cohering of his emerging stature as an Indian with no partisan promptings from Mother India, although the cultural and political resurgence of the Indian homeland and its independence in 1947 were germane to his ascendancy. But he also contrived to retain the support of most of the Indian commercial sector, Hindu and Muslim, despite his Marxist-Leninist creed over five decades. The subtle, but effective, dissemination of the 'otherness' of Africans was also integral to Jagan's politics. This was demonstrated, for instance, in the strategy of his PPP not to contest several unwinnable constituencies in the general elections of August 1961, ironically to aid the right-wing United Force of Peter D'Aguiar as a counter to Burnham's People's National Congress (PNC) – a wise strategy under the first-past-the-post electoral system.

II.   Jagan's 'Bitter Sugar' Campaign and the Discrediting of Ayube Edun's MPCA

Shortly after Cheddi Jagan was elected to the Legislative Council in November 1947, he was sanguine that although the franchise was still not granted to all adults, the fact that 71.5 per cent voted in the general elections was indicative of a new political culture in the colony. This was, in effect, Jagan's message (essentially a Marxist one) as he was about to become the legislator for Central Demerara:

> No longer can it be said that the people are not politically conscious. It is indeed a welcome sign that the people are ready for universal adult suffrage. Labour has been returned triumphant. The representatives of capital and privilege have been rudely awakened…One candidate in his victory speech pleaded that capital must have its share of profit, and labour must work hard to be assured of a decent wage. Such a statement forgets that all profits come from the sweat of labour, and that to tell labour that it must work hard for a decent wage is to fully misunderstand the real needs of labour. Labour wants now a decent wage for the present hard work carried on under conditions of malnutrition and poor housing.[3]

He and his wife, Janet Jagan (she lost), did not contest the elections under the banner of the loose so-called Labour Party, of whom the veteran trade unionist, Hubert Critchlow, was a principal mover. The party did not have any Marxists (there were very few, indeed, in the colony); many were opportunists who considered the label 'Labour' an asset in their political endeavour. The Jagans (Janet contested Central Georgetown) called themselves Independent Labour – a ploy to deflect known antagonism towards their Marxist beliefs. The so-called Labour Party won five of the fourteen seats; Dr J. B. Singh (then the most prominent Indo-Guyanese politician) won as MPCA Labour and Dr Cheddi Jagan as Independent Labour.

Cheddi was shrewd enough not to censure those who voted for the so-called Labour Party while indicating the necessity for a genuine party dedicated to addressing the grievances of labour. He did concede that race was a potent element in the elections, clearly so in his own constituency, yet he sought to discount its significance, as dictated by his Marxist tenets. He envisioned: 'Labour [the working class] did right to vote the way it did. But labour must begin to search now for its true leaders for the next election. It must look for those leaders within its own ranks and be able to pick the real labour men from its elected members [him, for instance]. If labour at the next election votes labour with this difference, then labour will prove that it is a force to be reckoned with.'[4]

Then this Marxist tenet that Cheddi could never relinquish – what Sylvia Wynter considers his obdurate base/superstructure foundation of knowledge, written in stone. It underlines his faith in Marxism from the inception of his political career:

> **Labour, however, will have to solve the question of race. This it can only do by replacing the question of race by one of class.** The rich and the poor of one particular race do not have the same interests. It is the poor and exploited of all races who have a common interest – that of improving working and living conditions. The slogan in British Guiana should be: WORKERS OF ALL RACES, UNITE [emphasis added]![5]

But Cheddi had struck a responsive chord already by locating the plight of the poor and the powerless at the core of his fledgling political mission. In British Guiana, where the chronic hydrological difficulties necessitated costly expenditure on drainage and irrigation, small-scale agriculture, often could not bear such a daunting imperative. This was the context in which a few large British companies had continually absorbed numerous small sugar estates facing bankruptcy. Besides, the volatility of sugar prices exacerbated the risk involved in producing cane sugar on small plantations. Therefore, unlike colonial Trinidad, where small farmers (many of them Indians) found the cultivation of sugar cane remunerative, British Guiana could not sustain a peasant cane-farming sector of even minimal proportion. Thus, did Booker become overwhelmingly dominant, the peerless colossus of sugar, owning around 80 per cent of the plantations after the Second World War; only their size enabled them to raise the capital required to persist with that product in so hazardous an environment. And with the Commonwealth Sugar Agreement of 1951 (in which Jock Campbell played a decisive role), guaranteed prices and quotas in Britain enabled the industry to thrive, and under Campbell's progressive leadership of Booker, to introduce a range of reforms on the sugar plantations. Cheddi Jagan played a significant part in accelerating change, but without the reforming intent and resolve of Campbell, the pace would have been markedly slower. Yet Indians, though the main beneficiary of these reforms, could never be reconciled to Campbell's culture of reform. 'Bitter sugar' was an inviolable mantra, with deep roots in another inviolable concept: the notion of Indian indentureship as 'a new system of slavery.'

It was Jagan's narrative of 'bitter sugar' only that evoked empathy from Indo-Guyanese – Campbell's reforms, though far-reaching, could muster no appreciation whatsoever. Jagan's masterstroke of a symbolic representation of the Indian's 'white man burden' was inextricably intertwined with his Marxist vision. The former had such resonance among all Indians (even among the middle class) that it attenuated, if not erased, the potentially negative impact of his Marxism. Indeed, for his Indian supporters (Hindus and Muslims), many still residing on the plantations in the 1950s–60s, his indictment of 'bitter sugar' was so redemptive that his devotion to communism never did become insufferable for them. Most did not comprehend the implications of his ideology, and the likelihood that it would have fatal consequences for them, in the context of the Cold War, hardly caused a stir because it remained largely unventilated and unexamined – barely fathomable – among themselves. Besides, Jagan did not have the freedom to implement a communist programme in colonial Guyana, between 1957 and 1964; therefore, his Marxism-Leninism remained largely innocuous, ventilated purely on a theoretical plane. Guyanese were thereby spared its potentially pernicious effects. This was conducive to his longevity.

Jagan, the Marxist-Leninist, never did rule!

When Peter D'Aguiar of the United Force was remorselessly pursuing his anti-communist crusade against Jagan (between 1961 and 1964), it was disregarded by most Indians as an elitist Portuguese campaign fomented against their hero, the underdog, for purely racial reasons. Even the peril inherent in Cheddi's embrace of a pro-Moscow communism, in 'America's backyard,' failed to kindle antipathy towards him personally, whatever reservations some, a minority of businessmen and professionals, harboured towards his creed. Cheddi's crusade against 'bitter sugar' and the 'sugar gods' (Booker in particular) was so consuming that he became a veritable Nehru to his Indian Guyanese supporters. In many Indian homes, framed pictures of Jagan took their place amongst those of a pantheon of Hindu gods and goddesses, along with Gandhi and Nehru: all being intrinsic to the Indo-Guyanese sensibility.

The passion and sincerity of Cheddi's crusade against sugar was also the source of his inflexibility – the hatred (no exaggeration!) for Booker, the British, and the American imperialists, the evil forces of capitalism. Yet deep though the source of his resolve, shaped by his birth and early life at Plantation Port Mourant, it was the virtual religious devotion to Marxism-Leninism that sustained his somewhat evangelical political vocation. This is how Jagan saw 'bitter sugar' and the 'sugar gods' in the early 1950s:

> Sugar has, indeed, played a major role in the agricultural economy of British Guiana [B.G.], so much so that the history of B.G. can truly be said to be a history of sugar. This history abounds with many instances of looting, bloodshed and murder. As late as 1948, at Plantation Enmore, five workers were killed and several others severely injured...Agricultural policy has always been determined

not so much 'in conjunction with' sugar but 'after' sugar. Sugar has indeed been 'king.' This has been possible because the sugar plantation owners are mostly absentee British Imperialists.

> Booker is the Symbol of British Imperialism in B.G....It is represented in all phases of economic life, so much that B.G. is sometimes colloquially referred to as Booker's Guiana. It controls a greater part of the sugar estates, and has a dominant position in commerce... The workers are sweated [totally exploited], and millions of dollars produced by them find their way into the pockets of sugar 'gods' in England [Booker being foremost]...As a socialist Party [Jagan's PPP], **nationalisation of the sugar industry, and indeed all major industries is our objective. In the interim, while we are still tied to British imperialism with limited constitutional powers, certain reforms have to be undertaken to break the back of imperialism...Join the fight against sugar imperialism**. Make B.G. British Guiana and not Booker's Guiana [emphasis added].[6]

It was a simple but powerful message that inspired, and stayed with, Cheddi's Indo-Guyanese supporters – not only the less enlightened ones, but among the more successful as well, most of whom would eventually migrate to countries of 'decadent capitalism': America, Britain, and Canada. However, one cannot comprehend the power and longevity of his 'bitter sugar' crusade if it is divorced from the widely accepted, but rarely examined, conception of indentureship as 'a new slavery.' The latter essentially posits that Indian indentured labourers were tricked or kidnapped into indentureship in the Caribbean, Mauritius, Fiji, and other plantation colonies in the Tropics. The underlying assumption is that they had no agency whatsoever in their departure from India, between 1838 and 1917; moreover, that conditions under indentureship and beyond on the sugar plantations were so inhuman and blatantly exploitative that it did constitute 'a new slavery.'

But this assumption tends to obscure the fundamental difference between Indian indentureship and the infinitely, and incomparably, more dehumanising enslavement of Africans (for life), although it is true that in the 1930s and 1940s living conditions on many plantations, encapsulated by the infamous logies or ranges where the resident workers lived, were often abominable. And Cheddi Jagan's campaign against 'bitter sugar' was, indeed, seminal in accelerating social change, but of no less importance was the fact that, from 1952, Jock Campbell (1912–94), with Fabian socialist tendencies, became the chairman of Booker. He had the inclination, imagination, and resolve to meet Jagan more than half-way. It initiated a period of reform in the 1950s to early 1960s that radically changed health, housing, wages, and recreational facilities on the sugar plantations. Many of the recommendations made by the Venn Commission (1949) for reforms on the estates (following the Enmore shootings of June 1948) were implemented.

But it is important to recall another impetus for reform: without the security of prices and quotas of the Commonwealth Sugar Agreement, very little would have been achievable.

Campbell first went to British Guiana in 1934, aged twenty-two (two years before Cheddi left for America) to work for the family's sugar company, Curtis Campbell, and he was aware immediately of how abysmal conditions were on their plantations (they owned Albion and Ogle). Campbell recalled the seminal experience thirty-five years later, in October 1969, in a talk to the Fabian Society in London:

> Conditions of employment in the sugar industry were a disgrace. Wages were low; housing unspeakable; workers were treated with contempt – as chattels not as human beings – animals and machinery were in fact cared for better than the workers because they cost money to replace…The plantocracy had great power in Government – did all they could to prevent other industries in order to maintain a surplus of labour. This was an industry founded on slavery, continued on the indenture system, maintained on the exploitation of African and Indian workers.[7]

Cheddi's mission to improve working and living conditions on the sugar estates was a noble one, but nothing Campbell did could have moderated the predilection of Jagan, whose 'bitter sugar' crusade was clear about its ultimate goal: 'nationalisation of the sugar industry, and indeed all major industries is our objective.' Therefore, he could never be reconciled to the fact that Campbell was pursuing an enlightened culture of reform to redress ancient wrongs on the plantations. **Of no less importance, Cheddi ought to have recognised that, certainly after 1957, he had a potentially priceless ally in Jock Campbell, who could have been decisive in his pursuit of the great prize: independence.**

It was an Indo-Guyanese autodidact, Ayube M. Edun (1893–1957), who had set an early example of a formidable challenge to the old order of the plantocracy. He started the *Guiana Review* in 1935 to document the generally poor working conditions of plantation workers. He also founded the Manpower Citizens' Association (MPCA), the first trade union to represent the predominantly Indian fieldworkers; it was registered on November 5, 1937. But as the *Guiana Review* observed on November 6, 1938 (the first anniversary of the MPCA), the union had a membership of 'not less than 10,000.' This cannot be verified, but the sugar planters were not enamoured of the union's persistence in ventilating the grievances of workers:

> its success has resulted in a kind of panic on the part of the Vested Sugar Interests [sic], and every conceivable kind of tactics – mean and otherwise – has been employed in order to crush the Association

in the bud. Our members had been victimised, repressed, black-listed and provoked, the Executive has been maligned, abused and cursed, and despite all these pernicious practices, the Association has emerged triumphant.

Edun's MPCA was recognised by the Sugar Producers' Association in early 1939, when the Moyne Commission was visiting British Guiana. The latter was delegated by the Colonial Office to examine living conditions in the British West Indies after a series of labour riots in several of the colonies, precipitated by generally poor economic conditions in the aftermath of the Great Depression and abysmal sugar prices in the early 1930s. The MPCA appeared before the Moyne Commission in February 1939, and they dramatised the objectionable circumstances under which some women fieldworkers (usually weeders) were made to function daily:

> Men and women have to wade and cross the canals and trenches to get to their work. As the men and women proceed in their hundreds on the dams, the women, as soon as they reach their destination [the cane-fields], will have to get into the trenches. These trenches are sometimes breast-deep and other times shallower, but in any case, they have to lift their clothing before they enter, and they tell the men: 'Brothers, hide your faces that we may cross.' Invariably it has been found that overseers, drivers and others have been in the habit of amusing themselves on the novelties of the unhappy scenes aback.

> Numerous complaints have been received by the Association [MPCA] and strong recommendations have been made with the result that boats have been recommended, but the process seems to be so slow that the abuses have not yet been eliminated on several estates. In addition to this abuse of women in the cane-fields, they are given tasks to weed the parapets of the trenches where they have to wade in breast-deep water for days and, strange to say, that with all the representation made, these pernicious systems are still in vogue.[8]

The MPCA was equally repelled by the state of the 'logies' or barracks in which the workers lived, often called the 'nigger yard' as many were built during slavery and had been patched up over many decades – some marooned in a sea of mud and refuse, unsanitary and derelict in appearance. The Union also deplored the lack of potable water, as residents had no option but to procure drinking water from canals in which the punts or iron tugs transported the cane from field to factory. These conditions rendered the workers and their children even more susceptible to malaria (chronic in some districts), hookworm, and intestinal diseases. The MPCA was graphic in depicting the revolting environment. It corroborates Jock Campbell's seminal recollection of the abominable 'logies' he encountered in British Guiana in 1934:

The latrines are built on open drains through which water runs. The excreta lie about, and pigs, ducks and fowls feed on them, and these roam about the compound of the barracks [logies] with the consequence that sewage is carried into the very homes of the workers. Further, the pigs and ducks enter into the open trenches and people are seen to bathe and wash clothing therein. It is not conceivable to find anything worse...

Apart from the defective latrine system, in the rainy season, as there are no roads leading to the workers' houses, the mud dams become liquid mud, and the mud also is carried into their houses. In hot seasons the barracks, covered as they are with galvanised roofs, are nothing but ovens. In the nights they are cold. While the staff compounds carry electric lights, the workers' compounds are devoid of light.[9]

The MPCA also identified the pervasive illiteracy among Indians on the sugar plantations as the 'chief obstacle' to trade unionism. They considered the limited opportunities for even a primary education a studied approach by the plantocracy because 'the less the workers were educated the easier it was for them to be controlled.' It was common for workers to walk seven miles before reaching their place of work on the sugar estate, apart from Blairmont, Port Mourant, and another plantation where a light railway relieved them of this onerous daily chore. The Union elaborated: 'In wet seasons the mud does become impassable and trudging in one or two feet of mud is a harrowing experience, with the result that when the destination is reached the worker is exhausted.'[10]

Ayube Edun's MPCA constituted a kind of revolution for the sugar workers: a recognised body articulating their grievances, with empathy and authority, to the hitherto sacrosanct White 'czars' on the plantations. These were festering grievances – not actuated by communists or other subversives, as some planters were inclined to assert. Cheddi Jagan was studying dentistry in America (from 1935 to 1943), so he could not have been indicted for fomenting subversion. Not yet! It was the sugar planters' own primitive human relations practices that had precipitated the strikes of 1934–35, thus hastening the formation of the MPCA in 1937. As the MPCA observed in their memorandum to the Moyne Commission in 1939: 'The system of work, of working hours in the fields and factories, are all based on irrational and traditional customs and usages of the past which do not allow room for modern progressive methods.'

The MPCA, to its credit, took a broader view: that the disaffection on the estates at the end of the 1930s was triggered by more than the workers' multitude of grievances. It was precipitated by a culture of repression, so the union sought to empathise also with the plight of the overseers on sugar estates, largely poor young Scots, 'mostly unmarried men living in barracks and open to all sorts of bad designs of sex.' There were apparently a few Eurasian children on the plantations, a testimony to these desperate men's 'adventures': exploiting their supervisory position to extract sexual favours from vulnerable young Indian women, in situ: the cane-fields. Jock Campbell had encountered several such men on their own plantations in 1934–35. They paid board to the managers who made 'handsome profits,' but nothing would have been spared for their putative offspring, if recognised at all. Yet, when Edun's union appeared before the Moyne Commission, they evinced amazing empathy with these overseers – in their telling phrase, 'the sucked oranges of sugardom.' The MPCA explained: 'As buffers between their bosses and the workers, they suffer mental agony, economic serfdom and grave social disabilities which are grossly unfair for human beings to endure.'[11] Likewise, the trauma of the Indian women who were exploited by these young White overseers remains an area of darkness that is almost as pronounced, and as defiant of apprehension, as the void that persists regarding the antecedence, in India, of the female indentured labourers.

This was the soil in which the 'bitter sugar' narrative germinated and assumed a compelling hold on the Indian imagination. But it was, overwhelmingly, of Indo-Guyanese resonance, as there were very few, if any, African residents in the 'logies' on the sugar plantations by the 1930s. The predominantly African workers in the sugar factories, many with ample sugar-manufacturing or allied mechanical skills, did not reside on the plantations; they tended to live in African villages within cycling distance of the factory. They had a different union, the British Guiana Workers' League (founded and led by a Barbadian-born African Guyanese educator, A. A. Thorne [1871–1956]), and recognised by the Sugar Producers' Association (SPA) since 1931. So, the workforce on the sugar plantations was divided both by class and ethnicity, as the factory workers were largely skilled African men on a comparatively higher wage-rate than the predominantly Indian fieldworkers. Therefore, Cheddi Jagan's 'bitter sugar' crusade, even in the late 1940s, did not necessarily resonate with the African factory workers, his fervent espousal of the class struggle against the 'sugar gods' notwithstanding. Furthermore, Africans in the villages and in urban areas, beyond the sugar estates, also found the 'bitter sugar' narrative indigestible. They were inclined to see it as another ruse to facilitate Indian hegemony – the fear of an impending Indian Colony, however subliminal, was obdurate.

Although Jagan did seek to engage with all sugar workers, his origins on a sugar plantation, Port Mourant, Corentyne (under four miles from Jock Campbell's family plantation, Albion), had imbued him with instinctual empathy for Indian fieldworkers. He was, in fact, treasurer of the MPCA for one year (1945–46), but was soon removed because, as he recalled, he had repudiated his colleagues for what he deemed 'their high level of expense allowances from the funds of a poor union.' Besides, as a Marxist, he judged the MPCA's method of bargaining with the SPA deficient in the requisite militancy. He believed the MPCA had already degenerated into a 'company union.' He pointed out that a few years before, one of the founding members of the union whom he did not name (it was C. R. Jacob, snr) had accepted a handsome monthly stipend of £100 from Booker.[11] I do recall seeing a Booker document to this effect where Jacob had approached Alfred Sherlock of Booker for financial help, as his son was studying medicine in London during the War.

In May 1990, I asked Jock Campbell about this matter. Jock was a young director of Booker when the bribe was made to Jacob (around 1940) to curb the militancy of the recently recognised MPCA. Jock responded:

> The allegations are true [about the SPA and C.R. Jacob]. I don't think I knew it then, but the SPA was much more worried about the MPCA than I was; I got on fairly well with Ayube Edun. I was in sympathy with the sugar workers wanting a union, and I think the MPCA was a responsible union. I was fairly junior in those days [when] the scandal came out, and it was certainly true that the SPA was paying Jacob. Sherlock never told me about it. He did it and then came back and reported it. I was appalled. I remember it distinctly.[12]

In the MPCA's organ of September 24, 1944 (renamed *Labour Advocate*), the union revisited the issue, as their reputation had clearly been undermined by it:

> It has been proved beyond any doubt that the Hon C. R. Jacob, during his term as President of the British Guiana East Indian Association and Treasurer of the Man-Power Citizens' Association used his offices to secure employment with the British Guiana Sugar Producers' Association [SPA] for £100 ($480) per month under a contract – the gist of which was published in the *Labour Advocate* of July 11, 1943, which Mr Jacob has made no attempt to deny or correct thereby establishing the veracity of the accusation.

Although Cheddi Jagan's tenure as treasurer of the MPCA was brief (1945–46), his expulsion from the union for challenging union leaders regarding their extravagance (as he saw it), redounded to his long-term advantage. The MPCA was severely tainted, in the minds of many workers, for being complicit in colluding with the SPA. The worst consequence of the Jacob Affair was the hardening of the sugar workers' conviction that they could never trust the evil plantocracy. Booker in particular, the old devil, was incapable of mending its rotten ways. The pejorative appellation, 'Booker's Guiana' (for British Guiana), was virtually ineradicable, the later resolve of Jock Campbell to embed a robust culture of reform within the sugar industry notwithstanding. Cheddi Jagan's 'bitter sugar' mantra thereby planted its enduring roots that fed his political mission for five decades.

The MPCA, as well as the BGEIA, could not erase the stain of the Jacob Affair. The upshot was that as early as the mid-1940s, the MPCA, although a pioneer in championing the sugar workers' cause, was enmeshed in an undercurrent of suspicion and diminishing credibility. And Ayube Edun, despite his indefatigable advocacy of the sugar workers' rights and the widespread appreciation of his personal sincerity in alleviating their grievances, never recovered fully from Jacob's perceived collusion with Booker. But he deserves recognition as the first Indo-Guyanese since the intrepid Bechu, in the late 1890s, to pose a reverberating challenge to the plantocracy (virtually single-handedly) by creating, first, a newspaper (the *Guiana Review*, superseded by the *Labour Advocate*) to ventilate the sugar workers' problems; then for taking the monumental step of founding a trade union in 1937 – and getting it recognised in 1939 – to rectify ancient wrongs. Edun was a pathfinder, but he has received barely any recognition for his sterling seminal contribution. (An eloquent silence has shrouded the work of virtually every Indo-Guyanese leader who preceded Cheddi Jagan – a lacuna in Guyanese history.) Baytoram Ramharack's recent comprehensive study of Dr J. B. Singh (2019), therefore, is a bold initiative to redress this shortcoming.

III. Governor Lethem's Quest for Reform Aborted: A Challenge to the Orthodoxy of the Sugar Plantocracy

The closing years of the 1940s brought a change in the content of the debate about colonialism. It was becoming clear that because of the immense debts incurred by Britain during the War, in addition to the Independence of India in 1947, the imperial centre could not hold for much longer. The Empire was already on dodgy legs. On the other hand, during the War, British Guiana had become sanguine regarding possibilities for economic transformation. A good deal of that buoyant attitude to reform was stimulated by a remarkably imaginative and empathetic governor of British Guiana, Sir Gordon Lethem (1886–1962). He held that office from November 1941 to November 1946, and a broad cross-section of Guyanese had petitioned the Colonial Office for him to be granted a second term. Such was the respect and confidence they reposed in him, yet the authorities in London did not accede to the request. It was widely believed in British Guiana that the sugar interests in London had intervened to block Lethem's return to the colony.

Lethem's devotion to the cause of drainage and irrigation for the coastland of Guyana was so resolute, that it won the support of all sections of the community, possibly with the sole exception of the sugar planters. It was the most bedevilling problem in the colony, but there was an unmalleable apprehension among these planters that if more land were empoldered (drained and irrigated), it would siphon off labour from the premier industry of British Guiana: sugar. Yet virtually everything Governor Lethem did in this difficult multiracial colony in the 1940s, during the War, lifted the spirits of the people. He was probably the most enlightened governor the colony ever had.

But Cheddi Jagan was rather sparing in his appraisal of Lethem:

> Sir Gordon was a progressive governor, certainly, as governors go. His [rather, the people's] efforts to have his term of office extended were blocked by the planters and the Colonial Office, for he was much too liberal and outspoken for their liking.

Hon Ayube Edun of the MPCA (nominated to the Legislative Council by Lethem in 1943) knew Governor Lethem personally; he was well-placed to make an informed judgement of his stewardship in British Guiana. On July 16, 1944, Edun gave a talk on radio station ZFY (Georgetown), focusing on Lethem's achievement. He was clearly animated by prospects that the most fundamental problem in British Guiana (the stubborn ethnic question apart), drainage and irrigation of the coastland, was on the verge of being partially resolved, in great measure because of Lethem's tenacity. I reproduce Edun's talk almost in its entirety because the vibrant sense of possibilities in the colony was a major factor in Cheddi Jagan's initial impact at the end of the 1940s. For Indians in particular (given their engagement with agriculture), a comprehensive drainage and irrigation programme was crucial to their welfare. They considered Lethem an instrument of progress and prosperity, unlocking the hitherto strangled potential of their enterprise in rice, market gardening crops and cattle.

Ayube Edun (speaking in Urdu) said:

> My Indian brethren...since the advent of Sir Gordon Lethem the consciousness of the people has awakened. He is endeavouring to place the country on a better economic footing — that is, to produce more and more sugar, rice, [ground] provision, cattle, milk and greens [vegetables], in the hope of stabilising the finances...He has placed on the tapis a comprehensive scheme in order to drain and irrigate the lands so as to ensure the crops. These schemes have been placed before the Secretary of State for the Colonies...It is essential that the peasants, and even the workers, should take advantage of time and prepare themselves for the occasion when land settlement would be a practical reality...I may give you an indication of what the comprehensive scheme means. Twelve million dollars will be spent; 500,000 acres of land will be released for cultivation; and 132,000 acres for pasturage. The money, it is hoped, will come from the Development and Welfare Act [of 1940]. In order to hasten this ideal His Excellency himself is proceeding to London...[where] the proposition would be fully considered in all its aspects.[13]

However, Governor Lethem's imaginative plan for a comprehensive drainage and irrigation scheme, particularly for the more salubrious and substantially less malarial Corentyne Coast – the Indian heartland of British Guiana – would soon encounter the potent resistance of the sugar monoliths who had long exerted inordinate influence on the political and economic agenda of the colony. The local head of Booker, Hon F. J. Seaford, was an elected member of the Legislative Council (on a very restricted franchise), as well as a member of the policymaking Executive Council. Sugar was therefore at the heart of colonial governance (hence the term plantocracy), but the head of Booker in London, Sir Alfred Sherlock, was even more instrumental in determining colonial policy because of his capacity to modify, if not determine, the thinking of the secretary of state for the colonies.

Jock Campbell recalls that Lethem was passionately committed to reforms in British Guiana, but he was confronted with extraordinary pressure from 'King Sugar':

> Lethem was very unusual, rather left-wing, very controversial; he really was shocked by what he found in British Guiana: the power of the plantocracy and the bad conditions, and he really wanted to do something about it. I felt I had an ally in him, and I think he felt he had an ally in me. He was a splendid Governor and, in fact, was not very popular at the Colonial Office because he tried to do too much too fast.[14]

Lethem was determined to challenge the economic orthodoxy in the colony, of subordinating virtually every other economic activity to the procrustean mould of sugar. He dared to reorient colonial policy toward the wider interest of the people, enunciated clearly in his despatch to the Colonial Office of September 23, 1943:

> If the position is that **everything** must be sacrificed to sugar, as Sherlock [Head of Booker in London] would argue, then of course no doubt government should have kept down and prevented all rises in prices of rice and ground provision [produced primarily by small cultivators]. I think any fair man will appreciate that that would have been outrageous…**If we are to sit back and do nothing except where sugar comes into the picture, this place will remain one of the blackest spots of the Empire** [emphasis added].[15]

F.J. Seaford had concurred with Lethem that the chronic hydrological problems of British Guiana must be 'put in order.' However, he retracted after his boss in London, Sir Alfred Sherlock, intervened with the conventional arguments countering development initiatives beyond the primacy of sugar. He was apprehensive that unlimited access to reclaimed land would divert a substantial amount of labour from the plantations, with devastating consequences for sugar. But Lethem challenged Sherlock's argument in his despatch to the Colonial Office:

> The fulminations of Sherlock against anything being done for non-sugar interests have been having effect, and Seaford himself is getting uneasy that schemes which will cater for rice, provisions, pasturage, etc., are going to mean more and more difficulties for sugar – shortage of labour...Seaford tends to harp pessimistically that...[a comprehensive drainage and irrigation scheme] can never carry any of the capital costs and probably never, for many years, fully carry maintenance charges. I am not going to deny this, but I would go on hoping that some of them would pull out not so badly, and I certainly don't want to be deterred from the obvious thing to do... **I am a little anxious lest sugar interests may try and pull every possible wire against any big drainage and irrigation projects which are not principally or largely sugar** [emphasis added].[16]

Sherlock and Seaford met officials at the Colonial Office towards the end of 1943, and they marshalled all the standard, well-rehearsed, objections in combating Lethem's drainage and irrigation scheme. They contended that the cost had been under-estimated. So too was the labour accessible in the colony for the crucial requirements of the sugar industry; besides, rice (the product pioneered single-handedly by Indians) could not be remuneratively produced except on a large scale. They were subversive of Lethem's resolve to broaden the base of the colony's economy, and they did everything in their power to undermine it. But Lethem persevered, submitting a comprehensive plan, in April 1944, for the drainage and irrigation of the potentially prosperous, less malarial, Corentyne Coast. The population of this district had increased from 58,260 in 1931 to 75,694 in 1942.

Lethem applied for a grant of $3,100,000 under the Colonial Development and Welfare Act (1940), for the empoldering of an area of 443 square miles between the Berbice and Corentyne Rivers, for rice, provision, food crops, and cattle. He adroitly observed that the scheme would be beneficial to the 'surplus' population on sugar estates which the planters were desirous 'to diminish.' He was subtly making the case that the sugar plantations were not short of labour, and that the provision of drainage and irrigation facilities was indispensable to the expansion of the agricultural base of the colony beyond its chronically inordinate dependence on sugar. But he was also intimating that the sugar planters were obsessed by the idea that creating alternative means of livelihood for their predominantly Indian workers in the Corentyne District would lure their resident workers away from the four plantations in the district, all Booker-owned by the late 1940s: Albion, Port Mourant, Skeldon, and Rose Hall (East Canje).

In April 1944, despite the strident antagonism of Sherlock and Seaford, Lethem sought to convince the Colonial Office that the Corentyne Coast was the most propitious environment to implement his drainage and irrigation scheme. His heart was still totally in it; he remained unfazed:

> [A feature of the Corentyne] is the increase in the East Indian population, several large villages being now practically entirely populated by East Indians. One of the reasons for the large scheme being so necessary is precisely to accommodate the growing population. The four large sugar estates in the area present a picture of well-drained and irrigated land, and these have had their reward in being among the most well-doing in the colony. The same satisfactory picture, however, does not apply generally to the lands apart from sugar estates [the African and Indian villages], and in times of flood, from rain in the rainy season and the over-flow of the savannah water in the back-lands, the picture in many of the villages is lamentable: not only provision lands suffering heavily, but sanitation being deplorable for a period of several weeks on end.[17]

Lethem was sanguine about his scheme, in this notably less malarial district with a high proportion of Indians whom he clearly regarded as energetic and ambitious:

> The Corentyne area [whence came Cheddi Jagan, born at Plantation Port Mourant in 1918] is in many ways the most promising agriculturally in the colony ... Not only have the sugar estates been doing well, but the rice crop has become more and more successful in recent years while some areas are particularly suitable for pasturage, as well as for certain kinds of ground provisions which do not do well elsewhere ... Large and expensive as the scheme put forward may appear, there is very substantial ground for belief that the economic as well as the sociological benefits will materialise not unsatisfactorily given due time, though this will mean a considerable period of years.[18]

It could not bear fruit overnight. It was a price worth paying.

However, the sugar interests were unrelenting in their hostility to Lethem's visionary plan for draining and irrigating the Corentyne. This was a time of lucrative prices for both sugar and rice, and, given their substantial power to influence colonial policy, the sugar planters were uncompromising. The price of sugar was $57.32 per ton in 1943 and $61.58 per ton in 1944. Meanwhile, the total value of sugar produced in such a short time had climbed from $7,519,000 to $10,962,000. The area cultivated rose from 192,733 acres to 201,060 acres. The intransigence of the sugar planters had hardened, too, because of a simultaneous expansion of the rice culture among the Indians in the colony. The export price of rice in 1943 was $98.95 per ton; the following year it had risen to $108.38, while the acreage climbed from 85,984 to 91,729, respectively.[19] It is incontestable that most of the resident labourers on the sugar plantations (Indians) wished to emulate their vastly more independent, and incrementally more prosperous brethren in the rice-growing and cattle-rearing villages: a potent substantiation of freedom after indentureship. Lethem's scheme would have opened the door to unprecedented land settlement opportunities that could, conceivably, have undermined the labour supply on the sugar plantations. It is hardly surprising, therefore, that Booker and the other plantation owners opposed it, root and branch.

Less than a month after Lethem's despatch to the Colonial Office (in May 1944), Seaford of Booker wrote to him to repudiate the Corentyne drainage and irrigation scheme. He did not believe that any source of taxation other than sugar could bear the burden of such an extravagant project of dubious viability. Consequently, he could see no merit in the scheme being executed until 'pressure of population warrants it, and when some economic crop suitable to the colony has been found to justify the large expenditure proposed.' Seaford conceded no credence to Lethem's allusion to the 'excess' resident population on sugar estates; he also repudiated the estimate of the population of the Corentyne, as stated by the governor, as an exaggeration. According to Seaford, the Corentyne had a population of only fifty-five thousand – not seventy-five thousand, as Lethem claimed; moreover, only eighteen thousand were available for employment. Creating alternative sources of livelihood would fatally undermine the reservoir of workers accessible by the sugar industry:

> Allowing for the expected natural increases of population, it will be many years before the area of the scheme can be even partially beneficially occupied – bearing in mind that the sugar estates on the Coast are today suffering from a severe lack of labour.[20]

Booker and the other sugar companies prevailed upon the Colonial Office to repudiate the widespread agitation, in British Guiana, that Lethem be granted a second term in the colony. This set the seal on scuttling the comprehensive drainage and irrigation of the Corentyne. Jock Campbell recalled for me what this meant:

> I think Lethem was trying to do what any sensible man would have done: he was trying to relieve conditions and pressure on the sugar estates. He was trying to make the plantocracy see the writing on the wall more clearly – that one day [soon] there would be political development and there would be Independence; so, they had to come to terms with reality instead of behaving like ostriches. That made him unpopular with the plantocracy. They really resented Lethem and all his views, which were for reforms because he understood the workers' resentment.[21]

In July 1945, in an address to the colony, Lethem expressed his earnestness for the evolution of democratic institutions. He also anticipated (prophetically and tragically, as it proved to be) some of the monumental leadership qualities essential for the evolution of the country as a vigorous democracy – maturity; the eschewing of sectional or private interests; the subordination of emotional appeal to reason – gravitas in its political culture:

> I am a most confident believer more and more of democratic institutions, for this means sharing responsibility and the participation in the ordering of our affairs throughout our community and on the common man. Yet in itself that contains no divine principle, and it can only successfully live for the common good if sustained by reasoning men working to serve with all their capacity; it is for people who are adult and have learned to judge for themselves and not betray their minds and their reasons to emotional appeal or private interests.[22]

The high hopes and subsequent dismay occasioned by the aborted Lethem scheme were deeply felt among Indians on the Corentyne, in the villages where rice and cattle had already provided many with a life of palpable security (even prosperity) – strikingly superior to the condition of Indians resident on the sugar estates. But even on the plantations, many workers found it 'more profitable' to cultivate their rice-plots and small patches of ground, on land apportioned by the planters for limited supplementary use. Therefore, after the petition soliciting a second term for Lethem (endorsed by various segments of local society) was repudiated by the Colonial Office, clearly having succumbed to the sustained lobbying by Booker and other sugar interests in London, Jagan's seminal 'bitter sugar' campaign was imbued with the will to garner the gravitas and vigour that would transform it into a potent political instrument. Yet Cheddi's primary vision of radical transformation on the sugar plantations was perceived, forebodingly, by many Africans as indicative of the primacy of Indo-Guyanese priorities even in his formative political thinking – thereby underscoring their trepidation regarding the impending granting of universal adult suffrage. The fear of Indian domination was more lacerating in the late 1940s than it was in the 1920s when the idea of an Indian Colony in British Guiana was ventilated with ominous intensity.

IV. Impending Universal Adult Suffrage and African Fear of Indian Domination

In July 1944, the Legislative Council debated the Franchise Commission Report, and it was beyond belief that Hon. Hubert Nathaniel Critchlow, the founder of the BGLU and president of the TUC, who had been the leading advocate of universal adult suffrage in the 1920s–30s, concurred with the mounting African apprehension regarding the latter, renounced his long-held principle and voted against it. He even countenanced 'reduction of the franchise.' Critchlow's rationale was straightforward:

> ...we have found out that many people believe that if we were granted universal adult suffrage the East Indians would out-vote us in this Council...I feel that if the [Franchise] Commission recommends that we should reach universal adult suffrage by stages, and that at present we should have a reduction of the franchise, I certainly agree with that because we cannot get all we ask for at once. We must accept what we are given and come back again. I see now that it is really a dangerous thing to allow certain people to exercise the franchise [illiterate Indians], and permit other people to tell them any kind of thing and fool them.[23]

Critchlow's *volte-face* (in 1944) had so infuriated Ayube Edun, a fellow nominated member of the Council and president of the MPCA, that he considered it a betrayal of Indian workers. Edun deemed Critchlow's repudiation of universal suffrage retrograde:

> How on earth will this labour leader expect East Indian labour to co-operate with the TUC when he, as its head, will change his opinion as if changing a coat? Maybe as a member of the Executive Council, now, he has had to fall in line with the majority bourgeois councillors, leaving the proletariat to fend for themselves. We are indeed perturbed about this volte-face of a man in whom we had implicit confidence.[24]

Hubert Nathaniel Critchlow (1884–1958), founder of the first trade union in British Guiana (BGLU), in 1919; a leading advocate of universal suffrage until the early 1940s, when he repudiated it for fear of Indian political domination

Edun stressed the racial prompting of Critchlow's change of heart: its sole motivation was to disenfranchise as many Indians as possible. This appalled him since most members of his MPCA did not have the vote by virtue of the literacy and income prerequisites: 'Because these illiterate persons are Indians and cannot read and write the English language, they are to be disregarded...Would relegating the sugar workers, many of whom are Indians and most of whom are illiterates, to the political scrap-heap be any gesture of uplift to equality of standard?'[25]

Ayube Edun was so perturbed by the matter that he felt impelled to emphasise his pride in his racial identity, in an editorial for his union's paper, *Labour Advocate* (July 23, 1944). At a time when leaders ought to have been advancing a commonality of purpose in pursuit of democracy, the bedevilling ethnic insecurity permeated the discourse. Edun remarked:

> I am proud of the fact, and take infinite pride in the fact, that I am
> a full-blooded Indian and a member of the British Commonwealth.
> I am proud to be an Indian and a British subject, but if as an Indian,
> there is this stigma against me and my people because they happen to
> be illiterate, though intelligent enough to work and carry on, I must
> oppose it.[26]

In the chapter titled 'Bitter Sugar,' in *The West on Trial*, Jagan alludes to the
fact that the ostrich-like attitudes of the plantocracy, specifically regarding their
intransigence in restricting access to empoldered land by the small farmer, gave
grist to his political mission against the 'sugar gods':

> In the face of the dwindling labour supply, the planters took steps to
> ensure that the labourers found it impossible to make a living in any
> other way than on the sugar plantations. Steps were taken to prevent
> the emergence of peasant agriculture or a literate peasantry. In a
> country with a low population density, there was grave land hunger,
> the average holding in 1943 [being] only three-and-three-quarters
> acres per family. Land policy was directed with the aim of keeping a
> cheap and abundant supply of labourers in the vicinity of the sugar
> plantations.
>
> The sugar planters...monopolised the land. They held a total
> of 170,000 acres of which more than half was leased from the
> government...But less than half of this holding in 1943 [the year
> Lethem started to promote his scheme] was used in the production
> of sugar. The planters were able to keep the land idle because of the
> low land rentals of between five to twenty cents per acre charged by
> the government...
>
> But land idleness was not the only factor in preventing peasant
> agriculture. There was water control. No money was spent on
> drainage [and irrigation] which did not directly benefit the sugar
> plantations. In consequence, village lands and all lands outside the
> sugar plantations could not be farmed successfully. The position had
> hardly changed over the years.[27]

This was not a totally accurate assessment of the question of drainage
and irrigation. As seen in the last chapter, a sizeable proportion of Colonial
Development and Welfare funds was indeed allocated to drainage and irrigation
in the late 1940s, although not on the scale anticipated by Lethem. It is arguable,
therefore, that this was Lethem's legacy to Guyana; besides, his untiring advocacy
of hydraulic works did lay the foundation for the construction of the Black Bush
Polder and Tapacuma Schemes when Jagan was in power in the late 1950s to
early 1960s, where the settlers were almost exclusively Indian. Moreover, the
recalcitrant attitudes of the plantocracy towards Lethem provided a cutting edge
for Jagan's politics of radical change. And it was this that led to the fight of the

Guiana Industrial Workers' Union (GIWU), in which the Jagans were leading lights, to replace Edun's MPCA as the sole trade union in the sugar industry. The latter culminated in the shooting of Indian workers at Plantation Enmore, on June 16, 1948, precipitating a post-Lethem thrust towards drainage and irrigation.

The development expenditure between 1947 and the end of 1950 amounted to $12,573,407, of which $5,945,000 (47 per cent) was expended on drainage and irrigation; the second highest area of expenditure was rural housing and land settlement, amounting to only $1,605,802 (12 per cent). Indian rice farmers were the principal beneficiaries of development expenditure in the late 1940s to early 1950s.[28] Therefore, vital political capital accrued to Cheddi Jagan because of the progressive leadership of Sir Gordon Lethem and his challenging encounter with the 'sugar gods.'

Notes

1. *Daily Chronicle*, August 2, 1936.
2. Ibid.
3. *PAC Bulletin*, No. 20, December 17, 1947.
4. Ibid.
5. Ibid.
6. Taken from a pamphlet by Cheddi Jagan: *Bitter Sugar* (Georgetown: The Author, n.d. [1953]).
7. Speech by Lord Campbell of Eskan [Jock Campbell] to the Fabian Society, London, *Mimeo*, October 22, 1969.
8. CO950/675, Memorandum of the Manpower Citizens' Association [MPCA] to the Moyne Commission, 1939.
9. Ibid.
10. Ibid.
11. Cheddi Jagan, *The West on Trial: My Fight for Guyana's Freedom* (London: Michael Joseph, 1966), 88–89.
12. Interview with Jock Campbell, Nettlebed, Oxfordshire, May 9, 1990.
13. *Labour Advocate*, July 23, 1944.
14. Interview with Jock Campbell, July 23, 1992.
15. CO111/785/60493 [1943], Lethem to Lloyd, September 23, 1943.
16. Ibid.
17. 17. CO111/785/60466/13 [1944], Lethem to O. F. G. Stanley, no. 74, April 7, 1944.
18. Ibid.
19. Dwarka Nath, *History of Indians in Guyana* (London: The Author, 1970 [1950]), 252, 257.
20. CO111/785/60466/13 [1944], F. J. Seaford to Lethem, May 10, 1944.
21. Interview with Jock Campbell, Nettlebed, Oxfordshirc, May 9, 1990.
22. CO114/237, 'Speech by His Excellency the Governor (Sir Gordon Lethem),' July 3, 1945.

23. Legislative Council of British Guiana, Debates, *The Franchise Commission Report*, July 7, 1944.
24. Leader, the *Labour Advocate*, July 30, 1944; see also *Report of the British Guiana Franchise Commission, 1941* (Legislative Council Paper, No. 10 of 1944), Minority Report by the Hon. A.M. Edun.
25. Legislative Council of British Guiana, Debates, *The Franchise Commission Report*, July 6, 1944.
26. Leader, the *Labour Advocate*, September 24, 1944.
27. Jagan, *The West on Trial: My Fight for Guyana's Freedom*, 75.
28. Anne Patricia Cook, 'Social Policy and the Colonial Economy in Guyana' (PhD Thesis, University of Surrey, Guildford, 1985), 191.

5.

The Political Affairs Committee, Race, and the General Elections of 1947

> Mr H.J.M. Hubbard (General Secretary of the TUC) was a Marxist in whom Dr Cheddi Jagan confided. I was introduced to Cheddi and Janet Jagan by Hubbard. We became close friends and worked together in the Political Affairs Committee, founded in 1946. I admired their dedication and devotion to working in the interest of the working class. This led them into the trade union movement. I consider them genuine, dedicated and hard-working in the interest of the labour movement...
>
> Marxism was the basis of their political philosophy. Janet fully supported Cheddi's political precepts in British Guiana. He was fortunate to have a wife who saw eye to eye with him in the area of political philosophy...Having regard to the source from which Dr Jagan emerged, it is fair to say that his objective was to elevate Guyana through the avenue of communism...His conviction was that the communist route would further advance the country.
>
> **– Ashton Chase to Oscar Ramjeet (email, May 2017)**

I. The *PAC Bulletin* (1946–49): Disseminating Cheddi's Communist Vision Inspired by the Soviet Union

It is reasonable to postulate that the plantocracy's triumph over Lethem was a catalyst for the initiation of the mission of Cheddi Jagan against 'bitter sugar.' The anger that the thwarting of Lethem's reformist policies engendered was canalised by Cheddi and Janet Jagan in shaping their political mission. On Wednesday, November 6, 1946, the last time Lethem presided over the Legislative Council, on the eve of his departure from the colony, four political neophytes issued a cyclostyled paper (the first of forty-three issues; the last was on December 26, 1949) – the *PAC Bulletin*, the organ of the Political Affairs Committee (PAC). This study group comprised the young US-trained Indo-Guyanese dentist and Marxist, Cheddi B. Jagan (1918–97); his Chicago-born wife (also a Marxist),

Janet Jagan (nee Rosenberg) (1920–2009); H. J. M. Hubbard (1911–72), a Marxist trade unionist of European Guyanese extraction; and Ashton Chase (1926–), a twenty-year-old African Guyanese trade unionist based in Hubert N. Critchlow's British Guiana Labour Union. Sometime during 1947, they were joined by Sydney King (1925–), a young African Marxist-oriented schoolteacher from the village of Buxton, East Coast Demerara, and shortly thereafter by the young poet, Martin Carter (1927–97). The *Bulletin* was issued by the PAC from 69 Main Street, Georgetown, the dental surgery of Cheddi Jagan. The PAC was definitively Marxist-Leninist in its ideological stance, a most unusual characteristic of political organisations in the British West Indies. For the next fifty years, Cheddi Jagan remained at the centre of the politics of Guyana – controversially so – as his orthodox communism, on the side of the USSR, led him ineluctably into the Cold War. This was suicidal in the context of the Western Hemisphere, America's self-proclaimed 'backyard.' Jagan and his little underdeveloped colony would pay a hefty price for his fidelity to his communist creed.

The *PAC Bulletin* was the medium through which Jagan articulated his Marxist vision of a new Guyana. He was a gadfly of the sugar planters, other capitalists, and the colonial authorities, ceaselessly decrying collusion between the colonial authorities and 'vested interests.' He saw himself as a partisan of the working class irrespective of their race. He was unsparing in his advocacy of the underdog, focusing continually on a range of grievances that afflicted them: high rent and the exploitation of landlords; land-hunger and insecurity of tenure; the plantocracy's perennial cry for labour; their unremitting resistance to land reclamation and the initiation of alternative industries; the alleged complicity between the recognised union (the MPCA) and management in the sugar industry; and the 'exorbitant' profits of those he castigated as the 'sugar barons' or the 'sugar gods,' extracting 'surplus value' from the workers. But it was the passion and pertinacity of his crusade against 'bitter sugar' that became the motif of his political mission. Cheddi Jagan's politics was permeated by the zeal of the crusader; incorruptibility while championing the sugar workers' cause; and an implacability in declaiming the 'evils' of the plantocracy and the colonial rulers – 'imperialist bloodsuckers,' as he disparaged them. His mission, from its inception, was inspired by a quasi-religious faith in Soviet communism as the perfect instrument for making a world of abounding freedom, prosperity, and happiness for humankind. But he also maintained that while the creation of the communist society was inexorable, it still required a protracted 'struggle,' guided by the 'scientific' doctrines of Marxism-Leninism and the 'glorious' example of the Soviet Union.

Cheddi had no equivalent in the British West Indies; few, indeed, among leaders in the colonial world shared his enduring devotion to the Soviet Union. In the first issue of *PAC Bulletin*, on November 6, 1946, he espoused his belief in 'scientific socialism' and the need for a disciplined political party guided by 'the theory of scientific socialism'– in other words, a Marxist-Leninist or Communist party. And from the early issues, it was evident that the USSR and the 'People's Democracies,' the Soviet Union's satellites in Eastern Europe acquired by virtue of the Red Army's 'liberation' of them from Nazi Germany, were the model for Jagan's conception of the free society. The masthead of the first four issues of the *Bulletin* read:

The aims of the Political Affairs Committee are:

> To assist the growth and development of the Labour and Progressive Movements of British Guiana, to the end of **establishing a strong, disciplined and enlightened Party, equipped with the theory of Scientific Socialism** [Marxism-Leninism];

> To provide information, and to present *scientific political analyses* on current affairs, both local and international; and

> To foster and assist discussion groups, through the circulation of Bulletins, Booklets and other printed matter [emphasis added].

The inaugural issue of the *Bulletin* favoured promoting cooperative societies in the colony, while rejecting the capitalist means of production as impelled by 'individualism and greed.' It is probable, however, that 'cooperative societies' were a smokescreen for what Jagan really intended: an orthodox Marxist approach to economic organisation, in which collective enterprises under state ownership, operated on the principle of central planning (in the context of five-year plans), as practised in the Soviet Union. Obviously written by Cheddi, the gist of the piece indicates that, from the start of his political engagement, he was motivated by this staple of Marxist political economy:

> The past has been dominated to a great extent by a philosophy of individualism and greed [capitalism]. More and more it is beginning to be realised that this acquisitiveness for personal gain has to be supplanted by co-operation for mutual gain.

> The capitalistic economy, its mode of production and distribution, is wholly inadequate. It has yielded a very low standard of living for the majority of inhabitants of British Guiana. This is primarily due to the fact that, on the one hand, its productive capacity is restricted either by antiquated methods of production or by production of raw materials only; and, on the other hand, that distribution is so constituted that the average worker-consumer has to pay large profits [surplus value] to a whole range of middlemen.

> It becomes imperative, therefore, that the various sections of
> the working class urge upon Government the vital necessity for
> the establishment of a well-planned collective [state-controlled],
> industrial economy; and in the meanwhile, to participate in the
> various phases of the cooperative movement [a half-way house to the
> centrally planned economy].[1]

Then, as if to point the way to the future economic development of Guyana, the same issue of the *Bulletin* carried a brief item on one of the 'people's democracies,' Czechoslovakia, where the oil refineries were being nationalised. They noted that no foreign capital would be permitted in key industries, and, implicitly, no local private capital either; all would be publicly owned: 'This is one way of safeguarding the country's independence from foreign big business.' For Marxists, foreign capital was inherently exploitative, a drain on national resources and subversive of economic development and the emancipation of the working class, wherever it had penetrated. But so too was local private capital. This was an inviolable mantra, and Jagan considered it sacrosanct.

This first issue of the *PAC Bulletin* concluded with a terse note that Sir Gordon Lethem 'will not be permitted to serve a year more as Governor of British Guiana in accordance with general policy.' He was being retired at the ripe old age of sixty, but no reference was made to the machinations of the sugar interests, at home and in London, in the decision of the Colonial Office to refuse him a second term in British Guiana. Lethem returned to his native Scotland, becoming vice-president of the Scottish Liberal Party. He contested the constituency of Banffshire in the general elections of 1950; he came third and promptly retired from public life. He died in 1962, aged seventy-five.[2] It is incontestable that Governor Lethem's radical posture in British Guiana, between 1941 and 1946, paved the way for the iconoclasm of Jagan. It is ironic, but totally comprehensible, that the district where Lethem's greatest ambition foundered was the environment that shaped the radical Indo-Guyanese political leader, the young Marxist, Cheddi Jagan of Plantation Port Mourant. Out of the withered hopes of those yearning for a drained and irrigated Corentyne Coast – the antithesis of sugar monoculture – sprung the green shoots of 'bitter sugar': the quintessential Indo-Guyanese narrative of historical oppression and the imperative of drastic change, dexterously woven by the irrepressible Cheddi.

The second issue of the *PAC Bulletin* was more transparent in their espousal of communism as the means of eradicating poverty in British Guiana. Responding to Governor Lethem's farewell address to the Legislative Council (on November 6, 1946) reaffirming his support for workers' rights and their resistance to entrenched interests, coupled with his appeal for racial unity if the colony were to advance, the *Bulletin* concurred that the latter was crucial in eradicating the endemic exploitation of the working class under the capitalist system. But the

PAC went beyond Lethem in implying that ethnic discord itself is transitory, because the communist society (as evidenced by the USSR) was imbued with the means, by virtue of its 'scientific' theoretical foundation and broader conception of human freedom, to erase primordial aggregations of identity based on race, religion, language, or tribe, fostered and exacerbated under the 'evil hand' of 'parasitic capitalists':

> As a basis for progress, Lethem stressed the unity between the various racial groups with special emphasis on the…African and the Indian. This point cannot be over-emphasised. With the rising class consciousness of the labour movement; with the ever-present danger of capitalistic unemployment and economic crises and depressions, the role of every worker and wage-earner, regardless of race, religion or colour is to unite with every other worker to form a collective working class with the object of vigorously opposing and removing the exploitation meted out by the capitalists and the capitalistic system.
>
> **Mention need only be made of the Soviet Union where various ethnic groups participate in their own cultural institutions, at the same time working together as comrades in the same socialistic economy, from which the evil hand of capitalistic exploitation has been removed** [emphasis added].[3]

The *Bulletin* contrasted the Soviet socialist idyll with the plantations of British Guiana, where the workers were deemed 'wage slaves.' Their onerous task in the fields was compensated by 'a mere pittance,' equivalent to a fraction of the value of their day's work; the remainder of their day's labour – surplus value – was appropriated by the 'absentee capitalist' [Booker and others]. The PAC embraced Lethem's advocacy of empoldered land for small farmers because this was a means of reducing capitalist oppression: '[The farmer] working for himself or in co-operation with other farmers on free or relatively free land does not produce any surplus value for parasitic capitalists or landowners.' Here again, the Soviet Union provided the template for the emancipation of the working class. There, all land had become the property of the workers' state (guided by the 'scientific socialism' of the CPSU under Comrade Stalin), therefore the property of all the people. The 'kulaks,' the land-owning class of big farmers (hence inveterate exploiters) had been 'eliminated.' Farmers were now producing collectively, with the process enhanced by the mechanical means and technical expertise afforded by the communist state. A mirage!

Lethem had deprecated the conduct of the commercial elite in British Guiana, stressing their unscrupulous methods in a poor colony: 'too large a class which has fattened in spite of the mass of poverty-stricken citizens…existing on imports from which the merchant importers have gleaned an easy harvest through percentages, commissions and profits.' But this reformist critique could not palliate the ideological fervour, the rabid anti-capitalist instincts of Cheddi. His beliefs originated in loftier Marxist certainties, the foundation of his sustaining vision – 'bitter sugar' – the central plank of his political mission:

> What the Governor failed to point out was that there is inherent in capitalism all these modes of exploitation, whether by the sugar and bauxite capitalists, the commercial, the land-owning or the money-lending class. All these parasitic exploiters are sharing among themselves in varying proportions the surplus labour value created in production by the wage-earning working class.
>
> **Only with the complete elimination of the capitalist mode of production and distribution, and its consequent surplus labour value and the substitution of socialistic means of production and distribution will this exploitation cease** [emphasis in the original].[4]

There could be no accommodation of even a reformist or social democratic strand of capitalism in Jagan's messianic vision of change in British Guiana. Marxism-Leninism alone possessed the key to the post-colonial socialist paradise. Arguing from what the PAC termed 'scientific' premises, they asserted that the productive process is dependent on four components – land, raw materials, equipment, and labour power. But labour is the only 'dynamic' one, the others being 'inert' or 'static' until labour power is organised to activate the latent value of land, raw materials, and equipment. Under the capitalist mode of production, however, man is alienated from the means of production, monopolised by the 'parasitic capitalist' who appropriates surplus value – the worker's wages being 'the minimum price required by him for performing the function of vitalising the inert elements.'

The received Marxist primer instructed the PAC that the capitalist exploiter is totally dispensable: 'He is not essential to the productive process.' The state alone perpetuates his parasitic role under capitalism. The socialist revolution would deliver total control of the state to the workers, with the productive process wrenched irretrievably from the 'evil hands' of this crooked element. For Jagan, the 'struggle' for the liberation of Guyanese, indeed all humankind, could be simplified thus – what he termed his 'credo':

> Society is divided into irreconcilable camps: the camp of the workers and the camp of the capitalists. This division is the only **real** and fundamental division in society although there are many other **apparent** divisions [racial, religious, caste, and tribal (among them), belonging to the 'superstructure']. This division of economic interest – a class division – finds expression in the political forms, and the whole structure of the state or the Government is built to serve the class that is in power [emphasis in the original].

> In a capitalist society the state is designed to maintain the power and
> influence of the capitalists and to protect them against the workers.
> The workers seek to protect themselves and their interests by setting
> up suitable collective organisations, the chief of which are trade
> unions. Later the workers set up political organisations [the foremost
> being the communist party] aimed at taking control of the state and
> Government apparatus out of the hands of the capitalist. The reality
> of the Social Organisation, therefore, is that the two classes confront
> each other and contest for supremacy.[5]

Jagan believed every word of this formulaic thinking – for the rest of his life.
He perceived the African-Indian ethnic problem as primarily a product of the
'divide and rule' policy of the imperialists; moreover, that it really does belong
to the superstructure. Guided by the communist party and 'scientific socialism'
(Marxism-Leninism), that 'apparent' pseudo-division will be erased:

> To disguise the reality of the fundamental division of society into
> classes, the capitalists use various methods. In British Guiana they
> use the method of encouraging the workers to believe in a division
> of interests among different religious and racial groups in the
> community. The workers must counter this method of disguising
> the reality of the struggle by exposing its reactionary character and
> setting up their own organisations on a class basis. They must begin
> by supporting their trade unions....[6]

For Cheddi, the reformist approach to change of Ayube Edun, Sir Gordon
Lethem (and Jock Campbell later) constituted half-measures that obscured the
fundamental and irreconcilable class division in colonial society, between workers
and capitalists, particularly the 'parasitic' foreign ones such as Booker. The logic
of the class struggle, based on 'scientific' principles (historical materialism),
determining the evolution of society, would transcend the 'apparent' or false racial
and religious divisions in British Guiana, bred and fed by capitalism to distort
and delay the final transition to the socialist/communist order. Therefore, the
first major step of the workers, imbued with class consciousness, is to aggregate
their collective resistance within the trade union movement against the capitalist
'bloodsuckers': a prelude to establishing the Communist Party. This is the recipe
for the acquisition of real power: control of the state and the means of production
by the socialist state (the embodiment of the will of the proletariat, the working
class). The 'dictatorship of the proletariat' is a state of transition from socialism
to the perfect communist society. The capitalists would resist to the bitter end,
but theirs was a futile intransigence against the inevitable communist utopia. For
Cheddi Jagan, this simple message represented an encounter with the truth – a
secular faith, but with the millenarian overtones of a religious calling.

In July 1947, the *PAC Bulletin* reacted robustly to an editorial comment in the
pro-business *Guiana Graphic* that stridently repudiated a series of recent strikes.

The latter argued: 'the time is surely approaching when the Government of British Guiana may be forced to step in and outlaw such action.' The *Graphic* cited the opinion of a 'socialist' MP from Clement Attlee's Labour Party to corroborate their case for constraints on 'irresponsible unionism.' But the *Bulletin* would have none of it, countering that 'many Labour Party men of Great Britain' preach socialism, but they 'actually practise capitalism and imperialism.' The response portended the ideological implacability, the entrenchment of the Marxist vision of Cheddi Jagan:

> The working class strikes not because it wants to stop production, but because it wants full employment, better wages, and an increased standard of living...It is inherent in capitalism that this struggle between capitalist and worker must continue. As long as the worker is working to put profits, no matter how small, into the hands of capitalists, so long will there be strikes. **Only under a changed political-economic system, as in socialism** [in the Soviet Union], **where the means of production are owned by society, where profits for individuals are eliminated, where there is no contradiction between production and distribution will there be an end to strikes. To outlaw strikes, we must first outlaw capitalism** [emphasis added].[7]

Cheddi Jagan's millenarianism was rooted in the supposedly triumphal, but severely flawed, Soviet experiment. The infallible scientific theory was yielding impeccable praxis, productive of rapid social and economic transformation of the working class. And, in the aftermath of the Second World War and the heroic role – the fortitude and monumental sacrifices – of the Soviet Union in the defeat of Nazi Germany, communists like Cheddi (all over the world) were euphoric that they were on the threshold of a new age – the perfect communist society of ultimate freedom from the seemingly eternal travails of capitalism, class exploitation, ethnic bigotry, and war. It was tantamount to a kind of religious awakening promising the perfectibility of humankind. The PAC envisaged the so-called people's democracies of Eastern Europe not as repressive states in the making, under the heel of Stalin's Soviet monolith, but as free societies already crafting a glorious alternative to the evils of capitalism. These Soviet satellites were erroneously perceived as being in a process of radical transformation, guided by the illuminating and selfless ('disinterested') comradeship of the Communist Party of the Soviet Union (CPSU).

British Guiana, the region (arguably), had never seen anything like Cheddi and Janet Jagan: youthful, handsome, and energetic – their ideological certainty, their sincerity and intensity of purpose – the sheer bravado in challenging the Goliaths of privilege. The PAC sought to foster educational groups 'to discuss the contents of the *Bulletin*'; apart from encouraging readers to respond to issues covered despite their lacking a letters column, being an A4 cyclostyled newssheet of only four pages. The principal prompting for this was their eagerness to create Marxist study groups throughout the colony. The PAC was also seeking the generosity of someone to provide space that could be utilised as a public reading room. They had built up a substantial collection of literature (Marxist primarily), much of it on the Soviet Union, published in London under the auspices of the Communist Party of Great Britain (CPGB) by the communist press affiliated to the party, Lawrence and Wishart.

Such radical literature was hitherto inaccessible in British Guiana. Besides, several instalments of the 'History of the CPSU' were carried from the fourteenth issue of the *PAC Bulletin* (August 6, 1947), prefaced by the following brief introductory note:

> The history of the Communist Party of the USSR is one in which it is believed PAC readers and the working class generally will be much interested. Based on the works of a Commission of the Central Committee of the CPSU, PAC presents, with pleasure, from this issue onward a summary of the history of the Communist Party. **The correct approach to many issues affecting the working class should be noted** [emphasis added].' Doctrinal purity!

The following excerpt, on the fundamental Marxist tenets, is an example of basic 'truths' the PAC was encouraging its readers to study for discussion in small groups:

> The basic teaching of Marxism was that the capitalist system would fall just as serfdom had fallen, and that capitalism was creating its own grave diggers in the person of the proletariat. It taught the proletariat to be conscious of its own strength, to be conscious of its class interest and to unite for a determined struggle against the bourgeoisie. It taught that it was impossible to get rid of the power of capitalism and to convert capitalist property into public property by peaceful means, and that the working class could only achieve this by revolutionary violence against the bourgeoisie, by a PROLETARIAN REVOLUTION, by establishing its own political rule – which must crush the resistance of the exploiters, and create a new, classless, Communist Society. Marxism further taught that the industrial proletariat was the most revolutionary and therefore the most advanced class in capitalist society, and that it was the only class that could overthrow capitalism. But in order to accomplish this, the proletariat must have a working class party – a Communist Party.[8]

Cheddi Jagan embraced this in its entirety; it was as clear a statement of his 'credo' as one could get; besides, it clarified that the PAC's Marxism was unreservedly congruent with the version emanating from Stalin's USSR. Theory and practice were guided by the example of the Communist Party of the Soviet Union. This was evident in their celebration of the public health provisions they claimed were available to all the Soviet peoples at the end of the Second World War:

> The Constitution of the USSR guarantees the working people the right to free medical services, security in old age, maintenance in the event of loss of working capacity or illness, and the right to state protection of the mother and child. And medical service, from first aid to the most intricate surgical operation, is free of charge to the working people of the Soviet Union. The Soviet citizen is given the care of the public health establishment from the very day of birth.[9]

The *PAC Bulletin* attributes what it depicts as a comprehensive and virtually flawless public health programme in the USSR, despite the enormous depletion of resources during the recent War (including possibly twenty-seven million deaths), to the superiority of the communist instrument of central planning geared totally to promoting the welfare of the working class. It speaks of a veritable utopia, already a vindication of the unimpeachable communist system, freed of the greed, material inequalities, and cultural alienation inherent in capitalism – creator of the new socialist man, winner in war and in peace:

> The entire public health system is based on preventive medicine. Effort and means are directed primarily towards preventing illness, and safeguarding the population against sickness. A centrally-directed, definitive state planning makes possible the proper utilisation of all the facilities of the country, the widespread application of the latest achievements in medical science and unified methods of work.
>
> Soviet public health work has been efficacious because of the very nature of the social and state system existing in the USSR, in which unemployment, destitution and poverty have been permanently done away with on the basis of the abolition of the exploitation of man by man. In a remarkably short period of time, the Socialist state has succeeded in raising the material and cultural level of the entire population enormously, thereby the firm foundation for successful work in the field of public health.[10]

A few months later, the *PAC Bulletin* addressed the role of the Leninist Party, the Communist Party of the Soviet Union and its exemplary leadership of the proletariat towards the making of the communist society. It is not enough merely to imbue the proletariat with class and ideological consciousness; the Communist Party, adhering to the hallowed tenet of democratic centralism, must maintain internal discipline, scrupulously precluding 'deviationism' to the left or the right. The Communist Party is 'the highest of all forms of organisation of the working class, and it is its mission to guide all the other organisations of the working class.' The party is everything: the 'vanguard' of the working class; 'paramount' over the state and its instruments – all gains would be forfeited without its supremacy. It is imperative, therefore, that nothing be done to vitiate the 'paramountcy of the Party,' its nobility of purpose in the communist endeavour. Behaving in such a manner – even to be suspected of, or reported for, a contrived transgression – is so abhorrent that any extreme or brutal sanction meted out by the party to dissidents/deviants is morally defensible. Yet the PAC and Jagan's PPP (later) never did repudiate Stalin's butchery or his Gulag designed to destroy body and mind – to annihilate non-persons perceived to have dared to challenge the infallibility of Stalinism and the CPSU, equated with Marxism-Leninism. The latter is rooted in the irrefutable laws of the development of society; consequently, one must be mentally impaired to be agnostic of the validity of such 'scientific truths.'

This is how the Leninist tenet on the paramountcy of the Communist Party was framed in his book of 1904, *One Step Forward, Two Steps Back: The Crisis in Our Party*. It became the guiding principle of the CPSU and all the parties that adhered to the Moscow line. It had the sanctity of scientific truth, but it was really a recipe for the evisceration of liberal democracy: the destruction of all 'bourgeois' freedoms and the entrenchment of totalitarianism – the foundation of Leninism-Stalinism. Lenin's dictum was reproduced in the *PAC Bulletin* of October 8, 1947 (about six weeks before the general elections of that year, contested by three of the founding members of the PAC, Cheddi and Janet Jagan, and H.J.M. Hubbard):

> The Marxist Party is a part, a detachment, of the working class. It differs from other detachments of the working class primarily by the fact that it is not an ordinary detachment but the vanguard detachment, a class-conscious detachment, a Marxist detachment of the working class, armed with the knowledge of the life of society, of the laws of its development, and of the laws of the class struggle, and for this reason able to lead the working class and to direct its struggle…It can lead the practical struggle of the working class and direct it towards one aim only if all its members are organised in one common detachment welded together by unity of will, unity of action and unity of discipline…
>
> The Party is the highest of all forms of organisations of the working class, and it is its mission to guide all the other organisations of the working class. The Party is the embodiment of the connection of the vanguard of the working class with the working class millions. The Party must be organised on the principle of centralism, having one set of rules and uniform Party discipline. To preserve the unity of its ranks, it must impose a common proletarian discipline, equally binding on all party members, both leaders and rank and file.[11]

II. The PAC and the General Elections of 1947

In the same issue of the *Bulletin*, it was announced that the general elections, the first since 1935, would be held on November 24, 1947. This was the first elections in which a substantial working-class element was enfranchised: everyone (man and woman), over the age of twenty-one, was entitled to vote provided they were literate in any language, and in receipt of earnings of at least $10 per month. In 1935, there were 9,514 voters; in 1947, 59,193 were registered, an increase of over 80 per cent. The PAC made an analysis of the type of candidates who would present themselves, and they counselled that a serious effort be made to scrutinise their bona fides. There was the capitalist who was proud to proclaim that his investment was the source of employment, but such a person must be rejected as inherently and compulsively exploitative: '...his primary motive is profit...[his being] the employer of labour is merely incidental to his making profits.' Repudiation of the capitalist candidate by the PAC was predicated on the Marxist assumption that he is superfluous to the production process – merely the appropriator of the 'surplus value' generated by the worker, who sells his labour power for mere subsistence while being the primary producer of goods and services.

They were categorical that any candidate deemed capitalist be ruled out of court, as 'his capital is the vampire which sucks the living blood of labour.'

But the PAC had no time either for the middle-of-the-road 'so-called liberal.' The latter is in favour of both labour and capital because he erroneously believes that co-operation between the two is indispensable. Therefore, Cheddi and Janet Jagan could not empathise with the liberal, even the social democrat (such as Ayube Edun of the MPCA or Hubert Nathaniel Critchlow of the BGLU), 'who goes hat in hand to beg for charity from the capitalists. He is merely content to fight for better wages and shorter hours, but at the same time leaving the capitalist system intact.' They also challenged the new voters to distinguish between the genuine Labour candidates from the fake ones usurping the label for short-term advantage at the polls. All the so-called Labour horns should be examined closely before they cast their ballot on November 24, 1947.

The following was the gist of the political message of the Jagans, a civics lesson permeated by their conviction that only socialism (communism) could create the new society for the emancipation of the working class:

> The main issue before the electorate is capital versus labour. The masses must support those candidates who faithfully represent labour, but must be able to distinguish between real labour and pseudo-labour. Many are the candidates who are claiming that they are

labour candidates, but their past activities and alliances can disprove the stand. We need militant labour representatives in the Legislative Council, men who will fight diligently against the capitalist economy which constantly oppresses the masses. **The immediate goal of the Labour candidate should be adult suffrage, a changed constitution and progressive labour legislation. The ultimate goal of the true Labour candidate is Socialism [Communism].**

The electorate would do well to examine the candidates very carefully and see in which of the above three categories they fall. Paying lip-service alone should not be enough. The candidate's background along with his class alliance must merit careful scrutiny. Who has consistently stood for Labour before the electioneering began? Many will suddenly spring from nowhere, and others will attempt to capture the votes through emotional appeal, racial appeal, dramatic speeches, false promises, bribery and corruption. The electorate is warned against these![12]

Already, at the core of the politics of Cheddi and Janet Jagan was the Leninist conception of the paramountcy of the Communist Party to the revolutionary transformation of society, from colonialism and capitalism to socialism and the communist utopia. When one examines the Leninist notion of democratic centralism, it becomes clear that such a party could not conceivably accommodate and integrate a plurality of views. Democratic centralism was fundamentally irreconcilable with liberalism or even moderate socialist democracy (as practised by segments of the old British Labour Party, led by Aneurin Bevan and his wife, Jennie Lee, or the Fabian socialists) because, at the heart of the tenet, was a rigid adherence to what the 'vanguard' of the party dictated, based on the supposed scientific premises of Marxism. The latter is written in stone, and to deviate from it is to court expulsion at best or, infinitely worse, as the tragedy of the Russian Revolution and its aftermath revealed, imprisonment and torture in the Gulag and mass slaughter of loyal 'comrades' as enemies of the working class or the workers' state, perpetrated by Comrade Stalin.

On the eve of the general elections in British Guiana in November 1947 (before nomination day), it was widely assumed that Cheddi and Janet Jagan would be contesting. And it was also highly probable, in view of the known Marxist orientation of the PAC, that they would encounter fierce opposition from the local press, the Christian denominations and other established segments of colonial society. But they were undaunted by the rising tide of anti-communism, taking it in stride, with Cheddi revelling in it. He was a true believer; indefatigable – nothing seemed to faze him. In late September 1947, Cheddi and Janet addressed a meeting at Buxton, in the Central Demerara constituency that Cheddi wished to contest. It is interesting that the newspaper reporter referred to Cheddi and the speakers at this meeting, sarcastically, as 'comrades':

an allusion to their perceived communist persuasion. Thus, 'Comrade' Cheddi reportedly said: 'There is Fascism in British Guiana. By that I mean there is a sort of Government control for the economic benefit of the few.' It was also noted that he 'wanted all the industries of the colony nationalised.' The report was captioned 'Janet Jagan went East to tell Buxtonians they are Free Individuals!' The provocative allusion to going 'east' was suggestive of her belief in Soviet communism, playing on the fact that she had travelled east from Georgetown to Buxton. 'Comrade' Janet counselled Buxtonians, as free individuals, not to be seduced by 'a little rum and a few favours like drops [rides] in a car' in exercising their franchise. The report concluded: 'She could stake her all that her Comrade husband was honest and able.'[13]

The central theme of their campaign was Cheddi's humble origins on the sugar plantation (his intimate experience of 'bitter sugar'), and his vision for, and dedication to, the liberation of the underdog. One Ramcharan of Bel Air (Boysie Ramkarran) was the first speaker at Buxton, and he struck precisely that chord with his remark that Cheddi was 'a man from down under – the gutter – and had risen the hard way.' At another meeting in Barr Street, Kitty, Ramcharan (Boysie Ramkarran) explained that he decided to support Dr Cheddi Jagan after he learnt that he was 'born on a sugar estate and had worked his way up; he was not ashamed of it, but had identified himself actively with the Labour movement on his return to the colony.' Cheddi reportedly spoke about himself. He was born at Plantation Port Mourant and had worked on the sugar estate before he left to study in the US. It was there that 'his ideas were opened up, but he had been identified with the working classes all his life. He knew their needs. They were entitled to a living wage. **Their fight was against class not race or religion** [emphasis added].' Janet Jagan also spoke, as did the veteran Indo-Guyanese legislator, Dr J. B. Singh, though not a communist.[14]

Interestingly, while several candidates contested under the banner of the so-called Labour Party, of which the esteemed founder of the British Guiana Labour Union, Hubert Nathaniel Critchlow (1884–1958), was the principal architect, Cheddi and Janet contested as Independent Labour, the only two under that name; Dr Singh fought as the candidate for MPCA Labour (named after Ayube Edun's trade union). It is reasonable to assume that Cheddi and Janet, as Marxists who subscribed to the communist doctrines as enunciated by the Soviet Union, perceived Dr Singh and Edun, as well as Critchlow and others in the Labour Party as 'pseudo-socialists': not 'scientific socialists' or communists. It is noteworthy, too, that while their *PAC Bulletin* espoused an unambiguous pro-Soviet communist line, they were discernibly discreet when articulating their ideology for radical change on the hustings. But their anti-communist enemies, who were many, were not duped by the softening of their rhetoric or by euphemisms, such as 'socialism,' 'independent labour,' or 'the class struggle.' H. J. M. Hubbard, the other member of the PAC, contested as an Independent. It is not clear why he did not contest as Independent Labour with the Jagans, but he appeared to have left the PAC just after the general elections of November 1947.

The *Daily Chronicle*, for instance, had a subtly sarcastic way of identifying Cheddi's extreme brand of socialism (communism), as in the following item:

> At Beterverwagting Government School, Comrade Cheddie Jagan [*sic*] told about 300 of his electorate to vote labour, and it was only a "Labour Government" that could serve the ills of British Guiana. He was a socialist and a true representative of labour.

He was not a 'pseudo-socialist' or an 'opportunist labour' candidate. A few days later, Jagan revisited the issue of bogus labour candidates playing to the gallery for electoral gain. Only twenty-nine years old, Cheddi was clearly warming to the challenges of the campaign, drawing on his humble background and his sincerity of purpose in pursuit of a radical political mission. The reporter captured his style which would become an enduring feature of Guyanese political folklore:

> At a warmish wayside meeting last Sunday, Dr C. B. Jagan gave his listeners a cursory review of his early life and his "tough uphill climb." He began calmly with his arms locked, like Napoleon, behind him; but when he came to "exploitation" [by capitalists], his avowed pet aversion, he unwound like an acrobat.

His animated references to 'exploitation' were usually allied to his central theme: 'bitter sugar.' Several sugar plantations were in his Central Demerara constituency: Enmore, LBI, and Ogle.

Cheddi contrasted his personal income with that of the average worker, damning his own professional practice, as a dentist, as exploitative. He observed that while he was earning $1 in five minutes, his patients probably had to toil two days for that dollar. He was henceforth solemnly committing himself to ameliorate such unconscionable privations in working people's lives. Cheddi continually admonished his own class of lavishly remunerated professionals (dentists, doctors, and lawyers); no wonder he was treated with repugnance by many of them. He was renouncing his class while unveiling the method and scale of their enrichment, such was his faith in his Marxist illumination as a universal force for the liberation of humankind from material greed and 'possessive individualism.' His devotion to his creed superseded his ample scope for acquiring wealth. This explains why, throughout his political mission of five decades, even his foremost enemies (and they were many) could garner no dirt whatsoever, regarding corruption or other methods of self-aggrandisement, to stick on this irrepressible combatant in the class struggle. As early as 1947, he was declaiming: 'The present system of Government allows professional men like myself to exploit the working man. There should be socialisation of the professions. Professional men, however hard they work, should not be classed with the labourers, for they usually invest their money in capitalistic businesses.'[15]

Someone in the crowd had challenged him regarding victorious candidates who routinely abjure solemn pledges made on the hustings. Cheddi was alert to this, as he was advocating a recall system to censure precisely such legislators for being deceitful and therefore unworthy of the people's trust: '...if a Legislative Council representative is found not to be loyal to his electorate, he could be recalled by a two-thirds majority. Real Labour men [Marxists like himself] have nothing to fear from this.' It is not clear how this recall system could have been implemented. Who would institute such a charge, and how could its validity be verified? How was the recall enforceable? Assuming that the charge of deceit or fraudulence was established against the legislator, who precisely was entitled to vote in the recall elections? Would the sitting legislature have a role in the process? The idea of a recall seemed morally defensible, yet it remained opaque.

Cheddi was already a charismatic figure on the platform, and many were clearly impressed with his declared resolve to become a genuine representative of the working class, while seeking no personal material advantage. The fact that his wife, Janet (just turned twenty-seven), too, was seen as politically adroit and committed, coupled with her youth, beauty, and whiteness, appealed to Indians in particular, given their ancient predilection for lightness of skin and other so-called Aryan physical attributes. Cheddi and Janet, even at the dawn of their Marxist crusade in the late 1940s, constituted a formidable unit with immeasurable political potentiality. They were both imbued with the passion, conviction, and resolution of true believers – Cheddi even more so. They harboured no reservations that Soviet communism was, indeed, the template for the eradication of ethnic and religious bigotry, imbued with the scientific knowledge and a moral imperative to create a classless society. I repeat: British Guiana, in fact, the British West Indies, had never witnessed anything like this radical Jaganite mission. It would last for fifty years, however flawed their Marxist-Leninist vision of reaching the mountaintop.

Yet on the eve of the general elections in November 1947, it was common knowledge that race remained a potent factor in the political discourse. An African Guyanese correspondent in Georgetown, Leo E. Small, had written about 'politics and pigment,' decrying several organisations with the 'temerity' to affirm sentiments that undermined their stated ethos. He did not name them, but he rejected any demonstration of racism:

> No force is too great to use to stamp out this new form of discrimination that is rearing its head as an indication of which direction the coming elections will be fought. It is not too late to change the course.

Another correspondent argued that 'racial arguments and tendencies should not be countenanced by candidates for political honours.' He rejected race-based politics, root and branch: '…there is no room for any Indian political organisation in this colony, nor least of all for any Indian organisation that has nationalist aspirations. The association has been wrongly conceived and will do harm and mischief to the general political body and that of the colony as a whole.'[16] He was referring specifically to an Indian organisation formed recently at Buxton, 'professing to be a branch of the Indian National Congress [in India],' and engaged in the campaign on behalf of a candidate for the Central Demerara constituency (possibly Dr Frank Jacob, an Indian). Cheddi was also contesting this seat, as were John De Aguiar, the incumbent, a Portuguese business executive in Georgetown, and H. L. Palmer, an African farmer and veteran village leader.

The question of race had become so virulent in some constituencies that the *Daily Chronicle* felt it warranted editorial censure. It was titled 'Gospellers of Hate'; and it rebuked the peddlers of prejudice emphatically, 'men who have the temerity to stand on a public platform and preach racial hatred with such careless abandon, and evil intent.' The tone of the editorial is evocative of a scale of racial intensity that, if unchecked, could set British Guiana on the road to chronic racial discord:

> … we cannot allow insidiousness aimed at any section of the community to go unchallenged, for the country must not be dragged down the road to ruin at the behest of perverted gospellers of race hatred. We have already warned electors of those candidates who play on their emotions by appealing to racial susceptibilities. We repeat that warning. It would be a dire tragedy for the colony were there returned to the Legislature an unbalanced coterie of racialists. Those who put race before country are not true Guianese.[17]

In fact, these 'gospellers of hate' were merely seeking to extract electoral advantage from racial apprehensions firmly embedded in the Guyanese psyche.

III. Cheddi's Radical Message and the Dawn of Anti-Communism

A few days later, at a meeting at Beterverwagting, Cheddi Jagan (assisted by Janet Jagan, Ashton Chase, Ramkarran, and a couple others) announced that he was contesting the Central Demerara seat because it was easily accessible from his place of work in Georgetown. He also sought to moderate somewhat his widely known antagonism to capitalism, claiming now that he was not contending that private capital and capitalists should be extirpated; rather, he wanted capital to give labour 'a square deal.' This, however, required the militant leadership of genuine representatives of labour because of the unpalatable reality that 'the capitalists were out to exploit the masses.' And, as if to advance his credentials for that task, he again proclaimed his working-class roots, having been born and brought up on a sugar plantation. He recalled that his father started work as a child labourer on the estate at Port Mourant, and although he had struggled his way up to the post of 'driver' (field foreman), his wage remained meagre. Therefore, he had to constantly supplement it with a variety of odd jobs. Cheddi himself was no stranger to hard work as a boy: planting rice, cutting grass for their cattle, and planting a vegetable garden to make ends meet in a very large family. This was the context in which he had left to study dentistry in America in 1936. Finally, he returned to his favourite theme, 'bitter sugar,' demanding improved social amenities on the plantations.[18]

Cheddi's campaign was the most vigorous and educative executed during the elections of 1947. He had returned to Buxton, a predominantly African village, so he was clearly making a resolute endeavour to bridge the racial divide being exploited by some candidates opportunistically. This was how the reporter sketched Jagan's second meeting:

> He did so again last Monday morning by the market place [at Buxton]. The principal theme in all his addresses is 'labour,' and **he treated his hearers to the salient features of Marxism, Communism and Socialism.** His platform associates requested their hearers to put down CAPITALISM and lift up LABOUR by ridding the Legislature of the present members who are known to support capital at the expense of labour [emphasis added].[19]

Cheddi's campaign was unique in its objective of apprising the electorate regarding the 'various forms of government'; essentially simplifying the classic Marxist formulation pertaining to the stages in the evolution of society, culminating in the classless communist society. His series of lectures was described thus: '…[it addresses] the politico-economic theories of the various forms of government – slavery, feudalism, capitalism, imperialism, fascism, socialism and communism.' They were delivered throughout his constituency, at Buxton, Vryheid's Lust, Plaisance, Beterverwagting and Kitty. British Guiana had never experienced a campaign in which a candidate was espousing Marxism-Leninism. With respect to the latter philosophy being the central plank in building a major political party, Cheddi Jagan has no parallel in the political history of the Anglophone Caribbean.[20]

Whatever Jagan's limitations as a politician, his capacity for hard work, honesty of purpose, incorruptibility, and sheer indefatigability (based on his belief in the tenets of Marxism-Leninism) rendered him a unique politician in the history of the region – possibly in the British Empire. As I have stated before, his political ideology was like a religion to him, with an inviolable moral authority to sustain him indefinitely, however massive the hurdles, indeed, the failures. 'History and time are on our side!'

A week before the elections, the *Daily Chronicle* rejected out of hand (without naming him) Jagan's 'pseudo-socialism' and his self-designation as 'Independent Labour' in the elections, which they construed as a mask for 'hot-blooded communism.' They also deplored his 'communism based on class warfare'; this, the paper asserted, was a dangerous road to travel. It was paved with 'a burning hatred, which may flare at any time into a…[combustible] bitterness that may well prove the ruination of the colony.'[21] Such was their trepidation of the communist virus at the start of the Cold War!

This editorial in the *Chronicle* is the first I have encountered that challenges Jagan's communist calling. I am therefore reproducing an extensive portion of it. Millions of words would be written, over the next several decades, repudiating his unwavering devotion to his Marxist-Leninist creed. These are among the first:

> There is being nurtured in our midst a doctrine of eternal rancour which credits none but the labouring classes with any honesty of purpose, and viciously asserts that Capital is the root of all trouble. Accompanied by violent language, it builds behind a facade of idealism, an envy and prejudice which can only prove to be a disruptive and subversive influence in this country. Accusing Capital of attempting to divide and rule, **this Communism preached in the guise of Socialism, seeks to break the bridges which have brought Capital and Labour together over a number of years, and substitute a dictatorship of the proletariat** – in which certain leaders will be cock of the roost!

> …the fomenting of industrial strife and class warfare which is obviously planned by the pseudo-Socialists [communists], could do the country an incalculable amount of harm. We face a period of development and expansion, in which we can triumph only if there is understanding between all classes, and the minimum of industrial friction. For this reason, it is wise that the Legislature should be composed of balanced individuals who will work together for the good of the colony, who will seek peaceful means to settle industrial disputes; and who have proved by their past behaviour that this is within their power and has been their practice. **We want good, responsible Labour leaders, and champions of the underdog. But we do not want the Comintern [control by Moscow] in British Guiana** [emphasis added].[22]

This leader in the *Chronicle* was precipitated by an incident in Georgetown the previous day. After Janet Jagan, a candidate for the Central Georgetown seat, had concluded her address, Cheddi made a 'theoretical intervention' supposedly on her behalf, but he thereby undermined her hitherto favourable impression and promising standing by a tactless remark. He reportedly stated that 'the time had arrived for open class warfare' in the colony. When Janet was asked whether she concurred with Cheddi's comment, she apparently said: 'naturally.' The reporter was unimpressed with her response, and he counselled voters in her constituency to bear this in mind when they cast their ballot.[23] Cheddi recalls the incident:

> At Janet's first public meeting … almost everyone who mattered in Georgetown, from high to low, was there. Janet made a magnificent speech which was **somewhat marred** by my intervention on a theoretical level with talk about the class struggle, while I was supposed to be helping her personally [emphasis added].[24]

It was a thoughtless intervention by Cheddi because the following day a local correspondent ('Fluorescent') responded thus:

> Many misguided persons confuse the doctrines and theories of Socialism with the principles of Democracy. While the shining principle of democracy is the greatest good for the greatest number, socialism [communism] is still merely a number of theories and doctrines which are now being tried out and are failing in all countries save those in which **a man's tongue may cost him his head** [an allusion to the abrogation of freedom in the totalitarian Soviet Union with its Stalinist barbarism].[25]

Although a communist herself, Janet could not have been impressed with Cheddi's lack of political nous. This failing – a lack of discernment – became a staple of his *modus operandi*. Yet Janet never tried to rein him in, or she was disinclined to do so. In any case, their loyalty to the creed would prove calamitous.

Meanwhile, Cheddi's fellow candidate for the Central Demerara seat, Dr Frank Jacob (a Christian Indian; son of C. R. Jacob formerly of the MPCA), had adopted a novel way of commencing his meetings: he read from the Bible (Exodus 18:21) to dramatise the godlessness of Jagan. Jacob exhorted the audience to reject 'unbelievers and choose men of truth. Throw out atheists and communists.' He argued that he was an official representative of the Labour Party; therefore, he would be able to exert more political clout than any individual outside of it, however sanctimonious the latter's profession of being a champion of labour. Jacob was evoking another means of undermining Jagan's political posture, as he and Janet could not be reconciled to the nebulous character of the Labour Party's working-class credentials: 'pseudo-socialists,' in their estimation. This was the reason why Cheddi and Janet decided to contest as Independent Labour. It is noteworthy that their fellow founding member of the PAC, H. J. M. Hubbard (a near-White Marxist), contested the North Georgetown seat as an Independent. After he lost by a huge margin, he left the PAC and politics for ten years and did not join Jagan's PPP until 1957. Was he the first in a long line of defectors, over many decades, from the Jaganite camp?[26] It is believed that Hubbard was deeply disillusioned by the racism that plagued the election campaign. Hubbard's Marxism could not protect him from the demoralising impact of Guyanese racism, for unlike Cheddi, he did not have the security of an ethnic base. He would have been perceived as a White man – already a handicap amid the ethnic passions provoked by the expanding electorate.

Nomination day was November 14, 1947. The *Daily Argosy*, in a subversion of conventional political categories, designated the forthcoming elections a contest between progressives and reactionaries. They did not identify Cheddi and Janet, but it is evident that, by the paper's idiosyncratic definition, these two radicals were consigned to the class of reactionaries. The *Argosy's* depiction of the politics of the Jagans seems more compatible with the *modus operandi* of anarchists, devoid of a constructive approach to governance while fomenting instability: '…[they] burn with a desire to upset everything around them – the even tenor of people's lives; and the security, as we know it, on which resolute men can build a better future into which we can go peacefully without encountering the mountains of strife and dark abysses of confusion…The essence of the successful conduct of human affairs is the work-a-day spirit of give and take [gradualism]. The fellow who wants everything his own way or tries to make other people believe they should have everything their own way cannot fit into the democratic ordering of our affairs for which we are striving.'[27]

Four candidates were nominated (at the Sparendaam Magistrate's Court) to contest Central Demerara, the most populous constituency in the county of Demerara. They were the incumbent John Ignatius de Aguiar; Henry Llewellyn Palmer; Dr Cheddi Jagan (proposed by Shivsankar Persaud and seconded by Pandit R. Sharma, both Indians); and Dr Frank Ramkissoon Jacob.[28] The *Argosy*, in reporting the nomination of Cheddi and Janet, struck a trenchant ideological note: 'Cheddie Jagan [sic], dental surgeon…[and] his better half, Janet Jagan, think the time is ripe for open class warfare.' In the adjacent column, the paper studiously placed a brief item, 'What is Communism?,' adumbrating the implications of 'open class warfare.' They quoted from a letter in a paper called *Truth* (most likely religious) to expand on the subject:

> Let it never be forgotten that there is no fundamental difference in principle and ultimate aim between Communism and Socialism; it is merely a matter of tactics. Communism and Socialism are the two false faces of the same bad penny of Collectivism: one face is the portrait of the highwayman, the other of a pickpocket. One inscription reads 'grab all,' the other 'sneak all.'[29]

This, of course, was meant as a repudiation of the Marxist Jagans, who with fellow PAC member, H.J.M. Hubbard (Georgetown North), were the only communists contesting the elections. The *Daily Chronicle*, too, was not enamoured of what they perceived as the extremist ideology of Cheddi, and on the twenty-eighth anniversary of the founding of the first trade union in the colony, the British Guiana Labour Union (BGLU), they deftly conveyed their preference for the 'moderate and responsible' leadership of H. N. Critchlow, the founder of the union in 1919, and the leading light of the Labour Party in the 1947 elections. Critchlow's 'reasonableness' as an 'able' labour leader of longstanding was extolled as an exemplar of responsible trade unionism in British Guiana, having established the modalities for conciliation, conflict resolution, and industrial stability between capital and labour. Critchlow's brand of unionism and its accompanying social democratic politics were infinitely preferable to the perils embedded in the perceived extremism, the communism, of the Jagans and the PAC.

The *Chronicle* was affirming the social democratic trajectory of the emerging political culture in the rest of the British West Indies:

> So far as we have been able to judge, it has been the policy [of the BGLU] to ensure that the spirit of reasonableness should be at all times apparent, and that no damage should be done to any employer that would surely prove detrimental to employees at a future date. This is common sense. What is won from the employer must not be so much that he is discouraged in his business and deterred from investing further capital in industry. Should this occur then the eventual sufferers are the workers themselves...

> [The BGLU]...has set an example of conscientious effort for the good of the country that few unions can rival, and has assured that its approach to employers shall always be well received, and secure the consideration that is merited. Labour unions have a very great responsibility in shaping the future of this great country, and should they shoulder that responsibility adequately, and with due regard to the rights to which employee and employer are entitled, we need have no fear for the future relationship between both parties. Only by co-operation shall the country achieve the destiny which looms brightly on Guiana's horizon.[30]

However, although Critchlow and Cheddi Jagan espoused a muscular working-class politics of differential socialist orientation, the political culture of the colony was still at an embryonic stage. While Critchlow's credentials as the pioneering trade unionist in British Guiana were impressive (and the driving force in the 'Labour Party'), there was no genuine political party in the colony because of the stipulated constitutional constraints of the colonial polity. This Labour Party had been contrived in a rush, solely to contest the elections of 1947.

It had no pretensions to a clarity of ideology or a programme for change; it failed to produce a manifesto (possibly because there was no executive and support staff to undertake such a project). Besides, most of the candidates representing the Labour Party shared few political goals. Until 1947, the electoral privilege was so circumscribed by income criteria that a fraction of the adult population had the vote; consequently, there was no incentive to form political parties because power was still exerted primarily by colonial officials, in conjunction with nominated members primarily from vested interests. Therefore, the elected representatives were free agents with little political authority or responsibility. But towards the end of the 1940s, with universal adult suffrage imminent (Jamaica was granted it in 1944, Trinidad in 1946), and British Guiana conceivably on the threshold of self-government, even independence, the political culture was at a watershed.

It was rightly assumed that the expansion of the franchise would engender authentic party politics, with incremental devolution of power. Cheddi Jagan's politics of radical change was taking shape in an environment of colonial transformation, energised by the recent Independence of India; it was also the context in which Janet Jagan (always less overtly ideological than Cheddi) was making her mark as a formidable political personality. On the eve of the elections, she gave a talk at the Empire Cinema in Georgetown, which was received with enthusiasm because of its sensible and reasonable tenor, with no overt reference to 'open class warfare' (a la Cheddi), yet she argued measuredly and shrewdly in support of the enfranchisement of the working class and the deepening of popular democracy. She wanted all nominated seats abolished, as the majority of them were allocated to partisans of capitalism; the time was ripe for the granting of universal adult suffrage; the lowering of the income qualifications of candidates to attract younger people to the legislature; the implementation of a system of recall to censure legislators who were dishonest with their constituents; and the reduction of the tenure of legislators from five years to three or four. Janet reportedly concluded: 'The Council just dissolved [1935–47] was governed by a small clique whose interests were not in the masses but [only in] a few. What they wanted were...candidates whose activities would be in the lively interests of the majority.'[31]

Yet, despite the prominence of the so-called Labour Party and the endeavour of the Jagans and the PAC to prioritise 'the class struggle' on the hustings, race remained the dominant factor in the elections. The results in the Central Demerara constituency underline the strength of the latter. It was won by Cheddi who polled 1,592 votes. H. L. Palmer, the African candidate and veteran village politician, got 1,471 votes; the Portuguese incumbent, J. I. de Aguiar, the head of the firm of J. P. Santos and Co., 1,299; while Dr Frank Jacob, an Indian and son of C. R. Jacob, a businessman and an elected member of the previous Council, 802 votes. Cheddi, therefore, had a slender majority of 121. He polled 30.8 per cent of the valid votes cast. Jacob said, after the results were declared, that 'one sad note is the question of race, and I hope that in the years to come such a thing will disappear.' However, Cheddi made no reference to the fact that an overwhelming majority of the votes polled by him were from Indians, while a similar proportion of those polled by Palmer were Africans.

Cheddi Jagan (Independent Labour) responded: 'I am overfilled with joy... My faith in the people and in democracy has been confirmed...We the people have won...Now will begin the struggle.'[32] The Labour Party won five seats: H. N. Critchlow (Georgetown South); Dr J.A. Nicholson (Georgetown North, defeating H.J.M. Hubbard); D. P. Debidin (East Demerara); W. O. R. Kendall (New Amsterdam); Theo Lee (Essequibo River). Dr J. B. Singh (Demerara-Essequibo) won as MPCA Labour, while there were seven Independent victors: John Fernandes (Georgetown Central, defeating Janet Jagan); C.V. Wight (West Essequibo); Dr G.M. Gonsalves (Eastern Berbice); J.P. Coghlan (Demerara River); Rev A.T. Peters (Western Berbice); C.P. Ferreira (Berbice River); W.A. Phang (North West District). The fact that seven seats (50 per cent) were won by Independents, while the so-called Labour Party won only five, underscores that it was a rudimentary political culture in which *bona fide* political parties were yet to emerge.

It is true that if one adds to the five Labour Party seats, Cheddi Jagan (Independent Labour) and J. B. Singh (MPCA Labour), 'labour' representatives, arguably, did win seven seats, the same as Independents. But the *Chronicle* carried a sobering editorial, 'The People have Spoken,' an ironic response to Cheddi's expression of similar sentiments after he won in Central Demerara: 'We the people have won.' However, it was the extent to which the people were swayed by racial predilection that was the most disturbing feature of the social and political reality of British Guiana, towards the end of the 1940s:

> **One thing is perfectly clear. The election has been fought, willy-nilly, on racial lines. Men and women have voted for their own kind – in some cases with little regard for the ability of the opposing candidates** [emphasis added].[33]

The *Chronicle* also alluded to the Jagans (principally), inveterate critics of the entire colonial order, who were promulgating 'class warfare' as indispensable for the emancipation of the working class of all races. The paper hoped that their much-vaunted advocacy of the 'class struggle,' arguably an uncompromising encounter between labour and capital, would be tempered, with legislative experience and wider knowledge, by sane judgment:

> Many…who have been bitter critics of various aspects of Guianese life, and have attacked the colony's economy and its industries may find that, once in the Council, things are not exactly what they seemed from outside. They will benefit from an enlarged knowledge and have available to them information which hitherto was denied. We trust, for the sake of the country, that they will use such information to the best advantage.[34]

A few days later, the *Chronicle* carried another editorial on the elections, lamenting the fact that many voters had rejected experienced, able, and selfless legislators (presumably E. G. Woolford [light coloured] in New Amsterdam and F. J. Seaford of Booker [European], in Georgetown North), for 'men of not half their political stature' purely on 'race and class' premises. They were unequivocal: **'There is no doubt that the colour of a candidate's skin played a large part in the number of votes he secured**…[emphasis added].' In addition, the 'class warfare' preached by some candidates could have had 'disastrous' consequences for British Guiana had there not existed palpable divisions within their ranks. But apprehensive of the long-term relationship between capital and labour, the paper cautioned that political maturity and a sense of proportion were pivotal to the progress of the colony. Permeating their response to the general elections was a deep-seated anxiety regarding the communist virus they felt the Jagans were spreading in the colonial body politic. But the neophytes had evidently struck a chord, and this would be magnified severalfold after the fatal shooting of five Indian workers at Plantation Enmore, in Cheddi's constituency, on June 16, 1948.[35]

It is not known how cognisant local authorities were of Cheddi and Janet's communist predilection, but they were already under surveillance by British intelligence, MI5. As the agency's files reveal, they were aware (as early as 1947) that Cheddi was in contact with communists overseas, seeking to build up a Marxist library collection to gain regular access to communist material for their fortnightly publication, *PAC Bulletin*, and to disseminate such literature widely and stimulate public engagement with aspects of it. The MI5 report states:

> The Jagans first came to notice in February 1947 when Dr Jagan was reported to have asked the Soviet Embassy in Washington for copies of the Embassy's Bulletin. Later that year, it was learnt that Jagan was receiving literature, including copies of the *Daily Worker*, from the headquarters of the British Communist Party [CPGB] in London. This literature was apparently intended to form a reference library to assist in the production of the duplicated Political Affairs Committee [*PAC*] *Bulletin*, which Jagan was producing in British Guiana…The Governor of British Guiana [Sir Charles Woolley (1947–53)] stated at the time that there was no evidence that Jagan was connected with foreign Communist organisations, other than the British Communist

Party, although it was believed that his wife was in contact with Communists in the United States.[36]

The same MI5 file notes of Janet Jagan:

> …born October 20, 1920, in Chicago…a white American by birth… In October 1941 the FBI investigated her because she had sent a letter to one Adeline Kohl, who was acting state secretary for the Young Communist League of Michigan [youth arm of the CPUSA]. No information came to light during the FBI inquiry which showed that she was a member of, or active in, any communist group. She forfeited US citizenship early in 1947 for having taken an active part in the political affairs of another country [British Guiana].

The fear of communism, at the beginning of the Cold War, became such an obsession in British Guiana that the problem of race, with its potential of becoming a cancer (it did) in the political culture of Guyana (it still is), was not given the undiluted focus it merited, including from the anti-communist *Daily Argosy* and *Daily Chronicle* – as well as Cheddi and Janet Jagan. Of course, as I remarked earlier, for Marxists like the Jagans in the PAC, the question of race belonged to the superstructure and, consequently, did not necessitate priority of consideration over the economic base or substructure: the latter being at the core of the Marxist materialist conception of history – historical materialism. For Cheddi and other Marxists, therefore, belief in the inevitability of the communist order rendered ethnic and religious prejudice, though real, transitory and totally eradicable by the tenets of historical materialism.

But as Professor Leszek Kolakowski argues, it is all a dream, a utopian fantasy:

> No student can fail to recognise that Marx's view of history, as he knew and analysed it, derived its meaning not from itself alone but from the future that lay before mankind. We can understand the past only in the light of the new world of human unity to which our society is tending – this is the Young Hegelian point of view, which Marx never abandoned. **Marxism, then, cannot be accepted without the vison of the communist future: deprived of that, it is no longer Marxism**…
>
> If it were true that the social degradation of the working class was bound to increase, the prospects for a world socialist revolution, as Marx's critics often pointed out, would not become any the brighter: how far could a class that was kept in a state of ignorance and debility, humiliated, illiterate and condemned to exhausting labour, find the strength to bring about a universal revolution and restore the lost humanity of mankind?…

> The idea that half a million years of man's life on earth and five
> thousand years of written history will suddenly culminate in a
> 'happy ending' is an expression of hope. Those who cherish this
> hope are not in a better intellectual position than others. Marx's
> faith in the 'end of prehistory' is not a scientist's theory but the
> exhortation of a prophet [emphasis added].[37]

IV.   Racism and the Demoralisation of H.J.M. Hubbard, Jagan's Seminal Communist Ally

Yet the millenarianism at the heart of Marxism did endow its true believers
with enormous faith to endure unimaginable setbacks and reversals – driven
by essentially another form of religious illumination. However, the strength of
Guyana's racial predilection, even as early as the general elections of 1947, could
not be obscured. This is how Jagan saw the elections:

> I was pitted against John D'Aguiar [sic], Frank Jacob and H.L.
> Palmer...In this contest, racism and cultism were used to blur
> the class issue...H.L. Palmer had a reputation in the field of local
> government. But he was quite advanced in age and thus did not have
> the advantage of my youth and vigour. His support came from the
> League of Coloured Peoples [LCP] whose particular weapon was
> Negro racism wherever it placed its support...I won over the workers
> on the sugar estates [Indians] by an overwhelming majority...My
> support came from the working class, except those who voted for
> Palmer [Africans] because of the racist appeal of the LCP....

It is noteworthy that Cheddi acknowledged the contribution of Sydney
King to his campaign: 'Of great help to me in the villages was one of my
protégés, schoolmaster Sydney King, of Buxton.'[38] King [Eusi Kwayana] was
just twenty-two years old in 1947, and he does not mention his own role in
Cheddi's campaign, but he identifies several who did, including Africans, thereby
suggesting that Cheddi was able to assemble a multiracial team, despite the
racial predilection at the core of the hustings. Among these were: Byron Lewis,
Doodnauth Tiwari, Edmund Jack, Balram Singh Rai (of Beterverwagting [aged
twenty-six]), Benjamin Proffitt (Plaisance), Ms Bertha Harry, Ms Vera Griffith,
and Rampersaud Sawh and his wife, Jasmat.[39] In a private communication with
me (email of April 9, 2010), Eusi Kwayana recalls that his political engagement
commenced in the context of Jagan's election campaign of November 1947. He
was inspired by Cheddi's radical message, hitherto unexampled in local politics:
'My own direct interest began in November 1947 when Dr Jagan came to Buxton
to launch his election campaign at the Olympic Cinema.' He declared, quoting
from *The Communist Manifesto*:

'Workers of the world, unite! You have nothing to lose but your chains
and a new world to win.' I had never heard anything in politics with
so much purpose…[But] I always had the impression that H.J.M.
Hubbard had been a Marxist before the return of the Jagans.

He was right.

Cheddi elaborates on the racial politics pursued by the LCP in Georgetown
as well:

> For example, in Georgetown North, the LCP carried out an extremely
> racist campaign against H.J.M. Hubbard [a Marxist of European
> extraction, a founder-member of the PAC] and succeeded in getting
> J.A. Nicholson [an African doctor] elected, even though Hubbard
> had a militant and creditable record as secretary of the TUC. In
> Georgetown South, the LCP caused [H.N.] Critchlow to lose his
> seat. He had won easily…but lost his seat soon afterwards on an
> election petition. The ground for the petition was an allegation made
> by the vice-president of the LCP, R.B.O. Hart, during the campaign,
> that Frances Stafford, a white Guyanese and member of the WPEO
> [Women's Political and Economic Organisation, founded in 1946;
> Janet Jagan and Winifred Gaskin were also leading members], one of
> the opposing candidates, had kicked a Negro servant down the stairs.
> The court held this to be a damaging lie….[40]

A noteworthy consequence of the 1947 elections – another ominous sign for
the future of race relations in the colony – was the departure of H.J.M. Hubbard
from local politics for ten years. In the elections for the Georgetown North
constituency, Dr J.A. Nicholson polled 949 votes; the incumbent, F.A. Seaford of
Booker 758; while Hubbard got just 163 votes, losing his deposit in the process.
The fact, as Cheddi recalls, that Hubbard was subject to an 'extremely racist'
campaign, seemed to have demoralised him immeasurably. He left the PAC
shortly after the elections and stayed out of politics until 1957, when the PPP
(led by Cheddi) won the general elections and nominated him as a member of the
Legislative Council. But, before I make a few more observations regarding race
and anti-communism in the 1947 elections, I wish to emphasise that Hubbard, a
rare Marxist in the colony in the late 1940s, was seminal to the political initiative
of Cheddi and Janet in launching the PAC in November 1946.

In an unusual personal reminiscence, Janet Jagan recalls the peculiar
circumstances of their first encounter with H.J.M. Hubbard and the consequences:

> The book that started this process was *The Problem of India* [1943]
> by R. Palme Dutt [1896–1974], who was one of the foremost
> theoreticians of the Communist Party of Great Britain. He wrote
> many wonderful books and was the editor of *Labour Monthly* which
> he founded in 1921. Cheddi and I were walking on Water Street,
> Georgetown, one day in 1946 when we passed a shop window that
> contained some books. We paused to examine the titles and saw, to
> our astonishment, this book of R. Palme Dutt. This was the very first

time we had seen any book other than those in our own library, about Marxist-Leninist theory, in British Guiana. Since Cheddi's return to his homeland, with me, in 1943…we had searched for someone with kindred beliefs in scientific socialism [Marxism-Leninism] but had so far found no one. During the two-and-one-half years [1944 to mid-1946] when we had become involved in the struggle of sugar workers [Cheddi was the treasurer of the sugar union, the MPCA, in 1945], we had been unable to meet any person who was interested in the ideology of Marxism-Leninism.[41]

Janet and Cheddi were enraptured by their amazing rendezvous, out of the blue, with a unique kindred soul, H. J. M. Hubbard. Imperishable!

We entered the shop, which proved to be a printery, and which also sold a small number of books. There we met H. J. M. Hubbard. In talking to him, we discovered that he had been reading the works of Marx and Lenin and evinced great interest in the subject. We arranged for further meetings. A little later we met Ashton Chase, who was then a very young man working with the British Guiana Labour Union [the assistant secretary, aged 20], and one of Hubert Nathaniel Critchlow's most able lieutenants. The four of us began talks about [British] Guiana and the need for some organisation and means of introducing socialist [communist] ideas in the country.

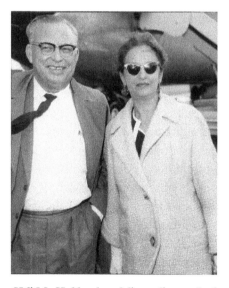

H.J.M. Hubbard and Janet Jagan (both Marxists), two of the founders of the Political Affairs Committee (PAC) in November 1946. The other two were Cheddi Jagan (elected to the legislature in November 1947) and Ashton Chase, a very young trade unionist. They received valuable assistance shortly afterwards from Sydney King [Eusi Kwayana] of Buxton and Ramkarran of Kitty

Out of these talks emerged the idea of forming the Political Affairs Committee, which would set as its goal the formation of a party based on the ideology of scientific socialism [Marxism-Leninism]. **We decided that this could best be achieved by issuing a bulletin which could reach out, contact and inform people…From 1947, events moved rapidly. Small study groups were formed in Buxton, Kitty and elsewhere. PAC's views were propounded by Cheddi in the Legislative Council and thereby gained a wider range of contact and understanding. The** *Bulletin* **was more widely distributed** [emphasis added].[42]

Back to the issue of race and the 1947 elections! Hubbard was not the sole victim of the permeation of racial prejudice in the general elections of 1947. As Guyanese historian Tota Mangar observes:

> ...[a] disturbing feature of the elections was the exploitation of ethnic differences for political advancement. In the urban constituencies many Labourites [the so-called Labour Party] pursued sectional [racial] voting preferences with undisguised vigour; in the rural constituencies both the MPCA Party [Indian] and some independent candidates [African and Indian] pursued a similar policy with identical enthusiasm.[43]

The role of racism in the elections was expressed in the *Daily Chronicle* by a contemporary correspondent (H. E. Cumberbatch), who had scrutinised the results in the constituency of Western Berbice, which probably had a slight majority of African voters over Indians. It was a three-cornered fight between Rev A. T. Peters (African), Peer Bacchus, the incumbent legislator (Indian), and Georgetown businessman, F. H. Martin-Sperry (European). The seat was won by Peters (913 votes) over Bacchus (789) and Martin-Sperry (232), the latter losing his deposit. Cumberbatch had no reservation in pronouncing that racial loyalty had predominated over every other consideration in the elections: '...we get the idea of racism at work. There is certainly no doubt that racial considerations were major factors to be reckoned with for or against a candidate.' At Cotton Tree, for example, an exclusively Indian area in the constituency, the Indian candidate, Peer Bacchus, secured an overwhelming majority; at Lichfield, an African segment, A. T. Peters polled most of the votes. Martin-Sperry was probably supported by the upper echelons (White or very light) at the two sugar plantations of Blairmont and Bath, but his humiliation was attributable to the inescapable racial predisposition of voters.

The correspondent also commented on racial voting in the Berbice River constituency. The seat was contested by C. P. Ferreira (Independent), a Portuguese businessman in New Amsterdam, and S. M. Shakoor, an Indian trade unionist (Labour Party). However, the Indian element in this constituency was in a distinct minority, so despite Shakoor representing Labour, the predominantly African electorate voted by a large margin for the Portuguese businessman. Ferreira polled 1,063 votes; Shakoor a paltry 455. Cumberbatch remarked on the fragility of the concept of labour (in fact, any ideology) and the tenuous grasp of party politics in the popular imagination. He concluded candidly:

> Labour Party politics is no real catch for the suffrage of the electorate. There are forces that can operate most convincingly against it. Racism is definitely the finest of them...The labouring population of the Berbice River district polled their votes heavily against a labour candidate [Shakoor] because he represented the very race [Indian] for whom they had no vote to give.[44]

This correspondent's conclusion regarding racism in the elections was also applicable to the constituency of Eastern Berbice, the region of Cheddi

Jagan's birth; however, it was manifested differently. This seat had the largest number of eligible voters, followed by Central Demerara, which Cheddi won. With a significant Indian majority, Eastern Berbice covered the entire Canje and Corentyne Districts, and it was contested by four candidates: Dr G. M. Gonsalves (mixed-race); Ayube M. Edun, an Indian (president of the MPCA, the sugar union); the eminent Indian lawyer, Lionel Luckhoo (a Berbician); and an Indian businessman, Robert Ganpatsingh of New Amsterdam. Dr Gonsalves was victorious, polling 2,266 votes, most cast by non-Indians, predominantly African and mixed-race; on the other hand, the three Indian candidates succeeded in splitting the Indian votes, almost in equal measure: Edun (1,687), Luckhoo (1,125), Ganpatsingh (1,049) – a classic example of ethnic electoral disaggregation. Ten per cent of the votes were spoilt, indicative of the high illiteracy rate among Indians in the constituency.

That Ayube Edun, a veteran labour leader of the largely Indian fieldworkers on the sugar plantations (the founder of the MPCA in 1937), did not do better was partly a consequence of the fact that his union's reputation had not recovered fully since the revelation that one of its leaders (C. R. Jacob) had been in the pay of the Sugar Producers' Association. But the bizarre circumstances whereby he (a Demerarian Indian) was contesting against two strong Indian opponents, both Berbicians of formidable stature in their respective fields, exacerbated Edun's difficulties. However, the non-Indian vote in Eastern Berbice stayed consolidated and was effectively mobilised to secure Dr Gonsalves an easy victory. The correspondent concluded, rightly, that 'the defeat of Labour in constituencies where nearly every vote was polled by labour [voters] shows that party-politics has not the grip on our cosmopolitan electorate as in other parts of the world.' Racial loyalty was, and still is, the stubborn kernel of Guyanese social reality – bending political parties and their leaders to its procrustean mould; and nullifying the efficacy of the loftiest Marxist certainties to consign it to the 'superstructure,' the periphery or 'into the dustbin of history' (Trotsky).[45]

V. Conceptualising the West Indies Federation and Its Racial Implications

In the wider society, ethnic insecurities were aggravated periodically by apprehension that one racial segment would be enabled inequitably to augment its numerical advantage, through various proposed colonisation schemes though none was ever realised. But the idea of an Indian Colony in British Guiana, as I have argued, did plant a seed of permanent anxiety among Africans, of a decisive demographic preponderance by Indians. Nothing had changed by 1947, but now Indians were becoming alarmed at the likelihood of large-scale African migration from the British West Indian islands, whether through a colonisation scheme or a West Indies Federation. The latter became lodged in the Indo-Guyanese imagination as synonymous with irreversible African domination through significant migration from the comparatively poorer smaller islands. Their angst was magnified because it was inconceivable that independent India would approve any immigration scheme to recruit Indian settlers for British Guiana, however generous the terms.

As early as 1927, Jawaharlal Nehru (1889–1964), then secretary of the All-India Congress Committee, had clarified the role he envisaged for Indians overseas, whether they migrated as 'a coolie or as a mercenary soldier':

> An Indian who goes to other countries must co-operate with the people of that country and win for himself a position by friendship and service...The Indians should co-operate with the Africans and help them, as far as possible, and not claim a special position for themselves.[46]

His stance never changed. In fact, on the eve of India's independence, a letter from the secretary of the government of India (May 22, 1947) clearly counselled Indians in British Guiana to remain there. (A ship with returning immigrants, the *Orna* did leave British Guiana for Calcutta in 1949; another, the last one, *The Resurgent*, left on September 4, 1955.) He firmly disabused those entitled to an assisted return passage to India of the assumption that they had anything whatsoever to gain, socially or economically, from returning.

I quote at length from the letter of May 1947, as it may be considered the watershed, anchoring Indo-Guyanese in British Guiana physically and psychologically – at last, a permanent presence, committed to their future there – as citizens, as Guyanese:

> Experience shows that the majority of...[the returnees] are either impoverished or physically unfit, and that return to India means destitution for many of them. In 1938 a shipload of 880 returned to India of whom 32 died during the voyage, 261 were destitutes, and 234 had only very small savings...On return to India these repatriates are faced with uncongenial [unwelcoming] rural areas and therefore tend to migrate to cities where employment is scarce...

> These immigrants have practically no roots in India and have lost all contact with their people. Quite a considerable number of returned immigrants have for several years been clamouring for return to the West Indies.

> The Government of India consider the present time most inopportune for immigrants returning to India and would be grateful if your Government could explain the present position to Indian immigrants, and induce them to stay on there or at least to defer their return until conditions are better [he meant 'let them stay where they are'].[47]

This was the context in which Cheddi Jagan emerged as the champion, first and foremost, of the Indian sugar plantation workers, and (with very few exceptions) of Indians irrespective of class or religion. Very few Africans supported him, his Marxist philosophy and his lifelong declaration of commitment to the working class, irrespective of race, notwithstanding. It is arguable, therefore, that the rise of Jagan was coterminous with, and demonstrative of, the consolidation of Indians as integral to the emerging Guyanese nationalism, however bifurcated or incoherent. Yet at the core of this embryonic Guyanese national identity was not its working-class basis for solidarity, but its ethnic insecurity and mutual suspicion, between Africans and Indians. This would become increasingly irreconcilable – indeed violent – as African repudiation of Guyana's independence, under Jagan's leadership, seemed on the verge of fruition by the early 1960s.

Earlier, throughout the latter half of 1947, talks between West Indian politicians and the Colonial Office regarding the creation of a West Indies Federation, with the probability of large-scale West Indian migration to British Guiana, were covered copiously in the local press. In July 1947, for instance, it was reported dramatically that W. A. Crawford, the deputy leader of the Barbados House of Representatives, was engaged in '**finding breathing space in British Guiana for their surplus population in Barbados** [emphasis added].' He was not amenable to the settling of displaced Europeans, including Jews, in British Guiana (then being considered by the Evans Commission). Such migrants, he argued, would encounter formidable social and cultural problems adapting to a tropical colony with cultures and attitudes significantly divergent from their own. Crawford observed that the population crisis in Barbados was precipitated by the fact that ten thousand of their migrant labourers had returned home within a short period. Yet he was optimistic that Barbadians could settle in the area around Atkinson Field (on the East Bank Demerara, in British Guiana), where they could become independent producers of food, with no compulsion to seek employment as paid labourers.[48]

Crawford welcomed the conference between West Indian legislators and the secretary of state for the colonies, Arthur Creech Jones (scheduled for Montego Bay in September 1947), to explore closer union. He was advocating dominion status for the British colonies united within the Federation. As he put it, 'Barbados is completely wedded to the idea of Federation...And I sincerely hope British Guiana will participate in the Federation.'[49] Thus was the idea implanted in the Indo-Guyanese imagination that Federation presaged unfettered West Indian migration, inescapably overwhelmingly African. Therefore, it is comprehensible why Indo-Guyanese were inclined to see Federation as subversive of their future, at a time when they were beginning to flex their political muscles and were anticipating the granting of universal adult suffrage. Federation, consequently, was conceived as the antithesis of their aspiration to effective dominance of British Guiana and, in due course, an independent Guyana.

The *Daily Chronicle* must have pleased many Indo-Guyanese when they cautioned the Guyanese delegates to the Montego Bay conference in September 1947 not to be mesmerised by the compelling oratory of Arthur Creech Jones, who was resolved to lure the people of the region to embrace political union within a federal framework. Contrary to the rose-tinted expectations of many West Indians, the paper was clearly not enamoured of the idea. The *Chronicle* concluded:

> By all means, let us co-operate with the British West Indies for any resulting mutual benefit, but let us not allow our common sense to be ensnared by political eloquence, even if it emanates from the highest pinnacle of the Colonial Office…Of political federation, insofar as British Guiana is concerned, we entertain grave doubts, being unconvinced of its practical value.[50]

Sir Eustace Woolford, the Guyanese legislator and one of the colony's delegates to the conference, stated that he was uncertain of the projected attributes of Federation. One of the pressing needs of British Guiana was population, but, inexplicably, although many Barbadian-born immigrants had done well there, it was still not a favoured place for the migration of their compatriots. Woolford concluded his speech in Jamaica thus:

> …in British Guiana [they are] hankering after expansion, with opened-armed readiness to admit…thousands of African men enduring conditions in Barbados of starvation and deprivation of every sort, while in a colony like B.G. if they want to be peasant farmers they can become so…yet every appeal that B.G. made to Barbados for large-scale immigration failed.[51]

This notwithstanding, the primary conception of Federation in the minds of Indo-Guyanese remained one of escalating West Indian migration.

African Guyanese, on the other hand, were inclined to view the idea of a West Indies Federation with approbation. It may be considered a belated counterpart to the idea of an Indian Colony – a means of augmenting the African population – a bulwark against Indian demographic predominance and their creeping economic and political ascendancy. The latter, arguably, had impelled Hubert Nathaniel Critchlow, despite being an advocate of universal adult suffrage since the 1920s, to vote against it in the Legislative Council in 1944. It was believed that this measure would enhance the electoral advantages of Indians decisively, to the long-term detriment of Africans. As seen earlier, anxiety concerning Indian supremacy if adult suffrage were granted, was aggravated towards the end of the 1940s with the virtual eradication of the dreaded malaria. This had instantaneously precipitated a demographic leap of the Indian segment of the population.

It is noteworthy that young Ashton Chase of the PAC was also the Assistant Secretary of Critchlow's British Guiana Labour Union, and when he spoke on Cheddi Jagan's election platform in late 1947, he advocated the granting of universal adult suffrage. This had prompted a correspondent ('Bewildered Voter') to pose a pertinent question:

> I see Comrade Chase planked for universal adult suffrage at Dr Jagan's [elections] meeting. I wonder if he consulted General Secretary Critchlow who so bitterly opposed it at the Franchise Commission and at a mass meeting at the Town Hall [Georgetown]....[52]

This fundamental premise of democratic governance was being vitiated by intractable ethnic priorities. Federation, also, with its prime connotation of rampant Black West Indian migration, could not elude this rigid ethnic mould. The divergent perceived self-interests of Africans and Indians tended to neutralise even Cheddi Jagan's Marxist creed, with its lofty aspiration of forging working-class unity against imperialism.

The anxiety surrounding Federation among Indo-Guyanese was exacerbated by the Settlement Commission (chaired by Sir Geoffrey Evans), which had spent two months in the colony in 1947, exploring the feasibility of 'settling surplus West Indian population and displaced European people' in British Guiana. Evans thought it crucial that the 'vast potentialities' of the interior of the colony be released, as the narrow coastal belt was approaching the limits of its capacity to sustain the local population. He felt that they had 'to find room not only for the population here but also the people who are likely to come in.'[53] The *Chronicle* carried a news item captioned:

Jamaica and Barbados can Supply BG with 50,000 Settlers But Want Assurances No Dumping in the Bush

Sir Geoffrey Evans had visited several West Indian islands, and he was convinced that 'there was a real land hunger in Barbados and Jamaica.' He encountered many who were very able farmers, but they were candid that educational facilities and other social amenities must be enhanced and be verified as accessible before they would contemplate settling in British Guiana. The question of European migration was devoid of credibility from the beginning; but at the end of 1947, it appeared as if both the West Indies Federation and the settlement of a significant body of Black West Indians were on the verge of coming to fruition. The boot was on the other foot! As far as Indo-Guyanese were concerned, this was a menacing eventuality, the likelihood of migration from India having evaporated completely. Independent India could give no credence to any colonisation scheme, however attractive and credible the guarantees: opposition to indentureship and the maltreatment of Indians overseas (especially Fiji and South Africa) had been a robust Gandhian strand permeating the anti-colonial movement.

This was the social and political context of Cheddi Jagan's entry into the Legislative Council, on Thursday, December 18, 1947, as the representative of Central Demerara. He was the first Marxist or communist to become a legislator in British Guiana, but the political trajectory of the country was not auspicious. Racial proclivities were shaping Guyanese responses to the debate on the proposed West Indies Federation, the settlement of West Indians in British Guiana, and, of course, attitudes to universal adult suffrage. Even then, with few exceptions, Africans and Indians were predisposed to adopting divergent stances on fundamental issues in British Guiana, based on the designated self-interest of their respective segments.

Yet Jagan never faltered in his conviction that Marxism-Leninism or 'scientific socialism' would, inevitably, resolve problems rooted in primordial loyalties, despite their monumental complexity and ancient provenance among humankind. This appeared to have made him complacent about the necessity for flexibility, to compromise and to build alliances, a *modus vivendi* even with one's enemies. It is an imperative of the political endeavour, an inescapable prerequisite of statesmanship. The Federation issue was irreconcilably divisive: invariably, Africans embraced it; on the other hand, Indians rejected it root and branch, however convoluted and evasive Cheddi's posture on the matter did become.

But there was a rare case of convergence between a prominent African and an Indian: R. B. O. Hart of the League of Coloured Peoples and Dr J. B. Singh (1886–1956), president of the BGEIA and the Hindu Maha Sabha. Dr Singh was a legislator (since 1930) and a representative of the colony at the Closer Union Conference at Montego Bay, Jamaica, in September 1947. Hart argued that an aggregation of all the people of the British West Indies would be more effective on the world stage than the disparate, diluted representation of the fragmented units. Hart felt that Guyanese should naturally seek integration with such a regional body: 'From our historical and ethnic background, we have a common heritage and kinship with **West Indians** and are *prima facie* suitable for partnership and community life...The country's bargaining power for the raising of big money on reasonable terms would be greater if we were partners of a Federal state. We need not only capital but population also.' R.B.O. Hart was fully aware that the likelihood of European refugees or Latin Americans migrating to British Guiana was remote. And the fact that he emphasised 'West Indians' as potential migrants, cited in bold in his letter, was indicative of his preference.[54]

After the Montego Bay conference, Dr J.B. Singh was reported to be 'definitely in favour of federation.' He was impressed by the 'happy atmosphere' that pervaded the interaction of men from the region, most of whom had never encountered each other before. For him, this alone bode well for closer political union, adumbrating the collaborative spirit that could be engendered when the various territories were federated. He explained: 'We have so much in common, we speak the same language, some of the islands are already eager to enter into trade relations with us, and we could get all the surplus West Indian population we desire.'[55]

How does one explain the unusual case of possibly the most prominent Indian politician at the time, Dr J. B. Singh, opting for Federation? It is possible that Dr Singh genuinely believed this was the way forward for the colony. But while not attributing Machiavellian motives to him, he was an astute politician, alive to the political implications of whatever he did or said. British Guiana was on the eve of general elections, scheduled for November 1947, and Dr Singh was contesting the Demerara-Essequibo seat against M. B. Khan, another Indian. It was a straight fight between the two of them; there was no African candidate in a constituency that was over 30 per cent African. He was highly respected in the constituency (having represented it since 1930), and he probably felt assured of polling a substantial proportion of the Indian vote. Is it possible, then, that he was seeking to win the bulk of the African vote by his stance in support of a political federation? I have seen no evidence that he articulated a pro-federation stance on any other occasion. Was it an expedient?

Dr Singh's position, however, was strikingly discordant from the known Indo-Guyanese stance against the West Indies Federation and West Indian migration. Yet, surprisingly, it was not an overt issue at the general elections of November 1947, although it was probably an underlying factor, consolidating the racial voting instincts that inhered in the electorate. Dr Singh, having fought on a MPCA-Labour ticket (as the sugar union's representative), won his seat with one thousand three hundred votes; M. B. Khan, an independent candidate, received 772 votes. Dr Singh, as noted above, was president of the BGEIA and the Hindu Maha Sabha, the two main Indian organisations in British Guiana. It is highly likely, therefore, that his recent overtures towards Federation, even if widely known, failed to persuade many Africans to vote for him. They must have voted overwhelmingly for Khan (with no known affiliation to any Indian organisation), as there was no African option on the ballot. Khan polled 37 per cent of the valid votes, roughly the same as the representation of Africans among registered voters. The aggregation of political sentiments primarily based on race pervaded the elections of 1947. But it is interesting to note that Dr Singh's star was on the wane, and this was accelerated as Dr Jagan's political appeal rose meteorically from the late 1940s, particularly among Indians, irrespective of their religious or class identification. Thirty-two years older than Cheddi, Dr Singh did succumb to the PPP juggernaut in the general elections of April 1953.

Baytoram Ramharack, the biographer of Dr J. B. Singh, observes that by the early 1950s he had modified his position on political union considerably; he was in favour of a federation

> premised upon economic co-operation, before a broader political federation could be established…He understood that given the political and economic divide that existed among the key players of the federation movement, it was important to first promote co-operation on soft issues, primarily social and economic issues, through a Customs Union, rather than tackle the more challenging issues that were generally associated with a political federation.[56]

VI.   Cheddi's Legislative Triumph, 1947: Enhancing His 'Bitter Sugar' Crusade and His Soviet Beacon, 'a Secular Religion'

Tota Mangar identifies another unsavoury aspect of the 1947 general elections: the virulent opposition by the church (Catholic and Anglican) to the campaigns of Cheddi and Janet Jagan, having 'mobilised its international resources and imported the anti-communist crusade into the colony.'[57] But the *Daily Argosy* and the *Daily Chronicle* also showed no restraint in their rabid anti-communism against the political mission of the Jagans. This crusade would accompany them, acquiring incremental virulence throughout their long political career, until the collapse of the Soviet Union and the communist world in the early 1990s. On the eve of the elections in November 1947, the *Chronicle* launched a frontal assault on the Marxist politics of the Jagans, attributing to its radical idealism 'communism preached in the guise of socialism' – with the potential to foment 'hatred' and the 'ruination' of British Guiana. They categorically censured 'industrial strife and class warfare,' asserting that such action was intrinsic to the politics of the Jagans, with the likelihood that they were being guided by the diktats of the Comintern.[58]

The reference to the Comintern was predicated on the *Chronicle's* assumption that Jagan's 'socialism' was made in the USSR and inspired by the universal goal of communism as defined by the international organisation of communists under Soviet hegemony: world revolution. Profoundly shaped by Leninism and the necessity to dismantle the capitalist state, the Comintern had laid down the central premise of the international communist movement, at its second world congress in 1920: 'to struggle by all available means, including armed force, for the overthrow of the international bourgeoisie and the creation of an international Soviet republic as a transition stage to the complete abolition of the state.' The *Argosy* also had pronounced against the communist virus (as they saw it) that was being spread in France, but it was really meant as a warning to be vigilant about Jagan's PAC:

> For those who may be without any vivid idea as to what communism stands for, we will quote from Lenin's *State and Revolution* [1917]. Lenin wrote: 'The liberation of the oppressed class is impossible not only without violent revolution but also without the destruction of the apparatus of state powers. The state must be replaced by a special repressive force of the proletariat for the suppression of the bourgeoisie'. 'Repressive force' is an ugly term aptly descriptive of the hideous monster of human subjugation. This is the evil thing trying to foist itself on France, one of the bastions of our western civilisation.[59]

However, Jagan and the PAC were not disconcerted by the spate of anti-communist denunciation with which they were persistently bombarded. In fact, they were inclined to absorb and relish the inordinate attention as a badge of honour for their little group, especially after Cheddi was elected to the legislature in November 1947. He was not deterred in the least in exhibiting his Marxist credentials. On April 14, 1948, *PAC Bulletin* carried an article on its front page, captioned 'A People's Government,' a tribute to the Soviet-imposed government in Czechoslovakia, under the draconian rule of the Communist Party. They were contemptuous of 'the capitalist class' for labelling it 'totalitarian,' and they erroneously asserted that 'the people' perceived it as 'a new and genuine democracy.' Supposedly, land was being 'handed over' to the peasantry (no one could own more than 125 acres); all businesses employing more than fifty persons would be nationalised, and the press was being brought under the control of trade unions, cooperatives, and political parties – not run by capitalists.

Cheddi Jagan believed that the Czechoslovak experiment and that of the other so-called people's democracies (Poland, Hungary, East Germany, etc.) were eminently worthy of emulation in British Guiana:

> Transposing this situation to British Guiana would mean that the present slave plantation system of the sugar estates would be completely smashed. The estate land would be divided up and the sugar workers, instead of merely working for miserable wages would be the producers of their own sugar cane on their own land. The sugar factories would be owned and operated by Government. The other large landed proprietors, who are today making an easy and comfortable living by money-lending, share-cropping and land-renting, would be forced to earn their bread by performing actual work. The local capitalist press now owned by, controlled and

operated for the preservation of private profit would be replaced by a people's press fighting for the real needs of the people.

Jagan's paramount example was, of course, the Soviet Union, totalitarian and at best authoritarian, yet redefined by the terms of his pro-Moscow Marxist vision as the essence of 'a new genuine democracy.' Dictatorial rule in Czechoslovakia, under Soviet diktat, was rationalised thus: 'Can the people of British Guiana expect that the capitalists will call such a government anything but dictatorship or totalitarian? Will the people of British Guiana call such a government anything but a genuine democratic government?' Josip Broz Tito (1892–1980) and Milovan Djilas (1911–95), the Yugoslav communists, visited Stalin in 1945, as the Red Army marched triumphantly across several countries in Eastern Europe. Djilas recalls Stalin's credo with respect to the Soviet Union and its conquered neighbours: 'This war is not as in the past…Whoever occupies a territory imposes on it his own social system. Everyone imposes his own system as far as his army has the power to do so. It cannot be otherwise.'[60] Communism was being imposed from above, with the compliments of Comrade Stalin and the Red Army. Yet, for Cheddi Jagan, this was 'a new genuine democracy' in Eastern Europe, and Janet would never seek to temper his excesses. Comrade Cheddi was on the road to nowhere! And he would make many enemies, some extremely powerful, on his high road to the communist utopia. He was firmly and irrevocably on the side of the USSR in the Cold War – from the beginning. The man was 'not for turning'!

Anne Applebaum argues that the Soviet model could not encompass the autonomy of civil society; obeisance was reserved for the omnipotence of the Communist Party of the Soviet Union. That party was the beacon: the source of illumination – inviolable!

> By 1945, the Bolsheviks had also developed a theory of civil society, albeit one that was entirely negative. In contrast to Burke, Tocqueville and their own Russian intellectuals, they believed, in the words of the historian Stuart Finkel, that 'the public sphere in a socialist society should be unitary and univocal.' They dismissed the 'bourgeois' notion of open discussion, and hated independent associations, trade unions and guilds of all kinds, which they referred to as 'separatist' or 'caste' divisions within society. As for bourgeois political parties, these were meaningless…The only organisations allowed to have a legal existence were de facto extensions of the communist party. Even completely apolitical organisations had to be banned: until the revolution had triumphed, there could be no such thing as apolitical organisations. Everything was political. And if it was not openly political, then it was secretly political.[61]

Despite slavery and colonialism, a liberal democratic political culture was taking shape in the British West Indies after the Second World War. But Cheddi and Janet Jagan rejected it as 'petit bourgeois,' essentially a variant of capitalism. Yet they would find it difficult to persuade a large segment of Guyanese society of the moral superiority of their 'scientific socialist' creed and its foremost exemplars, the Soviet Union and its satellites. Most who supported them did so despite the latter. They were impelled largely by racial loyalty and his hatred of the 'sugar gods.'

Notes

1. *PAC Bulletin*, No. 1, November 6, 1946.
2. The *Times* (London), August 20, 1962. See also the Obituary of Sir Gordon Lethem, the *Times*, August 16, 1962.
3. *PAC Bulletin*, no. 2, November 20, 1946.
4. Ibid.
5. *PAC Bulletin*, no. 9, May 7, 1947.
6. Ibid.
7. *PAC Bulletin*, no. 12, July 9, 1947.
8. *PAC Bulletin*, no. 14, August 6, 1947.
9. *PAC Bulletin*, no. 8, March 12, 1947.
10. Ibid.
11. *PAC Bulletin*, no. 18, October 8, 1947.
12. Ibid.
13. *Daily Chronicle*, September 26, 1947.
14. *Daily Chronicle*, October 13, 1947.
15. *Daily Chronicle*, October 16, 1947.
16. *Daily Chronicle*, October 15, 1947.
17. Leader, Ibid., October 18, 1947.
18. *Daily Chronicle*, October 20, 1947.
19. Ibid.
20. *Daily Chronicle*, October 31, 1947.
21. Leader, *Daily Chronicle*, November 7, 1947.
22. Ibid.
23. *Daily Argosy*, November 9, 1947.
24. Cheddi Jagan, *The West on Trial: My Fight for Guyana's Freedom* (London: Michael Joseph, 1966), 91.
25. *Daily Argosy*, November 9, 1947.
26. *Daily Chronicle*, November 10, 1947.
27. Leader, *Daily Argosy*, November 14, 1947.
28. *Daily Chronicle*, November 14, 1947.
29. *Daily Argosy*, November 16, 1947.
30. Leader, *Daily Chronicle*, November 17, 1947.
31. *Daily Chronicle*, November 18, 1947.
32. *Daily Chronicle*, November 26, 1947.
33. Leader, *Daily Chronicle*, November 26, 1947.
34. Ibid.
35. Leader, *Daily Chronicle*, November 29, 1947.
36. [The National Archives], KV2/3637, 'Cheddi and Janet Jagan up to and Including the First PPP Elections Victory in 1953,' top secret.

37. Leszek Kolakowski, *Main Currents of Marxism* (New York: W.W. Norton, 2005 [1978]), 304, 306–7.
38. Jagan, *The West on Trial: My Fight for Guyana's Freedom*, 93.
39. Eusi Kwayana, *The Morning After* (Georgetown: Guyana-Caribbean Politics Publications, 2005), 100.
40. Jagan, *The West on Trial: My Fight for Guyana's Freedom*, 92–93.
41. Janet Jagan, 'Thirty Years since the PAC,' *Thunder* (January–March 1976): 3–5.
42. Ibid.
43. Tota C. Mangar, 'The 1947 Parliamentary Elections in Colonial British Guiana,' *Stabroek News*, May 6, 2010.
44. H.E. Cumberbatch, 'Western Berbice's Place in the New Pattern,' *Daily Chronicle*, December 3, 1947.
45. Ibid.
46. Hugh Tinker, *Separate and Unequal: India and the Indians in the British Commonwealth, 1920–50* (London: C. Hurst, 1976), 93.
47. *Daily Chronicle*, October 10, 1947.
48. *Daily Chronicle*, July 14, 1947.
49. *Daily Chronicle*, July 19, 1947.
50. Leader, *Daily Chronicle*, September 13, 1947.
51. *Daily Chronicle*, September 14, 1947.
52. *Daily Chronicle*, October 1, 1947.
53. *Daily Argosy*, December 12, 1947; *Daily Chronicle*, December 12, 1947.
54. R. B. O. Hart to the Editor, *Daily Chronicle*, September 23, 1947.
55. *Daily Argosy*, September 27, 1947.
56. Baytoram Ramharack, *Jung Bahadur Singh of Guyana (1886–1956): Politician, Ship Doctor, Labour Leader and Protector of Indians* (San Juan, Trinidad: CHAKRA, Kumar Mahabir, 2019), 202–3.
57. Mangar, 'The 1947 Parliamentary Elections in Colonial British Guiana.'
58. Leader, *Daily* Chronicle, November 7, 1947.
59. Leader, *Daily Argosy*, December 6, 1947.
60. See Anne Applebaum, 'Introduction' to Milovan Djilas, *Conversations with Stalin* (London: Penguin Books, 2014 [1962]).
61. Anne Applebaum, *Iron Curtain: The Crushing of Eastern Europe* (London: Penguin Books, 2013 [2012]), 161.

6.
Jagan's Emerging Marxism, Enmore, and Its Aftermath
The Late 1940s

He was a man of faith – Marxism was like a religion.

> – **Dr Fenton Ramsahoye**

Enmore made us.

> – **Janet Jagan**

I.   Cheddi's Rising Star: The Eclipse of J.B. Singh, Ayube Edun, and Other Indo-Guyanese Politicians of the Old Order

Cheddi Jagan still holds a very special place in the Indo-Guyanese imagination. He came from the sugar plantation; he could empathise with the sugar workers and rice farmers (Hindus and Muslims). This gave him abundant political leverage over the most prominent Indo-Guyanese family, the Luckhoos, people of the legal and medical professions – Christians, who could not readily empathise, or be seen to, with the Indian 'coolie.' In fact, two of the Luckhoos were elected to the colonial legislature between the Wars: J. A. Luckhoo, was the first Indo-Guyanese to be so honoured, in 1916; his older brother, E. A. Luckhoo (father of Sir Lionel) was first elected in 1930. J. A. became identified with the idea of creating an 'Indian Colony' in British Guiana, the aborted scheme to secure more Indians for permanent settlement in British Guiana at the termination of indentureship. However, the latter had acquired such notoriety in India, the case for its abolition integral to the embryonic Gandhian nationalist crusade, that the idea of an Indian Colony had no chance of coming to fruition because the likelihood of the revival of immigration was minuscule.

J. A. Luckhoo was vilified, erroneously, for actively seeking to revive the discredited indentureship system. The Indo-Guyanese narrative of indentureship as 'a new slavery,' coupled with Jagan's potent construction (later) of the universe of 'King Sugar' and the *modus operandi* of 'the sugar gods' as 'bitter sugar' – an unfathomable hurt at the core of the Indo-Guyanese soul – remain sacrosanct. Whoever dares to challenge its veracity could be deemed a fifth columnist. Therefore, the upper-middle class, 'bourgeois' background of the Luckhoos rendered them ill-equipped as representatives of Indo-Guyanese, buoyed by the imminence of universal adult suffrage, and enthralled by the radical youthful charisma of Cheddi and Janet Jagan, towards the end of the 1940s.

Dr J. B. Singh, a conservative Hindu leader of the British Guiana East Indian's Association (BGEIA) and the Maha Sabha (the latter being an orthodox Hindu organisation), was the most prominent Indian politician in the colony in the 1930s–1940s. As seen in the previous chapter, Dr Singh contested the Demerara-Essequibo constituency in 1947 and was victorious. However, while he still evoked palpable respect among Indians, his political fortunes were fading. Substance does not always matter in politics, but charisma does. Dr Singh was thirty-two years older than Dr Jagan. He could not match the compelling handsomeness, the youthful exuberance, in addition to the persuasive vision and passion of Cheddi Jagan and his mission. This glamour was enhanced in the Indo-Guyanese imagination by his young beautiful White wife (Janet), intrinsic to their politics of revolutionary change. But Cheddi also crafted an enduringly persuasive message – against the detested 'sugar gods.' Dr Singh's politics, on the other hand, felt tired and rudderless compared with Cheddi's insurgent crusade – unencumbered by self-doubt and stridently assertive in righting ancient wrongs on the sugar plantations. The older man was put in the shade by the robustness of Jagan's Marxist faith, simplified in its appeal to Indo-Guyanese because it was pervaded by a consuming dichotomy: the narrative of 'bitter sugar' and the 'sugar gods' pitted against the downtrodden 'coolie.' Besides, in the aftermath of India's independence, Cheddi's anti-colonial campaign was inspired by the spirit and vigour of Indian nationalism, epitomised by the saintly

Dr Jung Bahadur (J.B.) Singh (1886–1956), the foremost Indo-Guyanese politician in the 1930s–40s, before he was superseded by the energetic, charismatic and seductively iconoclastic Cheddi Jagan from the early 1950s

Mahatma and the handsome and heroic Jawaharlal Nehru, who overcame the mighty British Empire without bullets. The fact that both Gandhi and Nehru had been to jail several times in their crusade for India's freedom had virtually elevated them to the Hindu pantheon of gods. This was never lost on Cheddi and Janet. Cheddi was a 'Nehru' in the making to the Indo-Guyanese people.

Meanwhile, Ayube Edun's star also was fading. He had championed the cause of the predominantly Indian's sugar workers since the mid-1930s, articulating their grievances in his *Guiana Review* and *Labour Advocate*, and he founded the Manpower Citizens' Association (MPCA) in 1937, which was recognised by the Sugar Producers' Association in 1939. But his union had lost considerable credibility, having compromised the workers' trust. It was disclosed that in the early 1940s one of its leaders, C. R. Jacob, was the recipient of a monthly stipend from Booker. Edun probably knew nothing of this infraction, yet he was severely tarnished by it. It is also conceivable that, being a Muslim, Edun encountered a Hindu backlash in the aftermath of the partition of India and the accompanying Hindu-Muslim mutual barbarism there. I surmise that there was some validity to this assumption as the secretary of the MPCA, Mohammed Shakoor, also, was Muslim. Richard Hart, the Jamaican communist and lifelong friend of Jagan, once told me that he felt this was certainly the case. He visited British Guiana in 1949 and had travelled to the sugar belt on the Corentyne; he was informed, at Plantation Skeldon, that the provoked religious sensibility among Indians was a factor in the increasingly negative response of the sugar workers to Edun and the MPCA.

Cheddi Jagan, on the other hand, by his continual declamation of a class-centred politics (however ineffective an antidote to African-Indian racial susceptibilities), did help to moderate, if not neutralise, the replication of the Hindu-Muslim bifurcation of the other plantation colonies in the Tropics, including neighbouring Trinidad, Mauritius, Fiji, and South Africa. Besides, as I have argued, the fact that around 40 per cent of the Indian population, Hindu and Muslim, remained co-residents in the derelict ranges or logies on the Guyanese sugar plantations, engendered and sustained a robust solidarity against the 'sugar gods,' perceptibly greater than elsewhere. But it is also true that Cheddi's indifference to, if not repudiation of, Hinduism in his personal life contributed immeasurably to the attenuation of the undercurrent of mistrust that could have impaired Indo-Guyanese cohesion, in the aftermath of the barbaric rupturing of India in 1947. In addition, his pursuit of a vigorous and unrelenting campaign against 'bitter sugar,' over many decades, dissipated the potential hazards of his non-religious Marxist-oriented politics among a deeply religious people. His embrace of a 'materialist conception' of change, as he would put it, placed him equidistant from Hinduism and Islam, hence credible to both. The 'bitter sugar' narrative transcended the discrete religious identities of Indo-Guyanese which remained, but Jagan's secular politics enabled him to negotiate the potential pitfalls.

His Marxism, if examined at all within the Indian community, was sublimated and accommodated, purely as the gospel of militancy to cut the 'sugar gods' down to size. It was a mission of radical change, aimed primarily and relentlessly at 'bitter sugar' – and imbued with a moral scrupulousness ever juxtaposed with the supposedly compromised and derelict principles of the MPCA. But its political ramifications were exploited ruthlessly, later, by leaders from other ethnic groups in British Guiana (such as Burnham and D'Aguiar), the Christian churches (particularly the Catholics), in addition to the three daily newspapers. They continually sought to undermine Jagan as subversive of Western democratic norms (inviolable in the British West Indies), and simultaneously as a pawn of Soviet communism – an instrument of totalitarianism. It became a veritable crusade against godlessness and the 'red menace.' Therefore, both internally and externally, from the beginning of his political career, as a declared communist (the euphemism was 'scientific socialist'), Jagan had to confront the consequences of being on the Soviet side of the Cold War in the Western Hemisphere. The birth of his political mission coincided with the genesis of the Cold War, and the antagonism of his imperialist enemies, who engineered his downfall and virtual exile in the wilderness of toothless Opposition politics for nearly twenty-eight years, terminated only when communism collapsed at the end of the 1980s.

II. The PAC's Declared Marxism-Leninism and Its Detractors

From the commencement of his political crusade, Jagan did not deny that his philosophy was 'scientific socialism,' that is Marxism-Leninism or communism. Often, however, until the mid-1960s (when he was in office under colonialism), Jagan preferred the term socialism, rather than the more loaded communism. But from the late 1960s (after his PPP joined the world communist movement in 1969, led by the USSR), he resorted to the latter more frequently, with a swaggering bravado. It seems absurd, therefore, that many still doubt that he was, indeed, a communist; or, no less inexplicable, that the Americans and the British would spend endless time appearing to agonise over his communist credentials and associations. The systematic interception and bugging, by MI5 and the CIA over many years, of Cheddi Jagan's correspondence, telephone conversations, in addition to his voluminous writings espousing communism, should have been conclusive enough. Yet, as Jock Campbell told me, the British always preferred Jagan to Burnham, and they hoped earnestly that maturity and responsibility in government would divest him of his Marxist utopianism.

In the issue of the *PAC Bulletin* (April 14, 1948), in which the 'people's government' of Czechoslovakia was cited with approbation for 'initiating a new and genuine democracy,' a correspondent (CAB) sought clarification with respect to the political orientation of the PAC:

> For some time now I have been receiving regular copies of the *PAC Bulletin* which I have read carefully and have so far found most enlightening; yet, today, I cannot determine whether PAC is Socialist, Communistic or Democratic in its outlook. I would be much obliged if you can clear this point up for me as early as possible.

The *Bulletin* responded:

> We rejoice that our reader has found the *PAC Bulletin* 'most enlightening', in itself a confession that said reader appreciates our outlook – which incidentally is, as we said as far back as November 6, 1946 [the first issue of the *Bulletin*], Scientific Socialism [Marxism-Leninism/communism].

Cheddi became a good friend later of the eminent African American singer, actor, and communist, Paul Robeson (1898–1976). In September 1948, clearly empathising with the latter's belief in communism as the philosophy for the liberation of humankind (despite his caution in articulating it, given his American citizenship), the *Bulletin* quoted, with evident concurrence, an excerpt from Robeson's testimony to the Senate Judiciary Committee:

> I consider communism as nothing but an extension of public ownership of the main means of resources, like the railroad worker said the other day. And the coal-mines? If they are that important to the people of the USA that every time there is a national emergency it is life or death to the American people, couldn't it occur to you that instead of beating the workers on the head that maybe the Government should own the railroad and the coalmines? Well, this is a whole struggle of which communism is a part. This is a part of the conception of the struggles of human beings for ages. And you can't rule communism out anywhere in the world.[1]

Later in the same year (1948), the *Bulletin*, striving to demonstrate the inherent superiority of the Soviet system over a degenerate Western capitalism, reproduced an article by A. Birman, 'Prices up under Capitalism; Down under Socialism.' He argued that since the War prices were escalating in capitalist countries, whereas in the Soviet Union, prices were stable, if not falling. This was because of central planning, coupled with the fact that its resources were owned by the people, hence surplus value was no longer being extracted to bloat the pockets of rapacious capitalists. Therefore, they could afford to keep prices down because the capitalist exploiter (utterly superfluous to the process of production, in any case) had been effectively eliminated. It was a foretaste of the utopia supposedly taking shape under the socialist system, engendered by the workers' state – indicative of incremental transformation in the Soviet Union towards the perfect communist society:

> Prices in the Soviet Union are regulated on entirely different principles. There are no capitalists here, and factory and other enterprises belong to the people and are run by the state. Prices in the Soviet Union are determined so as to cover the expenditure on the production of goods and to yield a certain profit, rarely exceeding 4 or 5 percent. Furthermore, the profit accrues to the State Budget [of the USSR], and, consequently, is also used to meet the requirements of the people. Thus, 39% of the expenditure of the USSR Budget for 1948 is allocated to the development of the national economy, and over 30% goes to public education, health services, the promotion of science and art, social security and social insurance. The Soviet Government's policy is to reduce prices as far as possible, thus raising the standard of living of the people…In the post-war years…prices in the capitalist countries keep rising, while in the Soviet Union they fall. This difference is one more manifestation of the difference between the two economic systems – capitalism and socialism [communism].[2]

This article was probably sourced from a magazine in the USSR. It was normal practice for the *PAC Bulletin* to reproduce excerpts of articles or brief news items emanating from the Soviet Union and Eastern Europe, thus vindicating (by concrete example of radical change) the Marxist vision/mission of Cheddi and Janet Jagan in British Guiana. And the fact that the USSR made a magnificent contribution, incurring an enormous toll in lives and resources, in the campaign to defeat Nazi Germany (widely acknowledged and acclaimed in the capitalist west), rendered their claims for the superiority of socialism/communism, by virtue of its solemn obligation to all humanity, morally unimpeachable. Marxism-Leninism had acquired the essence of a religious faith for Cheddi and Janet: inviolable tenets, scientifically grounded therefore rooted in the truth – a crusade, nothing less! They were indomitably primed to challenge their sternest critics.

In fact, soon after the shooting of sugar workers at Plantation Enmore (East Coast Demerara) on June 16, 1948 (to be addressed later), the Jagans were exhilarated that their little Marxist group, the Political Affairs Committee (PAC), was recently disparaged by Sir James Henderson-Stewart (1897–1961), a right-wing Scottish MP (of the Liberal National Party), which had broken away from the Liberals in 1931 and merged with the Conservatives in 1947. It was a source of immeasurable pride to the PAC that they had attracted such disapprobation at Westminster. For the record, Henderson-Stewart was responding to Cheddi

Jagan's PAC and their supposed role in fomenting subversion that led to the Enmore tragedy. But the PAC rejected 'Mr Stewart's' (*sic*) allegations although he did possess some first-hand knowledge, having visited the colony shortly after the shooting at Enmore. The *Bulletin* denounced his charge as 'nonsensical propaganda spread in England by the representatives of the friends of the Sugar Gods.'

The following is a part of Henderson-Stewart's statement to the Commons:

> The [GIWU] strike started at the end of April. From the start it was clearly a political agitation organised by Communists, fellow travellers and other good-for-nothings who hang about the roads and bridges on the coast. The agitation was designed not to improve the social conditions of the workers at all, but to incite a revolutionary spirit among all those who labour on the sugar estates, and to cause chaos on those estates. They issue the most poisonous propaganda which I have seen – with apparently the greatest freedom. These journals are being issued inciting people to all kinds of trouble, to withdraw their labour, to demonstrate against the estate managers and in every possible way to cause disturbance…According to my latest information, White women and children are in terror of their lives. I have a letter from one woman, the wife of an estate manager, who writes that for ten weeks she has been unable to leave her house because of the danger of attack from this lawless element in the country.[3]

Yet the PAC was not deflated by Henderson-Stewart's provocative intervention in the Enmore tragedy; on the contrary, they were energised by it. He had accorded this fledgling Marxist group a modicum of heartening recognition and gravitas in London, way beyond their imagination. The *Bulletin* was not irritated by the 'nonsensical propaganda' in the House of Commons, at their expense; on the contrary, they expressed gratitude to the MP for affording them precious publicity in that august institution:

> Although PAC [*Bulletin*] is not a newspaper, we feel that Mr Stewart [*sic*] has us in mind when he made these statements, for no other publication in B.G., to our knowledge, championed the cause of the sugar workers. PAC, however, is grateful for the recognition received in the English [*sic*] Parliament.

The PAC also challenged a Christian minister who had proclaimed that 'Communism and the Christian faith cannot walk together.' They countered:

> The Christian faith referred to has, of course, no relation to that proposed by Jesus of Nazareth, who is reported to have taken loaves and fish from one and fed them to a multitude; and later on, gave some money changers a severe thrashing.

They also noted that the *Daily Chronicle* 'continues to get excited about communism in B.G. and the "Pattern from Moscow," which they alleged local communists [the PAC] are following.' They responded to the 'Comrade Editor,' with evident sarcasm: 'The Comrade Editor seems confused when he states that "the true communism of Marx and Engels no longer exists – the Bolshevists have seen to that." Could it mean that the comrade is an advocate of Marxism?'⁴

In the same issue of the *Bulletin*, in July 1948, the PAC was no less exhilarated by the attention they were attracting from another local exponent of anti-communism. They responded to an editorial, from the *Daily Argosy*, thus:

> We stand up to the neck in gratitude and obligation to the leader-writer of the *Argosy* for his unreserved advertisement for our little bulletin. Thanks to his publicity our circulation is far exceeding our little bulletin. He calls us P(act) A(gainst) C(ommunism) in the title of his leader. Further on, he slates us for spreading "communist" doctrine. Such inconsistency! We wonder how our comrade editor has not been sacked by his bosses for advertising *PAC Bulletin*.'

The PAC was the target of incessant anti-communist attacks from other streams in the colony, beyond the three daily newspapers. One such group affiliated to the Catholic Church, the Sword of the Spirit, was unremitting in their denunciation of the communism of the Jagans. A prominent member, John Fernandes (1901–82), a popular Portuguese businessman in Georgetown, observed that in the Soviet Union 'a man may not select nor quit employment.' The *Bulletin* responded by citing the lack of choice in the sugar industry, where the cut-and-drop method of cane-cutting was being arbitrarily superseded by the more arduous cut-and-load method. This matter was, ostensibly, the principal grievance that had sparked the strike in the sugar industry, culminating in the shooting and death of the five workers at Enmore on June 16, 1948. The PAC posed the following question:

> Did Mr Fernandes ever hear of a capitalist depression with unemployment and starvation in the MIDST OF PLENTY or of the "unemployed reserve" in "normal" times? Is he aware of the thousands of workers in British Guiana who are forced by starvation to hold on to their undesirable jobs?⁵

The same issue of the *Bulletin* reflected on the inception of the Cold War, the division of the world into two irreconcilable ideological camps: the capitalist led by America and the socialist or communist led by the USSR. Even at that early stage, Cheddi Jagan's loyalty in the Cold War was not impaired by self-doubt or equivocation:

> The struggle for freedom has taken on a global significance. The world's forces are now slowly aligning themselves into two camps, one democratic, peace-loving [the eastern or communist bloc, led by Comrade Stalin], the other reactionary, fascist and war-minded [the western or capitalist]…In Europe, some countries (Czechoslovakia, Bulgaria, Hungary, Poland, Romania, Yugoslavia) are on the road to

progress and freedom; others have unstable governments (France, Italy)…In the United States, the Marshall-planners, the Wall Street grabbers and the Southern 'democrat-lynchers' are launched on a cruise of world imperialism with Great Britain on the tow.[6]

No vacillation or ambiguity with respect to whose side Cheddi embraced!

The *Guiana Graphic*, the newest daily newspaper, had carried an anti-communist article (clearly intended to discredit the PAC) asserting that communists 'must resort to force, violence and revolution [in order] to achieve power.' The *PAC Bulletin* (July 20, 1948) repudiated the *Graphic's* intervention, while savouring the publicity such criticism was garnering for them. Anti-communism was the standard instrument the press, the church and most politicians adopted in challenging the Marxist PAC. But none of this could detract Jagan from his sacred creed – the making of the classless society, bringing to the poor and the powerless peace, freedom, self-esteem, and an abundance of material needs (the perfect communist society), irrespective of race or nationality. The Enmore tragedy, therefore, was morally defensible because it was a vindication of the 'growing consciousness of the working class,' confronting the forces of repression, the capitalist exploiters and the colonial state, for trade union rights, seminal to making the communist party. The message was secular in appearance (and supposedly based on scientific principles), but it was firmly grounded in a kind of secular theology. This was what the PAC was disseminating in its *Bulletin*, in conjunction with the ample Marxist literature it was circulating among its comrades, in study groups at Kitty, Buxton and Plaisance (all in Cheddi's constituency).

In August 1948, the *Bulletin* carried a piece on 'Class Distinction and the Class Struggle,' in its 'Introduction to Political Economy' series on 'scientific socialism.' Their message to Guyanese is encapsulated in the following excerpts (most likely written by Cheddi):

> The basis of class distinction in human society is the simple fact that those who own the means of production find it expedient to keep in some form of subjugation those who do not. In this country we have the sugar companies, the bauxite companies, the gold concerns, the cattle companies and big merchants, etc. This class lives in luxury by making use of the labour of others for personal profit. This making use of the labour of others for amassing personal wealth is what we call exploitation of labour…The outcome of all class struggles will only mean that all the facilities [enjoyed by capitalists] will be at the disposal of every worker, of the sick and aged and not at the disposal of a few rich families….[7]

> The working class or the class of exploited people is now, in various ways, challenging the domination of the capitalist class or exploiters.

Trade unions, labour parties and similar organisations all bear witness of the growing consciousness of the working class. Now, during the dominance of feudalism a new class of exploiters arose from the very ranks of the feudal serfs [capitalists]. The character of modern capitalism is such, however, that no new class of exploiters develops. Workers in their common struggles against the capitalists are becoming more and more fitted to lead the reformation of society…

The study of society proves that history cannot be escaped. When history speaks, the truth is spoken. History will make no apologies. The working class, the socialist reformation, will not replace one minority of exploiters by another, but is made in the interests of the great majority and leads forward to a CLASSLESS SOCIETY (sic) [emphasis added].[8]

This virtual catechism was pivotal to Jagan's crusade against 'bitter sugar,' the sustaining vision of his long political mission. Fortified by his belief in the superiority of 'scientific socialism,' based supposedly on infallible historical and 'scientific' premises, with certainty of its realisation, every criticism was taken in stride as the effusion of reactionaries, doomed by historical materialism to irrelevance. It is not possible, therefore, to comprehend Cheddi Jagan's irreproachable certainty, indefatigability, and longevity in politics unless one grasps his belief in Marxism-Leninism as a science, flawless in its capacity for the total liberation of humankind – virtually a religious calling, as Dr Fenton Ramsahoye characterised it.

As late as 1990, while the Soviet system was crumbling precipitately, Jagan still retained his faith in his communist creed although, fortified now by Gorbachev's reforms and his radical 'revisionism,' he was emboldened to pronounce several former communist heroes, including Comrades Stalin and Brezhnev, villains. In reality, he was belatedly embracing the reformist Czechoslovak notion of 'socialism with a human face,' the source of the Prague Spring, crushed by Soviet tanks in August 1968 (under Comrade Brezhnev). The latter was greeted with approbation (at the time) by Jagan and his PPP:

Marxism-Leninism is a science, not a dogma. We used its principles as a guide to action…Scientific socialism, which was built on the foundations of religious reformism and utopian socialism, has like them the same immortal vision and ethical, moral and spiritual values. Today, many liberation theologists apply its tools of analysis: an internationalist worldview and a class and humanitarian approach. The goals of socialism [communism] must not be confused with the failures of those who tried to implement socialism. For instance, there is a vast difference between communists: Stalin and Lenin; Pol Pot and Ho Chi Minh, Brezhnev and Gorbachev…President Gorbachev has made it clear that he has not abandoned Marxism-Leninism and the goal of communism, that his fundamental reforms are intended to make a better socialism [emphasis added].[9]

But Jagan was such a decent man, perceived as incapable of malevolence whatever the circumstances, that it was impossible for most to identify him with any manifestation of tyranny. Moreover, it was impossible to conceive that he could ever emulate the evil reign of terror under Stalin or other bloodthirsty communist dictators, such as Mao, or (later) the butcher of Cambodia, Pol Pot. In addition, the fact that he was abstemious not only in his own life but also in his attitude to public resources, moderated the responses of many who were sceptical of his belief in the Soviet example as the inspiration for the world in creating the communist utopia.

III. The Birth of Jagan's GIWU and the Campaign for Recognition in the Sugar Industry over Edun's MPCA

Jagan's PAC prioritised control of the trade union as crucial in aggregating and mobilising the substantial force of the predominantly Indian field labourers on the plantations – the largest body of workers in any industry in the country – for his political mission. This inevitably placed him in collision with the recognised union, the MPCA. Consequently, he considered it imperative to his political advancement to establish a union that could supplant the MPCA in a very short time. Such a union would hasten the fulfilment of a principal plank of his Marxist endeavour: nationalisation of the sugar industry. The *PAC Bulletin* (July 9, 1947) alluded to the centrality of trade union militancy as a precursor to the construction of a disciplined communist party, a prerequisite for the dismantling of the capitalist state:

> As long as the worker is working to put profits, no matter how small, into the hands of capitalists, so long will there be strikes. Only a changed political-economic system, as in socialism [communism], where the means of production are owned by society, where profits for individuals are eliminated, where there is no contradiction between production and distribution, will there be an end to all strikes.

The biggest union in British Guiana was Ayube Edun's MPCA which, as noted earlier, was recognised by the SPA since March 1939 as the bargaining agent for the primarily Indian fieldworkers. Jagan, an Indian from the plantation, was readily drawn to the MPCA as he was to the BGEIA, after he returned to British Guiana in 1943, having studied in America, for seven years (1936–43), to become a dentist. Strange as it may appear, this dentist would play a most extraordinary role in the political evolution of Guyana. He became the Treasurer of the MPCA in 1945, during Lethem's progressive governorship although he was averse to 'reformism' both in unionism and in politics. It is hardly surprising, therefore, that he was soon revolted by a perceived lack of militancy in the union's negotiations with the 'sugar gods.' The fact that Jagan was already devoted to Marxism meant that he was naturally at odds with the 'moderate' political underpinning of the MPCA and the BGEIA – what he construed as their adherence to the old order – liberalism, not revolutionary socialism. When he was dismissed from the MPCA in 1946, he felt liberated to pose a radical challenge to the pervading orthodoxy of the principal Indian leaders, Dr J. B. Singh, Ayube Edun, and Lionel Luckhoo 'convinced of the necessity for having a ["scientific socialist"/Marxist] theoretical organ and political platform.' This was the backdrop to the creation of the PAC in November 1946.

Jagan recalled his initial turbulent encounter with the MPCA, but this would persist for thirty years, causing him fatal damage that rendered his political fortunes irretrievable:

> The union machinery was against me…Pressure was brought to bear upon me for two reasons. Firstly, because I objected to what I considered to be the high level of expense allowances from the funds of a poor union, and secondly because of the tendency to collaborate with the sugar planters. Actually, the MPCA was already set on its course of becoming a company union. A few years before [1940], one of its founder-members [C. R. Jacob] had been taken on to the payroll of Booker at £100 per month…This had shattered the confidence of members in the union. In 1945 I saw for myself that others in the leadership were inclined the same way. Round the bargaining table where I sat for brief intervals, I saw that the union leadership was not prepared to fight the workers' cause.[10]

Freed of the constraints of the moderate MPCA, Jagan and the PAC could pursue a militant campaign to dramatise and validate their assertion that the union leaders were in the pockets of the 'sugar gods.' And after the election of Jagan to the Legislative Council in November 1947, the capacity of the PAC to articulate a radical counterargument to the MPCA was enhanced immeasurably. It was essentially a project to discredit and eliminate the MPCA as the bargaining agent of the fieldworkers, largely Indian. The predominantly African factory workers were represented originally by another union, the British Guiana Workers' League, founded by A. A. Thorne in 1931. By the late 1940s, the latter was defunct, and the MPCA had become the bargaining agent for both field and factory workers. In January 1948, the PAC repudiated the 'low slave wages' on the sugar plantations; it was eight cents to twenty cents an hour, no incentive for people to do a full week's work. They reproached the government for allowing the 'iniquitous wage rate' to continue, a consequence of the stubborn 'plantation psychology' in British Guiana:

> A labourer lives in an estate house – in most cases dilapidated ranges. His small wage does not permit him a saving, with the result that he

perpetually lives in the fear of insecurity. Should he refuse to do any work to which he may be assigned, he can be given notice to quit [the range or logie]. This he cannot afford, consequently he submits to the dictatorship of the system, revolting only to the extent of mild passive resistance to the detriment of increased production.[11]

The PAC wanted the government to provide land for small farmers, in addition to providing credit, fertilisers and advice on marketing. They observed: 'Government is more bent on aiding the landed proprietors and capitalists than the farmers who actually need the help.'[12]

The PAC was instrumental in embedding the belief among sugar workers that the MPCA had 'sold out' to the sugar producers, Ayube Edun's personal integrity and impeccable pioneering work on behalf of the workers notwithstanding. And the fact that Edun was defeated in the East Berbice constituency (with four sugar plantations) in the elections of 1947, while Jagan was elected in Central Demerara (with seven plantations), was reflective of the latter's increasingly formidable leadership stature among Indo-Guyanese. The economic and cultural momentum among Indians (as I explained earlier) was already accruing to Jagan in a manner that represented a kind of ethnic political awakening. This was the context in which the Guiana Industrial Workers' Union (GIWU) was founded in 1948, with the primary aim of displacing the MPCA. Its two principal leaders were Dr J. P. Lachmansingh (president) and Amos Rangela (secretary). It is significant that they held the same positions in the main Indian organisation in the colony, the British Guiana East Indian Association (BGEIA). They could be considered Indian nationalists but were not radical or left-wing in the least – and definitely not Marxist.

Jagan, a communist, had little regard for the politics of the likes of Lachmansingh, Rangela, Edun, C. R. Jacob, Dr J. B. Singh, and most of the members of the BGEIA, seen as petty bourgeois, if not reactionary. But he was shrewd in recognising early that the best means of furthering his political mission was to secure the support of the sugar workers, indeed, Indians as a whole, whatever their religious allegiance. The mantra of 'bitter sugar' was a compelling one, and the GIWU (despite the character of its leadership) was an efficacious instrument for disseminating that message to the heart of the Indian community. As I have argued, indignation at their experience on the sugar plantation was integral to the Indian sensibility: it was encapsulated in notions of 'a new slavery' and 'bitter sugar,' and Jagan was peerlessly masterly at evoking it. But so, ironically, were the far-reaching reforms that Jock Campbell (the chairman of Booker, 1952–67) introduced in response to Cheddi's militant political crusade against 'bitter sugar,' thereby engendering a vibrant sense of possibilities. Yet the fact that Campbell did meet Jagan half way or more is scarcely appreciated; it is Cheddi's acclaimed single-handed challenge of the 'sugar gods' that pervades the Indo-Guyanese imagination – David and Goliath!

It is my contention that while Jagan trusted the presumed infallibility of his Marxist creed in winning the confidence of Africans (in the long-run), his grasp of *realpolitik* was astute in at least one fundamental respect – energising, aggregating, and retaining the pivotal loyalty of his Indo-Guyanese base. In this regard, his political acumen was finely tuned, and he was as adept a practitioner as Forbes Burnham of the politics of race. As Dr Fenton Ramsahoye observes, they were both leaders who deftly accommodated racism to enhance their political fortunes. They were racist leaders, the Marxism-Leninism of Jagan and the nebulous and eclectic brand of socialism of Burnham notwithstanding.

IV.   The Enmore Tragedy (June 1948) and Its Aftermath

Jagan recalls how his legislative responsibilities were harnessed to gain maximum political capital:

> On many vital issues some elected members supported the planters, and at times when it was too embarrassing to do so, they either abstained from voting or absented themselves. **They did not have the courage to stand up against Booker and Government House** [the Governor]. Early in my apprenticeship, therefore, it became clear to me that the struggle must be joined at the industrial [trade union] and political level outside the legislature…From 1948 the sugar workers marched under the banner of the Guiana Industrial Workers Union (GIWU) led by Dr J. P. Lachmansingh. To counter the influence of this union, the planters occasionally made concessions through their company-dominated MPCA [emphasis added].[13]

The GIWU was registered on April 5, 1948, and their early work centred on several estates on the East Coast Demerara: Ogle, Non Pareil, Lusignan, Vryheid's Lust, LBI, and Enmore. As the legislator for the constituency of Central Demerara (all these plantations were located there), Jagan quickly became deeply engaged with the GIWU. This was congruent with his resolve to eliminate the MPCA, despite his reservations regarding the non-Marxist leadership of the GIWU.

The GIWU, from its inception, sought to gain recognition from the SPA as the sole bargaining agent for both the predominantly Indian fieldworkers and the largely African factory workers. The SPA was not prepared to countenance this, as they felt obligated to the established terms of recognition of the MPCA. But, towards the end of the 1940s, the sugar workers' many grievances remained unresolved – lack of potable water ('trenches over which people bathed and washed their clothes provided drinking water'); the ranges or logies, invariably, were in a state of advanced dilapidation, an abomination; long distances to and from work, exacerbated by muddy dams and many hours in the fields; pregnant women working in water to their waist or breast, while weeding the parapets of canals; child labour on many estates; insufficient land allocated on the plantations for supplementary farming by resident workers. However, it was the replacement of the 'cut-and-drop' method of cane harvesting by the 'cut-and-load' method that the GIWU chose as the site to advance their case for recognition.

The change, introduced in 1947, transformed the character of cane-cutting. Previously, the cane cutters harvested the cane and left it in bundles *in situ*; others, the loaders, then fetched the bundles to the bank of the canal and deposited them in the punts, the flat-bottom iron tugs. Now cane cutters were required to perform both tasks at the combined pay of sixty cents per ton (forty-five cents for cutting, fifteen cents for loading). In February 1948, the MPCA held a conference where the delegates endorsed the cut-and-load method on condition that the SPA approved a hike in pay from sixty cents to $1 per ton. In mid-April, the MPCA, the SPA, and the commissioner of labour met and agreed to an increase of four cents per ton, in addition to a cost-of-living bonus from 30 to 33 per cent. This, in fact, represented an increase of seven cents per ton. The MPCA signed the agreement.

The GIWU repudiated it as yet another exemplification of the degeneration of the MPCA into a company union, and they proceeded to call a strike on April 22, 1948, to protest against adopting the cut-and-load method. Ashton Chase, a founder-member of the PAC, admitted that this issue was a ruse to advance the GIWU's pursuit of recognition against the MPCA:

> The Enmore strike was started…by cane cutters ostensibly over the system of cut-and-load as against cut-and-drop. The real object of the strike, however, was to secure recognition of the GIWU as the bargaining agent on behalf of field and factory workers in the sugar industry.[14]

Cheddi Jagan, the new legislator of the district, and his wife, Janet, were deeply involved in the strike, including the provision of strike relief. For Jagan, this was a cardinal plank of his political mission – replacing the MPCA with the GIWU, thereby controlling the largest union in the colony. This was a seminal step towards eventual control of the economy and the state in his vision of the communist society.

The *Daily Argosy* carried a leader a few days before the fatal shooting of five striking workers at Plantation Enmore. It was clearly alluding to the active engagement of the Jagans in the strike on the East Coast Demerara estates:

> It is no exaggeration to say that the situation would never have come about had a minor and ill-founded grievance not been seized upon,

> magnified and fanned into flame…Those with some knowledge
> of affairs will not have failed to notice in this affair the familiar,
> Communist-like strategy of first raising or fomenting trouble, then
> moving in as champions of the oppressed in the hope of discrediting
> the orthodox labour organisations. This need surprise no one who
> considers some of the individuals connected with or supporting this
> mushroom union [GIWU] – one, especially, who was originally
> at pains to deny his involvement, but has now come into the open
> [Cheddi Jagan].[15]

The paper was urging the workers to return to work so that the commissioner
of labour could facilitate a meeting between the SPA and the two recognised
unions (the MPCA and the British Guiana Workers' League [BGWL]) to address
their perceived grievances. If the workers no longer desired to be represented
by the recognised unions, the SPA could consider meeting with independent
persons whom the workers had approved.

But the *Argosy* was averse to any politician arrogating unto himself the role
of intermediary – another allusion to the energetic, idealistic, and charismatic
young Cheddi Jagan (just thirty years old): 'It is and must remain a principle
that labour and trade union questions are negotiated through their own media,
without political interference.'[16] This, of course, was anathema to the rationale
of Cheddi's politics: the sugar workers' cause was at the heart of his mission;
nothing could detract him from it. And he could never have acquiesced in
compartmentalising trade unionism and politics – indivisible by his Marxist *modus
operandi* for radical transformation. Militant trade unionism was the embryo of
the communist party and the workers' state – 'the dictatorship of the proletariat.'

Back to the tragedy at Enmore! When, by mid-June 1948, the strike appeared
to be flagging, the GIWU tried to engage the predominantly African factory
workers to present a broader ethnic coalition in their campaign for recognition.
This was the context in which, on June 16, several Indian fieldworkers at
Plantation Enmore (it is claimed) in attempting to contact African workers inside
the factory were shot at by the police, and five were killed. Armed policemen had
been dispatched earlier to the factory compound to protect it. When some Indian
fieldworkers crossed a canal encircling the factory and entered the compound,
apparently to persuade the African workers to join the strike, the police opened
fire. They alleged that the property and their own lives were endangered by the
strikers, supposedly armed and agitated into a state of hysteria by the GIWU,
including the Jagans. But there is no evidence to corroborate that these workers
were indeed armed. The five invading workers killed, reportedly, were frantically
trying to retreat across the canal whence they had come when they were shot in
the back by the police. What the Indian workers did was foolhardy, but the ferocity
of the response of the colonial police (Africans) seems totally unwarranted.

The funeral took place the next day, Friday, June 17, 1948. It was a very moving event as several thousand joined the funeral procession, from the East Coast Demerara plantations and villages to the Le Repentir Cemetery, outside of Georgetown to the south. The *Argosy* recorded the heart-wrenching experience thus:

> The procession, comprising men, women and children, trekked to the city on foot, bicycles, carts and motor-cars, but was prevented by armed police from entering the main sections of Georgetown, which had been proclaimed...From early morning men, women and children from Plantations Enmore, Non Pareil and villages as far as Belfield assembled at the Enmore hospital's mortuary for the funeral procession to the city. The hearse conveying the coffins of Pooran, Lalla Baggee and Rambarran [the other two died in the Georgetown Hospital] left the estate at about 8 o'clock, followed by hundreds on foot, while Hon D.P. Debidin, Dr J.P. Lachmansingh, Dr and Mrs Cheddi Jagan, Messrs C.R. Jacob, Amos Rangela, M.B. Khan, Pandit Sharma, Rev J.M. Eby and several others carrying black flags and mourning ribbons followed in motor-cars, bicycles and carts.
>
> The East Coast road was well-nigh impassable as the procession grew to huge proportions, and labourers from the various estates joined the crowd. The heat of a broiling sun took its toll. At various points along the route, sympathisers supplied water to the thirsty travellers...At 12.20 pm the procession reached the junction. Thousands strong, a milling crowd of men, women and children led by Dr Lachmansingh, Messrs Debidin, Jacob, Rangela, M.B. Khan and Jainarine Singh, and Dr and Mrs Jagan proceeded along Vlissengen Road flanked by the mounted police, to the cemetery. As the procession progressed, it grew larger as city residents joined in.
>
> With much weeping, and apparent resentment, the procession wended its way peacefully along Vlissengen Road, and at the junction with Regent Road a halt was made and prayers said, the large crowd, including labour leaders, standing with bowed heads. After a lapse of half-an-hour, the procession proceeded to the cemetery, where the interment was made. Amidst touching scenes, the victims were laid to rest side by side.[17]

The funeral of the five workers was a momentous episode in the consolidation of the anti-colonial movement in British Guiana. The perceived brutality of the police impugned the character of the colonial state while appearing to validate Jagan's indictment of it as an agent of oppression beholden to 'King Sugar.' It also reinforced the widely held assumption that the sugar interests, embodied by Booker, were an instrument of reaction resistant to change. It gave solidity and a visionary aura to Cheddi's 'bitter sugar' mission. Enmore brought sugar to the heart of the embryonic nationalist campaign. The intemperate reaction of the police was a gift to Jagan; the traumatic event became the enduring

'Enmore made us' (Janet): Cheddi addressing predominantly Indian sugar plantation workers, 1948 – the launch of his 'bitter sugar' crusade

motif of his nationalist crusade; it possessed the Indo-Guyanese imagination for the rest of his political career. Enmore encapsulated 'bitter sugar'; it would virtually neutralise whatever reservations the minority of informed Indians had of the ominous implications of his communism. The enslavement of Africans notwithstanding, sugar remained in the blood of Indians more potently because it was a living reality for Indo-Guyanese, hence more susceptible to evocative promptings. Cheddi and Janet Jagan were masterly at touching those sensitive pulses, thus provoking indignation against the 'sugar gods,' while canalising the aroused Indian rage for their wider political mission.

Enmore had given Cheddi Jagan's cause its cutting edge. And the *PAC Bulletin* readily grasped its potentiality with a compelling piece by its twenty-three-year-old activist from Buxton, Sydney King (Eusi Kwayana), evocatively captioned (as the latter has confirmed for me):

THEY ASKED FOR BREAD! THEY GAVE THEM BULLETS!

He wrote:

> The day after the shooting the three capitalist daily papers [*Daily Argosy*, *Daily Chronicle*, and *Guiana Graphic*] presented a united front, displaying a vast amount of creative genius. They claimed that the police were 'forced to shoot' in self-defence, as an 'armed mob assailed the police and attempted to destroy the factory'. None of them attempted to explain why so many were shot in the back!

King dramatised, movingly and with precision, the harrowingly painful personal strand in the tragedy:

> There was 30-year-old Lala Bagi who lay dead on the mortuary table. He was shot through the back 'assailing' the police. There was 19-year-old Pooran lying cold dead with a gaping three-inch

wound above the pelvis with his guts hanging out and another bullet through his leg. His bullet, too, came from behind. Rambarran's fists were clenched irrevocably, but there was no weapon in those dead hands. His leg had two bullet wounds. Dhookie died in the hospital the same day. Harry died the next day from a spinal injury. Lala Bagi left a young widow with three young children. Harry's unborn child will never see the father who died so gallantly. Two of the injured are not yet out of danger. Many of those in the hospital were hit from the back. Bayonets were used too. The papers say they were all attacking the police.

King's narrative of the funeral procession, from Enmore to Georgetown, captures its traumatic permeation of the public imagination:

At 8 am on June 17 a monster funeral procession left Plantation Enmore by foot taking the bodies for interment in the city, 16 miles away. As the procession got underway strikers from the seven estates along the coast swelled the crowd to more than ten thousand. Villagers along the way showed their sympathy and women came out with pails of water for the thirsty. As the procession neared Georgetown, the leaders were officially told that they could not proceed to the Public Hospital where they had hoped to take up the body of Dhookie. The police had escorted the coffin outside the city limits...At 3 pm the procession reached the cemetery. Here the human factor broke loose from its temporary prison and just stared you in the face and tore at your heart. Relatives and widows cried and wailed. Observers recall that on June 7 the Central Demerara representative [Cheddi Jagan] tabled a motion asking for the appointment of a committee to enquire into the dispute, the working and living conditions and into the profits of the proprietors.[18]

The strike continued for several weeks after the shootings on June 16, 1948. The GIWU was confident that most of the workers (Indian fieldworkers) were supporting them. It was, as noted earlier, primarily a campaign for recognition, to unseat the MPCA. On July 20 *PAC Bulletin* reported that six labour leaders were served with trespass notices for seeking to meet with workers on the striking estates. Among them was the legislator for the constituency of Central Demerara, Dr Cheddi Jagan. In effect, the two principal leaders of the GIWU, Dr J. P. Lachmansingh and Amos Rangela, were already being eclipsed by the thirty-year-old handsomely charismatic Cheddi. That he also had (to repeat) a young, attractive, and politically engaged White wife (aged twenty-seven), already identified as equally devoted to the welfare of the workers, enhanced his leadership stature immeasurably. His speeches in the Legislative Council, informed by meticulous research and a passion for justice and statistics, were framed by his radical views on the condition of the working class, premised (uniquely for that body) on Marxism-Leninism. This, of course, unfailingly evoked anti-communist venom from diverse sources: the press, the church, fellow legislators bar none, the security forces, including the security liaison officer of MI5 (based in Trinidad).

But none of this mattered to Cheddi's predominantly Indo-Guyanese supporters who saw in him another liberator, a freedom-fighter in the mould of their unimpeachable heroes, Gandhi and Jawaharlal Nehru. It was his widely acclaimed sincerity of motives that drew the bulk of the Indian population towards him. Meanwhile, Janet Jagan, as editor of the *PAC Bulletin*, skilfully undermined the credibility of the so-called Labour Party, a task rendered relatively straightforward by virtue of its void in ideological clarity, programme, or commonality of purpose; this lacuna quickly spawned a pronounced fissiparous tendency. Yet the fragile Labour Party still constituted an impediment to creating a genuine political party, based on 'scientific socialism,' to which the Jagans were committed.

Peter Simms, a British journalist who spent several months in Guyana in the mid-1960s and apparently secured unrestricted access to Cheddi and Janet, provides a rare account of the seminal political shrewdness, organisational skills, and *modus operandi* of Janet in neutralising the Labour Party as a potential rival:

> [Janet] used the *PAC Bulletin* in a most effective series of articles. Whenever a bill came up before the Legislative [Council] that could be presented as of major importance to the lives of her readers, she described its advantages and disadvantages in the clearest and strongest terms. If the issues were sometimes over-simplified, that was not, perhaps, as important as their being clear-cut. She then listed how the different members voted. She proved that Dr Jagan consistently voted for the people, while the Labour Party she showed to be hopelessly split and, by constant repetition, to appear as frightened and sycophantic followers of the ruling class.[19]

The PAC was adroit in depicting themselves as uncompromising partisans of the poor and the powerless. Peter Simms considers the Enmore shootings the watershed in the political ascendancy of Cheddi Jagan. After this tragedy the leaders of the MPCA, as well as those of the oldest Indo-Guyanese organisation, the BGEIA, were irrevocably identified with the moribund past, lacking the energy, the ideological clarity, the purity of motives, consistency of purpose and fortitude of Cheddi and Janet Jagan. In the process, the young Cheddi built a reputation as the only legislator who unfailingly challenged the Goliaths of privilege, particularly the 'sugar gods.'

In the wider society, it was a virtuoso performance by the young couple who seemed to have emerged from nowhere and, with passion, daring, diligence, and a capacious vision of possibilities driven by an iconoclastic politics, was rising inexorably. It was unreal – a kind of fiction. I repeat: the fact that Janet was White rendered the Jaganite mission surreal: subversively entrancing – the stuff of movies. Not the White lady in the great house! The White lady in the canefield!

Peter Simms observes:

> The PAC had achieved a major objective. Before Enmore, the PAC was a movement that could probably rally most of the Indian vote; it could also attract some of the progressive intellectuals of Georgetown, and hope to get the Negro vote. **After Enmore, Dr and Mrs Jagan were a power in the land. The Indian vote was solidly behind them, and they could start to plan for their party.** When Burnham came back [to British Guiana in 1949] he was to find that a national leader already existed…Janet Jagan, in a private conversation [with Simms], summed it up succinctly: **"Enmore made us"** [emphasis added].[20]

However, this was primarily an Indo-Guyanese narrative.

What Simms does not state, while Eusi Kwayana has done so repeatedly, is that although the agitation of Indo-Guyanese, on the plantations, was often passionate and at times tempestuous, it did not necessarily resonate with Africans. Enmore, therefore, embodied a robust strand in post-War Indo-Guyanese self-assertion. It belongs to the vibrant tradition of Indo-Guyanese resistance rooted in the latter third of the nineteenth century, with its master narrative of indentureship as 'new slavery'; augmented by the vigour and resonance of Cheddi's 'bitter sugar' crusade. Enmore was certainly the watershed in Indo-Guyanese political awakening – arguably the equivalent of the Amritsar massacre of April 1919 (in Punjab) to the Indian nationalist movement. Many Africans did empathise with the latter; Enmore, however, did not belong to the African Guyanese narrative within the country's inchoate, yet transparently bifurcated, nationalism. But Janet Jagan was right about Enmore and its aftermath: it gave the Jaganite political mission the necessary gravitas, along with a palpable millenarianism, which they proceeded to deploy most effectively. The momentum was with Indians when Forbes Burnham returned to British Guiana in 1949.

In his memoirs of 1966, Cheddi pondered on the profound personal impact of the Enmore shootings:

> The Enmore tragedy affected me greatly. I had personally known the young men who were killed and injured. My wife and I, Dr Lachmansingh [President of the GIWU] and the other leaders led the funeral procession…it became a tremendous protest demonstration. We left Enmore on foot and marched to the city [Georgetown] 16 miles away, taking the bodies there for burial. At the graveside the emotional outbursts of the relatives were intensely distressing, and I could not restrain my tears. There was to be no turning back. There and then I made a silent pledge – I would dedicate my entire life to the struggle of the Guyanese people against bondage and exploitation.[21]

Cheddi's politics now had a clarity of focus, almost simplistic in its certainty (this was not always made explicit) that Marxism-Leninism or 'scientific socialism' had all the answers to fundamental issues, such as race, economic organisation, wealth creation and its distribution, and the ultimate goal of the communist society devoted to peace, freedom, and the total emancipation of humankind. As he put it later, he had discovered in Marxism-Leninism 'total knowledge' of the world; its tenets were infallible; its realisation of the perfect human condition was inevitable; and this was realisable universally: 'proletarian internationalism.' For him, Marxism-Leninism was virtually religious in its inviolability and scientific in its infallibility. He was, as he saw it, in possession of the perfect formula for radical transformation. The fundamental problem of poverty and exploitation in British Guiana was epitomised by 'bitter sugar,' which gave him assiduity in assailing chronic injustices on the plantations. Shortly after the Enmore shootings, in an article titled 'Bitter Sugar,' the PAC was demanding government intervention to 'secure for the [sugar] workers...their civil liberties and the pursuit of happiness.'[22]

There could be no compromise, no middle road, definitely no *modus vivendi* with the 'sugar gods.' Jagan's visceral hatred of Booker and the smaller British sugar companies, allied with a compulsion that the trust and political allegiance of the predominantly Indian fieldworkers justified his becoming their principal political and trade union leader (the two roles were inseparable – not conflictual in his politics), constituted the fulcrum of his political mission. However, Jagan's conviction was animated not simply by the Indian ethnicity of most of these workers but, even more trenchantly, by what he considered a basic postulate of his Marxist creed – the ultimate ownership of the sugar plantations by the communist state: the state of all the working people. This would prove fatal for him and his country as he, virtually unique for the British West Indies, entered the Cold War, from the beginning, on the side of the Soviet Union and, later, in favour of Castro's Cuba as well.

Yet his 'bitter sugar' narrative did have its heroic phase, his early years in the Legislative Council, between 1948 and 1953, in the aftermath of Enmore (as Moses Bhagwan observes). Jagan had warmed to his self-imposed role as the quintessential gadfly – a provocative presence, indeed!

> I soon learned to play the game in the same determined way that F.J. Seaford did his job for Booker and sugar – sweetly and suavely with a smile...It was my task to find out how in a multitude of ways, covertly and overtly, the sugar 'gods' ruled. Mine was the role of 'politics of protest,' with the weapons of exposure and struggle. If the legislature was my forum, the waterfront, the factories, the plantations, mines and quarries were my battleground. I brought a new dimension to the politics of protest. A continuity between the legislature and the street-corner; the legislature was brought to the 'streets' and the 'streets' to the legislature...[the latter] at last became part and parcel of the struggle of the people.[23]

Ashton Chase (1926–), one of the four founder-members of the PAC, recalls Jagan's spirited participation in the Legislative Council (in his early thirties), between 1948 and 1953, as an irrepressibly militant voice in the wilderness. It was sustained by a genuine resolve to alleviate working-class grievances, buttressed by his unflagging Marxist beliefs. Chase enables us to feel the zeal, the passion of Jagan's iconoclastic political engagement. One could even conceive of him single-handedly transcending the stubborn racial susceptibilities of British Guiana by his unconquerable will: the power of his convictions 'replacing' race consciousness with a unified working-class identity. His amazing bravura, pitting himself against the high and mighty of colonial Guyana, was truly epic:

> The solemnity of the Legislative Council was rudely shaken by his vigorous advocacy of the cause of workers. He had a passion for statistics. He used these in his pungent and forceful arguments to expose reaction and to lay bare before the workers the vicious system that exploited them. At sitting after sitting, he assaulted the vaunted privileges of the capitalists. On many occasions single-handedly, but nevertheless most heroically and inspiringly, he fought for the workers' rights.[24]

Cheddi recalled the rigour and relentless focus he brought to the debates in the Legislative Council:

> At 29, I was the youngest member of the Council which included some of the most prominent personalities of the time. I entered my legislative work with great seriousness and a singleness of purpose. I devoted all my time and energy to my new task. Literally, almost anything – reports, documents, Hansards – I could lay my hands on, I read, and I buttonholed anyone who could throw light on any question…My service in the Legislative Council from 1947 to 1953 was a most rewarding and stimulating experience. I looked forward to the debates.[25]

Cheddi took his youthful energy and his hard-earned knowledge, garnered from extensive reading (notably the Marxist literature that he imported and distributed in the colony, as well as a range of official documents), to his legislative work, while continuing his dental practice (at 199 Charlotte Street, Lacytown, Georgetown) virtually full-time. His dental assistant was Janet. It was an extraordinary (still almost ungraspable) example of devotion to the political vocation – driven by a consuming cause – hitherto unexampled in British Guiana, the British West Indies as a whole. I have described Cheddi and Janet as being possessed by a kind of religious passion, but it was a secular religion based on Marxism-Leninism.

After the shootings at Enmore the strike on the plantations of East Coast Demerara was sustained for several months, with the plantocracy becoming more obdurate in resisting the GIWU's campaign for recognition. But Jagan's political mission was already elevating him way beyond the confines of his Central Demerara constituency; it was expanding into several rural districts, indicative of his goal of recognition on a broader political canvas. On August 26, 1948, at Grove, East Bank Demerara, Cheddi reportedly remarked that there were two kings in the colony, King George and King Sugar, and that the governor, Sir Charles Woolley, was beholden to King Sugar. Cheddi would have concurred with Dr Lachmansingh (president of the GIWU), who spoke next. The latter asserted that the strike would continue until they (presumably the union) were able to run the estates themselves. It was a most irresponsible and inflammatory intervention by the president that probably did nothing for the workers' cause, in the short-run or the longer-term:

> We are to strike and make as much trouble as possible until we get what we want...We are out to destroy the sugar industry either by giving each worker 5 acres of land; the worker plants the canes and sells to them, or ask Government to scrap the sugar estates and give us as land settlements. And we will grow rice and get good prices for our rice.[26]

Such was the immature rhetoric of the leadership of the GIWU!

The Jaganite vocabulary adumbrated inevitable collision with the 'sugar gods.' Sugar was a red rag to this usually charming man, who could become intemperate in a flash, whenever Booker or any matter pertaining to the sugar plantations was broached. On August 29, 1948, Cheddi told sugar workers at Good Intent, West Coast Demerara, that strikes were going to be the weapon for winning their rights, and that the next strike would last one year. He did not say how poor striking workers would survive for a whole year. He emphasised:

> **We have to hit the sugar producers one after the other; we are going to cripple the bitches. They say sugar does not pay; well, why the hell keep planting it – divide the land and give the people to plant their own canes and the mills will be owned by them or the Government** [emphasis added].[27]

As early as 1948, Jagan's Marxist faith made him visualise the future of the sugar industry solely in terms of its nationalisation – the vanquishing of the 'sugar gods.' Yet Jock Campbell, the young, liberal deputy-chairman of Booker, did believe genuinely that by pursuing a culture of reforms on the plantations the long, dark history of sugar could be redeemed substantially (though never erased), to the advantage of Guyana and its plantation workers. Campbell (aged forty) became chairman in 1952, and on two occasions (as I am inclined to repeat), in 1958 and in 1960, he even broached with Jagan the possibility that Booker and the government could forge a partnership as joint owners of the industry. But Cheddi was averse to any compromise with the 'sugar barons.'

This recalcitrance reached his Indo-Guyanese followers as a heroic attribute, rendering him a veritable Nehru – imbued with a similar nobility of purpose that had brought freedom (*swaraj*) to Mother India.

Yet Jagan's ideological inflexibility (while stemming from a sincerity of motives) would contribute significantly to his country's degeneration into racial strife, dictatorship, and poverty (under Burnham); and the continuous flight of its people, for over six decades, (ironically) to the northern heartlands of capitalism. Cheddi was a charming and incorruptible man. But he lacked nimbleness of mind, subtlety of perception and judgment; in fact, he did not possess the intellectual rigour and imagination to go beyond his mission as an intrepid and inveterate crusader. He was not an able politician, endowed with the cardinal attributes of statesmanship. In a biographical sketch of 1961, when Jagan was premier of British Guiana, it was noted that an American journalist had asked him if he desired to be like Nkrumah or Nehru. He replied: 'I always wanted to be a research scientist, but I am stuck with this, and I'll do the best I can.' His voluminous political writings, over a period of fifty years, probably had their source in his initial interest in becoming a 'research scientist.' The 'laws' of the development of society, provided by Marxism, satisfied his craving for mastery of the 'scientific.'[28]

It was a measure of the growing confidence of Jagan and the PAC, after Enmore, that they could assess themselves in the manner they did, in November 1948, on their second anniversary. It suggests their conception of self as being at the heart of a new awakening, and, by implication, the authentic recipient of the Enmore legacy: 'November 1946 saw the birth of British Guiana's foremost labour publication, the *PAC Bulletin*. There is no doubt that since that date, the PAC has stood in the vanguard of labour and has always guided workers along progressive lines. During this period...the publicity given us by the three daily newspapers [*Daily Chronicle*, *Daily Argosy* and *Guiana Graphic*] has resulted in our circulation jumping tremendously.'[29]

V. The Venn Commission Report (1949): Blueprint for Jock Campbell's Reforms on the Sugar Plantations

On July 20, 1948 (shortly after Enmore), the PAC expressed their eagerness for the Colonial Office to appoint a commission of enquiry to undertake a comprehensive study of the sugar industry. They put forward the following terms of reference: 'to enquire into and report on the organisation of the sugar industry, including means of production, profits and their distribution, and wages and condition of work.' Meanwhile, the PAC also suggested that pending the appointment of the commission the workers could return to work on mutually accepted terms, a primary one being that employers be made to recognise the union enjoying the majority of members [i.e. replacing the MPCA with the GIWU].[30]

They were claiming, unequivocally, that the GIWU was the authentic union of the sugar workers – the real bone of contention in the first place.

A week later, on July 27, 1948, the secretary of state for the colonies announced the appointment of a Commission of Inquiry into the sugar industry of British Guiana. Its terms of reference were virtually a carbon copy of what the PAC had suggested, a clear indication that even the Colonial Office had to accommodate the reality of the rising political stature of Cheddi and Janet Jagan among the Indian sugar workers in the colony: 'To enquire into and report on the organisation of the Sugar Industry in British Guiana, with particular reference to means of production, wages and working conditions and any other relevant matters, and to make recommendation.' There was, however, a notable divergence between the latter and that by the PAC: no reference to 'profits and their distribution.' The members of the commission were announced in October 1948: the chairman was Professor J. A. Venn, president of Queen's College, Cambridge and Gilbey (University), lecturer in the History and Economics of Agriculture, along with R. Sudell, agricultural journalist, and B. G. Smallman of the Colonial Office, as secretary.

The Venn Commission conducted its investigation in the colony from December 15, 1948 to February 19, 1949. The hearings were held *in camera*: 192 witnesses were examined in Georgetown and New Amsterdam. Many of these were workers, including several women; over three hundred thousand words of oral evidence were taken. Besides twenty memoranda were submitted by organisations and private individuals. The Commission inspected the main plantations to assess conditions in field, factories, hospitals, and the homes of workers on the estates. Dr Cheddi Jagan (the legislator for Central Demerara) appeared before the Commission, as did F. J. Seaford, the head of Booker in the colony and a nominated member of the legislature, as well as the SPA, the MPCA, the GIWU, and the BGEIA.

In his memorandum to the Venn Commission, Jagan recommended the breaking up of the sugar plantations into smaller holdings of twenty-five acres, each to be reallocated to small farmers, with the government assuming responsibility for drainage and irrigation and the disbursement of machinery. In the following exchange with R. Sudell (on January 14, 1949), he defended his argument for the dismantling of the plantation structure of the local sugar industry:

Jagan: The estates should be divided, and the small people have their own land, say 25 acres or so. If mechanisation comes, the people should be able to work on a bigger scale...The same mechanisation which is going to be used for the estate, should be taken over under Government's supervision and utilised to mechanise the smaller units. It must be under Government's supervision because if you leave the small farmers to themselves, they would not be any better off...

Sudell: I see your point Dr Jagan, although I cannot say I agree with it. I do not think it would be a wise policy to break up these large units into small-scale units. We have been on several estates, and we have seen much progress made along the lines of mechanisation, and I cannot see how it would be good to break them up.

Jagan: Take a small family having 25 acres, they will not be producing on their own, but they will be working according to a set plan under the supervision of government. I do not see how the efficiency of the industry will be impaired. It is being tried out in Puerto Rico and is working successfully there...I would like to refer to the absenteeism [of the sugar planters]...it is tied up with this point of dividing up the land. Very many people will be able to improve themselves, and more money will be left in the colony. Most of the capital is sent out of the colony at the present.

Venn: I do not think you should go beyond saying 'presumably sent out of the colony.'

Jagan: Well, sir, that must be investigated by you.[31]

The Venn Commission Report advocated far-reaching reforms that would soon transform life on the plantations because Jock Campbell, the chairman of Booker from 1952, was committed to pursuing a culture of reform. And he had written to R. R. Follett-Smith, the managing director of Booker in British Guiana, stressing the centrality of the report to that process:

> My personal reaction to it is that it is an absorbingly brilliant analysis of the British Guiana sugar industry and its environment. It seems to me to be a much better diagnosis and statement of the Industry than any other I have read...It is dispassionate and passes no moral judgement.[32]

Campbell observed that the Report was 'of far more value' than they were anticipating; and he advised that Booker should make 'the fullest use of it.' It was adopted as the blueprint for his wide-ranging reforms on the plantations, soon after he had played a significant role in negotiating the Commonwealth Sugar

Agreement of 1951, with higher prices and guaranteed quotas for sugar in the UK market: key to funding his programme of reforms. He underlined the utility of the Venn Report:

(1) [We must use] it as terms of reference for further action, improvement and development. I think that the three senior people on every sugar estate should have a copy of the Venn Report and study it.

(2) [We must use] it as the platform or base for establishing a new and better relationship between the industry and its environment, Government, Labour and 'the man in the street.'[33]

However, the bedevilling reality of Cheddi Jagan's irreconcilable Marxist stance with respect to Jock Campbell's culture of reforms, and its catastrophic consequences for Jagan and Guyana, were probably expressed most comprehensively by Peter Simms (the British journalist) in his book of 1966. The following extensive quote gets to the bottom of the dilemma for both Cheddi Jagan and Jock Campbell. I do not think it possible to improve on Simms's analysis:

Even in 1953 the long coastal strip where most of the wealth and the population lay was nothing more than a tropical Gorbals, an enormous slum from which the underprivileged – whether Indian, Negro, Chinese or Portuguese – could look across at the seemingly impregnable positions of the British and a carefully selected few Guyanese. Only in these terms can one understand the post-war swing to the left by both the intelligentsia and the worker, and only thus can one see why even people who are now his political opponents, say that modern Guyana must be divided into two periods: the pre-Jagan and the post-Jagan eras.

It was Jagan who showed that the positions were no longer impregnable; [and] who so put the fear of God into the directors of Booker that they appointed as their Chairman [in 1952] a young and junior member of the Board, Jock Campbell (now Sir Jock) [aged 40], a [Fabian] socialist whom they hoped would save something out of the cataclysm.

He was to do more than that. He completely changed the outlook of the company and the condition of the people on the estates. But once change has set in, not even the most radical innovation can catch up with people's wants; nor did Dr Jagan, riding the crest of the discontent he had aroused, ever feel that he could for more than a moment let it appear that real progress was being made. He could discuss co-operation between his government and Booker, but he could not let it be seen that together they were implementing a joint policy. For Dr Jagan the dichotomy of the past was the strength of the present, and he gambled on the hope that it would continue to be so in the future.

What Dr Jagan's policy finally brought was a state verging on civil war where all issues were reduced to race: the Indian against the Negro, with the other races throwing in their weight as they thought their best interests lay. Dr Jagan had forgotten that while he spoke in terms of class warfare, the people themselves were thinking of what they knew of the past and were wondering what each development meant for their future. In this the Indian and the Negro had different viewpoints.[34]

There was ample political space for Jagan to reach a *modus vivendi* with the reform programme of Jock Campbell, if he so desired, while retaining the support of his political base. It made social and economic sense for the latter's advancement; besides, it would have enhanced his stature as a statesman immeasurably among the principal actors in his political future: the Americans, the British and the West Indian leaders. There was also room for the Jagan government, between 1958 and 1960, to embrace joint ownership of the sugar industry with Booker, as Campbell had twice proposed to Jagan. But this would have contravened Jagan's communist creed: to sup with the 'sugar gods' was a profanity too far. In fact, nationalising the sugar industry was at the core of his political mission, and his control of the union in the sugar industry was a major prerequisite towards that end. It was a fatal error that would take Guyana on the road to self-destruction, and the country has not recovered from it since.

For Jock Campbell and Booker, it was a journey to nowhere because when the Indian sugar workers started to benefit from the reforms on the plantations, by the mid-1950s, not only did they attribute it solely to the militancy, on their behalf, of Cheddi Jagan, but they also conceded no credit whatsoever to Campbell or Booker. They were convinced that such improvement, as Jagan preached to them incessantly, was the tip of the iceberg: much more was owed to them, but it was routinely stolen by the 'absentee sugar gods' – their 'surplus value' – the true measure of their rate of exploitation. Indians, on and off the plantations, were under the spell of Jagan's mantra that 'the commanding heights of the economy' must be nationalised. Therefore, Campbell's reforms, paradoxically, advanced Jagan's political fortunes among Indians indelibly. This was a consequence of improving conditions on the plantations and optimism for better times, not starvation and despair – certainly not a static 'bitter sugar' milieu.

Eric Hoffer identifies the latter as a fact of the universal human condition, and one can apprehend its applicability to the 'bitter sugar' mantra of Cheddi and the futility of Jock's reforms on the plantations of British Guiana:

> Misery does not automatically generate discontent, nor is the intensity of discontent directly proportionate to the degree of misery. Discontent is likely to be highest when misery is bearable; when conditions have so improved that an ideal state seems almost within reach...In both France and Russia the land-hungry peasants owned

> almost exactly one-third of the agricultural land at the outbreak of the revolution, and most of that land was acquired during the generation or two preceding the revolution. It is not actual suffering but the taste of better things which excites people to revolt.[35]

Sydney King observed that most Africans, by the 1950s, could not identify with the 'bitter sugar' narrative and the impassioned anti-Booker Jaganite crusade. It was irrelevant to the source of their enduring ethnic insecurity, magnified by the granting of adult suffrage. In addition, Africans could not, as King was pointing out from the early 1950s, be reconciled to an Indian leader; so too Indians to an African leader (Forbes Burnham). When King left the PPP in late 1956, he was unperturbed by Jagan's communism, but he was implacably revolted by what he considered the racial trajectory of his politics: its blatant pro-Indian essence. The irreconcilability of Jagan and King – more than the Jagan-Burnham split in 1955 – attested to the inherent limitation of the Jaganite mission. This specific rupture unveiled its futility in the political evolution of Guyana: its incapacity, ever, to conciliate African insecurities while claiming to engage them in his nationalist agenda for independence, as equals. A Guyanese national identity remains elusive, as every 'nationalist' endeavour is inexorably undermined by the aggregating of discrete ethnic sentiments.

So even the Enmore tragedy of June 1948, suffused with historical plantation resonance which clearly catapulted Cheddi Jagan to political acclaim, remains behind an Indo-Guyanese *cordon sanitaire*, as David de Caires and Miles Fitzpatrick argue:

> Enmore was an experience felt on two levels, the political or economic or cultural. It was also, however, a traumatic shock that was experienced by the entire Indian community at the time...**Indian sugar workers were shot by African policemen, and those who wanted to make the most of it did so** [emphasis added].

> Enmore was saved from this level of debate largely through the effort of the PAC, and subsequently the PPP. Historically it has become a prime example of the oppression of the [Indian] sugar workers, and the PPP has always commemorated it in this light. With the break-up of the united party, however, our national memory has once more become sectionalised, and Enmore is hardly remembered, even on the most formal level, by the urban masses [African]. It has been reduced, in the minds of the Guyanese people, to a racial episode, mourned by one section of a shattered movement (PPP/[Indian]) and forgotten by the other (PNC/[African]).[36]

Guyanese history is littered with signposts that, rather than aggregating national consciousness, provoke responses of 'otherness' through non-identification, thus rendering them triggers for sectional identity – for segmental difference rather than a stimulus for a wider cohesion. This, perhaps, could explain the escape into absurdity of Guyanese politics of the late 1970s, when the three main political parties were all contesting for the mantle of being authentically Marxist-Leninist. On June 16, 1977, on the twenty-nineth anniversary of the Enmore shootings, Burnham's government was seeking to acquire something of its symbolic power. They created a monument to the memory of the five martyrs of Enmore. Cheddi Jagan was one of the invitees to the event and was scheduled to deliver an address. However, it was so obvious that the organisers were tendentiously appropriating Enmore's legacy to enhance the PNC's 'paramountcy' over the government, that Jagan walked out without giving his talk. This was delivered elsewhere, but he was still extolling Enmore as a seminal force in, and an enduring inspiration to, his political mission. As Janet said: 'Enmore made us.'

Notes

1. *PAC Bulletin*, no. 30, September 26, 1948.
2. *PAC Bulletin*, no. 32, November 22, 1948.
3. *PAC Bulletin*, no. 30, September 26, 1948.
4. *PAC Bulletin*, no. 28, July 20, 1948.
5. Ibid.
6. Ibid.
7. *PAC Bulletin*, no. 29, August 22, 1948.
8. *PAC Bulletin*, no. 30, September 26, 1948.
9. Cheddi Jagan, *Tracing our Path in a Changing World* (PPP Pamphlet), 1990, 23, 14.
10. Cheddi Jagan, *The West on Trial: My Fight for Guyana's Freedom* (London: Michael Joseph, 1966), 88.
11. *PAC Bulletin*, no. 21, January 14, 1948.
12. Ibid.
13. Jagan, *The West on Trial: My Fight for Guyana's Freedom*, 116.
14. Ashton Chase, *A History of Trade Unionism in Guyana, 1900–64* (Ruimveldt, Guyana: New Guyana Co. Ltd., n.d.), 112–13.
15. Leader, *Daily Argosy*, June 13, 1948.
16. Ibid.
17. *Daily Argosy*, June 17, 1948.
18. *PAC Bulletin*, no. 27, June 20, 1948.
19. Peter Simms, *Trouble in Guyana: An Account of People, Personalities and Politics As They Were in British Guiana* (London: George Allen and Unwin, 1966), 85.
20. Ibid., 94.
21. Jagan, *The West on Trial: My Fight for Guyana's Freedom*, 109.
22. *PAC Bulletin*, no. 28, July 20, 1948.
23. Jagan, *The West on Trial: My Fight for Guyana's Freedom*, 95.
24. Ashton Chase, *A History of Trade Unionism in Guyana, 1900–64*, 126.
25. Simms, *Trouble in Guyana*.
26. CO111/797/60270/5/5 [1948], 'Report of a GIWU Meeting held at Grove, East Bank Demerara, August 26, 1948.'
27. Ibid.
28. *Dr the Hon Cheddi Jagan, Premier of British Guiana: A Biographical Sketch* (A Government of British Guiana Publication, 1961), 10.

29. *PAC Bulletin*, no. 32, November 22, 1948.

30. *PAC Bulletin*, no. 28, July 20, 1948.

31. CO946/1, Evidence of Dr Cheddi Jagan (to the Venn Commission), January 14, 1949.

32. CO111/813/10, J.M. Campbell to J. A. Venn, December 28, 1949, personal (excerpts from letters by Campbell to R.R. Follett-Smith, Georgetown, reproduced in this correspondence).

33. Ibid.

34. Simms, *Trouble in Guyana*, 64–65.

35. Eric Hoffer, *The True Believer: Thoughts on the Nature of Mass Movements* (New York: Harper-Perennial Modern Classics, 2002 [1951]), 28–29.

36. David de Caires and Miles Fitzpatrick, 'Twenty Years of Politics in our Land,' in *On the Canvas of the World*, ed. George Lamming (Port of Spain: The Trinidad and Tobago Institute of the West Indies, 1999), 59. This article was first published in 1966 in the Guyana Independence Issue of *New World Quarterly* (edited by Martin Carter and George Lamming).

7.

Jagan's Marxist Vision in the Context of the Cold War – I
With Special Reference to the Suspension of the Constitution, 1950-54

Guyana has always been a land of fantasy. It was the land of El Dorado....

– V. S. Naipaul (1991)

The balance of power in the executive committee of the PPP is with the communists.

– Cheddi Jagan (1951)

However much we must regret suspension of any constitution, we should deplore far more the continuance of a Government that put Communist ideology before the good of the people.

– Grantley Adams (Barbados), quoted by secretary of state for the Colonies (Oliver Lyttleton), House of Commons, October 22, 1953

I. Courting Communist Allies in the 'People's Democracies': Jagan Visits East Germany and Czechoslovakia, 1951

In Guyana the sugar plantation was readily evocative of enduring hurts, but it was substantially more pronounced among Indians because memories of indentureship were fresh, and many of them still lived in the old slave-quarters, the 'nigger yard' (the common evocative designation), in 'logies,' or derelict ranges on sugar estates. In 1939 and 1948, at Plantations Leonora and Enmore respectively, Indian workers were gunned down by the colonial police, another manifestation of what had become a common feature in the Indian tradition of resistance.[1] The founding, in 1937, of the first trade union by an Indo-Guyanese, Ayube Edun, had begun to politicise Indian sugar plantation workers at the end of the 1930s. The intransigence of the plantocracy, which strangled embryonic unionism, had kindled Indian sugar workers' wrath. The shootings in 1939 at Plantation Leonora, while the Moyne Commission was in Georgetown investigating chronic social and economic deprivation in the British West Indies, precipitated the recognition of Edun's union, the Manpower Citizens' Association (MPCA) by the Sugar Producers' Association (SPA). Armed with its organ, *The Guiana Review*, Edun pursued a radical critique of colonial society generally, and the plantation in particular. In his book of 1935, *London's Heart-Probe and Britain's Destiny*, Edun advocated transforming the British Empire by creating a Rational-Practical-Ideal state, the 'inviolable controller' of production and distribution that would 'mobilise the citizens' to cater for 'each citizen's equal needs.' This ideal state would also assume sole responsibility for the education of children, virtually taking the place of parents. Permeating Edun's philosophy of reform was a utopian strand that would soon be advanced even more lavishly and indefatigably through the Marxist-Leninist beliefs of Cheddi Jagan, the principal beneficiary of Edun's seminal work on the sugar plantations.[2] Jagan was a communist.

In August–September 1951, Jagan spent nearly five weeks in East Germany (GDR) as a guest of several communist organisations, including the Berlin Youth Festival Committee and the Free German Democratic Trade Unions. He then travelled to Czechoslovakia where, on September 13, 1951, he wrote to the International Department of the Czechoslovak Communist Party, soliciting help to procure the machinery for a printing press for his People's Progressive Party (PPP), in addition to a stipend of about £80 pounds per month which

> could be rendered in the form of newsprint, books, pamphlets, and other communist literature printed in English. The sale of these would provide the funds for our Party and, at the same time, popularise what is taking place in the People's Democracies [the Soviet satellites in Eastern Europe], China and the Soviet Union. Films will also be of great help.

To enhance his case for support from the Czechoslovak communists, Jagan established his impeccable communist credentials and his empathy with the Soviet bloc in the Cold War. He stressed that his PPP had to continually counter the pro-Western loyalty of most of the politicians in the region, in conjunction with the virulent anti-communist press in British Guiana: three dailies that were

> continuously attacking the People's Democracies, China and the USSR. They consistently oppose our Party, and try to discredit us by calling us 'communist' because of *Thunder's* [the monthly organ of the PPP] support of the People's Democracies, the Soviet Union and China against the Anglo-American bloc; and also because of the sale by us of communist literature, such as British Communist Party pamphlets, Lawrence and Wishart books [affiliated to the

Communist Party of Great Britain (CPGB)], Soviet Union foreign languages publications (*New Times, Soviet Weekly, Daily Worker* [organ of the CPGB], *WFTU Bulletin*, etc, obtained from Central Books in London [also linked to the CPGB].[3]

Jagan traced the pursuit of his communist mission to his entry into local politics (in 1946), a project, he observed, that was being promoted and extended by the PPP, the paucity of funds notwithstanding:

> The PPP was started in January 1950. It grew out of the Political Affairs Committee, a small Marxist group, which was organised some four years before [in November 1946], with a small circulation of a monthly mimeographed bulletin [*PAC Bulletin*: 43 issues between November 1946 and December 1949]. The political organ of the Party is a monthly called *Thunder*. Membership [of the PPP] is now about 4,000 out of a population of about 400,000, but potential following is much greater than the present membership. It is the most militant and presently the strongest party. Weakness is on the organisational side. Because of lack of funds, there is no rented office, no paid secretarial staff or salaried officials. All work is voluntary. The Party has its official address at my dental surgery [199 Charlotte Street, Georgetown, British Guiana], which is also used as a bookshop. **The balance of power in the executive committee of the Party is with the communist**s [emphasis added].

> The secretary of the Party and editor of *Thunder* is my wife, Janet Jagan, who is also…secretary of the Women's Political and Economic Organisation (WPEO) and a member of the Georgetown (capital city) Town Council [elected in 1950]. *Thunder* was named after Willie Gallacher's 'Rolling of the Thunder.' [Gallacher (1881–1965) was a Scottish communist MP elected to the House of Commons in 1935; he did not write the poem, 'The March of the Workers,' in which the line appears; it was by William Morris (1834–96).] It started out in January 1950 with 2,000 copies; it now has a circulation of 12,000 copies per month. It is printed on a small, antiquated foot-operated treadle platen press. Other printers would not undertake the printing. Typesetting is done by hand, taking about two weeks to put out one issue of the paper. We can sell about 10,000 copies of a tabloid size weekly with a good press and staff.[4]

I do not know if Jagan did procure any financial assistance from the Czechoslovak Communist Party; if, indeed, he got a reply. But it is noteworthy that he suggested if they required a testimonial of him or the PPP, they should communicate with the Communist Party of Great Britain (CPGB) in London, and that they could do likewise if they wished to forward any confidential information to him. Jagan gave the CPGB as the intermediary because his principal ideological mentor and confidante was the Jamaican-born communist, Billy Strachan (1921–98), secretary of the Caribbean Labour Congress (London Branch) and the leading light in the West Indian section of the CPGB.[5] Billy would remain possibly Cheddi's closest friend and mentor for over four decades – arguably the person, Janet Jagan apart, in whom he confided most. He was essentially a disciple of Billy, harbouring implicit faith in his theoretical and political acumen, as documented in the MI5 files of the 1950s (see chapter 10).

II. The Ideological and Racial Origins of the Jagan-Burnham Rivalry in the Embryonic PPP

The contours of Guyanese politics were already discernible after India's freedom from British rule in 1947: race was becoming pre-eminent. Indians were in the ascendancy in British Guiana, but the colony's journey to independence was fraught with imponderables, of which conciliating ethnic susceptibilities and engendering a coherent Guyanese nationalism, in this ethnically diverse colony of limited resources, were the most daunting. However, the peoples of Guyana, with rare exceptions, have been unable to contemplate their ethnic prejudices – their racism – which could not be submerged for long. It was not enough to hate the British.

The definition of indentureship as 'new slavery' and the sugar planters or 'sugar gods' as ineluctably exploitative, bred a messianic craving for deliverance among Indo-Guyanese: the root whence sprang their communist leader, Cheddi Jagan. But this conception of 'bitter sugar' (as Jagan termed it) excited no such strident emotions from African Guyanese, most of whom had left the

Forbes Burnham and his sister Jessie, 1953. She was one of three women elected to the legislature; the others were Janet Jagan (1920–2009) and Jane Phillips-Gay (1913–94)

plantations and sought employment there strategically, for short periods, after the end of slavery. Moreover, the perceived ascendancy of Indians and fear of their potential economic and political dominance by the late 1940s, had tempered even the anti-colonial instincts of Africans. As Eusi Kwayana (formerly Sydney King), a comrade of Jagan from his early political campaigns in the late 1940s, recalls:

> I lived among very poor African people all of my life…They were very political…But I know also that they did not have strong feelings against colonialism – they had no strong feelings against colonialism – or against Booker because of their monopoly [of the sugar plantations] or their treatment of people. **The whole idea of rejecting the British was not very firm among Africans. Indians had it a lot firmer because of the Indian nationalist movement** [and the inspiration of Gandhi and Nehru].[6]

It is arguable, therefore, that Jagan's long-term political failure stemmed significantly from the intractability of the racial identity problem between Africans and Indians in Guyana and his personal incapacity to contemplate or comprehend African insecurities. On the eve of the first general elections under universal adult suffrage, in April 1953, the PPP, led then by Cheddi Jagan, an Indian dentist, and Forbes Burnham, an African lawyer with formidable oratorical gifts – certain of his intellectual sagacity over his co-leader – was really a loose coalition between the two major ethnic groups. This was the reason why Sydney King (Eusi Kwayana), supported by Martin Carter, the poet, had moved in the executive of the party that they should contest only eight seats. If they fielded candidates in all the constituencies, Kwayana argued, they would win the elections and therefore have to precipitately face the trauma of being in government. He did not believe that the PPP was ready for office because 'it was a kind of coalition…[some] racial unity was there but it was not well-grounded; it was tenuous.' He adds:

> I told Jagan and Burnham we would win the elections. They didn't believe me. They thought we would win about 8 seats [out of 24]. I moved a motion that we fight about 8 seats and try to do, in a multiple of eight, what Jagan had done alone [since 1947, in the legislature and in his constituency of Central Demerara], and really try to unite the country.[7]

Kwayana's fears were realised immediately – the PPP won eighteen of the twenty-four seats. As soon as the party's supposed victory was declared, Burnham challenged Jagan for sole leadership of it. The rivalry was there from the beginning. The legally brilliant and politically shrewd mind of Burnham could not be reconciled to being second to anyone, particularly Jagan whom he considered his intellectual inferior. As a non-communist (though nebulously socialist), Burnham was perceived as the leader of the right-wing of the PPP, ready to utilise that base to advance his case for leadership of the party away from its communist susceptibility.

It is revealing, therefore, that even before the general elections of April 1953, Janet Jagan was confiding in her communist guru, Billy Strachan in London, that she feared for the unity of the PPP. Sydney King was visiting the communist bloc as a guest of fraternal communist parties, and his prolonged absence seemed to have emboldened the Burnhamite right wing, as Janet remarked:

> We are terribly concerned here about Sydney [King]. No one has heard from him since the first week of January [1953], when a couple of postcards arrived from Hungary. His mother is frantic. The whole thing is ridiculous, and we are unable to understand what is happening…The right wing is becoming more powerful, especially with Sydney away. Give Sydney a good talking to, as the one you warned us about [Burnham] is already showing a few horns. At any rate, you can say 'I told you so.'[8]

Clearly, Billy Strachan must have expressed reservations to the Jagans regarding the political motives of Burnham, although it was Billy who had originally recommended Burnham to them. He was also instrumental in Burnham visiting Jamaica (in 1949 on his way back to British Guiana from his studies in England) to consult with people like Richard Hart on the organisational structure of Norman Manley's People's National Party (PNP). Hart recalls his initial encounter with Burnham and the context in which Burnham joined Jagan in founding the PPP in January 1950 (Burnham was only twenty-six at the time; Jagan was thirty-one):

> In 1949 we [Billy Strachan, prompted by Dick Hart] had formed the London Branch of the [Marxist] Caribbean Labour Congress (CLC)…It was soon after that that Billy wrote telling me about Burnham…an outstanding law student who was about to return to Guyana…It was the CLC in London who arranged for Burnham to come to Jamaica…
>
> [Burnham] had family connections with Dr Claude Denbow, leader of the League of Coloured Peoples (LCP) [in Georgetown]. When he arrived home from England, the LCP welcomed him first, and for about two or three months they thought that he was going to join them. He took part in the launching of the PPP [on Sunday, January 1, 1950], but I have no knowledge of any promise of leadership of the party offered to him at that time.
>
> **I do remember an early letter from Janet complaining about this protégé of mine – Burnham. She said that he came to meetings late, sat on the floor and was very flippant; and at 10 o'clock he used to say 'Well, I got to go. I got a date.' He would also not go out of Georgetown for meetings** [emphasis added].[9]

Burnham, as Ashton Chase observes, was incapable of being second to anyone. It was, from the inception, a discernibly tenuous relationship between Jagan and Burnham. The likelihood of an irreparable rupture in the PPP, between Cheddi Jagan and Forbes Burnham, was corroborated soon after the general elections of April 1953 by a PPP legislator, Fred Bowman, an African of working-class background. He, too, was confiding in Billy Strachan, the intermediary for possibly forty years between Jagan's PPP and the CPGB, as well as with communist parties in the Eastern bloc:

> No sooner than the jubilation [over the PPP's victory] was finished and the time for electing the ministers came, a brand-new trouble started. Burnham with his right-wing clique demanded that he be given the leadership of the Party in the House of Assembly, despite the fact that Cheddi was recently elected to that [post] by the Congress [of the PPP]. His [Burnham's] ultimatum was leadership or no ministry, and with him were his faithful disciples [Ashton] Chase and [Frank] Van Sertima and their followers.
>
> **The fact is that the Party is divided into two camps: the minority led by Burnham and the majority by Cheddi; and a split is likely to occur anytime** [emphasis added].
>
> Failing to achieve their aims, after resorting to some Hitlerite mob-tactics, they [the Burnhamites] are feverishly organising groups in [George]town, and at the same time demanding a special Congress with the hope of capturing control of the Executive, but we [the Jaganites] are standing firmly, observing only the principles by which we are guided and the rules of the Party Constitution.[10]

It is hardly surprising, therefore, that after just 133 days in office the British Government suspended the Constitution, invaded British Guiana and removed the PPP government, alleging that it was pursuing a communist agenda, with the objective of taking the colony into the Soviet bloc. The PPP did have a core of communists; it was led by Cheddi and Janet Jagan. As early as August 1952, for instance, the PPP's *Thunder* (edited by Janet) was offended by Jock Campbell's [of Booker] Chairman's Statement, and they rejected his assertion that Booker and other 'imperialist companies' were essential to the progress of colonial peoples. Their indignation was unmistakable; it embodied the communist creed at the core of the Jaganite conception of the PPP:

> Without the imperialist companies, 'there can be no colonial economic development, thus no social or political development [quoting Campbell].' The sequence has been turned upside down – the cart has been put before the horse. Surely every infant knows that in order to put their economy on a sound and democratic footing, the subject people must FIRST capture political power now in the hands of the rulers. The truth is that there has been no real economic development because of these companies and the loot and plunder, and the perpetual drain into the coffers of the British Treasury and into absentee owners of these plantations and trading companies.[11]

It is noteworthy that although the PPP of 1953 was a loose coalition of communists, non-communists, and even anti-communists, the communists were unfazed in disseminating their ideology. People like Cheddi and Janet Jagan and Sydney King were defined as 'extremist' or communist, and the literature distributed by the PPP in the early 1950s was overwhelmingly Marxist-Leninist and pro-Soviet. This reflects the inordinate influence of the Jagans, despite the diverse political perspectives within the PPP. But Burnham, Ashton Chase, and the two other ministers in the government, Dr J. P. Lachmansingh and Jainaraine Singh (four of six), were perceived as 'moderate' or non-communist, even anti-communist. Cheddi and Sydney King were the communists. It is arguable, therefore, that the composition of the cabinet was a concession to Burnham, to palliate him following his quest for leadership of the PPP.

However, the inchoate, even discordant, philosophy of the members of the early PPP could not be sublimated despite their stridently disparaging anti-British rhetoric, often crude and offensive. But there was no prospect that Cheddi Jagan would have renounced his Marxism-Leninism despite the necessity for a measure of *realpolitik* by any government in a colony; neither was he inclined to adopt a moderate ideological posture to conciliate Burnham's ominous challenge of his leadership. On July 24, 1953, for instance, Jagan provided the House of Assembly with a civics lesson in world politics:

> Communism and Socialism are in the same camp, so that to all intents and purposes the world is divided into two camps – the Socialist or Communist camp, which is the people's camp, and the camp which today calls itself the Democratic camp, but which is really the capitalist camp.[12]

Cheddi Jagan around 1953: young, fearless and already possessed by the utopian vision of the superiority of the Soviet system – the universal beacon for the liberation of humankind

In August 1953, he was more passionate on the subject. He conceded a role for local capitalists for some time but did not indicate where foreign capitalists stood in his Marxist scheme, neither did he offer them any reassurance. Yet he let the cat out of the bag when he intimated dire austerity for Guyanese, necessitating extraordinary measures and heroic sacrifices to counter the potential deleterious consequences of their nationalisation of foreign assets. And he alluded to the White Sea-Baltic Canal, built by Comrade Stalin and opened in 1933, with slave labour from the dictator's brutal Gulag, using primitive tools that eventuated in around twenty-five thousand deaths and unconscionable suffering to many thousands. It was not a clever example on which to draw despite its telling evocation: 'In the past, canals were dug and dams were constructed with bare hands. If we cannot get the money and the machines, we must undertake to do these things again with our bare hands.'[13]

III. Courting Suspension? Rebuffing the SPA's Offer of Recognition for Jagan's GIWU: The Principal Exemplification of the PPP's Recklessness in Government, 1953

A Pyrrhic victory! The short-lived, recklessly utopian but fissiparous, cabinet of the half-baked PPP Government, May-October 1953 (133 days); dogged from the beginning by the Jagan-Burnham rivalry for leadership, rooted in deep-seated racial and ideological suspicion – (left to right) J.P. Lachmansingh, Sydney King (Eusi Kwayana), L.F.S. Burnham, Janet Jagan, Cheddi Jagan, Jainarine Singh, Ashton Chase

Such was Jagan's faith in the Soviet experiment that no sacrifice was too demanding or unconscionable in pursuit of the communist utopia. Therefore, there was menace lurking in Jagan's passion and certainty – the potential for self-destruction. On August 9, 1953, he conducted another lesson on his creed, in a broadcast on Radio Demerara:

> Capitalism proved itself more efficient than feudalism and slavery and so replaced them. So will the capitalist system, in due course, be changed into a higher and more efficient socialist system. Likewise, socialism itself will evolve into the higher communist stage of society...**I am a great admirer of the Soviet Union, the People's [Republic of] China and the People's Democracies** [of Eastern Europe].[14]

This was the context in which the second claim for recognition by the PPP's union, the Guiana Industrial Workers' Union (GIWU), may be understood. Its president, Dr J. P. Lachmansingh, was the minister of health. On July 21, 1953, the PPP's minister of labour, Ashton Chase, wrote to the Sugar Producers' Association (SPA) seeking, as it had done unsuccessfully in 1948 (culminating in the Enmore tragedy), to replace the MPCA as the sole bargaining agent for all workers in the sugar industry: the predominantly Indian fieldworkers, in addition to the overwhelmingly African factory workers. After some delay, the SPA replied to Ashton Chase on August 20, 1953, indicating their willingness to recognise the GIWU as the bargaining agent for the overwhelming majority of the workers in the sugar industry, the fieldworkers, most of whom were Indians; while the MPCA would remain the union for the minority factory workers, most of whom were Africans (their original union, the British Guiana Workers' League was defunct since 1951). It is essential to emphasise the ethnic bifurcation permeating this issue.

The SPA's letter to Minister Ashton Chase stated:

> **...in the first instance,** the GIWU would represent the field workers [the overwhelming majority] and the MPCA the factory workers.' Alternatively, the two unions should merge as the bargaining agent of all sugar workers. They wished that the agreements negotiated with the MPCA would stand, but these were subject to renegotiation shortly, with effect from January 1, 1954.[15]

This was a momentous concession by the SPA, granted primarily because the Venn Commission Report of 1949 had recommended reconsideration of the recognition issue after a few years, providing the GIWU could demonstrate substantial support.[16] Jagan's ascendancy among Indian sugar workers (Indians generally) was demonstrated emphatically in the general elections of April 1953. Besides, Jock Campbell (chairman of Booker) told me that he was fully aware that Jagan had the support of the majority of the Indian sugar workers, and this warranted recognition of the GIWU. It is not clear, however, if the factory workers, predominantly African, approved of the calibre of representation of the MPCA and wished to retain this union as their bargaining agent with the SPA. But, as in 1948, they appeared not to be receptive to the PPP's GIWU.

The SPA was being very reasonable, apart from signalling a disposition to work with the PPP government. However, the PPP was not amenable to compromise; it was already out of control, lacking internal coherence, as different factions in this loose and unwieldy coalition pursued their respective, and conflicting, agendas. Consequently, the GIWU effectively rejected the SPA's offer of recognition without even the common courtesy of a response to that body. It was not just arrogance; it was a manifestation of the youthful irresponsibility and political immaturity of many members of the PPP (including the ministers: four of the six were thirty-five or under, with virtually no experience of administration of any sort), in conjunction with Jagan's incapacity to influence and reconcile the divergent ideological factions. He was a very fine crusader for change, at his best when agitating against perceived evils, but his limitations as a statesman – the rhetoric untempered by responsibility – were evident from those early years. As Professor Harold Lutchman observes of the PPP government of 133 days, in 1953:

> In terms of political experience they were neophytes. Perhaps, if they had experience in Government, over a longer period of time, they might have behaved differently. The PPP leaders didn't have a true appreciation of the forces against them in 1953.[17]

Sydney King was right: they were not ready to assume the authority of governance, whatever the character of the Constitution. It is necessary to reiterate that he had moved in the executive of the PPP, in early 1953, that 'we should not win a majority.' He knew that no PPP government would be up to the task because the deep-seated issue of racial insecurity (primarily among Africans) was routinely swept under the carpet, if not openly repudiated.

The principal architect of the rejection of the SPA's terms of recognition was Sydney King, the minister of communications and works, perceived as one of the foremost 'extremists' on whom Cheddi and Janet Jagan relied heavily. He was the most prominent African Marxist in the PPP; therefore, he was arguably more important to the Jaganite mission than the principal non-communist African, Forbes Burnham. King intervened at a meeting of the executive committee of the GIWU on August 30, 1953, and instructed the Union to call a strike the next day. It was not until September 5, however, that the Union informed the SPA of the reason for the strike.[14] They, ostensibly, were now demanding better wages and improved working conditions for various categories of sugar workers. As the Robertson Commission Report of 1954 observed:

> The letter [to the SPA] made no mention of recognition, and indeed the Union would obviously have found it difficult to justify a strike in support of recognition since discussions on the question of recognition had already been initiated by the Minister of Labour [Ashton Chase], and might very well have led to a settlement of the issue.[18]

But as the PPP was not predisposed to a *modus vivendi* with the imperialists, especially the 'sugar gods,' it was paramount to be seen to be waging an unrelenting struggle against the abominable capitalist system, vigorously in pursuit of its dismantling, root and branch. As with the Waddington Constitution, so with the recognition of the GIWU, the PPP was disinclined to, or even be seen to, co-operate with the imperialists in finding an immediate resolution of the putative problems. The PPP's leadership, in rejecting the offer of recognition of the GIWU as the bargaining agent for all the fieldworkers (well over 90 per cent of the sugar workers), was saying, in effect, that they were not amenable to a compromise. They desired to keep stirring the pot.

Ashton Chase (aged twenty-seven), the minister of labour in the short-lived PPP government from May to October 1953, recalls the recognition issue on the eve of the suspension of the Constitution. The SPA was, in fact, meeting the GIWU virtually all the way, but the recalcitrant PPP would have none of it:

> The GIWU came very close to the bull's eye of recognition but there was a slip between cup and lip. As a result of negotiations carried out by the author (as Minister of Labour) with the SPA…[they] agreed to recognise the GIWU for field workers [predominantly Indian] but to continue recognising the MPCA for the factory workers [overwhelmingly African]. This offer was rejected by the GIWU. It wanted unconditional recognition for all field and factory workers previously represented by the MPCA. The SPA's counter proposal included the acceptance by the GIWU of all collective agreements made with the MPCA and the execution by the GIWU of similar agreements…The GIWU rejected the condition; it reserved the right to negotiate and settle fresh agreements with the SPA.[19]

W. A. Macnie, managing director of the SPA, met Minister Chase on September 8, 1953, and told him that the alternative suggestion of an amalgamation with the MPCA was made on the assumption 'that it might ultimately lead to absorption of the MPCA by the GIWU.' He added that the apparent reservation of the GIWU regarding acceptance of the agreements signed with the MPCA was not insuperable. Macnie advised that the impression should be corrected that these terms were not negotiable. In fact, the SPA letter of August 20 to Minister Chase offering recognition, construed it thus:

> that the existing agreements with the MPCA should be accepted by the GIWU until new agreements could be negotiated with the latter

union and not that they should be accepted indefinitely...The SPA had contemplated that new agreements with the GIWU would be negotiated and come into force by January 1, 1954.[20]

Sydney King's reason for rejecting the SPA's offer of recognition is complex, but it was compatible with the broader objective: the class struggle as the principal instrument of forging racial unity. No one had the courage to confront the racial issue head-on, although King did endeavour to broach it, however circumspectly. As noted earlier, he had warned Burnham and Jagan in early 1953 that the PPP would win the elections. He was fearful of its being a Pyrrhic victory because the party was still a loose coalition between Africans and Indians; the class struggle was at a rudimentary stage; it could be overwhelmed easily by passions fed by racial insecurities. King (Eusi Kwayana) explains in a recent article his 'disagreement with the PPP attempting to win a majority in the 1953 elections':

> I was fully aware of the immature and therefore not very sturdy quality of interracial unity in the country...[consequently I] moved a motion [in the Executive Council of the PPP], supported only by Martin Carter, to the effect that the party should attempt to win no more than eight seats in the forthcoming elections. The argument was that the multiracial community, although promising, was still frail and not sturdy enough to withstand unforeseen shocks...Both Dr Jagan and Mr Burnham dismissed it with the identical statement: 'If you are fighting, you are fighting to win.'[21]

In addition, Burnham's challenge to Jagan for the leadership of the PPP immediately after their victory at the polls was declared, in April 1953, confirmed the accuracy of King's foreboding with respect to the fragility of the coalition. As he recalled, it was a massive undertaking for activists like himself to persuade Africans to endorse an Indian leader, as they instinctively defined Cheddi Jagan from the beginning. Consequently, King probably construed the SPA's withholding of recognition of the GIWU as the bargaining agent of the predominantly African factory workers as well, as another manifestation of the entrenched divide-and-rule tactic of the imperialists to retard the inculcating of class consciousness and stymie the lessening of racial discord between Africans and Indians.

King had extolled Jagan as a 'doughty champion' of the working class in his foreword to a PPP booklet, *Fight for Freedom* (in the early 1950s). He wrote of Cheddi:

> I cannot close without adding a word of tribute to this doughty champion of the working class and popular masses. His name has deservedly become a byword of resistance and of exposure of the ruling classes. On the lips of every loyal Guyanese of every race

and in the hearts of the oppressed, his name has become a banner behind which tramp the revolutionary and progressive masses of our country….[22]

Yet King's acute sensitivity to African apprehension of even an Indian leader of Jagan's stature underscores the power of ethnic passions and predilections to determine political choices.

Another reason for rejecting the generous terms of recognition of the GIWU by the SPA was the fact that 'bitter sugar' was a lucrative and historically resonant site for the PPP to wage an uncompromising 'struggle' against imperialism; as was their harping on the limitations of the Waddington Constitution with its tendentious provisions to emasculate the colony's burgeoning nationalism and the pursuit of Independence. It constituted a cathartic rebuff of the 'sugar gods,' while being conducive, supposedly, to the building of working-class consciousness between the Indian field and African factory workers. For the Marxists in the PPP, trade unionism and the strike weapon were crucial instruments in their mission to seize the state from the capitalist exploiters for the benefit of the workers. The strike in the sugar industry lasted twenty-four days, from August 31 to September 23, 1953. This was the decisive issue that impelled the British government to suspend the Constitution on October 9, 1953.

Jock Campbell, the chairman of Booker, based in London, was the recipient of several letters from senior Booker people in Georgetown denouncing the PPP leaders. Possibly the most important one was from Henry Seaford of Booker Shipping (brother of Sir Frederick Seaford, head of Booker in British Guiana), dated September 8, 1953, during the latest GIWU strike on the plantations. He was in a desperate mood and was deeply pessimistic regarding the implications of the communist machinations of the PPP for the future of Booker in the colony. His was probably essentially the voice of Sir Frederick, who had clashed with Jagan on many occasions in the Legislative Council on matters pertaining to sugar and communism:

> What the majority of the Ministers is trying to do is to cause chaos in the colony, then go to the Colonial Office and say that it is because they have not complete control, that these things are happening. Their aim is to get rid of all the white officials and make life so unpleasant for other whites that they will get out. Schools are to be taught communism, and those masters who don't agree will be fired. Can you imagine what this colony will be like in five years' time if this sort of thing continues? **Unless something drastic is done, Booker will cease to exist as a large firm in five years.** This is a serious statement to make, but I do it in all sincerity and because of my love for this firm. I consider that the future of Booker is at stake [emphasis added].[23]

235

Jagan's Marxist creed virtually ensured that Booker would have been nationalised at some point after independence. Campbell forwarded Henry Seaford's letter to Philip Rogers and N. L. Mayle of the West Indian Department of the Colonial Office, both of whom he knew well. He visited them on September 17, 1953, with the GIWU strike on the plantations already into its eighteenth day. Nothing definitive seemed to have emerged from the meeting other than Jock's ventilation of the panic the conduct of the PPP leaders had provoked among the ruling elite. The following day Campbell forwarded another letter from another desperate representative of sugar, H. L. Steele of the much smaller Demerara Company. He was appalled by the 'unscrupulous communist gangsters,' whose patron was Russia: they had allegedly created a 'cancer' in British Guiana. Campbell remarked in his covering note that 'H.L. Steele is a local "white creole". A letter not to be taken too seriously; but an interesting expression of local opinion.'[24]

In his letter to Campbell of September 8, Henry Seaford had also informed him that a deputation opposed to the PPP government was scheduled to visit the Colonial Office shortly, and that he would probably be requested to lead it. On September 15 Rogers minuted thus on the matter:

> It would be most unfortunate to give the impression to those sitting on the fence in British Guiana that if the constitution has to be suspended, the Secretary of State's decision was taken because of a deputation from one group concerned. He added: 'Mr Campbell fully agrees.'[25]

Jock Campbell was not enamoured of Jagan's Marxist philosophy, nor was he impressed with his brief leadership, or lack thereof, in government in 1953. And it is also true that the calling of the GIWU strike on August 31, at the instruction of Sydney King (arguably with the support of the Jagans), shortly after the SPA had indicated that they were prepared to recognise the GIWU as the bargaining agent for the fieldworkers, was the principal factor behind the decision to suspend the Constitution. It was perceived as the clearest vindication of communist intent to damage the economy and cripple the 'sugar gods,' paradoxically, as a means of forcing the hand of the Colonial Office towards an accelerated devolution of power. It was irresponsibility of the highest order, virtually seeking a confrontation with the colonial authorities, by a PPP that was rudderless. As the only communist in the cabinet, apart from Cheddi, Sydney King exerted immeasurable influence on the Jagans. But the latter could not be absolved of responsibility for this insanity perpetrated on the premier sugar industry – insurrection by the primer!

Campbell was clearly antagonised by the PPP's intransigence, as he had recommended that the GIWU become the recognised union for the majority fieldworkers, overwhelmingly supporters of Cheddi Jagan. It must have convinced him that the Marxists in the PPP were determined to nationalise the sugar industry, and it was futile to try to change their minds. He was right, as this was Cheddi's aim: 'the commanding heights of the economy' must belong to the people. Socialism/communism was not compatible with capitalist control of the economy, worse still foreign capitalists. Yet it is not verifiable that Campbell did recommend suspension of the Constitution when he met officials at the Colonial Office, although the option of suspension was intimated to him by Rogers and Mayle before their decision to proceed a few days later.

This is the Robertson Commission's verdict (in 1954) on the PPP's role in the GIWU strike of September 1953 – the straw that broke the camel's back, precipitating the suspension of the Constitution:

> [Para 180] On the evidence, including the evidence we had of Mr King's intervention in the GIWU meeting on 30 August, we find it impossible to resist the conclusion that the hot-heads ['extremists'] in the PPP, knowing of the discussions that had taken place and fearing that they might lead to an agreed settlement [recognition of the GIWU by the SPA, in their letter of August 20 to Ashton Chase], became anxious to precipitate an immediate industrial conflict which they intended to exploit for their own political purposes.

> [Para 181] We cannot believe that Mr Ashton Chase [Minister of Labour] and Dr Lachmansingh [Minister of Health and President of the GIWU], for example, were fully in sympathy with this intention. However, once the strike was called, it secured the full support of the PPP. No leader of the PPP publicly condemned the strike or advocated moderation in its prosecution. Several PPP Ministers (notably Mr King) who, as members of the Executive Council, were responsible for peace and order and the economic development of the country, together with many PPP Members of the House of Assembly, toured the sugar estates calling upon workpeople to support the strike and using language which was bound to encourage the strikers to acts of intimidation and of violence against those who refused to observe the strike call. The strike spread gradually throughout the estates, and by September 8 [the day Henry Seaford had written alarmingly to Jock Campbell] the industry was at a standstill. Altogether the strike lasted for 23 [24] days and in that period strenuous efforts were made by the leaders of the PPP, including several Ministers, to get the strike extended into a general strike…By September 23, however, it was clear that the strike had failed and it was called off on that day. On the following day, September 24, the Labour Relations Bill was introduced to the House of Assembly.[26]

On September 21, 1953, the Colonial Office minuted that the decisive argument in favour of suspension had come from two sources: the governor of British Guiana, Sir Alfred Savage (1903–80), in a letter of September 13;

the other was Sir Stephen (Timmy) Luke of the Colonial Office, writing from Barbados on September 12, following his visit to British Guiana. The minute was definitive:

> **It is becoming clearer every day that a break with the [PPP] Ministers is going to be, sooner or later, inevitable. We had already been coming to this conclusion in the Colonial Office and we have been confirmed in this view by two letters received today** [September 21 from Savage and Luke]…

> Sir Alfred Savage refers to the 'countless directions in which the foundations of society are being attacked insidiously almost without check'; and he concludes: 'I am rapidly coming to the conclusion that unless the opposition elements in the country rouse themselves quickly and wake up to their obligations and opportunities, then to retain British Guiana in the Commonwealth we shall have to go back on the new Constitution which would mean the use of force and the maintenance of military forces here for some considerable time.'

> Sir Stephen Luke refers to the thoroughgoing communist totalitarianism with which the Ministers and other leaders of the PPP are organising themselves. **It is not now so much a question of whether or not a break with Ministers is to come, but when and how that break is to be made** [emphasis added].[27]

IV. Suspension of the Constitution, with Special Reference to Jagan's Intimate Relationship with the Communist Party of Great Britain

On September 24, 1953, the Labour Relations Bill was introduced by the minister of labour in the legislature, a measure designed to secure a ballot of workers in any industry where there was jurisdictional dispute to ascertain the union of choice by the majority. That majority was stipulated at 52 per cent, and the validation of the case for a poll was the determination solely of the minister of labour. But the fact that the strike in the sugar industry that lasted twenty-four days was accompanied by this measure, created the impression that the PPP government had, in the communist tradition, embarked on emasculating the trade unions for political ends. Moreover, this was interpreted as a prelude to totalitarian communist rule, replicating the culture of unfreedom and chronic fear endemic in the Soviet bloc – the knock on the door in the middle of the night! It is most likely, therefore, that the Colonial Office's decision to suspend the Constitution was determined, finally, by the demonstrated recalcitrance of the PPP government despite the generous offer of the SPA to recognise their union, the GIWU, as the bargaining agent for most sugar workers.

The same day that the Labour Relations Bill was introduced and rushed hastily through all three stages in the Legislative Council (September 24), the secretary of state for the colonies sent a telegram to Governor Savage regarding their decision to suspend the Constitution. The PPP was not in a mood to compromise with the imperialists, and the latter were convinced that the objective of the core of the PPP leadership (the Jaganites) was to create a communist state:

Jagan and Burnham with Governor Sir Alfred Savage (centre), during their 133 days in Government when the 'ultra-left' faction in the PPP seemed resolved to making the constitution unworkable. This was the context in which the British suspended the constitution on October 9, 1953. The gulf between Jagan and Burnham was unbridgeable from the beginning

It has become increasingly clear to me from your recent reports, including your letter to Lloyd [Sir Thomas Lloyd of the Colonial Office] of 15 September [in fact, September 13] that there was no prospect of Ministers acting responsibly and foregoing their extremist [communist] aims. It was clearly right on the introduction of the new Constitution [Waddington] to try to do all that tact, patience and tolerance could achieve to win them away from the extremists and to see whether the responsibilities of office would make them see reason. It is, however, clear that they had no intention of working the present Constitution in the interests of the people of British Guiana as a whole, but are seeking a one-party totalitarian control of the country and a link-up with Russia which we obviously cannot contemplate...

[We] should make it clear that British Guiana was given its new constitution in the hope that it would seize this opportunity to advance along the road to responsible self-government within the British Commonwealth; that the constitution has been perverted by a small group of Communist sympathisers who sought to impose totalitarianism on the territory and were bringing the economic life of the country to a standstill [by the strike in the sugar industry].[28]

With the decision to suspend the Constitution approved by cabinet, the secretary of state for the colonies forwarded a speech (on October 4, 1953) to Governor Savage, for delivery when announcing the suspension. It is noteworthy that in the voluminous correspondence bearing on the issue, there is no suggestion whatsoever of American intervention at any stage of the crisis. But this should not detract from the potent impact of Cold War hysteria on British attitudes, fomented by the US and its infamously virulent variant of anti-communism, McCarthyism:

> Her Majesty's Government and I were well aware that some of the Ministers had extreme left-wing sympathies. We know that two of them had paid visits to communist countries in Eastern Europe [Cheddi Jagan in 1951; Sydney King in 1952–53]. Nevertheless, I have done everything I could to meet their wishes and to induce them by tact, patience and tolerance to carry out their responsibilities as Ministers...[They] have failed utterly to live up to their responsibilities and, regardless of your welfare, have devoted all their energies to perverting the Constitution for their own extremist ends...
>
> The leaders of the PPP have openly strengthened their links with communist countries, and have boasted of their preference for the Russian way of life...The Colony is being flooded with communist propaganda...I am convinced...that the Ministers and the Party are completely in the hands of an extremist clique with totalitarian aims planned from outside, and are taking measures which are being carried out by the classical communist technique....[29]

And then the clincher – the strike in the sugar industry despite the SPA's having indicated their willingness to recognise the PPP's union, the GIWU!

> The sugar strike was deliberately engineered by certain of the Ministers [Sydney King in particular] to secure the dominance of a particular union [GIWU] in the industry for their political purposes. Furthermore, they sought to spread the stoppage to other industries, including essential services, thus endangering the whole life of the community which it was their duty as Ministers to preserve. Foiled by their efforts to gain their ends by the strike, they were now attempting to achieve it by a proposed Labour Relations Ordinance, which would introduce measures quite contrary to British practice. They are seeking, in fact, to turn the workers and their unions into the political tool of an extremist clique.[30]

Moreover, the Colonial Office was alleging that the communist segment of the leadership of the PPP (the Jagans, Sydney King, and Rory Westmaas) was under the influence of the communist-dominated World Federation of Trade Unions (WFTU) based in Vienna; the latter was instrumental in funding trade unions in the colonies to foment labour troubles to spread the communist virus.

The British government white paper on the suspension of the Constitution observed that the WFTU Secretariat was augmented by the arrival of Ferdinand Smith (1893–1961), a US-based Jamaican communist and close friend of Cheddi Jagan's special friend, Billy Strachan, the Jamaican-born London-based communist and the CPGB's man responsible for the Caribbean. Ferdinand Smith was the assistant secretary at the WFTU Secretariat with special responsibility for American, Canadian and Caribbean affairs, and head of the WFTU Colonial Department. In the spring of 1952, Smith and Strachan visited Jamaica and Trinidad but were banned from entering British Guiana. This had precipitated indignation in Cheddi Jagan, which he vented in the Legislative Council.

The white paper substantiated Jagan's seminal links to the 'communist-controlled' WFTU, noting that he had attended its General Council meeting in Soviet-controlled Berlin in November 1951. He made the case then for the WFTU to actively support trade unions in the colonies by creating a colonial department. His submission was approved shortly thereafter by the General Council, as was his recommendation that the 'WFTU should send delegates to colonial territories in order to strengthen its links with these territories.' This was the prism through which the Colonial Office viewed the PPP's GIWU and its *raison d'etre*, the elimination of the recognised MPCA; likewise the PPP-sponsored strike lasting twenty-four days, shortly after the SPA had informed the minister of labour of its readiness to recognise the GIWU as the union of the majority of the sugar workers, the fieldworkers. Control of trade unions was perceived as a crucial weapon of the communists for destabilising the colony under imperialist rule, with the aim of acquiring power: the dictatorship of the proletariat.

The white paper also asserted that the Jaganite core of the PPP was inspired by, and affiliated with, several communist organisations in addition to the WFTU: the World Federation of Democratic Youth (WFDY), the World Peace Council (WPC), and the Women's International Democratic Federation (WIDF). The PPP's women's organisation, the Women's Progressive Organisation, was founded in May 1953, and it sought affiliation immediately with the WIDF. That same month, Janet Jagan attended the Third World Congress of Women in Copenhagen, organised by the WIDF. Having been elected to its presidium, she appealed to her comrades thus:

> We need guidance and help. We in the colonial world are tied economically and politically like the slaves of old. **Our people turn their eyes to the great Socialist countries which have been moving forward with great rapidity and success.** Help us to win freedom for all the oppressed colonial peoples of the world [emphasis added].[31]

241

But the PPP was not a communist monolith. It was an agglomeration of discordant political strands, on a capacious continuum from communist to capitalist. It was evocative of the Tower of Babel with the supposed leader (this was never definitive), Cheddi Jagan, lacking the authority and the resolve to rein in divergent tendencies, all seeking to outdo each other by their loathing of the British imperialists. On one hand, the right wing of the PPP, inspired by Forbes Burnham and including Ashton Chase, Dr J. P. Lachmansingh, Clinton Wong, and Jainaraine Singh, was virtually irreconcilable with Cheddi Jagan's communist core of the party that included Janet Jagan, Sydney King, Martin Carter, Rory Westmaas, Boysie Ramkarran, and Brindley Benn. It will be recalled that just after the election victory in April 1953, Burnham challenged Jagan for the leadership of the PPP. This was never resolved; it simmered – an uneasy truce. But, as Kimani Nehusi has argued, King, Carter, and Westmaas (the so-called 'ultra leftists,' as described by Jagan in March 1956) were not fully reconciled with the Jagans, for although committed to Marxism, they were perturbed by the growing issue of Indian racism in the PPP. They were supporters of a West Indies Federation and viewed Jagan's resistance to it as predicated solely on racial, if not racist, premises and self-interest.[32]

The divergent ideological strands notwithstanding, the fundamental problem within the PPP was African fear of Indian political ascendancy, in an independent Guyana led by Cheddi Jagan. One of Jagan's most loyal supporters at the time, Sydney King, was perturbed by this unexplored bugbear shrouded by the anti-colonial and Marxist rhetoric within the PPP.

However, the 'ultra leftists' appeared to want to focus primarily on using their Marxist learning to address grassroots mistrust between the two principal races. Unlike Jagan and Burnham, for whom the pursuit of power was the foremost and urgent goal in their politics, King, Carter, and Westmaas, as Kimani argues, were in for the long haul: building long-term unity across the racial chasm although that meant eschewing, for some time, the lure of acquiring power. And King himself, as he told Professor Frank Birbalsingh in 1993, harboured such foreboding regarding the fragility of the PPP on the question of race that he was not excited by its 'victory' in April 1953. The party was ill-equipped to assume office:

> I always believed that the seeds of disunity were already there. There was neither the ideological nor what I would call the racial unity that was necessary for the political undertaking in hand. I lived in a multi-racial society in Buxton. Before the election [of 1953] I argued that we should not fight to win. The movement needed to consolidate itself. The victory was too quick. I didn't expect it to founder, but the movement needed time to develop real integrity.[33]

Moreover, the fact that Burnham was earnestly challenging Jagan for the leadership of the PPP left a bitter taste, a gnawing incoherence. This must have engendered a feeling of absurdity about governing, as this inchoate group, primarily of young, inexperienced men high on indigestible leftist rhetoric of varying intensity, sought to undermine the Waddington Constitution. One way of looking at it is that there was no ideological or philosophical glue to hold the fragile PPP and its government together. Moreover, the bedevilling reality of Guyanese racial susceptibility (no less virulent today) was so inexorable, even Jagan's Marxist formulation to studiously prioritise class over race could not neutralise the power of the latter to draw people – even Cheddi – into its procrustean mould. The Jagan-Burnham rivalry for power in the PPP mirrored the chronic racial insecurities of the wider colonial environment, over several decades (as I argue in chapter 3).

And even an African Marxist like Sydney King could not escape the implications of the consuming ethnic frame of reference. As he put it, time and again, African politicians like himself encountered enormous obstacles in persuading African Guyanese that their interests were best served by an Indian leader, Cheddi Jagan. He recalls that Jagan was driving him out into the country one day, before the PPP candidates for the general elections of 1953 were selected, and he remarked to him that he was disinclined to contest because a substantial amount of work had to be undertaken at the grassroots, first, to moderate deep-seated mistrust among the people. Kwayana adds that Cheddi responded quickly that if he was not a candidate, he, too, would not contest. This was what led Kwayana to change his mind and contest the general elections of April 1953.[34]

Therefore, in hindsight, the irresponsibly abrasive anti-British, anti-White rhetoric of several of the PPP ministers and legislators appears like an affectation of a robust nationalism – unparalleled in the British West Indies, but it was really a charade to camouflage the ideological and racial chasm permeating the PPP. It could not obscure the built-in limitations, the half-baked character of the party's anti-colonial project: its lack of internal coherence; its ill-preparedness for leadership and governance; and, worse of all, it evoked a deep-seated fear among Africans that its *raison d'etre* was the political ascendancy of the Indian juggernaut. Jagan's ship was heading for the rocks. It was only a matter of time before Burnham and the right-wing desert it; and that was likely to precipitate the flight of the so-called ultra-left, with a predilection for bridging the ethnic chasm by a more rigorous application of Marxism, though no less sceptical of Indian hegemony. However, the 'ultra-left' did not constitute a discrete, numerically strong, unit with the means to effect a robust challenge of the perceived emerging Indian ascendancy within the PPP. Yet they were symbolically potent, and their departure sealed the identity of Jagan's PPP categorically as an Indian party.[35]

Cheddi Jagan, on the other hand, was a true believer in the 'Made in Moscow' brand of Marxism-Leninism. He would stick with it tenaciously, until the collapse of the Soviet Union, although most of his supporters were innocent of the international political and economic implications of his devotion to communism. But Cheddi and Janet were politically fortified, at home, by the fact that their 'bitter sugar' crusade, bolstered by effective campaigning and deft exploitation of Indian cultural idioms, had won them the unchallengeable loyalty of most Indo-Guyanese – those who stayed in Guyana, as well as the several hundred thousand who migrated voluntarily, ironically, to greener pastures, in the advanced capitalist world.

The setback of the Suspension in October 1953 notwithstanding, the Jagans were sanguine that they would regain power by virtue of the numerical strength of the Indian electorate, enhanced by the eradication of malaria in the late 1940s. This would eventuate in an unassailable majority under the first-past-the-post electoral system. Jagan did not need to reach an accommodation with the 'ultra-left' or any other party for that matter, such as John Carter's pro-capitalist United Democratic Party. Already, by 1956 (the year after the split with Burnham), Sydney King would conclude that the politics of the Jagans had become an expression of Indian racial power, with the potential to dominate an independent Guyana. Therefore, it is reasonable to contend that the PPP's 'victory' at the polls in April 1953 was, indeed, a Pyrrhic one because the fundamental problem of racial insecurity, at the core of the interminable political futility of Guyana, remained largely unexplored and unresolved.

One of the indictments the British government made of the PPP, in rationalising their decision to suspend the Constitution, was the arrogance of several members of the cabinet, especially Burnham and Sydney King. It was a real Tower of Babel in which it seems as if those on the right, as well as some on the left, were united in their resolve that the essentially flawed experiment that was Jagan's PPP – increasingly perceived by Africans as a project for the aggrandisement of Indians – must not succeed. It is not far-fetched to suggest, therefore, that Burnham in particular must have calculated that courting suspension was the best means of torpedoing Jagan and the 'extremists.' He was downright rude and crudely abusive to colonial officials; and the 'ultra-left,' comprising King, Carter, and Westmaas, was no less abrasive and unmindful of a peaceful transition to self-government. They were tilting at windmills and quixotic in their conception of the art of governance. They were so unflinchingly anti-British that one could interpret it as an absurdly suicidal challenge of imperial authority which only they comprehended. The legacy of this irrationality is still a millstone around the neck of the political culture of Guyana. Saner counsel would have inclined towards building bridges across the ethnic chasm, while fostering instruments of power-sharing within the PPP and working the Constitution towards self-government. As I have noted, this intransigence (perhaps an index of the racial futility) has no parallel in the rest of the British West Indies, not even in multiracial Trinidad.

As early as November 1951, Forbes Burnham wrote in *Thunder*, the PPP's organ, that the Waddington Constitution Report succeeded 'in illustrating that, indeed, the state is an instrument designed to maintain the dominance of the ruling class, and that there is no advance to be gained except by relentless and determined struggle.' In January 1952 Cheddi Jagan, speaking in the Legislative Council, rejected the new constitution as 'being merely a fake and another tactic of the British colonialists to perpetuate exploitation and maintain the old order. He urged the struggle for immediate self-government.' Around the same time, an official statement of the programme of the PPP also repudiated the Waddington Constitution as 'a new formula for the continued subjugation of our people.' *Thunder* (September 1952) was certain that the governor would use his veto powers to thwart the will of the people, but the PPP was resolved to 'never rest until these checks and veto powers are completely removed.'[36]

It was not a good omen despite the introduction of universal adult suffrage and the enfranchisement of 208,939, an increase of around one hundred and fifty thousand since the general elections of 1947. The limitations of the new constitution notwithstanding, it was a watershed transition that all adults acquired the vote in 1953, including around forty thousand who were illiterate, primarily Indians. But instead of focusing on the fundamental racial insecurities in Guyanese society and the ominous dissonance brewing within the PPP, the leaders sought to outdo each other in denouncing the Waddington Constitution. Odeen Ishmael was wrong when he argued that after the First PPP Congress (held in Georgetown) in April 1951, the PPP 'saw the welding of national unity in British Guiana. At that time strong unity prevailed.'[37] In fact, the urgent problem of ethnic insecurity, posed by Sydney King in the early 1950s, was relegated to the periphery of the PPP's political discourse. The most monumental problem for the future of the colony was studiously ignored – festering!

At the conclusion of their first congress in April 1951, the PPP made a statement on the progress of the party, having been in existence for fifteen months. They claimed that it was 'a different kind of political party with a strong organisational apparatus and **a guiding ideology** and grassroots support... the first mass party to appear in British Guiana [emphasis added].'[38] It was not totally accurate. Its organisational capacity was certainly unexampled, and it was gaining mass support. But this self-assessment obscured the fact that it was a very broad coalition of various races and classes, and while it did have a communist core led by the Jagans, this did not include most of the members of the executive committee. The 'guiding ideology' of the Jaganite faction was

Marxism-Leninism, but the Burnhamites, as well as several who belonged to neither faction, were not communists.

Of the following members of the PPP's first executive committee, only Cheddi and Janet Jagan, Sydney King, and Ramkarran could be considered Marxists: Cheddi Jagan (leader); L. F. S. Burnham (chairman); H. Aubrey Fraser (first vice-chairman); Clinton Wong (second vice-chairman); Janet Jagan (general secretary); Sydney King (assistant general secretary); Ramkarran (treasurer); and the executive members: Ashton Chase, Rudy Luck, Frank Van Sertima, Ivor Cendrecourt, Mary Thompson, Hubert Critchlow, E. Kennard, Theo Lee, Ulric Fingal, Jainaraine Singh, Dr J. P. Lachmansingh, Cecil Cambridge, Fred Bowman, Pandit S. Misir, and Sheila La Taste (the Trinidadian-born wife of L. F. S. Burnham). In reality, this was such a disparate group of voluble anti-colonialists, one could have driven a coach and horses through the whole lot. It was beyond Jagan's capacity as 'leader' (this was never definitive) to exert much discipline on this motley crew.

The PPP did not expect to get into office in 1953; the main objective appeared to have been to become an effective opposition, pursuing their anti-colonial 'politics of protest' in the Legislative Council and in the wider society. Catapulted into office and devoid of experience in administration, their prime asset was their rhetorical exuberance, yet the fissiparous tendency rooted in the racial futility of the country, and swept under the carpet within the PPP, remained strong. Disaster was surely around the next bend, as they were behaving like the Opposition, and a recalcitrant one to boot. Just five months in office, the PPP launched a campaign to get people to sign a so-called 'Patriotic Appeal' to the Queen, seeking a fundamental amendment of the Waddington Constitution. It was asking for a virtual revocation of the Constitution and the elevation of the status of British Guiana to being on the threshold of independence. It was indicative of the centrality of Sydney King in the Jaganite camp that he launched the 'Constitutional Amendment' campaign in his native village of Buxton on September 28, 1953. The *Daily Argosy* (October 2, 1953) reported the proceedings, captioning the article thus:

SYDNEY KING LAUNCHED 'CONSTITUTIONAL AMENDMENT'
CAMPAIGN AT BUXTON
ASKS PEOPLE TO SIGN SO-CALLED 'PATRIOTIC APPEAL'
TO THE QUEEN
REFERS TO THE GOVERNOR AS 'THAT MAN SAVAGE'

On October 2 the general secretary of the PPP, Janet Jagan, announced that the party was 'making a bold bid to secure for British Guiana a further step forward on the road to national independence.' She added that at the last general elections in April 1953, the PPP had told the electorate that they intended to pursue 'the fight for the attainment of national independence.' Towards that end, they were seeking immediate amendments to the Constitution, aimed at enhancing the elective and democratic component in the governance of their own affairs. Their principal demands encompassed such root-and-branch changes that it was tantamount to the PPP endeavouring to subvert the Constitution after only five months in office. These were the principal demands of their 'Patriotic Appeal':

1. the abolition of the Upper House [the State Council, all nominated with the PPP in a distinct minority];

2. the governor should have no power to dissolve the House except on the approval of two-thirds majority of the Lower House [the House of Assembly];

3. the vote at eighteen years of age;

4. the withdrawal of the three civil servants [the chief secretary, the attorney general and the financial secretary] from seats in the House of Assembly and Executive Council;

5. the recall...of any representative for whose removal appeal is made to the governor-in-council by a two-thirds majority of the electors on the existing voters list in respect of any district;

6. the abolition of the governor's veto;

7. all nominated seats in local government assemblies be abolished, and that all elections be on the principle of universal adult suffrage.[39]

Scholarly assessments, as well as informed popular opinion, have addressed the rivalry for leadership between Jagan and Burnham in the PPP of the early 1950s, with all its implications, in the colony, of the intractable problem of racial insecurity. But while the hazard posed by the communism of the Jagan faction of the PPP is recognised, it is dismissed frequently as a red herring perpetrated by the British imperialists, consonant with their pernicious imperial tradition of divide-and-rule. However, the MI5 files indicate that the communism of the Jagans and their international communist links (particularly with the Communist Party of Great Britain) were perceived as a serious threat to the colony; moreover, that the PPP, in government, seemed committed to fomenting discord to force the issue of independence, possibly through another general election. Therefore, the irreconcilable antagonism between Jagan and Burnham notwithstanding, the Jaganite vision of a rapid advance to self-government was still being pursued. And while Burnham certainly did not wish the country to become independent under the leadership of the Indian communist Jagan, he appeared (on the surface) not to have opposed the party's recalcitrance – indeed, he vented his own venom against the British imperialists, seemingly tactlessly but possibly with deliberation.

It is conceivable that Burnham reasoned that his best chance of supplanting Jagan would come if the confrontational approach of the PPP government (branded communist) collided soon with British imperial assumptions in the context of the Cold War, particularly their anti-communist agenda in the colonies. In America's 'backyard'! This was Burnham's strategy throughout, as he cleverly juxtaposed his amorphous politics with Jagan's widely confirmed pro-Moscow communist beliefs, thus reinventing himself, beyond the PPP, as America's man. This would eventually secure Anglo-American complicity and subversion on his behalf, thereby facilitating his acquisition of power in 1964; thus, he was railroaded on his path to independence in 1966. **Without Jagan's devotion to communism and his loyalty to the Soviet Union, Burnham's political career would probably have been consigned to the scrap heap, after his electoral defeat of August 1961.**

In July 1953, just a couple months after the PPP entered the government, Janet Jagan (general secretary of the PPP, editor of its organ, *Thunder*, a legislator and deputy speaker of the House of Assembly) attended the Women's International Congress in Copenhagen, held under the auspices of the communist-dominated Women's International Democratic Federation. At its completion, she visited Romania and then paid a short visit to London (arriving on July 8, 1953); she spent most of her time with West Indian communists of the Caribbean Labour Congress (London Branch), led by Billy Strachan, and affiliated to the CPGB. Janet stayed with a female member of the CPGB; she was under constant surveillance by agents of MI5.

When she met with the senior leadership of the CPGB (on July 9), their conversation was eavesdropped on by two resident agents of MI5, who worked for several years at the King Street office of the party. These agents were 'Swift' and 'North,' and in the MI5 report to the security liaison officer (SLO) in Trinidad (also responsible for British Guiana), it was noted that the detailed information regarding Janet Jagan's meeting with the communist leaders was based on 'reliable source of the utmost delicacy.' They requested the SLO to forward copies of their report to the governor of British Guiana (Savage) and to the Special Branch in Georgetown, but they cautioned that the material 'requires handling with utmost care and discretion.'

It is highly likely that this MI5 report was the definitive evidence the British government needed to establish that the core faction of the PPP, under the leadership of the Jagans, was deeply influenced by the CPGB and that Billy Strachan and the CLC (London Branch) were their vital conduit to the

Communist Party. Strachan (their 'guru') was hospitalised at the time, so Janet was accompanied by another Jamaican communist, Rolly Simms of the CLC:

> During the course of her stay here [in London], Mrs Jagan was able to meet leading members of the British Communist Party [CPGB], including Harry Pollitt [1890–1960], General Secretary, Rajani Palme Dutt [1896–1974], Head of the International Department of the BCP [and Idris Cox (1899–1989) of the same department]. It is known that during the course of their conversation Mrs Jagan went out of her way to ask the Party both for constructive criticism and advice as regards the tactics of the PPP in British Guiana. The BCP pointed out to Mrs Jagan that it would not be in the best interest of the PPP for the BCP to proffer written advice or directions as to how the PPP should conduct its affairs. The Party, however, was prepared to state its views when requested to do so, and in this connection, it is understood arrangements for the exchange of correspondence between the BCP and the PPP, through suitable intermediaries, have been made.[40]

This meeting between Janet and the CPGB leaders lasted about seventy-five minutes; it was eavesdropped on and transcribed by 'North,' the MI5 spy in the party office. The latter noted that the conversation was not always audible, but it was surmised that Janet was eager to access their learned Marxist counsel on matters of policy in government, as well as in sustaining a vibrant party culture and organisation that would engender active grassroots education and mobilisation. R. Palme Dutt and Idris Cox advised that although the PPP was saddled with the responsibility of governing, they must not slacken their resolve in fighting colonial capitalist exploitation in their ultimate struggle for self-government. But the CPGB was also concerned about 'reconciling' the differences within the party, a clear allusion to the Jagan-Burnham rift that was profoundly disturbing, if not debilitating. Janet responded with something about 'racial competition' in the colony, but nothing more was audible to the spy on the subject.

Rajani Palme Dutt, an Englishman of Bengali-Swedish ancestry, educated at Balliol College, Oxford, was a brilliant scholar of Marxism, author of many books, and the theoretical guru of the CPGB. The learning showed. He posed the crucial question to Janet: was the PPP 'conducting propaganda towards real, decisive power coming into the hands of Ministers'? Palme Dutt's query was prompted by the fundamental communist perspective: the illusion of power within the interstices of capitalism, on one hand, and the goal of proletarian power that was the only instrument of building the perfect communist society, on the other.

Palme Dutt suggested to Janet that they maximise their mass support to pursue civil rights issues, in addition to creating cultural organisations that could be instrumental in intensifying the class struggle. However, he reportedly cautioned:

> ... they could not actually tell her [as General Secretary of the PPP] exactly what she should do but would be willing to advise her on procedure...It would be fatal for her if the [Communist] Party were forced into sending written documents from this country.

Palme Dutt also spoke of Marxism and Marxist leadership: the necessity of 'combining the mass movement, the Party organisation and the trade union organisation with their parliamentary and ministerial roles.' Idris Cox observed that

> it's not a question of propaganda campaign against the [Waddington] Constitution, as I don't think that will carry any weight; but it's rather a question of raising issues in which the people are interested, in such a way that will arouse them to struggle, and from their own experience begin to realise what an obstacle the Constitution is.' The meeting concluded with their agreeing to informal means of active communication that would supposedly overcome most of the intelligence hurdles. Palme Dutt said: 'We'll be glad to do all we can to help.[41]

Professor Vincent Harlow, a member of the Waddington Constitution Commission of 1951, commenting on the suspension of the Constitution, stated that they had foreseen the 'danger of the present situation,' but they 'decided to take a risk.' He observed that the current crisis was a consequence of 'the non-Communist majority failing to organise while the Communist party [Jagan's PPP] became highly organised.' Harlow felt it was premature to introduce instruments of liberal governance unless there was a 'good citizen' class capable of practising it. I presume he meant the necessity for an appreciable educated middle class of differing political persuasions. He concluded: 'This was lacking in British Guiana. The only alternative was despotism.' This was the context in which the Waddington Commission exercised caution by incorporating the checks implicit in the nominated element (ex-officio and otherwise).[42] Harlow did not remark on the failure of the 'moderates' or 'socialists' in the PPP, of whom Forbes Burnham was considered the principal exponent, to rein in the communists controlled by Cheddi and Janet Jagan. However, he alluded to the paucity of civic responsibility in British Guiana, thus underscoring the vagaries implicit in extending the parameters of democratic governance.

The Robertson Commission Report (1954) observed that during the PPP's 133 days in office, the governor and the ex-officio ministers in the Executive Council were under 'terrific pressure' from the PPP ministers not only because of disagreements on government policy but also on account of the latter's uncompromisingly personal hostility towards their official colleagues, as demonstrated in their public criticisms. The report characterised the relationship as 'entirely impossible.' Janet Jagan and Sydney King in particular, both of whom had been exposed recently to the cherished Marxist illumination of the leaders of the CPGB in London, were the principal exponents of the escalation of the class struggle, from July 1953 – the trade union militancy centred on recognition of the GIWU, and the 'patriotic appeal' for radical constitutional amendment. This confrontational approach precipitated an irreconcilable dissonance with the governor and the ex-officio members in the House of Assembly, the State Council, and the Executive Council. It was subversive of any normality in governance. And it is conceivable that the 'patriotic appeal,' launched by Sydney King in late September 1953, was designed to make the Constitution unworkable and to accelerate the class struggle.

Towards the end of August 1953, Billy Strachan, the Jagans' communist confidante of the CLC (London Branch) and publisher of *Caribbean News*, cabled Janet Jagan regarding several reports in the local press (which had obviously reached London) that activists of the PPP had pulled down the Union Jack at a public meeting of the party, in connection with their calling the GIWU strike in the sugar industry. Janet was irked by this intervention by her most esteemed communist mentor, and her reply to Billy of September 1, 1953 (intercepted by MI5), reflects her irritation. She was assertive that the 'flag pulling incident' was a fabrication by the local press: 'As far as we can ascertain, **someone, to get a good story, made up this stuff about the Union Jack being pulled down. It didn't happen, so you, too, can't have a "good" story** [emphasis added].' It is strange, perhaps reflective of an affected arrogance seeking to paper over their internal fissures, that the PPP did not repudiate the story immediately, as downright fake, and they failed to respond even after the *Argosy* 'apologised for printing a false report,' as Janet claimed.

Janet was clearly following the esteemed counsel proffered to her by Rajani Palme Dutt and Idris Cox of the CPGB to escalate the class struggle despite being in office, to expose the limitations of the Waddington Constitution and accelerate the process towards self-government. The assumption, equally endorsed by Sydney King, must have gained credibility because it was perceived, erroneously, as the best means of bridging the chronic chasm between Indians and Africans which was having a most unsavoury impact within the PPP: the smouldering Jagan/Burnham imbroglio regarding the leadership of the party. It will be recalled that the GIWU strike in the sugar industry was called on August 31, 1953, even after the SPA's conciliatory recognition offer, but the PPP had rejected it because the MPCA would have remained the bargaining agent of the predominantly African factory workers for some time yet. This recalcitrance, apparently, did not gain the approval of 'moderate' ministers, such as Ashton Chase and Forbes Burnham.

In Janet's letter of September 1 to Billy Strachan she mentioned the PPP strike in the sugar industry:

> **The GIWU has called a colony-wide strike on the sugar estates for better wages and working conditions.** It is too early to report on it, for we are just now organising it. I leave for Berbice this afternoon to call them **off** [she meant '**out**']. If they answer the call, everything will be ok, as they are really the key. Will report to you later when I can give you a full story [emphasis added].[43]

Strangely, she did not mention the principal bone of contention: the recognition of their union, which should have been a non-issue after the SPA's recognition offer of August 20, 1953. The strike was ostensibly for 'better wages and working conditions.' They were playing with fire.

There were also ad hoc issues that the Jaganite faction identified periodically as appropriate sites for the anti-imperialist struggle. The Queen was scheduled to visit Jamaica in November 1953, and its government had extended an invitation for British Guiana to send two delegates. But the PPP government deemed the event an anachronism: they would not dare to fraternise with the imperialist enemy of whom the Queen was the highest representative. This, too, was another straw that broke the camel's back. I believe that Janet's communist predilection apart, as an American, she never did grasp the subtleties of British colonial rule; neither did Cheddi, who grew up on a Guyanese sugar plantation and spent his young adult years in America, not Britain. Burnham was by no stretch of the imagination an Anglophile; yet, like most middle-class Africans, he was more at ease with British colonial culture and its symbolic projection of power. It is not known how Billy Strachan saw their uncompromising stance, but Janet clearly was not in favour of sending a delegate to meet the Queen. She sought to explain to Billy:

> The question of sending a delegate to Jamaica to meet the Queen has also been causing some controversy here. The matter came up in the House of Assembly on August 28 [1953], when NDP's [National Democratic Party's] W.O.R. Kendall [1903–83] moved a dual motion calling for the House to pledge loyalty to the Queen and to send a delegate to see her in Jamaica. The debate began and Sydney [King] set the pace by saying that our Party members would abstain from voting on the first part but would reaffirm our position **not** to send a delegate. **He referred to the Opposition's plea to send a delegate, saying that they had 'displayed the culture of bondsmen and the intellect of grovelling worms**' [emphasis added].

> Cheddi criticised the Opposition for wanting to follow the traditions of the past automatically, and that 'we were steeped in too many

antiquated customs and conventions. It is time we think in terms of a new age.'

The Speaker, however, postponed the voting, so the matter has not been settled yet. Some brilliant speeches were made that day.[44]

Limited vision, indeed, on the part of the Jagans, King and the PPP!

The advice of the CPGB was that the PPP should not be detracted by the demands of office: they must simultaneously pursue a multi-dimensional anti-imperialist struggle to secure self-government, while creating the base for constructing a communist political culture. And as Janet informed Billy, they were also guided by proletarian internationalism:

> There will be an inaugural opening of a Committee of Cultural Relations with Foreign Countries on October 3–4 [1953] to honour China's Anniversary [of liberation on October 1, 1949]. There will be an exhibition of photographs, books, folk art and the playing of [Chinese] records.[45]

The Jaganite faction of the PPP was, indeed, adopting various forms of struggle to sustain the anti-imperialist momentum, thus obviating the likelihood of their becoming bogged down by the stultifying demands of the minutiae of governance, in a colony. In fact, the PPP appeared more at ease as a protest movement than it was in demonstrating its capacity to govern. They were out of their depth: a disparate group, with little in common other than a deep-seated anti-British/anti-White reflex, thrown overnight into a role for which they manifested little talent, and with no inclination or resolve to fulfil. The most they had anticipated, and probably desired, was to constitute the official Opposition; however, they polled 51 per cent of the votes but a disproportionate eighteen of the twenty-four seats (75 per cent) – a major defect of the first-past-the-post system, surely! It was a Pyrrhic victory, as the racial insecurity of Africans remained unredressed. But the Jaganites knew that their 'bitter sugar' mantra, particularly on the big sugar plantations in Berbice and Demerara, was 'the key,' as Janet put it – the tested instrument for mobilising Jagan's numerically expanding Indian base. This was consonant with the wise counsel given to Janet by the CPGB leadership on July 9, 1953. But this militancy on the sugar plantations was subversive of their relationship with the governor and the senior colonial officials in the colony to the point where any collaboration, as required by the Waddington Constitution, had become impracticable.

On September 2, 1953 (the day after Janet's candid letter to Billy Strachan), Governor Savage sent a telegram to the secretary of state for the colonies, deploring the sugar strike called by the PPP/GIWU. He insinuated that the PPP ministers had no desire to maintain a working relationship with the colonial officials, including the governor. It appears that the Jaganites concurred with their CPGB comrades that the class struggle and the anti-imperialist crusade were of the highest order. It could not simply be subordinated to the constraints of governance. This course, however, was a recipe for collision – incompatible with the widely accepted gradualist approach to self-government, implicit in working within the strictures of the Waddington Constitution.

With some PPP ministers actively promoting the strike in the sugar industry, Governor Savage was desperate, and he conveyed this to the Colonial Office. He could no longer work with the PPP ministers. I believe this was, indeed, the straw that broke the camel's back – what finally drove the British government to suspend the Constitution on October 9, 1953:

> I regret to say that the situation has deteriorated. All estates on the East Coast Demerara are now on strike, except two. In Berbice, Skeldon and Rose Hall are on strike as a result of agitation by Mrs Jagan and Ajodha Singh, members of the House of Assembly who are doing everything possible to spread the strike to the rest of the area. Estates on the West Coast [Demerara] and the West Bank Demerara are not seriously affected as yet, but it is understood that Dr Lachmansingh [President of the GIWU and Minister of Health and Housing] is visiting the area today to foment trouble. The demands have been presented by the workers to the management of the estates, and the basic objections vary between wage increases and recognition of GIWU.
>
> **There is no doubt that the motives behind the strike are purely political, and that the principal instigators are Mrs Jagan and Sydney King** [Minister of Communications and Works]…The Commissioner of Police considers that the local forces can control the situation even if all the sugar workers strike, but he is of opinion, which I share, that if the other industries and ports are affected, outside assistance may be required to maintain order.
>
> **In the last few days there has been an acceleration of the attacks on me, the ex-officio members and the State Council; and I cannot ignore the possibility that the extremists** [the Jaganites] **intend…to develop present situation and find excuse for the present Government to resign and seek a general election on the question of full self-government** [emphasis added].[46]

Governor Savage would have been fully aware that the chasm between Jagan and Burnham was unbridgeable; that it was inconceivable they could arrive at a common position. In fact, it is possible that the coarseness of the PPP's response to the colonial officials reflected an endeavour to mask the PPP's lack of internal cohesion and its chaotic ad hoc approach to governance. It was a journey to nowhere, as the SLO, C. A. Herbert (based in Trinidad), sought to explain to the director general of MI5, on August 11, 1953. He saw clearly that Cheddi Jagan's leadership was floundering, as he looked over his shoulder to his nemesis, Forbes Burnham:

> During the past month [July–August 1953] signs of confusion and lack of leadership became evident among the elected ministers of the PPP. No constructive legislative programme has yet been announced, and the only positive decision which was taken was to refuse the invitation to send two representatives to be present in Jamaica when Her Majesty the Queen visits that colony in November [1953]. Dr Jagan said briefly that British Guiana's public money could be put to better use.[47]

The SLO observed that 'the so-called moderate' ministers, Forbes Burnham and Ashton Chase, appeared to be 'at least as radical as their more extreme colleagues.' But, as I suggest, this was a façade because the Jagan-Burnham rift, with potentially negative implications for relations between Indians and Africans, was swept under the carpet in the PPP, obscured by the Marxist rhetoric regarding the paramountcy of the class struggle; the problem smouldered while the racial chasm expanded. The sublimated problem excited exaggerated compensatory anti-colonial rhetoric from the leaders of the PPP, as each faction sought to demonstrate their anti-British credentials. But Burnham was irreconcilable with Jagan's immutable pro-Soviet ideological stance, beyond moderate suasion. Besides, Burnham's overweening ambition could not accommodate his being second to anyone; worse, to one whom he considered intellectually his inferior.

The SLO also remarked that while Jagan was not implicated in the spate of 'attacks' on colonial administrators, he was 'clearly worried by his inability to get the unqualified support of his ministers.' Moreover, other members of the party, such as Assemblyman Fred Bowman, seemed to have had a free hand in fomenting strikes, using inflammatory language to 'incite workers to strike'; and he alluded to Cheddi's inability to exert authority in a PPP that was out of control. This was probably true, given the leviathan that was Burnham, but it is also true that the GIWU's message and *modus operandi* were congruent with the 'bitter sugar' narrative. An excerpt from Bowman's address to sugar estate workers follows:

> The autumn crop is about to start [in September 1953]. What I want you to do is to work for the first few weeks and save a few cents, because if we do not get what you want, you must be ready [to strike]. The white man say they are higher than us, they have big limousines to drive in. Even their dogs are driving in cars. Where did they get all this luxury from? It is from our sweat.[48]

The SLO observed that Jagan was present at this meeting, and he 'apparently acquiesced' in Bowman's remarks. He, too, reflected on the objective of the strikes in the sugar industry, suggesting they were designed to precipitate a constitutional crisis, thereby accelerating the process of self-government through popular agitation and mobilisation. The SLO concluded his report with a reference to Cheddi Jagan's apparent recalcitrance towards colonial officials:

'The B.G. [British Guina] Director of Agriculture, who passed through Trinidad a few days ago, told me that Jagan was making no attempt to co-operate with him and seemed content to allow the Department to slide into chaos.' The director of MI5 routinely passed on such material to the Colonial Office.[49]

At public meetings, PPP Ministers were accused of 'insolent and insulting references to the Governor and the ex-officio Ministers'; and the Robertson Report cited the case of Forbes Burnham. On August 30, 1953, at a public meeting at Kitty, this is how he referred to Attorney General F. W. Holder (a Barbadian), and the chief secretary, John Gutch:

> There is another fellow the Attorney General, he is the one who is to legislate the laws and he can do as he likes. We will also have to get rid of him too. The next person is the Chief Secretary…Yes, I am referring to [John] Gutch. I am sorry one of his security police is not here to report to him in the morning what I have to say now.

Burnham might not have known, but an undercover officer from Special Branch was usually present at all PPP meetings. One was clearly there at this meeting in Kitty. They also spied systematically on several members of the PPP, particularly Cheddi and Janet Jagan. However, MI5 seemed disinclined to spy on Burnham. I know not why.

On that same day in August 1953, Burnham (speaking at Bourda Green, in Georgetown) described Governor Savage 'as a charming fellow…who has too much power and is the servant of the British Imperialists.' On September 24, 1953, Burnham displayed his irreverent vein, at another public meeting:

> As for Gutch, his post can be filled from here [British Guiana]. Holder (Attorney General), that Barbadian boy…we will pack him up and chase him back to Barbados…As for Fraser (Financial Secretary), poor boy, we will get rid of him also…Who is Savage [the Governor] to be vested with all this power? Why can't our boys be given these powers? Poor boy, Savage, we will soon make him pack his bundle and take the boat.

Yet while Burnham was making these scurrilous remarks about his fellow members of the Executive Council, he was no less irreconcilable with Cheddi Jagan being seen as the presumed leader of the PPP – Cheddi's peerless spadework, from the PAC to the PPP as legislator, inveterate campaigner and Marxist agitator/theorist since 1947 notwithstanding.[50]

V.   The Robertson Commission Report and Burnham's Split from the PPP, 1954–55

The Robertson Commission Report observed that by August–September 1953 the principal policymaking body, the Executive Council, was being routinely undermined to a degree that rendered it barely functional. But it is plausible that given the open ideological discrepancy and simmering rift over leadership within the PPP, between Jagan and Burnham, the patent uncouthness of several PPP ministers and legislators towards colonial officials reflected psychological displacement. The Jagan and Burnham factions of the PPP, at this early stage in office, appeared

A façade: Jagan and Burnham, two irreconcilable leaders in the original PPP, depart Atkinson Field (airport), in late 1953, on their way to London and India to protest against the suspension of the constitution. It was an exercise in futility because Burnham was inherently incapable of being second to anyone, including Jagan.

to have sublimated their implacable rivalry; consequently, they were inclined to overreach each other in venting their anti-imperialist, anti-British (even anti-White) venom. But the Commission shrewdly ascertained and defined the divergent ideological thrust of Jagan, the communist, and Burnham, designated as 'socialist' or some such vague, but acceptable, approximation, his caustic anti-colonial sentiments notwithstanding.

Overall, they were accurate with respect to the irreconcilability of the two leaders of the PPP. It was not simply a matter of divide-and-rule by the imperialists, as many have argued. This is the assessment of the Commission of the communist Jaganite segment of the party:

> [W]e have no doubt that there was a very powerful communist influence within the PPP. At the time of the elections [April 1953] at least six of the party's most prominent leaders – specifically Dr Jagan (Leader of the Legislative Group), Mrs [Janet] Jagan (General Secretary and Editor of *Thunder*), Mr Sydney King (Assistant General Secretary), Mr Rory Westmaas (Junior Vice-Chairman), Mr B. H. Benn (Executive Committee member and Secretary of the Pioneer Youth League), and Mr Martin Carter (Executive Committee member) – accepted unreservedly the "classical" communist doctrines of Marx and Lenin: were enthusiastic supporters of the policies and practices of modern communist movements: and were contemptuous of European social democratic parties, including the British Labour Party.[51]

However, the Robertson Commission got it totally wrong that Jagan did not become a 'convinced communist' until after his visit to East Germany and

Czechoslovakia in the summer of 1951. As I have documented, Jagan became a Marxist-Leninist shortly after his return to British Guiana in 1943; this was what had given him (and Janet) the conviction and impetus to form their Marxist study group, the Political Affairs Committee, in November 1946. Janet, of course, was already a communist. But the report was acute in recognising that the Jaganite faction of the PPP was not in favour of working the Waddington Constitution and that they believed the imperialists had to be confronted to relinquish power through militant struggle. They were rather contemptuous of the British government's measured, incremental approach to granting self-government. Only a frontal assault on British imperialism, the 'class struggle' encapsulated in Jagan's 'bitter sugar' narrative, could rid the country of the arch-imperialists, the colonial regime and 'blood suckers' like Booker:

> [W]e are convinced that these people [the Jaganites] had been restrained by expediency rather than by principle from forming and leading an openly communist party. They had decided on balance that they could more speedily achieve their most important and immediate objectives – that of ridding British Guiana of British rule and influence – by remaining associated with others [like Burnham] who had a similar objective in a party with a wide popular appeal...
>
> **They did not believe that self-government for British Guiana could be earned in successive steps by revealed capacity for responsible government.** On the contrary, they believed that a dependent territory can normally expect to win self-government only by violent action little short of revolution. But they thought that with Great Britain still economically weak and weary of conflict and, as a great colonial power, morally on the defensive, a determined threat of sustained disruption with a strong hint of violence might well be enough to compel a British Government to concede self-government to British Guiana as the only alternative to repression by force [emphasis added].
>
> We do not doubt that these were genuine beliefs and that Dr and Mrs Jagan, Mr King and Mr Westmaas in particular were willing to stake their own and the Party's political existence upon them. Indeed, we are convinced that from the moment the PPP secured its majority, it was...only a question of time before these people made a concerted effort to get the Party embarked on a course of action which was deliberately intended to lead to a serious constitutional crisis as a means of forcing the British Government to capitulate to the demands of the PPP.[52]

Whatever reservations this militant approach evoked in Burnham, he brought combustible rhetoric of his own to the anti-British vitriol; although it was Jagan's Marxist faction that controlled the dominant narrative of the PPP in 1953. Burnham (a brilliant lawyer) often deemed 'ambiguous,' recognised that the

British government would have preferred him to lead the PPP rather than the avowed communist Jagan. Yet he considered it imperative to continually project his anti-colonial mettle while never endorsing Jagan's pro-Moscow communist stance. Burnham's strident anti-British posture gave him credibility locally, but he also knew that, in the end, he could make a persuasive political impression on the British imperialists, Conservative and Labour, who loathed communism in equal measure. In fact, it is not far-fetched to suggest that Burnham had a vested interest in undermining the leadership of Jagan, hence his crudely flippant attitudes towards the colonial officials on the spot, even if the consequence was imperial subversion of the PPP government. He would keep his powder dry for another day, and his day could come if Jagan persisted with his untenable communist ideology (in 'America's backyard') while the Cold War was ablaze. Thus, conceivably, independence could be withheld from Jagan, although Burnham (being a Guyanese nationalist) would unfailingly feign commitment to the principle of independence while sabotaging Jagan's advance towards it.

The suspension of the Constitution was not publicly welcomed by Burnham, but he probably construed it as a crucial eventuality in impeding, if not arresting, the ascendancy of the Jaganite Indian juggernaut. Yet, strangely, so deep was the faith of the Jaganites in the superiority of their Marxist creed that they, too, were prepared to push the British to the limit; to be equally intransigent with respect to working the Constitution, rather than accommodating its conventional limitations. The Marxists were instinctually averse to the British predilection for incremental change, constitutional or otherwise – 'the inevitability of gradualness,' in the Fabian socialist Sidney Webb's memorable phrase. The Jaganites were playing with fire, but they solemnly believed that history and time were on their side.

On September 25, 1953, Janet Jagan sent an article to Billy Strachan for the *Daily Worker*, the official organ of the CPGB; it was titled 'Crisis in Guiana.' The mail was intercepted by MI5. She commenced it thus:

> A constitutional crisis is rapidly developing in British Guiana. They took an uncompromising stance on the Waddington Constitution, having launched a 'Patriotic Appeal...calling for amendments to the constitution, abolishing all the features which undemocratically hold back the will of the people and calling for legislation against racialists and warmongers.

I am not sure what prompted the latter comment, but it must have been aimed at the imperialists and in defence of the Soviet Union. The PPP was active in the communist World Peace Council, the two young radicals, Rory Westmaas and Martin Carter – a law unto themselves – being the principal figures.

Janet also remarked on the end of the twenty-four-day strike by the PPP union, the GIWU. But she was not telling the truth when she stated that the SPA had refused to recognise the GIWU in favour of the MPCA, 'a company union affiliated to the western-backed ICFTU.' It will be recalled that the SPA, in August 1953, was prepared to recognise the GIWU as the agent for the fieldworkers, the overwhelming majority in the sugar industry, in the first instance. But the party still proceeded with the strike. Then, on September 24, the minister of labour presented a labour relations bill in the House of Assembly, a measure aimed at the recognition of any union with majority support demonstrated in a poll, wherever there was jurisdictional dispute between contending unions. The minister of labour asked the Speaker to suspend the standing orders of the House to expedite the three readings of the bill on the same day. This was most provocative and foolhardy: the TUC had no input in the matter, at any stage. It was indicative of the reckless arrogance, arguably a self-destructive indifference to consequences, permeating the inchoate party. The Speaker refused, and the PPP members walked out of the House.[53]

It is necessary to repeat (yet again!) that the SPA had agreed to the GIWU representing all the field workers (predominantly Indian), while the MPCA would continue to represent the minority factory workers (mainly African), but the latter situation was negotiable in the near future. It was a major concession. It was rejected by the PPP.

Sydney King (now Eusi Kwayana, aged ninety-eight) responded recently to allegations that the recalcitrance of the PPP, regarding the strike despite the SPA's recognition of the GIWU, was attributable to him. It is a candid revelation of the foundation of his negative response to the recognition by the sugar producers of the GIWU, in August 1953:

> This author has been blamed by observers...for rejection by the union of an offer by the SPA to recognise the GIWU for field workers [predominantly Indian] and the MPCA for factory workers [predominantly African]. It is true that this writer saw the offer, when it was made, as repeating the situation that led to the Enmore shooting of 1948 when a number of field workers [Indians] decided to enter the factory to appeal to factory workers [Africans] to join their strike. He opposed it because it would only have made formal the same situation that left power in the hands of the employer.[54]

The day before Janet Jagan sent her article to Billy Strachan (September 24, 1953), Cheddi wrote to Tom McWinnie, the representative in London of the communist front, pro-Soviet World Federation of Trade Unions (WFTU). The letter was intercepted by MI5. It pertained to the third World Trade Union congress in Vienna in October 1953, sponsored by the WFTU. And he was requesting that two trade unionists, Brentnol Blackman and Andrew Jackson,

Africans from non-PPP unions, be accredited as delegates, in addition to his trusted lieutenant, Ramkarran, a PPP member of the legislature. Cheddi's aim was to engage with unions that were pivotal in persuading the TUC to become affiliated to the WFTU, rather than the pro-Western International Confederation of Free Trade Unions (ICFTU). The control of trade unions was a fundamental aspect of the Cold War, and Jagan was unequivocally on the Soviet side. The WFTU, of course, as another communist-front organisation promoted by the Soviet Union was clearly a repository of its ideology and finance. Cheddi explained to Tom McWinnie the reason why he had intervened to ensure those two trade unionists did go to Vienna:

> The sending of Blackman and Jackson was entirely my responsibility. I felt it was absolutely imperative that they attend. Their respective unions are strategically very important. They both have shown opportunist tendencies [being non-Marxists], but without them there cannot be any hope for early national [TUC] affiliation to the WFTU.[55]

The Jamaican-born communist, Ferdinand C. Smith (1893–1961), was a senior official at the WFTU head office in Vienna. According to MI5, it was through him that funds were disbursed to communist trade unionists in the Caribbean, principal among them being Richard Hart (1917–2013), the Jamaican communist expelled from Norman Manley's PNP in 1952. A letter from the director general of MI5, dated September 26, 1953, observes that WFTU funds for the Jagans were sent by Smith to Hart to conceal its source:

> It seems to us that…Hart has been acting on behalf of Smith to avoid the possibility of any suggestion being made that the Jagans have been receiving direct subsidies from a representative of the WFTU. Our information indicates that Hart himself would be in no position to send funds from his own resources.[56]

Whether these reports of communist money going to the Jagans were correct or not, the fact that they emanated from MI5 must have rendered them credible at the Colonial Office. But an equally interesting item in the same MI5 note was their failure to ascertain the source of US$4,000 Sydney King reportedly took into British Guiana in early 1953. King had been in Eastern Europe for about three months in 1952–53, and he did take some money with him into British Guiana, but he told me it was a mere US$400.

It is noteworthy that Burnham's engagement with 'recent happenings' seems to have been marginal, apart from his vitriolic interventions against some of the highest colonial officials. Yet the Robertson Commission appeared not to have fathomed the true depth of the chasm – personal, ideological, and racial – between Jagan and Burnham; moreover, that Burnham's strident anti-British rhetoric was strategic to his pursuit of the leadership of the PPP, while never succumbing to the compromising communist tenets unfailingly espoused by Jagan. But they did dangle the carrot, forthrightly to Burnham, for him to make a clean break with the communist Jagan, if he was earnest about enhancing his political fortunes.

And this is what the Robertson Commission thought of Forbes Burnham, the 'socialist,' while urging him to moderate his wild rhetoric – thereby erasing any ambiguity with respect to his ideology and that of the communist Jagan. It was a timely intervention, in 1954, a significant one:

> Mr Burnham (Chairman of the Party) was generally recognised as the leader of the socialists in the PPP, and as such to be in rivalry for the moral leadership of the Party as a whole. He had, however, by the wildness of many of his speeches and by the irresponsibility of some of his actions created doubts in the minds of some of our witnesses as to whether his differences with Dr Jagan were not more personal and racial than political. Even among those of our witnesses who were keen supporters of the PPP, there were many who thought that as the recognised leader of the socialists in the PPP, Mr Burnham ought to have taken a much stronger line than he did in opposition to the more blatantly communist activities of the Jagans and their supporters.
>
> We came to the conclusion that, besides the ambiguous Mr Burnham, at least two of the most prominent leaders of the Party – specifically Mr Ashton Chase (Executive Committee member) and Mr Clinton Wong (Senior Vice-Chairman) – and a number of its less prominent leaders were socialists. They were as bitterly opposed as their communist colleagues to British colonial rule, but they were not communists. They too were familiar with and approved many of the orthodox theories of communist writers on imperialism and capitalism. But their dislike of imperialism and capitalism was based less upon Marxist interpretations of history than upon their own understanding of the history of colonial rule and the interpretations which they have placed upon experiences of capitalist enterprise in British Guiana. They were certainly extremists even by colonial standards, and we are not surprised that many of our witnesses were unable to distinguish between their socialism and the communism of some of their colleagues.
>
> **Yet we had no doubts that the socialists in the PPP were essentially democrats, and that left to themselves their preference at all times would have been that the Party should pursue its constitutional objectives by straightforward and peaceful means. We doubt, however, if they had the wit to see the essential difference between themselves and their communist colleagues or the ability to avoid being outmanoeuvred by them** [emphasis added].[57]

Jagan was correct that the Robertson Commission was cleverly attempting to aggravate the fissure in the PPP to precipitate a clean break by Burnham, the 'socialist,' from the Jaganite communists. Although Burnham was studiously vague regarding his brand of 'socialism,' it was assumed by the Colonial Office to be in harmony with the social democratic politics of Norman Manley and Grantley Adams of Jamaica and Barbados respectively, which they deemed responsible and moderate. Therefore, the Robertson Commission was, in essence, enticing Burnham to assert his non-communist credentials as a prelude to his definitive break with the Jagans and his own political ascendancy. Only thus could he become his own man and, by implication, Britain and America's logical preference in the Cold War.

The Robertson Report benefited from the learned and urbane local member of the Commission, Sir Donald Jackson (1892–1981), a distinguished African Guyanese lawyer with a thorough grasp of Guyanese society, its ineluctable partisan politics and fragmented racial dynamic. He was a headmaster before he went to England to read law; Burnham's father, James Burnham, was a headmaster also; they would have known each other, in Georgetown, through the vibrant teachers' union. Sir Donald (chief justice of the Windward Islands) was highly respected in the Colonial Service, as is evident in this excerpt from the following telegram of November 3, 1953, by the governor of the Windward Islands (E. B. Beetham) to the secretary of state for the colonies regarding the composition of the British Guiana Commission of Inquiry:

> I think Jackson would be an admirable choice. He is a quick and clear thinker...and has no (repeat no) illusions about the limitations of West Indians generally. He would furthermore be able to give other members much useful information from his own personal knowledge, and as a generally respected Guianese he should be able to obtain much additional information of value to the Commission denied to other members. He will remain calm and unruffled no matter what attitude...his fellow countrymen adopt towards the Commission. His integrity is beyond question.[58]

Another prominent African from that middle-class stratum of headmasters, journalists, junior civil servants, lawyers, and a few doctors was R. B. O. Hart. An educationist and journalist, he must have shared the vision of Sir Donald Jackson on the prospects of Forbes Burnham as a moderate African leader, one of their own (a seminal Guyanese response, then and now), with the intellectual gifts and capacity for leadership to supplant the Indian communist, Cheddi Jagan. Hart was the editor of a small newspaper, *Clarion*; and in its issue of July 25, 1954 (as Jagan stated) Hart anticipated or, conceivably, helped to shape the judgement of the Robertson Commission on Burnham's leadership potential. He wanted

Burnham to lead the PPP 'into safe channels,' beseeching him to 'cease being a figurehead and become the effective leader of his Party; [therefore] he must be able to control more votes on the Executive Committee. This means that the Executive must have on it a majority of sober men.'

A few days before Burnham finally broke with the PPP, in February 1955, Hart was proud to take credit for effecting it. He wrote thus in the *Guiana Graphic* of February 10, 1955:

> On July 25, 1954, I sold Burnham an idea which he is now putting into practice. I quote the *Clarion* of that date: 'You owe a duty to the people of this country [he meant Africans primarily] who have followed you blindly. So far you have been lucky. You have done nothing to merit their blind support and idolatry. How can you as a young man [aged 31] of any character and decency lead them astray again? You and Dr J. P. Lachmansingh would make a very effective team, and if you stood hand in hand would be able to keep the Party together while kicking the extremists out [Jagan and the communists]. Lachmansingh [aged 58] is no spring chicken himself, but he is one of the few men in your party of whom I would say 'he is not a communist.'[59]

Apart from being Indian and anti-communist, Lachmansingh was president of the PPP's union, the GIWU, which was dedicated (perpetually) to contesting the right of the recognised union, the MPCA, to represent the sugar workers. However, as demonstrated in the elections of 1953, Cheddi Jagan was incontestably the *bona fide* leader of the Indians; his verve, charismatic appeal, and his 'bitter sugar' crusade were unassailable. The older Dr Lachmansingh had no discernible political base among Indians, including the sugar workers. Nobody but Cheddi did, certainly by the early 1950s. So, R. B. O. Hart's counsel to Burnham that Lachmansingh would be an asset in shaping a multi-ethnic appeal was inherently flawed. Burnham did get two of his anti-communist Indian colleagues, former Ministers Lachmansingh and Jainaraine Singh, to follow him in the split of February 1955, but that could not be equated with Indian support for him by any stretch of the imagination. Jainaraine Singh became general secretary of Burnham's PPP, and in January 1957 he explained the principal reason for the split: 'We told the truth about the reason why there has been this split. We told the people that Communism was the basis of it all. We, not being Communists, could not support a Communist policy.'[60]

It is interesting, therefore, to ascertain how three of the key leaders of the PPP reacted to the Robertson Commission Report of 1954 on the suspension of the Waddington Constitution. Jagan did moderate his Marxist response, but he did not try to refute the allegation that he was a communist. Burnham, on the other hand, was vague as usual, circumventing the prime determination that the report had identified him as the leader of the 'socialists,' who should recognise the 'essential difference' between himself and the communists and proceed to establish his leadership of the PPP on that moderate premise. Sydney King was forthright in venting his Marxist perspective on the report, arguing that the Suspension was done mainly in defence of foreign capital, Booker in particular. His stance was in the mould of Jagan's rooted Marxist assessment, but it was at variance with Burnham's position as a 'socialist,' or as he probably preferred to be seen at the time, a social democrat. Burnham was more in step with the principal leaders of the British West Indies, who rejected the Marxist tenet that foreign capital was inherently evil and subversive of economic progress.

In November 1954 (in *Thunder*), Jagan rejected the central premise of the report: that British Guiana, given the recent 'subversion' of the liberal constitution despite its concomitant implication of incremental steps towards self-government, must be placed on a reset – thus 'marking time' constitutionally. Yet Cheddi was not intimidated by the Commission's definitive deprecation of his communist ideology, neither would he pander to Burnham's machinations. Moreover, he was never susceptible to renouncing his faith in communism in countering Burnham's much touted 'moderation,' already recognised by the West and in the region:

> Boiled down to the barest essentials, the Robertson Commission's dictum is this – you can vote, but you mustn't vote for the people who are going to fight for you…Only when you come to your senses by throwing out your militant leaders and changing your anti-imperialist policy, will you be given the right. This interpretation of democracy by the Robertson Commission is merely translating into practice [Colonial Secretary] Lyttleton's famous pronouncement: 'Her Majesty's Government is not prepared to see the setting up of Communist governments in any part of the British Commonwealth…' The PPP will mark time, but not at the tune of the imperialists.[61]

What is conspicuous, however, is Burnham's studied vagueness regarding the report, a finely honed feature of his writing and his speeches throughout his career. It was frequently unascertainable what he really stood for, although his impeccable diction and oratorical gifts were often mesmeric. Spiced with the vernacular and combined with measured Churchillian pauses, pace, and delivery, many were drawn to his meetings to be enthralled and entertained. In the same issue of *Thunder* carrying Jagan's reaction, in November 1954, L. F. S. Burnham also responded to the Robertson Report, and (as noted earlier) he cleverly circumvented their transparently partisan and seductive enticement regarding his 'socialism' – juxtaposed with Jagan's communist extremism that was increasingly unpalatable to the British. However, Burnham was already in the process of shrewdly engineering his split from Jagan:

> The people of British Guiana have enough political maturity (the members of the Commission will call it precocity) that even according to theoretical standards set by herself, Britain has shown every intention of stifling democracy here as elsewhere in her Empire. The fight therefore continues, and the day must come when we shall no longer be lectured by the representatives of our foreign masters or have our Constitutions written by our exploiters. Guiana shall be free, and we shall choose our own government.[62]

Two weeks later, Burnham, in an editorial for *Thunder*, still minimised the chronic ethnic insecurity that was at the root of the PPP's fragility, even deriding the widely feared imminence of a split. Meanwhile, Burnham was discretely framing his plan to break with Jagan's faction of the PPP to establish his own leadership of the party:

> That Indians and Africans represent two different race groups is a physical fact, but that they are all subject to domination and oppression under the British imperialist system is also a physical fact…Any racial antipathies perpetrated and transferred into the field of politics will give the British the excuse of remaining on our backs in the alleged interest of law and order…With the advent of the PPP the broad masses of [Africans and Indians]…were brought together politically in the interests of British Guiana…
>
> **Though several attempts were made to engineer a split, they were all unsuccessful, and this lack of success on the one hand, and sustained solidarity on the other, were a source of intense fear to those who sought to divide and rule…Thanks to the PPP, this will not happen. We have welded a Guianese nation on the basis of struggle against imperialism and the establishment of a free Guiana. The armies of racial division will not prevail against us** [emphasis added].[63]

Such were the Machiavellian manoeuvres of Forbes Burnham that while he was undermining Jagan's leadership on ideological grounds, he was simultaneously feigning repudiation of the charge of communism levelled disparagingly against Jagan's segment of the PPP by the Robertson Commission. The latter, of course, was unabashedly on Burnham's side. Yet Burnham, shamelessly, countered with the following blatant affectation:

> great use was made of the alleged communist ideology and 'extremist' leaders of the Party…[But] when one examines the Robertson Report and notes events which supposedly led to Her Majesty's sending troops and saving Guiana from ruin, it becomes obvious that the 'mistake' the PPP made was not any attempt to propagate the doctrines of Marx and Lenin, but rather their determination to put effective power in the hands of the people's representatives.[64]

But it was not just a matter of ideological incongruity between Burnham and Jagan – it was both communism and race. Burnham's supposedly moderate, socialist ideological prism did attract anti-communist Indians like Dr J.P. Lachmansingh and Jainaraine Singh, but the anticipated viable non-communist African-Indian alliance (under Burnham) never could materialise, as only a microscopic minority of Indians was prised from their hero from the plantation, Cheddi Jagan. Neither Lachmansingh nor Jainaraine Singh possessed the political acumen to cultivate a base among their Indian compatriots. Jainarine Singh, the first general secretary of Burnham's PPP, did win a seat in the 1957 general elections but only because of Burnham's African supporters, yet as early as 1959 he had left Burnham's PNC. Jainaraine told me, in Georgetown in August 1992, that Burnham had become increasingly racist after the elections of 1957, therefore he could no longer work with him, and the solidarity triggered by their anti-communist stance against Jagan was inadequate to sustain the alliance.

Just as the Marxism of Cheddi Jagan could not alleviate the mutual insecurities of Africans and Indians, the 'socialist' or ideologically amorphous, but perceptibly non-communist, politics of Burnham could not erase, or even attenuate, the centrality of race in the political culture. A week after the split in February 1955, R. B. O. Hart reflected candidly on Burnham's role in the post-Suspension politics of British Guiana:

> Burnham now emerges as a racial and sectional leader. He leads the African section of the population rather more than less. Jagan has greater claim to being a national leader, since in any showdown, Jagan will get ten times as many Africans following him as Burnham will get Indians.[65]

Starting from the latter's appallingly low base, it is not as impressive as it sounds.

Yet as Odeen Ishmael observes, such African support, however thin, owed little to Jagan's Marxism or his charisma; it was engendered through the irreproachable personal stature of Sydney King in the African villages on the East Coast of Demerara. The abstemious King was a hero of the rural African, and if his loyalty to Jagan held, in opposition to Burnham, a modicum of African support for Jagan was sustainable. But after King became alienated from Jagan in 1956–57, before the general elections of 1957, that sliver of support evaporated quickly. African support for Jagan was virtually non-existent after King became general secretary of Burnham's PNC in 1958 and editor of the party's organ, *New Nation*. Jagan, like Burnham, was now a 'racial and sectional' leader unmitigatedly.

VI. The 'Ultra-Left' in the PPP and the Affirmation of their Communist Creed: The Prison Testimonies of King, Carter, and Westmaas

King had been the Jagans' most stellar African Marxist ally in the PPP. He, Martin Carter, Rory Westmaas, and Lionel Jeffrey were later dubbed the 'ultra-left' by Jagan, yet he did nothing to restrain them before the 1953 elections, neither did he do so for the brief period the PPP was in government in 1953. In fact, the Jagans agreed with most of the Marxist pronouncements of King; they relied on his judgement and his sobriety, and the parting of ways was not transparent until 1956 when he came to the conclusion that Jagan's communist creed notwithstanding, it was retention of his pivotal Indian racial support that was his primary motivation.

King's response to the Robertson Commission Report in 1954 was essentially congruent with Jagan's stance on foreign capital, exemplified by his 'bitter sugar' crusade against Booker and other 'sugar barons' – 'robber barons,' by his definition. King remarked:

> [The Robertson Commission Report]…was saying that the presence of the PPP inside the Government machinery prevented foreign capitalists from investing in the country. Hence in order to satisfy the lusts of foreign capital, it was necessary to kick out the PPP. What the foreign monopolies seek is a situation in which they, the monopolies, can gain maximum concessions, can enter into conspiracies with the ministers against the native people.
>
> Foreign capital also seeks to dominate the economy. It is sugar (foreign capital) that has dominated the economy of this country for over a century and hampered development. Foreign capital attacks the working class, seeking to reduce its standard of living to nought; and seeking a political situation in which the dominant party will join with capital against the trade unions, tie the hands of the workers and crush their militancy by propaganda and legislation.[66]

It was this attitude to foreign capital that had also contributed to the minister of Communications and Works, Sydney King, rejecting the offer of recognition, by the SPA, of the GIWU as the bargaining agent of the fieldworkers. This was the origin as well of his directing the GIWU to go on strike on August 31, 1953, regarding general grievances – not recognition, as this was already on offer but had effectively been rejected. This intransigence, coupled with a confrontational posture that precluded any compromise, had forced the hand of the British government to suspend the Constitution in October 1953.

King and several 'extremists' in the PPP, including Martin Carter and Rory Westmaas, were detained after the Suspension. Others, such as Cheddi and Janet Jagan, also served brief sentences in jail for deliberately breaking their restriction orders. For Cheddi and Janet, however, going to jail placed them virtually at the same level of adulation as Gandhi and Nehru, in the eyes of most Indo-Guyanese. It is noteworthy that Burnham was not detained or jailed, neither were several of his supporters in the PPP, deemed 'socialists' as opposed to the Jaganite communists. On November 28, 1953, King responded to the Advisory Committee for Detained Persons, challenging the government's 'grounds of detention' presented to him. His remarks, as well as those of Carter and Westmaas, corroborated the British assertion regarding the 'extremist' core at the heart of the Jaganite PPP – that their goal was building a communist society in an independent Guyana.

In his inimitable manner, King thought it necessary to correct the authorities for the sake of historical accuracy: 'I have been distributing communist propaganda since 1948 and *not* since 1949.' He rejected allegations that he was planning 'to foster racial hatred' (against Whites), or that he envisaged using violence in pursuit of his communist designs:

> All the world knows that the philosophy of Communism is hostile to all forms of racism and race hatred … All the world knows that the communist view of proletarian revolution rejects out of hand such forms of struggle as arson, incendiarism and the killing of individual leaders.

King wrote thus under the prescribed heading 'background and past conduct':

> I should like to confirm my close association with Dr and Mrs Jagan. **I am an admirer of the Soviet Union**. I am, in fact, an admirer of all peace-loving peoples and of the finest in the cultures of all peoples. **But in the Soviet Union I see the first country to break the imperialist chain, a staunch defender of peace and the liberation of all oppressed humanity.**

> It is charged also that I am a convinced Communist. Now 'conviction' alone is not enough to make one a Communist. V. I. Lenin says that a communist must have a fair mastery of all human knowledge, of the sciences, arts, philosophy, of history, economics, anthropology, etc. I cannot pretend to have reached this eminence. **However, with this reservation, I am a convinced communist** [emphasis added].[67]

Another prominent member of the PPP detained was Rory Westmaas, junior vice-chairman of the party. His grounds for detention were like those of Sydney King, but it was also noted that he was, until he returned to British Guiana in 1952, a member of the West Indian section of the CPGB. The latter segment was led by Cheddi's friend based in London, Billy Strachan. Westmaas was also accused of displaying pictures of famous communists, Marx, Lenin, Stalin, and Mao, during the May Day parade in Georgetown on May 1, 1953. In addition, he was reportedly disseminating 'orthodox Communist propaganda' in British Guiana, material obtained from Eastern Europe and from the CPGB.

Rory responded to the governor's Advisory Committee for Detained Persons on November 30, 1953. He, like Cheddi and King, was not intimidated into renouncing his faith in communism, observing that the grounds for his detention

> have their roots in the vain attempts of two decadent imperialist hierarchies [Britain and America] to help in the securing of the maximum capitalist profit through the ruin, exploitation and impoverishment of the population of the given country through the enslavement and systematic robbery of the peoples of other countries, especially backward countries ....[68]

Rory confirmed that he was a member of the CPGB before he returned to British Guiana in 1952, and he was fulsome in his admiration of that party and what he foresaw as its vital role in the transformation of Britain into a communist society, free from the shackles of American imperialism. He was proud to be a communist and brim-full in his youthful idealism, something he shared with Martin Carter and Sydney King (all in their twenties):

> While a member of that organisation [CPGB], I strove to learn and apply the method and philosophy of dialectical and historical materialism – the guide to action…the tool with which the world can and will be interpreted and changed into the best possible place for human beings. I shall continue in my determination to wage a ceaseless war against the exploitation of man by man; against the enslavement and systematic robbery of peoples; against philistinism and against the debaucheries of human culture; against those who would turn science into a mockery; while on the other hand, to wage a ceaseless struggle for an end to class society, for the freedom of peoples and the release of the pent-up springs of human will, endeavour and joy; and for the development and enrichment of the people's culture and for the use of science as a weapon in the hands of man, permitting his ever-increasing control over the forces of nature for the creation of a society of truly human beings in a world at peace.[69]

This utopian vision of the young Marxists did not make for pragmatism in politics, and it marked the PPP, in the eyes of the colonial officials, as a disparate group in which the Jaganite 'communist clique' controlled the narrative of subversion. Rory Westmaas was certainly at the heart of this 'extremist' faction: '[T]he spectre of communism is haunting the world…My views are Communist views, and because I believe them to be right, I will continue to propagate them for as long as it is possible to do so.' Rory also responded forthrightly to the allegation that the 'Peace Committee Section' of the May Day procession in May 1953 displayed communist slogans and pictures of Lenin and Stalin. He was unapologetic:

The names and faces of such great leaders of the working class and oppressed peoples as Comrade Lenin and Stalin will always live on in the minds of men, and their writings will constantly be a call to action for the toiling masses, urging ever new tasks of skill and audacity in the struggle for complete human liberation. On May Day 1953, in Georgetown, I led the Peace Committee in the demonstration carrying portraits not only of Lenin and Stalin but also of Karl Marx, the founder of scientific socialism; Comrade Mao Tse-Tung, leader of the People's Republic of New China; and Comrade Sydney King, Assistant Secretary of the PPP, and subsequently a People's Minister in the House of Assembly.[70]

Forty years later, in an interview with Professor Frank Birbalsingh (July 19, 1994), Rory was not only cynical of the political vocation, but he could also see no future for Guyana:

Birbalsingh: You come from the Georgetown middle class whereas Cheddi Jagan was of rural plantation stock. Were you aware of a social difference?

Westmaas: Not social but racial difference. I foresaw the threat of racial polarisation from the very beginning. And that is exactly what happened…The politician has to tell lies. He has to say different things to different people. I could never defend politicians. They speak with a forked tongue…

Martin Carter (1927-97), Guyana's foremost poet and an early Marxist ally of the Jagans. Like Sydney King, he was deemed an 'ultra-leftist'; yet, ironically, after leaving the PPP, he joined Jock Campbell's Booker as an information officer, later editing the company's paper, **Booker News**

Birbalsingh: What may we expect from Guyanese politics in the future?

Westmaas: A race war.[71]

Martin Carter was also detained and imprisoned in the aftermath of the Suspension. Among the 'grounds of detention' meted out to him was the allegation that he was one of the 'extremists' in the PPP, 'a close associate' of Cheddi and Janet Jagan and Sydney King. He, too, was deemed to have 'been active in the dissemination of orthodox Communist propaganda material obtained from East European and British Communist Party sources.' The PPP was described by John Gutch, the chief secretary of British Guiana, as being 'completely under the control of a Communist clique'; and that the Peace Committee of British Guiana, of which Carter was chairman, was affiliated to the communist-controlled World Peace Council. Carter, therefore, was a dyed-in-the-wool communist. He certainly was proud of the Soviet example, as it was the foremost proponent of peace among all peoples; moreover, the Soviet people made a massive contribution, at unimaginably vast cost to themselves, in defeating the Nazi menace in the Second World War. As Martin Carter put it evocatively:

> In 1939 the fiend Hitler broke loose and soon the whole of Europe was groaning beneath the heel of the Nazi jackboot. Were it not for the moral strength of the peace-loving Soviet Union, the Nazi plague might well have overtaken the entire world like some poisonous fungus ... Stretching long tentacles over the world, American imperialism today threatens the world with the threat of war. War to the rulers of America is the only solution to the contradictions inherent in the system they foster.[72]

Like Cheddi, Martin Carter was not intimidated by the power of the colonial state to detain him to curb his militancy. He was confident that what he stood for, the idea of communism as a world system, was unconquerable. He responded (on November 28, 1953) to the governor's Advisory Committee for Detained Persons thus:

> I became an Assistant Secretary of the PPP in 1953, but I have been selling and distributing Communist propaganda before 1953, and I shall continue to do so as long as I possibly can. **I feel convinced that it is only by the adoption of the principles laid down by Marx and Engels, furthered and developed by Lenin and Stalin, that a people, colonial or otherwise as the case may be, can learn how to free itself from the tight bonds of imperialism and capitalist serfdom and go forward to the creation of a society in which the free development of all will be assured** [emphasis added].[73]

VII. The Pursuit of Moderation and Political Maturity: Jock Campbell's Appeal after the Suspension

This spectre of communism would follow Cheddi Jagan virtually for the rest of his life, at great cost to himself and his supporters, most of whom were completely ignorant of the content of his communist creed. Yet his idealism never faltered; it could not be extricated from its Marxist-Leninist procrustean mould. And while Forbes Burnham was not encumbered by similar ideological strictures, he, too, did not possess the reasonableness, imagination, and commitment to social democratic norms of, say, Norman Manley of Jamaica. Therefore, although Burnham and his more 'moderate' or non-communist supporters in the PPP did break away from the Jaganite faction in February 1955, as the Robertson Commission had sought to instigate in 1954, British Guiana was no less burdened by the rhetorical excesses and poverty of statesmanship of its anti-colonial leaders. This would leave the country with a bitter legacy which the head of Booker, Jock Campbell, had bemoaned at the time of the suspension of the Constitution in October 1953:

> [British Guiana] will not prosper until she can produce a leader of the calibre of those other British Caribbean leaders who have held ministerial office with high distinction; a Guianese who can form a clear vision of the good Guiana, strive for it, convey it to the public imagination, and, when he has gained election, lead government and people, constructively and progressively towards their goal – **with a true sense of responsibility and in terms of the possible** [emphasis added].[74]

In 1956, even after Burnham had created his own party, calling itself PPP (Burnham), the precursor to his People's National Congress (PNC) founded in October 1957, Campbell was still perturbed by the calibre of leadership in British Guiana. And although he would actively pursue a *modus vivendi* with Jagan after he won the general elections of August 1957, he was not enamoured of his 'communist-dominated PPP' on the eve of the latter; in fact, he was deflated by the palpable poverty of alternatives to Jagan and Burnham. Campbell reflected on Jagan's enhanced stature among Indians after the Suspension:

> [Not] more than a handful of people [in British Guiana] would vote for Communism or for the destructive features in the Party's programme – any more than they did in 1953, but...being human they would vote for the unattainable material promises of the PPP in default of a coherent Party with a straightforward, constructive, reasonably practical and intelligible programme likely to capture the public imagination; and in default of real leadership.[75]

Campbell was not asking for a conservative government in the colony; he wanted a radical one that could inspire Guyanese to work cooperatively and imaginatively, in pursuit of attainable goals. This was his aspiration in 1956:

> It is only by cohesion and concerted action that the many politicians of goodwill and good sense will be able to avoid a small Communist clique driving a horse and coaches through them at the next elections as they did in 1953 – to the disaster of British Guiana. We are not looking for some sort of conservative Government [here]. Nothing but a progressive, radical and nationalistic party – with virile leadership – can capture the imagination of the people. We shall make it our business to work with any such Government – and leader – that will work for the real good of the people.[76]

But Campbell's yearning for a social democratic party, like Norman Manley's People's National Party in Jamaica, proved futile. Cheddi's hold on the Indian imagination was unchallengeable. Racial allegiance was already the pervading motif of Guyanese politics; over six decades later, nothing has changed. Guyana has not been served well by its crop of political leaders. Ashton Chase (1926–), the minister of labour, was the youngest member of the short-lived PPP cabinet of 1953 (aged twenty-seven), but he was generally perceived as moderate, responsible, and effective. He was not a communist, and although he was a trade unionist, he was not an ideologically driven minister – no extremist, certainly. In an interview with Professor Frank Birbalsingh, in 1994, Chase was most censorious of the 'ultra-left' in the PPP of 1953, but he was probably not fully aware of the strong, ongoing links between the Jagans and Billy Strachan and the CPGB. He was also asked if Jagan's experiences as a student in America shaped his radicalism, as opposed to the other West Indian leaders (primarily social democrats) who were educated in Britain:

> I don't think so. I don't think studying in America…had anything to do with it. What had to do with it was Dr Jagan's commitment to Marxism and his communist leanings. Whichever country he was in, those ideas would have been the same. The fact of his being in the US made no difference.[77]

Chase was right.

Notes

1. See my *Sweetening 'Bitter Sugar': Jock Campbell, the Booker Reformer in British Guiana, 1934–66* (Kingston, Jamaica: Ian Randle Publishers, 2005), chapter 13.
2. Ibid., chapter 7: 'Ayube Edun, the *Guiana Review* and the Birth of the MPCA, 1936–39: Sugar Workers Find a Voice.'
3. Letter from Cheddi Jagan to the International Department, the Communist Party of Czechoslovakia, September 13, 1951. See http://digitalarchive/wilsoncenter.org/document/121125.
4. Ibid.

5. No biography of Billy Strachan exists, but I am grateful to Eric Huntley for the following booklet on Strachan published recently: David Horsley, *Billy Strachan, 1921–98: RAF Officer, Communist, Civil Rights Pioneer, Legal Administrator, Internationalist and above all Caribbean Man* (London: Caribbean Labour Solidarity, 2019).
6. Interview with Eusi Kwayana (formerly Sydney King), Georgetown, Guyana, September 22, 1992.
7. Ibid.
8. Janet Jagan to Billy Strachan, February 6, 1953, Billy Strachan Papers, Institute of Commonwealth Studies (ICS), Senate House, University of London.
9. 'Interview with Richard Hart,' in Frank Birbalsingh, *The People's Progressive Party of Guyana, 1950–92: An Oral History* (London: Hansib, 2007), 79–84.
10. Fred Bowman to Billy Strachan, June 24, 1953, Billy Strachan Papers, ICS, Senate House, University of London.
11. *Thunder*, August 1952.
12. Speech by Dr Jagan in the House of Assembly, July 24, 1953, an excerpt cited in the Report of the British Guiana Constitutional Commission, 1954 (Sir James Robertson, chairman), Cmd 9274 (London: HMSO, 1954), 81. Hereafter cited as the Robertson Report.
13. Taken from an unmarked Booker file (in the possession of the late Jock Campbell), n.d., [1953].
14. Text of Talk by Dr Cheddi Jagan Broadcast on Radio Demerara (Georgetown), (mimeo.), August 9, 1953.
15. W. A. Macnie (managing director, Sugar Producers' Association [SPA] to Ashton Chase (minister of labour, industry and commerce), August 20, 1953, in Macnie, 'Labour Unrest Commencing August 31, 1953,' strictly private and confidential, (mimeo.), September 15, 1953, 7–9.
16. See my discussion of the Venn Commission Report in *Sweetening 'Bitter Sugar,'* chapter 14: 'The Venn Commission Report of 1949: Blueprint for Campbell's Reforms.'
17. 'Interview with Harold Lutchman,' in *The People's Progressive Party of Guyana, 1950-92: An Oral History*, ed. Frank Birbalsingh (London: Hansib, 2007), 136.
18. Robertson Report (1954), see the section on the Labour Relations Bill, 58–63.
19. Ashton Chase, *A History of Trade Unionism in Guyana, 1900 to 1964* (Ruimveldt, Guyana: New Guyana Company Ltd, n.d. [1964]), 208.
20. Macnie, 'Labour Unrest Commencing August 31, 1953,' appendix III.
21. Eusi Kwayana, '65 Years after October 1953: A Report and Review by One Present at the Events,' (mimeo), 2018, 5, 12–13.
22. Quoted in 'Cheddi Jagan – 43 Years the People's Champion,' 1990 (mimeo.), CJRC, call no. 5044. Cheddi Jagan entered the colonial legislature on December 18, 1947.
23. TNA, CO1031/121, Henry Seaford to Jock Campbell, September 8, 1953.
24. See TNA, CO1031/118, for H. C. Steele's letter and Jock Campbell's covering note.
25. CO1031/121, minute, September 21, 1953.
26. Robertson Report (1954), 61.
27. CO1031/121, minute [James W. Vernon]. Savage and Luke's letters to the Colonial Office are in this file.

28. Secretary of State for the Colonies to Governor Savage, telegram, September 24, 1953, top secret:http//www.guyana.org/govt/declassified_british_documents _1953.html.
29. Text of Planned Radio Broadcast to be Made by Governor Savage to Announce the Suspension of the Constitution – prepared by the Colonial Office and sent by the Secretary of State for the Colonies, October 4, 1953. See note 26 for the source.
30. Ibid.
31. British Government White Paper on the Suspension of the Constitution of British Guiana, October 20, 1953, Appendix A, Contact between PPP Leaders and International Communist Front Organisations, 1950–53. See note 26 for the source.
32. See Kimani S. K. Nehusi, *A People's Political History of Guyana, 1838–1964* (Hertford: Hansib, 2018), chapter XXIII: 'Contradiction between Dr Jagan and the "Ultra Left": the Split in the Original PPP in 1956–57.'
33. 'Interview with Eusi Kwayana,' in *The People's Progressive Party of Guyana, 1950–92: An Oral History*. ed. Frank Birbalsingh (London: Hansib, 2007), 48.
34. Interview with Eusi Kwayana, Georgetown, September 22, 1992.
35. Nehusi, *A People's Political History of Guyana, 1838–1964*.
36. See Odeen Ishmael, 'Charting the Course for Democratic Change: The Waddington Commission Report and the First Congress of the PPP [1951]' – guyanajournal. com/waddington.html.
37. Ibid.
38. Ibid.
39. *Daily Argosy*, October 3, 1953.
40. The National Archives [TNA], KV2/3605.
41. Ibid.
42. *Daily Argosy*, October 11, 1953.
43. The intercepted correspondence between Billy Strachan and Janet Jagan is in KV2/3605.
44. Ibid.
45. Ibid.
46. TNA, KV2/3605, Governor Savage to the Secretary of State for the Colonies, telegram, September 2, 1953.
47. TNA, KV2/3605, SLO, Trinidad, to the Director General, MI5, August 11, 1953.
48. Ibid.
49. Ibid.
50. The Robertson Report (1954), 63–64.
51. Ibid., 36.
52. Ibid., 36–37.
53. TNA, KV2/3605, intercepted letter from Janet Jagan to Billy Strachan, September 25,1953.
54. Eusi Kwayana, '65 Years after October 1953: A Report and Review by One Present at the Events,' (mimeo.), 2018, 3–4.
55. TNA, KV2/3605, Cheddi Jagan to Tom McWinnie (WFTU representative, London), September 24, 1953.
56. TNA, KV2/3605, Director General of MI5, September 26, 1953.
57. The Robertson Report (1954), 37.

58. E. B. Beetham, Governor of the Windward Islands, to the Secretary of State for the Colonies, November 3, 1953: http//guyana.org/govt/declassified_documents_1953.html.

59. Quoted in Cheddi Jagan, *The West on Trial: My Fight for Guyana's Freedom* (London: Michael Joseph, 1966), 200.

60. *Daily Argosy*, January 22, 1957.

61. *Thunder*, November 6, 1954.

62. Ibid.

63. Editorial by LFSB [Burnham], *Thunder*, November 20, 1954.

64. L. F. S. Burnham, 'The Crime of Self-Government,' *Thunder*, November 13, 1954.

65. *Guiana Graphic*, February 20, 1955.

66. Sydney King, 'Foreign Capital and the People,' *Thunder*, November 27, 1954.

67. Sydney King to the Advisory Committee for Detained Persons, see http://www.guyana.org/govt/declassified_british_documents_1953.html.

68. Rory Westmaas to the Advisory Committee for Detained Persons, see http://www.guyana.org/govt/declassified_british_documents_1953.html.

69. Ibid.

70. Ibid.

71. 'Interview with Rory Westmaas,' in Frank Birbalsingh, *The People's Progressive Party of Guyana, 1950–92: An Oral History* (London: Hansib, 2007), 70, 72.

72. Martin Carter to the Advisory Committee for Detained Persons, see http://www.guyana.org/govt/declassified_british_documents_1953.html.

73. Ibid.

74. Jock Campbell in the *West India Committee Circular*, October 1953.

75. Jock Campbell, *The [Booker] Chairman's Statement, 1953*, 36.

76. Ibid.

77. Frank Birbalsingh, 'Interview with Ashton Chase,' in *The People's Progressive Party of Guyana, 1950–92: An Oral History* (London: Hansib, 2007), 43.

8.

Jagan's Marxist Vision in the Context of the Cold War – II

Race, Ideology, the Cuban Revolution, and Jagan's Fatal Encounter with President Kennedy, 1955–61

Everyone assumed that he was an avowed Communist. There was a lot of preparation that went into the briefing of Dr Jagan for his meeting with President Kennedy [in October 1961]. A lot depended on how he would answer only one question: 'Are you a communist?' But he never developed a formulation of words to give the right answer. He was too sincere in his commitment to Communism.

Cedric Joseph (1997)

Burnham had a vision of *realpolitik*. He was aware of the international context in which the Guyanese struggle was being waged...He played to different constituencies, letting each of them think he was their man. He was regarded as a pragmatic Socialist...whereas Cheddi was someone who would not change his principles, no matter what.

Robert J. Moore (2003)

To head whatever vital body he was directly connected with was Mr Burnham's aim. An important example was his contention and determination to be political Head of Government when the PPP won office in April 1953. His pursuit of personal power and glorification was evident to those who were in a position to observe. It nearly cost the PPP entry into Government in 1953. Fortunately, such a split was avoided then, but it reared its ugly head again in 1955.

Ashton Chase to Oscar Ramjeet, personal correspondence (May 2017)

I. 'On the Political Situation' in 1956: Jagan's Marxist Critique of the 'Ultra Leftists' and Their Contribution to the Suspension of the Constitution in 1953

Forbes Burnham was perceived by the British as being less ideologically driven than Cheddi Jagan, thought to be profoundly under the influence of his communist wife, Janet, an American of East European Jewish extraction. Though left-wing, Burnham was not considered a communist, so the British sought to cultivate him, prompting him to break with the hardliners, led by the Jagans. Burnham left the People's Progressive Party (PPP) in February 1955 and formed his own party (known from October 1957 as the People's National Congress [PNC]). In 1956–57, Sydney King (Eusi Kwayana), Martin Carter, and Rory Westmaas also left Jagan's PPP, largely on grounds that it was subordinating its Marxism to racial pragmatism. Jagan's PPP would henceforth be spurned by Africans as a party for Indians, yet he never redressed the source of that rudimentary issue – the bedevilling question of African insecurities. Basically, Jagan's unreconstructed Marxist mantra on the primacy of the class struggle assigned matters of race and other primordial loyalties out of existence: a false question.

Castigated as 'ultra-leftists' by Cheddi in his paper, 'On the Political Situation' (read by Brindley Benn), at the PPP Congress in New Amsterdam in March 1956, King, Carter, and Westmaas, though self-proclaimed communists at the time, were nowhere as sectarian as Cheddi in his adulation of the Soviet Union. They were inclined to a degree of eclecticism and were appalled by Nikita Khrushchev's revelation of Joseph Stalin's personality cult and his reign of terror, at the twentieth Congress of the Communist Party of the Soviet Union (CPSU), in February 1956. Their scepticism of Soviet communism was exacerbated by the Soviet invasion of Hungary in October–November 1956, when the endeavour by reformers to introduce change to an ossified communist structure in Hungary was thwarted. Cheddi and Janet Jagan, like their mentors in the Communist Party of Great Britain (CPGB), supported the Soviet Union with respect to their invasion of Hungary while remaining silent on the evils of Stalinism.

As Kimani Nehusi observes of King's response to the Soviet invasion of Hungary:

> …he openly condemned it while the PPP stayed silent. Dr Jagan's wooden, inflexible and received notion of Marxism demanded that the Moscow line be followed, religiously. This mode of thinking or not thinking had, in 1956, led the PPP leadership into passive and silent complicity with Soviet action that was identical to that previously suffered by the PPP itself and the Guianese people when the British invaded their colony in 1953 and evicted the PPP from office…The PPP leadership had condemned in the harshest possible terms the British invasion of Guiana…but complied with Soviet *diktat* when the Soviet Union invaded Hungary…The PPP's reaction to the 1968 Soviet invasion of Czechoslovakia illustrates a similar mindset. Such contradictions did not find favour with the…['ultra leftists,' including Sydney King]…The PPP leadership was partial and therefore inconsistent in its approach to such questions.[1]

The disenchantment of the so-called 'ultra-leftists' was aggravated by their perception that Jagan's opposition to joining the West Indies Federation was predicated on purely racial (possibly racist) premises – Indian fear that West Indian migration would nullify the likelihood of their imminent preponderance in the electorate. Besides, Jagan's apparent indifference to a united electoral front, as a mechanism for promoting ethnic concord, was interpreted as a winner-takes-all intransigence rooted in assumptions of an unassailable Indian economic and demographic ascendancy in the near future. Moreover, Jagan's identification of local Indian capitalists specifically as a 'progressive' force and, therefore, potential allies against imperialism, did not resonate with the so-called ultra-left, Sydney King in particular. He considered it the decisive affirmation of Jagan's capitulation to racial pragmatism.

While Jagan's paper to Congress was read 'behind closed doors,' a copy was received by Sydney King (restricted to his village of Buxton), three days later, on March 29, 1956. However, it did not appear in the public domain until December 22, when it was leaked to the *Daily Chronicle* and published in its entirety under the caption: RED MOVE TO TAKE OVER B.G. Whatever ambiguity or reservation lingered regarding Cheddi Jagan's communist motivations should have been dissipated by his Congress paper. The latter was characterised by transparently woolly thinking, not uncommon with this irrepressible exponent of the class war. He seemed overly concerned with not alienating local capitalists (primarily Indian), whom he surmised were naturally anti-imperialist, therefore recruitable in the struggle for independence, and towards this end, he declared war on the 'left deviationists' or 'ultra-leftists,' primarily King, Carter, and Westmaas. On the other hand, his wholesale reproduction of quotes from 'Comrade Stalin' and 'Comrade Mao' was a vindication of the assertion of his enemies, local and foreign (particularly the British imperialists), that he was a dyed-in-the-wool pro-Soviet communist. The latter was already established, as far as the British rulers were concerned, by virtue of MI5's interception of letters, bugging of telephone conversations, and eavesdropping (by their planted agents) on live conversations at CPGB headquarters in London (known as King St), between the Jagans and fellow communists. (Having read most of the MI5 files on Cheddi and Janet, between the late 1940s and early 1961 [the rest have not been declassified, given Anglo-American complicity in subverting him in 1962–64], it is not far-fetched at all to state that the Colonial Office knew virtually everything concerning their loyalty to their pro-Soviet creed.)

In his paper to Congress, Jagan sketched the composition of the PPP:

> The PPP is a national party, a broad alliance of various democratic sections – working class, peasantry, middle class, native businessmen and capitalists – opposed to imperialism. As such, communists [such as himself and Janet], social democrats, native capitalists, civil

servants, professional men can all play their part in, and belong to, such a party.

This was clearly a broad coalition of people many of whom he would probably have considered antagonistic to his fundamental Marxist-Leninist beliefs, even counter revolutionary. Yet, he maintained a *modus vivendi* with them while espousing a communist perspective that could no longer accommodate the so-called ultra-left, though vastly more compatible with his ideology than the rightists whom he instinctively despised.[2]

Jagan even challenged the PPP's constitution in his apparent initiative to project a more moderate posture. Yet this is incongruous with the tenor of his paper, which demonstrated a patently dogmatic allegiance to his communist creed. Therefore, it was a spurious moderation that was not substantiated by his evident inspiration by the wisdom of Comrades Stalin and Mao Tse Tung:

> This formulation is more precise and, therefore, more correct, than Rule 2(b) of our Party's constitution, which states that the object of our party shall be 'to promote the interests of the subject people by transferring British Guiana into a socialist [communist] country with a balanced agricultural-industrial economy.' While this is a long-term objective, nevertheless it gives the impression that the PPP is a socialist [communist] party.
>
> **Such a formulation has the danger that it will drive away from the party native capitalists [primarily Indian] opposed to imperialism, but mortally afraid of socialism-communism.** How is our Party different from other national parties such as [Norman Manley's] People's National Party of Jamaica [PNP]? Our Party is unique in the history of national movements in that from the very inception it was under left-wing, Marxist-inspired leadership uncompromisingly championing the cause of the working class. The right-wing [Burnham's faction] representing the middle and professional class and native capitalists was in the distinct minority. In Jamaica's PNP it was just the opposite...[there] the right-wing controlling the PNP, but fearing the left-wing supremacy [including Richard Hart, a communist], acted decisively and decimated the left [in 1952]. In British Guiana the Burnham right-wing, unable by constitutional means to gain supremacy, acted illegally to take over the Party [the split in the PPP of February 1955]...[emphasis added].[3]

Jagan then proceeded to censure those with 'left deviationist tendencies,' an obvious reference to Sydney King, Martin Carter, and Rory Westmaas specifically. It is clear from Jagan's disparaging treatment of them that he was more amenable to Indian capitalists, however right-wing, being drawn into the PPP than he was in palliating the 'ultra-left' by whom the party had 'suffered' politically:

> While our Party…had the distinct advantage of left-wing leadership, it suffered also from left deviationist tendencies. Some comrades on the left behaved in a mechanistic fashion, copying wholesale revolutionary tactics and slogans of left parties in the metropolitan, capitalistically advanced countries, without bothering to study carefully our concrete conditions and historical stage of development. Some communists in our party tended to act as communists in a communist party and to make our party into a communist party of an advanced country…Having failed to write our own books and pamphlets, we continue to base our theoretical studies on material from the independent, capitalistically advanced countries like the UK and USA. Young cadres particularly tended to swallow wholesale from these sources.

> This tendency towards left deviationism and adventurism must be combated. At times it was condoned in the past in order to protect left strength and unity against the onslaught of the right [the Burnhamites]. Such tendencies have had their toll on our party. And without carefully distinguishing between imperialist capital and native capital has frightened and therefore alienated native capital support for the party. By failing to take advantage of…the contradiction between native capital and imperialist-foreign capital, and to adjust our tactics accordingly, we drove back native and foreign capital into the arms of one party, the UDP [the anti-communist United Democratic Party of John Carter and W.O.R. Kendall].[4]

Jagan mustered all his ammunition against the so-called ultra-left, known for their scepticism of the omniscience of the Soviet comrades and their disciples in Eastern Europe – therefore, potentially conflictual with Cheddi's creed. He obviously was laying great store by the native commercial capitalists (largely Indian) – 'the revolutionary bourgeoisie' (Stalin's term) – whom he deemed anti-imperialist by virtue of their subordination to the foreign commercial capitalists in British Guiana. Cheddi sought corroboration from Comrade Stalin in repudiating the left deviationists because they were exaggerating the scope for revolutionary transformation in British Guiana:

> Comrade Stalin teaches that…one must not lose sight of two deviations … [one of which, left deviationism] … consists in overrating the revolutionary possibilities of the liberation movement and in underrating the importance of an alliance between the working class and the revolutionary bourgeoisie against imperialism. The communists in Java, who recently erroneously put forward the slogan of a Soviet government for their country, suffer, it seems, from this deviation. **This is a deviation to the Left, which threatens to isolate the Communist Party from the masses and to transform it into a sect** [emphasis added].[5]

Jagan felt fortified by the supposed doctrinal infallibility and affirmation of Comrades Stalin and Mao in ridding the PPP of the 'ultra-left' virus. The jargon he deployed against King, Carter, and Westmaas virtually assured that his estrangement from them was irreconcilable:

> It is clear from my analysis that in the period of our Party's ascendancy up to October 1953 [the suspension of the constitution after 133 days], we committed deviations to the left. We definitely overrated the revolutionary possibilities of our Party, the leader of the liberation movement. We allowed our zeal to run away with us; we became swollen-headed, pompous, bombastic. 'In order to smash these powerful enemies,' said Stalin, 'it is necessary to have a flexible and well-considered policy to take advantage of every crack in the enemy's camp and skill in finding allies.' We were attacking everybody at the same time. We tended towards what Mao Tse Tung called 'all struggle and no unity.'

> This is how Comrade Mao Tse Tung attacked the left dogmatists who during the 10 year (1927–37) civil war period advocated overthrowing everybody. He said: 'You cannot overthrow those in power, so you want to overthrow those who are not in power'…[Jagan continued, quoting Stalin]: We definitely 'underrated the importance of an alliance between the working class and the revolutionary bourgeoise against imperialism.' It is our task, therefore, to lay the basis for forging such an alliance.[6]

Politics by the primer! King, Carter, and Westmaas were receptive to the PPP's collaboration with other political parties to forge a united national front. They were apprehensive that the Jagan-Burnham split would plant the virus of racism in the body politic, thus rendering the African-Indian racial divide endemic to the political culture. Jagan agreed in principle that it was 'absolutely necessary that we secure allies in our struggle against imperialism.'[7] But he was confident that a built-in Indian majority, by virtue of the first-past-the-post electoral system, guaranteed his return to power, whatever the constitutional constraints. Consequently, he was circumspect about any alliance that included the sharing of seats, indeed, the sharing of power. For Jagan, henceforth, it was a zero-sum game, and he did not require African support to achieve this. However, as Burnham and (D'Aguiar later) knew very well, Jagan could not secure a majority under proportional representation (PR) for some time yet, remote though the likelihood of the realisation of the latter.

It was primarily to safeguard and enhance Indian electoral dominance under the first-past-the-post electoral system that Jagan was, conceivably, viscerally disinclined to joining the West Indies Federation. It will be recalled that the idea of an Indian Colony in British Guiana, in the 1920s, had precipitated African demand for 'ethnic balance' through migration from Africa and/or the British West Indies. Therefore, Jagan (like most Indians) viewed Federation with apprehension – primarily as an instrument to augment the African segment of the population, decisively, through large-scale migration of Black West Indians.

This is how Jagan, alluding to the so-called ultra-leftists, assessed the contentious issue of the West Indies Federation in his Congress paper of March 1956:

> ...they fail to take into consideration that if we support Federation now, unreservedly, we take the chance of losing our mass support [overwhelmingly Indian] and becoming not a mass party but a sect...In the West Indies as a whole [overwhelmingly African], with the exception of Trinidad's one-third Indian population, there is general support for Federation. The imperialists want it for better economic, political and administrative control; the native capitalists want it for protection; and the people want it because their leaders want it.
>
> What is the position in Guiana? Imperialism – Booker, the Sugar Producers' Association – has declared its support. The native capitalists (Peter D'Aguiar and other Portuguese businessmen) in the Chamber of Commerce join the imperialist representatives in this body in support of Federation, but for different reasons – protection in a wider home market. **The Indians, feeling as they do a sense of national oppression, are almost 100% opposed to Federation. This is why the native Indian capitalists who predominate in the Junior Chamber of Commerce go against their class interests and oppose Federation. The Indian capitalist up to this stage puts his 'national' [racial] interests before his 'class' interest. Consequently, he can be a resolute ally against imperialism within these considerations** [emphasis added].[8]

Jagan was, in reality, contending that the Indian capitalist was an Indian first – like most Indians (irrespective of class) mortally afraid of an African-dominated Guyana within the Federation – therefore, a natural or potential supporter of the PPP. Race had triumphed over class, and Jagan was accommodating that reality. He then sought to assess the response of Africans in Guyana to Federation, but the veracity of his assertion that 50 per cent opposed it is highly suspect. The African-Indian racial incomprehension, manifested in mutually incompatible perspectives on most issues, long predated the PPP; and this instinct as regards Federation specifically was accentuated by Burnham's split from the party in early 1955, as well as by the known commitment to the idea by Sydney King and others of the so-called ultra-left. Jagan remarked:

> Support for Federation also comes from the middle classes, the backbone of the civil service. Civil servants see in Federation further economic rungs. This explains why the middle class Negro who predominates in Government services, Portuguese and mixed race groups support Federation...The position of the African working class is somewhat different. I would say that about half [50%] support Federation because their leaders – League of Coloured Peoples, John

> Carter [UDP] and Forbes Burnham – support Federation. The other half is opposed to Federation, fearing undercutting and loss of jobs from West Indians who are prepared to migrate to our country. There has been direct experience with this particularly in the interior, in the wood grants and the quarries ...[9]

But Jagan was not prepared to forfeit what he considered the fundamental role of the PPP, as 'the leader of the liberation movement' inspired by Marxism-Leninism, unrivalled in its right – a virtual entitlement – to pilot British Guiana to Independence and, ultimately, to the free communist society. He was proud that no other political party in the region was endowed with such a nobility of mission; yet he was not oblivious of some aspects of *realpolitik* – appreciation of the centrality and indispensability of his core Indian base, irrespective of class or religious calling:

> These are the concrete realities not as we may desire them, but as they are [unanimous Indian opposition to Federation, for instance]. Are we to ignore them even if they are based on prejudices?...Some comrades [King, Carter and Westmaas], **taking the path of reckless adventurism want to brush away these realities, want to gamble with the existence and role of our party as leader of the liberation movement...**So strong are these realities that imperialism, which at one time was prepared to push British Guiana into Federation, has now decided that only an elected representative government can decide the question. And so, imperialism made a strategic retreat, realising that any force in favour of Guianese participation in federation will only strengthen its opposition ... [emphasis added].
>
> Your adventurists [the so-called ultra-left] are prepared neither to see nor to understand these shifts and contradictions. Where the imperialists are afraid to tread – to force Guianese participation into Federation – they are prepared to rush. They call us opportunists, we who support Federation in principle and say that the minimum condition of Guiana's participation must be dominion status and self-government for each unit; and who would leave the final decision to be expressed by way of a referendum. Is it opportunism to safeguard the life of our party, the leader of the liberation movement in Guiana and the only Caribbean working class-led party with mass following?[10]

II. Sydney King's Rebuttal of Jagan's Allegations and the Defection of the 'Ultra Leftists' from the PPP, 1956–57

Jagan clearly believed that Indian support alone would guarantee him victory in the next general elections, therefore the West Indies Federation was a potential millstone that could quickly erode the preponderance of the Indian vote, even

Sydney King [Eusi Kwayana (1925-)], one of the 'ultra-leftists', with his late wife Tchaiko after their marriage in 1971. He had ditched his Marxism for a robust African cultural nationalism that propounded the option of a racial partition of Guyana

under first-past-the-post. After Jagan's Congress paper of March 1956, it was inconceivable that King, Carter, and Westmaas could have remained in Jagan's PPP. In fact, King repudiated Jagan's paper, root and branch, shortly after it was delivered; he was well on his way to becoming the most formidable critic of what he saw as Jagan's racist agenda (never mind the Marxism!), to consolidate his pursuit of power by aggregating Indian support from all classes, including the local Indian capitalists. Moreover, Jagan's opposition to the West Indies Federation was denounced by the 'ultra-left' as essentially a ploy to keep out Black West Indians from British Guiana – to perpetuate an Indian majority in future elections: in effect aggrandising the Indian juggernaut towards independence and permanent Indian domination.

It is arguable that the disaffection/defection (the latter was never formalised) of Sydney King was a bitter blow to Jagan, as he had been his young Marxist protégé, confidant, and the most significant African in the PPP after Burnham, but substantially more invaluable to him because he considered him a communist ally. The loss of Martin Carter (ironically) to Jock Campbell's Booker later (1959–67) and Rory Westmaas to architecture – and both thereafter to lifelong political scepticism and transparent cynicism – was absorbed rather seamlessly by the Jagans. However, the defection of King to Burnham's PNC after the general elections of 1957 (he contested as an independent in Central Demerara and lost to the PPP's Balram Singh Rai), like Ranji Chandisingh's defection to Burnham's PNC nearly two decades later, could not really be mitigated.

After King's defection, Jagan's PPP was overwhelmingly regarded by Africans as the instrument for aggregating and consolidating Indian power to gain independence and permanent domination. And, as King remarked later, since Jagan was henceforth mobilising politically based on his Indian racial identity, he would proceed do likewise among his own African people. King was arguably crucial to Burnham's consolidation of his stature as the unassailable leader of

Africans after 1958, although he left the PNC in mid-1961 because he repudiated Burnham's apparent readiness, should he lose the general elections in August 1961, to acquiesce in Jagan's determined quest for independence. Burnham did lose, but the issue of independence became inextricably enmeshed in Jagan's suicidal Cold War stance against America – demonstrably on the Soviet/Cuban side. Ironically, it was Jagan who enabled Burnham, unimaginably, to be awarded the grand prize of independence, through Anglo-American duplicity in his destabilisation (1962–63), the Sandys delusion of 1963 (more later), and his engineered electoral demise in December 1964.

Sydney King had repudiated Jagan's 1956 Congress paper, 'On the Political Situation,' on several counts: his dogmatic Marxist theorising to uninformed peasants and workers; the transparency of his racially motivated anti-Federation rhetoric; his affirmation of local Indian capitalists while disparaging the 'ultra-left'; his insincerity on the creation of a United Front, supporting it eclectically to obviate any power-sharing formula – all tantamount to the pursuit of Indian supremacy (as King perceived it). From 1957, King would become the most robust embodiment of the moral conscience of African Guyanese and the indefatigable gadfly of Cheddi Jagan, matching his 'racial' politics with an unfaltering Afrocentric crusade pursued with self-abnegating zeal and eye-catching panache. King's paper was titled 'Observations on the Congress Paper "On the Political Situation" by Comrade Cheddi Jagan.' It was written shortly after Jagan's Congress paper, possibly in mid-April 1956, and the so-called ultra-left, comprising Sydney King, Martin Carter, Rory Westmaas, Keith Carter (brother of Martin), and Roddy Atherley, forwarded it to the Executive Committee of the PPP with a covering letter, dated April 17, 1956. They deemed Jagan's paper 'an attempt to expose the so-called ultra-left, to attack them without notifying them before hand, to muzzle them, to attach slander to their name and consequently to weaken their position in the movement.' Moreover, they could not accept that Jagan's paper was 'binding' on them, as it was 'an individual act' perpetrated without the approval of the Executive Committee of the PPP.

Sydney King, therefore, refuted Jagan's PPP Congress paper although it was already adopted, without amendment, by that body in New Amsterdam in March 1956. He was appalled that he and others Jagan had denounced as the 'ultra-left' were at no time apprised of the fact that he was about to mount a scathing repudiation of them. He added:

> My first reaction to such an unprincipled act is to ignore completely … his theories and confused outpourings, his mixture of scientific analysis and day-dreaming to the fate they deserve. But lest the movement should suffer, or be persuaded into accepting this hotch-potch for a real policy, I shall discharge my scientific duty by giving my views on the stab-in-the-back document…[comprising] 840 lines

of matter, [of which] 162 lines consist of quotations from what the author, Comrade Jagan, calls 'Communist sources.'[11]

King, at the time a declared Marxist, believed that he was, indeed, performing his 'scientific duty' in his critique of Jagan. He did not identify any fundamental flaw in the writings of 'the creative Marxists – Marx, Engels, Lenin, Mao and others.' But he was censorious of Jagan's rhetorical bombardment of delegates to the PPP Congress in New Amsterdam, very few of whom had any familiarity with the complexity of Marxist-Leninist thought:

> When should one quote from the creative Marxists…? Of course, one should quote from them when speaking to Communists who have read or are supposed to have read these books…To quote line upon line of Marxist theory to an audience comprising mainly of agricultural workers and peasant women who have not had the opportunity of being trained in these matters is to fit in with the local proverb: 'One-eye man a king in blind-eye man country.' But when people have to vote upon proposals put to them in such terms, unable to test them for themselves, not having been given the necessary training, it is clear that the authority of the Congress … is being used as a big stick to whip the so-called ultra-left … [However,] quotations alone will not convince us. All would-be theoreticians must present us with analyses based on the dialectics of reality if they wish to convince us of their theories.[12]

King also rejected the allegation by Jagan that the so-called ultra-left was guilty of 'swallowing wholesale' revolutionary slogans that attracted the opprobrium of many (including the British), apprehensive that the PPP was a communist party. It was ironic, indeed, that Jagan, no slouch himself in deploying Marxist dogmas, should have levelled similar charges at the 'ultra-left.' King did not let him get away with it:

> Who was it that spoke in and out of the Legislative Council from 1947 about Socialism [Communism], nationalisation of industries, etc, when he should have been consolidating the national movement for Independence [prioritising racial unity] and training cadres for the trade union movement – Comrade Jagan himself – and this at a time when some of the 'ultra-left' were in Britain [Rory Westmaas, Keith Carter and Lionel Jeffrey: members of the CPGB] and others were just beginning the study of Marxism-Leninism [Sydney King and Martin Carter]. Who was it that quoted in the Legislative Council from Communist papers – Comrade Jagan? Who was it, as late as 1953, put forward the people's democratic slogan of a 'People's Police' – Comrade Jagan? Who spoke on May Day 1953 of a People's Government having come to power – Jagan, Burnham and Chase? If we are to suppose that Comrade Jagan now realises his shortcomings, why does he not say so instead of trying to pin them on other people?[13]

The original PPP, elected to office in April 1953, was ill-equipped to assume even a modicum of responsibility for governance. It comprised a coalition of communists (its core led by the Jagans and Sydney King), socialists (possibly social democrats, including Forbes Burnham and Ashton Chase), capitalists/ Indian nationalists (Dr J. P. Lachmansingh and Jainarine Singh) – not a recipe for cohesion – a classic Tower of Babel. Moreover, it constituted a loose, and ominously fragile, coalition of two peoples historically suspicious of each other: Africans and Indians. Sydney King was particularly sensitive to the latter and had cautioned Jagan and Burnham regarding the potential pitfalls. The PPP of Jagan and Burnham, not unexpectedly, managed to secure an unprecedented, if infamous, legacy: the only British colony (on the verge of independence) where the Constitution was suspended and the elected government kicked out. This was a consequence not only of British (and American) resolve to preclude the emergence of a communist state in the Hemisphere, but also the utter futility of the PPP as a party of governance.

The endemic suspicion between Africans and Indians could not be papered over. The coalition, therefore, was stitched together, and as Sydney King had anticipated from the inception, it lacked the means to integrate its Indian and African components, embodied by Jagan and Burnham: rival leviathans irreconcilably in pursuit of power. But King felt that any such access to power should be obviated for the foreseeable future because the basis for a durable racial alliance did not exist yet. Consequently, the principal task for the PPP should be informed by that fundamental prerequisite: cultivating a broader, more inclusive, vision of national identity – a grassroots project of rigorous re-education across the ethnic chasm, however idealistic and necessarily protracted. King's Marxism, therefore, was infinitely less dogmatic, more nuanced, than Jagan's because he envisaged that it was paramount for the African people to be persuaded of the validity of the PPP's multiracial objectives. Led by an Indian, it was an enormous venture for King and others in the PPP to convince Africans that Jagan was a better option than one of their own: the brilliant and charismatic lawyer, Linden Forbes Sampson Burnham.

King found several strands in Jagan's Congress paper of 1956 reprehensible, including a few he deemed essentially racist in their prompting. It was especially repugnant to him that Jagan admitted the 'ultra-left' was 'condoned' (King reframed this as 'used') in the PPP only because they were crucial in fortifying the Jaganite left-wing (primarily Indian) against the Burnhamite right-wing (overwhelmingly African). But King was under immense pressure from his own loyal African base in Buxton specifically, and East Coast Demerara generally, to rationalise his remaining in Jagan's PPP after the departure of the foremost

African leader, Forbes Burnham, in February 1955. The multiracial image of the party was not sustainable, yet Jagan was certain that he could dispense with King and the other 'ultra-leftists' (independent Marxists, but a tiny faction), because he was confident that he commanded the loyalty of the totality of Indians. Under the first-past-the-post electoral system, as I have noted, Jagan was assured of a majority of seats independently of non-Indians.

It is evident that Jagan was suspicious of the *modus operandi* of the 'ultra-left' for some time. He contended that the latter had failed to recognise that sections of local capital were opposed to foreign capital, and that support from the former was lost to the PPP because it was alienated by the irresponsible rhetoric of the 'left deviationists.' Jagan had had enough of them, and he made this very clear indeed in assessing the role of native capitalists in the anti-imperialist struggle: 'It is important for us to retrace our steps and if necessary correct certain mistakes and errors of judgment, certain indiscretions of youthful exuberance.'[14]

In a letter of March 28, 1956, at the conclusion of the PPP Congress, Jagan (restricted to Georgetown) wrote to King (restricted to Buxton) explaining his rationale for attacking the so-called ultra-left. He framed it as a necessity to drain the swamp:

> You cannot be unaware of the fact that for a long time now there has been a corroding, insidious campaign of slander directed against me with the deliberate intention of undermining my position in the Party. That I am an opportunist, that I will sell out, that I may be a good leader for now but not after Independence, are all bits of the campaign. [These apparent fears of the 'ultra-left' sprang from reservations regarding what they saw as Jagan's Indian majoritarian politics.]…
>
> I invite discussion and open comradely criticisms. But I most definitely object to criticism which does not come out in the open, which takes the form of slander that develops into cliquism and factionalism. It was this type of behaviour and attitude which, to a great extent, was responsible for the split…My paper to the Congress is meant as open comradely criticism for taking the right course now and in the future.[15]

King interpreted Jagan's declared commitment to attracting local Indian capitalists to the PPP as an abrogation of his much-vaunted Marxism with its primacy of the class struggle. He deemed Jagan's new approach an intimation that henceforth his politics would be determined by the pursuit of power to facilitate Indian ascendancy – not the class struggle towards the communist society: 'No one who reads the paper "On the Political Situation" can fail to be struck by Comrade Jagan's preoccupation with the racial question. Personally, I do not mean by this that Comrade Jagan is slipping down to a racist position and is "deviating" to racism [he meant precisely that!]. Yet some of his conclusions and arguments raised great doubts as to whether he really approached the whole question from a class point of view or a racial point of view.'[16]

King's paper reflects his views on Jagan and race in his quest for power through a majoritarian electoral process. He responds to Jagan regarding the 'split' of February 1955; his stance on the creation of a united front towards independence and on the anticipated West Indies Federation. King found him wanting on all three issues. Concerning Burnham's split from the PPP, Jagan had remarked that 'generally the mass of Indians came over to us; most Africans, with the exception of the politically aware, went over to Burnham.' King's repudiation of Jagan's analysis of the racial realignment after the split was withering: 'No question of class, backward or politically aware Indians. Indians are Indians, argue Comrade Jagan. Are the Indians attacked in the whole or in part for 'coming over to us' for racial reasons? Oh no, Oh no! That is all to their credit once they follow Jagan. And this at a PPP Annual Congress. What a disgrace! This formulation of the question just shows how seriously involved Jagan is. When he should use scientific analysis, he argues like a shopkeeper, and when he should argue from concrete reality, he quotes line upon line of Stalin.'[17]

King then reproached Jagan for opportunism on the issue of a united front towards an electoral alliance. Jagan was in favour of a limited united front of the PPP and other anti-imperialist parties to accelerate constitutional reform and a return to representative government, but he was disinclined to contest the elections on a common platform because this would have eventuated in some form of power-sharing, of which King was strongly in favour. With the departure of Burnham from the original PPP, King was perturbed that the country would slide into a political imbroglio of rigid and enduring racial discord. Jagan, on the other hand, was confident that under the first-past-the-post electoral system the consolidated Indian vote alone (including Indian capitalists with their potential financial support) would give him a majority of seats and the key to returning to power and, soon, the big prize – independence. But King perceived a united front imperative to prevent a slide towards an impending racial chasm. This prompted him to pose the discomfiting question:

> Does Comrade Jagan…want allies in the extra-parliamentary struggle but not in the parliamentary struggle which carries with it 'sweets of office'? We, the 'left dogmatists,' however, favour, demand and are 100 per cent for a united front with an electoral alliance as the best method of keeping colonial despotism at bay … We are not prepared to give instructions to the united front as to how it should fight, but would rely on the creative forces of the people ....[18]

Finally, King, an avid exponent of the proposed West Indies Federation, could have no truck with Jagan's prevarication on this issue. It was probably the final straw that drove him to the conclusion that it was inconceivable that he could be reconciled with what he considered the Indocentric political motivation of Jagan. King did not mince his words regarding Jagan and Federation:

> Here again Comrade Jagan goes into a profoundly racial analysis of the situation which is nauseating: 'The Indians feeling as they do a sense of national oppression are almost 100% opposed to Federation.' Jagan, of course, does not criticise them for this. This is how a soldier of the international proletariat carries on. What if Africans, at the prospect of adult suffrage were to feel a 'sense of national oppression' and oppose adult suffrage [as the BGLU's Hubert N. Critchlow did in 1944]?...Jagan slanders the working masses. He says they do not want union with blacker people, and he is prepared to 'lead' them in these unfortunate prejudices...Is he a servitor of racism and racist prejudices? How strong is the party, supposed to be 'working class led,' which confessed to be full of racial prejudices? Jagan is only prepared to 'notice how strong these prejudices are,' but does not intend lifting a finger against them.[19]

On May 3, 1956, Jagan wrote to King regarding his unsparing criticisms of his Congress paper. He underlined King's 'ultra-left' role in the short-lived PPP government of 1953, attributing to him specifically some culpability for precipitating the suspension of the Constitution after only 133 days:

> Let me...admit that certain theoretical mistakes were made by me. But this did not seriously affect the practical workings or achievements of the Party. **Despite all my leftism, I did not achieve the reputation of wildness ... R.B.O. Hart [a reputable black local journalist] pointed out openly that it was not so much my 'communism' which caused the suspension of the constitution, but the pompous, erratic behaviour of King and Burnham.** A few nights ago, W.A. Raatgever, Chair of the Joint All Party Conference, spoke words to that effect that Jagan was all right, but the people he has associated with him [were irresponsible and reckless]...It is to correct those impressions, to remove the tag of wildness, that I devoted so much space [in the Congress paper] to [left] deviationism and adventurism [emphasis added].[20]

III. Sydney King and the Partition of British Guiana: His Robust Response to Jagan's Perceived Indian Majoritarian Pursuit of Independence

Yet King was disdainful of Jagan's stance: he believed the leader of the PPP (since Burnham's departure in 1955) was pursuing a political agenda inspired fundamentally by the majoritarian interests of Indians: zero sum politics. This was what impelled King later (as Eusi Kwayana in ASCRIA) to mobilise Africans, culturally and politically, to aggregate their discrete interests. Himself an austere, incorruptible man, Kwayana had arrived at a position of profound dissonance with Jagan. His recognition of African fear of Indian supremacy became central to his political mission after he left the PPP in early 1957. Ethnic insecurities could not simply be 'replaced' by the notion of the primacy of class – that is, conceptualised as 'epiphenomenal,' in the Marxist jargon.

Kwayana's argument remains as valid today as when I interviewed him in Georgetown, thirty years ago, shortly before the PPP's electoral victory in October 1992. It is fruitful to ponder at length the gist of his contention:

> The two major groups have stereotypes of each other. Africans tended to see Indians as clannish, as having more money, having an interest in land – many [Africans] were selling out their lands to Indians when they went broke. Although they were doing it voluntarily, it also harmed them. Then there was this rumour that someone from India had come and said that those who owned the land owned the country [possibly intertwined with the Indian Colony idea]…A lot of Africans were unable to go beyond that. They looked at the behaviour of Indians near to them in judging the PPP. If there was an aggressive [racist] member of the PPP in their district, this is how Africans tended to see the PPP. The PPP does not understand this until today.

> Jagan never dealt with these things at the subjective level, although he had a lot of rage against Imperialism. That problem was never dealt with; that's one of the reasons why I left the PPP. **The psychology of the leader is crucial. We had to fight to get Africans to accept an Indian leader [Jagan]. He didn't have that problem. He never had to accept a leader of another race, so he didn't know what it is like. He talks about revolution, but the personal revolution – nothing** [emphasis added]!

> He had a cultural problem. Having rejected colonialism and its [western] intellectual and cultural baggage, he had to take something from somewhere else [Russian communism]; he didn't rely on his own personality [cultural foundations]. If he had Hinduism, it would have made him a different person.[21]

But King (Kwayana) was more apprehensive of Jagan's factional political agenda than he was of his communism. And this had driven him to resign as general secretary of Burnham's PNC and editor of its organ, *New Nation*, on May 21, 1961. He was appalled (as noted earlier) that Burnham had declared his intention, should the PNC lose the general elections in August 1961, of supporting Jagan's bid for independence. The PNC was being very diplomatic on the eve of those elections, arguing that independence was 'the inalienable right of Guiana and the PNC, though it will always strive to protect the interests of all groups, will never stand in the way of independence regardless of the party in office.'[22]

In an open letter, King made it clear that as a partisan of his African people, he was revolted by Burnham's acquiescence in Jagan's racial independence mission – the leader of Africans was giving away the store. Yet he was still counselling Africans to support Burnham because he was their only viable leader, and he needed their weight of affirmation to bargain effectively on their behalf. But he had arrived at firmer ideas to ensure the protection of African rights before independence. It is incontestable that Sydney King was no less instrumental than Burnham in ensuring that Jagan and his Indian supporters did not march seamlessly to independence.

King has often been censured for advocating the partition of Guyana on racial lines, but that is not entirely true. He argued that because of the multiracial composition of the country, with Indians 'the largest and most united group,' the British concept of democracy could not be transplanted unalterably – a 'special solution' was indispensable. He proposed certain safeguards for Africans and Indians (as well as minorities), deemed indispensable to their peaceful co-existence in an independent Guyana. Among these were:

> (1) Joint and equal Prime Ministership according to LAW, between the Leaders of the Indian and African people;
>
> (2) An independent Watch Committee established by LAW, made up of people of all races and especially the minorities, to supervise the spending of government funds and the benefits derived by various races. The same Committee will keep a watch over jobs and employment at all levels to see that justice is done to all races;
>
> (3) A socialist system without foreign links; and a state neutral by LAW, of Russia and the USA. **By socialism must be understood a system of cooperatives in all fields, existing private enterprise and some state enterprise:** production for needs; respect for all religions and for the religious tradition of our peoples [emphasis added].[23]

But King did not trust Cheddi Jagan. Marxism was, he argued, a façade to deflect scrutiny of his principal goal of Indian supremacy. Therefore, if an independent Guyana could not guarantee freedom – equality of representation – for all its peoples, the option of partition of the country should be pursued before independence was granted. The fact that two men who embodied the embryonic hope of shaping a nation from its congeries of ethnic loyalties ended up as mortal enemies underlines the consuming nature of the Guyanese futility – then and now:

Jagan does not hide his attitude. He wrote of his people as 'nationally oppressed' among Guianese. **His Independence will be only for them** [Indians]...Burnham's statement [supporting Independence under Jagan] is dangerous to the African people and will give Indian racists unfair advantage over us. Such a plan leads direct to slavery. I cannot be any part of Burnham's plan. **I did not leave Jagan's party** [the PPP] **so as to help Jagan get Independence for his East Indian people who are 'nationally oppressed' in Jagan's opinion.**

We have known all along that the Indians would not trust a black leader, and that the Africans would not trust an Indian leader. We could see then that any attempt of the one to rule the other will lead to blood baths...Your people, Jagan, do not trust a black leader; and my people do not trust an Indian leader. Therefore, we must find a special solution and not pretend. Our problem is similar to that of India in 1947...[emphasis added].[24]

Painful, but essentially still true! This was the context in which King made his call for 'joint and equal Prime Ministership' between the African and Indian people. However, he had reservations that Jagan would ever agree to any form of power-sharing. King concluded his letter thus:

If the power-drunk Jagan, wanting to be top dog as usual, should agree to this plan, all well and good. If he rejected it, we should refuse to be ruled by him and call for a division of the country, before Independence, into three zones – an African zone, an Indian zone and a Free zone in which those who wish to live with other races may do so...That is the plan. Equality of rights and power as custodians of the whole [mandatory power-sharing]...Joint and equal Premiership. Partition as a last resort. This plan can end all cause of racial antagonism and mistrust. Our co-ops will lay the economic foundation for better race relations.[25]

Burnham was aided immeasurably by King's astuteness (his personal reservations notwithstanding) in counselling fellow Africans to vote for Burnham to boost his electoral strength and his overall bargaining position. King scolded and reasoned at the same time:

Burnham is your chosen Leader. No one must rival him. It cannot be tolerated in our situation. I feel he is playing straight into Jagan's hands. He thinks he is going to travel to London with Jagan. Never mind! ...You MUST vote Burnham. You MUST vote PNC. You have to vote [for them] even if they put up as candidates a lump of tar in the shape of a man. But if Burnham thinks that, in the case of defeat, he will hand you over to Jagan; and if Jagan thinks he is going to rule you, each of them is making a terrible mistake ... Use the elections to show that you stand fast and firm in a united block. After that, if Jagan wins he has lost as far as you are concerned.[26]

Burnham lost! And the possibility of Indian domination led King and his close ally, H.H. Nicholson ('Vigilance'), to create the African Society for Racial Equality (ASRE), founded at Buxton (King's home village) a few days after the PPP victory in the general elections of August 21, 1961. Though a small group, King and Vigilance's role in retrieving African self-esteem after the debacle of the Jagan victory in the elections is inestimable. They were again censorious of Burnham for indicating that he would have, if he did lose the elections, supported independence under Jagan. Yet it is highly likely that Burnham harboured no intention whatsoever of doing so. It was conceivably an aspect of the Machiavellianism of this master politician, as he quickly proceeded to unveil one of the glaring flaws of the electoral verdict; in so doing, he had struck upon a cardinal premise for a robust challenge to Jagan's mandate for independence.

As early as 1957, Burnham had indicated his preference for a change of the electoral system to proportional representation (PR). He felt inordinately disadvantaged since most of his supporters, Africans, were concentrated in urban constituencies, primarily Georgetown and its suburbs. Therefore, his PNC, of necessity, faced appreciable drawback under the first-past-the-post system, predicated on winning a majority of arbitrarily designated seats not on the proportion of votes polled throughout the country. Burnham henceforth routinely seized the opportunity to underscore that his PNC would be the principal victim, for the foreseeable future, of an iniquitous electoral system that was skewed in favour of Jagan's PPP.

He observed that in the general elections of August 1961, the PPP polled ninety-three thousand or 42.7 per cent of the votes cast and won twenty seats; his PNC polled eighty-seven thousand or 41 per cent and won just eleven seats; while Peter D'Aguiar's United Force (UF) got thirty-five thousand votes or 16 per cent and won four seats. Therefore, the PPP's seats were won at 4,650 votes per seat; the PNC's at 7,909 votes per seat; and the UF's at 8,750 votes per seat. Ironically, Jagan's PPP had tactically contested only twenty-nine of the thirty-five seats to ensure that Burnham's PNC was pressured into a two-cornered contest with the UF in constituencies the PPP could not win, the UF's virulent anti-communism/anti-Castroism notwithstanding. Consequently, the PPP's total votes were reduced by virtue of their not contesting six seats they deemed unwinnable; D'Aguiar's United Force was the beneficiary. They won Georgetown North and Georgetown Central because the PPP did not contest them, thus signalling to their Indian supporters to vote, tactically, for the UF against Forbes Burnham.

Burnham remarked that twice in four years (1957 and 1961) the first-past-the-post system had 'yielded anomalous results.' And he astutely hinted that this could have repercussions for the independence issue although Jagan was sanguine it would be resolved in his favour in 1962. Ominously for Jagan, and contrary to what King had dramatised effectively, Burnham had no intention of joining Jagan on the same plane to London to ensure the British grant independence to the colony. Burnham was never a pushover, as King had insinuated, thus impelling him to quit the PNC on the eve of the elections. Forbes Burnham was a dexterous and nimble political operator, a clever and ruthless politician who could run rings around Jagan at will. He was henceforth resolved to interpose a change of the electoral system to proportional representation (PR) as a precondition for independence, possibly in a referendum, which Jagan could not win. Burnham remarked: 'this might have to be put to the electorate when the question of Independence comes up.'[27]

Meanwhile, King was able to engender a sustaining vision among many Africans, through the grassroots Afrocentric cultural revival campaign of his ASRE, bleak though their political horizon in the aftermath of Burnham's defeat in August 1961. Their future seemed precarious in a Guyana on the verge of independence, which most observers believed was within the grasp of Jagan after the elections. It was a hazardous and uncharted road ahead for Burnham and his loyal African supporters. It required a monumental blunder on the part of Cheddi Jagan for Burnham to rise from the ashes of his second electoral defeat in four years. But Jagan's Marxist creed restricted his propensity and flexibility to identify and cultivate potentially strategic allies, such as Jock Campbell (1912–94), the chairman of Booker, a reformer by temperament evidently desirous of working with him after 1957; or Iain Macleod (1913–70), the liberal conservative colonial secretary (1959–61), who had gone against many in the Tory party and granted Jagan internal self-government in 1960 (with the likelihood of independence by 1962); or Norman Manley (1893–1969), a fine intellectual and leader of the People's National Party of Jamaica, inclined towards Fabian socialism; or Professor Arthur Lewis (1915–91), the region's most eminent economist, imbued with similar political sympathies as Manley and Campbell. Besides, Jagan's incapacity for clear and prudent thinking was exacerbated by his predilection for tortuously doctrinaire explications of his Marxist beliefs, in inappropriate circumstances, thereby alienating potential allies or significant others who still wielded enormous power over his political destiny. Such calamitous errors of judgement would prove fatal, thereby resurrecting the political fortunes of the supremely more astute Forbes Burnham, who was on the ropes after the elections of August 1961 and badly wounded as a political force.

After 1959–60, Jagan's ideological obduracy – his widely known communist sympathies – magnified by his unequivocal support for Fidel Castro's revolution in Cuba, gave Kennedy and the CIA the rationale and the resolve to destroy him.

Jagan's alignment with Castro provided more fodder than any other issue to the anti-communist crusade fomented against him, at home and abroad, that would devour him by the end of 1964. Many of his local enemies had been outraged and galvanised by the PPP's unconscionable victory parade across the country in August 1961, in which the elections symbol of Burnham's PNC, the broom, was dragged on the road behind Indian cars, trucks, buses, and tractors. Jagan (joined later by his wife) was at the head of a mammoth motorcade, from the Corentyne Coast to Georgetown, including through numerous predominantly African villages. It was a vulgar display of triumphalism that left a deep wound in the soul of Africans. Rupert Roopnaraine (aged eighteen) recalls the bitterness the PPP's tasteless parade left in his young mind:

> ... it was an act of the most extraordinary political insensitivity. I recall my extreme disenchantment when PPP supporters [Indians] spat on Afro-Guyanese bystanders on the roadside ... The 1961 elections simply entrenched the polarisation that had begun in 1957, and produced a situation where victory in democratic elections came to mean the victory of one race over another...It was actually one tribe conquering another.[28]

Cheddi and Janet Jagan in a post-election victory parade through a transparently disheartened African village, August 1961. Many deemed this an exercise in triumphalism that exacerbated the alienation of the African supporters of Forbes Burnham

The PPP's lack of magnanimity towards the feelings of Africans was maladroit. They construed the massive motorcade, led by a jubilant Cheddi (joined later by Janet), as a vindication of popular support for him, a sure affirmation of the case for immediate independence. For many it did represent a crude and tawdry display of Indian power of which Sydney King was warning – the decisive victory over Africans on the eve of independence. *Thunder*, the organ of the PPP, could not see beyond the exultation of the Indian moment:

> It was the biggest motorcade, **the largest demonstration of joy yet witnessed in British Guiana. The PPP victory motorcade superseded by far the motorcade when Princess Margaret was here [in 1958]...It was the greatest event in the history of B.G.** It was hot and dusty, but with a lot of humour. Old women and young children jigged in the street with joy beaming from their moistened eyes. At every point on the journey where people waited to greet the Premier-designate, Dr Jagan was stopped and garlanded [emphasis added].[29]

Sydney King was deeply pained by this exercise in racial ascendancy, and like most Africans was thereby energised to undermine the capacity of Jagan to lead British Guiana to independence, as seemed inescapable after the elections of August 21, 1961. King and his foremost collaborator in the ASRE (based at Buxton), H. H. Nicholson (alias Vigilance), issued a detailed response to Jagan's victory, a few days after the elections. It was titled 'In the Name of Freedom: An Appeal from the Africans of British Guiana to Send Observers to our Country,' dated August 28, 1961. It is permeated by a fear of Indian supremacy and the 'urgent' necessity to rescue the African people from Jagan's Indian juggernaut, as the British were determined to give him independence. They renewed their call for Partition before such eventuality. The paper is haunted by the old African apprehension of the 1920s: an 'Indian Colony' in British Guiana.

King and Vigilance observed, with evident pain:

> The Indians are indeed pitiless in their victory. For the PPP, victory is none other than an Indian victory over other races, and especially over the Africans...The capitalist press is silent. They all call for collaboration with the PPP Government which they know has been put there against the will of 57.3 per cent of the electorate.

They were particularly censorious of what they deemed the brazen racism permeating Jagan's politics, masked by his Marxist rhetoric. It was a final, desperate appeal by King and Vigilance to save the African people of British Guiana from becoming 'slaves of the East Indian people,' before the granting of independence. Partition was now the only option because Jagan would go the whole hog in effecting Indian domination:

The man who tells us he has a 'vision of socialism' has always had the support of the Indian capitalists who opened their money bags to him…We do not care whether Jagan is a capitalist, fascist, anarchist, a fire-worshipper or a socialist – **Jagan is an Indian, and he and all the other Indians wish to rule over us. They say they will never accept a black leader. We shall never accept an Indian one** [emphasis added].

King and Vigilance could conceive of no way of defeating the Indians because they were allegedly scheming to augment their numbers, to make the country overwhelmingly Indian, thus rendering Africans an impotent minority. The ghost of the Indian Colony!

We hope the British are not giving British Guiana Independence so that we become slaves of the East Indian people…It is an empty dream to talk of winning future elections, seeing that the East Indian vote will outnumber the African in every rural constituency. Besides talks have already been held with Mauritius [predominantly Indian] about Indian immigration from that country, making the Africans a feeble minority…Jagan, once hostile to [the West Indies] Federation, may soon be willing to accept it. British Guiana [B.G.] could well support…five million more Indians and many more…It is clear what Jagan and his Indian supporters are dreaming of. They will bring enough Indians into B.G. so as to dominate the entire West Indies. Then – federation!

The idea of power-sharing, which King had long advocated, was no longer practicable. Immediate independence would be calamitous for Africans. Partition of British Guiana, before independence, was the only hope for Black people. King and Vigilance concluded:

Our toil, tears, sweat and blood for 300 years have earned us the right to a piece of soil where the black people can build a home free at last…We have all the scholars and workers to build cities and villages…The Indians covet the entire 83,000 square miles. They know its wealth…The part we will get will be more than adequate for ourselves…

The Indians, everywhere, every day, since Jagan's 1957 election victory have promised the African people to enslave them. 'We'll chase you back to the Congo. We'll put you to pull punt. We'll kick you, you black dogs. We'll use your women before you can marry them.' Today the Indians perpetrate every outrage against our women, sparing not even the old. This is the 'Independence' the 'socialist' Jagan has promised…

It is a historic dream of the East Indians to set up an Indian outpost in British Guiana [an allusion to the old idea of an Indian Colony]…**The only salvation for its peoples is PARTITION** [emphasis added].[30]

IV.   A Fatal Attraction: Jagan's Ideological Implacability and His Declared Admiration for Fidel Castro, 1960–61

But the PNC, Africans as a whole, held few trumps in the aftermath of the general elections debacle of August 1961. It would require the man in possession of virtually all the trumps to forfeit his game – to contrive failure from the jaws of victory – for Burnham to be resurrected. By his ineptitude, dogmatism, and arrogance as a true believer in Soviet communism, Jagan managed to precipitate an unlikely scenario that eventuated in Burnham being awarded the big prize. Jagan's tactlessness – arguably recklessness – when he met President Kennedy (as will be seen later) was the most inconceivable gift bestowed on Forbes Burnham. Such was the colossal blunder of Jagan in Washington, in October 1961, all that was required of Burnham thereafter, to become America's chosen man, was to parade his anti-communist credentials, particularly his anti-Castro sentiments. Astoundingly, in a matter of months, he was endowed with all the trumps: the backing of President Kennedy and the CIA; Peter D'Aguiar's UF and the Catholic Church's relentless and bountiful anti-communist crusade against Jagan; the solidarity of the TUC (including, ironically, the recognised sugar workers' union, the MPCA); the local press (the *Chronicle*, the *Graphic*, the *Evening Post* and the *Weekend Post and Sunday Argosy*); and, of course, Sydney King's iconic role in communion with the soul of Africans, inconsolably devastated by their defeat in August 1961, and exacerbated by the PPP's indefensible (Indian) victory motorcade on Tuesday, August 22, 1961.

Jagan's communism and his lack of statesmanship ensured that the Americans saddled Guyana with the increasingly dictatorial regime of Forbes Burnham, from December 1964 to his death in August 1985. For some of his time as ruler of this doomed land, Burnham (as will be seen), with Machiavellian dexterity, affected a radical posture to consolidate and prolong his authoritarian rule. By strategically appearing to embrace Marxism and Fidel Castro – the core of Jagan's creed – he did steal the latter's thunder, leaving him with the crumbs of doctrinal purity. Jagan could, subsequently, merely luxuriate in being the self-proclaimed sole custodian of the authentic Marxist tenets: an arid doctrinal high ground yielding no discernible political capital. Moreover, Burnham, recognising that general elections in Guyana are essentially ethnic censuses (of adults) stacked against him, rigged them all: in 1968, 1973, 1980, and 1985 (the last by Mr D. Hoyte, his successor). Rigging was deemed inescapable to arrest Indian political and economic ascendancy that evoked in most Africans intense foreboding – a reflex triggered by long-standing fears: loss of their land (sold) to Indians because of need; the 'Indian Colony' idea in British Guiana, advanced by J. A. Luckhoo,

Dr W.H. Wharton, C.R. Jacob, and others; tangible Indian commercial and agricultural progress; their cultural effervescence and triumphalist identity with a free 'Mother India.' Impressive educational advances by Indians after the Second World War magnified those fears, as these challenged the last citadel of African supremacy: the professions of law and medicine and the civil service and, ultimately, the demographic explosion of Indians (with the eradication of malaria in the late 1940s) and the granting of universal suffrage by the British in the early 1950s.

Jagan's PPP won the general elections in 1953 and 1957. Burnham's PNC, founded after his humiliating defeat in August 1957 (still using the name PPP), was largely innocuous. Between then and in the aftermath of the elections of 1961, no one, including the British, Booker, and the Americans, considered Burnham a viable alternative to Jagan. But the British also recognised how flawed Jagan was as a leader, bewitched by his quasi-religious conviction that communism was a science for the perfectibility of humankind – flawless and attainable in his time.

The governor of British Guiana (1958–64), Sir Ralph Grey (1910–99), got to know Jagan very well. And he apprehended his deficiency as a political leader with precision: he was implacably tethered to his immoderate communist mantras. Just a few months after Governor Grey had been in the colony – in 1959 – he could grasp with immaculate discernment Cheddi's *modus operandi*. It is hard to improve on this:

Jagan's PPP returns to Government in August 1957, while Burnham's PPP (renamed the PNC in October) is vanquished. The five ministers are seen here with Governor Sir Ralph Grey (front row, centre) and several official members of the administration: (front row) Janet Jagan, Cheddi Jagan, Brindley Benn; (back row, second from left) Balram Singh Rai, (fourth from left) Ramkarran

Dr Jagan's government will always be weak in the sense that, like all communist leaders, he seems unable to keep with him intelligent lieutenants of independent mind…He will not accept, without suspicion, even professional advice of those outside his own [Marxist-Leninist] way of thinking, however distinguished. [And] he has almost nobody inside his party with the ability to help him to resolve his suspicions. He follows his star. He is forced to carry almost the whole intellectual burden himself. Instead of getting ahead with practical action, he causes delays and frustration by his opinions and antagonisms, by his dialectics and automatic theorising…

His government does not know how to win friends. It does not seem to want to win friends. It will take on anybody. Let them all come! It has the courage of its convictions. But its convictions are too often irrational obsessions…

There is no change to Dr Jagan's Marxism. **He fills his head with Marxist politico-economic theories. They seem to mean more to him than present realities. Perhaps he has faith that world communism will triumph even in this hemisphere early enough for him to try his theories.** But with all his theories and arguments and with all his obsessions and conceits, he has not insisted on any action which seems calculated purposefully to disrupt the economy and the present way of life [emphasis added].[31]

Like Jock Campbell (chairman of Booker), Governor Grey was exasperated by what he considered Jagan's incapacity to make decisions, to get things done: his 'unpracticality' informed, as he characterised it (uncharitably) on another occasion, by his 'scatter-brained policies.' And he wrote over and over to his superiors in London, to convey just how difficult it was to pursue a rational discussion with Cheddi without his communist certainties obtruding. This is Grey's reaction to Jagan's discussion with him (in February 1962) regarding the supposed 'failure of the capitalist system in Canada': **'The trouble with this chap is not that he is a communist or a communist sympathiser, but he just is not cut out to be a premier or a minister or anything else of a practical nature**

Cheddi Jagan with Governor Grey (in 1957), who cautioned him about the pitfalls inherent in his pursuit of communism in the Hemisphere

[emphasis added].'[32] A few months earlier, in November 1961, the Foreign Office (in an internal memorandum, clearly reflecting the views of the men on the spot) elaborated on what Grey's predecessor, Governor Renison, had considered Jagan's inclination to theorise while demonstrating little aptitude for practical administration:

> [Jagan] is madly industrious and probably sincerely devoted to his country's cause, but he is hopelessly unpractical...He is already infected with exaggerated ideas of his importance as a 'world figure,' and having had a taste of meeting with Prime Ministers and Presidents, is all for more of the same, rather than the painful and (less politically rewarding) business of trying to solve the problems on his desk. Dreams multiply and deeds diminish...It is this lack of practical ability, rather than any ideology that will cause Jagan to bring his country into trouble.[33]

This assessment was largely accurate, but they were underestimating the political implications, indeed the centrality, of Jagan's communism for President Kennedy's policy of preventing 'a second Cuba' in the Hemisphere. But Governor Grey knew that apart from the dearth of intellectual capacity in Jagan's PPP, there was a palpable absence of a democratic framework for decision-making in his party. The Jagans retained a proprietorial hold on the organisation and brooked no dissent from their pro-Moscow brand of communism:

> Dr Jagan and his insistent [inflexible?] wife dominate his party. Major decisions are made to his dictation in an inner circle consisting of him, his wife, Mr [Brindley] Benn and Mr Ram Karran. The party executive is then required to endorse these decisions. Those who are brave enough to resist and question are discredited among the membership.[34]

Thus did a sterility to the process of policy formation and its execution become entrenched, as Jaganite dogmas stifled a free ventilation of new ideas, thereby crippling the imagination. A culture of obscurantism had become ingrained in the PPP. The rule of the Jagans had already assumed a divine right. Only death could terminate it.

The PPP was self-contained and self-obsessed, looking into its narrow Marxist-Leninist, Soviet mirror and seeing only what they wished to see. The governor was correct: they lacked flexibility and made no effort to cultivate strategic alliances, at home or in the region. Their belief in scientific truths could not accommodate bourgeois compromises: *realpolitik* was anathema. The Jagans (they were essentially the PPP) did not think that compromises with people who did not share their creed merited serious consideration. It is arguable that this was the foundation of the disintegration of the coalition that was the PPP of the early 1950s: the 'rightist' split of 1955 (led by Burnham) and the so-called ultra-left deviation of 1956 (associated with Sydney King, Martin Carter, and Rory Westmaas). Therefore, despite the loyalty of his Indian supporters, philosophically the PPP of the Jagans increasingly assumed the dimension of a sect, eschewing serious relationship with those deemed to be bereft of their ideological purity and unwavering devotion to 'scientific socialism.' Even the bedevilling chasm between Africans and Indians – the virulent racism in Guyana – definitively embodied by Burnham and Jagan respectively, did not merit undue consideration, as the science of Marxism was imbued with the means of neutralising, in due course, any such excrescence.

In 1962–63, the Trinidadian economist, Lloyd Best, sought to counsel Jagan on aspects of development planning. He tried to persuade him to be less reliant on the irrefutable laws of 'scientific socialism' that consigned capitalism, with its chronic social degradation of the working class, to inevitable doom – the antidote to primordial loyalties, such as racialism, tribalism, and religious bigotry. Best could get nowhere with Cheddi: 'Jagan was perhaps a little too dogmatic [nothing but!]. A very nice man but not given to much discussion or debate or democracy in decision-making...Jagan was rigid. There was no intellectual life in the Party. It was all tired dogma.'[35]

Best (like Sylvia Wynter, the Jamaican intellectual who knew the Jagans well) could see no illumination emerging from Jagan's Marxist faith, nothing that offered resolution of his country's monumental problem of racism and ethnic insecurity:

> The big problem in Guyana was the fragmentation of the society: ethnic conflict fuelled by the crisis over political succession. It pitted Burnham against Jagan, Afro-Guyanese against Indo-Guyanese, blacks against Portuguese whites. The complete breakdown in 1963 focussed the issue of social integration. It also raised doubts about the ideological basis and economic policy on which that integration would be possible...It was in Guyana that I first began to confirm that ethnic cleavages were the much more relevant and much more seminal concept we needed rather than that of class war. Race in Guyana forced us to consider the fact that Burnham and Jagan were both socialists in the same PPP and yet they were so fiercely at each other's throat.[36]

This ethnic insecurity and dire mutual mistrust, papered over in 1953, had no chance of being addressed after the return to power of Jagan's PPP in 1957, when some detected a measure of ideological moderation on his part. This was an illusion. In fact, with the return to British Guiana in 1958 as the editor of *Thunder* (the organ of the PPP), of the orthodox communist theoretician, Ranji Chandisingh (1931–2009) of the Communist Party of Great Britain, a protégé of Cheddi's mentor, Billy Strachan, it was obvious that the Jagans were not about to ditch their allegiance to communism as dispensed by Moscow and the CPGB. Then, handed the doctrinal Hemispheric affirmation – the splendid gift of Castro's Revolution in 1959 with its heroic iconography of youthful vigour, daring and iconoclasm – the PPP was certain that their ideologically pure Marxist vision of the liberation of humankind was being vindicated in the region. The utopia was around the bend!

Cheddi was exhilarated by the victory of Castro and the Cuban Revolution in January 1959, and he embraced it as a good omen for the spread of Marxism-Leninism in the Western Hemisphere. Yet, by 1960, the PPP had redeemed itself in the eyes of the British, particularly the colonial secretary, Iain Macleod, who assured Prime Minister Harold Macmillan that 'there has been for some time the feeling that British Guiana has largely purged itself of its offence.' He meant that the Colonial Office was no longer inclined to see Jagan as a communist threat. In March 1960, at the constitutional conference in London, Macleod (a friend of Jock Campbell) rejected Burnham's case for proportional representation (PR) and granted Jagan internal self-government, with independence virtually guaranteed in about two years. But Cheddi tactlessly repudiated the 'imperialists' for not giving immediate freedom to British Guiana. He said he was 'totally dissatisfied with the outcome,' and he accused the Colonial Office of 'wielding the big stick.' He added that 'an unsatisfactory formula for independence had been forced down the throats of his delegation.'[37]

Independence was there for the taking, and internal self-government was an established prelude, yet Jagan denounced the transitional constitutional arrangements in language unbecoming of a statesman: 'They [the British] were prepared to adorn me with the title of Premier and I threw it back in their faces, because I was not asking to become Premier but to have cabinet status as in Trinidad.' It got worse. He wanted immediate independence; two years were far too long for him to wait: he was in a hurry to create his communist utopia, inspired now by his hero, Fidel. He announced, while he was still in London, that he would take his case for immediate independence to the UN. He even threatened to resign from the government in order 'to carry on the struggle, to increase the tempo both at home and abroad.' Jagan could not resist showing his trumps to the 'imperialists': he said that Castro had promised to help British Guiana, 'in keeping with his policy for the liberation of the hemisphere.'[38] Such was the lack of proportion, the paucity of rational thinking and political judgement of the man that Professor Arthur Schlesinger, after meeting him at the White House in October 1961, said was endowed with 'an unconquerable romanticism and naiveté.'

This was the context in which Jagan promptly declared that he was going to Cuba to learn from Fidel how things should be done. He said of his host: 'Fidel

Castro is not only the liberator of the American continent but also the liberator of this century.' Buoyed by what he saw there (he had discussions with Che Guevara, twice, in April and September 1960), Jagan mocked Prime Minister Macmillan's recent 'wind of change' speech of February 1960 (regarding Africa), intimating his renewed faith in the inevitable victory of his communist creed:

> The East wind is blowing over the West and because of this the West is forced to liberate colonial peoples. The British are breaking up fast, not because they want to make us free… Two years from now there will be no more colonies.[39]

He was, in fact, admitting that there was no need to 'struggle' for independence, no need to provoke a potentially suicidal ideological conflict with the imperialists. It was simply a matter of exercising the patience and caution of maturity – to know how to wait just a little bit longer. As Dr Fenton Ramsahoye put it to me in 1997: 'Independence was virtually in Jagan's bag. Why fuck around and let Burnham steal it from you!'

A fatal attraction! Jagan with Castro in Havana, April 1960. Contrary to Booker Chairman Jock Campbell's counsel to Jagan not to go to Cuba, Cheddi visited Castro twice in 1960, proclaiming him the greatest liberator of the twentieth century. Jagan had effectively taken his country into the Cold War against America.

V. The Fatal Meeting at the White House: Jagan Confirms His Marxist-Leninist Credentials to President Kennedy, October 25, 1961

Colonial Secretary Iain Macleod's offer of internal self-government was made despite the continued opposition of many in the Conservative Party to Jagan's communism. Macleod was an independent thinker, and as his deputy Nigel Fisher observed: 'he had the courage to take controversial decisions against official advice.' Therefore, Jagan's repudiation of Macleod's offer demonstrated not merely a lack of common sense, but a dearth of political discernment and tactical acumen – an immaturity that still astounds. The British were now largely on Jagan's side (against Burnham), so he must have infuriated them with his puerile rhetoric and tantrums, exacerbated by his affirmation of Castro's Cuba on the heels of the 1960 conference in London.

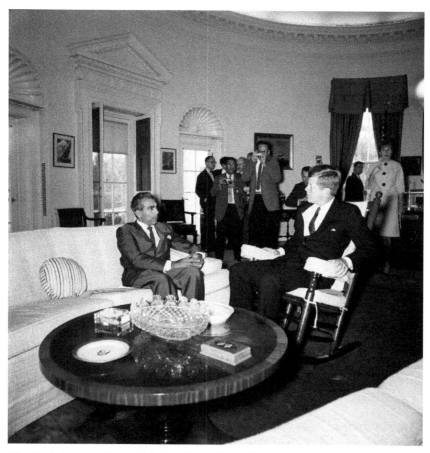

The fatal meeting! Jagan visits President Kennedy at the White House, October 25, 1961, and seeks to persuade him that his conception of Marxism was compatible with the basic freedoms espoused by liberal democracy

Yet when Macleod met Kennedy in early 1961 and the president cautioned him not to move precipitately to independence for British Guiana, he responded: 'Do I understand Mr President that you want us to decolonise as fast as possible all over the world except on your own door-step?' Kennedy laughed and said: 'Well, that's probably just about it.' Macleod replied that while he appreciated the president's reservations, their commitment to granting independence to British Guiana was irreversible.[40] The following year, in February 1962, Macleod (wrongly) sought to persuade Professor Arthur Schlesinger, Kennedy's chief political assistant, that their fears concerning Jagan's politics were unwarranted:

> Jagan is not a communist. He is a naïve London School of Economics Marxist filled with charm and personal honesty and juvenile nationalism … If another election is held before independence, Jagan will win … Jagan is infinitely preferable to Burnham. If I had to make the choice between Jagan and Burnham as head of my country I would choose Jagan any day of the week.[41]

Jock Campbell (1912–94), the progressive chairman of Booker (1952–67), who sought twice (in 1958 and 1960), but failed, to initiate a partnership with Jagan towards joint-ownership of the sugar industry

The latter sentiment was precisely what Jock Campbell of Booker was expressing publicly and privately, and he told me that after 1957 he had spoken on Cheddi's behalf whenever he met with people at the Colonial Office. He added that all the secretaries of state for the colonies, except for Duncan Sandys, consulted him from time to time. In a confidential address to the Booker Board in London on March 22, 1960, Campbell observed:

> We would be reactionary if we were not flexible and adaptable to the aspirations, the changed values, the hopes and the fears of Guyanese ... I think people [Indians] will continue to vote for Jagan and what he stands for, even if it can be logically shown that it is against their own interest as capitalists and landowners. As far as the small man is concerned, as long as he is still a peasant farmer, he will tend to vote for Cheddi, because Cheddi is a very attractive and effective politician, and everyone in this room who was not half-witted would vote for Cheddi Jagan if he lived in British Guiana, because there is effectively nobody else to vote for.[42]

Campbell clearly had no time for Forbes Burnham.

In fact, the governor of British Guiana, Sir Ralph Grey, had counselled Cheddi to be cautious in whatever he did or said on his mission to the US to meet with President Kennedy. Acutely aware of the potential pitfalls, Grey met with Jagan on September 23, 1961, imploring him to avoid 'acts or words likely to bring unfavourable publicity.' He was repelled that the American press instinctively placed every dimension of Jagan's politics beneath the cloud of communism, thereby precluding a rational comprehension of the colony. Cognisant that Kennedy would scrutinise Jagan about his communist beliefs, the governor advised Cheddi to be smart, to present himself as a statesman. Grey noted:

> If he wanted to be treated by the US administration as a person of consequence, he must behave like one. He made some demurring noise about being himself – I sympathise and said that it was not pleasant to have to be less than sincere in all one's dealings – but ... the pursuit of Absolute Truth is remarkably difficult and must in a man of affairs occasionally yield to expediency.

Grey sought desperately to alert Cheddi to a few tactical rudiments to impress the Americans that he possessed a statesmanlike gravitas; he was worthy of respect. He suggested to him that he should stay in a 'reputable hotel' and not with Felix Cummings, his somewhat unkempt representative in New York, to go up-market a tad.[43] After nearly three years in the colony, the governor should have known that Cheddi's creed was sacrosanct. Yet I do believe that, by the late 1950s to early 1960s, despite the American obsession with Castro's communism, the British (like Booker's Jock Campbell) had arrived at a clear preference for Jagan over Burnham and were genuinely trying to persuade him to adopt a modicum of moderation – a degree of common sense – indispensable to his survival in the context of the Cold War.

John Hennings was the colonial attaché at the British Embassy in Washington. He appreciated the sinister overriding motivation of the Kennedy administration; he scrupulously endeavoured to prepare Cheddi for his meeting with the president on October 25, 1961 – arguably the most fateful encounter of his political career. On October 21, Hennings explained to Cheddi why he was receiving such inordinate attention in Washington and the necessity for him to dispel apprehensions of his communism when he spoke with the president. Hennings, obviously, did not know his student very well:

> I told him that he now had...the opportunity to make a forthright and unambiguous statement on his political credo, which would sweep away these equivocations...I told him that he was an intensely controversial figure in this country, and he might wonder why America should appear to be so excited about such a small country as his. I said that Americans were not really interested in British Guiana as such; they were interested in it as a symbol [of communism]. Americans by and large were a very simple people: they saw things as broad issues, and they believed in action to fight wrongs; they believed, too, that America had the power, or should have the power to put matters right. They were therefore perplexed by the complex and threatening world scene [the perceived Sino-Soviet communist threat magnified by Fidel Castro]: they were exasperated that there were no quick answers to these problems; they were frustrated by not being the first nation to put a man into space which their belief in the superiority of their system of economic organisation suggested to them to be right and proper.[44]

Hennings also pointed out to Jagan that Kennedy was a liberal, but he was facing a small but vocal conservative segment in his country, who were perturbed by what they considered weak leadership against the communist enemy. Hennings did not say that this was exacerbated by the Bay of Pigs fiasco of April 1961, but he observed, presciently, that such people were looking for a soft target where a lesson could be taught to the enemy, thus restoring the credibility of the American way. Cheddi ought to have grasped readily the ominous tone in Hennings's grave prognostication:

> They were yearning for some small issue on which swift and firm action could be taken. British Guiana seemed to them such an issue – small, isolated and easy, if only the leaders of the country were brave enough to take the plunge.[45]

The British had definitely fathomed the significance of this meeting to Jagan's political future. And the fact that they expended considerable time (in Georgetown and in Washington) trying to coax him towards a degree of statesmanship, should dispel the popular assumption that they were spineless before American power or that British attitudes, since their suspension of the constitution in October 1953, were typified by unrelenting antagonism towards Jagan. On the contrary, Hennings even tried to persuade him that his political vocabulary – leftist idioms and their specific American connotation – should be eschewed if he were to avert the baleful ramifications. He gave Cheddi a few examples:

> A Communist, for example, was not a man who believed in scientific socialism as a method of economic organisation. When Mr Spivak [on 'Meet-the-Press'] asked him whether he was a Communist, he meant if he was a lackey of Moscow, Peking or Havana. It was therefore no use saying he was a socialist, rather than a Communist, because Communists also call themselves socialists, and the strongest believers in free enterprise in this country regarded any extension of Government endeavour as creeping socialism, which would lead inevitably to Communism. It was no good saying he was a democrat, because Communists called themselves that as well…To Americans generally, a Communist was the dedicated agent of an international conspiracy, controlled by Moscow and Peking, in the interests of the new Communist imperialism.[46]

John Hennings concluded with the observation that Americans were incapable of assimilating the potential validity of Marxist 'economic doctrines,' or the appeal of Castro's Cuba:

> Thinking Americans recognise the disequilibria and instabilities in Latin America; they recognised the Cuban Revolution was due to them, but they felt that Castro had betrayed the revolution. **I warned him against trying to score runs for Castro; he had enough troubles of his own and should concentrate on the interests of British Guiana** [emphasis added].[47]

Hennings was imploring Jagan to desist from any ideological discourse with the president. His appearance on 'Meet the Press' [on October 15, 1961] had already made a poor impression on Kennedy. Professor Arthur Schlesinger, the special assistant to the president, recalls that Jagan had 'resolutely declined to say anything critical of the Soviet Union.' He adds:

> This appearance instantly diminished the enthusiasm for helping his Government. The President who caught the last half of the show, called for a re-examination of all aspects of the problem, saying he wanted no commitments made until he had seen Jagan himself.[48]

The president and Professor Schlesinger, surely, must have been informed, certainly by the CIA (who would have been bugging him), that Jagan was a dyed-in-the-wool pro-Moscow communist. Besides, the American Consulate in Georgetown missed nothing and forwarded everything regarding Jagan to Washington. It is noteworthy, therefore, that during the recently concluded general elections of August 1961, Jagan had declared in a radio broadcast (on

August 17) that his communist ideology was winning; he had nothing to be apologetic for:

> The imprint of [Joseph] McCarthy [the notorious anti-communist] still lies heavy on that land [United States]. **Events in Russia and Cuba have deeply wounded their [American] national pride and made their fear of Communism psychopathic.** No wonder the great [British] politician Aneurin Bevan [1897–1960] wrote: 'Fear of Soviet Communism has led to the US and those who follow her lead to take a distorted view of the world situation and the forces which are at work in modern society [emphasis added].'[49]

Jagan and his disciples in the PPP were certain they were on the correct side of the evolution of society towards universal perfectibility, ideological and scientific. In fact, they did not compartmentalise politics and science, as is evident in their response to the Soviet Union's sending the first man into space: Yuri Gagarin (1934–68), on April 12, 1961. The PPP was ecstatic; this amazing achievement was embraced and celebrated as an affirmation of the supremacy of a vibrant communism – the irrepressible future of human perfectibility – over moribund capitalism. It gave them immeasurable pride to cite Professor Bernard Lovell (1913–2012), the first director of Britain's Space Observatory (Jodrell Bank), on Soviet leadership in the field: 'I think it most remarkable that a nation which was largely illiterate only a generation ago has succeeded in this immense task…the greatest scientific achievement in the history of man.'

Thunder, enlarging on Jagan's ideological fervour – the superiority of Marxism-Leninism over a dying capitalism – drew its own lesson from the pioneering accomplishment:

> The distinction of being the first man in space thus falls to a worker, a citizen of the first socialist country, a Communist, and his achievement made possible by the combined material and scientific resources of the socialist system.
>
> The world over, mankind acclaims this feat and marvels that **within the short space of 40-odd years** [since the October Revolution of 1917] **the socialist philosophy has been able to transform an illiterate and backward country into the world's leading space pioneer** [emphasis added].[50]

The year 1961 should have been a good year for Jagan. He was elated that because of his two visits to Castro's Cuba in 1960, they were providing him with loans allegedly cheaper than the rate at which they had borrowed the money, from communist countries. Jagan deemed Cuban benevolence a 'disinterested' expression of proletarian internationalism, while his enemies perceived it as a means by which Soviet funding was penetrating British Guiana, driven purely by nefarious ideological motives. But the relationship with Castro was pivotal in sustaining Jagan's inviolable image among the predominantly Indian rice growers specifically, and Indians generally. In March 1961 it was announced that the Cuban government had agreed to buy two hundred thousand tons of Guyanese rice over the next five years, at a higher price than that obtained hitherto in its traditional market, the British West Indies.

Jagan had thereby fortified the loyalty of a significant proportion of his crucial Indian electoral base by negotiating a secured and lucrative market for their rice. This deal with Cuba, in conjunction with the Black Bush Polder and Tapacuma land settlement schemes (completed during Jagan's regime of 1957–64, with British funding, primarily for rice), were perceived by a majority of his Indian supporters as demonstrative of Cheddi's loyalty to them. On the eve of the general elections of 1961, the Cuban rice deal was timely in consolidating his Indian support base. And he was immeasurably proud of the fact that he was the sole head of a government in the Hemisphere (granted of a colony) to endorse the Cuban Revolution as the model eminently worthy of emulation. He was not perturbed in defying the Americans, even alienating them. He was emboldened. History and time were on his side. The future belonged to communism:

> Cuba, much maligned and castigated by the daily press and the reactionaries in our midst, has signed an agreement whereby they will purchase this year 26,000 tons of rice at a higher price than that paid by the West Indies...Over the next five years, beginning 1962, Cuba will purchase 36,000 tons of rice, more or less per annum. British Guiana, therefore, has secured a market for all its foreseeable surpluses over the next few years. Not only the rice farmers or those directly involved in rice production stand to benefit. The whole economy and people benefit. The prophets of doom are shaken. They cannot find their voices...The agreement is a slap in the face for our detractors, and a vindication of the international relations pursued by the majority party [the PPP].[51]

In June 1961, Jagan was asked by the editor of the *Daily Argosy* whether capitalism could be reformed. With millions of workers acquiring shares in capitalist companies, was it not conceivable that a reformed 'people's capitalism' was already in the making? The latter, arguably, had some parallels with Jock Campbell's reformist capitalism: social reform allied with a *modus vivendi* between Booker and the government of British Guiana, Jock having broached with Cheddi twice, in 1958 and 1960, the possibility of joint ownership of Booker. This, however, was subversive of the fundamental Marxist conception of the creation and distribution of wealth. For Cheddi, 'people's capitalism' was bogus, 'a euphemism for monopoly capitalism.' It was because socialism was advancing universally that the 'adherents of the old order of capitalism and imperialism were peddling this new line.' A dying capitalism could not be mended. It had to make way for socialism/communism:

The propagandists for the capitalist class are busy trying to fool the working class. Some prattle about business democracy to stem the tide of socialism. They try to make workers into potential capitalists by schemes such as profit-sharing, gifts of shares, etc. Others [such as the Moral Re-Armament movement] take on the garb of preachers – capitalism is not bad; what is bad is greedy men; we must appeal to the hearts of the greedy …

[But]… the fault is with the system…**Not all the new garments, not all the perfumes of Arabia can save dying capitalism. The handwriting is on the wall. Socialism** [communism] **is winning. This will be the socialist century** [emphasis added].⁵²

In his pre-election radio broadcast of August 17, 1961, Jagan did concede that certain reforms had been achieved on the sugar plantations. But he attributed none of it to Jock Campbell's comprehensive programme of social reform. It was all due to him and his 'bitter sugar' crusade, yet he was unimpressed with these half-measures:

We have fought for freedom, and even as we fought, we won by-products of the battle … The fact that the sugar estate ranges [logies] have been tumbled down, that wages and conditions have somewhat improved, the fact…that your sons and daughters can now get jobs in Water St [the commercial centre] irrespective of their colour, the fact that British money has at last begun to flow into this benighted country – all of this is due to us.

This, however, was too little, too late for this inveterate exponent of class warfare: 'what they did was little compared with what you need for your ease and happiness. They gave a slice of bread to some, so as to save themselves the loaf. But the loaf is YOURS not theirs.'⁵³

It is noteworthy that while the Kennedy administration, in the aftermath of the Bay of Pigs fiasco, continued to express reservations regarding Jagan's relations with Castro and his potential danger to the Hemisphere, the British were still defending him. Only three days before the general elections of 1961, on August 18, British foreign secretary, Lord Home, wrote thus to Dean Rusk, the American secretary of state:

No one can say for certain how Jagan will behave if he is returned to power. **He is a confused thinker, and his mind is clogged with ill-digested dogma derived from Marxist literature.** But he has learnt a good deal in the last eight years; he has not, since 1957, proved as difficult to deal with as he was earlier. It is true that he has during the election campaign made it clear that he expects to strengthen his relations with Cuba, and he has at times shown an interest in the possibilities of trade and aid with the Soviet bloc. But he has also, during the elections, promised to seek further aid from the US; and, **if we in the West show a real willingness to try to**

315

help, we think it by no means impossible that British Guiana may end up in a position not very different from that of India [non-aligned, but not communist] [emphasis added].[54]

The Cuban Revolution's expression of 'proletarian internationalism' of which Jagan was a beneficiary; the pioneering Soviet mastery in space coupled with America's Bay of Pigs fiasco, both in April 1961, in addition to his own victory at the polls in August 1961, strengthened Jagan's conviction, on the eve of his meeting with President Kennedy, that the latter was the principal exponent of a decadent system that could not be reformed; it was destined for the 'dustbin of history.' Cheddi had no doubts that socialism/communism was, indeed, on the verge of supplanting capitalism universally. Meanwhile, the West Indies Federation, to which he was vehemently opposed, was unravelling irreversibly; and with 54.1 per cent of Jamaicans voting to leave it, in a referendum on September 19, 1961, he felt absolved. He was on top of the world, and that world was, in his view, moving irrevocably towards communism as exemplified by the Soviet Union. He had no misgiving regarding his belief that Marxism-Leninism was superior to capitalism, and he was inclined to proclaim it even to the American president. His belief was absolute.

On October 14, 1961, while Jagan was in America on the eve of his meeting with President Kennedy, the PPP's *Thunder* carried a leader reflecting their certainty of the impending supremacy of communism and its conquest of the universe by the end of the twentieth century – likewise were they conceited with regard to the granting of independence by the British in 1962:

> Today we stand on the threshold of Independence, led by **the same PPP, which has not gone back one thousandth of an inch in its programme and policies [Marxism-Leninism] advocated since its formation** [in January 1950]. The moral is clear for all to see: so long as people are prepared to fight for the improvement of living and working conditions in a given country; so long as the leadership is unbending in its resolve to lead the people correctly, they will win out ...
>
> **The PPP is prepared to move on towards Independence even if it has to drag the politically dead bodies of our opponents to that goal**...We have said time and again that we are entitled to our freedom; we reiterate this. The British have decided on a date for the independence of the West Indies Federation. With the secession of Jamaica, the British have more or less agreed that Jamaica may become independent outside the Federation. We claim that same right and immediately too [emphasis added].[55]

But neither Norman Manley, leader of the PNP, nor Alexander Bustamante, leader of the Jamaica Labour Party (JLP), was a communist. The British and the Americans had no problem whatsoever even with Manley, generally perceived as a Fabian socialist, therefore moderate enough and compatible with the left strand of the British Labour Party, led by Aneurin Bevan and his wife, Jennie Lee. But with Jagan, who had not changed his stance 'one thousandth of an inch' since the British evicted him in 1953 for his communist beliefs, the question of independence could still be problematical. Yet, by 1960–61, the British were inclined to give him the benefit of the doubt. And after his victory in the general elections of August 1961, even the Kennedy administration was persuaded to give Jagan a final chance. As Guyanese scholar Cary Fraser observes:

> Despite having reservations about Jagan's predilections, the Kennedy administration seemed to have decided that it had little choice but to collaborate with the British in working with the PPP as British Guiana took the final steps towards independence.[56]

Then Cheddi went to Washington, in October 1961, to meet with President Kennedy!

On October 15, 1961, a few days before Jagan visited the White House, he had attempted to vindicate his communist creed on American television (NBC's 'Meet the Press,' moderated by the renowned anti-communist Laurence E. Spivak) – and President Kennedy was watching:

> I do not believe in capitalism. I do not believe that free enterprise, which may have been very wonderful for, say, the United States of America, will in present day circumstances develop either my country or an [any?] underdeveloped country generally ....

In response to Spivak's probing whether democratic freedom really existed in the Soviet Union and China, Jagan gave a typically tortuous response that must have left Kennedy in no doubt that he was looking at the potential perpetrator of a 'second Cuba' in the Hemisphere. It was a dreadful performance:

> On the question of the Soviet bloc as such, there is a planned economy. In this sense I am interested in what is happening there. All I can say – I haven't been to China, I haven't been to Russia, but the experts who have been there have said – for instance, you have this chap who is a writer for the London *Observer*, I can't recall his name right now [Edward Crankshaw (1909–84), an authority on the Soviet Union], but he has said in his latest book [possibly *Khrushchev's Russia* (1959)] that **life in the Soviet Union is growing day by day better and better. The standards of living are improving, and as such, we are concerned. We want to know how this is done** [emphasis added].[57]

Jagan was then lured into an incriminating definition of his creed, which arguably confirmed, as far as the president was concerned, that an independent British Guiana, contiguous with Brazil and Venezuela and led by Cheddi Jagan, would become a 'second Cuba' – the beachhead for the Soviet communist penetration of South America. Jagan was a true believer, and he was disinclined, contrary to the counsel studiously rendered by the British, to eschew divulging his faith in the Soviet Union as the beacon of enlightenment:

> I would like to say from what I have read from the [Marxist-Leninist] textbooks, socialism means, or the slogan under socialism is, from each according to his ability, to each according to his labour, the work that he gives. Under communism as under the early Christian set-up, all persons were supposed to share equally, and so I see the communists say, in that period to come, there will be distribution according to needs. Each one will contribute according to his ability, and from my point of view this is good. This is a good thing that all persons should get from society what they need, regardless of whether he is a cripple or whether he is able to produce more or less.[58]

Lloyd Searwar recalls that

> Spivak shafted him. That was a mistake. Sir Hugh Foot, former Governor of Jamaica and Head of the British Mission at the UN, had cautioned me against it. They rather liked Cheddi and hated Burnham's guts. I should never have allowed Cheddi to go on that programme, but I thought it would give him a visibility which would have constrained Kennedy. It was a disaster.[59]

With the British essentially on his side, with Booker's Jock Campbell backing him unequivocally against Burnham, Cheddi was well placed to receive the gift of independence, possibly in 1962. But his communist creed was like a religious calling; he would not deviate from it, and this was magnified, fatally, by Castro's communist revolution in Cuba after 1959. Yet he did have a last chance to redeem himself when he met Kennedy at the White House on Wednesday, October 25, 1961. A devotee of communism as exemplified by the Soviet Union, Cheddi was suspicious of short-term pragmatism (as genuinely proffered to him by the British Embassy in Washington) because the universal triumph of communism was unstoppable; thus, the perfect society, releasing humankind from its ancient chains of oppression, was on the verge of fruition. Capitalism was decadent and doomed to extinction. There was no need to compromise with that evil system, however tactically defensible in the short run.

On October 24, 1961 (the day before Jagan met Kennedy), in an address to the National Press Club in Washington, Cheddi unveiled his political philosophy to the world, thus flying in the face of John Hennings's earnest entreaty of him for moderation and circumspection:

> **I believe that the economic theories of scientific socialism** [Marxism-Leninism] **hold out the promise of a dynamic social discipline which can transform an underdeveloped country into a developed one in a far faster time than any other system.**

> **We may differ from you in the way we organise our economic
> life. You have as your dominant philosophy private enterprise**
> [capitalism], **but let us not forget that your development took
> place in a different political historical epoch** [emphasis added].[60]

Jagan would soon squander the political capital of which he was the recipient, directly or indirectly, from Iain Macleod and Jock Campbell in 1960: the former, in granting him internal self-government, with every likelihood of independence by 1962; the latter with respect to his categorical preference for Jagan over Burnham, which he declared to the Booker Board, and which (he told me) he had conveyed to Macleod several times. On October 25, 1961, Jagan visited the White House and, again, disregarding British counsel to tread cautiously (to refrain from expressions like 'scientific socialism,' indeed, the word 'socialism' completely), he provoked an ideological exchange with Kennedy that placed him, in the eyes of the president, unambiguously in the communist camp. In his ninety-minute meeting with Kennedy **(an hour of which was between Kennedy and Jagan alone, with no notetaker)**, uniquely prolonged for a leader from an obscure South American colony, Jagan left the president in no doubt that he was deeply enamoured of the Soviet system – indeed, that he was a pro-Soviet communist.

Professor Arthur Schlesinger recalls that Jagan was 'personable and fluent,' but he was 'endowed, it seemed to those of us present, with an unconquerable romanticism and naivete.' Jagan had admitted to John Hennings that 'saying too much was a besetting sin of his.' And true to form, circumspection was not one of Cheddi's attributes on display that fatal day, in the presence of the president and his men. Yet he celebrated his fatally tactless performance in his memoirs, grandiloquently titled *The West on Trial*, published in London in early 1966. This was after Kennedy's machinations, precipitated by their encounter in October 1961, had contrived his demise, by December 1964, having afforded Burnham (deemed anti-communist by the Americans) the invaluable help of the CIA and its supporting apparatus. Jagan elaborated:

> I recall, on this question of underdevelopment, my hour and a half
> interview with the late President Kennedy in November [October]
> 1961 ... and my conversations with some of his 'Harvard brains trust'
> aides [Arthur Schlesinger and George Ball, for instance]. I gathered
> the impression that they were realists who understood the problems
> confronting them, and who as good defenders of the faith [capitalism]
> recognised the necessity for change to prevent a 'powder keg' from
> exploding.[61]

Jagan recalls his arguments with President Kennedy, as he tried to persuade him of the futility of adopting capitalism as the instrument for resolving the endemic problems confronting backward Guyana, in the short run. He was, in effect, instructing the president that his recent economic transactions with Castro's Cuba, and by extension the Soviets, offered infinitely better possibilities for the accelerated transformation of the economy of his chronically poor country. Moreover, that American capitalism was intrinsically inadequate for that purpose:

> Kennedy and his aides attacked me on the grounds of our trade with Cuba and associations with socialist countries [the Eastern bloc]. I took the counter-offensive and attacked them for preventing countries like British Guiana from making an economic breakthrough. I referred to their opposition to non-alignment as evidenced by their overthrow of the government of President Janio Quadros of Brazil, and pointed out that the increasing difficulties which faced poor countries...could easily be overcome by a planned, balanced industrial-agricultural economy and free trade with all countries ...

> I cited our negotiations with the Cuban Government which not only bought our rice at prices favourable to us but was prepared to lend us initially $5 million (US) for a wood-pulp project, and the steel, cement and generators for a $32 million (BG) hydroelectric plant. The $5 million was to be a soft loan at 2% interest to be paid in wood-pulp produced locally...I was told there were dangers in this kind of arrangement.[62]

Lloyd Searwar (1925–2006) was the assistant head of the Government Information Services, and he accompanied Jagan to Washington and the White House. He recalled that crucial meeting as nothing but a disaster; and he explains the context of Jagan's 'confidential' attack on the president with regard to the 'overthrow' of President Quadros. Jagan was alone with the president when he took him through the French windows to the Rose Garden for a decisive informal one-to-one discussion. What Jagan said to him during their extended meeting of nearly an hour was probably the final straw: it left the president with no doubt that Cheddi was the man most likely to present him with his worst nightmare – a second Cuba in the Hemisphere, thus aborting his chance of re-election in 1964 – if the British gave him independence, as planned in 1962.

Searwar elaborated for me:

> I was with Cheddi when he met Kennedy in October 1961. Kennedy had with him Pierre Salinger [press secretary] and Arthur Schlesinger [special assistant], but this meeting lasted a short time [about 30 minutes]. Then the President took Cheddi out through the French windows unto the lawn – out of earshot of anybody. And they talked at great length, for a long, long time. His staff became very upset because Robert Frost, the great poet [aged 87], was waiting to see him, and was kept waiting for the better part of an hour...Then Arthur Schlesinger and I had to produce some kind of a communique, but we found it hard to agree on a form of words...**Cheddi was naïve;**

he never acquired the sophistication of a statesman. He never really left the plantation [emphasis added].[63]

But there was no one present to take notes, so all we have on the obviously momentous one-to-one conversation is Jagan's brief recollection regarding his private exchange with the president. And Kennedy never did divulge the substance of their informal discussion and the impressions formed (I have seen no record of it), but it must have been largely negative – and fatal – given Jagan's virtually religious conviction that what he stood for, his Marxist-Leninist creed as dispensed by the Soviet Union, was flawless and unimpeachable. Jagan recalls one remark he made to the president, with no remorse at all:

> I referred to their [American] opposition to non-alignment as evidenced by their overthrow of the government of President Janio Quadros of Brazil [in August 1961]...I accused the US government [Kennedy] of overthrowing Quadros because he was pursuing a path of non-alignment in attempting to solve his economic problems. I was told [by the President] that the US had nothing to do with the overthrow of the Quadros government...I referred to our own position and asked Kennedy point-blank: 'What would you do, were you in our position?' I took the counter-offensive and attacked them for preventing countries like British Guiana from making an economic breakthrough ... **This philosophy of the West** [capitalism], **I argued, could not help the underdeveloped countries** ... [emphasis added].
>
> Kennedy and his aides [prior to the one-to-one], forced on the defensive, said they were not opposed to genuine non-alignment, not even to nationalisation...They said, however, that what they were opposed to was a total commitment to the Soviet bloc and the denial of freedom![64]

It is clear why White House officials deemed the talks 'delicate and controversial.' Consequently, the president made no definite commitment to grant Jagan any aid, his principal reason for the visit. On the other hand, the president had agreed to the meeting primarily because he wanted to make a final judgment on Jagan's widely known devotion to communism. An inane communique was eventually contrived to enable Jagan to save face. As Lloyd Searwar told me, he and Professor Schlesinger 'laboured over a form of words' afterwards, at his club in New York. Thereby Jagan did commit himself to abide by democratic norms, while the US promised to dispatch a team to examine the urgent economic priorities of British Guiana. But Kennedy's one-to-one conversation with Jagan left no doubts in the mind of the president that he was 'lost' to communism: a foremost enemy in the Cold War! Jagan was not amenable to yielding 'one-thousandth of an inch' (as *Thunder* put it) in pursuit of his utopian vision.

In the aftermath of the Bay of Pigs, it is highly likely that the first casualty of President Kennedy's paranoia regarding communism, was Janio Quadros (1917–92), a very left-wing president of Brazil, elected with a significant majority in late 1960, yet he lasted just seven months in office (the first seven months of Kennedy's presidency) before he was forced to resign. He was in office from January 31 to August 25, 1961. Shortly after Jagan had accused Kennedy of engineering the 'overthrow' of Quadros, the PPP's *Thunder* carried on its front page an article from *Daily Worker* (organ of the CPGB) on the subject. It alleged that 'US imperialism forced the resignation of former President Janio Quadros because he refuses to follow Yankee foreign policy.' Besides, they dismissed Kennedy's flagship Alliance for Progress initiative for economic reform in Latin America as pie in the sky: it would beget 'greater impoverishment, exploitation by tyrannical rule and the loss of independence and freedom.' The US Consulate in Georgetown missed nothing; this would have been communicated to the State Department.

Jagan could well have been right regarding the sudden resignation of Quadros after just seven months. He was determined to have an independent foreign policy that deviated from anything pursued hitherto by Brazil: he was in favour of opening relations with the Soviet Union, China, and Cuba. He was totally opposed to any attempt to overthrow Castro. He was even disinclined to collaborate with other Organization of American States (OAS) countries in forging an anti-Cuba alliance. In fact, Quadros was deemed a communist, and this indictment gained traction when he conferred Brazil's highest award for foreigners to Cuban revolutionary 'Che' Guevara.[65]

Earlier in the year, on April 29, 1961, days after the American-conceived-and-executed invasion of Cuba to overthrow Fidel Castro ended in disaster (the Bay of Pigs fiasco: Kennedy's worse nightmare!), Cheddi Jagan wrote an article in his party's paper, *Thunder*, celebrating the impending demise of 'imperialism.' He did not equivocate:

> Imperialism is dying. It used force to overthrow several democratic regimes…Fidel Castro is lucky. He has not only the people of Cuba on his side. History is on his side…The reactionary imperialist forces are fighting back. But the handwriting is on the wall. The death knell of imperialism is sounding on all fronts.

Cheddi had taken his little obscure colony into the Cold War.

In early May 1961, the Progressive Youth Organisation (PYO), youth arm of Jagan's PPP, mounted a picketing exercise in front of the US Consulate in Georgetown, against American imperialism, following the aborted Bay of Pigs invasion of Cuba the previous month. They contrasted the moral promptings of their action with that of the 'reactionaries' (the United Force and their allies the Defenders of Freedom, as well as the right-wing National Labour Front), for whom it was an occasion for congratulating 'world capitalist racketeer and mouthpiece, Kennedy.' However, they felt that for 'the overwhelming majority of Guianese it was an unthinkable crime of the antediluvian mentality of North American capitalism.' The PYO displayed placards inscribed thus: 'Long Live Fidel Castro!'; 'Long Live the Cuban Revolution!'; 'US Warmongers, Hands off Cuba!'; 'Down with Yankee imperialism!' Their solidarity with the Cuban people against foreign domination was inspired by the spirit of proletarian internationalism: 'In its moral terms of reference, the demonstration ranks with the greatest this country has ever witnessed [the picture shows about a dozen people!]. It was not lavish, but quietly excellent. There was no pomp, no pageantry (we're too poor to afford it), but it was a moral spectacle.'[66]

Around the same time, Shiv Gangadeen, a regular columnist on the *Sunday Chronicle* (owned by Peter D'Aguiar) and a staunch supporter of the United Force (UF), wrote a portentous article captioned: 'Inside the PPP: Little Rats in a Trap.' Described by the security forces as 'an ex-boyfriend of Janet Jagan,' the reputedly handsome Gangadeen observed:

> The Jagans…hear the death-knell of their hopes for a communist take-over of Guiana, and their dream of totalitarian power of a people they thought they could fool forever … And they also understand the meaning of the massive offensive – economic, technological, educational, social and ideological – which the US has launched against communism in the Western Hemisphere. These Reds know full well what they are facing. **They have trapped themselves. They may survive for a while yet, but their doom is certain …**

Gangadeen was contending that the Jagans and their PPP were enmeshed in the Cold War on the wrong side. They could not win in the Western Hemisphere.[67]

The day before Gangadeen's article appeared, Cheddi Jagan sought to explain the aims and objectives of his PPP. He noted that although it had a socialist (communist) bias, it was a national party encompassing various strata of the society: farmers, workers, native capitalists, professionals, intellectuals – people of all races and religions. He was saying that although the PPP was deeply influenced by communism, it was a broad-based party contesting democratic elections in a colony, therefore it was necessary to mobilise across class and race lines. However, since the departure of Burnham in early 1955, it could no longer be considered even a coalition of the two main races, as it was in 1953. Jagan's PPP was essentially an Indian party, as Burnham's PNC was an African party – retaining a sprinkling of Africans and Indians respectively did not a 'national' party make!

Yet Cheddi was never daunted or restrained by the anti-communist crusade of the UF, or the dangers inherent in his communist beliefs, as adumbrated in Shiv Gangadeen's article. Cheddi had an inviolable all-weather formula that no one, however mighty, could moderate, much less extirpate. His communist faith was indestructible, and with gaining independence he believed he would be free to pursue it without the severe restraints imposed by American and British imperialism. It was a simple and simplistic utopian communist mantra that was like a religious conviction (Jagan tended to use the sanitised term 'socialism'):

> Socialism means the ending of exploitation of man by man. It's to be achieved by public ownership of the means of production, distribution and exchange. In other words, ownership by the people, for the people, for the benefit of the people.[68]

Although Jagan's many enemies in the Cold War, at home and abroad, were resolved to destroy him, his faith in the communist utopia was undiminished. He had learnt nothing from the suspension of the constitution by the British in October 1953. He was recklessly indifferent to, possibly incapable of, the practice of *realpolitik*, despite the brutal reality that he was, from late 1961, a primary target of American imperialism – President Kennedy now obsessed with precluding the emergence of 'a second Cuba' in the Hemisphere. Cheddi's faith was irrepressible, whatever the consequences for himself and his devoted Indian supporters, most of whom (ironically) knew nothing whatsoever about the implications of his Marxism-Leninism or communism. What he stood for was infallible; it was winning; he was not about to change.

As Jagan asserted in May 1961:

> Both theoretically and practically socialism is superior. Capitalism is based on unplanned production and wasteful competition. Private profit and greed are its main force. It has led to private opulence side by side with public squalor on a wide scale. Feudalism replaced slavery. Feudalism in turn was replaced by capitalism. This was because the new system was more efficient than the one it replaced. In the same way socialism will replace capitalism. Socialism has always been a way of measuring the actual against the potential, the immediate against the possible condition of man.[69]

For Cheddi, pursuit of the communist utopia was, indeed, a quasi-religious calling. The jargon and the accompanying certainties were absorbed no less comprehensively than devout Hindus do the mantras and rituals that underpin their faith. It was well-rehearsed and could be recited *ad nauseum*, but his facility for critical thinking, filtering things with their inescapably daunting complexity, was deficient. Here again, Jagan is explaining the aims and objectives of the PPP:

> What about socialism and communism? What is the difference between the two? In socialism, the slogan is 'from each according

to his ability, to each according to his work.' In communism, the slogan is 'from each according to his ability, to each according to his need.' The difference between socialism and communism is that in socialism there are still not enough goods produced. The result is that distribution has to be made on the basis of work done. **In communism, productive forces would have been so advanced that all of man's material needs could be met by only a few hours of labour. In other words, man will have all that he needs in terms of food, clothing and shelter** [emphasis added].[70]

In January 1961, Dr Scott Nearing (1883–1983), an American Marxist economist who contributed regularly to *Monthly Review* (the reputable Marxist monthly journal in New York, edited by Paul Sweezy and Leo Huberman), visited British Guiana as a guest of the Jagans. He gave a lecture at Freedom House (the home of Jagan's PPP) titled 'The Socialist Century.' The millenarianism permeating Dr Nearing's message would have resonated with Cheddi's vision of human perfectibility:

> Before we get to 1999 we will be living in a century that will be dominated by socialism [communism]…The end of the 20th century will see the triumph of socialism as a system, though of course there may still remain pockets of capitalism just as pockets of feudalism had lingered on into this century.
>
> The United States has taken over 200 years to reach her position, while it has taken the Soviet Union 43 years, and China is achieving it in less time. **Socialism can use science and technology to reshape society, abolish poverty, and raise human society to a new level never before attained. This is the reason why the 20th century is bound to become the Socialist century** [emphasis added].[71]

Kennedy was humiliated by the colossal blunder at the Bay of Pigs in April 1961. For the rest of his presidency, he was preoccupied with the idea that no other communist state – no second Cuba – must emerge in the Western Hemisphere. Shortly after the debacle, Kennedy, as Howard Jones argues: 'quickly regained his hard-line Cold War composure and joined his brother [Robert, his attorney general] in a virtual vendetta against Castro. To restore US prestige, they would have to take a firm stand, not only in Cuba but also in Berlin, Vietnam, and other trouble spots. Cuba, though, was the centrepiece. Castro's removal became the top priority on the administration's agenda, for it would help to determine the course of the Cold War, refurbish the stature needed by the White House to pursue its ambitious domestic programme, and, no less important, satisfy the Kennedys' growing obsession with eliminating their Cuban adversary.' And the president communicated his resolve, unambiguously, to Hemispheric leaders (all, save Castro and Jagan, embedded in the American camp):

... if the nations of this Hemisphere should fail to meet their commitments against outside Communist penetration – then I want it clearly understood that this Government will not hesitate in meeting its primary obligations which are the security of our Nation.[72]

No second Cuba!

Yet Jagan did have a last chance to redeem himself in the eyes of the Americans, who had the power and the firm determination to destroy him. He chose not to. In fact, he took the president on – from the other side of the fence! During Jagan's visit to Washington in October 1961, Kennedy had heard enough from him to reinforce the long-held assumption that he was confronted with a dyed-in-the-wool communist. Therefore, the president concluded shortly after his meeting with Jagan, on October 25, that the British *must not* give independence to British Guiana under a government led by him. Yet Kennedy would give no hint that they were about to deploy the resources of the CIA to thwart Jagan's resolve to gain independence for his country in 1962, primarily because the British still preferred him to Burnham, as they had indicated to him on several occasions.

And Jagan – routinely oblivious of political nuances and not endowed with the attributes of statesmanship – failed to grasp that he had effectively declared to President Kennedy that he was on the side of America's foremost enemies, the Soviet Union and Cuba. It is strange, therefore, that Jagan could convince his comrades in the PPP that although the 'American imperialists' were implacably opposed to him, they had acceded to his right to follow a Marxist-Leninist path because he was democratically elected. And the basis of this assessment, paradoxically, was that Jagan's conversation with Kennedy – specifically his defence of Marxism – was so deftly and persuasively handled as to evoke a fundamental ideological rethink by the president: that despite the Cold War and the primacy of the Cuban factor, he was prepared to make an exception of Cheddi Jagan. Unimaginable, but true!

VI. The Consequences of the Jagan-Kennedy Encounter: Resurrection of the Fading Political Fortunes of Forbes Burnham and the Energising of the Anti-Communist Crusade of Peter D'Aguiar

Incredibly, just after his contentious meeting with Kennedy, Jagan told reporters that 'assurance was given to him that aid was forthcoming.'[73] Yet on November 3, 1961, he announced to the House of Assembly that the US had refused his request for financial aid and had thereby implied that he should 'get it where he could.' He added that it had been confirmed 'at the highest levels,' in the US and

Canada, that while they were concerned with the 'preservation of the democratic way of life in developing countries, it is no concern of theirs how these countries organise their economic life.' He was badly mistaken with regard to the latter. He had effectively blown it by virtually declaring himself a partisan of Castroism and an exponent of Marxism-Leninism, in his fatal encounter with President Kennedy.

The US government feigned surprise at Jagan's announcement, stating that they had opted for 'modest and venturesome financial support,' in an endeavour to retain him 'within the western fold and the inter-American system.' Jagan's statement that he had been refused aid and told to look elsewhere was rejected as 'not hopeful.' They considered it a ploy by him to ascertain whether the Communist bloc would provide aid to his country, due to become independent in a year or two.[72] In any case, Jagan would not have been overly perturbed by failure to procure American aid. He was already entranced by the notion of Cuban aid on preferential terms (in effect, Soviet aid with Cuba being the intermediary), and with independence imminent, he felt assured that such 'disinterested' aid, motivated purely by 'proletarian internationalism,' would flow unimpeded to the bountiful advantage of his country.

However, there were turbulent seas ahead for Jagan following what was, indeed, a calamitous encounter with Kennedy. But the ominous signs were not only external; his local enemies had apprehended a notable chink in his armoury after his White House debacle. Forbes Burnham and Peter D'Aguiar were energised by the perceived rebuff of Jagan by the Kennedy administration. Although it cannot be verified that the president had already opted for a replacement of the communist Jagan, implicit in Jagan's disclosure of his failure to procure American aid (given the high-profile nature of the visit), was the likelihood that the Americans were already contemplating a 'moderate' alternative to him before independence. It is not possible to ascertain what was communicated by the American consul-general in Georgetown to Jagan's enemies (much was probably informal and unrecorded), but it is noteworthy that only two days after Jagan announced his failure to get American aid, Burnham considered it opportune to advance a very strong case for a change of the electoral system to proportional representation (PR).

Burnham was already testing the ground in pursuit of a definitive, and potentially decisive, American affirmation. He was distancing himself from communism, and planting in the impressionable American Cold War mentality the most efficacious means of vanquishing the communist Jagan – PR. Thereby would the danger of 'a second Cuba' in the Hemisphere be obviated – the demise of Jagan through a potential electoral contrivance. As noted earlier, under the first-past-the-post system in August 1961, with 42.7 per cent of the votes, Jagan's PPP won twenty seats; with 41 per cent – only 1.7 per cent less than Jagan – Burnham's PNC got only eleven seats; D'Aguiar won four seats, with 16.2 per cent. Moreover, as Sydney King had argued before the elections, a victory by the PPP must necessarily be construed by Africans as purely an Indian victory, therefore invalid and unacceptable, as it could not reflect, or be empathetic with, their aspirations.

Burnham took heed of this, in his address to the PNC Congress in Georgetown on November 5, 1961. He must have been emboldened, just two days earlier, by Jagan's acknowledged failure in procuring funds following his mission to Washington:

> The PPP victory, regardless of what its leaders may say or think, represents to its adherents and supporters, as well as to their opponents, an Indian racial victory at the polls on August 21 [1961] … The PPP leadership has recognised that their victory has been victory of a minority in peculiar circumstances [the flawed first-past-the-post system].

Then, with potentially combustible imagery, Burnham dramatised what he projected as Indian racism at the core of Jagan's mission. And, like Sydney King, Burnham was not troubled by Jagan's contentious Marxist beliefs in the context of the Cold War. The latter would prove to be crucial capital that retrieved Burnham's political career from the abyss, but he (like King) was perturbed primarily by Jagan's politics of racial domination (as they saw it) – his stranglehold on the Indian electorate, under a voting system irredeemably stacked against Africans – that could soon take the colony to independence, for the sole benefit of Indians. Burnham drew on the racially impassioned idioms of King and 'Vigilance' to galvanise his African supporters for the anti-Jagan crusade:

> They have been pouring forth declarations about the necessity for a single nation, while the acts of their supporters and some of [the] lieutenants…of the PPP are in the habit of making such remarks as 'we pon top' [we are on top] – and more specifically to the African people – 'You been come fo' cut cane and pull punt [slavery].' On the other hand, we have had the bombast from the Minister of Natural Resources [Brindley Benn, a black man], on more than one occasion, that 'heads will roll.' In the midst of the bombast, he did not make the mistake of specifying any PNC [African] heads. That, comrades, is more than a coincidence. That is, I submit, because we of the PNC have shown such great solidarity and determination, have shown specifically on the Corentyne Coast [predominantly Indian] that we can give better than we take.[75]

It was a call to war! Burnham was clearly buoyed by the failure of Jagan's visit to Washington; whether he knew that Kennedy was already in pursuit of a safer, non-communist option – with every likelihood himself – is not possible to determine. But, contrary to what Sydney King had feared, Burnham was not going to accompany Jagan in any plane bound for London to collect the prize of independence. Burnham now had an exaggerated spring in his step; he was summoning his people to resist, indeed, to ensure that no such prize was on offer, not yet. The passion and sanguinity of an energised man, who had clearly recovered from his electoral debacle only a little over two months before, were transparent in his address on November 5, 1961.

Burnham was given a new lease of life by Jagan's dreadfully inept and suicidal performance in Washington:

> Comrades, there is one question I will ask you. Are you mice or men? Will we sit down and allow Jagan to rape our Constitution? If he attempts to make these changes without the referendum to the electorate, a revolutionary situation is created, and I believe that we can learn a lesson from our members and supporters on the Corentyne Coast [resort to violence]. That is why I continue to emphasise at all times and at all points that we have now entered a new phase of our struggle…You will recall that Jagan talked about sharpening cutlasses. We have been accused in the past of talking and not doing. Comrades, let us think and reason and let us be prepared to do when the time comes.[76]

Burnham would not acquiesce to Jagan on the fundamental question of a constitution for independence. That which was prepared by Jagan's attorney general, Dr Fenton Ramsahoye, and presented to the House of Assembly would not wash. Burnham insisted that only a constitution ratified by the people, in a referendum, could be accepted as the basis of negotiations for independence. Burnham was confident that Jagan could not get a majority for his constitution by such procedure. He was beginning to feel that the tide was turning in his favour. However, the British were, by 1960–61, prepared to give Jagan independence; they wished to be rid of their West Indian colonies, millstones with little to commend them. Only the Americans could save Burnham, King, and their Africans supporters from eternal Indian supremacy, as they envisaged it.

But, paradoxically, Cheddi Jagan did! He could have had the Americans on his side, thus shutting out Burnham and his African followers for good. He chose not to gain the support of President Kennedy; indeed, he virtually told him that he was on the Soviet side of the Cold War. This was also evident from his remarks on 'Meet the Press' and in his address to the National Press Club in Washington. He would not play ball with the arch-imperialists. He was, like a devout Hindu or Muslim, secured in his secular Marxist creed. He would not sacrifice his faith in Marxism-Leninism for American capitalism, for a system he deemed ineffectual for the development of his country – and he effectively said so to the president and the American media. In any case, he could not pretend, even tactically (as John Hennings of the British Embassy in Washington, as well as Governor Grey, had counselled him), to have any faith in a system he considered doomed. Such was not the nature of the man, punctilious though he was in cultivating and sustaining the loyalty of his Indian powerbase.

Jagan held firmly to his Marxist creed positing the inevitable conquest of racial bigotry through the inexorable class struggle. After all, the twentieth century was bound to end with the supremacy of Marxism-Leninism all over the world; capitalism was dying. The Soviet system was indestructible; it was winning. From this mindset, Jagan felt vindicated by an interview President Kennedy gave to the Soviet leader Nikita Khrushchev's son-in-law, Aleksei Adzhubei (1924–93), editor-in-chief of the Soviet newspaper, *Izvestia*. It took place at the family compound of the Kennedys at Hyannis Port, Massachusetts, on November 25, 1961 (precisely one month after the Kennedy-Jagan meeting). Jagan drew the erroneous conclusion that the president was reconciled to the democratic foundation of his electoral victory of August 1961, thus he was fundamentally redefining America's relationship with a Marxist leader such as himself – a *modus vivendi* – essentially a radical policy shift. But Jagan appeared not to have grasped the implications of Kennedy's foremost preoccupation: Castro's Cuba and the imperative of terminating the spread of the Soviet-disseminated communist virus in the Hemisphere. No second Cuba!

The interview was published in its entirety in *Izvestia* three days later, and the *New York Times* carried a report on it, on its front page, on November 29, 1961. It was, indeed, a high-profile interview, but it is noteworthy that the *Times* discerned a darker side to Kennedy's assessment of the perceived communist menace: 'President Kennedy told the Soviet people today that they could live in peace and plenty if their government [under Khrushchev] halted its efforts to promote conspiratorial communism throughout the world.' Therefore, Kennedy would already have determined that Jagan was a pawn in the Soviet scheme of world subversion, with Castro being their principal instrument in the Western Hemisphere. By no means was he inclined to make an exception of Jagan, as the latter would soon find out.

I reproduce the relevant excerpts of the exchange between President Kennedy and Mr Adzhubei:

Kennedy: Where we feel the difficulty comes is the effort by the Soviet Union to communise, in a sense, the world…It is this effort to push outward the communist system, on to country after country, that represents, I think, the great threat to peace. If the Soviet Union looked only to its national interest and to providing a better life for its people under conditions of peace, I think there would be nothing that would disturb the relations between the Soviet Union and the United States...

Adzhubei: As a citizen of the Soviet Union, as a member of the Communist Party, I cannot agree with you...that we are trying to 'communise' the world...Our government and our party believe that every people chooses such a system of government as they like...And we would be happy if you, Mr President, were to state that the interference in the affairs of Cuba was a mistake [the Bay of Pigs invasion, April 1961]. We hope that the Cuban people will consolidate their own way of life.

Kennedy: In the case of Cuba, let me remind you that the Castro revolution was originally supported by the great majority of the people. When Castro was leading the revolution, the statement was made that there would be free elections, and freedom for the people, and progress for the people. But Castro has not kept that commitment. Until the present government of Cuba will allow free and honest elections, in our opinion, it cannot claim to represent the majority of the people. This is our dispute with Cuba.

Mr Jagan, on the other hand, who was recently elected Prime Minister in British Guiana is a Marxist [communist], **but the United States doesn't object – because the choice was made by an honest election which he won. If the people of any country choose to follow a communist system in a free election, after a fair opportunity for a number of views to be presented, the United States would accept that ...** [emphasis added].

What we find to be objectionable, and a threat to the peace, is when a system is imposed by a small militant group by subversion, infiltration, and all the rest...[an allusion to Castro's Cuba]

Adzhubei: You mentioned that a Marxist came to power in British Guiana. Do you think that events occurred there according to our instructions?

Kennedy: ...if the people of these countries make a free choice, that they prefer the communist or socialist or any other kind of system, the United States and the people of the United States accept that. That is why I give the example of British Guiana...What we object to is the attempt to impose communism by force, or a situation where once a people have fallen under communism, the communists do not give them a fair opportunity to make another choice [another allusion to Castro's Cuba].[77]

CHEDDI JAGAN AND THE COLD WAR, 1946–1992

The president's contention was that Castro's Cuba represented a repudiation of choice; that by embracing communism, the Cuban Revolution had veered radically away from the democratic principles it claimed to have espoused originally. But it was not the latter that made the Castro regime unpalatable to the US. It was its perceived subservience to the Soviet Union, solely, that rendered it their irreconcilable adversary in the Cold War. Indeed, while Kennedy appeared robust in advancing the right of Cubans to a democratically elected government, he was eloquently silent about several brutal dictatorships in Latin America because they were anti-communist, definitively on the American side of the Cold War – allies. But this hypocrisy is of older vintage, encapsulated in Franklin Roosevelt's famous alleged remark (around 1939) on the Nicaraguan dictator, Anastasio Somoza: 'He may be a son of a bitch, but he's our son of a bitch.' It was all about defeating communism in the Hemisphere.

Therefore, although Kennedy was prepared to concede that the communist Jagan was freely elected, the underlying apprehension was that once his country became independent, he (a declared admirer of Castro and Khrushchev) would not just replicate the totalitarian *modus operandi* of communist regimes under the wing of the Soviet Union, but, more importantly, Guyana would become a staging post for Soviet penetration of the rest of South America. Therefore, Jagan would subvert the democratic principles and undermine the free institutions planted by the British, while becoming an instrument for the dispersal of the communist virus by virtue of his ingrained philosophical orientation. The dominoes would fall! Far-fetched? Possibly! But such was the logic or illogic of the Cold War. On the surface, it did appear as if Kennedy was, indeed, giving Jagan the green light to pursue his communist creed. The truth is much more complicated, as it was driven by machinations within the parameters of Cold War politics.

In December 1961, *Thunder* (the organ of Jagan's PPP) was over the moon that their leader's meeting with Kennedy had, as they interpreted it, redounded to the advantage of Cheddi. Their palpable triumphalism was precipitated by the president's apparent concession that Jagan was entitled to pursue his Marxist (communist) ideology because he was democratically elected. Jagan was therefore being prematurely credited with having defended his right to pursue his Marxist faith without genuflecting to the imperialists:

> During his visit to the USA ... [in October 1961] in the face of reaction in this greatest of all imperialist strongholds, Jagan reaffirmed his faith in socialism [communism], and the right of people to choose whatever government they wish. **As a direct result of his activities in the US, President John Kennedy in one of the most important Press interviews that he is ever likely to hold in his lifetime – we refer to the interview with the correspondent of Izvestia – said that irrespective what Jagan was, even if he was a communist,**

he has been elected by free ballot and deserved respect and assistance from the US and other countries.

Who could detract from the significance of this statement? Who could detract from the brilliance of this outstanding achievement on the part of a Premier of a country with a handful of people, without arms, without forces, without power to threaten anyone? **This statement of policy by the President of the United States will go a far way in assuring people all over the world of the recognition of the right to choose whoever they wish to lead them in free elections.**

We look forward to celebrating the Independence of Guiana in 1962 even if the British do not agree...**At the head of this struggle for freedom there is an unyielding leader** [Jagan], **one who will not swerve one-thousandth of an inch in his determination to free Guiana and to fight for socialism [communism] and peace not only in Guiana but for the whole world** [emphasis added].[78]

David and Goliath – Cheddi's crusade! This editorial comment ought to have clarified why with the independence of British Guiana within grasp – yet with everything to lose – Jagan still considered it imperative to risk persisting with his mission of promoting communism as the superior system for the governance of humankind, while virtually declaring this to President Kennedy and the American public on 'Meet the Press' and to the National Press Club. He would 'not swerve one-thousandth of an inch!' The Americans and the British understood this very well, the seemingly conciliatory passing remark of Kennedy to *Izvestia* notwithstanding. In reality, by revealing to Kennedy and the American public, in October 1961, that he was enamoured of the Soviet-Cuban philosophy of governance, he had virtually ensured his political demise, despite his declared certainty regarding Guyana's impending Independence. Contrary to *Thunder's* exultation over Jagan's American visit, he had done badly – bringing the Cold War home to British Guiana – with him being on the wrong side in America's hemispheric anti-communist crusade. His foes at home, Burnham and D'Aguiar, were given a lifeline – ironically, by Cheddi!

In fact, in its final issue of 1961, the PPP's *Thunder* was signalling that although Jagan had sought to prevail upon the British to grant independence to British Guiana in 1962, it was not necessarily plain sailing. Yet Jagan's New Year message for 1962 was clear: 'Make a reservation that 1962 must be our freedom year. Nothing can stop us. We must proclaim this on our banner.' However, the new colonial secretary, Reginald Maudling, was not on the liberal wing of the Conservative Party like his predecessor Iain Macleod. The PPP's organ had recognised this difference in a fashion, noting that Macleod had 'pushed the policy' of granting several colonies independence, depending on the 'personality of the local political leader' and the 'geographic situation of the territory.' This unnecessary qualification was at the heart of the PPP's dilemma: they dare not admit that after the independence of India, the British wanted to be rid of colonial millstones like British Guiana. A prolonged 'struggle against imperialism,' like the Gandhian/Nehruvian crusade for freedom, was superfluous, so was the monotonous invective against the 'sugar gods.' It would have been infinitely more salutary for the PPP to conserve and harness their energy for the most exacting task – of Himalayan proportion – the country's endemic racism.

What the PPP could not admit was that Jagan had failed the Kennedy 'test' by his obduracy and hubris in revealing to the American nation and the president that he would never change his spots – in effect, endorsing Marxism-Leninism (communism) as the best, scientifically grounded, philosophy for the rapid development of underdeveloped countries, specifically an independent Guyana. Besides, he set great store by the power of 'scientific socialism' to dissolve the chronic racial dissonance between Africans and Indians. Cheddi cited both the Soviet Union and Cuba as exemplars for his stewardship of a free Guyana. This was a perilous stance, precisely what Kennedy's anti-communist programme for Latin America was obsessed with eliminating. No second Cuba!

Stephen G. Rabe is a formidable authority on the subject, and he explains Kennedy's response to Jagan in that context:

> Not only national security anxieties but also domestic political calculations informed President Kennedy's approach to the region. The President was loath to face in his 1964 re-election campaign the same charge – losing a Latin American country to communism – that he had thrown at the Eisenhower-Nixon team in 1960. Throughout his tenure, Kennedy predicted disaster in Latin America. In January 1961 he told an aide 'the whole place could blow up on us.' In November 1962 he cautioned Argentina's General Pedro Eugenio Aramburu [President 1955–58; assassinated by the Montoneros in 1970] to be alert, observing that 'the next twelve months would be critical in Latin America with respect to renewed Communist attempts at penetration.' In October 1963, a month before his death, he warned that Latin America posed 'the greatest danger to us.'

> A few months earlier [at Birch Grove, in Sussex, on June 30, 1963], in a meeting with Prime Minister Harold Macmillan, Kennedy demanded that the United Kingdom postpone the independence of its South American colony, British Guiana. Kennedy alleged that British Guiana might become a Communist state. British Guiana would then join Cuba as a major campaign issue and jeopardise the President's re-election. The British ultimately succumbed to Kennedy's extraordinary pressure and postponed the colony's independence. **As** [his] **presidential adviser and biographer, [Professor] Arthur Schlesinger, put it, it was his boss's 'absolute determination' to prevent a second Communist outpost in the Western Hemisphere** [emphasis added].[79]

Cheddi Jagan's journey to Washington should never have been made. The British were not enthused by it, knowing his vulnerability and tactlessness. They had reached a point where they were prepared to take a chance with him whatever the risks, rather than opt for Burnham. In this respect, both Iain Macleod and Jock Campbell had played a pivotal role by 1960. But Jagan seemed determined to see the president, as if he simply wanted the meeting to fail, so that he could pursue, with freedom, the aid programme begun with Cuba in 1960, with the Soviet Union and the rest of the communist bloc. He was totally convinced that it was the best way forward for his country because communist aid was 'disinterested' and inspired by 'proletarian internationalism.' And when Kennedy told Khrushchev's son-in-law that because Jagan was democratically elected, he was free to choose his friends providing he was committed to democratic freedoms, Jagan and his PPP felt they had won the debate against the imperialists. They were wrong. Kennedy was, in fact, 'absolutely determined' to ensure that he was removed before the British grant independence to the colony. The president spoke with a forked tongue.

Notes

1. Kimani S. K. Nehusi, *A People's Political History of Guyana, 1838–1964* (Hertford: Hansib, 2018), 524.
2. Cheddi Jagan, 'On the Political Situation,' paper read to the Congress of the PPP (by B. H. Benn), New Amsterdam, March 1956, (mimeo.), confidential. (It was leaked to the press and published as 'Red Move to Take over British Guiana,' *Daily Chronicle*, December 22, 1956.)
3. Ibid., 4–5.
4. Ibid., 5.
5. Ibid., 8.
6. Ibid.
7. Ibid., 9.
8. Ibid., 15–16.
9. Ibid., 16.
10. Ibid.
11. Sydney King [Eusi Kwayana], 'Observations on the Congress Paper "On the Political Situation" by Comrade Cheddi Jagan,' (mimeo.), n.d., [mid-April 1956], 1.
12. Ibid., 2.
13. Ibid., 4.
14. Jagan, 'On the Political Situation,' 5.
15. Cheddi Jagan to Sydney King (Buxton), March 28, 1956.
16. King, 'Observations on the Congress Paper,' 5.
17. Ibid., 5–6.
18. Ibid., 9–10.
19. Ibid., 10–11.
20. Cheddi Jagan to Sydney King, May 3, 1956.

21. Interview with Eusi Kwayana, Georgetown, September 22, 1992.
22. *Daily Chronicle*, July 21, 1961.
23. *Daily Chronicle*, July 20, 1961.
24. Ibid.
25. Ibid.
26. Ibid.
27. *Daily Chronicle*, August 26, 1961.
28. Frank Birbalsingh, 'Interview with Rupert Roopnaraine (1996),' in *The People's Progressive Party of Guyana, 1950–1992: An Oral History* (London: Hansib, 2007), 157.
29. *Thunder*, September 2, 1961.
30. Sydney King and H. H. Nicholson ['Vigilance'], 'In the Name of Freedom: An Appeal from the Africans of British Guiana to Certain Governments to Send Observers to our Country,' Issued by the African Society for Racial Equality (Buxton), August 28, 1961 (mimeo). (A copy of this document is in the C. L. R. James Papers at the University of the West Indies, St Augustine, Trinidad.)
31. The National Archives (TNA), KV2/3634, Governor Sir Ralph Grey to Secretary of State for the Colonies [Alan Lennox-Boyd], March 10, 1959.
32. Quoted in Colin Palmer, *Cheddi Jagan and the Politics of Power: British Guiana's Struggle for Independence* (Chapel Hill: The University of North Carolina Press, 2010), 176.
33. Ibid., 177.
34. Ibid.
35. David Scott, 'Interview with Lloyd Best,' *Small Axe*, no. 1 (1997): 128, 130.
36. Ibid., 134.
37. *Daily Argosy*, April 1, 1960.
38. Ibid.
39. *Daily Argosy*, April 15, 1960.
40. Nigel Fisher, *Iain Macleod* (London: Andre Deutsch, 1973), 190.
41. Memorandum from the President's Special Assistant (Arthur Schlesinger) to the Ambassador of the United Kingdom, February 27, 1962.
42. Booker Brothers, McConnell and Co. [Jock Campbell], 'The Group Chairman's Visit to British Guiana and the West Indies, January–March 1960,' (mimeo.), confidential, 18, 23.
43. The National Archives, CO1031/4177, Governor Sir Ralph Grey to A.R. Thomas (Colonial Office), September 26, 1961.
44. The National Archives, CO1031/4178, J. H. Hennings (Colonial Attaché, British Embassy, Washington) to Governor Sir Ralph Grey, secret and personal, November 19, 1961.
45. Ibid.
46. Ibid.
47. Ibid.
48. Arthur M. Schlesinger, Jr, *A Thousand Days: John F. Kennedy in the White House* (London: Andre Deutsch, 1965), 665.
49. *Thunder*, September 2, 1961.
50. *Thunder*, April 15, 1961.
51. *Thunder*, March 25, 1961.
52. 'People's Capitalism – Myth and Reality,' *Thunder*, June 24, 1961.
53. *Thunder*, September 2, 1961.

54. Quoted in Cary Fraser, 'The "New Frontier" of Empire in the Caribbean: The Transfer of Power in British Guiana, 1961–64,' *The International History Review.* XXII, no. 3 (2000): 587.
55. Leader, *Thunder*, October 14, 1961.
56. Fraser, 'The "New Frontier" of Empire in the Caribbean,' 591.
57. The National Archives, CO1031/4177, 'Cheddi Jagan on "Meet the Press," Script of the Interview [NBC News],' October 15, 1961.
58. Ibid.
59. Interview with Lloyd Searwar, Georgetown, August 24, 2000.
60. Cheddi Jagan, 'Towards Understanding…,' The Text of an Address to the National Press Club, Washington, DC, USA, October 24, 1961.
61. Cheddi Jagan, *The West on Trial: My Fight for Guyana's Freedom* (London: Michael Joseph, 1966), 415.
62. Ibid., 415–17.
63. Interview with Lloyd Searwar, Georgetown, August 24, 2000.
64. Jagan, *The West on Trial: My Fight for Guyana's Freedom*, 417.
65. *Thunder*, November 11, 1961.
66. *Young Guiana*, May 1961.
67. Shiv Gangadeen, 'Inside the PPP: Little Rats in a Trap,' *Sunday Chronicle*, May 7, 1961.
68. Cheddi Jagan, 'Our Aims and Objectives,' *Thunder*, May 6, 1961.
69. Ibid.
70. Ibid.
71. Scott Nearing, 'The Socialist Century,' *Thunder*, January 28, 1961.
72. Quoted in Howard Jones, *The Bay of Pigs* (New York: Oxford University Press, 2008), 132.
73. *Thunder*, October 28, 1961.
74. *New York Times*, November 4, 1961.
75. The National Archives, CO1031/3714, 'Intelligence Report for the Month of November 1961,' [A. J. E. Longden], secret and personal.
76. Ibid.
77. See *New York Times*, November 29, 1961.
78. Leader, *Thunder*, December 23, 1961.
79. Stephen G. Rabe, *John F. Kennedy: World Leader* (Washington, DC: Potomac Books, 2010), 79–80.

9.

Anti-Communism at Home and Abroad

The Decline and Fall of Jagan in the Context of the Cold War, with Special Reference to Anglo-American Complicity, 1962-64

> We believe that Jagan is a Communist, though the degree of Moscow's control is not yet clear…Jagan's recklessness and impulsiveness are notorious, and could at anytime overrule his judgment.
>
> **CIA, 'The Situation and Prospects in British Guiana,'**
> **April 11, 1962**

> Latin America is still the most critical area in the world today… Together, **we are determined that there shall be no more communist states in this Hemisphere,** and we know that the only really effective means to this end is to remove the grave social and economic iniquities that are the breeding grounds of Communism.
>
> **President Kennedy (September 1963), as reported in the**
> ***Weekend Post and Sunday Argosy* (Georgetown),**
> **September 29, 1963**

PART 1.
1962

'Black Friday' and Its Aftermath: America's Resolve to Convince the British as Regards Their Alternative to Jagan: Forbes Burnham and Proportional Representation

I.   Kennedy's Obsession: No 'Second Cuba' in British Guiana

The idea of a 'nationalist struggle against imperialism' was a romanticising of local anti-colonial politics, dictated by Jagan's Marxist-Leninist creed that required unremitting confrontation with 'imperialism' for its validation – leaving well alone was not conceivable. Towards the end of the 1950s, one simply needed the patience to await the inevitable granting of independence to British colonial possessions. However, the fundamental problem of racism in colonial

Guyana – particularly escalating African insecurity regarding independence – remained chronically unconsidered, yet it could not be papered over. Besides, in the context of the Cold War in the aftermath of the Cuban Revolution, if one were a communist proclaiming the Soviet system as the prototype for the future of humankind, particularly in the Western Hemisphere, one was likely to be shafted by the Americans, in their perceived 'backyard.' Both of these factors, race and the Cold War, underpinning the incoherent nationalist agenda, would conspire to undermine Jagan's dedication to leading British Guiana to independence.

Iain Macleod, the colonial secretary (1959–61) was perceptibly amenable to Jagan in March 1960, granting him internal self-government, while rejecting Burnham's demand for PR and agreeing in principle to the colony's independence within a couple years at most. Yet he did harbour some reservations regarding Jagan's politics, but Jagan was disinclined to allay those fears. He promptly and, arguably defiantly, proceeded to consolidate his relationship with Fidel Castro and the Cuban Revolution (he visited Cuba twice in 1960), thus effectively undermining Macleod, who had countervailed a significant segment of the Conservative Party by his conciliatory engagement with Jagan. But it is also noteworthy that Macleod was still empathetic with Jagan even after the Americans had decided, by the beginning of 1962, to vigorously engineer his removal before independence. This was the context of the anti-Jagan riots in Georgetown on February 16, 1962 ('Black Friday'), fomented by the United Force (UF) and the Peoples' National Congress (PNC).

Yet on February 27, 1962, Macleod (by then chairman of the Conservative Party) told Professor Arthur Schlesinger, Kennedy's special assistant, that Jagan was not a communist:

> He is a naïve, London School of Economics Marxist filled with charm, personal honesty and juvenile nationalism.' Macleod suggested that the Jagan budget that sparked the riots on February 16 was 'not a Marxist programme. It was a severely orthodox programme of the 'Crippsian' [social democratic] type.

And, like Jock Campbell (with whom he was in regular contact), Macleod was still unequivocal in his preference for Jagan over Burnham: 'If I had to make the choice between Jagan and Burnham as head of my country, I would choose Jagan any day of the week.'[1] The anti-budget riots were really a ruse to subvert the Jagan government, as Burnham admitted, it was not the *causa belli* but a *casus belli*: not the cause of the upheaval, but an occasion for it.

However, with the liberal Macleod removed from the Colonial Office by early 1962, his two successors, Reginald Maudling and Duncan Sandys (on the centre-right and right wing of the party respectively), were patently more receptive to the imperatives of America's anti-communist Hemispheric agenda. Jagan had squandered his political capital: not for the first time! However, it is interesting that when Arthur Schlesinger met Maudling on March 1, 1962, in London, he also did express his preference for Jagan over Burnham. Schlesinger noted:

> Maudling does not regard Jagan as a disciplined Communist...He says that he would not trust Jagan ... [but] it is his understanding that Burnham is, if possible, worse. He is reluctant to take any action that would make Jagan a martyr. He does not believe that Britain can conceivably dislodge a democratically elected government. His [Maudling's] general view is that Britain wants to get out of British Guiana as quickly as possible. He said he would be glad to turn the whole thing over to the United States.[2]

Thunder, organ of Jagan's People's Progressive Party (PPP), observed that

> the [decolonisation] process has slowed down significantly and the new holder of the office of Colonial Secretary, Reginald Maudling, has shown every sign of digging in ... The British Guiana government has been the only one in this area which has chartered an unwavering course for Independence ... Yet it is precisely this country whose future Britain drags her foot on.

But the PPP government was committed to gaining independence, and they cautioned the British government not to be detracted by the 'antics' of the UF and the PNC, resolved to stall the inevitable march to freedom. Then, as if they had smelt a rat, they also warned that the prospective alternative, Forbes Burnham, was 'rotten rope' driven purely by 'personal aggrandisement': 'It is no use encouraging the PNC in their obstructionist tactics on the Independence constitution. The people will win out in the end, and that soon.'[3]

In fact, this was precisely what the Kennedy administration had embarked upon: supporting the UF and the PNC to foment violence against Jagan, thus creating a pretext for the British government to renege on its original plan to grant Independence to British Guiana in 1962. Following his abysmal meeting with Jagan in October 1961, Kennedy had made up his mind that Jagan must not lead his country to Independence. Yet Jagan was mistakenly clutching the mirage of a straw extended by Kennedy that he would tolerate an independent Guyana, led by a democratically elected communist. And Maudling's failure to offer Jagan a firm date for Independence talks had so riled him, that he was enticed into a circuitous, and potentially futile, path to independence. This should have been a walk in the park, but Jagan's communist creed and the president's obsession with precluding 'a second Cuba' in the Hemisphere, were the source of Maudling's departure from the freedom road that Macleod had virtually charted.

Jagan recalls the response of Maudling to his request for the British government to move quickly to independence in 1962, 'to fulfil the pledges given at the 1960 Constitutional Conference [by Iain Macleod]': 'When I saw...[Maudling] at the Colonial Office on December 13, 1961, he refused either to fix a date for independence or a date for a conference to decide on a date for independence.'[4]

Contrary to British counsel, Jagan sought and got permission from the Fourth Committee of the United Nations to present his case for independence. He appeared before them on December 18, 1961, citing the liberal sentiments towards him that Kennedy expressed to *Izvestia* on November 25 as the principal strand in his presentation. It was a futile exercise and it reinforced the widely held perception that Jagan was a communist:

> President Kennedy stated that the United States Government would respect and have friendly relations with any government, even communist, which had been elected at free and fair elections. **Did not President Kennedy signify his pleasure when he said that even though Marxist** [communist]**, I had won my position at fair elections** [emphasis added]?[5]

But events were moving fast. The president was mortally afraid that Cuba was becoming the medium for the diffusion of the communist virus in the Caribbean and Latin America. Besides, the Republican Party (increasingly under the influence of the militant anti-communist Barry Goldwater) was exploiting the Bay of Pigs fiasco to tarnish Kennedy for being 'soft on communism.' If the British gave Jagan independence in 1962, as appeared likely, that could well have presaged the realisation of 'the second Cuba' that would sink Kennedy in the elections of 1964. Jagan's British Guiana, therefore, had assumed a significance in the president's policy towards Latin America vastly beyond its insignificant position in the region as a whole.

This was the context in which the foreign ministers of the Organisation of American States (OAS) met in Punta del Este, Uruguay, in the last week of January 1962, to discuss the Cuban issue. A key outcome was the statement underlining **'the incompatibility of Marxism-Leninism and the present Cuban government with the Inter-American system** [emphasis added].'[6] Dean Rusk, the secretary of state, represented the US, and in his telegram to President Kennedy of January 31, 1962, he advised that he should stress 'the remarkable movement in the hemisphere in the past several months in recognising the dangers of communist penetration.' This was, he thought, a transformation in outlook, much more than they could have anticipated even a few weeks before. It is pertinent that Rusk also informed the president that 'smaller countries especially in and around the Caribbean feel themselves to be under direct Castro-Communist pressures and that the US felt it important that the OAS give these countries its full support.'

In June 1962, President Kennedy had discussions with the popular left-wing Mexican President Lopez Mateos in Mexico City. He agreed with the latter that improved economic conditions were the best antidote to the spread of communism in the Hemisphere, and that the Alliance for Progress would make a major contribution towards it. However, Kennedy said it would take about a decade for the latter to make a palpable impact on the standard of living in Latin America. Therefore, he was eagerly trying to ascertain what could be done in the short-run to arrest communist advance. Then, possibly alluding to Cheddi Jagan and an independent British Guiana, Kennedy observed: '...as Cuba shows, once a communist regime has fastened itself on a country, it is most difficult for the people to rid themselves of it.' The report of the meeting concluded thus:

> President Kennedy returned again and again to what...[the Mexican President] thought was the best way to deal with the obvious danger of communist influence in Latin America. President Mateos each time repeated his view that rapid economic development and social progress were the answer...President Kennedy stated that the United States wished to deal with the problem of communist penetration of the Hemisphere in co-operation with other Latin American states like Mexico. He said he wanted to keep in close touch with Mexico on this point, and to reach agreement on practical measures which could be taken by American states to deal with the threat. He said the United States had no plans at the present time for unilateral military action against the Castro regime.'[7]

II.   The 'Black Friday' Riots and the CIA

Professor Stephen Rabe is in no doubt that the CIA was involved in destabilising the Jagan government as early as the riots of February 1962. He argues that on January 12, 1962, President Kennedy sent officials out to British Guiana to assess the feasibility of a loan to the government of $5 million. Kennedy told the head of the Agency of International Development (Fowler Hamilton) that he simultaneously wished to 'intensify our observations of political developments in British Guiana, and by this and other means extend our programme of reinsurance in case the situation should show signs of going sour.' Hamilton later admitted that among the technical people sent out were CIA agents who had an urgent political role to play. On January 18, 1962, the consulate post was elevated to consul general to accommodate a larger diplomatic staff. Rabe contends that this was the context in which CIA personnel became active in Georgetown, as the Kennedy administration had 'intensified its contacts with Jagan's political opponents [Burnham and D'Aguiar], trade union officials in British Guiana and the AFL-CIO.'

In fact, union officials from the AFL-CIO, Howard McCabe and Ernest Lee (son-in-law of AFL-CIO President George Meany), were present in Georgetown during the strike and riots against the Jagan government in February 1962, ostensibly against the 'Kaldor Budget.' They assured Governor Grey that they were there for 'legislative purposes.' Rabe adds that McCabe was, in fact, a CIA agent working under the cover of the American Federation of State, County and Municipal Employees and its international affiliate, the Public Service International. McCabe arrived in British Guiana in the midst of the riots as a stowaway on an airplane carrying a blood bank from Suriname.

It is not possible to access the incriminating documents because the CIA claims that its records on British Guiana were destroyed, and US government censors will not release key documents. However, Rabe draws attention to Tim Weiner, a *New York Times* correspondent specialising in 'declassification issues,' who stated that he was informed by US government officials that

> still classified documents depict a direct order from the President to unseat Dr Jagan...The Jagan papers are a rare smoking gun: a clear written record without veiled words or plausible denials of a President's command to depose a Prime Minister.[8]

Two days after the 'Black Friday' riots in Georgetown on February 16, 1962, assistant secretary of state for European affairs, William R. Tyler, sent Secretary of State Rusk a memorandum (dated February 18) that summarises America's stance on the Jagan controversy:

> In response to pressure from Jagan, including action at the UN, the British have announced readiness to hold a conference in May to approve a constitution and set a date for British Guiana's independence. Independence would presumably occur before the end of 1962. We concurred reluctantly in the British timetable for independence, but in doing so strongly stressed the hope that new elections would be held. **The timetable may be stretched out as a result of the current disorders....**
>
> The policy of working with Jagan had not really been applied in practice subsequent to Jagan's visit to the US [in October 1961]... the US has not carried out the agreement on economic assistance reached during Jagan's visit. Factors beyond the control of State have also intervened [a likely allusion to President Kennedy's views based on his one-on-one chat with Jagan, in the rose garden of the White House]. Latest reports indicate that Jagan is increasingly suspicious of the US. **It is now doubtful that a working relationship can be established with Jagan which would prevent the emergence of a communist Castro-type state in South America** [emphasis added].[9]

The Kennedy administration had concluded that Jagan would, indeed, make an independent British Guiana a 'second Cuba.' He was a menace to the Hemisphere. He had to be removed.

The following day (February 19, 1962), Secretary of State Rusk forwarded to the US ambassador in London (David Bruce) the following definitive remarks establishing the Kennedy administration's rejection of Jagan as the leader of an independent Guyana. The letter was addressed to 'Dear Alex,' the British foreign secretary, Lord Home (later Sir Alec Douglas-Home, prime minister, 1963–64), and it corroborates that Cheddi did inflict fatal self-harm when he met President Kennedy on October 25, 1961:

> Subsequent to his [Jagan's] victory in the August [1961] elections, we agreed to try your policy of fostering an effective association between British Guiana and the West, and an Anglo-American working party developed an appropriate programme...In pursuance of this programme, the President received Jagan on his visit to this country in October [1961].

> **I must tell you now that I have reached the conclusion that it is not possible for us to put up with an independent British Guiana under Jagan.** We have had no real success in establishing a basis for understanding with him due in part to his grandiose expectations of economic aid. **We have continued to receive disturbing reports of communist connections on the part of Jagan and persons closely associated with him. Partly reflective of ever-growing concern over Cuba, public and Congressional opinion here is incensed at the thought of dealing with Jagan. The Marxist-Leninist policy he professes parallels that of Castro, which the OAS at the Punta del Este Conference** [in January 1962] **declared incompatible with the Inter-American system.** Current happenings in British Guiana indicate Jagan is not master of the situation at home without your support [an allusion to the riots necessitating the presence of British troops]. There is some resemblance to the events of 1953. **Thus, the continuation of Jagan in power is leading us to disaster in terms of the colony itself, strains on Anglo-American relations and difficulties for the Inter-American system...**

> **In the past your people have held, with considerable conviction, that there was no reasonable alternative to working with Jagan. I am convinced our experience so far, and now the disorders in Georgetown** [just three days before], **make it necessary to re-examine this premise.**

> **It seems to me clear that new elections** [by implication, under proportional representation (PR)] **should now be scheduled, and I hope we can agree that Jagan should not accede to power again** [emphasis added].[10]

The British did not acquiesce readily in the American scheme to remove Jagan before independence; initially, they sought to resist the sustained pressure from the Kennedy administration. On February 26, 1962, Foreign Secretary Home replied to Rusk's abrasive letter, which Prime Minister Macmillan characterised as 'pure Machiavellianism.' He asserted that the process of decolonisation was irreversible and that British Guiana could not be designated an exception purely on account of Jagan's communism. Home was forthright in challenging Rusk's unilateral proposition regarding the removal of Jagan before independence; and he sought to broach the difficulties implicit in effecting a constitutional coup against Jagan.

The British were clearly not enamoured of Forbes Burnham as a replacement for Jagan, as determined by the Americans:

> You say it is not possible for you to 'put up with an independent British Guiana under Jagan,' and that 'Jagan should not accede to power again.' How would you suggest that this be done in a democracy? And even if a device could be found, it would almost certainly be transparent, and in such circumstances if democratic processes are to be allowed, it will be extremely hard to provide a reasonable prospect that any successor regime will be more stable and more mature… So I would say to you that we cannot now go back on the course we have set ourselves, of bringing these dependent territories to self-government. Nor is it any good deluding ourselves that we can now set aside a single territory such as British Guiana for some sort of special treatment.[11]

But American pressure was relentless; nothing could, or would, detract them from what was their final solution: Jagan was a communist, and like his acknowledged exemplar, Fidel Castro, tied irrevocably to the Soviet Union; he had to be removed. President Kennedy phoned the British ambassador in Washington (his friend, Ormsby-Gore), on March 8, 1962, stating that 'he was worried about the future of British Guiana. He was not satisfied that information on developments there was correct.' Buoyed by American success in helping to foment violence against Jagan in February 1962, the president was resolved to convince the British that the equation had changed. He contended that Jagan was being challenged definitively by the robust anti-communist opposition in the colony (led by Forbes Burnham and Peter D'Aguiar); therefore, it was imperative to obviate the distinct possibility of a 'second Cuba' in the Hemisphere by divesting Jagan of power before independence.

The colonial secretary, Reginald Maudling, had, a few days before, told Arthur Schlesinger that 'responsible people' (presumably in British Guiana) had stated that the CIA had a role in fomenting the recent riots in Georgetown against Jagan. Schlesinger denied it; but in 1990 (in the presence of Jagan in New York) he did admit that the CIA was implicated in making the colony ungovernable in order to secure the removal of Jagan. And this anti-communist obsession on the part of President Kennedy (as I have been arguing), regarding Cheddi Jagan, was finally determined – and incorporated into policy – primarily by his one-on-one exchange with Jagan in the Rose Garden of the White House on October 25, 1961. The details may/will never be known, beyond Jagan's self-proclaimed hubris that he had, for instance, effectively put Kennedy in his place by accusing him of engineering the removal of the left-wing regime of Janio Quadros in Brazil after only seven months in office, in 1961; and that he had been frank with the president about his Marxist convictions (see below).

On September 5, 1962, the American consul general in Georgetown, Everett Melby, reported to the State Department on a meeting he had with Jagan that day. Cheddi stated that he was 'worried' the US believed that British Guiana could become 'another Cuba,' but he recalled that Castro had laughingly remarked to him that 'socialism had never come about without revolution.' Melby noted that Jagan did not intend to change his socialist/communist philosophy, but he was determined to pursue it by peaceful means:

> Jagan said he had openly discussed his socialist [communist] ideas with President Kennedy, as well as his determination to bring this about by peaceful means. All he is asking of the United States is understanding and assistance so that he can make British Guiana the first example of a socialist [communist] state created by non-violent means [emphasis added].[12]

III. America's Man: The Burnham Alternative

Clearly, after their intense scrutiny of Jagan in Washington in October 1961, the Kennedy administration was disinclined to acquiesce in the British line that Jagan, warts and all, was still the only credible person to lead British Guiana to independence. We will never know precisely what Jagan said that made the president conclude that he was the deadliest communist threat to the Hemisphere after Fidel Castro. All we have to corroborate the proposition is what Jagan recalled he said to Kennedy, as the two of them conversed alone for possibly an **hour** (as Lloyd Searwar related to me). But it appears that both his admission that he was a Marxist (as Melby has stated) and the unmistakable pro-Soviet/pro-Cuba sentiments of Cheddi's political aspirations, convinced the president that he must not lead British Guiana to independence.

Consequently, as Dean Rusk instructed the British, they should revisit their fixed assumptions regarding the lack of alternatives to Jagan. It was clear that the Americans wanted an urgent reassessment of L.F.S. Burnham. As Colin Palmer, who has written an excellent study of Jagan, observes, Burnham met thirteen US officials, at their invitation, in Washington on May 3, 1962, and he succeeded in persuading his hosts that he possessed the anti-communist credentials to be America's man. Known reservations the British held regarding Burnham's personality defects (his apparent arrogance, even flippancy on occasions; his amorphous political beliefs; his alleged hatred of White people) were clearly not replicated in his encounter with the Americans. This was make-or-break for Burnham – the last chance, equivalent to Jagan's fatal encounter with President Kennedy six months earlier – and he did not falter, according to Palmer:

> Their conversation lasted for ninety minutes. Seeking to ingratiate himself with the Americans, Burnham described the PNC as 'a social democratic party' as opposed to the 'communist' PPP. He said he knew 'from personal experience' that the PPP received 'instructions via the international communist movement' up to 1955, when he left the party. He stressed that if he won the next elections, he would not tolerate communists in the party. Burnham reported that there were several communists in the leadership of the PPP, and that these individuals had close ties with Cuba. Guianese students were being sent to Havana, East Germany and the Soviet Union to be indoctrinated and trained by the communists...
>
> **Burnham burnished his anti-communist credentials in his conversations with US officials, undoubtedly impressing them as a good alternative to Jagan...**He met with officials of the Department of State a second time in September [1962] to discuss the political situation in his country, repeating his allegations about communist penetration. Burnham expressed his support for the adoption of the system of proportional representation [PR] in the colony, predicting that the PNC and UF would form a coalition after the next election [emphasis added].[13]

The Americans were not unduly concerned with Burnham's lack of multiracial support. It was all about the Cold War and his declared disdain for communism. Burnham was their man, and a change of the electoral system to PR could do the trick in removing Jagan if the British delayed the granting of independence. Colin Palmer states that by the time of the inconclusive constitutional conference in London in October 1962, Burnham had established his anti-communist credentials (an easy task given his rival, the communist, pro-Castro Jagan), and thereby secured his place as America's man to replace the tactless Jagan.

Kennedy had sent Arthur Schlesinger on a secret mission to British Guiana, in mid-June 1962, to make a final assessment of Jagan. Schlesinger concluded:

> **There is considerable feeling here, which I am inclined to share, that British Guiana would be worse off with Burnham than with Jagan.** [Yet on 21 June 1962 he submitted the definitive judgement on Jagan to Kennedy, establishing that Burnham must be their man in their campaign to destroy their communist foe.] The evidence shows increasingly that Jagan's heart is with the Communist world. He is quite plainly a Marxist nationalist who sees the West in

terms of the old stereotypes of capitalism and imperialism and who is deeply persuaded of the superiority of the communist methods and values...The alternative to Jagan is Forbes Burnham...He made a good impression on his visit to Washington [in May 1962]. All alternatives in British Guiana are terrible; but **I have little doubt that an independent British Guiana under Burnham (if Burnham would commit himself to a multi-racial policy** [a ruse to placate the British]**) would cause us many fewer problems than an independent British Guiana under Jagan** [emphasis added].[14]

Professor Schlesinger corroborated the positive impression orchestrated by Burnham in Washington in May 1962, as he deftly juxtaposed his moderation with the communist proclivities of Jagan, long beholden to the international communist movement, as Burnham attested based on his former proximity to him, in the PPP. Burnham, not burdened by ideological strictures, told his influential hosts precisely what he knew they wished to hear. But it was Schlesinger who made the decisive evaluation of Burnham for the president. It is necessary to quote him at length:

> Thus far our policy had been based on the assumption that Forbes Burnham was, as the British described him, an opportunist, racist and demagogue intent only on personal power. One wondered about this though, because the AFL-CIO people in British Guiana [some believed to be CIA men] thought well of him; and Hugh Gaitskell [Leader of the British Labour Party, 1955-63] told me that Burnham had impressed him more than Jagan when the two visited Labour Party leaders in London.
>
> Then, in May 1962, Burnham came to Washington. He appeared an intelligent, self-possessed, reasonable man, insisting quite firmly on his 'socialism' [a nebulous concept when deployed by Burnham] and 'neutralism' but **stoutly anti-communist**. He also seemed well aware that British Guiana had no future at all unless its political leaders tried to temper the racial animosities and unless he in particular gave his party, now predominantly African, a bi-racial flavour.
>
> In the meantime, events had convinced us that Jagan, though perhaps not a disciplined communist, had that kind of deep pro-communist emotion which...the United States could not afford... when it involved a quasi-communist regime on the mainland of Latin America. Burnham's visit left the feeling, as I reported to the President, that 'an independent British Guiana under Burnham (if Burnham will commit himself to a multi-racial policy) would cause us many fewer problems than an independent British Guiana under Jagan.' [This quote, cited earlier, was the key to Kennedy's opting for Burnham.]
>
> And the way was open to bring it about, because Jagan's parliamentary strength was larger than his popular strength: he had won 57 per

cent of the seats on the basis of 42.7 per cent of the vote [in August 1961]. **An obvious solution would be to establish a system of proportional representation** [emphasis added].

This, after prolonged discussion [pressuring], the British Government finally did [contrived!] in October 1963; and elections held at the end of 1964 produced a coalition government under Burnham. With much unhappiness and turbulence [sponsored largely by the CIA], British Guiana seemed to have passed safely out of the communist orbit.[15]

The Americans and the British did not like Burnham. After 1957, the latter in particular never said anything good about him that I can recall. They both settled on Burnham, reluctantly, only because they were afraid of Jagan's devotion to Soviet communism, which was corroborated (year after year) by MI5's constant surveillance of him. It is highly likely that the CIA also spied on him. Therefore, it is interesting to examine the context of Professor Schlesinger's secret visit to British Guiana, in mid-June 1962. The riots and the fire that gutted the commercial centre of Georgetown led to the creation of the Wynn-Parry Commission of Inquiry to investigate the circumstances of the violent event in Georgetown in February 1962, perpetrated by the UF and the PNC, against Jagan's government. This prompted the Macmillan government to postpone the planned independence talks from May to the autumn of 1962. It is clear that violence (with the complicity of the CIA) had revived the political fortunes of Burnham and D'Aguiar, both of whom were later deemed culpable by the Commission with fomenting disturbance to halt the seemingly inevitable march of the colony to independence, in 1962, under Jagan. It energised the Opposition, with the active connivance of the Kennedy administration, to work assiduously towards this end.

And when Schlesinger was on his secret mission to British Guiana, the daily newspaper controlled by Peter D'Aguiar (the *Chronicle*) carried a leader in which the position of his UF was articulated unambiguously: 'Dr Jagan is an avowed Communist, and the majority of the people in this country fear that Independence under his regime would mean the loss of democratic freedom.'[16] On the same day, Jagan's former minister of home affairs, the very able Balram Singh Rai (recently expelled from the PPP), repudiated Jagan's communism in the Legislative Assembly. He reportedly remarked that 'they all know the type of state the PPP government wants to build – a Communist state in which they hoped to bend everybody's will to their own.'[17]

A few days later, the *Chronicle* carried a bold headline captioned:

'I AM A COMMUNIST,' SAYS DR JAGAN
ADMIRER OF CASTRO AND KHRUSHCHEV[18]

CHEDDI JAGAN AND THE COLD WAR, 1946–1992

This was based on their coverage of Jagan's evidence before the Wynn-Parry Commission on June 22, 1962. The following is a part of Jagan's testimony under interrogation by his arch-enemy, the brilliant Indo-Guyanese lawyer and failed politician, Lionel Luckhoo (1914–97), a rabid anti-communist and former leader of the right-wing National Labour Front:

Luckhoo: Dr Jagan, are you an admirer of Fidel Castro?

Jagan: I have said so, yes.

Luckhoo: Have you declared him to be the greatest liberator of the 20th century?

Jagan: Yes.

Luckhoo: You have. As an admirer do you endeavour to pattern your own government after his style and fashion?

Jagan: No, not necessarily …

Luckhoo: Are there any policies of Fidel Castro to which you do not subscribe?

Jagan: I am not aware of all the policies.

Luckhoo: Those that you are aware of?

Jagan: I am not aware of any …

Luckhoo: That you oppose?

Jagan: Yes.

Luckhoo: Are you an admirer of Nikita Khrushchev?

Jagan: Yes.

Luckhoo: And you have publicly proclaimed this?

Jagan: I have publicly said so, yes …

Luckhoo: Have you said in unmistakable language that the communist way of life is preferable? Admit it! Yes or No.

Jagan: Yes. **I have said already what I believe communism to be, and I said it is the aim of communism to bring about a society of equality.**

Luckhoo: **Yourself, Dr Jagan – in the Robertson Report [1954] – and Janet Jagan were named by the Commission as being ones who accept unreservedly the classical communist doctrines of Marx and Lenin. Now, do you accept the classical doctrines of Marx and Lenin?**

Jagan: **I believe in Marxism, yes.**

Luckhoo: **And Lenin?**

Jagan: **Yes** [emphasis added].[19]

Jagan could not resist expanding on his communist creed, and he did so before the Wynn-Parry Commission. In the process, he implicated himself further by his tortuous endeavour at explication:

> If you look at a Webster dictionary, one would find a definition of communism which will compel me to say that I am not a communist because the assumptions are that liberties and freedom will be denied under such a set-up … In this country the people who have been accusing us for many years on this question have always assumed that communism is evil. That is why I have always refused to give a 'yes' or 'no' answer to this very complicated question. I have always said that I am a Marxist. **Marxism is a science of the laws of development of society from one stage to the next … Now, sir, by saying that I am a Marxist, I could be at one and the same time an anti-colonialist, an anti-imperialist, a democrat, a socialist and a humanist and a communist** [emphasis added].[20]

It is interesting that in early July 1962, when the highly contentious matter of the independence for British Guiana under Jagan was receiving inordinate attention in the White House, President Kennedy reminded the world that at the Punta del Este Conference of Foreign Ministers in Uruguay, in January of that year, 'the nations of the Western Hemisphere…declared Marxism-Leninism incompatible with the American system.'[21] In fact, the conference in Uruguay was convened primarily to engender a commonality of response against the communist regime in Cuba. But the Americans were particularly disturbed that Jagan was a close ally of Castro, so they felt increasingly justified in committing themselves to the idea that 'a second Cuba' must not emerge in the Hemisphere. This required, first and foremost, rendering support to the PNC and the UF to foment disorder in British Guiana, by any means necessary, in order to forestall the imminent plan of the British to grant independence to Cheddi Jagan.

On July 12, 1962, Secretary of State Dean Rusk, corroborated the president's stance with respect to Jagan's Marxism and its incompatibility with the American-dominated system in the Hemisphere. However, if Jagan had been a right-wing dictator of the fascist type (like Somoza of Nicaragua or Duvalier of Haiti, for instance), he would have been accommodated automatically. It was about the Cold War exclusively; it had little to do with democracy or cherished freedoms. Rusk wrote to Kennedy:

> I believe we are obliged to base our policy on the premise that once independent, Cheddi Jagan will establish a Marxist regime in British Guiana and associate his country with the Soviet Bloc to a degree unacceptable to us for a state in the Western Hemisphere…It is also my view that a policy of trying to work with Jagan, as urged by the British, will not pay off.[21]

The next day (July 13, 1962) McGeorge Bundy, the president's special assistant for national security affairs, also wrote definitively to Kennedy regarding Jagan's communism: 'Jagan will indeed go the way of Castro, if he is not prevented. He would be weaker than Castro because he is even more inefficient, but he would also probably be more easily controlled from Moscow....'[22]

Then, on September 5, 1962, Professor Schlesinger, with his on-the-spot knowledge, having visited British Guiana, including Port Mourant (Jagan's birthplace), and with every likelihood that he met with Burnham and D'Aguiar, endorsed Bundy's stance that Jagan should not be supported. He had to be removed:

> The Administration cannot be put in the position of working to strengthen a quasi-Communist regime in British Guiana...Our covert plans [the CIA, whose presence he had denied to Maudling] in British Guiana will be much facilitated [... one line not declassified] with a minimum of continuing contact with the Jagan regime.[23]

Janet Jagan and Zhou Enlai, Beijing (Peking), 1962

Janet with Chairman Mao, Beijing (Peking), 1962

Peter D'Aguiar (1912–89), a rabid anti-communist (of Portuguese extraction), who founded the United Force in October 1960. He was dedicated to preventing Jagan from leading Guyana to independence. But, unwittingly, he made a significant contribution to the rise of Forbes Burnham and the consolidation of his dictatorship. Belatedly, from 1967, he endeavoured to repudiate Burnham's authoritarian rule. It was too late

IV. The Anti-Communist Crusade of Peter D'Aguiar's United Force: A Major Component in Burnham's Resurgence

At home, Peter D'Aguiar's United Force was obsessed with dramatising Jagan's enthralment with Castro and Khrushchev: his exemplars for the imposition of communism on an independent Guyana. Burnham was not a communist, yet he seemed temperamentally disinclined to engage openly in the anti-communist crusade pursued by D'Aguiar, between late 1960 and 1964. However, Burnham realised that only Kennedy's intervention, driven by his own anti-communist ardour, could halt Jagan's march to independence, as the British, by the late 1950s, were inclined to give Jagan the benefit of the doubt because they wished to be rid of the colony; besides, they were transparently not enamoured of Burnham, having dubbed him an opportunist and a racist. It was therefore imperative for Burnham to ensure that the anti-communist crusade of the UF and the Catholic Church was not stymied in any way. The prototype was the 'Black Friday' riots of February 1962: for Burnham, it was totally acceptable that D'Aguiar should virtually spearhead the anti-Jagan, anti-communist campaign while guaranteeing that his Black supporters were energised and mobilised to provide the bulk of the firepower, so to speak, for the violence in Georgetown. Burnham was thereby bound to be the foremost beneficiary of the UF's crusade against the communist Jagan. It was relentless. Jagan was cornered. Burnham was substantially indebted to the Portuguese, the light coloureds and the Catholic Church for the unsparingly crude anti-communist onslaught against Jagan, thus creating the environment for CIA intervention in order to foment violence. The Americans were in it right up to the hilt.

This obsessive orchestration, spearheaded by President Kennedy, rescued Burnham's faltering political career by anointing him their man to forestall the emergence of 'another Cuba' in the Hemisphere. The Americans did not realise they were buying a pig in a poke, as the British had cautioned them. As early as March 1962, Professor Schlesinger informed Kennedy that the relevant US government machinery was set in motion on the anti-Jagan project:

> ...both [the] State [Department] and the CIA are under the impression that a firm decision has been taken to get rid of Jagan... British Guiana has 600,000 inhabitants. Jagan would no doubt be gratified to know that the Americans and the British are spending more man-hours per capita on British Guiana than on any other current problem.[24]

In January 1962, with the negative fallout from Jagan's fateful and disastrous meeting with President Kennedy transparent, Peter D'Aguiar accelerated his anti-communist onslaught against Jagan's push for independence. The latter was sanguine regarding a constitutional conference in London to discuss the transfer of power to his government, and had drafted a constitution that included respect for the fundamental freedoms of a liberal democratic society. D'Aguiar, however, did not believe that a communist would ever uphold any such liberal principles, as all communist states routinely abrogated supposedly guaranteed basic freedoms:

> The problem as I see it, is not the shape or the form of the constitution. It is whether a constitution under a Marxist system is worth anything at all…[as] the reasonableness of the constitution does not mean that the government carries out its principles.[25]

Jagan was confident that after independence he would be the recipient, like the Castro regime, of substantial Soviet aid/subsidies. He contended that such aid was rendered with no ulterior motives in mind, presumably in a spirit of 'proletarian internationalism.' D'Aguiar gave no credence whatsoever to such 'disinterested' promptings:

> The Soviet Union has one single interest, and that is to further its own imperialist expansion. It is clear from the Cuban experience that Russia has taken out of Cuba far more than she has put in. She is paying less for Cuban sugar by 50 per cent than what the United States government was paying.

D'Aguiar concluded on a very pessimistic note, indicting Jagan for being a dyed-in-the-wool communist who would make an Independent Guyana a satellite of the Soviet Union. He was forthright:

> Jagan appears to be sweeping us from colonialism to satellitism. That is to say, in place of this country's being a colony of the United Kingdom, we will become a satellite of the Soviet Union. In the state of satellitism, we will be denied all the freedoms which have been enjoyed even in our colonial state, and thus we are on the verge of taking a step which, instead of making us proud and free men, is in danger of making us ashamed and enslaved.[26]

In fact, the UF was substantially more uncompromising in opposing Jagan's endeavour to lead British Guiana to independence; but they were also demanding of Burnham a firmer, less ambiguous, stance against early Independence. It is highly likely that by late 1961, in the aftermath of Jagan's fatal meeting with Kennedy, both the UF and the PNC must have been informed that US help was available (most likely through the CIA) to foment chaos to stall Jagan's seemingly unstoppable march to independence. Anti-communism would be the instrument to torpedo Jagan's progress.

The *Daily Chronicle* (owned by Peter D'Aguiar and integral to the anti-communist crusade of the UF) could find common ground even with Sydney King, although he was less troubled by Jagan's communism than he was by his 'racist' politics. However, the paper appreciated his resolve to prevent the British from granting independence to Jagan:

> Mr King's reasons...for opposing Independence under Jaganism are different from ours. Mr King feels that Independence under Jaganism would be Independence for a faction of the population only [Indians]. The *Chronicle*, while being critical of factional government, believes that Independence under Jaganism, while it would start out factionally, would end in communist slavery for everybody. We are convinced that Jaganism is only using race to achieve power for the communists. It is not factional government to be feared. It is communist government. However, the reasons for opposing Jaganism matters little. The principle that Independence is inopportune is the ground on which we find ourselves in agreement with Mr King.[27]

As seen earlier, in August 1961 (after the PPP victory in the general elections), a resolution was drafted by Sydney King (Eusi Kwayana) and Bertie Nicholson (Vigilance), on behalf of the African Society for Racial Equality (ASRE). The resolution was presented on August 30 by King and Nicholson to Governor Grey, who stated that King told him that having failed to build mutual political trust between Africans and Indians after fourteen years [1947–61], he was 'now convinced that it was impossible for Guianese of African origin to secure the co-operation of Guianese of Indian origin.' The ASRE resolution probably reflected the apprehension most African Guyanese harboured of an independent Guyana under perceived Indian rule, led by Jagan. But unlike D'Aguiar's UF and the Portuguese of Guyana, it was Indian domination in perpetuity, not Jagan's communism, that Africans feared.

In July 1962, the *Chronicle*, consonant with its stance of the previous two years or more, reiterated that Jagan's primary source of inspiration was Fidel Castro; moreover, that their 'comradeship' presaged the way towards a communist dictatorship in Guyana:

> In four years...dictator Castro has transformed his followers' ideal of the democracy of Lincoln into the Communist ideal of the so-called dictatorship of the proletariat. And further, he has imposed the Kremlin system of totalitarian authority, under the guise of collective leadership of the impotent masses, for the cause of Marxism-Leninism, and by their absolute master.[28]

This was congruent with the view from the White House on Cheddi Jagan; and this suited Burnham because it was more ammunition for Kennedy's anti-communist offensive against Jagan's communism.

V.   David de Caires and Burnham's Amorphous Politics

David de Caires was a young Guyanese intellectual of Portuguese extraction, possibly a supporter of the pro-capitalist UF during its very early period (1960–61). Yet, even then, he was inclined to take a broader view than most, arguing that Burnham's politics was nebulous and that his vague socialism, pitted against Jagan's decidedly Marxist beliefs, rendered him somewhat 'redundant.' D'Aguiar, too, despite his limited popular support, was identified unambiguously as a conservative and a capitalist. But, as late as July 1962, de Caires could not fathom what Burnham stood for; where, indeed, he was going politically, as without a coalition, either with Jagan or D'Aguiar, there was no way he could win a general election. He was not sanguine about his prospects. Burnham was apparently a very fine card player; in politics, too, he kept his cards very close to his chest while having the knack of reading those of his rivals.

I quote David de Caires at length because even a clever man like him could not envision Burnham's rising political capital with the post-Castro escalation of the Cold War in the Hemisphere:

> The actual policy of the PNC has never been clear. It will be recalled that the PNC went to the polls [in August 1961] on a secret economic policy. In fact, to a large extent, it is not a party, but a one-man institution, and as such suffers from the leader's ambivalence and dilettantism. It is difficult to see what Mr Burnham is aiming at. He must have recognised that he will never win the elections on his own. If there were some agreements with the UF, he might defeat the PPP, yet he points out, perhaps correctly, that such an agreement is not feasible: there can be no 'marriage' between such different partners even on the grounds of expediency.

> Up to the present, Burnham…has not been vitally important, as the PPP have been able to retain control at the elections despite his opposition. However, after Independence Burnham will be extremely dangerous as, having recognised that he is unable to win power democratically, his opposition will lose all sense of responsibility and he may be tempted to employ whatever means are available.[29]

But de Caires observed that the racial problem of the country was so intractable that economic development was unattainable without a coalition between Jagan's PPP and Burnham's PNC. He felt that Jagan should therefore make overtures to Burnham, in order to establish definitive terms for the creation of a viable coalition government. And if Burnham were not amenable to such an idea, the PPP should purge itself of the 'racial elements' in the party and resolve to transform itself into a 'genuine socialist party.'[30] The latter is not defined, but it is hardly likely that he meant a communist party, consistent with Jagan's pro-Soviet utopian vision. de Caires probably envisaged that such a party, left-wing and social democratic, could conceivably eradicate some of the evils of the current capitalist order, including racialism, poverty, and ignorance.

But de Caires recognised that any initiative on the part of Jagan for unity with the PNC could spell political suicide. He was so overwhelmingly dependent on racial support that an alliance with Burnham would undermine his stature as the Indian leader *par excellence*. However, as long as the PPP could win outright, under the first-past-the-post electoral system, they were disinclined to engage with non-Indians and conscientiously pursue a power-sharing constitutional arrangement. In the general elections of August 1961, for instance, the PPP contested only twenty-nine of the thirty-five seats because the rest were deemed unwinnable, being predominantly African or Amerindian or with a significant light-coloured and Portuguese component.

Their focus (understandably) was on winning a majority of seats, not a majority of votes as is mandatory under proportional representation. Ironically, however, the PPP did not contest two seats in Georgetown because they preferred Peter D'Aguiar's UF to win rather than Burnham's PNC. The UF won both (including D'Aguiar in Central Georgetown) arguably because Jagan's Indian supporters voted for them, thereby eclipsing the PNC.

VI. The Last-Ditch Stance by the British to Rescue Jagan: Kennedy's Aides Are Uncompromising in Their Anti-Communist Fervour

Yet, contrary to de Caires's questioning of the political relevance of Burnham, by July 1962 (as seen earlier), Professor Schlesinger had already recommended Burnham to Kennedy: the chosen one in the president's resolve to get rid of Jagan before independence. And that was predicated on convincing the British to withhold independence from Jagan – specifically by engineering the imposition of PR in British Guiana, under which Jagan's electoral defeat was virtually guaranteed. But even under PR, Burnham's PNC could not win outright, so it was imperative for them to cultivate a coalition with the conservative and capitalist UF, at some stage, before or after the elections. It was the central proposition on which Arthur Schlesinger's plan for Jagan's demise was being hatched.

Yet the British still retained a discernible preference for Jagan over Burnham. Even after the anti-Jagan 'Black Friday' riots of February 1962, the undersecretary of state for the colonies, Hugh Fraser, who had just visited British Guiana, was counselling top White House officials (including Assistant Secretary of State Tyler and Schlesinger) to offer Jagan financial aid in order to nudge him towards the centre. He was also forthright that independence for British Guiana was imminent: 'independence would come possibly at the end of 1962, but more probably in early 1963...It would be madness to attempt to delay independence.'

Fraser reportedly also noted that the sugar company, Booker, as well as the bauxite company, Alcan, were not 'worried about nationalization.' He added that

> Booker probably considered Jagan to be the best leader of the lot. Any attempt to dump Jagan or to manipulate the political molecules in the situation would be tricky and apt to be counter-productive. If proportional representation [PR] became part of the British Guiana constitution, this might help in affecting the outcome of a new election. He stressed, however, that such a solution could not be imposed by the United States or the United Kingdom.

But Fraser did hint at the possibility of a referendum in effecting 'some kind of adjustment in the present political machinery.'

Fraser had a meeting with Burnham on March 17, 1962. He remarked he was 'intelligent and opportunistic,' but that he could not win in the long run because of the entrenched racial character of local politics. There was no alternative Indian leader in the PPP to Jagan, and Jagan told him that D'Aguiar and the CIA were responsible for the recent riots. But, although the Kennedy administration had declared Jagan lost to communism, Fraser still sought to persuade them to adopt a more pragmatic stance, as 'he did not believe that the Jagan regime was communist.' Hugh Fraser was a Conservative, yet he reportedly concluded:

> The affairs of the colony were puffed up out of all proportion to their true importance. He felt that this was partially the fault of the British in sending troops and suspending the constitution in 1953. Jagan's visit to the United States [in October 1961] and the hostile American reaction to him had also contributed to the inflated importance of the colony...He felt we should all keep a sense of humour and proportion in considering the situation.
>
> Mr Alexis Johnson [Deputy Undersecretary for Political Affairs at the State Department] interjected to say that...we would not think it funny if another country in South America were to go communist.
>
> Mr Fraser stated that the racial tension between Africans and East Indians in the colony was the central problem. This made matters particularly difficult for the United Kingdom which planned to get out of the colony as soon as possible. He felt that the elections of August 1961 had been the last chance for Burnham and the Africans in the colony. From now on there would be more Indians of voting age than Africans. It was his understanding that by the middle of the 1970s there would be a ratio of almost two Indians to one African in the population...**He believed that the Indians were not naturally inclined towards communism. They were an acquisitive people and had a strong ethnic loyalty to their own kind.** This racialism had been stimulated by Burnham's African bias and by the actions of D'Aguiar [emphasis added].[31]

Fraser still envisaged a role for the US in moderating the political philosophy of Jagan, should they dangle a carrot of financial aid before him. He reasoned that

> the Indian commercial community might well put pressure on Jagan to move to the right if the United States adopted a more friendly attitude [towards him]. Mr Fraser had urged Jagan to move to the right and to indicate publicly that private capital was welcome in British Guiana. He urged Jagan to consider himself as the Premier of a country and not just the head of a political party. Mr Fraser explained his feeling that a delay in British Guiana's independence would not help matters.

But the Americans were consumed by anti-communist hysteria; they could not conceive of a *modus vivendi* with Jagan. That had evaporated with Jagan's disastrous visit to Washington in October 1961. For them, it was a single-minded project to pre-empt another Cuba at all costs; and they were resolved to exert any conceivable pressure on the British to remove Jagan before independence, the ameliorating preference for him (as opposed to Burnham) by Iain Macleod and Hugh Fraser notwithstanding. The allusion of the Americans to an Anglo-American 'political action programme' was, in fact, a veiled reference to their intent to engineer the termination of the political career of Cheddi Jagan:

> Mr Alexis Johnson said that the United States would like to feel more confident that...the granting of independence to British Guiana would not bring chaos and a communist-controlled government. He reminded Mr Fraser that we thought of this situation partly in terms of the Cuban experience. Castro had originally been presented as a reformer. We do not intend to be taken in twice. He felt it important that the United States and the United Kingdom work very closely at all levels on the problem of British Guiana in order to prevent catastrophe from taking place there. Mr Fraser agreed entirely but expressed the opinion that the problem of communism would get worse if a United States [economic] mission did not go to the colony soon. He felt there was a real possibility that the Soviets may decide to send such a mission if there was no constructive action by the West. Mr Johnson suggested the advisability of the discussions between the US and the UK about a political action programme. Mr Fraser did not respond.[32]

Arthur Schlesinger said the granting of aid to Jagan would be construed by the right-wing in America as a measure beneficial to communism. This could, indeed, provide ammunition to those already strongly opposed to Kennedy's foreign aid legislation before Congress. Besides, Dr Joost Sluis, a rabid anti-communist of the Christian Anti-Communist Crusade, who was active in the colony before and after the general elections of August 1961, had done much to tarnish Jagan's political image in America. And Schlesinger knowing precisely how Kennedy felt about Jagan after their one-on-one meeting in the Rose Garden of the White House, concluded:

> Jagan has made things very difficult by his behaviour in the United States. It would be helpful if he would take some action to better his US public image and destroy the parallel in the American public mind with Castro. It would help a great deal if Jagan would do something about this, or if some other figure were to arise as a leader of British Guiana.'[33]

Jagan would do no such thing to placate the imperialists.

That 'other figure' was already being sized up! He was the antithesis of Jagan. Burnham's political slate was essentially indeterminate – on which he could inscribe or erase whatever he deemed expedient in order to enhance his political fortunes. And in a society where most Africans (only marginally numerically less than Indians) perceived Burnham as their hero, the principal defender of their race against an ominously dominant Indian segment led by Jagan, it made sense to be studiously vague, politically nebulous at best, roughly equidistant from the communist Jagan (on the left) and the capitalist D'Aguiar (on the right). Yet Burnham was consistent in one respect: his rhetoric was unfailingly anti-colonial with a discernible veneer of undefined 'socialism.' He was a magnificent orator; yet his speeches were routinely slight in terms of content. However, unlike Jagan, he was not considered a communist or an admirer of Comrades Castro, Khrushchev or Mao. I'm aware he has been dubbed a Titoist; I appreciate the prompting – seeking a handle on his vagueness. But he was indefinable. Yet by mid-1962, politically ambiguous, amorphous or even devious L.F.S. Burnham was already being anointed as America's man. Cheddi Jagan was his greatest asset, but so too were Peter D'Aguiar and Sydney King.

Unlike Jagan's, Burnham's ideological posture (such as it was) appeared anodyne: from 1950, when he and Jagan formed the PPP, to 1964, when imperialism secured his accession to power and the supplanting of the communist Jagan. Burnham's cultivated nebulousness is reflected in the PNC's original Constitution regarding the party's principal objective:

> To transform British Guiana from an economically and culturally backward country into a developed country with a properly balanced economy and a flowering culture in which the interests of the working people and of the underprivileged, and an equitable distribution of the country's wealth will be the primary concern of the government when this party is in office.

In March 1960, shortly before the Constitutional Conference in London, the ill-defined character of the PNC's political philosophy was reinforced, but the anti-communist strand was evident. The following is from the organ of the

PNC, *New Nation* (edited by its General Secretary Sydney King [Eusi Kwayana]), elaborating on the excerpt from the PNC's Constitution cited above:

> [T]he PPP...bears upon its ugly brow the marks of communist, fascist and religious totalitarianism all at once...the clause [quoted above] is not formulated by a bunch of doctrinaire socialists who get up and declare that only Socialism can save British Guiana. Socialists of the democratic type there are in the ranks of the PNC in large numbers. These people are at the same time opposed to Communist dictatorship and to State domination of the economy of British Guiana or of control to such a degree as to stifle or appear to stifle the health and creative genius of the producers of wealth – workers, capitalists, financiers or entrepreneurs. As the PNC sees it, for British Guiana progress lies along the road of a rapid development of the productive forces by free enterprise, individual enterprise, state enterprise acting at times apart and at times in collaboration, but always in subjection to the best economic interests of the country and of its people.[34]

A week later *New Nation* revisited the question of the communist programme of Jagan's PPP, as it deftly sought to prompt Indian capitalists, many of whom were still supporting the PPP, to demonstrate courage by disengaging from the communist Jagans, and to recognise that their financial security would be undermined irretrievably if they did not do so. The leader (possibly written by the editor, Sydney King) was forthright in exposing what it saw as the communist machinations of Jagan; in such a state there will be no room for the local Indian capitalist despite the financial support he had been giving to the PPP for his own protection. The paper argued that the communist Jagan could not change his spots; there was no long-term security for Indian capitalists under his rule after independence.

It is noteworthy that these two editorials were written on the eve of the Constitutional Conference in London in March 1960. It is obvious that the PNC wished to disavow any sympathy for Jagan's communist philosophy – that they were, indeed, not communists:

> What the Indian capitalists do not understand is that the policy of milking them against 'Imperialism' is not being done in opposition to communist doctrine but IN OBEDIENCE TO PRINCIPLES LAID DOWN BY STALIN [*sic*]. In his work *Marxism and the National and Colonial Question*, Stalin laid down the line for Communist parties in colonies. First join with the working class, farmers and the 'national bourgeoisie' (that is you, Messrs capitalists) against the Imperialists, then with the working class and poor peasants against the bourgeoisie (in plain words, the Communists will then break up the common front and start moving)...

> If the Indian capitalists are able to find a leader to replace Dr Jagan and his charming lady [Janet Jagan] BEFORE IT IS TOO LATE [*sic*], and at the same time to maintain the party's hold on the Indian masses who gave it power all is well and good. But can they do it? That is the question.
>
> What seems to have happened is that the Indian capitalists who support Jagan have paid ransom money and have MANAGED TO SAVE THEIR OWN SKIN FOR THE TIME [*sic*]. In accepting their support on this basis, Jagan is ensuring that he remains in power so as to be able AS SOON AS HE CAN PUT ASIDE DEMOCRACY [*sic*], to fix up all capitalists – first those few who did not pay the party ransom money, next those who did. BUT THE MAJORITY OF INDIAN BUSINESSMEN DO NOT UNDERSTAND THIS, NOT HAVING STUDIED MARXISM-LENINISM-STALINISM AS THE ATROCIOUS DOCTRINE IS OFFICIALLY CALLED [*sic*].
>
> The PPP is 'uniting' with capitalists to milk them up and to gobble them up later on. The Indian capitalists think they are being 'protected' from the blacks and from West Indians by one of their own race. If they play the game long enough, they will find out the score.[35]

The PNC declared they were not anti-capitalist or communist like Jagan; and they were offering capitalists an environment conducive to the creation of wealth. They desired that local capitalists should 'blossom forth into a class of some stability, not to be eliminated or wiped out, but to be active in social and economic progress for all.' On the other hand, Jagan's PPP was enticing them into a 'union leading to final destruction.'[36]

The PNC did not deviate from this liberal capitalist and vaguely socialist stance for most of the 1960s. After 1961 (following his meeting with Jagan in the White House) President Kennedy pursued a policy of imploring and cajoling the British to get rid of Jagan before granting Independence to British Guiana. In a memorandum dated July 12, 1962, Secretary of State Dean Rusk informed President Kennedy that there was no doubt about Jagan's communist, pro-Soviet political loyalty; however, they should pursue their anti-Jagan policy with a more sympathetic British Ambassador in Washington (Ormsby-Gore), rather than through their Ambassador in London (David Bruce), thereby having to engage with the 'not so sympathetic Colonial Office.'

Rusk argued:

> We have been given by the FBI a report of the American Communist Party's intention to seek for Jagan economic assistance from the Soviet Bloc…[enclosed]. Attached [also] is a study we have prepared of contacts by the People's Progressive Party (PPP) with communists, communist fronts and the communist bloc since September 1961…

During cross examination before the Commonwealth Commission of Enquiry into the causes of the February riots, Jagan admitted on June 22, 1962 that he was a communist. This admission came after much muddled explanation by Jagan as to what the term 'communism' meant, and was qualified by his definition that communism was a system based on 'from each according to his ability and to each according to his needs.' Further questioning on Jagan's political beliefs was cut short on June 26, by the British Chairman of the Commission [Sir Henry Wynn-Parry], with the ruling that it was useless to pursue the subject since it had 'already been established beyond peradventure' that Dr Jagan was a communist.

In the light of all the evidence...I believe we are obliged to base our policy on the premise that, once independent, Cheddi Jagan will establish a 'Marxist' regime in British Guiana, and associate his country with the Soviet Bloc to a degree unacceptable to us for a state in the Western Hemisphere...It is also my view that a policy of trying to work with Jagan, as urged by the British, will not pay off. Jagan is too far committed emotionally and suspicious of our intentions...[emphasis added].[37]

Dean Rusk concluded his advice to the president with essentially a call for greater American involvement in subverting Jagan's government before independence:

I propose that we transfer the locale of the discussion with the UK on British Guiana to Washington, and that I call in the British Ambassador and speak to him in the lines indicated in the attached paper [attachment not declassified]. My thought in transferring the locale to Washington is to enable us to deal through a sympathetic British Ambassador [David Ormsby-Gore, a close friend of Kennedy] with the Foreign Office and the Prime Minister, rather than sending messages to our Embassy in London, which in practice usually discusses British Guiana with the not-so-sympathetic Colonial Office. It is further helpful to us to talk in Washington because we have available here people with the most up-to-date US information on British Guiana [the CIA], and we would be able to provide nuances of our current thinking to the British Ambassador.[38]

Kennedy's anti-communist campaign was aggravated by the Cuban missile crisis of October 1962; it rendered the removal of Jagan an US obsession. On March 14, 1963 the American Consul General in Georgetown, Everett Melby, wrote to the State Department arguing that it was imperative for the American government to actively pursue a change of the electoral system in Guyana to ensure that Jagan did not lead the colony to independence. He was endorsing precisely what the Opposition was demanding – proportional representation (PR) – although the State Department and the British government seemed to have already agreed to it in principle. The consul general saw PR as 'the most practical electoral device for replacing Premier Cheddi Jagan and the People's

Progressive Party (PPP) with a more democratic and reliable government. It is generally conceded that PR should be put to a referendum.'

It is evident that Consul General Melby perceived an independent Guyana, under the leadership of Jagan, inimical to US national security in the Hemisphere. The following is Melby's definitive judgement on Cheddi:

> Based on an appraisal of the local scene...unless definite action is taken, time favours Jagan. The longer the delay, the more difficult it will be to dislodge Jagan and Jagan's brand of 'socialism' from Government; extended delay presents the possibility of Cuba-like situation ['a second Cuba' in the Hemisphere]. Since it is definitely not in the best US interests to have either British Guiana or an independent Guyana ruled by Jagan's PPP, **the US Government should strive for an HMG** [British Government] **decision for an immediate referendum on PR...**
>
> **Granted that spheres of influence exist, an independent Guyana will be within the US sphere. It is not in the national interest to have a communist government on the mainland of South America. An independent Guyana with Jagan and the PPP in office represents such a threat and as such should be removed** [emphasis added].[39]

VII. American Endorsement of Proportional Representation: The Definitive Instrument to Vanquish Jagan

Melby could not have been more unequivocal. And he, like the PNC and UF, was confident that in any such referendum on PR Jagan could not win. The emphasis henceforth must be to secure the mechanism for the removal of Jagan while a Conservative government was still in office. They could not depend on Labour to facilitate the elimination of the communist threat, given the inclination of the British, since the late 1950s, to be discernibly conciliatory of Jagan, warts and all:

> It appears that for most of the last decade it has been the British approach to present the Guianese situation as one which, while neither tranquil nor in the best free world interest, is not as serious as might be supposed...**In the late 1950s it became HMG's policy to consider Cheddi Jagan and the majority of the PPP hierarchy as neither communist nor particularly** [communist] **bloc oriented...** [although] **there was no firm evidence to indicate a change of PPP philosophy...**
>
> **The UK will have no major political interest in an independent Guyana...**[therefore] **HMG wants to shed BG quickly, consistent with as graceful a departure as possible.** The private views of one Colonial Officer [obviously Governor Grey] seems to stress more

the awkwardness of an Order-in-Council for PR than its utilisation to remove Jagan…

A British Labour Government could be expected to be more inclined to grant independence under the existing government than would a Conservative one. **Therefore, US actions should be taken while the UK Government of the moment could be expected to be more receptive to the PR concept** [emphasis added].[40]

Melby was providing precisely the corroboration Kennedy wanted in order to validate and energise his campaign to defeat Jagan before independence. The president would henceforth intensify his pressure on the Macmillan government to ensure that they revoke their judgement of Jagan – their definitive preference for him rather than Burnham, in conjunction with their virtual resolve to granting Cheddi independence. Prevarication in ousting the latter could be 'dangerous' for US perceived national interest; and the imposition of PR before the next elections was central to this imperative:

Failure to act quickly provides Jagan with a chance to assume the initiative. For example, if the present situation continues, he might demand new elections under first-past-the-post. With the existing electoral districting, he could probably win a majority of seats. This would permit him to present a 'fresh mandate' for independence without PR. Lack of action probably provides the PPP with a morale boost and simultaneously tends to dishearten the opposition.

The presence of a British army battalion makes the possibility of renewed mass urban disorders most unlikely. Also, having learnt its lesson in January-February 1962, the government can take preventative action to avoid creation of the tension-filled situation which preceded 16 February 1962…

Continuation of the status quo permits Jagan to consolidate his gains in establishing PPP domination of all facets of BG life [a likely allusion to his determination to oust the MPCA by his own union, GAWU, as the bargaining agent in the sugar industry.] To the degree which the US Government and HMG fail to move to counteract this trend, they are providing support for his rule. Such support is dangerous.[41]

Consul General Melby was, in effect, recommending a concerted push by the Kennedy administration to ensure that the British government did not, under any circumstances, grant independence to Jagan. By implication, even the fomenting of urban disorder should be supported by the CIA (as in the case of 'Black Friday' in February 1962), as it could be the decisive factor, again, in dramatising to the British that Jagan did not have control of the local situation. It was imperative, therefore, that the US government prevail upon the British government to hold general elections before independence – under Proportional Representation. Consequently, changing the electoral system was pivotal in order to install, in an independent Guyana, a government compatible with the strategic hemispheric interests of America. In effect, Melby's counsel was unambiguous: Cheddi Jagan must be removed – and more violence, fomented by the PNC and UF, might be necessary and worthy of support by America in order to achieve its anti-communist goal.

And the collapse of the Independence Conference in London in 1962, postponed from May to October because of the orchestrated violence (in February) perpetrated by the UF and the PNC with the support of the Americans – as Jagan interpreted it – did not only sanction violence, but it planted in the opposition the conviction that their intransigence on the issue of independence would eventually award them the big prize. Jagan's assessment of the failed conference in 1962 is a valid one, and it presaged the fatal outcome for him in October 1963, yet he could not fathom the depth of American machinations in their obsession with ousting him as the leader of an independent Guyana:

> The talks broke down primarily owing to common interests of the British Government and our Opposition not to transfer residual powers to my government. The intransigence and the insistence of the British government on the principle of unanimity were two sides of the same coin...On the adjournment of the Conference Sandys declared that if the political parties could not come to an agreement, and if social and economic conditions deteriorated, HMG might have to consider 'imposing a settlement.' This was simply giving the greenlight to the Opposition for further obstruction and violence, as a result of which he would impose a settlement to his liking. As the Attorney General, Fenton Ramsahoye, aptly put it, the British Government, by acceding to the wishes of the Opposition and insisting on the principle of unanimity, had 'placed a premium on violence, looting, arson and murder.'[42]

Jagan, with Brindley Benn (his deputy) and Dr Fenton Ramsahoye (his attorney general), at the aborted constitutional conference, London, October 1962

PART 2.
1963

The Labour Relations Bill, the CIA, the Eighty-Day Strike, and Jagan's Fatal Error in Unwittingly Facilitating the Sandy's Plan to Impose Proportional Representation

I. The Labour Relations Bill and the CIA's Role in the Eighty-Day Strike: The Complicity of the TUC in the Subversion of Jagan's Government

In fact, if President Kennedy had not intervened personally and ferociously, obsessed with Jagan's communist creed – deemed synonymous with, and as virulent as, Castro's – the British were all set to relinquish the colony and give independence to Jagan. He ought to have known that. No 'struggle' against the imperialists was necessary. Why hand the prize to Burnham? But Jagan appeared not to have appreciated fully the decisive role of the Americans in cajoling the reluctant British to collude in their scheme to destroy him. And it is arguable that Melby knew that the PPP government was about to introduce the Labour Relations Bill, as it had done nearly ten years before, in order to secure a poll to ascertain the union that should be recognised by employers where there was jurisdictional dispute. In essence, it was designed specifically to oust the MPCA as the recognised bargaining agent in the sugar industry by the PPP's union, the Guyana Agricultural Workers' Union (GAWU). But it may be recalled that the Sugar Producers' Association (SPA) was prepared to recognise the precursor of this union (GIWU) as the bargaining agent for the predominantly Indian fieldworkers (the overwhelming majority) as early as August 1953. Yet the offer was rejected by ministers in the PPP government.

Jagan knew, as did Dr Fenton Ramsahoye, that Burnham and D'Aguiar were now endowed with all the trumps: the final Anglo-American solution was being hatched – accommodating PNC/UF violence that could make the colony ungovernable, thus providing the rationale for the imposition of PR. What Jagan found most galling, however, was that Richard Ishmael, president of the TUC and one of the architects of the violence against him in 1962, was, in fact, also president of the MPCA as well as being an ally of Burnham; his union was recognised by the SPA as the sole bargaining agent for sugar workers. But it was widely recognised that the overwhelming majority of those workers, Indians, were loyal supporters of Jagan's PPP. Besides, they constituted the largest body of workers in any industry in the colony; therefore, Jagan's GAWU could potentially have become a significant force in the TUC, which was militantly opposed to him.

This was what impelled Jagan to introduce the Labour Relations Bill in the House of Assembly on March 25, 1963. It read:

> This Bill seeks to ensure the compulsory recognition by employers as bargaining agents on behalf of those unions which, after due inquiry, appear to the Minister of Labour, to be truly representative of the workers in a particular industry, trade or undertaking.

The Minister could then authorise a ballot: if the union challenging the recognised one secured 65 per cent of the votes, he would then recommend that the employer proceed with its recognition.

This was the context in which the TUC, allied with Burnham's PNC, launched a general strike against the Labour Relations Bill in 1963. Being president of the TUC, Richard Ishmael was identified by Burnham as central to his pursuit of power. This strike could make the colony ungovernable, thus bolstering his and America's case (by now the same) for the removal of the communist Jagan. Political instability would virtually guarantee that the British did contrive a means of imposing PR with elections before independence, as Duncan Sandys (a compliant American puppet, unlike Macleod) had intimated at the constitutional conference of October 1962, which was orchestrated to fail.

This was not lost on the Americans and their man, Forbes Burnham. Jagan informed Sir Ralph Grey, governor of British Guiana (1959–64), that Burnham had told him that the Labour Relations Bill was not the *causa belli* but the *casus belli* – not the cause of the war (strike) but the occasion for it. The TUC backed Burnham unreservedly, and succeeded in prosecuting a general strike that lasted eighty days. Yet it is significant that the predominantly Indian sugar workers, ostensibly represented by Ishmael's MPCA, did not go on strike. This was conclusive evidence that their loyalty was to their political hero, Cheddi Jagan. This did not matter, however, as the prolonged strike, financed by the CIA, wrecked the economy. Total collapse was averted only because the Cubans and the Soviets supplied Jagan with oil and basic food items, thereby providing added fuel to the anti-communist crusade of Burnham, D'Aguiar, and their American sponsors.

America was involved up to the hilt in what was transparent complicity in this exercise of subversion to destroy Jagan. The CIA in league with the AFL-CIO and the AIFLD, provided about $1 million (US) to the TUC in British Guiana to sustain the strike. The Labour Relations Bill had to be withdrawn towards the end of May 1963, as the PPP was reduced to a minority because several of its members were suspended by the Speaker of the House for unbecoming conduct towards him. However, the strike continued until early July, as the energetic opposition, buoyed by Kennedy's financial support, grounded the feeble PPP government into the dust. The CIA, the AFL-CIO, and the British TUC were all engaged in funding anti-Jagan unions, as Robert Waters and Gordon Daniels (specialists on the subject) argue:

> British Guiana is an excellent test case for charges that the AFL-CIO's Cold War foreign policy was in bed with the CIA and that it privileged anti-communism over the needs of workers. The AFL-CIO did push tremendous resources into British Guiana because its leaders believed Cheddi and Janet Jagan were Communists intent upon destroying free labour once British Guiana became independent. Anti-communism was the key issue for the AFL-CIO and for the British TUC which also provided substantial assistance to the Guianese TUC...[43]

Throughout the eighty-day strike, racial violence fomented by the Opposition and powered surreptitiously by the terrorist campaign, the PNC's X-13 Plan, constituted a virtual civil war between Africans and Indians. This Plan was 'a detailed account of a PNC terrorist gang...a detailed document of the PNC line of command in planning and executing violence.' Jagan was wounded beyond recovery, precisely what the Americans desired in their implacable crusade to destroy him. The violence of February 1962, coupled with the orchestrated collapse of the Independence Conference in October 1962, had taken its toll on Jagan. In December 1962, Governor Grey informed Duncan Sandys that 'Jagan is very tired and depressed, and I think he would prefer to resign and go onto opposition rather than continue in office and try to put this unhappy country on its feet.'[44]

It is conceivable that the alleged infidelity of Janet Jagan (documented by the security agents who spied on her in the colony and in London) could also have undermined Jagan's self-confidence as a leader, if not his irrepressible ideological fidelity to Marxism-Leninism. But Janet was indispensable to his political mission; therefore, he was probably resigned to overlooking any deviation of which she was culpable. And the British, prodded relentlessly by President Kennedy since the 'Black Friday' riots of February 1962, reluctantly acquiesced in divesting Jagan of his political ascendancy of 1960–61 (when Iain Macleod, a friend of Jock Campbell, was colonial secretary); thereafter Burnham's leading the colony to independence was virtually assured. Cheddi had squandered his political capital through a series of unforced blunders.

Jagan's dark mood did not lift. It was virtually the end of the road for him. His ideological fervour; his face-to-face, candid and self-destructive private exchange with Kennedy; and his visceral repudiation of 'American imperialism' had pitted him as the enemy of the foremost capitalist country, in the heat of the

Cold War. But he lacked the ammunition for the fight. Yet on June 12, 1963, Jagan wrote to Sir Ralph Grey, the governor of British Guiana, accusing the Kennedy administration of complicity in the subversion of his government. His rage was palpable:

> The Opposition will use any pretext to subvert and destroy my Government. Unfortunately our situation is complicated by the fact that there is outside interference, particularly of the USA, in our affairs...Our trade unionists are working in close collaboration with the American Institute for Free Labour Development [AIFLD] sited in Washington, which is also working in close collaboration with the US State Department and the USAID. It is likely that there are CIA agents operating here in devious ways as information officers, trade unionists, etc. The Americans have built up a vast propaganda against my Government. The popular image in the United States is that British Guiana is going to be another Cuba and Jagan another Castro; consequently, every means is being used to subvert and destroy my Government...President Kennedy complained about communist subversion. What about capitalist, imperialist and fascist subversion?[45]

Jagan then challenged the veracity of the seemingly magnanimous statement, by Kennedy to *Izvestia* (in November 1961), that he had no problem with Jagan's Marxism because he was democratically elected. 'Fine words,' Jagan remarked sarcastically. The reality was that, in 1963, the Americans were 'directing the strike behind the scenes,' in a concerted plan to destroy him. Jagan asked portentously:

> Is it the intention to keep the pot boiling here so that the British government, goaded by the Americans, can use the 'situation' to delay indefinitely the granting of independence to this country, as it did last year with the February disturbances to delay the independence talks?' He was correct: the plot, made in Washington in the aftermath of his visit of October 1961, was unfolding precisely as he sketched it. In despair, Cheddi exclaimed to Governor Grey: 'This is western democracy in action'![46]

Repetition is warranted here! By 1963 Burnham, of course, knew that he was America's chosen man. Jagan had made that eventuality possible. After the 1961 elections, Burnham could, justifiably, have been pronounced dead politically. But Jagan's inept and unstatesmanlike presentation of himself at the White House and in Washington generally in October of that year, particularly in his one-on-one exchange with President Kennedy (this cannot be overstated), gave Burnham a new lease on his political life. In April 1963, for instance, on the eve of the general strike in which money from the US government played a major role, Burnham skilfully sought to underline the ideological distance between his PNC and Jagan's PPP: 'The governing party [Jagan's PPP] professes to be socialist but by its postures, its statements and the literature it distributes, leads one to the conclusion that its aim is to make Guyana a Soviet satellite.'[47] He had made his point deftly; and it was enough to reassure President Kennedy. But one still does not know where Burnham stood ideologically – arguably until today. This was clearly an attribute, in the context of the Cold War: although neither the British nor the Americans were enamoured of Burnham, he had done enough, bolstered by the infantile political blunders of Jagan himself, to convince the Americans that he was not a communist – he would do as their man.

At this time of delicate political sensitivities when Cold War susceptibilities were preeminent, the PPP's *Mirror* was transparently tactless, carrying numerous articles contemptuous of America while underlining their loyalty to the communist bloc. The PPP would have known that British and American intelligence kept tabs on their every word, but the party, like their leader, genuinely believed that 'history and time were on their side.' They may lose in the short-run, but they would never be deterred. They were in for the long haul. What they believed in was bound to win. It was infinitely more thrilling to travel than to arrive.

Two articles in April 1963 are reflective of the PPP's declared affinity with the Soviet bloc. One, captioned 'Writing on the Wall for Kennedy,' spoke of 'the vast influence' of the Cuban Revolution even on liberals in Latin America:

> They can scorn whatever is identified with communism in the Castro regime, but the fact that Castro has been the first to challenge the authority of the US, refusing to let himself be intimidated despite an economic situation which is extraordinarily difficult as a consequence of the American embargo, places that same Latin American liberal on Castro's side.[48]

Neither did *Mirror* enhance the stature of the PPP in American eyes when reporting the remarks of the Party's guest, American communist Scott Nearing, on the Cuban example:

> The Americans do not wish other Latin American countries to go the Cuban way because it is a threat to their imperial expansion… Mr Khrushchev's actions in the Cuban [missiles] crisis last October [1962] showed his statesmanship. He prevented a war which America wanted.[49]

Jagan was right, the eighty-days strike of 1963 was, indeed, subsidised by funds from the CIA channelled through the AFL-CIO and the AIFLD, obviously at the behest of President Kennedy. Colin Palmer argues that

> the Labour Relations Bill and the general strike provided the occasion for another assault on the [Jagan] government. As in February 1962, there were widespread acts of violence, arson, looting and racially based attacks. British Guiana, particularly its capital [Georgetown],

descended into disorder once again as the country's leaders displayed their enormous incapacities ... The twelve-week strike spluttered to an end on July 6, but not before the colony's psyche had been badly scarred.[50]

The general strike had achieved what the PNC, the UF, and their American sponsors wanted: chaos in order to establish definitively, to the British government, that Jagan no longer controlled the situation in British Guiana. It was therefore ungovernable by Jagan's PPP. A constitutional imposition was inescapable, one necessarily enmeshed in chicanery (even another suspension) to ensure that PR was introduced to oust Jagan, before independence was awarded to non-communists, Forbes Burnham and Peter D'Aguiar, in a feasible coalition. It was a Cold War story through and through, with the CIA pivotal to the process.

II. The Fateful Birch Grove Summit: Macmillan Accedes to Kennedy's Relentless Pressure to Impose Proportional Representation in Order to Destroy Jagan

In early July 1963, with the termination of the strike, Burnham called on Jagan to hold a referendum on PR so that all Guyanese could decide on the electoral system for the conduct of fresh elections. He knew Jagan would lose. But Burnham might not have known that President Kennedy, in his meeting with Prime Minister Harold Macmillan, in England on June 30, 1963, had already ensured that the British would impose PR in British Guiana as a prelude to elections before independence. Kennedy was actively fighting Burnham's corner, deemed crucial to his own crusade to halt the march of Castroism in the Western Hemisphere.

On June 21, 1963, at a meeting at the White House when Richard Helms of the CIA gave a briefing on 'the current situation in British Guiana' (John McCone, director of the CIA was also present), **President Kennedy was forthright that 'British Guiana...[is] the most important topic he has to discuss with the Prime Minister** [Macmillan].' **They also spoke of the 'desirability of inviting Duncan Sandys** [the Colonial Secretary] **to Birch Grove since he is a significant figure in any decision which HMG may make** [emphasis added].'

It is noteworthy that an attachment to this document, 'Points the President might make to Senator [William] Fulbright [Chairman of the Senate Foreign Relations Committee],' included a comment attributed to Janet Jagan, minister of home affairs, on June 20, 1963: 'British Guiana will establish closer relations with Russia and Cuba when it becomes independent; and the BG government is "deeply grateful" to Fidel Castro's Cuba for "helping us when we were stuck.'" It was also noted that the British government supported Jagan's government by having its Coldstream Guards protect Cuban and Russian vessels in Georgetown discharging food and fuel to break the strike. The latter was, of course, prolonged (eighty days) with funds from the CIA.[51]

The same day (June 21, 1963), Dean Rusk informed the US ambassador in London (David Bruce) that British Guiana was 'the principal subject' the president intended to discuss at the meeting. He then explained precisely what they wanted from Macmillan. They were after a final solution; and it had to be extracted before the Constitutional Conference in London, scheduled for October 1963:

> **Our fundamental position is that the UK must not leave behind in the Western Hemisphere a country with a Communist Government in control. Independence of British Guiana with a government led by the PPP is unacceptable to us. Our objective in London is to get HMG to take effective action to remove Jagan from government before Independence...**
>
> Last Fall [autumn] Macmillan agreed to this objective, but he has now reverted to the view that the UK should wash its hands of British Guiana by granting early independence, leaving the mess on our doorstep...**I would welcome your thoughts** [Ambassador

President Kennedy prevails upon Harold Macmillan that Cheddi Jagan must be removed from office before independence, Birch Grove, Sussex, 30 June 1963

Bruce] **on how best to convince our British friends of the deadly seriousness of our concern and our determination that British Guiana shall not become independent with a Communist government** [emphasis added].[52]

By June 30, 1963, when Kennedy met Prime Minister Harold Macmillan at Birch Grove, solely for that purpose, his advocacy of the removal of Jagan before independence had been pursued so passionately and relentlessly that, in the end, Macmillan caved in. (The prime minister, demoralised by the Profumo/Keeler Scandal, was most vulnerable to a bullying president.) Yet it is worth noting the tone of the response of the British foreign secretary, Lord Home, to Dean Rusk, the secretary of state, regarding the contentious issue of independence for British Guiana:

> Time and again you face us with situations in which you ask us to vote for resolutions which will undermine any chance we have to keep pace of independence for our remaining colonial territories under reasonable control. **Time and again you beg us on bended knees to prevent British Guiana from achieving independence within the foreseeable future, but everywhere else you make it almost impossible for us to maintain control. I do not seem to persuade your people that you cannot have it both ways** [emphasis added].[53]

Kennedy argued that if the British granted independence to Jagan, his country would become a communist state. Therefore, it was imperative to delay independence while imposing the system of proportional representation in order to secure the removal of Jagan by the ballot box. He underlined that Cuba would be the major issue in the presidential elections of 1964, and 'adding British Guiana to Cuba could well tip the scales, and someone would be elected who would take military action against Cuba.' Kennedy argued that Americans would not tolerate a situation in which the 'Soviet Union had leap-frogged over Cuba to land on the continent on the Western Hemisphere.'[54] The British were left with no doubts that the president considered the removal of Jagan vital to his re-election in November 1964. No second Cuba!

Duncan Sandys (son-in-law of Winston Churchill), the right-wing colonial secretary, then remarked to Kennedy and Macmillan that the best solution would be a Burnham-D'Aguiar coalition to which they would then grant independence – precisely the US's ultimate objective. Sandys added that they would need US support if they were to 'resume direct rule in the colony,' as they were apprehensive of the fallout if they were to suspend the Constitution a second time (the first was in October 1953). Kennedy assured him: 'It would be a pleasure…we would go all out to the extent necessary.' Sandys stated that the Constitution would be suspended, direct British rule introduced and PR imposed to secure the election of a non-communist alternative to Jagan: a coalition of Burnham and D'Aguiar in elections to be held in 1964.[55] As noted earlier, the CIA had already been subsidising an anti-communist campaign of violence unleashed by Burnham's African supporters (in league with Peter D'Aguiar's rabidly anti-communist United Force, the Catholic Church, and the trade unions), in 1962–63, in order to delay independence. Riots and strikes, fuelled with CIA funds, enveloped the colony to the brink of civil war. Jagan had wasted his trumps; his country had become ungovernable; he was a broken man; he had no non-communist allies who really mattered. All the leaders in the Caribbean, bar Castro, rejected communism and were antagonistic to Jagan.

Duncan Sandys was as resolved as Kennedy to destroy Jagan, but he was wary of world reaction to a plan that was patently contrived to oust a democratically elected leader. This was the context in which, in implementing Kennedy's anti-communist directive, Sandys devised, in the autumn of 1963, a means to trick Jagan into signing a document giving him sole authority to change the electoral system to PR purely to facilitate Jagan's defeat. It is enthralling, if depressing, to trace the Byzantine process by which Sandys succeeded in luring Jagan to acquiesce in his own demise.

III. Closing the Stable Door after the Horse Has Bolted: Jagan's Seeks to Mend Fences with the Americans

Having realised that the Kennedy administration was vigorously in pursuit of his political demise, Jagan contacted the consul general in Georgetown (Melby) three times in ten days, in August-September 1963, belatedly seeking to mend fences with the American imperialists. Melby conveyed to the State Department, on September 5, 1963, the desperate state in which Jagan found himself, convinced that the US government 'had now adopted as its policy the attitude of the right extremist, namely, Jagan must go.' Melby captured the gist of Jagan's apprehensions regarding his political survival; yet Cheddi, strangely, appeared to be oblivious of the brutal realities of the Cold War:

> America, Jagan said, is worried about B.G. becoming another Cuba. Castro, in reference to B.G., once laughingly asked if socialism had ever come about without revolution. **Jagan said he had openly discussed his socialist** [communist] **ideals with the President** [Kennedy on October 25, 1961]**, as well as his determination to bring this about by peaceful means. All he is asking of the US is understanding and assistance so that he can make B.G. the first example of a socialist** [communist] **state created by non-violent means** [emphasis added].[56]

The consul general could not offer Jagan any reassurance of assistance from the US. The situation had deteriorated beyond repair. And as Jagan naively admitted to Melby – obviously without realising its import – by declaring to Kennedy in October 1961 (during his one-on-one exchange with the president) his commitment to creating a communist state by peaceful means, he had set himself up as the prime target for American subversion, after Fidel Castro.

Jagan had revealed the crux of his fatal encounter with Kennedy – his belief in communism – in his belated fence-mending with Melby:

> I, of course, made no specific reply to Jagan's question as to what could be done to improve B.G.-US relations. I noted that when matters had deteriorated to the extent he described, it was usually a long way back to more normal relations, an observation that seemed to depress him. I also briefly reviewed the usual points about doubts in the US, both public opinion and government, on his ultimate objectives, his relations with Cuba and the communist bloc. As he talked much about his socialism [communism], I said the question in the mind of many Americans was precisely that: whether it was his socialism [communism] or socialism [communism] controlled by another power [the Soviet Union]. To this Jagan said he had once invited representatives of the US press and government to see for themselves who ruled B.G.; he was thinking of renewing this invitation.[57]

IV. The Sinister Sandys Plan: Jagan Tricked into Signing a Document Contrived Specifically for His Own Political Emasculation

Jagan was trying to close the stable door after the horse had bolted. On October 7, 1963, three weeks before the convening of the constitutional conference in London to discuss the issue of independence, Sandys held a meeting with his officials in the Colonial Office to underline the objectives of the conference – the removal of Jagan at all costs, as Macmillan had assured Kennedy at Birch Grove on June 30. Therefore, **they had to ensure that the conference ended in a deadlock to facilitate the imposition of the final solution: delaying independence until after elections were held, under proportional representation (PR).** The following are the verbatim notes of the meeting:

> (1) It was important to ensure (both at the conference and in the meantime) that Dr Jagan and Mr Burnham failed to agree either on the terms of reference or on the composition of any good offices commission. Mr Burnham should be encouraged to say that half the members of any commission must be drawn from countries having proportional representation, and **the Department should also make sure that there was someone present at the conference to advise Mr Burnham generally.**
>
> (2) **It was agreed that *when* the conference ended in deadlock, the British Government would announce the suspension of the constitution and the resumption of direct rule. At the same time,**

it would be announced that an election would be held under the new electoral system in 1964 [proportional representation]**, and that the British Government would review the situation in the light of its result.**

(3) The Secretary of State [Duncan Sandys] asked what progress had been made in encouraging alternative parties to form…It was reported that a Muslim party might soon be formed under the leadership of Hoosain Ghanie. The Secretary of State said that financial encouragement should be given to Mr Ghanie and no questions asked [emphasis added].[58]

Sandys was determined that Jagan and Burnham **must not** reach a compromise towards the formation of a coalition government, and that no UN or Commonwealth commission be approved by them to facilitate any such reconciliation. In fact, Macmillan had already advised Kennedy, in early September 1963, that it was essential that Burnham must not be lured by Jagan into any initiative for a UN commission to explore options for a united front government or any other conception of a coalition, for which Jagan had been canvassing. And he was leaving it to the president to ensure that Burnham arrived at the constitutional conference in London, in October 1963, adamantly opposed to any compromise with Jagan. Macmillan concluded: 'I assume…that your people will be doing what they can to discourage any joint moves, either for a coalition or for an outside enquiry, either of which might upset all our plans.'[59]

As the document above shows, the British, too, were prepared to provide counsel to Burnham to ensure that he was recalcitrant to any compromise, thus enabling the parameters for an imposition. However, suspending the Constitution of British Guiana for the second time in ten years in order to remove Jagan (again), who had won two democratic elections since the first suspension in October 1953 (in 1957 and 1961), would necessarily trigger a storm of international revulsion against the British, despite the steadfast support from Kennedy. On October 23, 1963, the day after the conference convened in London, Sandys adjourned the plenary session and met the three Guyanese leaders individually because, as premeditated, they could not reach agreement on the three key issues: (i) the electoral system (the British, the Americans, Burnham, and D'Aguiar supported a change to PR; Jagan the retention of the first-past-the-post system); elections before independence (only Jagan opposed this); and a change of the voting age from twenty-one to eighteen (advocated by Jagan only).

Sandys told Jagan that there were three options available: they try to reach agreement [he did not mean that]; they adjourn without an agreement [and a unilateral imposition by him]; **or the secretary of state was 'asked to make an arbitral decision** [imposition by invitation] [emphasis added].' **Jagan said** that he had 'more or less' come to the same conclusion. He added that he would make a final effort to reach an agreement with Burnham, failing which he was 'prepared to accept that the Secretary of State [Sandys] would have to impose a decision.'[60]

Sandys met Burnham later that day and he, too, was presented with the three options. Unfailingly shrewd and ever the supreme political operator, Burnham said that 'in private he accepted that there were only these three possibilities, but he could not accept the third in public.' (His nationalist pride would not allow him to be seen to embrace an imposition by the White imperialists. Yet he knew full well he was their man. They told him so, emphatically.) Burnham informed Sandys that Jagan was inclined towards acceptance of an imposition. Burnham realised it was imperative to ensure that Jagan did not change his mind. Therefore, it was incumbent on him to reach **no compromise** with Jagan, in the final hour, because (as he was counselled beforehand) a potential imposition by Sandys was the stratagem devised by Sandys to favour Burnham exclusively.[61]

Dr Fenton Ramsahoye, Jagan's attorney general (1961–64) and a member of his delegation at the conference in London, told me that, worn down by the violence fomented in Guyana by opposition forces (aided and abetted by the Americans and the British), and aggravated by the impossibility of a compromise with Burnham and D'Aguiar, the PPP delegates met at Lancaster House and agreed that they would defer to the Opposition on all three contentious issues, including changing the electoral system to PR and having elections before independence, providing Sandys would concede a date for independence. The PPP delegates felt that securing a date for independence, even with elections before independence – under PR – as a precondition, offered them a potentially decisive psychological advantage, significant though the concessions they were prepared to make. A date for independence would energise their campaign, and conceivably take them over the line, to another electoral victory, however slender. They were genuinely ignorant of the monumental resolve of the British and the Americans, at the highest level, to destroy Jagan in order to stall the road to independence. In retrospect, Ramsahoye thinks that the meeting room which they were allocated at Lancaster House was bugged by MI5 (this was standard practice). Therefore, Sandys was, in all likelihood, fully apprised of Jagan's revised stance – that he was ready to accede to Burnham and D'Aguiar on all the outstanding issues, save a date for independence, which they were prepared to advance as their sole *quid pro quo*.[62]

I concur with Dr Ramsahoye about the bugging of their deliberations (MI5 unfailingly intercepted Jagan's letters and telephone calls to the CPGB and other communists). Therefore, the intelligence services arguably were even more zealous in recording everything that Jagan did and said in London in 1963. (The relevant MI5 files, after early 1961, are not declassified.) Sandys must have been informed that Jagan's team would be obdurate on a date for independence as the sole precondition for making concessions on the other key issues. **Sandys would have known (from MI5) that the best way to ensure that Jagan did accede to the colonial secretary being the sole arbiter of the contentious issues, was to ensnare him with the illusion of the necessity to set a date for independence.** Sandys, consequently, devised a way to trick the unsuspecting Jagan, who (his Marxism and anti-colonialism notwithstanding) was inclined to accept the myth of British notions of fair-play and even-handedness, even in transactions with those whom they differed with fundamentally. If Jagan (a dentist by training) had relied on the learned counsel of his legal advisers (Dr Ramsahoye and Professor John Griffiths of LSE), he would probably have been more circumspect of the motives of the British and arguably have responded differently.

On the evening of October 24, 1963, Sandys contacted Jagan and requested that he should go alone the next morning to Lancaster House. Suspecting nothing untoward, Jagan went to see Sandys, accompanied only by the secretary of the British Guiana government Office in London, Lee Akbar (later Lee Samuel). She related to me the somewhat bizarre and disturbing atmosphere at Lancaster House that morning of October 25, 1963 (uncannily, precisely two years to the day of Jagan's fatal meeting with Kennedy at the White House). Burnham and D'Aguiar were there too, but, ominously, they had all their delegates with them, including their legal advisers. Lee Akbar sat behind Jagan, who was a lonesome spectator. A clever woman, Lee knew instinctively that something was being hatched, so she whispered to Jagan that she ought to go back to their office on Cockspur Street (not far away) and get Dr Ramsahoye, Brindley Benn, and his other PPP delegates to join him. He told her that was not necessary. Very unsettled by the atmosphere, she soon repeated her suggestion to Jagan, but he dismissed it again.

Lee Akbar recalls that a document was passed around shortly thereafter which Dr Jagan was the first to sign, followed by Burnham and D'Aguiar in that order. Her instincts regarding the palpable eeriness of Lancaster House that day left her with a deep foreboding, so much so that as soon as she returned to the office, she told Jagan's colleagues, who had no idea what had transpired, that the boss had just relinquished their future without even realising it.[63]

As Dr Ramsahoye told Mike Thomson of the BBC (Radio 4, August 30, 2010):

> When Jagan was called to a meeting [at Lancaster House] with Duncan Sandys and the other Guyanese leaders, and Sandys told him that he wasn't to bring anyone else with him – he was to come alone – I thought that something was afoot. If I were present, I would not have allowed him to sign that letter.

I wish to add that Lee Akbar told me that she accompanied Jagan everywhere he went in London for the duration of the Conference in October 1963. She said: 'I was his baggage lady.' She even speculated that Jagan's mind was clogged by the tortuous theoretical discussions he pursued with his communist friends in North West London, often well past midnight. Lee was referring to Cheddi's extended meetings with his old comrade and mentor, Billy Strachan, and other members of the CPGB, at Billy's home in Colindale Avenue, Colindale (NW9). Though fit and in good health, she was worn down by it; she felt that Cheddi, too, was exhausted by the exertions of those prolonged sessions of Marxist discourse. His capacity for clear thinking was impaired by what she considered an irrelevant distraction with detrimental consequences for his primary responsibility.[64]

This appears to be corroborated by the governor, Sir Ralph Grey, after Jagan signed the fatal document. Sandys had convened a plenary session on October 28, 1963, in order, ostensibly, to facilitate a final ventilation of views on the contentious electoral system. This is Governor Grey's assessment of their respective presentations:

> Burnham led off with a quiet and very competent argument against the present system and in favour of the West German type of Proportional Representation. D'Aguiar bumbled as usual; and overstated his case against first-past-the-post...**Jagan (who told me afterwards he was so tired he could hardly think) stumbled through a justification of first-past-the-post and his own record** [emphasis added].[65]

Jagan had given Sandys a blank cheque to do precisely as he had connived for British Guiana. But neither Kennedy nor Macmillan could have envisaged that an unsuspecting Jagan could conceivably have handed them such a gift, on a platter, without demurral. Miraculously, there was no necessity to suspend the Constitution; no imperative to impose direct rule, with the potential for exciting international outrage – high-handedness in the imposition of a PR solution. But as Lloyd Searwar, who had accompanied Jagan to meet Kennedy at the White House in October 1961, told me, Jagan was 'shafted by consent.'

The trick was perpetrated through this now legendary infamous document of October 25, 1963, drafted by Duncan Sandys and signed by the three political leaders:

TO THE SECRETARY OF STATE FOR THE COLONIES

> At your request we have made further efforts to resolve the differences between us on the constitutional issues which require to be settled before British Guiana secures independence, in particular the electoral system, the voting age, and the question whether fresh elections should be held before independence.

> We regret to have to report to you that we have not succeeded in reaching agreement; and we have reluctantly come to the conclusion that there is no prospect of an agreed solution. **Another adjournment of the Conference for further discussions between ourselves would therefore serve no useful purpose and would result in** *further delaying British Guiana's independence* **and in continued uncertainty in the country.**
>
> In these circumstances we are agreed to ask the British Government to settle on their authority all outstanding constitutional issues, and we undertake to accept these decisions [emphasis added].[66]

CHEDDI JAGAN
L.F.S. BURNHAM
P.S. D'AGUIAR

Sandys had lured Jagan into signing the document – he was the first to do so – by including the strategic sentence in bold in the second paragraph above. Read quickly by an unsuspecting, 'tired' individual in virtual isolation amidst a colony of enemies, and bereft of legal counsel, it is readily suggestive of the interpretation that Sandys's arbitration by invitation would serve **not to delay independence** whatever his verdict on the other two contentious issues. This suggestion of a possible date for independence (as was agreed by Jagan's team in the allocated room in Lancaster House, most likely bugged by MI5) must have struck a singular and decisive chord with Jagan.

Before Sandys had revealed his plan, Janet Jagan responded: 'I am surprised they [Cheddi] agreed to sign.'[67] **Cheddi explained why he agreed to Sandys's intervention:**

> **I am assuming that independence is obviously forthcoming...I have put my confidence in the hands of the British government and I hope decisions will be taken on the basis of constitutional principles, on British and Commonwealth precedents and conventions**...independence is absolutely necessary...for the country cannot get anywhere without it [emphasis added].[68]

However, Sandys adjudicated against Jagan on all the unresolved issues – he changed the electoral system to proportional representation (PR) without setting a date for independence; he rejected the reduction of the voting age to eighteen; and he ruled that general elections must be held (under PR) before another constitutional conference was convened. The British had delivered even more than the Americans were expecting – to Burnham and D'Aguiar. A month after the imposition, Alec Douglas-Home (formerly Lord Home, the foreign secretary), who had succeeded Harold Macmillan as prime minister in October 1963, joked with US Secretary of State Dean Rusk that it was 'slightly awkward that Dr Jagan had given so little trouble at the conference.' He added that without the support of several leaders in the West Indies for a change of the electoral system (in order to defeat Jagan), international pressure against their action would have been intense.[69]

Cheddi offers his irrepressible smile to Duncan Sandys (secretary of state for the colonies), utterly oblivious of the trick the latter had contrived for him, October 1963

Forbes Burnham (centre and standing tall) at the decisive constitutional conference in London, October 1963, when Jagan was lured into signing a document that empowered the colonial secretary Duncan Sandys to impose proportional representation, which eventuated in Burnham leading Guyana to independence in May 1966. The others (left to right): Neville Bissember, Winifred Gaskin, Llewellyn John, Eugene Correia and H.M.E. Cholmondeley

V. *Jagan's Vain Campaign to Overturn the PR Debacle: Burnham Gloats at His Monumental Blunder and Misplaced Optimism That the Labour Party Would Repudiate the Sandys Trickery*

Jagan's immediate reaction to Sandys's plan, brazenly framed to ensure that he was assigned to the political wilderness, was marked by impotent rage. He had misread Sandys's motives as badly as he had the infamous document that he signed. Too late was his discovery that the British, who had (after 1957) stuck with him for several years and would have defended him to the end if he had moderated his communist creed, were now in the pocket of the Americans:

> I do not feel bound to accept Mr Sandys's decision because independence was a condition of his imposing a solution **[not so!]**. Not to have a definite date for independence fixed is a betrayal of trust on the part of Mr Sandys. It is clear that this decision of the British Government is in keeping with the wishes of the United States Government and is subservient to it **[True!]**. Mr Sandys has decided to hold another conference after the elections. **This is a clear breach of faith, for it was understood when he was given the authority that the intention of all the participants was that this should be the last conference.** [Jagan did believe that Sandys would have set a date for Independence.] Mr Sandys has rigged the electoral system and by surrendering to the irresponsible Opposition in British Guiana, the British Government has placed a premium on intimidation, violence, looting, rape and arson.[70]

On November 7, 1963, seething over the trickery perpetrated on him, Jagan wrote to Prime Minister Alec Douglas-Home that Sandys's decision 'constitutes a breach of faith and is a betrayal of trust placed in the British government.' He repeated that in giving Sandys the authority to adjudicate on the contentious issues, he 'expected that the British government would act in good faith in transferring residual powers to my government and resolving differences on the basis of solid constitutional principles and precedent.' Jagan was obviously not cognisant of the capitulation of Macmillan to President Kennedy's implacable pressure at their Birch Grove summit on June 30, 1963. Moreover, he did not possess the intellectual acuity or the political adroitness to temper his Marxist philosophy, consonant with the fact that the British 'imperialists' had endeavoured to bat for him, for quite some time (virtually to the end), even as the Americans were demanding his head.

Burnham's response (in London) to his victory, though engineered through Anglo-American duplicity, was totally in character. He pretended that he had nothing to celebrate, downplaying the magical reality that his colonial masters had rescued his practically moribund political career, while continuing to flaunt his anti-colonial nationalist passions, seamlessly accommodated by his imperialist sponsors. He even affected repugnance at the imposition, pretending to be appalled that the British had not set a date for independence. In fact, Burnham was dancing on Jagan's utter humiliation – elated at his political suicide:

> I am pleased about nothing. A nationalist can never be pleased over the indignity of an imposition. We find no reason for jubilation because B.G. is still without a firm date for independence. [He was never in favour of Independence under Jagan, Sydney King's fears of his capitulation notwithstanding.] Perhaps Jagan should rethink his naïve statement in which he expressed great confidence in the British sense of fair-play and justice…I agree with Dr Jagan that the people of B.G. should stand firm in this hour of betrayal – of them by him.[71]

Burnham knew that Jagan was broken; and that he was the one desperate for an imposition by Sandys, deluded that independence was still in the offing. Burnham knew already what the score was: it was exclusively about his elevation; and he was fully aware that any imposition, even if it entailed suspension of the constitution, would necessarily grant him PR and elections before independence. That was why the British (Duncan Sandys specifically) had counselled him not to compromise with Jagan on any initiative towards a coalition; they had also provided him with an adviser to ensure that he followed the script designed to make him the top dog. Burnham's feigned aversion to an imposition by invitation, therefore, could not have been mistaken by many as an authentic response. It is doubtful, too, if Sydney King's stated opposition to imposition by invitation was genuine. He certainly had no desire to live in an independent Guyana led by Jagan, the leader of Indians bent on Indian domination after independence, as he perceived it. Surely, he would have appreciated that any imposition by the British (given America's consuming fear of Jagan's communism and Guyana becoming 'a second Cuba') would be advantageous to Burnham and Africans.

Sydney King argued:

> If what the Colonial Office release says is true, the request of the B.G. leaders is an abject surrender of manhood. For men who profess nationalism, nothing could be more shameful. Judged by their own standards, they are utterly bankrupt. Culturally and spiritually, we are on our death bed. There is, of course, another side to it. The whole world has been saying B.G.'s leaders cannot agree among themselves. This accusation now falls on the ground. They have disagreed in order to agree, achieving parity in disgrace. This performance is new evidence that a Guianese nation does not exist.[72] (It still does not.)

For King (like Burnham), his rejection of imposition by invitation was arguably an affectation of a spurious nationalism because only the British had the power to withhold independence from Jagan. Burnham had already cleverly reinvented himself as America's man to whom the British were now beholden, having been chosen to save Guyana from communism. That hour had come! It could only be Burnham's hour.

When Jagan agreed to the imposition by Duncan Sandys, his party's newspaper, *Mirror*, expressed consternation at his decision. They were clearly perplexed by it, as they groped towards an absurd explanation: 'Why this admission of Guyanese inferiority, and why the supine and humiliating acceptance of white supremacy, and acknowledgement of a master race? We hope that all is not irretrievably lost.'[73] When Sandys delivered his ruling – a flagrantly partisan judgement against Jagan on every count – *Mirror* sought solace in philosophical reflections, which they commended to their innocent leader. Diminished by the trickery on the part of the British in league with their unyielding anti-communist American friends, Jagan could not have been reassured by the sentiments of some of his demoralised comrades – possibly sarcastic: neither bouquet nor balm!

> In his hour of travail he [Jagan] must find the balm of consolation in the philosophical sayings and practical maxims which, through the centuries, have served to stimulate man's interest for good…'Sweet are the uses of adversity'; 'I am the master of my faith, I am the captain of my soul'; 'A man's reach must exceed his grasp, or what's a heaven for?'and 'The menace of the years finds, and shall not find me unafraid.'[74]

A sense of futility soon obtruded as *Mirror* sought to accommodate the reality that Jagan, having possessed virtually all the trumps in March 1960 at the conclusion of the Constitutional Conference in London (chaired by Iain Macleod), was about to face the likelihood of a prolonged post-colonial irrelevance in the political wilderness. *Mirror's* despair was eloquent in the aftermath of the Sandys imposition: 'There is hypocrisy. Guyanese know British hypocrisy to be the most odious in the whole world, and we blush for the decent British citizens who must live among Guyanese and justify the perfidy of their government.' Impotent rage!

David Smithers, the correspondent for the *Guiana Graphic*, interviewed both Jagan and Burnham in London after Duncan Sandys had, unashamedly, conceded everything to the latter. Yet, as he reported, Burnham was still professing that he had nothing to be grateful for or be exultant about. Smithers conveyed the slick essence of the man:

> …Forbes Burnham, who is almost as indignant about the 'Sandys Plan' as Jagan – because it sets no firm date for independence [*sic*] – is determined not to return to London for the next and final conference with the Colonial Office, which is projected for after the next elections. **He will insist that it must be held in Georgetown** [an absurdity!] **He even went so far as to say 'independence is sometimes a mere formality'**…[75]

Regarding the latter, Burnham was letting the cat out of the bag. All he would have to do is to turn up at the next conference; the big prize was reserved for him, whether Jagan was there or not.

Burnham was studiously deceptive. Independence was withheld from Jagan; the granting of PR virtually guaranteed that Burnham would accede to power in a likely coalition with the United Force; any 'final conference' would be essentially a rubber stamp to grant him independence. He had a lot to be grateful for: Jagan's communist creed and his poverty of statesmanship; D'Aguiar's and the Catholic Church's anti-communist crusade; Sydney King's Afrocentric cultural and political grassroots engagement; Kennedy's obsession with removing Jagan before independence to avoid 'a second Cuba'; and the Macmillan government's acquiescing to Kennedy regarding the latter. Such luck! But Burnham, ever relishing the role of the anti-colonialist and 'third world' nationalist (though light on ideology), never did fancy the perception of himself as having been anointed by the White men in power in Washington and London – their Uncle Tom!

Meanwhile, after the shock of Sandys's shamelessly partisan plan, Jagan was floundering. It was the end of the road for him with regard to leading British Guiana to independence. Jagan was henceforth largely irrelevant to the process. Burnham knew it, and he relished rubbing salt in Jagan's gaping wound with his legal astuteness and his penchant for mischievous ridicule. As David Smithers reported from London:

> Of the suggestion hinted at by Dr Jagan that the PPP might not participate in the next elections [under PR], Burnham declared: '**I cannot see how Dr Jagan who was most anxious to leave the matter to the decision of the Colonial Secretary can nullify an election which is the result of an imposition by the Secretary of State for the Colonies** [emphasis added]'.[76]

Jagan told Smithers that he intended to take the matter of the colony's independence back to the United Nations, but he wished to discuss it first with the Labour opposition leader, Harold Wilson. He had sent telegrams of protest promptly to the president of Ghana, Kwame Nkrumah, and the prime minister of India, Jawaharlal Nehru. Jagan was on a journey to nowhere.

Miles Fitzpatrick, a young intellectual who had quit the PPP by 1963, saw clearly that PR would exacerbate the racism in Guyanese politics; and he expressed incredulity that it could engender a genuine alliance between Africans and Indians. Yet he was hoping against hope for a last-minute compromise between Jagan and Burnham. Miles ought to have known that the prize was virtually reserved for Burnham; he had no incentive or inclination whatsoever for a reconciliation with Jagan:

The institutionalisation of racial politics will now be carried a stage further by the introduction of the system of PR. It is therefore highly unlikely that either of the two opposition parties [PNC and UF] can gain a majority of the votes. Thus, unless the PPP wins outright [highly unlikely], a PR election that is contested by all three groups will result in either a PNC-PPP coalition [inconceivable!] or a PNC-UF anti-socialist [anti-communist] front.

The failure of the two main parties [PPP and PNC] to reach agreement before, or at, the conference, the commencement of talks between the PNC and UF in London, and the obvious dynamics of an election fought on an anti-PPP ticket, all combine to make the latter alternative a definite probability.

There thus seems to be only one honest course to take – the two mass parties must combine to reject the colonialist imposition and mobilise support for a conference in Guiana that will settle their outstanding differences and fix a date for independence.

The infamous letter to Sandys must be immediately rejected as an unauthorised undertaking given under the influence of the wilful misrepresentation of the Colonial Office that a date for independence would be fixed by them.[77]

A pie in the sky!

Fitzpatrick had posed the question of Burnham's sincerity in expressing 'dissatisfaction' with the outcome of the conference. He did not know that the whole exercise was orchestrated, through Anglo-American subterfuge, to neutralise Jagan, the communist. But he did observe that Burnham's 'dissatisfaction' with the Sandys Plan was just 'a hypocritical smirk,' given his 'cynical manoeuvring' in London. It was precisely that. But Miles could not have known the magnitude of President Kennedy's angst, and that he had prevailed upon Macmillan (wounded by the Profumo scandal by the summer of 1963) to shaft Jagan. Besides, L.F.S. Burnham knew that tomorrow belonged to him. He would not have wanted anything to change, for he had risen from the ashes of defeat and despair in August 1961 to being on the threshold of power after October 1963. He had no need to collaborate with Jagan; the supposedly halcyon days of the early 1950s held no nostalgic appeal for him.

Yet Burnham persisted in mocking Jagan's decision to ask the British to impose a solution to the contentious constitutional issues at the London conference. Jagan had made allegations of Kennedy's instrumentality in the imposition of Sandys's rulings against him. Burnham responded with mischievous adroitness, as he sought to demoralise him further:

Let me concede, as a lawyer would, that that proposition is correct, and that the US Government was particularly interested in the outcome of the conference and preferred a particular outcome so far as the electoral system is concerned [PR, as Burnham and D'Aguiar wanted]. Is not this naïve of the same Dr Jagan, who says that the US Government would be interested in a particular outcome, to entrust the political future and the destiny of this country to the greatest friend of the US Government?[78]

He was right. More studied ridicule would emanate from the sagacious brain of this astute operator – possibly the best the region has ever produced. In February 1964, for instance, he told a mammoth crowd of his supporters in Georgetown of his efforts (spurious though it was) to reach an agreement with Jagan, 'before the fateful document was signed.' He jeered, before the cheering jubilant masses, at Jagan's signing of the document conceived by Sandys: 'Some people have learnt to write. They had a pen and there was ink!'[79] This was peculiarly galling, as it was suggestive of the belatedly literate Indian, the *arriviste* 'coolie,' juxtaposed with the pedigreed African scribe. For many of the Indian supporters of Jagan, the Sandys Plan was a kind of social death towards the end of empire.

But it is instructive to reflect on an event shortly before the fateful conference in London in October 1963. Lloyd Searwar was not a member of the delegation, but he accompanied Jagan as far as New York. (He had gone with him to the White House in October 1961.) His tale is revealing for the fount of goodwill many foreign capitalists still had for Cheddi; it also illuminates what Searwar meant when he characterised Jagan as 'closed up,' a man with 'hang ups' who 'never left the plantation' – honest but naïve, and lacking in statesmanship:

> Cheddi went through New York to the Constitutional talks at which he was tricked by Duncan Sandys. When we were in New York, Mrs Vijaya Lakshmi Pandit [1900-90], Nehru's sister and India's permanent representative to the UN, asked Cheddi to go and see her. He and I went to the exquisite Carlyle Hotel where the Indians were based. He had a chat with Mrs Pandit. She said that Lester Pearson, the new Canadian Prime Minister [1963-68], had been on to her. She gathered from him that the British were planning something to get Cheddi out of office, and that he ought to be very careful. Mrs Pandit [had]...the aristocratic bearing of the Nehrus, but she was warm and she came down to street level to see us off in our taxi. But Cheddi said to me as soon as we were in the taxi: 'Lloyd, you can't really bother with the Nehrus. They have always been rich, wealthy people,' or something to that effect. He wasn't addressing what she had just told him about British machinations. The woman had been almost motherly to him, but he could not see beyond her family's wealth and upper caste. That was Cheddi – very closed up. And, of course, he went on to London and was duly tricked.[80]

For Cheddi Jagan, however, this was a tactical blip in the supreme mission, the noble pursuit of communism: 'Difficulties there will be; the battle will be long and hard. But win we will. History and time are on our side!' The Marxist vision could rationalise such setbacks as transitory deviations in the inevitably triumphant struggle against a moribund capitalism; the apparent defeat would evoke a resurgent spirit to energise the true communist for the millenarian calling. In this battle, as he had done in 1948, 1953, and 1964, he would mobilise his Indo-Guyanese base, particularly the indefatigable sugar workers. They remained at the core of his political mission: no sacrifice was too great to demand of them. They were the steadfast foundation that sustained Jagan's communist faith. And he remained, to the end of his life, a very simple, ever accessible, charming man. Most Indians never failed to vote for him. Very few ever questioned his communist creed, even many for whom it was discordant with their entrepreneurial instincts.

The reality, however, was that Burnham was the victor. Violence had paid off. Jagan's defeat at the polls was virtually assured. There was no way he could secure a majority under PR. He urged his supporters to initiate 'a hurricane of protests' to get the British to revoke their 'iniquitous decision.' He contended that he was not bound to abide by Sandys's ruling 'because independence was a condition of his imposing a solution.' It was a 'betrayal of trust.' Belatedly, he recognised the foundation of the trick for which he had fallen:

> It is clear that the decision is in keeping with the wishes of the American government and is subservient to it…The machinations of the Imperialists cannot destroy the PPP. I call upon the people of Guyana to stand firm in this hour of betrayal.[81]

Having asserted that his enemies were rewarded for their violence, he would now seek to retaliate, in order to stall new elections under PR, scheduled for late 1964.

It was a strategy stimulated largely by misplaced optimism that the opposition Labour Party in the UK was opposed to the Sandys Plan, particularly the imposition of PR; moreover, that if Labour did get into office, in October 1964, they would abrogate it. Harold Wilson dubbed the Sandys Plan 'a fiddled constitutional arrangement.' Labour spokesman on colonial affairs, Arthur Bottomley, had also fed the illusion of a reversal when he remarked of the imposition that 'to change the system to a new one looks far too much like manipulation with the blatant purpose of ousting Dr Jagan.' The illusion was magnified by Cheddi's friend, the anti-colonial Labour MP and inveterate left-winger, Fenner Brockway (1888–1988). Writing in *Tribune*, in November 1963, Brockway attributed the 'deadly betrayal' of Jagan to the capitulation of the Conservative government to America's Cold War objectives. He then launched this pie in the sky: 'There is the hope that we may have the opportunity before the last stage of the Sandys betrayal is completed of getting rid of the government with which he shares the guilt. The immediate repudiation of his plan by Arthur Bottomley, Labour's Colonial spokesman, opens the door to a new start.' This fantasy had seduced the youth arm of Jagan's PPP to demand mobilisation of 'the patriotic forces to bring about the reversal' of the imposition and the 'retention of the first-past-the-post electoral system.'[82] A pipe dream, indeed!

The organ of the UF, the *Sun* (December 7, 1963), reported that a few days earlier Fenner Brockway was less sanguine about the prospects of a reversal of the Sandys Plan. It seems that he was confounded by Jagan's signing of the letter addressed to Duncan Sandys, as it did not state unambiguously that setting a date for independence was a precondition for Jagan's request for him to impose a solution. The paper, in an article captioned 'Brockway Slaps Jagan in the Face,' alleged that 'he condemned Jagan for lacking common prudence.' Brockway is quoted thus from *Colonial Freedom News*:

> The trouble is that Dr Jagan signed a letter to Mr Sandys in which nothing was said about these things [a date for independence]. The letter asked Mr Sandys to impose a solution. If Dr Jagan was only willing for Mr Sandys to impose a solution within certain limits, he should surely have defined these terms with some care in his letter. To do so would be no more than minimum prudence obvious to any businessman, let alone an experienced politician.

In fact, the letter was drafted by Sandys with no input from Jagan, who was the first to sign it, and without legal scrutiny from his attorney general, Dr Ramsahoye, who was not even in the building.

PART 3.

1964

Jagan's Anti-PR Campaign and Defeat! Failure of the GAWU Strike for Recognition in the Sugar Industry, Escalating Racial Violence, and America's Role in the Making of the Burnham-D'Aguiar Coalition Government

I. Mobilising His Indian Base against PR: A Futile March and the Evocation of 'Bitter Sugar'

'Bitter sugar' had made Jagan, as time and again, sugar workers struck in an endeavour to secure recognition for his sugar union, whatever its incarnation: GIWU, GSWU, or finally GAWU. The Labour Relations Bill of 1963 was another attempt to secure recognition for his union in the sugar industry. But the TUC, allied to Burnham's PNC, had used that bill as the pretext for an eighty-day strike that crippled the country. The support of the AFL-CIO and the CIA was instrumental in sustaining the strike, engendered primarily by the resolve to inflict irreparable political damage on Jagan. But the irony of the TUC strike that destroyed the Jagan government was its leadership by the president of the TUC, Richard Ishmael (an Indian), president of the MPCA, the old union in the sugar industry that was still recognised by the Sugar Producers' Association (SPA). This was abhorrent to Jagan because most of the sugar workers, Indians, supported him and his union, the Guyana Agricultural Workers' Union (GAWU), not Ishmael's MPCA that claimed to be their representative. Therefore, on the basis of a bogus legitimacy in the sugar industry, the latter was using violence to destabilise the Jagan government.

Towards the end of January 1964, with general elections under PR scheduled for later that year, Jagan sought to stall, if not reverse, the process he had agreed to abide by when he signed the infamous Sandys document. His union, GAWU, resurrected its claim for recognition by the SPA with a strike supported by most of the sugar workers, Indians exclusively. Even before the escalation of the violence triggered by the strike, Martin Carter, the poet and former 'ultra left' disciple of Cheddi, now editor of *Booker News*, had written a confidential internal paper on the GAWU strike, stressing its political foundations. He anticipated the PPP's course of action as early as February 1964:

> The forces of the governing party [PPP] are committed to whatever action is considered to prevent the British Government carrying out the plans announced by Mr Duncan Sandys in October last year. The strike in the sugar industry is mainly one phase of such action. Starting with cane burning as their way of attacking the British Government, anti-personnel violence will now be resorted to. Naïve enough, at first, to believe that the burning of cane…would exert immediate pressure on the British Government, the forces of the governing party will attempt to practise full-scale terrorism, directed to that section of society which appears to have power in civil, economic and commercial life.
>
> The idea being that this section will appeal to the British Government for protection and that the giving of any such protection will lead to so much dislocation of normal life that all plans for constitutional change will be delayed. The forces of the Opposition [PNC and UF] do not want to act in a way that would serve the interests of the governing party. In other words, they do not want to retaliate or take serious reprisals for fear that the British Government would be forced to intervene and take such action as might serve to delay elections under Proportional Representation later this year.[83]

Shortly after the calling of the strike, Jagan's PPP staged a countrywide march in order to galvanise their overwhelmingly Indian supporters to resist the implementation of PR and persist with their campaign for early independence. Peter D'Aguiar, leader of the UF, had reacted to Jagan's march with Burnhamesque derision:

> What can the PPP march achieve? It cannot wipe out Dr Jagan's signature from the letter (signed for Mr Sandys). It cannot change the decision of the British Government. If the PPP is dissatisfied with the decision made by the British Government, then they should remonstrate with Dr Jagan for asking the British Government to decide and agreeing to accept its decision. The march cannot do anything to speed up independence.[84]

The PPP's march only served to concentrate Indian minds on the despair of their political condition – evocative of Africans after the electoral defeat of the PNC in August 1961, with every likelihood of independence being granted to Jagan in 1962. The march was dismissed by the PNC and their African supporters as not worthy of disruption. It reflected the futility of Jagan's political mission following the imposition of PR. It was obvious that the PPP, hitherto ominously embodying Indian supremacy after independence, was clearly on the ropes. Suddenly, with Jagan's enemies the likely recipient of the gift of independence because of the Sandys Plan, Burnham cautioned his supporters not to be 'provoked' or 'baited' into retaliatory violence by the PPP's campaign of 'civil disruption' and 'hatred.' Violence had been the decisive instrument in the PNC/UF pursuit of PR and in delaying independence in 1962–63. But they had no desire, in 1964, to disrupt the path to elections (which Jagan could not win), as well as the virtual assurance of independence in its aftermath. **It was entirely logical for Burnham and D'Aguiar to become belated wagers of peace.**

The idea of the protest march in February 1964 across the coastland of Guyana was absurd. It could change nothing. It was arguably a manifestation of impotent rage by the leader of the PPP, who had squandered the abundant capital he possessed before his meeting with President Kennedy on October 25, 1961. He had entered the Cold War on the side of the Soviet Union and Cuba, and he virtually said so to the president. He and his loyal supporters paid a heavy price for his ideological implacability. Like the PPP's tactless staging of the triumphalist motorcade in August 1961 across British Guiana (after their election victory), the march of 1964 (totally Indian, with the rare exception) further polarised a fractured society.

At the conclusion of the march, on February 9, 1964, Jagan addressed several thousands of his Indian supporters, just outside of Georgetown. Bizarrely, he expressed interest in a PPP-PNC coalition in order to unite Africans and Indians and defeat the 'fascists,' the UF; he also advocated a new conference to fix a date for independence; and he demanded the repudiation of the Sandys Plan. What Jagan said beyond this, however, could be construed as racist fodder to entice his Indian support base to mobilise against elections before independence, under PR. His partisan remarks could not have been conducive to racial concord. In a volatile society, disfigured by racism, this was combustible – a virtual call to arms. I'm quoting him at length. Jagan speaks!

> Let those who think they can dominate Georgetown, New Amsterdam and Mackenzie [Africans] know that these places are not the whole of British Guiana. Let us tell them that we [Indians] also have strength. We have geographical distribution. There is no doubt that the two main crops of this country are produced by people in the PPP [Indians]. Take away rice and you will have starvation in this country…including Georgetown. Take away sugar and what will happen…Economically and politically we [Indians] are powerful. Let them [Africans] note that in all three elections [1953, 1957, 1961] we have won every time.
>
> Let those who preach and practise the psychology of violence and fear [Africans] note these facts that since 1953, when we [Indians] got into power, they [Africans] have tried to make normal government impossible, by instigating disturbances and violence and injecting fear in the minds of the people. Those people who do these things [Africans] must remember that if one side can do it the other side can also do the same. Two sides can play the game…We [Indians] have been humble and cordial, but it seems that some people [Africans] have taken humility and cordiality for weakness.
>
> Instead of respecting these virtues, these people [Africans] have inflicted abuse and beat our comrades [Indians] when they come to Georgetown. Well, comrades, I want to issue a warning to these people [Africans]. We [Indians] have pleaded for calmness for a long time, but it appears that these people [Africans] believe that because we [Indians] are humble and courteous, we are weak. They [Africans] have mistaken humility, courtesy and our peaceful intention for weakness. Your demonstration today shows that we [Indians] have strength also.[85]

It appeared that, momentarily, Jagan had let his Marxist dogmas slip as the racist rhetoric, the sectarian anger, absorbed the pain of political despair. Yet he quickly retrieved the tired nostrums when he vented his hatred at his old enemy, Booker and 'bitter sugar.' Jagan told his followers that there is a distinction between 'property for personal use' and property used 'to exploit the people.' He despised those who exploited the masses and stole their resources. There was no place in his country for Booker and other foreign 'exploiters.' He shouted:

> This nonsense must be stopped. What the PPP wants is the development of this country and the establishment of more industries. But we want those industries to be controlled by the local people. Our masters do not want to stop the exploitation of our people. But the time has come when we have to tell them we are not standing anymore of this. Foreigners bring in a few thousand dollars and take out millions. To hell with them!

II. Jagan's GAWU Calls Strike in the Sugar Industry: Racial Antipathy Ignited into Widespread Racial Violence and Murder

The impotent rage was ablaze as Jagan turned to Duncan Sandys, who had conned him into affixing his signature to his political death warrant. He said the imposition was 'a gross betrayal of a solemn pledge in 1960 by his predecessor, Mr Iain Macleod,' to grant the colony independence by 1962. (Yet, oblivious of consequences, Jagan had denounced Macleod's failure to grant him immediate independence as another act of deception by the imperialists.) He concluded his speech to the deluded marchers on an inconsequential note that belied despair: that Sandys wanted to perpetuate colonial rule; but 'we will show him that the people who are behind me – the people of British Guiana [in fact, only Indians] – will not let this nonsense stand.'[86] There was potential peril in Jagan's floundering scheme to force the British to discard the Sandys Plan.

The PNC, on the other hand, now confident of vanquishing Jagan by electoral means, was sober in their response. By 1964, they had no need to resort to violence, although their capacity to revert to such measures, if deemed necessary, was not diminished. They rejected Jagan's declared enthusiasm for racial unity as 'nothing new,' while recalling it was the PPP that had rescued the so-called fascist UF from electoral annihilation in August 1961. They counselled Jagan that his apprehensions for the future of British Guiana could be alleviated 'with the country achieving independence under PR.' The PNC was fortified by regional and international support; it was not prudent for them to collaborate with a fatally wounded Jagan. They would allow him to slide into ignominy in his desperate campaign to get PR revoked by the show of force – the GAWU-sponsored strike in the sugar industry, which degenerated into racial violence after the PPP march, between February and July 1964. Virtually a civil war, between Africans and Indians!

Peter D'Aguiar's UF was forthright in its denunciation of the GAWU strike, a ploy by the communists to foment disorder in order to pressure the British government to revoke the Sandys Plan. Their organ, the *Sun* (February 29, 1964), in a leader aptly titled 'Anarchy,' argued:

> The violence, the fires and the bombings which have broken out on the sugar estates are a fulfilment of the threat to unleash anarchy on the country [by Jagan]...The GAWU, the cat's-paw of the communist-backed PPP is being used as a tool...Since it is anarchy the PPP is after, the role of the GAWU is to demand the impossible – recognition – while the MPCA is the recognised bargaining agent for the sugar workers. It was for this very purpose that the GAWU was formed – to demand the impossible and when its demands are refused to spread terror and violence on the sugar estates...the final

aim being to show that 'popular resistance' to PR has caused the anarchy which Jagan predicted.

Forbes Burnham was unequivocal regarding the objective of the violence in 1964: 'The burning of the canes synchronises and coincides with the campaign of extreme agitation and hatred started by the PPP after the Sandys decision.'[87] He was categorical that this violence was provoked by them in a concerted campaign to postpone the elections under PR scheduled for 1964. In March 1964, Burnham observed that the strike for recognition of GAWU was purely political in its intent, as were the accompanying acts of terrorism fomented:

> GAWU is the handmaiden of the PPP – being supplied by the PPP with smokeless and noiseless hand grenades, to commit murder, including that of an innocent child [Godfrey Teixeira, son of a Booker employee at Enmore, killed in a school bus bombing]. The strike has little or no industrial significance, but aims at sparking political agitation and intimidation to prevent the holding of fresh elections this year…under a system of PR.[88]

But the US State Department was vigilant in connection with Jagan's machinations, and on May 13, 1964, they reassured their consul general in Georgetown, thus:

> **We concur with guidance to Burnham not to resort to counter-violence, and that he can be assured that if the PPP makes effort to take over the country by force, the US Government will not stand by and see the Opposition crushed by terror** [emphasis added].[89]

Burnham was guaranteed that the grand prize was there for the taking; he must not be lured into jeopardising it. His use of violence in 1962 and 1963, aided and abetted by the CIA, had achieved his aims, which were in harmony with America's Hemispheric imperatives. But, as observed earlier, were it not for the rabid anti-communist crusade of Peter D'Aguiar and his UF – the antithesis of Jagan's communist creed – driven by the consuming fear of D'Aguiar's many Portuguese supporters (primarily Catholics) that Jagan would pursue his 'godless' communism, the 'red menace,' and subvert private enterprise and freedom of speech and religion, it would have been substantially harder for Burnham to reach the mountain top. Besides, the strategic contribution of Sydney King in galvanising and sustaining African loyalty to Burnham between 1961 and 1964, whatever his personal reservations about the man, should not be underestimated.

Jagan, in despair, bemoaned in a radio broadcast on May 30, 1964, that the Opposition PNC and UF had been 'recompensed' by the British. He who had toiled for freedom had it stolen from him. Their 'illegal and unconstitutional activities yielded them rich rewards'; all he had fought for 'now hangs in the balance':

> Factional strife strides the land and our movement lies divided and weak. For many years, while others spent their time and leisure in the pursuit of wealth or pleasure and frivolity, I tread every nook and cranny of our wide country preaching the gospel of nationalism and freedom and seeking to infuse in our diverse groups a Guyanese consciousness which would transcend the bonds of race and creed. Today my hopes of national unity have been cast in the dust. I wish to appeal for the end of racial strife. Racial antagonism is not deeply rooted in this country. But it can easily become so if it is not promptly removed.[90]

By April 1964, the violence on the sugar estates and communal violence in rural areas had made the PPP's demand for recognition of the GAWU by the SPA invisible through the cloud of racial bigotry and violence stalking this inchoate society. Indeed, it had made the colony virtually ungovernable by Jagan's government. Having situated the colony's problems so definitively, if crudely, within the parameters of racial identity, in his speech to his Indian supporters at the termination of the march in February 1964, he sought to defuse the aggravated racist passions engulfing the country with a spurious intervention on the class struggle. Jagan, as usual, returned to his old stalking horse, Jock Campbell's Booker.

Addressing Indians on the West Coast Demerara, where racial atrocities were out of control, Jagan contended that African-Indian antipathy was 'an illusion, not a reality.' The real struggle should be 'with forces from outside.' He explained:

> The trouble in the country was mixed up with the role of the big companies, such as Booker, interested in having and owning everything and exporting big profits...**This is not a racial question. It is a question of the big shots, like Booker and those imperialists who want to ride on the backs of the poor people** [emphasis added].[91]

This was central to Jagan's politics after 1956, with the departure of the so-called ultra-left from the PPP: he would preach the primacy of class struggle while being an adroit practitioner of *realpolitik* with respect to his Indian base. He manipulated racial and religious symbols, pursued policies (such as land settlement schemes for rice cultivation), championed the rights of sugar workers – defensible yet (for Africans) perceived as geared specifically toward Indian priorities – a guaranteed winner under the first-past-the-post electoral system that Sandys had eliminated.

But Jagan, irrevocably deluded by his Marxist frame of reference, was certain he would eventually eradicate Guyanese racism: the chronic African-Indian incomprehension. The sugar strike by the PPP in 1964, staged essentially to pressure the British to scuttle the Sandys Plan, precipitated violence throughout the country. As the Intelligence Report for the period, March to June 1964, stated:

> It is difficult to escape the conclusion that much of the racial violence originated from deliberate provocations, designed to substantiate the PPP arguments [against the Sandys Plan]…Violence on the sugar estates continued, directed by strikers at non-strikers and at substitute labour brought in by estate management – largely African.

This ignited racial violence that the government was ill-equipped to handle. The report added with perspicuity that 'intimidation became increasingly terrorist and racial in character until, in mid-May, race rather than union membership became the issue; this caused the extension of disturbances outside the sugar producing areas.'[92] The most abominable crimes were perpetrated at Wismar, as well as on the Demerara River.

The atrocities at Wismar occurred on May 25, 1964, and the Intelligence Report attributed it to Burnham's PNC: 'Responding to events on the coastal strip, the African population at Wismar fell upon the Indian minority; before the disturbances came to an end 160 houses and seventeen shops, mainly Indian and some Chinese, had been destroyed, four people lost their lives, and approximately 1,500 Indians were evacuated to Georgetown.'[93] Jagan put these figures a bit higher, adding: 'Women and even children were raped and otherwise savagely maltreated.' There was a very savage retaliation for this atrocity, apparently, when about forty Africans died when the boat plying between Georgetown and the bauxite mining town of Mackenzie, near to Wismar, was blasted to bits on the Demerara River in early July 1964. On this Jagan was brief, noting that after an explosion on the *Sun Chapman*, 'more than two dozen persons, mainly negro workers and their families were drowned.'[94] This was believed to have been perpetrated by PPP terrorists. Later in the month Freedom House, headquarters of the PPP, and GIMPEX, its trading arm with communist countries, were bombed: two died. The three leaders were locked in 'peace talks' at the time![95] This was thought to be the act of PNC terrorists. 'Wismar' and *Sun Chapman* became the signature of the Guyanese futility, etched in its racial/racist collective memory.

At the end of May 1964, Jagan was insisting that recognition of the GAWU had to be resolved, as well as the constitutional issue. The Sandys Plan still caused him anguish: 'A constitution designed to bring about the defeat of a particular political party and to justify the demand of a foreign power [the United States] cannot provide a framework for peace and orderly development.'[96] So the strike continued. When it was called off in late July 1964, over 160 people were dead; many communities, multiracial for decades, had witnessed the flight of their minorities; new narratives of racial terror, segregation, and despair had been created: impenetrable barriers to the shaping of a national identity. Jagan's resort to violence was in vain, given Anglo-American Cold War urgencies. In this context, therefore, the Sandys Plan was sacrosanct – irrevocable!

Elizabeth Wallace, writing in late 1964, assessed the bitter legacy of the GAWU strike:

> The violence it has triggered off resulted in over 160 deaths, many more injuries, the destruction of over 1,000 houses, financial losses estimated at fourteen million dollars, and racial bitterness of a degree hitherto unknown even in British Guiana. When the strike finally ended, some thirteen thousand Guyanese, of both Indian and African descent, had fled from their homes and were living as refugees…The six months' sugar strike which precipitated the sorry chain of events in 1964, was overshadowed, almost from the outset, by the racial strife which it both reflected and accentuated. Indeed, long before it ended the strike had been almost forgotten.[97]

It is entirely explicable why Cheddi Jagan chose the sugar industry as the site to resist PR and general elections before independence. Despite his justifiable outrage at the non-recognition of GAWU, it was primarily the Indian sugar workers, since Enmore in June 1948, who had sustained his political mission. But **it is important to recall (yet again!) that the SPA had agreed to recognise the predecessor of Jagan's union, GIWU, in August 1953 (prior to the sugar strike that precipitated the suspension of the constitution). But the PPP rejected the offer. It was a stupid thing to do; so the 'bitter sugar' mantra remained at the heart of the Jaganite mission, even as it was in ruins.** As Janet Jagan said in 1965, of 'the largest group of workers in British Guiana…it is no secret that the PPP's strength, from 1953 to the present, has been based on this rock of working class support.'[98]

But the strike of 1964 and the ensuing racial carnage had broken Jagan, as Tony Tasker of Booker intimated, in July 1964, to Nigel Fisher, Sandys's deputy at the Colonial Office. He said that Jagan, obviously in despair at the anarchy, had told him: 'If we win, we lose; if we lose, we die.' It is significant that Tasker had suggested to Fisher that the question of recognition of Jagan's union, the GAWU, was more in the hands of the Opposition, as they had become the ascendant force by 1964. It was therefore potentially suicidal for them to accede to Jagan. As Jock Campbell told me, Burnham was getting 'tremendous support' from the Booker people in Georgetown and in London, his own authority having waned considerably by then: 'Tasker and the local Booker people were playing up to Burnham.'[99]

It is arguable that Jock's declining fortunes in Booker was a consequence of Cheddi's failure to reciprocate in any way to his culture of reforms on

the plantations. **Cheddi could not accommodate half measures. He wanted to be rid of the 'blood suckers,' root and branch.**

But Jagan's ideological rigidity had destroyed him as well; the aborted sugar strike was the final nail in the coffin. The future belonged to L.F.S. Burnham, adept at negotiating Cold War realities with infinitely greater tact and foresight than Jagan, who opted fatally for the wrong side in the Hemisphere. In 1948, Burnham had written to his mother regarding 'the attack I was supposed to have levelled at B.G.'s Indians,' adding 'I feel strong about the Indian attitude, but the time has not come yet for me to broadcast those feelings and muddy my water.' In April 1964, in the midst of the consuming racial violence, Burnham gave a London correspondent an insight into those raw feelings – a confirmation of what Jessie Burnham, his sister and a member of Jagan's PPP, saw as the 'dark stain of cruelty which only surfaces when one of his vital interests is threatened.' Forbes Burnham warned:

> **If it came to a showdown, the East Indians must remember that we could do more killing than they could. Everyone knows there are more East Indians than negroes. But let me say that in an all-out race war, Dr Jagan's numerical superiority would not be reflected in the results** [emphasis added].[100]

III. President Johnson Affirms Support for the Sandys Plan in the PR Elections: The CIA Persists with Its Resolve to Defeat Jagan

Burnham was, of course, energised and emboldened by the fact that he had the Americans fully on his side (by virtue of Jagan's communist creed), fighting his corner vigorously and without restraint. The Americans (President Kennedy in particular), finally, did prevail upon the Macmillan Conservative government regarding their dictate that their man, Burnham, must rule an independent Guyana. However, even after Colonial Secretary Duncan Sandys had tricked Jagan into signing the document (in October 1963) – a suicide note – the Americans did not relent in 1964. They were determined to secure Burnham's election to office, in a coalition with Peter D'Aguiar of the UF. In February 1964, Alec Douglas-Home (formerly Lord Home), the new British prime minister, was about to meet President Lyndon Johnson in Washington. Dean Rusk, the Secretary of State, sent a summary (on February 6, 1964) of the key points with respect to British Guiana the president should discuss with Douglas-Home. There must be no deviation from the Sandys Plan concerning PR and elections before independence, designed to realise a PNC-UF anti-communist coalition, that the British had promised Kennedy:

I recommend you make the following points to Sir Alec Douglas-Home regarding British Guiana:

1. You are as concerned as President Kennedy over British Guiana.

2. Emergence of another Communist state in this Hemisphere cannot be accepted; there is grave risk of Jagan's establishing a Castro-type regime should he attain independence.

3. Prime Minister Macmillan and President Kennedy agreed that British Guiana should not become independent under Jagan, and that a change of government must be sought.

4. **Jagan must be defeated in the next election** [emphasis added].[101]

The State Department confirmed that President Johnson and the British prime minister did discuss British Guiana during the latter's visit to Washington; and that they reaffirmed the agreements between Kennedy and Macmillan, at Birch Grove, England, on June 30, 1963, 'where the British proposed and Kennedy agreed that independence should be delayed, that a proportional electoral system [PR] be established, and that the alliance between the leading politicians opposed to Jagan be supported.'[102]

The general elections in the UK were due in October 1964, and the Americans were circumspect about how a Labour government would implement the Sandys Plan. Consequently, on February 19, 1964 officials of the State Department met with Labour's 'shadow' foreign secretary, Patrick Gordon Walker. William R. Tyler, the assistant secretary of state for European Affairs, did not mince his words about 'the menace represented by Jagan.'

> We could not live with a Castro-type government on the South American continent. [But] Mr Gordon Walker thought the US exaggerated the menace of Jagan...Mr Tyler added that we were worried about the Castro aspects – that British Guiana would be used as a base for subversion of the continent.

However, Labour was not likely to reject or amend the Sandys Plan whatever their reservations about the PR solution imposed to guarantee Jagan's defeat:

> Mr Gordon Walker replied that a bit of this sort of thing was bound to develop in Latin America. However, if a way could be found for the US to put its troops in British Guiana, the Labour Party would not object. Britain did not want to keep its troops there indefinitely. **Britain had no real reason of its own to stay** [emphasis added].[103]

In any case, the CIA was already entangled with both Burnham and D'Aguiar, manoeuvring them towards an anti-Jagan anti-communist coalition. As early as April, eight months before the PR elections of 1964, the deputy director of the CIA (Richard Helms) informed McGeorge Bundy, the president's special assistant for national security affairs, that they had despatched political advisers to British Guiana in order to facilitate 'an understanding between Burnham and D'Aguiar for co-operation during the election campaign and for the future coalition government.' Helms concluded that the two leaders had discussed cabinet posts in a future coalition government, but no agreement was reached. The CIA advisers reported that the meetings between the PNC and the UF leaders were 'harmonious.'[104] The US government was leaving no stone unturned in their resolve to engineer Jagan's defeat.

Meanwhile, the CIA was fully cognisant of the specific objective of the Jagan-initiated strike in the sugar industry – ostensibly for recognition of his union (the GAWU) and the derecognition of the MPCA – to foment chaos and, thereby, secure the postponement of the PR election in which his defeat was inescapable. The intelligence memorandum of May 12, 1964, noted:

> In an effort to prevent the holding of a UK-imposed proportional representation (PR) election, expected to be held late this year [December 1964], the Jagan regime has been resorting to intimidation and violence. What began some 12 weeks ago as a strike by the pro-Jagan sugar workers' union [GAWU] has developed into a campaign of beatings, bombings, and arson in which 19 persons have been killed and more than a million dollars worth of property and sugar cane have been burned. [When the strike was called off, in July, 160 people were dead.] This violence has exacerbated the racial tensions between the majority East Indians and the minority Negroes to such an extent that some officials fear the situation may get out of hand…
>
> As the PR election which threatens to oust Jagan from office draws nearer…Jagan's despair is deepening. In the hope that the election may be postponed, he has invited the Prime Minister of Trinidad [Dr Eric Williams] to try to mediate the differences between him and the leaders of the opposition parties. **It seems unlikely, however, that the opposition parties, hopeful** [confident?] **of victory in the PR elections, will agree to Williams's proposals** [emphasis added].[105]

The CIA was correct. Furthermore, the US consul general, Delmar Carlson, was punctilious in ensuring that Burnham and D'Aguiar did not retaliate openly against the belated perpetration of chaos, conceived by Jagan in 1964, by mobilising the Indian sugar workers to resist the Sandys Plan to which he had pledged compliance. Although the Opposition's execution of violence, in 1962–63 with the collusion of the CIA, had yielded ample dividends, it was prudent that they should not jeopardise their being gifted independence (as orchestrated by the Americans) by retaliatory violence. On May 13, 1964 the State Department wrote thus to the Consul General in Georgetown:

> We concur with guidance to Burnham not to resort to counterviolence, and that he can be assured that if the PPP makes [any] effort to take over the country by force the US government will not stand by and see the opposition crushed by terror…We are now exploring the

possibility of giving counterterrorist training to selected members of the opposition.[106]

A week later the CIA was forthright in reaffirming their resolve – an obsession – to ensure that Jagan, their designated communist enemy, did not get near the levers of power again:

> **Our principal objective is to defeat the PPP in the forthcoming elections, and to bring into power a coalition government of the People's National Congress [PNC], the United Force [UF], and alternative East Indian party(ies), headed by Linden Forbes Burnham. While retaining tactical flexibility, all our moves must be directed at attainment of this objective** [emphasis added].

> We believe that in terms of accomplishing our objective things at this time are going well, despite the current wave of violence…We should make every effort to adhere to the present schedule, i.e., elections under PR in early November [held on December 7, 1964], and to avoid being deflected from our present course.

> We believe that resumption of direct British rule at this stage would impede the attainment of our objective. Resumption could delay elections, make it easier for the British Labour Party, if it comes to power, to tamper with Sandys's decision, and give the PPP additional campaign issues.[107]

IV. Jagan's Political Mission in Jeopardy: Conveys Sense of Impending Demise to US Consul General Carlson

By May 1964, with racial hatred and violence beyond control, the ostensible original issue – the recognition of Jagan's union (GAWU) in the sugar industry – was completely submerged: the strike continued, but it was clearly an exercise in futility. The PPP-engineered violence, unlike that unleashed by D'Aguiar and Burnham in 1962–63, could achieve nothing because the US government was determined that Jagan must be defeated; that he must not accede to leadership of an independent Guyana. Consequently, Jagan was in despair, and this was evident during his meeting with the US consul general, Delmar Carlson. The latter reported that in a 'rambling exposition,' on May 24, 1964 (the day before the PNC-executed 'Wismar Massacre'), Jagan said:

> No matter what I try to do, I can get nowhere. I am opposed by everyone, including the CIA which, I suppose, is the American government. I laid my cards on the table to President Kennedy [that he was a socialist/communist], and he gave me to understand that he would help me, but he didn't. I can only conclude that he was a liar, or that he was influenced to change his decision.[108]

Carlson added that Jagan believed he had 'a successful visit to Washington [in October 1961],' but pressure was probably applied on Kennedy by right-wing groups and the CIA. Jagan told him that 'the only answer to the present situation was a grand coalition,' yet Burnham would not agree to such a measure because 'the United States would not let him.'[109] Of course, Carlson denied such was the case; however, Jagan was correct: the CIA was already actively engaged in British Guiana crafting the parameters for a Burnham-D'Aguiar coalition, in the aftermath of the PR elections later that year. They stressed that they did not want Burnham to confuse undecided voters by co-operating with Jagan in any way, even in a temporary pre-election peace initiative – and definitely not in a coalition. Hence the corollary: the US government would not collaborate with Jagan in any way; they would grant him no legitimacy.

On the same day Carlson met with Jagan, a memorandum from the National Security Council to the president's national security advisor, McGeorge Bundy, was sanguine that the current violence in British Guiana demonstrated that their anti-Jagan strategy was working in the colony: 'Cheddi Jagan and his people are beginning to feel that they are on their way out, and are stirring up trouble in the hope that they can reverse the trend. We will see more of this sort of thing in the next few months.' However, the memorandum advised that they should be 'preparing for a Labour Party victory' in the UK; and that if Labour won (in October 1964), 'our Ambassador should immediately talk to the new Prime Minister [Harold Wilson]…Our policy with respect to B.G. is the right one and we should stay with it. With a little more luck, events after November [December], with Jagan in opposition, will also be controllable.'[110] The Americans need not have worried about a Labour victory, their declared reservations regarding the Sandys Plan notwithstanding. It was inconceivable that Labour (fully apprised, through MI5, of Jagan's intimate links with the CPGB) would seek to subvert the concentrated American goal of unseating the communist Jagan. (Apart from Fenner Brockway, Jennie Lee, Ian Mikardo, and a few others on the far-left of the party, most found Jagan's communism and links with the CPGB indefensible.)

Meanwhile, as US Consul General Carlson reported on June 27, 1964, after Jagan had called him in again for talks, the country was mired in 'deplorable violence, senseless retaliation, and there seems no end in sight.' Jagan noted that he had made 'concession after concession for a coalition government, including parity in cabinet' to Burnham, yet he remained intransigent because he 'will not go against the wishes of the United States.'

Jagan stated that he had tried to understand why his relations with the US had 'gone sour,' but was unable to fathom it. He reportedly told Carlson that he had gone every year, between 1957 and 1961, to the US, and he thought 'personal relations were very good,' presumably with officials in Washington. Carlson added:

> In 1961 he had talks with President Kennedy, Chester Bowles, Arthur Schlesinger and other top officials. **They had probed him very deeply, and he had every reason to believe that he had passed the test. He had been quite frank with them about his socialist** [communist] **views.**

Jagan concluded that the obvious deterioration in relations was a consequence of the anti-communist propaganda, disseminated against him in the US, by the opposition leaders in B.G. (Burnham and D'Aguiar); this was compounded by the current US 'trouble with Cuba.'[111]

It will be recalled that Jagan had totally disregarded everything John Hennings, the colonial attaché at the British Embassy in Washington, had studiously counselled him in October 1961 – that he should eschew any reference to 'socialism' in his meeting with the president (on October 25) because it connoted despicable 'communism' in the American political vocabulary, nothing less. But Jagan also had chronic problems at home, stemming from his communist creed, as he explained to Carlson. He had tried to alleviate the fears of several civic bodies in the country that he was a communist; countering that their apprehension of 'regimentation, exclusion of private enterprise, and if independent, of an invitation by him to the Soviets and Cubans to come in' was without substance. He sought to reassure them that his record did not substantiate their apprehension that private enterprise was in danger. Moreover, he had 'publicly pledged to keep his hands off the sugar and bauxite industries.'[112]

Jagan was being disingenuous: for him, private enterprise, the essence of capitalism, is irredeemably exploitative, the source of 'surplus value' – an inherently flawed system detrimental to the welfare of working people. Therefore, as a staunch communist, he believed that the 'commanding heights' of the economy must be in the hands of the putative workers' state. Its nationalisation was imperative to the making of the perfect communist society predetermined infallibly by Marxism-Leninism. 'Bitter sugar,' in particular, and the Booker 'blood suckers' (as he termed them) had no place in the communist state, where everything would be resolved in favour of the paramount interest of the working class.

Yet, very late in the day, and doomed to political oblivion by the machinations of American imperialism, he appeared to have discovered an element of *realpolitik*. But this could not save him, as Delmar Carlson observed of their meeting of June 27, 1964, amidst the escalating racial carnage:

> Jagan gave a controlled performance. He was purposely calm, reasonable, most courteous, earnest. Only sign of tension was slight

shaking of hands at times; otherwise he seemed relaxed. It is obvious that he would give almost anything to obtain US support, and will leap at any possibility of favourable response. We can probably expect some more peace feelers.[113]

Jagan had told Consul General Carlson that he 'could see no end to violence without a coalition' between himself and Burnham. For ideological reasons he did not wish to include Peter D'Aguiar's UF in any coalition. But this was a lifeline the Americans were not prepared to extend to him, as Dean Rusk indicated to Duncan Sandys on August 4, 1964:

> ...we seriously doubt that Jagan, who has been using violence for political purposes, would be likely to forego such tactics if a coalition were formed. Apart from that...[there is] the very real possibility that a pre-election coalition would adversely affect the electoral prospects of the PNC and the UF by confusing the supporters of those two parties. **A coalition of the PPP and PNC and excluding the UF would endanger the hoped-for post-election PNC-UF coalition which at the moment is the only possibility of replacing the Jagan Government.** In short, we share your view of holding the elections later this year, but are concerned that nothing be done in the pre-election period, in the quest for order and security, which would jeopardise the currently hopeful electoral results...**The strike of the sugar workers has been ended in what amounts to a defeat for Jagan** [emphasis added].[114]

Duncan Sandys was on vacation, but his deputy (Sir Hilton Poynton) reported that with the end of the strike the risk of violence was 'diminished'; therefore, the case for a temporary coalition was 'less strong.' He was confident that Sandys would concur with Rusk's position regarding the necessity to ensure Jagan's defeat at the polls.[115]

On September 11, 1964, Delmar Carlson briefed senior officials of the State Department and the National Security Council in Washington. It is obvious that the obsession with removing Jagan (in favour of Burnham) was no less paramount under Johnson than it was under Kennedy. They agreed that 'something would have to be done if the PPP did win'; and 'the general feeling was that, despite his conciliatory noises, Jagan is the same unrehabilitated bad egg he has always been; he has not really been "educated" by the US/Cuban experience.' President Johnson's team was repeating the Kennedy mantra: that Jagan was a communist like Castro; they would not tolerate a 'second Cuba' in the Hemisphere; a Jagan victory constituted a threat to American national security; and they would destroy him if he proceeded to introduce communism should he win the elections under PR.

However, it is clear that the Americans, like the British, were not enamoured of Burnham. It was only because Jagan was perceived as an 'unrehabilitated bad egg,' inextricable from his communist creed, that they reluctantly opted for another 'rotten rope,' supposedly cohered from strands of a different texture. Delmar Carlson did get to know Burnham well, and he provided a frank assessment of him to his superiors in the Johnson administration, on the eve of 'their man' being anointed the recipient of the Anglo-American gift of independence. It would take several years for the Americans to discover they had bought a pig in a poke:

> ...while Burnham is now getting on well with the leaders of opposition parties [essentially Peter D'Aguiar of the United Force], we should not expect this to last forever. [Prophetic!] The anti-PPP forces are bound to have plenty of problems with one another in the future...**Burnham and the British do not get along. The Governor [Sir Richard Luyt] does not like Burnham, who twists the lion's tail whenever he can. We can expect to see a growing British/Burnham problem...Mr Carlson said that while he is trying to build a relationship with Burnham, it is tough to do so. Burnham, a racist and anti-white, remembers slights and repays them; at the same time, he takes advantage of people who treat him softly** [emphasis added].[116]

Burnham knew that Jagan's poverty of statesmanship had gifted him the winning American ticket; therefore, he was meticulous in toeing the American line. As Carlson noted: 'Burnham [told him] that if he gets into power, he will not recognise the USSR, and that he will have nothing to do with Cuba so long as he can find other people to buy B.G.'s rice.' If Jagan had adopted this posture when he met Kennedy in October 1961, he (not Burnham) would have been leading his country to independence. But Cheddi was incapable of changing his spots.

V.   America's Man at the Helm: The PR Elections and the Defeat of Jagan, December 1964

The day before the British general elections in 1964 (October 14), the State Department informed Ambassador David Bruce in London that he should meet with Harold Wilson urgently (should be become prime minister) to discuss the crucial British Guiana issue. They were seeking reassurance from Wilson that he would 'continue the charted course'; and they reiterated their resolve to be rid of Jagan:

> Latin America is an area of the greatest concern to us. The establishment of an independent [post-colonial] government in British Guiana, under a leadership which has been markedly receptive to communist ideas and vulnerable to communist subversion, would create an intolerable situation for the United States and other countries in the Hemisphere. Previous British Governments have

shown an understanding of this situation…The President [Johnson] hopes you will share with him [Wilson] the conviction that it should continue along present lines.[117]

The Americans were still sceptical of the Labour Party's reliability in executing the Sandys Plan against Jagan; hence they were palpably relieved when Harold Wilson got a majority of just four seats in the general elections. A memorandum from the National Security Council, two days later, noted that the State Department 'feels that the election was sufficiently close so that Labour will be chary of tampering with the present course of events in B.G.'. It was also remarked that the CIA was actively engaged in aiding the anti-Jagan parties in 'ensuring that the opposition parties turn out to vote on election day; to this end the CIA, in a deniable and discreet way, is providing financial incentives to party workers who are charged with the responsibility of getting out the vote.'[118]

Meanwhile, the US government was engaged in preliminary work to fund a 'non-Jagan government' in order to execute several infrastructural projects. However, they were aware that the British government could still insist on a PPP-PNC coalition if Jagan were to lose 'by a close vote.' But they were adamant that no such coalition must be entertained; they would offer no aid to any government that included Jagan; yet they were still peddling the fiction that 'a coalition government can be formed without the PPP and that it will be genuinely multiracial.'[119] No such outcome was attainable without the engagement of the PPP. However, it was not an issue that bothered the Americans.

Carlson had a meeting with Burnham on October 23, 1964, regarding the composition of a non-Jagan coalition. Burnham was amenable to a minority position in his cabinet for D'Aguiar's UF and ex-PPP minister Balram Singh Rai's Justice Party (possibly funded by the CIA). Carlson was already circumspect about Burnham's predilection for making the coalition 'unduly PNC-dominated with other parties' participation a kind of sham.' He discerned a distinct lack of enthusiasm on the part of Burnham for an inclusive government. But he deemed this 'very decisive' or the consequence could well be that he retained power for 'one term or less.'[120] Carlson was not factoring in Burnham's iron will to stay in power indefinitely by routine rigging of all future elections – an art in which he would demonstrate singular proficiency in the region.

The first general elections in British Guiana under PR were held on Monday, December 7, 1964. That same day the new British prime minister, Harold Wilson, and his team met President Johnson at the White House. The latter's notes included the necessity for him to raise several matters regarding British Guiana: their desire that independence should not be granted prematurely; that the US would provide no aid to a government that included Jagan; and that 'close co-operation and aid' could help to create 'a racially peaceful, democratic and non-communist British Guiana.'

Harold Wilson, on the other hand, was not enamoured of either Jagan or Burnham; he deemed both despicable; yet there was no reason to think that, in the end, the Labour Party would not comply with the comprehensive anti-Jagan Sandys Plan that the Americans ultimately extracted from the British in October 1963. Booker's virtual monopoly of sugar notwithstanding, Britain had no vital interests necessitating their long-term engagement with British Guiana. Wilson reportedly informed President Johnson that:

> He had told Jagan that whoever wins in BG, the UK would not grant B.G. independence, as there would be a bloodbath if they did so. He thought that if both Burnham and Jagan (the latter he described as a naïve Trotskyite [anything but, being a pro-Soviet communist!]) were out of B.G. it would be so much the better. **He didn't think a government could be entrusted to either of them, and the UK rather felt the US placed excessive trust in Burnham who was just as bad in his own way as Jagan was in his. In fact, interjected Patrick Gordon Walker** [British Foreign Secretary] **'they are both horrors** [emphasis added].'[121]

Earlier that day, Patrick Gordon Walker had met with Secretary of State Dean Rusk; he informed him that the British government would not grant British Guiana independence 'in the foreseeable future.' And he, too, observed that the US government 'had an excessively favourable estimate of Burnham.'

Yet the Americans and the British (the latter belatedly) gave Burnham a blank cheque to do as he pleased. However, the PPP had clung to a flimsy thread of hope that should the Labour Party win the general elections in the UK, in October 1964, they would abrogate PR. This was sheer fantasy, and they should have known it. In April 1964, Labour had moved a motion in the House of Commons to have PR rejected, but they withdrew it at the conclusion of the debate on the Sandys Plan. The Conservative government pleaded that such a measure would exacerbate the racial situation in the volatile colony if it were pressed to a vote. Jagan's last straw had slipped away. Yet the illusion that Labour would pull the PPP's chestnuts out of the fire was still being fed by Janet Jagan, who attended the debate in the House of Commons on April 27, 1964.

Janet had a meeting with Duncan Sandys, and she told him that his constitutional imposition on British Guiana was 'a negation of democratic practice, a betrayal of historical precedents, an oppressive Imperialist design, and a stain on Britain's honour.' Sandys, unsurprisingly, was imperturbable, countering that his formula was conducive to the flowering of 'every subtle shade of philosophy' in the political arena; it would conduce to the blurring of the lines of racial particularism.[122] Hogwash! Sandys could not have believed any of this. Strangely, Janet still insisted all was not lost because if Labour were elected, they would be 'more sensible' about British Guiana. Her silver lining originated in the exaggerated optimism of Fenner Brockway on the far left of the Labour Party. Perhaps the mirage was necessary in order to sustain their political mission, given the stark reality that a PPP victory in elections under PR, later that year, was unattainable:

> I believe that the Labour Party when it comes to power will take a very careful look at the whole B.G. problem and not just leap in as the Conservatives have done. It is clear that Mr Sandys hasn't produced an answer, and it is likely that Labour would be able to do better. After all it would be a feather in Labour's cap to get a proper solution for our country than tamely follow the Conservatives.[123]

As noted earlier, the Labour Party did win the elections in the UK, in October 1964, with a very slender majority of four. Many of Jagan's Indian supporters followed the elections closely, staying up all night for the results carried on local radio. Like Janet, they did not appreciate the bipartisan approach of the parties on colonial issues; and, that even if they were so inclined, the narrowness of Labour's victory precluded their pursuit of measures to retrieve the dwindling fortunes of a communist whose back the Americans were determined to see, and were resolved to hasten. Harold Wilson had assured President Johnson (in their meeting in early December 1964) that he had 'no intention of granting independence to strife-torn British Guiana until the contending Negro and East Indian communities have demonstrated an ability to live together in peace.'[124]

What Wilson really meant was that, should Jagan get 51 per cent of the votes under PR, a pretext would be hatched to delay granting him independence. Despite his reservations about Burnham, the leader of the Labour Party was as acquiescent as Macmillan and Douglas-Home to America's irrepressible bidding – that Jagan must not lead an independent Guyana under any circumstances. In the general elections held under PR on December 7, 1964, the PPP failed to get a majority although they polled the highest number of votes. President Kennedy was dead for just over a year, but the communist from an obscure colony in the Hemisphere, who had caused him inordinate anguish during his thousand days in the White House, was ousted. There would be 'no second Cuba.'

Jagan polled 45.8 per cent of the votes (twenty-four seats); Burnham 40.5 per cent (twenty-two seats); D'Aguiar 12.4 per cent (seven seats). The objective of the whole iniquitous Anglo-American anti-communist/anti-Jagan project was achieved. Burnham and D'Aguiar formed a coalition, as anticipated; they were thereby empowered to ensure that they were the anointed recipients of the gift of independence. The latter was not a culmination of a nationalist 'struggle,' such as the Gandhian crusade for independence in India; this was not necessary in the backwater of British Guiana. Jagan, a man of abundant passions and unwavering dedication to his creed, had forfeited his right to be the recipient of the prize. His ideological inflexibility in the context of the Cold War made him a mortal enemy of the Americans. They perceived Jagan through the prism of their consuming fear of communism, only marginally less than what they harboured for Castro, Jagan's greatest hero in the Hemisphere.

It should be noted, however, that on December 10, 1964 (just three days after the elections), Consul General Delmar Carlson remarked that the 'complete racial voting by Indians [for Jagan] apparently stems from fear and distrust of an Africanised government [led by Burnham].' He did not comment on racial voting among Africans (PNC) and Portuguese (UF), but he added that the PNC-UF coalition 'would have to govern without significant [any?] Indian representation.' This did not seem like a pressing concern for the Americans because the anti-communist coalition they craved, and had schemed relentlessly for, was on the verge of fruition – thus obviating the 'second Cuba.' However, Carlson appeared to caution that the rate of increase of the Indian segment of the electorate was bound to pose insurmountable problems for Burnham's re-election at the next election. He knew Burnham better than most (he met with him constantly), and he had a fine grasp of the Guyanese social and political landscape.

Yet Carlson was either uncannily prescient or he was already conniving with their man – to rig to eternity:

> Carlson was pessimistic about the depth of the racial cleavage in British Guiana. He speculated that while the Burnham administration would probably try to 'demonstrate responsibility, improved government and assistance to all Guianese,' it seemed unlikely that such an approach would lead to Burnham's re-election within the next few years, 'especially in view of the increased number of eligible Indian voters at that time. **Therefore, it might be expected that, before another election, Burnham's administration may seriously toy with more radical solutions, possibly, e.g., seeking to obtain Independence in order to tamper with the electoral system** [emphasis added].'[125]

British reservation regarding the granting of early independence to British Guiana notwithstanding, instant intimations were emanating from the American government of their readiness to advance Burnham's case for immediate independence. The State Department (on December 10, 1964) advised the consul general in Georgetown that he must speak with Burnham 'soonest' regarding the composition of the cabinet. He should convey to him their pleasure at the outcome of the elections; and suggest that his new government could include a few moderate PPP Indians, but there **must** be no room for Jagan:

> **We were gratified by the election outcome, for in our view it provides a basis on which B.G. can move forward toward independence without the danger of communist domination...** We were pleased by the report that a PNC/UF coalition appeared certain...We would not be opposed to Burnham trying to bring one

or two moderate Indians into the cabinet, but in this connection it must be clearly understood that the United States would not be able to provide assistance for a government which involved a PPP/PNC coalition of any kind or which included Jagan or his henchmen. We assume that Burnham will be on guard against approaches by Jagan to get the nose of the camel under the tent [emphasis added].[126]

Burnham was already cleverly pressing his case, with his American sponsors, for early independence – the only means to ensure that the communist Jagan was never returned to power in democratic elections. As Delmar Carlson informed the State Department, Burnham wanted immediate independence 'in order to tamper with [rig] the electoral system.' And the Americans, irrevocably haunted by the spectre of Jagan's communist creed, were ready to go to bat for their man. Carlson noted: Burnham's main concern was the 'means to overcome what he called "Jaganism"...' **Burnham 'urged the desirability of early independence and appealed to me to persuade the USG to use its influence to that end.'** Burnham stressed that he did not want to be 'hampered' by Britain's 'fair play,' and that 'if we do not down this "ogre Jagan" before too long, we will never be able to do so.'[127] The Americans concurred with that.

As early as December 17–18, 1964, US and UK officials met in London; the former wished to feel the pulse of the latter regarding independence for British Guiana. The British stance was that racial harmony was a precondition for the granting of independence; and as long as Jagan 'continues as leader of the Indian community racial harmony cannot be re-established without a rapprochement between him and Burnham.' The Americans 'took issue with this concept,' countering that 'Jagan's record does not justify any assumption that he can serve as a basis for the establishment of racial harmony. I believe we have in effect bought time which Mr Burnham can use to try to allay the Indian fears. If Burnham's actions bear out the intentions of his speeches, there may be some basis for hope.'[128] The Americans planned to 'counsel Burnham toward moderation and assist him where possible,' but Jagan must be excluded from the coalition.

It is also noteworthy that although Balram Singh Rai's Justice Party, the Indian capitalist party of Jagan's expelled former minister, polled only 1,334 votes or 0.6 per cent of the votes cast, the American officials were still making the case that it 'could continue to serve a useful purpose.' This arguably lends plausibility to the widely held belief that Rai's party was partly funded by the CIA in order to split Jagan's Indian votes. But the Indians, irrespective of religion or class, did not desert their racial leader, his communist creed notwithstanding.

In early 1965, Ernst Halperin, a distinguished American scholar of insurgency in Latin America, assessed the consequences of Jagan's irrepressible Marxism-Leninism in the cauldron of racism that was/is Guyana. He contends that Jagan's lack of intellectual and political discernment, magnified by his unmalleable devotion to communism, redounded to the detriment of Jagan's loyal, overwhelmingly Indian, supporters. Halperin argues:

> Although the PPP's appeal is increasingly racist, and its membership, apart from a few Negro and Coloured [mixed] figureheads, is wholly Indian, the PPP's policy [ideology: Marxism-Leninism] cannot be said to be in the interests of the Indian community. Guiana would already have achieved independence under Indian leadership if only Dr Jagan had clearly and unequivocally renounced his allegiance to the ideals and policies of world communism. The fact that he had not done so, even though it would have been highly profitable for him, his party and for the Indian community, is a clear indication of the strength of his loyalty to the Communist cause.[129]

Ernst Halperin is right; but he did not grasp the power of Jagan's hatred of the 'sugar gods,' his eternal crusade against 'bitter sugar,' congruent with his Indian people's master narrative of their encounter with sugar – an exaggeratedly tendentious tale of unremitting brutality after they were 'tricked' into leaving a benign India, whence they were supposedly wrenched, to British Guiana and 'a new system of slavery' – and, of course, 'bitter sugar' – with absolutely nothing compensatory in the process. This is fundamentally flawed, as anyone who knows anything about the following could testify: the degradation of the lower castes, historically as well as in contemporary UP and Bihar; the flight of lower caste people and women in particular (two-thirds of whom migrated on their own) to a caste-less world of possibilities however circumscribed; the acquisition of land by Indo-Guyanese after indentureship; the rise of villages and the development of the rice and cattle industries; the emergence of an Indian middle class in business and the professions, irrespective of caste; finally, the culture of reform and its benefits associated with Jock Campbell's Booker from the early 1950s. Jagan's communist creed thrived on the enduring fallacy of 'bitter sugar'; and it is the source of the alienation, dispossession, and virtual displacement that is still being played out. The exodus of entire villages, ironically, to the heartlands of capitalism! So, too, the 'socialist' experiments of Forbes Burnham and the PNC, for more than two decades!

The legacy of Jaganism and Burnhamism is a bitter one that will continue to retard possibilities for the making of a nation, despite the exaggerated dreams of 'Oil-Dorado.'[130]

Notes

1.   Memorandum from the President's Special Assistant (Schlesinger) to the Ambassador to the United Kingdom (Bruce), February 27, 1962, in *Foreign Relations of the United States, 1961-63, Vol. XII* (Washington: US Government Printing Office, 1996), 509.

2. Ibid., 550.
3. Leader, *Thunder*, December 30, 1961.
4. Cheddi Jagan, *The West on Trial: My Fight for Guyana's Freedom* (London: Michael Joseph, 1966), 250.
5. *Thunder*, December 30, 1961.
6. With reference to Cuba and the Punta del Este conference in Uruguay, January 2-31, 1961, see Resolution 6: 'Exclusion of the Present Government of Cuba from Participation in the Inter-American System': avalon.law.yale.edu/20[th]_century/intam17.asp.
7. Memorandum of Conversation on Communism in Latin America, between President Kennedy and President Mateos [of Mexico], Mexico City, June 29,1962.
8. See Stephen G. Rabe, *US Intervention in British Guiana: A Cold War Story* (Chapel Hill: The University of North Carolina Press, 2005), 91-93.
9. William R. Tyler (Assistant Secretary of State for European Affairs) to Dean Rusk (Secretary of State), memorandum, February 18, 1962: http://guyana.org/govt/declassified_documents.html.
10. TNA, PREM11/3666, Dean Rusk, Secretary of State, to Lord Home, British Foreign Secretary, February 19, 1962.
11. See note 1, 546-48: Letter from Lord Home, British Foreign Secretary, to Secretary of State Dean Rusk, February 26, 1962.
12. See note 1, 610: Telegram from the Consul General, Georgetown, to the State Department, Washington, September 5, 1962.
13. Colin Palmer, *Cheddi Jagan and the Politics of Power: British Guiana's Struggle for Independence* (Chapel Hill: The University of North Carolina Press, 2010), 262-63.
14. See note 1, 572-73: Memorandum from the President's Special Assistant (Schlesinger) to President Kennedy, June 21, 1962.
15. Arthur M. Schlesinger, Jr, *A Thousand Days: John F. Kennedy in the White House* (London: Andre Deutsch, 1965), 668-69.
16. Leader, *Daily Chronicle*, June 20, 1962.
17. Ibid.
18. *Daily Chronicle*, June 23, 1962.
19. TNA, CO887/8, Commission of Inquiry into the Disturbances in British Guiana in February 1962, Dr C.B. Jagan examined by Lionel Luckhoo, June 22, 1962.
20. Ibid. *Daily Chronicle*, July 6, 1962.
21. See note 1, 575: Memorandum from the Secretary of State Dean Rusk to President Kennedy, July 12, 1962.
22. Ibid., 577: Memorandum from the President's Special Assistant for National Security Affairs (Bundy) to President Kennedy, July 13, 1962.
23. Ibid., 582: Memorandum from the President's Special Assistant (Schlesinger) to President Kennedy, September 5, 1962.
24. Ibid., 548, Memorandum from the President's Special Assistant (Schlesinger) to President Kennedy, March 8, 1962.
25. *Daily Chronicle*, January 17, 1962.
26. Ibid.
27. Leader, *Daily Chronicle*, July 21, 1961.
28. Leader, *Daily Chronicle*, July 19, 1962.
29. David de Caires, 'Where Do We Go from Here,' *Daily Chronicle*, July 19, 1962.
30. Ibid.
31. See note 1, 558-64: Memorandum of Conversation between Undersecretary of State for the Colonies, Hugh Fraser, and Officials of the Kennedy Administration

(including William R. Tyler, U. Alexis Johnson and Arthur Schlesinger), Washington, March 17, 1962.

32. Ibid.
33. Ibid.
34. Leader, *New Nation*, March 12, 1960. This was the organ of Burnham's PNC, edited by Sydney King [later Eusi Kwayana].
35. Leader, *New Nation*, March 19, 1960.
36. Ibid.
37. See note 1, 575-76: Memorandum from Secretary of State (Rusk) to President Kennedy, July 12, 1962.
38. Ibid.
39. Ibid., 584-587: Consul General in Georgetown [Everett Melby] to the State Department, March 14, 1963.
40. Ibid.
41. Ibid.
42. See note 4 [Jagan], 269.
43. For a very fine treatment of the role of the AFL-CIO and the CIA in the 80-day strike of 1963, see Robert Anthony Waters, Jr, and Gordon Oliver Daniels, 'When you're handed money on a platter, it's very hard to say "where are you getting this?": The AFL-CIO, the CIA and British Guiana,' *Revue Belge de Philologie et D'Histoire*, Vol. 84, No. 4 (2006), 1,075–99. The quote is on 1,095–96. See also Gordon Oliver Daniels, 'A Great Injustice to Cheddi Jagan: The Kennedy Administration and British Guiana, 1961-63,' PhD Thesis, University of Mississippi, 2000, Chapter 6, 191-244.
44. TNA, CO1031/3714, Governor Grey to Duncan Sandys, December 8, 1962, secret and personal.
45. TNA, CO1031/4931, Cheddi Jagan to Governor Grey, June 12, 1963.
46. Ibid.
47. *New Nation*, April 19, 1963.
48. *Mirror*, April 14, 1963.
49. *Mirror*, April 21, 1963.
50. See note 13 [Palmer], 230-31.
51. See note 1, 604-05: Memorandum on White House Meeting on British Guiana, June 21, 1963.
52. See note 1, 606: Telegram from the State Department [Rusk] to the US Embassy in the UK [Bruce], June 21, 1963.
53. Ibid., Message from Foreign Secretary Lord Home to Secretary of State Rusk, July 29, 1963.
54. See note 1, 608, Memorandum of Conversation [Meeting of President Kennedy with Prime Minister Harold Macmillan, Birch Grove, Sussex, June 30, 1963].
55. Ibid., 609.
56. Ibid., 610-11: Telegram from the US Consul General, Georgetown, to the State Department, September 5, 1963.
57. Ibid.
58. TNA, CO1031/4495, Note of a Meeting in the Commonwealth Relations Office, October 23, 1963.
59. Ibid., 613: Telegram from the State Department, Washington [Rusk], to the US Consul General, Georgetown [Melby], September 7, 1963.
60. See note 58.
61. Ibid.

62. Interview with Dr Fenton Ramsahoye, London, July 25, 1992.
63. Interview with Mrs Lee Samuel, MBE (formerly Lee Akbar), London, June 12, 1997.
64. Ibid.
65. TNA, CO1031/4495, Governor Grey to David Rose (OAG, British Guiana), secret and personal, October 29, 1963.
66. *British Guiana Constitutional Conference, 1963*, Cmd. 2203, November 1963.
67. *Daily Chronicle*, October 26, 1963.
68. Ibid.
69. TNA, FO371/167690, Record of a Conversation between Home and Rusk, November 26, 1963.
70. *Daily Chronicle*, November 1, 1963.
71. Ibid.
72. *Daily Chronicle*, October 26, 1963.
73. *Mirror*, October 27, 1963.
74. *Mirror*, November 3, 1963.
75. *Guiana Graphic*, November 2, 1963.
76. Ibid.
77. Miles Fitzpatrick, 'Shame! But there is Still a Way Out for Us,' *Sunday Graphic*, November 3, 1963.
78. *Guiana Graphic*, February 20, 1964.
79. *Guiana Graphic*, February 9, 1964.
80. Interview with Lloyd Searwar, Georgetown, August 24, 2000.
81. *Daily Chronicle*, November 1, 1963.
82. *Mirror*, February 2, 1964.
83. Martin Carter, 'Some Implications of the Present [Political] Situation,' confidential internal paper, BSE (Booker Sugar Estates), n.d. [1964], mimeo.
84. *Mirror*, February 10, 1964.
85. *Mirror*, February 11, 1964.
86. Ibid.
87. *Guiana Graphic*, February 20, 1964.
88. *Guiana Graphic*, March 26, 1964.
89. Foreign Relations, 1964-68, Vol XXXII, Dominican Republic, Cuba, Haiti, Guyana: Telegram from the State Department to the Consul General in British Guiana, May 13, 1964.
90. *Mirror*, May 31, 1964.
91. *Guiana Graphic*, April 22, 1964.
92. TNA, CO1031/4758, Intelligence Report for the Period March 17-June 22, 1964, secret and personal.
93. Ibid.
94. Cheddi Jagan, *The West on Trial* (1966), 358.
95. *Guiana Graphic*, July 18,1964.
96. *Mirror*, May 31, 1964.
97. Elizabeth Wallace, 'British Guiana: Causes of the Present Discontents,' *International Journal*, Vol. XIX, No. 4 (Autumn 1964), 540, 543.
98. Janet Jagan, 'How Left is the New Left?,' *New World Fortnightly*, no. 21, August 20, 1965, 20.
99. Interview with Jock Campbell (Lord Campbell of Eskan), Nettlebed, Oxfordshire, February 18, 1994.

100. *Daily Telegraph* (London), May 1, 1964.
101. Foreign Relations, 1964-68, Vol. XXXII...Guyana [US Declassified Documents], Memorandum from Secretary of State Rusk to President Johnson, February 6, 1964.
102. Ibid., Memorandum of Conversation between President Johnson and Prime Minister Sir Alec Douglas-Home, February 12, 1964.
103. Ibid., Memorandum of Conversation [between officials of the State Department and Patrick Gordon Walker, Labour's 'Shadow' Foreign Secretary], February 19, 1964.
104. Ibid., Memorandum from the Deputy Director for Plans of the CIA (Helms) to the President's Special Assistant for National Security Affairs (Bundy), May 1, 1964.
105. Ibid., Research Memorandum from the Deputy Director of Intelligence and Research (Denny) to Acting Secretary of State Ball, May 12, 1964.
106. Ibid., Telegram from the State Department to the Consul General, British Guiana, May 13, 1964.
107. Ibid., Memorandum from the Deputy Director of Plans of the CIA (Helms) to the President's Special Assistant for National Security Affairs (Bundy), May 22, 1964.
108. Ibid., Memorandum of Conversation [between Cheddi Jagan and Delmar Carlson, the American Consul General, British Guiana], May 25, 1964.
109. Ibid [same as above].
110. Ibid., Memorandum from Gordon Ross of the National Security Council to the President's National Security Adviser (Bundy), May 25, 1964.
111. Ibid., Telegram from the Consul General in British Guiana to the State Department, June 27, 1964.
112. Ibid [same as above].
113. Ibid [same as above].
114. Ibid., Message from Secretary of State Rusk to the British Colonial Secretary (Sandys), August 4, 1964.
115. Ibid., [Sir Hilton Poynton, Deputy to Duncan Sandys to Rusk, August 17, 1964].
116. Ibid., Memorandum for the Record [Delmar Carlson's meeting with officials of the State Department and the National Security Council], September 11, 1964.
117. Ibid., Message from the State Department to the Embassy in the UK, October 14, 1964.
118. Ibid., Memorandum from Gordon Chase of the National Security Council to the President's Special Assistant for National Security Affairs (Bundy), October 17, 1964.
119. Ibid., Memorandum from the Director of the Office of British Commonwealth and Northern European Affairs (Shullaw) to the Assistant Secretary of State for European Affairs (Tyler), October 27, 1964.
120. Ibid [same as above].
121. Memorandum of Conversation [between President Johnson and Prime Minister Harold Wilson, the White House], December 7, 1964.
122. *Guiana Graphic*, April 23, 1964.
123. *Guiana Graphic*, May 1, 1964.
124. See note 4 (Cheddi Jagan, 1966), 391-92.
125. See note 102: Editorial Note, Carlson to the State Department, December 10, 1964.
126. Ibid. Telegram from the State Department to the Consul General in British Guiana, December 10, 1964.
127. Ibid.

128. Ibid., Memorandum from the Director of the Office of British Commonwealth and Northern European Affairs (Shullaw) to the Assistant Secretary of State for European Affairs (Tyler), December 21, 1964.
129. See Ernst Halperin, 'Racism and Communism in British Guiana,' *Journal of Inter-American Studies*, Vol. VII, No. 1 (January 1965).
130. I have taken this term from Guyanese journalist, John Mair.

10.

Burnham, Jagan's Communism, Billy Strachan and the Communist Party of Great Britain
The MI5 Files, the Early 1950s–1961

Burnham showed early signs of opportunism when he returned to British Guiana [in 1949] and did not contact Cheddi as Billy Strachan had arranged. He joined the League of Coloured Peoples [an African organisation based in Georgetown]…That was where Cheddi found him. Burnham wanted to create his own movement from the start… And it is this opportunism that drove him to demand leadership of the PPP and divide the party…

I don't know that Burnham was ever a serious Marxist. He certainly was not in the 1960s and much of the 1970s; he was virulently anti-communist. I have always taken his Marxism with a pinch of salt…

Billy Strachan was a lifelong friend of the PPP and many of its leaders including…[the Jagans], my father [Boysie Ramkarran], and Ranji Chandisingh. He influenced broad party policy mainly by personal discussion with party leaders who were passing through London.

– Ralph Ramkarran to Oscar Ramjeet (May 2017)

Billy Strachan was a member of the CPGB…He was de facto political ambassador of the PPP in London, and he served as a conduit to the CPSU and East European Communist Parties. He was unshakeable in his fidelity to Soviet hegemony and the CPSU line. The Jagans supported the Soviet invasions of Hungary, Czechoslovakia, and Afghanistan.

– Moses Bhagwan, personal correspondence (March 2019)

I. An Overview of Burnham, Jagan, and D'Aguiar: The Nebulous Socialist, the Avid Pro-Soviet Communist, and the Rabid Anti-Communist

Cheddi Jagan could not resist showing all his cards to anyone inclined to read his and his party's numerous publications. But Linden Forbes Sampson Burnham (1923–85), the African Guyanese leader, has often been described as 'nebulous' or 'ambiguous': it was difficult to elicit a straight answer from him on anything. I recall Jock Campbell telling me that Forbes once pointed out to him that the only positive thing he had ever said about him was that he was a fine orator. Jock retorted that it was 'the best thing one could say about you.' Eusi Kwayana (formerly Sydney King) was the general secretary of Burnham's People's National Congress (PNC) and the editor of his party's organ, the *New Nation*, from 1958 to 1961. He states that Burnham had honed his spectacular oratorical skills, using rhetorical devices that may be deemed Churchillian, particularly the modulation of intonation of his voice. Yet he was no less versatile in deploying the vernacular, spiced with biting and witty folk allusions, in his mesmeric hold on his audiences, even those not enamoured of him. They listened to him to be entertained, not necessarily to be informed. But Kwayana was also candid in his observation that a discernible emptiness about content and ideology pervaded his speeches and his writings.

In 1993, Professor Frank Birbalsingh interviewed Eusi Kwayana in Toronto; he asked him for his assessment of Burnham. Although they were not friends, Kwayana had served loyally for nearly four years in Burnham's PNC – after he left the People's Progressive Party (PPP) around early 1957 – and he remained an 'ally' for many more, primarily for racial reasons, although he never rejoined the PNC following his expulsion in mid-1961. I reproduce that section of the interview, as it elucidates Kwayana's perspective on a very complex man:

Birbalsingh: I get the impression that, from the beginning, you were never really an admirer of Burnham. Yet, it seems, circumstances conspired to push you into his camp.

Kwayana: That is correct. My response at that stage was racial, and I said that at the time. **I said I would join Burnham for racial reasons because the country was already divided racially, and if Jagan was organising Indians, I would organise black people** [emphasis added].

Birbalsingh: How long did your union with Burnham last, and how did it break?

Kwayana: I remained a member of the PNC for four years [1957–61], and I maintained a kind of alliance with Burnham that went on longer than that [arguably nearly ten years]. Again because of ethnic realities. I was expelled from the PNC, specifically for a proposal put forward in my name, although I was not the only contributor. The proposal was that, as a constitutional solution, there should be a joint and equal premiership between leaders of the Indo-Guyanese and Afro-Guyanese, and that minority groups should be represented in an upper chamber of the Parliament that had the power to remove discriminatory legislation and expenditure from the budget. If this did not work the country should be partitioned racially as a last resort. [The document, titled 'In the Name of Freedom,' was issued on August 28, 1961, by the African Society for Racial Equality of Buxton, and signed by Herbert H. Nicholson ('Vigilance') and Sydney King (Eusi Kwayana)].

We were sure the country was moving to racial violence. Our rationale was not any cultural differences...it was purely a question of power-sharing. Within the group, Nicholson favoured partition, but I refused to go along with partition: only as a last resort, and so the proposal for joint premiership was essentially mine.[1]

African Guyanese wanted their country to join the West Indies Federation, perceived as their natural ethnic and cultural home, but Indo-Guyanese (like Indo-Trinidadians) were dubious of this project, regarding it as deleterious to their growing demographic, economic and political ascendancy. Africans and Coloureds, including the so-called ultra-left who quit the PPP in 1956 (Sydney King in particular), were appalled that Jagan, for racial and political reasons, was determined to reject the Federation. Their apprehension was exacerbated by the likelihood that the British would grant independence to Jagan in 1962. Therefore, an independent Guyana would, inevitably, seal the fate of Africans as a permanent minority.

Could their African leader rescue them from the brink of the abyss? How did Forbes Burnham respond? He was loosely linked to the Communist Party of Great Britain (CPGB) while a law student in England in the late 1940s, but he was never a communist. Burnham did not espouse even a theoretical Marxism; he had no predilection for it. Neither was he enamoured of dogmas, but he was a fervent anti-colonialist, anti-British to the core and viscerally anti-White, and proud of his African antecedence. He was well-read, articulate, formidably clever, and inclined to arrogance about it. He was repelled by Jagan's dogmatic political vocabulary and his plantation obsessions, informed by the Marxist-Leninist primers. Burnham quit the PPP in 1955, and he contested the general elections in 1957, retaining the name of the PPP. It took him a few years to establish a distinct political identity credible enough to conciliate and consolidate African support for his new party, the PNC (founded in October 1957, after his ignominious defeat in the elections in August).

Jainaraine Singh, an Indian minister in the short-lived PPP government of 1953, who defected from the PPP at the same time as Burnham (in early 1955) and became secretary of his party, recalled in early 1957:

> We told the truth about the reason why there has been a split in the PPP. We told the people that communism was the basis of it all. We, not being communists, could not support a communist policy, and that is why we parted company at the time.[2]

In fact, shortly after the split, Burnham (writing in his *PPP Thunder* on April 16, 1955) disavowed any sympathy for Jagan's communism, as he defined the broad political orientation of the PPP (Burnham), the precursor to the PNC:

> Ours is not a communist party nor is the party affiliated to any communist organisation outside or inside the country. This does not mean that this party is prepared to launch a witch-hunt against persons who call themselves communists or who are in fact communists. What it does mean is that we will not and cannot permit persons who consider an international reputation for being communists more important than the success of our struggle to thereby slow up our movement and weaken it. Such persons who seem to be geniuses at isolating themselves and the cause they espouse are liabilities unless they are prepared to discontinue their wanton conduct and put the movement before their personal fancies. We are fighting right now to get the British off our backs and will direct our energies and efforts to that end instead of having them diverted to irrelevant issues [communism].

The British, following their suspension of the Constitution in October 1953, had intimated to Burnham that his political prospects could be propitious were he to disengage from the 'extremist' politics of Jagan and the communists and adopt a more 'moderate' stance. This was consonant with their *modus operandi* in relation to the Fabian socialism or the social democracy of two of the principal political leaders in the British West Indies: Norman Manley of Jamaica and Grantley Adams of Barbados, likewise anti-communist Eric Williams (all three Oxford-educated), who emerged shortly thereafter (in 1955–56), in Trinidad. Burnham was being lured into a distinctly non-communist posture, an antidote to the unpalatable extremism of the intransigent Jagan: the lone communist with political gravitas in regional politics. But Burnham was finding it challenging to embrace forthrightly their tantalising overture because of his passionate anti-colonial, anti-British, discernibly anti-White propensity. He had other problems: the low morale within his new party (still devoid of coherence: ambiguously called PPP [Burnham]), struggling to find its feet and its identity, after the split from the PPP in February 1955. This was compounded by a palpable inertia among Africans generally, set against the self-assurance and optimism (even triumphalism) manifested by Indo-Guyanese after the War.

Michael Swan, an English writer, visited British Guiana in early 1955 under the auspices of the Colonial Office. He had an audience with Forbes Burnham, but despite the recent split in the PPP, Burnham was tardy in articulating a coherent political philosophy beyond his known anti-colonialism and rejection of Jagan's pro-Soviet communism. Yet he appeared not to embrace the British, even tangentially, despite their carrot to him of adopting a moderate posture, with the possibility of his elevation as a credible counter to the communist Jagan. Moreover, he was disinclined to be defined primarily as an ethnic leader representing his African people. The Robertson Commission considered Burnham 'ambiguous'; a British politician (Labour's Patrick Gordon Walker) assessed him thus in 1954: 'His whole political approach is opportunistic...he will tack and turn as advantage seems to dictate.' He rarely ever showed his cards, but he was shrewd in seizing the moment, guided primarily by pragmatism and self-interest.

Swan observed:

> Mr Burnham is a leading Georgetown barrister, and I saw him in his chambers, a dilapidated wooden shack in the traditional manner of law offices in Georgetown. He was a tall handsome man of thirty-two, wearing gabardine drapes and a bow-tie...**He is a town man and his hatred of Sugar does not have the same root as Jagan's, being an extension of his violent anti-imperialism...**

> For Burnham the reason for the split was that there was too little emphasis on the national struggle in the colony because the issue of Communism had blurred everything. 'Communism is irrelevant to British Guiana at this stage,' he said, 'it's something only an independent country can think about. In British Guiana it's simply a matter of getting power and I don't see this coming for ten or fifteen years.' I asked him what his politics were...He smiled and said he had sympathy with some Marxist ideas and was against others [emphasis added].[3]

Forbes Burnham did badly in the general elections of 1957, winning only three seats: many Africans (particularly in rural constituencies) were despondent at his uninspiring campaign and did not vote (only 55 per cent of the eligible voters did so in 1957). Burnham was dispirited. On the other hand, with the consolidation of their Indian base, the Jagans had, in effect, inadvertently redefined the parameters of political mobilisation for Burnham — the primacy of race was now self-evident: an imperative. Consequently, Burnham soon sought to remake his rather nebulous political identity since the split of 1955 to project a more robust African posture. By amalgamating his PNC with the older, right-wing party of John Carter and W. O. R. Kendall, the United Democratic Party (formerly the National Democratic Party), in 1959, Burnham was beginning to shape a more coherent African profile. He also benefited immeasurably from Sydney's King's defection from Jagan's PPP in early 1957 and his assumption of the post of general secretary of the PNC and editor of *New Nation* in early

1958. King had solid African credentials rooted in his perceived asceticism, incorruptibility and continued humble residence and accessibility in the Black village of Buxton on the East Coast Demerara. Equally pivotal to Burnham's political reinvention was his studied projection of pragmatism – the cultivation and perfection of vagueness, the eschewing of a definitive ideological stance. His was a politics of eclecticism designed to allay any residual suspicion of his links with communism, and more reflective of the general social democratic run of West Indian politicians. In the process, Burnham was also building bridges with West Indian leaders; his stature was bolstered by his support for the West Indies Federation, a project that Jagan opposed on spurious grounds, widely perceived in the region as primarily racial premises, despite his continual rejection of such assertions.

But, following Jagan's electoral victory in August 1957 and up to around early 1961, the British were gradually reconciled to what they discerned as a more mature and moderate posture by Jagan, who appeared to have lessened his Marxist rhetoric while focusing on possibilities for economic development. Jock Campbell (the chairman of Booker) also had become more amenable to Cheddi, having abandoned his antagonism to his 'communist' *modus operandi* of the early 1950s, culminating in the suspension of the Constitution in 1953, which Jock is believed to have supported, if not recommended. He was a friend of Iain Macleod, the liberal Tory secretary of state for the colonies (1959–61). They were both of Scottish descent; they shared an old family friendship. Jock told me that he had conversations with Macleod (in 1959–60), and they concurred that there was no alternative to Cheddi Jagan leading British Guiana to independence. He had also forwarded to Macleod the confidential talk he gave to the Booker Board in March 1960, recommending long-term support for Jagan over Burnham.[4]

Like Jock Campbell, Macleod was not enamoured of Forbes Burnham. Jock said that he spoke with Cheddi shortly after Macleod had granted him internal self-government (in March 1960), with the distinct probability of independence in a couple years. Yet Cheddi was incensed, denouncing Macleod and the British government for not granting full independence immediately. After the conference, Jock invited Cheddi and his PPP delegation (including Balram Singh Rai) to dinner at his club in London, the Travellers Club (on Pall Mall), where he informed Cheddi that Macleod and elements within the British government were largely sympathetic to him despite lingering reservations about his communist predilection. He also pointed out that Harold Macmillan's 'Wind of Change Speech,' to the South African Parliament in Cape Town, on February 3, 1960, constituted a definitive change in attitudes towards independence for colonies like British Guiana. Consequently, he counselled Jagan to temper his passions against the 'imperialists' because the tide was already turning in his favour. But Cheddi was not amenable to persuasion by one at the core of his 'bitter sugar' crusade, although he did get on well personally with Jock, and was inclined to make a distinction between him and the leaders of Booker in Georgetown, such as F. J. Seaford, Follet-Smith, Edgar Readwin, and Tony Tasker.[5]

Cheddi promptly informed Jock that he was going to Cuba as a guest of Fidel Castro; he was eager to learn how he was transforming his country in the region. Jock tried to dissuade Cheddi from visiting Castro's Cuba because it would open a Pandora's Box for the Americans and many politicians in Britain, Conservative and Labour. Several were already ferociously apprehensive of Macleod's overtures towards Jagan, in the aftermath of the Cuban Revolution, defined as 'a red menace' in the Western Hemisphere. Jock feared that Cheddi's Cuban visit would revive the antipathy towards him by his many foes in the Conservative Party.[6]

Cheddi and Janet visited Cuba in April/May 1960, less than a month after the successful constitutional conference in London. The trip was arranged by Cuban officials in London, largely through the instrumentality of Billy Strachan (the Jamaican-born communist and secretary of the Caribbean Labour Congress), Cheddi's friend and confidant in London, the principal actor in the Caribbean section of the CPGB. The Jagans met Castro and 'Che' Guevara. It was the beginning of the process by which Cheddi took British Guiana into the Cold War definitively against the Americans.

By April 1961, in the aftermath of the Bay of Pigs debacle, the failure to overthrow Castro (conceived by the Eisenhower administration and executed with humiliating ineptitude by the Kennedy administration), it was clear that the Americans would not tolerate another communist regime in the Americas, and they told the British so. The failure fed an obsession on the part of President Kennedy – deemed a matter of the utmost national security – to get rid of Jagan before the British granted him independence, as they were inclined to do by 1962–63. Burnham had not fully reshaped his political posture to counter Jagan's communism, but he was distancing himself from Castro and Soviet communism and tilting towards the Americans.

However, it was the founding, in October 1960, of the rabidly anti-communist United Force (UF), led by Peter D'Aguiar (1912–89), a businessman of Portuguese ancestry (supported by the Catholic Church), that really brought the Cold War home, vilifying Jagan relentlessly as an agent of Fidel Castro and the Russians: a 'red menace' and a 'commie stooge.' It was an unsparing anti-communist crusade, pursued with an intensity and absence of restraint that Burnham probably could not have envisaged, and which, arguably, he was temperamentally and philosophically disinclined to initiate and execute. But it was an unimaginably bountiful gift to him, and he was canny enough to let the UF prosecute it while feigning indifference. The greatest beneficiary of the relentless 'anti-red' crusade of the UF was Forbes Burnham. Small in terms of its support-base but ideologically impassioned in its anti-communist loathing and paranoia over the impending 'godless communism,' the UF received the unstinted support of the Catholic Church, the Portuguese, and light coloureds, as well as the indigenous Amerindians, swayed by the inordinate influence of the Catholic missionaries in the interior of British Guiana.

In addition, Peter D'Aguiar controlled two newspapers that were indefatigable in fomenting anti-communism: the *Daily Chronicle* and the *Sun*, the latter being the weekly organ of the UF. Another rabid anti-communist, Peter Taylor (an Englishman), owned the *Weekend Post and Sunday Argosy* as well as the *Evening Post*. The organ of the Catholic Church, the *Catholic Standard*, played a similar role in the crusade. It was the irrepressible zeal of these papers – a visceral antipathy to communism – that really dramatised the Cold War in British Guiana, between 1961 and 1964. From the sidelines, Forbes Burnham must have relished this sustained onslaught that relentlessly demonised Jagan as a communist lackey of Fidel Castro and the Russians. Burnham was conspicuously less strident in his anti-communism, but this crusade piloted by D'Aguiar helped immeasurably in elevating Burnham categorically in the scheme of the Kennedy administration as their man: their anointed alternative to the communist Jagan.

Meanwhile, Guyanese racism had its own dynamic, oblivious of American obsession with the allure of communism in a colonial backwater. Even the foremost exemplars of early Marxist illumination, Cheddi Jagan and Sydney King, could not elude the Procrustean racial mould. In essence, no utopian philosophy promising the perfectibility of mankind, often seducing many enthralled by it to perpetrate heinous crimes for the elusive heaven on earth, could eliminate primordial loyalties: to one's racial, religious, tribal, linguistic, or caste group. One's identity is ineluctably shaped by these ancient aggregations of social organisation, possibly ineradicable and stubbornly resurgent, as the demise of the Soviet Union and its dreadful failure to erase ethnic particularism have underscored.

This explains why a man like Sydney King, the foremost African ally of Cheddi Jagan between 1947 and 1955, would return to his ethnic source as the wellspring of his politics, apprehensive not of Jagan's communism but of what he perceived as his political opportunism, premised primarily on Indian economic ascendancy, bolstered by the advantage of an ominous Indian demographic upsurge. The fragile experiment in the inclusively democratic politics of the early 1950s, in a racially insecure and increasingly fissiparous British Guiana, was short-lived. Yet, as with Peter D'Aguiar's anti-communist crusade, Burnham benefited immeasurably from King's Afrocentric cultural mission, shaped profoundly by the racial political environment – premised on racial solidarity with Burnham even after King was expelled from the PNC in mid-1961. Kwayana's mercurial politics, however convoluted, is reflective of the depth of the racial insecurity that permeates Guyanese society, then, now, and conceivably for a long time to come.

But throughout Burnham's political career, from his return to Guyana in 1949 as an English-trained lawyer to his death at the comparatively early age of sixty-two in August 1985, it was his oratorical gifts and his deftness in evading ideological labels (frequently inhibiting) that stand out. He was, indeed, the antithesis of the dogmatic Jagan. In 1960, Forbes Burnham was the leader of the Opposition, and with most assuming that the colony (under Jagan) was 'on the threshold of independence,' it was hard to imagine how his political career could be retrieved from its seeming inevitable nullity. In fact, with the eradication of malaria by the end of the 1940s and the consequent explosion of the Indian population on the coastland of the colony, it would have been delusory to anticipate anything but a terminal decline of Burnham's political vocation. But Burnham possessed special gifts that could make him a potentially effective politician.

V. S. Naipaul was travelling in British Guiana in late 1960, and he framed a telling portrait of Burnham, the consummate orator, at a public meeting in the town of New Amsterdam in Berbice:

> Mr Burnham, in a plain short-sleeved sports shirt, was speaking from a high platform...He spotted the chauffeur [Jagan's, who had taken Naipaul to the meeting] and made a comment too full of local allusion for me to understand...Mr Burnham is the finest public speaker I have heard. He speaks slowly, precisely, incisively; he makes few gestures; his head is thrust forward in convinced, confiding, simple but never condescending exposition; he is utterly calm, and his fine voice is so nicely modulated that the listener never tires or ceases to listen. The manner conceals an amazing quickness, all the more effective for never revealing itself in an acceleration of pace or a change of pitch...His speeches are known to be entertaining and the crowds come to be entertained, as the New Amsterdam crowd undoubtedly was...Unfortunately Mr Burnham had little to say.[7]

Compare this with a verbatim excerpt from a public address by Cheddi Jagan, in San Fernando (Trinidad), a few months earlier, in April 1960, en route from Castro's Cuba to British Guiana. This was no aberration – any such presentation by Jagan was permeated by examples drawn from various places around the world and augmented by copious statistical data, supposedly confirming the evils of capitalism/imperialism and the inexorable march to socialism/communism. It was a kind of religious mission. And he never relented:

> British Guiana in 1953 [the suspension of the constitution] was not an isolated event. It started with the Cold War. We in the West Indies were victims of the Cold War. In 1948, the oil companies overthrew the Romulo Gallegos government in Venezuela. That was the beginning. In 1951 Mosaddeq, who was not a communist, his government was overthrown in Iran, and he was put in jail. Our turn came in 1953, and the boys told me in Cuba – I met some Guatemalans there – that as soon as they saw our Government was overthrown, they knew their turn was coming, and it came in 1954 [the coup against Jacobo Arbenz (1913–71) by the CIA]. What I'm trying to say to you is that the freedom movement of the world today is not an individual problem. Freedom is indivisible, and wherever you are fighting for independence and economic emancipation, vested interest and the imperialists will come down on you like a ton of bricks.
>
> Let us take Latin America. From 1946 to 1955, 2 billion dollars of new investments went into Latin America, and 7 billion dollars were drawn out of Latin America in that period…Take [neighbouring] Venezuela, in one year, 1954, 1.25 billion dollars were invested, but in that year alone 1.5 billion dollars were made in profits…60% of Bolivia's exports come from tin; 84% of Colombia's exports from coffee; 59% of Brazil's from this product, and 69% of El Salvador's from it. Ecuador and Uruguay export respectively 56% and 52% of bananas; Chile, 56% of the economy is based on copper; and Venezuela 94% is based on oil.[8]

This is a sample of the density of empirical data that, without fail, characterised even Cheddi's seminal writings and speeches for the PAC and as a legislator, from 1946–47; he was already unique in the colony for the volume and diversity of the research that underpinned his presentations. These were consistently anti-imperialist (pontificating against the abominable exploiters, the Americans and the British), while ritualistically celebrating every facet of life in the Soviet Union and the 'People's Democracies' of Eastern Europe. Burnham, on the other hand, was profoundly anti-colonial and discernibly anti-White, but it was hard to pin a definitive ideological label on him. His whole approach was guided by *realpolitik*, with the sharpness of his legal mind navigating him dexterously around the Jaganite communist jargon that constricted his imagination. The irony was that most of Jagan's supporters, Indians, had no idea what communism was all about. Even today, they (including the certificated) still reject that he was a communist.

II. Billy Strachan of the Communist Party of Great Britain: Cheddi's Mentor and Foremost Guru in Pursuit of his Marxist-Leninist Creed

Billy Strachan (1921–98), the Jamaican-born communist and leading member of the Communist Party of Great Britain (CPGB), a Marxist theoretician and life-long mentor and confidant of Cheddi and Janet Jagan with strong links to the Soviet Union and its satellites

Richard Hart (1917–2013), the other Jamaican-born communist, another revered fount of Marxist inspiration to Cheddi Jagan. He briefly edited the Mirror, *the newspaper of Jagan's PPP*

Dr Fenton Ramsahoye, Cheddi Jagan's young attorney general in the turbulent years, 1961–64, has remarked on the ramification of Jagan's allegiance to the Soviet Union in the Cold War – the price he paid for being America's perceived enemy in their 'backyard.' It was a journey to nowhere for Cheddi:

> The Americans believed that Jagan was being financed by the Soviet Union, and that who paid the piper would call the tune. It is true the party had very strong ties with the Soviet Union. I also think the party was being financed by them. But how much the party got by way of finance was never known to members of the General Council. It was never discussed at our party meetings. We discussed how we would fight to get Independence from the British. And we would not have had to fight for Independence were it not that Cheddi Jagan was considered to be on the side of the Soviet Union in the Cold War. We would have got Independence at the Constitutional Conference, in London, in 1962.

> The reason why the British didn't give us Independence was this security scare that the Americans suffered from... [And] the United Kingdom was America's greatest ally. When we were ministers we were told, in correspondence from the Foreign and Colonial Offices in the UK, that we should not do things to become dependent on the Eastern Bloc. They were hinting that they didn't want us to ally ourselves in any manner or form with the Eastern Bloc, not even to trade with them. Whereas the other West Indian countries heeded that warning, we did not. And we paid dearly for it.[9]

Jagan had taken British Guiana into the Cold War, and he could not elude the dire consequences. Dr Ramsahoye implies that, by the early 1960s, independence was a gift routinely granted by the British: there for the taking. However, Jagan's devotion to Soviet communism (a kind of religiosity) virtually ensured that his 'imperialist' foes (creatures of his making, supposedly doomed by the laws of the evolution of society to be the losers) conspired to deprive him of the prize. The Americans did prevail upon the British to contrive a means of guaranteeing that Jagan did not rule an independent Guyana. Moses Bhagwan and Fenton Ramsahoye did not (or could not) elaborate on the process by which the financial link between the PPP and the CPSU was sustained, as it is not widely known that the main figure in the process, the conduit, was most likely the Jamaican-born communist and, for many decades, a member of the CPGB, Billy Strachan (1921–98). He lived in Colindale, north-west London, and the Jagans corresponded with him at least a couple times a month, over several decades. They were family friends. That 'comradeship' never ceased, not even during the decades when Jagan was in the political wilderness.

As the partial correspondence reveals (many letters are withheld, and Strachan's are not included), Cheddi and Janet considered Billy Strachan their ideological guru; they clearly regarded his learning in Marxism, his thoughts on most issues, and his solid links to the CPGB (therefore the CPSU and its satellites) as sacrosanct. It is highly likely that Billy was the intermediary for Soviet funding to the PPP, and the fact that the quarterly accounts of the PPP's trading arm dealing exclusively with communist countries, GIMPEX, were sent up to Strachan in London, without fail, gives credence to the assumption that he was, indeed, crucial to the link between the PPP and the communist bloc. GIMPEX sold merchandise that originated in the communist countries, and this was arguably a means by which some funds reached the PPP. The goods were generally shoddy but cheap.

David Horsley has commented on Billy's relationship with Cheddi and Janet Jagan:

> Billy was a great letter-writer, and his archive is brimming with letters replying to him, especially from the Caribbean. The majority are

from Cheddi and Janet Jagan, who were close friends of his as well as being political comrades...A most important role in Billy Strachan's life was as a mentor...His comrades from the Caribbean Labour Congress...acknowledged him as a mentor and teacher.

Cheddi and Janet Jagan, too, revered Billy as their Marxist-Leninist guru. Horsley adds that Billy once told his son, Chris Strachan, that 'if I hadn't discovered Marxism, I would have undoubtedly ended up in a mental institution.'[10] And like Billy, Cheddi also found in Marxism-Leninism the certainties and self-assurance that religion often gives to its devotees.

Strachan, bearing the authority of the CPGB, as head of its West Indian Committee and a member of its International Committee, was obviously highly respected by the Soviets. He was certainly instrumental in securing scholarships in the bloc for many young members of Jagan's PPP, as he was in facilitating visits to the Soviet Union and Eastern Europe for activists of the PPP. Virtually every member of the PPP who came to London or passed through the city, en route to Eastern Europe, made a pilgrimage to Billy's home in Colindale, north-west London. This relationship had deep roots in the pro-communist Caribbean Labour Congress (London Branch), of which Billy was secretary and Ranji Chandisingh, its president. Billy retained strong links with Jamaica, particularly the Marxist left of the People's National Party (PNP) in which Richard Hart was the leading light. Norman Manley expelled the communists in the PNP in 1952, but the comradeship of Billy and Dick Hart remained inviolable for the rest of their lives.

It was Strachan who had recommended Forbes Burnham, a clever law student in London, to the Jagans; he was also instrumental in arranging for Burnham, on his way home to British Guiana in 1949 after his studies in London, to visit Jamaica to be apprised of the organisation of the PNP. And it was Dick Hart (1917–2013), one of a small minority of communists in the PNP, who made it possible for Burnham to do a two-week course on the grassroots organisation of the PNP. Hart recalls:

> ...the PNP was the only party with a grassroots membership structure in the English-speaking Caribbean. Burnham came and did that course in 1949...I arranged it as Secretary of the Caribbean Labour Congress (CLC). I had previously persuaded Billy Strachan to take the initiative in launching the CLC (London Branch). It was soon after that that Billy wrote telling me about Burnham, and it was the CLC in London who arranged for Burnham to come to Jamaica. Then Janet wrote to say she and Cheddi were taking a holiday that included Jamaica. So, I arranged a similar course for them, and when they launched the PPP, they had acquired knowledge of the political structure of the PNP in Jamaica. That is how they were able to model the PPP on a similar grassroots organisation basis.[11]

This was a prelude to the founding of the PPP on Sunday, January 1, 1950. There is no evidence that Burnham was a member of the CPGB although he probably empathised with some aspects of their programme; he was, however, ferociously anti-British and apparently harboured a palpable antipathy towards White people generally. He was very proud of his African antecedents, and this would later be reflected in his unfettered solidarity with, and material support for, African liberation, particularly the anti-apartheid movement. But Strachan did recommend several communists to the Jagans, of whom Lionel Jeffrey, Keith Carter, Rory Westmaas, Ranji Chandisingh, George David, and Trevor Carter (a Trinidadian) all worked for, or were closely associated with, the PPP in Georgetown in the 1950s–60s; so did Dick Hart (as editor of the PPP's *Mirror* in 1965–66).

But the most far-reaching recommendation Billy Strachan made to the Jagans was Ranji Chandisingh (1930–2009), a Harvard-educated communist, a disciple of Billy in the Caribbean Labour Congress (UK branch) and the CPGB, and editor of *Caribbean News* (organ of the former, monthly then bi-monthly, between 1952 and 1956). Ranji was an urbane intellectual (he looked it) and erudite Marxist theoretician, who went to British Guiana in 1958 to edit the PPP's *Thunder*. He remained in the PPP, sustaining its Marxist flame until 1976. Widely believed to have been anointed by Jagan to succeed him as leader of the PPP, Ranji defected to Burnham's PNC in early 1976, possibly at the prompting of the Cubans. It was probably the most lacerating of the multitude of defections of close lieutenants Cheddi and Janet had to endure over several decades. How they survived Ranji's 'betrayal' is a miracle. But, as if to demonstrate the futility of Ranji's flight to a bogus belated Burnhamite adoption of Marxism, Cheddi became even more tortuously enmeshed in Marxist ideology – a kind of theology – arguably intensified specifically to counter the widely recognised cleverness of Ranji in Marxist philosophy and politics. But Cheddi's pursuit of Marxist purity, in contrast to the 'revisionism' of so-called Marxists (Marxism/Burnhamism), even the perceived independent Marxism of Walter Rodney, merely vindicated the futility of Jagan's pro-Moscow communist politics, which (as I argue) originated with the Political Affairs Committee in the late 1940s.

The principal West Indian communists in Britain were Billy Strachan (1921–98), Rolly Simms, and Ranji Chandisingh (1930–2009). They were the leaders of the Caribbean Labour Congress (London Branch), a communist-front organisation sponsored by the CPGB. George Padmore, a former communist from Trinidad, observed that funding to the CPGB came through the World Federation of Trade Unions (WFTU), based in Vienna with an office in London. Whatever funding went to communists in the West Indies would have gone from the CPGB, through Billy Strachan's CLC, to, say, Jagan's PPP. This would explain why both Cheddi and Janet Jagan corresponded over several decades with Billy Strachan, even during the most difficult years in British Guiana (1962–64), when the colony was experiencing virtual civil war. They shared their most important thoughts with Billy, while continually seeking his wise Marxist counsel, as they obviously saw it, on political matters and in establishing links with Moscow and its East European satellites.

Much of the telephone conversations between the Jagans and their communist friends in the CLC and the CPGB were bugged by MI5, and many of their letters were intercepted and copied before they reached their recipients. The security liaison officer (SLO) in Trinidad and Special Branch in British Guiana were also deeply involved in similar activities. It is clear from the files that this information was routinely conveyed both to the Colonial Office and the governor of British Guiana. From as early as the early 1950s, before the suspension of the Constitution in October 1953, the links between the Jagans and the British communists, such as Harry Pollitt and Rajani Palme Dutt, the two foremost leaders of the CPGB, were well documented. Further day-to-day sensitive information was also procured by agents planted by MI5 in the CPGB headquarters ('King Street'). Two of these, using the pseudonyms 'North' and 'Lascar,' reported regularly on conversations between visitors to the King St office of the CPGB and Pollitt, Dutt, and another communist, Idris Cox.

The CPGB was aware of the formation of the PPP in British Guiana in January 1950, when an emissary of Cheddi Jagan initiated links between the two parties. They wanted access to the material and ideological resources of the Communist Party at the heart of Empire. 'Lascar,' the MI5 spy planted in the CPGB, reported this initiative by the PPP thus:

> In 1950 'Lascar' reported that the CPGB's attention was drawn to the formation of the PPP in British Guiana when an emissary of Jagan, whose identity was not established, attempted to obtain the help of the CPGB with a view to:
>
> (a) buying a printing press;
>
> (b) reprinting articles from the *Daily Worker* [organ of the CPGB];
>
> (c) obtaining suitable supplies of books and pamphlets.
>
> The attitude of the CPGB appeared to be that it would give all possible support, but it did not wish to be openly involved for two reasons:
>
> (a) there would be opposition in the UK;
>
> (b) overt communist interference might alienate those in the colony who would otherwise join the party for nationalist reasons.[12]

The report also summarised the nature of Jagan's visit to the UK and Eastern Europe in 1951. He established contacts with the International Department of the CPGB (R. Palme Dutt and Idris Cox), and he also met with the manager of WFTU Publications. In August 1951, he attended the Third World Festival of Youth and Students in Berlin (a Soviet sponsored event) before going on to Prague, Czechoslovakia, where he 'denounced British Imperialism' on Prague Radio. When he returned to the UK in September, he 'offered his services' to the CPGB in the general election campaign. 'Lascar' reported that Jagan sought the help of the CPGB in contacting Soviet and 'satellite embassies' in London. This contact with the CPGB and the WFTU was, of course, strengthened immeasurably by the comradeship Cheddi and Janet maintained with Billy Strachan.

In fact, the Jagans hardly tried to conceal their communist connections. Janet became a regular correspondent for the organ of the CPGB, the *Daily Worker*. Cheddi wrote for *World Student News*, a Soviet-backed paper; and he sent fraternal greetings to the East German Trade Union Organisation as the president of the Sawmill Workers' Union in British Guiana. He was clearly invigorated by his travels and engagement with communists in the UK and Europe, as the MI5 report points out: 'When Jagan returned to British Guiana at the end of November 1951, the PPP sought greater publicity than before and Jagan himself declared his Communist sympathies openly, as was instanced by his support for the World Peace Council [WPC], the showing of films depicting life in Satellite countries [of Eastern Europe]; and in the Legislative Council he openly praised Russia and the Satellite countries [or People's Democracies, as he called them]...'[13] The WPC was another Soviet-front organisation, dedicated to the anti-imperialist campaign of the USSR.

Billy Strachan was so central to fostering relations between the PPP and the CPGB, as well as with the communist bloc, that even delicate internal issues of the PPP were broached with him. In a letter dated February 6, 1953 (cited earlier), Janet Jagan wrote to Billy about Sydney King; she was perturbed that he had been away in Eastern Europe longer than expected. Meanwhile, Forbes Burnham was apparently seeking to extend his political reach towards leadership. Janet was obviously alluding to the fact that Sydney King, as the second most influential African in the PPP and known for his strong Marxist views (more compatible with Cheddi than Forbes), was probably the only person with the racial, ideological, and personality capital, combined with his gravitas, to temper Burnham's militant pursuit of his leadership ambition, with potential for the eruption of a nasty racial split in the PPP – a rather precarious coalition – on the eve of the first elections under universal adult suffrage.

It is interesting that Billy Strachan had apparently warned the Jagans about Forbes Burnham's consuming quest for power within the PPP. Yet, as Billy also acknowledged, it was on his recommendation that Cheddi and Forbes were to meet in British Guiana, in 1949, after the latter had completed his legal studies in England. Billy also recalled, at the memorial for Cheddi Jagan on May 25, 1997,[14] that it was Forbes who had brought to his attention the *PAC Bulletin*, published by Cheddi and Janet since November 6, 1946, and 'clearly built on Marxist thought.' They were both impressed with the radical character of the *Bulletin* and were prompted to contemplate a political party inspired by its frame of reference. This was the context in which Billy and Forbes wrote to Cheddi, and it led to the decision to form what became the PPP. It is interesting, however, that Billy gives no hint of the political philosophy of Forbes Burnham nor his relationship with him beyond those initial encounters in London. His evident rapport with Jagan, on the other hand, sprang from a common belief in, and pursuit of, their communist creed. In fact, they would remain steadfast disciples of Marxism-Leninism adhering loyally to the vagaries of the Moscow line. The only other person in the region who would embrace the gospel of Moscow with similar fidelity was Fidel Castro.

Billy Strachan, though, was the ideological godfather of Cheddi and Janet Jagan: no other person, neither Fidel nor Khrushchev (later), could exert the supreme qualities as mentor to Cheddi and Janet. Shortly after Billy died in 1998, Janet wrote:

> Billy was my friend, my comrade, my mentor, for most of my adult life. He gave himself fully to our struggle. He was a genuine Caribbean man, always in the forefront of labour and political challenges of our time. I will miss him very much. Life without Billy is not the same.[15]

Like Billy, Cheddi was a true believer. They would never dare to question whatever edict emanated from the Soviet Union. And on matters pertaining to the People's Democracies of Eastern Europe, whether Hungary (1956) or Czechoslovakia (1968), the Soviet line was sacrosanct as was their belief in the perfectibility of humankind as enunciated by the USSR. To both men, Marxism-Leninism was a kind of theology that filled a peculiar void in their lives. It was cathartic; it provided a 'scientific' means of redressing the seeming futility of the human condition. I wish to repeat what Cheddi explained to V. S. Naipaul in 1991 that Marxism gave him

> **a total understanding** of the development of society. Until then all the various struggles…had been disjointed experiences. To put it in a way that was *totally* related to a socio-economic system came from the reading of Marxist literature. For instance, the woman question was dealt with in Engels's book, *The Origins of the Family*. The Marxist

> theory of surplus value brought a **totally** new understanding of the
> struggle of the working class – not only that they were exploited. It
> was exciting to me, an intellectual excitement, because a whole new
> world opened to me, **a total understanding of the world** [emphasis
> added].[16]

Coming from the sugar plantation, Marxism offered Cheddi the instrument to right ancient wrongs, perpetrated by 'the sugar gods.' It did take the place of his family's Hindu frame of reference. It offered 'total knowledge.'

Forbes Burnham, on the other hand, was from the lower middle class, the son of an African headmaster in Kitty, a suburban district on the north-eastern edge of Georgetown. His class comprised literate people and included the colony's African schoolteachers (men and women), the lower echelons of the colonial civil service, most of the clergymen of the nonconformist Christian churches, several lawyers, a few doctors and chemists, and many journalists – people who had mastered, or were at ease with, English colonial idioms: education, cricket, and Christianity. These African professionals were tutored to assimilate, and were cultivated to negotiate, most aspects of the imperial culture. Largely an urban people, they were palpably shaped by the mores and the etiquette fostered by their colonial education. This was not the case with most Indians, Hindus and Muslims, still steeped in their ancestral cultures and largely unhabituated to the emerging creole sensibility. (Indentureship was not terminated until 1920, two years after Jagan's birth.) Forbes Burnham's training as a lawyer (in London in the late 1940s), his whole make-up, enabled him to master the subtleties and the cultivated ambiguities and ironies of British political discourse. And like several British politicians at the time, Forbes also had a way with words – a compelling oratorical style and the lawyer's gift for articulating a position eloquently and delicately, without being constrained by a definitive, and potentially inhibiting, political label.

Burnham wrote several articles, including by-lined leaders for the PPP organ, *Thunder*, between 1950 and early 1955, when he left the original PPP claiming to be the authentic leader of that party. But an examination of a cross-section of his writing does not establish any congruence whatsoever, even a suggestion of empathy, with the Marxism-Leninism of Cheddi and Janet Jagan. Indeed, beyond a general, ritual denunciation of British colonialism and White racism, one discerns nothing ideological that could, by any stretch of the imagination, earn him the pejorative label of 'communist' by the colonial rulers or their American friends – the bane of the Jagans, from the end of the 1940s to the collapse of the Soviet Union and the death of communism at the end of the 1980s. But the Jagans, like Billy Strachan, never deviated from their loyalty to the CPSU. In recommending Ranji Chandisingh to Cheddi and Janet, Billy deemed him a Marxist theoretician of the highest order (pro-Soviet, of course), and from 1958 (when Ranji became the editor of the PPP's *Thunder*) to 1976, when he defected to Burnham's PNC, Ranji and Cheddi were the principal keepers of the communist flame in the PPP.[17]

Professor Harold 'Harry' Drayton (1929–2018), a friend of Strachan for many years in the UK, substantiates in his magisterial memoirs that Billy was the ideological foundation stone and confidant par excellence of Cheddi and Janet. Drayton recalls a meeting with Billy in Earl's Court, London, in late 1962, on the eve of his return from Ghana to Guyana, at the request of Cheddi, to pilot the creation of the University of Guyana in 1963. Billy had posed what Harry considered 'a strange question' that 'totally flummoxed' him: 'Harry, why is it that in all the years that you were a student in Edinburgh [1954–60], and lived in this country, you never joined the Communist Party [of Great Britain]?' Drayton sought to defuse the apprehensions Billy clearly held regarding his communist credentials, noting that the president of the Edinburgh University Communist Club had counselled him that he could exert more political influence if he did not belong to a political party. But Harry also reassured Billy that he had spoken frequently on many communist platforms in Edinburgh, besides collaborating with them in organising meetings and campaigns.

Harry ended his uncomfortably defensive response to Billy's disturbing reservation regarding his communist authenticity thus:

> I finally blurted that the only Party affiliation that I **did** treasure was with the PPP of British Guiana, which I had supported actively as a member since the year of its foundation in 1950, and in which I looked forward to working on my return to B.G. He had listened to all I had said without a single interruption, and when I had finished, all that I remembered Billy saying was: "Some people may still wonder, as I do, why you never took that final step." It was a statement that I did not think merited a response.'[18]

Like Billy, Cheddi had a virtually divine devotion to communism. And they could not really trust anyone who did not accept the creed comprehensively, no matter how sterling their contribution within or beyond the party.

It was only when Harry returned to British Guiana that he was able to fathom the 'critical importance' of Billy Strachan's scepticism regarding his communist credentials, that afternoon in London in November 1962. Only then did he grasp fully Billy's enormous influence on the politics of Cheddi and Janet Jagan. Harry Drayton provides a rare insight into the centrality of the relationship between the Jagans and the CPGB, and the critical role of Strachan in it:

> Each Comrade – in preparation for work within the PPP on returning home [from the UK] – was expected to join the British Communist Party. As Chairman of the West Indies Committee of

the Party, Billy was expected to give a report to Cheddi/Janet on each Guyanese returning home to work with the PPP. I have never seen any such report, but I would imagine that it would have included the duration of CPGB membership, responsible roles within the Party, positive attributes, character flaws, addictions, a general assessment of loyalty and trustworthiness, 'fraternisation' with 'enemies,' such as Trotskyites, Anarchists and even Labour Party members.

The problem with the PPP was that so many of those who had served their apprenticeship in the British CP, sooner or later ran foul of the PPP leadership by sins of omission or commission, and either left or were booted out of the Party. Most notable of all of them was the illustrious Ranji Chandisingh, who after working for some years with the Soviet News Agency (TASS), and serving as a good and faithful Comrade of the West Indies Committee [of the CPGB], and almost a deputy to Billy, eventually returned home [in 1958] and was a minister in successive PPP administrations, only to 'jump ship' eventually [in 1976, after 18 years in the PPP] to become Burnham's Minister of Higher Education, General Secretary of the PNC and Ambassador to Moscow.[19]

Having never joined the CPGB (the source of all light!), Harry could now appreciate the basis of Billy's palpable anxieties over his returning to British Guiana to serve in Jagan's government. He could understand the problem this created for Billy: '…he would have no evidentiary basis for his customary report to the PPP, and without such a report, my loyalty and trustworthiness would always be dubious to the Party leadership.' Dr Fenton Ramsahoye told me on several occasions that he (and Balram Singh Rai) were never genuinely acceptable to the Jagans because they were not communists. They were perceived essentially as 'capitalist-roaders' (Fenton's expression), provoking a pervading suspicion that was beyond redress.

The detail provided by Professor Drayton suggests that he was not ignorant of the character of such mandatory reports by the communists in London. After all, he knew many in the leadership of the PPP at a personal level, as he did West Indian communists in London. The process probably originated in the paranoid sect-like ethos of the CPGB and other communist organisations. This engendered a culture of doctrinal inflexibility and mistrust, with a penchant for shutting out – to see few, only the ideologically pure and anointed, as potential allies. Worse! It planted in the Jagans, Billy Strachan, and his young, most-trusted lieutenant, Ranji Chandisingh, the conviction that they possessed the 'scientific' truth, at the heart of the inviolable Soviet interpretation of the Marxist-Leninist tenets.

But, as Eric Hoffer observes of those who think they are 'in possession of the one and only truth…backed [by]…the law of history': 'By elevating dogma above reason, the individual's intelligence is prevented from becoming self-reliant.'[20] It is not conducive to the cultivation of competence in statecraft: the give and take of the art of governance – a degree of pragmatism that is *realpolitik*. It has another potential fundamental flaw: it is inclined to perceive primordial loyalties, such as one's own racial identity, even one's own racism, in Guyana, as 'epiphenomenal' – a false problematic that would, of necessity, be eliminated by the release of the productive forces from moribund capitalism and the pursuit of equality under communism: an inevitable outcome, by the laws of dialectical materialism. Billy was the most illustrious West Indian Marxist by the early 1950s. And he had pedigree: a light-coloured Jamaican, who had excelled as a pilot in the Royal Air Force during the Second World War. Cheddi was also close to Billy's fellow communist compatriot, Richard Hart, equally respected as an authority in Marxist theory.

As noted earlier, for nearly four decades, however monumental the hurdles confronting their political mission, Cheddi and Janet never ceased communicating with Billy, never faltering in their adulation of his Marxist wisdom. Many of the letters from the Jagans to Billy were hand-written; even confidential family matters were apparently shared with him. Harry Drayton recalls that a delicate matter was broached when he met Billy in December 1962; he had enquired about the situation within the PPP with Cheddi, Janet and other comrades:

> [Billy responded]: There have been serious marital infidelities at senior levels of the Party,' he pronounced in a pontifical tone. But though I pressed for details, he would tell me nothing unless I would promise never to repeat what he would tell me. I promised. And although Billy and a number of the leading PPP Comrades have since died, a few of the principal actors are very much alive, and I feel that I am therefore still bound by my vow of silence. In any event the players and the circumstances of their situation are already so well known in Guyana and overseas, there is no need for the story to be repeated here. Billy seemed to regain his composure after divulging perhaps the only secret tale of PPP 'immorality' to which he was privy....[21]

Harry Drayton first met Billy Strachan in 1952, in Jamaica, when he was doing his first degree at the University College of the West Indies. He got to know him well during his years of graduate studies at the University of Edinburgh. I give the final word to Harry on the centrality of Billy to the political mission of the Jagans:

> Billy became quite well-known in London for his political activism as a member of the Communist Party...and had taken the initiative to establish the Caribbean Labour Congress (CLC London Branch), and the newspaper *Caribbean News* [the latter two were really an extension of the CPGB]. As a lifelong member of the Communist

Party of Great Britain, Billy never deviated from whatever was the prevailing 'party line'; and he often seemed to me incapable, even after the events of 1956 [Khrushchev's speech on the notorious reign of terror of Stalin and the Soviet invasion of Hungary], of taking a nuanced view of the role of the USSR in the international socialist movement. For that quality he was often criticised by the independent-minded West Indian 'left-wingers' and was lampooned on one occasion by *Private Eye* magazine as 'the veteran CP hack.'[22]

Yet it was Billy's implacability, his steadfastness in pursuit of the communist utopia as envisaged by the CPSU, that endeared him, for nearly five decades, to the CPGB as well as to Cheddi and Janet Jagan, his two most loyal and eminent disciples – the only ones with access to power and the potential of exercising power in a sovereign state. As Harry Drayton explains:

> …those very qualities earned him [Billy] the trust of the CPGB's leadership [particularly Harry Pollitt, R. Palme Dutt, and Idris Cox], and of all those in the Caribbean who cherished the objective of building a socialist society in their home countries, and who sought access from time to time, to the Party's resources, advice and international links. In this context…Billy Strachan served as the 'gatekeeper' for admission to the PPP of Guyanese comrades, who having served an apprenticeship in the CPGB, could be accredited by him as 'trained', disciplined, loyal and industrious.[23]

This is at the core of the problem with the doctrinaire politics of Cheddi Jagan – at variance with the eclecticism of Forbes Burnham. One could never really be 'kosher' within Cheddi's inner sect, as in Billy Strachan's, if the sacred body of 'scientific socialist' learning was not embraced unreservedly. And, if the recurring allegations of Janet's infidelity are accurate, Cheddi must have felt that there were very few around him in whom he could ever have confidence. The communist faith was reinforced; it became the ultimate truth – an inviolable body of beliefs that transcended the frailties and fatal flaws of humankind. The creed could not be profaned. I have argued that Marxism-Leninism took the place of Hinduism to which Cheddi's family, his mother (Bachaoni) in particular, was devoted. Billy reportedly said that his communist faith inoculated him against sliding into madness. His candid self-assessment was probably no less germane to Cheddi's sanity and resilience. However, the political partnership between Cheddi and Janet was a profound and lasting one: mutual human frailties could be absorbed, if not neutralised, by the imperatives of the transcendental utopian vision – the cause that could not be profaned – beyond violation.

III. The Communist Party of Great Britain: The Enduring Beacon for Cheddi and Janet Jagan

If there was one person in the world in whom Cheddi reposed total confidence, it was Billy Strachan. After the suspension of the Constitution in October 1953, Jagan and Burnham left British Guiana and travelled to the UK and India, endeavouring to present their case against British imperialism while garnering international solidarity. MI5 followed all their movements, taped Jagan's telephone conversations (I have no evidence that they did the same to Burnham), and documented Jagan's contacts with the communists in the CLC (London Branch). In fact, a few days after the suspension, MI5 taped the verbatim conversation between Jagan (in Georgetown) and Rolly Simms of the CLC (in London). It is indisputable that MI5, which transmitted their intelligence to the Colonial Office, was infinitely more concerned with establishing Jagan's communist links than they were with ascertaining Burnham's ideological allegiance. It seems clear that they were not perturbed by Burnham's role in the post-suspension political manoeuvring of the PPP in England. They recognised him as radical and anti-colonial but not as a communist. The lack of evidence of a parallel surveillance of Burnham is rather strange. Is it conceivable that Burnham was already engaged as an ally, with some links to them and/or the Colonial Office?

An MI5 document, dated November 20, 1953, assessed the nature of the PPP campaign, noting that Billy Strachan could not be engaged in their activities, as he was in hospital in London. But their spies had established that Jagan did visit Billy in hospital, and that the chief theoretician of the CPGB, R. Palme Dutt, was also present. The following are excerpts from the document:

> While the British Communist Party itself has been conducting a national campaign demanding the withdrawal of troops from British Guiana and agitating against the suspension of the constitution, it has made no attempt to direct the activities of Jagan and Burnham. In the communist field, Jagan's and Burnham's connections have been predominantly with the leadership of the communist-dominated London Branch of the Caribbean Labour Congress (CLC) [led by Billy Strachan], an organisation of West Indians. They have also been in touch with a small number of communist trade unionists and youth organisers, as well as with the staff of the *Daily Worker* [the paper of the CPGB, 1930–66].
>
> As far as is known, however, Jagan has had only one short meeting with Rajani Palme Dutt, Head of the International Department of the British Communist Party. This took place at the bedside of Billy Strachan, a Jamaican communist resident here and presently a patient at a Ministry of Pensions hospital in London. A possible reason for the lack of contact between Jagan and Party Headquarters is that the Party realises that the establishment of a close relationship with

> Jagan and Burnham might prejudice the chances of the PPP leaders obtaining support in other left-wing quarters [such as Aneurin Bevan, his wife, Jennie Lee and Fenner Brockway, on the left of the Labour Party].
>
> Both Jagan and Burnham have been kept extremely busy addressing meetings both in London and the Provinces. Some of these meetings have been organised by communist elements, but most have been held under the auspices of the Congress of Peoples against Imperialism (COPAI).
>
> Jagan and Burnham have been staying at Kennington [south London] with an Indian doctor named Dr K.D. Kumria. Kumria is not a communist but is connected with COPAI.[24]

MI5 observed that the Jamaican communist, Ferdinand Smith, assistant secretary of the World Federation of Trade Unions (WFTU: a Soviet-front organisation) was in London briefly, and he had at least one meeting with Jagan. It was widely known that funding from the Soviet Union to the CPGB came through the WFTU, and that Billy Strachan's CLC (London Branch) was responsible for disbursing any funds allocated to West Indian communists. The Security Liaison Officer (SLO) in Trinidad noted thus in his quarterly review (January–March 1955):

> The PPP have received some outside financial help during the past quarter: 3,000 rupees from India and drafts of £150 and £100 from London. These last were forwarded to Jagan by the London Branch of the Caribbean Labour Congress [led by Billy Strachan] after the split had occurred in the PPP; this, as one might expect, shows that the British Communist Party recognised his group as the legal PPP.[25]

A few weeks earlier (March 18, 1955), the SLO informed MI5 Head Office in London regarding the draft of £150 sent to Jagan by the CLC. He noted: 'There would therefore appear to be no doubt that the Jagan group has been accorded recognition by the Communist Party in the UK as the real PPP.'[26]

The SLO in Trinidad, in a note to the MI5 Head Office in April 1955 regarding Billy Strachan and Cheddi Jagan, suggested that the WFTU (a front for the CPSU) was the source of the funds:

> It would in fact be quite impossible for the London Branch of the Caribbean Labour Congress [CLC] to subsidise Jagan to the extent indicated in your letters in view of its own extremely precarious position. An analysis of a number of recent and current reports by 'Label' and 'Land' [most likely MI5 spies planted in the WFTU office in London] indicates that we need not look further than the WFTU for the source of the money.
>
> The transmission of these funds does not, however, indicate any special renewal of interest by the WFTU in the situation in British

Guiana; the money was, according to 'Label,' first earmarked a year ago, but had been held because no safe and secure means of transmission could be found. Eventually Billy Strachan dealt with the matter on behalf of the WFTU…

The above material may be passed to the Head of Special Branch in British Guiana…and we should be grateful if you would ensure that our sources in this instance are given the maximum security protection.[27]

On the eve of the split in the PPP that led to the Burnhamite 'moderates' seeking control of the party from the Jaganite 'extremists,' MI5, based on a spy planted in the CPGB, reported (on February 10, 1955) that Jagan was contemplating breaking away from the PPP and creating a Marxist Party. Apparently, he had communicated this to the leadership of the CPGB towards the end of 1954, but they cautioned him to be circumspect, to await Burnham's action before taking any steps of his own, while not desisting from pursuit of a Marxist programme. But *he* should not initiate a split in the PPP.

The MI5 report notes:

> …it seems that Jagan asked for advice from communist circles in the United Kingdom [the CPGB] as to the advisability of such a step. The view of the British Communist Party is that Jagan would be making a serious tactical error to take the initiative in 'splitting' the PPP. In their view Jagan should bide his time and attempt to collaborate with his 'right wing' [Burnhamite] colleagues as long as possible, endeavouring at the same time to base Party policy on Marxist lines. The Party takes the view that Burnham himself might then be forced to come out in open opposition to the Jagan faction, in which case the latter might well be able successfully to exploit the resulting situation. There is certainly no point in Jagan exposing himself at this stage by labelling himself either as a Marxist or a communist.[28]

Cheddi Jagan passed through London on his way to Accra for the independence celebrations of Ghana on March 6, 1957. With the first general elections in British Guiana since the suspension of the Constitution (in October 1953) scheduled for August 1957, MI5 secured authorisation for the surveillance of Jagan in Ghana. He allegedly stated in Accra that he was overthrown in 1953 primarily because of opposition from the 'monopolistic sugar plantation owners,' but he was confident of returning to power in 1957 and of proceeding to self-government for his country. The following report on Jagan's meeting with Professor Arthur Lewis (1915–91), the eminent West Indian economist from St Lucia and later Nobel laureate (in Accra), demonstrates the futility of persuading Jagan to attenuate his Marxist frame of reference for a moderate posture, as the distinguished scholar evidently sought to counsel him. Pragmatism and intellectual ingenuity were not Jagan's forte:

> Jagan is reported to have met Professor A.W. Lewis and to have discussed politics with him. Jagan is said to have described himself as a 'Marxist-Socialist,' who did not take orders from Russia or anyone else. **Lewis is reported to have advised him to work as a nationalist for the independence of British Guiana, but Jagan asserted that it was against his conscience to say one thing and practise another. He criticised Dr Nkrumah for practising Marxist-Socialist methods yet claiming to be a Christian, describing such action as 'intellectual dishonesty.'** Jagan is also reported to have criticised Nkrumah for his policy of encouraging capitalist investment in Ghana [emphasis added].[29]

On his return to London from Ghana, Jagan met with R. Palme Dutt, now Head of the CPGB, on March 25, 1957. 'Lascar,' a MI5 spy based in the party office (King St), eavesdropped on the conversation and reported on a substantial portion of it. The following comment by Jagan on supposed differences between Africans and Indians in British Guiana was summarised by 'Lascar':

> Jagan commented on the difference between the Indian and African in the West Indies. He thought it had a lot to do with their 'social psychology': the Indians were emotional and highly…[word inaudible: 'materialistic'?], and the negro was a person who lived from day to day not knowing whether he would die tomorrow; they couldn't plan and had nobody to do anything for them. Whereas the Indians were basically people with a lot of family and had roots; therefore, there was more stability among them. Jagan then appeared to say [strangely, but he probably meant ideologically, with regard to Marxism]: 'You see, we'll never win Indians…I can win Africans.' And he added that 'our position' was very good in that respect, but they had to be very careful.[30]

The latter comment could have been prompted by Jagan's deep-seated Marxist assumptions, in addition to his desire to reassure R. Palme Dutt that rigorous class struggle would inevitably win over the African working class, presumably perceived by Jagan as less materially driven than Indians.

'Lascar' also reported on his eavesdropping on R. Palme Dutt's discussion with one Salmi of his meeting with Jagan. Dutt said that he had cautioned Jagan to steer a moderate course for the time being – no need for nationalisation of foreign assets as yet – as they did not wish to precipitate another Guatemala, an obvious reference to the overthrow of the Arbenz regime by the CIA in June 1954. He noted that Booker seemed prepared to work with any government in British Guiana. But there was no mistaking Dutt's dream of the extension of the communist agenda. 'Lascar' noted that Dutt and Jagan had discussed the recent victory of the communists in the Indian state of Kerala:

> Dutt said they had spoken of the position in British Guiana and Kerala. The only two places in the Empire (Dutt used this word)

where there's prospects of COMMUNIST governments on the basis of elected majorities of the people, and in both cases...INDIANS have done it.

Rajani Palme Dutt was, of course, of Indo-Swedish ancestry.[31]

Apparently Salmi had asked Dutt if Jagan expressed 'any difficulties' regarding the situation in Hungary, an obvious reference to the Soviet invasion and crushing of the revolt against the authoritarian regime in late 1956. Dutt said 'no, he is not that type.' He was probably alluding to the fact that Jagan was never inclined to deviate from the orthodox Soviet line. Salmi responded that Jagan 'is a statesman,' and Dutt agreed. Jagan was clearly a safe comrade by the orthodoxies of the CPGB and the CPSU.

Dutt's reported concluding remarks to Jagan to project a moderate posture, for the time being, while pursuing an educational programme to disseminate Marxism, are as follows:

> You don't need to make any proclamations on communism over there [British Guiana], but simply the good old liberal right of people to read whatever they want to read, in the same way people can read in England. That's all it amounts to. Of course, this lack of freedom has been the fatal thing [for propagating Marxism-Leninism]. It was clear that that was the essential thing because once literature can circulate, serious political education can go on, and that is the main thing, for that to go on developing, and to keep the leadership of the people.[32]

Meanwhile, MI5 never did cease its surveillance in connection with the communist links of the Jagans, particularly with Billy Strachan and the CPGB. In a position paper on the subject, dated January 9, 1961, several such contacts are cited in documenting the communist orientation of the PPP. They noted that at the beginning of 1958 Janet Jagan had 'enlisted the aid of Billy Strachan in London to persuade Ranji Chandisingh to return to British Guiana.' Chandisingh was, of course, the editor of *Caribbean News*, the newspaper of the CLC (London Branch), a close 'comrade' of Billy, and a Marxist theoretician of considerable stature. He became a formidable communist force in Jagan's PPP until he defected to Burnham's PNC in 1976.

MI5 also observed that when Cheddi Jagan visited Venezuela, in January 1959, he met with several communists in the region with the aim of forming a Caribbean Communist Party. Among these were John La Rose, a Trinidadian communist resident in Venezuela, Richard Hart (friend of Cheddi and Billy Strachan), the Jamaican communist, and Dr Gallegos Mangera, a prominent member of the Communist Party of Venezuela.

On a visit to London in July 1959, Cheddi Jagan met with Tom McWhinnie, head of the WFTU publications, 'to discuss what assistance the WFTU could give to British Guiana.' The latter (as noted earlier) was a Soviet-front organisation, widely believed to be the means by which Soviet funding was sent to the CPGB, then through Billy Strachan's CLC (London Branch) to Jagan's PPP. With respect to the study of Marxism-Leninism within the PPP, it was noted that the PPP's Research and Education Committee was 'resuscitated' on July 1, 1960, with several lectures by Miles Fitzpatrick, Ranji Chandisingh, Charles Jacob, Jnr, and Cheddi Jagan. They drew the conclusion: 'Since all of these are Communists or strong sympathisers, there is little doubt that these lectures would have been given with a Marxist slant.' This was nothing new: most of the books and literature sold by the PPP were Marxist-Leninist; the party's organ, *Thunder*, was similarly oriented, as were the books in the party's lending library. They also noted that both Cheddi and Janet were in regular correspondence with Central Books in London (intercepted by MI5), affiliated to the CPGB, to procure 'progressive publication' for the PPP library. As early as February 1952,

> a consignment of books was stopped by the British Guiana Customs which showed that Jagan was importing communist propaganda in large quantities from London [from Central Books]. There were, for example, 5,229 books printed in Moscow and a further 617 in other parts of the USSR.[33]

The MI5 report also noted that in November 1960 Hannah Greenwood, 'the well-known British communist, had been holding clandestine meetings at night with Janet Jagan and other members of the PPP [in the colony].' The report concluded:

> …in July 1960 Jagan met leading members of the Cuban Communist Party at the Party's newspaper offices (*Hoy*)… 'Lascar' [the MI5 spy in the CPGB] revealed in March 1960 [when Jagan was in London] that Idris Cox of the CPGB's International Department said that he thought of the PPP as an expression of the Communist Party in British Guiana.[34]

In early 1961, MI5 prepared a position paper on Cheddi Jagan personally, stressing the consistency and longevity of his communist contacts in the UK: the CPGB, the WFTU, and Billy Strachan's CLC (London Branch) particularly. The paper noted that there was a central core of communists in the PPP, and that the most confidential matters were 'entirely restricted' to this group – not accessible to the perceptibly less ideologically driven in the executive committee of the PPP. They did not name the members of the inner group, but it comprised Cheddi and Janet Jagan, Brindley Benn, Ramkarran, and Ranji Chandisingh: all known to have impeccable communist credentials. MI5 described it as 'a Party within the Party,' adding that 'this has always made it difficult to obtain precise information about them.'[35]

It is interesting what MI5 thought about the attempt of the Jagans to enhance the Marxist-Leninist orientation of the PPP, hitherto geared primarily to winning elections, essentially mobilising the Indian segment of the electorate that was strong enough to give the party a healthy majority, indefinitely, under the first-past-the-post system:

> In 1958 the Jagans attempted to increase Communist influence in the PPP by the recruitment of two British Guianese, Ranji Chandisingh and Miles Fitzpatrick, who had been trained by the CPGB. The intention was, that on their return to British Guiana, these two should take over the editorship of the PPP's organ, *Thunder*, and also that they should assist in a large scale 'education programme' which aimed to give political education to the masses. There is little doubt that this political education programme was to consist of Marxist classes, but probably because of the preoccupation of the Jagans with political affairs [being in government] and of the laziness of the two individuals concerned, the classes did not succeed in their purpose.[36]

The report addressed the question of the Jagans' ideological foundation and their commitment to enhancing the Marxist character of the PPP, 'to increase the number of left-wing and communist publications in the PPP's library.' It added: 'A survey of the literature in this library, which was made by the British Guiana Special Branch about a year ago [in 1960], showed that approximately 75 per cent of the literature fell into this category.'[37]

MI5 also stressed the commonality of the ideological beliefs of Jagan and the 'West Indian communist group in this country,' a transparent allusion to the CLC (London Branch) and Billy Strachan with their enduring links to the CPGB. They also observed that in all contacts between Jagan and the CPGB or with the WFTU, the intermediary was always Billy Strachan. But these communist organisations were deeply penetrated by MI5 spies. For instance, the meeting between Jagan, R. Palme Dutt, and Idris Cox, in the summer of 1959, took place in a supposedly 'safe' address, yet 'Lascar' the MI5 spy in the CPGB was able to give a comprehensive report on the conversation. The meeting between Jagan and Tom McWhinnie of the WFTU publications was also eavesdropped on by 'Lascar,' who revealed that one of the purposes of this meeting was 'to discuss the trade union situation in British Guiana. Jagan was particularly anxious to learn what assistance WFTU could give to British Guiana.'[38]

IV.   MI5 Corroborates Jagan's Entrenched Communist Credentials

Billy Strachan was never out of the picture. In January 1961, the SLO in Trinidad, in his Intelligence Committee Report for December 1960, noted that Jagan was being offered several scholarships for students from British Guiana to study at universities 'behind the Iron Curtain.' And he reflected on the role of Billy in the process:

> It would appear that Billy Strachan of the British Communist Party, to whom the recommendations [from the PPP] are made, is acting as an intermediary between Jagan and the persons or organisations from behind the Iron Curtain who have offered the scholarships.[39]

He was correct, as the correspondence between the Jagans and Billy corroborates. David Horsley, too, notes how instrumental Billy was in developing the scholarship programme:

> Another of Billy's major contributions was enabling young Caribbean students to study free of charge in the Soviet Union and the Socialist countries of Europe. Through his leading role in Caribbean politics in London and his connections with the World Federation of Trade Unions and the CPGB, he contacted colleagues in the West Indies to find potential students. These connections – particularly with Cheddi and Janet Jagan in British Guiana, Richard Hart in Jamaica and John La Rose in Trinidad – made it possible for many young men and women especially from poor backgrounds to have free university education that otherwise they never would have had.[40]

It was indicative of the stature of Billy Strachan in the politics of the Jagans that he expected an ongoing report from them (and invariably got it) on developments in the colony. A letter from Billy sent from his home in NW4, Colindale (London) to Dr and Mrs C. B. Jagan of 97 Laluni St, Georgetown, was intercepted by MI5. They summarised the contents of the letter thus: 'Strachan complains that he has not heard from anyone in British Guiana for over a month and has not received *Thunder* since December 10 [1960]. He asks Jagan to write soon and send the missing copies of *Thunder*.'[41]

The SLO in Trinidad liaised regularly with the governor of British Guiana, thereby did the latter secure confidential information on Jagan and the PPP, augmented by the routine reports submitted by Special Branch in the colony. Following his visit to British Guiana on December 22–23, 1960, the SLO noted that 'many members of the PPP are non-communist, and some are even opposed to the communists.' He thought that this should exert a moderating influence on the Jagans, but 'it cannot be assumed that this influence would be decisive.' However, he asserted that most of the friends of the Jagans overseas were 'either communists or near-communists'; and the SLO was alarmed at the obvious exemplary status of the Soviet Bloc in their conception of the future of their country:

> The Jagans appear at present to have an innate tendency to look to the Soviet Satellite Bloc and their Western friends [obviously the

CPGB] for help. It is at least possible that this tendency will increase rather than diminish as the Jagans progressively exercise more power within the Government of British Guiana.[42]

The MI5 files also reveal that the intelligence service was keen to ascertain, if not establish, the communist provenance of Janet Jagan. In a report dated February 21, 1961, the SLO in Trinidad noted that the governor of British Guiana, Sir Ralph Grey, had informed him that opponents of the Jagans were claiming that Janet Jagan was related to Julius and Ethel Rosenberg, who were convicted in 1951 and executed in June 1953 for spying for the Soviet Union: passing on technological and nuclear secrets to the communists. It was also rumoured that Janet had taken 'a course in subversion at a special Communist school' before she married Cheddi in 1943. Finally, it was alleged by enemies of the Jagans that Janet 'had been deliberately used as an agent for Communist imperialism and that her marriage to Jagan must be viewed in that light, as a deep-laid plot to subvert British Guiana.'[43]

Although these aspersions were widely disseminated, neither the governor nor the SLO (Trinidad) gave any credence to them. Janet's maiden name was, indeed, Rosenberg, and her parents did change it to Roberts, but 'it provides no grounds for believing that either they or she are related to the notorious Rosenbergs.' The SLO concluded with an apt quote from a letter by the commissioner of police, British Guiana, dated July 3, 1951, regarding the antecedents of Janet Jagan provided by the US consul in Georgetown:

> …information concerning Mrs Jagan's family in the United States indicates that her father was greatly opposed to her marriage to a Hindu [Cheddi] and requested the Department [of State] to prevent his daughter's departure for British Guiana by withholding [issuing] a passport, in the hope that if she could not join her husband the marriage could be broken off.

> Inquiries concerning her associations and activities in the United States revealed that, subsequently, at the Cook County School of Nursing in Chicago, her scholastic record was good, that she appeared to be an intelligent young woman, quiet and reserved and apparently very much interested in her work. Her teachers and the house mother saw no evidence of any interest in Communism. However, information from other sources indicates that during her student days she was a member of the Young Communist League.[44]

The SLO concluded that 'in an examination of all the available information there is nothing to substantiate the allegations made against Janet Jagan.' A few days later, on February 28, 1961, the SLO submitted a paper titled, 'An Assessment of the People's Progressive Party (PPP) and its Leaders,' to Governor Grey. The principal objective of the paper was to ascertain the nature of the PPP's contacts and activities, and to determine whether the party could be deemed communist.

The conception of communism on which this paper is partly predicated is the abolition of private property following the Marxist-Leninist notion of the proletarian revolution and the elimination of capitalist exploitation, conducing to the 'classless society' and the evolution of communist man. Besides, in the context of the Cold War, were the many enemies of the Jagans justified in indicting them with endorsing Sino-Soviet ideological penetration of Guyana and the world, in pursuit of the perfect communist society?

The SLO report asserts that Cheddi and Janet Jagan monopolised the leadership of the PPP; therefore, anyone who dared to challenge their untrammelled authority had no chance of survival in the party; in fact, 'without the Jagans, the PPP in its present form would not exist' – an allusion to its communist core. The principal means by which the PPP sustained 'fraternal relations' with communists in the Sino-Soviet bloc and in capitalist countries, in the previous two years, are identified thus:

(a) in looking for recruits for government posts in British Guiana from Communist sources;

(b) by seeking material aid for British Guiana from Communist countries [such as a loan and a rice deal with Cuba];

(c) by encouraging students from British Guiana to study behind the Iron Curtain [Billy Strachan was at the core of this programme];

(d) by personal contact with and support for known Communist international front organisations [the World Peace Council, the WFTU, and the Women's International Democratic Federation (WIDF), for example]…controlled by the Russians, which support Sino-Soviet policy, but which aim, usually without success, to present themselves as bona fide political or professional bodies with no hidden political allegiances;

(e) by collecting and disseminating Communist literature [such as from Central Books (London), affiliated to the CPGB];

(f) by extensive contacts with prominent individual Communists outside British Guiana [particularly Castro, Billy Strachan, and R. Palme Dutt of the CPGB].[45]

With respect to scholarships granted to members of the PPP in communist countries, the SLO noted that the Soviet Union, consonant with its propaganda initiative worldwide, had 'increased considerably, the number of scholarships it was offering to dependent territories' such as British Guiana. The report elaborated:

These scholarships often ostensibly concentrate on technical education but are also intended to train and indoctrinate intelligent young men to work for the Communist cause on their return to their home countries. The arrangements for these scholarships have not been handled by Jagan…The arrangements have been made through the Prague headquarters of the Communist controlled International Union of Students (IUS), through Billy Strachan, a Jamaican living in London who is publicly known as an active Communist… Jagan and his ministers know that Guianese are being awarded these scholarships and approve of the arrangement. Further, there is some evidence to show that Janet Jagan is taking a hand in the arrangement…[46]

In fact, Janet corresponded frequently with Billy on this matter.

The SLO (Trinidad) was alive to the propaganda work pursued by the PPP, including the procuring of communist literature for the party's library, as well as for sale in the wider community. MI5 regularly intercepted the correspondence between Cheddi and Janet with Central Books in London, 'the distributive organisation of the CPGB…[requesting] what they describe as "progressive publications."' He also noted that the Jagans were continually seeking help from their communist friends in the CPGB/CLC (London Branch), particularly Billy Strachan, in raising funds for the PPP; in helping to secure a printing press for the party; in making contact with Soviet/Satellite embassies in London in order to procure assistance of some sort; in arranging details of scholarships in communist countries; in seeking financial help from Soviet-controlled organisations such as WFTU. He adds: 'Help has been sought from American Communists and sympathisers to raise money in the US for the PPP; while visits to British Guiana of Communists, and more particularly those active in Communist front organisations have been encouraged.'[47]

It may be recalled that the British West Indian leaders were unanimously unsympathetic to Jagan when the British suspended the Constitution in October 1953. By 1959–60, it was widely held that Jagan, returned to office since August 1957, in all probability, would lead British Guiana to independence in a couple years. However, the SLO did not think that the West Indian leaders had changed their minds regarding Jagan's devotion to communism, nor their conviction that he posed a security risk to the region. This adverse appraisal of him was not alleviated by the widespread assumption that he was opposed to the West Indies Federation primarily on racial grounds, and their apprehensions of Jagan's political creed were, necessarily, exacerbated by the consolidation of Fidel Castro's pro-Soviet communist regime in Cuba. From his vantage point in Trinidad, the SLO observed:

> There is no doubt that Jagan, and more particularly his wife, are generally regarded throughout the West Indies as Communists; and, indeed, Sir Grantley Adams [Barbados], Mr Norman Manley [Jamaica] and Dr Eric Williams [Trinidad] have all privately said as much…[and] they undeniably regard the Jagans as a possible menace

to the stability of the area, and fear that the latter are likely to take a dangerously pro-Russian or a pro-Cuban line.

There are also clear indications that Jagan is regarded as a Communist by his Communist friends, who no doubt interpret his anxiety to use Guianese members of the CPGB in the PPP [primarily the brilliant, Harvard-educated Marxist theoretician and sidekick of Billy Strachan, Ranji Chandisingh] as evidence of his desire to organise his own party on Communist lines. On the other hand, there is some evidence to suggest that prominent members of the Labour Party in the UK [Fenner Brockway, Aneurin Bevan, Jennie Lee and Ian Mikardo, for instance], although looking suspiciously at Jagan, are by no means convinced that he is a communist.[48]

The SLO then cited excerpts from a personal and secret despatch by Sir Patrick Renison, governor of British Guiana (1955–58), dated February 6, 1958. He remarked that Jagan dreamt of a 'Marxist paradise,' being a 'devoted Marxist whose whole adult thinking and study, both economic and political, had been anti-colonial, anti-British and pro-Russian.' Renison could not conceive of Jagan ever renouncing his Marxist beliefs. However, he did entertain the notion that his Marxist excesses may yet be tempered by the responsibility of governance, coupled with the reality that the rank-and-file of the PPP, overwhelmingly Indian, were not communists. They were nationalists, therefore 'blatant communist action' by the Jagans could undermine that support. But how realistic was it that the Jagans could be restrained; indeed, that they could be persuaded to moderate their deeply held communist creed?

The SLO was pessimistic that the Jaganite Marxist mantras were susceptible to moderation. Moreover, even if Jagan's Indian supporters did realise, eventually, that his communist ideology was at variance with their economic aspirations, they were likely to be disinclined to accept an African leader, however compatible his politics with their perceived material self-interest, because they would still feel racially fortified to be ruled by an Indian:

The Indian rice farmers and sugar workers, among whom Jagan has his strongest support, are would-be property-owners [most were, in fact, already such, many quite prosperous] to whom the essential doctrines of Communism would be repugnant. But they do not understand these doctrines, and they do not see in the Jagans's contact with Communists evidence of activity which is hostile to their own interests.

They support Jagan as the leader most likely to give effect to the racial and political policies from which they would benefit, and although Jagan professes alarm at the spread of racialism in British Guiana and does not preach benefits for the Indian at the expense of the African, there is no doubt that Indians think that he will do more for them than say an African could or would, and that is his greatest single appeal....[49]

The SLO then pointed to the challenge, in late 1959, posed by Edward Beharry, an Indian capitalist minister in Jagan's government, to the PPP's chairman, B. H. Benn, an African communist and loyal disciple of the Jagans. Jagan was determined to retain an African as window-dressing for his party, and the fact that Benn was a communist endeared him to Jagan. Beharry and a few of his supporters (such as Fred Bowman) were expelled from the PPP, accompanied by the ritual denunciations of Jagan's communism, but this could not impugn the loyalty of his Indian supporters, already beholden to the incontestable leader of their race. The SLO remarked on the unassailability of the Jaganite stranglehold on the PPP and the political imagination of Indians, his Marxist-Leninist creed notwithstanding:

> ...[despite] these and similar troubles, the Jagans still control the Party machine, and there is little sign that public attacks on them because of their alleged Communist activities – some of which were well documented – have led to their losing any significant part of the support they command. Although, therefore, the Jagans are unlikely at least for the present, to secure any real support for Communist policies either from the masses or from the rank and file of their Party, it would be dangerous to assume that the influence of either could be decisive in turning Jagan away from Communism and contacts with Communist countries...It is certainly true of the Jagans that their interest in Communism and Communists has not abated over the years, and their contacts have grown no less.[50]

The SLO attributed the PPP's dithering in pursuing a communist programme in British Guiana to the probability that they had not educated their supporters adequately to appreciate the merits and the hazards of that monumental task; in addition to their apprehension that their many enemies, locally and abroad, could undermine their capacity to govern in a colony; finally, and arguably most decisively, that the British government still had the power to frustrate such a radical reorientation of policies, with the likelihood of another suspension as was the case in 1953, allegedly for the same reason. But he was not deluded into thinking that the Jagans were likely to retreat from their communist beliefs; indeed, contrary to most leaders in the colonial world, the exercise of power had failed to disabuse them of their solemn conviction that Marxism-Leninism was the key to a perfect system that would change British Guiana and the world into a veritable paradise on earth.

As the SLO argues, this partly accounted for Jagan's fixation with achieving independence separately – not emasculated by the capitalist-oriented parameters of the West Indies Federation. Once his country was released from the shackles of colonialism, he would give effect to his strongly held vision of joining the Sino-

Soviet Bloc, construed as sacrosanct ideologically, therefore possessed of the will and the means for radical transformation of the human condition. But Jagan's communist certainties could have deleterious consequences in the context of the Cold War if a 'second Cuba' did materialise in an independent Guyana, on the mainland of South America – ominously more strategically located than Cuba. The SLO's formulation was consistent with American fears that an independent British Guiana, led by Jagan, would precipitate Soviet penetration and subversion of the South American continent:

> It can be confidentially said that after Independence they [the Jagans] will take an increasingly Communist line…[establishing] close and friendly relations between British Guiana and both the Sino-Soviet Bloc and its friends, notably in Cuba…the Russians are everywhere pledged to secure the establishment of a 'socialist' system on the Soviet model under Russian direction…[therefore] they will try to extend their activities not only in British Guiana but also in those neighbouring territories where there are no Soviet missions; they will also engage in espionage….[51]

The SLO then addressed what was already the biggest bone of contention, Castro's Cuba as the beachhead for communist subversion in the Hemisphere, with the probability of its escalation by virtue of Cheddi's 'fraternal relationship' with Fidel. The Americans, of course, obsessed with the domino theory of incremental communist expansion if the virus takes hold of a specific country, exaggerated the perils of British Guiana's continental location – an instrument for its transmission to two of her neighbours, Brazil (the largest and most populous state in South America) and Venezuela:

> The Jagans's association with Cuba will bring other dangers because the present Cuban Government supports and nurtures exiles from many other Latin American countries who are usually Communists and who inevitably clamour for the overthrow, by force, of the existing regimes in their own countries. For some of these people British Guiana might be a more convenient base for operations than Cuba.
>
> In addition, British Guiana would be likely to be used as a venue for the operations and meetings of Communist front organisations, and from it would emanate a steady stream of propaganda material and other activities directed at neighbouring countries. Efforts by HMG or the Western powers to counter these Sino-Soviet moves would be unlikely to command much sympathy from the Jagans and might not receive even tolerance.[52]

The SLO concluded on a note reflective of America's Cold War imperatives in thwarting the 'red menace' in the Hemisphere, embodied by Castro and – no less virulently – Cheddi Jagan:

> Castro's Cuba poses a particularly virulent threat to the whole area, and particularly to Latin America; that threat is at present mitigated because Cuba is too far north to present a convenient base for subversive activity in the Southern Caribbean; joint activity directed from both Cuba and British Guiana would be a great deal more effective...It must be clear that if the Jagans remain in power after Independence, and if their activities and views remain unchanged, they will represent a threat to the stability both of British Guiana itself and of the neighbouring territories, and particularly of the West Indies Federation. They will also threaten the position of the Western powers in this part of the world.[53]

The surveillance of the Jagans by MI5 and their agents in the British West Indies and in British Guiana was relentless. The intelligence services obsessively garnered every crumb of evidence in substantiating their absorption by communism and their routine discourse with their communist friends. As I have noted, virtually all their mails to Billy Strachan and others in the CPGB were intercepted; their telephone conversations bugged; while 'Lascar,' the MI5 spy at the CPGB headquarters, eavesdropped whenever they visited with R. Palme Dutt and Idris Cox at 'King Street.' The following are excerpts from an intercepted letter, dated October 2, 1959, sent by Cheddi (97 Laluni St, Georgetown) to Billy (146 Colin Crescent, London NW9). It pertained to a public announcement Cheddi made in Georgetown regarding the possibility, not the certainty, of a big loan from the Soviet Union. It did not materialise, but he clearly had not thought through the Cold War implications of his potential dependence on Soviet loans. Meanwhile, it quickly attracted the opprobrium of his local enemies, such as Forbes Burnham and Rupert Tello of the TUC.

Cheddi wrote thus to Billy:

> We had a big meeting at Bourda Green [Georgetown] at which I made the announcement that I had every reason to believe that the Soviet Union would be prepared to make a loan of $100 million at a low rate of interest or no interest at all. This was quite a bombshell and it has created a certain amount of consternation in the camp of the Opposition [Burnham's PNC]. Burnham is clearly in a dilemma. By saying 'no,' he puts himself in a position to be criticised by his own supporters. If he says 'yes,' he is thereby laying the basis for a full-blooded Development Plan for which, no doubt, he believes we may claim credit. He took a long time to reply and ultimately came out with an ambiguous statement, more or less saying that we have done the biggest service to Communist Russia and that British Guiana should look to the West and the Commonwealth for support.
>
> Tello from the TUC has also come out against the acceptance of a Russian loan, but we have support from many quarters, for instance, the Junior Chamber of Commerce [predominantly Indian] which

is growing in strength. In addition, many of Burnham's supporters are now questioning his motives and sincerity especially when they see that Ghana, Guinea and Ethiopia are negotiating loans from the Soviet Bloc. We are making it clear to the people that we are not interested in the Soviet system, but we are interested in a straightforward business proposition. We expect later to carry out a countrywide agitation possibly with the signature campaign on this point [in favour of a Soviet loan].[54]

Cheddi's remark about the PPP not being interested in the Soviet system rang hollow, as *Thunder*, the party's paper, week after week without fail, extolled the superiority of Marxism-Leninism and the new world of peace, freedom, and socialism it was making in the Soviet Union and the 'People's Democracies.' But, surely, no straightforward business arrangement with the Soviet Union could be premised on loans at 'a low rate of interest or no interest at all.' It was arguably predicated on ideological conformity with the Soviet Bloc that, of necessity, would pit Jagan against the Americans in the Cold War. He was potentially on a perilous course.

A few days after Cheddi had written to Billy, the SLO observed that the British government was *not* likely 'to give its blessing to an approach to Russia [for loans]'; and, consequently, Jagan 'has adopted a negative approach to the subject.'[55] Yet it was evident that Jagan believed trade with, and aid and soft loans from, the communist countries were crucial to the development of his own. On November 10, 1959, a four-man trade mission from Hungary arrived in British Guiana. They were guests of the Ministry of Trade and Industry of which Jagan was the minister. Cheddi gave an interview to the press in which he explained the purpose of the Hungarian mission: 'to discuss arrangements for the establishment of a glass-making industry…using Hungarian equipment.' He added that if the deal were concluded they would need the services of Hungarian technicians for some time to train local personnel. The Russian loan did not materialise; neither did the Hungarian glass factory.[56]

Clearly, while Iain Macleod, the liberal colonial secretary, was strongly inclined to give Jagan the benefit of the doubt over Burnham, the conservative government of Harold Macmillan was not enamoured of the idea of him getting into major trade and aid deals with the Soviet Bloc. On December 9, 1959, Jim Callaghan, the shadow colonial secretary, wrote to 'My dear Cheddi' regarding a meeting he had with Macleod in which he told him that if the British government was not prepared to adequately fund the development programme for British Guiana, of which they had approved, such funding could well be sought (by Jagan) in the Soviet Union. Yet it is noteworthy that Callaghan was also counselling Cheddi to be circumspect because of the dangers of 'other countries becoming scared as a result of Russian capital coming into the country.' He advised:

> ...it would be well worth your while raising the matter again when you come to London in February for your talks. I think if pressure is put upon the Colonial Office, they will be willing to return to the Treasury to see if further finance cannot be made available.

This was the context in which Cheddi proceeded to Cuba after the constitutional conference in London, in March 1960, and secured both a market for Guyanese rice and well as a soft loan at 2 per cent (less than the rate at which the money was 'borrowed' from the Soviet Union). Is it not likely that this was money that came from the Soviet Union, through Cuba, specifically for British Guiana? In any case, it was indicative of the way Cheddi really wished to travel after independence: to the Soviet camp, whence he felt, with conviction all his life, 'disinterested' aid was procurable in the spirit of 'proletarian internationalism.'[57]

A trip to Jamaica by Cheddi towards the end of 1959 encapsulated his approach to the political vocation. He arrived there on November 20 and left four days later. He was followed closely by the intelligence people, as the SLO (Jamaica) relates. The principal reason for his visit was to discuss with government officials the importation of rice from British Guiana. However, it was his communist friends with whom he was primarily in contact. He was met at the airport by Dick Hart and Frank Hill, both well-known Marxists in Jamaica. On the evening of his arrival, he visited Hart's home in Kingston; there he met with Ferdinand Smith, the Jamaican communist with strong links to Moscow and the WFTU, one of the instruments for the transmission of Soviet funding to communist organisations outside of the Soviet Bloc. He also visited Hart at his home the following evening.

The SLO reported on Jagan's two visits to the University College of the West Indies (UCWI) on the same day, November 23, 1959:

> ...Jagan went to UCWI and spoke to students from British Guiana. Details of this meeting are lacking, but it is believed that he was invited to lecture that night under the auspices of the University Students Union. The lecture commenced at 7.45 pm. Richard Hart and Rolly Simms [a London-based Jamaican communist, close friend of Billy Strachan in the CLC (London Branch) and a member of the CPGB] were present at Cheddi's lecture at the College.
>
> During most of his lecture Jagan criticised the British Government. **He said that he was against encouraging foreign capital to the West Indies as this gave the capitalists the opportunity to milk the territories. He thought the Government should nationalise all industries to keep the profits in the country** [emphasis added].[58]

However, although MI5 and the Colonial Office (the 'secret' or 'top secret' intelligence of the former was routinely transmitted to the latter) were fully aware of Jagan's implacable devotion to his communist cause, the British government was still set to grant Jagan independence sometime in 1962, until Kennedy intervened, personally and relentlessly in the aftermath of Cheddi's fatal visit to America in October 1961, to ensure Jagan's removal. The MI5 files after February 1961 have not been released (there being no statutory obligation for them to do so); therefore, we have no way of ascertaining the precise details of the machination of the various actors during the turbulent years in Guyana: the subversion by the CIA and MI5 in particular, in fomenting violence in 1962 and 1963, culminating in the contrived electoral defeat of Jagan, through proportional representation, in December 1964. However, it is highly likely that the surveillance of Cheddi and Janet Jagan was augmented substantially after 1961. They were on the wrong side of the Cold War (and defined as America's enemies). In June 1963, Macmillan finally succumbed to the dictates of Kennedy, obsessed with preventing 'another Cuba' in the Hemisphere.

On April 3, 1961, shortly before the Bay of Pigs invasion of Cuba, the Kennedy administration issued a white paper on Cuba. Its table of contents constitute the crux of their case against the Castro regime that had seized power in January 1959 and was perceived shortly thereafter to have definitively aligned themselves to the Soviet side of the Cold War. The sections of the paper were headed thus: I. The Betrayal of the Cuban Revolution; II. The Establishment of the Communist Bridgehead to [Latin America and the Caribbean]; III. The Delivery of the Revolution to the Sino-Soviet Bloc; IV. The Assault on the Hemisphere. The Americans were not prepared to tolerate any regime in the Hemisphere that chose the side of their mortal enemies. Two weeks before the Bay of Pigs invasion, they had warned Castro:

> We call once again on the Castro regime to sever its links with the international Communist movement…If this call is unheeded, we are confident that the Cuban people, with their passion for liberty, will continue to strive for a free Cuba…in the spirit of Jose Marti.

They perceived Cheddi Jagan in exactly those terms and were determined to get rid of him before independence if he, too, were disinclined 'to sever [his] links with the international Communist movement.'[59] The Americans would never have allowed a 'second Cuba' in the Hemisphere. They could do little about Castro after the Missile Crisis of October 1962, but they were not prepared to tolerate an independent Guyana led by another pro-Soviet communist, Cheddi Jagan.

Notes

1. See Interview with Eusi Kwayana, in Frank Birbalsingh's *The People's Progressive Party of Guyana, 1950-92: An Oral History* (London: Hansib, 2007), 47–51.
2. *Daily Argosy*, January 22, 1957.

3. Michael Swan, *British Guiana: The Land of Six Peoples* (London: Her Majesty's Stationery Office, 1957), 133–35.
4. Jock Campbell's assessment of the political situation in British Guiana, and his recommendation of Jagan over Burnham is contained in the following document: Booker Brothers, McConnell and Company, Ltd., [Jock Campbell], 'The Group Chairman's Visit to British Guiana and the West Indies, January-March 1960,' [March 22, 1960], (mimeo.), confidential. Campbell's recollection of his exchange with Cheddi Jagan, at the Traveller's Club, London (in late March 1960), was related to me in my interview with him, July 23–24, 1992, Nettlebed, Oxfordshire. See also my *Sweetening 'Bitter Sugar'* [Chapter 18: 'Jagan (and Burnham) in 1960: Campbell's Confidential [Assessment],' 247–60.
5. For Jock Campbell's ideas regarding reform, see my *Sweetening 'Bitter Sugar,'* Chapter 19: '"Practical Idealism": Campbell's Philosophy on Reform,' 263–86.
6. Campbell's conciliatory gestures towards Jagan after the latter's electoral victory in August 1957 recur in several interviews I did with him at his home in Nettlebed, Oxfordshire, between May 9, 1990, and December 22, 1994, four days before he died, aged 82. Dr Fenton Ramsahoye, Jagan's attorney general (1961–64), took part in the last interview.
7. V. S. Naipaul, *The Middle Passage* (Harmondsworth: Penguin, 1969 [1962]), 143.
8. The National Archives [TNA], KV2/3637 [MI5 File].
9. See note 1 (p. 123), Frank Birbalsingh, Interview with Dr Fenton Ramsahoye, July 29, 1998.
10. See David Horsley, *Billy Strachan, 1921-98: RAF Officer, Communist, Civil Rights Pioneer, Legal Administrator, Internationalist, and ABOVE ALL CARIBBEAN MAN* (London: Caribbean Labour Solidarity, 2019), 28, 30.
11. Frank Birbalsingh, Interview with Richard Hart (July 25, 1998), in *The People's Progressive Party of Guyana, 1950–92*.
12. TNA, KV2/3637, 'Cheddi and Janet Jagan up and Including the First PPP Victory in 1953,' May 5, 1960, top secret.
13. Ibid.
14. See 'Remarks by Billy Strachan,' Cheddi Jagan Memorial Service, London, May 25, 1997, Cheddi Jagan Research Centre (CJRC), call number: B032 (1915).
15. Janet Jagan is quoted in David Horsley, 'Billy Strachan's was a Remarkable Life,' letter, *Islington Tribune*, May 23, 2019.
16. V. S. Naipaul, 'A Handful of Dust: Return to Guyana,' *New York Review of Books*, April 11, 1991, 18.
17. See Obituary of Ranji Chandisingh [1930–2009], *Stabroek News*, June 28, 2009.
18. Harold Drayton, *An Accidental Life* (Hertford: Hansib, 2017), 488–89.
19. Ibid., 489.
20. Eric Hoffer, *The True Believer: Thoughts on the Nature of Mass Movements* (New York: Harper Perennial, 1966 [1951]), 122, 128.
21. Drayton, *An Accidental Life*, 488.
22. Ibid., 533–34.
23. Ibid., 534.
24. TNA, KV2/3609.
25. TNA, KV2/3616/2, April 22, 1955, top secret.
26. TNA, KV2/3615, March 18, 1955.
27. TNA, KV2/3615, April 12, 1955.
28. TNA, KV2/3615, February 10, 1955.

29. TNA, KV2/3619, [no date] March 1957.
30. TNA, KV2/3620, March 15, 1957.
31. Ibid.
32. Ibid.
33. TNA, KV2/3637, 'Cheddi and Janet Jagan up to and Including the First PPP Electoral Victory in 1953,' May 5, 1960, top secret.
34. TNA, KV2/3638, January 9, 1961, top secret.
35. Ibid.
36. Ibid.
37. Ibid.
38. Ibid.
39. TNA, KV2/3638, January 16, 1961, secret.
40. Horsley, *Billy Strachan, 1921–98*, 26.
41. TNA, KV2/3838, January 7, 1961.
42. TNA, KV2/3638, December 28, 1960, top secret.
43. TNA, KV2/3638, February 21, 1961.
44. Ibid.
45. KV2/3638, February 28, 1961, top secret.
46. Ibid.
47. Ibid.
48. Ibid.
49. Ibid.
50. Ibid.
51. Ibid.
52. Ibid.
53. Ibid.
54. TNA, KV2/3636, Cheddi Jagan to Billy Strachan, October 2, 1959, top secret.
55. TNA, KV2/3636, Extract from the Local Intelligence Committee Report for October 1959 by the Security Liaison Officer (SLO, Trinidad), October 7, 1959.
56. TNA, KV2/3636, Extract from the Report of the SLO, Trinidad, November 19, 1959.
57. TNA, KV2/3636, James Callaghan to Cheddi Jagan, December 9, 1959, top secret.
58. TNA, KV2/3636, Extract from the Local Intelligence Committee for November 1959, forwarded by the SLO, Jamaica, December 15, 1959.
59. James G. Blight, Bruce J. Allyn, and David A. Welch, *Cuba on the Brink: Castro, the Missile Crisis and the Soviet Collapse* (New York: Pantheon Books, 1993), 38.

11.
The Cold War and Jagan's Politics of Futility, 1965–69

It is important that countries that are winning Independence understand which is the road to development: Cuba is an example… From what I saw, Cuba will be the happiest country in the Western Hemisphere in a few years…It will be a brilliant example for other countries that are exploited by imperialism…My greatest hope and desire is that the greatest number of people from my country can come here and see how they have been misled by Imperialist propaganda and opportunist and puppet leaders [Burnham and D'Aguiar].

> – **Cheddi Jagan ('on a goodwill visit to Cuba'),**
> *Guiana Graphic,* **April 11, 1965**

We would like to remind you, Dr Jagan, that Socialism and Communism are NOT the same. Mr Burnham broke with you on this very point…Dr Jagan, we are no longer your comrades because we reject Communism. We do not want a Castro here. We do not want our sons to be sent to Cuba to learn the trades of violence and terrorism. We do not want to be slaves of Moscow and be forced to do their bidding to repay their 'gifts.'

> – **'Open Letter to Cheddi Jagan,'** *New Nation,* **May 23, 1965.**

We live in the Western Hemisphere. We share certain democratic ideals. We…will never be partner to the setting up of a communist state or any foreign bases to threaten the security of our neighbours in our Hemisphere, but we will not be the satellite of any nation under the sun.

> – **L. F. S. Burnham,** *New Nation,* **April 25, 1965.**

I. Jaganism and Burnhamism: A Tarnished Legacy

General elections under proportional representation (PR) brought Burnham's People's National Congress (PNC) to power in December 1964 (in a coalition with the rabidly anti-communist United Force [UF] that collapsed after three years).

But it paved the way for the incremental destruction of the Guyanese economy, its democratic institutions (including the legislature and the judiciary), as well as its admirable colonial educational legacy. Moreover, by identifying himself categorically with the Soviet Union and Castro's Cuba – exemplars of his political mission – Jagan made it substantially easier for Burnham to establish a dictatorial regime in a region that is proud, and protective of, its liberal democratic tradition.

In late 1965, as promised to President Lyndon Johnson, the British held another constitutional conference in London in order, as expected, to present the gift of independence to L. F. S. Burnham, who still had the support of Peter D'Aguiar in the coalition, although their relationship was relentlessly fraught. Jagan boycotted the conference. Guyana became independent on May 26, 1966. On July 22, Burnham was the guest of his chief sponsor, President Johnson, who reaffirmed his support for his rule in independent Guyana: 'Remember you have one friend in this corner and his name is Lyndon Johnson.' A beaming Burnham (cigar between his fingers) celebrated by posing with the president for a picture in front of the White House.

The history of Guyana since the early 1950s has been painfully tortuous. The politics of nationalism and Jagan's and Burnham's ideological experiments spawned a static political tribalism in a

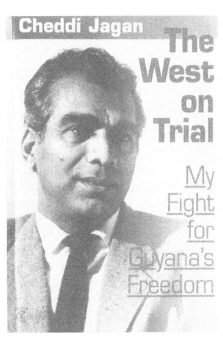

After losing power in December 1964, Cheddi Jagan grandiloquently put **The West on Trial** *in his memoirs published in London in 1966, on the eve of Guyana's independence from Britain*

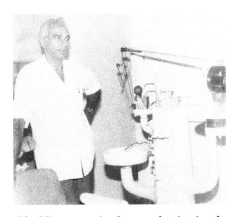

Cheddi was trained as a dentist in the United States (1936-43). After he lost power in 1964, he returned to dentistry part-time for a period in the late 1960s. His reputation for honesty and fine dental work was impeccable

fractured country that is still not a nation. How then does one assess the legacy of Cheddi Jagan? One of the most perspicacious verdicts of the man was made in 1998, the year after his death, by one of his young disciples from the late 1950s to early 1960s, Moses Bhagwan (1935–), in an interview with Professor Frank Birbalsingh. He argues that Jagan was confident Marxism-Leninism could resolve all of Guyana's social problems, including racism; therefore, he never gave serious consideration to the question of African racial insecurity:

> **He advocated Marxism because he thought it would solve the problems of Guyana, and he believed he could persuade the Americans to accept that...**He destroyed the so-called Indian leaders [such as the Luckhoos, C. R. Jacob, snr, Dr Jung Bahadur Singh, and Ayube Edun, of the 1930s–40s] because he opposed their [racial] politics...He [also] attacked the American and British imperialists. His whole plan was to unite the PPP into a national party. Yet the great irony is that he ended up as a symbol of ethnic disunity when he became a leader of Indians only...Jagan and Burnham reigned over a country that became tormented by ethnic conflicts of a level and intensity that never existed when they were denouncing Indian and African racism and British colonialism...

> It is a major failure of the PPP, in its early years, that it did not regard the Indian/African racial problem with due seriousness...[Jagan] had total, unremitting and relentless commitment to his party. He was democratically oriented and easy to get along with. He never kept grudges or carried out vendettas. He had integrity and did not use his position to accumulate wealth or power. He seemed incapable of corruption. He never made remarks to me that could be interpreted as racist. But **he could be calculating and ruthless when the interest of his party was at stake...**

> **I think Dr Jagan's greatest political contribution was made between 1943, when he returned from America, and 1953, when his first government was dismissed. From then, the impact of Jagan and Burnham, whether individually or jointly, has been negative** [emphasis added].[1]

Jagan was not a racist, yet he did exploit Indian primordial loyalties dexterously to retain their political allegiance. But he was a 'true believer' who was certain that Marxism-Leninism would resolve whatever problems Guyana encountered, including its monumental racist proclivities that remain resistant to erasure and the making of a nation.

One of Britain's most eminent contemporary thinkers, John Gray, Emeritus Professor of European Thought at the London School of Economics, notes the enduring power of 'ideas that promise a magical deliverance from human conflict,' but he cautions against the seductive utopian vision with pretensions to resolving all the problems of humankind. He was addressing the abysmal failure of Marxism-Leninism to supplant a supposedly moribund capitalism and transform the Soviet Union into a communist utopia:

> There is no reason to withdraw the claim…that the deadly mix of metaphysical certainty and pseudoscience that Lenin imbibed from Marx had a vital part in producing Communist totalitarianism. Pursuing an unrealisable vision of a harmonious future after capitalism had collapsed, Marx's Leninist followers created a repressive and inhuman society that itself collapsed, whereas capitalism – despite all its problems – continues to expand…Contrary to what Marx expected, nationalism and religion have not faded away and there is no sign of their doing so in the foreseeable future…[T]he vision of the future he imbibed from positivism…in which industrial societies stand on the brink of a scientific civilisation in which the religions and conflicts of the past will fade away, is rationally groundless – a myth that…has been exploded many times but seems to be ineradicable.[2]

Jock Campbell, the chairman of Booker, told me that he had warned Janet Jagan in the early 1960s that the millenarian vision, the communist utopia, was a dangerous fallacy that could lead to mass hunger and death for many Guyanese. She allegedly responded that such sacrifices were often necessary for the greater good: building the socialist alternative to capitalism. It is arguable, therefore, that if Cheddi Jagan had not been sabotaged by the Americans and the British in the early 1960s, he would have had the freedom, in an independent Guyana, to pursue his economic experiments, confident that the communist utopia, which sustained his political mission for fifty years, was attainable. With the dismal experience of the Soviet Union and its satellites as our guide, in conjunction with Guyana's own diabolical record under Burnham's unexampled 'cooperative socialism,' it is conceivable that Jagan's communist state would have eventuated in an equivalent abyss or worse. He was at least spared the indelible ignominy of the potential consequences of his Marxist faith by Kennedy's obsession with preventing 'another Cuba' in the Hemisphere. However, Guyana and several generations of Guyanese continue to bear the legacy of the ideological fantasies of Cheddi Jagan and Forbes Burnham. V. S. Naipaul is correct: 'Guyana has always been a land of fantasies. It was the land of El Dorado.'

Jagan lost the elections under PR on December 7, 1964. Burnham and D'Aguiar formed a coalition government, which was actively facilitated by the CIA. The communist Jagan, as the Americans had contrived it, was now ousted. He was impotent; he had squandered his considerable political capital, having been lavished with it up to the end of 1961. Relieved of responsibility, he embarked on a concatenation of nihilistic tactics, characterised by the boycotting of crucial events, with profound implications for the future of the country. He refused to enter the House of Assembly because several of his party's members were still in detention, Burnham's pretext being that this was imperative because of national security. He boycotted the Commission of Inquiry to British Guiana, appointed by the International Commission of Jurists in 1965, on grounds that their terms of reference were too diffused and did not focus adequately on what he propounded as the principal problem: racial imbalance in the security forces. He had advocated redressing racial imbalance in the latter specifically; the Burnham regime decided, however, that the question of racial imbalance be explored, in all its dimensions in the society, including land settlement schemes.

Jagan also boycotted the crucial constitutional conference in London in November 1965, when the British government duly granted independence to the Burnham-D'Aguiar coalition. He rationalised his absence as a protest against the deceit and violence fomented by Anglo-American imperialism to ensure that the prize was awarded to their lackeys. He told the BBC: 'I do not wish to lend support to the formal promulgation of decisions already taken [regarding independence] which are gravely inimical to the interests of the Guianese people.'[3] The date for independence was fixed for May 26, 1966. Jagan then boycotted the Queen's visit to Guyana in February 1966. His reason: '...solidarity with the 4,000,000 Africans in Rhodesia ... now suffering from white minority rule under Ian Smith.' The PPP accused Her Majesty's government of 'lacking in its duty to Africans to crush the rebellion ... [Smith's unilateral declaration of independence].'[4] Given Jagan's *modus operandi* since his electoral defeat of 1964, Burnham relished mocking him as a kindred soul of the Yorkshire and England batsman, Geoffrey Boycott, christening Dr Jagan 'Dr Boycott.'

II. Jagan's Obdurate Pro-Soviet Communism and the Internal Haemorrhaging of the PPP

But this cascading nihilism of self-inflicted non-engagement was reflective of an internal haemorrhaging in the PPP as early as mid-1965 when the great Jagan loyalist, Brindley Benn, a trusted communist, became estranged from the PPP, as did a few who were loyal to Benn, such as Victor Downer (the manager of Freedom House, the home of the PPP), Patricia Benn (wife of Brindley), and Thelma Reece, the latter two being the leading lights of the party's women's branch, the Women's Progressive Organisation. The main source of estrangement seems to have been Benn and his comrades' dissatisfaction with the Jaganites regarding their devotion to the made-in-Moscow brand of communism; they were inclined towards what they saw as a purer version of the product, made-in-Peking (Beijing).

I have argued that the history of the PPP was characterised by an unwavering devotion of Cheddi and Janet Jagan to the communist enterprise as inspired by the Soviet Union – virtually a faith. This made for chronic factionalism in the PPP, with accompanying defections or desertions, as someone or some group was ever on the verge of quitting because they could not be reconciled to the Jaganite Soviet orthodoxy. The loss of power at the end of 1964, aggravated the fissiparous tendency as possibilities for disbursing patronage by way of the resources of the state evaporated. The departure of B. H. Benn and Moses Bhagwan (chairman of the PPP and of the PYO respectively), by late 1965, was prompted by ideological dissonance with the Jaganite orthodoxy. Benn was clearly oriented towards the Maoist persuasion within Marxism-Leninism, which had become anathema to the Soviet orthodoxy. Bhagwan, on the other hand, was inclined toward a less sectarian approach to Marxism; he was expelled for not toeing the Soviet line. There could be no confluence or co-existence of diverse conceptions of Marxism within the PPP controlled by the Jagans and predicated on the primacy of Soviet communism.

Bhagwan explains the *modus operandi* of communist parties, such as the PPP, enmeshed in the Soviet sphere of influence:

> The Party was partially financed from Russia…The real reason for my expulsion from the PPP was because I appeared to be anti-Russian. The Russians would not tolerate anybody inside the leadership with whom they were not comfortable…In Third World [communist] parties, as soon as differences arise, somebody has to go. These parties are not structured to accommodate people with strong beliefs and feelings, or people who are prepared to change and work out new positions: they are distrustful of innovation, difference or criticism. These are not parties but proprietary interests. I became disillusioned when Cheddi revealed that orientation as party leader. As soon as the party was threatened or made vulnerable in any way someone had to go…These parties are so structured that they really cannot sit down with leaders and allow them to have different points of view….[5]

It got nasty as the foremost African member of the PPP, B. H. Benn, and his wife, Patricia, were no longer prepared to accept as gospel the mantras of the Jagans. It came to a head in mid-1965 when a reprimand by Cheddi of the manager of the PPP Head Office (Freedom House), Victor Downer, an ally of Benn, was leaked to the press. Janet Jagan wrote a letter to Benn, dated November 26, 1965 (it was forwarded to Billy Strachan in London). She quoted from a letter Benn had sent to her earlier: 'You see the Party as your personal property. You have no sense of comradeship. You keep whom you want and destroy them later. You have one face for Guyana and another for foreign socialist countries.'

Janet was transparently angry with Benn; any reconciliation was inconceivable:

> In these words, which I know you have been using against me all year, you merely express the same slander I was subjected to by SK

[Sydney King, later Eusi Kwayana] at one time and [Balram Singh] Rai at another. Why do you say I regard the Party as my personal property? Is it because I take serious objection to people using the Party for their own objectives – because I object to comrades running to the filthy capitalist press with inner party matters?

Is this a sign of lack of comradeship – because I severely chastised Comrade Downer for showing a confidential letter from the Leader [Cheddi] all over the place, including the hostile press?

The remarks in your letter are slanderous and not only contained in your letter but are used over and over again by you and your colleagues. If you believed in comradeship, you would not behave like this.[6]

Out of office and with little to offer 'comrades' beyond more 'struggle against the imperialists,' the PPP was severely wounded by the departure of Moses Bhagwan and several young 'comrades' from the PYO, in addition to Brindley Benn and his followers, all stalwarts of the PPP, such as Victor Downer, Patricia Benn, and Thelma Reece, while Burnham strolled merrily along towards independence. As noted earlier, Jagan boycotted the constitutional conference in London in November 1965, but the prize was awaiting Burnham's collection. This hitherto contentious issue of independence, at the heart of Anglo-American complicity in sabotaging Jagan's acquisition of it, while occasioning much pain, bloodshed, and enduring racial hatred, was embarrassingly anti-climactic – a walk in the park for Burnham and his reluctant partner in the coalition, D'Aguiar.

III. Jagan Boycotts the Independence Conference in London

Odeen Ishmael depicts the Independence Conference, chaired by Labour's Tony Greenwood (secretary of state for the colonies), as a rubber-stamped event – a farce. He is right:

> Just a few days before the conference began, a draft constitution prepared by the [PNC/UF] coalition government, without any input from the people, was published in Guyana. Absent from it were many of the reservations and safeguards they had argued for forcefully at the 1962 Independence conference.

> The Independence conference began on November 2 and by November 7 [1965] agreed that Independence would be granted on May 26, 1966. The British Government quickly agreed to the draft constitution which was adopted after very little discussion. Independence was thus handed over to the PNC-UF Government without any reservations by the British Government, which only up

to a year before had stubbornly resisted granting Independence when the PPP was in power. In doing so, it complied with the wishes of the American Government not to grant Independence until a pro-western 'friendly' administration was in power in Guyana. Shortly after the conference ended, Burnham returned to Guyana and received a grand welcome by his supporters who, only a year before, had stoutly opposed Independence.[7]

To recap: Guyana became independent at midnight on May 26, 1966. For nearly twenty years, Cheddi Jagan, of Indian extraction, buoyed by the independence of India and obsessed with the dominance of the British company, Booker, in the colony's plantation economy, had championed Guyana's 'struggle' for independence. Yet, on the big night it was the African leader of the PNC, L. F. S. Burnham, who was the recipient of the prize. His politics, though left-wing, was characterised by a cultivated pragmatism, strategic ambiguity – the facility to 'tack and turn as advantage seems to dictate…his whole political approach is opportunistic,' as a major British politician had assessed him in 1954.[8] With the aid of the Portuguese and Coloured middle-class (mixed-race) political party, the UF, led by Portuguese businessman, Peter D'Aguiar, anti-communist to the bone, in conjunction with the decisive intervention of President Kennedy himself and the CIA, in 1962–63, the PNC and UF resorted to violence to make British Guiana ungovernable. The latter proved effective in delaying independence, while Anglo-American collusion brought a Burnham-D'Aguiar coalition to power in December 1964, and independence in May 1966. But Jagan, ironically, was essentially a spectator to the celebration of his country's 'freedom.'

Speaking in the National Assembly on Independence Day, Jagan made it clear that this was not his Freedom Day. That still had to be 'struggled for': foreign control of the economy must be eliminated; only his party, the PPP, could achieve real liberation for the country. He meant disengagement from 'imperialism' and the capitalist system – pursuit of the communist utopia, inspired by the glorious Soviet Union. It was not an auspicious beginning for this troubled land:

> [P]olitical independence has been attained under the continuation and consolidation of foreign economic control and the maintenance of the colonial type economy, based on primary production and extraction. This has already detracted from the living standards of the working people…The PPP, the vanguard of Guyana's struggle for national liberation, is convinced that liberty is achieved only when it has been struggled for and won. It cannot be a gift of charity. For the people of Guyana, real freedom is still a prize to be won, and win it we will – as a reunited free people.[9]

On the eve of Guyana's independence, Percy Armstrong, a veteran anti-communist journalist, dramatised the implications for Jagan's loyal Indian supporters of his ritualistic boycott of crucial national events, following his loss of power in December 1964. His views mirrored those of many of Jagan's followers, disheartened by their creeping political marginalisation:

> All this means that the forthcoming celebrations, like those of the Queen's visit [in February 1966], will be largely a celebration by Africans, while people of the Indian community will perhaps huddle themselves in their homes, peeping through creases and cracks and giving furtive glances over their shoulders to see whether terrorists from amongst them…are lurking in the rear…The main aim behind all these boycotts is to convert the Indian community into a dissident group which will become an irritant in the body politic of the newly independent state of Guyana, to be used like putty by the Communist international organisations.[10]

IV. Reckless! Jagan Veers Outrageously to the Left, Attends the Tricontinental Conference, Havana, January 1966

Jagan's reaction to the independence prize being bestowed on Burnham at the conference in London in late 1965 was to veer outrageously to the left, thereby claiming the ideological high ground – infallible by virtue of its Marxist-Leninist authenticity and destined to supersede the moribund pro-imperialist and capitalist stance of the PNC-UF coalition. Jagan was, in fact, already rendering his supporters such fragile leadership that it would conduce to their incremental relegation to the periphery – indeed, electoral irrelevance and prolonged exclusion from power that engendered a culture of mass migration persisting until today.

Jagan boycotted the Independence Conference in London, yet he attended the Tricontinental Conference in Havana, from January 3–15, 1966, where long-term revolutionary tactics against American imperialism were addressed. A meeting of communist delegates from eighty-two countries, the general political resolution stated that 'the common enemy of all peoples is international imperialism, headed by US imperialism.' Reflecting on his experience at the conference in Cuba in a journal affiliated with the Communist Party of Great Britain (CPGB), *Labour Monthly* (edited by R. Palme Dutt of the CPGB), Jagan remarked:

> Cuba is the symbol of a small country successfully confronting the giant of the north and exploding the illusion and myth of US omnipotence and invincibility, as well as being a symbol of ideological unity. The Cuban Revolution encompasses revolutionary nationalism, socialism and communism.[11]

The Tricontinental Conference of the communist parties of Africa, Asia, and Latin America was convened by the Castro regime, with the unstinted support of the Communist Party of the Soviet Union (CPSU), to co-ordinate 'anti-imperialist' activities among communist parties loyal to the Soviet Union. As Castro told the conference:

> The Soviet delegation has arrived at this conference with the aim of giving all-round assistance to the unification of the anti-imperialist forces of the three continents in order to provide greater impetus to our common struggle against imperialism, colonialism and neo-colonialism – led by the US capitalists.[12]

The US government, naturally, followed the deliberations closely, and in a document prepared by the Senate Judiciary Committee, it was noted that the PPP was represented by Cheddi Jagan, Lalbachan Lallbahadur (a young PPP activist studying in Havana), and one other. The document stressed the Cold War underpinning of the conference, and observed that Moscow had scored a resounding victory over Peking (Beijing), in the battle to win communist minds:

> The USSR has much to gain by giving moral and material support to the Tricontinental Conference. The conference established an instrument through which the Soviet Union could effectively conduct subversive operations in every country of North and South America, Asia and Africa. Speakers at the Tricontinental Conference referred repeatedly to efforts being made to attract students, particularly those from Latin America, to attend the schools for subversion which have been established in the Soviet Union and its satellites. In its clash with Communist China, the Tricontinental Conference furnished an opportunity for a major Soviet propaganda victory over its Chinese rival.[13]

In March 1966, *Thunder*, the organ of the PPP, was emphatic that they were combatants in the Cold War and that 'immoral' America was not only Cuba's foremost enemy, but it was the PPP's as well:

> The delegates had, above all, a clear-cut objective – how in the face of a ruthless and immoral enemy to unite all the progressive forces for simultaneous confrontation…The establishment of a tricontinental organisation with provisional headquarters in Havana, Cuba, and a continental (Latin American) organisation was a stunning blow to US imperialism.[14]

President Kennedy and Duncan Sandys were clearly vindicated in respect of where Cheddi Jagan stood in the Cold War.

Jagan had played into the hands of Burnham, who kept seventeen PPP activists in detention in 1966, contending – erroneously – that they were agents of communist subversion trained in Cuba. The Burnham government continually renewed the state of emergency on grounds that it was essential in neutralising the seditious programme of Jagan's PPP. In fact, when Guyana became independent in May 1966, the state of emergency was still in place. In January of that year, Dr P. A. Reid, the deputy prime minister, speaking in the House of Assembly on the rationale for extending the emergency, observed: 'We want to make it known that this government has no one detained for political reasons. They are not political detainees. If we lift the emergency, we have no control over the movement of explosives which is the basis of the trouble.'[15] He was astutely defining them as terrorists precisely at the time Jagan was attending the Tricontinental Conference in Havana.

In April 1966, Prime Minister Forbes Burnham reinforced the government's designation of the PPP as an organisation committed to subversion:

> When lawlessness prevails, Government must exercise control of the source from which senseless and irresponsible acts are inspired... PPP member Dr Fenton Ramsahoye described the extension of the emergency as a disgrace for a country going into Independence... [But] it is not for those who participated in Tricontinental conferences [Jagan at the meeting of communists in Havana in January 1966] to criticise actions by the state, permitted by the constitution and aimed at protecting the community at large.[16]

Shortly afterwards, Jagan announced that the slogan of the PPP, for the independence celebrations in May 1966, was: 'Independence Yes! Celebrations No!' He explained the rationale:

> The PPP opposed the fraudulent constitutional arrangements [the Sandys Plan] which resulted in its removal from the government in 1964. It did not take part in the rigged constitutional talks in London in November 1965. And it was not consulted on the date for independence. The party's attitude to the independence celebrations is therefore coupled with mixed feelings. On the one hand it is happy that on May 26 our Guyana flag will replace the Union Jack, that we will have our own national anthem and coat-of-arms. But independence has meaning for us not only in symbolic terms. Above all we want also the substance of independence. The substance has been denied the Guyanese people.
>
> For the following reasons, we cannot celebrate independence. Firstly, full powers have been transferred to the puppets of the imperialists [the PNC and the UF] by a rigged constitutional arrangement. Secondly, the imperialists who have a stranglehold on our economy [Booker primarily] are being further strengthened. Thirdly, independence is being ushered in under a state of emergency. The main purpose is to silence the political opposition and to intimidate the working class. Fourthly, on Independence Day comrades who have fought vigorously for independence during the course of several years will be in detention.[17]

Jagan and his teenage son (Joey), accompanied by Ranji Chandisingh, his Marxist theoretician, and C. R. Jacob, Jr, his former minister of finance, did attend the flag-raising ceremony at midnight on May 26, 1966 – the totality of their participation in the independence celebrations. But they certainly were ill-equipped to plan or execute any subversion of the government. The truth is they were clueless, mired in jargon. They would henceforth claim the ideological moral high ground, proclaiming that they were the sole practitioners of a pure Marxism: the source of genuine liberation, the making of 'socialist man.' But this was reflective of their ineffectuality rather than their commitment to, and preparation for, revolution. Even the anti-communist *Weekend Post and Sunday Argosy* observed that the PNC's tendency to project on to the PPP insurrectionary intent after independence was a mirage; it was beyond their capacity even when they were in government.[18] Yet Burnham would harp incessantly on allegations of ill-conceived violence by the PPP, utilising the 'Tricontinental stick' to give credence to his assertions, in the absence of concrete evidence that they were fomenting revolution.

Dr Jagan's surfeit of revolutionary rhetoric notwithstanding – Dr Jargon, as characterised by one critic – the imputation of insurrectionary intent against the PPP had a ring of fantasy. In June 1966, Burnham addressed Jagan. Sheer farce!

> If ...[he] genuinely wishes to unify our peoples and insure their future happiness and well-being, he can readily do this by openly renouncing, once and for all, his penchant for looking outside our borders for solutions to the nation's problems: by renouncing violence, subversion and armed conflict which he affirmed in his recent utterances at the Tri-continental Conference in Havana; by henceforth ceasing to send his supporters and representatives abroad for 'ideological orientation' and financial assistance; by halting the training of his followers in guerrilla warfare, the manufacture of bombs and by openly giving up his ambitions as an international communist leader.[19]

Jagan was in office for seven years, from 1957 to 1964. If he had not been so engrossed by his communist dogmas, Burnham would never have got anywhere near the big prize. Jagan was an honest man, but a politician with severe limitations. He published his autobiography on the eve of Guyana's independence in May 1966. It was grandiloquently titled: *The West on Trial: My Fight for Guyana's Freedom*. Richard Gott, reviewing it for the *Guardian*, wrote:

> Unfortunately for him, his arrogance, intolerance and political misjudgement made him an easy target for criticism...[even] from those who were not predisposed to believe that he was a communist.' David Holden, reviewing it in the *Sunday Times*, was less charitable: '[I]ts author is an inept politician, with an inflated sense of his own

importance, a garrulous pen (and tongue) and a thoroughly woolly mind.[20]

As early as midnight of May 26, 1966, with most Indo-Guyanese (at the bidding of Cheddi Jagan) boycotting the independence celebrations, it was evident that while British Guiana was terminating its colonial links with Britain, a Guyanese nation was still to be born. It remains elusive: like so many 'nations' in the world, it is essentially a geographical expression. The various strands of Marxism (a useful device, as I have argued, to circumvent facing Guyanese chronic racism) have failed to bring the idea of a nation any closer to fruition. But Jagan's sanctimonious communist vision – manifested in his patent loyalty to the Soviet Bloc – the exemplar for Guyana's liberation, ensured that the US government was complicit in (or, at least, tolerated) Burnham's ritual rigging of the general elections, on a massive scale, to perpetuate his increasingly dictatorial rule.

Jagan, the real communist (other variants would blossom), would never be allowed to accede to power even when the Burnham regime became the world's first exponent of 'cooperative socialism.' In an address to comrades of his PPP, the foot soldiers, on August 27, 1966, Jagan cited two examples as the benchmark of the kind of society they were aspiring to build in an independent Guyana:

> For the people of the non-socialist world who are suffering from capitalist, imperialist, colonialist and neo-colonialist subjugation, exploitation and oppression, the Soviet Union is a shining example of what can be achieved when the system of capitalism – the exploitation and despoliation of man by man, is abolished...

> In Cuba, unemployment and hunger have been abolished and despite the imperialist blockade, the foundations of a great new future are being laid.[21]

V. 'This is Like Homecoming': Jagan's Pride as a Cold Warrior for the Soviet Union; Celebrates the 'Crumbling of the Capitalist Edifice'

The longer Jagan languished in opposition, marginalised by an electoral process subversive of democratic norms, the more immutable his wallow in the morass of Soviet futility. Therefore, the moral authority of his campaign for electoral transparency in Guyana was necessarily vitiated – the political culture he embraced being diametrically opposed to liberal democracy, which it maligned as 'bourgeois democracy': a fraud. The latter was found wanting juxtaposed with the purportedly flawless scientific instrument for the liberation of humankind from the evils of capitalism: Marxism-Leninism. Jagan believed that the Soviet

Union was creating the 'new man'; that the communist society was on the verge of coming to fruition. It was a quasi-religious conviction, not amenable to rational scrutiny – as if the butchery of Comrade Stalin, the Gulag, and the desecration of the creative spirit, then and thereafter, under communism were a fantasy contrived by the imperialists.

In April 1971, in his address to the 24th Congress of the CPSU in Moscow, Jagan extolled the superiority of the Soviet system, inspired by ideas rooted in 'natural science' not idealism – the infallible materialist conception of history:

> Time was when the representatives of the capitalist class not only called for the strangling of 'the communist infant in its cradle,' but also proclaimed that the legacy of the Great October Socialist Revolution would be starvation and oppression, which would bring down the Communist edifice. Now, instead, the world witnesses the crumbling of the capitalist edifice with hunger at the doorstep, and the twin plagues, unemployment and inflation, eroding the foundations...[22]

Jagan was so enthralled by the illusion that the Soviet Union represented the ultimate beacon towards the communist utopia, that he never dared to be reproachful of the CPSU, however odious the documented atrocities perpetrated by the party. And it did foment many horrendous deeds, while casually rationalising their unmitigated evil as indispensable to the heaven on earth they were convinced their practice of 'scientific socialism' would soon realise. Jagan, incredibly, did proclaim:

> **It is in the Soviet Union, the fountain-head of the Socialist World, where one breathes the air of real freedom; where substance, not just form, gives a new meaning to democracy; where unemployment and insecurity are mere memories; where socialist humanism values man as its most precious asset; where a new man is being forged on the communist ideal of 'from each according to his ability, to each according to his need' is on its way to fulfilment.**[23]

The Soviet project, putatively grounded in scientific rationality, was therefore endowed with the means to eradicate ethnic prejudices bred and perpetuated by capitalism to divide, rule, and oppress. It is predicated on the real material world of the means of production and relations of production: the class struggle; when this is resolved in favour of public ownership of the working people, under socialism/communism, all 'superstructural' barriers to the perfectibility of humankind, such as ethnic and religious bigotry (manifestations of false consciousness), will have been eliminated. Jagan believed that the Soviet Union was setting the example of peace, freedom, and socialism, as peoples of diverse nationalities were engaged in the glorious project of human emancipation from all its ancient fetters: the crafting of 'socialist humanism' – the radical transformation of the human condition:

Lenin has written: 'materialism has proved to be the only philosophy that is consistent and true to all the teachings of natural science'... Under the Leninist nationality policy, the once backward and oppressed peoples of the Soviet Union have been brought into positions of equality and fraternity. In the West, where racism, discrimination and material oppression are still potent weapons in divide-exploit-and-rule politics, brotherhood is reserved to the church for Sunday preaching. In the Soviet Union it has been put into practice.[24]

Homecoming! Jagan shaking the hand of his communist hero, Mikhail Suslov (chief theoretician of the CPSU), in the presence of Nikolai Podgorny (chairman of the Presidium of the Supreme Soviet), Moscow, June 1969

Out of office since December 1964, but certain that 'history and time' were on his side, Jagan felt emboldened, in June 1969, to embrace his ideological beacon, the Soviet Union. 'This is like homecoming,' he exulted, in his address to the International Meeting of Communist and Workers Parties in Moscow. 'Repeated attacks' from Churchill, Macmillan, Alec Douglas-Home, and the 'liberal' Kennedy, and 'betrayal' by the 'social democrats,' Clement Attlee and Harold Wilson, had not tempered his communist ardour. He had not 'somersaulted,' as most Caribbean leaders did once the Cold War was ignited by 'American imperialism' in the late 1940s. He was proud of that:

...not only theory but practice has taught us that this is where we belong...only the international communist movement can liberate the people of Guyana from imperialist exploitation and oppression. Our presence here will be the excuse for further attacks. But this does not frighten us.

Jagan explained that as early as 1946 his source of political inspiration was the CPSU:

We have long been faced with imperialism's biggest weapon – anti-communism. We were attacked more than two decades ago, when inspired by the heroic deeds of the Soviet people under the magnificent leadership of the Communist Party of the Soviet Union [under Comrade Stalin], we formed in 1946 the Political Affairs Committee and, in 1950, the People's Progressive Party, with a programme of national independence and scientific socialism [Marxism-Leninism] as our banner.[25]

Jagan condemned American and British imperialism for the fact that their puppet, Forbes Burnham, through electoral fraud, was foisted on the Guyanese people. He was addressing the World Communist Meeting in Moscow in the aftermath of the first fraudulent general elections, in December 1968 (aided and abetted by the Johnson administration) and after the Soviet invasion of Czechoslovakia, which he supported and considered a victory for the progressive forces of the world. Although Jagan was not fazed by the machinations of imperialism, he was still venting his indignation at the dark forces of Western capitalism and imperialism. The anger showed:

Guyana is the graveyard of imperialism's alleged good intentions. It is a case history of its hypocrisy and deceit, a laboratory of its tricks and stratagems...During the past 20 years, our people have learnt that despite the loud claims of the imperialists about their beliefs in freedom and democracy, Western democracy means naked force, bribery, gerrymandering, fomenting racial strife, manipulation of constitutions, rigging of elections, denial of constitutional guarantees, and militarisation of our politics. No doubt, these methods were adopted from time to time because our Party, though dubbed communist, has been able to win three consecutive elections [in 1953, 1957 and 1961]...And we would have been in the government today had it not been for the crudest practice of electoral manipulation, subversion, force and fraud.[26]

However, Cheddi was not dispirited because what he believed in was winning – indeed, it was bound to win: 'It is imperative that national liberation parties in other third world countries like Guyana quickly follow the lead of the PPP, begin to transform themselves from loose, mass parties into vanguard Marxist-Leninist type of parties and develop the closest links with the socialist system.' And, for Jagan, that system was infallible and beyond reproach. He told the meeting of world communists in Moscow that the Soviet 'entry' of Czechoslovakia (as Jagan downplayed the Soviet invasion) in August 1968 was totally justified, by contrast with the American invasion of the Dominican Republic in April 1965, which he deemed 'a violation not only of territorial integrity but of real sovereignty.' The same did not apply to Czechoslovakia, where 'reactionary' pro-capitalist forces had taken a backward step against an authentic workers' state, obviously another subterfuge of American imperialism.

As with Hungary in 1956, Jagan embraced the Soviet deception regarding Czechoslovakia unequivocally:

> Imperialism has never given up its aggressive intentions. It has changed its methods not its aims. It has become more cunning. Comrade Brezhnev has warned us of its many disguises. It practises new tricks and pursues different tactics...Comrade Husak [General Secretary of the Communist Party of Czechoslovakia] rightly drew our attention to the concept of the class content of sovereignty... If the entry of troops of the Warsaw Pact countries was similarly a violation of Czechoslovakia's borders, its objective was different from the American invasion of the Dominican Republic, done to maintain the neo-colonialist status quo and to prevent a social revolution. It [the Soviet invasion] was done to prevent a socialist state from reverting to capitalism, and to preserve the sovereign right of the Czechoslovak people, the right to be free from capitalist exploitation and all the other ills of capitalist society. Therefore, far from being a violation of internationalism. It was a duty.[27]

The Americans must have felt vindicated as regards their resolute subversion of Jagan. Not only had they eliminated a key communist leader in the Hemisphere (second only to Castro) without invading British Guiana, but Jagan had confirmed all their apprehensions regarding his loyalty to Soviet communism. And, by their definition of the situation, they had precluded Guyana from becoming a 'second Cuba,' potentially more menacing than Castro's Cuba by virtue of its strategic continental location, contiguous with the crucial states of Brazil and Venezuela.

On the twenty-fifth anniversary of the PPP, in 1975, Jagan critically revisited his seven years in government, between 1957 and 1964. What he said was pure fantasy. He believed they should not have stayed in office because they were precluded from pursuing their communist agenda. Rather, they ought to have prioritised party work, with special emphasis on re-educating Guyanese at the grassroots by the tenets of Marxism-Leninism, thereby erasing the pernicious legacy of their colonial miseducation:

> Only fools who do nothing make no mistakes. The main burden of their attack is that we should not have openly espoused Marxism and given support to the Cuban Revolution. What they fail to note is that had we not taken a firm patriotic position, a world-view [Marxism-Leninism]...we would not have been able to win over the masses

[presumably Africans: untrue!] from the traitors and collaborators [Burnham's PNC] **…The mistake we made was not the espousal of Marxism; it was that we did not fully implement it in practice. The PPP was a party geared to winning elections…**[emphasis added].

It was not until 1961 that we established an ideological school [Accabre College], and only in 1969 that we took a decision to transform our loose mass party into a disciplined Marxist-Leninist party. One of the difficulties encountered was that…there was not enough personnel to man both the government and party administration at the same time. The result was that party work suffered while we were marking time in government, without power and being sabotaged at the same time. The mistake we made was to have given priority to government rather than the party, staying in the government too long without Independence, assuming responsibility without real power, and thereby undermining our influence, cutting the ground from under our feet.[28]

L.F.S. Burnham did ensure that Jagan had the privilege and ample time – nearly twenty-eight uninterrupted years, from 1964 to 1992 – for little but 'party work'! Yet by April 1980, already fifteen years in the political wilderness, Jagan was proud to proclaim, in a lecture at Freedom House to mark the 110th anniversary of Lenin's birth, that his PPP was emulating the concept of the communist party promulgated by Lenin, with reference to its so-called democratic centralism and, by implication, the 'paramountcy' of the party over the government. There was no room for a plurality of parties in the Soviet Union and its satellites – a bourgeois concept:

> **Marxism-Leninism is not a lifeless dogma; it is a living guide to action. It is a science** that grows and develops in accordance with changing conditions and times…Lenin's genius lies in the fact that he comprehensively and creatively developed the science which Karl Marx and Friedrich Engels elaborated. He translated theory into practice, founded a party of the new type, guided the making of a socialist revolution and laid the foundations for a communist society [emphasis added].[29]

There was nothing democratic about the Leninist Party, the CPSU, that Jagan found so inspiringly transformative and worthy of emulation; Burnham, too (for obvious reasons), was enamoured of it. Jagan had said 'our experience shows the necessity for a vanguard party of the working class.' Burnham agreed: he determined that his PNC was that 'vanguard party of the working class.' The US government would view Jagan's PPP through the prism of potential communist subversion, thus ensuring Burnham's immunity from scrutiny in his routine rigging of the general elections and the consolidation of his dictatorial propensities by virtue of the 'paramountcy' of the PNC.

VI. American and British Sponsorship of Burnham: The Farcical Independence Conference, 1965

In fact, as soon as Burnham and D'Aguiar, coached by the CIA, had formed the coalition government in December 1964, the US Government (USG) of President Lyndon Johnson reaffirmed their mantra that Burnham must be fortified against potential defeat, through constitutional means, by the communist Jagan. What the Americans deemed most ominous was the likelihood that Indo-Guyanese, by virtue of their imminent numerical superiority, could unseat Burnham in democratic elections, even under PR. Consequently, they considered it a legitimate moral imperative to aid and abet Burnham in devising mechanisms for rigging future elections. The Johnson administration was not perturbed by any such flagrant repudiation of democratic norms, deemed indispensable if their anointed anti-communist man were to retain power in perpetuity. The Americans were central to Burnham's rigging of the first post-independence general elections, in December 1968 – indeed, to his mastery at staging fraudulent general elections, thereby institutionalising a crooked electoral tradition lasting nearly a quarter of a century. Yet none of the leaders of the region could summon the moral integrity to challenge the fragile political bona fides of Forbes Burnham. Jagan's communism apart, it was as if his repudiation of Federation, in the 1950s, had boomeranged.

Shortly after Burnham assumed office in December 1964, he told US Consul General Delmar Carlson bluntly that securing independence was the prerequisite for whatever 'radical' scheme he may conceive to stay in power indefinitely. And at no time, did his American benefactors attempt to dissuade Burnham from his pursuit of rigging as the principal means of establishing the foundations of a dictatorship, perceived as anti-communist. But independence first!

As early as January 4, 1965, the Johnson administration conveyed to the British that Burnham was a 'moderate' and responsible leader worthy of American assistance. They were already sowing the seeds for their man to lead an independent Guyana. At a meeting between assistant secretary for European affairs, William Tyler, and the director of the Office of the British Commonwealth and Northern European Affairs, Harold Shullaw (both of the State Department), and senior officials of the British Embassy in Washington, the former were cleverly advancing the case for Burnham. The British had long-standing apprehensions that Burnham was a racist and an opportunist; US Consul General Carlson concurred, but the primacy of their anti-communist crusade necessitated their continual allaying of such fears. Besides, the compelling truth that Jagan was entombed by his Marxist-Leninist creed alleviated their task, while presenting Burnham with an open goal:

> We believe that Burnham has not done badly since taking office, and that he has adopted a moderate and constructive line in his public statements regarding racial conciliation [with Indians]. We are under no illusions about Burnham's weaknesses and shortcomings. He is not ideal, but nevertheless he is the only [anti-communist] alternative at present to Jagan and the PPP.

> We have told Burnham that we would move ahead rapidly on an aid programme immediately after the B.G. elections. We are ready to do so and wish to send an AID official to Georgetown…Any delay, we are convinced, would have extremely adverse consequences. Such delay would destroy Burnham's confidence in us and make his relations with Governor Luyt difficult…We are asking, therefore, with great urgency that the Prime Minister and Foreign Secretary authorise our going ahead with the implementation of our aid programme.[30]

It was all about not offending their blue-eyed boy, Forbes! How things had changed since 1961, when most thought it was all over for him. Cheddi had indeed won the lottery – on Forbes's behalf! In a heavily redacted document from the National Security Council, in early February 1965, it was evident that the US government was conscientiously seeking to project a lofty image of their man. Their reservations in respect of Burnham's personality traits notwithstanding, they were virtually genuflecting to him, as if to safeguard that they did not forfeit their man to some segment of the communist world, given Burnham's nebulous socialism. But they were buying a pig in a poke:

> …there is a note of optimism in B.G. these days, even among East Indians…the Governor [Sir Richard Luyt] is pleasantly surprised by Burnham's performance thus far, and…the two men seem to be getting along quite well with each other…we can expect the PPP to come up with some kind of shenanigans during [Secretary of State for the Colonies] Greenwood's visit to B.G., now scheduled for about February 12–15 [1965].[31]

The CIA was methodically preoccupied with preparing the ground, determined to convince the British to grant independence to Burnham as early as possible. This explains the heavy redacting of the documents. One high-ranking CIA man visited British Guiana from January 16–19, 1965, but did not meet with Burnham. However, he did see Burnham in New York on February 3, 1965; the latter was en route to British Guiana from the UK. He had good news for the Americans. Burnham met Tony Greenwood in London, and he was pleased to report that he was 'not as pro-Jagan as he had originally assumed.' The overtures of the Americans to the new, and weak, Labour government of Harold Wilson was bearing fruit.[32]

Moreover, the US government was meticulous in covering all bases, systematically cultivating a convincing, if inflated, image of Burnham. The foremost reservation the British harboured of Burnham was his apparent lack of empathy for Indians; consequently, the State Department and the CIA modified, if not erased, this perception. A telling case related to the glut of rice following Burnham's termination of relations with Castro's Cuba, hitherto a significant market for local rice grown primarily by Jagan's Indian supporters. In a memorandum of February 26, 1965, Assistant Secretary of State Tyler wrote to deputy director of the CIA, Richard Helms, regarding 'a project involving the disbursement of up to $550,000 to subsidise the clandestine purchase of 5,000 tons of rice from British Guiana.'[32] The details are not available, but this action indicates that the Americans were leaving no stone unturned in their resolve to persuade the British to grant independence to Burnham.

The results were most encouraging, as Consul General Carlson reported following the visit to British Guiana of Tony Greenwood (secretary of state for the colonies) in mid-February 1965:

> The ... visit was very successful from our point of view. Jagan behaved like a petulant adolescent, while Burnham and D'Aguiar made a favourable impression. Carlson was particularly buoyed by the secretary's evaluation of Burnham: Greenwood agreed that Burnham had done well but thought that 'sooner or later Cheddi would win an election.' Greenwood said: 'I don't subscribe to the view, you know, that Cheddi is a Communist'; he was 'in his way brilliant although rather incompetent.' He then remarked: 'On the other hand, here is this other man [Burnham] who knows so quickly relationships, where British Guiana fits in the wider scheme of things, procedures, etc., whereas Cheddi just does not grasp those things.'[33]

Greenwood's assessment was predicated on their respective grasp of *realpolitik*: the politics of the Cold War.

In another message to the State Department, Carlson remarked that Burnham had made a salutary impression on Greenwood. The Americans clearly considered this crucial in securing a constitutional conference in London, later in the year, to grant independence to Burnham. The State Department responded to Carlson noting that Greenwood's visit

> was apparently more productive than we had anticipated. We agree with Governor [Luyt] that it is important to take advantage of Greenwood's goodwill and provide him with the basis for convincing the Labour Party that Burnham is more responsible than many Labourites had believed. You should, after briefing the Governor on our views, pass them on to Burnham in a manner you judge most likely to be effective.[34]

The State Department also informed Carlson of their receipt of a favourable report from HMG of Greenwood's visit to British Guiana, and they attributed it primarily to **'Burnham's astute statesmanship.' Greenwood was so**

charmed by Burnham, he revealed that 'he had no idea he was a man of such stature.' On the other hand, he considered the performance of Jagan and the PPP 'lamentable.' Apparently, Greenwood no longer felt a coalition between Burnham and Jagan was feasible or even desirable. Consequently, he was reportedly offering Burnham an easy path towards the big prize: 'if the racial imbalance question in the security forces [predominantly African] could be resolved, then a constitutional convention to prepare a way to Independence could be held.' The State Department was confident that if Burnham agreed to a commission of inquiry to examine racial imbalance in the public service, Greenwood would give the green light to a date for the Independence Conference. It was virtually in the bag.

The State Department was clear about what Burnham should do, and Consul General Carlson was instructed to get Burnham to 'seize this chance to make progress toward independence by, in effect, providing the tools he needs to do the job, i.e., authorise Greenwood to go ahead with the commission to examine racial imbalance, and work with him toward this end. We urge him to send Greenwood a message giving the authorisation Greenwood requested.'[35]

However, there was already a problem simmering within the PNC-UF coalition government that troubled the Americans: basic temperamental incompatibility between Peter D'Aguiar (minister of finance and leader of the UF) and Forbes Burnham, compounded by discordance pertaining to budgetary matters. D'Aguiar's aim was to balance the budget, but Burnham was driven by 'politically inspired spending increases.' D'Aguiar informed Carlson that he was going to resign from the cabinet because he had 'no political future,' as the PNC 'intended to merge with or swallow up his party [the latter: very true!].'[36] But the US govwernment regarded the coalition as pivotal to the perceived cohesion they deemed vital to the case for independence at the constitutional conference, preferably later that year in London. Interestingly, providing a date was set for independence, they intimated that D'Aguiar could do whatever pleased him. He was clearly dispensable. Burnham had already indicated to the Americans that he would introduce mechanisms for rigging the elections to ensure that the communist Jagan never did accede to office. And the Americans would acquiesce in facilitating his rigging. But independence must be obtained quickly before the next general elections.

Carlson did succeed in persuading D'Aguiar to remain in the coalition, stressing his attributes as the minister of finance, and his exemplary achievement as the spearhead of the anti-communist crusade over many years. The mission against communism should not be relinquished, and he was crucial to that exercise in the pursuit of freedom. Carlson had breakfast with D'Aguiar on April 11, 1965, to placate and entice him into compliance with the US/Burnham project:

> I decided to try a combination of flattery, pleading and strong
> language related to the horrible consequences of the breakdown
> of the anti-Jagan forces. I told D'Aguiar how much US entities
> appreciated his contribution to the Burnham administration...that
> I had just been to Washington and had given an optimistic appraisal
> of the stability of the Burnham administration, and that the US
> government on the basis of such reports had gone to extraordinary
> lengths to expedite aid and to make it substantial; that because of this
> stability and his presence in the cabinet potential foreign investors
> were being encouraged.

> And I could not believe that after all the effort put into saving B.G.
> from communism, including strenuous efforts by D'Aguiar (all those
> miles and all those speeches), it was going to be thrown away. I
> stressed it would be bad enough if he had to leave government, but
> to permit the UF to leave was to sell his country out; that with all
> the trouble spots the Secretary [of State] had to cope with, such as
> Vietnam, the Russians, Castro, the Chinese, were we now going to
> add B.G. to the list? I asked him to think about the consequences in
> B.G. itself, which would doubtless see the return to violence, possibly
> against his own supporters.[37]

For the Americans it was critical to ensure that the British did convene the constitutional conference in late 1965, and that independence be granted to Burnham shortly thereafter. They were dedicated to the proposition that Burnham, their bulwark against Jaganite communism, must retain power indefinitely, by any means necessary. It was essential, therefore, for Burnham to accede to the British regarding their proposed international commission to investigate racial imbalance in the security forces. It was also imperative to anchor D'Aguiar in the coalition until Burnham was given independence, thereby empowered to contrive a majority at the polls as he saw fit. The Americans were most apprehensive of the rapid growth of the Indian segment of the population and, consequently, that Jagan would soon secure a majority, even under PR.

Burnham was not keen on the commission, but, prompted by the Americans, he sanctioned it on condition that its terms of reference be broadened beyond specific focus on racial imbalance in the security forces (as Jagan had canvassed) to racial imbalance in the civil service, as well as in government-sponsored projects, such as land settlement schemes. The commission of inquiry by the International Commission of Jurists (ICJ) was constituted in July 1965 and they reported in October, before the constitutional conference was convened in London in November 1965.[38] Jagan boycotted the commission; in any case, it was a ruse – a façade by the Labour government of Harold Wilson to lend respectability to the fiction that the Burnham government was resolved to treat the chronic problem of racial insecurities in British Guiana as a matter of utmost importance.

It is noteworthy that by May 1965, before the ICJ Commission was constituted, Burnham was becoming anxious about the 'holding of a constitutional conference and fixing a date for independence.' He was increasingly suspicious of both the British and the Americans, that they were not more forthcoming on the matter. Apparently, press reports were circulating in the UK that the US was deeply concerned that 'an independent British Guiana might go communist,' possibly because of the escalating Indian demographics. But Burnham need not have been perturbed because the ICJ report would have no material bearing on the British decision to grant him independence. It was a smokescreen designed by the British to his advantage.

In a telegram of May 17, 1965, to the State Department, Carlson reported he had assured Burnham that reports regarding the US government's circumspection about early independence were 'completely false.' Besides, as the State Department confirmed in May 1965, the British had already reserved the prize for Burnham even before the purportedly crucial ICJ investigation of racial imbalance was constituted in July:

> The British have informed us that they expect to hold the promised constitutional conference as early as practicable, presumably, if all goes well, sometime towards the end of the year, but they have not been willing to be this explicit to Premier Burnham. Instead, they have told him that the conference could not be scheduled until there has been time to study a report on racial imbalance in the public services, which the British Guiana Government has requested from the International Commission of Jurists...We have suggested that since it is their intention to convene this conference this year, Premier Burnham might be advised of this fact.[39]

A damp squib! Burnham could resort to petulance, as he saw fit, because he was America and Britain's chosen man for the anti-communist mission against the irrecoverable disciple of Moscow, Jagan. It was all set up for Burnham. And he knew it. The ICJ Commission Report was a mere pretext, to create the illusion that the British (and Burnham) were concerned about the bedevilling racist predisposition of Guyanese that could emasculate the making of a nation out of its diverse irreconcilable peoples, particularly Africans and Indians.

As Governor Luyt implied to Consul General Carlson, Forbes Burnham had no reason to fear British motives. Cheddi Jagan, yesterday's man, was nowhere in the frame:

> Carlson reported that the Governor [Sir Richard Luyt] had confirmed his earlier assurance that the 'only stipulation [concerning timing] was that of the time to "study" the ICJ Report before the constitutional conference. And that there was no...[precondition], such as requiring its implementation.'

It was, indubitably, a façade. The ICJ report was throwing dust in the eyes of the Jaganites, who had been insistent on redressing the racial imbalance in the security forces. The prize was awaiting Burnham's appearance at the conference.[40]

On July 14, 1965, the US ambassador in London informed the National Security Council in Washington of Greenwood's anticipated announcement to the House of Commons the next day – that the British Guyanese constitutional conference would convene on November 2. The US government was eager for the British to leave the colony 'sooner rather than later.' They were concerned that if the British stayed Jagan 'feels he still has a chance': 'With the British in B.G. and the East Indian population growing [comparatively rapidly], there is always the chance that the British will change the rules of the game.'

VII. Ensuring the Survival of America's Man: Coaching Burnham to Rig the General Elections of 1968

America's man: Burnham with President Johnson at the White House, July 1966

Therefore, the USG was determined, at all costs, that Burnham must inherit the kingdom urgently and that the British be apprised of the necessity for this. It is astounding this obsession of the Americans to consign Jagan to urgent political oblivion:

> With the British gone, Jagan himself may decide to bug out. With the British gone, it is highly likely that Burnham will do what is necessary to ensure that Jagan does not get back into power on the wings of a growing East Indian population (e.g., import West Indian Africans; establish literacy tests for voters – these would hurt the PPP [Indians]. [A licence to rig, by whatever means!]

> The chances for violence probably won't increase significantly with independence. Generally speaking, the East Indians are timid compared to the Africans and, without the British to protect them, they might be even more timid.

> If Burnham does not get fairly early independence, his credibility as a national leader will be questioned…Once we assume that relatively early independence is probably not only inevitable but also desirable, it would seem to make sense to announce it…Best guess on date of independence is mid-1966.[41]

Much ado about nothing! The Americans and the British were in bed on this. Ever since Jagan signed that fatal Duncan Sandys document on October 25, 1963, he was finished politically. Of course, it all started on October 25, 1961, at the White House, when he basically told President Kennedy that he was a communist and that he was seeking the freedom to pursue his path to human perfectibility, in a democratic fashion. On July 23, 1965, the State Department received a brief from the British Embassy in Washington inviting them to a series of 'periodic discussions on policy toward Guyana as it approaches independence.' The first meeting between the two was held on July 30, 1965, when the Americans presented a paper on independence for British Guiana.

They were forthright in their expectation that Burnham would be granted independence soon: **'The US welcomes the intention of the British Government to convene the constitutional conference in November which will, among other tasks, fix the date for independence.'** The Americans accused Jagan and his PPP of gross irresponsibility in not meeting jointly with Burnham to discuss the racial imbalance issue with Tony Greenwood. In addition, they deplored the possibility that Jagan would not co-operate with the ICJ Commission, as well as the likelihood he would boycott the constitutional conference in London in November. Therefore, they were recommending that 'other persons in the Indian community in B.G. may be invited to assure this important section of the community be represented at the conference.'

The British responded to this suggestion later (September 3, 1965), rejecting it because they 'doubted whether they could invite other persons to represent the Indian community if the PPP refused to attend, since these special invitees could hardly claim to be democratically elected representatives.'[42] Of course, it mattered not to the Americans and the British whether Jagan did attend: they were virtually rid of their communist archenemy. Granting independence to Burnham would seal Jagan's fate as marginal, if not terminal, in the exercise of power in an independent Guyana.

However, despite the disregard for democratic norms by the Americans, evident in their complicity in Burnham's declared intention to rig future elections, they did fathom the depth of the racial antipathy between Africans and Indians. Sadly, what they stated in 1965 requires no revision, more than five decades later, because Guyana remains stultified by its chronic predilection for racial loyalty, at the expense of rationality, in its political discourse. The idea of a Guyanese nation defies realisation:

> The United States Government believes that the racial fears in B.G. will be difficult to assuage, based as they are on deep racial cleavages. These are not easily susceptible to rapid transformation and several generations may be required to effect more than marginal progress toward this objective. While efforts of government make a contribution toward this task, it should not be assumed that any government, no matter how well intentioned, will be able to eradicate long-standing suspicions. Only years of education, association and understanding can break down the wall of segregation on which racial fears rest.[43]

By early August 1965, the CIA noted that the ICJ was expected to publish its report by early October, ostensibly a prerequisite to the convening of the constitutional conference in London. The CIA was certain of the outcome of those talks, as was Burnham: 'The British Government has informed Burnham of its intention to convene a conference to devise a constitution for British Guiana and to set a date for independence .... and a date [for the conference] of November 2, 1965 is tentatively established.' The CIA was confident that 'British Guiana will achieve independence in the spring of 1966.'[44]

A rubber-stamp! Burnham was granted independence as predicted: Independence Day was Thursday, May 26, 1966.

But the Americans were also thinking of continuity: extending the rule of their chosen one way beyond the independence of the country. This was integral to their transcendent mission of conquering the 'red menace,' likely to be exacerbated because of Cheddi Jagan's undiminished stature among an ominously expanding Indian electorate. Consul General Carlson was curious to learn how Burnham viewed 'the central problem of assuring re-election in 1968,' but he also wanted the coalition to remain intact, to keep D'Aguiar on board at least until independence was granted. Implicit in the latter was the assumption that the latitude for rigging would thereafter be untrammelled. But in September 1965, Burnham still lacked a coherent plan for rigging:

> It is clear that Burnham prefers to hope that a significant fraction of Indians can be won over to his party or one he can work with. If...such development is not occurring, he strongly favours the importation of West Indian Negroes...If such a programme is not possible, I gather he would be willing to consider such ideas as unitary statehood with Barbados or, conceivably, disenfranchisement of illiterates. He finds such thoughts very distasteful, but he believes he would do so if convinced that there is no other way to survive politically against the PPP...

> There is increasing anxiety that Burnham might establish a police state. This is undoubtedly having an effect on D'Aguiar, but apparently that is only one aspect of what is bothering him...It is essential to seek to improve relations with D'Aguiar and try to go to London in general accord...[Carlson counselled Burnham to try to cultivate D'Aguiar assiduously until the London Conference was concluded.] Perhaps have him to dinner or other private meetings weekly until the London conference; seek his opinion and advice on various subjects, even if your mind is already made up; compliment him privately and perhaps publicly in a press conference just before leaving for London.[45]

In early October 1965, Consul General Delmar Carlson met Gordon Chase of the National Security Council in Washington. It is obvious that their preoccupation with Jagan's communism had not diminished, and they were still agonising over their inability to identify a 'moderate' alternative Indian leader. Gordon Chase reported 'Del' Carlson's views on the subject:

> Del said we are so far getting nowhere with respect to building up an alternative East Indian party...The big hope is that we can locate an alternative East Indian leader...[but] no one of any stature appears to be on the horizon. A lesser hope is that Burnham will, by sensible and progressive policies, be able to win the East Indians over to his side. Burnham, however, is not at all confident that he can ever translate East Indian acceptance of his regime into East Indian votes. Neither is Del.

> Del added that even if the East Indians cannot be wooed away from Jagan, Burnham will probably do whatever is necessary to win the elections in 1968. This could take the form of importing Negroes from other Caribbean countries or, in a pinch, establishing literary tests for Guyanese voters. Literacy tests would hurt the East Indian population more than the Negro population.[46]

Balram Singh Rai (1921–2022), on whom the Americans (including the CIA) had pinned their hopes to garner some Indian votes at the expense of Jagan, in the elections of December 1964, did not win a single seat and was terminally damaged by the implacable Indo-Guyanese invective hurled at him during the campaign. Arguably a bright anti-communist, but not a robust political animal, Rai was soon claimed by reclusiveness and, later (1971), voluntary exile in London. Certainly not the sole aspirant to leadership of Indo-Guyanese broken by the Jaganite juggernaut! In July 1966, following Guyana's independence in May, Carlson conceded to the State Department that he could detect no silver lining regarding an alternative Indian leader to challenge Jagan:

> At the present time, the prospects in this area are not particularly encouraging. The anti-Jagan East Indian Justice Party [of B.S. Rai: polled 1,334 votes in the entire colony (0.6 per cent) in 1964] and the Guyana United Muslim Party [of Hoosein Ganie: polled 1,194 votes (0.5 per cent)] have been discredited, and consequently offer little, if any, hope of being able to contribute substantially to any future anti-Jagan initiative. However, if nothing new appears before 1968, and there is reason to believe that these basically defunct organisations can still play a useful role, consideration should be given at that time to pumping blood into their emaciated bodies.[47]

Meanwhile, the two key issues for the Americans and the British were the granting of independence to Burnham and to help him, by whatever means necessary, to ensure that he retained power indefinitely. Two weeks before the constitutional conference was convened in London on November 2, 1965, the secretary of state for the colonies (Greenwood) met US Secretary of State Rusk in Washington to reassure him that independence would be granted to Burnham. He erroneously believed that Jagan and the PPP would attend, but they would walk out at some point. In fact, Jagan was already indicating that he would boycott the conference, convinced it was a rubber stamp to grant independence to Burnham. And Greenwood virtually confirmed the latter to Rusk. He expressed satisfaction with Burnham's leadership since he assumed office in December 1964: 'a good Prime Minister,' whose performance 'has been above expectations.' But his references to Jagan were reportedly 'unsympathetic,' noting his deteriorating position because of internal differences in the PPP.

Greenwood stated that Burnham wanted independence in February 1966, but he thought June or July was more realistic. It is significant that at a meeting at the White House, McGeorge Bundy of the National Security Council had informed Greenwood of 'continuing Presidential interest in British Guiana.' Greenwood complimented Bundy on the work of the US consul general in the colony (Delmar Carlson). Bundy responded: 'we have taken particular pains in our selection of personnel for all agencies [including the CIA] in British

Guiana.'[48] He meant that they had unfinished business there; the work would continue after independence – contriving the means of institutionalising the indefinite rule of Burnham: the bulwark against their communist foe, waiting in the wings if the next elections were free and fair. The latter must be averted.

Jagan did boycott the London conference; D'Aguiar supported independence despite his interminable conflict with, and aversion to, Burnham. And, as expected by most, the date for Guyana's independence was announced: May 26, 1966. The deputy director of the CIA (Helms) was pleased with the outcome, as he intimated to Bundy on December 10, 1965:

> A number of compromises were worked out between Premier Forbes Burnham and Finance Minister Peter D'Aguiar which, hopefully, would ease some of the strains between them. The conference did not, however, succeed in bringing the two leaders much closer together; **they remain basically incompatible on both personal and political grounds and are united only in mutual defence against the threat posed by Cheddi Jagan** ...[emphasis added].[49]

Helms acknowledged that Jagan and the PPP would retain the support of the overwhelming majority of Indians; this, he felt, could pose a threat to an independent Guyana. He was, of course, alluding to Jagan's communism. Yet he was appreciative of the 'good judgement of the British Government in granting independence to a government led by a representative of a minority racial grouping [Africans]...in British Guiana.' Between late 1961 and Burnham's death in 1985, he was in possession of the winning ticket gifted him by the pro-Moscow communist ideologue, Cheddi Jagan. Burnham could run rings around Jagan at will.

The CIA document of December 10, 1965, cited a conversation between Burnham and someone (the name is redacted) on November 20, 1965. It was the day after the conclusion of the constitutional conference; Burnham was still in London, so that person was probably the long-serving US ambassador to the UK (1961–69), David Bruce, at the heart of Anglo-American shenanigans in making Burnham America's man. The deputy director of the CIA remarked:

> Forbes Burnham stated that his immediate objective is to launch his economic development plan so that he will be able to induce large numbers of West Indians of African descent to settle in Guyana prior to the December 1968 elections. **His purpose is to radically alter the racial balance now existing in the electorate in sufficient time to enable him to win a plurality in the 1968 elections.** Burnham stated that he will seek aid both from the British and American Governments for this purpose. He said further that he was confident his scheme was feasible, and that it was the only possible course of action which would prevent Jagan returning to power with the support of the Indian community [emphasis added].[50]

With the prize firmly in his hand, Burnham reportedly also stated that the British had granted him independence to 'salve their own consciences.' It is unclear what he meant (possibly an allusion to British enslavement of his African ancestors), but he was often deemed anti-British and anti-White. Both the Americans and the British considered Burnham a racist. They had settled on him only because his bitter foe was one of their two foremost enemies in the Hemisphere (Jagan and Castro). However, Burnham was feigning circumspection of British motives in awarding him the prize. It was a studied affectation, fortified by the astounding fact that Jagan had cultivated no friends in the West, beyond perennially marginalised communists and inconsequential ultra-leftists. Yet, although Burnham's pragmatism and eclectic socialism, bolstered by the definitive power of American patronage, had culminated in British subterfuge in gifting him PR in October 1963 and independence in May 1966 – thus vanquishing Jagan – his overweening racial pride impelled him to evade the unassailable truth that it was White men – John F. Kennedy, Harold Macmillan, Duncan Sandys and – massively – Peter Stanislaus D'Aguiar, who had delivered him from impending political oblivion: from the abyss to the mountain top.

However, Burnham was resolved that having been anointed heir to the White man's seat of power, the Indians must never be allowed near to the levers of power again. He must assume the all-powerful persona of the 'white man on horseback' – like massa on the plantation – in total control! Not only was he inclined to use West Indian migration to fabricate electoral invulnerability, but he was also set to introduce 'absentee voting' to contrive victory in the general elections of December 1968: registering real and fictitious Guyanese in Britain and America, exclusively African, to 'vote' for him. It was barefaced and crude, but it created the template for fraudulent elections by the PNC that persisted for many years.

The CIA document (December 10, 1965) states that Burnham dismissed the constitutional safeguards from the inception, alleging the British were conscious that such measures would soon facilitate the empowerment of Indians to gain political control by constitutional means. He was deftly reinforcing the anti-communist obsession of the Americans that – given the prolific incremental increase of the Indian segment of the population – a valid electoral process was essentially the instrument to entrench Indian domination, Jagan's communist control of Guyana. But Burnham reportedly stressed that he would never allow this to happen: '[the British] fully expected that the constitutional safeguards would lead to East Indian control by constitutional methods, which he [Burnham] said was "not going to come about."' Burnham was forthright: 'under the new constitution absentee voting would be permissible.'[51] In the general elections of 1968, he would use the largely bogus overseas vote to rig the process to his advantage – here again, with Anglo-American complicity.

In April 1966, a month before Guyana's independence, the CIA prepared a report on 'the prospects of Guyana over the next year or two.' They anticipated accurately that the transition to independence would be 'relatively smooth,' but that 'racial suspicions' between Africans and Indians 'will continue to dominate Guyanese politics.' However, they had reservations regarding the survival of the PNC-UF coalition while predicting a 'neutralist posture in foreign affairs' by Burnham. Yet they were clearly resolved to persevere with their man indefinitely (despite his mercurial behaviour) because of the rigidity of the countervailing narrative: Jagan's communist creed. The CIA document states:

> The governing coalition of Burnham, a professed but pragmatic socialist [not a communist], and the conservative United Force leader, Peter D'Aguiar, will continue to be a tenuous one. Friction between the partners over patronage and fiscal issues will probably be intensified after independence, but the chances are that a common fear of Jagan will hold the coalition together.

> Guyana's economy will need substantial foreign capital, much of it from the US. The need for aid will keep Burnham on tolerable terms with the US, UK and Canada, though his administration will incline toward a neutralist posture in foreign affairs. If Jagan came to power, he could, because of his Marxist sympathies and his connections in Communist countries, count on some help from these countries. However, they probably would furnish only token quantities of aid.[52]

After the euphoria over Guyana's independence had subsided, the Americans became engrossed with devising an effective mechanism for rigging, to the sole advantage of Burnham's PNC. Ambassador Carlson forwarded such a plan, 'designed to ensure the government's victory in the next election.' They were determined to keep Burnham in power despite harbouring several reservations about him personally, including the nature of his socialism. Of course, fortified by Anglo-American sponsorship and solidarity, Burnham was disinclined to relinquish power ever again, as Ambassador Carlson observed:

> **Burnham has confided to close colleagues that he intends to remain in power indefinitely – if at all possible, by constitutional means. However, if necessary, he is prepared to employ unorthodox methods [rigging] to achieve his aims. In these circumstances, probably the best that can be hoped for at this time, is that he might…take the most effective and least objectionable course to attain his goals** [emphasis added].[53]

In other words, the US ambassador was counselling their man to rig, but to do so with discretion. The intractable problem that rendered stealing the elections indispensable to the US project – perpetuating Burnham's rule – was the unpalatable truth that Indians were overwhelmingly disinclined to desert Jagan, his Marxist philosophy notwithstanding. Besides, ominously and inexorably, the demographic growth of Indians would soon make them an unassailable and decisive electoral force:

> The East Indian people, as a whole, dislike the African, distrust him, especially fear him, and believe they must stay together, particularly as a voting unit, if their rights are to be protected and their aspirations achieved. The East Indians, generally, believe that if they maintain their solidarity, they can, by virtue of their rapidly increasing numbers, win any future election.

> Most East Indians do not think, and will not be easily convinced, despite a plethora of anti-Jagan propaganda, that Cheddi Jagan is anything less than an altruistic leader who, although perhaps capable of error, loves his people and is motivated by a desire to act in their best interest. His charismatic appeal continues basically undiminished, although apparently some of the gloss has gone from his image.[54]

Ambassador Carlson did not believe there was adequate time to pursue Burnham's proposal for West Indian migration to resolve his impending electoral predicament: 'As a short-term election device, immigration does not seem to be very practical.' However, he was amenable to enabling Guyanese resident overseas (he meant Africans only), particularly in the UK and the US, to vote in the general elections. His preference for this specific means of rigging assumed that it was substantially easier to execute, in a short time, in subverting the process to the sole advantage of Burnham:

> ...[they should have] **election experts conduct a study and make detailed recommendations as to how best (preferably in the simplest and most fool-proof manner) the government might proceed to rig, if necessary, the next election. Particular attention should be given to the absentee ballot which would seem to lend itself to manipulation, as well as to any manoeuvre in Guyana** [emphasis added].[55]

Carlson had been instrumental in arranging a private meeting between Burnham and President Johnson on July 22, 1966. He explained forthrightly to the State Department that it was being done purely to boost Burnham's ego and the president's diary had the following terse notation on the trip: 'there was no substantive reason for the meeting.' Burnham told Carlson afterwards that the president 'strongly supports him,' having affirmed it thus: 'Remember you have one friend in this corner going for you, and his name is Lyndon Johnson.' Burnham, in turn, indicated his solidarity with the president on Vietnam, 'expressing wonder as to how the Communists always seem to get away with their case before much of the world.' He also related to Johnson his notion of West Indian migration as a means of augmenting his electoral strength. The president reportedly evinced a 'sympathetic attitude' to the idea.[56]

By 1967–68, the US government was actively engaged in counselling and funding Burnham on matters pertaining to the orchestrated rigging of the elections scheduled for December 1968. In March 1967, for instance, a memorandum prepared for the 303 Committee of the National Security Council was unambiguous in outlining their strategy for rigging those elections:

> **It is established USG policy that Cheddi Jagan, East Indian Marxist leader of the pro-Communist PPP in Guyana, will not be permitted to take over the government of an independent Guyana.** Jagan has the electoral support of the East Indians, who are approximately 50% of the total population of Guyana. It is believed that Jagan has a good chance of coming to power in the next elections unless steps are taken to prevent this [emphasis added].
>
> Prime Minister Forbes Burnham…is aware of the problem and has stated that he is fully prepared to utilise the electoral machinery at his disposal to ensure his own re-election [by rigging]. Burnham has initiated steps for electoral registration of Guyanese at home and abroad, and has requested financial assistance….[redacted] for the PNC campaign. It is recommended that he and his party be provided with covert support in order to assure his victory at the polls.[57]

On September 16, 1967, Burnham met with….[name redacted], possibly a CIA agent in the American Embassy in Georgetown, and he requested money for various election purposes, including a programme

> to identify and register all Guyanans [Guyanese] of African ancestry in UK, Canada and the US in order to get their absentee votes in the next elections. 'Conversely,' Burnham acknowledged with a smile, 'East Indians living abroad may have trouble getting registered and, if registered, getting ballots.'[58]

Therefore, overseas voting was adopted as the principal means of perpetrating extensive electoral fraud to secure a PNC majority. Burnham was in an uneasy alliance with Peter D'Aguiar since December 1964; the latter resigned from the coalition in September 1967, but his UF had weakened considerably since he joined the government. Burnham did not intend to be hamstrung by another coalition. He would rig decisively, buttressed by the financial and technical support of the US government. The latter was committed 'to influencing the course of the election,' central to its definitive anti-communist mantra that Jagan must not rule Guyana again:

> The US Government determined in 1962 that Cheddi Jagan would not be acceptable as the head of government of an independent Guyana. When elections were scheduled for December 1964…

> [redacted: the CIA] was instructed to ensure Jagan's defeat by the provision of guidance and support to Burnham and D'Aguiar…This was accomplished. Burnham and D'Aguiar established a coalition government which is now in power. This is, however, an uneasy arrangement and Burnham desires a PNC majority in the Assembly to result from the forthcoming elections.[59]

It is beyond doubt that Burnham was working in collusion with his American sponsors to achieve his goal. In a meeting with Ambassador Carlson, in June 1967, he expressed confidence that 'overseas vote figures could be manipulated pretty much as he wished.' Carlson concluded it was obvious that 'he intends to follow a number of election tricks to add to the PNC total and detract from the PPP votes…He was well aware of the need that these election tricks be done smoothly and without controversy.'[60]

In December 1967, a CIA document rationalised the assistance they were giving Burnham to defeat Jagan. It was

> predicated on the assumption that Jagan is a Communist…and that his becoming Prime Minister of Guyana would be disastrous for Guyana, would prove a dangerous stimulus to Castro, and would introduce an unacceptable degree of instability into the Caribbean area…as Prime Minister Jagan would be an instrument of Communist influence in Latin America…Some 90 PPP youths were currently being trained (educated?) in [Eastern] Bloc countries…In Guyana Jagan's Accabre College was training Guyanese youth in Marxist thought.[61]

Another CIA document a day later, in December 1967, observed that Burnham was 'working on various schemes to enlarge the Negro vote. He will try to obtain a substantial number of absentee votes from Negro Guyanese residing abroad.' It was noted earlier that Burnham had concurred with the Americans that this was an efficacious means of orchestrating extensive rigging in a short time. But they also speculated on Jagan's fate should he win the general elections. It is evident that the US government would have supported any measure Burnham adopted to preclude this 'enthusiastic Marxist-Leninist' from ruling; conceivably, even endorsing the Venezuelans' reassertion of their territorial claims with the eventuality of military action against Jagan. No 'second Cuba' in the Hemisphere!

> **If Jagan's party won, he would probably not be permitted to exercise power. Burnham could use force to keep him out, or suspend the Constitution and rule by fiat** [a coup!], **or even press for a grand coalition which he himself would seek to head. Alternatively, he could permit Jagan to take office – only to subvert his government at a later date** [emphasis added].

> In the unlikely event that Jagan did take and hold power, the Communist orientation of the government, more than its actual capabilities, would make it a more disturbing factor in hemispheric

affairs, especially in the Caribbean area. Communist countries would make considerable propaganda capital of the fact that such a government had come to power by free elections. The USSR and some other Communist governments would move quickly to establish diplomatic or trade missions in Georgetown. Both the Soviets and Castro would probably provide Jagan with small amounts of aid.

A Jagan administration would, however, be beset by powerful internal opposition [as in 1962–63, with CIA sponsorship], and would not have the resources for an adventuresome programme abroad. Thus, Jagan would not try to launch an independent Communist revolutionary effort on the continent or in the Caribbean, though he would probably co-operate in the overt and clandestine activities sponsored by the USSR and Cuba. **Such actions would encourage Venezuela to press its territorial claims against Guyana and perhaps even to undertake military action** [emphasis added].[62]

On January 23, 1968, Burnham (in Washington for a medical check-up) met with Secretary of State Rusk. (President Johnson saw him for twenty minutes the previous day.) Burnham told Rusk he was 'quietly confident' about the outcome of the elections later in the year. All plans for rigging having been finalised, there was no further discussion on the subject. However, he did indicate to Rusk that Jagan had assumed a defeatist posture: '[He] was already setting the stage, among his followers, for a defeat by claiming that the elections would be rigged, and he would not be allowed to assume power.' Jagan was probably ignorant of the fact that Burnham and his American 'Cold War' sponsors were resolved that he must never accede to power again. Could he not foresee that all elections henceforth were bound to be crooked, predicated on the American rationalisation that this was imperative in countering the 'red menace,' in defence of 'freedom' in the Hemisphere?

I reproduce below a substantial portion of a memorandum (dated June 12, 1968), prepared internally for the special assistant to President Johnson, Professor W. W. Rostow. It is titled 'Plan by Burnham to Rig the 1968 Election.' It reveals that Burnham had augmented his repertoire of instruments for internal rigging, beyond the planned bogus overseas voting exercise. Besides, it substantiates further that this was undertaken with the approbation of the Johnson administration to guarantee the defeat of Jagan. Indeed, even when Burnham himself adopted a nebulous form of socialism in 1970, 'cooperative socialism,' it was never deemed 'communist' by the West. Jagan's loyalty to Soviet communism and Castroism ensured that Burnham's culture of rigging was insulated from regional censure as well, and replicated with impunity until the fall of the Soviet Union and its satellites at the end of the 1980s.

> In a meeting of high-level government and PNC leaders...Forbes Burnham...gave instructions to rig the elections scheduled for late

1968...in order to permit the PNC to win a clear majority...Burnham said that the registration of East Indians, who traditionally vote for the PPP should be strictly limited in order to keep their number of eligible voters as low as possible. He also gave instructions to his party leaders to increase the size of the PNC electorate by registering some PNC adherents who are between the age of 17 and 20 years of age [the legal age was 21]. He said he plans to have written into the electoral law a provision for increasing the use of proxy votes.

Through these means...Burnham said he hopes the PNC will receive approximately half the total votes cast in Guyana. In order to provide the winning margin for the PNC, he has arranged for Guyanese who reside overseas to vote in the Guyanese elections. He believes there are sufficient PNC adherents overseas to give the PNC a clear majority. If it appears that the overseas registration is not sufficient to provide this majority, Burnham said he has instructed his campaign organisers to provide enough false registrations to give the PNC the desired majority.

In April 1968 Burnham stated that he will not form a government if he has to continue to depend on his coalition partner, Peter D'Aguiar...after the elections. **In order to avoid having to depend on D'Aguiar, Burnham said that he will rig the elections in such a way that the PNC will win a clear majority** [emphasis added].[63]

The 'elections' were held on December 16, 1968. The Americans 'won.' Burnham had stolen the elections with their unstinting collaboration, but he did it with a modicum of discretion – not as outrageously and absurdly as he would in subsequent ones. The PNC 'polled' 174,339 votes or 55.8 per cent (thirty seats); the PPP were allocated 113,991 votes or 36.5 per cent (nineteen seats); the UF got 23,162 votes or 7.4 per cent (four seats). Burnham awarded himself thirty out of fifty-three seats, or eight more than he won in the free elections of 1964. He had contrived the majority he craved and did not need a coalition after December 1968. He was virtually set, in keeping with American preference, to wield power for life. Little did the imperialists realise that their man had tricked not just the Guyanese electorate, but he would soon trick those who paid the piper as well.

Odeen Ishmael has remarked on Burnham's inaugural electoral fraud of 1968, including the overseas voting hoax:

The PNC 'won' more than 90 per cent of the 'overseas votes,' amounting to 6 seats in the National Assembly, [where he had a majority of 7]. This was expected considering the heavy padding with fictitious names [and fabricated addresses, including a field where horses graze]. The rigged 'ballots' from the UK were personally and proudly transported to Georgetown by Guyana's High Commissioner Sir Lionel Luckhoo.

Significantly, among the first governments to send messages of congratulations to Burnham were those of the US, the English-speaking Caribbean and the UK. In glowing platitudes extolling the victory of 'democracy' [sic] in Guyana, these governments expressed firm support for the PNC administration, thus giving encouragement for the perpetuation of a long period of undemocratic rule in the country.[64]

A memorandum of the 303 Committee (responsible for oversight of covert affairs and chaired by the director of the CIA) of May 23, 1969, documented conclusively that the CIA was instrumental in funding the subversive activities of the PNC and the UF against Cheddi Jagan, as early as the riots of 1962 and as late as the general elections of 1968. But it also established that by 1967, they were questioning whether money for this purpose was defensible, as the budget allocated hitherto for the anti-communist project against Jagan had been exhausted. They did agree, however, to continue the funding of the 1968 elections only because their fear of a 'second Cuba' remained as potent as it was in 1961 or 1962:

> The US government determined in 1962 that Cheddi Jagan would not be desirable as the head of government in Guyana. The CIA was instructed to provide guidance and support to the PNC and to the small, conservative United Force (UF) in the 1964 campaign…New elections were scheduled for December 1968 and, as a result of a 303 Committee decision of April 7, 1967, the CIA was again instructed to support the PNC and UF. **In the 1968 elections the PNC used its control of the government to pad the electoral rolls and win a slim majority of the vote** [yet a comfortable parliamentary majority of 7]…The leaders of the PPP and the UF attacked the elections as being dishonest, but their charges had little effect in Guyana and stirred almost no interest abroad…[emphasis added].[65]

The CIA was given approval by the 303 Committee 'to provide financial support to the [redacted: probably the PNC and the UF] in 1962 and 1963, and the CIA was instructed to support the UF and the PNC in the 1964 elections.' As noted earlier, the CIA was also deeply involved in the 1968 rigged elections, as they had determined that 'Burnham would lose to Jagan in an honest election.' Therefore, their assistance in 1968 was primarily to facilitate the rigging. It was also observed that there was no exposure of the 'US [government] or CIA involvement in the 1964 and 1968 elections.' The only 'significant adverse publicity' had come from two TV programmes in the UK, produced by Granada TV: 'The Trail of the Vanishing Voters' (December 1968) and 'The Making of a Prime Minister' (January 1969), which documented widespread fraud in the registration and polling of overseas Guyanese voters in the UK. Yet the

Americans had emerged totally unscathed, as the broadcasts 'did not mention the involvement of the US [government] or the CIA, and they had little impact.'[66]

The Burnham mould with respect to the conduct of fraudulent general elections, unexampled in the Anglophone Caribbean, was established. After 1968, habituated and seasoned to rigging, Burnham did not need, neither did he appear to seek, the counsel or material resources of the Americans to rig with impunity. The Americans preferred him to rig with discretion, but he was totally oblivious of the consequences. He was right; there was none. But Jagan's devotion to his narrow pro-Soviet brand of communism did not antagonise only the Americans, but it also alienated most of the best and brightest in his party, who defected, deserted, or were expelled, incrementally – fealty to the creed being the principal attribute of most of the residue of true believers.

As Dr Joshua Ramsammy (1928–2009), marine biologist and radical gadfly of Burnhamism (who survived an assassin's bullet in 1971) observes, the legacy of Jaganism and Burnhamism is rather dismal:

> I admired his [Cheddi's] steadfastness in advancing the socialist ideology that dominated his party; but as a result of [his Marxist-Leninist] ideology, a lot of good people [non-communists] were left by the wayside, and Cheddi was surrounded by those who told him what they felt he would like to hear.
>
> Political stability was upset by racial polarisation, and racial polarisation was exacerbated by the hold that two charismatic leaders had over their respective racial groups. Burnham's charisma drew Afro-Guyanese support from the [original] PPP. Cheddi's charisma maintained an Indo-Guyanese constituency for the PPP. This was further exacerbated by the period of rigging from 1968 to 1985 in which Afro-Guyanese supported the fraudulent system out of racial necessity. They had to close ranks behind their racial leader. The Indo-Guyanese did the same. **So unlike other places, politics was not fought on issues. Politics became an emotional contest between two races** [emphasis added].[67]

Two irreconcilable tribes! Nothing has changed in the fifty-seven years since independence. Guyanese racism remains venomous.

Notes

1. See Interview with Moses Bhagwan, in Frank Birbalsingh's *The People's Progressive Party of Guyana, 1950–92: An Oral History* (London: Hansib, 2007), 114–21.
2. *The New York Review of Books*, May 9, 2013.
3. *Mirror*, November 5, 1965.
4. *Mirror*, January 26, 1966.
5. Bhagwan, in *The People's Progressive Party of Guyana, 1950–92*, 114–21.
6. Janet Jagan to B. H. Benn, November 26, 1965, in Billy Strachan Papers, Institute of Commonwealth Studies Collection, Senate House Library, University of London.

7. Odeen Ishmael, 'The 1965 Independence Conference' – see Guyana.org/features/guyanastory/chapter179.html.
8. This quote is by the Labour Party's Patrick Gordon Walker (1907–80), cited in Cheddi Jagan, *The West on Trial: My Fight for Guyana's Freedom* (London: Michael Joseph, 1966), 202.
9. 'Speech by Dr Cheddi Jagan in the National Assembly, May 26, 1966 (Independence Day).' Accessed from the CJRC website.
10. *Weekend Post and Sunday Argosy*, May 8, 1966.
11. See 'The Havana Conference: New Stage in the Struggle against Colonialism, Neo-Colonialism and Imperialism,' *Thunder*, March 1966.
12. *The Tricontinental Conference of African, Asian and Latin American Peoples* by the US Congress, Senate Judiciary Committee (Washington: US Government Printing Office), 33.
13. Ibid, 10.
14. 'The Havana Conference: New Stage in the Struggle against Colonialism, Neo-Colonialism and Imperialism,' *Thunder*, March 1966.
15. *New Nation*, January 16, 1966.
16. *New Nation*, April 3, 1966.
17. See 'Message from Party Leader: Independence Yes! Celebration No!' *Thunder*, March 1966.
18. *Weekend Post and Sunday Argosy*, April 3, 1966.
19. *Sunday Chronicle*, June 3, 1966.
20. Ibid.
21. Cheddi Jagan, 'Address to Comrades, August 27, 1966,' Cheddi Jagan Research Centre (CJRC), call number 1371.
22. Cheddi Jagan, 'The Soviet Union Leaps Forward,' Address to the 24th Congress of the Communist Party of the Soviet Union (CPSU), April 20, 1971, CJRC, call number 1493.
23. Ibid.
24. Ibid.
25. See Cheddi Jagan, 'Address to the Meeting of Communist and Workers' Parties, Moscow, June 1969,' *Thunder*, October–December 1969, CJRC, call number 2039.
26. Ibid.
27. Ibid.
28. See 'Address to the 25th Anniversary Conference on behalf of the Central Committee of the PPP by the General Secretary, Dr Cheddi Jagan, August 3, 1975,' *Thunder*, September–December,1975, 3–35.
29. Cheddi Jagan, 'Leninism in the 1980s,' Lecture at Freedom House, April 23, 1980, CJRC, call no. 2355.
30. Memorandum of Conversation (between British Embassy officials, Washington, and Assistant Secretary of State William Tyler), January 4, 1965, in *Foreign Relations of the US, 1964–68, Vol. XXXII: Dominican Republic; Cuba; Haiti; Guyana*, accessed at history.state.gov/historicaldocuments/frus1964-68v32.
31. Ibid., Memorandum from Gordon Chase of the National Security Council to the President's Special Assistant for National Security Affairs (Bundy), February 8,1965.
32. Ibid.
33. Ibid., Memorandum from the Officer-in-Charge of B.G. Affairs (Cobb) to the Director of the Office of British Commonwealth and Northern European Affairs (Shullow), February 19, 1965.

34. Ibid., Telegram from the State Department to the Consul General (Carlson), Georgetown, February 25, 1965.

35. Ibid.

36. Ibid., Telegram from the Consul General in B.G. to the State Department, April 11, 1965.

37. Ibid.

38. See *Racial Problems in the Public Service: Report of the British Guiana Commission of Inquiry Constituted by the International Commission of Jurists* (October 1965).

39. See note 30: Memorandum from the Assistant Secretary of State for European Affairs (Davis) to the Secretary of State (Rusk), May 21, 1965.

40. Ibid.

41. Ibid., Memorandum from Gordon Chase of the National Security Council to the President's Special Assistant for National Security Affairs (Bundy), July 14, 1965.

42. Ibid., Paper Prepared by the State Department, July 30, 1965.

43. Ibid.

44. Ibid., Memorandum from the Deputy Director for Operations of the CIA (Helms) to the President's Special Assistant for National Security Affairs (Bundy), August 6, 1965.

45. Ibid., Telegram from the Consul General in B.G. (Carlson) to the State Department, August 6, 1965.

46. Ibid., Memorandum from Gordon Chase of the National Security Council to the President's Special Assistant for National Security Affairs (Bundy), October 5, 1965.

47. Ibid., Telegram from the Ambassador to Guyana (Carlson) to the State Department, July 15, 1966.

48. Ibid., Memorandum of Conversation (between Secretary of State Rusk and the Secretary of State for the Colonies Greenwood), Washington, October 18, 1965.

49. Ibid., Memorandum from the Deputy Director of the CIA (Helms) to the President's Special Assistant for National Security Affairs (Bundy), December 10,1965.

50. Ibid.

51. Ibid.

52. Ibid., National Intelligence Estimate [by the CIA], April 28, 1966.

53. Ibid., Telegram from the Ambassador to Guyana (Carlson) to the State Department, July 15, 1966.

54. Ibid.

55. Ibid.

56. Ibid., Letter from the Ambassador to Guyana (Carlson) to the Assistant Secretary of State for Inter-American Affairs (Gordon), August 4, 1966.

57. Ibid., Memorandum Prepared for the 303 Committee [of the National Security Council], March 17, 1967.

58. Ibid.

59. Ibid.

60. Ibid., Telegram from the Ambassador to Guyana (Carlson) to the State Department, [day missing] June 1967.

61. Ibid., Memorandum from the Deputy Director for Coordination of the Bureau of Intelligence and Research (Truehart) to the Director and Deputy Director [of the CIA], December 6, 1967.

62. Ibid., Special National Intelligence Estimate (CIA), December 7, 1967.

63. Accessed at: http//www.guyana.org/govt/latest _declassified.html.

64. Quoted in Odeen Ishmael, 'How the American Government Helped Burnham to Rig the 1968 Elections.' See www.guyana.org/features/postindependence/chapter 1.html.
65. Memorandum for the 303 Committee, Washington, May 23, 1969 (Proposal for Support to the People's National Congress of Guyana), in *Foreign Relations of the United States, 1969–76, Vol. E-10*. See http//history.state.gov/historicaldocuments/frus-76ve10.
66. Ibid.
67. Interview with Joshua Ramsammy, in Frank Birbalsingh's *The People's Progressive Party of Guyana, 1950–92: An Oral History* (London: Hansib, 2007), 173.

12.
'Scientific Foresight'
Jagan's Utopian Marxist Vision and Burnham's Amorphous Socialism

To some, out of the very purity of his Marxist vision, he has conspired against both the interest of his supporters and his own political success.

– **V. S. Naipaul (1991)**

Forbes Burnham, the charismatic and ideologically nebulous African leader, who benefited immeasurably from Jagan's doctrinaire pro-Soviet communism. Having secured power through Anglo-American complicity, Burnham later befriended many of Jagan's communist friends, captivated by their politics of untrammelled rule by virtue of 'the paramountcy of the Party', although he defined his imposed national ideology as 'co-operative socialism'

I. Burnham's Eclectic Socialism: A Façade to Entrench the Stealing of Elections and Dictatorial Rule

Around 1993, Cheddi Jagan strived to explain why his People's Progressive Party (PPP) survived as a credible political force during the 1964–92 period, nearly twenty-eight years in opposition. He attributed it to what he alluded to as a philosophical methodology endowed with 'scientific foresight,' accompanied by 'appropriate modes of struggle,' which the PPP embraced and pursued all those years in the wilderness. In Jagan's view 'scientific foresight' involved thorough 'concrete analyses,' including 'class analysis,' of both the domestic and global environment in order to determine 'how the world will develop'; then on the basis of the conclusions of such 'scientific' analyses, programmes appropriate to the requirements of the situation 'were formulated and proposed as alternatives to the pro-imperialist policies of the [People's National Congress] PNC Government.'[1]

In September 1970, Cheddi Jagan addressed the 16th Annual Congress of his PPP at Anna Regina on the Essequibo Coast. He argued that the American imperialists in league with their lackeys, like Eric Williams in Trinidad and Forbes Burnham in Guyana, were inclined to use the 'carrot' rather than the stick to project a façade of reform and social change. He was contemptuous of this 'reformism,' especially as embodied in Burnham's pursuit of 'cooperative socialism,' his instrument for economic transformation to a socialist society. Neither was Jagan impressed with the notion of joint-ownership, or 'meaningful participation,' between the state and foreign capital invested by imperialist companies. This was another palliative of 'reformism' – certainly not compatible with revolutionary transformation guided by 'scientific socialism' or Marxism-Leninism.

This is how Cheddi repudiated the reformism of Burnham's PNC and its accommodation by their sponsors, the American imperialists:

> Now that the past decade has brought the realisation that political independence has been only nominal and that revolutionary change is necessary, imperialism's new strategy is partnership and cooperatives, instead of public ownership.

> We must combat this reformist fraud. Lenin long ago warned against the dangers of reformism. He said: 'Reformism, even when quite sincere, becomes a weapon by means of which the bourgeoisie corrupt and weaken the workers.' The experience of all countries shows that the workers who put their trust in the reformists are always fooled.[2]

Therefore, throughout the latter half of the 1970s and the 1980s, as the PNC reinvented itself as 'cooperative socialist' or, at times, even Marxist-

Leninist (however nebulously), Jagan would assert his singular possession of the communist ideological purity, by virtue of his enduring loyalty to the creed. On the other hand, he affixed the disparaging badge of reformism on Burnham, not the philosophically exalted Marxism-Leninism that was his prerogative. After all, it was the PPP that had demonstrated the courage of its conviction by aligning with 'the world socialist system' led by the Soviet Union, at the International Conference of Communist and Workers' Parties, in Moscow in June 1969. As far as Jagan was concerned, that occasion, 'a kind of homecoming' (by his definition), represented the decisive event in the consummation of his PPP – the ultimate validation of his fundamental and unwavering belief – his faith in Marxism-Leninism, which he had espoused since the late 1940s:

> Recent class battles have struck a blow at the illusion spread by partisans of neo-capitalism and reformism and have given fresh proof of the basic propositions of Marxism-Leninism...Socialism [communism] has shown mankind the prospect of deliverance from imperialism. The new social system based on public ownership of the means of production and on the power of the working people is capable of ensuring the planned, crisis-free development of the economy in the interest of the people, guaranteeing the social and political rights of the working people, creating conditions for genuine democracy, for real participation of the broad masses of people in the administration of society, for all-round development of the individual, and for the equality and friendship of nations.
>
> **It has been proved in fact that only socialism [communism] is capable of solving the fundamental problems facing mankind...**
> The socialist world has now entered a stage of its development when the possibility arises of utilising, on a scale far greater than ever before, the tremendous potentialities inherent in the new system [emphasis added].[3]

However, by the early 1970s, Burnham's PNC was beginning to inch their way to a form of socialism that did not unduly alarm the Americans, while securing the affirmation of Jagan's comrades in Cuba and, possibly, even those in the USSR. The Cubans, in particular, were keen to build alliances with governments that, even if not mildly definable as socialist, were adopting a consistent anti-American posture on many issues. Castro's Cuba was in eager pursuit of diplomatic recognition in the Caribbean region and were inclined to be less censorious in embracing new friends (such as Forbes Burnham), however vague their ideological pretensions. But the political flexibility, the evident pragmatism of his Cuban comrades was disconcerting to Jagan, and it tended to push his PPP even further to the left as he continually sought revalidation in his tested fidelity to the authentic Marxist-Leninist creed – a perceived return to the source. And, as Ralph Ramkarran has speculated (but with much inside knowledge), it is highly likely that the Cubans were instrumental in persuading the PPP's chief Marxist theoretician, Ranji Chandisingh, to join the PNC in 1976. This was the context also in which the PPP was cornered earlier into extending 'critical support' for Burnham's fraudulently 'elected' government in 1975. But the PPP did not do so with conviction, as they launched yet another strike in the sugar industry for recognition of their union, the Guyana Agricultural Workers' Union (GAWU) – a perennial exercise in political manoeuvring.

And they succeeded, at last. The PPP's union was allowed a free vote by the government in December 1975, which they won overwhelmingly with 97 per cent of the votes. Besides, Jagan also realised his greatest dream: the strangling of 'bitter sugar' and the 'sugar gods.' Burnham nationalised the sugar industry in 1976. Booker, the foremost enemy of Jagan throughout his political career, was finished in Guyana. It was Jagan's reward for his 'critical support' of the government. Yet the GAWU/PPP would call a 135-day strike in 1977, claiming it was aimed at forcing the PNC government to agree to a profit-sharing formula, for the benefit of the workers. In fact, it was primarily a vigorous flexing of their trade union muscle, now imbued with political clout – the mobilisation of the Indian sugar workers to exert economic damage on the floundering PNC regime.

However, the espousal of a form of socialism by Burnham was designed primarily to institutionalise the paramountcy of the PNC over the government. After all, this was the established mechanism by which the ideological kin of the PPP, the Leninist communist parties in Cuba, the USSR, and her satellites, perpetuated their draconian control. Yet the PPP never did repudiate this principle of totalitarian rule in communist states, dominated by the Leninist parties. On December 20, 1989, with the Soviet system in tatters, Jagan announced that

> the PPP rejects the doctrine of paramountcy of the Party under which the ruling PNC has become indistinguishable from the state, and the Government has become the Executive arm of the PNC. The PPP rejects this principle and will ensure the complete separation of the ruling party or parties from the state.[4]

The PPP had also committed itself, from as early as 1977, to a winner-does-not-take-all political culture. Moreover, they pledged that even if they did secure a majority in free elections, they would construct a government embracing a 'plurality of political and ideological beliefs.'[5]

The PNC, however, continued to rig elections wantonly, while seeking to refute the unimpeachable allegations by the PPP (and other small political parties, including their erstwhile coalition partner, the United Force) that the results of all the general elections since independence were not a representation of the popular will. Burnham, with the complicity of the Americans (resolved to keep the pro-Moscow communist Jagan in the political wilderness), had initiated the charade in the elections of 1968. Henceforth, Burnham, fortified by the fact that he was continually driving Jagan further to the left – and that his PNC government was thereby inoculated against any conceivable American subversion – became totally shameless in his manipulation of the electoral process.

In 1973, he arrogated to himself 70.1 per cent of the votes or thirty-seven seats; he kindly reserved 26.6 per cent or fourteen seats for Jagan. He exceeded himself thereafter, oblivious of whatever the Americans thought, by delaying the next elections from 1978 until 1980. In July 1978, he held a referendum to change the Constitution to give himself untrammelled power: he claimed to have polled 97 per cent of the votes! The new 'socialist' constitution was promulgated in 1980, thereby consolidating his dictatorial rule. When he eventually staged the general elections in December 1980, he awarded himself 77.7 per cent of the votes and forty-one seats, granting Jagan a mere 19.5 per cent of the votes and ten seats. The travesty was not terminated with the death of Burnham in August 1985, as his successor, D. Hoyte, blatantly rigged the elections of December 1985. The PNC awarded themselves 78.5 per cent of the votes or fort-two seats; they gave Jagan's PPP a paltry 15.8 per cent or eight seats. Another monumentally crooked exercise!

Such a glaring contravention of democratic electoral norms, by Burnham and Hoyte, has no parallel in the Anglophone Caribbean, steeped in the liberal democratic tradition (the Grenadian aberration, under Gairy and Bishop, notwithstanding). Yet the political leaders of CARICOM stayed eloquently silent and non-committal despite the flagrant abrogation of democratic rights in a member state. The US government, though angry that their chosen man (Burnham) had become blatantly recalcitrant, fraternising ostentatiously with Castro, Kim Il-sung, Chou-en-Lai, and other communists, and despite extricating themselves from the later riggings by the PNC, also maintained their silence. Burnham was particularly enamoured of the brand of totalitarianism inflicted on the North Koreans by their maximum leader, Kim Il-sung (1912–94). Burnham appropriated the *Juche* idea of Kim, with emphasis on an iron discipline, self-reliance, and the theatrical staging of mass games, enforced through 'paramountcy of the Party,' as he indoctrinated the masses into reverence for the 'Great Leader.'

Moe Taylor has examined the relationship between Burnham and the North Korean dictator, Kim Il-sung, between 1974 and Burnham's death in 1985. Suzy Kim, an authority on North Korea at Rutgers University (New Jersey), concurs with him on several of his conclusions. And she draws specifically on Taylor's argument that Burnham was deeply impressed with the stern discipline and prodigious effort Kim extracted from his workforce, who seemingly manifested total devotion to their 'Great Leader':

> According to Taylor, Burnham was most impressed by the hardcore discipline embodied by the North Korean workers, such that 'when fellas bent their backs at seven [to work in the fields: Suzy Kim], they didn't get up until they took a break' [presumably a quote from Burnham]. Such levels of discipline were attributed to their devotion to the leader, and Burnham sought to adopt North Korea's work ethic in order to implement his vision of cooperative socialism by emulating the cult personality and a system of education that placed priority on collective discipline.

> This was most visible in the Mass Games, a grandiose choreographed gymnastics extravaganza with the participation of tens of thousands, all of which moved in unison. A North Korean team visited Guyana for nine months in 1979 in order to train personnel from the Ministry of Education as Mass Games instructors, which culminated in the 1980 performance of Guyana's first Mass Games to commemorate the 10th anniversary of Burnham's 1970 proclamation of the Cooperative Republic. By 1982 Mass Games training became part of the physical education in the Guyanese public school system, remaining so until the early 1990s.[6]

Burnham's bizarre 'comradeship' with Kim was arguably prompted and sustained by a shared ingrained megalomania, yet it elicited scarcely a discernibly critical reaction regionally or beyond. The Caribbean leaders, as well as the Americans, were averse to Cheddi Jagan ever regaining power; he was deemed indissolubly yoked to Moscow and seduced by their mantra of 'proletarian internationalism,' which the West construed as world domination by the Soviets in the context of the Cold War. Consequently, virtually every Burnhamite excess was insulated from censure by the fact of Jagan's perceptibly more extreme and objectionable communist creed, definitively Soviet-inspired.

In December 1974, Burnham had promulgated his much-heralded Declaration of Sophia, espousing socialism as the instrument for the liberation of the working people: 'making the little man a real man.' His brand, cooperative socialism, possibly first conceived by Eusi Kwayana, identified the cooperative as the 'principal institution for giving the masses control of our economy.' He made no reference to Marxism-Leninism – I cannot recall him ever doing so, at any time – but there were allusions to a commitment to abolishing exploitation, eliminating production for profit that bulged the pockets of individual capitalists. And Burnham did underline the fundamental distinction between the socialist man he wished to create, on one hand, and the exploited, alienated man under rapacious capitalism, on the other. The latter involves the 'production of goods and services for profit to the individual,' whereas socialism is infinitely more altruistic: 'production for the use of and service to people.' Burnham explained further that under socialism 'surpluses are sought in certain operations and undertakings. These surpluses, however, are not intended to be pocketed and owned by private individuals as a means of enrichment and power, but rather to be further invested in development and/or deployed to provide services to the people.' He added that it was a protracted process to eradicate capitalism and capitalist attitudes; it could not be done overnight. It was towards this noble objective that the PNC was creating the Cuffy Ideological Institute to re-educate party activists for the task of building socialism. The capitalist, therefore, could not lead a socialist party or lead Guyana to socialism.[7]

On August 18, 1975, Burnham addressed another congress of the PNC at Sophia; its theme was 'Towards the Socialist Revolution.' It was characterised by the familiar vagueness that always permeated his speeches: impressive in its delivery and rhetorical flourish but rather light on content. As usual, unlike Jagan, there was no suggestion whatsoever of a Marxist-Leninist/communist or Soviet component to Burnham's socialism. I am quoting at length how Burnham defined the socialist revolution he professed to be initiating in Guyana – the first Cooperative Socialist Republic in the world (by his designation):

> Socialism is an ideology. It describes a social and economic system with clearly defined features and relationships between people and people and between people and the means of production, distribution and exchange. To my mind there cannot be different types of Socialism.
>
> Different socialist parties and different countries, however, while sharing each other's experiences and learning from each other will use, and have used in their own objective circumstances, various and varied means, instruments and techniques to achieve the objective of Socialism.
>
> When, therefore, the People's National Congress speaks of Cooperative Socialism, it is merely stating two propositions in one for the sake of easy reference. **First, we believe in Socialism as an ideology and are striving to establish that system in Guyana. Second, we are using and intend to use the Cooperative as the main vehicle or tool for achieving that goal** [emphasis added].
>
> We have identified the Cooperative for a number of reasons. It is rooted in the social and economic history of our peoples [African? Marginally!]. In its proper operation, it values each member as the same, for when decisions are to be taken each man has one vote and not each share one vote.
>
> It also offers to each member a direct opportunity to be involved in important decision-making and avoids the alienation that one finds under the capitalist system, and in many cases of centrally controlled and directed state ownership, where decisions are made from above without consultation or involvement of the workers.

It further emphasises for us in Guyana groupness as distinct from individualism, and its members work together and enjoy the sharing experience.[8]

Groupness! Not much good came out of this the most ambitious strand of Burnhamite philosophy. Most cooperatives, such as they were, turned out to be disastrous as the prime instrument 'towards the socialist revolution.' Yet, occasionally, apologists of the PNC (aware of the PPP's ridiculing the concept as bogus, or as 'a fraud' by Cheddi) would define cooperative socialism as being totally compatible with Marxism-Leninism. One such was George Morris (in October 1979), who even retrieved a quote from Lenin in making his case: 'Cooperative socialism, as envisaged by the Vanguard Party [PNC], is not a distortion of Marxism-Leninism as some detractors would like to make out, for Lenin in his cooperative plan had observed that co-operation as a democratic form of distribution and production, prepares the material prerequisite for socialism...Lenin explained: "Since political power is in the hands of the working class, since the political power owns all the means of production, indeed, the only task that remains for us is to organise the population in cooperative societies".'[9]

II.   Jagan's Ideological Rigidity: His 'Possession of a Pure Marxist Way'

One 'comrade' from Jagan's PPP, however, was less charitable, describing cooperative socialism as 'total unadulterated skunt': mumbo jumbo. But, by and large, Burnham's cooperative socialism did give the PPP, repeatedly cheated in rigged elections and marginalised by their Marxism-Leninism in the region and beyond, the backdrop to contrast their theoretical acuity and credentials of communist authenticity and recognition by the international communist movement (led by the Soviet Union), with the eclectic and nebulous 'socialist posturing' of the PNC. It was a ritual in sterility, but it brought the PPP's true believers in communism a measure of self-belief and self-abnegation, as if imbued with a kind of religious purity. It was manifested by their resolve to suffer and 'struggle,' at a low standard of living (most riding bicycles), for a just cause which is preordained by historical materialism to materialise and succeed: the law of the evolution of societies. The associated rituals were self-affirming: annual party conferences attended by fraternal delegations of communists from the USSR and its satellites, as well as those from fraternal communist parties, even smaller sects, in various parts of Asia, Africa, and Latin America. The Chinese were beyond the pale shortly after the beginning of the Cultural Revolution of 1966–67; they were not invited to PPP congresses, and their literature disappeared from the party's bookstores from around 1968.

This unwavering devotion to the creed sustained Cheddi Jagan for five decades, while the young comrades around him (in the 1970s–80s) – disciples who owed everything to his wisdom – were unfaltering in their devotion to him and his wife, despite the puny material rewards. Meanwhile, the most intellectually endowed comrades tended to jump the PPP ship, seduced by the lure of Burnham's PNC, with the means to offer a higher standard of living: a lucrative post in government was guaranteed indefinitely. The incentive to endure privation with the Jagans in the PPP was an unattractive proposition. It required extraordinary sacrifice and Herculean loyalty. This made for a kind of cult psychology in the PPP of the 1970s–80s. But those within it genuinely felt that they were the chosen ones, recognised by Cheddi and Janet Jagan as the genuine class warriors. After the continual haemorrhaging of the PPP for ideological or personal reasons, at last, these younger comrades around Cheddi and Janet – the noble votaries of Marxism-Leninism – repaid with astounding personal devotion and self-sacrifice, to them and the cause. It bred internal solidarity, but fostered suspicion of the outsider, both those outside of the PPP in Guyana, as well as the several hundred thousand who had escaped to the heartlands of capitalism under Burnhamism.

V. S. Naipaul recalls his re-encounter with the irrepressible Cheddi in 1991, nearly twenty-seven years after Anglo-American complicity had orchestrated his removal from office:

> Through all of this…Cheddi Jagan has sat at his post, the leader of his party, always there, the possessor of a purer Marxist way, waiting to be called. His support has always come from the Indians, but he has never accepted that he is just a racial leader. In the hardest times of African oppression [under Burnham's rule], he has supported whatever legislation came up that could be seen as socialist or Marxist [including nationalisation of 80% of the economy – and demanding more!]. So, **to some, out of the very purity of his Marxist vision, he has conspired against both the interest of his supporters and his own political success** [emphasis added].[10]

What is not examined in this assessment, however, is that both Cuba and the Soviet Union, in the context of the *realpolitik* of the Cold War, were reconciled to the assumption (around 1973–74) that Burnham's PNC government, however inconclusive the evidence of its professed socialist/communist credentials, was genuinely and demonstrably anti-imperialist. Yet these two communist countries could co-exist with both Burnham's PNC and Jagan's PPP, although the latter still highly prized the consistency, longevity, and unimpeachable integrity of their Marxist-Leninist pedigree, including their ideological identification and solidarity with Cuba and the USSR (at considerable cost, as Naipaul points out). Their unfaltering loyalty, surely, had earned Cheddi and Janet Jagan and the

PPP a more robust reciprocation of fraternal solidarity from their communist friends.

Therefore, when comrades from the communist parties the world over attended their annual congress or sent messages of fraternal solidarity in admiration of their common pursuit of 'proletarian internationalism,' the party felt vindicated. Thus, on the twenty-fifth anniversary of the founding of the PPP, in 1975, the Central Committee of the Communist Party of the Soviet Union (CPSU) sent a message that read in part:

> The PPP has gained the respect of the fraternal parties by its devotion to the principles of Marxism-Leninism and proletarian internationalism, by its allegiance to the cause of consolidating unity and cohesion of the international communist movement and of all anti-imperialist forces.

But the CPSU was covering all bases when it recognised that the PPP was committed to the unity of the international communist movement, in addition to their work in the cohesion of 'all anti-imperialist forces.' The latter is an allusion to what was interpreted as a discernible political change in Guyana after 1972–73, with the recognition of Cuba by the Burnham regime. This was perceived in Moscow as a bold initiative in the consolidation of an anti-imperialist/anti-American front in the region: America's 'backyard'! And coming in the aftermath of the US-supported coup against the government of the Marxist Salvador Allende in Chile in September 1973, the Cubans and the Soviets must have been exhilarated by overtures of reconciliation by Jagan's PPP towards Burnham's PNC: its likely Cuban-prompted 'critical support' of 1975.[11]

Jagan was cognisant of the strategic ideological fluidity that had emerged since he took the PPP into the communist movement, in Moscow in June 1969. But he was not enamoured of the precipitate Cuban-Soviet softer line towards Burnham, tantamount to an appeasement. Jagan's PPP was enraged and implacably antagonised by the rigged elections of 1968 and 1973, the latter being even more unashamedly blatant as the armed forces seized the ballot boxes, impounded them at their headquarters, and proceeded to criminally tamper with, and massively inflate, the ballot in favour of Burnham's PNC. It was an agonising tight rope for Cheddi Jagan to walk: this shifting dynamic, the new pragmatism in the communist world, must have been unimaginably dispiriting for him. Yet Cheddi did not lose an iota of faith in his inviolable communist creed; this was evident in his address to the 18th Congress of the PPP, at Leonora (West Coast Demerara) in August 1974. He was fortified by the longevity and solidity of his credentials as a communist; unlike the ambiguous Burnham, his were not marred by ambivalence or motivated by opportunism. His Marxism-Leninism was permeated by an ideological certainty that communism would revolutionise the experience of humankind, erasing all the ancient prejudices that corrode the human spirit, while creating a new man imbued with the vision to remake humanity by the 'laws' of communist perfectibility. Cheddi was the first Guyanese to commit his life unreservedly to the communist mission. He did see himself as 'the possessor of a purer Marxist way,' as Naipaul framed it. Quintessentially so!

Jagan's faith in the Soviet Union as the beacon inspiring humankind to build the communist utopia – the antithesis of moribund America – remained undiminished. As usual, he cited figures in profusion (a habit of several decades), often drawn from Soviet or East European sources, to proclaim that the days of capitalist America were numbered. He was a true believer in the inevitable supremacy of communism; that it was gaining ground all over the world, irreversibly so. The future belongs to Marxism-Leninism:

> Unemployment is increasing in the developed capitalist states. In 1973 there were three million more unemployed than in 1970. In the USA the unemployment rate rose from 4.8 percent in December 1973 to 5.2 percent in January 1974, with a prediction of 6–7 per cent for the rate of the year.
>
> **Imperialism is dying. Let's redouble our efforts to bury it** [emphasis added].
>
> By contrast, socialist countries do not face such crises. **In the Soviet Union, for instance, all prices are stable, while real incomes rise by some 5 per cent annually** [emphasis in the original]. Medical services and education are free. House-rent amounts to about 5 per cent of the wage, and taxes about 8 percent. There is no unemployment. And the retirement age for pension is 60 for men, 55 for women and still lower for workers in heavy and hazardous occupations.
>
> Between 1950 and 1969 public and private consumption in the Soviet Union and the Eastern European states increased by 6.5 per cent as compared with only 4 per cent in the European capitalist states. The overall increase per capita in socialist [communist] countries was roughly 2.33 per cent over.
>
> **To socialism** [communism] **has passed the historical initiative. Its moral prestige has grown and the world balance has shifted in its favour** [emphasis in original].[13]

Cheddi did acknowledge that the Soviet Union and its satellites in Eastern Europe, guided by Marxism-Leninism, had not yet attained their full utopian promise, but all the indicators were that the great transformation, offering a fulfilled life for remaking a new, enlightened, selfless communist man was imminent. To him, such was the magnitude of the advancement in the communist countries allied with the 'moral prestige of the world socialist system since 1969' that 'imperialism has been forced to restrict its aggressive policy and to abandon its outright violence.' It was the time of détente, with Nixon and Brezhnev committing their nations to peaceful co-existence. Cheddi argued: 'In place of the Cold War and economic blockade, there are now peaceful competition and economic agreement.' The American embargo on trade with Cuba remained, and the Cold War was far from over, but Cheddi was sanguine and keen to convey to his supporters that the improving relations between the US and the USSR was a vindication of the Soviet Union's 'growing economic strength and moral prestige...particularly during the past two years.'[13]

Therefore, in August 1974, Jagan felt fortified in asserting that Burnham's overtures to Cuba and the Soviet Union did not stem from an authentic conversion to Marxism-Leninism, nor was it actuated on his own initiative. It was a pragmatic tactic driven by America's recognition that the vibrant socialist economies were a reality of international trade. Therefore, the imperialists were impelled to grant concessions for their lackeys, such as Burnham and others in the region, to trade with Cuba. In addition, Jagan was claiming credit for his 'vanguard' party, the PPP, for its relentless pressure on the PNC to move towards the left:

> The PNC's recent establishment of diplomatic relations with Cuba should not be viewed as an act of independence...The PNC regime was obviously given the 'green light' on Cuba and China [supporting the latter's seating at the UN] by its US overlords. Having accepted peaceful co-existence with the USSR and China, US foreign policy could gain little from the continued blockade of Cuba...The PNC clearly does not follow a principled course but moves pragmatically and opportunistically. Its anti-imperialist pose is the result of a variety of factors – [but essentially] consistent ideological pressure from our vanguard [communist] party...The PNC's foreign policy must be seen therefore as a product of countervailing pressures. Basically, it operates after consultation with imperialism and within the limits imposed by it, in accordance with its changing strategies and tactics.[14]

But it was primarily the irreversible economic dynamism of the Soviet Union (centrally planned), conducing to its impressive contribution to world trade, that would redound to the advantage of communist parties the world over. Jagan added: 'May the Soviet Union grow from strength to strength. Long live the heroic Soviet people!' He obviously had in mind the difficulties, indeed, the impenetrable opposition he encountered from America and Britain when, as a colonial leader, he was desperate to trade and procure aid from communist countries because their motivation was supposedly 'disinterested,' actuated solely by proletarian internationalist convictions. However, Jagan was correct in that

Burnham was never constrained by definitive ideological principles of any sort. Burnham was an exponent of statecraft as the art of the deal: to vanquish one's enemies in pursuit of power by any means necessary. This, inevitably, requires Machiavellianism: the gift to manoeuvre and meander in the endeavour to outwit one's enemy before the final hurdle and to neutralise their capacity for a resurgence – indeed, never to mount an effective challenge for power again. For Burnham, principles are an instrumental device, necessarily amenable to revision, strategic distortion, even wholesale and blatant repudiation – not immutable 'laws' dictated by ideological imperatives, as Jagan perceived Marxism-Leninism. Basically, he was ready to tactically adopt any left-oriented ideology endowed with the philosophical rationale and accompanying political accommodation of totalitarian rule. Castro's Cuba offered a regional exemplification of this as did Kim Il-sung's North Korea – comrades both!

III. American Reappraisal of Their Intractable Man: Settling for Benign Neglect

The US ambassador in Guyana (1969–74), Spencer King, knew Burnham well, as is evident from the following excerpts from his comprehensive telegram to the State Department of May 28, 1970:

> Burnham is a complex and difficult personality. He is intensely proud and does not like asking for anything, especially aid from white people. He is sharply conscious of his colour and of the inferior position of black people and black nations around the world...The rich nations and the white man also bear moral responsibility for injustices and evils of the past, especially slavery and colonialism. Thus, whatever they do in less developed countries, in their own self-interest, is evil. **Burnham is an avowed socialist** [not a 'communist': reserved for Jagan] **with a socialist's attitude toward capitalism and private investment.** Since these are predominantly white, he probably also considers them evil, especially if they control the economic life of his own country.
>
> Burnham is intensely ambitious and restless, and he is frustrated. Guyana is probably too small for his ambitions, and his people, including his cabinet, are too slow for his restless energy. We have seen evidence of his efforts to assume leadership in the Caribbean. He is, no doubt, also concerned with his image among the leaders of the Third World...
>
> Burnham is an experienced and consummate politician, expert in the ways of manipulating his people, individually and collectively...He is a plunger who will take great risks if he sees a long-term advantage. **His determination to 'make the small man a real man' and to 'seize control of the commanding heights of the economy' can**

**thus be seen in the context of efforts to undercut the appeal
of Jagan's call for nationalization of the means of production...**
Burnham is also undoubtedly nettled by Jagan's constant charges
that he is a puppet of US imperialism, and feels he must prove his
independence to his own people...

**He aims to build a homegrown ideology to counter Cheddi
Jagan's Marxism...**Burnham understands parliamentary democracy,
perhaps better than most of his colleagues, **and he probably values
the esteem of the democratic leaders of the Commonwealth
enough to retain at least a semblance of a democratic system.
But he is touchy, does not relish criticism, does not face a
responsible opposition** [the PPP], **and is determined to press
ahead with his revolution. He will crush those who stand in his
way** [emphasis added].[15]

Crushed them, he did. The US ambassador provided a most perceptive
assessment of Burnham, but at no point did he label him a communist. Not
so Jagan, whom he accused of 'subservience to Moscow.' The previous year,
1969, the Nelson Rockefeller Mission to Latin America identified communist
subversion, inspired by the Soviet Union largely through their agent, Castro's
Cuba, as a virus threatening America and America's interests in the Hemisphere.
The report was also forthright about the perceived threat of Cheddi Jagan's
communist creed. This was their judgement under the heading, 'US-Guyana
Relations':

> Guyana is not a politically stable nation. Its political sphere reflects
> both the strength of a Communist party [PPP] and the depth of racial
> tension...A Communist victory would completely change Guyana's
> foreign policy. It is therefore of crucial concern to the United States
> and other nations of the Western Hemisphere as well as Great
> Britain...Brazil in particular has indicated its concern in this area.[16]

Rockefeller's observation did not dampen Jagan's communist ardour, as he
proudly reproduced it in his address to the PPP Congress in 1974. It was a
badge of recognition, from the arch-imperialists, of the solidity of his Marxist
credentials. In fact, this judgement by the Rockefeller Mission was made in
the immediate aftermath of Jagan's hitching the PPP to the world communist
movement, in Moscow in June 1969. It was arguably a visceral reaction to the
proliferation in Latin America of the guerrilla movement inspired by Castroism,
despite the killing of Che Guevara in Bolivia, in October 1967. This was the
impassioned Cold War context in which Jagan's PPP would be functioning
throughout the 1970s and 1980s. Besides, the American rule of thumb was
that whatever Burnham's ideological diversions or excesses – including his
belated promulgation of socialism from the mid-1970s, and his tilting towards
Castro and the North Koreans – he was infinitely more tolerable than the

hardcore pro-Moscow communist Jagan. Although Burnham was increasingly refractory towards the 'moderate' posture that had made him America's man, the imperialists never contemplated dislodging him, whereas they did conceive such drastic action if Jagan should win the elections under PR in 1964 or thereafter. The Americans could envisage no options. Therefore, they treated Burnham with palpable incremental indifference. Consequently, they never did revoke their relegation of Jagan to the political wilderness – a pariah to the end of the Cold War.

Yet while Jagan protested America's high-handedness, earning appreciable empathy within liberal democratic circles in the west, he regarded it as a noble accolade that the mortal enemies of communism, the American imperialists, had settled on him as a foremost enemy in Latin America – second only to Comrade Fidel.

It is necessary to recall that the CIA had funded the campaign of violence by Burnham's PNC and Peter D'Aguiar's rabidly anti-communist United Force (UF), in 1962 and 1963, to pressure the British to get rid of Jagan before granting independence. The CIA had also aided them in the elections of 1964 that ousted Jagan, and they rendered Burnham material and moral support to rig the general elections of 1968. Burnham was still their man, but now that he was beginning to demonstrate discernible independence of, and recalcitrance towards, the US, they were no less adamant that their paramount stance regarding Guyana was to ensure that Jagan never acceded to power again. The domino theory was a dominant strand in America's foreign policy, and Guyana's contiguity to two of the most important countries in South America, Brazil, and Venezuela, remained the definitive premise on which American perceptions of Jagan were predicated.

I wish to quote at length, again, from the extended telegram sent by the US ambassador in Guyana to the State Department on May 28, 1970. It replicates the assessment by the Rockefeller Mission to Latin America regarding Jagan's communism:

> There is no need here to discuss Jagan at any length. **His subservience to Moscow has been established.** He repeatedly calls for economic and political ties with the Soviet bloc and Cuba, and an end to western domination of the country and immediate nationalisation of the means of production. **Jagan in power would pose a real and immediate threat to the basic US interest in Guyana.**

And what was the fundamental US interest in Guyana? The embassy's report is categorical:

> **To deny control of the country to communists or other groups that are systematically hostile to the US and other friendly governments in the Hemisphere...**US commercial interests and investments are relatively small and Guyana's international power

and influence are negligible [emphasis added].' Therefore, it was exclusively a geo-political matter.[17]

Cheddi Jagan's communist creed was the sole reason for America's preoccupation with this insignificant backwater, long after the Kennedy obsession:

> The basic interests of the US in Guyana are essentially limited to denying it to international communism...Jagan's subservience to Moscow has been established. This leaves Burnham. He is proud, complex, difficult, determined, impulsive and sensitive. He is an accomplished politician, sensitive to significant currents and pressures. **He is a socialist, but a non-communist socialist...**He is leading Guyana into the Third World [the non-aligned movement] and launching an economic revolution in search of economic independence to go with political independence; and a restructuring of the economy to gain control of the country's resources so that they can be exploited by Guyanese for Guyanese.

> His chosen instrument is the cooperative, with government control. To him, his revolution is the answer to Black Power, and the sacrifices it demands are the price of 'avoiding another Trinidad' [the revolt against Eric Williams in early 1970]. **There is a trend toward increased authoritarianism. The USG [US government] will not like much of what Burnham will do and how he will do it, but there is no feasible alternative to Burnham. It must continue to help him.** In the process, it has an opportunity to show whether it can support change, which is inevitable, and identify itself with a Government that is seeking its own solutions in the interests of the masses of the people [emphasis added].[18]

Several things are clear from this verdict on Burnham's 'socialist revolution' in Guyana in the early 1970s. Foremost, the Americans were prepared to stick with him because the alternative was the dyed-in-the-wool communist, Jagan, firmly anchored in the pro-Moscow camp, therefore incompatible and irreconcilable with the fundamental democratic values of the US. Yet they would tolerate, even aid and abet, Burnham's rigging of elections because he was deemed the lesser evil in terms of their hemispheric strategic interests. Burnham, they observed, was mindful of the abortive Black Power revolt against Eric Williams in Trinidad in February 1970, and he was focused on precluding a similar eventuality in Guyana. He was promulgating 'cooperative socialism,' a home-grown philosophy that would accelerate the social and economic upliftment of the masses.

The Americans believed also that Burnham's independent socialist thinking was distinctly at variance with Jagan's Marxism-Leninism, of established Moscow vintage. The latter rendered it imperative for them to continue to support Burnham indefinitely. There was no option. The Americans were not impressed with Burnham's notion of 'cooperative socialism,' yet they empathised with his earnestness in addressing the combustible problem of economic inequality and poverty. Although they ridiculed Burnham's so-called cooperative socialist revolution, they still deemed the politics of Jagan so utterly reprehensible, in the context of the Cold War, that no reconciliation with him could be envisaged. They were, as a result, committed to accommodating the eclectic, mercurial, and comparatively opaque politics of Burnham. And they were prepared for the long haul on behalf of Burnham if Jagan remained the alternative.

One cannot be certain of the gravity of Burnham's pronouncement when he identified his experiment as the 'first cooperative socialist republic in the world.' It was aimed primarily at his 'African brothers,' particularly Nyerere of Tanzania and Kaunda of Zambia, seen as transformative leaders for whom he had considerable respect (they both visited Guyana). But he also allayed any potential American apprehension inclined to equate his 'cooperative socialism' with communism. The following is from the long report on Burnham (cited above) by the US Embassy in Guyana:

> While Burnham professes, sincerely we believe, a desire to find a uniquely Guyanese framework within which to reactivate the economy of the country, he most certainly is influenced by the examples of his African brothers. Burnham's chosen instrument is the cooperative. **There has been much rhetoric, most of it meaningless, to the effect that cooperatives have traditionally been Guyanese and that they therefore provide a 'Guyanese solution.'**
>
> It is fairly clear that what Burnham has in mind is a form of cooperative organisation largely imposed from the top by the Government (Party?), rather than the voluntary associations of groups of individuals with common interests and objectives which have existed in the past. He sets his goal as ending unemployment, ending poverty and vesting control of the economy in Guyanese hands. He seeks economic independence to go with the political independence attained four years ago [May 1966]. **He also aims to build a home-grown ideology to counter Cheddi Jagan's Marxism.** But what Burnham really wants is for the Government (and his party) to have access to the allegedly vast profits being made by the producers of bauxite and sugar and the private interests that now control imports. Only then will he 'control the commanding heights of the economy [emphasis added].'[19]

IV. Burnham Outmanoeuvres the Obdurate Pro-Soviet Communist

However amorphous his socialism, Burnham was sensitive to Jagan's relentless goading him into 'nationalising the commanding heights of the economy.'

Therefore, what Burnham was embarking on, however piecemeal, would almost inevitably secure the approbation of Jagan. But, of no less significance, it could potentially gain the empathy of Jagan's great founts of inspiration, the Cubans and the Soviets. This was also Burnham's means of enhancing his stature as a radical Black leader of the Non-Aligned Movement where he genuinely felt he belonged. Ever nimble in his tactical steps, he was mindful not to appear to embrace the Soviet camp, thus ensuring that the Americans remained cognisant of the distinctive ideological content between his 'cooperative socialism' and the doctrinaire pro-Moscow communism of Jagan.

Burnham was continually provoked by Jagan, who derided him as a 'lackey of American imperialism.' Even after he nationalised the Canadian bauxite company, DEMBA in 1971, Jagan was challenging him to embrace the Soviet Union and its satellites, including Cuba, essentially to join their camp:

> Clearly, the imperialists are willing to accommodate even nationalisation so long as it is within the framework of imperialism and the maintenance of the international status quo…[This explains why] mere nominal diplomatic relations have been established with the Soviet Union; why instead of developing the closest political, cultural and economic links with the socialist world, the Burnham regime spreads its own special brand of anti-communism and anti-Sovietism by propagating false ideas about the self-interests of the two super-powers, the USSR and the USA; and about third world inter-dependence and self-sufficiency.[20]

The latter was a reference to Burnham's vigorous engagement with the Non-Aligned Movement for which Jagan manifested no discernible enthusiasm. He considered the central premise that had prompted the creation of the movement, its declared equidistance from the two super-powers, fundamentally flawed. For him, the Soviet Union was essentially beyond reproach, 'disinterestedly' providing international aid and various forms of fraternal assistance, consistent with a basic Marxist principle: proletarian internationalism. Therefore, for Jagan, the Non-Aligned Movement had dubious goals compared with the lofty and clear-cut aims of international communism, under the inspirational leadership of the CPSU. Tito of Yugoslavia was a principal architect of non-alignment; he was a renegade of the communist movement, deemed a revisionist, a deviant from the Marxist-Leninist orthodoxy that Jagan considered sacrosanct. Anything lacking the imprimatur of the CPSU was inherently sacrilegious. This is why I argue that Jagan's faith in Marxism-Leninism, in conjunction with his untrammelled devotion to Soviet communism, are the secular equivalent of a religious calling. It was rooted in inviolable tenets that he would not dare to profane.

Writing in the special issue of *World Marxist Review*, in April 1970, on the centenary of Lenin's birth, Jagan repudiated the founding principle of non-alignment – that both the US and the Soviet Union were motivated, first and foremost, by imperialist self-interest in pursuit of world domination. Jagan was aiming specifically at Burnham's faith in the concept of non-alignment:

> By refusing to make any real distinction between the imperialist and the socialist world system, by equating western imperialism with what they refer to as 'Soviet imperialism,' they help to prop up the main ideological pillar of US imperialism, namely, anti-Sovietism, the modern garb of anti-communism, and at the same time to create disunity in the struggle against imperialism.

> Charges of Soviet 'imperialism' are closely related to the specious idea that imperialism and socialism have some 'common features.' One hears in response to the specific charge of conditional, 'tied' aid from the Western imperialist states that all nations have egoistic objectives and are motivated primarily by self-interest.

> This observation does not take into consideration that the policies of the socialist countries are influenced by the trenchant dictum of Marxism that 'no nation can be free if it oppresses other nations.' And this sets them apart from the policies of imperialism.[21]

Burnham's allegiance to non-alignment, with its implicit anti-Sovietism, was abhorrent to Jagan, but he was also disdainful of Burnham's piecemeal approach to nationalisation of the 'commanding heights' of the economy. Jagan was contemptuous of joint-ownership, partnership with imperialist-owned companies, such as Booker. His challenge to Burnham to nationalise the whole hog was tenacious, and it acquired a compulsion for him tantamount to a moral imperative. It was politics by the primer: a fundamental of Marxism-Leninism, deemed unimpeachable by the CPSU. Jagan argued: 'In Guyana, while the imperialists control the commanding heights of the economy – sugar plantations, bauxite mines, banking, insurance and foreign trade – the government engages in tokenism and state capitalism, and emphasises cooperatives, community development and self-help.'[22]

This was the context in which Burnham proceeded to steal Jagan's thunder, although he was not affiliated to the world communist movement dominated by the USSR (China and Albania, like Tito's Yugoslavia, were outside the Soviet sphere of influence by the late 1960s). However, by moving to the left and initiating diplomatic and trade relations with Cuba in 1972 and Russia by 1975, Burnham was incrementally undermining Jagan's claim to singular access to, and identity with, the Eastern bloc, but he could not appropriate, nor could he nullify Jagan's abiding conviction of being in sole possession, in Guyana, of the pure Marxist-Leninist vision. Meanwhile, Burnham was also instrumental in persuading Barbados, Jamaica, and Trinidad to extend diplomatic recognition to Cuba by the end of 1972. Castro was deeply appreciative of Burnham's initiative, as it marked the beginning of the end of his isolation in the Caribbean region, in America's so-called backyard. Burnham was systematically encroaching on, if not unravelling, the sacred links to the communist world that Jagan had been cultivating and were at the core of his messianic political mission. Yet this did not induce Jagan to rethink, to seek even a partial or incremental rapprochement with the West that could have saved him from the abyss of chronic powerlessness and political irrelevance. On the contrary, it compounded his compulsion with parading his Marxist-Leninist purity, as the PPP became irretrievably mired in an unfathomable theoretical quagmire that lasted until the collapse of the Soviet system and its empire at the beginning of the 1990s.

It is one of the most bizarre exercises in communist futility anywhere in the world – possibly unique for a leader who lost power for the cause and was actively denied further access to power by the Americans because of his devotion to the communist creed. The Americans started to undermine Jagan in 1962; they did not modify their antipathy to him until the collapse of the Soviet Union nearly thirty years later. But there is an underlying tragedy to the story: Jagan's Indo-Guyanese supporters, largely ignorant of communism and its lethal implications during the Cold War, stayed loyal to him. Even the multitude of them, whole families, whole villages in numerous cases (a few hundred thousand), who fled to capitalist/imperialist America, Canada, and the UK (from the late 1960s) rarely deviated from their allegiance to Jagan. It was a racial loyalty with its source in the 'bitter sugar' narrative and the perceived incorruptibility and sincerity of purpose of Jagan. But it was also prolonged by the fiction that the 'imperialists' had done him a great wrong because he stood up for the underdog, particularly the sugar workers. As I argue, the latter is the lineal descendant, the modern exemplification, of the 'bound coolie' – seminal to the shaping of the Indo-Guyanese imagination, and integral to their sustaining vision. Therefore, the obsession of the Americans with Jagan's communism was largely incomprehensible within the Indo-Guyanese frame of reference, beyond his disciples in the PPP exposed to Marxism-Leninism.

Indian racial loyalty certainly kept Jagan politically afloat for nearly three decades, despite the rigged elections and his exclusion from power, but his Marxist dogmas (often indigestible but high-sounding) kept the fiction of his mission on behalf of the entire working class alive among his own supporters. Yet, of no less importance to him was the need for periodic affirmation from his comrades in the communist world controlled by the Soviet Union. It should be noted that Cheddi and the PPP never did give serious consideration to embracing Maoist philosophy or support for Communist China against the USSR. At the top of the list in terms of communist affirmation (along with the Soviets) was Fidel Castro whose revolution in 1959 is arguably the turning point in the political demise of Jagan; after the British had genuinely taken British Guiana to the threshold of independence (possibly in 1962), Cheddi announced to the world that Castro was the greatest liberator of the twentieth century and the greatest liberator of the Hemisphere. Though the premier of a colony, he started to trade with Cuba thus breaking the American blockade. He was deemed by the Americans as the potential creator of 'another Cuba' in the Hemisphere, therefore an archenemy of the Inter-American system.

Yet after 1972, when Burnham established diplomatic relations with Castro's Cuba (and persuaded Trinidad, Barbados, and Jamaica to do the same), thus conferring respectability and legitimacy to Cuba in the region for the first time, it was clear that Fidel considered Forbes a genuine ally. However, Burnham was astute enough to frame this belated comradeship as indicative of the vibrancy of the Non-Aligned Movement in the Caribbean – not a manifestation of Soviet subversion, as the Americans defined it when applied to the long-standing Castro-Jagan ideological solidarity. Burnham's overtures to Castro constituted an ironic reorientation, having been hitherto defined as America's man. In fact, while Jagan drew closer to Castro in the early 1960s, Burnham had collaborated with Peter D'Aguiar (leader of the UF) and the Catholic Church in mounting a virulent anti-communist crusade to oust Jagan before independence. The irony is that after 1972, Castro considered Burnham so important to his stature in the region that he virtually abandoned Cheddi Jagan as an irrelevance, despite the latter's unimpeachable devotion to him – the principal cause of his political decapitation. No 'second Cuba'!

I noted earlier that Burnham's tilt towards Castro was an aspect of his embrace of the Non-Aligned Movement, as he sought to boost his image on a wider canvas, in Africa and the rest of the Third World. But it is also conceivable that his new-found friendship with Castro was reflective of his skilful aggregation of the main regional leaders to enhance his stature as a statesman – thereby pre-empting and neutralising potential censure as he orchestrated the rigging of the general elections, on a massive scale, in mid-1973. Burnham was in pursuit of a two-thirds majority, essentially the basis for his creation of a dictatorship in which Jagan would be further marginalised. His aim was to reduce Jagan to a cypher, with virtually no allies that mattered. He knew that the Americans would not challenge the crooked results because the alternative was their implacable enemy; neither would the Black leaders of the English-speaking Caribbean (Eric Williams, Michael Manley, and Errol Barrow), all ill-disposed to Jagan's pro-Moscow communism. Now, with Castro in his tent along with the key regional leaders, Burnham could proceed to rig the general elections big time, with every likelihood that it would evoke barely a whimper. (He awarded himself 70 per cent of the votes; he gave Jagan 26.6 per cent. Castro was silent, as were the regional leaders.)

Burnham must have been buoyed by his design to further peripheralise Jagan, as evident from the response of the US Embassy in Georgetown. In a telegram to the State Department, dated July 25, 1973, a few days after the fraudulent elections (on July 16) of which the Americans were fully aware, they admitted:

> The US could not really have wanted it otherwise…Jagan appears washed up but will continue to be a source of trouble for some time to come [because of his communism]. **Burnham has everything just about his own way now. But we can still work with him if we accept his government 'as it is'** [emphasis added].[23]

American machinations that led to the removal of Jagan in December 1964 and the election of Burnham have been told already. In the next elections, in December 1968, the Americans were heavily complicit in securing Burnham's re-election, in rigged elections. As the embassy acknowledged:

> We helped Burnham get into office in 1964 and to stay there in 1968, on both occasions viewing him as highly preferable to the alternative, i.e., the pro-Moscow and self-avowed Communist leader of the People's Progressive Party (PPP), Dr Cheddi Jagan.[24]

Theodore J. C. Heavner was deputy chief of mission at the US embassy in Georgetown from 1969 to 1971. He, too, has confirmed the rigged elections in Guyana, commencing in December 1968, and America's unabated fear of Jagan's communism, even after Burnham proceeded to move radically to the left from the early 1970s:

> I think [America's] interest in Guyana was out of all proportion to the importance of that country…because we had seen it, as indeed I think the British did, as a potential Cuba. There was a very strong communist party there [PPP], with the support of the majority of the population. The communist party leader, Cheddi Jagan, had been elected repeatedly during the British colonial period [but was defeated in 1964], and after independence he expected to be re-elected. This was a concern because of our chagrin about Cuba, our concern that a second communist party in this hemisphere would spell dominoes…
>
> Jagan was still waiting in the wings and expecting to be elected at the next election [after independence, in 1968], not unreasonably so, since he was the undoubted leader of the Indian population in that country…the majority group, and he had virtually 100% support from them. He was a very charismatic figure in the Indian community. **Burnham, however, in power** [since 1964] **was repeatedly able to arrange that the elections didn't come out that way. They were rigged and we knew they were rigged, and that was fine with us. We thought we could not risk having a second communist country in our hemisphere** [emphasis added].[25]

Heavner recalled that the American embassy in Guyana was a 'fairly big' one. Jagan believed, and rightly so, that the embassy harboured several agents of the CIA, but Heavner, as expected, claimed he was not aware of that. However, he did admit that 'our concerns first of all [was] about this being a second Cuba... and we wanted to support the free democratic system [ironically, characterised by rigged elections they were aiding and abetting!] versus the Cheddi Jagan model of the communist system.' Heavner has given a rare account of America's assessment of Burnham's radical shift to the left in the 1970s, having chosen him as their man in the early 1960s. This is his version of what the Americans made of their man and his *modus operandi* (I quote at length):

> Burnham was an intellectual, a very, very brilliant man. He read constantly, going through a couple books at night after he had done all his other stuff. He would sit up reading and devouring the books and talk about them...This is a man who would have been a successful leader probably anywhere. It was his fate that he was born into this small inconsequential country. Nevertheless, he had enormous ambitions, and I think he did it [moved radically to the left] because he saw it as a way to become prominent on the international stage, playing a really important role in world affairs that he otherwise wouldn't have had if he was just a friendly US satellite. This is, I think, his motivation, but he was such a complex personality that you could probably explain it in many ways.[26]

Heavner was in no doubt that although the Americans were frustrated (and conceivably betrayed) by Burnham's embrace of Castro, yet they adopted a posture of transparent indifference to his socialist experiments and Third World adventures. But they were never repelled sufficiently, in the absence of an alternative, to instigate his removal, as they did perpetrate against Jagan – most unscrupulously – between 1962 and 1964. At no time did they envisage extending any overtures to Jagan or effecting a *modus vivendi* with this inveterate pro-Moscow communist. Burnham could carry on just as he pleased, although Spencer King, the US ambassador in Georgetown from 1969 to 1974, did temper Burnham's escalating leftist theatrics.

Jagan was therefore marginalised into ineffectual Marxist-Leninist rhetorical excesses for the duration of the Cold War. Heavner recalls:

> Essentially, we turned the other cheek. Our options were Burnham versus Jagan, and we still thought Burnham was a better bet. We thought he was making a lot of mistakes. We certainly didn't like the militant Third World stance he was taking and especially his gestures to Cuba. It fell to Spencer King to try to moderate Burnham's increasingly leftist behaviour. I don't think Spencer had much success. Burnham...increasingly felt, with some justice, that the US was a paper tiger and wasn't going to do anything that was very difficult, regardless of his own stances, statements and behaviour. So,

Spencer had a pretty tough job. Spencer wasn't an intellectual like Burnham either…

[Yet] we still kept Jagan at arm's length. It was still clear to us, or so Washington still thought, that Burnham was preferable to Jagan… We were concerned about Jagan essentially taking over by violence. He had been trained [more by the CPGB than the CPSU] and patronised by the Soviets. He went regularly to Moscow where he was lionised. He was clearly at all times following the Soviet line on all questions of any international importance. He seems to be almost a rubber stamp for the Soviets. His wife [Janet] was probably the more astute politician…I think she is the brains behind Cheddi in many respects.[27]

Therefore, Burnham's belated affectation of a nebulous Marxist-Leninist posture notwithstanding, it was generally perceived as the lesser evil, possibly of vaguely Titoist prompting, rather than by the proscribed Soviet inspiration of Jagan. Burnham's Marxist pretensions could be minimised, even overlooked, because located further to his left, and robustly defensive of his ideological beacon (the USSR), was the real 'red menace.' This contributed to the aggravated irrelevance of Jagan, congruent with the strategic objectives of Burnham. So Jagan and the PPP were left with little beyond their doctrinal purity: their claim to the unadulterated Marxist-Leninist tenets, virtually from the mid-1960s until the collapse of the Soviet Union and its satellites in 1989. 'Jargon competing with jargon,' as Naipaul framed it in another context. The Guyanese tragedy!

V. Burnham Rigs with a Vengeance: The Fraudulent Elections of July 1973

Things had changed prior to the general elections of July 1973. Burnham was not seeking American assistance to rig merely to get over the line. He was resolved to engineer a two-thirds majority, to create virtually a one-party state. It appears that the Americans were averse to sanctioning so extravagant a loot of the ballots; in any case, they probably concluded, correctly, that Burnham was determined to steal it anyway. He was now equipped to orchestrate such an outcome on his own. It is also interesting that the Americans seemed to have reached the conclusion that they had no vital economic interests to protect in Guyana. Their sole concern was that the dyed-in-the-wool Moscow stooge (as they saw him), the communist Jagan, be denied power in order to protect the country and its big neighbours, Brazil and Venezuela (economically and strategically significant to America), from the scourge of communism. They had no option but to tolerate Burnham. He would probably pursue stronger relations with Cuba and the Eastern bloc, but he was not deemed a communist or a geopolitical menace. The irrepressible pro-Soviet communist, Jagan, would provide the greatest insurance to Burnham, guaranteeing that he stayed in power in perpetuity. The latter's premature death at only sixty-two, on August 6, 1985, deprived this master manipulator of that dream.

This was the scenario even after Burnham had won the confidence of Jagan's most contentious communist friend in the Hemisphere, Fidel Castro, as he did momentously by the mid-1970s. There is no person in the world who paid a greater price for his unstinted loyalty to Fidel Castro than Cheddi Jagan, from the beginning of the Cuban Revolution (1959–60), through the Bay of Pigs (April 1961), the Missile Crisis (October 1962), the Tri-Continental Conference [of Communists] in Havana (Jagan attended, in January 1966), the death of Che Guevara (October 1967), and beyond. Jagan was shafted by President Kennedy primarily because of his devotion to Castro. It is fair to say, therefore, that Jagan was betrayed by his old friend, fellow communist Fidel, solely in pursuit of *realpolitik*. Burnham exploited this to the hilt although he was never a communist, and, to reiterate, he had colluded in a virulent crusade against Castro, with Peter D'Aguiar's right-wing UF (founded in 1960 primarily to defeat communism). Anti-Castroism was a potent weapon that resonated with the Americans, and it was used relentlessly to discredit and subvert Jagan, with the help of the CIA.

To put it bluntly: Jagan had sacrificed the imminent independence of British Guiana (gift-wrapped and ready for collection in 1962) for his sincere belief in Castro and the Cuban Revolution.

I wish to quote a few excepts from the US embassy's report of July 1973, to emphasise that Jagan remained Burnham's ultimate safety valve:

> Burnham asked for our help [to rig] in the elections again [1973] and it was turned down...In making these requests [for loans], he asked pointedly: 'Do you want Cheddi?' Our reasons for refusing were perfectly valid...This time Burnham did it on his own, [he rigged] without our help. We may question the way he did it and the magnitude of his victory, for there is considerable substance to the opposition's accusations of election fraud [less than one line not declassified] and police and Guyana Defence Force intervention, and the two-thirds majority he now has in parliament may make him even more difficult...Burnham will certainly note the absence of any formal USG congratulatory message following his election victory.

> And what of Cheddi? When my Canadian colleague paid a farewell call on Jagan a few days before the election, he found him in high spirits and exuding confidence. He professed...that he could win an overwhelming majority in a free and honest election...He obviously had grounds for optimism about his followers...[based] on the time-tested racial appeals...if not about how the elections would be contested...Jagan reacted to the election results by saying his party could never accept them, just as he did in 1968...

He has refused to provide the elections commission the names of fourteen party members to occupy the seats in parliament *allotted* to him…Cheddi is probably about washed up. He must know this. Hence his great anger and frustration. He can still cause trouble nevertheless, and we do not see real tranquillity in Guyana for some time ahead…

The political scene will thus continue to be dominated by Burnham and Jagan, as it has been for two decades. No viable alternative to either appeared during the election. But Burnham clearly has the upper hand now, and Jagan's ability to influence events is declining and will continue to do so, even though he still has the capacity to cause unrest and violence. **Burnham is now very close to having it all his own way** [emphasis added].[28]

Jagan was clearly exasperated that the elections were so shamelessly rigged against him; worse, that he was utterly powerless to do anything about it. He had no allies in the region; even his foremost comrade, Castro, was now in Burnham's tent. In any case, he was not enamoured of 'bourgeois elections.' Understandably, Jagan was not prepared to accept the paltry fourteen seats 'allotted' to him (as the Americans put it); this would have conferred a degree of legitimacy on the travesty. The ballots were counted only after the boxes had been tampered with by the Guyana Defence Force. The whole exercise was bogus. And the Americans, knowing in advance that Burnham wished to rig on a massive scale, opted out of the scheme, unlike 1968 when they were deeply mired in the fraud. However, as early as July 1971, with two years to go to the elections, the Americans had no doubts that Burnham would rig it, and they seem totally compliant to keep out the communist Jagan, seen to be 'totally at Moscow's bidding.'

A memorandum prepared by the National Security Council (July 9, 1971), to review renewal of funding to Burnham for organisational purposes, to camouflage the fraudulence of the electoral process, observed:

The outcome of the next election…would not be in real doubt; Burnham will win, if necessary by rigging the election. Our purpose in providing support would be to help make the voting result look more plausible through funding a sufficient level of pre-election organisational activity by Burnham's party to lend credence to the victory. Burnham's party will have to engage in a wide range of election campaign activity, including such things as a major effort in organising the overseas vote in the United States and Great Britain as he did in 1968 [totally fraudulent, yet it required funding to execute]. The plausibility of the result will be important in gaining at least passive tolerance of Burnham's government among the East Indian population, who constitute more than half of the population.[29]

Surely, the Americans must have known that it was easier for Burnham to go through the eye of a needle than for Jagan's Indian supporters to accept the legitimacy of the election results. But that was not their motivation for conniving with the mercurial Burnham. It had everything to do with their implacable fear of communism:

> Cheddi Jagan, who is totally at Moscow's bidding, still poses a serious threat in Guyana; his East Indian supporters comprise a majority of the population and are increasing in numbers at a faster rate than the negroes. **Burnham is still clearly preferable from our point of view** [emphasis added].[30]

But by 1972–73, the Americans realised that the 'plausibility' of the result could not even be contemplated because Burnham was embarking on a monumentally fraudulent exercise to give himself a most implausible majority. Burnham had hosted the conference of non-aligned foreign ministers, in Georgetown in August 1972. His very able foreign minister, Shridath Ramphal, played a pivotal role in this, and it redounded magnificently to the enhancement of the stature of Burnham in the Non-Aligned Movement. During the conference, a monument to the four founders of the Non-Aligned Movement, Nasser, Nehru, Nkrumah, and Tito, was unveiled in Georgetown. Burnham knew he had Jagan cornered and was inclined to act independently of his hitherto dependable American sponsors. He felt free to execute the electoral fraud without fear of consequences. And Jagan's communist comrades, including Comrades Castro and Brezhnev, had no moral authority to expound on the subject. In the elections of 1973, ballot boxes were not counted at the place of polling but were seized by members of the Guyana Defence Force (GDF) and taken to their headquarters where they were detained up to ten hours before being released for counting. The boxes were tampered and augmented with ballot papers premarked to the exclusive advantage of Burnham's PNC.

A cable from the US Embassy in Georgetown to US Embassies in Barbados, Trinidad, and Jamaica, dated July 19, 1973 (released by Wikileaks), reflected on the 'blatantly rigged' elections:

> In attempting its forecast of this election, the Embassy had not really expected the PNC to abandon all pretence of honest election. In event, however, this is what appears to have happened... From all reports ballot boxes were delivered by a variety of means Monday night [July 16, 1973] to the Guyana Defence Force (GDF) Headquarters in Georgetown where they remained under armed guard for upwards of 10 hours before vote counting began. The PPP evidently succeeded only too well in alarming the PNC by its last-minute exhortations to its followers to prevent removal of ballot boxes to three counting locations. **(Evidently) plans to engage in ballot-box stuffing and switching while the boxes were being**

> **delivered, as had apparently been the original intention, were abandoned and the stuffing and switching seems to have taken place while the boxes were held at GDF Headquarters before delivery to three counting locations** [emphasis added].[31]

On the Corentyne Coast in the county of Berbice, a Jagan stronghold (the region of his birth), two PPP supporters (Jagan Ramessar and Bhola Nauth Parmanand) were killed on the evening of polling, July 16, 1973, while resisting the removal of the ballot boxes by the armed forces from the place of polling, as the PPP had instructed their party workers.

It is telling that at the conclusion of the massively crooked elections, the American ambassador to Guyana, Spencer King, did not deem it appropriate to recommend to the US government that they send a congratulatory message to Burnham. He wrote:

> In view of the blatantly fraudulent nature of those elections, and of the potentially tense racial situation which that fraud might provoke, we now have serious reservations about such a message. We do not plan to send congratulatory message to Burnham…In attempting its forecast of this election the Embassy had not really expected the PNC to abandon all pretence of honest elections. In event, however, this is what appears to have happened…Rigging does seem to have gotten out of hand.

Yet the cable concludes that having expended much time and resources to keep Jagan out of office, 'we should perhaps not be too disturbed at the results in this election. Jagan is still out, and Burnham is still in.' This, despite the Ambassador's acknowledgment that the elections were 'blatantly fraudulent'![32]

After the electoral travesty, in a 'victory' speech on July 22, 1973, Burnham brazenly invited Jagan to meet with him to 'discuss the way ahead for Guyana.' Then (betraying the insincerity of his overture) he asserted instantaneously that it was in no way a reflection of weakness on his part. He attributed his 'landslide' (his word!) to a range of progressive policies pursued by his government, while contrasting his record of stability with the 'mayhem, fires, arson and murder of the sixties' (implying Jagan's sole culpability), as if he could conceivably be absolved of the chaos for which he was an arch-architect and the principal beneficiary. He proceeded to 'ridicule' Jagan's statement that he could not accept the results as valid. Burnham dismissed this as innocuous nonsense for 'the PPP has neither the power nor the capacity to do anything about it.'[33] He was right. He could be arrogant and shameless; he was accountable to no one, and he intimidated anyone who dared to challenge the transparent fraudulence of the entire electoral process. He had rigged outrageously and most abominably, yet he was beyond reproach.

It is arguable that following the nationalisation of DEMBA (the Canadian bauxite company) in 1971, the Americans realised that Burnham was embarking on total control of the economy by the state and his party. The man for whom they had strived tenaciously, by consistently foul means, to install and keep in power to counter their communist foe (Jagan), was already appropriating much of the latter's programme. But the Americans could find no alternative whatsoever to Burnham. Jagan was definitely not in the frame, as he was even more determined to assert the purity of his Marxism-Leninism (compared with Burnham) while retaining his iron grip on his Indian support-base. He was immovable though mired in a politics of indigestible jargon, thus magnifying the futility of his communist creed in 'America's backyard.' Meanwhile, ironically, Jagan's disaffected Indian supporters, in their thousands, sought greener pastures in the heartlands of capitalism and imperialism, including his own children. Consequently, Burnham did face an open goal from the time he was chosen as America's man and engineered into office, in December 1964, until his untimely death in August 1985 – nearly twenty-one years of megalomania!

VI. In the Aftermath of the Blatant Electoral Farce: The 'Grounding' of the Brothers, Comrades Fidel and Forbes, September 1973

It is noteworthy that Burnham was intensely irritated by the rejection of his request, in February 1973, to meet with President Nixon (a desired photo op) as he was by the refusal of the Americans to approve his application for two loans. He then turned to Mao's China which did give him a line of credit, and that seemed to have convinced him that there were, indeed, greener pastures in the communist world. He was never a communist, but he envied the totalitarian control of their societies by communist parties in power, the absence of a credible opposition, and the silencing of dissent. Although the Americans perceived Burnham as the sole alternative to the 'Red Jagan,' they were not really enamoured of the man. They could see through his Machiavellianism: his being very bright to the point of arrogance; in addition to his agonising astuteness in debate, his amorphousness and vagueness of ideology – all things to all men – the consummate political animal. But there was no moderate Guyanese leader (Fabian socialist or social democrat), like Norman Manley, Grantley Adams, Errol Barrow (even Eric Williams), to counter the two millenarian racial juggernauts, Burnham and Jagan. This mattered not. Each a hero to his 'tribe.' Burnham, in particular, was a master of grandiloquent rhetoric, much of it ornamental, but provocative and enthralling – to the less educated, even to the more enlightened. So, the

Americans settled for what they considered the marginally less rotten apple: the rising dictator, Burnham, although he had outgrown his Yankee sponsors and was inclined to shun them. Their Frankenstein's monster! Their 'son of a bitch'!

Such was the bizarre character of the politics of this little tropical backwater (population around six hundred thousand in the 1960s), which the British and Americans had elevated to unwarranted geopolitical significance and menace. Comprehensible in the context of the Cold War, yet surely excessive. But the Americans had come to realise, belatedly, that Guyana was not very important despite the geopolitical factor that magnified its capacity to influence hemispheric affairs.

Spencer King, the American ambassador, had met with Burnham on September 1, 1973, the day before Comrade Fidel's fleeting visit to Guyana. Burnham, Castro, and Michael Manley (now comrades all) would be leaving Trinidad on September 3, in a Russian Illyushin plane, for the Non-Aligned Movement conference in Algiers. Burnham told King that both he and Castro would benefit from the visit and their flight together:

> Castro would gain respectability [in the region], and he [Burnham] would put another nail in Cheddi Jagan's coffin. I commented that this was exactly what disturbed Washington – that Castro would gain respectability and acceptability...Burnham argued that every head of government had to do what he considered best for himself and his country. He was undercutting Jagan and isolating him from his followers. Furthermore, he hoped to develop trade.[34]

Burnham also told Ambassador King that 'Castro's advance party had sought clearance to meet with Cheddi Jagan. The government of Guyana concurred and arrangements were made...[but] apparently they only saw Janet Jagan, who argued unsuccessfully that Castro should not come to Guyana and betray his true friends here.' Castro's brief visit must have been unimaginably infuriating and demoralising to Cheddi and Janet Jagan, coming as it did just a few weeks after Burnham had stolen the elections by unashamedly crude rigging, while manifesting unbridled hubris towards, and disdain for, Cheddi. He frequently did, belittling him as if he were unlettered and mesmerised by indigestible communist jargon. The truth is that he often treated Jagan with distinct superciliousness, in his speeches, as if he were a Johnny-come-lately: the peasant come to town!

When Castro visited his new-found comrade in Guyana, in September 1973, he was received with great pomp and ceremony by Burnham at the airport. On the way to Georgetown, Burnham and Castro reportedly stopped at Diamond Estate where they engaged in an 'animated conversation on the sugar industry' – evocative of a commonality, given Cuba's massive dependence on sugar. Burnham had not only stolen Cheddi's narrative about Fidel, but he had also engaged

Fidel, symbolically, in the narrative of sugar, thereby usurping a central plank in Cheddi's politics. Burnham was already contemplating its nationalisation, seeking to silence Cheddi's consuming tale of 'bitter sugar,' so germane to his local mission and his mesmeric hold on Indians, as well as his crusade against the imperialists. Yet Jagan was eloquently missing from the picture. One could have apprehended Cheddi's pain occasioned by the surreal spectacle unfolding before his eyes: Comrade Fidel embracing Comrade Forbes, to the adulation of the fawning multitudes in Georgetown. So, having decided to boycott the fraudulently constituted Parliament, Jagan probably concluded that he could not sup with Comrade Fidel whose every gesture was an affirmation of his enemy. Indeed, Cheddi must have refused to meet with Castro's advance party, delegating Janet instead. She having failed to persuade the Cubans that Castro should not visit Guyana, it is wholly comprehensible why there was no meeting between Castro and Jagan in Georgetown.

Jagan's decision to boycott the bogus Parliament was announced shortly after the fake results were declared. Burnham had awarded himself thirty-seven of the fifty-three seats based on nearly 70 per cent of the votes. Cheddi was 'allotted' (the expression of the American ambassador) fourteen seats. It is hardly surprising, therefore, that Jagan did not meet with Comrade Fidel even for a handshake or a bear hug during his brief visit with Comrade Forbes. Conversely, it is likely that Comrade Fidel did not wish to meet with Cheddi given the candid counsel of Janet Jagan that he should not visit Guyana, thereby validating Burnham's illegitimate regime.

Times had certainly changed! On September 3, 1973, Castro toured Linden, home of the recently nationalised bauxite company (DEMBA) and an impenetrable stronghold of Burnham's PNC. He gave unstinted endorsement to the government of Guyana as a bastion in the fight against imperialism. Comrade Cheddi would have found Comrade Fidel's words of praise disgusting:

> ...you workers no longer produce for capitalism and imperialism but for the good of the Guyanese people. I am sure that you now work harder than before and I congratulate you on your successes, since with your efficiency you are teaching imperialism that the working class is able to handle industries with efficiency and quality. Here, as in Cuba, the capitalists and imperialists tried to make the workers believe that they could not run the concerns, but they failed and the workers are winning. Here is an intelligent working class, hard-working and enthusiastic, and to you, in the name of the Cuban workers, I say you can always count on Cuban support, friendship and solidarity.[35]

This remarkable proletarian victory was, of course, necessarily attributable to Comrade Forbes. Interestingly, apart from Janet Jagan endeavouring to dissuade

Castro from granting legitimacy to the illegal Burnham regime, the American ambassador (Spencer King) had sought to dissuade Forbes Burnham from hosting Castro and from agreeing to travel with him, in a Russian-supplied Illyushin 18 turbojet, to the Non-Aligned conference in Algiers. (The plane was a stunt to impress West Indians: it was too big to land in Guyana; it did in Trinidad, whence Fidel boarded a smaller plane to Guyana.) The ambassador's argument was that any alignment with Castro was contrary to the principle of non-alignment. King had consulted Burnham's 'moderate' foreign minister, Shridath 'Sonny' Ramphal, on the matter, but he reportedly said that the decision was irreversible because if Burnham did not travel with Castro, Jagan would. This was absurd, as Jagan (not being the head of government) could not conceivably have been invited to the conference in Algiers.

The Americans had shafted Jagan because his was the lone voice of a head of government (harder in a colony) proclaiming its support for the Cuban Revolution from the beginning. It was consolidated by Cheddi's visits to Cuba twice in 1960, while inaugurating a range of trade deals that contravened the American embargo on trade with the communist state. This was fatal for Cheddi, as the PPP's foreign minister, Ms Carolyn Rodrigues-Birkett, recalled with precision, in the National Assembly in January 2013, nearly forty years after Castro's visit:

> While diplomatic relations with Cuba was established on December 8, 1972, Guyana's relationship with Cuba started close to two decades before that. Indeed, our relations began following the Cuban Revolution in 1959 under Dr Cheddi Jagan, who desired to pursue a political and commercial relationship with Cuba…
>
> It was under Dr Jagan's leadership, in 1961…despite the pressures of this period…that we [first] exported rice to Cuba, representing 6 per cent of our exports. This act of trade, therefore, made us one of the first countries to break the economic blockade [imposed by the Americans]. Cuba, in turn, provided cement and oil (oil which they received from the Soviet Union) I am advised.
>
> It will be remiss of me if I did not recognise that the political fortunes, or indeed the political misfortunes of the PPP, which were engineered by forces in foreign lands [US and Britain] including the removal and prevention of the PPP from returning to government [in 1964], had a lot to do with the principled and good relationship we enjoyed with Cuba, and the fact that we shared similar ideas [Marxism-Leninism] on what we wanted for our people.[36]

Cheddi paid a great price for his fortitude – or his folly – guided by 'proletarian internationalism' towards Comrade Fidel, thus defying the dictates of the American imperialists. The CIA had been subsidising Burnham for several years, and after they assisted him to rig the elections in December 1968, it was obvious, very early, that the new Republican administration would not deviate from the policy of the Democratic presidents, Kennedy and Johnson, of aiding Burnham to keep the communist Jagan out of power by any means necessary. The following summary is from a US government 'editorial note' for the period 1969–72 that encapsulates CIA funding for Burnham and the context of its termination:

> The Administration of Richard M. Nixon continued the Johnson Administration's policy of covert opposition to Cheddi Jagan, the Marxist leader of Guyana's PPP. The USG had attempted, through covert means, to prevent Jagan from coming to power since 1962 by providing covert assistance to Jagan's political opponent, the PNC (headed by Forbes Burnham), from 1964 to 1968. After Burnham's election in 1968, US covert assistance continued.[37]

In fact, Burnham had requested US$10,000 per month from the US government, in early 1969, to ensure that his PNC was revamped as a vibrant force to counter the communist Cheddi Jagan. Burnham still appeared to relish his role as the anti-communist bulwark: it provided him with an open goal, unrestrained politically. However, the US ambassador to Guyana, Delmar Carlson, recommended that US$5,000 per month was an adequate sum for the task. The 303 Committee approved a subsidy of US$5,000 per month, for two years, to enable the PNC to carry out its supposed anti-communist assignment, as well as the highly improbable initiative aimed at wooing Indian support away from Jagan. The funds were disbursed to the PNC from July 1969 to July 1971. But it was determined by the 40 Committee (successor to the 303 Committee), in June 1971, that there was no need for the subsidy to Burnham to continue after it elapsed the following month.[38]

On December 8, 1972, Burnham's government (as well as that of Trinidad, Jamaica, and Barbados) recognised Cuba. As noted earlier, Burnham had spearheaded this initiative, and on December 12 the 40 Committee decided 'it was not in the United States interests to provide covert financial support to Prime Minister Forbes Burnham during the 1973 Guyanese elections.' In mid-January 1973, the People's Republic of China (PRC) filled the breach, offering Burnham £50,000 for his elections campaign. The CIA report on the latter noted:

> A high-level member of Burnham's government who furnished this data to the CIA [agent in Georgetown] was disturbed by Burnham's acceptance of the Chinese offer and felt that, by virtue of the favour, the PRC would eventually be able to attain a significant level of influence in Guyana.[39]

This CIA agent made a projection of the Indian response to the likelihood of a 'fraudulent' election. He felt that their support for Jagan would be undiminished, although they 'may not agree with Jagan's ideology [communism].' In any case, they could not envisage Jagan winning the elections. They were clearly thoroughly inured to Burnham's rigging machinery after 1968, reinforced by his equally bogus local government elections of 1970, and they were certain he would 'win' by 'fraudulent means.' It is noteworthy, however, that the CIA indicated it would continue to monitor the situation, and if they determined that Jagan could pull off an 'electoral upset,' they would request that the 40 Committee revisit its stance regarding the termination of electoral funding to Burnham.[49] In a word, however flagrantly and radically Burnham had deviated from America's designation of him as their anti-communist bulwark, the basis on which they embraced him as their man, the Americans were no less committed to their resolve that Jagan must never be allowed to assume office again, even if he were democratically elected.

The assumption was that the PNC was sufficiently resilient and firmly entrenched in power to overcome any potential challenge from the communist enemy. As the American ambassador to Guyana argued in his telegram to the State Department of May 28, 1970, Burnham was already unconquerable:

> He has consolidated his control over the Government and its security forces, and rules unchallenged as the leader of the governing party, the PNC, which he has greatly strengthened. He is charting Guyana's future course and few [no one] dare to advise or disagree with him.[41]

V. S. Naipaul revisited Guyana in 1991, after thirty years. His unsparing eyes caught an apt symbol of the Guyanese political absurdity – inseparable from its racial futility. His essay is appropriately titled 'A Handful of Dust':

> Georgetown, the capital, once one of the most beautiful wood-built cities of the world (with the great hardwood forests just a few miles inland), is weathered and decayed. Over the run-down city there now rises at the end of one of the principal avenues, an extraordinary, mocking monument to the Cooperative [Socialist] Republic: a giant African-like figure, long-armed and apparently dancing, with what looks like cabalistic emblems on its limbs. This figure of African re-awakening is said to honour Cuffy, the leader of a slave revolt in Guyana in 1763, but there are black people who believe that – whatever the sculptor intended – the figure was also connected with some kind of obeah working on behalf of Forbes Burnham, the Guyanese African leader. Mr Burnham is believed to have, in the end, mixed his Marxism with obeah, and to have had an obeah consultant.[42]

By the late 1970s, the three main political parties in Guyana all espoused a variant of Marxism. In a region where Marxists have, traditionally, remained dormant on the periphery, congenitally unelectable, this strange place on the north-eastern shoulder of South America (of it, but not belonging to the continent) was probably unique in the world. Naipaul was correct: 'Guyana is a land of fantasies; it was the land of El Dorado.'

I end with the concluding remark on Burnham by the American ambassador, two decades before Naipaul's return to Guyana in 1991. It anticipated Naipaul's discerning encapsulation of the futility of the place – as he could identify no one better than Burnham to govern or misgovern Guyana:

> While the immediate future in Guyana does not look bright, the vital interests of the US are hardly threatened (except, of course, for the investment of Reynolds Metals [nationalised by Burnham in 1975]). The real problem to be faced is that Burnham must not fall so flat on his face as to make Jagan a more attractive alternative for the Guyanese people. The US, while it may not like much of what he may do, will thus have to continue to help Burnham, often despite Burnham, for there is no acceptable alternative to Burnham in sight. And the help will have to be in tune with where he thinks he wants Guyana to go.[43]

This was the mantra that guided America's treatment of Burnham, even as he stole Jagan's thunder after 1972, befriending Castro, Kim Il-sung, Brezhnev, Gaddafi, and others of similar ilk – a far cry from the man that Kennedy spent an inordinate amount of time in the White House scheming to empower to counter the communist virus in British Guiana. That other American presidents could still see this incompetent megalomaniac and serial rigger of elections, who betrayed their trust, destroyed the democratic institutions inherited from the British, and brought impoverishment to his people (several hundred thousands of whom, of all races, fled to America and Canada) because of his nebulous 'cooperative socialist' experiment, as worthy of ruling Guyana indefinitely, is attributable to one man: Cheddi Jagan – the dyed-in-the-wool Moscow man.

Notes

1. Sallahuddin, *Guyana: The Struggle for Liberation, 1945-92* (Georgetown: The Author, 1994), 310–11.
2. Cheddi Jagan, 'Address to the 16th Annual Congress of the PPP, September 1970,' in *Transactions of the XVI Congress of the PPP* (Georgetown: a PPP publication), 40.
3. *Documents Adopted by the Conference of Communist and Workers' Party* (Moscow: Novosti, 1969), 37, 31–32.
4. Cheddi Jagan, *Tracing our Path in a Changing World* (Georgetown: a PPP publication, August 1990), 30.
5. Ibid., 29.
6. Moe Taylor, '"One Hand Can't Clap": Guyana and North Korea, 1974–85,' *Journal of Cold War Studies* 17, Issue 1 (Winter 2015); and the review by Suzy Kim of Taylor's article, accessed at: http://tiny.cc/AR624.

7. *Declaration of Sophia*, Address by L. F. S. Burnham at a Special Conference to mark the 10th Anniversary of the PNC in Government, Sophia, December 14, 1974, 16–17.

8. L. F. S. Burnham, *Towards the Socialist Revolution* (Georgetown: a PNC publication), Address by Forbes Burnham to a Congress of the PNC, Sophia, August 18, 1975, 29.

9. *Guyana Chronicle*, October 28, 1979.

10. See V.S. Naipaul, 'A Handful of Dust: Cheddi Jagan and the Revolution in Guyana,' in V.S. Naipaul, *The Writer and the World: Essays* (London: Picador, 2003 [2002]), 488.

11. *Thunder*, April–August 1975, 2.

12. Cheddi Jagan, 'Address to the 18th PPP Congress,' *Thunder*, July–September 1974, 3–4.

13. Ibid., 4–5.

14. Ibid., 19–20, 22.

15. *Foreign Relations of the United States, 1969–76, Vol E-10*, Telegram from the US Embassy, Georgetown, to the State Department, Washington, May 28, 1970.

16. Jagan, 'Address to the 18th PPP Congress,' 23.

17. Ibid.

18. Cheddi Jagan, 'Balance of Forces,' in his *The Caribbean Revolution* (Prague: Orbis Press Agency, 1979), 97.

19. Cheddi Jagan, 'Lenin in our Time,' *World Marxist Review* 13, No. 4 (April 1970): 54–55.

20. Cheddi Jagan, 'New Imperialist Strategy,' in his *The Caribbean Revolution* (1979), 96.

21. *Foreign Relations of the United States, 1969–76*, Telegram from the US Embassy, Georgetown, to the State Department, Washington, July 25, 1973.

22. Ibid.

23. Theodore J. C. Heavner was deputy chief of mission at the American Embassy, Georgetown, 1969–71. He was interviewed by Charles Stuart Kennedy (May 28, 1997) for the Association of Diplomatic Studies and Training Foreign Affairs Oral Project. It was accessed at: adst.org/OH%20TOCs/Heavner.%20Theodore%20J.C.toc.pdf.

24. Ibid.

25. Ibid.

26. *Foreign Relations of the United States, 1969–76*, Telegram from the US Embassy, Georgetown, to the State Department, Washington, July 25, 1973.

27. *Foreign Relations of the United States, 1969–76*, Memorandum from the National Security Council, July 9, 1971.

28. Ibid.

29. Wikileaks, Cable from US Embassy, Georgetown to US Embassies in Barbados, Trinidad and Jamaica, July 19, 1973.

30. *Foreign Relations of the United States, 1969–76*, note 21, Spencer King (US Ambassador, Georgetown) to Henry Kissinger (Secretary of State, Washington), cable, July 25, 1973.

31. Ibid., July 24, 1973.

32. *Foreign Relations of the United States, 1969–76*, Spencer King's report on his visit with L. F. S. Burnham at his home, September 1, 1973.

33. Ibid.

34. Ibid.
35. 'Castro Speaks to Guyanese Mineworkers,' in Castro Speech Data Base, Latin American Network Information Centre (LANIC): Accessed at: http//www1.lanic.utexas.edu/project/castro/db/1973/19730903.html
36. *Guyana Chronicle*, January 6, 2013.
37. *Foreign Relations of the US, 1969–76, Vol. E-10*, Documents of the American Republics, 1969–72, Editorial Note.
38. Ibid.
39. *Foreign Relations of the United States, 1969–76, Volume E-11*, Memorandum of the Deputy Director of Plans, CIA, (Karamessines) to the President's Assistant for National Security Affairs (Kissinger), February 6, 1973.
40. Ibid.
41. See note 15.
42. See note 10 [Naipaul], 487–88
43. See note 15.

13.

'I am a Socialist; You are not a Socialist' – I
Burnham's Cooperative Socialism v Jagan's Marxism-Leninism

There is a tinge of irony in the title of Jagan's magnum opus, *The West on Trial* [1966]. While Jagan was trying the West, the West was trying him.

> – **Rashleigh Jackson (Foreign Minister of Guyana, 1978–90), email to Oscar Ramjeet, July 11, 2017**

I did not try to fool the United States Government or anybody. Perhaps it is just that I have an ability to concentrate on one objective at a time. In the early stages, my priority was to gain independence for Guyana, and I was against any activity or posture that tended to delay that objective. But I was always a Socialist, and I said so in a speech I made in 1955. [At the time he also stated very clearly that, unlike Jagan, he was not a Communist.]

> – **L. F. S. Burnham, the *New York Times*, May 25, 1976.**

'Grounding with his Brothers': Forbes with Fidel and two other belated Cuban 'comrades', Georgetown, August 1973

Comrade Forbes with Comrade Fidel in Havana, April 1975, when he was given Cuba's highest honour, the Jose Marti Award

Forbes Burnham with Comrade Zhou Enlai, Beijing, ca. 1975

Forbes Burnham with the North Korean dictator, Comrade Kim Il-Sung, Pyongyang, late 1970s

PART 1.
Stealing Jagan's Marxist Ideological Thunder

I.   Burnham's Road to Damascus Marxist Challenge to Jagan's Communist Purity: Undermining His Case for Adherence to Liberal Democracy

All his political life, Jagan believed that Marxism-Leninism, as practised in the Soviet Union, was the most perfect and humane system of governance ever devised by humankind. Strangely, by the mid-1970s, L. F. S. Burnham, too, was intimating (at times) that he was an adherent of some variant of Marxism-Leninism, although much vagueness and palpable incredulity pervaded his supposed conversion. However, Jagan now felt vindicated that his sacred beliefs, which Burnham had vilified routinely (to extraordinary advantage since his split from the People's Progressive Party [PPP] in early 1955), were winning. And on the twenty-fifth anniversary of the founding of the PPP, in 1975, Cheddi celebrated both his ideological implacability (despite its consigning him to the wilderness for nearly three decades), as well as its presumed scientific infallibility – creating great societies for the liberation of the working class, such as the Soviet Union, the 'People's Democracies' of Eastern Europe, and Castro's Cuba.

Jagan saw his prompt recognition of Castro's government (the first in the Hemisphere to do so) as the expression of 'genuine proletarian internationalism,' and a vindication of his ideological convictions, despite the dire consequences for him in the Cold War:

> Standing steadfast to principle, the PPP was the only party in the Caribbean which did not join the US Cold War bandwagon. It did not tack and turn and make deals with imperialism. It did not assume an opportunistic position even in the face of grave difficulties [a transparent allusion to Burnham]…The Yankee imperialists in the early 1960s attacked the PPP government because it did not join the wolf-pack in blockading Cuba. But time has vindicated our stand. We are proud that we played a role, however small, in bringing… socialism to Cuba. Today, when we see so many flocking to Cuba and embracing the Cuban Revolution and the great Cuban leader, Comrade Fidel Castro…we can proudly say that we were right; that we were pioneers…Above all, we were the first to propagate the ideology of Marxism-Leninism. Today, the erstwhile anti-communists have suddenly taken on this mantle. It is not without amusement that we note that policemen who not too long ago were instructed to seize Marxist books, such as Lenin's *State and Revolution*, in their raids on homes and to harass their PPP owners, are now exhorted to study Marxism-Leninism.[1]

But Burnham's belated radical transformation (if not affectation) did not mean that he was about to share power with Jagan, or that he was less inclined to rig the general elections (as he did in 1968 and, more blatantly, in 1973) to ensure that the PPP did not gain power again. On the contrary, it is conceivable that the exceptionally shrewd Forbes, ideologically nebulous and politically crafty from the inception of his career in the PPP in 1950, had calculatedly adopted elements of Cheddi's Marxism-Leninism primarily because of its basic tenet regarding 'the paramountcy of the party [the PNC]' over the government – the instrument for indefinite rule. This Leninist formula, the rationale of all the ruling communist parties, was the model naturally embedded in Cheddi's ideological precepts.

It is also plausible that Burnham's *volte-face* was devised to make it untenable that Jagan, the unreconstructed pro-Soviet communist, could espouse 'free and fair elections' with any more justification than him. As professed Marxists, irrespective of the variant or the challenge of their *bona fides*, 'bourgeois elections' could not be naturally sacrosanct to either of them, therefore hardly defensible. Jagan had, with conviction, extolled totalitarian regimes under communism as 'people's democracies,' having repudiated popular protests for liberal democratic reform in Hungary (1956) and Czechoslovakia (1968) as utterly 'bourgeois' and counter-revolutionary. 'Free and fair elections' were, indeed, repugnant to the Marxist politics of Jagan's foremost heroes – Lenin, Stalin, Khrushchev, Mao (until around 1966–67), Brezhnev, Castro, Mikhail Suslov (the theoretician of the CPSU), Rajani Palme Dutt (the theoretician of the CPGB), and Billy Strachan (his communist guru and confidant affiliated to the CPGB). But Burnham had astutely stolen Jagan's Marxist garb, while appearing to secure the approbation of Jagan's seemingly loyal communist friends in Cuba and the USSR. Yet, unlike Jagan, a certain nebulousness prevailed regarding Burnham's Marxist awakening, and he could never be tagged 'made in the USSR' or 'made in Cuba.' Jagan was irrevocably stamped with that abiding stain as far as the Americans were concerned.

Burnham had further boxed in Jagan into an ideological morass, however unwittingly, as the latter (the self-proclaimed pure Marxist) felt he, solely, had earned the moral and intellectual right to interpret and propagate the tenets of 'scientific socialism': Marxism-Leninism. Consequently, he felt legitimately empowered, by virtue of his unwavering fidelity to the creed since the late 1940s, to instruct the opportunistic, and ideologically tainted, latecomers – his erstwhile 'right-opportunist' allies in the original PPP inspired by the ambiguous Burnham – towards a modicum of theoretical understanding and (possibly) incremental validity as communists.

But, in effect, Burnham was cleverly neutralising Jagan's moral authority to impugn his electoral legitimacy, in addition to other widely known infringements such as the erosion of civil and political liberties. But by the Marxist-Leninist yardstick, these are 'bourgeois rights' – bogus freedoms – deemed superfluous because emanating from 'bourgeois democracy' under a tainted capitalist order. Moreover, how could a seasoned pro-Moscow communist like Jagan, and widely perceived as such, have a leg to stand on regarding 'bourgeois democracy' given his immersion in a Soviet frame of reference? How much legitimacy could Jagan garner in the West, in the context of the Cold War, irrespective of how far to the left Burnham chose to wander in the context of detente? In fact, Burnham had induced Jagan to concede that the imperialists, whose machinations were designed specifically to empower Burnham indefinitely while mortally wounding him, had, indeed, become their mutual enemy over whom they should both exert vigilance. Such was the power of yet another artfully contrived device by Burnham.

Jagan had been outsmarted yet again by his erstwhile comrade of the early 1950s. Burnham had succeeded in stealing Jagan's ideological thunder, however circumspect or downright suspicious many were of the former's belated identification with Marxism-Leninism. On April 13, 1975, while on a state visit to Cuba, Burnham received the highest award granted by the government of Cuba to heads of state: the José Martí National Order. It is conferred on leaders deemed to 'have distinguished themselves for their international solidarity in the struggle against imperialism, colonialism, neocolonialism and for their friendship with the Socialist Revolution of Cuba.' The citation to Burnham's government honoured its

> progressive and independent leadership…on the international sphere and its solidarity with Cuba's revolutionary process, its condemnation in the international forums of the policy of blockade followed in regard to our country; and its initiative of establishing diplomatic relations with Cuba by the Caribbean states are eloquent proof of the consistent nationalism and progressive position taken by Prime Minister Burnham. His friendship towards Cuba and his action in strengthening relations with our country are confirmed by his official visit to our country.[2]

II. Jagan Undeterred: The Proliferating Jargons of a True Believer

This must have stirred despair in one of the staunchest and unwavering allies of the Cuban Revolution from its first days: Cheddi Jagan. Yet a couple months after Burnham's big honour in Havana, Jagan attended the Conference of Communist Parties of Latin America and the Caribbean, in Havana, from June 9–13, 1975. It is most likely that Burnham's People's National Congress (PNC), never recognised as a communist party by the world communist movement led by the Soviet Union did not receive an invitation (as far as I know). This would have been a source of crucial reassurance to Cheddi because he now had only two countervailing claims in challenging Burnham's socialist momentum: his record of unsparing embrace of the Cuban Revolution, at immense personal cost – political suicide; and the longevity of his communist authenticity, predating his engagement with Burnham in the original PPP of the early 1950s, manifested in his founding of the Political Affairs Committee (PAC) and the *PAC Bulletin* in November 1946, guided by 'scientific socialism.'

Jagan felt vindicated by his communist moral ascendancy over the vague, opportunistic Marxist affectations of Burnham: he had earned the right to belong to this august meeting of communists, in Cuba. And in the aftermath of the recent victory of the Vietnamese people against his mortal enemy, American imperialism, he could see clearly now that the latter's days were numbered. Of this he spoke with unfaltering certainty and moral authority:

> Our meeting is taking place at a very important juncture in the
> history of human development. We Communists the world over can
> be particularly proud of the role we have played, the foundations we
> have laid and the sacrifices we have made.[3]

Jagan conceived his fidelity to communism as a mission for universal perfectibility, inseparable from, and integral to, his immediate struggle against imperialism in Guyana. His obligation to 'proletarian internationalism' encompassed solidarity with the advancement of communism throughout the world. His speeches and writings were saturated with examples of what he construed as positive manifestations of the struggle everywhere for 'peace, freedom and socialism.' This meant that setbacks provoked by imperialism, such as his own, could be taken in stride (even as a badge of honour): transitory yet inescapable in the noble task of eradicating the evils of capitalism and imperialism. Besides, he could also celebrate and appropriate the triumph of comrades elsewhere, while finding inspiration for his own meandering journey towards the communist utopia:

> Imperialism is in retreat and rent asunder by internal convulsions. In
> our own hemisphere, its aggressive policies and machinations have
> failed against the free territory of the Americas. Revolutionary Cuba
> stands as a bastion of socialist strength – a constant reminder that
> there is an alternative road leading to peace, freedom and socialism…
> In the face of a deepening crisis of capitalism, new developments are
> taking place in our continent…under the influence of the growing

strength of the world socialist [communist] system, at the heart of which is the mighty Soviet Union…The main enemy of the peoples of the Americas is US imperialism; it is the duty of all the Latin American Communist Parties to take the lead in uniting all the possible forces against imperialism; to isolate, weaken and destroy it.[4]

Yet for Jagan, visiting Havana in June 1975, just two months after his Cuban comrades had given Burnham their highest national award, the agony of perceived betrayal must have been most wounding. He was subverted by American imperialism in the early 1960s and removed from office in 1964 largely because of his solidarity with the Cuban Revolution, in breaking the American blockade. Moreover, Burnham had successfully pursued an anti-communist agenda – anti-Castroism specifically – in collaboration with Peter D'Aguiar's United Force (UF) and the Catholic Church (between 1962 and 1964), in winning support from the Americans and the CIA to sabotage the Jagan government. This was the context in which the British were pressured relentlessly by President Kennedy to change the electoral system to proportional representation to defeat Jagan in the general elections of December 1964. Yet the Cuban government awarded their most prestigious prize to Burnham. Only Jagan's incontestable faith in Marxism-Leninism could have sustained him – arguably, the equivalent of a fundamentalist religious belief in an infallible doctrine bearing the truth. Of course, 'the truth **will** set you free!' This quote was placed above the editorials in the *Mirror*, the PPP newspaper.

Jagan, the idealist, could not grasp the political adroitness and pragmatism of Comrade Fidel – the primacy of *realpolitik* in his relationship with Burnham. Yet although the Cuban comrades had fallen for Burnham, Cheddi was not deterred: he had the pedigree, having been in sole possession of the Marxist-Leninist tenets for three decades, at immense personal cost and that of his largely unsuspecting, predominantly Indian, followers. He was no Johnny-come-lately, like Burnham and the vacillating PNC; his Marxism is deeply rooted (in the PAC of 1946), predating even Comrade Fidel's embrace of the creed. Amidst genuine communists representing the authentic communist parties of Latin America and the Caribbean (including his PPP), Jagan sought to convey the spuriousness of Burnham's belated espousal of Marxism-Leninism. He expressed reservations regarding both his nationalisation initiative and the premises on which his diplomatic recognition of Cuba was based. It is somewhat amusing that Jagan was also berating the Burnham regime for their subversion of what Marxists, including the Cubans, routinely disparaged as 'bourgeois rights and freedoms':

> It is important not just to look at the establishment of diplomatic and other relations with the socialist states and the expansion of the public sector by some nationalisation. Equally important is

consideration of the nature of the state. In Guyana, for instance, nationalisation is leading to state and bureaucratic capitalism, coupled with corruption, extravagance, racial and political discrimination and without basic democracy at the trade union, industrial and central and local government level. A minority regime is rapidly expanding the military-bureaucratic apparatus, not so much to defend national sovereignty and territorial integrity, as to hold down the vast majority of the people and to deny them their fundamental rights.

Cheddi was really telling his Cuban comrades that they had given their highest national award to a man whose Marxist-Leninist credentials were not only dubious, but also that their honoured recipient was flagrantly trampling on the mandate of the Guyanese people, perverting the electoral process to perpetuate his rule indefinitely. How ironic, therefore, that Jagan was arguing for the sanctity of civil and political freedoms at a forum – and in a country – where such 'bourgeois' rights were abrogated as superfluous to a deeper, more comprehensive, proletarian or people's democracy. He then offered an interesting explanation why the Burnham regime had given diplomatic recognition to the Cuban Revolution. He did not confer any agency on Burnham himself, even if actuated by political expediency. Jagan construed it as an initiative sanctioned by the imperialists, a flexibility precipitated by recurring crises and their declining economic stature. They were therefore compelled to abandon 'confrontation,' and adopt 'engagement,' with the 'socialist world' – thus adumbrating 'peaceful co-existence and detente' (culminating in the Helsinki Accords of 1975). He could not have conceived that the latter would contribute towards the unravelling of the entire Soviet system in fifteen years.

Jagan argued in June 1975:

> The recent recognition of Cuba by Guyana and other Caribbean states which previously had a hostile attitude to the Cuban Revolution must also be seen against the changed position of US imperialism to the question of peaceful co-existence in general with the socialist world. As regards Cuba, political considerations weighed more heavily than purely economic considerations for the US ruling class, and thus there were contradictions and vacillations with respect to the lifting of the US blockade on Cuba. In the Caribbean, however, because of the small size of the CARICOM market (about 4½ million) US subsidiaries...and the local bourgeoisie wanted the door opened to the expanding Cuban market. In such a situation, and in the face of popular internal pressure [alluding to the role of his PPP], the recognition of Cuba became a political necessity.[5]

Yet Jagan could not get it out of his mind that the Cubans were revelling in their auspicious condition that the governments of Guyana, Trinidad, Barbados, and Jamaica had accorded diplomatic recognition to their country, despite the US blockade remaining water-tight with no prospect of its revocation anytime soon. And Castro was not likely to split hairs whether the leaders of these countries were actuated primarily by the economic imperatives of US subsidiaries in the region or by the emerging accommodative political spirit of détente, on one hand, or by the objectives of the Non-Aligned Movement, on the other. Burnham was certainly anchoring his overtures to Cuba within the latter, whereas Jagan sought to debunk the legitimacy of the concept of non-alignment because (to him) the Soviet Union harboured no imperialistic motives. Soviet obligation to proletarian internationalism could not be equated with American imperialism driven by its implacable hegemonic obsessions. Hence there could be no conceivable rationale for any political distancing from the USSR. Castro himself was pragmatic enough, although heavily dependent on the Soviets for survival: he, Burnham, and Michael Manley were all proponents of the non-aligned movement.

Yet though recalcitrant, Jagan was being nudged towards a *modus vivendi* with Burnham, arguably because his Cuban and Soviet comrades were motivated by *realpolitik* with respect to their perceived self-interest in the Western Hemisphere. Therefore, they were inclined to be less judgemental of the Marxist *bona fides* of Burnham's 'cooperative socialist' programme of transformation in Guyana. Moreover, the fact that he was hitherto defined as America's man in the 1960s must, indeed, have rendered him a big catch in the eyes of many of Cheddi's communist friends.

Understandably, the rapprochement between Burnham and Castro had left Jagan in a spin. This was evident in his convoluted response (in Havana, to Latin American communists in June 1975) regarding Burnham's overtures to Cuba. Jagan remarked that his communist party, the PPP, was the 'vanguard,' so while he was offering 'critical support' to Burnham's PNC, he could not countenance any measure designed to liquidate, or amalgamate, his PPP by the belated 'revolutionary nationalism' of 'petty-bourgeois regimes' like Burnham's. Besides, he could give no credence to the 'cooperative socialism' of the PNC. It is highly likely that Jagan's conundrum was precipitated by instructions primarily from his Cuban comrades to forge a working relationship with Burnham, following the latter's initiatives towards the left, his anti-imperialist stance:

> …revolutionary nationalism [an allusion to the PNC] is taking steps against imperialism. Whatever the motivation for those steps, they must be regarded as positive; they help to weaken imperialism and must be supported. Such support, however, must be critical support, to ensure that the Communist Party [his PPP] plays its vanguard role, and is able continuously to exert pressure so as to influence the course of future development. It must be the duty of all fraternal communist parties to ensure that basic democracy is preserved and that no steps are taken…to liquidate the Party.[6]

Jagan was suggesting that the PNC could well have as its primary objective the elimination of his PPP, already effectively marginalised by Burnham's politics of chronic electoral fraud. Therefore, he was exhorting his Latin American and Caribbean communist comrades (from marginal parties invariably), contrary to their fundamental beliefs, to embrace the upholding of 'bourgeois democracy' in Guyana. Liberal democracy is rooted in the notion of the people's will being expressed through a plurality of parties, often with diverse philosophies, in periodic free elections. The fraternal communist parties Jagan was beseeching for solidarity, on the other hand, were disinclined to confer legitimacy on such elections even if they did participate in them. And even if any should accede to power – never attained through a transparently democratic electoral process – their first act was to suppress the articulation of the popular will. It is absurd, then, that Jagan could seriously have expected Comrade Fidel and his Hemispheric guests 'to ensure that basic democracy is preserved.'

However, Jagan did imply that there was a sliver of hope that Burnham's PNC, pressed relentlessly by his PPP, could complete 'the national anti-imperialist revolution' – a theoretical fantasy – the prelude to the building of the socialist/communist society. Presumably, the latter could not be achieved without his PPP, the 'vanguard,' as he harboured grave reservations about Forbes Burnham credentials as a Marxist-Leninist. Permeating the following quote from Jagan's speech in Havana were clear signs that he had little trust in Burnham, and that 'critical support' was an empty slogan to placate the Cubans and the Soviets:

> Certain anti-imperialist steps have been taken [such as nationalisation of the bauxite company and the diplomatic recognition of Cuba] which we have helped to bring about. We see as our duty constantly to apply mass pressure for the completion of the anti-imperialist national revolution. Unfortunately, demagogy in the form of 'cooperative socialism,' namely that the false idea that socialism will be achieved by means of cooperatives, offers the excuse for not dismantling the imperialist socio-economic structure. It also poses the danger of developing a new form of capitalism.[7]

Jagan was pushing Burnham relentlessly to move further to the left, to nationalise virtually the whole economy, certainly every business that was foreign-owned. Foreign capital was inherently evil. The bulk of the bauxite industry, owned by the Canadian DEMBA, was nationalised in 1971, and Jagan continued to apply intense pressure on the Burnham regime that culminated in the nationalisation of the British-owned Booker, in 1976. By the late 1970s, 80 per cent of the economy of Guyana was in the hands of the state that was essentially Burnham's for life. And by claiming to be guided by Marxism-Leninism (Jagan's mantras), he was able to strengthen his dictatorship to the point where his PNC exerted 'paramountcy' over the state: the government was the executive arm of the party, and in 1978 Burnham rigged a referendum massively to introduce a new constitution. Burnham had appropriated the veneer of Jagan's communism to subvert civil and political rights, the independent institutions of the state, such as the judiciary and the elections commission, and had consigned Jagan's PPP further to the periphery of Guyanese politics. Burnham had effected a potent means of rationalising his disregard of 'bourgeois democracy.'

Jagan became marooned in a morass of indigestible Marxist jargon, while even his communist friends of many decades were increasingly receptive to Burnham's socialist revolution, something with which they could live. Yet Jagan's 'critical support' for the regime notwithstanding, he could discern barely anything admirable in Burnham's belated Marxist-Leninist programme for radical transformation. He would rail against Burnham's historical anti-Castroism and anti-communism, his collaboration with the CIA that had scuppered Cheddi, in addition to his embrace of 'state capitalism' and his refusal to join the communist camp (opting for non-alignment) as indicative of his fundamental aversion to communism. Yet Burnham's supremacy over the political process was so unmitigated that Jagan became a mere purveyor of a 'pure' Marxism from the sidelines, powerless to reverse the authoritarianism of the PNC and the PNC-controlled state.

Jagan became adept at devising complex ad hoc Marxist interpretations of the Burnham state, virtually the owner of the whole economy, as Jagan had advocated all along. Meanwhile, the country became a basket case, thousands (irrespective of race) migrating every year to greener pastures, ironically, the capitalist West (Canada, US, UK), to escape the escalating disintegration of the economy and the impoverishment of its people. Yet Jagan could still envision possibilities for a patriotic alliance of all anti-imperialist forces to defeat the Americans comprehensively, while building the socialist/communist utopia he craved. It was as if his possession of the sacred Marxist truth would inevitably take him to the mountain-top; whatever setbacks were encountered en route, it would test the mettle of true communists whose time was bound to come by virtue of unremitting class struggle.

Jagan would seize every opportunity to expose the fraudulent Marxism-Leninism of the PNC, while exuding unbridled confidence in the new order that was destined to succeed in Guyana. He was certain of that because 'scientific socialism,' communism, could not be conquered, the 'balance of forces' continues to tilt in favour of socialism. But, in the short run, they would probably have to endure the vacillations and ideological meanderings of Forbes Burnham. In reality, Jagan would probably have to live with Burnham's flip-flops while ensuring that he never desists from pursuit of the anti-imperialist struggle.

Jagan's unfaltering devotion to 'scientific socialism' endowed him with the moral superiority (as he saw it) to engage and illuminate Burnham's hitherto misguided African Guyanese working-class supporters, detracted by the PNC's anti-communism and tainted by their collaboration with imperialism. But the infallible theory, founded on scientific truth, would have its day.

III. Boxed into a Quagmire: Jagan's So-Called 'Critical Support' for Burnham

Several excerpts cited below are from Jagan's address to mark the twenty-fifth anniversary of the PPP, in August 1975. These emphasise that although Burnham was asserting the 'paramountcy' of the PNC over the government based on his supposed new-found Marxist beliefs, Jagan was sanguine that what he stood for, unfalteringly for thirty years, was winning all over the world. Buoyed by the flight of the American imperialists from Vietnam in April 1975, he boasted that Guyana could, indeed, become a 'second Cuba.'

> For 25 years they [the African supporters of the PNC] have been hearing from the PPP that only socialism holds the answer. And no doubt they have been influenced by the positive gains made by the working people in the Soviet Union, Cuba and other socialist states. They may know little or nothing about the theory and practice of Marxism-Leninism (it cannot be otherwise in view of the previous outright anti-Marxist, anti-Communist stand of the PNC). But they realise that in more than one-third of the world where that philosophy is embraced and scientific socialist ideas have been put into practice, an end has been brought to unemployment, backwardness, hunger and misery...

> ...our main enemy was Anglo-American imperialism; and anti-communism, anti-Sovietism and anti-Castroism were used against us. **The PPP government was subverted in 1962-64 because of the hysteria created [by the PNC and the UF] that an independent Guyana, under the PPP, would become a second Cuba...**

> The new development...can initiate a process which even the PNC will find difficult in halting. It opens the door for a dialogue with the PNC rank and file [African Guyanese]. It must be our task to raise their understanding and consciousness of the theory and practice of scientific socialism, of Marxism-Leninism...

> [Today] **the possibilities exist for a real breakthrough in Guyana, of really going rapidly through anti-imperialism to socialism. The PPP, the majority party, is constantly exerting pressure in this direction. And conditions are very favourable, better perhaps than any country in Asia, Africa and Latin America, that Guyana has the possibilities of becoming a second Cuba** [emphasis added].

But let us not be lulled into a false sense of security because of this positive possibility. We must be on guard. We must remember that with the intensification of the international class struggle, and the balance of forces shifting in favour of socialism [communism], imperialism is becoming more flexible and cunning: it is devising new tactics and strategies. As Marxism-Leninism grips the masses, imperialism will try to distort and derail it.[8]

Then this note on the PNC, which suggests Jagan's grudging ambivalence regarding the 'socialist' claims of a few in that party, including Burnham. Jagan observed: 'The PNC leader and a few socialists in the PNC hierarchy (they can be counted on the fingers of one hand) are therefore forced to attack capitalism and advocate socialism and Marxism-Leninism…We are glad that the PNC has been forced to swallow its anti-communist, anti-Cuba sentiments and to advocate Marxism-Leninism.'[9] With the Soviet and Cuban comrades apparently concurring that Burnham was, indeed, disengaging from the American camp in the Cold War – to non-alignment – Jagan felt constrained to intimate that he was not averse to giving Burnham the benefit of the doubt: to consider a means of co-operating with him however unpalatable the proposition.

Ralph Ramkarran has noted that Cheddi was forced into granting 'critical support' to the PNC regime by his Cuban comrades, who were, by the mid-1970s, enamoured of Burnham, who initiated the process in the region of according diplomatic recognition to Cuba, in 1972. Therefore, not only had Burnham boxed Cheddi into the quagmire, but the Cuban and Soviet comrades also had left him no room for manoeuvre against Burnham. This was the context in which Jagan decided to give the fraudulent government 'critical support.' His definition of this nebulous concept, in his PPP's twenty-fifth anniversary address on August 3, 1975, is almost apologetic – as if it were a reluctant concession to an alien prompting.

This was a measure forced on Jagan by Burnham's supposed adoption of Marxism-Leninism, with the PPP changing their stance from 'non-cooperation and civil disobedience' (precipitated by the blatantly rigged elections of 1973) to 'critical support.' At the same time, Jagan was warning his communist friends in 'the fraternal parties' to be circumspect about Burnham's apparent change of heart, while reminding them that he, on the other hand, was their steadfast 'comrade,' in season and out of season, at immense personal cost:

> Critical support does not mean unconditional support. It means just what it says – giving support for any progressive measure, opposing any reactionary moves, and criticising all shortcomings…
>
> The PNC is carrying out insidious propaganda that there is no difference between the PPP and the PNC. No doubt this is being done to justify for itself the vanguard role for establishing a minority authoritarian one-party dictatorship.

> We must maintain our identity as the PPP. We must vigorously fight
> against any or all attempts to liquidate our Party.[10]

Yet, formidable though the PNC's programme for undermining, if not liquidating, Jagan's PPP, he could still hold on to some sustaining crumbs. Other political leaders might have succumbed to the PNC's relentless campaign to destroy the PPP, but Cheddi was a true believer in Marxism-Leninism. Nothing did faze this unrelenting warrior in the class struggle. He had few, if any, parallels in terms of ideological certainty and political resilience anywhere. His mission (lasting fifty years) was imbued with the intensity of a religious zealot. It is noteworthy that the Soviets did not send a delegate to the PPP's twenty-fifth anniversary conference in August 1975, but the Central Committee of the CPSU dispatched a message that recognised the PPP's contribution to the international communist movement. It read, in part: 'The People's Progressive Party has gained the respect of the fraternal [communist] parties by its devotion to the principles of Marxism-Leninism and proletarian internationalism, by its allegiance to consolidating unity and cohesion of the international communist movement and of all anti-imperialist forces.' The CPSU also thanked the PPP 'for the uniting of all anti-imperialist forces of the nation...for the cause of peace, democracy and socialism.' The latter was an unmistakable allusion to their rendering 'critical support' to Burnham's PNC, a step that was probably taken as a result of forthright prompting from the Cubans and the Soviets.[11]

Although the Cubans did attend the PPP's twenty-fifth anniversary conference, the absence of the Soviets must have been very disappointing, even painful, to Cheddi. But he could not afford to alienate his spiritual leaders (and partial financial backers); he was therefore sedulous in ensuring that he said nothing to jeopardise whatever goodwill the CPSU still harboured for him. They would have recognised the longevity of his devotion to Soviet communism, at immense cost to himself, his country, and those who gave him unconditional support, primarily Indo-Guyanese.

And, to underscore that his PPP was still the 'vanguard' party in Guyana, Burnham's assertion of the 'paramountcy' of his PNC notwithstanding, Jagan argued that if the latter were genuinely socialist, they should concentrate on eliminating fundamental 'evils' still persisting. They would undertake, first and foremost, root-and-branch nationalisation of most of those sectors of the economy remaining in private ownership. The exploiters had to be erased from the Guyanese economy, principal among them being Booker – the cornerstone of his 'bitter sugar' crusade commencing thirty years before.

IV. American Response to Burnham's Solidarity with Castro after His Receipt of the José Martí Award in Havana (1975)

In fact, after Burnham received the José Martí Award in April 1975, it was remarked by the American Embassy in Georgetown that Burnham and several of the PNC leaders were assuming a distinctly radical, Marxist position. They were certain that Burnham was on the verge of creating a one-party state, following the example of Castro's Cuba. In a telegram dated June 2, 1975, the embassy informed the State Department of the strengthening of links between Burnham and Castro:

> Prime Minister Burnham's recent visit to Havana, the first by a Western Hemisphere chief of government other than Chile's Allende since Castro's accession to power [in 1959], illustrated the growing ties between Guyana and Cuba. Cuba has now probably become the Western Hemisphere nation with which top political leaders of the Government of Guyana as well as some top technocrats feel most closely politically attuned. PM Burnham and other top PNC leaders have since his return from Cuba [April 1975] spoken increasingly of Guyana's commitment to orthodox socialism [Marxism-Leninism]. PNC Chairman and Deputy Prime Minister Ptolemy Reid and Labour Minister Carrington have defended dictatorship of the proletariat as appropriate for Guyana, and they and Burnham have vehemently denounced the concept of free enterprise....[12]

The embassy was correct in their evaluation that Castro's recognition of Burnham as a genuine ally, crucial to granting legitimacy to the Cuban Revolution in the region, was the basis of their honouring him as an authentic socialist, even if doubts lingered about his Marxism-Leninism. And it is arguable that after the Cubans gave Burnham the José Martí Award, he became more confident in his use of socialist rhetoric; indeed, that he seemed to feel that he had the mantle of communist authority in the region to proceed towards a virtual one-party state. It was believed, too, that the meeting of communist parties of Latin America, in Havana in June 1975 (attended by Jagan but not Burnham), also endorsed support for 'progressive' parties in the region even if they were not communist or Marxist. The following is from the US Embassy's telegram of June 2, 1975:

> Cuba has already begun to be spoken of as a model for Guyana... Cuba is Caribbean, widely perceived locally as successful, contains a substantial African element, and is ideologically attractive to the professed radical Socialists who are leading Guyana...The government-owned press, while denouncing the training of Guyanese labour leaders in the West (echoing Burnham and other PNC figures) has editorialised in favour of such training in Cuba.

> Since Guyana is moving toward a one-party state and a de facto self-proclaimed dictatorship of the proletariat, and since subordination of the Government of Guyana [GOG] to the PNC is progressing rapidly, this developing tie with the PNC (which now proclaims a doctrinaire Socialist ideology) could be highly significant in the context of GOG-Cuba bilateral relations.[13]

Burnham was emboldened by the fact that he had gained the untrammelled respect of Castro by virtue of his being awarded the highest national honour of Cuba. And, as the Americans believed, possessed of the unstinted affirmation of Fidel (by the mid-1970s), Burnham felt he had the political capital to assume that the 'paramountcy' of his party, the PNC, was no less legitimate than the paramountcy of the Communist Party of Cuba. But Castro was Jagan's hero *par excellence*, for whom he had sacrificed the future of his country after 1960 – and lost. I am arguing, therefore, that in pursuit of his transcendent communist creed, which was a quasi-religious calling, Jagan was reckless with the long-term security of his supporters (almost exclusively Indian). Yet all his supporters could see was a Gandhi-like quality in his perceived sincerity of purpose, incorruptibility and his unfaltering crusade against the White 'sugar gods': Booker!

Moreover, as Ralph Ramkarran argues, the Cubans were instrumental, possibly in early 1975, in persuading the deputy general secretary of the PPP (Jagan's deputy), Ranji Chandisingh, to defect to Burnham's PNC:

> After years of hostility to the Cuban Revolution, the Burnham Government opened diplomatic relations with Cuba in 1972. Close political relations quickly developed as the Guyana Government moved to the left. It appears as if the Cuban analysis of Guyana went something like this. The PNC is a friend of Cuba and is on the left. It is entrenched in power, which it will not share. Cuba's fraternal party, the PPP, should therefore support the PNC and strengthen its capacity to resist imperialism.
>
> The PPP's fundamental objection to this analysis was that the PNC held power undemocratically, and socialism cannot be built without democracy. Also, unconditional support for the PNC Government would have undermined their own support. The Cubans' disapproval of the PPP's posture was evidenced by Castro's visit to Guyana in [September] 1973, just after the egregious rigging of the [July] 1973 elections in which the PNC gave itself a two-thirds majority, and the brutal killing of three [two?] PPP supporters and not meeting with Cheddi Jagan.[14]

In any case, Jagan should have known that Castro, an ardent communist like himself, had no empathy whatsoever with 'bourgeois democratic' rights, such as free elections, freedom of expression, a free media, and the like. Likewise, Jagan ought to have appreciated that many in capitalist societies could not empathise with him when, as a communist who admired Castro and Brezhnev, he sought to indict Burnham for perpetrating a crooked electoral process. Moreover, Jagan should have known that by the early 1970s, Castro was no longer a protagonist of violent revolution (espoused by the late Che Guevara) as an effective instrument for radical transformation in Latin America. The failure of various guerrilla movements, in addition to 'Soviet pressure,' had impelled him to be more accommodative of non-communist parties or governments in the hemisphere. Cheddi was a doctrinaire communist idealist; Fidel was a crafty communist statesman (more like Burnham), now guided by 'flexibility and pragmatic calculation,' and inclined to promote lucrative commercial deals 'without regard to ideology.'

The following excerpt from a CIA document, dated November 1, 1974, on 'the status of Cuban subversion in Latin America,' is revealing:

> Castro's shift from violent to more conventional methods in recent years reflects a fundamental shift in his view of Cuba's role in the hemisphere. He now collaborates with governments and groups that conform to his loose definition of 'patriotic and independent,' having withdrawn from his previously intimate relations with the revolutionary factions of the 1960s. Castro is not likely to endanger the gains he has made in the region for the sake of any marginal group…Subsequent efforts to extend Cuban influence through more conventional means succeeded dramatically, and a significant change in Castro's view of his role in the region became apparent…
>
> By the early 1970s he…[was keen to embrace] 'patriotic' regimes 'independent of the US'…[For instance], **as bilateral ties with the Burnham government in Guyana have expanded, Castro's previously close ties with Cheddi Jagan's Marxist Opposition Party have suffered**; and when Cuba and Panama renewed relations in August [1974], Havana did not even notify the local Communist Party. There is no evidence of Cuban meddling in the internal affairs of Barbados, Jamaica and Trinidad and Tobago, the remaining countries in the region that have official ties with Havana [emphasis added].[15]

Castro, motivated now primarily by *realpolitik*, could not countenance any obligatory solidarity with Jagan over Burnham (already ten years in power with no probability of his being unseated), despite the former's devotion to Marxism-Leninism or, conceivably more persuasively, his fatal loyalty to the Cuban Revolution – the first leader in the hemisphere (British Guiana) risking all by embracing Comrade Fidel against the Americans. He was shafted by Anglo-American imperialism primarily because of his declared admiration for Fidel and the Cuban Revolution. But the CIA stressed that Castro, by the early 1970s, was no longer fomenting revolution in the Hemisphere; his focus was on consolidating the Revolution:

> At 48 [in 1974], Fidel is no longer the romantic revolutionary that he was during his early years in power [from 1959, aged 32]. Instead he has increasingly demonstrated a desire to find compromise solutions for Cuba's problems. Today ... preoccupied with domestic development priorities and the institutionalisation of the revolution, he appears to have little interest in quixotic policies or personalities at home or abroad.[16]

The CIA was correct: Fidel had grown up. The same could not be said of the irrepressibly 'romantic' and 'quixotic' fifty-six-year-old Cheddi, eight years Fidel's senior.

V. The Defection of Ranji Chandisingh (Jagan's Marxist Theoretician and Foremost Confidant) to Burnham's PNC and Their Initiatives towards the Non-Aligned Movement

The weakening of Fidel's 'comradeship' with Jagan, superseded by his strategic fraternal alliance with Burnham (now firmly entrenched in power, though fraudulently), boosted the latter's reputation in the Non-Aligned Movement. This was enhanced by the fact that Jagan's trusted deputy, Ranji Chandisingh, his Marxist theoretician, was persuaded to abandon his stunted habitat in the PPP for Burnham's greener pastures, at the behest of the Communist Party of Cuba. Interestingly, when Ranji defected to the PNC in 1976, he was made the director of studies of Burnham's ideological school, the Cuffy Ideological Institute. Therefore, the lingering reservations regarding the authenticity of Burnham's adoption of Marxism-Leninism notwithstanding, the jumping of ship by Ranji, the most learned communist in the PPP (possibly its last intellectual with gravitas), did confer some Marxist legitimacy on Burnham. At the same time, Burnham was in pursuit of a significant profile within the Non-Aligned Movement,

Comrade Ranji Chandisingh (1930–2009), the communist theoretician of Jagan's PPP for 18 years. He defected to Burnham's PNC in 1976, allegedly at the prompting of the Cuban leadership

and ideological proximity to Castro (if not convergence), paradoxically, was conducive to his more exalted goal. As the US Embassy in Georgetown had observed, the Guyanese or even the wider Caribbean political space was inadequate for the capacious ambition of Burnham. The flight of Ranji from the PPP was probably the bitterest blow Cheddi ever faced, in a career that was replete with periodic defections of virtually all his closest and brightest colleagues, invariably on some ideological premise. This really did expose the rudderlessness and futility of Jagan's crusade for communism, mired in a sterile assumption of a Marxist purity that Castro, clearly, had dismissed as peripheral to his productive pragmatism in the region.

Ranji was a communist steeped in Marxist-Leninist theory, cerebral by temperament and utterly devoted to the Soviet Union as the beacon of the perfect society in the making. But by early 1975, it was becoming clear that Ranji was drifting away from the PPP, so it was hardly surprising when he resigned his position as assistant general-secretary of the PPP shortly thereafter. Ranji had become estranged from the PPP, and it was widely known that he was on the verge of defecting to Burnham's PNC at the prompting of the Cuban comrades. It must have been precipitated also by the austerity he endured, for ten years, because of his immersion in Jagan's static politics on the periphery.

The last issue of *Thunder* (the theoretical journal of the PPP) in which Ranji is cited as editor (April–August 1975), carried Cheddi's speech in Havana to Latin American communists in early June 1975. It is significant that this issue also carried the text of a lecture Ranji delivered at Freedom House to PPP members. It is titled 'Socialism and Democracy,' but there is no indication when he gave the talk. Therefore, it is likely that the article was published to embarrass him, an impending renegade, as it is a searing critique of Burnham's 'cooperative socialism.'

Ranji had rejected the PNC's doctrine of cooperative socialism as the principal instrument for socialist transformation, supposedly the prelude to a communist society in Guyana. While welcoming the PNC's belated purported eagerness to be guided by Marxism-Leninism in this process, he could not affirm their 'socialist' project. The PPP, on the other hand, was unremitting in their pursuit of 'scientific socialism,' inspired by the Soviet Union, the pioneering and most developed socialist society. The great Soviet example embodied 'socialist democracy' – 'the dictatorship of the proletariat,' as opposed to the spurious bourgeois democracy of the West. All the Soviet peoples, encompassing the various nationalities, were empowered to engage in the governance of the workers' state. Ranji, arguably the foremost theoretician of Marxism-Leninism in Guyana, was not only addressing his comrades at Freedom House, but he was also offering the PNC's novices a masterclass in authentic socialist democracy towards the communist utopia:

> Marxists are justified in saying that the dictatorship of the proletariat is much more democratic than bourgeois democracy. The former extends democracy and freedom for the many, while in the latter, democracy is enjoyed by the few.
>
> The basis of bourgeois freedom is private ownership of property in the means of production, distribution and exchange. Working class rule does not destroy 'freedom.' It only destroys bourgeois freedom to own and exploit. It extends freedom for the masses, who now own the means of production, distribution and exchange. They own and run the press, radio and other media. They plan the economy in their own interest and enjoy **concrete** freedoms – which go beyond the *formal* ones of bourgeois democracy – such as full employment, health, education, leisure, equality of women and nationalities... Socialist democracy is a qualitatively higher type of democracy. The whole aim of socialist democracy is to effect the greatest participation of the people in the administration of the state and in public affairs. And this is, in fact, what is being brought about to an even greater degree in the Soviet Union.[17]

Ranji (like Cheddi), a staunch pro-Moscow communist, was stating nothing new; it was the standard Marxist-Leninist rebuttal of the liberal democratic critique of the Soviet system: that the totalitarianism or, at best, the authoritarianism of the rule of the CPSU could, by no measure, be equated with a genuine articulation of the will of the people; that periodic elections, deemed free and fair, and contested by a plurality of political parties is a more accurate reflection of it; that a free press and other media, in addition to free speech, are indispensable to the expression of diverse opinions and the shaping of official policy, fundamental to democracy; and that state ownership of most of the economy did not automatically translate into ownership by the people, the assumed pivot of the superior 'socialist democracy.' Equally robust was the charge that the Communist Party did not tolerate internal democracy or the free will of its members, as the concept of 'democratic centralism' was a means of stifling internal dissent while aggregating and enforcing whatever the coterie of communist leaders in the Politburo determined was good for the people. The sacred notion of the 'dictatorship of the proletariat,' therefore, was really a dictatorship over the working class and a stifling of the imagination and creativity of everyone.

Yet, ironically, Ranji and his mentors in the CPGB, including his and Cheddi's revered comrade, the Jamaican-born communist, Billy Strachan, conscientiously endorsed the upholding of so-called bourgeois freedoms in capitalist societies. Cheddi, for instance, never ceased protesting that these bourgeois freedoms were being abrogated by the Burnham dictatorship, and as noted earlier, he was entreating his communist comrades in Latin America, including the Cubans (no defender of bourgeois freedoms), for their solidarity in retrieving such rights in Guyana. It was a bizarre proposition, but it was rooted in the arrogant assumption that communism was for the ultimate good of humankind; that it was inevitable by the laws of the evolution of society; and that by usurping the sole right to chart the future of the working class, the communist party was endowed with a special entitlement. It was preposterous that bourgeois democracy should be defended to hasten the socialist revolution that was committed to the abrogation of such rights.

Communists wish to eat their cake and have it! Ranji explains why bourgeois freedoms, paradoxically, were sacrosanct to the communist agenda in non-communist states:

> It may appear that the working people and their party [the communist party] are not concerned with the form of democracy or the form of rule in a bourgeois state. This is not the case. **We have a great interest in the form of the bourgeois state, and struggle to defend bourgeois democratic rights from erosion by the bourgeoisie and their agents themselves. The working class has better opportunities for organising and spreading its ideology** [Marxism-Leninism] **in a state with bourgeois freedoms than in a fascist or bourgeois military dictatorship. So, it is vital to struggle to preserve and extend even those formal rights** [emphasis added].

> The difference between liberals and Marxists in this respect is that liberals see in bourgeois democracy the essence of 'pure democracy,' while Marxists seek to utilise bourgeois democratic rights to organise and mobilise the working people for winning people's power, and on this basis building genuine people's democracy and socialist democracy, that is the transformation of democracy for a few into democracy for the masses.[18]

Ranji stressed the fraudulence of the mandate of the PNC to govern. He was unequivocal:

> One of the most notorious and glaring features of Guyanese society in recent years is the heavy rigging of elections, from the 1968 general elections, culminating in the army intervention of the July 16, 1973, elections. The same applies to the local government elections of 1970, and the significant postponement of fresh elections when they were due to be held…This means that the will of the masses was systematically thwarted at all levels of representative government…The military-bureaucratic state machine [was used] to deny the masses of working people a representative government of their choice. In essence, we see a minority regime manoeuvring

and utilising certain aspects of socialist phraseology and concepts to serve ends that are diametrically opposite to the development of real people's democracy and socialism.[19]

In other words, Ranji was saying that an illegitimate government, having usurped Marxist tenets to sustain dictatorial rule, was not likely to hold free and fair elections anytime soon.

He also sought to unmask the shallowness of the PNC's 'cooperative socialism' and its sudden embrace of Marxism-Leninism. Only the PPP, having absorbed the legacy of the Great October Socialist Revolution, could legitimately bear the mantle of 'scientific socialism' or Marxism-Leninism. The PNC was not a party genuinely committed to the liberation of the working class. I quote Ranji at length because his conception of the socialist/communist endeavour was at the heart of Jagan's mission. Ranji, more than any other member of the PPP, articulated Cheddi's vision of Marxism-Leninism; he had no more loyal, and learned, exponent of communism in his political career up to the mid-1970s and beyond:

> Political power may be said to be in the hands of a petty-bourgeois nationalist intelligentsia and bureaucratic capitalist elite. And they are bent on diverting effective power away from the working people, of preventing power from falling into the working people's hands. The use of petty bourgeois socialist slogans and concepts can be seen in this context...
>
> Only a party guided by Marxism-Leninism can be effective in building socialism...What is the PNC's ideology? We are told it is co-operativism or 'cooperative socialism.' It is true that certain PNC leaders are now making references to Marx, Engels and Lenin. Naturally, we would like to hope that they would really get down to taking Marxism-Leninism and interpreting it correctly, and more so, applying its principles in practice.
>
> But, for the moment, **we can only observe that 'cooperative socialism' is an undiluted fraud being perpetrated on the people who take it seriously.** This cannot but complicate matters ideologically for those sections of the working class who follow the PNC in arriving at a proper understanding of their historic mission in society [emphasis added].
>
> At best, we can say that the PNC's idea of socialism is that of a petty-bourgeois conception, a non-class approach that embraces all classes – including the capitalists and bureaucratic capitalists. The whole thing is shrouded in vagueness and ambiguity...The PNC's hurried dash to cash in on socialism and even Marxism-Leninism is to be welcomed. At the same time, we must draw attention to its inconsistencies, to the eclectic manner of picking up bits and pieces of Marx and Lenin and tying them in a pepperpot mixture to justify non-Marxist and even anti-Marxist policies.[20]

As I noted earlier, I do not know precisely when Chandisingh gave this lecture at Freedom House, but it was probably early 1975, so the question of enticing senior PPP members over to the PNC was already being pursued, arguably with the collusion of the Cubans, as two prominent PPP members have suggested: Ralph Ramkarran and Odeen Ishmael. Chandisingh wanted socialists in Guyana to emulate Fidel's *modus operandi* towards the socialist revolution, yet he was not writing off the PNC. He believed that the real socialists in that party could, indeed, guide Guyanese to the promised land of communism a la Fidel. And there is even the suggestion that the PNC could get there on its own. Therefore, by implication, you either remained out in the cold, shut out from power indefinitely (like the PPP), or you bite the bullet and join them:

> Instructive in this respect is the example of revolutionary Cuba and of Fidel's constant explanation – not just on the basis of emotions and vague slogans, but by taking the people in confidence, relying on them, and explaining in a factual manner the goals, the stages and the methods. Thus the people are mobilised themselves to build socialism…There are undoubtedly those in the PNC, and [those] who support the PNC, who genuinely aspire to socialism; who, indeed, might have been rather embarrassed in the past by their party's total oblivion to socialism. And for them will come the realisation that socialism cannot be built without genuine socialists at the helm, and at all levels of leadership. The pseudo-socialists who ensconce themselves on the bandwagon are a heavy drag on the working class achieving its aims. Contradictions will undoubtedly arise between the genuine and the pseudo-socialists within the PNC. The quicker this takes place the sooner Guyana will emerge on the path of true socialist development.[21]

Was this a signal to Comrade Forbes that this inveterate champion of the class struggle was available for the crossing? Ready for the call! *Realpolitik* invariably conquers. The Cubans, actuated primarily by their self-interest in the region, were already pressuring the PPP to seek a *modus vivendi* with Burnham's PNC, and with Ranji veering towards the latter (after years of living rather austerely, and powerlessly, within the PPP), it is inconceivable that Jagan possessed any means of restraining, and retaining, his foremost Marxist theoretician in the history of the PPP, hitherto impeccably loyal to him personally. But this was virtually impossible to sustain henceforth, given the PNC's markedly leftward drift in 1975–76, enhanced by their evident capacity to dangle ample material enticement, from the resources of the state, to potential renegades.

Although Burnham had flagrantly and brazenly stolen the elections of July 1973, the Cuban communists (Jagan's heroes), were solidly behind the fraudulent Burnham regime. Ironically, Jagan was shafted by the American and British imperialists because of his devotion to the Cuban dictator when it was perilously unfashionable to do so. He had squandered the virtually unassailable prospect of his leading Guyana to independence in 1962–63 because of his admiration for, and devotion to, Comrade Fidel. Therefore, with the connivance of the Americans, the British and now the Cuban communists, driven by *realpolitik*, Burnham was empowered and emboldened to ride roughshod over Jagan, relegating his PPP to the political periphery – a rump on the margins, clutching its Marxist purity.

Burnham was also confident now to focus on elevating himself as a Third World leader of the highest order, beyond his little country invisible to most of the world. Burnham had pledged US$50,000 annually to the liberation fund of the Organisation of African Unity for countries like Angola and Mozambique fighting Portuguese colonialism. This would become a cardinal plank defining Burnham's relationship with the continent, enhancing his profile in Africa and beyond, particularly within the Non-Aligned Movement.

It was also a most effective means of ethnic self-affirmation among his own African Guyanese base at home, the closest approximation to the Gandhian nationalist struggle in the aggregation of Indo-Guyanese consciousness and self-esteem. Burnham's message on World Solidarity Day, in May 1972, resonated with his African supporters. He was responding to those, possibly in the PPP, who contended that he should have sought the approval of Parliament for his annual contribution to the African liberation fund. To this, Burnham responded: 'RIP!' He elaborated:

> I am a black man. And though I bear no ill will towards any ethnic group, I am Prime Minister and a black man who cannot be oblivious to the fact of persecution and oppression which black men throughout the world are being subjected to. The fact that I am Prime Minister makes me no less a black man and a human being who is hurt and affected by the hypocrisy of the big powers these days and their alacrity to voice noble sentiments which are not mirrored in acts…It is my view, my conviction that only force, only blood can settle the score in Africa…and while our African brothers shed their blood, let us give them support and money to get materials.[22]

By late 1975, Burnham had enhanced his 'socialist credentials' with the Cubans and the Soviets by his co-operation in permitting Cuban planes transporting their soldiers to the civil war in Angola to refuel in Guyana. This was a major strategic stance by Burnham, as it augmented his political capital not only with the Cubans and the Soviets but also within the Non-Aligned Movement, particularly the Africans. Burnham's persona animated the rebel African imagination as an implacable champion of African liberation, particularly in South Africa, Namibia, Mozambique, Zimbabwe, and Angola. Burnham was spreading his wings far beyond his little country, unlike the communist Jagan, still deeply loyal to Comrades Castro and Brezhnev, but marginalised into passivity – an innocuous exponent of what he construed as the purest version of Marxism-Leninism.

The Angolan civil war had acquired a moral dimension because of the active intervention of apartheid South Africa on the side of the National Liberation Front of Angola (FNLA) and the National Union for the Total Independence of Angola (UNITA), seen to be in alliance with the imperialists. Cuba, the USSR, and several important African countries were determined to secure victory for the People's Movement for the Liberation of Angola (MPLA), deemed the radical, authentically socialist, of the three movements that were vying for control of oil-rich, post-colonial Angola. For Ranji Chandisingh, this also must have vindicated the authenticity of the PNC's commitment to the socialist revolution. The fact that Cuba and the Soviet Union had placed considerable trust in Burnham, elevated his stature among several frustrated senior members of the PPP, who probably felt disengaged and disconcertingly irrelevant. The latter were demoralised by the party's diminished stature after a decade in opposition, with every likelihood that it would languish in the wilderness indefinitely. With Burnham moving so definitively to the left, the PPP must have seemed to them as if it were on the verge of being liquidated, or at best becoming an ineffectual sect. Besides, they were ground down by the subsistence level at which they existed from day to day, materially and intellectually. The PPP had been reduced to fourteen seats in the legislature by the rigged elections of July 1973, and were boycotting the Parliament ever since; for over two years they were bereft of even that engagement as they pursued their tactic of 'non-cooperation and civil resistance.'

PART 2.
Consolidating Burnham's Dictatorial Rule

I.   Seeking to Steal Jagan's 'Bitter Sugar' Mantle: Conceding Recognition of Jagan's Sugar Union while Consolidating the 'Paramountcy' of the PNC

In turn, the affirmation of the PNC's socialist programme by several defecting Marxist stalwarts of the PPP, such as Ranji Chandisingh, Vincent Teekah, and Halim Majeed, was a significant shift in the political compass of the country. It undermined Jagan's claim to sole possession of the Marxist-Leninist tenets and exacerbated his political impotence as the PNC consolidated its 'paramountcy' over the government. It enhanced and validated the PNC's claim to the socialist mantle implicit in their nationalisation of 'the commanding heights of the economy' – Jagan's goal for revolutionising the Guyanese economy, adopting the model established by the Soviet Union and its satellites in Eastern Europe and Cuba. The far-reaching reforms initiated by Jock Campbell in the sugar industry from the 1950s, following his negotiating the guaranteed prices and quotas under the Commonwealth Sugar Agreement (1951), had made no impression whatsoever on Jagan. He was immovable in his mantra that the 'sugar gods' were 'blood-suckers.' There was no place for them in his conception of the great panacea: the socialist revolution. Castro had done precisely that; Jagan would have nothing less and he continually pushed Burnham in that direction. Therefore, by 1975, Burnham was resolved to go for the biggest fish, Jagan's 'bitter sugar,' which it did the following year with the nationalisation of the assets of the Booker conglomerate. He had stolen Jagan's thunder, his greatest ambition: to eradicate the evil of the 'sugar barons.' But Burnham was mindful that Jagan had total control of the overwhelmingly Indian sugar workers; therefore, he could cause considerable mischief for the industry if his union, the Guyana Agricultural Workers' Union (GAWU), remained unrecognised to the advantage of the long-discredited, but recognised, Manpower Citizens' Association (MPCA).

In June 1948, as seen earlier, Guiana Industrial Workers' Union (GIWU) had called a strike, seeking to supersede the MPCA. This culminated in the shootings, at Plantation Enmore (in Jagan's constituency of Central Demerara), when five strikers were killed. This tragedy was seminal in the making of Cheddi Jagan – as the foremost enemy of 'bitter sugar' and champion of the sugar workers, against the 'sugar gods.' Already, by 1948, the reputation of the recognised union (the MPCA) was tarnished, as the perception took hold that it had become 'a company union.' Cheddi's political persona as David challenging the Goliath of 'bitter sugar' was taking shape; his standing among his Indian compatriots would remain inviolable despite his fatal political errors, precipitated by his irrepressible devotion to communism. In August–September 1953, the PPP-backed GIWU (the precursor to GAWU) had again called a strike for recognition as the sole bargaining agent of workers in the sugar industry. Initiated and given legislative support by the PPP's first government (the Labour Relations Bill), this was the decisive factor in the suspension of the Constitution, on October 9, 1953. Ten years later, the PPP was still endeavouring to unseat the MPCA and gain recognition for its union (GAWU), as it introduced another Labour Relations Bill (piloted by Ranji Chandisingh). It precipitated the eighty-day strike, led by the TUC and funded by the CIA, which brought the Jagan government virtually to its knees.

This was the context in which the Americans intervened decisively to prevent the communist Jagan from ever leading an independent Guyana. And in 1964, with the GIWU re-baptised GAWU, Jagan's union had called a strike to pressure the British government to revoke their decision to impose proportional representation (PR), a drastic measure pursued relentlessly with the British, by President Kennedy specifically to remove Jagan before the colony was granted independence. This strike led to the escalation of racial warfare, virtual civil war, yet the British did not revoke PR. The sugar union (GIWU or GAWU) was always manipulated by Jagan as the principal instrument to advance his political agenda.

But it is also noteworthy that the PPP's union in the sugar industry, GAWU, still unrecognised, had called strikes during the 'spring' and 'autumn' crops of seven- and six-week duration respectively, partly to claw back some of the windfall from high sugar prices in 1974, which the government had imposed on the industry – but primarily to gain recognition for their union, a matter of perennial controversy. The GAWU strike had resulted in the loss of $150 million in foreign exchange. This, therefore, was the context in which the Burnham government agreed to a poll in the sugar industry for the workers to finally decide whether they wished to have Jagan's union as their bargaining agent or continue with the old MPCA (backed by the PNC) and irreconcilably opposed to Jagan.

For nearly three decades, the Indian sugar workers had sustained the political credibility of Jagan, in reality, his communist mission of which most had little, if any, comprehension. His perceived incorruptibility and devotion to the small farmers and sugar workers rendered him sacrosanct in the eyes of his Indian supporters – in the mould of Nehru, their great Indian hero. This was at the root of his political longevity, however absurd his belief in the Soviet system as the model for his country's development, in America's 'backyard.'

Odeen Ishmael, a faithful member of Jagan's PPP, recalls the stunning triumph of GAWU in the free poll of December 31, 1975, and the political implications of it:

> …the sugar workers voted overwhelmingly for the GAWU, giving it 98 per cent of the votes cast. This poll, in which 83 per cent of the workers turned out to vote, demonstrated three facts: first, that the GAWU had the confidence of the majority of the sugar workers, as it had always asserted; second, the PNC's claim that it had made inroads into PPP strongholds (especially the sugar estates) was spurious – a claim based on the 71 per cent which it took at the 1973 elections with the help of the army; and third, it clearly exposed the fact that the PNC rigged the 1973 elections since the PNC-backed union [MPCA] could not obtain more than 2 per cent of the sugar workers' votes.[23]

Nonetheless, the Burnham regime needed the support of GAWU as it was about to embark on the nationalisation of the sugar industry, always at the heart of Jagan's political mission. The latter was achieved in 1976.

In 1974–75, as Burnham accelerated his socialist agenda, Venezuela had become more assertive in its claim to two-thirds of Guyana's territory. Meanwhile, it was widely believed, as the Burnham government had propounded, that Venezuela and Brazil (the latter a right-wing anti-communist regime) were carrying out military manoeuvres on their borders with Guyana. This was conveyed as a prelude to a potential invasion of Guyana to thwart the anti-imperialist and socialist programme of Forbes Burnham. The latter had again boxed Jagan into a corner, as the PPP was made to revoke its tactical stance against the crooked general elections of July 1973, from 'non-cooperation and civil resistance' to that of 'critical support' for the PNC's illegitimate regime.

Odeen Ishmael states that Ranji Chandisingh, the deputy general secretary of the PPP and the second ranking person in the party after Cheddi Jagan, was constantly pressing the leadership to give full support, not 'critical support,' to the Burnham government. By 1975, Ranji was persuaded that the PNC was undergoing a transformative leap towards Marxism-Leninism and that the PPP should acknowledge this and seek a *modus vivendi* with the PNC against imperialism and its aggressive reactionary neighbours. Ishmael feels that the possibility of an imminent Brazilian invasion was being exploited to effect a rapprochement.[24] He, too, like another trusted PPP member, Ralph Ramkarran, detects the hands of the Cubans in Ranji's evident drift towards the PNC, and it underscores Castro's belated, but genuine, comradeship with Burnham, rooted in the latter's initiative in securing diplomatic recognition of Cuba in the region – and firmly cemented, in late 1975, by Burnham's acceding to the Angolan-bound Cuban planes being refuelled in Guyana. In effect, Burnham, paradoxically, had joined the Cold War on the side of Cuba and the USSR.

As an informed correspondent remarked, the Cubans intervened to force Jagan to 'modify' his non-cooperative resistance towards Burnham, swayed by the latter's newfound socialist credentials:

> ...the international socialist movement took the position that the PNC administration was on the road to Marxism-Leninism and Guyana came to be regarded as a 'fraternal' country. When Cheddi Jagan went to Havana, Cuba, to attend a conference of Latin American communist parties [June 1975], therefore, he came under pressure from the Cuban Vice-President, Carlos Rafael Rodriguez, and members of the Political Bureau of the Communist Party of Cuba to modify the PPP's hostility to the PNC. At its [the PPP's] 25th anniversary conference, in August 1975 at Annandale, Jagan announced a change in its political approach from one of 'non-cooperation and civil resistance' to one of 'critical support' for the PNC administration.[25]

The PPP had little room for manoeuvre, as Odeen Ishmael observes:

> The PPP offer of 'critical support' [in August 1975] was also meant…
> to display its patriotic duty in defence of the nation's territorial
> integrity…During this period the PNC regime gave great publicity…
> that the Brazilian military forces were being built up on the Guyana
> border…and were therefore posing a real threat…The hugely state-
> controlled media created genuine fears in Guyana that Brazil – then
> strongly anti-communist and pro-American – would have staged a
> military intervention…with the main intention of forcing the PNC
> to reverse its pro-socialist tendency and to follow again the capitalist
> path to development…[fake news!]

> Significantly, inside the PPP, the Deputy General Secretary, Ranji
> Chandisingh, exaggerated the so-called Brazilian threat and tried to
> pressure the Party leadership to give unilateral support, instead of
> 'critical support' to the PNC. He did so shortly after he returned from
> a visit in 1976 [possibly 1975] to Cuba where he held consultations
> with leaders of the Cuban Government. At that time there also
> existed very close relations between the Cuban and the Guyana
> Governments, and most likely Chandisingh was convinced by the
> Cubans that the PPP, as a party having strong links of friendship with
> the Cuban Communist Party, should render unilateral support to the
> PNC Government. But after Chandisingh failed to get the PPP to
> support his stand, he, soon after [March 1976], resigned from the
> party and joined the PNC.[26]

But there was something more ominous than the PNC's profession of
Marxism-Leninism, of leading the socialist revolution in Guyana: an underlying
ruse not totally secreted. It was inspired by the Leninist mantra, the 'paramountcy
of the party' over the government – essentially an instrument for the supreme
leader to appropriate the PPP's own Marxist-Leninist rhetoric to marginalise
them further, while imposing a dictatorship *over* the proletariat. It is arguable,
therefore, that from early 1975, in the aftermath of the Sophia Declaration
of December 1974, what was being hatched could be deemed **Burnhamism
wrapped eclectically in the garb of Marxism-Leninism.** This was pursued for
four principal reasons: (1) to exploit the latter philosophy's disregard for liberal
democracy, termed 'bourgeois democracy' – to install a dictatorship in which
not only was the party paramount over the government, but the supreme leader,
in turn, was paramount over both the party and the government; (2) to employ
Marxist-Leninist rhetoric to undermine the stature of Jagan and the PPP, a
counter-claim of his being in sole possession of the tenets of the doctrine; (3) to
secure the affirmation of the Cubans and other communist countries in order to
validate the PNC's posture as a 'socialist' party and government, thereby further
eroding the legitimacy of Jagan's PPP, conceivably even to liquidate it as an
autonomous party; and (4) to utilise their radical, pro-African liberation stature
to enhance their credentials in the Non-Aligned Movement.

This pattern was certainly discernible in the organ of the PNC, *New Nation*, throughout 1975. The stage was being set for their 'Comrade Leader' to become a version of Comrade Fidel; besides, the Cubans manifested no incredulity of, or resistance to, Burnhamism, despite their long-standing comradeship with Cheddi Jagan. In fact, they helped immeasurably to validate the process as it was considered compatible with their enhanced profile in the Caribbean region. Having been stigmatised as the pariah because of their communism and their isolation by American imperialism, the Cubans perceived Comrade Forbes as a genuine convert who was prepared to walk with them that extra difficult mile, however hazardous. But to give Burnham's socialist credentials some plausibility, even credibility, it is arguable that he could have prolonged the support of his American sponsors indefinitely, if he so desired, given Jagan's unreconstructed pro-Moscow communism.

Yet the fact that Burnham abandoned this option although he was made and sustained by the Americans, lends veracity to what the American Embassy in Georgetown had explained to the State Department: that Guyana was too small a place for the intellect, ego, bombast, and ambition of Forbes Burnham; that he yearned for a wider canvas. This was actuated by the radical politics of the Non-Aligned Movement (NAM) and the vibrant liberation movement of Southern Africa (particularly apartheid South Africa), coupled with the inspiration of the revolutionary profile of Fidel in the region and in the Third World generally. But all along, even from his earliest days in Guyanese politics, Burnham always felt intellectually superior to Jagan whom he ridiculed often for lacking imagination, for being hidebound and mired in self-defeating dogmatism. He could outmanoeuvre him whenever he deemed it necessary, and he often deployed his amazing oratorical gifts, his versatile intellect and his eclectic political posture towards this end.

The conferral of the José Martí National Order by the Cubans, in April 1975, gave Burnham the ultimate accolade, the validation he needed to project his new radical persona in the NAM. Moreover, psychologically, he had also been provided with a crucial instrument to further undermine the validity of Jagan's claim to sole custodianship of the sacred Marxist-Leninist tenets in Guyana. Burnham was, indeed, on the road to Havana: consolidating his dictatorship a la Fidel, while deploying the ideology of socialism/communism to establish his paramountcy over his party and the state. And like Fidel, Forbes did not have to bother about preserving the façade of 'bourgeois democracy' because, as Ranji Chandisingh argued, the latter was primarily a means, exploitable by communists in capitalist states, to advance their pursuit of the 'dictatorship of the proletariat.'

As early as June 1972, Ken Bancroft, a feature writer for the PNC's *New Nation*, was rebutting the following remark from an editorial in the PPP's paper (*Mirror*, May 17, 1972): 'In the Soviet Union, when there is need for a change in the leadership, this is done by discussions, debates and voting at the various levels of the Communist Party.' Bancroft rejected this allusion to genuine democracy in the Communist Party of the Soviet Union. And he countered that the PPP, as disciples of communism, were on thin ice, indeed, when they lamented the lack elsewhere of what they cynically dubbed 'bourgeois freedoms,' such as the two-party system underpinned by free and fair elections. Bancroft was appalled by the hypocrisy of the PPP's underlying political assumptions:

> All of us are accustomed by now about these jokers and their utterances…This Communist-Marxist party knows that Communism-Marxism does not allow for the two-party system. For, according to them the one-party state allows for a greater democracy. One does not forget easily when, during the regime of the PPP [1957–64], they openly boasted that come independence we would be subjected to Communism-Marxism in all forms. They would have made history by being the first Communist Government in the world to be elected through the most honest form of democracy and the people's will – the ballot box.[27]

Bancroft was correct. As a communist and unwavering devotee of the Soviet system since the late 1940s, Cheddi Jagan did not really have the moral authority to challenge Burnham's repudiation of what Cheddi and Ranji considered 'bourgeois freedoms' that underpinned a flawed liberal democratic political tradition. Neither could Jagan's revered comrades, Castro, Brezhnev, and others of the same ilk in Eastern Europe, muster the democratic credentials to make a case for honouring key components of 'bourgeois democracy.' Burnham, ever sagacious, would not let this pass. And having gained the highest honour from Comrade Fidel, who did not meet with Jagan when he visited Burnham in Georgetown in September 1973 (after the rigged elections in July), he felt anointed to create what was effectively a one-party state from the latter half of the 1970s until the demise of communism in the late 1980s.

II. The Crusade for a New Constitution: A Bogus Referendum and the Virtual Elimination of Liberal Democracy

By 1975, therefore, Burnham was immeasurably confident to advance his notion of cooperative socialism (embodied in the Sophia Declaration, similar to the Arusha Declaration of 1967 by Tanzania's Julius Nyerere), as the instrument to forge his socialist revolution. What the latter really meant remained nebulous, but various leaders of the PNC would convey the impression that it was a Marxist-Leninist project, with similarities to the Cuban Revolution. Jagan was never persuaded of the validity of the claim; and his 'critical support' was itself nebulous. **Yet everybody in Guyana was now a socialist. This was reflective of the futility of a place imprisoned by its racism yet lacking the resolve and the political will to confront the miasma.** The Marxist-Leninist vocabulary could rationalise or obfuscate just about any political conduct, however racially determined or irrelevant to the reality of a country that is still not a nation. Being Guyanese still means being chronically hyphenated: African- or Afro-; Indian- or Indo-; or Amerindian-, the indigenous people who until now, by default, have placed their trust in other ethnic segments – unwisely!

But there was a bigger hoax underpinning this ideological nullity: 'time for a new constitution,' the editorial of *New Nation* pronounced on January 5, 1975. Their contention was that with the PNC's declaration of its adoption of 'cooperative socialism' as the instrument for socialist transformation, it was imperative to devise a constitution that was consonant with that fundamental goal. This was nonsense, but it was characteristic of the supreme leader that he should clothe his authoritarian ambitions with the rubric of socialism. Whatever the form of his socialism, Burnham's primary aim was to procure for himself maximum power as president of the world's first (and possibly last) Cooperative Socialist Republic, unrestrained by any institutional checks and balances. To repeat: this was, indeed, a ruse to become the Castro of the Anglophone Caribbean. And the anti-democratic foundation of Marxism-Leninism rendered it an ideal vehicle to institutionalise his dictatorial proclivity. Therefore, he would run rings around Jagan, as most of the latter's long-standing comrades, in Cuba and the USSR, were increasingly inclined to give credence to Burnham's claim to being Marxist-Leninist. And because he monopolised political power comprehensively, and arguably indefinitely, the foreign communists in power increasingly sought a *modus vivendi* with Burnham. The powerless Jagan, immersed in his dogmas, was left out in the cold: consigned since 1964 to the Opposition (or 'minority party'), as Burnham redefined the PPP.

But it is noteworthy that in the issue of *New Nation* where the case for a new constitution was being made, the seven 'Objects of the PNC' were cited as bullet points, but there is no reference whatsoever to Marxism-Leninism. I cite the two key points that refer specifically to the ideological underpinning of the PNC:

- To secure and maintain through **the practice of cooperative socialism** the interest, well-being and prosperity of ALL the people of Guyana.

- To pursue our commitment to the Socialist ideal and more particularly to ensure that the people of Guyana own and control for their benefit the natural resources of the Country.[28]

It was Burnham, in the Declaration of Sophia, in December 1974, who first made the case for a new constitution. It was the instrument that would grant him the untrammelled power that many of Jagan's communist friends exerted in their one-party states. Castro, Brezhnev, and the Soviet puppets in Eastern Europe had no compulsion to adhere to the 'bourgeois freedoms' Jagan still expected Burnham to uphold. The latter had no residual empathy for his tenuous ally of the early 1950s and was supercilious in his ritual ridicule of what he perceived as Jagan's mediocre intellect and blind immersion in communist dogmas. Burnham was flagrant in his pursuit of personal power, subverting whatever vestige of liberal democracy he deemed expedient in the process. Besides, he was so assured that Jagan was stuck in a sterile Marxist-Leninist orthodoxy, a quagmire of jargon (Dr Jargon), that in comprehensively rigging the general elections in July 1973, he had effectively consigned him to political nullity.

Burnham had been masterly in utilising sophistry, which enabled him to win the race for independence when Jagan was in striking distance of the winning post, and he would use amorphous language, rooted in no definitive ideological premise, to continually outsmart his inflexible foe. Burnham seemed to have found a belated flaw in the independence constitution, as he did in the imperialists who had cultivated him, connived in his favour, and made him the man he became, at the expense of the communist Jagan. But he deprecated being dubbed America's man – created by, and beholden to, White men, yet if Jagan had moved strategically, marginally to the centre, and his politics had assumed a more moderate posture (as Jock Campbell had intimated), it is conceivable that Burnham would not have abrogated his relationship with his erstwhile American sponsors to the extent he did after the mid-1970s.

Burnham wanted a new constitution to give himself the authority to rule autocratically, unrestrained by the strictures of 'bourgeois democracy.' By claiming the mantle of socialism, though belatedly – indeed, Marxism-Leninism, however eclectically – compared with Jagan's secured Marxist credentials, Burnham had licence to behave like any communist dictator, while vitiating Jagan's assumption of the theoretical high ground. Burnham was determined to have his new toy. And he was certain that with the alternative being the communist Jagan, the coast was clear for him to do just as he wished, picking holes in the independence constitution based on liberal democracy, framed to protect 'bourgeois rights.' As he indicated in December 1974, he was all set to tear it up because it was permeated by the 'ideology of our former colonial masters' – created at the bidding of the White oppressor:

I spoke [earlier] of the typical Independence Constitution with all its inhibitions and checks and balances, which we had to accept as part of the package in 1966. Certainly, it is clear that this patchwork of amendments from time to time is both unsatisfactory, untidy and unaesthetic, and that the moment has arrived for the review and rewriting of the Guyana constitution. The drafting and subsequent promulgation of a new constitution will, therefore, be undertaken shortly, that is from January 1975. This is a project in which the Party [PNC], the public and the parliament will be fully and openly involved.

As we complete our tenth year in office, and proceed to the country's tenth anniversary of independence, we cannot do so with a constitution out of step with modern trends, and our own ideas and ideologies; a constitution which reflects for the most part the beliefs and ideology of our former imperialist masters; a constitution which was taken out of the drawer, so to speak [it was, in fact, the product of Burnham's and Sonny Ramphal's sagacious legal brain, not his 'imperial masters'!]…with the minimum relevancy to the Guyanese peoples' needs, aspirations and thrusts. The Constitution must go, and in its place a new and relevant constitution must be substituted.[29]

This was how Burnham's *New Nation*, having adopted his spurious argument uncritically, proceeded to rationalise the necessity for a new constitution. It was essentially a ruse, the case for a socialist ethos at variance with 'bourgeois democracy':

The time has come when…[having] set not only our goals but the ideology which will inform our attainment of these goals [cooperative socialism], we must ensure that the Constitution allows for the realisation of these goals in keeping with our ideology.

The [present] Constitution, a work of art in itself, was designed to appease the former colonial bosses that there was a guarantee that their [bourgeois] values and concepts would be given the greatest protection that could exist in the country and, indeed, in fairness to the framers of the Constitution, it reflected the orientation of the majority of Guyanese at a time when Guyanese had not begun to savour the responsibility of nation-building nor articulated the concept of Cooperative Socialism…

The Constitution was designed for a capitalist-oriented society; and the sanctity of private and personal property clearly inhibits, except through tedious and lengthy amendment, the realisation of the concept of public property which we have formulated for the years where lands shall be primarily in the hands of the State, and the transference of property and land would be subject to careful scrutiny and control.

The Constitution of Guyana, now, is particularly concerned with protecting the rights of citizens from encroachment by the State or, indeed, from other groups, and little mention is made, if any, about the responsibility that citizenship imposes upon the people of the country. There are many who feel that the Constitution has served well, and that it can be used to achieve by amendment whatever new thrust is desired.

There are those who feel that it should be completely scrapped as being too inhibitory…for the achievement of the revolution on which we have embarked. The truth might well be that there are some features which ought to be retained and many which ought to go. The truth might well be that the basic difference of ideology between the present Constitution and the desired one is too profound to enable it to serve a different society.[30]

III. Burnham's Cooperative Socialism – A Mirage: An Experiment in Futility

There was no concession to liberal democracy or 'bourgeois freedoms' in the 'cooperative socialist' order Burnham sought to create. In this respect, it ought to have struck a chord with his old enemy, the unfaltering communist Jagan: both harbouring visceral aversion to liberal democracy, while certain that their specific path to the socialist utopia was attainable. In reality, the circuitous argument regarding the necessity for a new constitution, advanced by the PNC, was a stratagem primarily to give Burnham untrammelled power, to rule autocratically, for life. If he had not died in 1985, at the comparatively early age of sixty-two, it is inconceivable that this crafty practitioner of the pursuit of power could ever have been ousted by the ballot, even with the end of the Cold War which made America amenable to the neutered communist Jagan. This new constitution was the instrument that would be used to enthrone Forbes Burnham, in the manner communist leaders like Castro, Brezhnev, Kim Il-sung (a hero of Burnham), Ceausescu, and a host of enemies of 'bourgeois freedoms,' ruled in their dictatorships *over* the proletariat. The whole apparatus of governance was framed to invest the supreme leader with the halo of infallibility; therefore, if one dared to challenge the legitimacy of the noble one, one had to be mentally unbalanced. It was entirely rational to seek to restrain, if not eliminate, such deluded ones: a danger to themselves!

In February 1975, *New Nation* tried to explain the Comrade Leader's vision of utopia. This organ as well as many senior comrades (by this time all Guyanese were addressed as 'comrades') would continually struggle to grasp precisely what the concept of cooperative socialism meant. Apparently, this notion of the cooperative was first identified by Eusi Kwayana (Sydney King) as the instrument adopted by the freed African people, after emancipation, to build their village communities. The accuracy of this assumption is in doubt, as many freed people were compelled to pool their resources to acquire land, as one hundred acres was the minimum purchasable by any individual from the colonial state. The latter was contrived to undermine the freed people's quest for independence through landownership, thereby forcing them to return to plantation labour. It was to circumvent this draconian stricture on land purchase that many freed Africans participated in joint ventures – pooling their resources cooperatively – not primarily because of a philosophical commitment to cooperatives as the instrument of development.

Therefore, the communal acquisition of land did not translate into a vibrant cooperative movement, the principal historical and ideological assumption on which Burnham's cooperative socialism was predicated. It is true that the freed African people made enormous sacrifices to acquire land communally (the cost of land was at least $100 per acre); they felt it was indispensable to their independence of the plantations and pivotal to their realisation of genuine freedom. But the cooperative venture was dogged by failure during its short duration. There were proprietary villages where people had separate titles to their land, but the communal villages where people bought abandoned plantations, and then subdivided the land, were hampered by much internal discordance, culminating in the speedy disintegration of the collective enterprise.

Significant capital was expended on villages such as Friendship, Buxton, Beterverwagting and Plaisance, on the East Coast Demerara; and the average price was more than $112 per acre, an exorbitant charge. The late Alan Adamson (1919–2015) is the authority on this period of Guyanese history. This is his assessment of the abortive communal villages, aggravated by a colonial environment that was not amenable to their progress:

> But even at $100 per acre, it is small wonder that the communal villages ran into difficulty. The shareholders lacked experience in cooperative enterprise, and they had exhausted all their capital in land, leaving nothing to maintain the estates in sound operating condition. In British Guiana sugar production of any kind required a steady current outlay on irrigation, drainage and sea defence. After emancipation, sugar production at a profit demanded steam engines, vacuum pans and centrifugals…a continuing investment in technical renovation. None of this was available to the communal villages…

> Most communal villages were run by voluntary agreements under which each shareholder was required to make monthly subscriptions to help meet the costs of roads, bridges, sluice gates, dams, trenches, and so on. These agreements began to break down as early as 1845 [just seven years after Emancipation]. In 1851 the first ordinance was passed converting a communal village (Buxton) into a village composed of individually held plots. Thus, fragmentation began, and

> the communal estates added themselves to the proprietary villages in the formation of a new peasantry…Peasant subsistence and plantation monoculture collided head-on. The history of the fifteen years between 1838 and 1853 is in large part the history of that clash and of the ultimate victory of the sugar planters, or at least that part of the sugar industry which managed to survive the crisis.[31]

It was not a sound premise, therefore, to extrapolate from this tenuous communal experiment that cooperative societies could conceivably be the principal instrument for the radical transformation of the Guyanese economy towards the socialist revolution. Moreover, given the chronic problems of drainage and irrigation on the coastland of Guyana, requiring the complex construction and meticulous maintenance of costly hydraulics works, only large-scale industrial organisation could ever manage the sugar industry remuneratively. That was why the fragmenting of the estates was not a practicable proposition; why a peasant cane-farming sector never did emerge (as in Trinidad); why, too, Booker became the colossus it did in this backward colony. Only Booker, with access to foreign capital and technology, and the consequent economy of scale they attained, could have made sugar profitable on the hazardous coastland of Guyana. Both Jagan and Burnham were dreamers who really believed they had all the answers to defeat the White imperialists; that the sugar industry was making astronomical profits (not true!); and that they had the acumen to administer the sugar industry better than the White 'sugar gods.' In fact, without the guaranteed quotas and prices facilitated by the Commonwealth Sugar Agreement (Jock Campbell was a major player in negotiating it), the sugar industry would probably have folded shortly after the Second World War. Jagan and Burnham were both bombastic men – one a master of jargon; the other a gifted orator of frequently empty rhetoric – who could not 'run a cake-shop,' a common judgement of many Guyanese.

On February 23, 1970, Burnham announced that that Guyana was becoming 'the first Cooperative Republic in the world.' And it was then that he instructed that this vague instrument, which had played no discernibly significant role in the advancement of any of its diverse peoples, would be the means by which Guyana could reach the mountain top: the socialist utopia. And in his Declaration of Sophia, on December 14, 1974, the tenth anniversary since the American and British imperialists had conspired to make him their man to lead British Guiana to Independence, he turned against his White sponsors. Burnham had used them all along, ever since they had hinted, in the Robertson Commission Report of 1954, that they were ready to anoint him as their man, despite their never being at ease with him, suspecting him of being 'ambiguous' ideologically and for being instinctually anti-White.

The Declaration of Sophia was the turning point, indicating definitively that Burnham was moving away from his imperialist benefactors. He craved recognition as a Third World leader of world stature, not merely the leader of a Third World backwater. Liberal democracy had been presenting him with recurring problems of legitimacy in Guyana. Because of racial voting, if the elections were free and fair, Jagan (whatever his ideological stance) would always win. But in none of the communist countries that Jagan revered as creating the 'new man,' were elections free and fair (if held at all); neither did they subscribe to the sanctity of other so-called bourgeois rights: freedom of speech and the press, intellectual and creative freedom, and an electoral system based on a plurality of political parties. They were, without exception, one-party totalitarian states. Consequently, Burnham reasoned, why not adopt some core features of that ideological framework, whatever his reservations about Marxism-Leninism? Burnham's relationship to any definitive ideological frame of reference, from his early days in the PPP in the 1950s, was always amorphous. As I have mentioned before, he never claimed philosophical affinity with Marx, Engels, Lenin, Mao, or any of the founding fathers of communism to whom Cheddi Jagan was devoted. Several articles Burnham did write for the PPP's paper, *Thunder* (in the early 1950s), were eloquently anti-colonial but devoid of ideological content.

And in the Sophia Declaration of December 1974, his definitive adoption of 'socialism,' not once does Burnham make reference, or allude, to Marxism-Leninism or Jagan's hypnotic spiritual homeland, the Soviet Union. This is what Burnham said about cooperative socialism – the hogwash that engendered the Naipaulian disdain of Third World absurdities:

> Ours is not the first or only government in the developing world to place major emphasis on the use and development of the cooperative as an instrument of development or in the thrust towards socialism.

> We, however, named Guyana a Cooperative Republic to highlight the fact that the Cooperative will be the principal institution for giving the masses the control of our economy, to emphasise the fact that we aim at making the Cooperative sectors the dominant sector and that the Cooperative is and will be the mechanism for making the little man a real man.

> ...any party member or leader who does not hold this as an article of faith and act, work and behave accordingly, is untrue to his membership of the Party. In fact, he is unfit to continue holding such membership...Learning from the mistakes and failures... we can undertake the revolutionary changes that are necessary if the Cooperative Sector is to become the dominant sector and the means of involving the little man in the process of self and national development...Each member must be grounded in the ideology and programme of the Party. He must be not merely a member, but an active member of a cooperative.[32]

Burnham was ever set to eradicate pernicious attitudes implanted by the White colonial exploiters – fetters on his nebulous 'cooperative socialist' revolution. It was aimed at the erasure of so-called bourgeois freedoms to give himself unbridled power. Time and again, he would proclaim 'ours is a war' against the legacy of colonialism only to undermine another strand of liberal democracy. But the worse of it all was his utterly shameless rigging of the elections in 1968, 1973, 1978 (the referendum to change the Constitution), 1980, and the one after he died, in December 1985 (just as blatantly rigged by D. Hoyte). Jagan's repeated engagement with this travesty, knowing full well that all elections were orchestrated by the PNC – a farcical ritual – did give it a shred of legitimacy, to the satisfaction of the inveterate rigger.

Forbes Burnham wanted to re-educate Guyanese for the cooperative socialist experiment that was his big post-colonial idea – another journey to nowhere! Yet, for racial and ideological reasons, the West Indian leaders failed to repudiate, however mildly, Burnham's fraudulent electoral practices, totally at variance with the cherished liberal democratic tradition of the Anglophone Caribbean. Consequently, he had an open goal in promulgating his 'cooperative republic' of the damned. He was dismantling the education system that was the foundation of the brilliant lawyer he was, as were others of his generation and the one after. He was 'revolutionising' the colonial mind for the socialist revolution – the rationale for his dictatorship. It is an argument that would have resonated with Jagan's PPP if only they were initiating the re-education towards the Marxist-Leninist utopia.

Back to Forbes! Still no reference to Marxism-Leninism in his Sophia Declaration, but no scope either for 'bourgeois freedoms'!

> The Party, through Government [the former being 'paramount'] has already begun the process of revolutionising the formal education system, a process aimed at eradicating the old colonial and capitalist values and introducing and emphasising new and relevant ones…To this day, there are still some misguided teachers and lecturers who have no concept of and are even resistant to Cooperatives. They prefer to inculcate in their wards and emphasise selfish individual objectives, instead of those directed at the progress of the group, the community and the nation as a whole…
>
> A massive campaign has now been launched in which there can be no place for the disinterested and nonconformist who envisages freedom in terms of indulging in the practices and attitudes which were part of the old colonial order. We did not win political freedom from colonialism to protect the freedom of colonialism to poison and mislead our society and divert us from our national goals.[33]

It was, therefore, the role of the PNC's organ, *New Nation*, to re-educate the masses to appreciate that capitalism was a 'non-starter' as it led to the division of society into antagonistic classes, with economic and political power 'in the hands of a selected few.' In February 1975, the paper was essentially regurgitating Burnham's message at Sophia, chanting the merits of cooperative socialism. Interestingly, there is no suggestion that the leader's philosophy was grounded in Marxism-Leninism; it was being defined as a natural legacy of the historical 'struggle' of Guyana's peoples. This was a distortion, as I remarked earlier, but no one could dare to challenge the dictator's power to define.

This is *New Nation's* rationale for cooperative socialism, based on a misreading of Guyana's history – a flawed instrument of economic transformation, at conception:

> Cooperative Socialism is the model chosen by the People's National Congress to give force to the Party's socialist philosophy. The PNC has identified the Cooperative as the vehicle by which the transfer of economic power to the small man would be effected.

> The cooperative has been present in our society from the early periods of our history. Our early settlers organised all their economic activities in their villages on a cooperative basis. The freed slaves used this type of organisation to purchase villages in their effort to retain some degree of economic independence from their erstwhile masters. The East Indians also made use of this type of economic organisation, when they too had to struggle to escape the harshness of the indentured labour system.

> Co-operativism breeds an attitude of mind, which inspires a willingness among people to work together, and it dampens the destructive competitiveness that capitalism breeds...It is this new attitude of mind which must pervade the society, and it must therefore be consciously forged...The cooperative sector will be the dominant one in the economy of Guyana.[34]

But parallel with this 'thrust' towards cooperative socialism and the resolve to tear up the independence constitution was the underlying reality that a personality cult, centred on Burnham, was being cultivated. R. O. Bostwick, for instance, saw Burnham not just as the messiah of Guyana, but also as a source of inspiration to many developing nations. He alluded to Jagan's undiminished status as the leader of Indo-Guyanese, yet, ominously, he was advocating granting to the messiah Burnham substantially more powers, as he should be totally trusted to rule wisely, being 'a genuine champion of democracy.'

The stage was being set for the establishment of a virtual one-party state, ruled by the supreme leader. Bostwick entreated Guyanese to conceptualise Burnham in similar terms as Stalin, Mao, or Castro, supposedly the epitome of national pride and honour:

> Guyana cannot hope to survive as a divisive society continuously racked by political rivalry. We need now, as never before, unity as a

nation in order to quickly achieve our national objectives. This is the age of fervent nationalism which cannot thrive on dual leadership.

> The young nation of Guyana must acclaim its national leader irrespective of ideology, race or creed just like how the Romans acclaimed their Caesar; the French their Napoleon and de Gaulle; the British Churchill; the Russians their Stalin; the Chinese their Mao; the Cubans their Castro. Why not Guyanese their Burnham?[35]

Bostwick wanted Guyanese to grant Burnham a blank cheque because his time had come; he was the messiah; he could do no wrong. He was, in fact, sketching the template that would mark the next ten years of Burnham's increasingly dictatorial rule in which he opportunistically adopted aspects of Jagan's Marxist ideology while reducing him to being an innocuous onlooker, as the foundation of 'bourgeois democracy' was being gravely uprooted.

A final note from Bostwick. His specious counsel is the echo of his master's voice:

> Democracy becomes of very diminished value if people accept the alien conceived adage about absolute power and its corruptibility [an allusion to Lord Acton's dictum: 'Power tends to corrupt; absolute power corrupts absolutely']. The vast dimensions of the Guyana revolution that open promising vistas of an egalitarian society do not provide easy fodder for the abuse of power. And even if it did, on the basis of spotless performance and integrity, aided by a very Christian upbringing [*sic*], our revolution could be in no better hands than the Prime Minister's – a genuine champion of democracy [despite the stolen elections of 1968 and 1973!].[36]

A few weeks later, in March 1975, Burnham and his entourage were on their way to a state visit of China. When Burnham was America's man, he had voted against the admission of Mao's China to the UN; now that he had moved to the left, he voted for its admission. This was the context in which the state visit was being accommodated by China. Interestingly, by virtue of the PNC's eclectic conception of socialism, it could even rationalise the Chinese model as being compatible with Guyana's cooperative socialist revolution. But *New Nation* was also acutely aware of the fact that the virtual deification of Mao was something their own Comrade Leader craved enormously. The cult of Mao [like that of Burnham's hero, Kim Il-sung of North Korea] was highly prized, worthy of being pursued:

> That such a society can and does exist must be an inspiration to him [Burnham] and inspire in him that hope which springs eternal for a similar transformation of society in Guyana, and provide a great fillip for his endeavours. Sight of this huge nation of dedicated enthusiasts, at this crucial moment in their nation's history, imbued with a faith in their leader, Chairman Mao – a faith such as can move mountains

> – must mean to him [Burnham] far more than all the splendours
> of oriental civilisation with which he and his comrades must be
> captivated and charmed.[37]

It will be recalled that shortly thereafter, in April 1975, Burnham paid a state visit to Cuba where he was given Cuba's highest national award. I have already discussed the significance of this in terms of Burnham's profile in the Non-Aligned Movement and his role in aiding African liberation movements in southern Africa. And on the eve of Comrade Forbes's visit to Cuba, Shridath 'Sonny' Ramphal, Burnham's minister of foreign affairs, explained the significance of it. His interpretation is noteworthy in view of the grave reservations that still prevailed in the PPP and other left-wing circles in the region regarding Burnham's cooperative socialism. The Cubans, according to Ramphal, considered Burnham an authentic socialist and were prepared to go the whole hog with him:

> …the visit must be seen against the background of Guyana's socialist
> philosophy and thrust, and in this regard the promotion of relations
> with socialist countries whereby Guyana could learn from the
> experience of such countries which have similar hopes and aspirations
> in terms of nationalism, economic growth, higher standards of living
> of the masses, and creating equal opportunities for all. Cuba is also
> an important Caribbean territory, and in consonance with Guyana's
> attempt at regionalism and regional unity, it is relevant that Guyana
> fosters closer relations with territories of the Caribbean.[38]

Fidel, as Ramphal suggested, had found in Comrade Forbes (his African credentials consolidated) a viable entree not only to the Caribbean integration movement, but the wider, then prestigious, Non-Aligned Movement. This was enough for Castro to overlook the fact that Burnham never – not once – ever defined himself as a Marxist-Leninist or communist; neither did he adopt the jargon of that ideology in articulating his nebulous conception of cooperative socialism. His was a cleverly honed ambiguity that most recognised but could not pin down. This aspect of Burnham's politics was unalterable, even when he consolidated his authoritarian regime from the mid-1970s, and some of his disciples felt emboldened to resort to Marxist rhetoric from time to time.

A week after Castro had given Burnham the José Martí Award, the latter was interviewed on 'Night Ride' on GBS Radio (Georgetown) by Ron Sanders and Mohamed Hamaludin. What he said must have been painful indeed to Comrade Cheddi, seeing the impostor (as he saw it) being feted by communists around the world. Burnham explained the source of the chemistry between himself and Comrade Fidel, although he also spoke about his visits to Mao's China and Ceausescu's Romania. But Burnham was particularly keen to stress the warmth of the relationship he shared with Castro:

> [We] are after the same objectives of putting power – economic power
> – into the hands of the people and making their lot a better one…We
> hit it off. We speak freely and frankly with each other. We disagree
> sometimes, but I believe the Cuban Leader and Government and
> people recognised what the People's National Congress is doing…

Burnham underlined that he and Castro were also pursuing 'identical policies' internationally, as demonstrated in the Non-Aligned Movement and at the United Nations. Burnham was asked to elaborate on why he and Comrade Fidel 'get along so well.' He reportedly remarked that Fidel appreciated what the PNC was doing: 'putting power in the hands of the masses and making the economy serve them.'[39]

Burnham also addressed the relevance to Guyana of the socialist experiences of the three countries he had visited recently: China, Romania, and Cuba. He identified the centrality of planning in their socialist reconstruction and their remarkable discipline and commitment (China in particular). He added:

> planning must be done and must be rigidly carried out. The main
> lesson was that people must be involved through an understanding
> and not through being ordered; goals must be ruthlessly pursued;
> and **there must be the paramountcy of the party over the
> government** [emphasis added].[40]

As I have argued, the latter was the most seductive underpinning of the communist *modus operandi* to the Comrade Leader: it gave the dictator uninhibited latitude to do whatever he desired in maximising his personal power. Yet there remained a stubborn vagueness to Burnham's socialism that defied a definitive conceptualising of it. Possibly the nearest he came to expounding what he meant by socialism was in a lecture he delivered in May 1975, 'A Socialist Guyana in the Caribbean,' to the Jaycees of Linden (the small bauxite town, formerly Mackenzie, was renamed in 1970, after himself: Linden Forbes Sampson Burnham). He admonished them that if they wished to participate in the socialist revolution in Guyana, they had to dissociate themselves from their parent-body in Canada, or rewrite one of their received objectives: 'that economic justice can best be won by free men in free enterprise.' He repudiated this assertion as fundamentally flawed, as the erroneous juxtaposition of the adjective 'free' with the capitalist system could not modify its inherently exploitative character. He also submitted that many in the region and beyond (alluding to the Brazilians and the Venezuelans) were determined to undermine the socialist revolution to which Guyanese were devoted. But while he assured his listeners that socialism would triumph as a world system, capitalists everywhere would resist it to the bitter end. Yet it was 'a natural development: just as slavery was followed by feudalism, and the latter superseded by capitalism, the socialist transformation was inevitable.' But, unlike Jagan, I cannot recall Burnham ever speaking of socialism as a precursor of the communist utopia. The latter was arguably one step too far for this sagacious operator, for whom 'paramountcy of the party' and 'nationalisation of the commanding heights of the economy' were the backbone of his socialist endeavour.

As for theorising on Marxism-Leninism a la Jagan – not a word from the Comrade Leader! And never a word either about the 'glorious' Soviet Union! This is how he reportedly explained his version of socialism:

> [Burnham] made it clear that his concept of socialism was in no way different from that of any other socialist, and the only new element was that socialism in Guyana could best be achieved through the instrument of the cooperative, hence the philosophy of cooperative socialism...The Comrade Leader explained that cooperative socialism meant the PNC was intent on establishing a socialist state, a state where production was for the people's use and benefit, **where classes are abolished, and where equality of opportunity was created and there was control of the economy by the proletariat** [emphasis added].[41]

The Comrade Leader always combined grandiloquence with the threat of 'condign treatment' to those who dared to challenge what he pronounced as the orthodoxy of the moment. He was not remiss. But it is important to note that while claiming no difference between his conception of socialism and, one presumes, that of the wider communist world, he never ever identified himself as a 'communist or a Marxist-Leninist.' This cannot be overstressed:

> There are many people who believe that cooperative socialism is a new type of socialism. And there are many capitalists, and grasping businessmen, **free enterprise rascals** [mainly Indians], who join the PNC because they say the PNC is not socialist, so they can join the PNC and overcharge the people for milk and this and that and hope that the PNC card will save them from jail...If there be anyone who believes that because we talk of cooperative socialism, our objective in so far as establishing socialism is different from any other socialists, you are mistaken. And if you do not want to share the socialist objective, then, until we have educated you, the PNC is not the place for you.[42]

Burnham's cooperative socialism was hollow at the point of conception, his occasional allusion to congruence between it and international communism notwithstanding. And I believe that the historically flawed foundation of his contrived concept of cooperative socialism was of a piece: inseparable from Burnham's cultivated political pragmatism with its intrinsic amorphousness with respect to ideology. His way with words and the refined diction, allied with his legal dexterity, had long been his greatest strength.

Therefore, it seems as if Humpty Dumpty, in his clever exchange with Alice, had anticipated Forbes:

Humpty Dumpty: When *I* use a word, it means just what *I* choose it to mean – neither more nor less.

Alice: The question is whether you can make words mean so many different things.

Humpty Dumpty: The question is, which is to be master – that's all.

PART 3.
The Mind of L.F.S. Burnham

I. Ashton Chase, Once a Close Friend and Ministerial Colleague of Burnham in 1953, Assesses the Personality and Politics of This Adroit Operator

Ashton Chase, as I noted earlier, has endeavoured to get to the bottom of Burnham's *modus operandi*. He has no reservation, premised on a personal relationship with the man in the 1950s, in the PPP and the British Guiana Labour Union (BGLU), that it was all about tactical instrumentalities designed to gain for himself supreme power – to remake the place in his own image. It became a wasteland under his stewardship, but as many

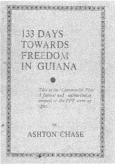

Left: Ashton Chase (1926–2023) in his eighties: the youngest member of the PPP cabinet of 1953, but arguably the most rational and responsible. He was not a communist

Right: Ashton Chase's booklet on the short-lived PPP government of May-October 1953

Guyanese would have concluded, the brightness of the man was indisputable, yet he patently lacked the temperament, imagination, and skills to rule for the good of his people. It was essentially a universe of words. Another pursuit of utopia. In this respect, he shared an ineradicable flaw with Jagan that inflicted a mortal wound on their country, as the best and brightest, of all races, religions, and class, sought greener pastures in the lands of 'free enterprise rascals' *par excellence*: the capitalist/imperialist North. With very few regrets.

Provoked relentlessly by Jagan to nationalise the 'commanding heights of the economy' and sever links with the imperialists, Burnham would force all the major industries, bauxite and sugar (including the giant Booker Company), under state control – and quickly on the road to ruin. Yet the PNC continued to propagate the faulty doctrine that the cooperative was the instrument to facilitate workers' control and management of the state-owned enterprises. Moreover, that it was the means to abundant productivity in all economic ventures while conducing to the eradication of individual greed – thereby would a culture of collective endeavour enhancing the lives of the working class come to fruition. But it was never believed by most Guyanese that such an absurdity, the biggest idea to emanate from the brain of the great leader, could ever deliver its projected bountiful harvest to the eternal satisfaction of the 'proletariat.' Burnham's Cooperative Socialist Republic, the first in the world, would also be the last such experiment in the world. In fact, even in the villages of Guyana, the cooperatives as an instrument for making 'the small man a real man' never did take off, while the large state enterprises became stymied, an irreversible drain on the country's resources, as poor management and the politicisation of decision-making destroyed the once thriving sugar and bauxite industries. Burnham had said that the Kuru Kuru Cooperative College would become the principal means of training cadres for the administration of cooperative societies, but this too was on its last legs by the time Burnham died in August 1985. Cooperative socialism died, and was buried or cremated, with the Comrade Leader.

Ashton Chase was a founder-member of the PAC/PPP, and like Jagan, Burnham, and Sydney King, a minister of the short-lived PPP cabinet of 1953, but he demonstrated greater maturity than all of them though only twenty-seven. He was not a communist and was inclined to empathise with the comparatively 'moderate' ideological posture of Burnham at the time, and for some time thereafter. But Chase never did join Burnham in his PPP (Burnham) or his PNC (after 1957), possibly because he was wary of his slickness, his seductive superficiality. He was fully aware of Burnham's predilection for self-aggrandisement and the pursuit of absolute power – an aspect of communism that 'tickled' him. Chase has tried, therefore, to penetrate Burnham's guile in his flirtation with Marxism:

> Because of Mr Burnham's ability – and he was unquestionably an able man – his flirtation with Marxism, both in England and in Europe as a student [1944–48], was enough to give him a firm grip of its principles and **it tickled his fancy to observe and comprehend the communist monolithic control in Eastern Europe at that time. But he was never absorbed into the communist movement or trusted by its leaders** [particularly Billy Strachan and other prominent leaders in the CPGB]. **He was too slick and amorphous, but he was later able to have friendly cooperation with some of them** [Castro and Kim Il-sung certainly].[43]

Chase apprehended also that Burnham (they were the two most senior executives in the BGLU) was, by instinct, a pragmatist for whom principles were flexible – malleable instruments that could be adjusted in pursuit of power.

In this respect, he was prepared to play ball with the communists but could never really join the club, in the manner of the doctrinaire Jagan. He would also play ball with the imperialists and desert them when he felt the time had come to ditch 'bourgeois democracy,' as he did from the early 1970s. Chase made an astute assessment of Burnham that remains valid in comprehending the enigma he was. In his time, some form of socialism (a vague term) was almost mandatory in many post-colonial societies. Burnham knew this very well, but he was also aware that to get power in America's backyard it was imperative not to antagonise the imperialists before adopting whatever version of socialism one chose to embrace. His rhetoric was invariably empty, but he was never likely to undermine his political aspirations by joining the communist side in the Cold War, definitely not before independence. He would never jeopardise his political ascendancy for any creed, unlike the naively reckless and suicidal abandon of Cheddi Jagan.

Burnham cultivated both the British and American imperialists in pursuit of power; he thereby had it delivered to him by them, and he utilised it to marginalise Jagan (through rigged elections). He then virtually abandoned his imperialist sponsors as he moved to the left to neuter Jagan, while gaining the affirmation of many of Jagan's communist allies. Chase argues:

> [Burnham] learnt and appreciated how the State machinery operated and where the corridors of power lay. He soon realised that in displacing the capitalists and by taking firm control of the public organs of communication he could control the State machinery and its citizens' very existence and their thought processes.

It was an expert stroke despite the fact that it was creating a nullity that would leave little credit for his legacy or Jagan's for that matter. Chase knew Burnham as well as anyone in the original PPP; in fact, probably only he could have persuaded Forbes to moderate his stance for total leadership of the PPP after the general elections that took a fragmented, vulnerable, and rudderless PPP into office, for 133 days in 1953. Ashton Chase tells it better than anyone:

> At a very early stage, even before entering the political arena in his native land [British Guiana]…[Burnham's] pragmatism led him to the conviction that open embrace of this dogma [communism] in the western hemisphere could not be the foundation of enduring political achievement and success. **So he adopted a devious approach with the ultimate objective…that he remained supreme and subservient to none. But first political power was necessary; for without it, all plans were mere dreams.** [Chase could well have been addressing Jagan posthumously.]
>
> Accordingly, Burnham fashioned and chartered his course, biding his time, deflecting impulses and images that sought to identify him

with Marxism, so as to be thought a safe ally by the colonial rulers…
[emphasis added].[44]

Burnham looked down on Jagan because he deemed him inferior to his own
widely acclaimed intellectual and political sagacity. Besides, it is arguable that as
the Indians seemed on the verge of economic and political supremacy after the
War, Burnham perceived his foremost political task as ensuring that Jagan did
not lead British Guiana to Independence – that Indo-Guyanese euphoria and
self-assurance over India's independence (*swaraj*) did not eventuate in an Indo-
Guyanese *swaraj*. Burnham's cultivated ambiguities and studied nebulousness
were choreographed, and underpinned, by the chronic ethnic insecurity of
Africans. As early as the short-lived broad coalition that was the PPP of the early
1950s, he was driven by the urgency to attain leadership of the anti-colonial
movement.

It is noteworthy that Jagan himself recalls that, virtually from the formation
of the PPP in January 1950, Burnham was manoeuvring to secure the leadership
for himself. And he states that as early as 1952, at the party's third congress,
Burnham was seeking, determinedly, to get himself elected leader. Jagan adds
that one of Burnham's foremost opponents then was Sydney King, who in
'an impassioned speech' denounced the manoeuvre: 'This is a motion of no-
confidence in our leader [Jagan]; why such a motion of no-confidence in our
leader; why such a motion at this time?'[45]

It is clear, therefore, that it was only a matter of time before the racial
insecurities permeating the wider society undermine the fragile organisational
structure of the PPP. Yet the question of racial identity, its underpinning and its
ramification, which still bedevil Guyana today, were never ventilated in the PPP
but simply papered over. And in 1955 it came to a head with the departure of
Burnham and his lieutenants (a few of whom were Indians), and then in 1956,
even stalwart defenders of Jagan, such as Sydney King, Martin Carter, and Rory
Westmaas (the so-called ultra-left, considered Marxists) deserted Jagan. King
would meander his way to the PNC for 'racial' reasons; Carter would seek
employment with Booker (and was a minister in the PNC government from
1967–69), and Westmaas left politics for good, disillusioned with politicians and
cynical about the political vocation.

In the context of the Cold War and Jagan's intractable pro-Moscow
communism, Burnham's mission was made infinitely easier. Ashton Chase was
at the heart of the early manoeuvres by Burnham within the PPP, to wrest its
putative leadership from Jagan. 'Leader or nothing,' he demanded:

> Mr Burnham soon showed his true colours when he claimed
> leadership in the House of Assembly, and there were rivalry and

confrontation with Dr Jagan who had been leading the independence struggle since 1948, and was at one time the lone PPP representative in the Legislative Council [elected in 1947 while in the PAC; the lone PPP legislator, 1950–53]. This embarrassing deadlock was only resolved on my private initiative with Mr Burnham, resulting in his withdrawing his challenge, thereby facilitating the PPP entering the House of Assembly and the executive office [Executive Council in May 1953]....[46]

That, up to this point and even the suspension of the Constitution in October 1953, there was no official leader of the PPP, was reflective of how contentious, and potentially calamitous, an issue it was. The question of leadership underlined the extent to which the original PPP was a very loose coalition, and it encapsulated the debilitating implications of the ethnic insecurities of this tenuously constructed colonial backwater. Chase noted that while the first PPP government lasted a mere 133 days before the British government suspended the Constitution, allegedly to forestall a communist plot to take over the country, Burnham was always circumspect about communism and 'left adventurism' within the PPP. He was, even at the age of thirty, the consummate pragmatic politician, never inclined to show his hand:

> The British Government's action...was presaged by leftist adventurism within the Party – in which he [Burnham] **took no part, and in fact cautioned moderation. The consequences of this extreme left posture – often demonstrated by infantile acts – were there for all to see. Although none of us, including him, expected such a sharp reaction from the British Government, he felt a sense of inward satisfaction that, had his approach of not riling the establishment been adopted, there would not have been such a sterile ending to the PPP's first ascent to office** [emphasis added].[47]

In an interview with Professor Frank Birbalsingh in July 1994, Ashton Chase recalled that Burnham's drive to become leader was a consuming dimension of his personality, but he also gives Burnham credit for his pragmatism, for recognising that the idea of practising communism while still a colony was not only absurd but also politically perilous. Burnham, never a communist although he was inclined to brandish a leftist phraseology, did see through the static communism of Jagan – 'his commitment to Marxism and his communist leanings' – as well as the puerile but incrementally ruinous, bombast of the so-called ultra-left, comprising principally Sydney King, Martin Carter, Keith Carter, and Rory Westmaas. Chase, a central figure in the first PPP government, contends that the intemperate behaviour of several members of the party and government, on the far left, precipitated the suspension of the Constitution:

Birbalsingh: I assume that in 1953 Dr Jagan was fully in control of the party [PPP]. He was leader?

Chase: Well, he had no position which you could describe as one man controlling the party. There was a top leadership of which Dr Jagan was certainly one of the leading participants.

Birbalsingh: The ideology of the party was social democratic?

Chase: There was much more than that. **There were strong communist influences in the party...**

Birbalsingh: I am told that Burnham may have thought that his British education and culture gave legitimacy to his bid for party leadership.

Chase: That is hogwash. It had [everything] to do with character: Burnham wanted to be head and leader. It was personal and had nothing to do with his British training...**The man's personality did not permit him to play second fiddle to anyone. He wanted leadership and that was that** [emphasis added].[48]

It may be recalled that Ashton Chase (aged twenty-seven) was minister of labour, industry and commerce in the PPP government of 1953; while Burnham (aged thirty) was minister of education. And, interestingly, Chase was general secretary of the oldest union in the colony, the BGLU, while its president was Burnham. Chase was at the heart of the storm, which he felt was brewing since the PPP entered the government in May 1953:

Birbalsingh: How did the disintegration of the party [the PPP government of 133 days] occur? Were there mistakes that could have been avoided...?

Chase: The British were very alarmed by the communist ideology that appeared to take over the leadership of the party and felt constrained to nip the menace in the bud...I am not saying the party had to do what it did in 1953. The party should not have been guilty of such amateurish displays at the time. It was absolute nonsense to try to establish communism in British Guiana at the time, without the necessary clout, support, and foundation, and without having independence. The thing has to be put in proportion. You couldn't jump straight from colonialism to communism. Those who thought they could, made a colossal error of tactics in the matter. The tactics were hopelessly wrong.

And Burnham said so. He lost credit for that. The extremists in the party took a course of action that provoked the British to react. I think they alarmed the whole western world. And later the Americans took a position that was so hostile to the PPP and exercised such influence on the British that there was no hope of establishing communism in the region.

Birbalsingh: The extremists failed to see the situation in a sufficiently global perspective?

Chase: Cheddi might have been able to control them [the ultra-left] but he did not. Perhaps he did not want them to think he was less Left than them. So, they just carried on.[49]

Words! Words! Words! There was much talking within the PPP in the early 1950s, yet at no time was the race issue which was already suffocating the party ever discussed (in the general council or in the party's organ, *Thunder*); neither was the possibility of creating an instrument for power-sharing within the PPP. It rankled and poisoned the politics of the party and the country as a whole. And, even when Burnham created a party with its distinctive identity, in late 1957, his PNC did not address this fundamental problem – the eternal curse of the place. Both the PPP and the PNC were racial parties and have remained so until today. Their solution was a synthetic one, mere window dressing: selecting a few people of the other ethnic group to create a façade of inclusion: the Brindley Benn syndrome (PPP); the Sonny Ramphal syndrome (PNC).

Chase has also written on the devastating consequences of Burnham's nationalisation of 80 per cent of the economy by the end of the 1970s (fully supported by Jagan, of course), and the rapid decline of the two key industries, bauxite and sugar. Between 1971 and 1985 (the years of Burnham's vigorous nationalisation programme), sugar production fell from about 311,000 to 243,000 tons; and calcined bauxite declined from 693,000 tons to 487,000 tons, while alumina dropped from 312,000 tons to 245,000 tons. And, ominously, poor management and the utter neglect of basic preventative maintenance were exacerbating this downward trend.

Ashton Chase's argument (in his book on Burnham), regarding the impact of nationalisation applies, in equal measure, to Jagan, a true believer in the concept. Moreover, Jagan was an indefatigable proponent of this mantra of Marxism-Leninism, challenging Burnham to escalate and expand his policy of state-control of 'the commanding heights of the economy':

> Production in all the important sectors of the economy declined. The international implications of taking control and ownership of bauxite and sugar were not properly addressed. The *modus operandi* of the transnational corporations that managed these concerns was not fully grasped. By way of example, Booker was an integrated body with

Fletcher Stewart and Co (UK), and it was out of this axis that the machinery for the sugar factories and spare parts were produced and were forthcoming. Little or no attention was paid to the continued servicing of the sugar factories or the bauxite plants, the draglines and rolling stock in the mines…

So stress on machines was one factor that helped curtail production and productivity. But this stress emanated from poor planning and inadequate provision for maintenance and rehabilitation. With the lack of democracy also came the flight of skills and experience, another contributory factory.[50]

Chase could have added that Jagan, impelled by a visceral antipathy towards the 'sugar gods,' was even more disinclined to see any merit in the *modus operandi* of such imperialist 'bloodsuckers' as Booker. Jagan was more obsessed than Burnham to be rid of the 'exploiters,' his conviction being that it was solely by sheer 'loot' that they made 'super profits'; indeed, as a communist, he saw all profits as evil: the 'surplus value' extracted from the exertions of the real toilers. These foreign capitalists, by his 'bitter sugar' mantra, had made no contribution worthy of recognition to the astounding achievement that was the sugar cane culture – not even the complex and costly hydraulic system they built and sustained or their scientific research and innovation in agronomy and engineering or their administrative rigour fed by a resolve, to which Chase gives justifiable credit. In fact, Chase believes that Burnham nationalised sugar not because it was integral to his socialism – rather, it was driven by the ego of a man who 'wanted more power.'

It is appropriate to recall what Dr Fenton Ramsahoye told me several times: Jagan and Burnham had 'no idea how money works'; they were impractical in devising viable initiatives for the creation of wealth; they were supercilious about their presumed acuity, that they were smarter than those with proven business acumen, and both were united in their hatred of the White capitalists.[51] Beyond their conceit, the inevitable wasteland. Ashton Chase elaborates:

Cursory examination of the systems used by transnational companies that operate here could have shown that they placed a high priority on the periodic maintenance of equipment and a certain ratio of spare parts to rolling stock…Every piece of machinery or equipment has an estimated working life. With care, it makes it; without care, it collapses much before it has even covered the initial capital outlay for its acquisition.

Such a loss business cannot afford. Businesses run in the manner in which these corporations were run would have collapsed [much earlier]…but because they were all backed by Government with an almost limitless capacity to tax, and to print currency notes, their inefficiency and incompetence were shielded and they survived far longer than could private enterprise similarly run.[52]

Burnham's nationalisation programme was an unmitigated disaster, and when combined with his ban on the importation of various basic foodstuff, such as flour, dal, garlic, onion, canned meat, **including sardines (a contraband supply of the latter was delivered to me regularly at 2–3:00 a.m., which I hid in rice husk in a barrel),** in addition to a wide range of consumer durables, the privation people endured in the world's first (and last) cooperative socialist republic could be imagined. This was exacerbated by the absurdity that a glorious sunshine awaited them at the end of the cooperative socialist tunnel. In reality, Burnhamism led to the impoverishment of a large segment of the population, irrespective of race or religion, while most of the best and the brightest deserted in droves, for the capitalist north: the US and Canada. The legacy of Burnham's nationalisation project (endorsed by Jagan who wanted even more of it) is encapsulated in the dismal fact that for a small country like Guyana its principal export since independence in 1966 has been its people. In 1980, Guyana's population was about seven hundred and eighty thousand; in 2018, it was roughly seven hundred and eighty-four thousand.

The ridiculous Grenada Revolution notwithstanding, there is no parallel in the Anglophone Caribbean to remotely match the Guyanese futility: the carnival of words, particularly the Marxist jargon, that has done nothing to enhance the place or to resolve the entrenched racist predisposition of its peoples. Just about every issue is ineluctably pressed through the sieve of racial proclivity, however solid the will for a rational discourse. The racist instincts soon kick in without even the supposedly enlightened realising it. In fact, the cascading socialist rhetoric of the three main political parties, in the late 1970s to early 1980s, had a knack for circumventing the Guyanese peoples' racism. In the end, they reaped the whirlwind: the economy disintegrated, and the last vestiges of liberal democracy evaporated. It is an experience that has ravaged the soul of this country which still eludes nationhood, fifty-seven years after the British handed it over to Burnham's PNC with a combined total of thirty-three years in power, and after twenty-five years of rule by Jagan's PPP. Alternating rule by two antagonistic tribes.

Ashton Chase, obviously reflecting on its omission from any serious consideration in the heady days of the fledgling multiracial PPP in the early 1950s, underlines the centrality of racial prejudice in the Guyanese discourse:

> The constructive approach to the racial question ought to have been an open consideration…instead of literally sweeping it under the carpet, pretending it does not exist. There should be open consideration of the subject, recognising that Guyanese society is so closely interwoven socially and economically that it would be impossible to harm or ignore any section of it without hurting all.

> One must therefore accept the thesis that racial understanding is a prerequisite to political progress. But racism…will be the bugbear of our society for a long time to come.[53]

Cheddi Jagan solemnly believed that capitalism would soon be eradicated from the face of the earth; that 'the commanding heights of the economy' must be controlled by the state; that Marxism-Leninism was the supreme philosophy for the radical remaking of society towards the ultimate social and economic liberation of humankind; and that the Soviet system was the prototype in forging a future of eternal peace, freedom, and happiness. Socialism/communism, with its postulated scientific foundations, provided a rationale to evade confronting Guyanese racism; a façade, too, for the practise of racist politics at which both Jagan and Burnham were artful practitioners. Dr Ramsahoye is correct: they were both racist leaders whose popularity and political longevity owed nothing to Marxism-Leninism or whatever variant of socialism they advocated in Guyana. And their legacies cannot redeem the country they misgoverned and misled, mired in a quagmire of racism that provokes futility even in the most sanguine.

Notes

1. See Cheddi Jagan, 'Address Delivered to the 25th Anniversary Conference of the PPP on behalf of the Central Committee of the PPP, August 3, 1975,' *Thunder*, September–December 1975, 6–9.
2. 'Citation by the Cuban Council of Ministers in awarding the Jose Marti National Order, Cuba's highest honour, to Forbes Burnham in April 1975,' in *People's National Congress Reform: 60th Anniversary Souvenir Magazine, 1957–2017*, 58.
3. 'Speech Delivered by Dr Cheddi Jagan at the Conference of Communist Parties of Latin America and the Caribbean, Havana, June 9–13, 1975,' *Thunder*, April–August 1975, 20.
4. Ibid., 20–21.
5. Ibid., 25–26.
6. Ibid., 26.
7. Ibid., 28–29.
8. Jagan, 'Address Delivered to the 25th Anniversary Conference of the PPP on behalf of the Central Committee of the PPP, August 3, 1975,' 9, 20, 23, 28.
9. Ibid., 28.
10. Ibid., 27–30.
11. See *Thunder*, April–August 1975, 2.
12. *Foreign Relations of the US, 1969–76, Vol E-11*, Telegram from the US Embassy, Georgetown, to the Department of State, Washington, June 2, 1975.
13. Ibid.
14. Ralph Ramkarran, 'Fidel Castro,' *Stabroek News*, November 27, 2016.
15. *Foreign Relations of the US, 1969–76, Vol E-11*, Part 1, Documents on Mexico, Central America and the Caribbean, 1973–76: Interagency Memorandum, Washington, November 1, 1974.
16. Ibid.

17. Ranji Chandisingh, 'Socialism and Democracy,' *Thunder*, April–September 1975, 37–38.
18. Ibid., 39–40.
19. Ibid., 41.
20. Ibid., 44, 46–47.
21. Ibid., 46–47.
22. *New Nation*, May 27, 1972.
23. Odeen Ishmael, 'The Offer of "Critical Support" by the PPP,' September 2006. Accessed at: guyanajournal.com/critical_support.html.
24. Ibid.
25. Anon., 'Ranji Chandisingh: The Enigma of a Trilemma,' *Guyana Review*, June 30, 2009.
26. Ishmael, 'The Offer of "Critical Support" by the PPP.'
27. *New Nation*, June 17, 1975.
28. *New Nation*, January 5, 1975.
29. *Declaration of Sophia*, Address by Forbes Burnham at a Special Congress to Mark the 10th Anniversary of the PNC in Government, December 14, 1974, 19.
30. Leader, *New Nation*, January 5, 1975.
31. Alan H. Adamson, *Sugar without Slaves: The Political Economy of British Guiana, 1838–1904* (New Haven: Yale University Press, 1972), 36, 40.
32. *Declaration of Sophia*, 9, 30–31, 26.
33. Ibid., 26.
34. *New Nation*, February 9, 1975.
35. R.O. Bostwick, 'The Shape of the Guyana Revolution,' *New Nation*, January 26, 1975.
36. Ibid.
37. Leader, *New Nation*, March 16, 1975.
38. *New Nation*, April 6, 1975.
39. *New Nation*, April 20, 1975.
40. Ibid.
41. *New Nation*, May 25, 1975.
42. Ibid.
43. Ashton Chase, *Guyana: A Nation in Transit: Burnham's Role* (Georgetown: The Author, 1994), 8–9.
44. Ibid., 9.
45. Jagan, *The West on Trial*, 137.
46. Chase, *Guyana: A Nation in Transit: Burnham's Role*, 11.
47. Ibid.
48. Ashton Chase interviewed by Frank Birbalsingh, July 20, 1994, in the latter's *The People's Progressive Party of Guyana, 1950–92: An Oral History* (London: Hansib, 2007), 43.
49. Ibid., 43–44.
50. Chase, *Guyana: A Nation in Transit: Burnham's Role*, 84–86.
51. Interview with Dr Fenton Ramsahoye, Georgetown, August 8, 1997.
52. Chase, *Guyana: A Nation in Transit: Burnham's Role*, 86.
53. Ibid., 12–13.

14.

'I am a Socialist; You are not a Socialist' – II

The Absurdity of Jaganism and Burnhamism, 1976-79

> Its Socialist pretensions apart, the PNC…would be quite incapable
> of achieving its vaguely stated objective of 'making the small man a
> real man.' It has neither the will nor the capacity to do this because it
> is devoid of any Socialist convictions…
>
> The Marxian Socialist realises that it is only the small (or exploited)
> man who can transform himself into a real (or free) man, that is,
> emancipate himself from capitalist wage-slavery…This he will
> do without the 'help' of false and conniving political and labour
> 'leaders,' once he becomes conscious of the cause of his poverty and
> degradation. He will then act in concert with all the other members
> of his class [irrespective of race] to remove that cause – capitalism –
> and establish socialism.
>
> The People's Progressive Party (PPP) is the only Guyanese
> organisation providing the knowledge that will enable the entire
> working class to unite and use its considerable power to establish a
> just (or Socialist) society.
>
> **–'"Cooperative" Republic,' Leader, *Thunder*,
> (October–November 1969)**

I.   A Cascade of Marxist Dogmas: Every Stray Dog's a Socialist!

I return now to Forbes Burnham's creation of the first (and last) 'Cooperative
Socialist Republic' in the world. Jagan lampooned it, so did many Guyanese
in virtually every segment of the society – neither fish nor fowl. I have noted
time and again that Burnham could not bring himself to characterise his
cooperative socialist experiment – the grandest 'big idea' from his brilliant mind
– definitively as Marxist-Leninist. It was as if such vocabulary reeked of tainted
Jaganite communist jargon: inherently flawed. Even in the early 1950s, when he
was chairman of the People's Progressive Party (PPP) and wrote regularly for
its organ, *Thunder*, he could not be boxed in by any such doctrinaire ideological
strictures. But by the mid-1970s, with his rule unassailable following his extensive

rigging of the 1973 elections, he deftly proceeded to befriend the Castro regime, the Chinese, the North Koreans, the Romanians, even the Soviets. Virtually overnight, the nose of Burnham's camel was in the tent of most of Jagan's communist friends.

Amazingly, Burnham also transcended the irreconcilable divide within the communist world, having found a way to court the Chinese simultaneously. Yet Burnham would eschew the standard communist lexicon; nothing remotely parallel to Jagan's voluminous Marxist-oriented writings celebrating the glory of the Soviet Union and the communist utopia ever did emanate from his eclectic mind. He would leave the belated Marxist-Leninist ideological posturing to his underlings – in the PNC, including several former senior leaders in Jagan's PPP, apparently counselled to cross the floor at the behest of the Cuban comrades. None was more illustrious than Cheddi's second in command and foremost Marxist theoretician, the lifelong communist, Ranji Chandisingh (1930–2009).

Before I address the defection to the PNC of Ranji, Burnham's prize catch, I wish to address the posturing of two Johnnies-come-lately 'Marxists': Comrade Ptolemy Reid (1918–2003), the deputy prime minister, and Comrade 'Kit' Nascimento, minister of state in the Office of the Prime Minister, the latter formerly a rabid anti-communist in Peter D'Aguiar's United Force (UF). Appearing on the GBS programme, 'Night Ride,' in mid-August 1975, Comrade Reid cast doubt on the authenticity of Jagan's pronouncement, a few days before, that the PPP was shifting from 'non-cooperation and civil resistance' to 'critical support' of Burnham's dictatorship. And Comrade Reid was reportedly quick in utilising standard Jaganite jargon to make his case for the socialist revolution: '… it was his belief that the country was on an irreversible path towards socialism but that while the PNC was a socialist party, the whole country was not yet socialist and the people must be on guard for subversion from imperialism.'

He added that Jagan had pursued his negative campaign for two years; it had obviously been a failure, as the people were in favour of embracing positive ideas for their self-improvement. The PNC was doing precisely that. Jagan's change of tactic, then, was precipitated by the possibility that his party could be facing its demise.

In fact, Burnham was essentially liquidating the PPP by appropriating, if not absorbing, Jagan's entrenched ideological rationale. Reid was asked to comment on the PNC's conception of cooperative socialism. He responded that the PNC believed in 'one socialism, based on the findings of Marx and the works of Lenin.' He added that 'the PNC was using the cooperative as the chief means of establishing a socialist society in Guyana because the country had a history of people working together in cooperatives…Since they have this historical background, we will build it up and use that as the means to help carry the socialist ideology.'[1] Untrue! But it was the dictum handed down by the Comrade Leader that, supposedly, would set all the people free.

Comrade Reid was asked how socialism could become the instrument for the liberation of West Indians specifically, known for their 'traditional openness.' Presumably, his interviewer had in mind the general aversion to communism in the Anglophone Caribbean where it lacked even a peripheral presence. The comrade responded that 'socialism would free the people's culture from the shackles of domination since capitalism used culture to keep them in subjection, not only by destroying their own culture but also by imposing an alien culture on them.'[2]

But it was the final point made by the Comrade Deputy Prime Minister which, arguably, underpinned his, as well as the Comrade Leader's, belated embrace of socialism: the 'paramountcy' of the People's National Congress (PNC) over the government of Guyana. This was the crux, and (as I contend) Marxism-Leninism provided the doctrinal affirmation for imposing the dictatorial rule of Burnham on Guyana. Of course, he was aided and abetted by the beliefs of, and interminable promptings from, the 'genuine communist,' Cheddi Jagan, to take control of 'the commanding heights of the economy.' Reid reportedly concluded 'that decisions taken by the PNC Congress would be binding on the government, which is regarded as one of its executive arms.' Speaking of paramountcy of the PNC over the government, he argued, in his inimitably prosaic manner, that 'this paramountcy made people perform better...It is not a paramountcy for idleness and laziness and ignorance. It is a paramountcy for greater efficiency.'[3]

A true measure of the absurdity of the socialist revolution launched by the PNC, was the fact that a principal advocate was Comrade 'Kit' Nascimento. He was one of the most formidable crusaders against Jagan's communism in the early 1960s, both as the leading youth leader of Peter D'Aguiar's UF and as the editor of the virulently anti-communist *Daily Chronicle*, owned and controlled by D'Aguiar since around 1960. But by the early 1970s, the UF was practically defunct; therefore, Comrade Kit seamlessly hitched his wagon to the PNC. So meteoric was the transformation that he accompanied Comrade Forbes when he received the José Martí National Award in Havana in April 1975.

Now, in late July 1975, Comrade Kit was pontificating on 'socialism as a worldwide phenomenon.' He appeared to be over the moon that most of Europe was already socialist (communist), as was 'almost all of Asia' and 'the greater part of the continent of Africa'; even South America, long characterised by right-wing dictatorships, was 'undergoing a revolutionary transformation in the direction of Socialism.' He was sanguine that Marxism-Leninism was the guiding philosophy for the liberation of the people of Guyana from want and the gross inequalities of capitalism. Comrade Kit's Marxism was substantially more theoretically robust than Comrade Forbes's: '...the means of production, distribution and exchange must be organised, planned and controlled in the interest of the people and the nation as a whole.' He also recognised Marx and Engels's massive contribution to theory and practice, 'an undeniable imprint on the development of mankind.' But their philosophical wisdom could not be replicated as if it were written in stone; it must be judiciously adapted if it were to be efficacious. As he put it, Marxism had to be 'examined, modified, and applied within the context of each nation's differing histories, social, political and economic backgrounds and priorities.'[4]

Unfailingly astute, Comrade Kit was covering all bases, particularly the sacred ground occupied by the Comrade Leader, the fount of ultimate wisdom. He addressed Burnham's peculiar contribution to Marxism, although the latter was consistently, or deliberately, vague about the place of Marxism-Leninism (if any) in his intellectual provenance. Kit was, of course, referring to Comrade Forbes's cooperative socialism. At the same time, he stressed that the Comrade Leader was not imprisoned by immutable ideological orthodoxy – an allusion to Cheddi Jagan's pro-Moscow communism:

> It is this philosophy which has directed the Comrade Leader of the PNC to identify cooperative organisation, in the context of Guyana, to be the instrument for bringing about the small man's involvement in the economic life of the nation. It is for this obvious reason that the PNC has refused to be placed in a straightjacket in so far as the means, strategies and tactics we apply to arrive at the establishment of a socialist society in Guyana are concerned...It is through the deliberate emphasis on the part of the Government in favour of cooperative organisation and enterprise that the PNC intends that the nation's resources will come under the control of and will be placed at the disposal of the masses of people.[5]

Burnham himself had disavowed any proclivity for the Marxist jargon that clogged Jagan's rhetoric for radical transformation, asserting that his notion of cooperative socialism was not predicated on 'the dreams of the visionary but on the solid foundations of reality.'

II. P.D. Sharma's Poetic Caricature of the Socialist Absurdity; and a Belated Toady's Ode to the 'Comrade Leader'

It was in this surreal context, in 1975–76, that P. D. Sharma wrote a poem that captures the Guyanese absurdity, in which the failure to face the chronic ethnic insecurity at the heart of its futility, was replaced by the bizarre condition in which virtually everyone – even stray dogs, as well as erstwhile reactionaries – was proclaiming his socialist creed. I wish to suggest that Sharma could also have titled his poem 'Comrade Kit'; he called it 'Struggle,' a derisory play on the primary prompting of the Marxist vocation. I reproduce it in its entirety, as its sheer triteness conveys (in the manner of the audience's response at a pantomime), with biting acuity, the nullity of the Burnhamite/Jaganite/Rodneyite politics of the 1970s–80s, as each school arrogated to itself sole possession of a version of socialist/communist wisdom – but definitively out of bounds to any bourgeois tendency! In fact, the latter (such as had survived the 'socialist' certainty) was forced to bolt its doors and stay indoors, away from the windows framed by a culture of rampant Marxist exuberance. Unlike the rest of the Anglophone Caribbean, Guyanese society, unremittingly stunted by its racism, ironically, had engendered a habitat in which every major political party defined itself as socialist or communist. Yet this did not spring from a uniquely radical temperament; it reflected a deep-seated apprehension to face reality – the country's racist underpinnings. Marxism-Leninism was a variant of the El Dorado fantasy, at the core of the Guyanese psyche.

Sharma speaks:
Struggle

'I am a Socialist'
'You are not a Socialist'

'I am a Socialist'
'You are not a Socialist'

'Yes I am a Socialist'
'No you are not a Socialist'

'I am'
'You are not'

'I am, I am'
'You're not, you're not'

'Yes I am'
'No you're not'

'Yes I am'
No you're not'

Yes I am'
No you're not'

'Yes yes yes I am'
'No no no you're not'

'I am a socialist'
'You are not a Socialist'[6]

Meanwhile, no less powerfully, Sharma prefaces the section of his poems captioned 'Flight' with a quote from V. S. Naipaul. It speaks to the strange shape of the politics where every Tom, Dick, and Harry Lall had, overnight, become a 'comrade' ready to fight imperialism to create the socialist utopia. Yet, ironically but with unruffled equanimity, many of these stalwarts of the socialist revolution with their children, as well as many victims of their misguided policies, were in pursuit of a new life – not in Guyana, but by flight northwards – seeking their place in the sun in the land of the imperialists: 'I left them all and walked briskly towards the aeroplane, not looking back, looking only at my shadow before me, a dancing dwarf on the tarmac.'[7] This dancing dwarf dogged by uncertainty, invariably, did find his or her place in the sun, even before communism collapsed in the Soviet Union and in its satellites or while the world's first cooperative socialist republic was already a failure – barely off the ground and floundering – the butt of easy ridicule.

The following from Sharma's 'Flights of Fancy' epitomises the strangled soul of the socialist revolution that never was:

When the stark truth
cannot be spoken
the trite obvious
becomes profound.[8]

And, in the next stanza, in a doubly sarcastic reference to 'our enemies,' the imperialist exploiters of the capitalist North, the poet is rescued from the socialist nullity by a real flight from his homeland, misgoverned by 'our comrades' (the cooperative socialists), paradoxically, to the land of 'our enemies,' the land of the imperialists:

And blessed be our enemies, O Lord,
for saving us from our comrades [emphasis added].[9]

Powerful, indeed!

The PNC, its profession of socialist rhetoric notwithstanding, would continually chide Jagan for lacking imagination, for being enslaved by dogmas: an ingrained incapacity to think creatively. In early 1975, Jagan had attacked the PNC government (in a regional newspaper) for a deteriorating economy on the road to ruin: chronic food shortages; pervasive malnutrition; a rising crime rate; misappropriation of public funds; escalating prostitution – appalling material and spiritual deprivation.

In a letter to *New Nation* (the PNC's organ) in early January 1975, a correspondent, G. A. Lashley, accused Jagan of treason for slandering the cooperative republic, 'despite our great progress.' And he rebuked him for his subservience to the Soviet Union:

> Dr Jagan talks about the curtailment of freedom in Guyana, yet he does not seem to realise that because Guyana is free that he can say such things so freely. Jagan is an unapologetic supporter of his masters in Russia. Is he oblivious of the fact that if he was living in Russia, it would have been well-nigh impossible for him to condemn his country and remain alive? He probably would have been sent to the salt mines.[10]

In fact, all the failures sketched by Jagan would soon become magnified in the cooperative republic, as a multitude of foodstuffs and myriad consumer durables were banned because of the country's dire shortage of foreign currency. Sharma puts it, in a poem laced with sarcasm and evocatively titled after two popular banned items, thus:

SARDINES AND SALTFISH

Behold! Utopia cometh

The greatest act of the revolution

the dialectical quintessence [an allusion to the carnival of Marxist dogmas]

of the co-operativist thrust [the latter word, a staple of Comrade Forbes]

the thundering herald

of the socialist millennium

the climactic zenith

of the proletarian epoch

sardines and saltfish banned.[11]

After the revolutionary grandiloquence, the vacuous rhetoric – the puniness of the harvest! Sardines and saltfish, simple iconic Guyanese food items, banned by the decree of the Comrade Leader. No less symbolic of the futility of the Jaganite pursuit of the communist utopia.

Guyana was reaping the bitter fruits of Burnhamism. Yet by the tenth anniversary of Burnham's rule, there was no paucity of lackeys, effusive in their homage to the 'great leader, the guiding light to Guyana's destiny.' One such sycophant, in March 1975, was J. C. Chandisingh (an uncle of Ranji Chandisingh), principal of the Corentyne High School, located in Jagan's birthplace, Port Mourant, on the Lower Corentyne. The following comprises excerpts from the obsequious remarks of this belated fawning disciple of Comrade Leader Burnham:

> ...ten years are over. And as yet another star joins the brilliant galaxy of his achievements, Prime Minister Forbes Burnham, in his gigantic humility, holds aloft the guiding lamp to Guyana's destiny. It is time to pause awhile in wonderment at the problems solved, and the progress made...

> At first, we moaned bitterly over our loss of imported foods [including sardines and saltfish]...But we all saw the light, and heard our Prime Minister's resolute call – 'Awake, arise and follow.' And we arose and followed, and we already can see, even in the midst of the agonies of change, a heartening promise and a hope inspired.

> The foundations on which the new Guyana rests and thieves [*sic*] [thrives?] have been soundly planned. The phase [base?] from which the various projects rise to reality is immovable. Let us now stand on this base and look...at the fruits of our efforts looming in the picture...And standing firmly on the base designed in the past ten years and pointing ahead into the shining light of the future, our Prime Minister Forbes Burnham shows us the way. Let us now honour anew our Republic, and him who guided us. Let us acclaim in sentiments born of a love sublime that swirls in the silence of grateful hearts.[12]

III. Whose is the 'Vanguard Party'?: The Guyanese Futility Magnified

It was against this absurd backdrop that Jagan was subject to pressure from a few of the senior leaders of his party, as well as his Cuban comrades, to terminate his 'non-cooperation and civil disobedience' campaign, launched two years before in the aftermath of the fraudulent general elections of July 1973. It precipitated his decision to offer 'critical support' to the Burnham government, based on its anti-imperialist posture and supposed embrace of Marxism-Leninism – rendered urgent by an apparent threat of imminent invasion by the reactionary Brazilians, acting in collusion with the imperialists. Yet neither the PNC nor the PPP manifested a resolve for a plausible *modus vivendi* in the interest of unity across the enduring racial chasm. Burnham addressed the First Biennial Congress of the PNC on August 18, 1975, but he demonstrated no conciliatory intent. Responding to Jagan's offer of 'critical support,' he asserted that the PNC was, without doubt, the 'vanguard party' exerting 'paramountcy' over the government.

It was transparent that Burnham did not put much store by Jagan's recent expression of 'critical support' for the PNC government. The concept had little chance of materialising because he construed it in disparaging terms – as reflective of the political fragility, the diminished stature, of Jagan. Moreover, Burnham established that the PNC was, indeed, the 'vanguard party,' and he was offering no olive branch, no rapprochement, to a moribund Jagan:

> ...since the Declaration of Sophia [December 1974] there has been unceasing interest shown in the PNC by friends new and old, as well as by enemies and detractors new and old. We have seen hitherto intractable foes [Jagan's PPP] purporting to change their line and generously offering 'critical support'...More recently, a certain political group [Jagan's PPP] has put forward the claim that it, and not the PNC, is the vanguard party. We who live in Guyana can recognise the falsity of such a claim. In non-technical terms, that group has been steadily reduced in the number and loyalty of its members [Untrue! It retained its racial support base.] This, its own leader has in fact admitted, at least by inference when he refers to the possible isolation of his Party and actual subversion and defection. All these amount to confessions of weakening.[13]

Burnham went further: instead of trying to build bridges, he was ardently debunking the assumption that the PPP was the majority party. Besides, he was brazenly enticing Jagan's senior lieutenants to desert him for his PNC, the authentic socialist party; therefore, he was disinclined to collaborate with a waning Jagan, stagnating into irrelevance, as he habitually mocked him. Burnham then made a rare, somewhat incongruous, expedition into Jagan's familiar terrain of jargon – his reference to 'theory' and classes does not belong; it has a discordant ring. I cannot take it seriously because I cannot get out of my mind: Sharma's sardonic response to the absurdity of it all – the Guyanese futility – the juxtaposition of the 'socialist millennium' and his 'sardines and saltfish' imagery. It was 'sardines and saltfish' politics with a gutter aspect, the stench of which permeates the racism in Guyanese politics until today.

What was Burnham's rare theoretical intervention?

> When a socialist states that a particular party is the vanguard party, he must be deemed to be saying that that party is based on and enjoys the firm support of the proletariat or industrial working class [non-existent in Guyana] which is by definition the leader of the socialist revolution, **otherwise he does not understand his theory...**

> When a socialist claims that a particular party is a majority party, he must be deemed to be saying that that party not only enjoys majority support, but also that that majority is based on the majority of the proletariat, rural working class, poor peasants and intelligentsia... [indeterminable because Burnham's elections, bar none, were crooked]

> Further, a socialist cannot, without forsaking his theory, boast that the party of which he [Jagan] is the proponent and leader [PPP], is a majority party because of a wishful and unrealistic anticipation of ethnic [Indian] support. What then differentiates such a party from an outspoken and unapologetic communalist and/or racist political grouping?[14]

Burnham was saying that he alone occupied the socialist high ground; Jagan was not only leading the minority party, but he was also irrelevant. Therefore, it made sense that the few in the leadership of the PPP, endowed with genuine socialist beliefs, should desert the sinking Jaganite ship and come aboard the PNC if they wanted to engage in the socialist revolution ('the true course'), rather than wallowing in theoretical nullity:

> Those who wish to support and quicken the pace of the socialist revolution taking place in Guyana, must do so straight-forwardly and not behind a maze of half-truths and rationalising. Socialists, like good Christians, must admit their faults and misjudgements and then embark upon the true course. Our party on the other hand must and will be prepared to welcome the converted and hitherto misguided, not the unrepentant purveyors of self-serving analyses and falsehoods [the foremost being Jagan]. So far as the PNC is concerned, co-operation and/or unity must be based on principles and ideology, not on opportunism and skin saving.[15]

IV. Burnham Appropriates Jagan's 'Bitter Sugar' Motif but Cannot Undermine His Racial Base

Burnham was not prepared to allow Jagan any space in his political firmament; he was determined to let him dangle in the wind, his proffering 'critical support' in August 1975 notwithstanding. Moreover, by veering definitively to the left and gaining the support of Fidel, Chou-en-Lai, and Kim Il-sung in the process, he was undermining the admirable gravitas Jagan had earned, among communists, for his implacability in espousing his Marxist-Leninist creed. On the ground as well, Burnham had garnered tangible respect, even from some PPP leaders, for his comprehensive nationalisation programme, which would soon result in 80 per cent of the economy being in the hands of the state. Burnham's single most dramatic measure in this process was in 1976 when he nationalised the sugar giant, Booker, the company that, more than any other, encapsulated for Jagan the predatory nature of imperialism: 'bitter sugar.' As argued earlier, even the far-reaching reforms conceived and piloted from the 1950s by the progressive head of Booker, Jock Campbell (with a Fabian socialist outlook), could make no impression on Jagan. He had pressured Burnham relentlessly to take control of 'the commanding heights of the economy,' to eradicate exploitative private capital, particularly foreign capital. The latter had no redeeming features for him.

Burnham executed his master stroke on the tenth anniversary of independence, May 26, 1976. By nationalising Booker, he claimed his party was redressing the imbalance of centuries, 'vindicating our forefathers.' But it was aimed primarily at stealing Jagan's most resounding thunder. By taking control of the sugar industry, Burnham was seeking not merely to extirpate what Jagan always contended was at the heart of Guyanese backwardness – 'bitter sugar' – but also to undercut the most resilient plank of Jagan's politics that resonated with his unassailable base: the Indian sugar-worker.

Burnham's posturing notwithstanding, he was fully aware that Jagan's Indian support base was not diminished one iota by the nationalisation of Booker. This was expressed most emphatically in the elections among the sugar workers, on December 31, 1975, to resolve, at last, the question of the recognition of the union controlled by Jagan's PPP, Guyana Agricultural and General Workers' Union (GAWU). As Odeen Ishmael rightly points out, by polling 98 per cent of the votes (a rare case of free elections in Burnham's Guyana), GAWU had vindicated that Indian loyalty to Jagan remained unimpaired, thus negating the assumption that the PNC had eroded his base to any material extent.[16]

Burnham knew that recognition of GAWU meant that although the sugar industry was owned by the state from 1976, Jagan now had a potent instrument at his disposal. He could readily deploy the union as an instrument of his politics, as he did in 1977, with the 135-day strike, to secure a profit-sharing formula. Time and again, GAWU would be the PPP's weapon to challenge the government on one issue or another. But the latter had become a dictatorship, particularly after the 1980 Burnham constitution was promulgated. He had, in essence, rejected the 'critical support' of the PPP, but Jagan now had the means of creating severe economic damage, as was evident with the strike in 1977, in addition to successive minor strikes over ad hoc grievances.[17]

But Burnham continued to dominate the political space, essentially appropriating Jagan's political programme, while rigging the general elections again, in 1980, thus denying him power until several years after his death in 1985. Yet it was his nationalisation of Booker that Burnham envisioned could conceivably lessen Jagan's ardour. When Burnham addressed the nation on the tenth anniversary of Guyana's independence (May 1976), his main subject was the recent takeover of the assets of Booker. He exploited it to the hilt, as if it presaged the elimination of the sustaining 'bitter sugar' motif at the core of the Jaganite mission for thirty years, thereby administering the final act in consigning Jagan to political oblivion.

I quote Burnham at length because this was the single most momentous act Jagan would have yearned to perform: the elimination of the 'sugar gods'; the end of 'bitter sugar'; placing the sugar estates in the hands of the people. Burnham's masterly oratory was enhanced further when he was righting ancient wrongs, evoking guilt from the White imperialists for their and their ancestors' sins, harking back to the unrequited brutalities of their great and great-great-grandfathers. The following excerpts illustrate the extent to which racial memory, of enslavement, retained its hold on the Comrade Leader. He could never really transcend it; it was inextricable from his self-definition as the redeemer – integral to the megalomania, too:

> There is no Guyanese, save those agents of the imperialists, the Judases of our time, attracted by the glitter of the silver pieces, who does not feel a certain exultancy over the Booker take-over.
>
> We feel that we have redressed the imbalance of centuries. We feel that we are vindicating our forefathers. We justly feel we have made the most significant declaration of independence…
>
> Our nationalisation of Booker is at once our greatest triumph and the greatest threat to our country and our sovereignty. **To us Booker was symbolic of the frustration, the exploitation, the degradation of colonialism, neo-colonialism and capitalism** [emphasis added].
>
> To our enemies who would keep us economic slaves; to our enemies who believe in the divine right to rule over and direct the lives of us lesser breed without the law; to our enemies who believe God ordained them to exercise dominion over palm and pine [Rudyard Kipling], Booker is also symbolic.
>
> I speak not necessarily of the representatives of Booker. They are reasonable mortals. I speak of the system and those who control the levers of power and domination in the capitalist, imperialist and neo-colonialist world. For them we have moved too fast; we have been too independent. We are setting a bad example, and puny though we are in size, we, in their minds, can contribute to the dissolution of the old system of greed and exploitation. We have been too resolute and too successful…
>
> Further, are we not the descendants of brutalised slaves and indentured labourers – a little lower than the animals? Was it not ordained, from the beginning of time, that we should be poor, mere hewers of wood and drawers of water? Are we not those whom the Almighty cursed and decreed that this chosen people should smite?[18]

Burnham had stolen Jagan's most sacred idiom, the ultimate source of his political inspiration, credibility, and longevity: 'bitter sugar.' And he had done so with the approbation of several of Jagan's communist friends, particularly

Castro – the most unpalatable aspect of it all. Only Cheddi's quasi-religious faith in Marxism-Leninism, coupled with the legitimacy fortified by his undiminished racial support, could have sustained him through such dispiriting travails.

Reading Burnham's triumphalist speech reminds me vividly of what Jock Campbell (1912–94), the chairman of Booker, told to me in the early 1990s: even if he were the Archangel Gabriel and had instituted the most radical transformation in the sugar industry in British Guiana, it would have made no difference whatsoever to Jagan and Burnham. On December 22, 1994, four days before Jock's death, Dr Fenton Ramsahoye (1929–2018), Jagan's attorney general (1961–64), and I lunched with him at his home in Nettlebed, Oxfordshire. The following is a brief excerpt from a long conversation of about two hours:

Seecharan: Fenton, what Jock did, was it a case of too little, too late? If the reforms had been speeded up in the 1950s to early 1960s, would it have made any difference to the political evolution of Guyana?

Ramsahoye: I don't think that any attempt to speed up the process of reforms would have made any difference to the sort of culture the political parties were endeavouring to create in Guyana. The basis of the PPP's political culture, in the end, was the nationalisation of the sugar industry, and whether the reforms were speeded up or the welfare programme speeded up, would in no way have altered their fundamental political philosophy. It would have remained the same whatever the pace of social development in the industry.

Campbell: By the time I'd got enough seniority in Booker to start things moving [after the War], I wasn't thinking politically at all. I was always thinking of the unpaid debts and the appalling scars of slavery and indenture…I thought the sugar industry would probably be nationalised, so we weren't trying to buy anybody off; we were genuinely trying to behave far better. Everybody hated Booker, and my business was to try to make people, if not **like** Booker – I said it was always easier for a Campbell to go through the eye of a needle than for a big company to be loved, but it could at least be understood and respected…I entirely agree with Fenton, it wouldn't have made any difference: anything we did at any stage.

To local politicians and others, it was axiomatic that sugar profits were unremittingly astronomical, and that the 'sugar gods' were 'bloodsuckers' (Jagan's characterisation). They could not wait to get their hands on the assets of Booker, the source of guaranteed massive wealth, presumably redounding to the prosperity of all Guyanese. Unfortunately, they got it wrong. Very wrong.

The narrative of sugar, understandably, still evokes painful memories and strong emotions, but the reality of sustaining the cane sugar industry in a transformed market with sucrose substitutes, little or no European compulsion or empathy to subsidise the industry any longer, in addition to the dearth of managerial and technical ingenuity, have rendered the cane sugar industry increasingly precarious, possibly terminal, in Guyana. Like most aspects of Guyanese political culture, the grand language of Burnham and the Marxist utopianism of Jagan overshadowed their capacity to judge or to lead. Besides, they were racial leaders with little credibility beyond their base.

V.   Burnham Catches the Big Fish: Ranji Chandisingh; Denounces the Arid PPP as 'Not yet a Marxist-Leninist Party' and Defects to Burnham's Greener Pastures

Meanwhile, although allegiance to Marxism-Leninism never did emanate from the mouth of Comrade Leader Burnham (it might have had a false ring after his ritual denigration of Jagan's communist dogmatism), yet some of his underlings appeared to have had licence to pledge their loyalty to the doctrine, however fluid its conceptualisation by the PNC. It was used sparingly and often strategically, primarily (it seems) as a device to undermine Jagan's stature as an internationally recognised communist. This was often the case when the PNC was interacting with the fraternal Communist Party of Cuba, such as in December 1975 when the PNC sent three delegates to their congress in Havana. The PNC stressed their common solidarity with the African liberation movements, as well as their joint initiatives in the Non-Aligned Movement in quest of a new world economic order.

Then came this startling affirmation of a commonality of purpose with their newfound Cuban comrades: **'Guyana is firmly committed to the establishment of a Socialist society inspired by Marxism-Leninism, and in this task finds useful lessons to be learned from the Cuban experience. Guyana is happy to count Cuba among her friends** [emphasis added].' The PNC's message added that Cuba's 'victory against imperialism struck a shattering blow to capitalist structures in Latin America and the Caribbean,' but cautioned that the 'bloody overthrow' of Salvador Allende (1908–73) in Chile in 1973 'demonstrated that the capitalists will do their utmost to destroy a truly Socialist government, and is a warning to us all to be ever vigilant to preserve the cause of Socialism.'[19] The Cubans would have had no doubt that Comrade Burnham's camel's nose was now under their tent. Some blow to Jagan!

This was soon followed by the biggest blow of all to Cheddi: the defection of the PPP's deputy general secretary (the deputy to Jagan) and Marxist theoretician of long-standing, Ranji Chandisingh (1930–2009), to the PNC, in March 1976. It is transparent that he was being courted to jump ship, having resigned his position of deputy general secretary earlier, in August 1975. He was appalled that the PPP, instead of recognising that the PNC was embarked already on the socialist revolution, guided by Marxism-Leninism (thus meriting unstinted collaboration), could only offer grudging 'critical support.' Having been (along with Cheddi) the PPP's most intellectually advanced communists for eighteen years, he had reached the conclusion that the PPP was diminished as a Marxist-Leninist party, and that they were being superseded ideologically by the PNC. His letter of resignation, sent to Jagan and the Central Committee of the PPP, was lacerating, and it must have wounded his erstwhile comrades severely. For the party's chief theoretician to challenge the communist credentials of the PPP, nearly seven years after it was admitted to the communist movement in Moscow (Jagan and Chandisingh were there in June 1969), was most debilitating, notwithstanding the periodic haemorrhaging that afflicted the PPP from as early as the early 1950s. In 1969, the PPP declared at the meeting of communist parties in Moscow, before Comrades Leonid Brezhnev, Nikolai Podgorny, and Mikhail Suslov, thus: 'a Marxist-Leninist party was essential to the attainment and retention of revolutionary, anti-imperialist political power and the building of a socialist society [and] decided to transform itself from a loose, mass party into a disciplined Leninist-type party.'[20]

But Chandisingh was arguing now that the PPP was being left behind by the PNC, which was becoming more theoretically advanced, with even greater potential, because the latter, as the governing party, could readily apply Marxist-Leninist principles to its policymaking process. He equated the PPP's scepticism regarding the PNC's transformation as a Marxist-Leninist party to that of the minority anti-Soviet Trotskyists – a damning repudiation of the entrenched pro-Moscow communism of Cheddi and Janet Jagan:

> Presented – almost on a plate [by the PNC] – with the best opportunities ever in the history of the movement for laying the foundations for socialist development in our Guyana, it has galled me to see the resistance put up by so-called socialists in a supposedly Marxist-Leninist party [the PPP]...It would appear that certain leading members in authority are less concerned with the real possibilities for socialism than with the prospect of achieving personal power and prestige – and this, in my opinion, inhibits objective analysis and distorts the policies that should flow from such analysis.
>
> The situation reminds me, in a way, of the Trotskyists and their attitude toward the building of socialism in the Soviet Union. They

refused to see that real socialism was being built when they lost out to the Leninists [/Stalinists] and continued, right up to the present day, to charge that what exists in the Soviet Union is not real socialism but state capitalism and the rule of a bureaucratic minority. Their hatred blinded them from seeing the truth. I hope the PPP does not take this particular leaf out of the Trotskyist book – political bankruptcy and isolation from the mainstream of socialist construction.[21]

Ranji also contended that while he had been engendering 'a communist outlook' in the PPP, the inculcation of Marxist-Leninist principles in building a party of the Leninist type, they remained recalcitrant on almost every count:

> For the past several years I have consciously considered it to be my specific task in the Party to help develop cadres with a communist outlook, loyal to Marxism-Leninism and the principles of proletarian internationalism. This was in keeping with the proclaimed aim of the Party to be transformed into a party of the new (Leninist) type...
>
> It seemed we were making some headway in this process, albeit slowly – and with a long way to go to becoming a real Marxist-Leninist party, ideologically and organisationally...We arrived at the point where we were able to proclaim Marxist-Leninist theoretical principles and slogans, in a more or less general form, but to some extent had not yet captured the full spirit of Marxism-Leninism, and certainly fell short on Leninist strategy and tactics. **We had not reached the stage in our development where we could apply the general laws and principles to the concrete historical conditions of our own country** [emphasis added].[22]

Ranji argued that the annual PPP congresses which attracted comrades from fraternal communist parties around the world had become a show, lacking Marxist-Leninist substance. It was sheer 'image building.' He was challenging the very *bona fides* of the PPP's Marxism-Leninism:

> We seem to be unduly concerned with impressing fraternal visitors, with the large numbers at our congresses and conferences, and with the artistic design of our banners proclaiming "Marxism-Leninism and Proletarian Internationalism", rather than with the quality of attendance and the content of such meetings. In other words, we have cultivated the technique of showmanship to impress others but have fallen short of what really matters – the building of a real vanguard party of the Leninist type [like the CPSU]. While basking in the glory of being the vanguard Marxist-Leninist party in Guyana – which was rendered relatively simple for many years because of the open positions taken by the PNC – our membership by and large and, to a large extent, the leadership of the Party, had not adopted a truly Marxist-Leninist class outlook...My view is that the PPP is not yet a Marxist-Leninist party...In the light of what I now observe taking place within the Party, I can hardly have much optimism about its future as a real, mature Marxist-Leninist party.[23]

Ranji was convinced that the PNC had, indeed, become the vanguard party, leading the country towards the socialist revolution, thereby relegating the PPP as a mere purveyor of shibboleth. He asserted:

> Strange it is that the vaunted Marxist-Leninist vanguard [the PPP] cannot yet see – or doesn't it want to see? – who is really pushing whom? It seems to me that it is the PNC that is taking all the concrete initiatives in terms of social transformation, while the PPP is merely reacting petulantly and seeking in some cases to go one better in words. Perhaps it is because the PPP is not in the seat of government and is under no pressure to have to concretise its thinking on the ways and means to bring about social and attitudinal changes.[24]

Ranji was unsparing to his erstwhile comrades:

> There can be no doubt that the PPP has played a historic role in Guyana. Shall it be recorded, however, that at such a crucial and glorious period in Guyana's history the PPP, which had done so much in the past was unable to rise to the occasion, to shoulder its responsibility, and was found wanting? Shall history record that having run well in the early stages of Guyana's race into the future, to socialism, the PPP eventually played itself out, and then the PNC took hold of the golden baton of socialism and carried it forward in the next stage of the great race?[25]

His reasoning was rather strange, as the PNC historically was never known to have embraced Marxist-Leninist principles, and their Comrade Leader, as far as I am aware, had never ever declared himself a Marxist-Leninist or communist. He was, on the contrary, anti-communist. That is why he became America's man! Moreover, his vaguely conceptualised cooperative socialism could not, by any stretch of the imagination, have been equated with Marxism-Leninism.

For Ranji (now in his mid-forties), having languished in Opposition in a stagnating PPP for over ten years, at incalculable personal cost in earnings and his family's standard of living and with all likelihood that Jagan would vegetate on the periphery indefinitely, it must have been irresistible (when a carrot was dangled in front of him) to seek greener pastures in the PNC. A conversion on the road to Damascus! And the fact that the Cubans, most likely, were instrumental in his decision to embrace the PNC, would have given him a special place as a convert. Moreover, he was the deputy to Jagan, and identified as his potential successor: the PNC could have made no bigger catch. Henceforth, Burnham would give Ranji free rein to articulate his orthodox Marxist-Leninist beliefs, which the Comrade Leader himself would never venture to ventilate.

'To go one better in words,' Ranji said of the PPP! He was right. Jagan had no trumps left; words, but words deemed pure – the Marxist-Leninist truth – were his sole asset, having been marginalised by rigged elections in 1968 and 1973. This was exacerbated with the defection of his chief communist thinker in 1976. Things were to get worse for Jagan in 1978, as Burnham accelerated his relentless quest for supreme power. He wanted to create a new constitution to institutionalise total control, in the office of presidency of the country. This required the abrogation of article 73 of the independence constitution, which required a referendum to remove certain entrenched provisions, designed as restraints against autocracy. Therefore, to end all referenda, Burnham contrived a referendum on July 10, 1978, to enable him to alter any of the entrenched provisions in the Constitution by a simple two-thirds majority in the legislature, which he had stolen already in the fraudulent elections of 1973. As expected, Burnham 'won' the 'rig-erendum' (as some dubbed it) by an astronomically absurd 97 per cent alleging, only slightly less ridiculously, that 70 per cent of the registered voters had participated in the farcical exercise. The Opposition was nearer the truth when they asserted that no more than 10–14 per cent actually voted. Burnham had his wish: the general elections due in 1978 were postponed to 1980 (that, too, massively rigged), and in 1980 his attorney general (M. Shahabuddeen) produced a constitution that gave Burnham total power virtually for life. It was a travesty, shameful to Burnham; no less so to his lieutenant, M. Shahabuddeen.

Ranji himself was no slouch with words or Marxist theory. And words could be manipulated to distort and cleanse any reality, however tyrannical or destructive of the spirit. He could match his old mentor, Cheddi, in any contest involving Marxist rhetoric. And by 1979, as a member of the Central Executive Committee of the PNC and the director of studies at the Cuffy Ideological Institute, the PNC's school for training party cadres, he was free to replicate the Marxist-Leninist tenets he had purveyed at the PPP's ideological school, Accabre College. (Cuffy and Accabre were rebel leaders of the Berbice Slave Rebellion of 1763.) In a paper presented to the third biennial congress of the PNC, in August 1979, Ranji, having extolled his Comrade Leader Burnham as 'our skilful, capable revolutionary leader,' endorsed his resolve to have his new constitution drafted and adopted. He concurred that it was indispensable to the ethos of the socialist revolution; that it would be 'more relevant for a Guyana in transition to socialism,' precisely the rationale offered by the Comrade Leader. The fact that the *raison d'etre* of the new constitution was the enhancement of the latter's status to virtual president for life obviously could not be broached.

Ranji's paper was punctuated by quotes from Lenin and specific references to Russian history and the Communist Party of the Soviet Union (CPSU). This indicates that he recognised similarities between the rise of communism in the Soviet Union and the revolutionary political trajectory he attributed to Burnham and the PNC. He also saw parallels between counter-revolutionary activities in the Soviet Union and what he perceived as the subversive politics of local 'counter-revolutionary bandits' opposed to the PNC. Chandisingh argued that certain 'bourgeois freedoms' had to be sacrificed to ensure that the counter-revolutionaries did not subvert the 'revolutionary transformation' the PNC was pursuing. This invariably mild-mannered, measured, and discernibly patrician man evinced palpable anger in his defence of the Comrade Leader's socialist revolution, while castigating the alleged terrorism of the small party, the Working People's Alliance (WPA), manifested in the burning down of the Ministry of National Development (really the PNC administrative office) in Georgetown, for which Walter Rodney, Rupert Roopnaraine, and other WPA activists were charged:

> Freedom and democracy must not be allowed to degenerate into license to subvert, to destroy – and in the revolution, we cannot allow ourselves to be unduly troubled over certain 'niceties' [bourgeois freedoms]. There are times when strong measures must be taken – swiftly and decisively. In this hard struggle for revolutionary transformation, we cannot expect to go through the process smoothly, without sacrifices, without losses – but **we must be prepared to make these losses rather expensive for the counter-revolutionary bandits.** They have to be challenged wherever they appear – and by whatever means necessary…It is imperative to deal firmly and ruthlessly with enemies who hatch plots and conspiracies, who incite for the violent overthrow of the people's power, who sabotage, bomb and burn, who incite and commit acts calculated to lead to internecine warfare, who disturb the peace so painstakingly built up since the accession of the PNC.[26]

Meanwhile, Burnham remained ideologically fluid regarding the character of his socialism and his socialist revolution. Yet Ranji was granted a sacred space in the PNC firmament, as director of the Cuffy Ideological Institute, not because of his Marxist-Leninist creed primarily, but because it ate into the soul of the Jagans and the PPP. For Jagan to have lost his erudite communist theoretician of nearly two decades to Burnham must have occasioned hurt beyond imagination. Besides, such was the intellectual stature of Ranji, that it is totally comprehensible why Comrade Leader Burnham would give him a blank cheque to interpret cooperative socialism as he deemed appropriate, within his Marxist frame of reference.

Ranji went the whole hog and transplanted the Marxist-Leninist precepts he had deployed without circumspection in the PPP, in its entirety, to the PNC. Ranji was framing the latter as essentially a communist party while denouncing his comrades of nearly two decades in the PPP as bogus communists. He asserted that the PNC was building 'a real socialist society,' in addition to their sterling 'contribution to the world revolution' towards the communist utopia.

Such was the absurdity of the post-colonial reality in Guyana. Actually, it was a grandiloquent façade to detract from the monumental racial bigotry and futility of the place, essentially ungovernable by standard liberal democratic norms.

Back to Comrade Ranji!

> Our Party's [PNC's] ideological guide is Marxism-Leninism, and its direction is the application of this theory to the concrete conditions of Guyana…The revolution proceeds through the class struggle. In the transition period the class struggle is intensifying…Unlike some others who boast and brag at the slightest opportunity about their Marxist-Leninist credentials [Jagan's PPP], but who, on closer analysis, reveal themselves as an agglomeration of charlatans and racists, outright counter-revolutionaries and perhaps some well-meaning but deluded elements – our Party [the PNC] eschews such posturing….[27]

Ranji was dismissive of those on the right who yearned to retrace the backward step to unbridled capitalism; neither did he have time for 'the extremist ultra-left,' a reference to his former PPP comrades, who were deceiving people that the alleged economic and other difficulties in the society stemmed from the fact that 'the PNC was not really socialist.' Ranji repudiated the Jaganites, thereby essentially abjuring who he was hitherto:

> [They] promise what amounts to magical remedies, proclaim general formulas that have no relation to the concrete situation in the world and in Guyana, and spread utopian fairy-tales about how socialism was actually being built or is being constructed in other countries. Furthering their own opportunist images, they sing praises to 'socialism,' 'Marxism-Leninism,' the Soviet Union and other Socialist countries, while objectively they obstruct our real efforts at socialist transformation at every opportunity…These fire breathers of 'ultra-socialism,' when they get down to the practicals, are running desperately to catch up with the PNC…They have nothing to offer but deceptive 'revolutionary' words. The PNC offers not words but its record of 14 years of practical achievements for the Guyanese people…There is only one force in Guyana that has the **capacity** and the political **will** to lead our people towards socialist transformation and development. That is the PNC, ably led by the architect of the revolution – Comrade L.F.S. Burnham![28]

That Ranji was denouncing his old comrades in the PPP for claiming the ideological high ground, primarily on the premise of their philosophical propinquity to the Soviet Union and its satellites, should have occasioned no surprise. He was himself an avid proponent of this mantra prior to his recent defection and had revelled in the longevity of the PPP's Marxist-Leninist credentials – at variance with the wishy-washy cooperative socialism of the PNC and their belated synthetic Marxist pretensions. And because the PPP always paid obeisance to the CPSU as the virtual avatar of their political mission –

the custodian of the inviolable Marxist-Leninist tenets – they never deviated from that fount of scientific truths until the system collapsed. In fact, Ranji the renegade probably engendered in the Jagans and their young disciples an inviolable resolve, from 1976 (when Ranji jumped ship) to 1991 (when the Soviet Union and its communist project finally disintegrated), to adhere infallibly to the orthodox tenets.

VI.   Jagan Counters 'the Chief Defector,' Asserts That His PPP is the 'Revolutionary Vanguard'

Therefore, although Jagan had ostensibly offered the PNC 'critical support' in August 1975 (at the prompting of the Cubans and Ranji), just a year later, at the nineteenth Congress of the PPP, at Tain, Corentyne, Jagan was decrying the flimsy foundation of Burnham's socialism. And, as was the tradition in the PPP, Cheddi commenced with an encomium to the upholder of his utopian dream – the Soviet Union:

> To Socialism has passed the historical initiative. Its moral prestige has grown and the world balance has shifted in its favour…Since the Great October Revolution of 1917, socialism has become increasingly a world system exercising a new and decisive influence for progressive change. It has demonstrated, in moral and material terms, its superiority over capitalism and its ability to hold the imagination of people and to inspire their day-to-day activities. It has forged bonds of brotherhood, mutual trust and respect and sown the seeds of progress as no other value-system has done in the history of the world. In the land of Lenin, perfectly in accordance with the vision of the founders of the Soviet Union, prices are stable while incomes are rising; education and medical services are free; rent amounts to about 5 per cent of the worker's wage; there is no unemployment; there is security in old age and hope for the youth… We proudly hail the land of Lenin. Marxism-Leninism is invincible.[29]

Therefore, for Cheddi Jagan (in 1976), the Communist Party of the Soviet Union was advancing towards the communist utopia that was the lifelong inspiration for his political mission. From the late 1940s to the late 1980s, he had no doubt, however monumental the setbacks (and there were numerous, many of his making), that what he stood for was superior, in 'moral and material terms,' to capitalism; indeed, to every 'value-system…in the history of the world'; it was 'invincible.' Marxism-Leninism was beyond reproach, and the PPP was the only party in Guyana guided by that unimpeachable fount of knowledge, 'scientific socialism,' as perfected by the keeper of the flame, the CPSU.

'Critical support' had a brief shelf-life, for by August 1976 (with Ranji having defected to the PNC), Jagan was expressing deep reservations about the nationalisation programme of the PNC, as well as the socialist credentials of that party. In fact, as he recalled, the notion of 'critical support' had come 'from the lips of the chief defector,' Chandisingh, in early 1975. With him gone, the PPP had no stomach for a rapprochement with the PNC. Jagan did not mention the Cuban comrades, who appeared to have been at the heart of the initiative to collaborate with the PNC.

Jagan's PPP always believed they alone had the ideological pedigree, the unsullied authority to lead Guyana to the communist utopia. However, the PPP had, incrementally (by virtue of periodic defection of its key leaders, bar the Jagans), become a Marxist sect that believed only they had a legitimate engagement with the essence of the philosophy, the supposedly unadulterated version of which the CPSU was the sole custodian. But with the PNC rigging the elections with impunity to secure uninterrupted control of the state, the PPP's principal asset was its assumption of singular mastery of the pure tenets of Marxism-Leninism, and that, ultimately, they would be rewarded with state power for unimpeachable loyalty to the scientific truth. It was a fantasy that similarly possessed and sustained many splintered religious sects for whom their assumed monopoly on purity was everything. And the reality that they were excluded from power for nearly three decades while still being led by the same true-believer meant that bereft of the experience of governance and the necessity for pragmatism – to compromise, to adapt theory to practice; to cultivate allies in order to create wealth and devise means of self-sustaining growth – the PPP did become a Marxist sect. Yet, paradoxically, they retained their Indian support base – purely for racial reasons. Guyana was awash with ideology. But this had virtually no impact on the racial predilection of Guyanese.

Jagan's address to the PPP Congress at Tain in August 1976, like Ranji's deeply wounding rationale for his defection, is an exercise in which jargon competes with jargon. A transparent rebuttal of Ranji, it is permeated by a singular objective: to establish that the PNC was anything but Marxist-Leninist, socialist, or communist. To do this at the PPP Congress, before visiting delegates from fraternal communist parties, must have been immeasurably self-satisfying – cathartic!

> At the ideological level, the PNC has had a hodgepodge, eclectic position…[But recently] the PNC declared that its ideas are based on Marx, Engels and Lenin. We welcome this development [hence 'critical support']. However, it is not enough for the PNC to claim to be Marxist-Leninist. Far more important is the formulation of the scientific theory, and the creative application of the tenets of Marxism-Leninism.[30]

Jagan argued further that the PNC's declared adoption of non-alignment as their overarching ideological stance, maligned the inviolable stature of the Soviet Union, erroneously equating it with exponents of great-power chauvinism, the US and China. He quoted from a manual prepared by the Burnham government in which the following sacrilegious conclusion was drawn: 'Non-alignment is vital if we, in the developing world, are not to become political and economic satellites of the super-powers in the East or the West.' For Jagan, any suggestion that the Soviet Union harboured selfish imperialist motives in its pursuit of proletarian internationalism was despicable. No genuine Marxist-Leninist could subscribe to such an utterly distorted and heretical proposition: 'What is the PNC's brand of Marxism-Leninism? It is anti-communist and reactionary, claiming that under "communist systems the workers are mere servants under state monopolies"…The PNC's anti-communism also takes the form of anti-Sovietism…Proletarian internationalism [inspired by the Soviet Union], another basic principle of Marxism-Leninism, comes in for attack by the PNC.'[31]

Jagan could discern no imperfection whatsoever in the communist mission in the Soviet Union and the 'People's Democracies' of Eastern Europe, routinely censuring dissident writers and artists as traitors (Anna Akhmatova, Boris Pasternak, Alexander Solzhenitsyn, Andrei Sakharov, and the rest), fatally compromised by American imperialism. Neither could he concede any validity to the PNC's 'utopian cooperative socialism' – essentially a gimmick by Burnham, designed solely to steal the PPP's thunder precisely at a time when the balance in the world was tilting decisively towards communism, led by the invincible CPSU:

> Whatever this is, it is not socialism according to Marx, Engels and Lenin. Little wonder that one PNC ex-regional minister called it 'people's capitalism'…The PNC is not a vanguard Marxist-Leninist party: it is a nationalist party. Its leadership is basically right-wing, largely petty-bourgeois, bureaucratic-bourgeois and professional… The 'right wing' is desirous of keeping Guyana on the capitalist path, albeit in a changed form. The reactionary petty-bourgeoisie and bureaucratic-bourgeoisie is not willing to surrender privileges… The PNC leadership with a left trend recognises the bankruptcy of a capitalist path. But it is caught in a real dilemma: how to pursue a socialist-oriented course and at the same time maintain elitist privileges?…The PNC's ideology is a revisionism of Marxism-Leninism, and its cooperative socialism…is utopian. Friedrich Engels long ago, in his *Socialism – Utopian and Scientific*, praised Robert Owen, Fourier and Saint Simon, for their humanitarian qualities in advocating cooperative socialism, but condemned them for wrong methodology, for being day-dreamers and renouncing the class struggle as the way to socialism.[32]

Jagan admonished the PNC for utilising state funds to bribe 'renegades' like Ranji Chandisingh and Vincent Teekah to defect from the PPP. But such 'underhand practices' could not succeed or deflect the PPP from its pursuit of communism. The party had pioneered Marxism-Leninism and stayed the course, despite serial defections and recurring intrigues between internal and powerful external enemies to liquidate it. Jagan's faith in the Soviet Union as the untarnished exponent of communism with its goal of the liberation and empowerment of the working class, was in no way attenuated by the 'right opportunist "Marxists"' who were slandering the PPP, propagating the big lie that the PNC was guided by the ideas of Marx, Engels, and Lenin. The PPP was the only genuine communist party in Guyana, contrary to the recent assertions of opportunists and 'the chief defector' (Cheddi's assignation), Ranji Chandisingh, who in late 1974 or early 1975 had dismissed the PNC's identification with socialism as spurious: 'with all its vagueness and superficiality, its eclectic hodgepodge of bits of Marx and Lenin linked with outright anti-democratic and anti-socialist practices.' Jagan remarked that Chandisingh had done 'a complete somersault' since he jumped ship:

> The PNC is put in a position of the Communist Party of the Soviet Union, the great party of Lenin, and we [the PPP] are accused of behaving like the Trotskyites after the Great October Socialist Revolution. The fact is that our Party has been and continues to be in the forefront of the struggle against Trotskyism, Maoism and ultra-leftist dogmatism and sectarianism.[33]

The claims of Jagan's PPP to ideological supremacy over the PNC's 'utopianism and revisionism' were consumed by the Guyanese absurdity regarding whose socialism was kosher – the genuine article. This was exacerbated by the PNC's fraudulent grip on power that remained unchallenged in the region or by Jagan's self-defined mortal enemies, the Western imperialists. Yet Cheddi's contention was that, unlike the PNC, they were consistent in their espousal of Marxism-Leninism, and by steadfastly adhering to the CPSU version of the creed (the 'Party of Lenin,' as he put it), were demonstrating affinity with the legitimate tenets: scientific socialism. He had no doubt that he stood on impeccable Marxist foundations; therefore, he could declaim on his credentials as a votary of the authentic communist creed.

By the 1970s, Jagan considered himself the foremost custodian, in Guyana and the Anglophone Caribbean, of the sacred tenets of Marxism-Leninism. No other politician in the region could make such a claim – a source of palpable pride to himself – a kind of divine affirmation:

> We were the first to propagate the ideology of Marxism-Leninism. **Marxism-Leninism is central to our creative, revolutionary work. We consider as our principal task its defence and the**

conduct of ideological struggle. Today, more than ever, this form of struggle is most essential. Our party [the PPP] fights against pragmatism, sectarianism, deviationism and opportunism. It has condemned Maoism and has carried on an unceasing battle against the utopianism and revisionism of the PNC and its ideologues.... [emphasis added].[34]

And to counter Ranji's contention that the PPP was still deficient in their theoretical grasp of Marxism-Leninism, Jagan stressed that 'ideological struggle' was inextricable from the PPP's immersion in their political mission. The fact that their young cadres were being rigorously trained ideologically, at home and in the Soviet Union, was demonstrative of the sanctity of Marxist-Leninist scholarship to their political work:

> Our Party also recognises that its strength and fighting capacity is largely dependent on the level of political and ideological consciousness of its members, activists and leaders. Towards this end, we lay great stress on ideological-educational work and the training of cadres [communist party workers]...Courses [in Marxism-Leninism] are given at the Party's ideological school, the Accabre College of Social Sciences [formerly led by Ranji Chandisingh]. And every year, a number of our students go overseas to the socialist countries, particularly to the Soviet Union, for political economy and trade union courses. Those who have been so trained make up the great majority of our functionaries working in the political and trade union fields and among the farmers. They are also well-represented in our highest policy-making bodies. In this way, we are methodically transforming the Party.[35]

Jagan was proud that the PPP was not just the incontestable champion of communism in Guyana, but that they also were fortified by the certainty they were ideologically more advanced than any other party in the Anglophone Caribbean. The PPP was imbued with the purest measure of the philosophy that, on scientific premises as confirmed by Lenin and the CPSU, was destined to supersede a dying capitalism doomed to extinction. Nothing could stem the revolutionary optimism of Cheddi; even the defamation of 'the chief defector' (Ranji), however unimaginably wounding, was already neutralised by the ideological purity of the mission. Therefore, he appeared unperturbed (to his disciples), regardless of how many 'rats' deserted the ship (and they were many) because the PPP was unsinkable:

> Whatever our enemies and detractors say, we will remain steadfastly loyal to the tenets of Marxism-Leninism...The PPP is the revolutionary vanguard of the [Indian?] working class and is constantly and persistently championing the cause of the Guyanese working people for economic progress and social justice...Marxists have always played the leading role in our Party. As such, the PPP is different from the other mass-based political parties of the English-

speaking Caribbean – a fact which has contributed to the Guyanese working people being the most politically and ideologically developed in the region, and Guyana today is playing the leading and guiding political role in the English-speaking Caribbean.[36]

The racial polarisation, the most intractable problem in Guyana for more than a century, engendered by Indian indentureship and its aftermath, is ignored totally. The assumption was that the scientific veracity of the Soviet brand of Marxism-Leninism would, in due course, reconcile even the working class in Guyana, though fused into its discrete ethnic components. After all, as Cheddi perceived it, the Soviet Union had resolved the potentially calamitous national question in the dauntingly ethnically diverse state, the USSR. He said time and again that Marxism-Leninism had completely obliterated the nationality issue, rendering it one of the most revolutionary achievements in the history of humankind. As he saw it, even the Central Asian Republics, steeped in their Islamic heritage, were now seamlessly integrated into the USSR while contributing their cultural richness to the emerging communist state – the leader of the unprecedented experiment in the transformation of the world. This was, indeed, the future, and Jagan's pride in it was inexhaustible because they were on the side of the authentic socialist revolution. The future belonged to him and the PPP in Guyana. It was a messianic vision. But because of the racial chasm in Guyana, he had a monopoly on the Indian segment of the electorate only – yet a stable and significant racial base, despite massive Indian migration to the lands ruled by the arch-imperialists. Indeed, Jagan's communist creed had no bearing whatsoever on the longevity and indissolubility of their loyalty to him. And the fact that their steadfast allegiance could not translate into access to power was immaterial. He was sustained by an unwavering trust in his creed that was indefatigable.

Therefore, Jagan's Congress speech in 1976 may be seen both as a refutation of 'the chief defector,' as well as his ridicule of Burnham's half-baked 'cooperative socialism.' Although repeatedly cheated of power through blatantly rigged elections, he was confident that his brand of Marxism-Leninism, tried and tested in the Soviet Union and the 'People's Democracies' of Eastern Europe, was bound to win. As Cheddi put it at the end of *The West on Trial*: '...although defrauded and cheated, we remain the strongest force in the country. Difficulties there will be; the battle will be long and hard. But win we will.' That was in 1966. He never changed his mind through all his years in the wilderness, until he got back into office after nearly twenty-eight years, ironically because of the intervention of the American imperialists with the collapse of the Soviet Union.

Jagan had a quasi-religious belief in the universal triumph of his pro-Moscow brand of Marxism-Leninism. Therefore, his PPP possessed impeccable pedigree and would stay the course; besides, their ideological 'implacability' was driving the PNC towards the left, flawed though the latter's conception of Marxism-Leninism. But they could not afford to sacrifice, and possibly liquidate, themselves on the opportunistic altar of Burnham's dubious socialism, as Ranji Chandisingh wanted them to embrace unconditionally:

> Those who defected from our Party must be isolated. To have followed their unscientific and adventuristic lead would have meant our Party divorcing itself from the [Indian] masses, and virtually liquidating itself...The fact is that **in no other country is there an ideologically-developed and organisationally-strong party like ours**...History is full of examples where, with communist parties liquidated or emasculated, the revolutionary process has been halted or turned backwards...The defectors...want unity and no struggle; like the PNC, they want us to take a position of **uncritical support**... [emphasis added].[37]

Jagan cited a PNC ideologue's statement that the PPP was endeavouring to duplicate 'Russian processes of socialist transformation.' But he did not refute this allegation, merely noting that this was 'the old propaganda line that the PPP takes orders from Moscow.' He was disinclined to take this triviality seriously; he had bigger fish to fry because of his redoubtable communist credentials juxtaposed with the PNC's flimsy, vacillating political record. Not only did he have history and time on his side; he had science as well:

> Let there be no doubt of our position. We are members of the International Communist and Workers Movement, and we are proud of it. Together we formulate the general political line of the Movement and are guided by it. Marxism is not a dogma but a guide to action; as a living science, it involves a concrete analysis of a concrete situation – national and international.
>
> There are general laws of scientific socialism which, like the law of gravity, cannot be ignored. In observing the application of these laws, the Communist International in its early days was able to guard against sectarian and right-opportunist tendencies among young Communist parties, which arguing on the basis of 'particularism' and 'exceptionalism,' fell prey to bourgeois nationalism. At the same time there are specific conditions, national peculiarities, which also cannot be ignored.[38]

Jagan had commenced his 1976 Congress Address of nearly sixty pages paying obeisance to the fount of communism, the Soviet Union. He quoted Comrade Brezhnev (at the 25th Congress of the CPSU) to underscore that the PPP never deviated from the unerring footsteps of the party of Lenin. This was the credo by which authentic communists were inspired in the glorious crusade against capitalism and imperialism. Brezhnev remarked:

> In their struggle, Communists proceed from the general laws governing the development of the revolution and the building of socialism and communism. Reflected in the theory of Marxism-Leninism and confirmed in practice, these laws were collectively and comprehensively formulated at international conferences of fraternal parties. A deep understanding of these general laws, and reliance on them, in combination with a creative approach and with consideration for the concrete conditions in each separate country, have been and remain the inalienable and distinctive feature of a Marxist-Leninist. And we say this with assurance: **a concession to opportunism may sometimes yield a temporary advantage, but will ultimately do damage to the party** [emphasis added].[39]

Cheddi felt vindicated. He never could countenance even mild concessions to the imperialists, even though his intransigence culminated in their denying him the opportunity to lead British Guiana to independence. The latter remark (in italics above), from the sagacious communist mind of Comrade Brezhnev, was clearly applicable to Forbes Burnham, the pseudo-communist/socialist – a 'right opportunist' to the bone, as Cheddi always designated him. Jagan said that the PPP was profoundly influenced by the guiding principles of international communism, yet he was also sanctimonious that the safeguarding of 'bourgeois rights,' systematically eroded by the PNC regime, must be pursued relentlessly because the socialist revolution was *not* inseparable from them. How does one square this circle? Why should communists enjoy the privilege of such 'bourgeois rights' as freedom of speech, freedom of the press, free and fair elections, etc., to facilitate the building of a system committed to the abrogation of what it rejects as 'bourgeois freedoms,' pseudo-democratic values?

Jagan, like his 'chief defector,' concluded:

> The fight for democratic liberties and rights is an essential part of the struggle for socialism. Without democracy, socialism cannot be built [tell that to Comrades Brezhnev and Fidel!]. Nor can the nation be successfully defended without the people's involvement at all levels… Whatever our enemies and detractors say, we will remain steadfastly loyal to the tenets of Marxism-Leninism…The PPP's position with respect to the Soviet Union is influenced [principally by the notion that]…in the struggle against imperialism for necessary deep-going economic and social transformations, the help of the socialist community headed by the Soviet Union is vital. To take any other position is not only stupid but dangerous.[40]

VII. 'A Kind of Political Tonic': Jagan is Sustained by the Inspiration and Fraternal Recognition of the Communist Party of the Soviet Union and by His Visits to the Ideological Motherland (the USSR)

Jagan's address to the PPP Congress of 1976 was, indeed, seminal: apart from dispelling the bile occasioned by the defection of erstwhile Comrades Chandisingh, Vincent Teekah, Halim Majeed, Lalbachan Lalbahadur, and others, it set the tone for the PPP's occupation of the Marxist-Leninist high-ground, as economic depression in Guyana became chronic and the PNC floundered towards a political and ideological wasteland. Cooperative socialism was dead by the time Comrade Burnham died prematurely, on August 6, 1985, aged just sixty-two. Succeeded by D. Hoyte, the PNC moved transparently back to a capitalist frame of reference in the late 1980s. But Comrade Cheddi was not ready for a U-turn. He did not retreat from his pro-Moscow vision of the communist utopia despite his marginalisation under an entrenched authoritarianism at home.

Meanwhile, the PNC dictatorship had become consolidated as it rigged the referendum of 1978, obscenely, to have Burnham enthroned as the executive president. No general elections were held between 1973 and 1980, and when the latter was orchestrated for December 15, 1980, the PNC rigged it – massively. They awarded themselves 77 per cent of the votes or forty-one of the fifty-three seats; they allotted the PPP a mere 19.5 per cent or ten seats. Yet Jagan never did contemplate relinquishing his post as leader of the PPP (general secretary, by the communist appellation), although he was effectively excluded from power, with every likelihood of its prolongation to the end of his life. However, for him, approbation by the CPSU and the Communist Party of Cuba remained of enormous significance – indispensable to his ideological gravitas. Despite the rapprochement between the Cubans and the Burnham regime since 1972, the meeting in Havana of the Communist and Workers Parties of the Caribbean, in May 1977, comprised the following: the Communist Party of Cuba, the Guadeloupe Communist Party, the PPP of Guyana, the Unified Party of Haitian Communists, the Martinique Communist Party, the Puerto Rican Communist Party, the Dominican Communist Party [Dominican Republic], with the Communist Party of Venezuela as observer. (No People's National Congress! No communist parties from the Anglophone Caribbean! In reality, none of substance existed.) The Havana Communique noted that these parties 'belonged to the international communist movement in the Caribbean sub-region.'[41]

The same issue of Thunder (April–September 1977) in which the Havana Communique appeared, carried an editorial repudiating the Burnham regime for a flip-flop towards American imperialism, once more challenging its Marxist-Leninist *bona fides*:

> For a regime to enforce solutions against the people, such a regime will have to turn to the western powers. This is exactly what the PNC regime in Guyana has done, despite its assertions that it is 'Marxist-Leninist,' 'socialist' and 'working class.' All efforts are now being made to woo American capital on a massive scale, because of the serious difficulties facing the economy. The floodgates have been thrown open already in many ways, and the red carpet of welcome rolled out…
>
> Rather than make democratic and revolutionary changes within the country, the regime has put a brake on the anti-imperialist process and is now making very penitent and pathetic postures towards the US imperialists. The overall purpose is to get financial aid whatever the cost may be, and to achieve short-term solutions to the current economic crisis. The US imperialists, no doubt, expect short-term benefits for their crucial short-term help. These 'benefits' cannot be in the interest of the Guyanese people.[42]

But it was communion with, and periodic affirmation by, the 'proletarian international' heart of Soviet power, in the Kremlin in Moscow, for which Cheddi always yearned: 'a kind of political tonic.' The 25th Congress of the CPSU, from February 24 to March 5, 1976, attended by 4,998 delegates from ninety-six countries, made such a great impression on Cheddi that he was still imbued with faith that capitalism and imperialism would soon be vanquished; that the time for his creed to triumph was just around the next bend:

> On my return journey from Moscow, I said…that the 25th Congress of the Communist Party of the Soviet Union (CPSU) will go down as a landmark in the history of human progress. During question time, one journalist asked what relevance has the Congress to our struggle in the Caribbean?
>
> First of all, I said, **for people like me who are in the 'firing line,' to be in Moscow and taking part in the Congress was an inspiration – a kind of political tonic. You are filled with revolutionary optimism and confidence. You cannot help observing: our side is winning out. And you leave confident that in spite of your own difficulties and problems, you too will win; the tide of history is on your side** [emphasis added].[43]

Jagan was energised by what he unfailingly perceived as the colossal achievements of the CPSU; he accepted the communist creed as it was presented by the Soviets. He could see no flaws in what they were supposedly doing to construct the supreme alternative to capitalism and imperialism – the great socialist revolution across the universe:

> Our task in the face of a constant barrage of capitalist propaganda
> is to 'sell' socialism, and to make the anti-imperialist and socialist
> revolutions. In Moscow, the opportunity was presented to learn from
> the rich experience of the CPSU, how to make revolution and build
> a new society, how to organise life and develop a new type of man
> under socialism as compared with capitalism, and how many-faceted,
> inter-connected policies and positions…create favourable conditions
> for the furtherance of the world revolutionary process…The 25th
> Congress of the CPSU also afforded the opportunity to communist
> leaders from all over the world to meet in Moscow, to get acquainted,
> to engage in bilateral discussions and to rejoice in the feeling that
> we belong to the biggest brotherhood, the international communist
> movement. Above all, the successes of the Soviet Union instilled
> in us an internationalist pride in our common cause. Because they
> increase socialism's force of attraction and example, they make our
> tasks easier.[44]

Cheddi turned sixty on March 22, 1978; it was therefore a tremendous honour that the Soviet Union recognised his personal milestone. The Soviet ambassador to Guyana presented him, at Freedom House, with the Order of Friendship of the Peoples, decreed by the presidium of the Supreme Soviet of the USSR. It was signed by the general secretary of the CPSU, Comrade Leonid Brezhnev. And the Central Committee of the CPSU sent a message to Jagan which read in part: 'Your active participation in the struggle against imperialism for Marxist-Leninist cohesion of the Communist Movement, your fruitful activity for many years in the peace movement have found well-deserved appreciation by the Soviet communists.' Cheddi replied that the personal accolade was accepted by the PPP as recognition, too, of the collective struggle they were waging 'against imperialism and to build in Guyana a socialist state.'[45] For Cheddi, his award from the Soviet Union surpassed in prestige the José Martí National Award that Castro bestowed on Burnham in 1975. It had emanated from the soul of the Soviet endeavour – unexampled in the universe of communism.

In December 1978, Cheddi travelled to Moscow to formally receive the Order of Friendship of the Peoples. He was proud to recall that in the early 1960s, when the CIA intervened to ensure that he did not lead Guyana to independence, the Soviet Union was instrumental in granting vital aid to his government in British Guiana. He noted that

> valuable Soviet assistance was rendered to the Guyanese people in
> the face of Anglo-American aggression and CIA intervention in our
> domestic affairs. For us in the PPP and most of the Guyanese people,
> friendship with the Soviet Union has been and will continue to be a
> cornerstone of our policy. We deeply treasure our friendship with the
> Soviet people.[46]

A few months later (May 1979), Cheddi Jagan delivered his May Day address at a Trade Union Congress (TUC) rally in Georgetown, his first since 1976, when 'critical support' for the Burnham regime, though frayed from the inception, still had some traction, having secured recognition for the PPP's sugar union, the GAWU, in December 1975. Meanwhile, by mid-1976 the PNC regime was in the process of nationalising Booker, arguably Jagan's most strongly held means of bringing an end to 'bitter sugar' – the primary motif of his political mission. Then he and Burnham were, briefly, 'confronting imperialism and [apparently] forging anti-imperialist national unity.' By 1979, however, Cheddi was depressed about the future of Guyana, with the economy in terminal decline and shortages of basic food items a chronic problem (many banned), and most people heavily reliant on 'barrels' of gifts (including food) dispatched by relatives in the US, Canada, and the UK. Cheddi was unequivocal that the PNC had ditched its pretensions to socialism; their tenuous Marxism-Leninism had long evaporated. Therefore, he was emboldened, given the honour he had recently received from his Soviet comrades, to re-emphasise that he and his PPP were the sole genuine proponents of the socialist revolution.

He began his address, in May 1979, with discernable triumphalism, convinced that his faith in Soviet communism was winning:

> In the socialist community, headed by the Soviet Union, there is steady progress. The working people hold their heads high. They are proud of their achievements, secure in the political power they wield, and confident of their future. Long live Socialism! Long live Marxism-Leninism! By contrast, world capitalism is in permanent and ever worsening crisis. Unemployment and inflation have become chronic. More and more people are on the dole. Alienation increases and crime escalates. There is the danger of neo-fascism. And the welfare state has become the warfare state.

A true believer, the 'laws' of Marxism-Leninism led him to accept the demise of capitalism as inevitable. His side was bound to win![47]

He also condemned the PNC regime for not adopting a forthright stand against the Chinese invasion of Vietnam, rather than demanding Vietnamese withdrawal from Cambodia (it invaded to eliminate the genocidal regime of Pol Pot) as a quid pro quo for Chinese departure from Vietnam. Jagan readily interpreted this as vindication of the Burnham regime's 'retreat into the embrace of imperialism and the transnational exploiters.' The PNC government perceived the Sino-Vietnamese conflict as a clash of interest between two communist states. As a devoted pro-Moscow communist, however, Jagan considered this an indefensibly reactionary stance since he had repudiated China for being a non-communist aggressor: 'China is now part of the world reactionary pro-imperialist bloc; it has abandoned Marxism-Leninism and betrayed socialism.'

Jagan felt that the PNC was in the grip of the International Monetary Fund, with the working people pressed to the wall, the cost-of-living driving many to penury; practically all subsidies on non-essential commodities and services having been withdrawn. The portion of the national cake going to the working class was contracting menacingly. By 1979, Jagan had written the obituary of Burnham's brand of socialism:

> Socialism cannot be built without class struggle. The government wants not class struggle but class collaboration. It would like the workers to lie down like sheep to be slaughtered by the state, cooperative and private capitalists. There is a lot of rhetoric about socialism. But it has not been translated into practice. Social reformism is being sold as socialism, while 'cooperative socialism' has become 'cooperative capitalism' and 'state capitalism.'[48]

Then in accounting for the massive decline in production, productivity, and the terminal state of the economy in the aftermath of large-scale nationalisation (at least 80 per cent), consistently demanded by Jagan and his PPP, he attributed it, ironically, to the absence of 'bourgeois democracy.' In fact, Jagan wanted the PNC to nationalise even more of the economy, including the banks and the insurance companies. If he were in power, Jagan would have left little under private ownership because he was fundamentally opposed to any form of free enterprise, dismissing it as inherently exploitative and injurious to the interest of the working class. Therefore, his damning indictment of the PNC government could have been, plausibly, no less applicable to him because of his visceral abhorrence of private enterprise. But Cheddi did not accommodate pessimism or fallibility in his communist frame of reference: 'In Guyana…the revolutionary tide cannot be stopped; the working people [of all races] will win.' Yet, again, no reference to the chronic African-Indian incomprehension!

The following is Jagan's analysis of the economic decline under the Burnham regime by the end of the 1970s:

> The crisis of production is a long-term phenomenon. Lack of democracy, bureaucratic-administrative and police-military method of rule, denial of human rights and civil liberties, militarisation of politics and industrial relations, refusal to establish democratic management and workers' control at state enterprises, non-recognition of truly democratic mass organisations, political and racial discrimination in the allocation of jobs, land, credit, houses and consumer goods at state outlets, political patronage, corruption and extravagance have acted directly and indirectly as breaks on the productive forces, thus adversely affecting production and productivity…

> This government has failed the nation…During the past two years [1977–79] it has embarked on a course of national betrayal. It is piling

up more debts. Last year alone about $500 million was borrowed, skyrocketing national debt from $128 million in 1964 to nearly $2,000 million [$2 billion] at the end of 1978…Already by 1976, Guyana was borrowing not for development, but for the payment of debts. In 1976, loans were $94 million and repayment $118 million; in 1977 loans were $76 million and repayment $125 million.[49]

To the imperialists, the 'cooperative socialist' experiment, particularly the wholesale nationalisation of all foreign assets, was no less reprehensible. The fact that Burnham was now disparaging the sugar spoon with which the imperialists had pampered him – the source of his unconstrained, increasingly authoritarian, rule – must have been a bitter pill for his Anglo-American sponsors to swallow. After all, they had reluctantly settled on Burnham as their man because they were mortally afraid of Jagan's communism – the central plank being his friendship with Castro and his commitment to the nationalisation of their assets in the colony in the arbitrary manner of Castro. Burnham's Anglo-American sponsors did not expect to reap the whirlwind. **But he was still preferable to Jagan.**

VIII. The USG States that Guyana Does Not Threaten Their Strategic Interests: There's 'little threat of the Moscow-line communist-controlled PPP gaining power'

I will end this chapter with the reaction of the USG to Burnhamism in 1975–76. The first is an analysis of the state of US-Guyana relations in early 1975 by the American Ambassador to Guyana (1974–76), Max Krebs (1916–2006); the other is a long discussion between the US secretary of state, Dr Henry Kissinger (1923–), and the foreign minister of Guyana, Fred Wills (1929–92), on February 12, 1976, in Washington.

Despite Burnham's overtures to Castro, Kim Il-sung, China, and the Soviet Union, Ambassador Krebs did not see Guyana as a threat to the strategic interests of the US or her South American allies. This was a radical departure from the 1960s, when they defined the communist Cheddi Jagan as their mortal enemy – a Hemispheric threat second only to Castro. This, of course, was the context in which they sabotaged and removed Jagan's government in the early 1960s and helped the PNC to rig the general elections in 1968 to secure the permanent rule of Burnham, perceived as anti-communist. Now, in early 1975, the US government was dispirited with Burnham's leftward posturing and his incremental estrangement from them; however, they were reassured that their old unreconstructed enemy, Jagan, had no chance of assuming office again. Ambassador Krebs argued:

Guyana's importance to the United States has continued to decline. Its small population, GNP, size and location make Guyana of little strategic importance to our national defence interests. **Guyana is an unlikely source of potential subversion to its three South American neighbours (because of poor communications [to the frontiers], the relative internal strength of two of them – Brazil and Venezuela – and language/cultural isolation)...**

Aside from calcined bauxite, Guyana is not a major source of any strategic material, and its other exports are not of a quantity to be of significance to the US. There is no large-scale US investment remaining in Guyana, and the level of imports from the US is among the lowest of the Americas, with little prospect of marked improvement. There are only a few hundred US citizens in Guyana, no known narcotics flow to the US, no serious human rights problem [rigged elections, apparently, did not merit censure], no appreciable starvation or natural disaster potential, and **little prospect of the Moscow-line Communist-controlled PPP gaining power over the short or middle term** [emphasis added].[50]

The ambassador did note that there was some limited drilling for oil, and if Guyana were successful US investment in the country could be reactivated. He was not enamoured of Burnham's socialism ever becoming a 'Socialist bellwether' for the Anglophone Caribbean, but he felt that the US had 'minimal ability to deflect Guyana...from a radical Third World line.' Therefore, providing the pro-Moscow communist Jagan was denied access to power indefinitely, by whatever means (implicitly), they should be prepared to tolerate closer relations between Burnham and China, Cuba, the Soviet Union, and other communist countries as a matter of fact.

Ambassador Krebs was saying that Burnham's enhanced stature as a radical Third World leader was a reality they had to accommodate – for this, he owed much to the intellectual and diplomatic gifts of Shridath Ramphal. However, the likelihood of Jagan ever regaining power was so remote that the US should simply live with the enigma that was L. F. S. Burnham, however unpalatable his radical adventures. In short, their man had turned out to be a rather paradoxical, cantankerous, and mercurial ally, but Guyana was not important to America economically or geopolitically – no longer perceived as a security threat in the Hemisphere, as in the early 1960s.

Moreover, because Burnham had diminished Jagan to 'near impotence,' the US could readily ignore whatever ideological escapade Burnham fancied. They were, in essence, inclined to condone his palpably dictatorial rule – such was their residual aversion to Jagan although they now regarded him as terminally innocuous:

On the international scene, Guyana will be a small but prickly thorn in our side as it becomes more and more integrated into… groupings such as the Non-Aligned Movement. Thanks largely to the charisma and talent of Foreign Minister [Shridath] Ramphal, Guyana now ranks as a spokesman/leader for the Third World in several organisations…

On the domestic Guyanese front, the bugaboo of a takeover by the PPP under Jagan, and the conversion of Guyana into a hostile Soviet-oriented satellite has receded even further into the realm of the improbable. Forbes Burnham has consolidated his hold on power more impregnably than ever, reducing both Jagan and the Black Power elements on the left to near impotence.

As Burnham and the PNC enter their second decade of government, they are free to focus on how they will exercise power. The emerging political shape of the future Guyana is that of a *de facto* one-party state, increasingly authoritarian, arbitrary and hostile to criticism, real or imagined. Socialist development, with economic power concentrated in state corporations and state controls, will take on the guise of an ideology….

In spite of his pervasive power, Burnham faces real obstacles in his endeavour to build a strongly regimented Socialist society with an undisciplined Caribbean people. He will have to contend not only with the apathy of the general populace and the alienation of the East Indian majority, but also with lethargy and corruption among his own supporters produced by ten years of enjoying the benefits of power.[51]

Ambassador Krebs believed that Burnhamism was antithetical to core American values because of the control of every aspect of the society by the state; its general authoritarianism: regimentation of thought and the attenuation of individual freedom; in addition to its dogmatism against 'capitalist imperialism.' But America's vital interests were no longer threatened by this insignificant backwater. Therefore, he was recommending that 'our approach in dealing with Burnham should emphasise openness and frankness, but studiously limit our actions and reactions to matters which touch our interests directly and significantly.' In other words, leave well alone. The ambassador could not have been clearer on this point: '…at the present time, with many urgent claims on the US taxpayer's resources from other quarters and other countries, Guyana seems to be a place where our interests would be adequately served by a low level of involvement.'[52]

On February 12, 1976, the foreign minister of Guyana, Fred Wills, met with the secretary of state, Dr Henry Kissinger, in Washington. From a long conversation (a portion of which I am reproducing), the US government, though not enamoured of the Burnham regime's relations with Cuba and the Soviet Union, was not likely to intervene to restore 'bourgeois freedoms,' as Jagan would have preferred. And the perennial bottom line was Jagan's unmalleable 'made in Russia' communism. Jagan's overwhelmingly Indian supporters paid a heavy price for his creed:

Kissinger: You have been terrifying our Ambassador [Max Krebs] who has been striving to have good relations with your country.

Wills: I do not intend to terrify Max…

Kissinger: We have no interest in a confrontation with Guyana, and we hope Guyana does not wish to confront us. We understand that our social and domestic views are not identical. Whatever system you may decide to follow will not undermine our structure. Likewise, we are not out to undermine Guyana. Let us act like adults and pursue a mature relationship…**We have no overriding national interests in Guyana. Is there anything you want from us** [emphasis added]?

Wills: Well, Max said our relationship has soured.

Kissinger: That is the case.

Wills: I should like to inform you, Mr Secretary, that Guyana will not allow itself to be used as a Soviet base.

Kissinger: What about a Cuban base?

Wills: That also goes for Cuba, and we will not permit Cuba to use Guyana to export revolution. We are an unaligned country, and no one will dictate to us what foreign policy to follow – not you, Moscow, Peking or Havana.

Kissinger: Philosophically, we have no problem with your unaligned position. I want you to know that we cannot expect you to support us all the time. We, however, believe that, as a non-aligned country, you can support us from time to time rather than always adhere to the Soviet-Cuban line.

Wills: We, Black Caribbean people, see ourselves as having much in common with Cuba. There are a number of Blacks living in Cuba, with whom we can identify. We have also noted that the bulk of the Cuban troops in Africa are Black. We are concerned, however, over Castro's mistreatment of Blacks and the disadvantaged status of Blacks in Cuba.

Kissinger: Does Castro mistreat Blacks?

Wills: Philosophically, Castro will say no, but in reality, the Cuban Blacks have not really benefited from the revolution. Guyana's close ties with Cuba have been dictated by special circumstances. Our major opposition party [Jagan's PPP] is Marxist-Leninist in origin, and its main sources of support were from the USSR and Cuba. The present government [of the PNC] has been forced to establish ties with these two countries to reduce financial support to the opposition. Now the opposition has given 'critical support' to our policies, and we cannot reverse ourselves. We, in Guyana, do not look to Cuba as a Soviet satellite. We see Cuba as a country that has long suffered under colonialism and imperialism.[53]

This essentially was the position of the US government towards the Forbes Burnham dictatorship until the time of his death in August 1985 – a benign neglect, despite the PNC's continued overtures to several communist regimes. Yet Fred Wills ensured that America's obsession with Jagan's communism did not wane. He had a valid reason for it. Indeed, the enduring fear of Jagan, the pro-Moscow communist, insulated Burnham from potential Western pressure or sanctions with respect to 'bourgeois freedoms' (as in the rest of the Anglophone Caribbean), thus facilitating his fraudulent electoral machinations (begun in 1968) and the consolidation of his dictatorial rule. But it was never Burnham's desire to remove Jagan from the political sphere: the preservation of an impotent Jagan was integral to the perpetuation of his authoritarian regime.

Notes

1. *New Nation*, August 17, 1975.
2. Ibid.
3. Ibid.
4. *New Nation*, July 27, 1975.
5. Ibid.
6. P. D. Sharma, *The New Caribbean Man: Poems, 1972–76* (Hayward, California: Carib House, 1981), 34.
7. Ibid., 51.
8. Ibid., 26.
9. Ibid.
10. *New Nation*, January 12, 1975.
11. Sharma, *The New Caribbean Man*, 14.
12. *New Nation*, March 16, 1975.
13. *Towards the Socialist Revolution*, Address by the Leader of the PNC, Prime Minister Forbes Burnham at the First Biennial Congress of the Party, August 18, 1975.
14. Ibid., 6–7.
15. Ibid., 7.
16. Odeen Ishmael, *From Autocracy to Democracy in Guyana: Aspects of Post-Independence Guyana's History, 1966–92* (Georgetown: GNI Publications, 2012), 133.
17. Ibid., see chapter 22: 'The 135-Day Sugar Strike,' 190–201.

18. *The Pursuit of Perfection*, Address to the Nation by Cde. L. F. S. Burnham, Prime Minister of Guyana, on the Occasion of the 10th Anniversary of Independence, May 25, 1976, 37, 39.
19. *New Nation*, December 28, 1975.
20. See Cheddi Jagan, 'The World Communist Meeting [Moscow, 5–17 June 1969],' *Thunder* (October–December 1969), 53–66.
21. *Why I Left the PPP: Cde. Ranji Chandisingh Explains* [1976], 5–6.
22. Ibid., 7.
23. Ibid., 8–9, 12.
24. Ibid., 13–14.
25. Ibid., 14.
26. Ibid., 22.
27. Ibid., 23.
28. Ibid., 23–24.
29. 'Report of the Central Committee of the PPP, Delivered by General Secretary Cheddi Jagan at Tain, Corentyne, August 1976,' *Thunder*, (July–September 1976), 1–2.
30. Ibid., 39.
31. Ibid., 40–42.
32. Ibid., 44–46, 48.
33. Ibid., 50.
34. Ibid., 47.
35. Ibid., 53.
36. Ibid., 49, 46, 50.
37. Ibid., 54, 51.
38. Ibid., 48.
39. Ibid., 49.
40. Ibid., 57–59.
41. See 'The Havana Communique,' *Thunder* (April–September 1977), 46–48.
42. Editorial, ibid., 1–2.
43. Cheddi Jagan, Straight Talk: '25th Congress of the CPSU – Landmark of Human Progress,' *CJRC*, Item 2261.
44. Ibid.
45. *Mirror*, March 24, 1978.
46. 'Speech by Cheddi Jagan on Receipt of the Order of Friendship of the Peoples, at the Kremlin, on December 20, 1978,' *CJRC*, Item 2299.
47. Cheddi Jagan, 'May Day (1979) Speech at TUC Rally.'
48. Ibid.
49. Ibid.
50. *Foreign Relations of the US, 1969–76, Vol E-11, Part 1, Documents on Mexico, Central America and the Caribbean, 1973–76*, Country Analysis and Strategy Paper by Ambassador Max V. Krebs [early 1975].
51. Ibid.
52. Ibid.
53. Ibid., Memorandum of Conversation between US Secretary of State, Dr Henry Kissinger, and the Foreign Minister of Guyana, Fred Wills, Washington, February 12, 1976.

15.
'What I Stand for Is Winning in the World'
Dedicated Man, Inflexible Mind, 1980–91

The West is a sea of crippled souls. What prospects does this inhuman system hold for the ordinary man? Modern capitalism is a society without ideals, without a future – hence its moral disintegration, its spiritual emptiness.

– Leonid Brezhnev, April 1970

We arrived in Moscow from Tiflis [Georgia] and when, in the evening we began to feel hungry and tried to buy something, we found there was nothing to be had in any of the shops…Then, as now, I would have been prepared to put up with any amount of hunger and live in the worst poverty if only our rights had been respected, and we had been subject to human law, not the law of wild animals.

– Nadezhda Mandelstam, 1972

Marxism did not fail anywhere. It's a thriving political ideology. Stalinism failed in the USSR and the socialist countries because of Stalinism. What failed in Guyana was the economy.

– Ralph Ramkarran to Oscar Ramjeet, personal correspondence, May 2017

I.   Professor Clive Thomas on Jagan's Political Credo

Shortly after the death of Cheddi Jagan (on March 6, 1997), ironically at the Walter Reed General Hospital, the US army medical centre in Washington, DC (the capital of capitalism/imperialism), Professor Clive Thomas, the eminent Guyanese economist, provided an overview of the politics of Jagan and his People's Progressive Party (PPP). He observed that by the early 1970s Burnham also was espousing a form of socialism (communism), and that Jagan's sponsors, the Soviet Union, had constrained him to be more empathetic with Burnham's People's National Congress (PNC). It was an absurd situation – every stray dog in Guyana was now a socialist – yet entire villages were actively disengaging from Burnham and Jagan's socialist mirage, decamping (largely with minimal restraint) to the heartlands of capitalism: the US and Canada primarily, augmenting the thousands already in the home of the old imperialist enemy, England.

An excerpt from Professor Thomas's long interview of 1997 follows:

> Politically, Dr Jagan and his PPP were active members of the Soviet group of Communist Parties, until the break-up of the Soviet Union. He was in Opposition...in Guyana for 28 long years; and in keeping with his international affiliation during this period his party adopted very pro-Soviet positions. In particular he also applied the 'official' theses of Soviet communism about the nature and policies for Third World societies to Guyana. Thus, he was a strong upholder of the 'non-capitalist path of development.' **He viewed the expansion of the state sector in Guyana as necessary for constructing socialism, and called for more and more nationalisation of foreign businesses...**From time to time this perspective led him into incongruous situations. Thus he gave 'critical support' to the Burnham regime because, as he argued, the regime had embarked on nationalising the two leading industries in Guyana: bauxite and sugar [emphasis added].[1]

Professor Thomas also noted that the Soviets (like the Cubans) were inclined to view Burnham's nationalisation of foreign-owned enterprises as a vindication of his 'socialist' credentials. Consequently, they 'sought to restrain Jagan and the PPP's opposition to' the Burnham regime. This is the backdrop to Jagan's offering 'critical support' to the regime.

In other words, the two old enemies (Burnham and Jagan) had reached an involuntary, but transitory, point of convergence whereby they were deemed to be in the same ideological frame: Soviet/Cuban and anti-American. Therefore, the Cold War should have been over in Guyana long before it was really over as a universal phenomenon. The politics of Jagan and Burnham, by the late 1970s to early 1980s, meant that the US had, in effect, 'lost' in this impoverished place, stunted by its stubborn racial insecurities, yet bizarrely manifesting a supposedly Marxist-Leninist anti-imperialist political culture on the part of virtually every political party. But, on a wider political canvas, the capitalists/imperialists were winning in a more profound way that prefigured the triumph of their system by the end of the 1980s.

Vast numbers of Guyanese, including ardent supporters of Jagan and Burnham, were seeking and finding greener pastures in the land of the arch-imperialists, the US and Canada primarily – and tacitly affirming their new capitalist, democratic homelands by sending remittances and barrels of numerous banned items to food-starved Guyana. A substantial amount of Jagan's Indian supporters settled in the borough of Queens, New York, recreating an Indo-Guyanese community centred on the Liberty Avenue commercial centre. Even the children of Cheddi and Janet Jagan found their place in the sun, in capitalist North America; so did those of Forbes Burnham, outside of Guyana.

However, no scholar has adequately explored Burnham's political philosophy: his tempering of his nebulous 'socialism' that, as he sought (strategically) to become America's preference in the early 1960s, he defined as being distinct from, and diametrically opposed to, Jagan's pro-Soviet communism. Burnham then distanced himself from his American allies who had anointed him; aided and abetted his ascension to power through President Kennedy's unrelenting pressure on the British, accompanied by the intervention of the CIA; then by sanctioning or deliberately overlooking rigged elections to preclude the communist Jagan from ever regaining power. All dictated by the Americans' perceived imperatives during the Cold War. Yet the geopolitical argument that the Americans advanced obsessively in subverting the communist Jagan, soon evaporated despite Burnham's embrace of Castro, Kim Il-sung, the Soviets, the East Germans, and other communist regimes with a despicable human rights record. However, America's residual apprehension of Jagan's pro-Soviet allegiance was not susceptible to erasure. It took the end of the Cold War (his communist utopia imploded) before the Americans (largely through Jimmy Carter) acceded to Jagan's return to office in October 1992 (aged seventy-four), after nearly twenty-eight years in the wilderness.

II. Mr M. Maxwell's Insightful Letter Regarding the Political Nullity of Jaganism and Burnhamism

I retrieved recently a letter I filed some years ago because it had made an impression on me. Written by a regular correspondent to *Kaieteur News* in Guyana, M. Maxwell (a pseudonym), it is captioned 'Cheddi Jagan and Forbes Burnham were terrible, failed leaders'; it appeared on August 10, 2012. I reproduce two excerpts from Maxwell's letter on the pernicious utopianism of two men, both of whom were congenitally unpractical. A carnival of words! 'They had no idea how money works; no conception of wealth creation,' as the late Dr Fenton Ramsahoye put it to me on several occasions. In older capitalist societies such men, if they were to gain power solely by the power of their rhetoric, could be restrained by the countervailing force of their robustly independent institutions, the professionalism of the civil service, and a vibrant free media. However, the less fortified institutional safeguards in post-colonial Guyana were quickly corroded because of the professed socialism/communism of the post-colonial order: contemptuous of just about everything of British provenance and at variance with the established liberal democratic norms in the rest of the Anglophone Caribbean, barring the New Jewel Movement in Grenada in 1979–83, another Marxist-Leninist travesty.

Maxwell's provocative assessment of Jagan and Burnham merits serious consideration:

> The Guyanese people had a natural propensity for capitalist entrepreneurship and commercialism. In fact, what Jagan (from 1957 to 1964) and Burnham (from 1964 to 1985) [28 crucial years despoiled] did was to cripple the natural Guyanese inclination to wealth creation, commercialism and capitalist energies by establishing state-controlled economic structures. In Burnham's case, the costly experiment...led to the complete destruction of African entrepreneurship and capitalist endeavours, which led to further impoverishment and economic marginalisation of Africans. If Cheddi Jagan had obtained power in 1964, Indians would have suffered the same fate under a Jagan communist government. Ironically and shamefully, these men are still celebrated by their ethnic communities as legends. Burnham and Jagan...did not think of the nation first, but of ideology and self before nation.

Maxwell's point about the creation of wealth is a pertinent one because both Jagan and Burnham believed that capitalism is intrinsically exploitative and fundamentally evil. Jagan, the inveterate ideologue, genuinely thought that the 'commanding heights of the economy' must be owned by the state and that the 'paramountcy' of the communist party over the state (as in the USSR and Cuba) was sacrosanct. The problem with this basic premise of his communist beliefs is that it has no tradition of accommodating a plurality of parties, certainly none espousing capitalism. It is also premised on permanent rule by the communist party as the sole instrument piloting social forces towards the inevitable communist utopia of permanent happiness.

Burnham recognised in the totalitarian foundation of communism the means of establishing himself and his party as the sole ruler of the country, permanently entrenched as in the Soviet Union and its satellites. After several rigged elections, a largely demoralised PPP, instructed or persuaded by the Soviet Union and Castro to render support to a 'progressive anti-imperialist' Burnham regime, was effectively neutered. In fact, while Burnham was stealing Jagan's radical clothing, the ineffectual Jagan became increasingly preoccupied with displaying credentials of Marxist-Leninist ideological purity. His self-proclaimed theoretical rigour and authenticity were contrasted with the 'eclecticism' of Burnham – a term of condescension and arrogant disapprobation by genuine Marxists. The consequence of this ideological palaver was a wounded national soul inflicted by the doctrinaire socialist adventures of Jagan and Burnham.

I am therefore drawn again to Maxwell's unsparing verdict on the legacy of Jagan and Burnham, 'derelict personalities' by his definition, and to his interesting perspective on why Burnham rejected the Americans, despite possibilities for a substantial amount of aid to undermine the appeal of the communist Jagan:

> Cheddi Jagan was an ideologue. Communism dominated his thought, life and decision-making. Forbes Burnham was a megalomaniac. The pursuit of personal power was his dominant philosophy in life. One

was all about the ideological cause; the other was all about himself. These two themes that consumed the two men wreaked destruction on Guyana…Instead of expanding and improving an existing capitalist model, they sought to impose a foreign ideology on an economy that was unprepared for it – the communist or socialist utopia in a society divided on racial lines. Burnham and Jagan have left us a legacy of racial division…The scar continues to run deep.[2]

Maxwell also addressed Burnham's *volte-face* from the early 1970s, in his long reign of nearly twenty-one years, his apparent appropriation of Jagan's Marxism:

Many facets of Burnham's rule were closer to communism than socialism. I strongly believe that despite the opportunity presented by the Americans to infuse massive capital in Guyana, Burnham chose socialism over capitalism because it was easier for him to gain maximum power through the state-control structure of socialism. Capitalism would have made Guyana wealthier, but also have made Burnham more vulnerable politically. Socialism was a means of greater personal power for a megalomaniac like Burnham.[3]

I have not encountered any of Burnham's writings or speeches suggesting that he endorsed Marxism, apart from the obvious allure of the Leninist doctrine of the 'paramountcy of the party' in building socialism (essentially a rationalisation of dictatorial rule). This contrasted with Jagan, who continually cited sources (especially Western ones) that substantiated the superior achievements of the Soviet Union and its satellites.

Burnham was a pragmatist by temperament, copiously gifted with the legal talent, oratorical brilliance, and political adroitness to play that role to perfection. And it never did escape him that even if he were so inclined, he could ill afford to be judged a political enemy by the Americans – indispensable to his principal ambition of leading Guyana to independence. Politically sagacious and apprehensive of the impending demographic superiority of the Indians in British Guiana (loyal to Jagan almost to the man and woman, Hindu and Muslim), Burnham recognised early that it was imperative to preclude the British from granting independence to Jagan, as most expected in 1962. Therefore, his only likelihood of ever gaining power was to exploit to the hilt Jagan's admiration of, and solidarity with, Fidel Castro, coupled with his devotion to world communism as exemplified by the Soviet Union and its satellites (systematically documented by MI5 and the CIA).

In this once-in-a-lifetime venture, Burnham was facilitated immeasurably and decisively by Peter D'Aguiar, the Portuguese capitalist, pro-American, and rabidly anti-communist leader of the United Force (UF). Burnham deftly exploited the latter's (and the Catholic Church's) crusade in the early 1960s against the 'communist virus,' in effecting his campaign against Jagan, thereby making himself America's chosen one. D'Aguiar's vitriolic anti-communism in the early 1960s constituted a stridently anti-Castro/anti-Jagan mission of which Burnham was, arguably, the sole beneficiary.

David de Caires argues that D'Aguiar's uncompromising anti-communism was substantially more instrumental in fomenting the violent demonstrations against the Kaldor Budget of 1962, which marked the start of the CIA's resolve to remove Jagan from office before the British granted independence:

> D'Aguiar's imperative was to unseat Cheddi Jagan. There is no doubt about that...I understand 1962 [the anti-Jagan riots: the widespread looting and burning of the commercial heart of Georgetown] purely in ideological terms. D'Aguiar got involved with the CIA too. There is no doubt in my mind that he was instrumental in planning to overthrow Jagan. Certainly, in 1962, he played a more active role than Burnham in this respect. D'Aguiar and his followers were the real activists...They were very, very vocal. It was D'Aguiar who was making the early running with very hostile speeches, deliberately attacking Jagan and advocating the anti-communist cause. Burnham was ambivalent on that issue because he still saw himself as a democratic socialist. He was tagging himself opportunistically on D'Aguiar's coattails. Then the CIA and the unions got involved [in 1963] and it became a more complex operation.[4]

III. Jagan Advocates 'Genuine Scientific Socialism,' Defines Burnham's Socialism as Fake – 'A Special Brand of Capitalism'

Yet Jagan still believed that history, time, and 'the laws of scientific socialism' would inevitably vanquish imperialism and its 'pseudo-socialist' minions like Forbes Burnham. Therefore, Jagan's PPP, throughout the late 1970s and most of the 1980s (until the fall of communism), continually cast doubt on the *bona fides* of Burnham and the PNC's belated assumption of a socialist or Marxist outlook. Speaking in the National Assembly on March 21, 1979, Jagan remarked that they had been rebuffed by the PNC when they made a proposal for national unity and 'to take a firm position against imperialism': their call for a National Patriotic Front Government. He argued that with the nationalisation of most of the economy (around 80 per cent), a new class formation was emerging – the ascendancy of a new elite. He referred to this group as 'a bureaucratic bourgeoisie.' Jagan was saying that Burnham was not interested in power-sharing, having already forged the means to rule the roost; neither was he prepared to join the Cold War against American imperialism. Yet Jagan was not deterred from engaging his morally unimpeachable ideological purity in defence of the Soviet system:

> If you want to build socialism [communism] you have to fight
> imperialism; anti-imperialism is the gateway to socialism. Socialism
> is not built by verbiage. They [the PNC] say so in the statement: 'We
> continue to strive for the orderly transformation of our country into a
> socialist state.' Hocus pocus, these are only words to fool the gullible.
> You cannot go to socialism unless you take an anti-imperialist course
> firmly, in domestic policy and foreign policy [essentially pro-Soviet].
> Tell us which country in the world, in both domestic and foreign
> policy, took a pro-imperialist course and arrived at socialism. Tell us
> which one.[5]

A little over four years before, when Burnham was already in close embrace
of his new-found friend Fidel, and a little before the latter had apparently
counselled Jagan and Chandisingh to collaborate with Burnham, Jagan (with an
intimate and prolonged exposure to the mind of Burnham) was categorical that
his belated Marxism-Leninism was fraudulent:

> When the PPP was in government [1957–64], the PNC advocated
> democratic socialism. It [allied with Peter D'Aguiar's United Force]
> used the weapon of anti-Marxism and anti-communism to incite its
> supporters against the PPP which it falsely accused of wanting to
> destroy freedoms and to abolish elections.
>
> Now that it cannot win an election under the proportional
> representation system, which was specially designed to bring it to
> power, it has abandoned democratic socialism and demagogically
> speaks of Marxism-Leninism. This is merely an excuse to adopt
> the politico-economic form, but not the content, of socialism as
> institutionalised in the socialist states.[6]

What Jagan probably could not apprehend was his implication that Burnham
was adopting aspects of Marxist-Leninist form (not its content) to circumvent,
if not negate, the troublesome issue of free elections – 'bourgeois democracy,'
by Jagan's pejorative labelling of it in other circumstances. Burnham, as Jagan
suggested unconsciously, wanted to appropriate the advantages accruing from
the totalitarian form of socialism institutionalised in the Soviet Union and its
satellites. Castro could therefore empathise with Burnham's stance very well:
he, too, was no stickler for general elections and other staples of 'bourgeois
democracy.' These so-called people's governments under the Soviet system,
including Bishop's Grenada, never did trust the working class to the extent they
would concede their right to exercise the franchise in free and fair elections.

Jagan could grant no validity to Burnham's initial nationalisation, particularly
the bauxite industry, as it did not constitute a socialist initiative per se. Yet he was
continually pushing Burnham to nationalise virtually everything with the sullied
mark of private enterprise. He believed totally that the acquisition of private
wealth connoted complicity in exploitative methods. He could not credit private

enterprise with the attributes of initiative, innovation, imagination, industry, and risk-taking; he perceived it as virtually a genuflection to mammon – with connotations of evil. Jagan's Marxism, as Dr Fenton Ramsahoye often said, was a faith: self-contained; infallible; unchallengeable because it is supposedly based on scientific premises – laws of the development of society. Although Jagan always felt Burnham's nationalisation was not congruent with authentic socialist transformation, he continually pontificated on the necessity for him to commit to nationalising private enterprise because the idea in itself – public ownership of the means of production – was fundamental to his Marxist tenets. The faith was always paramount; it gave him the moral authority and the energy to persist, year after year, in the wilderness. A virtual religious calling.

> [The PNC's] 'cooperative socialism,' 'Marxism-Leninism' and state intervention in the economy, including nationalisation, provide the cover for establishing a partnership with imperialism, and for building state capitalism and bureaucratic capitalism…In this era when imperialism is becoming increasingly concerned about shortages of raw materials, it is prepared to condone partnership (joint ventures with 51 per cent) government ownership and even nationalisation and/or sales contracts, and the raw materials.

> And what is being witnessed at the Guyana Bauxite Company [nationalised in 1971] is not socialist, but state-capitalist, nationalisation. There is no workers' control. And huge salaries and allowances are paid to the bureaucratic elite [the new class].

> Side by side with state capitalism is the development of bureaucratic capitalism. Fat salaries and allowances in the state machine, whether administrative or business, permit the accumulation of wealth in the hands of the PNC elite, which is then invested. Private and corporate business, which PNC leaders own and control, are masquerading as cooperatives and in the process, derive state patronage and avoid income tax…

> While the struggle for human rights and a people's democracy continues, there must be relentless pressure to force the PNC regime to break the imperialist domination of the economy [more nationalisation!]. Whatever steps are taken in the direction of a principled, consistent democratic and anti-imperialist policy must be supported.[7]

This was the context of Jagan's 'critical support' of mid-1975 for the PNC's socialist programme (however flawed), epitomised by large-scale nationalisation of just about everything, and the miniaturising of private capital. And Jagan was proud to acknowledge his role in this. It did not matter that nationalisation by the PNC spawned, as Jagan saw it, 'state and bureaucratic capitalism.' It did not matter that the nationalisation of 80 per cent of the economy opened the floodgates to the destruction of the economy, the impoverishment of the nation, the proliferation of horrendous violence against individuals and their property, all conducing to the flight of several hundred thousand Guyanese of all races. At least Jagan's mortal enemies, the 'sugar gods' (Booker in particular), were driven out by 1976.

But he was always ready with his learned admonition, based on genuine Marxism-Leninism, to tell the bogus Marxists in the PNC where they were going wrong; why, indeed, they were incapable of leading Guyana on the road to the Promised Land, guided by the infallible example of the Soviet Union and the People's Democracies of Eastern Europe. Jagan was proud that it was his PPP that had 'carried the ideological struggle' to move decisively to nationalise DEMBA (the Canadian bauxite company) in 1971. The PNC was heading for a reformist approach, joint ownership, with the government acquiring 51 per cent of the assets. The PPP rejected this as being compatible with, and subservient to, 'official US imperialist policy': a halfway house to stem socialist ownership of the means of production, distribution, and exchange.

Jagan recalled the sustained ideological offensive by the PPP, cognisant of the poverty of socialist theory and a void in a radical political imagination that inhered in the pragmatic, vacillating, and opportunistic PNC. It gave Jagan immense satisfaction that he was, consistently, on a higher philosophical and ethical plane guided by the tenets of Marxism-Leninism:

> [We]...pointed out that nationalisation alone was not socialism [communism]; that there were also capitalist nationalisation and reformist nationalisation; that without socialist nationalisation and workers' control, there would be state capitalism with bureaucratic management....[8]

Jagan made a distinction between socialism, the working-class ideology for which the PPP stood, and state capitalism that was the *raison d'etre* of the PNC. He identified the foundation of real socialism as its grounding in democracy – democratic centralism in the Communist Party and the wider society, and its commitment to production in worker-controlled industrial and agricultural entities, the aim being the valid redistribution of the surplus created by the workers – that is returning it to themselves, directly or indirectly through social amenities:

> Under socialism [communism], there is democracy – people's democracy during the transition period to socialist democracy during the socialist period – at the level of the state, party and industry. State power is held by the working class in alliance with the peasantry (farmers) and intellectuals who constitute the majority of the population. There is internal democracy within the party. A Communist or Workers' Party is guided by the principle of

democratic centralism – democratic on the basis of discussions from bottom to top and vice versa – and centralism for the purpose of unity and discipline on the basis that decisions once democratically made must be carried out by all.[9]

This was straight out of the textbook of the Communist Party of the Soviet Union (CPSU). Jagan was continually didactic towards Burnham, instructing him on how genuine working-class democracy worked in the people's factories, under communism. There were no loopholes for crooked party leaders to enrich themselves on the surplus generated by the workers. Cheddi's conception of democracy was rooted in Marxist-Leninist assumptions of the perfectibility of society, inspired by the unassailably lofty goals of the Communist Party. But this could not be realised if the party was corrupt, corrupting and pseudo-socialist like the PNC: 'At the factory level, there is industrial democracy through workers' participation and control. The workers through their trade unions elect management committees which together with the managers are in decision-making and management.' The utopia under communism ultimately was attainable only under the impeccable stewardship of the communist party:

> In a socialist society, the surplus produced by the workers and taken in the form of profits and taxes is returned to them directly and indirectly in the form of social and economic benefits – full employment, increase in wages, reduction in prices, subsidised rentals, free education, free medicine, security in old age, culture and sport, etc.[10]

Burnham's PNC was intrinsically lacking in the ideological credentials to create the perfect communist society. Therefore, Cheddi could discern nothing redeeming in their belated adoption of Marxism-Leninism. It was a fraud, and he must have felt vindicated in view of the extraordinary personal sacrifices – at an exorbitant, and irredeemable, cost to his supporters – that he made over the years for his creed:

> The surplus is clearly not going for development or for the people. It is being misused for the enrichment of the PNC leadership. And under the PNC, there is no real democracy at the level of the state, party or industry...**Guyana needs nationalisation of all foreign enterprises if we are to achieve national liberation** [more nationalisation!]. But there will be no liberation if foreign and local capitalism is replaced by PNC state capitalism and bureaucratic capitalism masquerading as cooperative socialism. **Guyana needs genuine scientific socialism** [(communism); emphasis added].[11]

The Communist Party, the sole repository of wisdom, in a one-party state. No reference at all to a plurality of competing political ideas or political parties or the question of ethnicity. And no mention of 'bourgeois freedoms,' such as free and fair elections, freedom of speech and of the press, under the socialist order. The Communist Party, with a higher form of 'internal democracy,' would become the custodian of socialist democracy, which transcends the much-vaunted 'bourgeois democracy' under capitalism. Yet Jagan, a true believer in Soviet and Cuban communism, was making the case relentlessly for 'bourgeois freedoms' in challenging the legitimacy of the regime of Forbes Burnham, now affecting its belief in 'cooperative socialism' or, from time to time, even Marxism-Leninism.

Burnham was tormented by the fact of the escalating Indian demographics: if afforded the franchise in free elections, Indians would precipitate his and his African people's banishment to the political wilderness for eternity. This had driven the Jagans' most trusted erstwhile African ally, Sydney King (Eusi Kwayana), to adopt an aggressively racial stand on behalf of his African people, from 1957 to 1964 (during Jagan's colonial term in office). He, like Burnham, was mortally apprehensive of ominous Indian dominance culturally, economically, politically – irreversibly.

Ultimately, despite the tortuous ideological rhetoric permeated by one or other variant of Marxism (arguably a means of circumventing the ethnic futility), Guyanese politics is underpinned by the formidably resilient issue of racial insecurity. Moreover, this problem is so intimidating it was infinitely more seductive to seek flight in utopian visions of human perfectibility – a conception of rapid economic growth with equality of access to abundant wealth that would herald the socialist/communist paradise; thus, would the transitory virus of Guyanese racism and chronic ethnic insecurity be eradicated. Marxism, therefore, was a kind of magic bullet.

In 1982, on the sixtieth anniversary of the founding of the USSR, Jagan celebrated what he considered their 'greatest success': a socialist society in which its dauntingly diverse nationalities (well over a hundred) were fully integrated into the Union – free, engaged, and confident in articulating and contributing their unique cultural attributes, while (in turn) being enriched by the collective Soviet enterprise in the making of communist man. For Cheddi, the USSR was the prototype for the resolution of whatever short-term ethnic or economic problems Guyana was experiencing. The Soviet Union was El Dorado.

> Among the greatest successes of the Soviet Union is the solution of the nationalities question on the firm principles laid down by Lenin. After the October Revolution, all the once oppressed peoples in the colonies of Tsarist Russia were freed. The once backward peoples of Asia joined the Union and today bear ample evidence that it is possible to by-pass the capitalist road and leap into a socialist future. The Union was founded on friendship, equality and mutual co-operation in all fields. **This remarkable experience shows the vitality of socialism in solving the nationalities question in a matter of years, which capitalism has been unable to do in centuries** [emphasis added].

Since December 30, 1922, the peoples of the USSR have developed as one family of nations...The 100 different nationalities today live harmoniously in freedom. Above all, the Soviet Far East, the Central Asian Republics, and the other once backward areas of Tsarist Russia offer an example to the developing countries. In 1906 an educational newspaper estimated that it would take at least 4,600 years to wipe out illiteracy among Central Asian peoples. Soviet power banished illiteracy in two decades...

As long ago as 1915, the immortal Lenin wrote: 'We must link the revolutionary struggle for socialism with a revolutionary programme on the nationalities question.' This has borne fruit. It has given the Soviet system a vitality which is indestructible.[12]

IV. The PPP Upholds the Inviolability of 'Bourgeois Democratic' Rights yet Pronounces Marxism-Leninism the Sole Instrument for the Emancipation of the Working Class

The Constitution of the PPP was adopted by the 20th Congress of the Party, at Annandale in August 1979. And as the preamble indicates, the party was defining itself as a full-fledged communist party, 'the vanguard of the working class and all working people of Guyana.' No mention was made of the chronic ethnic problem; therefore, the presumption (customary with the PPP) was that the party spoke not only for its overwhelmingly Indian supporters, but also for other segments of the working class, African and Amerindian. The sanctity of their socialist/communist creed, one supposes, entitled them to assume the ultimate right to aggregate and represent all the working people. And there was no ambiguity either regarding the PPP's doctrinal resolve to nationalise the entire economy, guided by Marxism-Leninism; this was manifested in their unremitting pressure on the PNC for total nationalisation in the 1970s. There was no niche in Jagan's conception of the great communist society for exploitative private enterprise:

[The PPP's] objective is the creation of a socialist [communist] society in Guyana in which the means of production, distribution and exchange will be socially owned and collectively used for the benefit of all. Only a socialist Guyana armed with the theory and practice of Marxism-Leninism will end exploitation of man by man, eradicate imperialist and neo-colonialist presence and fight for and preserve the full democratic rights of the people.[13]

Presumably, the communist party that the PPP aspired to become would be the sole custodian of 'full democratic' rights. The latter, however, was incompatible with the totalitarian ethos of the communist parties in the Soviet

Union, Cuba, and elsewhere. Yet Jagan, time and again, would pledge to uphold 'bourgeois democratic rights,' including the plurality of political parties; in fact, that Marxism-Leninism, in its Guyanese incarnation, would never subvert such fundamental freedoms. But not many beyond the Indian community (for racial reasons) were credulous of Jagan's continual assertion of Guyanese exceptionalism. It was easier for a camel to go through the eye of a needle than for the other political parties and diverse civil society organisations in the country to put their faith in Jagan's sanctimoniousness regarding liberal democracy. Their incredulity was magnified because the PPP's Marxist-Leninist creed was couched in the phraseology of orthodox communist parties, with their appalling record of extirpating 'bourgeois freedoms' wherever they had catapulted themselves into power.

The PPP Constitution states:

> The PPP is guided by Marxism-Leninism, the ideology of the working class, and is organised on the basis of democratic centralism. Its international work is based on the principles of proletarian internationalism under which fraternal relations are strengthened with communist and workers' parties and militant solidarity is extended to the socialist countries, the national liberation movements and the peace, democratic and progressive forces in capitalist countries.[14]

In Cheddi Jagan's collection of articles from the *Mirror* (republished in a booklet in January 1984), *Unmasking Enemies of the Guyanese People*, he is emphatic that Burnham's socialism was fraudulent and that the US was prepared to allow the PNC to continue along its path of bogus socialism because it gave genuine Marxism-Leninism a bad name. Jagan underlined the authenticity of his creed, arguing that 'US imperialism is the enemy of mankind. And this includes Guyanese.' He admitted that while the US government, in recent times, had blocked USAID and IADB loans to Guyana, that paled into insignificance by comparison with their virulent ideological crusade against genuine Marxist governments, as in Cuba, Nicaragua, and Grenada (prior to the US invasion of the latter in October 1983). Jagan was certain that such pressure as applied by America on the Burnham regime was motivated by non-ideological criteria, for it was still deemed capitalist, however aberrant. Guyana was not pursuing a revolutionary agenda actuated by communism, and the imperialists knew it:

> And what is Guyana being pressured for? Certainly not because there is an ongoing socialist revolution as the PNC claims, or that Guyana is in a state of transition from capitalism to socialism, as is stated in the 1980 Constitution. Imperialism is fully aware of the fact that there is no socialist construction in Guyana. But it does not object to the PNC bandying the form [rather than the substance] of socialism. Actually, it is glad, as it served and is serving the interest of imperialism to

have the socio-economic-political order called socialism. In this way, socialism gets a bad name. Economic pressure is being applied to the PNC regime not because it is socialist, but because it is practising a particular brand of capitalism – state bureaucratic, cooperative and parasitic capitalism.[15]

Jagan was contending that the Ronald Reagan administration wanted Burnham's government to retrace its steps, reverting to the orthodox capitalism in Latin American countries such as Argentina, Brazil, Chile, Mexico, and Venezuela. For Jagan, the latter was the worse form of capitalism: 'dependent, distorted capitalism...which breeds underdevelopment and worsening living conditions for the working people.'[16]

If one concedes that there was nothing socialist or Marxist-Leninist or communist about Burnham's break with Western capitalism and American imperialism, then did he still have faith in capitalism? Yes, according to Jagan, but it was a more convoluted strain of capitalism. It follows that Burnham was neither fish nor fowl. Therefore, Jagan's 'critical support' of the PNC regime, very short-lived (indeed microscopic), had little substance. It was probably prompted (as noted before) by his Cuban and Russian comrades as a desperate means of securing a rare ally in the hemisphere, America's backyard, however ambiguous Burnham's socialist or Marxist credentials. Yet, to many, he was genuinely anti-imperialist, because he was perceived as ditching erstwhile allies whose machinations had elevated him to power at the expense of Jagan, in 1964, and had also aided and abetted Burnham's first rigged elections, in December 1968, to defeat the communist Jagan.

All through the late 1970s to early 1980s, Jagan never did depart from his central theme: Burnham's socialism is fake socialism. What he really meant was that Burnham was not a genuine Marxist-Leninist; he was not a communist. Therefore, the Americans were never inclined to move against him because the alternative was an authentic 'socialist': the communist Jagan. In January 1984, Jagan restated that there was no hope for Guyana under the PNC: 'Burnhamism – state, bureaucratic, cooperative capitalism – is not the answer. Neither is dependent, distorted capitalism under Reaganism. The way forward is Socialist Orientation. This means a democratic, anti-imperialist state which is serving the masses of the people of Guyana.'[17]

The Report of the Central Committee of the PPP to the 22nd Congress of the Party, at Annandale, in early August 1985 (it concluded the day before Burnham died on August 6), fortified Jagan's contention that Burnham was a bogus socialist. Consequently, the American imperialists were disinclined to abandon 'their political love-hate relationship' with the PNC. The PPP, on the other hand, were vindicated by their fidelity to their inviolable creed. They were the only authentic Marxists-Leninists in Guyana, and that accounted for the Americans not daring to sanction the removal of the dictatorial PNC regime.

Jagan's PPP – like a sect – continued to brandish their ideological purity as a badge of honour. But they were also sceptical of the socialist *bona fides* of the Working People's Alliance (WPA), the party of Dr Walter Rodney, which also claimed to be Marxist:

> [Burnham's] Guyana is not 'a Marxist pro-Soviet state.' But that is the perception of the Reaganites. That is why the PNC no longer claims that its ideas are based on Marx, Engels and Lenin; instead the regime's emphasis now is on 'co-operativism' and not Marxism-Leninism and class struggle for the 'construction of socialism.' This is an attempt to make itself acceptable to the ideologues of the Reagan administration. This is why the WPA [also] is presently engaged in revising their 1979 programme, *For a Revolutionary Socialist Guyana*, which proclaimed its adherence to Marxism-Leninism. Now, it claims that it is independent Marxist, whatever it means.[18]

The report was also censorious of small political groups, such as Paul Nehru Tennassee's Democratic Labour Movement (DLM), which were arguing that as long as the PPP remained wedded to Soviet communism 'the United States will not allow it to come to power.' The PPP also rejected equating the PPP's socialism/communism with the PNC's nebulous version, and for submitting that 'socialism is no good; it has failed in Guyana.' The Central Committee of the PPP disabused both the left and the right of their anti-Soviet stance while corroborating Jagan's conviction that Burnhamism was, in fact, a form of capitalism – they being the sole exponents of a pure Marxism-Leninism:

> We have repeatedly stated that the PNC is neither socialist nor communist; that it is not socialism that has failed in Guyana but Burnhamism, a special brand of capitalism. We have been pressing for the building of the firm foundations – the political, economic, ideological, cultural and institutional prerequisites – of socialism. That is the essential difference between the PPP and the PNC. To the PNC we say: democracy is vital [presumably 'bourgeois democracy']; deepen the struggle against imperialism; and lay firm foundations for advancing to socialism. To the opposition forces we say democracy alone is not enough; the Guyanese revolution, as the WPA said in 1979 in its [original] political programme, must have 'an anti-imperialist and socialist focus'; imperialism is the main enemy of the Guyanese people. This is what the political struggle in Guyana is all about.[19]

This is muddled thinking and reflected the PPP's hubris regarding their being the quintessential apostle of the Marxist-Leninist creed. However, it is inconceivable that the PNC could have been persuaded to restore 'bourgeois democracy,' primarily free and fair elections (by the PPP's definition), which they were likely to lose. Neither was it plausible that Burnham's party would have embraced the PPP's concept of Marxism-Leninism, an unabashedly 'Made in Moscow' brand that flew in the face of the Americans in their 'backyard.' This preoccupation of the PPP, nearly twenty-one years in the wilderness and essentially the property of Cheddi and Janet Jagan, sustained largely by their obsequious younger disciples (most virtually thirty years younger than the two deities), rendered the party essentially a sect of inconsequential ideologues.

This was reflective of its prolonged poverty of imagination: an ingrained dogmatism spawned by the prolonged powerlessness of the PPP. It was compounded by the ideological eclecticism of Burnham, switching from West to East and vaguely in-between – a philosophical nihilism driven purely by self-preservation and self-aggrandisement. Of course, Burnhamism was facilitated largely by Jagan's own unquestioning adherence to every doctrinal pronouncement emanating from the CPSU that left minimal space for flexibility or originality of thinking – thus was the PPP marooned in a political quagmire by the late 1970s–1980s. It made them look clueless in their ineffectual pontifications against the Burnham dictatorship, the butt of derision even by many who still supported Jagan, purely on racial ground:

> The United States has not carried out a strident political crusade against the Burnham regime as it has done against Grenada…and is still doing against Cuba, Nicaragua and other revolutionary states. It is fully aware of the political realities of Guyana and the fact that it does not have a viable rightist alternative political force here… The imperialists know too that such a crusade might drive the PNC toward the PPP and the socialist [communist] world.[20]

So where precisely did the PPP place the PNC in the political spectrum by mid-1985, when Burnham died? They had re-consigned them to the camp of their old odious sponsors, the imperialists:

> Imperialism realises that the PNC had retreated in the 1977–82 period with its Letter of Intent to the IMF in 1978 and to the World Bank in 1982; that it was objectively on the same side with Anglo-American imperialism…In the present complex situation of Guyana, imperialism does not necessarily have as its immediate aim the removal of the PNC regime; it has more limited but precise objectives: the application of economic pressures to change its domestic and foreign policy as in the 1964–70 period: from bureaucratic-state, cooperative and parasitic capitalism to dependent/distorted underdeveloped capitalism. While working with the regime of the PNC, imperialism is at the same time strengthening the rightist, pro-imperialist elements inside and outside the ruling party. To this end it is channelling aid to the private sector.[21]

According to this bizarre analysis by the PPP, by the mid-1980s the Americans were resurrecting a right-wing force in Guyana. Yet they, as well as the imperialists, knew that this strand of thought was miniscule, virtually non-existent with the demise of Peter D'Aguiar's UF by the late 1960s and the mass exodus of the Portuguese and the coloured middle class to North America. Strangely, this putative right-wing was deemed to be aided and abetted by the local enemies of Cheddi Jagan: the indigenous 'parasitic capitalists' determined to halt the dawn of the communist utopia. By this interpretation, therefore, Burnham himself was susceptible to the menace of a rightist coup. Yet he appeared oblivious of this eventuality. He was making no military preparations for a potential right-wing coup that could liquidate Burnham as well as the PPP.

By this convoluted reasoning, the Central Committee of the PPP concluded that a political solution, between the PPP and the PNC, ought to be pursued vigorously. Given this possibility, the PPP was caught in yet another quandary in lending support to the PNC. But there was no discernible compensatory salutary dimension to the Burnham regime, such as its anti-imperialist stance or genuine commitment to 'proletarian internationalism,' solidarity with the 'fraternal socialist states' and revolutionaries elsewhere. But the PPP could still discern a residual anti-imperialist strand in the politics of the PNC. It was unimaginably surreal – a sterile political culture warped by its debilitating racial foundations, with no moral courage to confront it.

The PPP could not have been earnest in its counsel to Burnham to create a people's militia, engaging the 'whole people' against a possible 'ultra-rightist coup.' The truth was deflating: the PNC, fortified by untrammelled power for two decades, could run rings around Jagan any day of the week. The following demonstrates the rudderlessness of the PPP by the mid-1980s:

> We cannot be complacent. We must still be on guard as an ultra-rightist military coup would be aimed not only against Burnham's Presidency, but also against our Party [the PPP]. In this regard, a grave responsibility falls on the President. He has supreme powers in his party and government, but he has failed to train and arm the whole people, especially a genuine country-wide People's Militia, which is the only way to forestall an ultra-rightist coup. He has not done so for fear that the guns might be turned against him. Only a political solution will resolve this dilemma...The whole world, including Guyana, is faced, in the present grave international and regional situation, with nuclear annihilation. The world communist and revolutionary movement therefore sees Guyana's present stance in the anti-imperialist struggle, although qualified, as important. Of the Commonwealth Caribbean countries, Guyana has the most forward-looking anti-imperialist position.[22]

In adumbrating a *modus vivendi* with the Burnham regime, the PPP was, in fact, demanding of potential allies their adoption of a Marxist-Leninist programme in combination with a liberal democratic one. This contradiction always dogged the politics of the PPP: its communist purity, on one hand, in asserting its moral and political superiority in Guyana guided by Soviet Marxism; on the other, their tireless repudiation of the PNC for abrogating 'bourgeois democratic' principles. It could be construed, therefore, that the primary motivation of the PPP was their self-confidence that a built-in Indian majority would deliver them a decisive victory, if free elections were ever held. But the PNC was behaving as if it were, indeed, a communist party by adhering to what were the accepted norms of such parties in power. How could the PPP dare to demur? Comrades Fidel Castro and Leonid Brezhnev did not believe in 'bourgeois freedoms.' They themselves had barely any residual liberal democratic capital, evinced by the sanctity of 'democratic centralism' in the PPP:

> For political development to take place, there is need for the recognition of pluralism and a democratic political culture. This is laid down in the Guyana Constitution, but it is not practised by the State. This is because, under the PNC regime, the PNC party and the state have become indistinguishable [as in the Soviet Union, its satellites, Cuba and all other communist countries]. And under the doctrine of PNC paramountcy, the 'government is merely one of the executive arms,' and the critics of the party have been deemed 'the enemies of the State.'[23]

V. The Working People's Alliance: The Walter Rodney Enigma and the Ideological Vanity of the PPP

Left: Walter Rodney (1942–80), the young Marxist historian and radical political leader of the Working People's Alliance (WPA), assassinated on 13 June 1980

Right: Cheddi with Walter Rodney, Georgetown, mid-1970s.

This must have had a familiar ring to anyone with even minimal knowledge of governance in the communist countries: the prototype being the CPSU. But Jagan was so assured that he possessed the holy grail of communism that he could spare no credence for the Marxism of Walter Rodney's Working People's Alliance (WPA). The WPA recognised fully that Burnham's dictatorial regime was not subject to censure by the American and West European governments because the sole alternative was Jagan's PPP, a pro-Moscow communist party that they obviously considered reprehensible. In its publication, *Arguments for Unity against the Dictatorship in Guyana* (August 1983), the WPA explained how difficult it was to collaborate with the PPP because of its pretensions to Marxist-Leninist purity and Jagan's devotion to his 'Mecca,' the Soviet Union. The WPA tried to moderate the pro-Moscow creed of the PPP, endeavouring to convey internationally that they were shaping a viable alternative to the authoritarian Burnham regime. But the PPP, according to the WPA, continually placed hurdles in the way. They were not committed to building a durable coalition because they were assured that if free and fair elections were held, they would secure a majority. Thereby, the contentious issue of power-sharing, with the necessity for compromise (including the moderation of its sacred pro-Soviet sentiments), could be obviated.

By August 1983, the WPA did not wish to be identified with any of the two power blocs. They were disinclined to denounce American imperialism unless a measure of racial cohesion was consolidated. Even so, they indicated a preference for challenging the American system 'socially' (presumably, by means of competing ideas and winning minds) – in a non-confrontational context. In short, while the WPA was 'an independent Marxist party' advocating radical social and economic transformation, they clearly had no propensity for immersion in the Cold War. It is debatable, however, if their declared equidistance from the two superpowers was sustainable in the Western Hemisphere. Jagan, on the other hand, was impermeable to such vaunted neutrality; his political practice was conditioned by a definitive subservience to the CPSU, whatever the subject at issue. Moreover, Jagan was a rabid foe of American imperialism, and he was identified as such by successive presidents, to the advantage of Burnham. Consequently, by 1983 the WPA could not concur with Jagan's flagrantly hostile posture towards the Americans, fearing that any emulation of Grenada's ideological inflexibility (regarding Cuba and the Soviet Union) and transparent abrasiveness towards imperialism in the Hemisphere would eventuate in a calamity – collision with the might of the US – with dire consequences:

> At the present stage [August 1983; the US invaded Grenada in October 1983], it appears that the US financial and political system as a whole, and to some extent the EEC [European Union], are

fully aware of the collapse of all things under Burnham – except his regime. [Yet] they continue to ensure his survival because they are convinced that the only alternative is a Marxist-Leninist, and more, a pro-Soviet alternative [Jagan].

The WPA sees itself as an independent Marxist party…[It] has declared itself a partisan…of a genuine multi-racial power of the working people…The WPA is not over-active in foreign policy… our party should not be seen as an agency of a rival bloc, namely, in today's terms, the Soviet Union. The WPA has discussed its position with the PPP…The WPA does not apologise for not making use of the PPP type of language which can often be written in advance of the PPP on any one issue…[unfailingly pro-Soviet]

The WPA is not a member of the international grouping of communist and workers' parties, and does not wish to be seen as a member. With the remarkable thinker, Lenin, we believe it is wrong to dress the national liberation movement in communist clothing. What is wrong with a weak national liberation movement which has a million problems on its hands, taking care not to be seen as inviting a clash with US imperialism?[24]

It is true that the Soviets and the Cubans were still in favour of maintaining 'fraternal' relations with the PNC, as a 'progressive' force in the region. Consequently, they would most likely have instructed the PPP to be cognisant of such features as Burnham's anti-imperialism, support for liberation movements in Africa, and solidarity with Cuba. But it had angered the WPA that the PPP could express the following sentiment about the PNC, in their paper titled 'All Party Talks' (1982):

Guyana under the PNC, despite vacillations, still plays an international role, though muted, in the cause of world peace, liberation and development…As a result of the regime's role in the international struggle, particularly after 1974 and despite lack of democracy, corruption, discrimination, and a form of terroristic rule by the PNC, Guyana is not viewed by progressive and revolutionary states in the UN, the Non-Aligned Movement, OAU, etc. and liberation movements in the same way as dictators in Haiti, etc.[25]

The PPP document does not state that most of those governments still empathising with the PNC regime did not subscribe to free and fair elections or other expressions of liberal democracy: what the PPP and other Marxists disdainfully termed 'bourgeois democracy.' Moreover, as the WPA observed, Western liberal democracies, too, did not censor the Burnham dictatorship because of their perception that Jagan's PPP was an instrument of Soviet communism, expected to govern precisely like the PNC with regard to the abrogation of liberal democratic norms. Yet the PPP continued to manifest a palpably supercilious attitude towards smaller parties like the WPA and the DLM. They were sanguine that if general elections were ever free and fair, the PPP would win an overall majority, with the support of the minnows (as they saw them) rendered superfluous. But the WPA did remind them, however optimistically, that one of the reasons they had transformed themselves into a political party was because 'the PPP had failed to advance as a political party which could lead a multiracial struggle on a mass scale.' Its legitimacy, like that of the PNC, was rooted wholly in Indian and African racial solidarity respectively – definitely not on its Marxism-Leninism.

However, the PPP claimed to be in favour of a winner-does-not-take-all proposition in its campaign for free elections. But the WPA had doubts about their sincerity on this score. Apart from the PPP's inflexibility about their Marxist-Leninist tenets, their commitment to power-sharing also was in doubt. The following was extracted by the WPA from the PPP's 'All Party Talks' (1982):

> We [the PPP] are willing to make compromises in the interest of unity, but not to sacrifice fundamental principles. If we cannot find agreement now on a democratic, anti-imperialist, socialist oriented programme, we may very well find ourselves at war again after the PNC's ouster and an election. **We are confident that we can win such an election. But as we have said in the past, winner-does-not-take-all politics is** *not* **the best for our situation, and we will adhere to this position** [emphasis added].[26]

The WPA was eagle-eyed, observing that the sentences I have placed in bold meant that the PPP was not really interested in power-sharing, having asserted to potential allies that they would win outright, on their own, in any free and fair elections. They added sarcastically: 'Since then the PPP has been helping the cause of unity by making this declaration in the *Mirror* and at every public meeting. Is this a slip that lets the cat out of the bag?'[27]

The WPA also stressed that the PPP was missing a crucial point because of their ostrich-like attitude regarding racial insecurity, the most intractable problem in the country. Yet they were still driven primarily by a majoritarian agenda, although the country was best served by an inclusive, consensual democracy – a prerequisite to confidence-building for the gigantic task of alleviating the persistent mutual suspicion between the two major ethnic groups. The WPA cautioned the PPP:

> To pretend to treat the political economy of Guyana and to leave discussion of the race issue out of the political economy while boasting about one's ability to win elections, raises, among other things, questions of intent. What is the single most important factor for the advance of the anti-dictatorial struggle led by the Guyanese working people? It is the racial factor. So also is it for the reconstruction,

> development and transformation of the society into one in which
> public power is genuine multiracial power of the working people.
> How can the PPP avoid discussion of the race issue?[28]

Ever since the formation of the precursor to the PPP, the Political Affairs Committee (PAC) in 1946, Cheddi and Janet Jagan were disinclined to address the question of race and the chronic racial insecurities of the ethnic segments of Guyanese society. But fortified by the seemingly inexorable ethnic preponderance of the Indian vote in electoral politics, the PPP concentrated on the mobilisation of that perceived built-in majority while perpetuating the fiction that their Marxist or 'scientific socialist' creed would eradicate the virus of mutual racial incomprehension. Despite the early split of 1955 (when Forbes Burnham quit the PPP) and periodic haemorrhaging of the party thereafter, the Jagans always felt assured that their solid Indian base would hold. Nevertheless, they continually evoked their Marxist-Leninist creed to emphasise that the class struggle and the fight against imperialism were still central to their political mission. And, by implication, that racial insecurities conducing to entrenched partisan electoral preferences, though recurrent, would be eroded incrementally by the primacy of the class struggle.

Therefore, unabashed opportunism in exploiting an ethnic agenda could even be rationalised as a short-term expedient, to be superseded by the transcendent long-term objective: the communist utopia. The latter was worth the sacrifice, however agonising, as it was bound to yield boundless freedom, prosperity, and the enhancement of the human spirit untrammelled by class, racial, tribal, or other inhibiting primordial loyalties. Marxism-Leninism is a science: there is an inevitability in the outcome, however protracted its fulfilment. Jagan had inexhaustible faith in the millennium, hence his mantra: 'Difficulties there will be; the battle will be long and hard. But win we will. History and time are on our side!' The utopian vision fed a resilient smugness, rendering it virtually impossible for them to compromise – to build alliances with anyone who did not subscribe to their infallible creed.

The PPP was imprisoned by the erroneous conception of the perfectibility of humankind by their ideology of 'scientific communism.' And the source of this faith within the PPP (and its precursor, the PAC), for fifty years, was Cheddi Jagan: a true believer. It is likely that his training as a dentist (a very fine one, apparently) did not necessarily enhance his critical faculty, and this has induced me to ponder frequently on his thought process. I believe that if he were trained as a lawyer (like Forbes Burnham, Norman Manley, Grantley Adams, and Errol Barrow) or as a historian (like Eric Williams or Walter Rodney), he might never have been persuaded that Marxism-Leninism provided 'a total understanding of the world.'

Enthralled by the Soviet example despite its fundamentally flawed conception of its capacity for universal good, Jagan could not apprehend the pitfalls of his volatile political environment. As I have argued, even when he held most of the trumps (including the sympathy of the Colonial Office), around 1960, he still contrived to trip on his own banana peel. Jagan was, arguably, deficient in statesmanship: the flexibility required for building alliances; the need to modify or even change one's position tactically, prompted by the vagaries of the political equation. His idealism was not tempered by *realpolitik* – his sacred beliefs often written in stone – a limitation that Burnham exploited dextrously, in the context of the Cold War. Jagan had absolute faith in the superiority of the Soviet system. The latter point cannot be overstressed because, even today, many still seriously contend that Jagan was not a real communist; that there were no grounds for defining him as such. It is beyond belief that many people (particularly Indo-Guyanese) are still swayed by incredulity that Cheddi was, indeed, a dyed-in-the-wool pro-Moscow communist for fifty years. This probably reflects their instinctual individualistic self-realisation – more at ease with being left alone to pursue their preferred economic interests: largely capitalist by temperament. What is accurate, however, is that Jagan was never afforded the opportunity to shape policies according to his Marxist-Leninist creed. He was precluded from such measures by the strictures of colonial rule (1957–64), and communism had collapsed (no longer a viable proposition), when the Americans intervened, at the end of the Cold War, and facilitated his return to office in 1992.

Indians are proverbially wary of the *sarkar* (any manifestation of centralised authority), and would normally have repudiated Jagan's communism, with its imperatives of totalitarian control by the party and the state. But racial loyalty invariably triumphs over class identity in Guyana. Yet Jagan would have treated assertions of his non-communist credentials with derision: certainly, after he was removed from office in 1964, and felt no compunction to conceal his fidelity to communism. Moreover, if one examines his writings throughout his long political career (from the late 1940s), there is no doubt that he was totally committed to Marxism-Leninism from the inception and never did waver. Besides, MI5 with the connivance of the Colonial Office had established, by covert means, his very close relationship with the leadership of the CPGB (his principal link to the CPSU), long before he announced his 'homecoming' to Soviet communism in Moscow in 1969.

The WPA found it difficult to maintain a dialogue with the PPP (in the 1980s), which it described as 'a factory of slogans,' alluding to their doctrinaire political culture through which the dogmas of the CPSU were refracted. The WPA was convinced that because the PPP was effectively a communist party after 1969, having pledged their loyalty to the Soviet Union, the Americans would never have allowed Jagan (deemed another Castro) to rule, even if he were democratically elected. Before the end of the Cold War, at the end of the 1980s, the US would probably have subverted or invaded any such state in the Hemisphere and dislodged its perceived communist government (as they did with Allende in 1973 and Bishop in 1983). No American president, not only Kennedy, would have tolerated 'another Cuba' in the Hemisphere. And Jagan's comrades, in the Soviet Union, would not have dared to defend him militarily, in America's backyard; neither would the Cubans.

Cheddi Jagan was apprehensive of the political potential of Walter Rodney (1942–80), particularly among younger Indians – demoralised by Jagan's marginalisation by Burnham and frustrated by his garbled communist posturing and chronic ineffectualness, languishing in Opposition for nearly three decades. Jagan did recognise the intellectual stature of Walter Rodney, but the widespread curiosity in, and apparent popular appeal of, the latter in 1979–80 in both communities (before his assassination in June 1980) had precipitated palpable anxiety in the PPP. They were perturbed that the WPA, comprising several bright young intellectuals, such as Rodney and Rupert Roopnaraine (African and Indian respectively), would undermine their traditional Indian base, particularly the Indian youth. It is arguable, too, that similar fears were shared by Burnham with respect to Rodney's potential impact on young Africans.

Both entrenched racial leaders were rattled by the Rodney enigma, at the end of the 1970s. Yet the fact that the three principal leaders were espousing a variant of Marxism-Leninism (Burnham's eclecticism notwithstanding), gave the political culture of Guyana a ridiculously surreal character. For Jagan in particular, proud of his unfaltering devotion to Marxism-Leninism, Rodney's scholarly command of local history, in addition to his formidable grasp of Jagan's Marxist-Leninist ideology, must have rendered him a daunting challenge. Therefore, the assassination of Rodney was, conceivably, to the advantage of both Burnham (who effected it, according to the COI Report of 2016) and his outwitted, largely innocuous rival, Jagan.

After the death of Rodney and the collapse of talks (around 1982) between the PPP, the WPA, and a few smaller parties (with regard to forging a coalition against the Burnham dictatorship), Jagan felt less constrained in reasserting the authenticity and superiority of his pro-Moscow brand of the creed. He had denounced the PNC as fake Marxists; it was now the turn of the WPA to feel the rod of correction from the most ideologically robust communist in the country, as he clearly saw himself. Jagan pointed out that when Maurice Bishop headed the government in Grenada, President Reagan had indicted him for spreading 'the Marxist virus.' After the assassination of Bishop, and the subsequent invasion of

Grenada by the Americans, in October 1983, Jagan observed that 'communism is being put on trial.' In fact, he accused several in Guyana, including the WPA, of joining 'the anti-communist crusade.'[29]

Among those Jagan considered 'reactionaries' or 'anti-Marxists' were the *Catholic Standard*, the public intellectual, David de Caires, along with the WPA. While this charge was justifiable for the *Catholic Standard* in the 1950s–60s, by the 1970s (under its fearless editor, Father Andrew Morrison) it was, indeed, an intrepid champion of what Jagan at times dismissed as 'bourgeois democratic rights,' including free and fair elections. They paid a high price for their courage in challenging the Burnham dictatorship: the *Standard's* photographer, the Jesuit Father Bernard Darke (1925–79), was murdered by thugs from Rabbi Washington's House of Israel (agents of the Burnham regime), as he was taking pictures of their violent attack on peaceful protestors in Georgetown on July 14, 1979. It is correct to conclude, therefore, that the *Catholic Standard* was on the frontline of the fight to preserve basic democratic rights. It is entirely accurate to add that they were among the many robust defenders of freedom who made it possible for Jagan to return to government after nearly twenty-eight years of PNC rule. And he did so essentially on a winner-takes-all formula, contrary to what he had promised; consequently, he alienated many who had campaigned, at great risk, to retrieve some 'bourgeois democratic rights' from the Burnham dictatorship.

Mike James, the former assistant editor of the *Catholic Standard*, noted the progressive role played by the paper under the editorship of Father Andy Morrison (1919–2004), during the most harrowing years of the Burnham dictatorship, in the late 1970s to early 1980s. It certainly does not corroborate Jagan's critical perception of the *Standard* in 1984:

> Under Father Andy the articles and editorials in the *Catholic Standard* increasingly focused on the concerns of individuals and communities whose rights were being violated. Western Governments tacitly supported the Burnham government, arguing that any alternative was better than an avowed Communist government, even a fairly elected one. The *Catholic Standard* under Andy Morrison increasingly took the position that the concrete and blatant denial of the people's rights could never be defended [what the Marxists called 'bourgeois freedoms']; and that the right of people to choose their Government in fair elections was far more important than the ideological credentials of different parties. The paper also continuously exposed the hypocrisy of the claim by Western democracies that in Guyana, the denial of democracy should be tolerated in order to save people from losing their democratic rights under a Communist regime that would come to power if free elections were held.[30]

To repeat! Father Andy Morrison, like numerous others whom Jagan dismissed as reactionaries, was instrumental in creating the conditions that facilitated a free and fair poll in October 1992. But Jagan found it extremely difficult to build alliances with people across the political spectrum because they did not empathise with his brand of Marxism-Leninism. Yet it took people of varying religious and political persuasions, in and out of Guyana, to secure a free poll after four rigged elections and a rigged referendum, between 1968 and 1985. Father Morrison noted the part the *Standard* played in that process:

> ...from being rabidly anti-Jagan and what he stood for [communism], the [Catholic] Church ended up by linking arms with the Jagans, Walter Rodney, Eusi Kwayana and others of the political left in Guyana in opposing the 1978 fraudulent Referendum, the rigging of elections and other human rights violations, in working for the free and fair elections which brought Jagan back to power in 1992.[31]

Another brave soul who stuck his neck out against the Burnham dictatorship was David de Caires (1937–2008). (He and Miles Fitzpatrick, as I have noted, had edited and published fifty issues of the highly respected critical journal, *New World Fortnightly*, in the 1960s.) David founded *Stabroek News* in 1986, which courageously confronted the PNC regime to secure 'bourgeois rights.' Yet Jagan believed (as he did all his political life) that if you were not with him, if you dared to deviate from his notion of the superiority of 'scientific communism,' you were against him – a

> 'reactionary' and a lackey of imperialism. This is Jagan's assessment of David de Caires: 'He is basically pro-capitalist, pro-imperialist and anti-communist. He...counterposed communism to democracy, taking the CIA propaganda line that socialism/Marxism-Leninism (scientific communism) is not democratic, and by implication capitalism and imperialism are democratic. This is a distortion of the truth.'[32]

Jagan also censured the WPA for retreating from the robust Marxist-Leninist perspective of its Draft Political Programme of 1979; and he attributed this partially to its affiliation with the Socialist International (SI). He considered the SI 'basically anti-Marxist-Leninist and anti-communist'; and that the WPA had moved to the right since 1978 when it had declared itself Marxist-Leninist committed to fighting imperialism and the PNC regime, the latter defined as an instrument of imperialism.

The longer Jagan languished in the political wilderness, the more convoluted did his ideas become, as he constantly sought to parade his 'ideological implacability.' The following two quotes illustrate his atrophied thought process as he drew parallels between the WPA and the PNC, in debunking their Marxist-Leninist credentials. First, he remarks on the rightward drift of the WPA:

> In 1978, the labour/socialist, anti-imperialist tendency in its petty-bourgeois leadership was dominant. There was a clearer perspective.

This brought the WPA politically close to the PPP at that time. Now, the WPA says that the 1978 Programme ['Toward a Revolutionary Socialist Guyana'] was only a draft, and it has not been ratified by a congress. This is clearly a rationalisation for a retreat to the right. The anti-labour, pro-capitalist tendency of the petty-bourgeois duality seems to be on the ascendancy. That is probably why the WPA is now emphasising that it is not anti-American, that liberation movements must not carry out a crusade against imperialism, and conservative elements must not carry out a crusade against socialism.

This is a hodgepodge, eclectic neither-fish-nor-fowl position, similar to the PNC. It virtually corresponds to the PNC's 'equidistant from the two super-powers' non-aligned position... [emphasis in original].

Jagan equated the 'pragmatism' of the WPA with the 'rightist opportunism' of the PNC in the early 1960s, when the latter was in league with the UF under the sponsorship of Anglo-American imperialism:

The WPA is clearly moving to an opportunist position, like the PNC when in opposition in the early 1960s. That party had made itself acceptable to imperialism and its local allies [the United Force] as 'the lesser of two evils.' But look where the if-you-can't-fight-them-join-them attitude has landed Guyana under a PNC regime placed in power by Anglo-American imperialism!...

The progressive labour/socialist and anti-imperialist tendency in the WPA must fight to push the Party back to its 1978 position. There is no future for pragmatism and rightist opportunism either for the WPA or Guyana [emphasis in the original].[33]

Jagan held tenaciously to the notion that he possessed the moral high ground against imperialism because what he stood for was winning, claiming this legacy as of right, being the pioneer of Marxism-Leninism in Guyana. What is also noteworthy is Jagan's characterisation of the leadership of the WPA, in both phases of its short history, as primarily people he deemed 'petty-bourgeois.' He was, in fact, rejecting the party's Marxist credentials, suggesting that the social background of its leaders (many of whom were left-wing middle-class intellectuals) precluded the WPA from being a genuine champion of the working class. Jagan alone possessed the criteria for leading the Indian and African working class, inspired, of course, by the glorious example of the Soviet Union. But in the aftermath of the assassination of Walter Rodney (in 1980), widely thought to have been perpetrated by the Burnham regime, the invasion of Grenada by the US, and the termination of the Marxist-Leninist regime of Maurice Bishop and Bernard Coard (in 1983), the WPA was circumspect about the pursuit of that contentious ideology in the region. Jagan ought to have empathised with their stance, given his fatal experiences in the early 1950s and the early 1960s when the Americans and the British connived in his demise, as well as thereafter with the elevation of Burnham to prolonged authoritarian rule in Guyana and his chronic marginalisation.

VI.   Jagan's Mantra: The Soviet Example is Above Reproach, 'Capitalism is on the decline to oblivion'

Jagan, however, was notoriously deficient in his capacity for *realpolitik*. He always sought to win the ideological argument by parading his doctrinal sagacity. But try making sense of this exposition of his from 1984!

> **Marxist-Leninist science teaches that 'class dictatorship' exists in a bourgeois (capitalist) a transitional (petty bourgeois, bureaucratic and military strata) and a proletarian (working class) state. 'Dictatorship of the proletariat' is a specific form of state rule at a particular period in the revolutionary process, the transition period from capitalism to socialism. In essence, it is a higher type of democracy than bourgeois democracy (dictatorship of the minority capitalist class) since it has replaced the rule of the minority capitalist class by the majority working class and its allies, the peasantry, (farmers) and other non-proletarian strata of working people. This revolutionary process evolved as in the Soviet Union into a socialist democracy, a state of the whole people** [emphasis in the original].[34]

It was virtually obligatory for leaders of the PPP to convey their gratitude for the inspiration and infallible example of the CPSU. In December 1982, on the sixtieth anniversary of the founding of the communist state, Janet Jagan represented the PPP in Moscow. On December 23, she spoke at a meeting of the Moscow Area Branch of the CPSU. Janet expressed her party's sense of privilege in participating in the 'sparkling salute' of this great experiment in the advancement of humankind, as she defined it:

> Your labour is for the cause of humanity. We are confident that your country will pave the way to Communism and a bright future for all mankind. And most importantly, you continue to inspire the people of the world in the solution of the greatest problem facing the world – the preservation of world peace and socialism![35]

Janet, with evident approbation, reproduced a quote from the speech by the general secretary of the CPSU, Yuri Andropov – an excerpt from Kalinin's remarks on the founding of the USSR in December 1922:

> For thousands of years humankind's finest minds have been struggling with the theoretical problem of finding the form that would give the people the possibility, without the greatest torment, without mutual strife, of living in friendship and brotherhood. Practically speaking, the first step in this direction is being taken now, this very day.

This utopian insight was followed, of course, by a blood-stained legacy: Comrade Joseph Stalin's reign of terror. Yet Janet obviously perceived the USSR as the exemplar in creating peace, progress, and prosperity among its diverse nationalities, apart from its capacity to mould a world inspired by its supreme goal, 'the perfection of developed socialism.' The butchery of Comrade Stalin and other atrocities thereafter notwithstanding, the utopian vision of the CPSU remained seductive to the PPP, even into the 1980s.[36]

In mid-1983, the PPP's secretary for education (the party's Marxist theoretician after Chandisingh), Feroze Mohamed (1946–2020), remarked that 'right-wing forces' were being mobilised with the covert assistance of the US Embassy in Guyana. He claimed that these reactionaries were waging 'vicious propaganda against socialism [communism].' He did not specify who the right-wingers were, but this seems like an exaggeration, if not a distortion, as such elements were sparse on the ground after the virtual disintegration of Peter D'Aguiar's UF by the late 1960s. However, Mohamed was simply following Cheddi who, after his experience of CIA destabilisation in the early sixties, was ever spotting CIA agents in his political universe. Among the counter-revolutionary activities Mohamed identified in the 'ideological campaign' in Guyana, were the 'muting' of the class struggle, cessation of criticism of American foreign policy, and the 'discrediting of existing socialism particularly in the Soviet Union.'

But, like Cheddi Jagan, Feroze Mohamed was not disheartened because what the PPP stood for was winning all over the world; it was based on 'the laws of social development,' hence irrevocable – to the dismay of the imperialists. As the chairman of the PPP, Brindley Benn, put it picturesquely and with much conviction, in the early 1960s: 'It is easier to stop tomorrow than to stop communism.'

Feroze argued:

> It cannot be disputed that the 20th century has given prominence to ideology and the ideological struggle. It is a century where the fierce encounters between the two diametrically opposing ideologies have led to victory, over and over again, of one – Marxism-Leninism. Bourgeois ideologists are being roundly defeated. They are wading against a strong tide but not yet totally helplessly…The decade of the 1980s has begun with disturbing developments. Imperialism, like a wounded tiger, has become more vicious. Desperately, it is working to impede, stop and reverse the march of the world revolutionary forces…[pursuing] a hysterically conducted ideological offensive.

> …a fierce war of ideas is going on in Guyana as well, as the various forces within are in the thick of it. Ideology exists whether we like it or not…The prompting for the PPP to submerge its ideological stand in the face of the masses' misery implies that ideology and the solutions to the people's difficulties are unrelated…

> For us, ideology is not a set of abstract, high-flown ideas, unconnected
> to life, to be reflected upon by the idle. Different from the bourgeois
> conception, ideology to us (true of the working class) is linked to the
> general experiences and struggles of people; it sees development as a
> law-governed process and serves as 'a guide to action.'[37]

For Mohamed and his mentor, Cheddi Jagan, Marxism-Leninism is
predicated on irrefutable scientific laws. It constitutes an irreproachable body
of thought, profound truths, that would liberate humankind from poverty,
ignorance, and bigotry – the remaking of a new human being, endowed with
freedom in its most lofty conception that springs from material and spiritual
fulfilment. By Mohamed's understanding, 'Marxism-Leninism is a mighty,
invincible weapon in the working people's hands, important for their victory
in the class struggle fought within our society and globally.' It is, he argues, the
means for the emancipation of the working class from the 'historically obsolete
capitalist system.' Capitalism is doomed; it has had its day.[38]

On the centenary of Marx's death, in April 1983, an International Scientific
Seminar on Karl Marx was held in East Berlin, the German Democratic Republic.
The PPP was represented by Comrades Cheddi Jagan and Feroze Mohamed.
Proud of the superior scientific reasoning engendered by their Marxist-Leninist
learning, they were effusive in acclaiming the founding father of communism. In
addition, they were fortified in their 'anti-imperialist struggle' in Guyana by the
sterling example and irrepressible ascendancy of the expanding socialist world,
led by the Soviet Union:

> The historic significance and majestic scope of that great revolutionary
> genius came out in all its glory as statesman after statesman took the
> rostrum to pay tribute to him. No one has ever influenced the epoch
> as Karl Marx has done. **His ideas are winning out all over the
> world. The revolutionary and liberation forces armed with his
> theories and with Lenin's tactics are on the march invincibly.**
> Much of the world has changed since 1917 when the great October
> Socialist Revolution triumphed in Russia. **The balance of forces
> has tilted long ago in favour of Socialism. Capitalism is on the
> decline to oblivion** [emphasis in the original].[39]

Thunder carried an abridged version of the speech delivered at the conference
by Cheddi Jagan, 'Guyana's earliest pioneer of Marxism,' as they described him.
He argued that Marx's thoughts constitute a revolution in man's perception
of himself, thus expanding the scope of human potentiality beyond anything
hitherto conceived. It is not utopianism. Marxism has scientific foundations
rooted in 'the laws of social development.' This explains why Marxism-Leninism
was supposedly winning minds universally as the philosophy best suited to the
emancipation of humankind, while capitalism – based on exploitative human

relations and lacking the scientific premises for the advancement of the human condition – was revealing moribund symptoms and heading for the 'dustbin of history.' Jagan felt vindicated that he possessed the 'scientific' truth that led inexorably to the 'summit,' and that he was privileged to belong to the side that was winning. This released a kind of religious exaltation in him:

> As inheritors of Marx's rich legacy, we have come here not only to revere his name but to express our gratitude for his priceless liberating ideas. Marx revolutionised human thinking and shed new light in social thought, thus, in Marxism, man is afforded the possibilities of attaining such summits. The rounded scientific philosophical world outlook elaborated by Marx served to lift socialism from the realm of utopianism while providing answers to the burning questions then posed by history.[40]

Jagan was assured that the 'Socialist Community,' led by the Soviet Union, was setting the universal benchmark for the inexorable advancement of the human condition, while enhancing the scope for 'socialist orientation':

> With its tremendous achievements, real socialism is exerting a strong influence and an irresistible appeal on the world's peoples who have not yet taken this path. These developments…irrefutably show the impact and dynamism of Marx's ideas and the vitality of Marxism-Leninism…**In order to overcome the economic backwardness, poverty and illiteracy they inherited, developing countries are increasingly consulting Marxism for guidance and answers.** Many are set on the path of Socialist Orientation. They are learning from the rich multi-faceted experiences of existing socialism, and are benefiting substantially from the selfless, many-sided assistance received from the Socialist World. In this one sees the steadfast observance and realisation of the important principle of proletarian internationalism, one of the pillars of Marxism-Leninism…[emphasis in the original].[41]

Jagan also felt vindicated that the travails he (and his people) encountered in his pursuit of Marxism-Leninism were not in vain because capitalism, as Marx predicted, was certainly in terminal decline. He accepted as faith that the demise of capitalism was irreversible, as he did its obverse, the communist utopia, as inevitable:

> The obsolete, moribund character of this exploitative system has become abundantly clear. The promise it once held out has not proven to be durable. **As Marx foretold, we are witnessing… the capitalist world being stripped of its glitter and appeal. Its inherent antagonistic contradictions so methodically presented in Marx's life-long and renowned work *Kapital* are bared for all to see. This has been our experience in Guyana. Marxism-Leninism has proved its invincibility, as Lenin so astutely recognised when he wrote: 'Marxism is omnipotent because it is true'** [emphasis in the original].[42]

Jagan concluded his talk on the centenary of Karl Marx's death with an allusion that he was, indeed, 'the earliest pioneer of Marxism' in colonial Guyana. This gave him abundant self-satisfaction, as if his political scars (and there were many) sprang from a nobility of purpose. What he stood for was unconquerable, despite the monumental boulders planted in his path by imperialism and the heart-rending setbacks suffered. But history and time were definitely on his side.

> The ideology of Marxism-Leninism made its appearance in [British] Guiana in the mid-40s [through Jagan's PAC]. At the beginning of the 50s, with the formation of the People's Progressive Party, Marxism-Leninism guided and continues to guide its work and activities. It proved to be the most valuable weapon to defend the working class. Having withstood the early vicious attacks from the colonialist, anti-communist forces, our Party is currently engaged in a battle with demagoguery and the more subtle and skilful formulations used by those who, on imperialism's insistence, stand dutifully opposed to socialism, the Soviet Union and social progress generally. However, the experience of the world revolutionary movement gives us the assurance and fortify our conviction that no crusade of reaction can for long stand up to the potent and powerful scientific weapon provided us by Marx, Engels and Lenin.[43]

All his political life, commencing in 1946 with the PAC, and including his terms in government – briefly in 1953 (133 days), as well as his seven years (1957–64), when the Indian vote under the first-past-the-post system nearly carried his PPP across the line to independence, Jagan was on the horns of a dilemma. His unwavering faith in communism was confronted by the unpalatable reality that he was leading a government in a British colony, in the American sphere of influence, at the height of the Cold War, gravely exacerbated by the rise of Fidel Castro. And although Cheddi would continually seek to waffle his way around his communist creed, deep within himself was a true believer who could not deny the latter with any conviction: eschewing his belief, even for short-term pragmatism, was inconceivable. And his imperialist enemies were fully aware of this because they, obsessively, routinely spied on him, intercepting his mails; his telephone calls; tracking his every movement when he visited the UK (including his rendezvous with his communist girlfriend, Noreen Johnson from Bromley, Kent); even using spies planted in the CPGB to eavesdrop on his communication and conversation with his communist friends. At home, too, Special Branch never ceased its surveillance of him and his wife. Therefore, it must have given Jagan immeasurable relief – a kind of liberation – after he was removed from office in December 1964 (through Anglo-American machinations), to identify with, and embrace, his many communist friends all over the world – free, at last, to be a communist devoted to Soviet communism.

But the transition of his PPP to a full-fledged communist party was a protracted affair, as if such an exalted status had to be earned in the heat and turbulence of the class struggle, with its inescapable reverses. Therefore, although the PPP declared its allegiance to the world communist movement, headed by the CPSU, in Moscow in June 1969, it was not until the 22nd Congress of the Party, at Annandale (Guyana) on August 3–5, 1985, that they felt confident to announce that they were 'a Marxist-Leninist type of Party [communist] because "socialist construction is inconceivable in any country in the absence of" such a party.' The PPP was proud to proclaim that 'they were organised on and guided by Leninist principles and standards, with the ultimate aim of "making it a mass Communist Party."'

This is how the PPP defined its principal task just four years or so before the collapse of the Soviet system. They were still guided by what they deemed the 'scientific' premises of Marxism-Leninism – the benchmark for the making of communist man:

> Leninist norms and standards of Party life must prevail at all levels, and any violation or deviation from this course should be vigorously countered. Every member must now consider it obligatory to develop a rounded, scientific world outlook and constantly seek to strengthen his grasp and deepen his understanding of Marxism-Leninism. We must set in train a more considered, concentrated and conscious policy for cadre development and aim at constantly increasing the number of Party cadres.[44]

A mirage!

Notes

1. See 'Cheddi Jagan's Politics and Legacy: An Interview with Clive Y. Thomas,' *Against the Current*, no. 70 (September–October 1997).
2. M. Maxwell to the Editor, *Kaieteur News*, August 10, 2012.
3. Ibid.
4. David de Caires (Interview with Frank Birbalsingh), in the latter's *The People's Progressive Party of Guyana, 1950–92: An Oral History* (London: Hansib, 2007), 147.
5. Cheddi Jagan, *National Assembly Speeches, Vol. 6, 1976–80* (The Caribbean Press, 2011), 223.
6. Cheddi Jagan, *The Struggle for a Socialist Guyana* (Georgetown: PPP booklet, 1975), 3.
7. Ibid., 5–6.
8. Ibid., 8.
9. Ibid., 19
10. Ibid.
11. Ibid., 21.
12. Cheddi Jagan, 'The Soviet Union: A Mighty Force,' (1982), *CJRC*, call no 2403.
13. *The Constitution of the PPP*, 1.
14. Ibid., 2.

15. Cheddi Jagan, *Unmasking the Enemies of the Guyanese People* (Georgetown: PPP booklet, January 1984), 27.
16. Ibid., 28.
17. Ibid.
18. See *National Unity for Democracy, Peace and Progress* (Georgetown: PPP booklet, 1986), 76.
19. Ibid.
20. Ibid., 77.
21. Ibid., 77–79.
22. Ibid., 79, 81.
23. Ibid., 84.
24. The Working People's Alliance (WPA), *Arguments for Unity against the Dictatorship in Guyana* (Georgetown: WPA, August 1983), 24–25.
25. Ibid., 26–27.
26. Ibid., 35.
27. The Working People's Alliance (WPA), *Arguments for Unity against the Dictatorship in Guyana* (Georgetown: WPA, August 1983), 24.
28. Ibid.
29. For Cheddi Jagan's denunciation of many who were campaigning to restore democracy in Burnham's Guyana, see his *Unmasking Enemies of the Guyanese People*, (Georgetown: PPP booklet, January 1984). It is a collection of his 'Straight Talk' articles, originally published in the *Mirror* in 1983–84.
30. See Mike James's article, 'How the *Standard* Became a Voice against Political Injustice,' reproduced in Fr Andrew Morrison, *Justice: The Struggle for Democracy in Guyana, 1952–1992* (Georgetown: The Author, [1998]), 66–68.
31. Ibid., 65.
32. *Mirror*, May 20, 1984, reproduced in Cheddi Jagan and Clement Rohee, *Guyana: A Bed of Thorns* (Georgetown: a PPP booklet, August 1984), 15.
33. Ibid., 16–17.
34. Ibid., 16.
35. Janet Jagan, 'Sparkling Salutes to the Soviet Union,' *Thunder* (April–June, 1983): 24.
36. Ibid., 21.
37. Feroze Mohamed, 'No Ideology is an Ideological Weapon,' *Thunder* (April–June 1983): 8–9.
38. Ibid., 6–7.
39. Cheddi Jagan, 'Karl Marx and our Time,' *Thunder* (April–June 1983): 25.
40. Ibid., 27.
41. Ibid., 28–29.
42. Ibid., 29.
43. Ibid.
44. Report of the Central Committee to the 22nd Congress of the PPP, Presented by Dr Cheddi Jagan, General Secretary of the PPP, Annandale, Guyana, August 3–5, 1985, 104–5.

16.
The Fall of Communism and the Jaganite Mission

Everything grows, nothing good or permanent has been accomplished overnight. All improvisation carries the seeds of its own decay, and it is always the attempt to transform things by the wave of a magic wand – to change them abruptly and violently – that is the central crime of revolutions. Every country and nation and association has its own traditions, not exportable abroad…

– Isaiah Berlin

The great misfortune, the root of all the evil to come, was the loss of faith in the value of personal opinions. People imagined that it was out of date to follow their own moral sense, that they must all sing the same tune in chorus, and live by other people's notions, the notions which were being crammed down everybody's throat.

– Boris Pasternak, *Doctor Zhivago*

I. Gorbachev's Endeavour to Reform a Corrosive Soviet Communist System and the PPP's Accommodating Response

The 22nd Congress of the PPP unanimously adopted the resolution of the Central Committee that the party be deemed 'a Marxist-Leninist type of Party,' with the goal of building a communist society in Guyana, the day before Forbes Burnham died (August 6, 1985). The resolution was permeated by triumphalism:

> We are generally recognised as, and are accorded the status of, a communist party by all other fraternal parties. When we took our momentous decision in 1969 [to join the Soviet bloc], we hardly envisaged the tremendous achievement which we would have made. Despite the slanders of our detractors, anti-communism is no longer a force in Guyana. The PNC has been forced to go a long way to wrest control of our resources from foreign ownership…The right-wing in Guyana is no longer a major organised force to reckon with, though constant vigilance is necessary to combat rightist influences and to prevent rightist elements from developing a following. The prestige of our Party, both locally and internationally, has never been

higher. **We can say with confidence at this 22ⁿᵈ Congress that our Party has been transformed into a Communist Party.**[1]

However, the PNC government of the new president, D. Hoyte, was in no way intimidated by the People's Progressive Party's (PPP's) spurious triumphalism. Hoyte soon abandoned Burnham's disastrous 'socialist programme,' having adopted the Economic Recovery Programme (ERP) sponsored by the International Monetary Fund, to resuscitate the capitalist orientation of the economy. But the PNC did not dispense with their ingrained capacity for staging blatantly fraudulent elections, with no pretensions to subtlety in its execution. In fact, Hoyte (on December 9, 1985) successfully orchestrated a marginally more farcical outcome than Burnham did in 1980. The People's National Congress (PNC) gave themselves 78.5 per cent of the votes supposedly cast, or forty-two of the fifty-three seats in Parliament; they allotted the PPP 15.8 per cent or eight seats; the United Force (UF) was given one, and the Working People's Alliance (WPA) one. Twenty-one years after Anglo-American complicity in removing Jagan from office through proportional representation, the Marxist-Leninist PPP had nothing left but its ideological purity, and its purportedly more enlightened and stalwart communist cadres. Yet this presumed mastery of the tenets of communism was highly prized because the PPP believed that what they stood for was, indeed, winning all over the world. Their time would soon come.

Therefore, when Mikhail Gorbachev (1931–2022) became general secretary of the Communist Party of the Soviet Union (CPSU) in 1985 and embarked on *perestroika* (restructuring) and *glasnost* (openness), eager to facilitate the desperate necessity to reform the ailing economy of the Soviet Union and its juggernaut of a bureaucracy, the PPP (as usual) instinctively, and uncritically, grasped that which was falling from their masters' table. On the seventieth anniversary of the October Revolution, Clement Rohee articulated what was essentially the PPP's position on Mikhail Gorbachev's programme of reform of the Soviet system: the 'renewal and renovation' of communism. But no one could have envisaged, as late as 1987, that his much touted, and perceptibly audacious, endeavour to reform the chronically flawed system would soon eventuate in a cataclysm: the precipitous disintegration of Soviet communism by 1989.

Yet it is interesting how Comrade Rohee meanders around the fundamental issue, a ponderously centralised Soviet system corroded by bureaucratic inertia, which impelled Gorbachev to countenance the imperative of reform. Too little, too late. Yet, clutching at straws, Rohee argues that the PPP should educate people regarding the 'advance' in science, technology, economy, and social life in socialist countries, particularly the Soviet Union. He deemed this essential in winning 'broader sections of the population over to socialism.' However, implicit in his sleight of hand is the concession that the Soviet political system was irreparably impaired, as he virtually stipulated that the PPP must no longer take matters regarding the building of socialism at face value; that no one country should ever be embraced as the inviolable prototype: the sacred exemplar. There was need for a more nuanced and critical approach to the building of socialism. In fact, Rohee's counsel constituted a spurning of the hitherto obsequious reflex of the PPP towards the Soviet Union and its satellites:

> In these times when the World Communist Movement is going through a period of renewal and renovation; in these times when the philosophy of 'new thinking' is finding its way as a determining element in international relations; in these times when the Soviet Union is going through a process of reconstruction [*perestroika*] and openness [*glasnost*], it is incumbent upon our Party and its cadres to do away with all stereotypes, dogmatic and idealist views and notions about socialism.

> We must do away with the thinking that lead many of us to believe that ruling parties in socialist countries have a monopoly on truth and are the sole authorities in respect of interpreting Lenin, the Marxist-Leninist theory and in determining what is good and what isn't good for socialism's advancement.

> Our party and its cadres must avoid making the mistake of singling out a particular socialist country's experience in socialist construction and putting this experience up as a 'model' for others to follow or as the 'standard' for measurement of progress in one area or another.[2]

Yet Rohee did express approbation of the 'bold initiatives and innovative measures' on which Comrade Gorbachev had embarked to accommodate 'reconstruction and openness' in the Soviet Union. Clearly, he, like others in the leadership of the PPP, was sanguine that Gorbachev's belated rehabilitative effort was adequate to the monumental task of saving the decrepit Soviet system. There was no suggestion, as late as 1987, that the socialist/communist world was in terminal crisis; indeed, that its demise was impending. Instead, Jagan and the PPP were still ritualistically declaiming against the evils of the capitalist system and its dismal prospects. In the same issue of *Thunder* in which Rohee's article appeared, the journal carried notes titled 'Marxist Philosophy: Forms of Transition.' It states, in part, that 'the question of the concrete forms of transition to socialism by various countries acquires great importance in our age, **the age of inexorable movement to socialism.** Creative Marxism proceeds from the premise that the forms of transition from capitalism to socialism, depend above all on the correlation of class forces.'[3]

But the PPP could no longer pretend that the blazing sunshine they unfailingly located over the communist universe of the Soviet Union and its satellites was not becoming opaque. The fact that Gorbachev had launched a veritable crusade against the chronic defects of the Soviet system was evidence enough that it was untenable to parrot the tired platitudes regarding the glorious Soviet Union as the universal beacon for the creation of the communist utopia. Still, it is curious how the PPP appeared so seamlessly reconciled to Gorbachev's advocacy of *perestroika* and *glasnost*, as if it were natural and integral to the advancement of socialism and, therefore, entirely defensible. Although the PPP had, time and again, decried the notion of 'socialism with a human face' as an imperialist ploy to malign an incomparably superior system, finally (in 1988) they conceded that the Soviet system of governance had to become 'more democratic' in order to appeal to people the world over. Until the initiation of Gorbachev's reforms, the PPP would have repudiated any intimation of the need for openness and reconstruction within the Soviet system as simply the routine calumny of a dying imperialism.

The Report of the Central Committee of the PPP to the 23rd Congress of the Party, at the Empire Cinema, Georgetown (July 30–August 1, 1988), is most revealing regarding *perestroika* and *glasnost*. Delivered by Cheddi Jagan, they expressed confidence in the future of communism because of the 'process of renewal' initiated in the Soviet Union and in the fraternal 'socialist democracies' of Eastern Europe. The PPP also observed that even former foes of communism in the West were becoming attuned to Gorbachev's 'new thinking.' They did not seem to apprehend that any such appreciation was probably predicated on the hope that the lumbering and repressive communist juggernaut would be definitively reformed and humanised by the 'new thinking.'

Despite Clement Rohee's critical intervention in 1987, the PPP appeared not to have recognised that Gorbachev's reforms did constitute a monumental repudiation of the Soviet system – of their long-held, sacrosanct model for radical transformation to 'peace, freedom and socialism' (their slogan), in Guyana and everywhere else:

> These policies, as we understand them, have a single aim: to strengthen socialism economically, politically and ideologically; and **to make the new social system more democratic** [*sic*], more attractive and more vibrant for all the world to see and feel. Today the words *glasnost* (openness) and *perestroika* (reconstruction) are on the lips of millions of people around the world, and Guyanese are no exception. So popular have the two words become that certain politicians of varying political and ideological shades are using them to suit their own partisan and political interests [emphasis added].

> We believe that the process of openness and reconstruction now underway in the Soviet Union is a healthy development, a step in the right direction. The dynamics of the new process have opened

up new areas of study for investigation and debate. While applauding the new breath of life being given to socialism in the USSR, we have been following with deep interest the rectification process initiated by the Communist Party of Cuba. And just as we welcome the new approaches being pursued by the Soviet authorities, in the same way we are confident that the rectification process in Cuba will contribute to the strengthening of socialism in that sister Caribbean country.[4]

In reality, Gorbachev's reforms had opened a can of worms – 'reconstruction,' 'openness,' 'rectification' (in Cuba) – all such euphemisms could not conceal the chronic decay at the core of the glorious communist experiment. For many it reignited a seething anger because the flawed system was the source of some of the most horrendous perpetration of barbarism on humankind and degradation of the human spirit in the twentieth century. This is encapsulated by the proverbial knock on the door in the silence of night, and the vicious desecration and disintegration of mind and body in the Gulag, so brilliantly and harrowingly documented by Alesandr Solzhenitsyn, Eugenia Ginzburg, Varlam Shalamov, and others. Such atrocities, in addition to Hungary (1956) and Czechoslovakia (1968), were never condemned by Jagan. Now Gorbachev's indictment of the Soviet system left Jagan and the PPP in a predicament. It was inconceivable that one could rationalise Gorbachev's 'new thinking' without simultaneously casting a dark shadow on the communist project in its entirety. The exercise was also bound to evoke the uncompromising moral vision of liberal democracy ('bourgeois freedoms'), juxtaposed with the ineluctable evisceration of democratic freedoms as well as the spirit of the individual under communism – the scourge of totalitarianism.

The necessity for an agonising introspection permeates the following excerpts from the Report of the Central Committee of the PPP in 1988. The debilitating rottenness at the heart of the communist experiment is transparent, but the totalitarian temperament was, by definition, ill-equipped for the adjudication:

> Questions pertaining to the self-development and renewal of socialism have assumed such topicality and importance in today's world that it would only redound to our benefit to make a study of them and their relations to Guyana, in order to arrive at concrete conclusions that could help us in our struggle for socialism at home. We cannot underestimate the impact which these developments are having on countries like ours, especially in the ideological sphere where the struggle to win the 'hearts and minds' of people over to socialism has become more demanding. At the national and international levels, the ideological struggle has become more complex, more sharp. Questions are being posed as to the reasons for the reforms in the USSR. Answers need to be given in a clear, precise and honest manner. A lot depends not only on the positions adopted by the ruling [Communist] parties concerned, but on our ability to

articulate those positions to our members and supporters as well as
to those who do not coincide with us ideologically.[5]

They were their brothers' keeper. The PPP was confronted, virtually overnight, with the realisation that their glorious example for the universal emancipation of humankind (the Soviet Union), which they had embraced unconditionally for four decades, was shot through with rudimentary flaws. These stemmed from its totalitarian political and economic foundations, so they were desperate to recoup a modicum of credibility. The basis for their utopia, the superiority of the Soviet system as the instrument of unfettered human liberation, was in tatters. Jagan, hounded by the American and British imperialists, betrayed by Comrade Fidel and, to some extent, his Soviet masters, was vainly cobbling together a rationale for what was effectively a root and branch challenge, from within, of their presupposition of incremental Soviet perfectibility, built on scientific communist principles.

But the Soviet reality was dispiriting: the emperor had no clothes. It is painful, even at this remove, to revisit the PPP's exercise in futility by mid-1988. Their ideological compass had gone awry virtually in a flash, and they were in a spin regarding a means of interpreting the crisis of self-confidence in the Soviet Union. Yet they still sought to retrieve from the ruins some legitimacy for a presumably purer, unsullied, and nuanced, form of Marxism-Leninism:

> It is becoming more and more effective to take a comprehensive approach to any discussion about existing socialism and to avoid putting up one or two countries as models to follow [the Soviet Union and Cuba presumably]. Emphasis should be placed on the fact that each country, socialist or non-socialist, has its own national specifics and peculiarities. It is the non-recognition of this phenomenon that has led many to draw wrong conclusions that there is one and only one way of arriving at socialism and that socialism is a uniform society incapable of rejuvenation and renewal.

> There are many who still see socialism as something drab, dull, sad, a system without life that takes more from the people than it gives to them. Some people still see authoritarianism, rationing and regimentation as synonymous with socialism. Bourgeois propagandists are the chief culprits who paint this false picture of socialism. The difficulties in overcoming these distortions are immense.[6]

There was more than a kernel of truth in the 'distortions.' Yet, as late as 1988, the PPP was still sanguine that Marxism-Leninism was the most perfect and humane philosophy ever conceived for the liberation of humanity; they harboured no apprehension that it could ever be extinguished as the 'scientific' instrument for the emancipation of the working class. And, in the Guyanese context, they still perceived themselves as the premier, if not sole, custodian and purveyor of the communist creed. The PNC was undergoing a process of 'de-ideologising' since the death of Forbes Burnham in August 1985, but it still monopolised the limited means of communication in the country, yet the PPP was not intimidated. They held steadfastly to their faith in the infallibility of Marxism-Leninism:

> We need to stress the fact that the socialist social system remains the more humane, just and ever-developing society built up by man. Unlike capitalism, which has no solution to unemployment, juvenile delinquency, drug abuse, crime, etc., socialism, by its very nature, has already demonstrated its inner capacity to solve these problems.[7]

But it is challenging to fathom the PPP's stance regarding the necessity for reforms in the Soviet Union – the 'new thinking' – as adumbrated by Comrade Gorbachev. It is unclear what they meant by 'aberrations of socialist democracy' or 'violations of the norms of communist party life' and 'the creative application of science.' What precisely are these values and when did they discover that these presumably stellar attributes of communism were being undermined, if not transgressed, within the Soviet system? Were they, in fact, endorsing the introduction of aspects of 'bourgeois democracy' in the Soviet Union and its satellites, including Cuba? Did they really want free and fair elections in these countries, as they were striving pertinaciously to regain in Guyana?

Or was the Soviet crisis just an 'aberration of socialist democracy' – nothing the 'creative application of [the] science [of Marxism]' could not resolve? The PPP's attempt at illumination led to obfuscation – a further muddle in their flawed model:

> [S]ince socialism is no utopia, it is only natural that problems are bound to arise from time to time. On top of this, problems arising from social contradictions inherent in the new social system must surface occasionally. New experience has demonstrated that the emergence of certain problems under socialism is not consistent with the class nature of the new social system; rather, they arise out of aberrations of socialist democracy. At the same time, it is only natural to expect that other problems of a different nature are bound to arise as a result of such aberrations.
>
> Socialism has also proven that it has the capacity to overcome and resolve such aberrations once it relies on the creative application of science and the unlimited potential of the working people. The complexities and sometimes difficult struggle for socialism, notwithstanding, we in the PPP have complete confidence in its future. Thirty-eight years ago [1950], we pledged ourselves to the task of 'winning a free and independent Guiana; of building a just socialist society in which the industries of the country shall be socially

owned and managed for the common good [nationalised]; a society in which security, plenty, peace and freedom shall be the heritage of all.' Our Party remains committed to this lofty objective.[8]

Then came the PPP's endorsement of Gorbachev's 'new thinking' as a 'fresh wind' heralding a new dawn in the protracted, but ultimately triumphal, universal struggle for the communist utopia. It was bound to be delayed because the forces of reaction embedded in moribund capitalism would resist to the bitter end, but science and time were still on their side:

> Today, strong fresh winds are blowing into the sails of world socialism. And even as it weathers rough storms, we are confident that one day, by dint of our people's own struggles and sacrifices, Guyana will form part of this inexorable force of world peace and social progress... The proponents of the capitalist system and their propagandists use certain adverse developments to denigrate the socialist system; **they deliberately confuse aberrations of the system and violations of the norms of communist party life with the system itself. These aberrations and violations have hindered socialist development and social progress...The new Soviet leadership had the courage openly to admit aberrations and violations, and to take steps to correct them** [emphasis added].[9]

The PPP, strangely, envisaged that as a consequence of Gorbachev's resolve to reform a moribund system, the world was 'poised on the threshold of momentous developments.' It was essential, therefore, for the PPP to reinforce its 'struggle against anti-communism,' a backward strand in Caribbean politics that could only intensify 'the psychology of dependence on imperialism.' Yet there hovered a disturbing ambiguity regarding what aspects of the communist system were broken and, by the judgment of Gorbachev and the CPSU, required urgent remedial measures to engender its revitalisation.

The Central Committee of the PPP cited an excerpt from Gorbachev's speech in Poland, in July 1988, to confirm that more democracy was essential for the reform of communism. This implied, however, that the PPP was deluded all along, as it had unfailingly commended the 'democratic centralism and paramountcy' of the CPSU as the prototype – the exemplar – of genuine socialist democracy, in contrast with the erroneous pretensions to freedom of 'bourgeois democracy' under capitalism. Moreover, they were never persuasive with respect to how dictatorial rule under the Soviet system could be reconciled with the free and fair elections they were relentlessly demanding from the PNC regime; how, in fact, the monopoly of power by the CPSU (and other 'fraternal parties') could accommodate, even theoretically, the multi-party system (and other 'bourgeois rights') the PPP professed to be committed to unequivocally – indefinitely. This is Gorbachev's summary of his policy of *perestroika* and *glasnost*, with which the PPP obviously concurred:

> We are convinced that it is only through democratisation that we
> can achieve vigorous advance, tap the tremendous possibilities of the
> socialist system and the entire wealth of the human personality, and
> build a society with an advanced economy, science and technology
> and at the same time a very humane society.[10]

Gorbachev's 'new thinking' suggests that aspects of liberal democracy, hitherto maligned by communists as 'bourgeois,' therefore invalid by the Soviet conception of freedom, were being conceded a belated redeeming niche. Moreover, it implies, however mutedly, that their sacred doctrine of democratic centralism underpinning the communist party was patently deficient in engendering the critical temperament Gorbachev now deemed a prerequisite for the modernisation of the Soviet Union and its satellites. But by 'democratisation' did Gorbachev (and the PPP) really mean aspects of 'bourgeois democracy'? Was the CPSU ready to open the political sphere to 'bourgeois' parties committed to 'bourgeois freedoms'? Hardly likely. It is necessary, therefore, to follow the PPP's arguments to ascertain what they meant by opening the window to let in the air of democracy, to counter the 'aberrations' that 'hindered socialist development and social progress.'

The PPP did not think they had to make any overtures to capitalist democracy; in fact, they saw this as a contradiction, as by its basic motiving principles capitalism and imperialism constitute exploitative class rule by the bourgeoisie. It was incapable of creating an environment conducive to democratic freedoms for the working class. Only the fundamental tenets of Marxism-Leninism could do this, and the PPP could not concur with those who contend that Gorbachev's reform initiative was a distinct tilt towards capitalism. They felt that it represented a vigorous and imaginative endeavour to pursue the 'ideals of freedom and equality and a better life.' They noted that Gorbachev had told the Poles that corruption and an abrogation of the basic principles of the Communist Party had had a corrosive effect on the pursuit of the unimpeachable goals of communism. The reforms did not presage the abandonment or the lessening of the high aspirations embedded in the communist political endeavour; on the contrary, it was about its renewal: '*perestroika* means not less, but more, socialism.' The PPP quoted Gorbachev: 'Today, time sets the following question before us: what should be done to advance more vigorously, to tap fully, the possibilities inherent in socialism, to give a second wind to it?'[11] Little did they know that time was not on their side. Like Humpty Dumpty a fundamentally fractured system, infamous for its lack of democracy and its savagery to millions of dissenters, real or imaginary, could not be put together again. Once tinkered with, it would turn to ashes.

In fact, the PPP was arguing that the tenets of Marxism-Leninism were totally supportive of democratic norms, yet they did not explicate their precise conception of the latter. They contended that Lenin was an advocate of democracy in politics. Therefore, it was an aberration to depart from what was a fundamental Leninist attribute of governance:

> We have repeatedly stated that socialism and democracy are inextricably linked. This is a basic principle of Marxism-Leninism. Years ago, Lenin made it clear that socialism cannot be built without democracy. He said: 'Whoever wants to reach socialism by any other path than that of political democracy will inevitably arrive at conclusions that are absurd and reactionary both in the economic and the political sense....'

> Western propagandists have gone on to say that socialism has failed also in the socialist community of states. This lie must also be nailed, not because we are the spokesmen and defenders of the socialist countries, but because **our Party and the communist and workers' parties in those countries believe in the same doctrine of Marxism-Leninism, and the same goal of socialism with its high ethical and moral values** – the ending of exploitation of man by man; equal opportunity and the building of a secure future for all; the creation of a new type of man, highly developed culturally and spiritually [emphasis added].

> The proponents of the capitalist system and their propagandists use certain adverse developments to denigrate the socialist system; they deliberately confuse aberrations of the system and violations of the norms of communist party life with the system itself.[12]

For Cheddi Jagan (still the principal architect of the PPP's communist agenda), there was nothing intrinsically flawed about Marxism-Leninism as the philosophy for the liberation of the working class. There were minor aberrations, as in the Soviet Union of the late 1980s, that temporarily hindered the progress of socialism, as he was claiming that the 'socialist community' still boasted a rate of growth twice that of the major capitalist countries. He also asserted that unemployment, a cancer in capitalist societies, had been 'eliminated' in the communist states. He quoted a supposed BBC source who predicted that the three or four of ten unemployed in the imperialist nations could become seven of ten by the end of the twentieth century. This depiction of the capitalist versus the communist reality, at the end of the 1980s (in the context of Gorbachev's campaign for reform), could only have been a figment of the imagination of a true believer in the creed.

II. The PPP's Central Committee Report of 1988: Unrepentant with Respect to their Communist Creed

The Central Committee Report of 1988 was permeated by Jaganite rhetoric, unfailingly apologetic of the communist system. The PPP persisted with a myth of their own: that they still held the key to the magical transformation of society, its perfectibility under communism. It is absurd that even as they painfully sought to comprehend the potential unravelling of the Soviet myth, they were still unrepentant regarding the superiority of Marxism-Leninism, while repudiating the PNC's brand of socialism – a flawed experiment (by their assessment) introduced initially under the nebulous rubric of 'cooperative socialism,' in the early 1970s. The following is vintage Jagan, the theoretician:

Cheddi Jagan, the indefatigable communist! For him it was not the ideology that failed, but the so-called practitioners who violated its 'scientific' truths – the inviolable doctrine of liberation for humankind

> Unfortunately, the [PNC's] 'commitment to the socialist ideology' was merely rhetorical. Rhetoric was not translated into reality. Burnhamism or bureaucratic/state, cooperative and parasitic capitalism was identified with socialism in general and 'cooperative socialism,' in particular. But because Burnhamism was essentially anti-working class, even in its positive anti-imperialist movements (1974–78 and 1983–85) living and working conditions of the masses deteriorated, and socialism was given a bad name...
>
> Socialism has not failed. What has failed in Guyana is dependent capitalism, albeit a hybrid variety (bureaucratic/state as distinct from free enterprise, 'market place' type), which has been masquerading, under the guise of 'cooperative socialism,' as socialism...
>
> Socialism has not been tried in Guyana; the basic prerequisites (political, economic, ideological, institutional and cultural) for the advance towards socialism had not been laid. Consistently, we have been pointing this out since 1970 when the PNC came out with 'cooperative socialism.'[13]

The PPP remained confident that the future belonged to communism, inspired by the 'enormous strength of socialism as exemplified in the achievements of the USSR and the rest of the socialist countries':

> It was not by chance, nor a matter of mere sloganeering, that imperialism has been condemned time and again as the common enemy of mankind. We should never forget that it is imperialism that gives birth to fascism, the system of political terror and death camps; that wherever it can, imperialism wages an offensive against democratic rights and freedom. It tramples underfoot human dignity and promotes racism. It is imperialism that is responsible for the hardship and suffering of hundreds of millions of people around the world...compelled to live in abject poverty, disease, illiteracy and under archaic conditions and relations...This is the legacy which today's young generation has inherited; and that is why they are impelled to continue to fight against the common enemy of mankind.[14]

As late as 1988, Soviet communism, clearly, was still the inspiration in the PPP's pursuit of 'democratic rights and freedom.' Yet not a word about the wanton destruction of millions in the Gulag and in famine, including lifelong dedicated comrades, by Comrade Stalin. Not a word about the moribund state of the Soviet Union and its satellites – the political and economic decay that was the foundation of Gorbachev's last-ditch endeavour to revitalise the communist system. And while recognising that *perestroika* and *glasnost* were bound to have reverberations for all communist parties, the PPP still appeared assured that these would redound to the advantage of themselves and the international communist movement.

The following bore the mark of Jagan's sacred belief in the Marxist-Leninist creed, from the late 1940s to the late 1980s. It was infallible because of its scientific foundations. It was a secular religion to Cheddi:

> The new Soviet leadership had the courage openly to admit aberrations and violations, and to take steps to correct them... Among the peoples of the world, a fresh and positive interest has been kindled in the Marxist-Leninist theory and in the practice and advancement of socialism. Initiatives taken by the socialist countries themselves have led to this renewed and deep interest in socialism. Our Party welcomes this. Moreover, we consider that the new issues and questions appearing in our times must be dealt [with] within our overall educational work.[15]

Not a word (as usual) on the tormenting African-Indian antipathy in Guyana, although their supporters were still virtually all Indians. As in the early 1950s, when the racial question was papered over by the Jagan/Burnham PPP, it remained erased from their tedious theorising, as if the superiority of Marxism-Leninism would, in due course, inevitably eradicate racial prejudices, as was ostensibly the case in the multi-national USSR. *Perestroika* and *glasnost* did nothing to diminish Jagan's and the PPP's faith in communism. They were true believers to the end in the 'science' of Marxism, until all had crumbled around them by 1991. This encapsulates the tragedy of Guyana:

> We make no apologies whatsoever for being what we are. In fact, were we different, we would not be the PPP – the staunch, consistent fighter and defender of the legitimate interests of the entire Guyanese working people...**The science to which we adhere provides us with the necessary instruments to carry out our investigations in an objective and methodical manner, and to ensure that we arrive at correct conclusions...Defence of our working class ideology against harmful bourgeois and petty-bourgeois ideas is always a Party duty to be responsibly carried out by all members**...[emphasis added].[16]

In August 1988, Jagan concluded the Central Committee Report to the 23rd Congress of the PPP thus: 'Clearly, capitalism, not socialism, is bankrupt and moribund... **Time is on our side...The future is bright and it belongs to us... Long live the world communist movement** [emphasis added]!'[17] Astounding. Yet this was the conception of Marxism-Leninism that sustained Jagan for fifty years. In his budget speech in the Parliament, in 1988, Jagan condemned the ERP of the PNC as bogus. This was the initiative by President Hoyte (in collaboration with the International Monetary Fund) to reintroduce aspects of free enterprise as an antidote to the disastrous socialist experiment of the late Forbes Burnham. Jagan was unimpressed, arguing that Gorbachev's reforms in the Soviet Union represented a strengthening of Marxism-Leninism, whereas Hoyte's ERP was predicated on the embrace of a moribund capitalism:

> I am accused of turning my back on the need for reforms now in progress in the USSR and of being a Stalinist. Actually, this accusation should be hurled at the [PNC] Government and not me and the PPP...The Government talks about reconstruction; but like its 'cooperative socialism,' it is only a slogan; it has nothing in common with Gorbachev's **perestroika. In the Soviet Union, reconstruction is based on scientific socialism not dependent state/bureaucratic capitalism** [as with the PNC]. **At its core, is democracy and the human factor – not authoritarianism as exists in this country**...[emphasis added].

> In the Soviet Union, *glasnost* means openness and free discussion. In Guyana, despite the repeated propaganda...free discussion is stifled in the state-owned and state-controlled media; and openness can lead to instant dismissal.[18]

In November 1988, Jagan presented a paper at a conference at Harvard University on the US and anti-communism. He was still commending the Soviet communist example as an alternative model worthy of emulation in what he termed the ongoing 'ideological warfare,' between capitalism/imperialism and communism. He was evidently unfazed in his Cold War certainty:

In the battle to win men's mind, anti-communism, particularly its anti-Soviet brand, is propagated. The objective is to create confusion in the ranks of the working class, the national liberation movements and peace forces [usually pro-Soviet front organisations], and to isolate Cuba and the Soviet Union which offer an alternative social order, and provide a "stick" to suppress any progressive movement against colonialism, neo-colonialism and imperialism.[19]

III. *Realpolitik* after the Demise of the Soviet Union: Mending Fences with the Arch-Imperialists George H.W. Bush and Jimmy Carter

Within a matter of months, the whole communist edifice had disintegrated, with no possibility of its rehabilitation. And as Jagan himself stated in the Report of the Central Committee to the 25th Congress of the PPP (at Queen's College), December 3–4, 1994, it was the fall of communism and the termination of the Cold War in 1989, ironically, that hastened America's support for free and fair elections in Guyana (the first since that of 1964 when he was ousted). But Jagan also noted, on this occasion, the contribution of diverse forces, political and civil at home and abroad, which had continually agitated for liberal democratic freedoms in Guyana. He remarked:

> The battle for democracy advanced on many fronts. The political parties opposed to the PNC joined forces in the Patriotic Coalition for Democracy [PCD] to press demands for electoral reform. This show of unity at the political level stimulated broad sections of the population in civic, social and professional bodies to join actively the battle.

In November 1986, Jagan had endorsed the call of the leader of the opposition in Barbados, Henry Forde, for 'possible economic sanctions' on Guyana because of the massively rigged elections of December 1985. Jagan argued: 'The time is ripe for ostracism by all who cherish fairplay, democracy and freedom. Guyana, under the authoritarian PNC regime, must be treated as a political pariah.'[20] In December 1989, the president of Guyana, D. Hoyte, was invited to represent Guyana at the one hundreth anniversary celebrations of Costa Rica's democracy. Only democratically elected heads of government were invited; where they were deemed to have gained power fraudulently, opposition leaders were invited. In the circumstances, Cheddi Jagan felt he should have been invited. He wrote to President George H. W. Bush to that effect because Hoyte was president of Guyana by virtue of the blatantly fraudulent elections in December 1985.

Jagan noted that his letter did have an impact on the Americans, in combination with the 'winding down of the Cold War' in 1989. In his Republic Day message to the government of Guyana, in February 1990, President Bush expressed his desire that the elections scheduled for later that year be conducted on the democratic norms which both countries shared. Emboldened by this transformative gesture, Jagan visited the US twice, in late 1990, and must have made an impression – at last – on some American legislators. This was the context in which six senators and eight congressmen wrote to the State Department urging that aid should be withheld from Guyana unless the PNC government was committed to free and fair elections. They also recommended a reconstituted elections commission and the counting of ballots at the places of polling.

On one of those visits to America, Jagan took part in a seminar with Professor Arthur Schlesinger (1917–2007), at the office of the left-wing *Nation* in New York. On that occasion the latter, who was President Kennedy's special assistant with special responsibility for Latin American affairs and was instrumental in the choice of Forbes Burnham (as America's man) over Jagan, conceded that a grave wrong was perpetrated on Cheddi. He alluded to the machinations of the CIA, its active subversion of Jagan's government in the early 1960s, culminating in his removal from office at the end of 1964. Yet, it is paradoxical, but true, that had it not been for the disintegration of the Soviet system by the early 1990s, Jagan would probably never have been enabled to return to power through free and fair elections.

The Americans had intervened to shaft him in the early 1960s; at the end of the Cold War, they facilitated his return to office. Yet, all the while, Jagan had lingered in Guyanese politics, his devotion to Marxism-Leninism resolute. However, his overwhelmingly Indian supporters were largely oblivious of his communist creed, or its ramifications in the context of the Cold War, and even those with intimations of its perilous implications were disinclined to challenge Cheddi because of his messianic persona. They all stayed loyal to him, despite entire villages migrating to their perceived capitalist paradise, North America – a process that has no end. An exodus: no exaggeration! Even in exile under 'oppressive capitalism' (as Jagan saw it), their devotion to him rarely wavered. Most were, in fact, doing well in a system their leader never failed to calumniate as an abomination to human progress and the human spirit. But despite a majority of the best and the brightest Guyanese fleeing routinely, Jagan never did encounter any credible Indian challenge during his twenty-eight years in the political wilderness, nor did he during his four-and-a-half years in office, between October 1992 and March 1997. In Cheddi's last years, his Marxism-Leninism was sublimated, but it remained ingrained, virtually a religious faith defying rational explanation.

Jagan acknowledged the decisive role of President Jimmy Carter in persuading President Hoyte to allow a free and fair electoral process. He explained:

> **President Jimmy Carter's entry on the electoral stage was
> crucial.** Before his arrival in October 1990, Desmond Hoyte had
> categorically stated that ballots would not be counted at the place of
> poll. Carter made it clear, however, that vote counting at the polling
> place was an essential ingredient for free and fair elections, and
> without that his Council of Freely Elected Heads of Government
> might find it difficult to observe the elections. Hoyte conceded
> [emphasis in the original].

I wish to point out that when Jimmy Carter was president (1976–80), *Mirror*,
the PPP's paper, usually referred to him as 'James Carter.' They did not wish to
convey any suggestion of empathy with the 'arch imperialist.'

Hoyte (following internal and external pressure) also conceded that the
elections scheduled for December 1991 be postponed until the compilation of
a new and more accurate voters' list was completed. The elections, supervised
by President Carter's international team, were held on October 5, 1992, and
Jagan's PPP won twenty-eight of the fifty-three seats with 53.5 per cent of
the votes; the PNC won twenty-three seats with 42.3 per cent. Voting was on
racial lines; therefore, with the PPP's victory and Jagan becoming president, an
African Guyanese government was replaced by an Indo-Guyanese one. Nothing
had changed in twenty-eight years in terms of the racial spine of the political
culture of the country. The work of Walter Rodney and the WPA; the sterling
campaign of the coalition of parties in the PCD to secure free and fair elections;
the continual assertion by Cheddi Jagan that even if his PPP won the elections,
he would still ensure that winner-does-not-take-all, had made no difference
whatsoever to the racial predisposition of the Guyanese electoral tradition. The
PPP formed a government as PPP/CIVIC, but this was a façade in which a
few non-political professionals, including a few Africans, were incorporated to
project an impression of multiracialism. The Africans in the so-called CIVIC
component of the Jagan government had no support base whatsoever among
African Guyanese.

With the demise of communism, Jagan belatedly did reconcile himself to
realpolitik: recognising that without the support and intervention of his mortal
enemies, the American imperialists, he could never have regained power; that
it was imperative for him to adapt to the reality that the IMF/World Bank-
sponsored Economic Recovery Programme (ERP), initiated under the Hoyte
regime, could not be obviated; moreover, that it was pointless for him to persist in
proclaiming Marxism-Leninism as the instrument of economic transformation.

In an address to businesspeople and professionals in Georgetown (on June 8,
1991) Jagan, eschewing his communist frame of reference, assumed a uniquely
conciliatory posture. Prompted by entrepreneurs such as Yesu Persaud, he

appeared to renounce his inviolable tenet regarding the evil of foreign capital and the inherent exploitative nature of indigenous private capital:

> **In so far as multinational corporations are concerned, the PPP recognises that they will bring with them capital, technology, management, expertise and markets needed in our revival drive....**
>
> Last July [1990] I told a group of about a dozen American businessmen in Washington...that they would be welcomed, preferably in joint ventures, to play a partnership role in our economic development; further, that they would have, under a changed government, an advantage in real political stability. I said it must be clear that our economic, social and environmental objectives must be fully recognised, and due regard is given to our laws, our independence and sovereignty.
>
> ...we want foreign participation, but not as in the days when I grew up on the sugar estate, and British Guiana was called 'Booker Guiana' [an allusion to his 'bitter sugar' mantra]...**we want foreign capital-led economic growth to be in consonance with our national goals and tempered with social justice** [emphasis in the original].

He argued that economic and political partnership was indispensable for 'confidence building,' crucial to the task of national reconstruction. However, Jagan said nothing about genuine power-sharing in the aftermath of anticipated free and fair elections. His partnership with the CIVIC group of professionals did not necessitate his PPP (confident of winning) having to compromise with actors of diverse political persuasions, such as those in the PCD:

> ...**we believe that our Party's dream for Guyana is the same dream of the businessmen, the professionals as well as the working people**...It is because of this common dream and destiny, of the vison of what is good for Guyana, that the PPP has decided to involve representatives of various socio-economic organisations...in the planning and execution of our programmes for reconstruction, economic growth and human development. It is also for this reason that my Party rejects 'winner-takes-all' politics, and is including **a CIVIC component on its electoral slate** [emphasis in the original].[21]

Marxism-Leninism was extinguished as an option, and Jagan acknowledged this, as was enunciated in the Report of the Central Committee of the PPP delivered by him at their 24th Congress on July 6–7, 1991. It is interesting, therefore, to observe how the PPP rationalised the necessity for a *modus vivendi* with American imperialism. The sleight of hand protrudes awkwardly:

> Mikhail Gorbachev paved the way with *perestroika* and *glasnost* for the ending of the Cold War. **His new thinking removed ideological struggle from the realm of international relations, and**

> reintroduced the Leninist concept of peaceful friendly relations
> with all states, regardless of their socio-economic systems...
> [emphasis added].

> Internally, Gorbachev moved to establish a law-governed state: the
> separation of party from state and democratisation at all levels of
> government, management and party [surely, reflective of chronic
> flaws at the core of the system!]. Criticising bureaucratic and
> command methods of government and management, he advocated
> revolutionary reforms – democracy and openness and the replacement
> of 'bureaucratic socialism' with a superior 'humane and democratic
> socialism.'[22]

'Communism with a human face.' In examining the PPP's assessment of Gorbachev's 'new thinking,' one wonders what was really credible of all those inviolable attributes of communism that the PPP, over many decades, deemed so intrinsically superior to decadent capitalism. Now the 'new thinking' was redressing the deep-seated inadequacies of the system: the paramountcy of the party over the state, indeed, all aspects of society; the chronic inefficiency of the Soviet bureaucracy and the consequent corrosive nature of the productive process; the pervasive absence of even the rudiments of a democratic culture at all levels, including sites of production (an ostensibly paramount asset); the displacement of 'bureaucratic socialism' by a 'superior humane and democratic socialism.' **Was this fundamentally deficient Soviet system that Jagan staked everything on worth the dire consequences for the Guyanese people – the degradation of its democratic values; nationalisation of 80 per cent of the economy and consequent economic disaster; the flight of most of the best and brightest of all races to the heartlands of capitalism?**

The collapse of their *raison d'etre*, virtually overnight, left the PPP in a quandary, groping frantically for a reasonably credible rationale for their old creed. By 1991, it was a futile endeavour; accommodation with capitalism was inescapable:

> Since our last Congress [1988], there has been a big shift in the
> world's balance of forces towards capitalism. In Eastern Europe the
> communist parties lost power. The Warsaw Pact and the Council
> for Mutual Economic Co-operation (CMEA) ceased to exist...With
> the disintegration of the socialist bloc in Eastern Europe, many
> western ideologues have pronounced the death of socialism, an end
> of ideology and a capitalist millennium....[23]

IV.   The End of Ideology?

But the PPP was not about to succumb to despair despite the unravelling of their creed, as they did not discern unbridled glory in the camp of the capitalist/

imperialist foe. The latter was still burdened by many of their recurring systemic woes of old, even if no longer determined as terminal by the post-Soviet Marxist re-evaluation. Therefore, the PPP could explore niches of co-existence with the old enemy, such as ending their ideological crusade ('the end of ideology'), for decades mistakenly, and fatally, sustained by their arrogant certainty of universal success based on 'scientific socialism.' The 'end of ideology' offered the possibility of free and fair elections in Guyana, actively supported by the Americans. The PPP's side had fallen, but, ironically, it gave them their best chance, in twenty-eight years of their return to power. No one could have scripted such a bizarre eventuality in the tides of the late twentieth century.

In February 1997, a month before Cheddi's death (on March 6), he gave an interview to NACLA (North American Congress on Latin America). They pointed out that the US press had dubbed him 'an unabashed Stalinist and a Moscow-inspired purist'; on the other hand, some considered him 'a former Marxist who has seen the light.' They wished to know how he had evolved in his ideological thinking. He reaffirmed his faith in his Marxist-Leninist creed, but he acknowledged the failure of those who had sought to transform the human condition based on Marxist principles (including Comrades Brezhnev, Kosygin, Podgorny and Suslov obviously):

> For me, Marxism neither was nor is dogma, but a scientific guide to action. It gave me strong ethical beliefs in social justice, particularly in helping the poor, the underprivileged and the exploited…Today I would say that it's fashionable to talk about the collapse of Marxism and socialism, **yet it is not Marxism that has collapsed, but some of its practitioners.** There is a great distinction between theory and principles on one hand, and practice on the other [emphasis added].[24]

Jagan was also asked whether he still envisaged a role for socialism in Guyana. He was categorical that socialism/communism was no longer on the agenda. They were endeavouring to build what he called a 'national democracy,' essentially a capitalist economy with the support of the US. But he was committed to redressing the problem of poverty and growing inequality in the world, the shaping of 'a new global order.' This was his endeavour to alleviate an unimaginable trauma, the implosion of the inviolable Soviet exemplification of his faith – a virtual religious centre of gravity not only an ideological frame of reference:

> I would say that socialism has suffered a setback with the collapse of the world's socialist system. However, there are experiments going on in different parts of the world…a struggle is being waged between those who still want some form of socialism and those who want to pursue a capitalist course. So that struggle is going to continue. I would say that the contradictions are now being sharpened between

Marxism and the neo-liberal model which is currently dictated by the West.[25]

Jagan was tired. He had committed political suicide in pursuit of Marxism-Leninism, nailing himself to the cross of the Soviet Union and Cuba, in the Cold War, in America's backyard. He and his loyal supporters paid a very high price: decades in the political wilderness. Squandered years that robbed his country of most of its well-educated, industrious, and ambitious of all races. And, for such a small place (less than a million people), it possessed an astounding segment of talented people in diverse fields – a testimony to the calibre of its colonial education and myriad dedicated educators, despite the curricular limitation.

Seventy-four when he won the first free elections since that of 1964, Jagan must have had enough. He was, in old age, persuaded at last of the merits of *realpolitik* – playing ball with his old enemy, the American imperialists. Though harbouring residual circumspection, he had no alternative but to be accommodative:

> [The Marxist versus neo-liberal model debate] is not the most important struggle that we have going on now. The most important struggle is to seek a new international balance of interests in this period of globalisation and liberalisation. Developing countries will continue to be marginalised if we do not collectively seek a new global order. **Let me just say that socialism** [communism] **is not on the agenda in Guyana.** We can speak of a period of national democracy [emphasis added].[26]

Jagan remarked that they had inherited the PNC's ERP programme, dictated by the IMF and the World Bank, but they needed balance of payments support from these institutions of $40–45 million per year. There was no viable alternative. Therefore, Guyana had to comply with the austerity measures accompanying such support. Yet, the potential hazards of such a programme notwithstanding, the new PPP government opted for pragmatism – going against the grain of Jagan's Marxist creed of four decades that engendered a fatal recklessness. Therefore, his belated new posture felt awkward when, in October 1992, he won the first free elections since independence:

> At our Congress two years ago, we said that we had to walk carefully, skilfully and scientifically between conformity and transformation. Absolute compliance with the IMF and World Bank will lead to the death of many countries, as we have already seen…[But] our relations are very good with the United States. We are working to achieve a partnership with the North and the South of the world, particularly with the United States, Latin America and the Caribbean. I have praised the United States; the past is the past. The Cold War was a historical process that was going on at the time, and we became the victims. I have no recrimination against the US and Britain even though they helped to destabilise my government on two occasions [1953 and 1962–64].[27]

This is how the PPP, in July 1991, rationalised their *modus vivendi* with the capitalist ascendancy, in the aftermath of the disintegration of communism. It did represent an 'end of ideology.' But they could not desist from identifying a chink in the old enemy's armour:

> Socialism has suffered setbacks. But so has world capitalism. The industrially developed capitalist countries are presently going through one of their recessionary cycles, with increasing unemployment and insecurity. 'Welfarism' is being eroded and the gap between the rich and the poor is widening. Meanwhile, the dependent capitalist countries in the third world, especially in Latin America and the Caribbean, are generally facing a grave crisis. And the gap between the centre and the periphery of the world capitalist system is also widening.[28]

Yet while performing the obligatory cataloguing of the endemic flaws of capitalism, it is significant that the ritual conclusion did not materialise on this occasion: no reference to the inevitable conquest of 'scientific socialism' with its obverse – moribund capitalism, destined for the 'dustbin of history.' Then this necessary climb-down. With the death of communism, there was no credible half-way house. Therefore, the PPP was now reconciled to the fact (however reluctantly) that without the affirmation of the American imperialists, they could never procure a legitimate electoral process. And Jagan, confident that he would, in such circumstances, secure the decisive totality of Indian votes, was ready to compromise with his traditional enemies because only they could persuade Hoyte's PNC to facilitate a free poll, with Jimmy Carter (whom Jagan first contacted in 1990) and his international team as observers – indispensable guarantors of free and fair elections. Overnight, Jagan's agenda was being presented as a pragmatic social democratic one, after more than four decades of recalcitrant faith in Moscow's brand of Marxism-Leninism.

If Jagan had come earlier to this rational and infinitely less contentious position, many fewer Guyanese would have felt impelled to escape the chronic sense of futility spawned by the flawed utopianism of himself and the other 'socialist' fantasist, Forbes Burnham:

> ...the worldwide democratisation process is impacting favourably on the situation in Guyana. We must ensure our people's freedom so as to play our role in the serious challenge facing humankind to provide food for one billion more people by 2000, without destroying the world's precious natural environment. We must struggle to bring an end to the wasteful expenditure of human and material resources for military purposes, and fully to mobilise science and technology for the benefit of man. Humanity needs North-South cooperation and interdependence. We need....a New International Economic Order...

> The South needs the North just as much as the North needs the
> South in our interdependent world…This means an end to the
> unjust and inequitable international trading terms, the curtailment
> of protectionism through tariff and non-tariff barriers in the
> developed capitalist states; reform of the trade-distorting [western]
> subsidised agricultural products in the third world, thus destroying
> agricultural self-sufficiency and food security; observance of the UN
> code of conduct for the transnational corporations; and respect for
> the sovereignty, territorial integrity and independence of all nations,
> especially the young and generally vulnerable third world states.[29]

It was entirely appropriate, therefore, that Jagan should articulate the theme
of reconciliation and reasonableness in view of the triumph of capitalism/
imperialism in the Cold War – and, moreover, that he did this at a conference on
global development at the Carter Centre in Atlanta, Georgia, as it was President
Carter (more than any other) who was instrumental in persuading the PNC to
concede free and fair elections in October 1992. Jagan argued thus:

> It is necessary to think globally. In our interdependent world, the
> North and the South are interlinked and interacting. Recovery in the
> recession-ridden industrialised nations cannot be attained in the face
> of underdevelopment, hunger and misery in the South and vice versa.
> I fully agree that a better world is within our grasp. With the resources
> at our disposal and the application of science and technology, hunger
> and misery can be eradicated. And **for the attainment of human
> development, it is correct that rhetoric should be transcended
> by realism and action**, and the agenda of actions should focus on
> "what to do" and "how to proceed" [emphasis added].[30]

After so many decades of rhetoric on the superiority and invincibility
of communism, it took its disintegration to bring Cheddi Jagan to realism.
Fortunately for him, he never did have the freedom to pursue his Marxist-
Leninist philosophy during his seven years in office in British Guiana (1957–64).
He often recalled that he was in office but not in power: he was constrained by
the Colonial Office. But his country and his people did suffer massively from
the fact that he held the communist ideology as a faith, a kind of religion, and
both the Americans and the British were fully aware of this, hence their support
(the latter reluctantly) for Forbes Burnham, deemed of less risk to their national
security.

However, Jagan could not acknowledge the evil spawned by the practice of
Marxism-Leninism in the Soviet Union and its satellites (such as the barbarism,
the satanic Stalinist butchery of millions, even of loyal comrades); besides, even
when he finally conceded the abysmal failure of the system and evinced a kind
of social democratic posture, he never renounced his faith in the creed. But he
did demonstrate rare pragmatism, way beyond expectation, after the collapse of
communism around 1989–90 and his death in 1997. However, he still believed

that communism was never really strived for and that when, at some indeterminate time, it was revitalised and realised, it would eliminate all the ills of humankind. Hitherto, it became warped in its passage from theory to practice: the instrument (primarily the CPSU) that sought to deliver it became corroded – but not the grand idea for radical human transformation. For Jagan, Marxism-Leninism remained a humane and lofty aspiration, not beyond universal realisation.

I give the final word on the character of communist rule and its demise to the late eminent Bulgarian-French thinker, Tzvetan Todorov (1939–2017), who grew up under a totalitarian communist regime in Bulgaria, before studying in Paris and settling in France. He speaks from experience:

> …a political system that suppresses and scorns individual freedom… must eventually collapse. Seventy-four years [1917–91]…is merely a moment in history. Communism died for a whole set of political, economic and social reasons, but also because of a change in the mentalities of both ordinary people and the leadership. Everyone had come to aspire to forms of the good life that the communist regime could not provide – personal safety and peace, material plenty and individual freedom.
>
> Of course, **democracy does not offer collective salvation nor does it promise happiness on earth, but it does guarantee that there won't be a knock on the door before dawn, and that men in grey uniforms won't take you off for interrogation.** The prospect of arrest [and incarceration in the Gulag and possible death] is not really attractive even to party cadres with all their special privileges. In addition, democratic regimes keep the store shelves full. And we should not be so foolish as to despise people who would rather have this particular side effect of capitalism than the shortages endemic to communist societies [emphasis added].[31]

Todorov also reflected on the deleterious consequences of the 'paramountcy of the communist party,' as well as 'democratic centralism' within the party – fundamentals of the system, not aberrations, and he concluded that at every level democracy was ravaged. In addition, the institutions of the putative innovating society were corroded, thus leaving virtually no guiding principles, no framework, to sustain delivery of even the basic needs of its people. It was beyond reform, as Gorbachev learnt the hard way. The whole edifice, like Humpty-Dumpty after the fall, could not be put together again. Todorov is clear about the anatomy of the demise of communism:

> The [communist] party had usurped the authority of the state, and as a result the fall of communism made it plain that there was no state any longer. Having no state is far worse than having a bad one: its absence creates an open house for brute force and for a terrifying rising tide of crime. Much the same could be said of all the values of the public sphere: tainted by the fraudulent uses made of them under

communism; they have become unusable today…The regime has corrupted political institutions, but also, as we discovered only after its fall, it had ravaged the environment, the economy and human souls. Children will perforce pay for the errors of their parents for many years to come.[32]

Ravaged human souls! Some epigraph!

Yet beneath Cheddi Jagan's belated pragmatism, there lurked an immovable boulder – his devotion to Marxism-Leninism. It got him into one disaster after another, wandering into minefields of his own planting. But he genuinely believed that the creed would resolve all the problems of the world, including those of little Guyana (not even a million strong), with its persistent, but manageable, issue of race that paled into insignificance in the universal frame. Yet he did not appreciate that the PPP needed to collaborate with others in shaping a form of governance that could mobilise a wider range of people, irrespective of their political orientation, to tackle the problems of post-independence Guyana. The history of the PPP was one of periodic haemorrhaging of most of its able leaders, who eventually collided with the inflexible pro-Moscow communist orthodoxy of the Jagans. By the late 1970s, it was widely perceived as an Indian party of irrelevant jargons, bereft of power and people with leadership credentials. Yet Indians still saw Jagan as their redeemer. Racism breeds illogicality: rationality pales before the Procrustean passions of identity politics. This was replicated among Africans in their adulation of Burnham. **These two inordinately flawed leaders are revered by their respective racial communities until today.**

In 1977, with the Burnham regime floundering in the wake of its half-baked socialist experiments, the PPP submitted a proposal to create a national front as the basis for a national front government. It seemed like an inspired idea, but it was premised on a contradictory notion: only parties or groups identifiably pro-socialist, would be accommodated. This is quintessential Jagan, promoting reconciliation but heedless of the susceptibility of potential allies, many dismissed out of hand as 'reactionary,' ideologically repugnant:

> What is now required is a political solution based on the creation of a National Patriotic Front and a National Patriotic Front government, including all parties or groups which are progressive, anti-imperialist and wish to see Guyana take a socialist-oriented or non-capitalist path of development…[like the Soviet Union and Cuba]. It will exclude all reactionary, pro-imperialist, racialist parties or groups…
>
> In keeping with the realities of Guyana, it is necessary to devise a system where 'winner does not take all,' and the two major parties and their allies are involved in the process of governing.[33]

It was a flawed idea from the beginning, as the PPP was always averse to power-sharing (claims to the contrary notwithstanding) because they were certain that the Indian vote would get them over the line, providing the poll was free and fair. Time has made no difference to this mantra. As a despairing Jimmy Carter observed as recently as May 2015: 'There is a "winner take all" custom in Guyana and the efforts of the Carter Center to change this system to a greater sharing of power have been fruitless.'

Eleven years after Jagan's pronouncement on the character of a national front government, the Report of the Central Committee of the PPP to the 23rd Congress of the Party (July 30–August 1, 1988) assessed their position within the PCD. The latter represented a broad cross-section of political perspectives loosely linked in opposition to the PNC, and the PPP was clearly perturbed by the fact that several members of the coalition did not espouse a socialist or communist line. Yet the party claimed that the PNC was 'mortally afraid' of the PCD because it was a 'progressive multi-ethnic coalition striking at its divide-and-rule strategy of maintaining political power.' The PPP was alluding to the possibility that the PCD had the potential to undermine the African base of the PNC.

This was wishful thinking: in Guyana racial affinity is so preponderant a force in life and politics that to be seen to empathise with the political party or programme of 'the other' is to court social excommunication – to be set adrift from one's racial moorings for dubious recognition or transitory gain from the racial enemy. In this context, therefore, Guyanese are inclined to acquiesce instinctively in whatever the racial political leader dictates, imbued with the unchallengeable wisdom deemed indispensable to one's racial security. This kind of instinctual groupthink is not conducive to rational discourse, neither is it amenable to persuasion, however reasonable and conciliatory the counterargument. Racial self-definition, often unconscious, aggregates around most issues in the public sphere; this is not compatible with cultivating a liberal democratic temperament. It is at the root of the Guyanese malaise.

But the PPP, self-absorbed by the purity of its Marxism-Leninism, was disdainful of the PNC charlatans, unschooled in scientific socialism and trying overzealously to impress by citing elements of the creed eclectically, in an embarrassingly 'undialectical' manner:

> Since 1978 we have indicated our belief in 'winner-does-not-take-all' politics': namely, that even though we feel that we could win a free and fair election, the PPP alone would not form the government. For economic, ethnic/cultural and security considerations, we consider that a broad-based government of all left and democratic forces is essential for peace and social progress in Guyana...Our Party is working strenuously to strengthen the unity, organisation and effectiveness of the PCD...It is also considering the tactics and strategy to be adopted towards a political solution and the formation of an alternative government.

> Regrettably, we did not succeed in organising a left front. We will
> continue our efforts in this direction. Such a front is necessary, firstly,
> because of the retreat of the PNC [to the right]; and secondly, because
> the PCD, comprised of various ideological currents, has been finding
> it difficult to hammer out a single ideological/political line.[34]

The PCD was doomed because, as far as Cheddi Jagan was concerned, if any
group or party could not be located within the Marxist-Leninist frame, it was
necessarily construed as a potential fifth column. Yet Jagan purveyed the tale
that the country had bridged the chasm of racial animosity of the early 1960s,
towards an inclusive working-class vision. This was inaccurate: Guyana was no
less polarised, between Africans and Indians, than it was during the turbulent
years of the early 1960s:

> Over the past decade and a half [from the mid-1970s], racial unity
> has been forged at the political, trade union and religious levels.
> And the working people, including both the Afro-Guyanese and the
> Indo-Guyanese, have realised that the state, under the PNC regime,
> serves not the working class but the PNC neo-comprador elite and
> the super-rich corrupt big capitalists and landlords.[35]

Very few in Guyana would have recognised this characterisation of the state
of race relations. It was a case of the imposition of the classic Marxist analysis
on a social reality that was no less scarred by its old racial insecurities. Besides,
by 1991, with just about every dog and cat under state control in the country,
to claim that the PNC was serving 'corrupt big capitalists and landlords' was
an absurdity that even the dedicated comrades of the PPP must have found far-
fetched. It was, indeed, a fantasy world, with jargon competing with even more
indigestible jargon for the dubious mantle of Marxist purity.

In July 1991, the PPP committed themselves again to the notion that 'winner-
must-not-take-all':

> We have made it clear that the elections will be a race not between
> the PNC and the PPP but between the PNC and the whole people...
> **We intend to establish a race-balanced and class-balanced
> alliance government, with guarantees of racial equality through
> constitutional and institutional measures** [emphasis added].[36]

The PPP rejected the Leninist notion of the 'PNC's doctrine of paramountcy
of the ruling party over the state,' while affirming that they would pursue a
policy of affirmative action, in conjunction with promoting joint activities
between multi-ethnic and cultural groups, at the grassroots, in order to forge a
more robust national identity.[36]

Yet there were potentially insurmountable contradictions, the principal
one being the deep-seated Marxism-Leninism of the PPP, despite their Soviet
beacon being extinguished. Was the PPP really serious about a national patriotic

government? They seemed inclined to revisit their orthodox (pro-Soviet) Marxist-Leninist rigidity, the prime source of the chronic splits within, and defections from, the PPP ever since its formation in 1950. As late as 1991 (the year before the first free elections since 1964), they were still ambivalent about the scale and nature of the ideological revision required. Besides, ominously, they were already speaking as if the idea of 'winner-must-not-take-all' was no longer a compelling prerequisite of the elections:

> The enormity and rapidity of changes in the USSR and Eastern European countries have opened new discussions on the questions of ideology and the path of social development. For parties like ours, inspired by the ideals of a socialist society, new assessments are now necessary, but, with matters still in flux and many issues still unsettled in these countries, it would be premature to arrive at definitive conclusions.[37]

> Our embrace of Marxism-Leninism lies in our commitment to build a society free from exploitation and governed by those who produce the wealth. But we feel it is necessary to make a very studious re-examination of the numerous specific propositions on which the general theory and practice of socialism has been based. It will be necessary to review even some of the deeply entrenched previously unquestioned tenets of scientific socialist theory…[38]

> As we approach the elections…hopes of victory for the PPP will grow and the response of the Guyanese people will swell. In that situation we must not be complacent…The future PPP government must succeed. And the only way it would is when our Party organisation is strong politically, organisationally and ideologically…to face the challenge of nation-building.[39]

V. Winner-does-take-all! The PPP/Civic Wins the 1992 General Election, the First Valid One since 1964: Victory at Last, with the Decisive Help of the Imperialists

The PPP contested the elections in October 1992 as PPP/CIVIC, the latter being mere window dressing of a few non-PPP members to provide a multiracial façade – a tested communist stratagem of East European vintage. Jagan became president of Guyana, while Sam Hinds, an African Guyanese from the CIVIC component, was the prime minister. The concept of 'winner-does-not-take-all' did not inform the composition of the new government – essentially an Indian one was replacing the African one. And this is how most Guyanese would have seen it. Yet Jagan and the PPP continually disseminated the absurd notion that

Ending the Cold War: out of the wilderness after 28 years, with the compliments of the US Government: President Cheddi Jagan being sworn in, Georgetown, October 1992

theirs was a government of national unity with the authority to represent the African people. Sam Hinds and the few Africans in the CIVIC had no credibility whatsoever in their ethnic group. Jagan had regained the leadership of the government after nearly twenty-eight years, a remarkable story. This, arguably, was a unique opportunity for him to create a genuine multiracial government of national unity, as the PPP had promised over several years, but this did not happen. Having secured twenty-eight of fifty-three seats (the PNC got twenty-three) – thus confirming the unaltered racial pattern of voting – the PPP was going into office essentially alone. Racial unity had not been forged, contrary to Jagan's claim. But he had waited long to get there: power was too seductive to share, reminiscent of the Burnham Constitution of 1980 that endowed the executive president with extraordinary powers.

Meanwhile, the demise of communism was still being circumvented by specious arguments regarding a 'New Global Human Order,' because it did seem that Marxism-Leninism, though discredited, was not being jettisoned. It was rather nebulous. Yet with their Soviet mentors and sponsors powerless and rudderless, the PPP appeared strangely liberated: ironically, power had been regained because of their demise and the loyalty of Indo-Guyanese to Jagan. Ideology, for the first time since the late 1940s and the PAC, could be shelved for another day.

Delivering the Report of the Central Committee at the 25th Congress of the PPP, in Georgetown in December 1994, Jagan argued from the self-assurance of power, that he was leading a working-class government of all classes and all races, but with the freedom to engage his Marxism as he pleased, untrammelled by the behemoth that was the CPSU:

> **This PPP/CIVIC unity provides for racial/ethnic and class balance and ideological pluralism in a national-democratic state.** Some have adduced that the PPP/CIVIC government is not constituted on the basis of the PPP's winner-will-not-take-all policy of 1977, because the Cabinet does not include all the political parties in Parliament...[emphasis in the original]
>
> **Any serious analysis must be rooted in science and dialectics. It must not be forgotten that political parties represent classes in society. And the state is an instrument of class rule.**
>
> **Consequently, the PPP/CIVIC alliance, representing all classes and strata creates the basis for a government of national unity.** This is fortified by regular and meaningful consultations with the opposition political parties, inside and outside of parliament, the private sector organisations, the trade unions and non-governmental groups, including the religious/cultural bodies...within the context of parliamentary democracy and the supremacy of parliament.[40]

No reference is made to the void in authentic African representation in his government. Yet Jagan foresaw the dawn of a new age, for although his communist frame of reference had crumbled, this 'Gorbachev before Gorbachev,' as he described himself, still felt equipped to counter whatever brickbats were hurled at him. For all his fidelity to communism, he was fortified in his pursuit of parliamentary democracy by his unwavering Indian support base, a formidable electoral advantage which Burnham failed to undermine. Yet he believed sincerely, to the end, that his Marxist tenets would eventually dissolve the ostensibly intractable mutual racial incomprehension between Africans and Indians in Guyana:

> We do not share the view that politics in Guyana is cast in rigid racial/ethnic compartments and that allegiances would never change. ...Those who see only race/ethnicity in politics in Guyana, as others who see tribalism and religion in other countries, are not viewing reality comprehensively, objectively and scientifically...Although the two major racial/ethnic groups are culturally different, they are not uni-class...Both groups are largely made up of working people. As such, the PPP/CIVIC, with its working class sympathy, can lay the foundation for unity in diversity....[41]

Throughout his twenty-eight years in the political wilderness, Jagan never betrayed any scepticism that scientific socialism would, in due course, win over the African working class to the PPP. In December 1994 (despite the extinguishing of his Soviet beacon) he was equally sanguine that his unsullied creed was the most potent means of eroding racial and religious bigotry:

> In time with the PPP/CIVIC government's commitment to, and attainment of, further economic growth and human development, fears of racial/ethnic insecurity will disappear, and the ground will be prepared not only for national unity but also for racial/ethnic and working class unity.
>
> Objectively, conditions for unity will mature, not only because of the PPP/CIVIC Government, but also because the heavy arm of the PNC-controlled state can no longer bribe and coerce Afro-Guyanese to remain aligned to the PNC.
>
> And within the new developing situation, a new cultural awakening is evolving on the basis of multi-culturalism, diversity and unity [emphasis in the original].[42]

Jagan's communist world had collapsed before his eyes, but he was preternaturally disinclined to be overwhelmed by setbacks of any sort, whether actuated by the natural vagaries of politics or effected by chronic Burnhamite electoral fraud. For nearly five decades he had subscribed, with tenacity, to the notion that Marxism-Leninism would liberate and transform the world from capitalist and imperialist subjugation to the communist utopia. Returned to power in 1992, his personal post-Soviet reinvention included espousal of a modified philosophical frame for relaunching his old mission. He did not abandon his communist creed, but he was devising a pragmatic approach, in the short run, that would in no way vitiate his faith in the resurgence of Marxism-Leninism sooner or later. This short-term instrument he called a New Global Human Order. It was really another version of his old beliefs, sanitised to facilitate his engagement with, even accommodate for now, the singularly ascendant capitalist/imperialist system, although he treated it (in 1994) as if it were terminally ill:

> The world socialist system had been seen by the working people of the world as the great hope for the achievement of social justice through the instrument of a workers' state in individual countries, as an alternative to the capitalist state...The collapse of the socialist states in the former Soviet Union and Eastern Europe has given rise to the widespread notion that these events have proven capitalism as the only path for the peoples of the world...
>
> Armed with scientific principles, theory and practice of the development of society [scientific socialism], it is necessary to undertake an in-depth study of the causes for the failure of communist rule in the East and capitalist rule in the industrially developed West. Theoretical tools are now needed to understand global disorder, the newly-emerging, interconnected structures of the global economy and international relations, and the multiple new sources of instability, integration and inequality that are developing.[43]

This fetish for supposed theoretical rigour could not obscure the fact that the racial politics in Guyana is a zero-sum game. As late as the latter half of the

1980s, the PPP still possessed a blinkered vision. Despite working with others in the PCD, they always felt they were in essence the PCD by virtue of their longevity and theoretical maturity, in addition to their prospect of winning an outright majority should the elections become legitimate. The PPP was confident that despite the mass exodus of Indians to the heartland of capitalism, most of the Indian votes were necessarily theirs; this bred intransigence within a majoritarian Indian mould. The party could not build enduring alliances or they would not genuinely endeavour to do so. Even in the early 1950s, before the Jagan-Burnham split of 1955, the PPP could not bother to confront the bedevilling matter of African insecurity that was discernible as early as the 1920s, in the context of the proposed Indian Colonisation Scheme. They always underestimated this monumental issue as if it were unnecessarily exaggerated – therefore resolvable by virtue of good governance by the PPP, unencumbered by class or racial prejudice. This still inheres in the party of Jagdeo.

It is reasonable to conclude that the long-term limitations of Jagdeo's PPP are rooted in the fact that while its *modus operandi* in office, from 1992 to 2015, was unabashedly capitalist and motivated markedly by self-aggrandisement, it is still imprisoned by its old communist structure – the dominance of the central committee governed by the principle of 'democratic centralism.' This unpalatable facet of Jagan's legacy has left the PPP with a defective mechanism for cultivating internal democracy: imaginative ideas for governance in a country ravaged by racism, with little aptitude for engendering day-to-day operational fluidity – a state of chronic stagnation.

For most of his life, Cheddi Jagan touted the Soviet Union as the exemplar for the liberation of humankind: its capacity for fulfilling material needs in abundance, in tandem with its enlightened communist vision for the transformation of the human personality. While the collapse of communism impelled him towards *realpolitik* and compromise with capitalism/imperialism, it did not erase his faith in the creed. For Jagan, the power of Marxism-Leninism to create the communist man universally was inviolable; he did not recant even after the disintegration of the Soviet Union in the early 1990s. But, as the eminent historian of Soviet communism, Martin Malia (1924–2004), observes, it was all an illusion:

> Until 1991, the Soviet presence was a daily part of our lives, and indeed a major touchstone of political life throughout the world. One reason was that the Soviet Union had pretensions that were unique in twentieth-century politics. Most major nations made claims to have exceptional significance for the rest of the planet... The Soviet Union, however, went beyond this and claimed to be the sole model of the good society, the gold standard of human affairs, and the perfect polity at the end of history; and it found millions throughout the world to believe in these pretensions.[44]

There were millions of true believers in the sanctity of the Soviet system, one of whom was Cheddi Jagan. Even when it had turned to dust, he still believed solemnly in the creed which he considered inviolable. Its time would come again. Not in his lifetime, but genuine Marxism would come to fruition someday because it is based on the imperishable scientific truth for the ultimate good of humanity.

In 2017, the former president of Guyana (2011–15), Donald Ramotar, gave an interview to Oscar Ramjeet. It is clear that Cheddi's Marxist vision survives in at least one member of the PPP:

Ramjeet: Did Marxism fail because it could not bring the two main races together?

Ramotar: No! Marxism is still the most potent tool for analysing society and actions in both international and domestic affairs. Those who say Marxism failed are people who are dogmatists...who do not understand that Marxism is a science. But look at how creatively the Chinese Communist Party has used Marxism to build China and to contribute to international development despite recent setbacks internationally of Socialism. Look at how Vietnam is rapidly rebuilding, after decades of devastating wars, using Marxism as their tool.

Ramjeet: Why did virtually every political party claim to be Marxist by the late 1970s in Guyana?

Ramotar: It was the great success of the socialist countries and the anti-colonial national liberation movements. At that time, one felt the whole world was going socialist rapidly.[45]

Notes

1. See 'PPP is Marxist-Leninist,' *Thunder*, (July–September 1985), 5–6.
2. See Clement Rohee, 'The October Revolution and Guyana,' *Thunder*, (September–December 1987): 35.
3. Ibid., 49.
4. Report of the Central Committee to the 23rd Congress of the PPP, Presented by Cheddi Jagan, General Secretary, July 30–August 1, 1988, in Odeen Ishmael (compiler and editor), *The Campaign for Socialism and Democracy in Guyana: Source Documents of the PPP (1965–91)*, 2010, 327. Accessed from: jagan.org/links/PPP_Book_GNI.pdf. Hereafter cited thus: Odeen Ishmael (2010).
5. Ibid., 328.
6. Ibid.
7. Ibid.
8. Ibid.
9. Ibid., 329, 367.

10. Ibid., 367.
11. Ibid.
12. Ibid., 366–67.
13. Ibid., 366.
14. Ibid., 332.
15. Ibid., 380.
16. Ibid., 382, 388.
17. Ibid., 388.
18. Cheddi Jagan, 'Budget Speech in Parliament,' 1988, Accessed from Cheddi Jagan Research Centre (*CJRC*) website, call no. 2601.
19. See Cheddi Jagan, 'Address at International Conference on Anti-Communism and the United States,' Harvard University, Cambridge, Massachusetts, November 11–13, 1988, *CJRC* website, call no. 3838.
20. Cheddi Jagan, Straight Talk: 'Burnhamism without Burnham,' *Mirror*, December 7, 1986.
21. Cheddi Jagan, 'Our Footsteps and Our Vision for a Free Guyana.' June 8, 1991.
22. 'Report of the Central Committee to the 24th Congress of the PPP,' July 6–7, 1991, 390, in Ishmael (compiler and editor), *The Campaign for Socialism and Democracy in Guyana*.
23. Ibid.
24. See 'Interview with Cheddi Jagan,' February 1997, *NACLA Report on the Americas* 31, no. 1 (1997).
25. Ibid.
26. Ibid.
27. Ibid.
28. 'Report of the Central Committee to the 24th Congress of the PPP,' July 6–7, 1991, 390, in Ishmael (compiler and editor), *The Campaign for Socialism and Democracy in Guyana*.
29. Ibid., 391.
30. See 'Address by His Excellency Dr Cheddi Jagan to the Conference on Global Development,' The Carter Centre, Atlanta, Georgia, December 4–5, 1992. Accessed from the *CJRC* website, call no. 5971.
31. Tzvetan Todorov, *Hope and Memory: Reflections on the Twentieth Century* (London: Atlantic Books, 2005 [2000]), 46–47.
32. Ibid., 47.
33. 'Proposal for a National Front Government,' August 1977, in *The Campaign for Socialism and Democracy in Guyana*, ed. and comp. Odeen Ishmael (Georgetown: GNI Publications, 2010), 207.
34. 'Report of the Central Committee to the 24th Congress of the PPP,' July 6–7, 1991, 207, in Ishmael (compiler and editor), *The Campaign for Socialism and Democracy in Guyana*.
35. Ibid.
36. 'Report of the Central Committee to the 24th Congress of the PPP,' July 6–7, 1991, 365, in Ishmael (compiler and editor), *The Campaign for Socialism and Democracy in Guyana*.
37. Ibid.
38. Ibid., 407.
39. Ibid., 415.
40. Report of the Central Committee to the 25th Congress of the PPP,

Georgetown, December 1994, 23.

41. Ibid.
42. Ibid., 24.
43. Ibid., 26.
44. Martin Malia, *The Soviet Tragedy: A History of Socialism in Russia, 1917–91* (New York: The Free Press, 1994), 521.
45. 'Face Off: Oscar Ramjeet with Former President Donald Ramotar,' *The Thinker* 2 (July–December 2018): 75. See also Ramotar's article in the same issue of this journal: 'Karl Marx and the Future Society.'

Conclusion: A Journey to Nowhere

Anybody who knows the Soviet Union at all has known for years the communist idea has long ceased to be an active faith.

– Edward Crankshaw (1959)

Faith is truly faith only when it is blind; once it looks for justification it is done for.

– Isaiah Berlin

Dead bodies were a common product of the Stalinist system. But minds did not do well either. They had to endure a continuous barrage of untruth.

– Robert Conquest

The official Soviet world-view forbade speaking in many tongues. It suppressed all individuality. At the same time it almost destroyed social truth by killing off language. Official language, instead of picking out the diversity of life-as-it-was-lived, petrified everything it touched. Reality was completely obscured by ideological fabrications.

– Lesley Chamberlain

And in order to do good to others he needed, besides the principles that filled his mind, an unprincipled heart – the kind of heart that knows no general causes, but only of particular ones and knows the greatness of small causes.

– Boris Pasternak, *Doctor Zhivago*

Cheddi and Janet: a partnership of over 50 years in pursuit of their communist vision of the perfect society, deeply inspired by the example of the Soviet Union

What is the legacy of Jagan and Burnham? In May 2019, David Hinds, a Guyanese political scientist at Arizona State University, alluded to this with discernment. It is a corrosive assessment that does not inspire hope that Guyana will be possessed of the rudiments of a national identity anytime soon, the grand expectations of 'Oil Dorado' (as John Mair styles it) notwithstanding:

> Guyana's biggest challenges lie in its institutionalised poverty, in its entrenched ethnic insecurity, in its overpowering authoritarian state and in an insane government's intolerance of dissent. After almost six decades of Independence, we have not mustered the necessary will and vision to arrest these endemic problems. Party politics and its attendant ethno-political tribalism have stood in the way of this will and vision....

> The movement towards a plural form of government...the [APNU+AFC] Coalition, promised to break with the old politics and pave the way for the necessary creative social and political engineering. But the experience of the last four years [2015–19] has shown that we have not reached that level of maturity in our politics....

> The challenge for us as a country is still what it was when it achieved self-government decades ago [1966] – how do we balance ethnic fears and pride with our civic responsibility to hold our government accountable.[1]

Marxism-Leninism, which the three major Guyanese political parties espoused, variously, in the late 1970s to early 1980s, clearly, was ineffectual in tempering the primacy of racial identity over class consciousness, thus attenuating, if not neutralising, the much-anticipated anti-capitalist panacea: the class struggle. If anything, this peculiar pervasiveness of utopianism in politics was symptomatic of the reluctance to confront race and racism – conceivably a studied evasion – while counterposing a pseudo-science that landed Cheddi Jagan in particular, fatally, on the wrong side of the Cold War. So much was sacrificed for a dubious belief system that has left Guyana with a bitter legacy: its best and brightest decamped to the heartlands of capitalism; chronic underdevelopment and the end of ideology, yet with no new ideas or vision for social and economic transformation; ingrained corruption at every level of governance; an educational tradition, once the envy of the rest of the region, despoiled; a civil service that has long been denuded of its residual colonial standards of professionalism – and, most demoralising, tenacious ethnic insecurity and rampant racism vastly more pernicious than under colonialism.

Jagan and Burnham had a good deal in common as regards the colonial legacy of their country. In rejecting colonialism and imperialism root and branch, they arrogantly undermined even its generally appreciated attributes, such as the admirable colonial education system and the professionalism of the civil service that produced able Guyanese of all races, who had attained universal standards of excellence in their respective fields. The tainted legacy of these two men, racial leaders, will stunt the Guyanese imagination for a long time. But, most appallingly, racism remains so deeply entrenched that it is inconceivable a nation can be forged out of such unpropitious propensities. This makes the pursuit of democratic governance necessarily a facade, as ideas, however refined and demonstrably enlightened, cannot break out of the cocoon of instinctual racial insecurities and loyalties.

Oil, lots of it, is coming! But is this little country – still defying the notion of a nation – with a very fragile social structure and a void in a transformative vision, equipped to utilise its inestimable impending wealth for the betterment of its diverse ethnic citizens? Will this fortune alleviate the monumental mission of creating a nation out of its contentious disparate segments? Or will it exacerbate the fissiparous tendencies, as each ethnic group is tempted to get its communal hands on the seductive abundance of riches?

On May 19, 2019, *Kaieteur News* carried a leader, appropriately captioned: 'Guyana must search its soul.' It drew attention to a terse, profound remark by a Piedmontese statesman, novelist, and painter – a leader of moderate liberal sympathies, wisdom, and imagination: 'In 1861 the Prime Minister of Piedmont, Massimo d'Azeglio [1798–1866], said: "We have created Italy, now we must create Italians." A Guyana of sorts was created decades ago, now it is time to endeavour to create Guyanese (not hyphenated ones).'

It is imperative, therefore, to concentrate Guyanese minds on the Himalayan task ahead – the shaping of a national identity – if their country's promise of becoming one of the richest, materially and culturally, is ever to materialise. This could conceivably go a far way in redeeming the deeply flawed legacy of Cheddi Jagan and Forbes Burnham: racial leaders who, in pursuit of power, exacerbated the prejudices of the country's ethnic segments while doing nothing 'to create Guyanese.' A colony was granted Independence on Thursday, May 26, 1966 – no 'struggle' was really required against the British imperialists – but a nation is yet to be made.

The racial fault line is entrenched in Guyanese history and politics. Therefore, like the immortal and majestic Kaieteur Falls of Guyana, Jagan was not just unstoppable, but monumental: the Indian leader *par excellence*. This was so although Burnham's blatant serial electoral rigging, aided and abetted by America initially and condoned thereafter only because of Jagan's communist creed, meant that the possibility of his ever-regaining power seemed to have evaporated. Yet Jagan carried on, decade after decade, largely unchallenged.

Dick Hart (1917–2013), the Jamaican communist and a close comrade of Cheddi from his seminal years in politics (like fellow Jamaican communist, Billy Strachan of the CPGB in London), identified the interplay between the idealist and the pragmatic dimensions of Jagan's politics as the fount of his longevity:

> I am told that in the 1953 electoral campaign, he was deluged with invitations from Indian religious groups, and also invitations to Indian weddings, which he refused because he was conscious of the danger of being promoted as an Indian leader. But Cheddi subsequently did not maintain this position. Looking at the situation after the split with Burnham [in early 1955], it made sense for Cheddi to be willing to change and accept the blessings of Indian religious groups or to respond to invitations and attend Indian weddings....
>
> **He realised that to maintain his electoral support, he couldn't afford to antagonise people who wanted to embrace him as an Indian leader. It made sense...** [emphasis added].[2]

Professor Frank Birbalsingh had asked Dick Hart, in July 1998, what 'kept him [Cheddi] going for such a long time [1964 to 1992 in Opposition] in daunting and despairing conditions.' Hart, from first-hand experience (including editing the PPP's *Mirror*, in Georgetown, in 1965–66), replied:

> **I think it must have been his Marxist foundation: the belief that history progresses in a certain way and that the [communist] future is inevitable. Not just inevitable: it has to be struggled for. But the future is coming. It is assured if you keep struggling. I think it must have been his basic acceptance of historical materialism that kept Cheddi going** [emphasis added].[3]

The millenarianism is illimitable. It partly springs from the El Dorado syndrome, deeply rooted in the Guyanese psyche, as it does from his rejection of his family's Hinduism. Cheddi's Marxist creed was like religious faith, but his 'secular religion' was sustained by the fallacy that the vaunted certainty of the communist millennium was predicated on scientific premises: the laws of the evolution of society. Cheddi would assert this mantra of his faith ad nauseam because he was captivated by the vision that the perfect communist society – essentially heaven on earth – would materialise, of necessity. Yet Marxists must never desist from the class struggle, and they should also exhibit patience. Cheddi was endowed with an abundance of the latter, but he was contemptuous of 'left deviationism' – a 'tendency' deemed cavalier in their provocation of imperialism, being recklessly disdainful of its residual powers to subvert, confuse, and delay, though ultimately ineffectual in terminating, the incremental ascent to the pinnacle: the communist utopia.

However, Cheddi was profoundly misguided, as Isaiah Berlin (1909–97) argues, with respect to the utility of science in predicting the trajectory of collective human behaviour and the evolution of society towards ultimate perfectibility:

> Whatever can be illuminated, made articulate, incorporated in a proper science, should of course be so…[But] not everything in practice can be – indeed a great deal cannot be – grasped by the sciences. For, as Tolstoy taught us long ago, the particles are too minute, too heterogeneous, succeed each other too rapidly, occur in combinations of too great a complexity, are too much part and parcel of what we are and do, to be capable of submitting to the required degree of abstraction, that minimum of generalisation and formalisation – idealisation – which any science must exact…There is no natural science of politics any more than a natural science of ethics. Natural science cannot answer all questions….[4]

David de Caires (1937–2008), the late Guyanese public intellectual, co-editor of *New World Fortnightly* (in the mid-1960s), and founder of *Stabroek News* (in 1986) was a redoubtable exponent of liberal democratic values. With the collapse of communism, de Caires's newspaper submitted a few pertinent questions to Cheddi Jagan to which he responded at length, seemingly unfazed by what surely was a personal tragedy of incalculable demoralisation. The PPP published this in a booklet in August 1990, 'Tracing our Path in a Changing World!' *Stabroek News* made a sterling contribution to the campaign for free elections in Guyana, yet in the introduction to the booklet, Clinton Collymore, a PPP member of Parliament and Marxist activist of many decades, described that paper thus: 'This [*Stabroek News*] is a newspaper situated on the right of the ideological spectrum, and which is apparently firmly committed to Christian Democracy.' This was not meant as a compliment.

Collymore's response to de Caires typifies the PPP's attitude – its ideological fixity – regarding thousands of people of all races, diverse nationalities, and political persuasions (at home and abroad), who dared to challenge the Burnham dictatorship (a few at the cost of their lives). Yet they collectively facilitated Jagan's election as president of Guyana in October 1992 (in the first free elections since 1964), backed to the end by his loyal Indo-Guyanese base, swayed, of course, by their racial susceptibilities and perceived long-term communal self-interest. Democracy was restored, but the virulence of Guyanese racial insecurity and racism was not lessened. It was (and still is) a zero-sum game: the African-backed PNC was in power for nearly twenty-eight years (1964–92); the Indian-backed PPP ruled for nearly twenty-three years (1992–2015); the PNC (in a coalition dominated by them) was in power from 2015 to early 2020, and they did seek belatedly – through a shamelessly incompetent rigging exercise that lasted five months – to preclude any further banishment. They failed.

The PPP is back in office with a one seat majority. The African-Indian antipathy remains as venomous as it has ever been (possibly worse) – ineradicable unless there is a definitive demographic reconfiguration, effected primarily through random migration, enticed by the allure of 'Oil Dorado' but definitely not state-orchestrated. On February 5, 2021, *Kaieteur News* carried a leader permeated by melancholy regarding the current relationship between Africans and Indians. It does not augur well. 'Oil Dorado' could, indeed, become a mirage, while aggravating the ethnic insecurities and resurgent anger of those who feel vehemently that they are excluded from governance indefinitely:

> The rifts have never been so wide, so ugly, and so oozing with the pus of ethnic hatreds...A deep chill characterises the relationship between the two major ethnicities of Guyana...Instead of digging deep for the strength to confront and conquer, there is satisfaction with leaving things alone and merely getting by as we have always done with our racial baggage unopened and untouched. We are too frightened as to where the underlying truths could lead. So, we content ourselves with maintaining the imbalanced and unworkable racial status quo that pleases approximately one half and disgust the other segment. It is recipe for tragedy.

This is the Guyanese reality fifty-seven years after independence.

Assessing Cheddi Jagan's legacy in Guyanese politics is no easy task. But I wish to cite, at length, a studied reflection that encapsulates my argument in this book. I commend the following excerpts from David de Caires's interview with Professor Frank Birbalsingh, in November 1998, the year after Jagan died:

David de Caires (1937–2008), a public intellectual of moderate leanings and integrity, of whom his friend and legal partner, Miles Fitzpatrick (1936–2019), remarked in November 2013: 'David de Caires had a rendezvous with the truth as he saw it, which usually was what it was in fact'

David de Caires: I'm convinced Jagan was never corrupt; he always spoke very frankly, but he certainly did have certain blind spots. He was very sensitive about his Marxist credentials...[But] I don't believe he had a highly developed understanding of Marxism: he had a religious worldview which was Marxist. He accepted Marxism as a faith....

David de Caires then addresses what is the fundamental irony at the heart of Jagan's political mission – his quasi-religious devotion to Marxism-Leninism and the Guyanese albatross, its racial futility:

> What I saw as a paradox was for the charismatic Indian leader [Jagan] of what had become an ethnic party [the PPP] to profess Marxism as his ideology. It was such a fundamental contradiction because many Hindus and Muslims

were strongly against Marxism [for religious and economic reasons]. This variance between the formal ideology of the leader and his charismatic racial appeal is interesting for what it says about politics – that it's about symbols [of racial identity personified] and not necessarily about messages. There were several efforts by right wing Indians [pro-capitalist, such as Lionel Luckhoo, Jainaraine Singh and Balram Singh Rai] to break Cheddi's stranglehold but none could establish himself.[5]

Frank Birbalsingh: There is no doubt at all about the unwavering faith of most of the Indian Guyanese electorate in Cheddi.

David de Caires: When Cheddi died, there was an enormous outpouring of affection for him not only from Indo-Guyanese, but from left, right, centre, black, and white. There was a feeling that whatever his failings and inadequacies, he had devoted his life to Guyana; and **he was a decent man who didn't think meanly of people. Yet I feel he was deeply flawed. If you see him purely as a victim, you may say that he was overwhelmed by historical circumstances. But he partly created the circumstances. He created them by having a brand of politics** [pro-Soviet communism] **that was almost certain to lead to confrontation** [emphasis added].[6]

To repeat! Cheddi Jagan was in the political wilderness for nearly twenty-eight years, yet he became president in October 1992, in the first legitimate general elections during that period. His political longevity and his final triumph (about four-and-a-half years before he died), ironically, were a consequence of two main factors: a high proportion of his disenchanted Indian supporters had a safety valve – flight to the capitalist north: America, Canada, and the UK (Jagan's disdain for their political system notwithstanding); but more importantly, with the disintegration of the Soviet system, between 1989 and 1991, the 'imperialists' (the Americans), finally, were amenable to Jagan regaining power because they no longer considered him a communist threat to the security of the Hemisphere. The Cold War was over! Those who had destabilised him in 1953 and in 1964 gave him a last chance to govern Guyana, in 1992. By then there was little left of Marxism-Leninism in his practical politics or of the communist world that had so enchanted him into true belief and recurring fallibility: political suicide. Yet the mesmeric appeal of communism still possessed Jagan's soul – one day the utopia will, indeed, come to fruition.

David de Caires was right: 'He had a religious world-view that was Marxist.'

I retrieved, recently, the text of remarks by Dr Fenton Ramsahoye (1929–2018), Jagan's attorney general (1961–64), at the launch (at the Institute of Commonwealth Studies, University of London), in early 2005, of my book,

Sweetening 'Bitter Sugar,' which covers some of the ground in this study. This is Fenton's verdict on Cheddi, 'bitter sugar' and the Cold War:

> Because of the progress which was being made in Jock Campbell's policy of 'Guianisation' [of Booker], the sugar industry was ripe for public participation. This was offered to Jagan by Jock Campbell who was willing to allow the government, the unions and local capitalists the opportunity to acquire 51 per cent of the shares in Booker. There was no response to the offer which was made [twice], in 1958 and in 1960.

> The truth was that Jagan was [only] interested in the nationalisation of the industry. He did not want half measures. That was always his position, and accounts for his support for Burnham in 1976 when Burnham forced the take-over in circumstances in which Booker could not resist.

> The Cold War had a serious impact on the welfare of Guyana. Jagan was a potential ally of the Soviets in the Cold War. This caused the Americans to fear for their security and led them into designs for his overthrow after he was re-elected to government in 1961. The British had at first supported Jagan. They gave the country internal self-government in 1961. It came with a promise of early independence.

> But Jagan's addiction to Marxist dogma and the idea that the main industries, including sugar, were liable to be nationalised, caused economic insecurity and loss of potential investment…Internally, he called for control over the productive sectors ['commanding heights'] of the economy. Jagan was not a thief. He ran an honest government while in office, but his politics made sure that the base for private investment would not exist…Sugar would not have been allowed to remain in private ownership under Jagan. He was happy when Burnham took control over bauxite as well.

Dr Ramsahoye concludes that both the British and the Americans would have preferred to support Jagan over the evasive and ambiguous Burnham, but Jagan's loyalty to the Soviet Union was not susceptible to modification:

> Burnham was never fancied by the British rulers…He came into prominence when the Americans saw him as the alternative to Jagan in the period 1962 to 1964 and ensured an alliance between him and Peter D'Aguiar. The alliance was fertilised by subversion actively supported by the United States, which financed disruption, and by racial violence, which Professor Seecharan shows had originated at a much earlier time in feelings between Africans and Indians in Guyana.

> **The seeds of division existed long before the sixties. They came to the fore because politicians seeking power in the sixties found racism an instrument which could be acquired at no cost to themselves** [emphasis added].[7]

I wish to elaborate on Dr Ramsahoye's point regarding Jock Campbell's consistent effort to forge a partnership with Jagan after 1957, in an endeavour to accommodate, if not neutralise, his 'bitter sugar' crusade. The first initiative was in 1958, in Georgetown, when he suggested to Cheddi (confidentially) that Booker, the government of the colony, local capitalists, and trade unions could all have a stake in the sugar industry. Campbell recalled for me in 1992:

> I did have a long talk with Cheddi (I don't think this is recorded anywhere), but I said to Cheddi: 'Look, suppose I try to work out a scheme whereby the sugar industry of Guyana is owned 51 per cent by trust in Guyana, in which the government and the unions are represented and we own the other 49 per cent and we manage it… There would be a two-tier board as in Germany…the shareholders' board – there would be shareholders who consist of sugar workers, political parties, the unions, individual Guyanese could have shares – and they would have the controlling interests in the industry and the other Board of Directors would lay down the policy; and then there would be a practical management board on which the top board would be represented as well.' I remember it well, in Follett-Smith's office [in Georgetown] – I turned him out of it – and Cheddi and I talked for about two hours. Cheddi said: 'Well, I'll think about it.' But I never heard another word.[8]

This was a massively innovative formula that would have reduced the Booker monopoly substantially while paving the way for the accretion of trust in Jagan, in Britain and in America, as a responsible leader, even a statesman, equipped to lead British Guiana to independence. Campbell repeated the idea of joint ownership of the sugar industry in March 1960, after the conclusion of the Constitutional Conference in London when the colony was granted internal self-government. He hosted a reception for Jagan, and the informal offer was made again to him in the presence of two of his ministers: B.H. Benn and Balram Singh Rai. This is Rai's brief recollection of Jock's offer:

> Jagan refused to explore an informal offer made by Sir Jock Campbell, Head of Booker, to make over 49 per cent or 51 per cent of their sugar estates to the government to be paid out of profits in ensuing years, despite my urging him to do so. This offer was made at a dinner given by Campbell at the Travellers Club in London for the British Guiana delegation.[9]

But Jagan, obsessed with eradicating the White 'sugar gods' root and branch, was implacably dedicated to total nationalisation of the sugar industry, as dictated by his Marxist creed. In 1991, I asked Jagan whether he could recall the offers made to him by Campbell. He replied bluntly that he could not. My description of the context of the offers (as stated above) failed to jolt his memory. Some years later, I discovered, however, that he had, under cross-examination by Lionel

Luckhoo, revealed to the Wynn Parry Commission in Georgetown, on June 26, 1962, Campbell's offer of joint ownership of Booker. Cheddi appeared before the Commission, accompanied by Dr Fenton Ramsahoye as his legal adviser:

Luckhoo: May I remind you [Dr Jagan], you wrote a book called *Forbidden Freedom*... and on page 29 it says: 'Nationalising of the sugar industry and, indeed, all industries is the ultimate aim. B.G. is still tied to imperialism. Certain reforms should be undertaken to break the back of imperialism.' Do you still adhere to this?

Jagan: I still adhere in the main...There are some persons in this country, immediately on thinking of nationalisation, think of expropriation, think of confiscation without compensation...As regards sugar, the Chairman of Booker [Jock Campbell] suggested to me – I don't know if it was done in a jocular manner – that the government should take 50 per cent shares in Booker.

Luckhoo: Sir Jock [Campbell] said that?

Jagan: I said I don't know whether this was done jocularly?[10]

Shortly before the first general elections under PR, in December 1964, the New World group of radical intellectuals offered an appraisal of Cheddi's political contribution, and how he could conceivably benefit from the probability of imminent defeat. They proposed that he should temper, if not abandon, his enchantment with the 'tired' Marxist dogmas, implying that he may yet be reconciled to the idea of politics as the art of the possible rather than falling again for the communist mirage:

> It cannot be denied that Cheddi Jagan is the man to whom the country owes its awakening and the development of political consciousness. This is a great debt and for this alone he must play a major role in Guianese history...Starting from a left-wing position, nurtured both by his actual experiences and his acquaintance with Marxist writing, he expressed himself in dogmatic, anti-colonial terms...He is still captivated by the marxist-socialist vision but has been unable to translate it into concrete terms [in a colony]...
>
> Even if he does not secure a majority at the elections [he did not], this is clearly not the end of his political career...Perhaps this will give Jagan the opportunity to think out his position more clearly, and to get a better idea of what he really wants to do. **The tired slogans have worn thin, and they need new interpretation and a new inspiration. The real question is whether Jagan can learn from his experience and discard irrelevant dogmas and come to grips with the real problems confronting him. It is this, in the final analysis, that caused him to fail. It is the necessity to change this that he must recognise** [emphasis added].[11]

However, anyone who knew Jagan would have appreciated that he could never change his spots. On the contrary, he was soon articulating the counter-argument that being out of office presented his PPP with a wonderful opportunity to educate enough cadres ideologically, for 'propaganda' work – to transform itself into a genuine communist party, guided by the tenets of Marxism-Leninism. No one could ever prise Cheddi from his creed, to the end of his life. So, too, is the case with the former president of Guyana, Donald Ramotar, a disciple of Cheddi. As recently as 2018, the bicentenary of the birth of Karl Marx, despite the demise of the Marxist-Leninist project in the Soviet Union and its satellites, he was (strangely) celebrating the flowering of the creed in contemporary China:

> China's success is due to its creative application of Marx's theory in the building of socialism … Many other countries are now looking at this model of constructing socialism and building the new man. Marx's methodology in constructing the new society is being proven to be correct … China's experience is the best example of the creative application of Marxism in the building of the new society… developing the new socialist man.[12]

Isaiah Berlin stated that the brilliant nineteenth century liberal Russian thinker, Alexander Herzen (1812–70), was repelled by the message preached sincerely by many socialists in his time, that 'vast suffering in the present must be undergone for the sake of an ineffable felicity in the future.' Guyana will long be scarred by the tarnished legacies, the wild utopianism, of its two seminal leaders. What Herzen stood for needs no modification as an enduring indictment of Jaganism and Burnhamism.

> That the goal of life is life itself, that to sacrifice the present to some vague and unpredictable future is a form of delusion which leads to the destruction of all that alone is valuable in men and societies – to the gratuitous sacrifice of the flesh and blood of live human beings upon the altar of idealised abstractions.[13]

Like Herzen, Berlin, and Jock Campbell, I have no faith in the perfectibility of humankind. Our goals must be infinitely less ambitious yet inspired by the pursuit of incremental reform – enlightened pragmatism or what Jock termed 'practical idealism' – but not revolutionary or cataclysmic transformation driven by the 'ineffable' utopia. As that great luminary of the twentieth century, Sir Isaiah Berlin put it:

> Immanuel Kant, a man very remote from irrationalism, once observed that 'Out of the crooked timber of humanity no straight thing was ever made.' And for that reason, no perfect solution is, not merely in practice but in principle, possible in human affairs, and any determined attempt to produce it is likely to lead to suffering, disillusionment and failure.[14]

In October 1958, the great Russian poet, Boris Pasternak (1890–1960), won the Nobel Prize in Literature for 'his important achievement both in contemporary lyrical poetry and in the field of the great Russian epic tradition.' His famous novel, *Doctor Zhivago*, was rejected for publication in the USSR in 1955; it appeared first in Italy in 1957. The Soviet government denounced it as a 'malicious libel on the USSR.' Pasternak accepted the award but was forced to reject the prize because of unrelenting pressure from the communist state. Broken physically and mentally, he died two years later. In early 1959, the *Guiana Graphic* defended Pasternak, stating that he had 'won the award on merit.' The PPP rejected this immediately, claiming that the Nobel Academy had no interest in Pasternak the artist but in Pasternak 'another cold war crusader…who had earned the indignation of his people.'[15] Therefore, it was as an enemy of the Soviet Union that he was being exalted.

It seems appropriate, therefore, that I end this book with an excerpt from Pasternak's *Doctor Zhivago* that conveys, with power and precision, the intellectual wasteland that was the Soviet experiment. It yielded not just ravaged minds, but it also reaped many millions of dead bodies. It is a tragedy that Cheddi Jagan was prepared to sacrifice the future of his country 'for the sake of an ineffable felicity in the future,' as Herzen put it in the nineteenth century. Pasternak gave this candid reflection on the Soviet reality to his protagonist, Yuri Zhivago. It was a perilous thing for Pasternak to do. He was awarded the great prize, but he paid a grave price:

> … the idea of social betterment as it is understood since the October Revolution doesn't fill me with enthusiasm…It is so far from being put into practice, and the mere talk about it has cost such a sea of blood, that I am not sure at all if the end justifies the means. And lastly, and above all, when I hear people speak of reshaping life it makes me lose my self-control and I fall into despair.
>
> Reshaping life! People who can say that have never understood a thing about life – they have never felt its breath, its heart – however much they have seen or done. They look on it as a lump of raw material which needs to be processed by them, to be ennobled by their touch. But life is never a material, a substance to be moulded. If you want to know, life is the principle of self-renewal, it is constantly renewing and remaking and changing and transfiguring itself, it is infinitely beyond your or my theories about it.[16]

I have written an account of events informed by historical documents accessible at this time. New sources (Soviet and Cuban specifically) are bound to be found that may warrant a revision of aspects of this narrative. However, the absurdity of Guyanese politics – its abiding futility – has left me drained and in despair. I believe this tragedy could be captured more efficaciously in fiction.

My greatest wish is that this book could be instrumental in stimulating, if not shaping, such a potentially spectacular exercise of the creative imagination.

Sceptical? Cheddi and me at my home, Fillongley, Warwickshire, England, May 1989

Notes

1. David Hinds, 'The APNU+AFC after Four Years and Why the PPP Should not Come Back,' *Kaieteur News*, May 12, 2019.
2. Richard Hart, interview with Frank Birbalsingh, in the latter's *The People's Progressive Party of Guyana, 1950–1992: An Oral History* (London: Hansib, 2007), 82.
3. Ibid., 84.
4. Isaiah Berlin, 'Political Judgment,' in *The Sense of Reality: Studies in Ideas and Their History*, ed. Henry Hardy (London: Pimlico, 1997 [1996]), 48–49.
5. David de Caires, interview with Frank Birbalsingh, in the latter's *The People's Progressive Party of Guyana, 1950–1992: An Oral History* (London: Hansib, 2007), 143–44.
6. Ibid., 147–48.
7. Dr Fenton Ramsahoye, 'Sweetening Bitter Sugar,' *Stabroek News*, January 30, 2005.
8. Interview with Jock Campbell, Nettlebed, Oxfordshire, July 24, 1992.
9. I am grateful to Dr Baytoram Ramharack of New York City, the biographer of Balram Singh Rai, for this reference.
10. CO887/8, Commission of Inquiry into Disturbances in British Guiana in February 1962, Dr C. B. Jagan cross-examined by Lionel Luckhoo, June 26, 1962.
11. Portraits of the Leaders: Dr Cheddi B. Jagan,' *New World Fortnightly*, no. 3 (November 3, 1964): 22–23.
12. Donald Ramotar, 'Karl Marx and the Future Society,' *The Thinker* 2 (July–December 2018): 40.
13. Isaiah Berlin, *Russian Thinkers*, ed. Henry Hardy and Aileen Kelly (London: Penguin, 1979 [1978]), 194.
14. Isaiah Berlin, *The Crooked Timber of Humanity: Chapters in the History of Ideas*, ed. Henry Hardy (London: Fontana Press, 1991 [1990]), 48.
15. *Guiana Graphic*, January 7, 1959.
16. Boris Pasternak, *Doctor Zhivago* (London: Collins and Harvill Press, 1958), 305–6.

Select Bibliography

I. PRIMARY SOURCES

Cheddi Jagan Documents

[Cheddi Jagan Research Centre (Georgetown) and the CJRC website; National Archives, Guyana; National Library (Georgetown); The Alma Jordan Library, University of the West Indies Library (St Augustine, Trinidad)]

Articles, Books, and Pamphlets by Cheddi Jagan

'The Right to Vote.' *The Labour Advocate*, August 6, 1944.

'The Need for Consumers' Cooperatives.' *Indian Opinion*, June 2, 1945.

'The Cooperative Way.' *Indian Opinion*, Xmas Number, 1945.

'Memorandum on the Sugar Industry.' (Submitted to the Venn Commission in 1948). *Mimeo*.

Fight for Freedom: Waddington Constitution Exposed. Georgetown: self-published, 1952.

Bitter Sugar. Georgetown: PPP, n.d., [1953].

Is Imperialism Dead? Georgetown: PPP, 1953.

What Happened in British Guiana. London: Union of Democratic Control, n.d., [1954].

Forbidden Freedom: The Story of British Guiana. London: Lawrence and Wishart, 1954.

'Dr Jagan's Open Letter to Mr. D'Aguiar.' *Daily Argosy*, October 15, 1960.

'Address by the Honourable Dr Cheddi Jagan, Premier of British Guiana to the Great Neck Forum, [New York],' n.d., [October 1961].

'Towards Understanding.' Text of an Address to the National Press Club, Washington. *Mimeo*, October 1961.

British Guiana's Future: Peaceful or Violent? Georgetown: PPP, 1963.

'Guiana Crossroads.' *Labour Monthly* (September 1963).

'Dr the Hon. Cheddi Jagan at the Conference of Heads of Government of the Commonwealth Caribbean Countries held in Jamaica.' *Mimeo*, January 1964.

'Broadcast to the Nation by the Premier, Dr the Honourable C. B. Jagan on his Return from the Conference of Commonwealth Caribbean Countries held at Kingston, Jamaica, in January 1964.' *Mimeo*, February 8, 1964.

Cheddi Jagan Speaks at Freedom Rally, 9 February 1964. Ruimveldt: New Guyana Co, Ltd, 1964.

'Growing Support for Drastic Reforms in Emergent Nations.' Text of a Broadcast ... over Radio Demerara. *Mimeo*, April 4, 1964.

'The Racialists of Guiana.' *Mimeo*, April 21, 1964.
'Address to the United Nations Committee of Twenty-Four.' *Mimeo*, April 1964.
'Text of Broadcast by the Premier, Dr the Honourable C.B. Jagan.' *Mimeo*, June 6, 1964.
'The Four Freedoms' (Straight Talk). *Mirror*, September 6, 1964.
The Anatomy of Poverty in British Guiana. Georgetown: PPP, 1964.
The West on Trial: My Fight for Guyana's Freedom. London: Michael Joseph, 1966.
US Intervention in Guyana. Georgetown: PPP, 1966.
'The World Communist Meeting [Moscow, June 5–17 June].' *Thunder* (October–December 1969).
'Lenin in Our Time.' *World Marxist Review* 13, no. 4 (April 1970).
A West Indian State: Pro-Imperialist or Anti-Imperialist. Georgetown: PPP, 1972.
[Jagan] and Ramkarran, *Race and Class in Guyana*. Georgetown: PPP, 1974.
'Address to the 18th PPP Congress.' *Thunder* (October–December 1974).
Non-Alignment: A Force for Peace and Social Progress. Georgetown: PPP, 1983.
Unmasking Enemies of the Guyanese People: Straight Talk. Georgetown: PPP, 1984.
Guyana: A Bed of Thorns (with Clement Rohee). Georgetown: PPP, 1984.
The Caribbean – A Zone of Peace. Georgetown: PPP, 1985.
'Great Injustice Done to Jagan – Schlesinger.' Editorial. *The Nation*, June 4, 1990.
Tracing our Path in a Changing World. Georgetown: PPP, 1990.
Our Footsteps and Our Vision for a Free Guyana. Georgetown: PPP, 1991.
'Cheddi Jagan's Address at PPP/CIVIC Seminar.' Freedom House, Georgetown, March 7–8, 1992.

PPP Publications

Manifesto. Georgetown: PPP, [April 1953].
Manifesto, Programme and Policy. Georgetown: PPP, August 1957.
Independence Now! Georgetown: PPP, 1960.
Manifesto, General Election, 1961. Georgetown: PPP, 1961.
Hitler's Force in Guiana (By Moses Bhagwan), n.d., (1962). Georgetown: PPP, 1962.
Manifesto, General Election, December 7, 1964. Georgetown: PPP, 1964.
This Too is USA Georgetown: PPP, 1965.
Guyana's Road to Socialism; Political Programme of the People's Progressive Party. Adopted by the 20th Congress of the PPP, Annandale, East Coast Demerara, August 6, 1979.
Constitution of the People's Progressive Party. Adopted by the 20th Congress of the PPP, Annandale, August 6, 1979; amended at the 21st Congress, Mon Repos, August 2, 1982.
1983: The Year of Karl Marx — The Greatest Revolutionary of the Epoch!
The Road to National Unity. Georgetown: PPP, 1983.
Strengthen the Party! Defend the Masses! Liberate Guyana! Central Committee Report to the 21st Congress of the PPP, July 30–August 2, 1982.
National Unity for Democracy, Peace and Social Progress. Report of the 22nd Congress of the PPP, August 3–5, 1985.
Elections Crooked as Barbed Wire! Georgetown: PPP, 1988.

PNC Publications

Declaration of Sophia. Address by Forbes Burnham at a Special Congress to Mark the 10th Anniversary of the PNC in Government, December 14, 1974.

Towards the Socialist Revolution. Address by the Leader of the PNC, Prime Minister Forbes Burnham at the First Biennial Congress of the Party, August 18, 1975.

Symbol of Freedom. Address by the Leader of the PNC, Prime Minister Forbes Burnham, at the Unveiling of the 1763 Monument on May 23, 1976.

The Pursuit of Perfection. Address to the Nation by Comrade L. F. S. Burnham, Prime Minister of Guyana, on the Occasion of the 10th Anniversary of Independence, May 25, 1976.

Colonial Office and MI5 Documents
(The National Archives [TNA], Kew, London)

CAB129/163 – C. (53)261. Memorandum by the Secretary of State for the Colonies. Oliver Lyttelton to Cabinet, September 30, 1953. Top secret, September 25, 1953.

CO111/474. (Individuals). [Sir G. W. DesVoeux], November 2, 1894.

CO111/509. (Individuals). [Henry K. Davson to Secretary of State for the Colonies], February 15, 1898.

CO111/509. (Individuals). [W. M. Campbell], August 6, 1898.

CO111/517. Sendall to Chamberlain, no. 53, February 15, 1900.

CO111/518. Sendall to Chamberlain, no. 71, March 15, 1900.

CO111/525. (Individuals). W. M. Campbell, March 9, 1900.

CO111/525. (Individuals). H. K. Davson, March 13, 1900.

CO111/527. Sendall to Chamberlain, no. 203, June 6, 1901.

CO111/687/75080 [1930]. British Commonwealth Labour Conference, 1930: British Guiana Labour Union, Memoranda.

CO111/689/75141, encl., C. F. Andrews. 'Impressions of British Guiana.' *Mimeo*, [1930].

CO111/726/60036 [1935]. 'Report by County Inspector, J. Nicole, on the Labour Unrest on the Sugar Estates on the West Coast Demerara, during September 1934.' *Mimeo*.

Ibid. C. Douglas Jones (OAG) to Cunliffe-Lister, no. 29, January 24, 1935.

Ibid. Northcote to MacDonald, no. 238. Telegram (confidential), October 17, 1935.

Ibid. Northcote to MacDonald, no. 241. Telegram (confidential), October 23, 1935.

Ibid. Northcote to H. Beckles (Colonial Office), December 4, 1935.

Ibid. Beckles to Northcote, January 13, 1936.

CO111/732/60036 [1936]. 'Report of the Commission of Inquiry into the 1935 Disturbances.' Legislative Council Paper, no. 15 of 1936.

Ibid. Minute. S. Caine, January 22, 1937.

CO111/762/60270 [1939], encl. 'Report of the Leonora Enquiry Commission, 1939.'

Ibid. 'Note of an Interview with F. J. Seaford, O. B. E. (Booker Bros.), Elected Member of the Legislative Council of British Guiana, 20 June 1939.'

CO111/778/60493 [1943], Lethem to Lloyd, September 23, 1943.

Ibid. Lloyd to Lethem, personal, December 20, 1943.

Ibid. 'Notes of a Conversation in Mr. Beckett's Room…Friday, November 5, 1943.'

Ibid. Lethem to Lloyd, February 26, 1944.

CO111/785/60466/13 [1944]. Lethem to O. F. G. Stanley, April 17, 1944.

Ibid. F. J. Seaford to Lethem, May 10, 1944.

CO111/796/60270/5, (Ordnance no. 20 of 1947) and B. G. Smallman (CO minute), August 17, 1949.

CO111/797/60270/5/5 [1948]. 'Report on a GIWU Meeting Held at Grove, East Bank Demerara, 26 August 1948.'

Ibid. 'Report on a GIWU Meeting Held at Good Intent, West Coast Demerara, 29 August 1948.'

Ibid. W. S. Jones to Woolley, July 15, 1948.

Ibid. Campbell to G. F. Seel (Colonial Office), July 20, 1948.

Ibid. G. F. Seel to Campbell, July 21, 1948.

CO111/813/10, J. M. Campbell to J. A. Venn. Personal, December 28, 1949.

Ibid. J. E. Markham (Colonial Office) to Woolley, February 18, 1950.

Ibid. Woolley to J. E. Markham, April 3, 1950.

CO114/237. 'Speech by His Excellency the Governor (Sir Gordon James Lethem), 3 July 1945.'

CO318/421/3. Northcote to J. H. Thomas, no. 66, March 5, 1936, encl.: 'Report on the Sugar Industry of British Guiana' by J. Sydney Dash (February 24, 1936).

CO946/1. Evidence of Sanichari, January 10, 1949.

Ibid. Evidence of Cheddi Jagan, January 14, 1949.

Ibid. Evidence of Lionel Luckhoo, January 17, 1949.

Ibid. Evidence of Baichanie, January 19, 1949.

CO946/3. Jock Campbell to Dr J. A. Venn, April 1, 1949.

Ibid. W. M. Bissell to B. G. Smallman, May 21, 1949; June 8, 1949.

CO950/649. Memorandum of the Sugar Producers' Association (SPA), [1939].

CO950/675. Memorandum of the Manpower Citizens' Association (MPCA), [1939].

CO1031/118. H. L. Steele letter from Georgetown and Campbell's covering note, September 18, 1953.

CO1031/121. Henry Seaford to Jock Campbell, September 8, 1953.

Ibid. Sir Stephen Luke to the Colonial Office, September 12, 1953; Governor Savage to the Colonial Office, September 13, 1953.

Ibid. CO minute. E. F. for P. Rogers, September 15, 1953.

Ibid. CO minute. James W. Vernon, September 21, 1953.

Ibid. Ralph Grey to A. M. Mackintosh (Colonial Office). Secret, September 2, 1960.

CO1031/3714. 'Intelligence Report for the Month of October 1961.' Secret and Personal.

Ibid. 'Intelligence Report for the Month of November 1961 [A.J.E. Longden].' Secret and Personal.

Ibid. Grey to Sandys. Secret and Personal, December 8, 1962.

CO1031/3907. W. F. Dawson (Colonial Office) to R. E. Parsons (American Dept., Foreign Office). Confidential, September 7, 1960.

Ibid. W. M. Revell (Colonial Office) to R. E. Parsons (Foreign Office). Confidential, September 13, 1960.

Ibid. Copy of a translation of interview of Dr Cheddi Jagan with *Revolucion* [Havana], September 1960.

Ibid. Brief [by Foreign Office] for Secretary of State's talks with Mr Hester (American Embassy, London), on September 18, 1960, confidential.

Ibid. A. M. MacKintosh (Colonial Office) to Ralph Grey. Secret and Personal, October 28, 1960.

Ibid. W. F. Dawson (Colonial Office) to M. Johnson (Foreign Office). Confidential, November 14, 1960.

Ibid. British Embassy (Washington) to Governor Grey, November 29, 1960.

Ibid. J. D. Hennings (Colonial Attaché, British Embassy, Washington) to A. M. Mackintosh (Colonial Office). Secret, January 24, 1961.

Ibid. Extract from copy of a letter from Ralph Grey to Colonial Attaché, Washington, [Hennings], dated February 16, 1961, recording discussion with Mr Foster of US State Department.

Ibid. Extract from a letter, dated February 28, 1961, from Mr Thomas (Foreign Office) to Mr MacKintosh (Colonial Office). Secret and Personal.

Ibid., T. B. Williamson (Colonial Office) to F. C. Mason (Foreign Office). Secret and Guard, April 2, 1961.

CO1031/4178. J. H. Hennings to Ralph Grey. Secret and Personal, November 19, 1961, encl.

CO1031/4402. President Kennedy to Prime Minister Macmillan. Top Secret, September 10, 1963.

Ibid. Macmillan to Kennedy. Top Secret, September 27, 1963.

CO1031/4495. Note of a Meeting held in the Commonwealth Relations Office, October 23, 1963.

Ibid. Grey to David Rose (O.A.G., British Guiana). Secret and Personal, October 29, 1963.

CO1031/4567. R. W. Piper (Colonial Office) to R. E. Luyt. Secret and Personal, July 23, 1964. (A brief note of a talk at the Colonial Office between George Bishop and Edgar Readwin [Booker] and Piper and Ian Wallace).

Ibid. Note of a Meeting in Mr Nigel Fisher's Room [Colonial Office], on July 27, 1964, between Antony Tasker [Booker] and Fisher, Sir Hilton Poynton, Ian Wallace and R. W. Piper.

CO1031/4568. R.E. Luyt to Colonial Office, February 25, 1965; March 21, 1965.

CO1031/4758. 'Intelligence Report for the Period, 17 March–22 June 1964.'

CO1031/4931. Jagan to Grey, June 12, 1963.

KV2/3600-3638 MI5 Documents on Cheddi and Janet Jagan, 1950–61.

PREM11/3666. Record of a Meeting in the State Department, April 6, 1961.

Ibid. Reginald Maudling to the Prime Minister, January 10, 1962.

Ibid. Rusk to Home, February 19, 1962.

Ibid. Maudling to Macmillan [PM (62)15]. Secret, March 2, 1962.

Ibid. Macmillan to Sir N. Brook. Top Secret, May 2, 1962.

United States Government (USG) Foreign Relations Files on British Guiana, 1961–63 [reproduced in *Stabroek News* (Georgetown), December 1996–January 1997, in a series captioned 'Window on the Sixties']; FRUS documents relating to Guyana (online). For comprehensive access to these, see the following files on the CJRC website: US Declassified Files, 1961–63; 1964–68; 1969–76

USG. 'Prospects for British Guiana.' Special National Intelligence Estimate, March 21, 1961.

USG. Message from Foreign Secretary Home to Secretary of State Rusk, London, August 18, 1961.

USG. Telegram from the Dept. of State to the Embassy, UK, August 26, 1961.

USG. Memorandum from the President's Special Assistant (Schlesinger) to the Deputy Under-Secretary of State for Political Affairs (Johnson), September 7, 1961.

USG. Information Airgram from the Dept. of State. 'US Programme for British Guiana,' October 4, 1961.

USG. Memorandum of Conversation. 'Call of Premier Jagan of British Guiana on the President,' October 25, 1961.

USG. Telegram from the Dept. of State to the Embassy, UK, February 19, 1962.

USG. Memorandum from the President's Special Assistant (Schlesinger) to the Ambassador to the UK (Bruce), March 1, 1962.

USG. Memorandum from the President's Special Assistant (Schlesinger) to President Kennedy, Washington, March 1962.

USG. Telegram from the Dept. of State to the Embassy, UK, June 7, 1962, (encl., Letter from Macmillan to Kennedy, May 30, 1962).

USG. Memorandum from the President's Special Assistant (Schlesinger) to President Kennedy, June 21, 1962.

USG. Memorandum from Secretary of State (Rusk) to President Kennedy, July 12, 1962.

USG. Record of Kennedy's discussion with Ormsby-Gore (UK Ambassador, Washington), July 21, 1962.

USG. Consulate General, Georgetown [Melby] to the Dept. of State, March 14 ,1963.

USG. Letter from Premier Jagan to President Kennedy, April 16, 1963.

USG. Memorandum on White House Meeting on British Guiana, June 21, 1963.

USG. Telegram from Dept. of State to the Embassy, UK, June 21, 1963.

USG. Meeting of Kennedy and Macmillan, Birch Grove, England, June 30, 1963.

USG. Telegram from the Consulate General (Georgetown) to the Dept. of State, September 5, 1963.

USG. Telegram from the Dept. of State to the Consulate General (Georgetown), September 7, 1963.

FRUS. Foreign Relations of the United States, 1964–68

FRUS. Foreign Relations of the United States, 1969–76, Vol E-10, Documents of the American Republics, 1969–76.

FRUS. Foreign Relations of the United States, 1969–76, Vol E-11, Part 1, Documents of Mexico, Central America and the Caribbean, 1973–76.

Reports (in chronological order)

Report of the West India Royal Commission (H. W. Norman, chairman). London: Her Majesty's Stationery Office, 1897.

Report of the West Indian Sugar Commission (Lord Olivier, chairman). London: His Majesty's Stationery Office, 1930.

———. Vol. II, Evidence, etc., Relating to British Guiana.

Report by County Inspector, J. Nicole, on the Labour Unrest on the Sugar Estates on the West Coast Demerara, during September 1934. Mimeo, [CO111/726/60036 (1935)].

Report of the Commission of Inquiry into the 1935 Disturbances. Legislative Council Paper, no. 15 of 1936 [CO111/732/60036 (1936)].

Report of the Leonora Enquiry Commission, (John Verity, chairman). Legislative Council Paper, no. 10 of 1939 [CO114/230].

The Royal Commission in British Guiana, 1939. Georgetown: The Daily Chronicle Ltd, 1939.

Report of the British Guiana Franchise Commission, 1941. Legislative Council Paper, no. 10 of 1944.

Report by Dr F. C. Benham, Economic Adviser to the Comptroller for Development and Welfare, on the Economic Position of the Sugar Industry. Legislative Council Paper no. 11 of 1945.

Report of the West India Royal Commission, 1938-9 (Lord Moyne, chairman). Cmd. 6607. London: His Majesty's Stationery Office, 1945.

Report of the Enmore Enquiry Commission. Legislative Council Paper, no. 10 of 1948.

Report of a Commission of Inquiry into the Sugar Industry of British Guiana (J. A. Venn, chairman). Col. no. 249. London: His Majesty's Stationery Office, 1949.

British Guiana, Report of the Constitutional Commission, 1950-1 (Sir E. J. Waddington, chairman). Col. no. 280. London: His Majesty's Stationery Office, 1951.

Frank A. Brown, *Report on Land Settlement Problems in British Guiana with Particular Reference to the Coastal Belt. Mimeo*, December 24, 1953.

British Guiana, Suspension of the Constitution. Cmd. 8980. London: Her Majesty's Stationery Office, 1953.

Report of the British Guiana Constitutional Commission, 1954 (Sir James Robertson, chairman). Cmd. 9274. London: Her Majesty's Stationery Office, 1954.

Report on Social Security in British Guiana by J. Henry Richardson. Georgetown: Government of British Guiana, 1954.

Report on Local Government in British Guiana by A.H. Marshall. Georgetown: self-published, 1955.

Report to the Government of British Guiana on Employment, Unemployment and Underemployment in the Colony in 1956 [compiled by Edward McGale]. Geneva: ILO, 1957.

Report of a Commission of Inquiry into the Causes of a Disturbance which Occurred at Skeldon on 13 February 1957... (Kenneth S. Stoby, chairman). Georgetown: Government of British Guiana, 1957.

Report of the British Guiana Constitutional Conference Held in London in March 1960. Cmd. 998, (Rt. Hon. Iain Macleod, chairman). London: Her Majesty's Stationery Office, 1960.

Report of a Commission of Inquiry into Disturbances in British Guiana in February 1962. Col. no. 354, (Sir Henry Wynn Parry, chairman). London: Her Majesty's Stationery Office, 1962.

British Guiana Conference, 1962. Cmd. 1870, (Rt. Hon. Duncan Sandys, chairman). London: Her Majesty's Stationery Office, 1962.

British Guiana Conference, 1963. Cmd. 2203, [Prepared by Duncan Sandys]. London: Her Majesty's Stationery Office, November 1963.

'Memorandum by the Government of British Guiana on the Decision by the Secretary of State for the Colonies on the Independence of British Guiana, November 1963.' Sessional Paper, no. 3 of 1963.

British Guiana, Report by the Commonwealth Team of Observers on the Elections in *December 1964*. Col. no. 359, (Tek Chand, chairman). London: Her Majesty's Stationery Office, 1965.

Report to the Government of British Guiana on Planning Agricultural Development by Rene Dumont. Rome: Food and Agriculture Organisation, 1963.

Report of a Commission of Inquiry into the Sugar Industry in Guyana (G. L. B. Persaud, chairman), *Mimeo*, September 1968.

Newspapers [British Library, St Pancras, London, primarily; the National Archives, Guyana]

Booker News

The Daily Argosy

The Daily Chronicle

Guiana Graphic

Guiana Review

Indian Opinion

The Labour Advocate

Mirror

The New Daily Chronicle

New Nation

New World Fortnightly [journal]

New York Times

PAC Bulletin

PPP Thunder [Burnham]

The Sun

Thunder

The Times (London)

The Tribune

Weekend Post and Sunday Argosy

Interviews

Bhagwan, Moses (former head of the PYO and a PPP legislator), March 2019.
Campbell, Jock [Lord Campbell of Eskan], Nettlebed, Oxfordshire, May 9, 1990; July 23, 1992; July 24, 1992; February 17, 1994; February 18, 1994.
Campbell, Jock, and Dr Fenton Ramsahoye, Nettlebed, Oxfordshire, December 22, 1994.
Chand, Komal (trade unionist, GAWU), Georgetown, September 11, 1992.
Das, Premchand, (trade unionist, GAWU), Georgetown, September 9, 1992.
Jagan, Dr Cheddi, London, August 8, 1991; Coventry, May 10, 1992; Georgetown, September 8, 1992.
Kwayana, Eusi (formerly Sydney King), (politician and writer), Georgetown, September 22, 1992.
Ramsahoye, Dr Fenton, (former politician [Attorney General of British Guiana, 1961–64]), London, July 25, 1992; Georgetown, August 8, 1997.
Samuel, Lee, [formerly Lee Akbar], MBE (former secretary, British Guiana Government Office, London), London, June 12, 1997.
Searwar, Lloyd, (former government information officer), Georgetown, August 24, 2000.
Singh, Jainaraine, (former trade unionist [GIWU] and politician), Georgetown, September 10, 1992.

Interviews by Oscar Ramjeet (Georgetown), March 2017:

Chase, Ashton. Former PPP legislator and trade unionist.
Ishmael, Odeen. Former Guyanese ambassador to the US.
Ramotar, Donald. Former PPP activist and President of Guyana.
Ramkarran, Ralph. Former speaker of the National Assembly and editor of *Thunder*, organ of the PPP.

Billy Strachan Papers, Institute of Commonwealth Studies Collection, Senate House Library, University of London

Primarily correspondence between Cheddi and Janet Jagan and their principal communist mentor in the UK, the Jamaican-born Billy Strachan of the CLC (London Branch) and the CPGB.

II SECONDARY SOURCES

Books and Pamphlets

Aaronovitch, David. *Party Animals: My Family and Other Communists*. London: Jonathan Cape, 2016.
Adamson, Alan H. *Sugar without Slaves: The Political Economy of British Guiana, 1838–1904*. New Haven: Yale University Press, 1972.

Andrews, Margaret. *Doing Nothing is Not an Option: The Radical Lives of Eric and Jessica Huntley*. London: Krik Krak, 2014.

Barnet, Richard J. *Intervention and Revolution: The United States in the Third World*. New York: World Publishing, 1968.

Berlin, Isaiah. *Russian Thinkers*, edited by Henry Hardy and Aileen Kelly. London: Penguin, 1979 [1978].

_____. *The Sense of Reality: Studies in Ideas and their History*, edited by Henry Hardy. London: Pimlico, 1997 [1996].

Besancon, Alain. *The Intellectual Origins of Leninism*. Oxford: Basil Blackwell, 1981.

Birbalsingh, Frank. *The People's Progressive Party of Guyana, 1950–92: An Oral History*. London: Hansib, 2007.

Blight, James G., Bruce J. Allyn, and David A. Welch. *Cuba on the Brink: Castro, the Missile Crisis and the Soviet Collapse*. New York: Pantheon Books, 1993.

Bolland, O. Nigel. *On the March: Labour Rebellion in the British Caribbean, 1934–39*. Kingston: Ian Randle Publishers, 1995.

British Guiana Trades Union Council. *The Communist Martyr Makers: The Account of the Struggle for Free Trade Unionism in British Guiana in 1964*. Georgetown: BGTUC, 1964.

Brown, Stewart, ed. *All Are Involved: The Art of Martin Carter*. Leeds: Peepal Tree Press, 2000.

Burnham, Jessie. *Beware My Brother Forbes*. Georgetown: self-published, 1964.

Burrowes, Reynold. *The Wild Coast: An Account of Politics in Guyana*. Cambridge, Mass: Schenkman Publishing Co, 1984.

Butler, John. *The Red Dean of Canterbury: The Public and Private Faces of Hewlett Johnson*. London: Scala Publishers, 2011.

Chandisingh, Ranji. *Why I left the PPP* [1976].

Chase, Ashton. *133 Days Towards Freedom in Guiana*. Georgetown: self-published, n.d. [1954].

_____. *A History of Trade Unionism in Guyana, 1900 to 1964*. Ruimveldt. Guyana: New Guyana Co, n.d. [1964].

_____. *Guyana: A Nation in Transit – Burnham's Role*. Georgetown: self-published, 1994.

Dallek, Robert. *Camelot's Court: Inside the Kennedy White House*. New York: Harper Perennial, 2014 [2013].

David, Wilfred L. *The Economic Development of Guyana, 1953–1964*. Oxford: Clarendon Press, 1969.

Despres, Leo A. *Cultural Pluralism and Nationalist Politics in British Guiana*. Chicago: Rand McNally and Co, 1967.

Drayton, Harold. *An Accidental Life*. Hertford: Hansib, 2017.

Dyett, Harry. *Enigma of Development: Guyana 1900 to 1989 – An Unrealised Potential*. Georgetown: Institute of Development Studies and Faculty of Social Sciences, University of Guyana, 1994.

Edun, Ayube. *London's Heart-Probe and Britain's Destiny*. London: Arthur H. Stockwell, 1935.

Fisher, Nigel, *Iain Macleod*. London: Andre Deutsch, 1973.

Fraser, Cary. *Ambivalent Anti-Colonialism: The United States and the Genesis of West Indian Independence, 1960–64*. Westport, Ct: Greenwood Press, 1994.

Gallacher, William. *The Case for Communism*. Harmondsworth: Penguin Books, 1949.

Garner, Steve. *Guyana, 1838–1985: Ethnicity, Class and Gender*. Kingston, Jamaica: Ian Randle Publishers, 2008.

Glasgow, Roy A. *Guyana: Race and Politics among Africans and East Indians*. The Hague: Matinus Nijhoff, 1970.

Gopaul, Nanda K. *Resistance and Change: The Struggles of the Guyanese Workers (1964 to 1994), with Emphasis on the Sugar Industry*. New York: Inside News Publications, 1997.

Gordon, Andrew. *Communism is Evil*. Georgetown: The Argosy Co. Ltd., 1960.

Hoffer, Eric. *The Tue Believer: Thoughts on the Nature of Mass Movements*. New York: Harper Perennial, 1966 [1951].

Horsley, David. *Billy Strachan, 1921–98: RAF Officer, Communist, Civil Rights Pioneer, Legal Administrator, Internationalist, and ABOVE ALL CARIBBEAN MAN*. London: Caribbean Labour Solidarity, 2019.

Hubbard, H. J. M. *Race and Guyana: The Anatomy of a Colonial Enterprise*. Georgetown: The Daily Chronicle, 1969.

Ishmael, Odeen, ed. and comp. *The Campaign for Socialism and Democracy in Guyana: Source Documents of the PPP, 1965–91*. Georgetown: GNI Publications, 2010.

———. *From Autocracy to Democracy in Guyana: Aspects of Post-Independence Guyana History, 1966–92*. Georgetown: GNI Publications, 2012.

Jagan, Cheddi. *Forbidden Freedom: The Story of British Guiana*. London: Lawrence and Wishart, 1954.

———. *The West on Trial: My Fight for Guyana's Freedom*. London: Michael Joseph, 1966.

———. *The Caribbean Revolution*. Prague: Orbis Press Agency, 1979.

———. *The Caribbean: Whose Backyard?* Self-published, [1985].

———. *National Assembly Speeches, 1947–87*, 7 Vols. Caribbean Press, 2011.

Jayawardena, Chandra. *Conflict and Solidarity in a Guianese Plantation*. London: The Athlone Press, 1962.

Johnson, Hewlett. *The Socialist Sixth of the World*. London: Victor Gollancz, 1939.

Jones, Howard. *The Bay of Pigs*. New York: Oxford University Press, 2008.

Knowles, William H. *Trade Union Development and Industrial Relations in the British West Indies*. Berkeley: University of California Press, 1959.

Kolakowski, Leszek. *Main Currents of Marxism*. New York: W. W. Norton, 2005 [1978].

Kwayana, Eusi, *Guyana: No Guilty Race*. Georgetown: Free Press, 1999.

———. *Next Witness: An Appeal to World Opinion*. Self-published, 1999 [1962].

———. *The Morning After*. Georgetown: Guyana-Caribbean Politics Publications, 2005.

———. *Walter Rodney: His Last Days and Campaigns*. Birmingham: R. Ferdinand-Lalljie Publishers, 2009.

Lamb, Richard. *The Macmillan Years, 1957–1963: The Emerging Truth*. London: John Murray, 1995.

Leffler, Melvyn P. *For the Soul of Mankind: The United States, the Soviet Union and the Cold War*. New York: Hill and Wang, 2007.

Lewis, W. Arthur. *Labour in the West Indies: The Birth of a Workers' Movement* [Fabian Society, Research Series, no. 44]. London: Victor Gollancz, 1939.

Lutchman, Harold A. *From Colonialism to Cooperative Republic: Aspects of Political Development in Guyana*. Rio Piedras, Puerto Rico: Institute of Caribbean Studies, University of Puerto Rico, 1974.

Macmillan, W. M. *Warning from the West Indies: A Tract for the Empire*. Harmondsworth: Penguin, 1938 [1936].

Mandle, Jay R. *The Plantation Economy: Population and Economic Change in Guyana, 1838–1960*. Philadelphia: Temple University Press, 1973.

Mangru, Basdeo. *A History of East Indian Resistance on the Guyana Sugar Estates, 1869–1948*. Lewiston, NY: The Edwin Mellen Press, 1996.

Mars, Perry. *Ideology and Change: The Transformation of the Caribbean Left*. Detroit, MI: Wayne State University Press, 1998.

———, and Alma H. Young. *Caribbean Labour and Politics: Legacies of Cheddi Jagan and Michael Manley*. Detroit, MI: Wayne State University Press, 2004.

Morrison, Andrew. *Justice: The Struggle for Democracy in Guyana, 1952–92*. Georgetown: self-published.

Nath, Dwarka. *A History of Indians in Guyana*. London: self-published, 1970 [1950].

Nehusi, Kimani S.K. *A People's Political History of Guyana, 1838–1964*. Hertford: Hansib, 2018.

Newman, Peter. *British Guiana: Problems of Cohesion in an Immigrant Society*. London: Oxford University Press, 1964.

Palmer, Colin A. *Cheddi Jagan and the Politics of Power: British Guiana's Struggle for Independence*. Chapel Hill: The University of North Carolina Press, 2010.

Pierce, Paulette, *Noncapitalist Development: The Struggle to Nationalize the Guyanese Sugar Industry*. Totowa, NJ: Rowman & Allanheld, 1984.

Premdas, Ralph R. *Ethnic Conflict and Development: The Case of Guyana*. Aldershot: Avebury, 1995.

Rabe, Stephen G. *Eisenhower and Latin America: The Foreign Policy of Anti-Communism*. Chapel Hill: The University of North Carolina Press, 1988.

——— . *US Intervention in British Guiana: A Cold War Story*. Chapel Hill: The University of North Carolina Press, 2005.

——— . *John F. Kennedy: World Leader*. Washington, D.C.: Potomac Books, 2010.

Ragbeer, Mohan. *The Indelible Red Stain: Destruction of a Tropical Paradise – A Cold War Story*, 2 Vols [Published by the Author, no date].

Ramcharan, Lily. *The Cold War in the Third World: Guyana, 1953–89* [Published by the Author, 1997].

Ramharack, Baytoram. *Against the Grain: Balram Singh Rai and the Politics of Guyana*. San Juan, Trinidad: CHAKRA, 2005.

——— . *Jung Bahadur Singh of Guyana (1886–1956): Politician, Ship Doctor, Labour Leader and Protector of Indians*. San Juan, Trinidad: CHAKRA, 2019.

Reno, Philip. *The Ordeal of British Guiana*. New York: Monthly Review Press, 1964.

Rodney, Walter. *Oye: His Last Speech on the Mall, Georgetown* (June 6, 1980).

Sallahuddin. *Guyana: The Struggle for Liberation, 1945–1992*. Georgetown: self-published, 1994.

Schlesinger, Arthur, Jr. *A Thousand Days: John F. Kennedy in the White House*. London: Andre Deutsch, 1965.

Seecharan, Clem. *'Tiger in the Stars': The Anatomy of Indian Achievement in British Guiana, 1919–29*. London: Macmillan, 1997.

———. *Bechu: 'Bound Coolie' Radical in British Guiana, 1894–1901*. Mona, Jamaica: University of the West Indies Press, 1999.

——— . *Sweetening 'Bitter Sugar': Jock Campbell, the Booker Reformer in British Guiana, 1934–66*. Kingston, Jamaica: Ian Randle Publishers, 2005.

———. *Muscular Learning: Cricket and Education in the Making of the British West Indies at the End of the 19th Century*. Kingston, Jamaica: Ian Randle Publishers, 2006.

———. *Mother India's Shadow over El Dorado: Indo-Guyanese Politics and Identity, 1890s–1930s*. Kingston, Jamaica: Ian Randle Publishers, 2011.

———. *Finding Myself: Essays on Race, Politics and Culture*. Leeds: Peepal Tree Press, 2015.

Service, Robert. *Comrades: A World History of Communism*. London: Macmillan, 2007.

Shahabuddeen, M. *From Plantocracy to Nationalisation: A Profile of Sugar in Guyana*. Georgetown: University of Guyana, 1983.

Sharma, P. D. *The New Caribbean Man: Poems, 1972–76*. Hayward, California: Carib House, 1981.

Simms, Peter. *Trouble in Guyana*. London: George Allen and Unwin Ltd, 1966.

Singh, Jai Narine. *Guyana: Democracy Betrayed – A Political History, 1948–1993*. Kingston: Kingston Publishers Ltd, 1996.

Smith, Raymond T. *British Guiana*. London: Oxford University Press, 1962.

Southgate, John. *The Commonwealth Sugar Agreement, 1951–1974*. London: C. Czarnikow, Ltd, 1984.

Spinner, Thomas J. *A Political and Social History of Guyana, 1945–1983*. Boulder, Colorado: Westview Press, 1983.

St. Pierre, Maurice. *Anatomy of Resistance: Anti-Colonialism in Guyana, 1823–1966*. London: Macmillan, 1999.

Swan, Michael. *British Guiana: The Land of Six Peoples*. London: Her Majesty's Stationery Office, 1957.

Thomas, Clive Y. *Plantations, Peasants and State: A Study of the Mode of Sugar Production in Guyana*. Los Angeles: Centre for Afro-American Studies, UCLA, 1984.

Tucker, Robert C. *The Soviet Political Mind: Stalinism and Post-Stalin Change*. London: George Allen and Unwin, 1972 [1971].

Vatuk, Ved Prakash. *British Guiana*. New York: Monthly Review Press, 1963.

WPA. *Government of National Unity and Reconstruction of the Working People's Alliance* (October 1979).

WPA. *Arguments for Unity against the Dictatorship in Guyana* (1983).

WPA Manifesto: For the Redemption, Reconstruction and Rebirth of Guyana (1985).

Williams, Denis. *Giglioli in Guyana, 1922–1972*. Georgetown: National History and Arts Council, n.d.

Articles, Unpublished Papers, and Theses

Articles and Unpublished Papers and Speeches by Jock Campbell:

Campbell, Jock. Chairman's Statements [Booker], 1947–66. In *Report of the Directors and Statement of Accounts* for these years. (They were all written by Campbell personally and reflect his style, apart from the Statement for 1960, when he was ill).

'British Guiana.' Letter to the Editor. *The New Statesman and Nation*, October 24, 1953.

'British Capital in the Changing Conditions of the Colony.' Paper delivered at the University of Cambridge, July 12, 1954.

'People are More Important than Ships and Shops and Sugar Estates.' Script of a broadcast given by J. M. Campbell over Radio Demerara, on the British Guiana Government Information Services Programme, 'Sunday-at Noon,' March 4, 1956.

'Development and Organisation of Booker Bros., McConnell and Co., Ltd.' Paper delivered at the London School of Economics, November 24, 1959. *Mimeo*.

Booker Bros, McConnell and Co, Ltd. 'The Group Chairman's Visit to British Guiana and the West Indies, January–March 1960.' Confidential. *Mimeo*, March 22, 1960.

'The Clash of Immigrant Coloured Races in British Guiana.' Text of Address to the Ministry of Education Commonwealth Course. *Mimeo*, April 15, 1966.

'Speech by Lord Campbell of Eskan to the Fabian Society, London.' *Mimeo*, October 22, 1969.

'People are More Important than Ships and Shops and Sugar Estates.' [Jock Campbell, interviewed by David de Caires]. *Stabroek News*, July 8, 1989.

'The 1976 Nationalisation did not Take us by Surprise.' [Jock Campbell, interviewed by David de Caires]. *Stabroek News*, July 15, 1989.

Chandisingh, Ranji. 'Socialism and Democracy.' *Thunder* (April–September 1975).
———. 'Education in the Revolution for Socialist Transformation and Development.' Presented at the Third Biennial Conference of the PNC, August 22–26, 1979.

Cook, Anne Patricia. 'Social Policy and the Colonial Economy in Guyana.' PhD thesis, University of Surrey (Guildford), 1988.

Daniels, Gordon Oliver. 'A Great Injustice to Cheddi Jagan: The Kennedy Administration and British Guiana, 1961–63.' PhD thesis, University of Mississippi, 2000.

Fraser, Cary. 'The "New Frontier" of Empire in the Caribbean: The Transfer of Power in British Guiana, 1961–1964.' *The International History Review* XXII, no. 3 (September 2000).

———. 'Janet Jagan: An Important and Complex Political Legacy.' *Stabroek News*, March 30, 2009.

Halperin, Ernst. 'Racism and Communism in British Guiana.' *Journal of Inter-American Studies* VII, no. 1 (January 1965).

Hinden, Rita. 'The Case of British Guiana.' *Encounter* II, no. 1 (January 1954).

Hintzen, Percy C., and Ralph R. Premdas. 'Race, Ideology and Power in Guyana.' *The Journal of Commonwealth and Comparative Politics* XXI, no. 2 (July 1983).

Jagan, Janet. '30 Years since the P.A.C.' *Thunder* (January–March, 1977).

Kwayana, Eusi. '65 Years after October 1953: A Report and Review by One Present at the Events.' *Mimeo*, 2018.

Lewis, Gordon K. '[Review of Jagan's] *The West on Trial: My Fight for Guyana's Freedom.*' *Caribbean Studies* 7, no. 4 (1968).

Lutchman, Harold A. 'Historical Perspective of Race and the Public Service in Guyana.' *History Gazette*, no. 54 (March 1993).

Mars, Perry. 'The Significance of the Disturbances, 1962–1964.' *History Gazette*, no. 70 (July 1994).

Meisler, Stanley. 'Meddling in Latin America.' *The Nation*, February 10, 1964.

Naipaul, V. S. 'A Handful of Dust: Return to Guiana.' *The New York Review of Books*, April 10, 1991.

The Nation. 'Great Injustice done to Jagan — [Arthur] Schlesinger,' editorial, June 4, 1990.

New World Fortnightly. 'Portraits of the Leaders [Jagan, Burnham, D'Aguiar],' no. 3 (November 30, 1964).

———. 'Reply to Mrs. Jagan,' *New World Fortnightly*, no. 21 (August 20, 1965).

Potter, Lesley M. 'The Paddy Proletariat and the Dependent Peasantry: East Indian Rice Growers in British Guiana, 1895–1920.' *History Gazette*, no. 47 (August 1992).

Ramotar, Donald. 'Karl Marx and the Future Society.' *The Thinker*, no. 2 (July–December 2018).

Ramsahoye, Fenton. 'Sweetening Bitter Sugar.' *Stabroek News*, January 30, 2005.

Rose, James G. 'British Colonial Policy and the Transfer of Power in British Guiana, 1945–64.' PhD thesis, University of London, 1992.

———. 'The Enmore Incident of 1948.' *History Gazette*, no. 69 (June 1994).

Rose, James, and John Williams. 'International Perceptions of the People's Progressive Party by 1953.' *History Gazette*, no. 72 (September 1994).

'The Real Challenge of Guiana,' [Leader]. *The New Statesman and Nation.* October 24, 1953.

'The Story of British Guiana: Putting the Clock Back in the Colonies.' *The New Statesman and Nation.* October 17, 1953.

'Time when Malaria Wreaked Havoc in Guyana.' *Guyana Graphic* (Independence Souvenir). May 1966.

Thomas, Clive. 'Sugar Economics in a Colonial Situation: A Study of the Guyana Sugar Industry.' n.d. [1970]. *Mimeo.*

———. 'Sugar and Liberation: An Outline Programme,' n.d. [1975], *Mimeo.*

Walker-Kilkenny, Roberta. 'The Radicalization of the Women's Movement in British Guiana, 1946–1953.' *Cimarron* 1, no. 3 (1988).

———. 'The Leonora Strike of 1939.' *History Gazette*, no. 46 (July 1992).

Wallace, Elisabeth. 'British Guiana: Causes of the Present Discontents.' *International Journal* XIX, no. 4 (Autumn 1964).

Waters, Robert Anthony, Jr, and Gordon Oliver Daniels. 'The World's Longest General Strike: The AFL-CIO, the CIA, and British Guiana.' *Diplomatic History* 29, no. 2 (April 2005).

———. '"When you're handed money on a platter, it's very hard to say where are you getting this?"' *Revue Belge de Philologie et D'Histoire* 84, no. 4 (2006).

Index

A

Abyssinian issue, 96, 97–100, 109

Accabre College: and ideological education, 58

Africa: Afro-Guyanese and, 92–93, 101–02

African identity: in British Guiana, 78–79, 88, 100–02, 110

African-Indian problem, 75, 87–91, 104–05, 109–10, 125–28, 178–86, 225–30, 293–95, 678; Jagan and the, 154–55

African Society for Racial Equality (ASRE): King and the creation of the, 296, 355

Afro-Guyanese: and Burnham, 39; and the Italian invasion of Ethiopia, 92–97; and the idea of an Indian colony, 87–91; fear of Indian supremacy, 36–43, 78–80, 101–102, 104, 106, 113; Jagan and the, 71–72, 118–119; and the PPP, 36, 54; and slavery, 4–5; and the WI Federation, 181–182

Akbar, Mohamad: and Indian nationalism, 114–115

American Federation of Labor and Congress of Industrial Organization (AFL-CIO): and Jagan, 367–371

American Institute for Free Labor Development (AIFLD): and destabilization of BG, 370–371

American trade blockade: against Cuba, 59

Angolan Civil War: Burnham and the, 562–563

Anti-communism: dawn of, 164–174,185–188; and suspension of the BG constitution, 240–244; USA, 308–60; 366–378

B

Bacchus, Peer: and the 1947 general elections, 177

Barbados: and the WI Federation, 180–181

Bauxite: nationalisation of, 33, 518, 529, 532, 548–50, 641

Beharry, Edward: and the PPP, 452

Benn, Brindley, 31; and Marxism, 56, 63; and the PPP, 452, 464–65

Berbice Rebellion, 4

Berbice River Constituency: and the 1947 general elections, 177

Best, Lloyd, 47; and Jagan, 305–306; on Janet Jagan, 46–47, 53, 69

Bhagwan, Moses: and a Guyanese national identity, 126; on Jagan, 462; and the PPP, 42–43, 55, 75–76

Birbalsingh, Professor Frank: interview with Chase, 588–89; interview with Jagan, 30, 50–51

Birch Grove Meeting: between Kennedy and Macmillan, 374–75, 400

Birth rates: increase in, 118

Bishop, Maurice: communist leadership, 51–52, 55

Bitter Sugar: Jagan's mission of, 5, 6–7, 30, 48–51, 118, 128–37, 145–46, 186–88, 192–94, 211–13, 258, 564

Black Bush Polder Scheme, 72, 145

Black Friday riots: CIA and the, 343–47

Black South African migrants: in countering idea of an Indian colony, 87–88

Booker Company: domination of sugar industry, 129–130; Jagan an the, 131–131; nationalisation of, 33, 548, 603–06; and the PPP, 235–38; and sugar industry, 4, 48, 119

Booker's Guiana, 136

Bostwick, R.O: on Burnham, 578–83

Bowman, Fred: and PPP Leadership, 255–56

Brazil threat: to Guyana, 567

British Government: and BG independence, 308–34, 339–50, 461–62; and BG politics, 399–402, 407–12; and Burnham, 349, 478–79; and Jagan, 53, 372–82; and imposition of PR, 372–82, 385–86

British Government white paper: on suspension of BG constitution, 241–42, 244–45

British Guiana (BG): plantation economy, 4

British Guiana Colonisation Deputation, 81–85

British Guiana Constitution: suspension of the, 241–42, 244–56, 377

British Guiana East Indian Association (BGEIA): 79, 81, 100, 125, 202

British Guiana Labour Union (BGLU), 93, 169

British Guiana Workers' League (BGWL), 135, 201, 205

British intelligence: and the Jagans, 172

Britton, H. Aaron: and the invasion of Ethiopia, 95–96

Bundy, McGeorge: and BG politics, 403, 488–89

Burnham, Forbes: and Afro-Guyanese, 39, 54; and Angola, 562–63; and British government, 349, 372–80, 383–84, 488–97; and Castro, 526–29, 531–33, 539, 540, 580–82; cooperative socialism, 508–10, 573–82; and Cuba, 33, 513–14, 519–21, 526–30, 551–56, 563–69; death of, 34, 622; D'Aguiar coalition, 463–64, 486–87, 496–97; and deCaires, 356–57; dictatorship, 548–50; and electoral fraud, 491–98, 505–06, 525–30, 548–49; and Enlai, 540; the GAWU strike, 395–96; and the 1961 general elections, 294–96; and the 1962 elections, 2; and the 1964 general elections, 407–12; and the 1973 general elections, 528, 596;

550–52, 565; Jagan's critical support of, 550–52, 565; Jagan rivalry, 225–30, 242–50, 256–67, 355–78, 471–72, 518–24, 540–43, 600–613; and independence, 329, 383–86, 488–95; and Johnson, 491–92, 495; and the José Marti National Order, 543–44, 553–55, 568; and Kennedy, 72, 346–47, 370–72; and Kim Il-sung, 506–07, 540; legacy, 703–12; and Marxism, 56, 218, 506–07, 540–82, 603; nationalisation campaign, 33, 518, 529, 532, 548–50, 603–606, 639–41; and the new constitution, 571–73; overview of, 418–23, 426–28, 502, 514–15, 530–31, 637–38; and the PPP, 40, 47, 71 228–29, 255–67, 279; and PR in BG, 367–71, 391–96; reformism, 503–507; socialism, 507–14; socialist constitution, 506–507; and state of emergency, 470; US sponsorship of, 399–400, 406–10, 469–71, 478–97, 514–17

Burnham, James, 261

Burnhamism, 567–68; Jagan on, 645–50, 677–78; US reaction to, 627–31

Bush, President George W. H.: and calls for free and fair elections in Guyana, 680–81

Bustamante, Sir Alexander, 316

C

Cameron, Norman Eustace: on idea of African Homeland, 101–102

Campbell, Jock, 5–6, 22, 119, 564; and the CSA, 48, 129; and Jagan, 6–7, 32, 46, 49, 53, 131–32, 309–10, 314, 606–607, 709–10; on Janet Jagan, 69; on Lethem, 139; and the PPP, 235–38, 272–73; and the Venn Commission, 216–20; on working conditions on plantations, 132–33

Canterbury, Archbishop of: and the Italian invasion of Ethiopia, 99–100

Capitalism: Jagan and, 636–37; PNC and the move to, 623–25

Carew, Jan, 73, 74

Caribbean Labour: and Burnham, 227

Caribbean Labour Congress (CLC): and
communism, 431–33, 441
CARICOM: and electoral fraud in
Guyana, 506
Carlson, US Consul General Delmar:
and BG independence, 478–95;
and D'Aguiar, 481–82; and Jagan,
402–406, 478–85
Carter, President Jimmy: and the 1992
general elections, 3, 681–83, 687–89
Carter, Martin: and communism, 63, 66;
detention of, 272; and reversal of PR,
391–92
Castro, Fidel: and Burnham, 33, 526–29,
531–33, 539, 540; and Jagan, 59,
301, 306–307, 313–15; and Kennedy,
325–26
Catholic Church: anti-communist stance,
424–26
Catholic Standard: anti-communist stance,
425, 564, 657–58
Central Books, 59
Central Committee Report to the PPP
Congress: 23rd, 679; 24th, 683–85;
25th, 680–82, 694–95
Central Demerara Seat: and the 1947
general elections, 164–65, 170
Central Intelligence Agency (CIA): and
BG politics, 59, 400–402, 479–90,
533–36; and Cuba, 555–56; and
the Black Friday riots, 343–47; and
Jagan, 308–34, 367–71, 488–98
Central YMCA College: Jagan and the,
25
Chandisingh, Ranji: and Cuba, 567;
and electoral fraud, 559–61; and
Marxism, 56, 231–32, 431, 435–37,
444, 505; defection to the PNC, 554,
556–63, 566, 567, 607–13, 616
Chase, Ashton: on Burnham, 584–91;
and the GIWU, 204, 233–35; and
Jagan, 212; and the PAC, 148, 149;
and the PPP, 274; and universal adult
suffrage, 182
Che Guevara: Janet Jagan and, 55
China: and the 1973 general elections,
534–35
Christian Church: anti-communist
stance, 193, 196–97

Chronicle: and the 1947 general elections,
169, 171–72
Class struggle: Jagan and the, 75–76,
198–200
Classless society: communism and the,
54, 62
Closer Union Conference: Montego Bay,
183–84
Coastal Guyana: sugar industry, 48
Cold War: Burnham and the, 507; and
Guyana-US relations, 3, 308–78; and
internal politics, 19–20; Jagan and
the, 47–48, 53, 60, 468–97
Collet, Governor Wilfred: and the idea of
an Indian colony, 79, 86
Colonisation Deputation to India, 88
Colonisation Scheme: and the idea of an
Indian colony, 86, 87–91, 100–101
Colonial Development and Welfare
Grant: and drainage and irrigation,
119–21, 139, 140, 145
Commission of Enquiry to British
Guiana: International Commission of
Jurists, 464
Commonwealth Sugar Agreement (CSA),
48, 129, 564, 575
Communal villages: post-emancipation,
573–76
Communist International (Comintern);
and the 1947 general elections,
185–87
Communist Party of Great Britain
(CPGB), 156; Jagan and the, 224–25,
440–45; and the PPP, 430–39,
440–46, 449–56
Communist Party of the Soviet Union
(CPSU): Jagan and the, 64–67, 155,
156–58, 473–85, 624–26: Janet Jagan
and the, 660–61; and the PPP, 511
Communist Party of the USA (CPUSA):
Janet Jagan and the, 28
Communist state: PPP and creation of a,
238–56
Conference of Communist Parties of
Latin America, 544
Constitution: new Guyana, 571–82;
suspension of the BG, 239–56, 565,
586
Constitutional Amendment Campaign:

King and the, 246–48
Constitutional Conference, 261, 485–87
Cook, Ann: on benefits of drainage and
    irrigation programme, 119–20
Cooperative socialism: death of, 622;
    PNC and, 508–10, 547–48, 573–82
Corentyne: proposal to drain the, 140–42
Corentyne district: and the 1947 general
    elections, 178
Cox, Idris: and PPP, 249–52
Crawford, W.A.: and migration of
    Barbadians to BG, 180–81
Creech-Jones: and the WI Federation,
    180–81
Cricket: at Port Mourant, 22–23
Critchlow, Hubert: and the Labour Party,
    128, 169, 175; and universal adult
    suffrage, 143–46, 181–82
Cuba: Burnham and, 33, 513, 519–21,
    531–33, 543, 551–56, 567–68;
    Jagan and, 59, 72, 504–508, 510–11,
    531–35, 544–50; USA and, 341–48,
    550–56
Cuban Revolution, 59–60; Jagan and
    the, 306, 314, 545–48; Caribbean
    recognition of the, 546–47
Cuban rice deal, 314
Cuffy Ideological Institute: Chandisingh
    and the, 612; PNC and the, 508
Cumberbatch, H.E.: and the 1947
    general elections, 177
Czechoslovakia, 32, 194, 199; Jagan's visit
    to, 223–24; Soviet Union and, 476

D
D'Aguiar, Peter: anti-communist stance
    of, 18–20, 352–55, 395, 424–28,
    637–38; Burnham coalition, 460–61,
    463–64, 481–83, 489–90; Carlson
    and, 481–82; and the GAWU strike,
    394–95; and PR in BG, 379–81
Daily Argosy; and the Constitution
    Amendment campaign, 246–48;
    and the Enmore tragedy, 204–208;
    on Gandhi and Indian nationalism,
    104–105, 112–13; and 1947 general
    elections, 168, 185–88
Daily Chronicle: anti-communist stance,
    166–67, 196–97, 425; and the 1947
    general elections, 162, 177, 185–87;

and Indian nationalism, 112; and the
    WI Federation, 181–82
Daniels, Gordon: on AFL-CIO
    destabilisation of BG, 368–70
de Aguiar, John: and the 1947 general
    elections, 164, 170–71
Death rates: decrease in, 118
de Caires, David: and Burnham, 356–57,
    658; on Jagan's legacy, 706–07; and
    Stabroek News, 705
DEMBA: nationalisation of, 518, 529,
    532, 548–50, 641. See also Bauxite
    industry
Demerara Rebellion, 4
Democratic centralism, 160
Dictatorship of the Proletariat, 660
Drainage and irrigation: expenditure on,
    119–20, 138–42, 146
Drayton, Harry: on Jagan, 436–39
Dutt, Rajani Palme: and Janet Jagan,
    249–52, 431, 434, 439, 440–44

E
East Indian Association, 16, 39
East Indian Young Men's Association, 16
Economic Recovery Programme (ERP):
    Hoyte and the IMF, 668, 679, 682,
    683–84, 686, 687
Education and Research Committee of
    the PPP: Marxist Leninist ideology
    of the, 57–58
Edun, Ayube, 192; and the 1947 general
    elections, 178; and Jagan, 63; on
    Governor Lethem, 138–40; and
    reform of colonial society, 223–24;
    and trade the union movement, 21;
    and working conditions on the sugar
    estates, 133–35, 136; and universal
    adult suffrage, 144–46
El Dorado: syndrome, 3–7, 37, 41, 69,
    84, 113–16
Electoral fraud: Burnham and, 48, 474,
    488–98, 505–506, 523–30, 547, 548–
    50, 559–61; Hoyte and, 48, 506–508,
    668, 680; PNC and, 622–25, 668,
    680
Emigration: Indo-Guyanese, 2–3, 634–35
Enmore tragedy, 118, 131–32, 195–96,
    197, 198, 203–13, 219–20, 564
Enlai, Zhou: and Burnham, 540; and

Janet Jagan, 55
Ethiopia: Italian invasion of, 92–93, 95
Ethiopianism: and Africans in the
  Americas, 93–97
Ethnic balance: Afro-Guyanese and,
  100–102; Burnham and, 464; NPC
  and, 86, 87–91
Ethnicity: and a national identity, 125–26
Evans, Sir Geoffrey: and settlement of
  West Indies in BG, 182–83
Evening Post: anti-communist stance of
  the, 425, 622–23
Ferreira, C.P: and the 1947 general
  elections, 177
Fitzpatrick, Miles: and PR in BG, 386
Forde, Henry: and economic sanctions
  against Guyana, 680
Forsythe, Dennis: on the second invasion
  of Ethiopia, 95
Franchise Commission Report, 143–46
Fraser, Hugh: and Burnham, 356–58
Fredericks, E.F.: and Afro-Guyanese
  identity, 88–89; death, 92–93
Free and fair elections: Jagan and calls
  for, 680–81

G
Gajraj, H.B.: and the BGEIA, 100; and
  Mother India, 103
Gangadeen, Shiv: on the Jagans and the
  PPP, 322–23
Gandhi, Mahatma: and Indian
  emigration, 88; and Indian
  nationalism, 103, 104–105, 110; and
  Jagan, 192
Ganpatsingh, Robert: and the 1947
  general elections, 177
Garvey, Marcus: and the return to Africa,
  94–95; visit to British Guiana,
  109–11
Garveyism: and the NPC, 90–91; race
  first philosophy and, 91–102,
General elections: 1947, 159–64; 1961,
  296–97; 1962, 2; 1980, 668; 1985,
  680; 1992, 681–84; PR and the 1964,
  407–12; and the 1973, 496; and
  ethnic balance, 296–300, 301–305,
  410–12
Gibson, Isabelle, 13, 22
Gibson, J.C., 13, 22

Gonsalves, Dr G.M: and the 1947
  general elections, 177
Gorbachev, Mikhail: and the Soviet crisis,
  668–76, 683–93
Great Depression, 89, 96, 98
Greenwood, Tony: Secretary of State and
  Burnham, 480–82, 488–89
Grenada: US invasion of, 55
Grey, Sir Ralph: and Jagan, 302–304, 310
  370; and PR, 380
Groupness: vs individualism, 509
Guevara, Che: and Janet Jagan, 55
Guiana Graphic: anti-communist stance,
  198; and workers' strikes, 154–55
Guiana Industrial Workers' Union
  (GIWU), 146, 202–205; and the
  SPA, 231–38, 250–55, 260–64; sugar
  workers' strike, 232–34, 238–44,
  259–65, 564, 565
Guiana Review: and colonial society,
  223–24; Edun and the, 132
Gupta, Charu: and the millenarian vision,
  113–14
Guyana: and the Brazilian threat, 567;
  and cooperative socialism, 508–10,
  547–48, 573–82; Cuba relations,
  550–56, 561–63; electoral fraud
  in, 48, 474, 488–98, 505–506,
  523–30, 547, 548–50, 559–61; Krebs
  assessment of, 628–29; Marxism
  in, 535–37, 541–43, 553–55; US
  relations, 2, 53, 57, 59,308–47, 399–
  400, 406–10, 469–71,478–85, 474,
  488–98, 505–06, 514–17, 523–30,
  547, 551–56; Venezuela relations,
  566
Guyana Agricultural Workers Union
  (GAWU), 367, 564–66, 604–06;
  sugar workers' strike, 394–99
Guyana Defence Force: and the 1973
  general elections, 528–29
Guyana United Muslim Party, 488
Guyanese national identity: ethnicity and,
  125–28. *See also* National identity.

H
Haile Selassie: exile of, 109, 110;
  Rastafari and, 95–96
Hale, C.M.: and Indo-Guyanese
  ascendancy, 81

Hares: and sugar workers' riot, 98

Harlow, Vincent: and the Waddington Commission, 250

Hart, R.B.O.: and the WI Federation, 183, 263

Hart: Richard: and Burnham, 227, 430; on Jagan, 704; and the WFTU, 261

Heavner, Theodore: and US involvement in Guyanese elections, 523–25

Hellbeck, Jochen: on Stalin, 68–69

Helms, Richard: and the BG-Russia situation, 372–73; and BG independence, 489–90

Henderson-Stewart, Sir James: and Jagan, 195–96

Hennings, John: and Jagan, 311–12, 404

Herbert, C.A.: and the PPP leadership, 254–56

Hindus: and colour, 71

Hindu caste system: Jagan and, 14–15

Hindu-Muslim relations: in BG, 192–93

Home, Lord Douglas: and BG independence, 374–75; and BG politics, 299–402; and Jagan, 315–16

Hoyte, Desmond: and electoral fraud, 48, 506–508, 668, 680; and ERP, 668, 679; and the 1992 general elections, 682; succeeds Burnham, 622

Hubbard, H.J.M: and the 1947 general elections, 162, 167–69, 175; and the Jagans, 175–76; and the TUC, 148

Hungary: Soviet invasion of, 279–81

I

Identity: Afro-Guyanese, 100–102; in British Guiana, 78

Immigration ordinance, 81

Independence: Britain and BG, 308–34, 339–40, 343–46, 356–82, 408, 461–62, 467, 483; Burnham and, 377–81, 461, 467, 483; D'Aguiar and, 379–81, 467 489; Jagan and, 306–308, 316–18, 329–34, 378–82, 489; PNC and 294–97; PPP and, 246–48, 316, 470–72; race and the Cold War and, 339–40. *See also* Central Intelligence Agency, United States of America.

Independence Conference: collapse of the, 366; Jagan boycott of the, 466–68

India: independence from Britain, 117; and return of indentured Indians, 179–80

Indian-African problem, 42–43, 75–76, 86–97, 104–105, 109–10, 125–28, 177–86, 678; Jagan and the, 154–55, 225–30, 283–86, 293–96; USA and the, 483–85

Indian centenary: in British Guiana, 112–22

Indian colony: idea of an, 86, 87–91, 100, 112; Luckhoo and the creation of an, 78–79

Indian indentureship: a new slavery, 131–32

Indian middle class: emergence of, 117,

Indian National Congress (INC), 84, 85–86, 101, 103, 164

Indian nationalism, 112–22

Indian Opinion, 86, 101: and Indian nationalism, 114–15

Indo-Guyanese: ascendancy, 8–9, 15–16, 79–85, 117–20; emigration, 2–3, 634–35; and Jagan's Bitter Sugar campaign, 5, 6–7, 30, 48–51, 118, 128–37, 145–46, 186–88, 192–94, 211–13, 258, 564; identity, 104, 110, 115–16; and indentureship, 49–50; nationalism of, 38; plantation struggle, 118; political awakening, 3, 114; support of the PPP, 2 –3, 12, 38–40, 47, 58, 63 70–72, 129–30, 521–23, 681; and Mother India, 102–109; opposition to the WI Federation, 283–85

Internal self-government, 306

International Commission of Jurists: Commission of Enquiry to British Guiana, 464, 482–85

International Meeting of Communist Workers Parties: 634–35; and Jagan and the, 474–75

International Monetary Fund (IMF): and ERP in Guyana, 668

International Scientific Seminar on Karl Marx, 662

Ishmael, Richard: and the TUC sugar workers' strike, 367, 391

Italian invasion: of Ethiopia, 92–93, 95

J

Jackson, Sir Donald: and the Robertson Commission Report, 263–64

Jacob, C.R., 69, 72: and Indian nationalism, 112–13, 117; and the SPA, 136–38, 192–93;

Jacob, Dr Frank: and the Central Demerara seat, 167, 170–71

Jagan: Cheddi's father, 10–11, 23

Jagan, Bachaoni, 10

Jagan, Cheddi: and Afro-Guyanese insecurity, 118; bitter sugar campaign of, 5, 6–7, 30, 48–51, 118, 128–37, 564; and the Booker Company, 131–32; on Burnhamism, 645–50; and the caste system, 15–16; Castro, 301, 306–307, 313–16, 545–47, 551; and the Central Demerara seat, 164–65; communist leadership, 51–57, 148–58, 193–200; Congress paper, 286–87, 289–90, 292; critical support for the PNC, 550–52, 565, 614–18; death of, 633; education, 14–18, 21–22, 24–25; and the Enmore tragedy, 206–13; family background, 1, 8–15; and the 1964 GAWU strike, 394–399; and the 1947 general elections, 159–74; and the 1964 general elections, 407–12; Indo–Guyanese loyalty to, 47, 48–49, 58, 120, 127; and independence, 329, 376–82, 385–88, 460, 463, 470–71; and Kennedy, 72, 301, 310, 318–21, 326–27, 340–41, 351–53, 485–87; legislator, 60–61; legacy, 703–12; and Lethem, 151–54; and Arthur Lewis, 441–42; Marxist awakening, 2–3, 12–13, 16–17, 26–27, 258–60; Marxist commitment, 37–40, 50–70; 151–58, 197–200, 212–13, 229–30, 279–80, 324–26, 434–39, 468–85, 509–14, 541–50, 614–21, 662–65, 667–68, 676–80, 704–06; and the MPCA, 200–202; and Naipaul, 68; Order of Friendship of the Peoples awarded, 624–25; overview of, 423–25, 462–66; and PNC, 550–52; political inflexibility, 13–14, 50–51, 316; and PR, 391–93; and race,

37, 40, 127, 128, 280–84, 290–92; and Sandys, 376–90; on the US invasion of Grenada, 55; and the Venn Commission, 215–16; and the Waddington Constitution, 245; and the WI Federation, 280–84, 286–87; writings, 59–60. *See also* Central Intelligence Agency, Kennedy, President John F., Scientific socialism.

Jagan, Janet: and the Central Georgetown seat, 166–67; and the CLC and CPBG, 248–50, 251; communist ideology, 26–30; and the CPSU, 660–61; and the 1947 general elections, 170–71; influence on Cheddi, 46–48, 69–70, 71; and King, 17–18; marriage to Cheddi, 26, 28, 448–49; and the PPP, 3; meeting with Sandys, 408–409; *Thunder* editor, 63; and the Third World Congress of Women, 241–42

Jagan–Burnham rivalry, 225–30, 242–50; 256–67, 290–300, 328–30, 359–72, 487–88, 541–43, 600–613

Jailall, Ivy: on Gibson, 22

James, C.L.R: play on Haitian Revolution, 97–98

Jeffrey, Lionel: and communism, 66

Johnson, Rev. Hewlett: and communism, 61–62, 64–67

Johnson, President Lyndon: and Burnham, 461, 478–80; and Guyana politics, 399–402

José Marti National Order: awarded to Burnham, 543–44, 553–55, 568

Justice Party: and the 1964 general election, 411–12, 488–89

K

Kennedy, President John F.: and Burnham, 356–57; and Castro, 325–26; and the CIA in BG, 343–47; and Guyana politics, 2, 19, 40, 59, 72, 308–34, 366–76; and Jagan, 318–27, 331–34, 351–52, 368–71, 485–87. *See also* Central Intelligence Agency, United States of America

Khan, M.B., 183

Kim Il-sung: and Burnham, 506–508, 540

King, Spencer: and Burnham, 514, 531–32; on electoral fraud in Guyana, 529

King, Sydney: on Jagan, 17; and Janet Jagan, 17–18, 19; and the PAC, 149. *See also* Kwayana, Eusi.

Kissinger, Dr Henry: and Wills, 629–31

Kolakowski, Leszek: on the USSR and Marxism, 66–70, 173–74

Krebs, Max: on US-Guyana relations 1970s, 627–29

Kurmis: characteristics, 8–10

Kuru Kuru Cooperative College: and training in cooperative socialism, 584

Kwayana, Eusi: on Afro-Guyanese fear of Indian supremacy, 36–43, 120; and Afro–Guyanese support, 267; on Burnham, 419–20; defection from the PPP, 286–99; detention of, 269; and the Enmore tragedy, 207–208, 210; and the 1947 general elections, 174: and a Guyanese national identity, 126, 127, 425–27; and independence 355, 384–86; and Marxism, 56, 63, 66; and the PPP, 225–30, 242–43; and the Robertson Commission, 268–69; and the SPA, 234–35; and sugar workers' strike, 232, 240, 251, 260–61, 268; and the WFTU, 261

L

Labour Advocate: MPCA's newspaper, 136–37; and universal adult suffrage, 144–46

Labour Party, 128; and the 1947 general elections, 161, 169–72

Labour Party (British): and BG politics, 407–12

Labour protests: in the sugar industry, 21–23. *See also* Strikes and Sugar industry

Labour Relations Bill, 238, 260, 564; PPP and the, 367–71, 390–95

Lachmansingh, Dr J.P., 63, 264, 267

Land reclamation: and impact on slavery, 4–6

League of Coloured Peoples (LCP), 174; and Burnham, 227; racial politics of the, 175–76

Lenin, Vladimir: cooperative socialist philosophy of, 509; influence on Jagan, 29–30, 64–67

Leonora Plantation: shootings, 222, 223

Lethem, Sir Gordon: Jagan and, 151–55; stewardship of BG, 137–42, 146, 148

Lewis, Sir Arthur: meeting with Jagan, 441–42

London Conference: Jagan's boycott of the, 489

Love, Dr Robert: and Ethiopianism, 94–95

Luckhoo, Edward: and BGEIA, 79, 190

Luckhoo, J.A.: and the creation of an Indian colony, 78–80, 87, 190–91; and the race first philosophy, 92

Luckhoo, Lionel, 52, 61, 63; and the 1947 general elections, 178; interview with Jagan, 350–51

Luke, Sir Stephen: and the break with the PPP, 238

M

M15: surveillance of the Jagans, 172, 247–50, 259–67, 280–81, 431–35, 439–57

Macleod, Iain: and Guyana's independence 306; and Jagan, 308–10, 339–40

Macmillan, Prime Minister Harold: and BG independence, 374–75; and Guyanese politics, 2, 40. *See also* British Government

Macmillan, Professor W.M.: on creolisation among Africans in the WI, 96–97

Mangar, Tota: and the 1947 general elections, 185–86

Manley, Michael: and Non-aligned Movement, 531

Manley, Norman, 316–17

Manpower Citizens' Association (MPCA): and the GIWU, 203–204, 251–53, 367–71, 564; Jagan and the, 135, 36; sugar worker' union, 132–35, 192, 193, 200–203, 231–38, 260–64

Martin-Sperry, F.H: and the 1947 general elections, 177

Marxist awakening: Jagan's: 2–3, 12–13, 16–17, 26–30, 68

Marxist commitment: Jagan's, 30–43, 50–70, 155–58, 159–64, 279–81, 324–26, 509–14, 535–37, 544–50, 654–57

Marxist-Leninist ideology: in Guyana, 35, 56–57, 535–37, 541–50; and race, 54; and the USSR, 65–70. *See also* Marxist commitment.

Mateos, President Lopez: and Kennedy, 340–41

Maudling, Reginald: and Jagan, 340, 345

Maxwell, M: assessment of Burnham and Jagan, 636–38

McCabe, Howard: CIA agent in BG, 342–43

McWinnie, Tom: and the WFTU, 260, 444–46

Melby, Everett: and Jagan, 375–76; and PR for BG, 263–365

Michael Ford Bookshop, 59

Millenarian vision: Indo-Guyanese, 113; Jagan's, 155–58

Moore, Brian: on creolisation of Indo-Guyanese, 91

Moscow is Not My Mecca, 74

Mohamed, Feroze: Marxist Leninist ideology, 661

Mother India: and nationalist crusade, 91, 101–102; shadow of, 102–109

Moyne Commission, 117, 119; and the MPCA, 133–36

Mussolini, Benito: Italian invasion of Ethiopia, 95

N

Naipaul, V.S.: and Guyana, 535; and Jagan, 20, 68, 510–11

National identity. *See* Guyanese national identity, Afro-Guyanese identity and Indo-Guyanese identity

National Liberation Front of Angola (NLFA), 563

National Patriotic Front Government: Jagan and a, 638, 692–93

Nationalisation: of bauxite, 33, 518, 529, 532, 548–50, 641; of Booker, 33; Jagan and, 6

Nearing, Dr Scott: Jagan and, 325

Negro Progress Convention (NPC): and ethnic balance, 86, 87–91,92, 109, 110, 125

Nehru, Jawaharlal: Jagan and, 70, 192; and return of Indo-Guyanese to India, 179–80

Nehusi, Kimani: on Jagan's inflexible Marxist stance, 66

Nelson Rockefeller Mission to Latin America: and communism in Guyana, 515–16

New Global Human Order (NGHO): Jagan and the, 686–97

Nicholson, H.H. (Vigilance): and the ASRE, 296

Nicholson, Dr J.A.: and the 1947 general elections, 175

Nunan, J.J.: and the idea of an Indian colony, 84, 87

Non-Aligned Movement: Burnham and the, 531–33, 547

North American Congress on Latin America (NACLA): Jagan and the, 685–86

O

Order of Friendship of the Peoples: Jagan and the, 624–25

Organisation of African Unity: Burnham and the, 562

Organisation of American States (OAS): and communism in the Caribbean, 341

P

PAC Bulletin, 63; and the 1947 general elections, 161, 172–74, 186; and Jagan's Marxist vision, 148–58, 194–200,

Palmer, H. L: and the 1947 general elections 164, 170–71, 174–75

Patriotic Appeal: and the Waddington Constitution, 246–48

Patriotic Coalition for Democracy (PCD): and the 1992 general elections, 682, 683–84; Jagan and, 680–81, 691–93

People's Government (Czechoslovakia), 32

People's Movement for the Liberation of Angola (PMLA), 563
People's National Congress (PNC): and capitalism, 623–25; and Chandisingh, 556–63, 607–13; and cooperative socialism, 508–10, 547–48, 553–56, 561–63, 573–82; and Cuba, 566, 607–608; and electoral fraud, 48, 474, 488–98, 505–506; 527, 547, 548–50; and the ERP, 668; formation of the, 40, 273; and the 1964 general election, 407–412, 460–462; and the 1980 general election, 668; and the 1992 general elections, 682; and independence, 293–297; Jagan's critical support of the, 550–552; Marxist-Leninist ideology, 50; nationalisation campaign, 639–640; objects of the, 570–571; paramountcy of the, 550, 552, 554, 563, 582, 596, 601, 637, 649, 692; and imposition of PR in BG, 367–71, 391–96; reformism, 503–507; UF coalition, 460–61, 463–64, 481–83; x–13 plan, 369–70
People's National Party (PNP): Burnham and the, 431–32
People's Progressive Party (PPP): Afro-Guyanese and the, 54; and Benn, 464–67; and Bhagwan, 465; and Burnhamism, 645–50; calls for free and fair elections, 36, 680–82; 23rd Central Committee Report, 679; 25th Central Committee Report, 680–82; Chandisingh's defection from the, 556–63, 567, 607–13; 1976; Congress, 611–22; constitution, 644–46; critical support for the PNC, 550–52, 565, 602; and demise of Marxism, 683–93; dissension within the, 56–57, 242–50, 256–67, 285–301, 464–65; and the 1947 general elections, 175; and the 1953 general elections, 226; and the 1961 general elections, 296–300; and the 1964 general election, 407–12; and the 1992 general elections, 682, 692; and the GIWU, 231–38; government, 289–300, 302–308, 693–98; Hubbard

and the, 148; and independence, 246–48, 316, 340, 470–72; and Jagan, 1–2, 21–22, 53–54; Marxist– Leninist ideology, 33–36, 223–25, 238–50, 279–81, 431–57, 468–77, 504–508, 547–49, 567–69, 616–21, 654–57, 667–68, 676–80; and scientific foresight philosophy, 503–505; socialist constitution, 506–508; and the Soviet crisis, 671–76; and suspension of the BG Constitution, 254–56, 587–88; and the ultra–left faction, 280–83, 285–99. *See also* Jagan, Cheddi, Scientific socialism
Peters, Rev A.T.: and the 1947 general elections, 177
Plantation struggle: Indian, 118
Podgorny, Nikolai: Jagan and, 474
Political Affairs Committee (PAC): and the general elections of 1947, 159–64; Jagan and the, 1, 7, 63, 148–58, 201–203; Marxist-Leninist stance, 193–200, 258–60
Political longevity: Jagan's, 47–51
Politics: and ethnicity, 2; and ideology, 18–20; and race, 17–20, 36–43, 75–76, 128–30, 164, 167
Port Mourant, 10, 13–14, 22–23
PPP Bookshop, 59
PPP(Burnham), 273
PPP/CIVIC: and the 1992 general election, 682, 683–84, 693–98
Progressive Youth Organisation (PYO), 42, 322–24
Proletarian internationalism, 63
Proportional Representation (PR): Burnham and, 296–97, 306, 378–82; 1964 general elections and, 260–62; Jagan and, 391–92; Melby and, 363–65; Schlesinger and, 356–57, 359; US endorsement of, 364–66
Protest: against imposition of PR, 391–93

Q
Quadros, President Janio: Jagan and, 322
Queen's College: Jagan and, 12, 23
Queen's visit: to Jamaica, 252–53

R
Rabe, Professor Stephen: and US

destabilisation of the Jagan government, 342–44

Race: communism and, 425–27; and economic environment, 4; Jagan and, 17–18, 54, 63; and politics, 2, 17–20, 36–43, 75–76, 128–30, 164–68, 167, 171–72, 174–76, 266–67, 280, 286–87, 464–65

Race first philosophy: Afro-Guyanese and, 91, 92, 96

Racism: in British Guiana, 7–8, 36–43, 49–50, 125–28, 679, 703

Racial violence: GAWU strike and, 397–99, 403–06

Rai, Balram Singh: and the 1964 general election, 411–12

Rao, P Kodanda: visit to British Guiana, 100, 102–03

Ramayana: and the El Dorado syndrome, 113–14

Ramkarran: and communism, 63; on the PPP and race, 41; and the PPP, 56

Ramkarran, Boysie: support of Jagan in 1947 general elections, 161

Ramotar, Donald: commitment to Marxism, 698

Ramphal, J.I.: and national identity, 125–28

Ramsahoye, Dr Fenton: on racism in Guyanese politics, 127; on Jagan's legacy, 707–09

Reformism: Jagan on Burnham's, 503–07

Referendum: rigging of the 1978, 622

Renison, Governor: and Jagan, 304

Rice production: and drainage and irrigation, 119–21; expenditure on, 146

Riots: on sugar estates, 97–98. *See also* Labour riots, Strikes and Sugar industry

Robertson Commission Report, 121; and Jagan-Burnham rivalry, 256–67; on the PPP and the GIWU strike, 137–38, 232, 237, 250–51

Robeson, Paul: and play on Haitian Revolution, 97

Rodney, Walter, 50, 650, 651–54; assassination, 659; and Marxism, 56, 612

Rohee, Clement: Marxist-Leninist ideology, 668–70

Roopnaraine, Rupert: and Marxism, 56, 612

Ruhomon, Joseph: and the BGEIA, 79

Ruhomon, Peter: and Indian nationalism, 115

Russian Revolution: Stalin and the, 160

Rusk, Dean: and communism in BG, 373–75; and BG politics, 399–402

S

Sandys, Duncan: and BG independence, 374–75, 378–82; meeting with Janet Jagan, 408–409; and PR in BG, 366, 367–71, 391–93, 394

Sandys Plan: for imposition of PR in BG, 366, 367–71, 391–93, 394, 399–402

Sawh, Parbu: and the idea of an Indian colony, 84

Savage, Sir Alfred: and the break with the PPP, 237–38; and suspension of the BG constitution, 239–56

Schlesinger, Professor Arthur: and Burnham, 347, 356–58, 681; and Jagan, 319–20, 340; and PR in BG, 356–59

Scholes, Dr Theophilus, 93

Scientific socialism: Jagan and, 26, 34, 40, 41, 51–52, 53, 54, 62, 64, 70, 150, 148–55, 193, 199–200, 637–42, 654

Seaford, Hon. F. J: and colonial policy, 139, 140, 142; and the 1947 general elections, 175

Searwar, Lloyd: and Jagan, 321–22, 388–89

Settlement Commission: and migration to BG, 182

Shakoor, S.M.: and the 1947 general elections, 177

Sharma, P. D.: caricature of Guyanese socialism, 597–601

Sherlock, Sir Alfred: and colonial policy, 139, 140, 142

Simms, Peter: on the Enmore tragedy, 209–10

Singh, Dr J.B., 39, 63, 191–92; and the 1947 general elections, 161; and the WI Federation, 183–85

Singh, Jainaraine, 63, 267
Singh Rai, Balram, 63, 488–89. *See also* Justice Party
Sinha, Lord: and the British Guiana Colonisation Deputation, 81–85
Slave experience: Guyana, 3–5
Smith, Ferdinand: and the WFTU, 241, 261
Socialism: Burnham and, 507–10
Socialist Constitution: Burnham's, 506–507
Socialist revolution: Burnham's, 508–10
Socialist Sixth of the World, The, 64
Sophia Declaration, 569–71, 575–77, 602
Soviet crisis: PPP and the, 671–76
Soviet Union: Jagan and the, 61–62, 63–64, 473–85, 510–11; support of the Tricontinental Conference, 469–72. *See also* Marxist-Leninist commitment.
Stabroek News: and democratic elections, 705; and the PNC, 658
Stalin, Joseph: and the resolution of nationalities, 64–65, 68–69; and the Russian Revolution, 160, 661
State of emergency: renewal of the, 470
Strachan, Billy: and Burnham, 225–26, 433–34; and the CPGB, 241, 250–55, 418, 428, 430–39, 447–57
Strike: GAWU/PPP, 505; GIWU, 232–34, 238–40, 254–56; against Labour Relations Bill, 367–71
Subversive Literature Bill, 52, 61
Sugar industry, 4–5; hydrological challenges of the, 129–30; nationalisation of the, 505; and Venn Commission, 214–20; working conditions in the, 132–35, 152–53
Sugar Producers' Association: and C.R. Jacob, 136–38; and the GIWU, 203, 231–38, 250–55, 260–62; and the MPCA, 133
Sugar workers: Jagan and, 200–203; strike, 212–14, 232–34, 238–40; and universal adult suffrage, 143–46; working conditions, 132–135, 152–153, 203–205
Sun, The: anti-communist stance of the, 425

Sunday Argosy: anti-communist stance of the, 425
Suslov, Mikhail: Jagan and, 474

T
Tapacuma Scheme, 145
Thapar, Romila: on Indo-Guyanese utopianism, 113
Third World Congress of Women: Janet Jagan and the, 241–42
Thomas, Professor Clive: overview of Jagan and the PPP, 633–35; and Marxism, 56
Thorne, A.A.: and the BGWL, 135
Thunder: PPP newsletter, 57, 58, 63, 223–24; and the Cold War, 469–70; and the Waddington Constitution, 245
Todorov, Tzvetan: On the demise of Marxism, 689–92
Trade Union Congress (TUC): Critchlow and the, 143, 144; Jagan's address to the 1979, 625–26; strike, 367–71, 390–91
Tri-Continental Conference: Castro's, 60; Jagan attends the, 468–71
Tribune: Afro-Guyanese newspaper, 90, 93, 95, 96; and awakening of Africa, 97; and colonial rule, 107–108; and Indian nationalism, 105–109; and Rao visit, 100–101
Truth: on communism, 168–69

U
Ultra-left faction: in the PPP, 280–83, 285–99
Undesirable Publications Bill, 52
United Force (UF): anti-communist crusade, 352–55, 424–28; ideology, 18–20, 56; PNC coalition, 460–61, 463–64, 481–83
United States of America (USA): and Burnham, 399–400, 406–10, 469–71,478–85, 514–17, 523–27, 551–56, 627–31; and Cuba, 341–45; and democratic elections in Guyana, 680–89; and electoral fraud, 474, 488–98, 505–06, 523–30, 547; and Jagan, 2, 53, 57, 59,308–47 467–97;

endorsement of PR in BG, 364–71.
See also Central Intelligence Agency,
Cold War, Kennedy, President John
F., Johnson, President Lyndon.
Universal adult suffrage: debate, 143–46
Universal Negro Improvement
Association (UNIA), 93, 110

V

Vanguard party: PPP or PNC, 602–603,
616–21
Venezuela: Guyana border issue, 566
Venn Commission, 119, 131, 214–20; and
the GIWU, 231

W

Waddington Constitution Report, 243,
245, 254–56
Waters, Robert: on AFL-CIO
destabilisation of BG, 368–70
Webber, A.R.F.: on shaping Guyanese
identity, 78–79, 88–89
Weekend Post: anti-communist stance of
the, 425
West India Royal Commission: Indian
nationalism 116–22
West Indians: and Ethiopianism, 94–95
West Indies Federation: Jagan and
the, 72, 283–86, 292, 316; racial
implications of the, 178–86
West on Trial, The, 145, 461
Western Berbice Constituency: and the
1947 general elections, 177
Westmaas, Rory: and communism, 63,
66; detention of, 269–72
Wharton, Dr William Hewley: and the
idea of an Indian colony, 79, 80–85,
87
White Guyanese: and colonial privilege,
107–108
Williams, Henry Sylvester: Ethiopianism,
94
Wills, Fred: and Kissinger, 629–31
Wilson, Prime Minister: and BG politics,
408
Wismar Massacre, 397, 402
Women's International Democratic
Federation (WIDF), 241

Women's Political and Economic
Organisation (WPEO), 175
Women's Progressive Organisation
(WPO), 241
Woolford, Sir Eustace: and the WI
Federation, 181
Working People's Alliance (WPA):
and Guyanese leadership, 651–59;
Marxist-Leninist ideology, 50, 612
World Communist Party: Jagan and the,
475–77
World Peace Council (WPC), 241, 433
World Federation of Democratic Youth
(WFDY), 241
World Federation of Trade Unions
(WFTU); and PPP leadership,
240–42, 260–61, 431–33, 441–42
World Marxist Review: and the PPP, 59
Wright, T. A.: and Garvey's visit to
British Guiana, 110–11
Wynter, Sylvia: and Jagan's Marxist
paradigm, 73–76, 129

Y

Young Communist League: Janet Jagan
and the, 29

Z

Zedong, Mao: Janet Jagan and

Milton Keynes UK
Ingram Content Group UK Ltd.
UKHW030638280124
436805UK00008B/195